LONDON ILLUSTRATED 1604–1851

Frontispiece   Transept of Westminster Abbey from
Malton's *Picturesque Tour* of 1792 (72/9).

LONDON ILLUSTRATED
1604-1851

A SURVEY AND INDEX OF TOPOGRAPHICAL BOOKS AND THEIR PLATES

Bernard Adams

An artist, after a time, will find London more
interesting than any other place, for nowhere else
are there such atmospheric effects on fine days, and
nowhere is the enormous power of blue more felt in
the picture; while the soot, which puts all the stones
into mourning, makes everything look old. . . . In fact,
if the capitals of Europe are considered, London is
one of the most picturesque.

(AUGUSTUS HARE, *WALKS IN LONDON,* 1878)

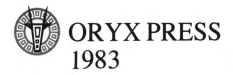 ORYX PRESS
1983

The rare Arabian Oryx is believed to have inspired the myth of the unicorn. This desert antelope became virtually extinct in the early 1960s. At that time several groups of international conservationists arranged to have 9 animals sent to the Phoenix Zoo to be the nucleus of a captive breeding herd. Today the Oryx population is nearing 300 and herds have been returned to reserves in Israel, Jordan, and Oman.

London Illustrated 1604–1851 is published in the United Kingdom in a limited edition of 1000 copies by Library Association Publishing, London and in the United States of America in a limited edition of 500 copies by The Oryx Press, Phoenix.

Published by The Oryx Press
2214 North Central at Encanto
Phoenix, AZ 85004

Published simultaneously in Canada

Designed and produced by Mechanick Exercises, London.

Library of Congress Cataloging in Publication Data

Adams, Bernard.
   London illustrated, 1604–1851.

   Bibliography: p.
   Includes indexes.
      1. London (England) in art.   2. London (England)
—Buildings—Pictorial works.   3. Prints—England.
I. Title.
NE954.3.G7A3   1983   769′.499421   83-2334
ISBN 0-85365-734-3

In memory of
Muriel Everard Evered
(†1978)

CONTENTS

INTRODUCTION

Nobody who looks into windows of secondhand booksellers, antique dealers or gift shops can have failed to notice a sideline of these businesses in the shape of local topographical prints, either original or in facsimile, black and white or coloured, unframed and framed, or made up into place-mats, desk-tidies, coffee tables and the like. Most of the genuine engravings so offered were by no means intended for framing but started life as illustrations in books of historical, antiquarian or architectural interest, while some of the larger sizes belonged to sets of prints kept for browsing in library portfolios.

Before the Second World War such books were within reach of quite modest purses and a standard early nineteenth century local history, complete with engraved views, would often be given a place in the family bookcase. In recent years, however, the private ownership of such books has become increasingly rare, principally because an astronomical increase in the cash value of such books has encouraged executors to dispose of them and at the same time discouraged private buyers, who would have been willing to acquire them at a reasonable price for the sake of their local associations.

Some are now only available at prices which even well-endowed institutional libraries may baulk at: for instance, several thousand pounds for a fine copy of Malton's *Picturesque Tour through the Cities of London and Westminster*, or a slightly lesser sum for an early printing of Ackermann's *Microcosm of London*. One would need a virtually inexhaustible bank account to build up the sort of London collection amassed by Major Abbey, Lord Nathan of Churt or Sir Mayson Beeton before the Second World War, when they acquired such volumes in fine condition at a price which would hardly purchase a new art book today. Private collectors

likewise think twice before investing a hundred pounds upwards on books illustrated with steel-engravings which were published in large numbers, such as Elmes's *Metropolitan Improvements* and Tombleson's *Thames*, and which in the first quarter of this century were abundantly and quite cheaply available in secondhand bookshops.

While some of these volumes have in recent years been bought at auctions for libraries or private collectors for the most part they have been acquired by dealers who, aiming to bring the greatest happiness to the greatest number, have broken them up, sending text and bindings for pulping and offering the plates for sale individually, either untreated or washed, tinted and mounted. Thus a new breed of collectors has grown up which, while not affluent enough to purchase or find house room for the complete volumes, is none the less eager to possess specimens of their illustrations, suggesting the whole work as a figured Persian tile suggests the wall from which it was abstracted. Such purchasers may actually derive more pleasure from an engraving displayed in isolation than if it were buried with its fellows in a binding surrounded by the accompanying text, which often proves to be boring, jejune and sadly uninformative on the subject of the pictures.

Inevitably then the sale of isolated plates—both to such collectors and to foreign and provincial visitors in search of an up-market souvenir—has become an increasingly profitable business and more and more of the books they were designed to illustrate, having been purchased at a premium, are discarded like empty pea-pods. So, in spite of the much larger editions possible as the result of the use of engraved steel plates after about 1825, the total available stock of illustrated books issued prior to

1851 must by now be very much eroded and the more popular volumes extremely hard to come by in an unmutilated condition. For even when apparently lodged in safety in the closed access of public, academic or national libraries plates have been lost over the years through delay in rebinding and, most regrettably, through the recent wave of print pilfering.

At this juncture, therefore, it seems imperative to include in the description of such works a detailed catalogue of the optimum number of separate plates with which each was originally published. Here this is attempted for some two and a half centuries of illustrated books on London.

The best general London bibliography is the printed guide to the GLC History Library, *London history and topography* (1939), but it is only a short entry catalogue, without collations. *The London region: an annotated geographical bibliography* (1981), by Philippa Dolphin, Eric Grant and Edward Lewis, although more recent is less complete for topographical works. For information on specific plates bibliographies on the larger geographical unit of Great Britain must be consulted. Colour plates are well documented in two works: *Scenery of Great Britain and Ireland in aquatint and lithography, 1770–1860 from the library of J.R. Abbey* (1952) and R.V. Tooley's *English books with coloured plates* (1954); both include collations and a check-list of plates transcribing subject, names of artist and engraver and publication date. In the previous century William Upcott in his *Bibliographical account of the principal works relating to English topography* (3 vols, 1818) included all works that came to his notice, whether illustrated or not, and endeavoured to list all plates whether coloured or monochrome. John Anderson's *Book of British topography* (1881) also embraces all types of books but disregards individual plates. Both Upcott and Anderson were wholly dependent on the stock of the British Museum Library and missed items not available there. Of these six works the Abbey catalogue alone indexes artists, engravers and publishers.

The several great public collections of London prints and drawings all include many engravings that were originally book illustrations. The Guildhall Library Print Room maintains the most exhaustive catalogue, on cards, in which prints are entered both under their subject and their artist and engraver, and often refers to the title of a book from which a particular plate has been abstracted. The chief function of such collections, however, requires them to arrange their material in a topographical classification so that a search for plates of a particular date or from a particular published work would involve turning over the contents of almost every box or portfolio they comprise. The present work, therefore, aims to supplement them in the following ways:

1 By providing a check-list of titles of books illustrating London.
2 By providing an inventory of plates useful to collectors, booksellers and auctioneers.
3 By acting as a subject and name (artist, engraver, architect) index to plates in books held by libraries and private collectors.
4 To relate plates bought without pedigree to their book source and thus to help date items lacking publication-lines or running titles.
5 To assist the discovery of illustrations of particular sites or buildings and to assess their actual as opposed to their nominal dates. It is shown that the same plates were used in successive works, sometimes over a century or more, and that the second half of the eighteenth century saw a great deal of slavish copying of plates from earlier works. This gives a curiously static appearance to illustration at that time and any assumptions as to the date of a view mut be based on the knowledge of its earliest engraving which in its turn may be taken from a drawing which had been for some years in the possession of the printseller or publisher. Moreover early nineteenth century antiquarian interest encouraged the publication of plates based on work of the two previous centuries sometimes engraved so carefully as to deceive the unwary.
6 By means of the publication histories to cast light on serial and subscription publication of illustrated works in the late eighteenth and early nineteenth centuries.

Acknowledgements

First and foremost I am indebted to Ralph Hyde, Keeper of Prints and Maps at the Guildhall Library, without whose unflagging enthusiasm and unstinted help this book would never have seen the light of day. Thanks are also due to his Guildhall colleagues whose cheerful patience in looking out scores of prints, drawings and books has greatly eased my task.

Other librarian benefactors to whom I am grateful for access to the collections in their care and for their specific help are: Sir Robin Mackworth Young and Mrs Moira Dowell of the Royal Library, Windsor; Miss P.M. Baker who has charge of the Bromhead Collection of London books in the University of London Library; Miss Dorothy Parsons, formerly Librarian of the Department of the Environment branch library housing the Mayson Beeton Collection of London books; Miss Cobb of the GLC History Library where the Burns and Harben London Collections include many fine illustrated volumes; Miss Scull of the Soane Museum Library which owns the extra-illustrated Fauntleroy Pennant; Mrs Bailey of the Tower of London Library; Nick Savage and Miss Thambimuttu of the British Architectural Library; John Hopkins, Librarian of the Society of Antiquaries; and Dr Celina Fox and Miss Galinou of the Museum of London. I have a long-standing debt of gratitude to the staff of the British Library, particularly to those in the North Library who over the years have produced for my inspection innumerable tomes from the Grenville and King's Libraries, and in the Map Room where the King's Topographical Print Collection is kept. Also I owe to the kindness of Peter Moore, formerly of the British Museum Department of Prints and Drawings, an acquaintance with the riches of the Crace, Crowle and Marx Collections and of the many bound volumes and printed catalogues relevant to my topic which are owned by that department. Finally I have received much help from the London Library, with its ever attentive personnel and considerable stock of early nineteenth century books, and from the Victoria and Albert Museum Library with its admirable reference collection.

For information on specific topics I am grateful to a number of individuals who have kindly helped me. These include: Peter Jackson, whose prodigious knowledge in the matter of London illustration added some titles to my list; Donald Hodson, who supplied transcripts of advertisements for Part publications found in eighteenth century news sheets; Mrs Sarah Tyacke of the British Library Map Room, who made available photocopies of early map and printsellers' lists; John Phillips, whose book *Shepherd's London* (1976) is a mine of information and with whom I have had a number of useful discussions; Stephen Marks, who allowed me to examine his complete set, in wrappers, of the two works comprising T.H. Shepherd's *London in the Nineteenth Century* and who supplied an invaluable transcript of the lettering on the wrappers, the pagination of each Part and the captions, credits and publication dates of individual engravings; Dr E.S. de Beer, who provided details of the view of Whitehall in his copy of Coronelli's *Viaggi*, which is missing from the British Library copy; H.M. Colvin, who measured the relevant plates in his copy of the rare *Vitruvius Britannicus, Volume the Fourth*, generally available only in reduced facsimile, and whose *Biographical dictionary of English architects* (1954), with its thorough indexing, helped me to identify the architects of a number of the buildings featured in engravings; Gavin Bridson, who advised me on the dating of engravers in my index; and Jonathan Ditchburn, who has generously shared information derived from his editorial work on the catalogues of the 'Images of London' series.

To the late George Suckling I owe the initial impetus for compiling this work, since not only did he give me 'carte blanche' to rummage, unattended, through the enormous stock of topographical illustrations kept in ancient portfolios and brown paper parcels in the basement of his Cecil Court bookshop but upstairs would impart all sorts of fascinating reminiscences of many decades in the trade together with anecdotes of the print collectors whose interests were nobly served by himself and his father.

Despite all this encouragement and help this book no doubt omits details of editions with illustrations significantly different from those listed, and there must certainly be other titles which have completely escaped the notice of the compiler. Such omissions are entirely due to his own shortcomings and he accepts full blame for them, but he would very much welcome notification of any corrections and additions to the work.

B.P.F. Adams
July 1982

LONDON ILLUSTRATED 1604–1851: A HISTORY

(Numbered books are cited in the chronological list on p xxv)

Pioneers and Prospectors

From the middle years of the seventeenth century until the year of the Great Exhibition books illustrated with plates showing London views or elevations of London buildings were published at an average rate of one a year. The antiquary William Dugdale was fortunate enough to have at his disposal the great Bohemian artist and etcher Wenceslaus Hollar when he published his *Monasticon Anglicanum* (no 6) and *History of St Paul's Cathedral* (no 8). The last named in particular was nearly all the work of Hollar and, with its exhaustive and painstaking illustrations of the mighty, doomed Gothic church, was both the first example of its particular genre and one which was not matched until the nineteenth century when Edward Brayley and J.P. Neale collaborated in their handsome *History and Antiquities of the Abbey Church of St Peter, Westminster* (no 123).

Many of the illustrated books published in the interim were, however, far more mundane, being designed to serve a variety of practical purposes and to cater for all sorts of needs. The influence of Hollar (no 5) is very apparent in the collections of small 'Prospects', such as those collected by Samuel Pepys, which were particularly popular from the Restoration to the mid-eighteenth century and which mostly consisted of line-engravings or etchings of familiar London 'sights' unaccompanied by letterpress. These plates were often issued in a numbered or lettered sequence and preceded by an engraved title-page, while some had an historical explanation engraved beneath each separate view. Such are Robert Morden and Philip Lea's *Book of the Prospects of the Remarkable Places in and about the City of London* (no 15), Henry Overton's *Prospects of the Most Remarkable Places in and about the Citty of London* (no 26) and John Bowles's *British Views* (no 28). Colnaghi's *Select Views in London and Westminster* (no 76) and the miniature *Lester's Illustrations of London* (no 127) are later examples. These, albeit much more modest in scope, are the English counterparts of the 100 views of *Le Fabriche e vedute di Venetia* engraved by Luca Carlevaris and published in Venice in 1703 as a souvenir for tourists. The nearest latter-day equivalent are those batches of postcard views for sending to stay-at-home friends, and like holiday postcards the small engravings often served to decorate the bare walls of humble living rooms.

Souvenirs worthier of a 'gentleman's library' were produced by printsellers who bound up sets of larger 'one-sheet' and 'perspective' views listed in their catalogues. Their collections sometimes cover a considerable time-span and include stocks bought in from rival firms, and are co-ordinated by means of over-printed running numbers and a general title-page. It was such a souvenir, probably bought from John Bowles's shop in St Paul's Churchyard, that Leopold Mozart took back with him to Salzburg in 1764, after displaying the genius of his prodigious son to London music lovers. Examples surviving intact are the Sutton Nicholls plates published by John Bowles as *London Described* (no 29), Sayer's collection of 'Views' by Chatelain, Maurer and Thomas Bowles, dated 1752–3 (no 217), which were peak years for this type of topographical engraving, John Boydell's *Collection of Views in England and Wales* (no 47), Samuel and Nathaniel Buck's *Antiquities* (no 54), R.H. Laurie's *Views of the City of London executed about 1730 to 1770* (no 191) and Francis West's *Collection of Views of Old London and its Environs* (no 193). Some of these collections were reissued with the addition of new prints, while the old showed signs of advancing senility.

Pictorial Guidebooks

Guidebooks to London, or to England as a whole, are a fertile source of small engraved illustrations. Some of these were published on the Continent for purchase by foreign tourists and written in French, the then international language. *Mémoires et Observations faites par un Voyageur en Angleterre* (no 19), attributed to Henri Misson de Valbourg and published at the Hague, is a duodecimo illustrated with a plan and folding views derived, both in subjects and style, from the Morden and Lea *Prospects*; his view of Bedlam elicits a dry, Gallic comment: 'Tous les Fous de Londres ne sont pas là dedans'. The fourth volume of the enticingly entitled *Les Délices de la Grande Bretagne* (no 20) by one James Beeverell, published in Leiden, is generously supplied with delicately engraved derivative London views, the limitations of the duodecimo format being overcome by allowing each print a double-page spread. Two further guidebooks in French were published in Paris: *Londres et ses Environs* (no 65), attributed to De Serres de Latour, which also overcame its size limitations by including a few excellent but somewhat vulnerable folding plates, notably one of 'Le Couvent Jardin'; and a later *Description de Londres* (no 103), by J.-B. Barjaud and C.P. Landon, which is more fully illustrated, with a map and 42 small views for which the engraver, Beaugean, has drawn largely upon the work of English predecessors for *London and its Environs Described* (no 41). A selection of these same Beaugean engravings was later incorporated in *Souvenirs de Londres en 1814 et 1816* (no 119) from the Imprimerie Crapelet.

Samuel Wale, one of the founder members of the Royal Academy, working with a skilled team of engravers, provided the numerous plates for the above mentioned *London and its Environs*, an illustrated guide-gazetteer issued in six small octavo volumes by Dr Johson's publisher, R. & J. Dodsley of Pall Mall. The skill of draughtsman and engravers is sufficient to convey a lively sense of place, even within the narrow confines of 8 × 14cm borderlines. But this well-illustrated book was a rare phenomenon since most London guides were either totally unillustrated or adorned with a few token engravings or with woodcut pictures only.

Such was *The Picture of London* (no 85), first published in 1802 by Richard Phillips, with two maps, a prospect from Greenwich and pictures of the three Thames bridges. It ran into numerous editions equipped with maps and, up to the fourteenth, with a varying handful of about five or six small engravings. Part guidebook, part history, was the same publisher's *Modern London* (no 89), in a larger format and more lavishly illustrated, not only with good exteriors and interiors engraved by E. Pugh after S. Rawle but also with a set of hand-coloured 'Itinerant Traders' in identified local settings such as 'Whitehall—Knives to Grind'. The *Picture of London* produced a good crop of imitations, none of which made much attempt to illustrate the text. *Tegg and Castleman's New Picture of London for 1803–4* (no 86), for instance, contains only one plan and four views eccentrically chosen. The title-page of the 1818 edition of a popular guidebook, *Leigh's New Picture of London* (no 126), claims that it is 'embellished with upwards of one hundred elegant engravings'; this is strictly true but in practice it contains only six folding plates, each of which carries up to 22 thumbnail engravings, some no larger than 4 × 4cm.

It is quite otherwise with Nathaniel Whittock's *Modern Picture of London, Westminster and the Metropolitan Boroughs* (no 183), which is illustrated with 92 separate steel-engravings. This exception may be explained by the fact that Whittock, the author, was also a topographical artist and an engraver whose name is associated with a facsimile of the Ashmolean Wyngaerde panoramic drawing of London. He also drew most of the London views for Thomas Allen's *Picturesque Beauties of England and Wales—Surrey and Sussex* (no 158) and, in all probability, for the same author's *Panorama of London, and Visitors' Pocket Companion* (no 162), liberally illustrated with small steel views engraved by J. Rogers.

Perambulators and Juveniles

A class of book intended rather for the resident Londoner than for the foreign or provincial visitor is the 'Perambulation', which has an enduring popularity as the more recent London books of Augustus

Hare, Stephen Bone and Sir Nikolaus Pevsner bear witness. The first notable London perambulator was Daniel Lysons, who gathered the observations made during his protracted stumpings round the neighbouring villages in the four volumes of *The Environs of London* (1792–6), but others adapted his method to describe the central area. Under the pen name of 'Dr David Hughson', David Pugh published in six volumes *London: being an accurate History and Description ... from an actual Perambulation* (no 93); this is illustrated with woodcuts, line-engravings and pretty vignetted half-titles decorated with sketches by Richard Corbould of the turnpike entrances. Vignetted sketches drawn and engraved by John Greig are an attractive feature of the same author's later *Walks through London* (no 121); each is accompanied by a tiny route map. More extensive explorations were to spring from James Dugdale's four-volume *New British Traveller* (no 130), but most of its London views (in vols 3 and 4) were also the work of John Greig or his partner James Storer.

For young readers Messrs Darton, Harvey & Darton published *Perambulations in London and its Environs* (no 102) by Mrs Priscilla Wakefield which, with its handful of line-engravings, was intended to promote observation and instil historical knowledge. It was preceded by a set of four miniature volumes from another well-known children's publisher, E. Newbery, *The Curiosities of London and Westminster Described* (no 49), of which each volume was illustrated with half a dozen engravings measuring 5 × 8cm. Even smaller views were included by John Harris, proprietor of the 'Juvenile Library', in a rather more racy book, *London Scenes, or a Visit to Uncle William in Town* (no 145), which so far indulged childish foibles as to include subjects such as 'Mad Ox on Blackfriars Bridge' and 'The Dancing Sweeps'. A curiosity, also intended for the juvenile and popular market, is John Marshall's *Views of the Principal Buildings in London* (no 101) in two minute volumes; these are themselves unillustrated but were sold in a slipcase together with 15 crude engravings on cards, very roughly coloured by hand, like the 'twopence coloured' theatrical prints.

Street Views

Allied to this perambulation class of book, although specifically published as a trade directory and advertising medium, are *Tallis's London Street Views*. Like Hughson's *Walks* they are illustrated with miniature street plans and these, together with their 88 architectural elevations or street panoramas and inset views, enable us to stroll in imagination down all the main thoroughfares, identifying on the way each individual dwelling house, shop, church, chapel or public building as it appeared at the accession of Queen Victoria. It is now an extremely rare collection since it was published at about 1½d per copy in paper-wrapped Parts which were ephemeral both because of their fragility and for their advertising and commercial associations. Fortunately a complete facsimile of this interesting series consisting of the original panoramas (1838–40) and of some supplementary ones (c 1847) was published in 1969 in association with the London Topographical Society. Concurrently with his *Street Views* John Tallis was publishing Thomas Dugdale's *England and Wales Delineated* (no 186), an illustrated gazetteer issued in Parts. When these were bound up the article on London straddled volumes 7 and 8 but the London views are to be found in each of the 11 volumes, the same plates sometimes serving for both of the Tallis publications. On some of these the name of the artist T.H. Shepherd is to be found, while others without credits are marked by his style. The publisher claimed to have sold 27,000 copies and in the 1850s he ventured on a second edition with additional Shepherd plates. Soon after, 'in commemoration of the Great Exhibition of all nations in 1851', was published *Tallis's Illustrated London* (no 215) in two volumes with a text by William Gaspey. So that it should appear a new work Tallis added a few up-to-date plates but the greater part were taken over from the stock of E.T. Brain, for whose *Illustrated London* (no 207) they had originally been engraved. Among the Tallis novelties were four views of the Great Exhibition and one of Colney Hatch Lunatic Asylum whose foundation stone had recently been laid by the Prince Consort.

Historians

A large number of illustrations are also to be found in works entitled 'Survey' or 'History', interchangeable titles since both invariably use as their source book John Stow's inimitable *Survey of London* (1603) which, alas for Elizabethan topography, is not itself illustrated. Between 1720 and 1775 adaptations and continuations by John Strype, William Maitland, John Mottley and others succeeded each other in numerous editions; all are illustrated with engraved views of varying quality and most with regional maps as well. The views no less than the texts are often derivative since it was clearly cheaper to copy existing plates than to commission a completely new set of drawings from which to engrave. Nevertheless their views and elevations do, in the aggregate, give a fairly good idea of those aspects of the mid-eighteenth century architectural London scene which were at the time most highly esteemed.

When the Rev John Entick, a schoolmaster of St Dunstan, Stepney, compiled a revision of Maitland's *History* (no 38), entitled *A New and Accurate History and Survey of London* (no 44), his publisher set the engraver T. Simpson to copy most of its plates from Dodsley's invaluable *London and its Environs*. When however the publisher of John Noorthouck's *New History of London* (no 51) borrowed views from the same source and printed them two or three to a quarto page his engraver omitted all mention of the original artist. Moreover nearly all the ward maps he included, decorated with charming rococo cartouches and miniature views, were originally designed, probably by Thomas Bowen, for the *London Magazine*.

Historical and topographical books at this period were mainly published by subscription in weekly Parts, each accompanied by one or two engravings. Foremost in this line of business was John Cooke whose *New and Compleat History and Survey of the Cities of London and Westminster* (no 48) was alleged to have been written by 'A Society of Gentlemen; revised, corrected, and improved by Henry Chamberlain of Hatton-Garden Esq.' The first Part came out in March 1770 and each of the plates issued with the letterpress was engraved with two or more historical or topographical subjects. These Parts when bound became successful 'coffee-table books' of the time, for Cooke was encouraged to publish only five years later *A New and Universal History, Decription and Survey of the Cities of London and Westminster* (no 57) with the name of Walter Harrison on the title-page. This was lavishly, albeit economically, illustrated since a large number of the plates from the earlier book were used again with minor alterations and the excision of their characteristic beaded framing. Cooke's former journeyman and rival, Alexander Hogg, not to be outdone launched in 1784 *The New, Complete and Universal History, Description and Survey of the Cities of London and Westminster* (no 61) which also stated that it was written by a 'Society of Gentlemen', but in this case 'corrected and improved by William Thornton Esq. assisted by George Smith L.L.D. and the Rev. Alex. Townsend M.A.' Hogg reissued the identical text in 1796 but all was now attributed to one Richard Skinner.

Indeed, a favourite pastime of both these publishers was the invention of elegant aliases for the authorship of their topographical 'sixpenny Numbers' which must in fact have owed their existence to the attic labours of a consortium of sweated Grub Street hacks. In Cooke's stable were 'Nathaniel Spencer Esq.' (*The Complete English Traveller*, no 52) and 'Charles Burlington Esq., David Llewellyn Rees, Gent. and Alexander Murray, M.A.' (for the English, Welsh and Scottish contributions to *The Modern Universal British Traveller*, no 60). In Hogg's were 'G.A. Walpoole' (*The New British Traveller*, no 62), 'Henry Boswell Esq. F.A.R.S. Assisted by Robert Hamilton, L.L.D. and other ingenious Gentlemen' (*Views of the Antiquities of England and Wales*, no 63) and 'William Hugh Dalton' (*The New and Complete English Traveller*, 1794).

To return to genuine authors, perhaps the most unimpressive qualification for writing an 1806 *History and Survey of London* (no 96), a book containing numerous engravings after a popular magazine artist, T. Prattent, is to be found on its title-page: 'by B. Lambert, editor of Bertholet's Chemical Statics'. The Rev Henry Hunter's *History* (no 107) was a potboiler isued in Parts from 1796 and completed at last in 1811; it is only worthy of note for its plates engraved from the drawings of Edward Dayes. An extremely prolific British topographer, Thomas Allen, was the author of a *History and Antiquities of London* (no 152) published in four volumes by George Virtue and including plates drawn and engraved by the author. Finally Edward Brayley, an FSA who in association with John Britton had made important contributions to London history and topography, with his *Londiniana* (no 155) went on to produce a popular historical, topographical and antiquarian medley illustrated with a series of specially commissioned engravings conformable to its modest format. Since many of these were reduced from plates in the 1720 Strype edition of Stow's *Survey* (no 25), the publications of the Society of Antiquaries (no 36) and other engravings of the seventeenth and eighteenth centuries they form a useful miniaturized print catalogue.

Antiquaries

The illustrated antiquarian books in circulation towards the end of the eighteenth century owe their origins to the collaboration of Sir William Dugdale and Wenceslaus Hollar in the *Monasticon Anglicanum* and *History of St Paul's Cathedral*; they were the first of many books designed to appeal to gentlemen with antiquarian leanings and what might be called the 'conservationist lobby' of the day. In Crull's *The Antiquities of St Peter's* (1711) and John Dart's *Wesmonasterium* (no 27) the monumental contents of the Abbey are recorded in uninspired detail; much finer engravings of the royal tombs were made from drawings by H.F. Gravelot and George Vertue for *The Heads of the Kings of England* (no 31). Vertue, as official engraver to the Society of Antiquaries, also produced many large-scale line-engravings of threatened or condemned buildings, such as the Whitehall Gates, and some of these were collected in the first volume of their *Vetusta Monumenta*. Old churches were the speciality of the draughtsman Robert West and the engraver W.H. Toms and in their oblong folio *Perspective Views of all the Ancient Churches* (no 32) they depicted 24 such London buildings which they thought in danger of collapse or replacement—and rightly, since about half of them have by now been superseded or demolished. In the last quarter of the century a series of plates made under the supervision of the artist and antiquary Francis Grose was issued in Numbers between 1773 and 1787 as *The Antiquities of England and Wales* (no 50). The small engraved plates are printed on the same folio sheets

as the letterpress below and the balance struck between the typeface chosen and the etched image lends a special charm to these pages.

John Carter, official draughtsman to the Society of Antiquaries, when introducing his miniature etchings, *Specimens of Ancient Buildings in England* (no 64), published in six little volumes, explains that he has segregated elsewhere drawings of 'other subjects of antiquity besides views'; unfortunately this practice was not followed by other antiquarian series whose engravings represent a jumble of museum objects and ancient monuments and buildings. Antiquarian interests are prominent in the writings of James Peller Malcolm, whose parochial history *Londinium Redivivum* (no 83) and his *Anecdotes of the Manners and Customs of London during the Eighteenth Century* (no 100) are illustrated almost entirely by his own etched drawings or by facsimiles of early prints. Miscellanies issued in the first two decades of the nineteenth century, *The Antiquarian and Topographical Cabinet* (no 118) and *The Antiquarian Itinerary* (no 113), include a few small engravings of mediaeval London buildings but they are mainly bent on illustrating 'the Druidical Cromlech or Logan Stone, the sculptured Font, the elegant Cross'. Credits in the former series include Edward Dayes, Samuel Prout, Storer and Greig and there were also pictorial contributions from local amateurs such as resident clergy.

For the London topographer, however, the most impressive of these collections in terms of both the size and number of its plates is *Londina Illustrata* (no 131). It was published in Parts between 1808 and 1825, at first by William Herbert as a purely antiquarian publication when it reprinted old prints, plans and drawings but subsequently by the printseller Robert Wilkinson who made use of the series to issue exterior and interior views of surviving ancient buildings, possible victims of plans for rebuilding, which were carefully engraved from drawings by accomplished draughtsmen such as Frederick Nash, George and T.H. Shepherd, William Capon and R.B. Schnebbelie. Although the authenticity of some of its Elizabethan theatre views must be called in question more recent stage history is well served by a number of good contemporary theatre engravings. William Herbert launched a further series of antiquarian views, *London before the Great Fire* (no 120), in conjunction with Boydell & Co, but this series was short-lived. These series, together with similar plates issued by the publisher of the *Encyclopaedia Londinensis* for its 'London' volume (no 114), also provided for the needs of extra-illustrators, particularly of the Pennant history of London (no 67).

Pennant and the Picturesque

Collections of engravings which were purely antiquarian in content can have had little popular appeal and their sales must mainly have been confined to the clergy and country gentlemen since the antiquities discussed and depicted were generally ecclesiastical or relevant contributions to parochial history. There was a much wider demand at the turn of the century, however, for illustrated London books, sold either in Parts or as bound volumes. This may be attributed both to their less pedantic nature and even more to the extension of the hobby of print collection among the discerning middle classes. Moreover in book illustration the aridly and fragmentarily archaeological was giving place to the cult of the Picturesque, to a more discriminating approach to architecture and interior decoration and to a taste for street views and building interiors peopled by animate human beings instead of lay figures inserted simply to set the scale of the objects engraved.

In the van of this improvement was the author and draughtsman John Britton who, with his friend Edward Brayley, was responsible for launching that remarkable series of illustrated Numbers entitled *The Beauties of England and Wales* (no 104) which came out during the first 15 years of the nineteenth century and accumulated ultimately into an 18 volume set. For the plates illustrating this work he, in his own words, 'sought a new style of embellishment in which accuracy of representation should be combined with picturesque effect'. The success of this endeavour is apparent from the Middlesex volume, in which the topographical artists J.P. Neale, Frederick Mackenzie, Frederick Nash and George Shepherd are represented, and from the prevailing high standard of the engravings. Additionally the work was one of the first intended for general consumption to incorporate intelligent criticism of architecture.

There was also a technical innovation which did much to improve the aesthetic quality of topo-

graphical illustration, namely the use of aquatint backgrounds in conjunction with line-etching. The first entrepreneur to grasp the full potential of this revolution in technique and public taste was Rudolph Ackermann, the German coach-builder turned fine art publisher. By engaging distinguished artists to produce his aquatinted plates, and by employing the cheap émigré labour which was a by-product of the French Revolution to colour them after models, he was able to publish in sizable editions books which gave the appearance of being individually illustrated with water-colours by such talented draughtsmen as Rowlandson, Augustus Pugin, Frederick Mackenzie, William Westall and T.H. Shepherd. Yet, although artistic excellence and the joint attractions of subtle gradations of tone combined with skilled application of colour which were exploited by a new generation of publishers were largely contributory to the boom in London illustration, there is no doubt that the widespread collecting of prints and illustrated volumes owed much of its impetus to a single volume, itself not lavishly illustrated, Thomas Pennant's *Of London*, first published in 1790.

This work by a Flintshire naturalist, the 'Tourist' whose powers of observation were praised by Dr Johnson, is a sober and traditional one-volume history of central London full of allusions to royal and noble persons. It was supplied by its publisher, Robert Faulder, with only a handful of antiquarian plates which were mostly etched by John Carter. Its appearance however coincided with the craze for extra-illustrating historical works which was inspired by the publication of the Rev James Granger's *Biographical History of England* (2 vols, 1769). This book gave rise to a number of portrait collections apparently published solely that they might be cut out and laid down on the blank sheets of interleaved copies, facing the biographies of their subjects, much as in more recent years foreign postage stamps were stuck down in albums on a page printed with useful information concerning their country of origin. Thus was born the hobby of 'grangerizing', a clipping, matching and pasting operation which must have helped many a Regency family circle to pass winter evenings with pleasure and instruction. In due course similar treatment was meted out to Pennant's book, and publishers, artists, engravers and printsellers all joined forces to encourage this new pastime, which may be christened 'pennantizing'. For at least four decades from its first publication collections of views and illustrated books on London were published with an eye to the needs of such collectors who continually sought fresh engravings to swell the corpulence of their ever expanding interleaved sets of volumes. A side effect of this pursuit was to create a fresh market for some of the 'Granger' portraits because Pennant was an obliging historical name-dropper.

In January 1791, hard upon the publication of *Of London*, the engraver John Thomas Smith completed the first plates of his series *Antiquities of London* (no 70) whose title-page alludes to 'the much admired works of Mr. Pennant, Stowe, Weaver, Camden, Maitland etc.' He further hedged his bets by allusions on some of the individual plates to the books by Strype, Lysons and Granger. He was on familiar ground since he had long been making drawings of London scenes for the collector William Crowle, whose vast extra-illustrated Pennant was to become a 'pièce de résistance' of the British Museum Department of Prints and Drawings, where Smith himself became Keeper. By 1800 he had completed 95 plates in the series which was subsequently issued as a bound volume. In 1810 he embarked upon another set of plates, *Ancient Topography of London* (no 115), which gave specific page references to Pennant's volume and in 1815 was equipped with a printed title-page for binding. In the interval between these two collections Smith published his *Antiquities of Westminster* (no 98). This contains 100 plates: some facsimiles of older prints and some original work reproduced in various mediums such as line, aquatint and even one inky lithograph, claimed to be the first application of this technique to book illustration. Some hand-coloured plates of antiquities in St Stephen's Chapel are particularly interesting and the whole attractive collection is a distinct landmark in the history of topographical illustration; it is not therefore surprising that the plates were much in demand for extra-illustration and one of their captions refers to 'the late ingenious & accurate Pennant'. Print dealers' cellars were scoured for old copper plates which could be re-engraved and printed off. In 1815 Robert Wilkinson had on offer a folio of 'Forty-Nine Plates engraved by Hollar, for Dugdale's *Monasticon* and *History of St Paul's Cathedral*'.

Pennant's own publisher, Faulder, issued a miscellany of *Illustrations to Mr Pennant and Mr Lyson's History* (no 77), some of the plates used being apparent survivors from Morden and Lea's *Prospects*, with instructions as to where they were to be pasted into Pennant's third edition, specially printed on Large Paper in 1793. About 20 years later John Bowles's *British Views* was reprinted with other Bowles plates and issued as a multi-purpose extra-illustration kit (no 105) accompanied by a table of volume and page references to the fourth edition of Pennant, to Strype and Maitland and to Malcolm's *Londinium Redivivum*. Vernor & Hood, who had published some *Select Views of London and its Environs* (no 90) etched by James Storer and John Greig, proceeded to reissue the plates, without their accompanying texts, as *Pennant's Account of London Illustrated*. In this collection the engravers introduced vignetted subjects, a hallmark of their partnership, which helped to break the monotony of the customary rectangular prints. This device became very popular in early Victorian book illustration.

An octavo set of Pennant illustrations, both topographical and portrait, was published by J. Coxhead in January 1813 and reissued the year after in book form, with title-page and explanatory text as *The History and Antiquities of London* (no 111). With the issue of further editions of Pennant in 1805 and 1814 printed on Large Paper, the latter specifically intended 'for the illustrator', the scene was now set for the wholesale cannibalization for collectors of books both new and old. In due course a thin trickle of text became completely submerged under a mass of pictorial addenda.

Two outstanding examples of this collecting craze contain a cross-section of London book illustration from Hollar onwards, together with specially commissioned contemporary water-colour drawings. They are the 15 volume set of Pennant illustrated by William Crowle before 1801 and now in the British Museum and the six-volume set once belonging to the notorious banker Henry Fauntleroy, hanged for fraud and forgery in 1824, which was subsequently acquired by Sir John Soane in whose library it still remains. Later collectors, such as the interior decorator Frederick Crace and John Edmund Gardner, found it more convenient to dissociate their illustrations from any text and preferred to keep them more conveniently in portfolios, arranged topographically. Crace's collection, which was catalogued by his son, has been kept together in the British Museum, but the eventual dispersal of Gardner's collection released a veritable flood of prints and drawings for a new generation of collectors. It is described briefly by Philip Norman in the preface to the Burlington Fine Arts Club London exhibition of 1919:

He began when little more than a boy by the purchase for five guineas of an extra-illustrated Pennant and continued buying steadily through a long life. He passed away December 29th, 1899 at the age of 82, having occupied himself with his beloved portfolios on that very day. Among his more important purchases were almost all the original drawings, about 200 in number, made for *Londina Illustra* and 28 folio volumes of sketches by John Carter. Not very many years ago the late J.P. Emslie, who with C.J. Richardson and others carried on the work of previous generations, told the present writer that he had just completed his one thousandth drawing for the Gardner Collection.

Among the beneficiaries of this dispersal was Hermann Marx who, from 1935 to 1942, sought from art dealers and bookshops all the fine London illustrations they could supply. The wheel was brought round full circle when he then caused them to be laid down in an interleaved copy of the 'illustrator's edition' of Pennant's *London*. Thirteen volumes of this work, magnificently bound with illuminated, calligraphic indexes, eventually joined the other treasures of London topography in the British Museum Print Room.

The Age of Aquatint

Two years after the appearance of Pennant's first edition and three after William Gilpin's influential *Observations relative to Picturesque Beauty*, the first London book with aquatints in colour was published, significantly entitled *A Picturesque Tour Through the Cities of London and Westminster* (no 72). Its artist, engraver and publisher was Thomas Malton, the son of an architectural draughtsman, much admired for his delicately tinted drawings of London and numbering among his pupils Thomas Girtin and Turner. He applied to the popular cult of the Picturesque the relatively unknown process of aquatint engraving, admirably adapted for reproducing the delicate gradations of water-colour, and opened a subscription list for a book to be issued in 24 Numbers 'illustrated with the most interesting

scenes of all that adorns and dignifies the metropolis'. Plates were accompanied by an architectural commentary and might be had with or without colour washes; the first Number appeared in June 1792 and the last in March 1801. Samuel Ireland published his own modest sepia aquatints, *Picturesque Views on the River Thames* (no 71), in 1791–2 but was immediately outstripped by the firm of J. & J. Boydell who superseded John Boydell's own earlier line-engraved Thames views, published in his *Collection* (no 47), with a set of 30 drawings by the academician Joseph Farington expertly aquatinted by J.C. Stadler, *An History of the River Thames* (no 75), offered either in monochrome or translucently tinted with thin water-colour washes. Two sets of outsize aquatints of Thames scenery in inner London were executed by William Daniell of the celebrated family of topographical artists: *Six Views of the Metropolis* and *Views of the London Docks* (no 92) were published between 1801 and 1808 and, on account of their large size, are more likely to be found loose in portfolios than bound up with their title-pages. Daniell's most important work, *A Voyage Round Great Britain*, published during the next two decades, surveyed the coastline and includes no London views.

At the head of the subscription list for Malton's *Picturesque Tour* was a 'Mr. Ackermann', no doubt Rudolph Ackermann who at this period had not yet set up shop as a printseller and publisher in the Strand. It was not until 1808 that he opened his own subscription-list for the first, and greatest, of his aquatint-illustrated books, the *Microcosm of London* (no 99), which was issued in monthly Numbers completed for binding into three volumes by 1810. It was through his organizing genius that characters as diverse as Augustus Pugin and Thomas Rowlandson were able to collaborate in apparent harmony in producing plates over so long a period. It is possible that each of these artists engraved his share of the subject, Pugin the architecture and Rowlandson the staffage, directly onto the plates, which were then passed to an experienced team of aquatint engravers. After the plates had been printed off a small army of hand colourists applied washes as indicated on the original sketches. All this had to be achieved within a tight schedule of monthly Numbers, each containing four plates with accompanying text. The same two artists also inaugurated a set of 18 much larger aquatint views of London which emanated from the same publisher between 1811 and 1822 (no 221).

Ackermann followed up his *Microcosm* with *The History of the Abbey Church of St Peter's Westminster* (no 108), which he described as a continuation. Subscription arrangements were similar (the first Number being published in May 1811) and so were the production methods; Pugin was again responsible for some of the drawings, and much the same team of aquatint engravers was engaged, but Rowlandson had no part in this sequel. Pugin was still working for Ackermann in 1816 when he produced sets of aquatint plates of nine public schools, issued collectively as *The History of the Colleges* (no 116). Thirty years later these three fine Ackermann books were still available, and at a quarter of their published price, from the bookseller Nattali of Covent Garden.

Among the engravers employed on this *History* was Daniel Havell of a family whose members were associated with topographical art and aquatint engraving. Other famous plates of his illustrate E.W. Brayley's *Historical and Descriptive Accounts of the Theatres of London* (no 148), and he collaborated with his son Robert in the series *Picturesque Views on the River Thames* (1812, from Windsor up stream only). Twelve aquatint views drawn and engraved by Robert and his son of the same name, *Public Buildings and Bridges in London* (no 133), were published by Colnaghi in 1820–1 and the younger Robert also engraved a 14 foot *Panorama of London taken from Nature*, extending from Putney down stream to Greenwich, which was published in the next year and was in the tradition of the 'Long View' by Samuel and Nathaniel Buck (no 54) and Henry Aston Barker's aquatint 'Panorama' of 1792. Finally a nephew of Daniel, F.J. Havell, contributed steel-engravings to Elmes's *Metropolitan Improvements* (no 154). Again the Thames was the theme of miniature aquatints by John Hassell published in 1823, *Excursions of Pleasure* (no 140) and of the last aquatint book published by Rudolph Ackermann senior, William Westall's *Picturesque Tour of the River Thames* (no 157); both were issued in hand-coloured editions.

More of the Thames

The Cookes were a family who had originally made their name with topographical engraving on copper before they adapted their talents to steel plates. The brothers, George and William Bernard, were skilled craftsmen who engraved for Britton and Brayley's *Beauties of England and Wales* and George's son Edward was a talented draughtsman and painter of maritime and riverine subjects, delighting specially in detailed accounts of shipping and tackle. In 1811 William Bernard engraved Samuel Owen's sketches for *The Thames* (no 106) and in 1822 both brothers produced a seond edition for which they engraved extra drawings by De Wint, Francia, Turner and others. Both these editions consist chiefly of views up and down stream from London but include also a few urban riverside views, a formula settled on by Boydell for his line-engravings, adopted by most publishers of Thames aquatint books and repeated in Tombleson's *Thames* (no 178), a set of steel-engravings distinguished by their delicate ornamental frames appropriate to and yet subordinated to each subject. The year of George Cooke's death saw the completion and publicaton of his *Views in London and its Vicinity* (no 149) for which he had engraved on copper drawings by Clarkson Stanfield, Samuel Prout, John Sell Cotman, his own son Edward and others. Edward's outstanding contribution to London topographical illustration is the series of etchings *Views of the Old and New London Bridges* (no 172), as complete an artistic record as one could desire of the demolition and erection that took place between 1830 and 1832.

The peak of the early nineteenth century river cult is reached in a set of lithographs by William Parrott, *London from the Thames* (no 198). Sumptuously coloured by hand, they depict views from Greenwich up stream to Chelsea and, although unaccompanied by text, must be reckoned the most delightful dozen Thames illustrations of any period.

Architectural Illustrations

Ackermann, throughout the entire period 1809–29 which saw the publication of his magnificent illustrated books, also published a monthly magazine, *The Repository of the Arts*. In this also the illustrations were the centre of attraction and included small aquatinted plates of topographical and architectural subjects individually coloured by hand. This particular series must have been well received since the publisher thought it worth reviving it in book form as *Select Views of London* (no 117) with historical and descriptive comments by J.B. Papworth. Like Pugin, Papworth was an architect and was the designer of Ackermann's second showroom at 101 The Strand. These professionals were employed by him because he correctly judged the current widespread interest in architectural aesthetics and his business acumen told him that the time was ripe for urban topographical books to be written and illustrated by authors and artists with some understanding of the subject.

In the previous century architects had not been much concerned with such works, with the exception of Thomas Malton, the first topographical illustrator with specifically architectural training, and Paul Sandby, skilled both as an etcher and a military surveyor. Austere measured plans and elevations of London buildings did indeed appear in professional compilations like Colen Campbell's *Vitruvius Britannicus* (no 24) and its sequels (nos 34, 45) and in architects' pattern-books such as William Kent's *Designs of Inigo Jones* (1727) or James Gibbs's *Book of Architecture* (1727–8), but in general the preference of that age was for the birds-eye view popularized by L. Knyff and J. Kip in *Nouveau Théâtre de la Grande Bretagne* (no 22). These were succeeded by 'perspective' or 'optical' views designed to afford stereoscopic entertainment, in which backgrounds, foregrounds and staffage were added to the outlines of the buildings to lend realism to the picture. Benjamin Cole, the illustrator of Maitland's *History* in its second edition, went in for drawing as spare as Campbell's but much less accurate and the descriptive text accompanying his plates astonishingly makes no reference whatever to the names of the architects.

A fashion for architectural subjects in roundels, as though viewed through an 'oeil-de-boeuf', was perhaps set by the eight circular compartments on the walls of the Court Room of the Foundling Hospital which were filled in with views of London hospitals contributed by celebrated painters who included Gainsborough, Richard Wilson and Samuel Wale. S.W. Fores published 24 such roundels, engraved, with the title *Principal Build-ings of London* (no 73), and another collection pompously entitled *The Public Edifices of the British Metropolis* (no 135) reprinted roundels engraved originally for the periodical *The Temple of Taste* between 1794 and 1796. These small illustrations are less notable for accurate rendering of architectural detail than for their decorative qualities, almost as if they had been intended as designs for tiles or dinner plates. They were in the drawing-book tradition of outlines for amateur colourists.

In 1810 H. Setchel & Son started issuing a series of engravings with the title *Architectural Series of London Churches* based on water-colours by George Shepherd, John Coney and William Pearson. These were collected in 1819 in a folio volume published by John Booth, *Architectura Ecclesiastica Londini* (no 129), and provide an invaluable record of the appearance of nearly all the churches then in existence. In 1812 John Britton included in his series *The Fine Arts of the English School* Edmund Aikin's descriptive essay on St Paul's Cathedral illustrated with measured drawings by another architect, James Elmes, and he was at the same time engaged on editing *The Architectural Antiquities of Great Britain* (no 97), which includes essays on the Temple Church and Henry VII Chapel in Westminster Abbey. The whole of the Abbey was soon to be portrayed in detail for E.W. Brayley's *The History and Antiquities of the Abbey Church of St Peter Westminster* (no 123) in which fine etchings from drawings by J.P. Neale convey even more strikingly in black and white the 'genius loci' than do Ackermann's coloured aquatints after Pugin. It was Pugin who was joint editor with Britton of a work, published like the *Architectural Antiquities* by J. Taylor of the Architectural Library, entitled *Illustrations of the Public Buildings of London* (no 146), whose text is visually enlivened by delicate outline-etchings of elevations, interiors and plans drawn by Pugin, his pupils and other architecturally trained draughtsmen. Its subjects include chapels, churches, theatres, hospitals and other institutions and also private houses—a wide range of buildings both new and old—so that it is really a precursor of Sir Nikolaus Pevsner's volumes on London.

Among its engravers was John Le Keux, who specialized in architectural work and was consistently associated with Britton's publications. He also worked on the numerous steel-engravings in *The Churches of London* (no 189) whose text was written by an architect, George Godwin, assisted by John Britton. These exterior and interior views from drawings by Robert Billings and Frederick Mackenzie, variegated with vignetted woodcuts, perfectly set the scene for Dickens's essay 'City of London Churches'. An old church which had just been replaced by its modern successor is the subject of J.F. Denham's *Views Exhibiting the Exterior and Interior of St Dunstan in the West* (no 166) with lithographs by W. Gauci after drawings by T.T. Bury, who was an architect. Britton once again joined forces with E.W. Brayley for *The History of the Ancient Palace and late Houses of Parliament at Westminster* (no 181), another title from the Architectural Library, which set out to record for posterity by measured drawings what remained after the conflagration of October 1834, which was so glowingly depicted by Turner. Its outline-etchings were mainly based on drawings by a pupil of Britton's, the architect Robert Billings, who to forestall the demolition squad must have installed himself with his drawing-board among the still warm ashes of the Palace.

The Age of Steel

Just as Ackermann's *Microcosm* established aquatint engraving as the ideal process of illustration for expensive topographical works with a limited circulation so, 20 years after, did *London in the Nineteenth Century* (nos 154, 161) launch engraving on steel as the perfect medium for reproducing views in books intended for a larger and more popular audience. Its success may be largely attributed to the artistry, topographical accuracy and tireless application of its draughtsman, Thomas Shepherd, who in four years produced all the drawings on which were based the engravings of its two component volumes, *Metropolitan Improvements* and *London and its Environs in the Nineteenth Century*. The association of the architect James Elmes with the work was some guarantee of mere pictorial authenticity but to this Shepherd added a new dimension which makes the 'antiquarian' style of J.T. Smith, Storer and Greig and of many of Robert Wilkinson's engravers look decidedly old-fashioned. He humanized the architectural settings by introducing into them really lifelike men and women, children, horses, dogs and conveyances, all

going about their business or amusement, yet the topographical accuracy of the streets is in no way impaired because they are washed with the tide of weekday animation. In no book since the *Microcosm*, on which two artists were engaged, had London been shown as such a lively capital. Moreover the durability of the new medium of steel enabled the publisher to multiply impressions in response to the demand resulting from its well-deserved popularity.

An earlier work by a pioneer of steel-engraving was Charles Heath's *Views of London* (no 147). His 45 views, after De Wint, William Westall and Frederick Mackenzie, were engraved on small plates in a style anticipating that of the 'Keepsakes' and 'Books of Beauty' with which he later made his name. This charming work was almost first in the field for steel-engraved London views, being preceded only by five even smaller plates engraved by William Cooke junior for Sholto and Reuben Percy's *London* (no 142).

Royal Palaces and T.H. Shepherd

Interior views of buildings, so attractive an innovation in Ackermann's *Microcosm*, play a preponderant part among the fine aquatints in *History of the Royal Residences* (no 132), which was not his publication but was written by one of his literary collaborators, W.H. Pyne. The state apartments, however, are depicted with soulless formality, populated primarily by framed oil paintings and furniture and totally lacking the animation typical of *Microcosm* interiors. Such animation is to be found in the drawings of T.H. Shepherd for the steel plates of *London Interiors with their Costumes and Ceremonies* (no 195), for they are replete with the human interest that characterizes all his work. He has wonderfully captured not only the Victorian interior but also Victorian sentiment in, to take an instance, 'Commander in Chief's Levee, Horse Guards', a poignant group of a soldier's young widow heavily veiled in weeds presenting her schoolboy son to the bluff and kindly Colonel Newcome of an officer.

The name T.H. Shepherd has constantly recurred in this narrative not only for the quantity and quality of his own work but also on account of its considerable influence on other illustrators. He was himself responsible for the drawings on which were based the small engravings published as a booklet by John Harris, *The Public Buildings of the City of London Described* (no 170), and probably also those in the companion volume, *The Buildings of Westminster Described* (no 169). He was chief draughtsman for C.F. Partington's *Natural History and Views of London* (no 177) for which he supplied literally hundreds of diminutive sketches engraved on steel by J. Shury, five miniatures to each plate. Although Woods's *History of London* (no 188) was published on the threshold of Victoria's reign its illustrations bear a strong family resemblance to those of a decade earlier in Shepherd's *London in the Nineteenth Century* both in their style of drawing and engraving and even in the dimensions of the area worked. This is not a matter for surprise since Shepherd did himself draw some of its views and his fellow artists both emulated his style and injected into their street scenes that human interest which he so successfully brought to bear on topographical illustration. Also it is noteworthy that one of these artists was Hablot Browne, already at this time associated with Charles Dickens and soon to win fame as his illustrator 'Phiz'; so here indeed is an evocation of Mr Pickwick's London. Two other artistic contributors to Woods's *History*, Robert Garland and John Salmon, had already been associated with Browne in H. and B. Winkles's *Cathedral Churches of Great Britain* (no 184) to which, at the age of 20, he had contributed illustrations of St Paul's Cathedral.

A complementary set of plates, often bound up with Woods's *History*, is the *Select Illustrated Topography of Thirty Miles Round London* (no 190). Most of these are from drawings by Charles Marshall, whose profession of scene-painter might be deduced from the theatrical 'Vauxhall Gardens' view. The combined plates from both works were reprinted and, together with an augmentation of the text by Fearnside, reissued by Thomas Holmes at the time of the Great Exhibition as *Holmes's Great Metropolis* (no 211). A synonymous title was given to another book published specifically for the same occasion, *The World's Metropolis or Mighty London* (no 213). This sumptuous memento for Great Exhibition visitors consists of a text accompanied by about 80 steel-engravings of scenes in London and its environs (of which over a quarter are based on T.H. Shepherd's drawings), a map and a variable

number of lithographs of interiors and exteriors of the Crystal Palace in which the exhibition was housed. The work was published simultaneously in London and Paris and issued originally in Parts. At about the same time George Sidney Shepherd, Thomas's brother, drew for Rudolph Ackermann's son a series of ten views of London and its environs (no 209) which were lithographed by Thomas Picken and published as uncoloured or hand-coloured lithotints.

The most beautiful and widely known lithographic views of London were published at the beginning of the previous decade and it is fitting that an account of books illustrating general London topography should be brought to a close with a mention of the splendid folio entitled *London as it is* (no 196). This consists of 26 unsurpassed views of early Victorian London issued either in monochrome or coloured by hand, with commentary by Charles Ollier. Now a very rare book, its plates are nevertheless widely known through copies and facsimiles and no other picture book gives a more vivid impression of the architectural splendours and the medley of high and low life, juxtaposed luxury and wretchedness, which made up the Victorian street scene.

'Souvenir Programmes' and Special Topics

One further category of London illustrations which calls for mention is that of sets of occasional prints, celebrating some royal or national event such as a coronation, military victory, peace conference or state funeral. Such mementoes usually took the form of a single inscribed engraving, or perhaps a pair, but sometimes they were published as a kind of souvenir programme with descriptive text and a number of illustrations. As was only fitting the artist tended to pay more attention to the important persons and their attendants than to the topographical background but there are instances of sufficient local colour being sketched in to lend the plates some topographical interest. One of the earliest of these descriptions, with a text by Puget de La Serre, was a record of the state visit of Marie de Medici to her daughter, Queen Henrietta Maria, *L'Histoire de l'Entrée de la Reyne Mère* (no 3), which besides engraved views of St James's Palace and the Pool of London contains a famous panorama of Cheapside. The arrival in England of Catharine of Braganza, in August 1662, was celebrated in seven large line-engravings by Dirck Stoop, of which the last depicts the aquacade arriving at Whitehall Stairs (no 10). Francis Sandford's *History of the Coronation of James II* (no 16) is illustrated with interiors of Westminster Abbey and Hall after William Sherwin's sketches. There were also souvenirs of the coronation of James I (no 1) and Charles II (no 9), produced respectively by Stephen Harrison and John Ogilby, but they have little topographical significance since they were intended chiefly as a graphic record of the triumphal arches erected by the City of London to cheer the monarchs during their sluggish progress towards Westminster.

Edward Orme published a lavish commemoration of Lord Nelson, with illustrations of his funeral (no 220), and eight years later a souvenir of the junketings in Hyde Park to celebrate jointly the peace with France and the Jubilee of the House of Brunswick (no 112). This latter comprised six coloured aquatints engraved by M. Dubourg who was also responsible for some of the magnificent plates in Sir George Nayler's splendid folio,

Coronation of George IV (no 232). Soon after he was engaged on further plates for *An Impartial Historical Narrative* (no 226) of the unhappy sequel to that coronation in which the King tried, unsuccessfully, to divorce Queen Caroline.

A very different event, the aftermath of the burning down of the Armoury of the Tower of London in October 1841, was drawn on the spot by J. Cater and W. Oliver and published in six lithotints by Colnaghi & Puckle (no 197). A well-illustrated account of the Tower had been published some 20 years before, John Brayley's *History and Antiquities of the Tower of London* (no 136), with good engravings by John Pye with the collaboration of Frederick Nash and the architect Edward Blore. There are three other important publications concerned with particular localities: two on the Inns of Court, Samuel Ireland's *Picturesque Views* (no 81), illustrated with his own sepia aquatints, and *Antiquities* (no 88) by William Herbert with etched plates by James Storer and John Greig, and an interesting Ackermann folio, F.I. Mannskirsch's large aquatints in colour, *Views of Parks and Gardens* (no 110).

CHRONOLOGICAL NUMBERED LIST OF BOOKS

LIST OF ILLUSTRATIONS

EXPLANATION OF THE CATALOGUE

The catalogue describes 238 books and sets of prints published over two and a half centuries and containing over 8,000 plates which illustrate London by means of line-engraving, etching or lithography. Excluded are books illustrated by wood-engravings printed with the letterpress or solely by an engraved frontispiece or map.

'London' for the purposes of this work embraces approximately the area shown on Shury's Plan of 1832, presented to *United Kingdom Newspaper* readers and recently reissued in facsimile by the Greater London Council; this coincides approximately with the area covered by the Crace Collection of maps, plans and views of London in the British Museum. It embraces the Cities of London and Westminster with Bloomsbury and extends southward to Lambeth, Southwark and Bermondsey and northward to Marylebone, Clerkenwell, Finsbury and Tower Hamlets. These limits are adhered to strictly only when selecting plates from those books which cover a wider area (eg Surrey or Great Britain), whose headings are distinguished by an asterisk. All plates in books covering both the environs and the central area are enumerated but no books are included which are concerned exclusively with the environs, as for instance Lyson's *Environs of London,* Ellis's *Campagna of London,* Cromwell's *Walks through Islington* or Westall's *Twenty-Five Views on the Thames.* The suburban scene is gradually being described in the current series 'Images of London' (Ackermann Publishing), and books on the Thames, other than Westall's, usually survey its whole course including the City, Westminster, Lambeth and Southwark and so are eligible for listing 'in toto' here.

Collections of early views purporting to illustrate London are usually based on the general work *Nouveau Théâtre de la Grande Bretagne* and thus often include provincial makeweights from as far afield as Ripon Cathedral, Stainborough Hall in Yorkshire and Longleat in Wiltshire; these, for the sake of completeness, are listed along with the London views.

In order to confine the catalogue within manageable bounds the following have been left out:

(a) Works of predominantly antiquarian, rather than topographical or architectural, inspiration.
(b) Monographs on the work of a single architect (eg Gibbs's *Book of Architecture*).
(c) Almanacks, annuals and magazines.

Maps of the central London area have been listed where they occur but are more thoroughly described in *Printed maps of London circa 1553–1850* by Ida Darlington and James Howgego and in Ralph Hyde's *Ward maps of the City of London.*

Book Descriptions

These take the form of:

(a) Notes on the volume's publishing history and its illustrations.
(b) A transcript of the title-page, omissions from wordy titles being indicated by an ellipsis and line endings indicated for engraved titles.
(c) Collation, including the page measurement of an average copy in millimetres.
(d) Check-list of London plates, each described in appropriate detail from the following:

1 Reference to the page of text opposite which the plate is bound in a standard copy.

2 Transcription of the caption, with indication of position other than in the bottom margin.

3 Credits for artist, engraver, architect.

4 Publication-line, with ellipses substituted for the formulas 'As the Act directs' or 'According to Act of Parliament'.

5 Measurements in millimetres of the engraved area and plate-mark (where measurable) in the form '210 × 324/220 × 330mm', implying an engraved area 210mm in height and 324mm in breadth, within a plate-mark of 220 × 330mm. The first two measurements exclude marginal lettering. When the view is in an engraved frame the frame measurements are inserted before the plate-mark. When the work has no geometrical boundary line only the plate measurement is given. Variable shrinkage of the damp paper, when it dries after printing, limits the accuracy of such measurements to within about 5mm.

6 A note further defining the subject or its date, when this is necessary (eg London Bridge, 'Viewed from the E.', or Goldsmith's Hall, 'built 1748').

7 The plate number assigned by the publisher, if different from the catalogue item number.

8 The Part or Number with which the print was included, in publications issued over a period.

9 Summary of keyed references engraved on maps or long views.

10 An indication, when helpful, of catalogues or iconographies which refer to the print or to the drawing on which it is based, or of the collections in which they are to be found. Details of books and catalogues referred to are given in the bibliography.

11 References to predecessors for plates related to a view published in a former work. (However, in any given list reference to the relevant catalogue number is only made at its first mention in that entry, which frequently occurs in the notes on the volume's publishing history. In order to ascertain a catalogue number for a predecessor, etc it is therefore sometimes necessary to refer back.)

Identification of Prints

Correspondence of a selection of these factors enumerated should make it possible to identify the source of plates separated from the books with which they were published, while the topographical index and the index to credits, titles and selected publishers provide ready access to the individual items. Undated plates can be dated approximately from the title-page of the work they illustrate or from the date of the publisher's Number with which they were first issued.

For 'points' which help to date impressions of colour plates reference should be made to the Abbey catalogue, *Scenery of Great Britain, in aquatint and lithography, 1770–1860*, and to R.V. Tooley's *English books with colour plates 1790–1860*.

1 Detail of William Kip's engraving of one of the seven triumphal arches put up to welcome James I to his new capital. This model of the City crowned that in Fenchurch Street (1/2). *Guildhall Library, City of London*

2 Another royal occasion, pictured by the court painter Stoop: the landing of Charles II and his Portuguese bride at Whitehall Stairs in 1662 (10/7). *Guildhall Library, City of London*

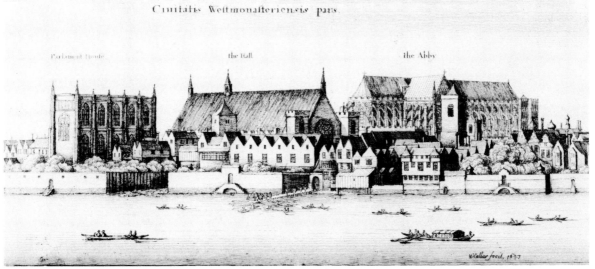

3 The most familiar of eight numbered London views engraved by Hollar in 1647. It shows Westminster Palace dominated by St Stephen's Chapel, the Hall and the Abbey with only rudimentary western towers (5/5). *Guildhall Library, City of London*

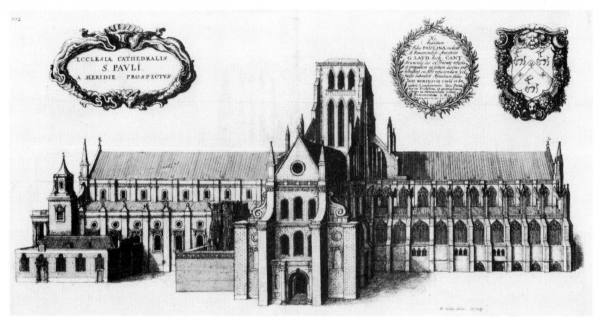

4 Hollar's plate, from Dugdale's *History of St Paul's* shows the medieval cathedral, now spireless, viewed from the south, the decorated Gothic chapter house looking out of place beside Inigo Jones's casing of nave and transept (8/36). *Guildhall Library, City of London*

5 Fanciful view of the Tower of London from the first considerable set of London prospects, engraved for Robert Morden and Philip Lea (15/11). *Guildhall Library, City of London*

6 Based on Morden and Lea's set are the plates issued by the Dutch publisher Van Bulderen with Misson de Valbourg's English travels, such as this one of the Royal Exchange (19/4).

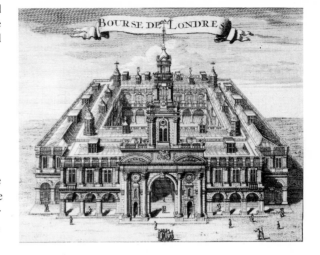

7 The decorative qualities of the engravings used by the Leiden publisher Van der Aa in his *Délices* volumes are shown by this view of the 'Holbein' Gate on a 'trompe-l'oeil' scroll in a park setting (20/28). *Guildhall Library, City of London*

Part of WHITE-HALL to the THAMES

8   A Dutch view of Whitehall Palace prior to the fire of 1698. The royal barge of King William and Queen Mary is leaving the Stairs (17/10). *Guildhall Library, City of London*

9   Old Somerset House, the palace of Queen Catherine of Braganza, drawn by Knyff and engraved by Kip for the *Nouveau théâtre*. Moored in the foreground is the houseboat or 'Folly' which provided music, drink and prostitutes (22/6). *Guildhall Library, City of London*

10   The great gateway designed by Colen Campbell in 1718 for Lord Burlington's house in Piccadilly, as engraved by Hulsbergh for *Vitruvius Britannicus*; it appears also in the popular satirical print 'Taste or Burlington Gate' (24/42).

11   Birds-eye view of the Charterhouse, typical of the plates engraved by J. Kip for the first illustrated edition of Stow's *Survey* published in 1720 (25/14).

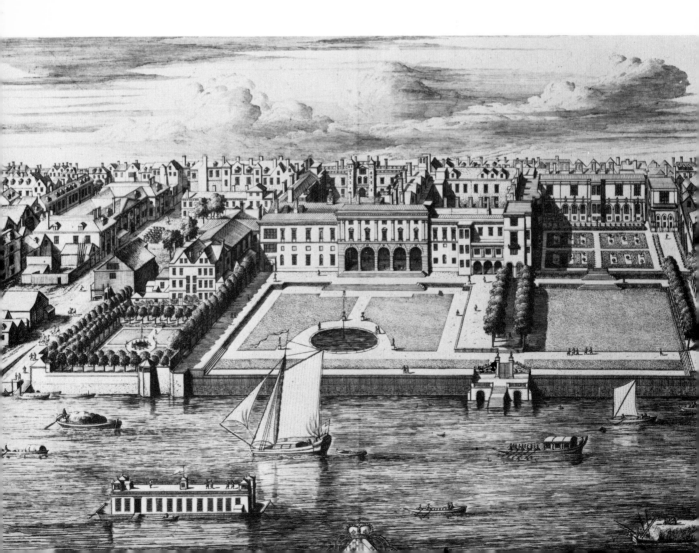

Le grand Porte de Maison Burlington dans Pickadilly a Londres.

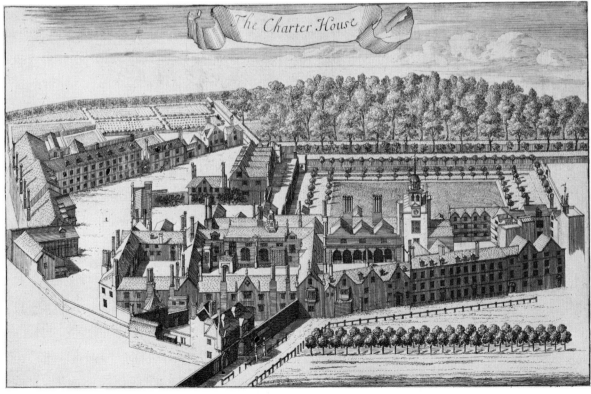

The Charter House

PROSPECTS
of the most remarkable places in and about the City of London, Neatly Engraved

Veues des toutes les endroites que est plus remarquable aussi bien celles dans le Ville de Londre que d'alentour, Gravé fort Curieusement.

Printed & Sold by Hen. Overton at ye White Horse without Newgate 1739.

12   Engraved bilingual title, dated 1739, to Henry Overton's large collection of views in London and elsewhere, with a standard panorama from a Southwark viewpoint (26/1).

13   Anonymous engraving of the Mansion House, in the 'Prospect' tradition, apparently specially commissioned to illustrate *Londres et ses environs* of 1788 (65/3).

14   John Bowles's *Prospects*, contemporary with Overton's, included in the engraving a short history of the subject, as on this Guildhall interior (28/18).

15   Sutton Nicholls's birds-eye view of Covent Garden and Soho from John Bowles's 1731 collection *London Described*, which also includes similar views of the squares later used in the second illustrated edition of Stow's *Survey* (29/26). *Guildhall Library, City of London*

Inside of Guild Hall.

This Hall is very Spacious and Stately, suited to the greatness & magnificence of the City. It is adorn'd with several Standards & Banners &c: taken at the Battle of Ramillies in 1706. The Intercolumns are embellished with the Pictures of 18 Judges, who determined the difference between Landlord & Tenant in rebuilding the City. At the East end are if Portraits of K. William, Q. Mary, Q. Ann & K. George. Over the Steps going into the Mayors Courts, at some height stand two Giants of Monstrous height and bigness, the one holding a Pole ax, the other a Halbert. Upon the Capital of the Pillars against the Walls, are the Royal Arms, The Arms of the City, and of the twelve Companys &c. This Spacious Receptacle for the Citizens being damaged by the Great Fire, was afterwards repaired at the Expence of £.2500.

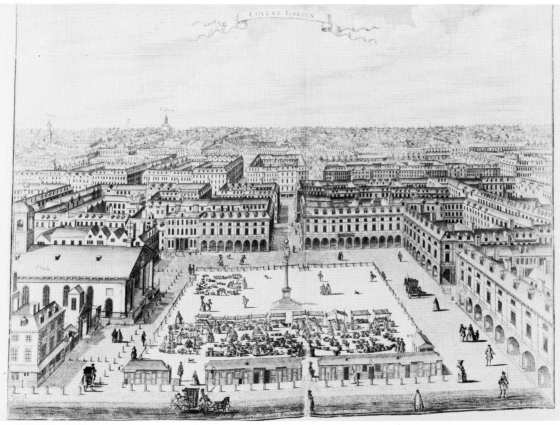

COVENT GARDEN

GUILD HALL

16 Thomas Bowles, the brother of the printseller John Bowles, in this plate of the Guildhall forecourt, engraved for Seymour's *Survey* of 1734, has improved upon the view by Kip in the 1720 edition of Stow (30/9).

17 St Dunstan in the West. One of two series of a dozen plates, each published by Robert West and the engraver W.H. Toms between 1737 and 1739; a unique source for churches which survived the Great Fire (32/17). *Guildhall Library, City of London*

18   This charming engraving, after a painting by Joseph Nichols, shows Middle Temple Hall and the fountain, then enclosed with railings to form a Benchers' garden. It was published by Boydell in 1753 and collected in 1770 (47/44). *Guildhall Library, City of London*

19   W.H. Toms engraved many of the plates for Maitland's *History*, first published in 1739; in this one he greatly magnifies the tower and steeple of Wren's St Mary-le-Bow (38/65).

20   A mid-century Venetian spectacle on the shores of the Thames at Ranelagh with the Rotunda in the background, drawn by Canaletto and engraved by N. Parr for the printsellers Sayer and Overton (191/59). *Guildhall Library, City of London*

21 New Square, Lincoln's Inn, looking in 1761, apart from the central basin and obelisk, much as it does today. Engraved by Fougeron from Wale's wash drawing for Dodsley's illustrated gazetteer (41/48).

22 One of 24 'Public Edifices' engraved in roundels, first published in Charles Taylor's magazine *The Temple of Taste* and reissued in 1820 as a collection (135/2).

23-4 This undistinguished, anonymous view in Whitehall was issued in an engraved, beaded frame by John Cooke with Chamberlain's *New and Complete History* of 1770. Five years later he reused this plate and others in Harrison's *New and Universal History* after the engraver had burnished out the frames and extended the views to fill the vacancy, as may be seen here (48/54; 57/65).

London, Publish'd by C.Taylor Holborn Dec.r 1, 1795

SIDE VIEW OF St PAULS, LONDON.

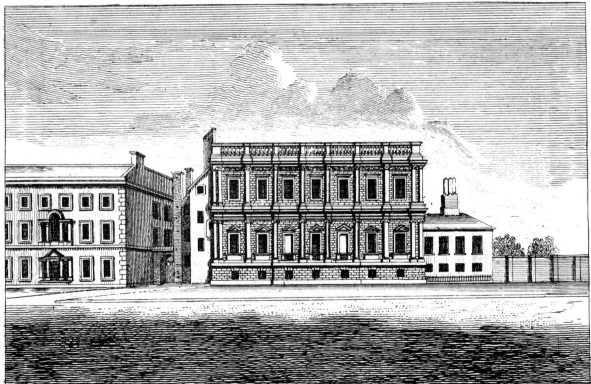

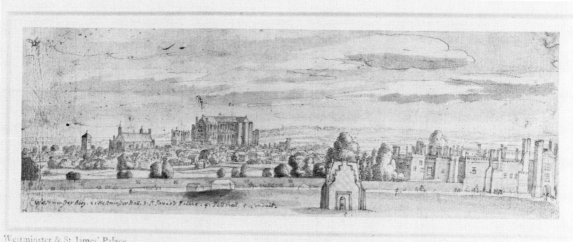

Westminster & St James' Palace

25-6 The remarkable Hollar drawing from the Royal Collection, taken from a viewpoint approximating to the present St James's Square, shows seventeenth century Westminster, dominated by the Hall and the Abbey, as if it were a cathedral city surrounded by open country. Engraved by R. Godfrey in 1775 and published by Francis Grose in his *Antiquarian Repertory* it was immediately taken up by John Cooke and other popular publishers. (56/5). *pl. 25 reproduced by gracious permission of Her Majesty the Queen; pl. 26 Museum of London*

(ROSAMOND'S POND.)

27 From J.T. Smith's first collection, *Antiquities of London*, in which most of the plates are austere, antiquarian etchings. Here, however, the elegiac mood of the copperplate inscription below is reflected in the gloomy, etched foreground of the view and its soft, billowing, aquatinted clouds (70/23).

28 Thomas Malton drew and engraved for his *Picturesque Tour* four aquatints of the Adam brothers' Adelphi which, after a financially shaky start, was by now a fashionable address; this one views the block from the Thames, looking towards Westminster (72/29). *Guildhall Library, City of London*

29   One of a set of plates published by Colnaghi; in the foreground are the domed entrance hall and Ionic portico added by Henry Holland in 1787, and the southward continuation of Whitehall is shown, dividing into Parliament Street and King Street (76/3).

30   In his second collection, *Antiquities of Westminster*, J.T. Smith was more adventurous in choice of medium. Aquatint was particularly suitable for reproducing this idyllically rustic scene of market gardening off Millbank in 1807 (98/95).

31   Ackermann's *Microcosm of London* is probably of all illustrated London books the most widely appreciated. Yet its brilliant plates always produce a fresh shock of pleasure; Rowlandson has found in the quarrelsome fishwives a subject after his own heart (99/9). *Guildhall Library, City of London*

32   The view by Edward Dayes down Fish Street Hill shows the Monument, St Magnus Church and the niched footway across old London Bridge. This is a case of illustrations by an able topographical artist being used in a second-rate book (107/7). *Guildhall Library, City of London*

33   St Dionis Backchurch, a Wren church which stood at the corner of Lime Street and Fenchurch Street, was demolished over 100 years ago. The excellent engravings of *Architectura Ecclesiastica Londini* portray 123 London churches, many of which, like this one, have ceased to exist (129/36). *Guildhall Library, City of London*

34 The Gothic conservatory, leading from the dining room to the garden of Carlton House. Designed by Henry Holland with interior by Gaubert, it had aisles, armorial stained-glass windows and fan-vaulting filled with clear glass in lieu of vaulting stones. Notice the hexagonal lanterns for use after dusk (132/99).

35 R.B. Schnebbelie, the principal draughtsman for Wilkinson's *Londina Illustrata*, made the drawing for this print of Furnival's Inn, a former Inn of Chancery, when it was being converted into sets of chambers by the contractor William Peto. Waterhouse's pink Prudential Insurance Company now occupies the site of these former Holborn buildings (131/114). *Guildhall Library, City of London*

36, 37 The 20 or so years that separate two important collections of engraved views are manifest in these title-pages, the earlier being decorated with a romantically lighted etched vignette of Temple Bar and the later with a businesslike, squared-up steel-engraving of the Marble Arch, front gate until 1847 to Buckingham Palace (104/3; 186/49).

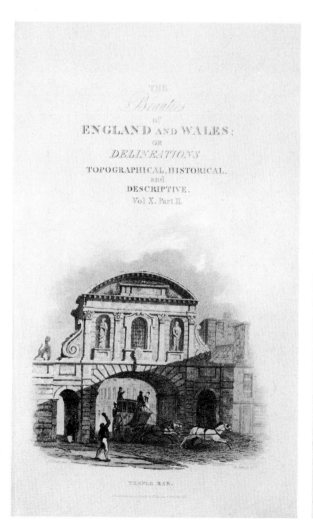

38-9 *Metropolitan Improvements* is largely a celebration of John Nash's shining new West End. His Regent Street (nos 106–30 on the east side) is here shown, both in T.H. Shepherd's original sepia drawing and in the engraved version. The start of the Quadrant shopping arcade is visible beyond Glasshouse Street (154/138). *Museum of London*

40-1 A contrast between the rusticated Watergate, then leading straight down to the bucolic, rushy Thames, as depicted by T.H. Shepherd for *London in the Nineteenth Century*, and the urban elegance of John Le Keux's delicate steel-engraving of a room in Sir John Soane's house, still happily intact in Lincoln's Inn Fields (146/63; 161/37).

42 A good example of John Preston Neale's magnificently atmospheric illustrations to Brayley's history of Westminster Abbey. The engraver has managed to suggest even the motes in the slanting, morning sunbeams (123/32).

43 In this steel-engraving from Tombleson's *Thames* not only is Billingsgate swathed in sails but even the margins of the print are draped in nets and other fishermen's tackle (178/57).

44 Edward Cooke's exhaustive record of the demolition of old London Bridge and the building of the new is exemplified by this plate, engraved by his father, which shows the works in mid-1827 (149/2).

45   The towering massiveness of Hawksmoor's St Anne, Limehouse well conveyed by Robert Garland's drawing and supplied with a funeral party by the Dickens illustrator Hablot Browne (188/23).

46   The quality of Frederick Mackenzie's architectural draughtsmanship is apparent in this light-bathed interior of Wren's finest parish church, St Stephen, Walbrook. It shows how gracefully the columns rose from the top level of the now discarded pews (189/108).

47   *London as it is*, drawn on stone by 'T.S. Boys 1841', as announced on the pedestal of Charles I's equestrian statue. This plate shows Northumberland House, demolished in 1874, and behind Morley's Hotel building, which was replaced in 1933 by South Africa House, and Nash's West Strand development pepperpots, still in evidence (196/20). *Guildhall Library, City of London*

48 The Pool of London, one of William Parrott's splendid set of lithographs showing the Thames from Chelsea to Greenwich. In 1841 paddle-steamers mingle with the usual fishing smacks, merchantmen and barges (198/11). *Guildhall Library, City of London*

49 Parrott's preparatory sepia wash sketch for the lithograph above. Before transferring his design to the stones he made some revisions, such as replacing sailing vessels by pleasure steamers and somewhat distancing the shore (198/11). *Guildhall Library, City of London*

50 The youthful John Gilbert had the entrée to the royal palaces to illustrate them for the very topical *London Interiors*. Here he depicts the Queen and her Consort watching the court artist Winterhalter as he paints their two and a half year old firstborn, little Princess Victoria (195/44).

Abbreviations used in the Catalogue

anon	without credits	lc	left centre
b	born	mm	millimetres
bc	bottom centre	N.	North
Bk	Book	nd	no date
bl	bottom left	No	Number of a part work
BL	British Library Reference Division	no	number of the work in this catalogue
bm	bottom margin	p, pp	page(s)
BM	British Museum, Department of Prints and Drawings	pinx.	pinxit (painted)
		pl.	plate
br	bottom right	Pt	Part
coll	collection	publ.	published
Crace	Crace Collection of maps, plans and views of London (BM)	r.	right
		rc	right centre
Crowle Pennant	Crowle Pennant (BM)	ref, refs	reference(s)
del., delin.	delineavit (drew)	RIBA	British Architectural Library (formerly Royal Institute of British Architects' Library)
dirext.	direxit (under the direction of)		
E.	East		
ed	edition, edited	sc., sculp.	sculpsit (engraved)
engr	engraved, engraver, engraving	sig, sigs	signature(s)
excud.	excudit (printed, published)	t	top
fec.	fecit (etched, engraved)	tc	top centre
front.	frontispiece	tl	top left
GLC	Greater London Council	tm	top margin
inv.	invenit (designed)	tr	top right
K. top.	King's Topographical Collection (BL Map Room)	vol.	volume
		W.	West
l.	left		

LONDON ILLUSTRATED 1604–1851

All books, regardless of their intellectual content,
are specimens of printing, deserving of
bibliographical analysis for what it may disclose
about the printing and publishing practices of the
time.

(From G. Thomas Tanselle's second Hanes Lecture in
the history of the book, quoted in *TLS,* 5 June 1981)

THE CATALOGUE

1 · HARRISON'S ARCHES OF TRIUMPH [1604]

This is not, properly speaking, an illustrated topographical work but a kind of souvenir programme which also illustrates the stage carpentry contributed by Stephen Harrison to the much delayed formal entry of James I into his new capital city and is thus a suitable curtain-raiser to *London Illustrated*. Moreover it was the first book to publish an engraving, other than cartographical, purporting to record the actual appearance of the City at a given date. Its first plate shows a triumphal arch in Fenchurch Street crowned with what was apparently a three-dimensional model of the capital as it then stood. The baptism of a Stephen Harryson on 25 May 1572 was entered on the register of St Dionis Backchurch in Lime Street, but all that is otherwise known about him is that he collaborated with John Webster and Thomas Dekker and designed the settings for the series of entertainments devised to greet the King and Queen and Prince Henry on their triumphal progress through the City.

Harrison combined the skills of architect and joiner. In the second capacity he persuaded the engraver to include on the first plate a small diagram showing the joints used to assemble the component parts of the arches and he continually refers to the arches themselves as 'pegmes', that is jointed scaffolds or platforms which could be assembled for temporary use in theatrical pageants. His set-pieces provide a fitting overture to a reign in which the Court devoted so much time and energy to presenting and being entertained by masques. Inigo Jones, who was to design the sets for many of these performances, was at this time still at the court of Christian IV of Denmark but by Christmas 1604 he was back in England, preparing to present Jonson's *Masque of Blackness* at Whitehall. By then the 'pegmes' would have been dismantled but Kip's pictorial record of them would be circulating at Court as a potential inspiration for the scenic artist. When the masque *Oberon* was presented in January 1611 under Prince Henry's patronage Jones's design for the fairy palace, described by Sir John Summerson as 'nonsense architecture', surely reminded the young prince of those triumphal arches under which he had passed with his parents seven years earlier.

The book must have been much consulted as a precedent by John Ogilby, whose record of the 'Entertainment' (no 9) he provided on a similar occasion in 1662 for James I's grandson includes another such set of triumphal arches engraved by David Loggan.

As stated on the title-page, the procession took place on 15 March 1603 (1603–4) but had been delayed for nearly a year because at the time of the King's arrival from Scotland he had found the City plague-ridden. He therefore prudently bypassed the ceremonial welcome and made his way instead by water from Whitehall to the Tower and thence to Westminster Abbey for his coronation on 25 July 1603. By the end of the year the plague had receded and James decided to make his public entry into London in the following March. Four

3

hundred pounds was raised by the Livery Companies for furnishing the pageants and stands for the occasion, the streets were swept clean and the dropping of litter was prohibited for the three days of the celebration.

The postponement must have caused some dismay to the organizers of the pageant for, in Harrison's words:

These five Triumphall Arches were first taken in hand in the beginning of Aprill 1603: presently after his Maiesty was proclaimed (24 March 1602–3). It being expected that his passage would have bene through his honorable City and Chamber to his Coronation upon St Iames his day following. But by reason of the sicknesse, it pleased his Maiestie to be solemnely Crowned at Westminster without sight of these Triumphs: Notwithstanding the businesse being set on foote, went on with all expedition: till Bartholmew-tide.

The 300 or so workmen employed on building the first five arches downed tools in August because of the spread of plague and resumed work only in February of the following year when the arches at West Cheap and Temple Bar were added. Harrison stage-managed the proceedings, designing all the arches save two which were 'invented' by their sponsors: in Gracechurch Street by the Italian merchants and in Cornhill by the Dutch and Flemish. He gives an interesting itinerary of the procession with its attendant junketings:

His Maiestie departed from the Tower betweene the houres of 11 and 12 and before 5 had made his royal passage through the Citie, having a Canopie borne over him by 8 Knights. The first Object that his Maiesties eye encountered (after his entrance into London) was part of the children of Christ's Church Hospitall, to the number of 300, who were placed in a Scaffold, erected for that purpose in Barking Church-yard by the Tower. The way from the Tower to Temple-Barre was not onely sufficiently gravelled, but all the streetes (lying betweene those two places) were on both sides (where the breadth would permit) rail'd in at the charges of the Citie, Paules Churche-yard excepted. The Liveries of the Companies (having their Streamers, Ensignes and Banerets, spred on the tops of their railes before them) reached from the middle of Marke Lane, to the Pegme at Temple Barre.... The Conduits of Cornehill, of Cheape, and of Fleetes-treete that day ran Claret wine very plenteously: which (by reason of so much excellent Musicke, that sounded foorth not onely from each severall Pegme, but also from diverse other places) ran the faster and more merrily downe into some bodies bellies.

His apologia for the book reads as follows:

Lectori Candido.
Reader, the limmes of these great Triumphall bodies (lately disioynted and taken in sunder) I have thou seest (for thy sake) set in their apt and right places againe: so that now they are to stand as perpetuall monuments, not to be shaken in peeces, or to be broken downe, by the malice of that envious destroyer of all things, Time. Which labours of mine, if they yeeld thee either profit or pleasure thou art (in requitall thereof) to pay manie thankes to this honorable Citie, whose bounty towards me, not onely in making choise of me, to give directions for the intire workmanship of the five Triumphall Arch's builded by the same, but also (in publishing these Peeces,) I do here gladly acknowledge to have bene exceeding liberall.

(*Title-page* pl. 1)

Folio, 362 × 260mm.   1604

COLLATION   Title-page; dedication to Sir T. Bennet, Lord Mayor, dated 16 June 1604, celebratory odes by Thomas Dekker and John Webster (2pp, sig B); Arches of Triumph, explanations and poetical tributes interpolated with plates (14pp, sigs C–I); address to the reader (1 leaf with colophon 'Imprinted at London by Iohn Windet, Printer to the Honourable Citie of London and are to be sold at the Authors house in Lime Street, at the signe of the Snayle, 1604').

The title and seven plates are engraved by William Kip, presumably a Dutchman who engraved a map for Norden's *Speculum Britanniae* in 1598 and in 1607 collaborated with William Hole in over half the maps for a new edition of Camden's *Britannia*. It is tempting to assume that he was a progenitor of Johannes Kip who, in the next century, engraved the first major British topographical collection, *Britannia Illustrata* (no 22). A wood-engraved headpiece of variable length is used to head the dedication, the odes and each page of explanatory text. There are no Kip credits on the plates themselves (apart from the title), only Harrison's, and no captions apart from the text headings. Measurements given are those of the plate-marks.

1 (engr title with strapwork ornaments, birds, masks and carpenter's tools, etc) The Arch's of Triumph/ Erected in honor of the High and/mighty prince James the first of/that name, King of England, and the Sixt of Scotland, at his/Maiesties Entrance and/passage through his Ho:/norable Citty & Chamber/of London upon the/15th day of march/1603/ Invented and published by Stephen Harrison/Joyner and Architect:/and graven by/William/Kip.... (cartouche bc beneath lion mask) Monumentum Aere Perennius. 290 × 205mm. Later issues add an

imprint: 'Are to be sould at the white horse in Popes head Alley, by John Sudbury and George Humble.'

2 (C The first Pegme was erected in Fanchurche-streete, the backe of it so leaning on the East ende of the Church, that it overspread the whole streete.... The Gate of Passage, then (into which his Maiesty made his first entrance) was derived from Tuscana (being the principal pillar of those 5 upon which the Noble Frame of Architecture doth stand).... most worthy to support so famous a Worke as this Fabricke was, considering that upon his Rusticke Pillars, the goodliest Houses, Turrets, Steeples &c within this City, were to be borne: and these Models stood as a Coronet on the forehead or Battlements of the Great and Magnificent Edifice.) (below the scale of feet is a diagram of the tenon and mortise used in the construction) S H Excud. 265 × 237mm.

A double-arched structure with a gallery from which 'the sound of loud Musicke (being the Waites and Hault-boyes of the City) was sent forth'. The musicians are flanked by the royal and City arms. 'The speakers were onely Thamesis and Genius, who uttered these speeches following....' Crowning the double-arch is a crenellated parapet with the word 'Londinium' centered in a strapwork cartouche and behind it the 'models' of the City waterfront from St Bride's Church in the W. to Fishmongers' Hall in the E. Scouloudi (p 18) places this in a category of its own as being the earliest dated view of its kind.

The viewpoint from the S. Bank seems to be almost opposite the Cathedral so that the tower of the pumping engine which appears on Visscher's view of c1600 as being to the W. of St Paul's here is almost opposite its E. end. On Visscher's view the tower of St Paul's has an invisible flat roof but in this view it is roofed with a shallow pitch exactly as shown by Hollar in his 'True and Exact Prospect' of London before and after the Great Fire (*Hind* 19). Buildings are carefully outlined and a number can fairly confidently be named. From W. to E. in the front rank: St Bride's, St Anne Blackfriars, St Andrew by the Wardrobe, Baynard's Castle, the pumping engine by Queenhithe, St Martin Vintry and Allhallows the Great (both with pinnacled towers), St Laurence Pountney, the Old Swan, St Michael Crooked Lane and Fishmongers' Hall. On the easternmost edge is a curious round building with an onion dome which is prominent but inexplicable in Visscher. On a level with the Cathedral from W. to E. appear St Vedast, St Mary le Bow, the Royal Exchange and the slender flèche of Austin Friars. No doubt other buildings can be identified but these suffice to show that, even though landmarks have been somewhat condensed for the purpose of model-making, this earliest of dated views has considerable topographical interest. It was, after all, exposed to the critical view of thousands of Harrison's contemporaries who lived among the structures he was celebrating.

3 (D The Italians Pegme stood in Gracious-streete.)

(below scale of feet) Stephen Harison Excude:. 300 × 205mm. A baroque arch 'garnished with foure great Corinthia Columnes with naked Portractures (in great) with artificiall trumpets in their hands at 4 corners'. 'The second Triumphall Arch was erected by the Italians: the cost theirs: the Invention their owne.... The Italians Speech–the same in English'.

4 (E The Pegme of the Dutchmen.) (below scale of feet) Stephen Harison Excude. 355 × 205mm. Above a lower stage of the Corinthian order an armorial display of the 'Seventeen Provinces' of the Netherlands, balustrades, allegorical figures, obelisks, all topped by Divine Providence supported on the tails of dolphins. 'The third welcome that his Maiesty receiude, was from the Belgians, who had builded a stately Triumphall Arch ... neere the Royall Exchange in Cornehill'.

5 (F The Device called,/*Nova foelix Arabia.*) (below, ground plan, scale of feet) S.H. Excudit. 285 × 205mm. An Ionic portal with round-headed postern gates on each side topped by giant obelisks; above the portal an allegory of 'dead limmes' and 'lively and stirring parts'; above these a balustrade, strapwork and triumphal columns. 'This Pegme presented itself above the great Conduit in Cheape'.

6 (G The Device called/*Hortus Euporiae* Garden of Plentie.) (below, an ornamental scale of feet and) S.H. Excud:. 305 × 235mm. 'The fift Pegme was a sommer Arbor, and seemed to growe close to the little Conduit in Cheape, which ioyning to the backe of it, served (or might bee supposed to have bene) as a Fountaine to water the fruits of this Garden of Plenty. This greene bower ... having two Gates ... borne up with foure great French termes, standing upon Pedestals. Sylvanus and his followers ... gave entertainment to his Maiestie, in these speeches following....' Three fauns emerge in the foreground from a central staircase.

7 (H The Device called/*Cozmoz Neoz* New World.) (within the portal a scale of feet, a ground plan with its own scale) (br) S.H. Excu:. 310 × 225mm. 'The sixt Triumphall Arch was ... erected above the Conduit in Fleetestreete. The two Posternes ... were cut out of two round Towers'. A 'gothick' gate with a Composite portal, baroque frieze and segment-headed niches and lantern arcades. 'The lively garnishments to this Building were 23 persons ... Zeale was the Presenter of this Device, who spake thus ....'

8 (I The Device called,/*Templum Iani* Temple of Janus.) (below, scale of feet) (br) S H Excu:. 320 × 170mm. 'The seventh and last Pegme (within the Citie) was erected at Temple-barre, being adjoyned close to the Gate: the Building being in all points like a Temple, and dedicated to Ianus Quadrifrons. Beneath that Four-fac'd head of Ianus was advanced the Armes of the Kingdome, with the Supporters cut out to the life ... All the Frontispiece (downeward

from those Armes) was beutified and supported by twelve rich Columnes ...

2 · GOTTFRIED'S NEUWE ARCHONTOLOGIA COSMICA* [1638]

Matthew Merian the elder, a Swiss engraver on copper, was born in Basle, studied in Paris and the Low Countries, and finally settled in Frankfurt where soon after 1623 he succeeded to the great publishing house of De Bry. It specialized in illustrated books of travel, notably a great collection of voyages in the East and West Indies partly inspired by Hakluyt. Merian brought this to a conclusion in 1634, himself illustrated Gottfried's *Neuwe Archontologia,* published in 1638, and with his sons Matthew and Caspar provided etchings for Zeiller's *Topographia* (Frankfurt, 1642, etc). It was in Frankfurt that the 20 year old Wenceslaus Hollar served an apprenticeship with hin in 1627.

Neuwe Archontologia Cosmica Das ist Beschreibung aller Kayserthumben, Königreichen und Republicken der ganzen Welt ... verfasset durch Johann Ludwig Gottfried.... auch mit den vornehmsten in Kupfer gestochenen Landt-Taffeln und Stätten gezieret und verlegt von Matthaeo Merian. Franckfurt am Mayn, in Wolfgang Hoffmans Buchtruckerey, M.DC.XXXVIII.

Quarto, about 320 × 200mm.   1638

COLLATION   Title-page; dedication (4pp); foreword signed by J.L. Gottfried and M. Merian (19pp); contents (3pp); introduction (14pp); pp 1–760, Neuwe Archontologia; index (23pp).

The section on Great Britain includes a map of the kingdom and a panoramic view of the capital city, both the work of Merian. The panorama extends from Whitehall to St Katherine by the Tower on the N. and from Paris Garden to beyond St Olave's in Southwark on the S. but is not acceptable as a contemporary record. Indeed Scouloudi (pp 42–4) argues that the scene shown is nearer to that of the year 1600, as depicted by Visscher and his followers from about 1616.

1 pp   286–7 Magnae/Britanniae/et/Hiberniae/Tabulae. M.Merian fecit. 266 × 340/270 × 350mm.

2 pp 290–1 (in sky between tl Royal Stuart arms with the Garter and tr City arms in laurel wreath) London. 2 sheets, each 208 × 345/228 × 347, overall 208 × 690/228 × 694mm. Keyed refs 1–43 in bm to numbers worked above landmarks.

3 · DE LA SERRE'S HISTOIRE DE L'ENTREE DE LA REYNE MERE [1639]

Histoire de l'entrée de la Reyne Mère du Roy Très-Chrestien, dans la Grande-Bretaigne Enrichie de Planches. Par le Sr de La Serre, Historiographe de France. (ornament) A Londre, Par Jean Raworth, pour George Thomason, & Octavian Pullen, à la Rose, au Cimetière de Sainct Paul. M. DC. XXXIX.

Folio, about 381 × 241mm.   1639

COLLATION   Title-page; dedication to Charles I and Henrietta Maria (12pp, sigs):(1–3); The Progress (49pp, sigs A–O).

The etched plates lack credits and publication-lines but the topographical views are captioned in capitals along lm. The three portraits in this work and the portraits and allegories in Puget de la Serre's companion volume of the same date, *Histoire de l'entrée de la Reyne Mère ... dans les Pays Bas*, are ascribed to Hollar who was at about this time appointed drawing-master to Charles, Prince of Wales. The anonymous views are spirited renderings of a royal progress with abundant staffage and buildings carefully delineated; considerable trouble has been taken over the skies which are varied with cloud and sunshine and even, over Colchester, a shower of rain. The book is unpaginated and the plates unnumbered, so their position is indicated by the signatures opposite which they are bound in the BL copy (G. 10865). Joint publisher with Pullen was George Thomason, a bookseller whose chief claim on posterity is his bequest of the great collection of ephemera which he formed between 1641 and the Restoration and which happily escaped the Great Fire of London. Three of the plates were copied by Basire, slightly reduced, for Bowyer and Nichols's reprint of 1775.

Description des royaulmes d'Angleterre et D'Ecosse Composé par Estienne Perlin, Par. 1558. Histoire de l'Entrée de la Reine Mère dans la Grand Bretagne. Par P. de la Serre, Par. 1639. Illustrated with Cuts and English Notes. London, Reprinted by W. Bowyer and J. Nichols: For T. Payne and W. Brown. MDCCLXXV.

Quarto, about 267 × 203mm. 1775

COLLATION   Title-page; pp i–xxiii, preface; pp 1–42, Description (unillustrated); pp i–xii, preface, ode; pp 3–58, dedications, Histoire (with 3 plates).

1 (engr title) Histoire de l'Entree de la Reine/Mere du Roy tres Chrestien/Dans la Grande/Bretaigne/Par Sr de la Serre (inscribed on two banners supported severally by an angel with a trumpet and by Britannia who also supports a crowned, oval cartouche of the arms of Marie de Medici; below, two draped maidens hold above an altar a laurel wreath with three crowns and the monogram 'MM') A Londre/Imprime par Iohn Raworth pour George Thomason et Octavian Pullen, Au Cimetiere St Paul a la Rose. 240 × 184/262 × 188mm.

2 sig):(2.1 (Portrait of Marie de Medici attended by Britannia holding a spear and gorgon head shield, with these lines in lm)

   La vertu se faire voir
   Sestant peinte surce visage

   Cette Grande Reyne fort sage
   Luy sert tous les jours de miroir
                                    /La Serre.

244 × 188/263 × 190mm.

3 sig):(3:1 (Charles I offers his sceptre, Henrietta Maria offers her crown and a man kneeling offers a sword to Marie, with verses lm)

   Tes Enfancs ravis de te voir
   Toffrent leur sceptre et leur couronne

   Ils te resignent leur pouvoir
   Par cette Espee quon te Donne
                                    /La Serre.

244 × 186/263 × 190mm.

4 sig):(3.2 (Charles I, holding a pair of scales, is crowned with laurel by the blindfold figure of Justice, with these lines in lm)

   Il ne jamais porte quun Sceptre de Iustice
   Et pour les Crimines et pour les Innocens

   Car aimant la Vertu autant quil hait le Vice
   Recompense les bons et punit les meschans.

240 × 185/260 × 190mm.

5 sig B1 L'Heureux des Embarqement de la Reyne au Port de/Harwich 244 × 188/272 × 193mm.

6 sig C2 L'Entree de la Reyne dans la Ville de Colchester. 244 × 188/282 × 193mm.

7 sig E1 Comme le Roy de la Grande Bretaigne estant venu au/devant de la Reyne sa Mere a Midlemead la salue. 248 × 185/274 × 190mm. 1775 ed p 19. (tr) 'Pl.1'. Reduced in size and copied. 210 × 184/241 × 190mm.

8 sig E2 La Sortie de la Reyne Acompaigne du Roy de la/Grande Bretaigne son Beau Fils du Chateau de/Gilde Halle. 240 × 187/270 × 195mm. Caption garbles Gidea Hall. 1775 ed p 24. (tr) 'Pl.II'. Reduced in size and copied. 210 × 185/245 × 190mm.

9 sig F Entree Royalle de la Reyne Mere du Roy Tres-Chrestien dans la Ville de Londres. 273 × 775/292 × 787mm overall, from two sheets, 273 × 387/292 × 394mm and 272 × 390/280 × 392mm. Panoramic view of Cheapside with the procession passing Cheap Cross; in the foreground an inn with its 'bush' and the sign of a horse's head; two spires shown, to the N. probably a church, to the E. possibly Gresham's Royal Exchange. This plate, less the staffage, was often copied and became the standard image of the pre-Fire City. 1775 ed p 29. (tr) 'Pl.III'. Re-engraved by Basire. 260 × 768/279 × 775mm overall, on three sheets.

10 sig L1 Comme la Reyne dAngleter Acompaignee de ses Enfans/se Iette aux Pieds de la Reyne sa Mere a son Arivee/dans le Palays de S.Iames. 247 × 185/275 × 190mm. Shows the gatehouse and courtyard of St James's Palace.

11 sig L2 Le Cercle de leurs Magestes dans la Chambre de/Presence=a=S.Iames. 245 × 190/274 × 195mm. In this and the two other Palace interiors extreme austerity is depicted: bare floorboards, scant furniture and hangings, and an almost total absence of pictures. Perhaps the official artist had to imagine the scenes and his imagination failed him after he had drawn likenesses of the royal personages.

12 sig M1 Representation des Feus de Ioye qui Furent Faicts sur/l'Eau dans Londres a l'Honneur de la Reyne la Nuict/dIour de son Entree. 240 × 188/268 × 195mm. Looking W. from Pool of London towards London Bridge with beacons or fireworks burning from the corner turrets of the Tower in the foreground, also on two church spires (one perhaps St Laurence Pountney) in the middle distance and on the spireless tower of old St Pauls in the background; nearby a broadside fired by large seagoing vessels is answered by the Tower guns.

13 sig N2 Comme Messieurs du Conseil Prive viennent saluer la/Reyne dans sa Chambre. 245 × 187/275 × 195mm.

14 sig 01 Comme le My Lord Mayor Accompaigne de ses Collegues/Vient Saluer la/Reyne luy Faire ses Presens. 242 × 185/272 × 192mm.

4 · HOLLAR'S PARLIAMENTARY MERCIES* [1642]

The eight plates which comprise this pamphlet must be ascribed to Hollar's efforts to support himself in September 1642 after his patron, the Earl of Arundel, had left for exile in the Netherlands and before he had enlisted as a soldier in the Royalist army. Each consists of two subjects but they were first issued without any text other than the engraved title-page and descriptive captions.

(engr on obelisk) All/the me=/morable/& wonder=/strikinge=/PARLIAMEN=/TARY MERCIES/effected & affor=/ded unto this/our ENGLISH/NATION within/the space of lesse/than 2 Years past/Ao 1641 & 1642/ Are to be sould by Thomas/Ienner in his shop at the old Exchange. 120 × 95mm. (The figures of Time and Truth carry scroll quoting *Isaiah* 54, 8 and 6, 3. Above a tablet quoting *Revelation* 16, 10 is the figure of 'Envie'.)

Small quarto, 185 × 133mm.   1642

COLLATION   Engr title-page; 8 plates (no text)

These plates were published by Thomas Jenner in 1646 in conjunction with a printed text of 29 pages, attributed to John Vicars, three extra plates and an amended title:

A/Sight of ye/Trans=actions/of these latter yeares Emble-ma/tized with engraven plats when men may/read without/spectacles.

Small quarto, 190 × 140mm.   1646

COLLATION   Engr title-page; pp 1–21 (ie 1–29), A Sight of ye Transactions; 8 plates.

Finally in 1648 most of the plates again appeared, all the worse for wear and two of them bisected, in a 42 page volume with printed title-page:

True Information of the Beginning and Cause of all our troubles: how they have been hatched, and how prevented ... London, Printed in the Yeare 1648.

Small quarto, 180 × 130mm.   1648

COLLATION   Title-page; pp 1–42, True Information; 11 plates.

The free style of these etchings forms a contrast with Hollar's usual tightly controlled burin strokes and careful hatching, as for instance in the 'Four Seasons' of 1641. They convey an impression of immediacy and participation, precursors of Hogarth's topical satires and the actuality of the graphic journalism practised by the mid nineteenth-century wood-engravers.

Of the eight plates first published, four include subjects with identifiable outdoor London locations and on the three extra plates added in 1646 are three such subjects, making seven in all (*Hind* 24–5, 31, 93, 108). Within each plate-mark of approximately 130 × 98mm are two small subjects of 64 × 95mm.

1 pl. 2b The rising Prentises and Sea-men on South/wark-side to assault the Archbishop of Canter/bury's House. (The rabble assembled in St George's Fields on the morning of 11 May 1640 and when the train-bands retired for the night it marched to Lambeth Palace; Archbishop Laud escaped by water to Whitehall.) 1646 and 1648 eds p 5. (*Hind* 108)

2 pl. 5a The Earle of Strafford for treasonable practices/beheaded on the Tower-hill. (On 11 May 1641.) 1646 ed p 11, 1648 ed p 9. (*Hind* 24)

3 pl. 7a The Citie Train'd Bands and the brave Sea-men/with Barges and Long-boates adorn'd with strea/mers drums & trumpets/... guard the/Lords & Commons safely to Parl: by land & water. (St Stephen's Hall and the clock tower seen from the river. The occasion was perhaps the grand review of the train-bands in Finsbury Fields before both Houses of Parliament on 10 May 1642.) 1646 ed p 19. (*Hind* 93)

4 pl. 8a The Bishops imprisoned in the Towre of London/for protesting against the Parliament. (Exterior view of the White Tower.) 1646 ed p 15. (*Hind* 25)

A Sight of ye Transactions

5 p 21 The 2 of May 1643 ye Crosse in Cheapside was pulled/downe, a Troope of Horse wayted to garde it ... —10 of May the Boocke of Sportes upon the Lords day was bu=/rnt by the Hangman in the place where the Crosse stoode/& at Exchange. 92 × 73, 92 × 50/95 × 127mm. 1648 ed p15. (*Hind* 31).

6 p 25 Sr Alexander Carew, Sr John Hotham, Captn Hotham &/the Archbishop of Canterbury, beheaded on Tower=/hill for Treason ... 1645. 98 × 60mm. (Laud was beheaded on 10 January 1645.) 1648 ed p 21).

5 · HOLLAR'S PROSPECTS [1647]

Although, strictly speaking, these prints fall outside the scope of this work, since they are equipped neither with a title-page nor with a running series title, they are exceptionally included both because they are uniquely important to our knowledge of the appearance of London in the seventeenth century and because each has a serial number engraved br in the margin. These numbers are missing in earlier states and must have been added to help sell them as a series. All eight are familiar images, which by dint of repeated reproduction have become almost clichés of book illustration, but their original impact survives and re-examination of them never fails to bring to light some telling detail. Moreover there are fortunately still in existence a number of those original drawings which Hollar must have taken with him to Antwerp when he took refuge there from the Civil War in the years 1644–52. They provided him with the copy for etching these and other views and maps during his exile from his adopted country. Four of these related drawings are referred to below by their number in E. Croft-Murray's *Catalogue of British drawings* vol. 1.

In some of these drawings, says Martin Hardie in his *Water-colour painting in Britain* vol. 1 (pp 59–60):

we certainly have the beginnings of the unbroken tradition of English topographical drawing, the close record of architecture and landscape, which was to be a central feature of 18th century art. With his faithful and accurate representations which add so much to our historical knowledge of the 17th century London and its suburbs, Hollar stands at the start of this tradition. In drawings and etchings he was a recorder first and foremost, but at the same time he had an eye for the pure beauty of the English scene.

In the same vein is A.M. Hind in his *Wenceslaus Hollar and his views of London and Windsor*, to which reference is made in the list: 'For a general idea of what London looked like at this period there could be no securer guide than Hollar. Apart from his diligent sketching from nature, and his study of the city's architecture, every plate that he did is redolent of the atmosphere of his adopted city'. He assigns the views, according to their size and shape, to two original sets: pl. 3–6 which are about 330mm in width and pl. 1,2,7 and 8 which are about 252mm. Significantly the first batch are also to be found cut down to about 290mm, bringing them closer to the dimensions of their companion plates in the consolidated set. Pl. 4 and 8 lack credits and only pl. 1, 5 and 6 are dated (1647). Some 40 years later Morden and Lea copied directly no fewer than six of these etchings for their own *Prospects* (no 15).

Some of the copper plates survived into the nineteenth century. In their 1775 catalogue Sayer & Bennett still offered 'Hollar's Original Prints, Just now re-printed (the Plates being carefully cleaned, and printed on very good Paper). Several Sets and some odd Ones of Hollar's Original Prints, much esteemed by the Curious'. The 'cleaning' no doubt refers to the re-engraving of worn lines. They also had for sale a bound volume which probably included some of the London prints: 'A Collection of Hollar's Prints, on 146 Copper-Plates, including his Views, Habits, Sporting Pieces, &c. &c. Price half-bound, 16s.' As an advertisement it is the more tantalizing since it seems likely that all copies of this collection were soon broken up by the extra-illustrators; no grangerized Pennant (no 67) seems to be complete without these eight London views and to supply the demand numbers were printed off on wove paper at the turn of the century by printsellers such as Laurie & Whittle.

1 (in sky along tm) S. Marie Overs in Southwarke. (above old St Paul's) London. W. Hollar fec. 1647. 144 × 254/150 × 260mm. From S., with old St Paul's in the distance. Hollar made a larger engr of this subject in 1661 for Dugdale's *Monasticon Anglicanum* (no 6). (*Hind* 26)

2 (in sky along tm) Piazza in Conventgarden. W. Hollar ('W H' in monogram) fecit. 145 × 252/150 × 258mm. Coach and pair coming into picture from l.; centre of square marked out by posts. (*Hind* 79)

3 (in sky along tm) Palatium Archiepiscopi Cantuariensis propae Londinum, vulgo Lambeth House. W. Hollar ('W H' in monogram) fecit 1647. 143 × 322/150 × 330mm. The Palace and St Mary's Church from the river. (*Hind* 107)

4 (in sky along tm) Palatium Regis prope Londinum, vulgo Whitehall. 143 × 323/150 × 335mm. Shows the Inigo Jones Banqueting Hall, the old Hall with a central cupola and the Palace apartments fronting on the river. A close-up view apparently based on a portion of the British Museum pen, ink and water-colour drawing (*Croft-Murray* p 351, no 7). (*Hind* 85)

5 (in sky along tm) Civitatis Westmonasteriensis pars. (above buildings) Parliament House – the Hall – the Abby. W. Hollar ('W H' in monogram) fecit 1647. 142 × 322/150 × 328mm. The three buildings are viewed from the N.E. This aspect is supplemented by the following Hollar drawings:

From E.S.E. in pen and ink (V & A, E. 128–1924).

From S.S.E. in pencil, pen and ink and water-colour (*Croft-Murray* p 350, no 6), corresponding to the aspect chosen for Hollar's panoramic etching 'Prospect of London and Westminster taken from Lambeth' (*Hind* 18).

A distant view of the same stretch of river from Lambeth Palace in pencil, pen and ink (*Croft-Murray* p 349, no 5).

A view from due N. looking towards Parliament and Lambeth Palace, in pen and ink (Barber Institute of Fine Arts, Birmingham, B.167). (*Hind* 86)

6 (in sky along tm) Sala Regalis cum Curia Westmonasterij vulgo Westminster Hall. W. Hollar ('W H' in monogram) fecit 1647. 145 × 322/150 × 330mm. New Palace Yard with the clock tower, the conduit and Westminster Hall from N.N.E. (*Hind* 90)

7 (on swallow-tailed banderole trailed across sky by putto) Byrsa Londinensis vulgo the Royal Exchange. W. Hollar ('W H' in monogram) fecit. 145 × 252/152 × 260mm. Showing the courtyard of Gresham's Royal Exchange in vacation time with children playing, viewed from the N. Hollar etched a larger and more formal view from the E. showing the courtyard crowded with merchants on a business day (*Hind* 29). (*Hind* 28)

8 (in sky along tm) Castrum Royale Londinense vulgo the Tower. 144 × 254/150 × 260mm. Viewed from river level, S.S.W. A Hollar drawing from the same viewpoint, but including on each side extra buildings, is in the BM (*Croft-Murray* p 349, no 4). (*Hind* 22)

6 · DUGDALE'S MONISTICON ANGLICANUM* [1655–73]

Roger Dodsworth, the Yorkshire antiquary, had for some time been assembling copies of baronial and monastic records as materials for a history of the monasteries of northern England when, in 1639, on the recommendation of Sir Christopher Hatton, he made the acquaintance of William Dugdale, a newly appointed Herald whose zeal for the project and assistance with transcripts from

documents in the Bodleian Library and Oxford colleges persuaded him to extend his range to monastic England as a whole. Dugdale started in 1649 preparing the work for the printer and spent the greater part of 1651 away from his native Warwickshire in London—'so great a task,' as he explained, 'have I had to bring Mr. Dodsworth's confused collections into any order and perfect the copy from the Tower and Sir Thomas Cotton's library'. No bookseller could be induced to publish this austere book all in Latin, so the joint authors themselves raised the cost of printing, Dodsworth engaged a printer and by 1654 the manuscript of the first two volumes was ready for the press. Printing had only just commenced when Dodsworth died in August 1654 and the first volume, consisting largely of charters of foundation, donation and confirmation granted to monastic establishments, was published in the following year; a second edition which appeared in 1682 was virtually a reprint. The second volume appeared in 1661 with an adulatory address to Charles II and was reissued in 1673. From the title of the third, published in 1673, Dodsworth's name was finally dropped. Two shortened versions followed, one a mere epitome in 1693. The other, a more satisfactory English abridgement, anonymous but assumed to be the work of John Stevens the translator and author of a two-volume supplement to the *Monasticon* (1722–3), was published in 1718 and included some of the original topographical plates. Finally an enlarged six-volume edition edited chiefly by Henry Ellis, the Keeper of Manuscripts at the British Museum, came out in 54 Parts between 1 June 1813 and 1830 (no 122).

Monasticon Anglicanum, sive Pandectae Coenobiorum Benedictinorum Cluniacensium Cisterciensium Carthusianorum A Primordiis ad eorum usque dissolutionem. Ex MSS. Codd. Ad Monasteria olim pertinentibus.... digesti per Rogerum Dodsworth, Eborac. Guilielmum Dugdale, Warwic. Londoni Typis Richardi Hodgkinsonne, M.DC.LV.

Folio, about 345 × 220mm.   1655

COLLATION   Title-page; preface (32pp); introduction (8pp); pp 1–1052, Monasticon Anglicanum; pp 1053–1151, index, errata.
(There is also an engraved title-page showing monasteries, with statues of St Gregory and St Augustine in an architectural setting, 'Wenceslaus Hollar Bohem. fecit Londini', and a frontispiece of a tree of the monastic orders stemming from St Benedict.)

Editio Secunda auctior & Emendatior.... Londini Impensis Christopheri Wilkinson, Thomae Dring & Caroli Harper, in vico vulgo vocato Fleet-street, 1682.

Folio, 345 × 220mm.   1682

COLLATION Title-page; introductory verses, preface (19pp); introduction (7pp); pp 1–1052, Monasticon Anglicanum; pp 1053–159, index.

Monastici, Anglicani, Volumen Alterum, de Canonicis Regularibus Augustinianis, scilicet Hospitalariis, Templariis, Gilbertinis, Praemonstratensibus & Maturinis sive Trinitarianis. Cum Appendice Ad Volumen Primum ... A Primordiis ad eorum usque Dissolutionem, Ex MSS. Codicibus ad Monasteria olim Pertinentibus ... digestum Per Rogerum Dodsworth Eboracensem, Gulielmum Dugdale Warwicensem. Londini, Typis Aliciae Warren, anno Domini MDCLXI. (The 1673 reissue substitutes 'Volumen Secundum' for 'Volumen Alterum'.)

Folio, about 345 × 220mm.   1661, 1673

COLLATION Title-page; dedication to Charles II (3 pp); introduction, contents (14 pp); pp 1–1057, Monasticon Anglicanum; index, errata (56 pp).

Monastici Anglicani, Volumen Tertium et Ultimum: Additamenta ... necnon Fundationes, sive Dotationes Diversarum Ecclesiarum Cathedralium ac Collegiatarum continens; Ex Archivis Regiis, ipsis Autographis, Ac diversis Codicibus Manuscriptis decerpta, Et hic congesta Per Will. Dugdale Warwicensem Norroy Regem Armorum. Savoy: Excudebat Tho. Newcomb, & Prostant Venales Ab. Roper, Joh. Martin, & Hen. Herringman ad Signa Solis in Fleetstreet, Campanae Coemeterio Paulino, & Anchorae Bursa Nova. MDCLXXIII.

Folio, about 350 × 220mm.   1673

COLLATION Title-page; dedication to Charles II (1 leaf); foreword (2 pp); pp 1–378, supplement to vol. 1; pp 379–92; index; errata (1 leaf); pp 1–209, Ecclesiae Collegiatae; pp 211–18, index.

Monasticon Anglicanum: or, the History of the Ancient Abbies, Monasteries, Hospitals, Cathedral and Collegiate Churches ... in England and Wales ... Containing a full collection of all that is necessary to be known concerning the Abby-Lands, and their Revenues; with a particular Account of their Foundations, Grants and Donations; collected from Original MSS.... Illustrated with the Original Cuts of the Cathedral and Collegiate Churches, and the Habits of the Religious and Military Orders. First Publish'd in Latin by Sir William Dugdale, Kt. Late Garter Principal King at Arms.... The Whole Corrected ... by an Eminent Hand. London: Printed by R. Harbin; for D. Browne and J. Smith in Exeter-Change, G. Strahan, in Cornhill; W. Taylor, in Pater-noster-row; R. Gosling, in Fleet-street; W. Mears, J. Browne, and F. Clay, without Temple-bar. MDCCXVIII.

Folio, 453 × 283mm.   1718

COLLATION Title-page; pp i–xvi, preface, glossary, introduction; pp 1–375, Monasticon Anglicanum; index (8pp).

This massive work was illustrated with a large number of plates drawn by Hollar, Daniel King, Thomas Johnson, Richard Newcourt and others and engraved by Hollar, King, J. Collins and Robert Vaughan. They were intended to attract buyers who might not relish the learned text unadorned and they still greatly add to the attraction of the work. Dedications show that sponsors were found for individual plates from the families whose arms or tombs were depicted but otherwise the engraving and printing of them after the death of Dodsworth devolved entirely upon Dugdale and actually cost him more than the printing of the letterpress. His diary for 1656 gives particulars of the charges paid in that year and these include £33 to Hollar, artist and engraver, and £45 to Mr and Mrs Reeve for 'working off the plates with his Rolling Press'.

Here we are concerned with a mere handful of London subjects, all the work either of Hollar or his imitator Daniel King of whom Dugdale had no high opinion. In the first volume, dated 1655, are four plates of Westminster Abbey, two by Hollar and two by King. The second volume, of 1661, contains three Hollar plates including the fine composite 'St John of Jerusalem' and the third (1673), which takes in collegiate churches and cathedrals, contains a plate by Hollar of St George's Chapel, Windsor and six originally published in Dugdale's *History of St Paul's Cathedral* (no 8, abbreviated as *D* followed by page number), plus a nave interior which would almost certainly have illustrated that work had not a larger plate been substituted.

Some of these plates were also published independently by King, to begin with in their original state with a title-page unornamented and engraved in bold lettering:

The Cathedrall and Conventuall Churches/of/England and Wales./Orthographically delineated/by D K/Anno/ MDCLVI.

Dugdale may either have borrowed these plates for publication in his first volume or, more probably, commissioned the drawings from King and afterwards permitted him to use the plates for his own work. King subsequently published a larger collection with the same title, but undated and surrounded by a double frame decorated with the arms of cathedrals and monastic foundations. These were in a later state with fairly consistent serial numeration br and captions in the vernacular added to the existing Latin ones. It is in this second state that the plates were again used for the *Monasticon Anglicanum* (vol. 1, 2nd ed 1682 and the 1718 abridgement in English) as noted below. The publisher of the 1718 abridgement also drew upon King's collection for alternative and additional illustrations. The numbers of the plates as engraved in King's later collection are shown with the abbreviation *K* but, as Hind explains, plates with this numeration unaltered, or corrected in MS only, are also to be found in the later *Monasticon* editions.

VOL. 1 (1655, etc)

1 p 54 (on cartouche tc) Areae Westmonas=/teriensis Ecclesiae Ichnographia. Ric. Newcourt delin. D.King sculp. 215 × 310mm pl. mark. *K* '16' adds: 'The Ichnography of the/Church of Westminster'. Thus also 1682 ed and 1718 ed p 16.I. (*Hind* 99)

2 p 56 (tr) Westmonast: Ecclesiae/conv: facies aquilonalis. W. Hollar fecit: 1654. 215 × 330 pl. mark. Name of donor on cartouche tl. *K* '18' adds: 'The North Prospect of the/late Conventuall Church of Westmynster'. Thus also 1682 ed and 1718 ed p 16.III. (*Hind* 99)

3 p 58 (tl) Westmonasteriensis Ecclesiae conv:/facies australis. D. King delin. et sculp. 175 × 315mm pl. mark. *K* '19' adds: 'The South Prospect of the Conventuall/Church of Westmynster'. Thus also 1682 ed and 1718 ed p 16.IIII.

4 p 60 (tc) Westmonasteriensis/Ecclesiae (quondā Con/ventualis) facies occi/dentalis. (in cartouche tc) P.S. Ne memoria Pe-/tri (Pauli modo)/cum mole ruat./P/Wenceslaus Hollar/E: Bohem. 250 × 170mm pl. mark. *K* '17' adds: 'The West Prospect of the/late Conventual Church/of Westmynster'. Thus also 1682 ed and 1718 ed p 16.II.

VOL. 2 (1661, etc)

5 p 460 (along tm) Conventualis Ecclesiae Hospitalis S. Catharinae Iuxta Turrim London: a Meridie prospectus. W. Hollar fecit 1660. 190 × 290/200 × 300mm. Name of donor on cartouche. (*Hind* 21)

6 p 504 (composite pl.) (tl) Hospitalariorum Militum Sti Ioh: Hierosol./Domus olim excelsae, in suburbio civitatis Londin:/portae Australis a Circio prospectus. 105 × 192mm. (tr) Ejusdem Domus (quanti nunc superest) cum occidentali Capellae/facie ab Affrico prospectus. 105 × 175mm. (above lower strip)

Praefatae Domus à retrò ab Euro-aquilone prospectus. 122 × 370mm. Wenceslaus Hollar delin: et sculp: 1661. 325 × 375mm pl. mark. Arms and name of donor on cartouches. (*Hind* 70)

7 p 940 (in cartouche tl) S. Mariae Overie olim Conventualis Ecclesiae ab Austro prospectus. W. Hollar delin: et sculpt: 1661. 217 × 295/225 × 305mm. Name of donor on cartouche. Hollar also etched a pre-Fire view of this subject (*Hind* 26). (*Hind* 27)

VOL. 3 (1673)

8 p 297 (in oblong engraved framework tl) Ecclesiae Paulinae Prospectus/qualis olim erat ... W. Hollar sculp. 1657. 255 × 358mm pl. mark. Page no added bl, otherwise as *D* 133.

9 p 297 (along tm) Areae Ecclesiae Cathedralis Sti Pauli Ichnographia. Wenceslaus Hollar dimensit, delineavit et aqua forti aeri insculpsit, A° 1657. 235 × 340mm pl. mark. Page no added bl, otherwise as *D* 161.

10 p 297 (in oval cartouche tl) Ecclesiae Cathedralis/Sti Pauli/A Meridie Prospectus. W. Hollar delin: et sculp:. 205 × 380mm pl. mark. Page no added bl, otherwise as *D* 162.

11 p 297 (in oval cartouche tl) Ecclesiae Cathedralis/Sti Pauli/ab Occidente Prospectus. W. Hollar delin. et sculp. 228 × 270mm pl. mark. Page no added bl, otherwise as *D* 164.

12 p 297 (tc) Ecclesiae Cathedralis Sti Pauli Lond:/ab Oriente Prospectus. W. Hollar delin: et sculp:. 195 × 250mm pl. mark. Page no added bl, otherwise as *D* 166.

13 p 298 (tc) Navis Ecclesiae Cathedralis S. Pauli/Lond: Prospectus Interior. 290 × 215/300 × 223mm. Arms of Philip Howard, Earl of Arundel, with dedication tr. 1718 ed p 328. Hind believes that this was a rejected plate, replaced by the larger one of the same vista published as *D* 167. (*Hind* 43)

14 p 368 (illustration to Lydgate's 'Dance of Death' printed with letterpress) W. Hollar fecit. 145 × 182/160 × 188mm. Credit added, otherwise as *D* 290.

Ecclesiae Collegiatae

15 p 87 (cartouche tc) Capellae Regiae ac Collegiatae/St Georgii/in Castro de Windsore/A Meridie Prospectus/In piorum olim Fundatorum memoriam/Decanus et Canonici ... /hoc posuere A° 1671 (above lower half) Areae ejusdem Capellae/Ichnographia. W. Hollar delineavit. 160 × 355, 135 × 355/305 × 360mm. Elevation and plan with refs 1–10. (*Hind* 119)

1718 abridgement (additional plates)

16 p 323 (tl) Ecclesiae Cathedralis Sti/Pauli facies Aquilonaris/(tr) The North Prospect of ye Cathedral/Church of St Paul in London. W. Hollar delin. Daniell King sculpsit. 215 × 370mm pl. mark. *K* '68';

although based on the same drawing there are differences in detail between this and Hollar's engraving (eg King shows round-headed niches on each side of the N. door, Hollar square). cf with *D* 163.

17 p 325 (tl) Ecclesiae Cathedralis Sti Pauli latus occidentale. The West Prospect of the Cathedral Church of/St Paul. Daniell King sculpsit. 255 × 180mm pl. mark. *K* '65', in lieu of the Hollar plate, item 11 above.

18 p 327 (along tm) The East Prospect of the Cathedral Church of/St Paul. 260 × 185mm. No credits. *K* '67' before letters. In lieu of Hollar plate, item 12 above.

19 p 352 The South Prospect of the Royal Chapel of St Georges in Windsor Castle. Sutton Nicholls sculp. 197 × 300/204 × 308mm. In lieu of item 15 above. Nicholls also contributed a view of Eton College Chapel to this volume (p 368).

7 · HOWELL'S LONDINOPOLIS [1657]

James Howell (1594?–1666) was a diplomat who, while in Madrid, wrote accounts of Prince Charles's courtship of the Infanta of Spain. Confined to the Fleet as a Royalist prisoner in 1643–51, he wrote most of the work by which he is generally remembered, *Epistolae Ho-elianae: Familiar Letters*. Gough dismisses the present text as 'Stolen from Stowe almost to a paragraph'.

Londinopolis; an Historicall Discourse or Perlustration of the City of London, The Imperial Chamber, and chief Emporium of Great Britain. Whereunto is added another of the City of Westminster, with the Courts of Justice, Antiquities, and new Buildings thereunto belonging. By Jam. Howel Esq; 'Senesco, non Segnesco'. London, Printed by J. Streater for Henry Twiford, George Sawbridge, Thomas Dring, and John Place ... 1657.

Quarto, about 270 × 180mm. 1657

COLLATION Title-page; epigraph, dedication, 'advertisements', contents (8 pp); pp 1–124, 301–407, Londinopolis; index, catalogue (8 pp). (Text apparently complete despite irregularity of pagination and sigs, 'R' followed by 'Aa'.)

The view in this book of London from the South Bank, which extends to the N. from Whitehall to St Katherine by the Tower and to the S. from Paris Garden to beyond St Olave, Southwark, contains a number of topographical anachronisms which puzzled A.M. Hind (*Hind* 17) and which were analysed by Scouloudi (pp 55–6). From the style the authorities infer that it was engraved by Hollar and at about the time the book was published. However it shows the Swan Theatre which had disappeared by 1632 and the buildings N. of London Bridge which were burned in 1633 and fails to record the alterations to St Paul's Cathedral made by Inigo Jones, 1631–42. None of these inconsistencies is observable in Hollar's famous long view from Bankside of 1647 (*Hind* 16), which makes it the harder to understand why he should have chosen to engrave either from a drawing which he must have known was out of date or possibly from the engraving made by his former master, Matthew Merian, for inclusion in Gottfried's *Neuwe Archontologia Cosmica* (no 2) published in 1638.

1 front. (portrait of the author beneath an oak tree, with his achievement of arms and motto 'Heic tutus obumbror') C. Melan et Bosse sc. 205 × 143/206 × 145mm.

2 p 1 (on central cartouche in sky supported by heraldic lions and surmounted by the City arms between C-scrolls) London/London the glory of Great Britaines Ile/Behold her Landschip here and tru pourfile. 188 × 312/237 × 318mm. Keyed refs 1–46 bm to nos engr above landmarks in work.

8 · DUGDALE'S HISTORY OF ST PAUL'S CATHEDRAL [1658]

Ths book is suitably dedicated to Lord Hatton since it was largely through his influence that William Dugdale extended his antiquarian and topographical research beyond his native Warwickshire. On a visit to London in 1635 he obtained an introduction to the Comptroller of Charles I's household, then Sir Christopher Hatton, who gained access for him to the records in the Tower and the Cottonian Collection, helped him to obtain an appointment as a Herald and advised him to get in touch with Roger Dodsworth. Dodsworth was gathering materials for a history of the antiquities of Yorkshire and of the foundation of monasteries in northern England when Dugdale offered his help. His transcripts of documents (many of them made in the Bodleian Library and college libraries from 1643 to 1646 when he was with the Court at Oxford) and his enthusiasm for the project induced Dodsworth to broaden the scope of his work and so *Monasticon Anglicanum* (no 6) was born. Meanwhile Hatton, apprehending the desecration of past glories inherent in a Puritan regime, commissioned Dugdale to visit Westminster Abbey, St Paul's Cathedral and some provincial churches taking with him a draughtsman, William Sidgwick, to make drawings of the monuments and armorial bearings while they were still intact and to transcribe epitaphs. The making of these records, which remained with the Hatton family, must have inspired him with the zeal for the conservation of ancient monuments to which we owe most of our knowledge of the fabric of the Gothic St Paul's. As a contemporary put it:

> Were't not for Books where had
>   thy Memory been?
> But that thou art, in Dugdale's learned Story
> And beautious Illustrations to be seen,
> Thy name had been as lost
>   as is thy Glory.
>
>   (F. Wright, 1668)

In about 1656, having finally set in order the material gathered by Dodsworth for the first volume of the *Monasticon*, printed in 1655, he went to work on documents relating to St Paul's and the results of these labours were printed in 1658.

No doubt some of the sheets of this edition perished in the Great Fire of 1666, perhaps in the very bowels of the building it eulogized. Certainly by 1685, when work on Wren's new cathedral was more or less halted for lack of funds, old Sir William Dugdale, now a knight and Garter King of Arms, was asked to help raise the wind by preparing a second edition of his book with an appendix describing the progress of the new works and a list of subscribers to the Fund. The revision was cut short by his death in the following year but his copy of the book, corrected, enlarged and continued in his own hand, ultimately came into the possession of the Rev Edward Maynard, an antiquarian precentor of Lichfield Cathedral, who published the second edition in 1716. Finally Sir Henry Ellis's third edition of 1818 (no 125) brought the history up to that date.

The History of St Pauls Cathedral in London. From its Foundation untill these Times: Extracted out of Originall Charters, Records, Leiger Books, and other Manuscripts. Beautified with sundry Prospects of the Church, Figures of Tombes, and Monuments. By William Dugdale.... London, Printed by Tho. Warren, in the year of our Lord God MDCLVIII.

Folio, 335 × 215mm.   1658

COLLATION   Title-page; dedication to Lord Christopher Hatton dated from Blythe Hall, Warwickshire 7 July 1657 (3 pp); pp 1–136, 157–299, History (p 157, sig Nn1 follows on from p 136, sig Mm2 verso; pp 174 and 293–7 are misnumbered 192 and 263–7); index, errata (5 pp).

Two pages are subtitled:

(p 59) A View of the Monuments Situate in and about the Quire, Side-iles, & Chapels Adjacent; As they stood in September Anno D.MDCXLI. With their Epitaphs exactly imitated of which In regard to every Eye, the Character is not so legible, I have added the Copies ... London, Printed in the year, 1658.

(p 175) Appendix in Historiam Ecclesiae Cathedralis S. Pauli; Diversa Ad majorem istius operis illustrationem Continens. Londini, Impressum Anno Domini MDCLVIII.

The History of St Pauls Cathedral in London. From its Foundation untill these Times: Extracted out of Originall Charters, Records, Leiger Books, and other Manuscripts. Beautified with sundry Prospects of the Old Fabrick which was destroyed by the Fire of that City, 1666, as also With the Figures of the Tombs and Monuments therein, which were all defac'd in the late Rebellion. Whereunto is added, A continuation thereof, setting forth what was done in the Structure of the New Church, to the Year 1685 ... By Sir William Dugdale Knt, Garter Principal of Arms. The Second Edition corrected and enlarged by the Author's own Hand. To which is prefixed his Life written by himself. Publish'd by Edward Maynard D.D.... Printed by George James for Jonah Bowyer, at the Rose in Ludgate Street MDCCXVI.

Folio, about 425 × 275mm. (Large Paper)   1716

COLLATION   Title-page; list of subscribers, errata, directions to the binder (4pp); pp i–xxviii, To the Reader, life of Dugdale, introduction; pp 1–147, History (the imprint of the subtitle on p 59 altered from the 1st ed to 'London, Printed for Jonah Bowyer ... MDCCXIV'); pp 148–71, History continued; pp 172–210, list of contributions to the fabric; pp 1–75, appendix (with 1715 imprint); pp 1–88, Historical account of York, Durham, Carlisle (mistakenly attributed to Dugdale—with a 1715 imprint).

The importance of this book for London topography lies not so much in Dugdale's learned transcriptions, cataloguings and comments as in the magnificent plates by Hollar which illustrate them. Thanks to these it is the first printed book to delineate in considerable detail an English building. Although its scope is confined to a single cathedral it is also the first acceptably illustrated book in the library of London topography and, therefore, the real starting point for this survey. Moreover it is an accurate graphic record of that fortunately unique phenomenon, an English Gothic cathedral which was to be reduced to rubble. For size and careful representation its plates were not equalled in book illustration until Johannes Kip's first volume of birds-eye views was produced in the early years of the eighteenth century (no 22) and for artistry and skill not until Malton published his *Picturesque Tour* (no 72) towards the end of that century.

Wenceslaus Hollar, born in Prague in 1607, was taught by Egidius Sadeler, engraver to the Imperial Court, and by 1627 was apprenticed to Matthaeus Merian, a Frankfurt engraver of topographical landscapes, city plans and architectural designs. During the following years he was at work in Strasbourg, Cologne and Holland and then, by a chance which was indeed fortunate for British topography, he joined the suite of the art connoisseur and collector Thomas Howard, Earl of Arundel when in 1635 he was travelling as an envoy to the Imperial Court. Indeed the Earl collected the person of Hollar and, on his return home to Arundel House in the Strand, gave him house room and a studio to work in—represented, it is believed, in Hollar's etching of the courtyard (*Hind* 83).

As a Royalist Hollar was involved in the Civil War and is said to have been present at the siege of Basing House, but by 1644 he had managed to get to Antwerp where he joined the Guild of St Luke and worked for engraver publishers on portraits after contemporary artists and the Old Masters. During these years he also etched, from drawings he had brought out with him, the most famous of his London plates. For these his 'annus mirabilis' was 1647 when he etched the six plates of his panoramic birds-eye view from Bankside, the first topographically reliable engraving of its sort, and the set of eight small plates (no 5) which established a precedent for the collections of 'Prospects' so popular in the next century.

In 1652 he was invited back to England and was arrested on arrival for his former activities, but by the intervention of Dugdale he was released again. He shared quarters near Temple Bar with a fellow artist, William Faithorne, and made a living by engraving at sweated rates of pay for publishers such as Peter Stent, John Overton and John Ogilby. In due course he and his imitator Daniel King were supplying illustrations for two of Dugdale's major works, the first volume of *Monasticon Anglicanum* (1655, no 6) and *The Antiquities of Warwickshire* (1656).

The plates in Dugdale's *St Paul*'s which followed are, however, nearly all from his own pen, etching-needle and burin; the majority even of those lacking credits are ascribed to him by Hind on account of their freedom from mechanical hatching and his characteristic use of 'flicks' to express shadows and textures. They are paginated in sequence with the text, the folding plates being counted as one page only, and on most the page number is engraved either just within or just without the work tl. Smaller single-leaf plates are printed on the verso of letterpress pages, a technically difficult operation since it involved keeping the plates aligned with the printed page on the recto as they went through the rolling press. Most of the plates carry a dedication from which it can be deduced that, as was the case with the *Monasticon Anglicanum*, the dedicatees subsidized the cost of engraving.

In the second edition four plates by John Harris were substituted for Hollar originals (pl. 34–5, 38, 40) and the pagination of a number of plates was altered to fit the revised text. These changes are signified in the notes on the individual plates which follow. Reference is made throughout to A.M. Hind's *Wenceslaus Hollar and his views of London and Windsor* which should be consulted for more detailed descriptions and comparison of states and for photographic reproductions.

Many of the plates survived in a degraded condition for more than 150 years: first to illustrate the 1753 edition of 'Seymour's' *Survey* (no 30) and subsequently in a Hollar collection issued in 1815 for extra-illustrators by Robert Wilkinson. This, according to William Upcott, consisted of 49 impressions of which 31 were from plates etched in 1657 for Dugdale. It is not surprising that for Ellis's edition published in 1818 (no 125) W. Finden was engaged to copy all Hollar's plates.

1 front. Gulielmus Dugdale/Ætatis 50. A. MDCLVI ... Wen. Hollar delin. et sculp. 216 × 166/260 × 175mm. 1716 ed adds publication-line.

2 p 40 (label tc) Capella Thomae Kempe Lond. Ep. 225 × 250/235 × 260mm. 1716 ed p 42. (*Hind* 47)

3 p 52 (tm and label tc) Inter Ecclesiae navim et alam Australem/Tumulus Iohannis de Bellocampo militis ... W. Hollar fecit. 250 × 180/265 × 185mm. (*Hind* 48)

4 p 60 (above each tomb) In superiori parte Chori prope Altare – in medio Chori prope Altare – in Choro prope introitum. 275 × 180mm pl. mark. Tombs of Robert Fitzhugh, William Grene and Dean Evere. (*Hind* 49)

5 p 62 (tc) Inter Chorum et alam australem. 300 × 165mm pl. mark. The shrouded effigy of John Donne, the only one to have survived the Great Fire. (*Hind* 50)

6 p 64 (tl) Inter Chorum et alam Australem. 280 × 200mm pl. mark. Monument with cadaver to John Colet, Dean and founder of St Paul's School.

7 p 66 (tc) Inter Chorum et alam australem. 305 × 170mm pl. mark. Tomb of William Hewit. Printed by mistake on the verso of p 67 instead of that of p 65; corrected in 1716 ed.

8 p 68 (tc) Inter Chorum et alam australem. 285 × 190mm pl. mark. Monument to William Cokain. Printed by mistake on the verso of p 65 instead of that of p 67.

9 p 70 (tc) In Choro ex opposito Monumenti Pembrochiani. 283 × 195mm pl. mark. Monument to Nicholas Bacon.

10 p 72 (tc) In australi ala ex adverso Chori. W. Hollar fec. 280 × 195mm pl. mark. Tomb slabs of Bishop John King, John Acton and Symon Edolph. (*Hind* 51)

11 p 74 (tc) In Australi ala/a latere Chori. W. Hollar fecit. 305 × 160mm pl. mark. Tombs of Thomas Okeford, William Rythyn and Richard Lichfield. (*Hind* 52)

12 p 76 (tc) In Australi Insula a latere Chori. 235 × 200mm pl. mark. Tomb slabs of Dean William Worsley, Roger Brabazon and Dean Valentine Carey. (*Hind* 53)

13 p 78 (tl) In australi Insula a latere Chori. W. Hollar fecit. 260 × 185mm. Tomb slabs of John Newcourt and another unnamed ecclesiastic. (*Hind* 54)

14 p 80 (on labels tl and tr) Henricus de Wengham ... – Eustachius Ffauconberg ... W. Hollar delin et sculp. 203 × 270/210 × 275mm. Tomb chests under Gothic canopies of Henry de Wingham and Eustace de Fauconberge, both Bishops of London. (*Hind* 55)

15 p 82 (tc) Inter Orientalem partem Ecclesiae et alam australem. 275 × 205mm pl. mark. Monument to Sir Christopher Hatton, d 1591.

16 p 84 (above each tomb) Tumulus Henrici de Lacie/Comitis Lincolniae – Tumulus Roberti de Braybroke Lond: Episcopi.... W. Hollar delin: et sculp:. 275 × 185mm pl. mark. (*Hind* 56)

17 p 86 (tc, below dedication and armorial bearings wreathed with bays) Inter alam aquilonalem et Chorum/Tumulus Rogeri Cognom: Nigri/Londoniensis Episcopi. W. Hollar fecit. 230 × 170,85 × 170mm on separate pl. 1716 ed omits smaller plate with dedication to Edward Waterhouse. (*Hind* 57)

18 p 88 (tc) Inter alam aquilonalem et Chorum. 285 × 195mm. Monument to William, Earl of Pembroke, d 1569.

19 p 90 (tc) Monumentum Iohannis Gandavi/ensis Ducis Lancastriae et Constantiae/uxoris eius. 310 × 170mm pl. mark. The most impressive of the monument plates, showing John of Gaunt's tomb with his tilting lance and shield and cap of maintenance. (*Hind* 58)

20 p 92 (on label tc) In fornice aquilonalis muri ex opposito Chori. W. Hollar delin. et sculp. 195 × 255/198 × 260mm. Tombs of King Sebba and King Ethelred. 1716 ed p 94. (*Hind* 59)

21 p 94 (tc) Monumentum Septentrionali/Muro Chori affixum. 285 × 185mm pl. mark. Tomb of John Mason, d 1566. 1716 ed p 96.

22 p 96 (tc) In Pariete Aquilonali/ex opposito Chori. W. Hollar delin. et sculp. 300 × 165mm pl. mark. Monument to William Aubrey. (*Hind* 60)

23 p 98 (on label along tm) In aquilonali muro ex adverso Chori. W. Hollar delin. et sculp. 168 × 230/175 × 235mm. Tomb of John de Chishull, Bishop of London. (*Hind* 61)

24 p 100 (in centre of pl.) Tumulus Radulphi de Hengham/in aquilonali muro, ex adverso Chori. W. Hollar delin: et sculp. 280 × 188mm pl. mark. Lower engraving with tomb chest under a canopied arcade, upper shows tomb slab. 1716 ed p 102. (*Hind* 62)

25 p 102 (tc) Tumulus Simonis/Burley Militis, In Septen-/trionali muro ex opposito/Tumuli Iohannis Gandavi/ensis, Ducis Lancastriae,/prope summum altare. W. Hollar delineavit et sculpsit. 285 × 193mm pl. mark. 1716 ed p 104. (*Hind* 63)

26 p 104 (tc) In ala boreali, ex adverso Chori. 275 × 160mm. Tomb slab of John Mullins and memorial to Sir Simon Baskerville. 1716 ed p 106. (*Hind* 64)

27 p 106 (tc) Tumulus Iohannis Wolley Eq. Aur./In Capella St Georgii. 266 × 184mm pl. mark. 1716 ed p 108. (*Hind* 65)

28 p 108 (Monument of Thomas Heneage, d 1594, in the Lady Chapel) 285 × 195mm pl. mark. 1716 ed p 110.

29 p 110 Ex aquilonali latere Ecclesiae/ab Orientali parte Chori./Alexandri Noelli,/Ecclesiae Paulinae Decani/Monumentum. 265 × 182mm pl. mark. Unpaginated, but 1716 ed p 112. (*Hind* 66)

30 p 112 (on label tc) Clausura circa Altare/S. Erkenwal-/di/sub feretro ejusdem. W. Hollar fecit 1657. 235 × 170/240 × 175mm. 1716 ed p 114. (*Hind* 67)

31 p 114 (tc) Templi Parochialis S. Fidis/(scil. areae ejusdem) Ichnographia. W. Hollar delin: et sculp 1657. 205 × 300mm pl. mark. Ground plan with refs to tombs 1–16. 1716 ed p 116. (*Hind* 32)

32 p 115 (on label tc) Ecclesiae Parochialis S. Fidis/ Prospectus Interior. W. Hollar delin. et sculp. 188 × 330/200 × 333mm. Verso blank. p 117 added in 1716 ed (*Hind* 33)

33 p 127 (on label tc) Domus Capitularis Sti Pauli a/Meridie Prospectus. W. Hollar delineavit et sculpsit. 193 × 288/197 × 290mm. Detailed engraving of the Chapter House and S. cloister. 1716 ed p 128. (*Hind* 34)

34 p 133 (in oblong engraved framework tl) Ecclesiae Paulinae Prospectus/qualis olim erat ... W. Hollar sculp. 1657. 255 × 358mm pl. mark. Showing the cathedral with its spire, struck by lightning and consumed by fire in 1561. 1716 ed p 133 is a substitute engraving by I. Harris. (*Hind* 35)

35 p 161 (along tm) Areae Ecclesiae Cathedralis Sti Pauli Ichnographia. Wenceslaus Hollar dimensit, delineavit et aqua forti aeri insculpsit A° 1657. 235 × 340mm pl. mark. Ground plan showing the position of the tombs and monuments etched on some of the previous plates. Refs 1–50. Copied by John Harris for 1716 ed. (*Hind* 36)

36 p 162 (in oval cartouche tl) Ecclesiae Cathedralis/Sti Pauli/A Meridie Prospectus. W. Hollar delin. et sculp:. 205 × 380mm pl. mark. Not in 1716 ed. (*Hind* 37)

37 p 163 (in oblong festooned frame tr) Ecclesiae Cathedralis/S. Pauli/A Septentrione Prospectus. W. Hollar delineavit et sculp: Londini 1656. 200 × 380mm pl. mark. To be placed between pp 134–5 according to 1716 ed binder's instructions. (*Hind* 38)

38 p 164 (in oval cartouche tl) Ecclesiae Cathedralis/Sti Pauli/ab Occidente Prospectus. W. Hollar delin. et sculp. 228 × 270mm pl. mark. Copied by John Harris in 1716 ed. (*Hind* 39)

39 p 165 (tc) Ecclesiae Cathedralis Sti Pauli Orientalis Facies. W. Hollar delineavit et sculpsit 1656. 248 × 172mm. Not in 1716 ed. (*Hind* 40)

40 p 166 (tc) Ecclesiae Cathedralis S. Pauli Lond:/ab Oriente Prospectus. W. Hollar delin: et sculp:. 195 × 250mm pl. mark. Substitute plate by Harris in 1716 ed. (*Hind* 41)

41 p 167 (on label tc) Navis Ecclesiae Cathedralis S. Pauli./Prospectus Interior. Wenceslaus Hollar Bohemus hujus Ecclesiae quotidie casum expectantis delineator et olim admirator memoriam sic preservavit A° 1658. 365 × 345/400 × 350mm. Numbered as p 145 in 1716 ed, to be inserted between pp 134–5. The finest of the interior views. (*Hind* 42)

42 p 168 (on label tc) Partis exterioris Chori ab Occidente/Prospectus. W. Hollar delineavit et sculp. 218 × 318/235 × 323mm. Numbered as p 146 in 1716 ed, to be inserted between pp 134–5. (*Hind* 44)

43 p 169 (along tm) Chori Ecclesiae Cathedralis S. Pauli Prospectus Interior. Wenceslaus Hollar delineavit et sculpsit. 308 × 220/320 × 225mm. Numbered as p 147 in 1716 ed, to be inserted between pp 134–5. (*Hind* 45)

44 p 170 Orientalis Partis Eccl: Cath: S: Pauli Prospectus Interior. W. Hollar fecit. 290 × 212/305 × 215mm. Numbered as p 148 in 1716 ed, to be inserted between pp 134–5. (*Hind* 46)

45 p 290 (printed with letterpress as illustration to Lydgate's 'Dance of Death', with dedication to John Porey) 145 × 182/160 × 188mm.

---

9 · OGILBY'S ENTERTAINMENT OF CHARLES II [1662]

John Ogilby, a man of parts, had been in turn dancing-master, tutor to the Earl of Strafford's children, theatre director and Deputy-Master of the Irish Revels, self-educated translator of the classics and publisher. At the Restoration the versatility of this talented individual came to the notice of Charles II who put him in charge of the public rejoicings of 22–3 April 1661 marking the event and celebrating his coronation. No doubt he drew inspiration for the street decorations from Stephen Harrison's record of the trimphal arches erected in 1603 to welcome the King's grandfather to London (no 1), but his pageantry was much admired and the device on the arch in Leadenhall Street earned a mention in Dryden's coronation poem. Ogilby credited the 'architectural part' to Peter Mills, City Surveyor, but drawings for the arches in the Burlington-Devonshire Collection (RIBA IV 13(1–4)) are attributed to Sir Balthazar Gerbier. He made haste to publish, in the same year, by way of souvenir, an account of the proceedings entitled *The Relation of the Entertainment of His Majesty Charles II in His Passage through the City of London to his Coronation*. On royal orders the text was revised by Sir Edward Walker and a commemorative folio appeared in the following year.

The Entertainment of His Most Excellent Majestie Charles II, in His Passage Through the City of London to his Coronation: Containing an exact Accompt of the whole Solemnity; the Triumphal Arches, and Cavalcade, delineated in Sculpture; the Speeches and Impresses illustrated from Antiquity. To these is added A Brief Narrative of His Majestie's Solemn Coronation: with His Magnificent Proceedings, and Royal Feast in Westminster Hall. By John Ogilby. London, Printed by Tho:

Roycroft, and are to be had at the Author's House in Kings-Head Court within Shoe-Lane. MDCLXII.

Folio, about 425 × 280mm.   1662

COLLATION Title-page; imprimatur of Garter King of Arms dated June 1662, dedication to the monarch (2 pp); pp 1–165, The Entertainent; half-title; pp 167–92, Narrative of His Majesty's Coronation.

Ogilby, both as writer and publisher, had already exploited the talents of the greatest illustrator of the day, the Bohemian engraver Wenceslaus Hollar. Full-page plates by this artist adorned both his 1654 translation of Virgil, in folio, and his *Iliad* version of 1660. Hollar was also well known to the restored monarch. In 1640 he had made fine etchings after Van Dyck portraits of Charles I and his Queen and been appointed drawing-master to the future Charles II. He had, moreover, contributed portrait and allegorical plates to an earlier London royal progress, that of Marie de Medici on a visit to Charles I's Queen, her daughter—La Serre's *Histoire de L'Entrée de la Reine Mère du Roy très Chrestien dans la Grande Bretaigne* (no 3)—and was an old friend of Sir Edward Walker who, as Garter King of Arms, was in overall charge of the coronation ceremony. He was thus the obvious choice as official artist to record the royal procession and the Westminster Abbey coronation scene. His magnificent etching of the latter, in its faithful rendering of the solemnity of the occasion and its admirable attention to detail, provides a fitting climax to the earlier illustrations in this handsome volume.

The other illustrator was David Loggan, a Scotsman born in Danzig and best known for the plates of Oxford and Cambridge colleges published during the next decade. His engravings of the four triumphal arches through which the King passed on his way to Westminster must have been one of his first commissions, predated only by his rendering of Daniel King's panorama of London with views of Old St Paul's (*Scouloudi* p 56) dated 1658 and published as a broadsheet by John Overton with verses by Edward Benlowes. The plates are unnumbered, without check-list and mostly without captions; descriptions in brackets are quoted from the text. Some of the plates have been cropped in binding and so lack plate-marks. In addition to those enumerated are small plates of Roman coins and medals for which spaces have been left in the letterpress.

1 front. Dieu et Mon Droit. W. Hollar fecit. 292 × 197/305 × 230mm. Royal Stuart arms with supporters, the Garter and elaborate mantling.

2–6 p 1 The Cavalcade in His Maiesties Passing through the City of London towards his Coronation. Five plates, engraved by Hollar, each printed on a two-page opening and consisting of 20 strips numbered in sequence, measuring 95 × 483mm. Pl. marks 367 × 490mm. Participants of the cavalcade shown without topographical background.

7 p 13 (In Leaden-Hall-Street, neer Lime-Street End, was erected the first Triumphal Arch, after the Dorick Order.) D. Loggan sculp. About 420 × 290mm. Commemorates 'Monarchy Restored' and the King's landing.

8–9 p 24 Trophea Marii de Bello Cymb Putat: ad Aed. D.Cvsebrom Romae. Each 400 × 250mm pl. mark. Two engravings of Roman trophies.

10 p 43 (Near the Exchange in Corn-hill, is erected the Second Arch, which is Naval) About 490 × 300mm. Commemorates 'Loyalty Restored' with two orders of architecture, garlanded Ionic and Corinthian. On the base of the upper order are small views of the Tower and the Royal Exchange, each 24 × 30mm. At the summit Atlas supports a globe and a ship.

11 p 111 (The third Triumphal Arch stands near Wood-Street end, not far from the place where the Cross sometimes stood.) About 425 × 295mm. A Corinthian Temple of Concord. The proof engraving in the BM (*Crace* 38.48) includes a partial credit: 'D. Log sculp.'

12 p 139 (In Fleet-street, near White-Friers stands the fourth Triumphal Arch, representing the Garden of Plenty: it is of two Stories, one of the Dorick Order, the other of the Ionick. The Capitals have not their just Measure, but incline to the Modern Architecture) 420 × 290mm.

13 p 162 (Rain & fire falling upon the tents of the Romans) 140 × 150/145 × 166mm. Printed with letterpress surrounding.

14 p 165 (The Coronation scene in Westminster Abbey—Charles II is crowned surrounded by his Peers on raised stands. View from the Crossing towards the Presbytery) 360 × 480/385 × 490mm. (*Hind* 101)

15 (The Coronation Procession) 6 strips, each 70 × 535mm in pl. mark 425 × 545mm.

10 · STOOP'S EMBASSY TO LISBON [1662]

This large folio was intended as a record of the Earl of Sandwich's mission to Lisbon with the object of conducting Catherine of Braganza, Charles II's consort, to London. In addition to these seven engraved plates the Earl also had printed a map of Lisbon, as recorded by Pepys (24 August 1663): 'There come to him (ie Lord Sandwich) this morning the prints of the river Tagus and the City of Lisbon, which he measured with his own hand, and printed by command of the King'. The plates are mainly a record of marine pomp and processions and, as with La Serre's *Entrée de la Reyne Mère* (no 3), they are of very minor topographical interest. The last engraving only has a London setting.

Dirk Stoop, a native of Utrecht, accompanied Catherine to England as court painter and apparently latinized his name to suit his circumstances. He was not nearly so proficient an etcher as Hollar but no doubt had to produce these plates in virtue of his office.

Each plate has a caption engraved in the sky in both English and Portuguese. All but the sixth have in their bm a dedication to a dignitary and a numbered key to persons, ships, etc represented. Dedications and credits are combined in one of the following alternatives: 'Dedicat Theodorus Stoop suae Matis Reginae Angliae Pictor', 'Dedicat V.C. Rodrigo (or 'Roderigo') Stoop', or 'Dedicated by their most obedient and humble servant Ro. Stoop'.

1 The Entrance of the Lord Ambassador Mountague into the Citty of Lisbone the 28 day of March 1662. 170 × 558/195 × 565mm.
2 The publique proceeding of the Queenes Matie of Greate Britaine through ye Citty of Lisbone ye 20th day of Aprill 1662. 165 × 535/190 × 548mm.
3 The manner how her Matie Dona Catherina imbarketh from Lisbon for England. 175 × 555/195 × 565mm.
4 The Duke of York's meeting with ye Royall Navy after it came into the Channell. 170 × 555/195 × 565mm.
5 The maner of the Queene's Maties landing at Portsmouth (and Portuguese title with date '25 majo') 165 × 540/193 × 553m.

6 The coming of ye King's Matie and ye Queenes from Portsmouth to Hampton Court. 162 × 538/185 × 550mm. No engr letters in lm.
7 Aqua Triumphalis (and below the beribboned shields of the City of London and the 12 major Livery Companies, six a side) The Triumphal Entertainment of ye King and Queenes Matie/by ye Right honble ye Lord Maior and Cittizens of London/at their coming from Hampton-Court to Whitehall (on ye River of Thames)/Aug: ye 23 1662. (lm) To the right Honble Sr John Frederick Kt, Lord Mayor of ye Citty of London: and to his right worfull Brethren ... This Plate is most humbly dedicated by theyre most obedient servant Rod: Stoop. 165 × 530/190 × 540mm. In the foreground is the royal barge about to land at Whitehall Stairs. Accompanying it are other ships and the Company barges, each identified by name and each laden with an allegorical pageant or a demonstration of some trade process. On the r. in the background are Westminster clock tower, St Stephen's, Westminster Hall and Westminster Abbey. On the l., Lambeth Palace and, in the distance, 'Chelsi'.

11 · SANDFORD'S INTERMENT OF THE DUKE OF ALBEMARLE* [1670]

The death of George Monck, the general-in-chief instrumental in restoring Charles II to his throne, was the occasion for Francis Sandford, genealogist and Herald, in his office of Rouge Dragon Pursuivant to which he had been appointed in 1661, to organize a state funeral. It was also the occasion for this his first printed work, a detailed record of the ceremonies.

(*Title-page* pl. 1)

Oblong folio, 350 × 470mm.   1670

COLLATION Title-page; The Order and Ceremonies (6pp); 21 plates.

Only two of the engravings in this folio have any topographical significance, one numbered '1' and the final one, unnumbered. The 19 intervening plates, engraved by Robert White from drawings by Francis Barlow, are a graphic record of the funeral procession with calligraphic names or titles above the heads of the mourners but without background, in the tradition of John Ogilby's record of Charles

II's coronation (no 9). The title-page also is designed by the animal painter Francis Barlow, and White engraved both it and the two other plates under consideration. He was a skilled engraver in line, chiefly known for some 400 portrait plates in this manner of most of the notabilities of the day including Lord Clarendon, Henry Purcell, George Herbert and Samuel Pepys. He was a pupil of the topographical engraver David Loggan and in 1679 the second Part of a new edition of Guillim's classic *Heraldry* was illustrated with his plates.

1 (engr title) The Order/and Ceremonies Used for, and at/The Solemn Interment of/The Most High, Mighty and most Noble Prince/George Duke of Albemarle ... /Ao 1670/ Collected by Francis Sandford/Gent: Rouge-Dragon, one of His/Maties Officers at Armes; and Published/by His Maties especiall Command. F. Barlow Invent: Roert White sculpsit. 220 × 320/245 × 345mm. Title engraved within two scrolled cartouches backed with a trophy of pikes, banners, drums, cannon and armour; tc a bust of the Duke is flanked by two female figures, the one representing Peace and Plenty and the other War who crowns him with olive. Below top cartouche two putti with dolphins, anchors and sea-shells. Supporting lower cartouche two fettered allegorical figures, perhaps Envy and Sedition.

2 pl 1 A prospect of the Chamber and Bed of State in which the Effigies of the Duke of Albemarle lay in Somerset House. R.White sculpsit. 235 × 315/250 × 330mm. The bed is set between three windowless walls bare but for candle sconces and the shields of arms which were part of the funeral trappings.

3 A Prospect of the Hearse in which the Effigies of the Duke of Albemarle lay in State, in the Abbey of Westminster. R. White sculpsit. 248 × 360/265 × 367m. Looking E. The hearse lies under the crossing with the effigy tilted for visibility. The armour is still preserved in the Abbey museum.

12 · SANDFORD'S GENEALOGICAL HISTORY* [1677]

This fine folio is the most important work of Francis Sandford, a Royalist from an old Shropshire family appointed at the Restoration to the College of Arms in the office of Rouge Dragon Pursuivant and promoted to Lancaster Herald in 1676. In this latter capacity he produced the official account of the coronation of James II (no 16) which, like this *Genealogical History*, contains Westminster Abbey engravings. This book is dedicated to Charles II who encouraged him in its composition and was written in collaboration with Gregory King, Sandford's successor as Rouge Dragon.

A Genealogical History of the Kings of England, and Monarchs of Great Britain, &c. From the Conquest, Anno 1066 to the Year, 1677. In Seven Parts or Books, containing ... Monumental Inscriptions With their Effigies, Seals, Tombs, Cenotaphs, Devises, Arms, Quarterings, Crests and Supporters; All Engraven in Copper Plates.... By Francis Sandford Esq; Lancaster Herald of Arms. In the Savoy: Printed by Tho. Newcomb, for the Author, 1677.

Folio, 365 × 230mm.   1677

COLLATION   Title-page; royal licence dated 3 January 1677, dedication to Charles II (6pp); seals and genealogical tables (4pp); pp 1–578, The Genealogical History; index of names and titles, errata (11pp).

The work is illustrated by numerous plates, many being of monumental effigies. Like those in Dugdale's *St Paul's* (no 8) and *Monasticon Anglicanum* (no 6) they are mostly ornamented with cartouches of dedication tl and of arms tr. They are generally paginated tr but have no captions or publication-lines. Only eight out of the 22 listed have credits and these are for the notable engravers Wenceslaus Hollar and his pupil Richard Gaywood and for Francis Barlow, Gaywood's friend and draughtsman. The finest is undoubtedly Hollar's beautifully finished etching of the bronze parclose which guards Henry VII's tomb chest, apparently in its pristine condition with statue-filled niches.

This selection is confined to Westminster Abbey monuments (and one from St Paul's), here depicted before spoliation by tourists and metropolitan vandals in the next century. Sixty years later George Vertue and the other illustrators of Rapin de Thoyras's *History of England* and its by-product *The Heads of the Kings* (no 31) were obviously dependent on these plates for their unmutilated versions of these royal icons.

1 p 92 (Tomb of Henry III) 230 × 172/270 × 182mm.

2 p 104 (Tomb of Aveline Countess of Lancaster) W. Hollar fecit 1666. 270 × 180/285 × 190mm. (*Hind* 103)

3 p 106 (Tomb of Edmund, Earl of Lancaster) 320 × 190mm. Attributed to Hollar. (*Hind* 104)

4 p 131 (Tomb of Eleanor of Castile) 295 × 180mm.

5 p 137 (Tomb of Edward I and the Feretory) R. Gaywood fe(c)it. 242 × 168/270 × 175mm.

6 p 154 (Tomb of John of Eltham) 295 × 135mm.

7 p 173 (Tomb of Philippa of Hainault) 235 × 172/290 × 180mm.

8 p 176 (Tomb of Edward III) R. Gaywood fecit. 273 × 165/280 × 178mm.

9 p 203 (Tomb of Richard II and Anne Neville) R. Gaywood fecit 1665. 295 × 190/305 × 205mm.

10 p 230 (Tomb slab of Thomas of Woodstock, Duke of Gloucester) R. Gaywood fecit. 280 × 178mm.

11 p 249 (Tomb of John of Gaunt in St Paul's Cathedral) R. Gaywood fecit 1664. 312 × 170mm. cf with item 19 in Dudgale's *St Paul's* (no 8).

12 p 281 (Chapel of Henry V) F. Barlow Delin. R. Gaywood fecit. 302 × 200mm.

13 p 282 (Tomb chest and effigy of Henry V) 130 × 183mm.

14 p 320 (Tomb of Margaret Beaufort) 175 × 175mm.

15 p 364 (Tomb of Philippa, Duchess of York) 175 × 175/220 × 180mm. Attributed to Hollar. (*Hind* 105)

16 p 403 (Memorial to Edward V and Richard, Duke of York, the 'little princes') 200 × 185/280 × 193mm.

17 p 442 (Parclose screen of Henry VII's tomb chest) W. Hollar fecit aqua forti Ao 1665, Aetat: 58 compl:. 280 × 360/295 × 375mm. (*Hind* 102)

18 p 443 (Tomb chest of Henry VII) 252 × 350mm.

19 p 471 (Altar tomb of Edward VI formerly in Henry VII's Chapel) 320 × 192mm.

20 p 493 (Tomb of Queen Elizabeth) R Gaywood fecit. 296 × 178mm.

21 p 506 (Tomb of Mary, Queen of Scots) 305 × 190mm.

22 p 536 (Memorial to the children of James I) 280 × 160mm.

---

13 · BURTON'S HISTORICAL REMARQUES [1681]

Nathaniel Crouch, the publisher of this book, was also its author under the pseudonym of Richard Burton which he used in full, or in its abbreviated form 'R.B.', on the many publications, mainly on historical subjects, he put out between 1678 and 1712. A freeman of the Stationers' Company, he specialized in compiling small shilling books of popular instruction which attracted the attention of Dr Johnson who described them as 'very proper to allure backward readers'. John Dunton says of him in *Life and errors*: 'I think I have given you the very soul of his character when I have told you that his talent lies at Collection. He has melted down the best of our English histories into twelve-penny books, which are filled with Wonders, Rarities and Curiosities'.

The *Historical Remarques*, first published in 1681, was brought out in two Parts, the first a Survey and the second a History of London with a separate title-page. These were separately paginated and signed but reprinted in the same year with continuous pagination and signatures. Crouch published a third edition in 1684, improved by the addition of topographical engravings made for Delaune's *Present State of London* (no 14). A fourth appeared in 1691 illustrated only with woodcuts and a fifth in 1703 illustrated with frontispiece and woodcuts. In 1730 a much expanded posthumous edition appeared newly illustrated with wood-engravings printed with the text. Finally, in 1810, an antiquarian reprint of the first edition printed on thick laid paper with woodcut illustration was issued by Machell Stace as part of a collected edition in quarto of Burton's 'Historical Works' intended to attract the grangerizers and pennantizers of the day.

Historical Remarques, and Observations of the Ancient and Present State of London and Westminster. Shewing the Foundation, Walls, Gates, Towers, Bridges, Churches, Rivers, Wards, Palaces, Halls, Companies, Inns of Court and Chancery, Hospitals, Schools, Government, Charters, Courts and Priviledges thereof. With an Account of the most Remarkable Accidents, as to Wars, Fires, Plagues, and other Occurrences which have happened therein for above Nine Hundred Years past, till the Year 1681. Illustrated with Pictures of the most considerable Matters curiously Ingraven on Copper Plates; With the Arms of the Sixty Six Companies of London, and the time of their Incorporating. By Richard Burton, Author of the History of the Wars of England. London, Printed for Nath. Crouch at the Bell next to Kemps Coffee house in Exchange Alley, over against the Royal Exchange in Cornhil. 1681.

(second tp) Historical Remarques and Observations of the Ancient and Present State of the Cities of London and Westminster With an Account of the most considerable Occurrences, Revolutions, and Transactions, as to Wars, Fires, Plagues, and other remarkable Accidents which have happened in and about these Cities, for above Nine Hundred Years past, till this present year 1681. Illustrated with Pictures. The Second Part. By Richard Burton. London, Printed by Tho. Snowden for Nath. Crouch. 1681.

The two title-pages of the second edition are the same but in the next edition the dates of the imprints are altered and the main imprint reads: 'The Third Edition Enlarged. London: Printed for Nath. Crouch at the Bell in the Poultry, near Cheapside, 1684'. In the fourth edition both imprint dates are altered and the first title-page terminates: 'By Richard Burton. The Fourth Edition. London, Printed for Nath. Crouch at the Bell in the Poultrey, near Cheapside, 1691'; the second title omits the words 'till this present Year 1681'. The fifth edition, reset throughout, has only one title-page, reading:

Historical Remarques and Observations Upon the Ancient and Present State of London and Westminster. Shewing the Foundation, Walls, Gates, Towers, Bridges, Churches, Rivers, Wards, Palaces, Halls, Companies, Inns of Court and Chancery, Hospitals, Schools, Government, Charters, Courts and Privileges thereof. With an Account of the most Remarkable Accidents, as to Wars, Fires, Plagues, and other Occurrences which have happened therein for above Nine Hundred Years past till this Time. Illustrated with Pictures of the most considerable Passages, and the Arms of the Companies of London, with the time of their Incorporating. By R.B. The Fifth Edition. London, Printed for Nath. Crouch at the Bell in the Poultrey, near Cheapside, 1703.

Duodecimo, about 145 × 80mm.   eds 1–5:
                        1681(two),1684,1691,1703

COLLATIONS
(1681 a) Title-page; To the Reader (2pp); pp 1–116 (sigs A–E), Historical Remarques (part 1); title-page; pp 1–116 (sigs Aa-Ee), Historical Remarques (part 2).

(1681 b) Title-page; To the Reader (2pp); pp 1–234 (sigs A–K), Historical Remarques.

(1684 and 1691) To the Reader (2pp); pp 1–233, Historical Remarques.

(1703) Title-page; To the Reader (1p); pp 3–156, Historical Remarks.

The illustrations in the first two editions consist of an allegorical frontispiece and 14 small historical scenes crudely engraved, two or three to a plate with captions above each subject. In the text are heraldic woodcuts of the arms of the City, three Merchant Companies and 62 Livery Companies which follow closely those in Delaune's *Present state of London*. The third edition adds to these topographical plates originally published in Delaune, indicated by *DEL* in the list below which is based on an apparently complete BL copy (577.a.8(a)). By the time the fourth and fifth editions were published the only surviving plate seems to have been the frontispiece.

This juxtaposition of a History and a Survey illustrated by naively dramatic historical scenes, by 'tourist attractions' on copper and by heraldic woodcuts was to set a pattern for over 100 years' output of popular London books, culminated in elaborate folios issued in Numbers, such as Harrison's *History* (no 57) with its numerous plates, and bore fruit in the engravings published on behalf of extra-illustrators of Pennant's *London* (no 67) during the first quarter of the nineteenth century.

Plates in the 3rd ed (1684) with references to the first two

(The placing of the plates may not be uniform for all copies of the first two editions because there are no binder's directions and facing page numbers are only inked in; those given in the references are from the BL first edition G.13203 and the London Library second edition.)

1 front. (in sky above each allegory) London in Flames – London in Glory. London: Printed for Nath. Crouch. (each 56 × 65) 117 × 65/127 × 75mm. The first allegory is backed by ruins and the second by the Royal Exchange and Monument. 1st and 2nd eds front.

2 p 12 (in compartments tc) The Tower – Ald-Gate. (each 67 × 71) 135 × 71/137 × 75mm. *DEL 6*.

3 p 13 (in compartments tc) Bishops-Gate – Moore-Gate. (each 67 × 70) 135 × 70/137 × 75mm. *DEL 19*.

4 p 14 (in compartments tc) Cripple-Gate – Alders-Gate. (each 67 × 71) 135 × 71/140 × 75mm. *DEL 13*.

5 p 16 (in compartments tc) New-Gate – Lud-Gate. (each 67 × 71) 135 × 71/137 × 75mm. *DEL 12*.

6 p 20 (t each design) Wat Tyler kil'd by ye Lord-Mayor – K. Richard Resigns his Crown – King Richard 2 Murdered. (each 35 × 65) 115 × 65/125 × 80mm. 1st ed 1, p 38; 2nd ed p 20.

7 p 80 (on banderoles in sky) Westminster Hall – The Royall Exchange. (each 64 × 70)133 × 70/140 × 75mm. *DEL 159*.
p 84 (City arms held by two matrons with sword and shield; above two putti with laurel wreaths supporting on a swag a blank cartouche) Wood-engraving in text. Thus 1st and 2nd eds. *DEL 1*.
pp 85–95 (Arms of three Merchant Companies and 62 Livery Companies) Wood-engravings in text. Thus 1st and 2nd eds. *DEL 302–29*.

8 p 108 (on banderoles tc) Phisitians College – Lord Shaftsbury House. (each 63 × 70)131 × 70/137 × 75mm. *DEL 104*.

9 p 111 (on banderoles tc) White Hall – The Temple. (each 63 × 70)132 × 70/140 × 75mm. *DEL 113*.

10 p 113 (in compartments tc) New Bedlam – Bride Well. (each 67 × 70)135 × 70/140 × 75mm. *DEL 81*.

11 p 119 (on banderoles tc) Clarendon House – Covent Garden. (each 64 × 70)133 × 70/140 × 75mm. *DEL 154*.

12 p 188 (t each design) K. Henry 6 Murdered in ye Tower – K. Edward 5 & his brother Murdered – Q. Elizabeth Prisoner in the Tower. (each 37 × 66)120 × 66/127 × 75mm. 1st ed 2, p 102; 2nd ed p 188.

13 p 217 (t each design) The Kings Restoration 1660 – The Regicides Exec: at Charing Cross – The Insurrection of Venner &c 1660. (33 × 65,35 × 65, 38 × 65)118 × 65/135 × 75mm. 1st ed 2, p 99; 2nd ed p 217.

14 p 232 (t each design) The Tryall of the L. Strafford in W.Hall – His Execution on Tower hill. (76 × 65,31 × 65)119 × 65/130 × 72mm. The execution engraving is keyed A-H. 1st ed 1, p 114; 2nd ed p 232.

One rather unedifying plate, present in the first two editions, was afterwards omitted:

15 vol. 2, p 23; 2nd ed p 165 Iews Crucifie a Child in England – K. Willi: Rufus Kil'd in Hunting – Iohn Poysoned by a Monk. (each 35 × 65)120 × 65/130 × 75mm.

Two further editions, that of 1730 and the reprint of 1810, are strictly speaking outside the terms of reference of this catalogue since they are illustrated only by woodcuts. They are, however, included in order to complete the history of this pioneer guidebook:

A New View and observations on the ancient and present state of London and Westminster. Shewing, The Foundation, Walls, Gates, Towers, Bridges, Churches, Rivers, Wards, Palaces, Halls, Companies, Inns of Court and Chancery, Hospitals, Schools, Government, Charters, Courts and Privileges thereof. Also Historical Remarks thereon. With an account of the most Remarkable Accidents, as to Wars, Fires, Plagues, and other occurrences which have happened therein for above 1400 Years past, brought down to the present Time. Illustrated with Cuts of the most considerable Matters; with the Arms of the Sixty Six Companies of London and the Time of their Incorporations. By Robert Burton, Author of the History of the Wars of England, continued by an Able Hand. London:Printed for A. Bettesworth, and Charles Hitch, at the Red Lion: and J. Batley, at the Dove, in Pater-noster-Row 1730.

Duodecimo, about 165 × 95mm.   1730

COLLATION Title-page; To the Reader (3pp); pp 1–312 (sigs B-N), New View of London; pp 145–240, 385–468 (sigs O-R, S-Z), Historical Remarks of London from 527 to 1730. (Text complete despite irregularity of pagination and sigs.)

The woodcuts with the exception of the frontispiece are all printed with the text. The heraldic blocks survive from the earlier editions but the other cuts are original.

1a front. (Royal arms and City arms) 32 × 63, 65 × 70mm. City arms from earlier eds p 84.

2a p 17 (Ald-gate) 106 × 70mm.

3a p 21 (Bishop's Gate) 106 × 70mm.

4a p 24 (Moor-Gate) 106 × 70mm.

5a p 26 (Cripple-Gate) 106 × 70mm.

6a p 28 (Alders-Gate) 106 × 70mm.

7a p 30 (New-Gate) 106 × 70mm.

8a p 34 (Lud-Gate) 106 × 70mm.

9a p 40 (Temple-Bar) 106 × 70mm.

10a p 42 Tower. 75 × 125mm.

11a p 120 The Arms of London. 66 × 70mm. From earlier eds p 84.

12a pp 121–31 (Arms of three Merchant Companies and 62 Livery Companies) From earlier eds pp 85–95.

13a p 152 (Bethlem Hospital) 75 × 133mm.

14a p 157 Sr Thomas Gresham. 95 × 70mm.

15a p 162 (Royal Exchange) 100 × 70mm.

16 p 173 The Monument. 130 × 75mm. Shows only the base.

17 p 179 Charles II. 100 × 70mm. The statue at the Stocks-Market.

18 p 196 Guild Hall. 75 × 125mm.

19 p 220 St Pauls Cathedral. 125 × 75mm. From W.

20 p 229 Queen Anne's Statue. 97 × 70mm. W. end of St Paul's.

21 p 288 Charles I. 97 × 70mm. The statue at Charing Cross.

22 p 291 The Cock-Pit-Gate. 130 × 75mm. ie the 'Holbein' Gate.

23 p 299 George I. 95 × 70mm. The horseback statue in Grosvenor Square.

The title-page of the nineteenth century reprint, printed in red and black, is virtually a transcript of that preceding the second part of the first edition up to the words 'Nine Hundred Years past'; then it reads:

till the year 1681. By Richard Burton. A New Edition, with additional wood-cut portraits, and a copious index. Westminster: printed for Machell Stace, No. 5, Middle Scotland Yard, By George Smeeton, St Martin's Lane, Charing Cross. 1810.

The original text is reproduced but the two Parts are reversed, the History preceding the Survey. Woodcuts of nine architectual subjects from the third edition copper plates are, as near as possible, facsimiles. They are supplemented by portraits of worthies in antique style—all printed with the text.

Small quarto, about 203 × 160mm.   1810

COLLATION Title-page; pp1–165, Historical Remarks; pp 167–78, indices

1 front. Sir W. Walworth, Knt. Byfield sc. 145 × 115mm.

2 p 18 Menassah Ben Israel. 80 × 80mm.

3 p 22 Duke Robert. Oval, 70 × 57mm.

4 p 56 W. Wallace. Oval, 70 × 57mm.

5 p 61 John Wickliff. Oval, 70 × 57mm.

6 p 63 John Gower. Oval, 85 × 70mm.

7 p 66 Lord Cobham. Oval, 72 × 56mm.

8 p 73 Jane Shore. Oval, 75 × 57mm.

9 p 79 Mrs Turner. Oval, 75 × 57mm.

10 p 84 P. Holland. Oval, 73 × 57mm.

11 p 90 The Tower. 65 × 71mm. 3rd ed p 12.

12 p 91 Aldgate. 67 × 71mm. 3rd ed p 12.

13 p 92 Bishopsgate. 65 × 70mm. 3rd ed p 13.

14 p 93 Moorgate. 65 × 69mm. 3rd ed p 13.

15 p 93 Cripplegate. 65 × 69mm. 3rd ed p 14.

16 p 94 Aldersgate. 65 × 69mm. 3rd ed p 14.

17 p 95 Newgate. 66 × 70mm. 3rd ed p 16.

18 p 97 Ludgate. 65 × 70mm. 3rd ed p 16.

19 p 125 D. of Ireland. Oval, 70 × 58mm.

20 p 126 D. of Glocester. Oval, 70 × 58mm.

21 p 135 H. Middleton. Oval, 74 × 58mm.

22 p 151 Sir T. Gresham. Oval, 70 × 57mm.

23 p 165 Clarendon House. 63 × 68mm. 3rd ed p 119.

14 · DELAUNE'S PRESENT STATE OF LONDON [1681]

Thomas Delaune, the author of this early London guide, was a non-conformist convert from Catholicism of Irish stock, who settled in London and kept a grammar school and whose polemical writings got him into trouble with the authorities, so that from November 1683 until his death in 1685 he endured great poverty and was confined in Wood Street Compter and Newgate Gaol. There is nothing controversial, however, in this businesslike publication except perhaps for the first lines of the introductory acrostic:

> T his is that City which the Papal Crew
> H ave by their Damn'd Devices overthrew
> E rected on her old Foundations, New
>
> P ourtrayed once by Stow and now again
> R ebuilt, and Re-reviv'd by thee, Delaune.

It is a systematic account of the sights of the City of London and Westminster, much of it in the past tense because of Great Fire casualties. It also lists Lord Mayors and Sheriffs from 1189 to 1680–1 and Merchant and Livery Companies, expounds the government of London and catalogues, in alphabetical order of their destinations, the carriers, wagoners and stage coaches arriving at inns in London, Westminster and Southwark. From St Albans, for instance, 'Widow Trott's Wagons come to the Cock in Aldersgate-Street, on Mondays and Fridays and goes out on Tuesdays and Saturdays'. A copy was owned by Pepys.

A second, and posthumous, edition was published in 1690.

The Present State of London: or, Memorials comprehending A Full and Succinct Account of the Ancient and Modern State thereof by Tho. De-Laune, Gent. (epigraph) London: Printed by George Larkin, for Enoch Prosser and John How, at the Rose and Crown, and Seven Stars, in Sweethings Alley, near the Royal Exchange in Cornhill. 1681.

Duodecimo, about 145 × 80mm.   1681

COLLATION Title-page; epistle dedicatory to Sir Patience Ward, Lord Mayor, dated 24 June 1681 (4pp); To the Reader, etc (4pp); contents (2pp); pp 1–360, 385–478 (sig R omitted), Present State of London.

Angliae Metropolis: or, The Present State of London: with Memorials comprehending a Full and Succinct Account of the Ancient and Modern State thereof.... First Written by the late Ingenious Tho. Delaune Gent. and Continu'd to this present Year by a careful hand. (epigraph) London: Printed by G.L. for John Harris at the Harrow in the Poultrey, and Thomas Howkins in George Yard in Lumbard-Street. MDCXC.

Duodecimo, about 145 × 85mm   1690

COLLATION Title-page; epistle dedicatory, signed 'S.W.', to Sir Thomas Pilkington (Lord Mayor 1689–90), preface, bookseller to the reader, contents (12pp); pp 1–444, The Present State of London.

The anonymous illustrations of the first edition consist of topographical line-engravings on tipped-in plates and of heraldic woodcuts printed with the text. The plates are unnumbered, have no page references and are unlisted, so that their placing was subject to the whim of the binder. This list follows their placing in the BL copy (G.3670). The jobbing engraver responsible has introduced into most of them staffage consisting of rather wooden-looking human and animal figures. They are up to date enough to include the steeple of St Mary le Bow completed by Wren in the previous year. The woodcuts are of the arms of the City, twice used, of three Merchant Companies and of 12 major and 49 minor Livery Companies.

The second edition contains only one plate, a copy of the original frontispiece, but it reuses the woodcuts throughout, only substituting a different woodblock for the City achievements.

1 front. The Lord Mayor & Court of Aldermen. 133 × 83/140mm. 2nd ed 130 × 80/137mm.

p 1 (tc) London. 65 × 70mm. Woodcut of City arms, two female supporters holding sword and shield; two putti above suspend blank tablet from ribbon. The arms in the 2nd ed have dragon supporters and the motto under.

2 p 6 (in compartments tc) The Tower – Ald-Gate. (each 67 × 71) 135 × 71/138 × 75mm. Traitors' Gate and White Tower from the river.

3 p 12 (in compartments tc) New-Gate – Lud-Gate. (each 67 × 71) 135 × 71/137 × 75mm.

4 p 13 (in compartments tc) Cripple-Gate – Alders-Gate. (each 67 × 71)135 × 71/140 × 75mm.

5 p 19 (in compartments tc) Bishops-Gate – Moore-Gate. (each 67 × 70)135 × 70/137 × 75mm.

6 p 25 (on banderole t) Westminster Abby & Parlament Hovse – (on banderole tc) The Monument. (each 64 × 70)133 × 70/140 × 75mm. The Westminster view shows St Stephen's Chapel and the Abbey as in the Hollar view (*Hind* 86) but Westminster Hall has been squeezed out. Both views have staffage.

7 p 40 (in compartments tc) The K. at the Stocks Market – The K. at Charing Cross. (each 67 × 70)135 × 70/140 × 75mm. Two statues: the first, of Charles II, was erected by Sir Robert Vyner, Lord Mayor in 1675, the horse being brought over from Rome and the pedestal and two figures probably sculpted by Jasper Latham; the second, of Charles I, by Hubert Le Sueur.

8 p 48 (on banderole t) St Mary Overies Church – (on banderole tc) Bow Steeple. (each 64 × 70)132 × 70/137 × 75mm. The first view follows Hollar's (*Hind* 26) and has staffage. Wren's steeple shown in the second was completed only in 1680.

9 p 81 (in compartments tc) New Bedlam – Bride Well. (each 67 × 70)135 × 70/140 × 75mm. Bethlehem Hospital in Moorfields, designed by Robert Hooke and completed July 1676.

10 p 104 (on banderoles tc) Phisitians Colledge – Lord Shaftsbury House. (each 63 × 70)131 × 70/137 × 75mm.

11 p 113 (on banderoles tc) White Hall – The Temple. (each 63 × 70) 132 × 70/140 × 75mm. The Whitehall view is extracted from Hollar's (*Hind* 85) and has staffage, that of the Temple is a miniature birds-eye.

12 p 154 (on banderoles tc) Clarendon House – Covent Garden. (each 64 × 70) 133 × 70/140 × 75mm. Clarendon House, built for the Earl by Roger Pratt in 1664–7, was demolished in 1683. The Covent Garden view is based on Hollar's (*Hind* 79) but shows the dial erected about 1668 in the centre of the Piazza.

13 p 159 (on banderoles tc) Westminster Hall – The Royall Exchange. (each 64 × 70)133 × 70/140 × 75mm. The Westminster view is a very poor rendering of Hollar's (*Hind* 90) with staffage. The Royal Exchange shown is Edward Jarman's, completed in 1671.

pp 302–29 (Woodcuts of shields of arms of three Merchant Companies and 12 major and 49 minor Livery Companies) The 2nd ed uses these woodblocks on the same pages.

p 331 (Woodcut of City arms as on p 1) The 2nd ed also repeats its different version on the same page.

15 · MORDEN AND LEA'S PROSPECTS [c 1687–92]

Robert Morden and Philip Lea were map and printsellers trading respectively at the Atlas in Cornhill and the Atlas and Hercules in Cheapside near the corner of Friday Street. Morden was the publisher of treatises on geography and navigation, of map pocket-books, of military maps in conjunction with William Berry and of Hollar's 1675 map of London with Robert Green. It was perhaps as a result of the sale of William Morgan's maps and books conducted by Berry and other stationers at Garraway's Coffee House (*London Gazette* 2235, 18–21 April 1687) that Morden became the publisher, in partnership with Lea, of two later issues (c 1692 and 1720) of William Morgan's 1681–2 map *London Actually Survey'd* (abbreviated *LAS*), complete with its 13 inset views, ornaments and a carefully drawn long view of London from the Thames. The map and its appendages are described in detail in Lea's undated *Catalogue of Globes, spheres, maps, Mathematical Projections, books and instruments*, probably compiled at the turn of the century, but by the date of their second issue both publishers had been dead for nearly 20 years and the widow Anne Lea was carrying on the business. This catalogue also advertises, under the head 'Books of Maps &c. by Philip Lea', *The Prospects of London, Westminster, and Southwark, in 35 Leves, price 2s 6d.*

A total of no more than 31 plates, including the engraved title, can be mustered from the three bound collections examined. Pepys collected ten of these; they are laid down in his first album of London prints. Twelve are certainly related to the views surrounding the Morgan map and, from this evidence and that of watermarks, it may be inferred that the *Prospects* were first issued between 1687 and Morden and Lea's earlier publication of the map of which they appear to be a by-product.

(*Title-page* pl. 1)

Oblong folio, about 195 × 265mm.   c 1687–92

Two of the plates, 10 and 31, bear the credit of John Dunstall, a drawing-master living in Black-friars who was employed by booksellers to engrave frontispiece portraits and views of buildings. Earlier states of pl. 12 and 29 also have Dunstall credits. He was a pedestrian imitator and copier of Hollar and, assuming that all the *Prospects* plates are his work, eight of them (11–14, 24, 28–30) are definitely after Hollar (no 5).

Nineteen of the original plates survived until at least about 1800, when they were reprinted by Robert Faulder, the publisher of Pennant (no 67). They formed part of a collection for the use of pennantizers and were printed on wove paper artificially yellowed to simulate age.

There is no text, nor any check-list of plates which are unnumbered and therefore bound together in no fixed sequence. This listing follows the arrangement of the BL copy (Maps: 29.a.23) but adds pl. 31 present in the GLC History Library copy.

1 (on swallow-tailed banderole in sky) A Prospect of London. (title, on tablet with allegorical figures holding shields of the Royal Stuart and City arms and the City regalia; their background is a panorama based on Merian's view, showing the N. bank of the Thames from St Paul's Cathedral to the Tower and the S. bank from Winchester House to St Olave, Tooley Streeet): A Book/of the/Prospects of the Remarkab-/le Places in and/about the City of London/By Rob: Morden/at ye Atlas in Cornehil/ and By Phil: Lee at the/Atlas & Hirculus in/Cheapside. 137 × 195/142 × 200mm. The Cathedral is quaintly represented by a Gothic tower surmounted by a small sphere. A copy in the Nathan Collection (*Sotheby* 1962, no 226) had John Seller

(whose line appears on item 21 below) as publisher and 'R. Adams' as the engraver's credit on the title. In a later state the title is re-engraved to read: 'A Book/of/Prospects/of the most Remarkab/=le Build-ings in/London and Westmins/ter.' 135 × 190/142 × 200mm. This re-engraving includes an amendment to the Cathedral which, while keeping its Gothic infra-structure, now appears topped with a dome and W. towers more or less as erected. It is found either with the publication-line burnished out entirely or (*Crace* 38.31) with the line 'Sold by R. Butter'.

2 (tc in sky) Bow Church. 135 × 195/140 × 200mm. Shows the steeple, completed 1683.

3 (on tasselled banderole) Guild Hall. 135 × 195/140 × 200mm. There is a central lantern supported on inverted consoles with a sundial on its hexagonal base. cf with 115 × 150mm engraving on *LAS*.

4 (tc in sky) Mercers Chapel. 130 × 194/140 × 200mm. cf with 100 × 160mm engraving on *LAS*.

5 (tc in sky) The Statue of King Charles II. at the/Entrance of Cornhill. 133 × 195/140 × 200mm. The pedestal and figure were probably sculpted by Jasper Latham in 1672; the horse was imported from Rome. cf with 230 × 145mm engraving on *LAS*.

6 (on swallow-tailed and tasselled banderole) The Hospitall of Bethlehem. 134 × 194/137 × 200mm. A water-colour drawing of this building of 1676, by Robert Hooke (130 × 159mm), signed by John Dunstall, in BM.

7 (on swallow-tailed and tasselled banderole) The Monument. (below) The figure of ye Columne Erected for ye Perpetual Memory of ye most famous City of London that was almost laid wast/by fire in ye Prodigious/yeare 1666 which from a basis of 17 foot square is Elevated with its head 202 feet high. 135 × 195/140 × 203mm. With scale of feet. Erected 1671–6.

8 (tc in sky) The Royall Exchange of/London. 136 × 180/145 × 190mm. Identical, but for reversal of shadows, with the 115 × 150mm engraving on *LAS*.

9 (tc in sky) The Marble Statue of King Charles the 2d in the/Royall Exchange. 132 × 195/135 × 200mm. Carved by Grinling Gibbons, 1683.

10 (on swallow-tailed banderole) The Custom House. John Dunstall/fecit. 130 × 195/135 × 200mm. Wren's building of 1669–74.

11 (on swallow-tailed and tasselled banderole) The Tower of London. 133 × 193/137 × 197mm. Based on the Hollar print (no 5, item 8 and *Hind* 22) but exaggerates the ogee domes and vanes on the corner turrets and adds to the r. of the White Tower the cupola of Wren's new Armoury (1685–92) and other new buildings on the extreme l.

12 (on swallow-tailed banderole) St Marie Ouers in/Southwark. 136 × 195/140 × 200mm. Based on the Hollar prospect of 1647 (no 5, item 1 and *Hind* 26) but elongates the pinnacles and adds a spire to old St

Paul's Cathedral in the background. Another state, with the Dunstall credit, in BM (*Crace* 34.122).

13 (on swallow-tailed and tasselled banderole) Lambeth House. 130 × 195/135 × 200mm. Follows Hollar's 1647 print (*Hind* 107) fairly closely, showing St. Mary's Church tower and the buildings beyond.

14 (tc in sky) The Cathedral Church of St Paul as it was before ye fire of London. 135 × 195/140 × 200mm. From the N., reversed from Hollar's plate of 1656 (*Hind* 38) in Dugdale's *St Paul's* (no 8), p 163.

15 (on swallow-tailed and tasselled banderole) St Paul's. 135 × 190/140 × 200mm. This apparently fantastic representation of what the engraver supposed were Wren's intentions for the Cathedral is based on the 235 × 310mm engraving on *LAS* and features in the long view issued with that map. It also bears a strong resemblance to the distant outline shown by Hollar in his *Prospect of London and Westminster from Lambeth* (*Hind* 18). It is taken seriously by Viktor Fürst (*The architecture of Sir Christopher Wren*, 1956, pp 100–2, 199) whose analysis of the authentic portions of the substructure to the cornice and the circumjacent guesswork causes him to date the original drawing to some time between the spring of 1679 and the spring of 1681.

16 (tc in sky) The Entrance of the Royall/Colledge of Phisitians. 135 × 185/140 × 195mm. Hooke's building of 1672–8.

17 (tc in sky) The Royal Colledge of Phisitians London. 133 × 198/140 × 215mm. The courtyard.

18 (on swallow-tailed banderole) Thanet House in Aldersgate Street. 132 × 197/140 × 205mm. Residence of the Tuftons, Earls of Thanet and subsequently of the family of Anthony Ashley Cooper (d 1683) after whom it came to be called Shaftesbury House. Another version (145 × 195mm), numbered '2', 'Johannes Dunstall delineavit', has a cartouche tc: 'Tennet House in Aldersgate Street'.

19 (on swallow-tailed and tasselled banderole) The Temple. 135 × 195/140 × 200mm. The earliest extant birds-eye engraving of the subject, perhaps taken from the same original as 'A View of the Temple as it appeared in the year 1671 when James Duke of York was a member of the Inner Temple ... re-engraved Ano 1770'. 444 × 864/489 × 889mm (BL Maps: *K. top.* XXV.18a).

20 (tc in sky) Temple Barr/The West Side. 135 × 192/140 × 200mm. cf with 180 × 130mm engraving on *LAS*.

21 (on swallow-tailed and tasselled banderole) St Paul's Couent Garden. Couent garden Iohn Seller Excud. 137 × 195/140 × 200mm.

22 (on swallow-tailed and tasselled banderole) Somerset House. 132 × 195/142 × 200mm. cf with 100 × 205mm engraving on *LAS*.

23 (tc in sky) The Statue of King Charles I./at Charing Cross in Brass. 132 × 195/140 × 200mm. Erected 1675. cf with 235 × 150mm engraving on *LAS*.

24 (on swallow-tailed and tasselled banderole) Whitehall. 135 × 195/140 × 203mm. River view based on Hollar's print (*Hind* 85) from a set published in 1647, surprisingly since there is a more up to date view on *LAS*, 110 × 315mm, apparently copied for the similar prospects published by De Ram (no 17).

25 (tc in sky) The Banqueting House. 135 × 195/140 × 200mm. An elevation. cf with 110 × 145mm engraving on *LAS*.

26 (tc in sky) The King's Gate at Whitehall/leading to Westminster. 135 × 195/140 × 200mm. The 'Holbein' Gate. cf with the elevation, 215 × 125mm on *LAS*.

27 (tc in sky) The Entrance of Westminster Hall. 135 × 195/143 × 205mm. cf with the 125 × 145mm engraving on *LAS*.

28 (on swallow-tailed and tasselled banderole) Part of Westminster. (in sky above buildings) Parlament House – the Hall – The Abby. 135 × 200/140 × 205mm. Based on Hollar's 1647 engraving (*Hind* 86).

29 (on swallow-tailed and tasselled banderole) Westminster Hall. 135 × 193/140 × 200mm. Based on Hollar's 1647 engraving (*Hind* 90), but omitting the covered fountain near the Clock Tower; a copy dated 1648 and with credits 'Dunstall del. Seller sculp.' is in the BM (*Crace* 15.68).

30 (tc in sky) Westminster Abbey. 135 × 195/140 × 200mm. Based on Hollar's view from the N. for Dugdale's *Monasticon Anglicanum* (no 6), p 56, dated 1654 (*Hind* 99) but reversed so that Henry VII's Chapel appears at the W. end. The similar view, 125 × 310mm, correctly oriented on *LAS*.

31 (on swallow-tailed and tasselled banderole) Clarendon House at St James's. John Dunstall fe. 133 × 196/146 × 216mm. Built for Edward Hyde by Roger Pratt, 1674–7, purchased 1675 by the Duke of Albemarle; demolished 1683. A larger engraving (160 × 225/175 × 230mm), captioned 'Albemarle House' and credited 'Johannes Dunstall delineavit', in the Harley Collection at the Society of Antiquaries (vol. 6, no '4').

16 · SANDFORD'S CORONATION OF JAMES II* [1687]

On the accession of James II the then Earl Marshal must have turned with gratitude to the record of the proceedings of the previous coronation prepared by John Ogilby and published as an illustrated folio in

1662 (no 9). So also the Lancaster Herald of Arms, Francis Sandford, appointed as official historian of the new coronation ceremony, must have welcomed this model on which to base his own account. On the publication of his handsome folio, in which he had the assistance of Gregory King, he was paid £300 by a grateful monarch who was to enjoy for only three years the throne on which he was then installed.

The/History/of the/Coronation/of the Most High, Most Mighty, and Most/Excellent Monarch/James II ... /And of His Royal Consort/Queen Mary:/Solemnized in the Collegiate Church of St Peter in/the City of Westminster, on Thursday the 23 of April, being/the Festival of St George, in the Year of our Lord 1685./With an Exact Account of the several Preparations in Order thereunto, Their/Majesties most Splendid Processions, and their Royal and/Magnificent Feast in Westminster-Hall:/the Whole Work Illustrated with Sculptures./By His Majesties Especial Command (plate with achievement of Royal Stuart arms impaling those of Mary of Modena. 85 × 135/90 × 148mm) By Francis Sandford Esq; Lancaster Herald of Arms/In the Savoy: Printed by Thomas Newcomb, One of His Majesties Printers. 1687.

Folio, 438 × 280mm.   1687

COLLATION   Title-page; dedication to James II, royal licence, preface, contents (8pp); pp 1–135, History of the Coronation.

Charles II was fortunate in having the ceremony of his crowning recorded in the magnificent Hollar engraving which illustrated Ogilby's account. William Sherwin who performed the same office for his brother was not so talented but produced nonetheless a satisfactory print of the occasion for inclusion in Sandford's folio. He was allied by marriage to the Duke of Albemarle, had produced line-engraved portraits of members of the royal family, had been taught the art of mezzotinting by Prince Rupert in person and was able to style himself 'engraver to the King by patent'. His chief contribution to London topography is a trio of large line-engravings of Jarman's Royal Exchange made in about 1668 on its completion (Crace 22.43–5). His coronation scenes were copied with very little alteration, except as to the scale, by Thomas Bowles and published over 40 years later to celebrate the coronation of the Hanoverian George II in his London Described (no 29), item 8.

The other illustrators of this book are: James Collins and N. Yeates who, not long before, had collaborated in an impressive line-engraving of Cheapside and the newly finished St Mary le Bow (Crace 21.14), John Sturt, a specialist in miniature and calligraphic engraving who later contributed to the 1720 edition of Stow (no 25) and to Nouveau Théâtre (no 22), and S. Moore.

Facing pp 36 and 40 are engravings by Sherwin of the regalia. Between pp 80 and 81 are plates numbered 1–19, each measuring about 220× 495/230×505mm, showing the order of the processions; these are engraved by Sherwin, J. Collins and N. Yeates. In addition there are headpieces, decorative initials and coronation medals impressed from small plates by J. Sturt and S. Moore and the following:

1 p 56 (in frame br) A Groundplot of part of the City of Westminster/Containing Westminster Abby ... But more particularly the way from the Hall to the Church as it was ... on the Day of the Coronation. 340 × 430/385 × 450mm.

2 p 81 (in frame tr) The Ground Plot of/the Collegiate Church of/St Peter in Westminster/ ... on the day of their Majesties Coronation,/Scilt 23 Apr. 1685. 365 × 515 pl. mark. Plan with 27 keyed refs and section showing scaffolding for stands.

3 p 81 (tm) A Prospect of the Inside of the Collegiate Church of St Peter in Westminster, from the Quire to the East End, With the Furniture thereof,/as it appeared before the Grand Proceeding entred; Showing the Position of the Altar, Theatre, Thrones, Chairs, Pulpit, Benches, Seats and Galleries. S. Moore delin. et sculp. 360 × 480/400 × 505mm.

4 p 93 (tm) A Perspective of Westminster Abbey from the High Altar to the West end. Shewing the manner of His Majesties Crowning. W. Sherwin sculp. 358 × 480/380 × 508mm.

5 p 103 (tm) The Inthronization of their Majesties King Iames the Second and Queen Mary. 365 × 480/398 × 510mm. Keyed refs A–V in bm.

6 p 109 A Ground Plott of Westminster Hall ... on the day of their Majesties Coronation, 23 Apr. 1685. 360 × 475/375 × 495mm. Keyed refs A–P in bm.

7 p 119 (tm) A Prospect of the Inside of Westminster Hall,/Shewing how the King and Queen, with the Nobility and Others, did Sit at Dinner on the day of the Coronation, 23 Apr. 1685.... S. Moore fecit. 360 × 495/405 × 520mm.

8 p 121 (bm) The Manner of the Champions Performing the Ceremony of the Challenge. Yeates fe. 200 × 245/230 × 265mm. Keyed refs A–H in bm.

17 · DE RAM'S VIEWS OF LONDON [c 1690]

The Guildhall Library possesses a bound collection of London views without text or title-page but which were obviously issued as a set (A.6.1.19). They are unnumbered and unlisted but they are uniform in the dimensions both of the work and of the plates; also each is framed by wreathed bays, broken into by a title bc. There are no credits but on the plate of the Monument there is a publication-line 'I. de Ram Exc. Cum Privil:'. Pepys collected these piecemeal and all but the Tower view are laid down in his first album of London prints.

Johannes de Ram was an Amsterdam engraver and publisher (1648–96) and local interest in London, aroused by the accession of William of Orange to the English throne, must have induced him to issue a collection of views on the lines of Morden and Lea's *Book of Prospects* (no 15), indicated by *ML* in the list below. They are, however, larger than the *Prospects* and have much more incident, such as the arrival of the royal barge at the Whitehall landing-stage, bearing Queen Mary and her consort seated side by side, and a royal procession through the gate to the N. of the Banqueting Hall. Staffage in the Temple Bar and Guildhall views has been reduced to midget proportions. Clouds billow in the skies.

De Ram also issued a map with portraits of William and Mary in medallions and a panorama of London based on Merian's view, *Londini Angliae Regni Metropolis* (*Darlington and Howgego* 40). This, like the *Views*, is undated but no doubt both were published soon after the Glorious Revolution.

1 The Monument. I. de Ram Exc. Cum Privil: 160 × 190/165 × 195mm. Same viewpoint as *ML* 7 only closer, and more staffage.

2 The Tower. 160 × 195/165 × 198mm. Birds-eye, more closely related to the relevant section of William Morgan's 'Prospect' issued with the 1681–2 map *London Actually Survey'd* than to *ML* 11.

3 St Peters church of Westminster Abbey (and tl) Henry VII Chapel. 164 × 197/167 × 200mm. cf with larger view issued with *London Actually Survey'd* and reversed in *ML* 30.

4 Somerset House. 162 × 194/165 × 195mm. Birds-eye.

5 Temple Barr—The West-Side. 162 × 192/165 × 195mm. The arch is made to look enormous on the scale of the miniature but lively staffage, a feature totally lacking from the outline-engraving of *ML* 20.

6 The South Prospect of the Royall Exchange. 162 × 192/165 × 195mm. Another state of this pl., undated, bears the credit 'R. & J. Ottens', map publishers. The direction of the shadows of the arcades suggests a derivation from the view on *London Actually Survey'd*; otherwise like *ML* 8.

7 Westminster-Hall. 162 × 194/165 × 195mm. More foreground staffage and sky detail than in *ML* 27.

8 The Royal Banqueting-House in Whitehal. 164 × 193/166 × 195mm. The most animated plate filled with dogs and every type of conveyance. In centre foreground is a sedan chair and a man carrying a curious two-tier umbrella, no doubt a civil servant. A procession winds through a double row of pikemen towards the Palace gate.

9 The South Prospect of Guild Hall. 163 × 193/165 × 195mm. Greater detail in sky, architecture and staffage than in *ML* 3.

10 Part of White-Hall to the Thames. 163 × 192/165 × 195mm. The architectural detail is taken from the view attached to *London Actually Survey'd* of 1681-2 but the scene in the foreground, which shows a party in a skiff hailing the royal barge in which the King and Queen are conspicuously enthroned, suggests a date around 1689.

11 St Paul's Cathedral. 160 × 190/165 × 195mm. This may be compared with the elevation of William Morgan's 'Prospect' issued with the 1681-2 map. Both are a brave guess at the appearance of the building when completed. This is also similar to *ML* 15.

18 · CORONELLI'S VIAGGI* [1697]

Viaggi del P. Coronelli. Parte Seconda ... In Venetia per Gio: Battista Tramontino M.DC.LXXXXVII.

Small octavo, 165 × 110mm.   1697

COLLATION   Title-page; subtitle: 'Viaggio d'Italia in Inghilterra', dedication (6pp); pp 1–208, Viaggi part 2; pp 209–32, index; list of 57 plates (2pp).

Six little plates, illustrating the passages in this Venetian book of travels describing London, are unskilled local copies of the work of an Amsterdam engraver and publisher, Johannes de Ram (1648–96), who issued a map and a series of views of London soon after the accession of William III to the English throne. They include a fantastic pre-figuration of the rebuilt St Paul's Cathedral, which de Ram based on the 'Prospect' issued with William Morgan's London map of 1681–2.

Each plate has engraved, tr, the volume number and page opposite which it is to be bound, and numbers are assigned to the plates in the table at the end of the volume.

Only the measurements of engraved work are given as plate-marks have been cropped by the binder. *DER* references are to the De Ram *Views* (no 17)

 1 p 158 Cathedralis S.Pauli Londini—St Pauls Cathedral. 125 × 160mm. pl 44. *DER* 11.

 2 p 160 (on banderole in sky tl) Monument. 125 × 175mm. pl 45. *DER* 1.

 3 p 163 Borsa Reale di Londra—The Royall Exchange of London. 125 × 180mm. pl 46. *DER* 6.

 4 p 164 Westminster Hall. 125 × 170mm. pl 47. *DER* 7.

 5 p 166 White-Hall. 120 × 166mm. pl 48. *DER* 10.

 6 p 167 Somerset House. 127 × 175mm. pl 49. *DER* 4.

19 · MISSON DE VALBOURG'S MEMOIRES ET OBSERVATIONS [1698]

In a preface, signed with his initials and dated London, 12 September 1697, Henri Misson de Valbourg describes himself modestly as 'un Officier relégué depuis trop longtemps dans sa Garrison, & un homme qui n'a guère plus d'étude qu'on en fait au Collège'. He says he was requested to write on the most noteworthy things in England, and particularly in London, and had intended to work his jottings into a narrative. But he found this too onerous a task and so set them out for the printer in alphabetical order. The latter managed to insert even his afterthoughts in the shape of shoulder-notes. His observations are not always colourless, as when he says of Bedlam: 'Tous les Fous de Londres

ne sont pas là dedans' and of the Royal Exchange statue of Charles II: 'On en voit deux autres de ce même Roi; l'une équestre & furieusement laide au marché qu'on nomme Stock Market: & l'autre dans le Quarré de Soho'. Van Bulderen's Hague edition of 1698 in French was followed in 1699 by an edition in Dutch, published by Antony Schouten of Utrecht, and by an English edition translated by Ozell but unillustrated, published by D. Browne in 1719.

Mémoires et observations faites par un voyageur en Angleterre, Sur ce qu'il a trouvé de plus remarquable, tant à l'égard de la Religion, que de la Politique, des moeurs, des curiositez naturelles, & quantité de Faits historiques. Avec une Description particulière de ce qu'il y a de plus curieux dans Londres. Le tout enrichi de Figures (allegorical ornament) 'Lege sed Elige'. A La Haye Chez Henri van Bulderen, Marchand Libraire, dans le Pooten, à l'Enseigne de Mézeray. M.DC.XCVIII.

Duodecimo, about 152 × 96mm.   1698

COLLATION Title-page; foreword, list of English and Welsh counties, dedication dated September 1697 (4pp); pp 1–422, Mémoires; index (38pp).

Gedenkwaardige Aantekeningen Gedaan een Reisiger In de Jaaren 1697 en 1698 van geheel. Engeland, Schotland, En Yrland.... Tot Utrecht, By Anton Schouten, 1699.

Octavo, about 160 × 95mm.   1699

COLLATION Title-page; foreword, list of English and Welsh counties, directions to binder (12pp); pp 1–454, Gedenkwaardige; index (42pp).

The plates illustrating these volumes reflect the close cultural relations existing between England and Holland, at least in the world of booksellers and printsellers, during the reign of William III. Like his Amsterdam contemporary De Ram (no 17) Van Bulderen copied all the views, which are confined to London, from Morden and Lea's *Prospects* (no 15); these are referred to in the listing as *ML*. They are all but facsimiles, with only a slight reduction in width due to the placing of the border-lines and the occasional addition of staffage or a more realistic sky. The pages opposite which they are to be placed are engraved tr on each plate. In the Dutch translation, because the text is longer, these have been scraped out, as have also the French captions, to be replaced by Dutch ones. The re-engraved captions and the Dutch text page numbers from the check-list are indicated after each item.

1 engr title (within border-lines, allegorical females of whom one wears on her head the Tower of London, the second a pentacle and the third a crown while she points to London on a map of England. A togaed historian writes and on a draped table above an allegory of Father Thames appear the words) Memoires/d'Angleterre. (bm) A La Haye/Chez Henri van Bulderen, Marchand Libraire,/dans le Pooten, à l'Enseigne de Mézeray. 1698. I.Y. d'Avele inv. f. 120 × 80/140 × 85mm. 1699 ed:'Tot Utrecht/ by Antony Schouten 1699'.

2 p 1 (tr, beneath Royal Stuart arms) La/Carte/des Royaumes/d'Angleterre/Escosse/et d'Irlande. 203 × 143/205 × 145mm. 1699 ed with Dutch caption.

3 p 29 (on swallow-tailed banderole in sky) Bedlam. 128 × 164/135 × 170mm. 1699 ed p 29. After *ML* 6. Viewed from N.

4 p 34 (on swallow-tailed banderole in sky) Bourse de Londres. 130 × 162/135 × 170mm. 1699 ed p 47: 'Beurs van Londen'. After *ML* 8. Viewed from S.

5 p 96 (on swallow-tailed banderole in sky) La Douane. 130 × 163/150 × 170mm. 1699 ed p 82: 'Het Tol-Huis'. After *ML* 10. Wren's building viewed from the river.

6 p 236 (on swallow-tailed banderole in sky) Hostel de Ville. 130 × 165/150 × 170mm. 1699 ed p 145: 'T Stad-Huis'. Staffage added to *ML* 3.

7 p 255 (on curtain tl) Laitière de May. 130 × 163/150 × 180mm. 1699 ed p 366: 'Melk-Tyd van May'. Two milkmaids dancing to a kit, one with head-dress of silver plate.

8 p 277 (on swallow-tailed banderole in sky) Hostel de Lambeth. 130 × 163/140 × 180mm. 1699 ed p 228: 'T Gasthuis van Lambeth'. After *ML* 13. Viewed from the river.

9 p 281 (on curtain tl) Plan/de la Ville/de/Londres. 132 × 175/150 × 183mm. 1699 ed p 262: 'Kaart/van de/Stad/ Londen'. On curtain tr the City arms in a cartouche. Along the base of the map is a miniature long view of London from Southwark, 20 × 175mm. (*Darlington and Howgego* 43)

10 p 298 (on each side of steeple) Tour de Ste//Marie le Bow. 130 × 70/145 × 85mm. 1699 ed p 220: 'Toorn von Ste Maria de Bow'. Background cross-hatched, tower only, reversed from *ML* 2.

11 (on swallow-tailed banderole) Le Monument. 130 × 165/143 × 185mm. 1699 ed p 87: ' 'T Monument'. With altered staffage, after *ML* 7.

12 (on swallow-tailed banderole) Temple Barr. 130 × 165/150 × 180mm. 1699 ed p 304: 'De Kerk Barr'. After *ML* 20.

13 p 361 (in work tc) Coacres et Coacresse/dans leur assemblées. 130 × 165/140 × 175mm. 1699 ed p 313: 'De Kwaakers en Kwaaker-essen'. A Quaker meeting-house.

14 p 388 (tc) Charles II/au milieu de la Bourse. 130 ×

165/140 × 175mm. 1699 ed p 30: 'Karel de II./in't midde van de beurs'. Statue only, after *ML* 9.

15 p 389 (on pedestal of statue) Charles I. 130 × 165/145 × 175mm. 1699 ed p 30: 'Karel den I'. With clouds added, otherwise as *ML* 23.

16 p 389 (on pedestal of statue) Charles II. 130 × 165/145 × 173mm. 1699 ed p 30: 'Karel de II'. In the Stocks Market. Cloudy sky added, otherwise as *ML* 5.

17 p 403 (on swallow-tailed banderole in sky) La Tour. 130 × 165/156 × 173mm. 1699 ed p 383: 'Den Toor'. Tower, from river, as *ML* 11.

18 p 414 (on swallow-tailed banderole in sky) St. Pierre de Westmunst. 130 × 165/150 × 173mm. 1699 ed p 223: 'St Pieter van Westmunster'. Staffage added, otherwise as *ML* 30.

19 p 414 (on swallow-tailed banderole in sky) Facade de la Grande Sale de Westmunster. 130 × 165/145 × 173mm. 1699 ed p 425: 'Voorgerel van le Groote Zaal van Westmunster'. Surrounding buildings replaced by cloudy sky, otherwise as *ML* 27.

20 p 416 (on swallow-tailed banderole in sky) La Sale des Banquet. 130 × 165/145 × 170mm. 1699 ed p 430: 'De Banket-Zaal'. Sky detail and staffage added, otherwise as *ML* 25.

21 p 420 (bm of each engr) Oposon – Serpent à Sonnette. 70 × 70,60 × 70/145 × 80mm. 1699 ed p 435: 'Oposon – Bel Slang'. Animals seen alive at the Royal Society.

20 · BEEVERELL'S DELICES DE LA GRAND'BRETAGNE* [1707]

The celebrated Leiden book, map and printseller and publisher Pierre Van der Aa dedicated the first edition of this work to Queen Anne being, as he says, 'd'une Nation qui a l'honneur d'être étroitement alliée à Votre Majesté', and thus introduced it to his public: 'Apres avoir ci-devant publié les Délices de l'Italie, de l'Espagne & du Portugal, présentement j'offre au Public un ouvrage de la même nature touchant l'Angleterre, l'Ecosse et l'Irlande'. The *Italy* came out in six duodecimo volumes in 1709 and the *Spain and Portugal* by Don Alvarez de Colmenar was also issued in six duodecimo volumes. By 1727, when the second edition appeared, he added to his score 'de Rome ancienne & moderne, de la Suisse, de la ville de

Leïde'. The *Switzerland* was by Gottlieb Kypseler de Munster published in four duodecimo volumes in 1714 and the *Leyden* was one octavo volume of 1712.

Of the author, Beeverell, nothing seems to be known save this particular work and his presumed British extraction but a contemporary, John Macky the government spy, seems to question the latter when, in the dedication to his *Journey Through England* (1714), he calls him 'James Borrel' and says of the *Delices*: 'the Author of it certainly had never been in England himself: for the whole is only a wild Rhapsody collected from *Cambden*, and some other Authors who have wrote the *Natural History* of distinct Counties'. Beeverell in his preface duly acknowledges his debt to Camden and also to Speed and John Chamberlayne.

Both editions were in eight volumes but the publisher claims that the second has been thoroughly revised and brought up to date by the original author. Evidences of this revision are: a reference on p 883 to the London mortality of 1722, on p 928 to an act of 1724 (9 Geo 1, c 29) suppressing the right of sanctuary in the Mint, Southwark, on pp 1060–72 a 'Blue Book' list of peers of the realm and bishops corrected to 1721.

Les Délices de la Grand'Bretagne & de l'Irlande; où sont exactemen décrites les Antiquitez, les Provinces, les Villes, les Bourgs, les Montagnes, les Rivières, les Ports de Mer, les Bains, les Forteresses, Abbaies, Eglises, Académies, Collèges, Bibliothèques, Palais; Les principales Maisons de Campagne & autres beaux Edifices des Familles Illustres, avec leur Armoiries, &c.... Par James Beeverell, A.M. Le tout enrichi de très-belles figures, & Cartes Géographiques, dessinées sur les originaux. Tome Premier (etc) ... A Leide, Chez Pierre Vander Aa, MDCCVII. Avec Privilège.

Small octavo, about 160 × 95mm.   1707

COLLATION   Vol. 1. Title-page; engr title (pl. 1a); dedication (14pp); Avertissement (6pp); author's preface (6pp); contents, licence (16pp); pp 1–248, Délices. Vol. 4. Title-page; engr title (pl. 1b); pp 737–872, Délices.

The second edition title-page reads identically but terminates: 'Nouvelle Edition, retranchée, corrigée & augmentée. A Leide, Chez Pierre Vander Aa, MDCCXXVII.

Small octavo, about 155 × 95mm.   1727

COLLATION   Vol. 1. Avertissement, author's preface (10pp); contents (22pp); pp 1–278, Délices. Vol. 4. Title-page; pp 815–977, Délices.

In both editions the publisher stesses the importance and quality of the 150 or so plates and acknowledges the 'plans' of country houses which have been supplied by their owners:

D'Ailleurs, je n'ai rien négligé de tout ce qui peut plaire aux personnes curieuses; ni rien épargné pour embellir cet Ouvrage par des Tailles-douces, d'autant plus estimables, qu'elles ont été gravées par les meilleurs Maîtres suivant les desseins faits sur les lieux mêmes, ou suivant les estampes publieés en Angleterre, dont j'ai même fait retoucher & corriger quelques-unes à mes dépens, qui étoient moins exactes.... On trouvera chacune de ces planches placée dans son ordre, & dans le lieu qui lui est propre.

Plates are mostly anonymous with the exception of the frontispieces which are credited to J. Goeree (b Middleburg 1670, d 1731), a pupil of the more notable Gerard de Lairesse (1641–1711). Certain features of the frontispieces, with their landscape and architectural backgrounds, are also to be found in the topographical plates, suggesting for some of them a common authorship; in particular the elegant, fashionably clothed figures. Van der Aa must have commissioned many hundreds of plates for the numerous illustrated works in his catalogue, including ten multi-volume titles in the *Délices* series; he is known to have employed his brother Hildebrand (fl 1692–1728) as a house engraver and had many outsiders working for him. The title-page of his publication *La Galerie Agréable du Monde* (no 23) mentions—besides Goeree—Luyken, Mulder, Baptist and Stopendaal. His advertisement suggests that most of these worked in Holland from existing engravings which were no doubt readily accessible in his own large, international printseller's stock. But they are by no means slavish copies and the addition of well-drawn staffage, 'trompe l'oeil' frames and a variety of foregrounds and caption labels differentiates them from their no-nonsense British predecessors (see especially items 9, 19, 20, 28). Considerable activity is also depicted: a dog-fight at Temple Bar (item 21), fisticuffs and a chained bear in St Mary Overy's churchyard (item 35), gallant court vessels bobbing on the Thames swell at Whitehall (item 26) and 'carriage-folk' drawing up ostentatiously at the Abbey's north porch (item 30).

There is a London panoramic background to the vol. 1 frontispiece but all other London views are to be found in vol. 4. There is no check-list of plates but each has engraved tr the number of the page opposite which it is to be bound. In the second edition, because of textual revision, higher page numbers have been re-engraved. The listing, which is from the first edition, notes this second state of each plate. All these plates, together with some from the other *Délices* volumes, were also printed on heavier paper and published under the same imprint in an oblong folio with an undated title *Vües des Villes de Londres, de Canterbury, de Colchester et autres lieux circonvoisins*.

As many views as possible were taken from a single collection. Just as Loggan's engravings provided models for Van der Aa's British university views, so he relied for most of his London ones on the *Book of Prospects* published by Robert Morden and Philip Lea about 1690 (no 15). Eighteen of the plates are from this source, abbreviated *ML*, and four more from a collection contemporary with it which came from the Amsterdam publisher De Ram (no 17). In a notice prefixed to *La Galerie* Van der Aa names David Mortier as one of the booksellers whose goodwill he has purchased and it was the first volume of his *Nouveau Théâtre de la Grande Bretagne* (no 22) that he ransacked for views of royal and noble seats. These were copied in a reduced format from the double folio plates of Knyff and Kip; nine of them are referred to below, abbreviated *NTGB*. Finally four plates of old St Paul's Cathedral are reduced from those of Hollar in Dugdale's *History* of 1658 (no 8), abbreviated *DUG*.

VOL. 1 (1707 and 1727)

1a front. (on the side of a tomb chest on which are hung shields of arms of Suffolk, Huntingdon, York and Durham) Les/Délices/de la/Grand' Bretagne et de l'Irlande,/Ouvrage très utile et très curieux./En Huit Tomes,/Par/James Beeverell, A.M./Tome Premier. /A Leide chez Pierre Van Der Aa. J. Goeree In. et Fec. 122 × 158/130 × 165mm. On the tomb chest sits Father Thames with a cornucopia and a pair of rabbits; he is flanked by a tree, a stag with his doe and a broken obelisk. He leans on a medal of Britannia and holds a bulrush, a crown and a vase from which pours water labelled 'Themes' in reverse. Behind him is a panorama of London from the S. bank with the Bear Garden and Globe Theatre to the l. of him and Bridge Gate and St Olave, Tooley Street to the r. In the background is the N. bank from the Temple to St Lawrence Pountney and from Billingsgate to the Tower. It derives from the panorama by Matthew Merian the elder (*Scouloudi* VIII, A), of about 1638. The second ed adds the date MDCCXXVII after the imprint.

VOL. 4 (1707 and 1727)

1b front. (on cylindrical pedestal) Les/Délices/de la/ Grand' Bretagne/et de/L'Irlande/Tome Quatrième. J.Goeree in. et Fec. 123 × 160/128 × 165mm. On the pedestal, accompanied by a sheep, a mitred and vested Church Father holding a book; to his r. two putti with a drawing board, a shield of arms labelled 'Cantuaria', fruit and agricultural implements labelled 'Cantium' and a dog seizing a hare; to his l. a farm-labourer, a foppishly dressed gentleman, a tonsured priest; at the foot of the pedestal more agricultural implements, a sheaf of corn and a mariner's compass; a rocky seascape with a house perched on the cliff in the background.

2 p 741 (label on wall in foreground) The South Prospect of the Cathedral and Metropolitan/Christ Church of Canterbury. 122 × 156/130 × 165mm. 2nd ed p 280.

3 p 750 (label on wall with veined surface) A Prospect of Grenwich Hospitall for Seamen as designed/and advancing Ao 1699. 121 × 157/127 × 165mm. 2nd ed p 830. A birds-eye view of the river front with only half the Queen Anne and King Charles blocks built but, prematurely, both domes completed. This and the Chelsea Hospital view (item 36) form a pair based on the same source, apparently, as the plates in the 1720 Stow (no 25) Bk 1, pp 214–15.

4 p 781 (on veined wall in foreground with achievement of royal arms, Queen Anne, 1702–7) Windsor Castle. 121 × 154/133 × 165mm. 2nd ed p 867. *NTGB* 4.

5 p 785 (on pedestal raised above foreground parapet) London. 123 × 152/127 × 159mm. 2nd ed p 871. Map of London with refs 1–24 on the parapet; inscribed on river 'La Tamise Fluv.' (*Darlington and Howgego* 54: 'possibly engraved by Johannes de Ram, d 1696')

6 p 802 La Tour de Londres. 130 × 162/135 × 167mm. 2nd ed p 890. Seen from river, with exaggerated wind vanes. *ML* 11.

7 p 808 (on cusped label against foreground parapet) La Douane, ou Costume House. 122 × 153/135 × 160mm. 2nd ed p 896. *ML* 10.

8 p 809 Le monument érigé en memoire du grand incendie de Londres. 130 × 162/140 × 165mm. 2nd ed p 897. Copied, with new staffage, from *ML* 7.

9 p 811 La Bourse de Londres. 130 × 160/133 × 165mm. 2nd ed p 900. Staffage and flanking buildings added, otherwise copied from *ML* 8.

10 p 812 (814,837) (on cartouches beneath each statue) Charles I en bronze/à Charing-Cross – Charles II/Dans le milieu de la Bourse – Charles II/Dans le marché de Stock. 121 × 152/127 × 155mm. 2nd ed pp 902, 902a, 935. Reduced from *ML* 23, 9, 5.

11 p 814.1 Bow Church. 127 × 157/130 × 164mm. 2nd ed p 902b. St Mary le Bow. *ML* 2.

12 p 814.II Vue de Guild Hall du Côté du Midi. 127 × 155/133 × 159mm. 2nd ed p 903a. *ML* 3.

13 p 815 (on cartouche below) Vüe de l'Eglise Cathédrale

de/S. Paul du côté de l'occident. Avant le feu de 1666. 121 × 154/130 × 165mm. 2nd ed p 904. After Hollar (*Hind* 39), reduced from *DUG* 164.

14 p 815.2° Mercers Chappel. 126 × 157/133 × 160mm. 2nd ed p 903b. *ML* 4.

15 p 818.1 (on oval tablet within work) Vûe du dedans de la Nef de l'Eglise/Cathédrale de S.Paul, Avant le feu de 1666. 123 × 154/130 × 164mm. 2nd ed p 906. Hollar's view (*Hind* 42) reduced and filled out with side panelling. *DUG* 167.

16 p 818.II (on cartouche bc) Vûe de la partie exterieure/ du choeur, du côté d'Occident/Avent le feu de 1666. 122 × 153/130 × 163mm. 2nd ed p 907. A St Paul's view after Hollar (*Hind* 44), reduced from *DUG* 168.

17 p 819 (on cartouche bc) Vûe du dedans de l'Eglise Paroissiale/de Sainte Foi, Avant le feu de 1666. 123 × 154/129 × 165mm. 2nd ed p 908. After Hollar (*Hind* 33), reduced from *DUG* 115-16.

18 p 827 (on label bc) Section du dedans de l'orient à l'Occident de l'Eglise Cathédrale/de S.Paul. 124 × 155/133 × 165mm. 2nd ed p 916. Wren's cathedral, section looking N. through the nave, dome and choir. The cone which ultimately supported the lantern not shown.

19 p 828 L'Entrée du Collége Royal des Medecins. 130 × 160/135 × 165mm. 2nd ed p 917. Framed in a trompe-l'oeil setting as a print with torn edges held to the wall by tacks, from *ML* 16.

20 p 831 Hôpital de Bethlehem. 125 × 156/127 × 165mm. 2nd ed p 928. Staffage added in foreground of *ML* 6.

21 p 834 Temple Barr du Côté du Couchant. 125 × 158/133 × 160mm. 2nd ed p 931. Framed in a trompe l'oeil setting of a print against a wall, with a cockled lower edge. Staffage of aggressive dogs added to *DERAM* 5.

22 p 835 (on convex of curving parapet bc) L'Hotel de Sommerset,/ou Sommerset House. 123 × 153/130 × 163mm. 2nd ed p 933a. Birds-eye view from river side, showing maypole in the Strand. *DERAM* 4.

23 p 835 Le Temple. 130 × 160/135 × 165mm. 2nd ed p 933b. Birds-eye view with St Dunstan in the West tc. *ML* 19.

24 p 837 (on a label surmounted by Queen Anne's arms as Princess of Denmark fixed to a wall in foreground) St James's House. 123 × 155/130 × 165mm. 2nd ed p 935a. *NTGB* 2.

25 p 837 (on a label fixed to a wall in foreground, surmounted by the royal arms previous to 1707) St James Palace and Park./1. Gate to Chelsea. 2. Admiraltie Office. 3. Cock Pitt. 4. Tilt Yard. 5. Horse Guards. 122 × 155/130 × 165mm. 2nd ed p 935b. Plan reduced from *NTGB* 3.

26 p 838 (on a label hanging from panelled wall in foreground) Partie de White Hall, qui fait face à la Tamise. 123 × 155/130 × 165mm. 2nd ed p 936. A fine

view of the Palace with royal yacht cheered by the occupants of other craft. The staffage has been altered but architecture based on *DERAM* 10.

27 p 839 La Maison apellée Banqueting House. 130 × 163/133 × 167mm. 2nd ed p 937. Midget staffage added to *ML* 25.

28 p 840 (on cockled bottom edge of trompe l'oeil print) The Kings Gate, ou Porte Royale/de White-hall, qui conduit à Westminster. 123 × 155/130 × 165mm. 2nd ed p 938a. The view appears to hang from a tall park wall terminated by an urn and a peacock. To the r. an attractive park vista with a retreating male figure. r. foreground two ladies and a man in high Queen Anne fashion with leverets. A much embellished version of *ML* 26.

29 p 840 (on cartouche bc fixed to brick wall with stone coping in foreground) Vûe de Westminster-Hall. 123 × 155/130 × 160mm. 2nd ed p 938b. Based on Hollar's 1647 view (*Hind* 90). *ML* 29.

30 p 841 (on scrolled cartouche fixed to parapet in foreground) Eglise de S.Pierre, ou Abbaye de West-minster./1. Chapele d'Henry VII. 123 × 153/130 × 165mm. 2nd ed p 939. Based on Hollar's engraving (*Hind* 99), with added staffage, from *DERAM* 3.

31 p 847 (on cartouche fixed to coping of parapet in foreground) Partie de Westminster./A.Maison du Parlement. B.La Sale. C.L'Abbaye. 123 × 153/130 × 165mm. 2nd ed p 946. After Hollar's 1647 engraving (*Hind* 86), from *ML* 28.

32 p 848 (on eared cartouche bc decorated with swags) Sale de Westminster,/ou Westminster-Hall. 123 × 153/130 × 165mm. 2nd ed p 947. View from N. *ML* 27.

33 p 850 (in wreath of bays bc against foreground embankment) Maison de Lambeth,/ou Lambeth House. 123 × 155/130 × 165mm. 2nd ed p 949a. Viewed at ground level from W.bank. *ML* 13.

34 p 850 (on label bc with archiepiscopal arms fixed to wall in foreground) Lambeth Palais des Archévêques de Cantorbery. 123 × 155/130 × 165mm. 2nd ed p 949b. Birds-eye view with City skyline in background, including a conjectural outline of St Paul's Cathedral. Reduced from *NTGB* 8.

35 p 851 Eglise de St.Marie dans South Wark. 127 × 155/130 × 165mm. 2nd ed p 949c. After Hollar (*Hind* 26). Old St Paul's in the distance but with spire added to Hollar's 1647 version. Also added is lively staffage, including a bear, a beggarman and a brawl, not on *ML* 12.

36 p 853 (on label bc fixed to wall with veined surface) Chelsey Colledge. /1 The Wards. 2 The Governours Kitthin and Wash-house. 3 The Gardeners Lodge. 4 The Guard-house. 123 × 158/130 × 165mm. 2nd ed p 952. Birds-eye with the following lettering on work, above to below: The River Thames, The Governor's house, The Barbers house, The Light House, The Infirmary, The Wash-house and Bake-house, The

Guard house, The Officers of the House, The Chapel, The Front to the Road, The Hall, The Master Butler's Apartment, The Master Cookes Apartment, The Porters Lodge, The Guard House. A pair with the Greenwich view, item 3 above. (*Longford* 65)

37 p 871 (on label bc with achievement of royal arms, Queen Anne 1702–7, all against a wall in foreground) Hampton Court. 121 × 158/130 × 168mm. 2nd ed p 974. Birds-eye view reduced from *NTGB* 5.

VOL. 4 (1727, contains four additional views of London and its environs)

38 p 869d (on label bc with achievement of the arms of the Duke of St Albans against a wall in foreground) A Prospect of the House at Windsor. 123 × 155/133 × 165mm. Birds-eye view of the Duke of St Albans's house showing the Castle in the middle distance. Reduced from *NTGB* 10.

39 p 977c (on label bc with achievement of the arms of the Rt Hon Charles Boyle against a wall in foreground) Burlington House in Pickadilly. 123 × 160/130 × 165mm. Birds-eye view reduced from *NTGB* 11.

40 p 977d (on label with Beaufort achievement of arms against wall in foreground) The House att Chelsey in the County of Middlesex. (along horizon) Holland House – Camden House – Kingsinton House. 121 × 160/130 × 165mm. Reduced from *NTGB* 9. (*Longford* 245)

41 p 977e (on label bc with achievement of arms of the Rt Hon Charles Boyle against a wall in foreground) The House att Chiswick in the County of/Middlesex. 123 × 158/130 × 165mm. Birds-eye view, a pair with 977c, reduced from *NTGB* 12.

21 · BRÜHL'S VIEWS [after 1707]

This scarce set of views of Great Britain engraved by Johann Benjamin Brühl of Leipzig was numbered by the engraver, bl or br in the margin or tr within the work, N1, N2, etc. Neither of the sets seen has a printed or engraved title but the Guildhall Library album (A.1.2. no 45) opens with a manuscript title and check-list of plates.

They are not original work but copies, often on the clumsy side, of the Dutch engravings made for James Beeverell's *Délices de la Grand'Bretagne* (no 20). Those plagiarized from the London portion (vol. 4) of that work are referred to as *BEEV*, with item number, in the list below.

The originals were slavishly followed, even to the setting of captions against brick or marble walls in the foreground and the occasional 'trompe l'oeil' setting. Only the coats of arms, central to some of the captions and inherited from *Nouveau Théâtre de la Grande Bretagne* (no 22), have occasionally been ignored.

The Guildhall album contains 46 views, mostly of London, of which ten carry Brühl's credit and the twelfth and thirteenth plates have had their numbers altered in manuscript. Another copy seen contained nine further views including one of London, namely St Paul's Cathedral. There are no publication-lines.

1 Banquet Hauss. I.B.Brühl Sc. Lips. 130 × 157/135 × 165mm. *BEEV* 27.

2 Kauffleutte Haus. I.B.Brühl Sc. 125 × 153/135 × 160mm. Mercers' Hall. *BEEV* 14.

3 Bow Kirche. IBB Sc. Lips. 125 × 153/135 × 165mm. *BEEV* 11.

4 Prospect des Theatri Sheldoniani von der Mitternacht Seite. 120 × 157/135 × 165mm.

5 Der Hafen Douvre. 122 × 160/135 × 165mm.

6 Theatrum Sheldonianum Zu Oxford von Mittage Seite. 121 × 158/135 × 170mm.

7 Das Haus Zu Chelseÿ. (along horizon)Holland House – Camden House – Knigsinton House. I.B. Brühl Sc. Lips. 121 × 155/130 × 165mm. *BEEV* 40. (*Longford* 245)

8 Königl.Palast Zu S.James. 121 × 152/140 × 170mm. *BEEV* 24.

9 Das Leuch Haus vor Plÿmouth. 118 × 155/130 × 165mm.

10 Marlbourch Palast Bleinheim. 130 × 195/140 × 200mm.

11 der Tower in London. 122 × 153/130 × 160mm. *BEEV* 6.

(12) Auditoria und Bibliotheca zu Cambridge. 123 × 157/135 × 165mm. Numbered in manuscript this is a substitute for 'St Pauls Kirche. I.B.Brühl Sc. Lips.' (140 × 184/146 × 190mm).

(13) Das Haus Windsor. 120 × 155/130 × 165mm. Numbered in manuscript and substitute for 'Prospect des Schloss zu Edinburg'. *BEEV* 38.

14 Die Stone Henge oder Mons Ambrosii. 120 × 150/130 × 160mm.

15 Theil von Westminster/1 Parlaments Hauss – 2 der Saal – 3 die Abtey. 120 × 151/130 × 165mm. *BEEV* 31.

16 Carolus I zu/Charin-Cross – Car/olus II/mitten in der börse/Carolus II/auf dem Stock Marck. 120 × 155/135 × 160mm. *BEEV* 10.

17 Lambeth-hauss. 120 × 155/130 × 165mm. *BEEV* 33.

18 Guildhal. 125 × 156/130 × 165mm. *BEEV* 12.

19 Eingang zum Königl Collegii Medici. 123 × 155/130 × 165mm. *BEEV* 19.

20 Der Tempel. Brühl Sc Lips. 127 × 160/130 × 165mm. *BEEV* 23.

21 Tempel-Barr von der abendt seite. 120 × 158/130 × 163mm. *BEEV* 21.

22 Dauane oder Zoll Hauss. 120 × 152/125 × 162mm. *BEEV* 7.

23 Das Monument. 127 × 160/135 × 165mm. *BEEV* 8.

24 Hampton Court. 120 × 155/125 × 160mm. *BEEV* 37.

25 Chelseÿ Collegium/ 1 der Wacht – 2 der Obersten Kuch u.Wasch haus – 3 der/Gärtners haus – 4 das Wachthaus. 122 × 160/135 × 167mm. *BEEV* 36. (*Longford* 65)

26 Die Boerse zu London. Brühl sc. 127 × 163/135 × 165mm. *BEEV* 9.

27 Ein Theil von White Hall/nach du Thems zu. Brühl sc. 120 × 153/127 × 160mm. *BEEV* 26.

28 Prospect der Bodlejanisches Bibliothec. 120 × 153/130 × 165mm.

29 Die Insul Bass. 120 × 150/130 × 160mm.

30 Prospect von Westminster Hall. 120 × 150/130 × 160mm. *BEEV* 29.

31 Kings' Gate. Brühl sc. 120 × 150/130 × 162mm. *BEEV* 28.

32 Westminster Halle. 120 × 150/130 × 160mm. *BEEV* 32.

33 Sommerset Haus. 123 × 152/130 × 160mm. *BEEV* 22.

34 Das Hospital Greenwich vor/invalide Seeleute. 120 × 155/130 × 165mm. *BEEV* 3.

35 Die Abteÿ Westminster oder Peters Kirch/ 1 Capelle Henrici VII. Brühl sc. 120 × 150/130 × 165mm. *BEEV* 30.

36 Die Auditoria zu Oxford. I.B.Brühl sc. 120 × 158/130 × 165mm.

37 Das Schloss zu Windsor. 120 × 155/130 × 160mm. *BEEV* 4.

38 Lambeth Palast der Erzbischöffe zu Canterberÿ. 120 × 155/130 × 170mm. *BEEV* 34.

39 Cambridge. 120 × 155/130 × 160mm.

40 Das Narren Hospital Bethlehem. 123 × 160/130 × 170mm. *BEEV* 20.

41 Lac Derg in Donegal. 122 × 158mm.

42 Oxford. 122 × 158mm.

43 Kleidung und Zierahten derer Ritter von Hosenband. 120 × 158mm.

44 Auditoria publica der Univers Oxford. 120 × 158mm.

45 Die Bodleianische Bibliothec und Auditoria. 122 × 158mm.

46 Das Auditorium Theologicum zu Oxford. 120 × 158mm.

22 · MORTIER'S (SMITH'S) NOUVEAU THEATRE DE LA GRANDE BRETAGNE (BRITANNIA ILLUSTRATA)* [1707, etc]

This work, chiefly noted for its birds-eye views of country seats, is also indispensable to the London topographer for its many views of palaces, great houses, public buildings and churches. Moreover it contains the two best panoramic views from the South Bank to be published since those by Hollar and by Morgan (*London Actually Survey'd*) of the previous century. The most comprehensive edition appears to be that of 1724 issued in four volumes under the title of *Nouveau Théâtre* by Joseph Smith who was also joint publisher of two other important architectural works in folio, Campbell's *Vitruvius Britannicus* of 1717–25 (no 24) and the 1718 edition of Dugdale's *Monasticon Anglicanum* (no 6). A supplement, which includes some 20 views of Audley End, was published in 1728 by J. Groenewegen and N. Prévost in the Strand. Proposals for a sixth volume were advertised in 1730 but seem not to have borne fruit. Smith, who traded from his 'Pictor-Shop', the Inigo Jones's Head next to the Fountain Tavern at the West end of Exeter Exchange in the Strand, says in his introduction to the first volume that he is reissuing all the plates originally published by a neighbour, one David Mortier, whose place of business was at the sign of Erasmus's Head, also near the Fountain Tavern. Mortier was born in Amsterdam in 1673. He set up in the Strand as a bookseller in 1698 and having married an English wife and obtained British nationality settled in London for the rest of his life, with an interval between 1711 and about 1721 when, on his brother Pierre's death, he helped his widow run the Amsterdam bookshop. It was natural that he should choose to employ immigrant Dutch artists to produce the plates which make up the first volume of this collection: Leonard Knyff, born at Haarlem in 1650, and the engraver Johannes Kip, born at Amsterdam in 1653, who were both settled in Westminster by the last decade of the century. His first volume, which consisted of 80 plates (11 of London and its environs), except for insignificant changes in their order, remained constant from 1707 throughout all its subsequent appearances, singly or as part of a set, with its original Latin/English title *Britannia Illustrata* or its alternative French title *Nouveau Théâtre de la Grande Bretagne*. To these, explains Smith, he has added in his four-volume edition an up to date map of London and certain extra plates: 'les Planches qu'on y (a) ajoutées tant d'Eglises, de Palais, que de Maisons de Plaisance, dont plusieurs sont faites par les mêmes Excellens Messieurs Kip et L.Knyff'.

Because so many of the first set of plates published were the work of one engraver the whole collection came to be known familiarly as 'Kip'; nevertheless later volumes were made up from the engravings of several other artists, originally published by printsellers other than Mortier or Smith. The title-page of one of the issues which appeared in 1709 conjoins the names of Daniel Midwinter and Henry Overton with those of the first publishers and by 1749 it was John Bowles who was publishing the first 80 plates; his 1753 catalogue lists the volume priced at £1 11s 6d.

Plates extra to the initial 80 were bound up in the succeeding volumes and came out over the years in various permutations and editions until they attained the dignity of the ultimate five tall folios of 1724–8 in which some 400 are bound. A detailed account of the intervening stages, with the states of individual plates and their replacements, would require a separate bibliographical study, so for the purpose of recording the London illustrations the following summary list of editions must suffice. It has been drawn up with reference to those recorded in the *US National Union Catalogue* and E.G. Cox's *Reference guide to the literature of travel* and to the holdings of the British Library, the British Museum (Department of Prints and Drawings), the Royal Institute of British Architects, the Royal Library, Windsor, the Society of Antiquaries, the Victoria and Albert Museum (Department of Prints and Drawings) and the Guildhall Library. Editions cited are distinguished by abbreviated London locations to which reference is made from the list of plates, press-marks being added where necessary.

1 1707. Britannia Illustrata. 1 vol., 80 pl. D.MORTIER. *1707 BI* (RIBA)

2 1708–13. Nouveau Théâtre. 2 vols, 80 and 67pl. D.MORTIER. (Vol 2, 'Villes, églises, cathédrales, hospitaux, ports de mer,...') *1708–13* (Soc Ant, vol. 1 in Royal Library)

3 1708–17. Nouveau Théâtre. 4 vols, 272pl., 40 maps. D.MORTIER.

4 1709–15, 16 or 17. Britannia Illustrata. 2 vols., 80 pl. each. J.SMITH. (Vol. 1, 'printed for Joseph Smith at ye Pictor Shop ye West end of Exeter Exchange in ye Strand' (Soc Ant), but RIBA copy 'printed for David Mortier at the Erasmus Head in the Strand, Daniel Midwinter at the Three Crowns in St Paul's Church Yard, Henry Overton at the White Horse without Newgate & Joseph Smith ...' Vol. 2, 'Views of the Nobility and Gentry ... with ... coats of arms ... printed for Joseph Smith'.) *1709–15 BI* (RIBA)

5 1714–15. Britannia Illustrata. 2 vols, 80 pl. each. J.SMITH. *1714–15 BI* (Soc Ant)

6 1716, 1714, 1715. Nouveau Théâtre. 3 vols (in 4), 80, 64, 67, 80pl. and atlas. D.MORTIER. (Tome 1 is in 2 vols, the first dated 1715 or 1716, the second 1716 or 1717. Tome 2, 'Villes, églises, cathédrales, hospitaux, ports de mer', is dated 1714 or 1715 and so is Tome 3 which contains, in addition to views, G. Valck and P. Schenk's 'Atlas Anglois'.) *1714–16* (RIBA)

7 1715, 1714, 1715. Nouveau Théâtre. 3 vols, 80, 58, 61 pl. (less tables). D.MORTIER. (Very similar in contents to the above except that the first tome is dated 1715 and is in one vol. only. The third tome lacks four of the listed London plates but has two substitutes, for St George's Chapel, Windsor and Hampton Court, and an additional plate of the environs at Twickenham.) *1714–15* (V & A)

8 1720, 1740. Britannia Illustrata. 2 vols, 80,102pl. D.MORTIER. *1720,1740 BI* (BL:191.g.15)

9 1722. Britannia Illustrata. 2 vols, 80 and ?pl. J.SMITH.

10 1724,1728. Nouveau Théâtre. 4 vols and suppl., 80, 69, 58, 84, 84pl. J. SMITH, suppl. J.GROENEWEGEN and N.PREVOST. (Vols 1 and 2, Palais du Roy, Maisons des Seigneurs & des Gentilhommes. Vol.3, with engr title-page dated 1719, Archevechez & Evêchez, Cathédrales, Eglises. Vol.4, Villes, Palais du Roy, Ports de mer. Suppl., Audley End, Atlas Anglois, Ecosse.) *1724–8* (BL:G.2713) *1724* (BM: 173.c.1)

11 1724,1729,1728. Nouveau Théâtre. 4 vols and suppl. as above but vol.4 dated 1729 is differently compiled

and contains a few alternative plates. J.SMITH.
1724–9 (BL:191.g.10; Royal Library)

12 1737. Nouveau Théâtre. (Advertisement in the *Daily Post* of 24 February for a four-volume edition printed for T.MILLWARD, J.BRINDLEY, R.WILLCOCK, C.CORBETT, WARD & CHANDLER, P.DENOYER.)

13 1749. Britannia Illustrata. 1 vol, 80 pl. J.BOWLES.

In a note appended to the check-list of plates published with *1707 BI* the prints are offered for sale by Overton 'either in compleat sets or single', and a similar note in the first volume of *1714–15 BI* runs: 'All these Printed for and Sold by J. Smith in Exeter Change. Where may be had all sorts of Prints & Maps for Halls, Parlours, Staircases, Wholesale & Retale'. Henry Overton in his 1717 catalogue lists the individual prints 'on Imperial Paper' and notes that they are 'sold singly as well as in sets'. The whole collection, with its alternating title and relatively fluid content, provided the printsellers with a vehicle for disposing of copies of topographical engravings issued over a considerable period of time by a number of publishers: Mortier's and Smith's own publications together with others from the stocks of Thomas Bowles, John and Henry Overton and Thomas Taylor. Also the purchaser who did not wish to adorn his parlour or staircase with them was spared the trouble of making a selection of prints and housing them in unwieldy portfolios. Many of the engravings though were singularly unsuited for binding, being printed on imperial size paper or often consisting of two sheets gummed together so that even a tall folio can accommodate them only at the expense of awkward and vulnerable folds at the head and fore-edge.

The list that follows is arranged according to the contents of *1724–8* but is supplemented with descriptions of London plates found in other editions. The first two volumes illustrate royal and episcopal palaces and noblemen's houses, but the second is not detailed here since it is concerned with places other than London. The third, with an additional title-page engraved and dated 1719, collects London views of the Cathedral and Abbey and of some churches and chapels. It omits or replaces nine of the plates which occur in *1714–16*, descriptions of which are included here in brackets with plate numbers in Roman. London views in the fourth volume, as in the first, consist of royal palaces and noblemen's houses with in addition public buildings, hospitals and the elaborately worked long panoramic views of the City and Westminster from across the river. Many of them are retained from the 1714–16 edition but in this volume also there are omissions and substitutes; once again London plates found in other issues have their descriptions interpolated in this list and distinguished from the 1724 content by brackets and Roman plate numbers. The subsequent issue of volume four, dated 1729 in *1724–9*, rearranges the plates and omits six of the London views. The variable nature of the contents and arrangement of this volume in particular is evident from a comparison of *1724–8*, with *1724*; title-pages and dates are identical but the BM volume contains six London plates not to be found in the BL copy. Such discrepancies easily slip through the net of standard bibliographical description and it is hoped that this census, although it can only be provisional, will enable owners to check their copies for London views which have so far eluded the compiler.

The supplementary volume dated 1728 includes an 'Atlas Anglois' previously published under Mortier's imprint (*1714–16*) but now under Smith's and 27 plates worked in the previous century by Henry Winstanley. There is only one view of London interest, the Howland Dock.

Confusion in catalogue entries sometimes results from the adoption for their own lesser publications of the Latin title *Britannia Illustrata* by two publishers who had also an interest in the major work, Henry Overton and John Bowles. Their sets of *Prospects* (nos 26 and 28), bound into oblong folios, without many credits and of modest proportions to appeal to a popular market, did however boast some plates reduced from their more splendid contemporay.

Although Kip, described by Hind as 'one of Hollar's worthiest successors in the etching of topography in England', is undoubtedly the collection's chief engraver credits for no fewer than 16 other artists are to be found, among whom Henry Hulsbergh was also engraver for Smith's *Vitruvius Britannicus* (no 24) and James Cole for his *Westmonasterium* (no 27). John Harris was almost certainly responsible for reduced engravings of some of the plates to suit the scale of Overton's *Prospects*, and Sutton Nicholls who contributed the well-known double view of London Bridge was soon to be heavily engaged on a rival series, John Bowles's *London Described* (no 29), which also employed H.Terasson. Work from the previous century is represented by the Clarendon House view by Johann Spilbergh, a German artist who died in 1690, that of the Monument by William Lodge who died in 1689 and the fine engraving by Robert White celebrating the completion in 1671 of Jarman's Royal Exchange. Finally there is a valuable contemporary record of the stunning impact of Wren's crowning achievement in the magnificent plates of St Paul's, originally issued in 1702 by the architect-draughtsman William Emmett and in those by John Harris. Some of these early plates are among those that Pepys had acquired for his collection by 1703, the year of his death (items 2, 6–8, 11, 21, 23, 50).

The publisher, Smith, added his name and address to some of the earliest collection of plates which were issued by Mortier without publication-lines.

VOL. 1

Nouveau Théâtre de la Grande Bretagne; ou Description Exacte des Palais du Roy et des Maisons les plus considérables des Seigneurs & des Gentilhommes du dit Royaume. Le tout dessiné sur les lieux, & gravé sur 80 Planches où l'on voit aussi les Armes des Seigneurs & des Gentilhommes auxquels elles appartiennent. Tome Premier. (achievement of royal arms, tabled as pl.1) A Londres, Chez Joseph Smith, Marchand Libraire proche d'Exeter Exchange, à l'Enseigne d'Inigo Jones, dans le Strand. MDCCXXIV.

Folio, 525 × 340mm. (Royal Library ed, dated 1708, 555 × 350mm) 1724

COLLATION Title-page; preface, descriptions and alphabetical list of plates, naming landowners and referring to nos engr on br of each plate (10pp); 80 plates.

The title-page of the 1708 edition reads 'de la Reine' for 'du Roy' and so, anachronistically, does that of the 1716 edition. Other variations are: 'de la Grande Bretagne' for 'du dit Royaume', 'quatre-vingt' for '80', 'A Londres, Chez David Mortier, Marchand Libraire dans le Strand, à l'Enseigne d'Erasme' for 'A Londres, chez Joseph Smith ...'; also 'MDCCVIII', 'MDCCXV', or 'MDCCXVI' for 'MDCCXXIV'.

The same collection of plates was published under the alternative title:

Britannia Illustra or Views of Several of the Queen's Palaces as also of the Principal Seats of the Nobility and Gentry of Great Britain Curiously Engraven on 80 Copper Plates. London, Sold by David Mortier, Book, Map & Print Seller at the sign of Erasmus's Head near the Fountain Tavern in the Strand, 1707. *1707 BI*

It was reissued under the same title in 1709 with alternative imprints:

... London, Printed for David Mortier at the Erasmus Head in the Strand, Daniel Midwinter at the Three Crowns in St Paul's Church Yard, Henry Overton at the White Horse without Newgate & Joseph Smith at ye Pictor Shop ye West end of Exeter Exchange in ye Strand, M.DCC.IX. *1709–15 BI*

or merely 'Printed for Ioseph Smith at ye Pictor Shop ...', which also appears in the 1714 edition but in this case 'Vol. 1' is inserted after 'Plates' on the title-page.

In the 1720 edition the title reads 'Royal Palaces' for 'Queen's Palaces', 'Elegantly Engraven on LXXX Copper Plates. Tom.1' for 'Curiously Engraven ...', and 'MDCCXX' for '1707'. There is no imprint, only a note appended to the table to say the plates are sold by David Mortier at the Erasmus's Head. The title of the second volume follows that of the first, with the amendment 'CII copper plates. Tom. II. London, Printed in the year MDCCXL'. No imprint is added but two plates retain Smith's publication-line.

1 (on title-page, the royal arms, George I) H. Hulsbergh fecit. 97 × 175/102 × 180mm. Earlier eds with royal arms 1707–14 but without credit.

2 pl.2 St James's House/le Palais Royal de St James. L.Knyff delin. I.Kip sculp. Printed & Sold by J.Smith at ye sign of Exeter Change in ye Strand. 325 × 470/355 × 480mm. Caption centered on arms of Queen Anne as Princess of Denmark bc. Cavalcade with coaches advancing down the Mall. Two other views, items 38–9, in vol. 4.

3 pl.3 (tr) Le Palais et Park de St James./St James's Palace and Park. L. Knyff de. I.Kip sculp. 345 × 480/355 × 490mm. Map, with identifications of: Gate to Chelsea, Admiraltie Office, Cock Pitt, Tilt Yard, Horse Guards. tc royal arms 1702–7.

4 pl.4 Windsor Castle/Le Chasteau de Windsor. L.Knyff del. I. Kip sculp. Printed & Sold by J. Smith at ye sign of Exeter Change in ye Strand. 320 × 475/350 × 490mm. Caption centered on royal arms 1702–7 bc. From the N., haymakers in foreground. pl.7 in Mortier eds. Two other views, items 43–4, in vol. 4.

5 pl.5 (br on tablet under royal arms 1702–7) Hampton Court. L.Knyff del. J. Kip sculp. 340 × 480/350 × 490mm. View from W. with birds-eye plan of Park. pl.6 in Mortier eds. Two other views, items 61–2, in vol. 4.

6 pl.6 Somerset House/la Maison de Somerset. L.Knyff del. I. Kip sculp. Printed & Sold by J. Smith ... 330 × 480/355 × 490mm. Caption centered on arms of Queen Catherine of Braganza on lozenge; she died in 1705. pl.4 in Mortier eds.

7 pl.7 The Tower of London Commanded in Chief by the Earl of Lincoln/La Tour de Londres. L. Knyff delin. I.Kip sculp. Printed & Sold by J. Smith ... 320 × 470/325 × 485mm. Caption centered on arms of dedicatee, Henry, Earl of Lincoln, Constable of the Tower 1722-5. *1708* names Lord Lucas as the Commander and an undated state of the plate (BL Maps: *K. top.* 24.23.dI) is dedicated by J. Smith to Col Williamson. pl.5 in Mortier eds.

8 pl.8 Lambeth, His Grace the Lord Archbishop of Canterbury's Pallace—Lambeth, Maison de l'Archevesque de Canterbury. L.Knyff delin. I. Kip sculp. Printed & Sold by J. Smith ... 323 × 477/350 × 485mm. Caption centered on the Archbishop's arms with the date '1697' bc. With skyline view of London including the elevation of the Cathedral shown on pl. 15 of Morden and Lea's *Prospects* (no 15).

9 pl. 13 The House att Chelsey in the County of Middlesex one of the Seats of the most Noble and potent Prince Henry Duke of Beaufort ... L. Knyff D. I.Kip scu. (in work, on skyline) Holland House – Camden House – Kingsington House. 330 × 475/360 × 485mm. Caption centered on Beaufort arms bc. Henry Somerset, the 2nd Duke from 1700, died in 1714. (*Longford* 244)

10 pl.14 A Prospect of the House at Windsor Belonging to his Grace Charles Beauclerk Duke of St Albans ... L. Knyff del. I.Kip scu. 323 × 470/345 × 475mm. Caption centered on Royal Stuart arms debruised by a bend sinister bc. The Duke, Charles II's natural son, died in 1726. Windsor Castle in middle distance, viewed from S.

11 pl.29 Burlington House in Pickadilly Belonging to the Rt Honble Charles Boyle Baron Clifford of Londesborough and Earl of Burlington ... L. Knyff del. I. Kip scu. 325 × 475/355 × 483mm. Caption centered on Boyle arms bc. The 3rd Earl, Richard the architect, succeeded to the title in 1704.

12 pl.30 The House at Chis Wick in the County of Middlesex one of the Seats of the Rt Honble Charles Boyle, Baron Clifford of Londesborough and Earl of Burlington ... L.Knyff de. I.Kip scu. 318 × 475/340 × 485mm. Caption centered on Boyle arms bc.

VOL. 3

Nouveau Théâtre de la Grande Bretagne ou Description Exacte Des Archevêchez & Evêchez d'Angleterre de leur Fondations, Cathédrales, le Nombre d'Evêques qui y ont siégez, avec les Revenus & Armoiries des Diocèses, & autres Eglises: Representés en soixante-six Planches. Le tout dessiné sur les lieux & gravé par les plus habiles Graveurs. Auquel on a ajouté une Table Généalogique & Chronologique de la Ligne Royale d'Angleterre, depuis Guillaume le Conquérant jusqu'au Roi George à présent Régnant. Tome Troisième. (royal arms 1702–7) A Londres, Chez Joseph Smith Marchand Libraire à l'Enseigne d'Inigo Jones, proche Exeter Exchange, dans le Strand. MDCCXXIV. *1724–8*

Folio, 525 × 340mm. 1724 (1719)

COLLATION Title-page; pp 1–8, descriptions and list of plates; pp 1–24, Historical Account. (The table lists 58 plates with nos which are not engr on the prints.)

The 'Tome 2' title-page of the 1714–16 edition reads:

Nouveau Théâtre de la Grande Bretagne ou Description Exacte des Villes, Eglises, Cathédrales, Hôpitaux, Ports de Mer &c. de la Grande Bretagne. Le tout dessiné sur les lieux, & gravé par les plus Habiles Graveurs. Auquel on a ajouté une Table Généalogique & Chronologique de la ligne Royale d'Angleterre depuis Guillaume le Conquérant jusqu'à l'établissement de la Succession dans la Maison d'Hanover par Acte du Parlement de 1701 (*1714–15* V & A variant: 'Avec les Grands Sceaux de tous les Rois depuis Guillaume le Conquérant jusqu'à la Reine Anne ...') Tome second. (royal arms 1707–14) A Londres, Chez David Mortier, Marchand Libraire, MDCCXIV (or '1713'). *1714–16.*

COLLATION ('Tome 2') Title-page; descriptions and lists of plates (14pp); 67 plates (upon which Smith drew for his vols 3 and 4).

The 1724 title-page promises 66 plates but is contradicted by the table (numbered 1–58) and by the engraved title which, in French, promises but 40. Confusion arises because a single view, if it is made up from two separately printed sheets, may be allocated two numbers in the table. None of these London church views bear Knyff's credit and only one, pl. 42 of St Clement Danes, carries Kip's name. Most seem to date from about 1713–20, but those of St Mary le Bow and St Dunstan in the East come from cruder and perhaps earlier Mortier stock. The plate of St Clement Danes has reached its final state in this edition, having passed through an intermediate state since the 1714 edition. If this plate is compared with the Westminster Abbey engraving by James Collins it will be seen that a selection of identical staffage occupies the foreground of both, perhaps drawn from a Kip sketchbook, so clearly they were originally intended for separate publication. Nine of the plates from the 1714–16 edition (vols 2–3) are republished but one of St Bride's Church and six of the Cathedral have been dropped; the table gives the publisher scope for switching these since it collectively describes items VII–X as 'Plates of St Pauls'.

13 front. (engr calligraphic title-page, 'J. Cole sculp.') Ecclesiarum Angliae et Valliae Prospectus or Views of all the Cathedrals in England and Wales, of the Collegiate Churches of Westminster and Southwell, & of the Royal Chapel of St George at Windsor Accurately Engraved on Copper Plates by the best Artists and printed on Imperial paper. To which is prefixed an Historical Account of each of them (followed by French title specifying) ... Exactement gravées sur quarante Planches. (a N.W. view of St Paul's Cathedral. 'H. Hulsbergh sculp.' 125 × 200/135 × 210mm.) London, Printed for Joseph Smith at his shop at the West End of Exeter Exchange in the Strand, 1719 (imprint also in French) 460 × 250/470 × 260mm.

14 pl. 2–3 (in cartouche rc) A New and Exact Plan of the Cities of London & Westminster and the Borough of Southwark with all ye Additional New Buildings to ye Present Year.... Printed for and sold by I. Smith Print & Map Seller next ye Fountain Tavern in ye Strand. 575 × 935/580 × 940mm overall, on two sheets. '1725' added to 'Present Year' in *1724*(BM). (*Darlington and Howgego* 71)

15 (pl.ix The Foundation or Ground-plat of St Paul's Church. Sould by Tho. Bowles in St Pauls Church-Yard. 705 × 470mm. *1714–16* vol.2.)

16 pl.4 (in sky) The North West Prospect of the Cathedral Church of St Pauls London 1720. (bm)Prospect of the Cathedral Church of St Paul's London. (and in French) A d'Puller fecit. Printed for J. Smith in Exeter Exchange in the Strand. 550 × 850/555 × 855mm overall, on two sheets. No sky caption on pl. in *1714–15*(V & A). *1714–16* vol.3, xiii.

17 pl.5 (on panels with drapery tl) The/Cathedral Church/of St Pauls/In London. (tr)A Section of the Cross Isle from North/to South with a Prospect of/the Choir & Dome. Will:Emmett sculp. Printed & Sold by Jos. Smith in Exeter Change in the Strand. 610 × 810/615 × 815mm overall, on two sheets. *1714–16* vol.2,vi–vii.

18 (pl.viii A Section of the Inside of St Pauls. 435 × 615/445 × 625mm. *1714–16* vol. 2.)

19 (pl.xv The Inside of the Cathedral Church of St Paul's London. 435 × 555/465 × 565mm. Inside of nave looking E. *1714–16* vol. 3.)

20 pl.6 (in sky) The East Prospect of St Pauls Church London. (bm caption in French and Latin) Printed for J. Smith in Exeter Exchange in the Strand 1720. 240 × 220/265 × 225mm. With scale of feet bc.

21 (pl.v (on cartouche) St Pauls/The East Prospect/ (and in French) Wm. Emmett Fecit. J. Simon sculpt. Sould by Tho. Bowles in St Pauls Church-Yard. 520 × 465/610mm. *1714–16* vol. 2.)

22 pl.7 (in sky)The South Prospect of St Pauls Church London. (bm caption in French and Latin) Printed for J. Smith in Exeter Exchange in the Strand 1720. 197 × 295/220 × 300mm. The French caption adds: 'Commencé sous le Roy Charles II en 1670 et achéve sous la Reyne Anne en 1702'.

23 (pl.iv St Pauls. (on curtain, with two putti blowing trumpets) The South Prospect of St Pauls London/The Foundation of the Noble Structure/Began to be layed in ... 1670 ... /And now Published ... 1702. Will: Emmett Fecit. Sould by Tho. Bowles in St Pauls Church-Yard. 450 × 680mm. *1714–16* vol.2.)

24 pl. 8 (in sky) The West Prospect of St Pauls Church London. (lm caption in French and Latin) Printed for J. Smith in Exeter Exchange in the Strand. 240 × 220/260 × 225mm.

25 (pl.iii The Front or West End of the Cathedral Church of/St Pauls London. (and in French) Wm. Emmett fecit. Sold by Thomas Bowles in St Paul's Churchyard. 515 × 465/655mm. *1714–16* vol.2.)

26 (pl.xiv The South East Prospect of the Cathedral Church of St Paul's London. B. Lens delineavit. I. Harris sculpsit. 430 × 655/465 × 675mm. Indian ink and wash original (406 × 648mm), by Bernard Lens (II, 1659–1725), offered for sale by Appleby Bros in 1963. *1714–16* vol. 3.)

27 (pl.xvi The Chapter House of the Cathedrall Church of St Paul's London. Ino Harris deliavet (!) et fecit. 445 × 570/475 × 580mm. The Chapter House was completed by 1713. *1724* 'pl.8'. *1714–16* vol.3.)

28 pl.39 The North Prospect of Westminster Abbey. J. Collins sculp. Sold by J. Smith near the Fountain Tavern in the Strand, London. 450 × 670/485 × 685mm. Alternatively as a separate print 'Sold by Capt Rhodes in St Dunstans-Court Fleet-street'. Staffage resembles that on pl. 42 below. Without publication-line in *1714–16* vol.2, xiii.

29 (pl.40 The Royal Chappel of St George in Windsor Castle where ye Knights of ye Garter are Install'd.... Tho. Bowles sculp. (arms of Lord Willoughby of Broke) Printed & Sold by Jos. Smith at Inigo Jones's Head, next ye Fountain Tavern in ye Strand. 405 × 540/450 × 555mm. Viewed from S. Without dedication, credit or publication-line in *1714–16* vol.3, x.

30 (pl.x The South Prospect of the Royal Chappel of St George in Windsor Castle. 422 × 560/460 × 570mm. *1714–15* (V & A) vol.3.)

31 pl.42 (tm) St Clement's Church in the Strand. Ino Kipp delineavit et fecit. (bm Kip's dedication to Brownlow Cecil, Earl of Exeter, with arms) Printed and Sold by J. Smith. 520 × 580/560 × 590mm. Brownlow Cecil, the 8th Earl, succeeded to the title in 1722. Staffage resembles that on pl.39 above. There are three states of this print:
(i) Showing the tower of five stages crowned by a wooden cupola, as it was left by Wren. 385 × 580/430 × 600mm. Dedicated to the Earl of Exeter in *1714–16* vol.2, xxxvii.

(ii) Showing the tower with the top three stages rebuilt but of the steeple only the first of three stages added by James Gibbs in 1719–20. 390 × 545mm.

(iii) A strip, 130mm deep, engraved with the two upper stages of the steeple has been added for pl.42.

States (1) and (ii) have the caption tm 'The South Prospect of the Church of St Clements Danes'. The buildings shown to the W. of the church in (i) were eliminated for (ii) and (iii).

32 pl.43 The new Church in the Strand London 1719. (and in French) Dd Lockley sculp. Sold by J. Smith at Inigo Jones Head near Exeter Change in ye Strand. 545 × 438/580 × 440mm. St Mary le Strand, built by James Gibbs, 1714–17. Copied from one of the official engravings made by John Harris (*Crace* 17.124).

33 pl.55 L'Eglise de St Mary le Bow a Londres. (and in Latin) 235 × 205/260 × 210mm. No credit or publication-line but apparently uniform with pl. 58 below, as in *1714–16* vol.3, xvii.

34 pl.56 Her Majesty's Royal Banqueting House of Whitehal London 1713. H. Terasson delin. et sculp. 1713. 380 × 565/425 × 580mm. Royal arms 1707–14 bc. Listed in the table as 'Chapel Royal'; it was so fitted out by Wren when the original chapel was burned in the fire of 1697-8 and the King first worshipped there on Christmas day 1698. As in *1714–16* vol.3, v.

35 pl.58 L'Eglise de St Dunstan a Londres. (and in Latin) a Amsterdam Chez la Veuve de P. Mortier. 235 × 208/255 × 215mm. Elevation of St Dunstan in the East. Pierre Mortier of Amsterdam, mapseller and publisher, died in 1711. As in *1714–16* vol.3, xviii.

36 (pl.xxxviii The Elevation or Prospect of the West end of the Steeple of St Bridget als Brides in Fleetstreet (also showing the Inside and Outside thereof.) 570 × 430/620mm. With a 'Ground-platt'. *1714–16* vol.2.)

VOL. 4

Nouveau Théâtre de la Grande Bretagne; ou Description exacte des Villes, Palais du Roy, Ports de Mer &c du dit Royaume. Le tout dessiné sur les lieux, & gravé par les plus Habiles Graveurs. Tome Quatrième. A Londres, Chez Joseph Smith, Marchand Libraire proche d'Exeter Exchange à l'Enseigne d'Inigo Jones, dans le Strand. MDCCXXIV (alternatively 'MDCCXXIX').   *1724–8*

Folio, about 525 × 340mm.   1724(1729))

COLLATION Title-page; pp 1–12, descriptions and list of plates. (The 1724 table lists 86 plates, the 1729 table lists 79 but nos are not engr on the plates.)

Of the 33 London plates in this list only 18 are included in *1724–8*, five being added from *1724*, four from *1714–16*, two from *1714–15*(V & A), three jointly from *1714–16* and *1724–9* and one jointly

from *1714–16* and *1724*. Five of the plates make a further appearance in the apparently late edition of *Britannia Illustrata, 1720,1740 BI.*

37 pl.1–2 (on banderole in sky supported by four putti; a fifth tc, suspends the arms of Westminster Abbey) La Ville de Westmunster. (bc) A Prospect of Westminster. 1720. Printed and Sold by J.Smith in Exeter Exchange in the Strand. 450 × 1120/490 × 1125mm. On two sheets numbered br '1' and '2'. Keyed refs bl:A-Q, R-Z, a-l. *Crace* 2.76 lacks publication-line and date but the catalogue advances 'J. Kip, 1710' not incredibly since St Clement Danes is shown without the Gibbs steeple added 1719–20, W. of this the Maypole is shown where St Mary le Strand rose 1714–17, and St Anne, Soho appears without the spire added by Talman in 1717. *1724* thus, but *1724–9* numbers this pl. '3–4'. Less publication-line, in *1714–16* vol. 3.

38 pl.3–4 The Royal Palace of St James's. (and in French) Robt. Inglish delineavit. J. Sturt sculpsit. Printed & Sold by Tho. Bowles, Print & Mapseller next to ye Chapter House in St Paul's Church Yard London. 450 × 655/475 × 663mm. The same subject engr by Kip, vol.1, no 2. (*Crace* 12.3; catalogue gives 1714 as date)

39 (pl.iii-iv (on banderole upheld by four putti in sky) Her Majesties Royal Palace & Park of St James's. 515 × 880/550 × 900mm overall, on two sheets. Looking N. over the canal. bm dedication to Queen Anne, royal arms 1707–14. Keyed refs: 1 Queens Palace, 2 St James's Chapell, 3 Duke of Marlboroughs House, 4 The Lord Godolphin's House, 5 The Canal, 6 The Mall, 7 The Horse Guards, 8 The Banquetting House, 9 Whitehal, 10 The Admiralty House, 11 Spring Garden, 12 Charing Cross.)

40 pl.5 (tm)The Prospect of Whit Hall. (bm, with royal arms, George I) Vüe du Palais Royall de White-hall comme il est à present 1724. J. Kip delineavit et sculp. 385 × 580/470 × 600mm. Banqueting House, Horse Guards and 'Holbein' Gate, with staffage of cavalry, coaches, sedan chairs. Numbered '20' in *1724–9*.

41 pl.6–7 (on banderole upheld by four putti in sky) Her Majesties Royal Palace at Kensington. (bm, with royal arms 1707–14) To Her Most Serene and most Sacred Majesty Anne by ye Grace of God Queen of Great Britain France & Ireland &c. Printed for and Sold by J. Smith in Exeter Change in ye Strand. 515 × 850/550 × 900mm overall, on two sheets. In *1724–9* numbered '9–10' and in *1720,1740 BI* vol. 2 '51'. Previously published *1714–16* vol.3, vi–vii.

42 (pl.vi–vii The Royal Palace of Kinsington. (and in French) Mark Anthony Hauduroy Delineavit. Printed & Sold by Tho. Bowles, Print & Map Seller, next ye Chapter-House in St Paul's Church Yard, London. 432 × 630/470 × 650mm. Only found in *1724*.)

43 pl.8–9 The Royall Palace and Town of Windsor. (and in French) Mark Anthony Hauduroy delineavit. J. Kip

sculp. Printed & Sold by Tho. Bowles, Print & Mapseller, next ye Chapter-house in St Paul's Church Yard, London. 450 × 650/490 × 665mm. In *1720,1740 BI* as '99' vol.2.

44 (pl.viii-ix (on banderole upheld by five putti) The Royall Palace and Town of Windsor. 520 × 890/560 × 895mm. bm dedication to Queen Anne with 1707–14 royal arms. In *1714–16* vol.3.)

45 pl.10 Buckingham House in St James's Park belonging to ... John Sheffield ... Duke of ... Buckingham. Printed for and Sold by J.Smith in Exeter Exchange in ye Strand. 430 × 590/475 × 595mm. Built by William Winde in 1705. The Duke died in 1721; his arms, impaling those of his wife Catherine Darnley, bc. Also in *1714–15 BI* vol.2, x and *1714–16* vol.3, xxxiii. (*Crace* 13.4; catalogue gives 1714 as date)

46 pl.11 The South West Prospect of his Grace ye Duke of Marlborough's House in St James' Park. Jams Lightbody delin. Iohn Harris Fecit. Printed & Sold by J. Smith in Exeter Change in ye Strand. 440 × 565/480 × 585mm. Built by Christopher Wren, 1709–11. In *1724–9* numbered '25'; as in *1714–16* vol.3, xxviii.

47 pl.12–13 (in sky)The Royal Hospital of Greenwich. (lm dedication to Philip Stubbs, Chaplain Royal to the Hospital)Prospectum Hunc D.D.D. Jacobus Collins. Printed and Sold by Henry Overton at the White Horse without Newgate London. 435 × 665/490 × 675mm. From the river, with the front incomplete and the Queen Anne and King Charles blocks without their outer flanks facing respectively E. and W. (the E. flank was completed by Hawksmoor in 1715). A similar but larger engraving by John Harris after Kip (*Crace* 8.134), dated 1711, is related to Kip's engraving for the 1720 Stow (no 25, Bk 1, p 215) which, however, shows the blocks completed. In *1714–15* (V & A) the façade is also incomplete but the print shows the flanking buildings. Also in *1714–16* vol.2,liv.

48 (pl.xxxix The Royal Hospital at Greenwich. 358 × 498/398 × 505mm. From the river with the façade completed. In *1724–9* numbered '39' and *1720,1740 BI* vol.2 '37'.)

49 pl.14 The North Prospect of Mountague House. James Simon Fecit. Printed for and Sold by J. Smith in Exeter Change in ye Strand. 440 × 590/478 × 600mm. In *1714–15 BI* vol.2, xli and *1714–16* vol.3, xxxii. (*Crace* 27.75; catalogue gives 1715 as date)

50 (pl.xv Prospectus Celeberrimae Domus Ilustrissimi Ducis ab Albemarle. J. Spilbergh del et exc. Cum Privil. Regis. W. Skillman sculp. 495 × 690/510 × 695mm. On a banner in the sky supported by three putti a dedication to the Duke of Albemarle, son of General Monck and Lord-Lieutenant of Devonshire who in 1675 bought the house, Clarendon House, from Lord Chancellor Clarendon's heirs. The misleading 'Description' says 'Hôtel bâti par le Duc d'Albemarle fils de General Monck—depuis sa mort passé à la Maison des Cavendish, Ducs de Devonshire'. Built

1664–7 by Roger Pratt for the Chancellor, it is here shown before its demolition in 1683, with contemporary staffage of men, horses, dogs, beggars and a beadle to guard the gates. Only found in *1724*.)

51 (pl.xvi The East Prospect of Dr Flamstead's House in Greeenwich Park. I. Simon sculp. Printed and Sold by Henry Overton at the White Horse without Newgate London. 383 × 535/410 × 550mm. The Royal Observatory. Staffage in Queen Anne period costume, rabbits, deer. Only found in *1724*.)

52 pl.18–19 (on banderole upheld by seven putti, three of them also holding a blank shield) The Royall Hospitall at Chelsey. Printed for and Sold by J. Smith in Exeter Change in the Strand. 510 × 880/550 × 890mm overall, on two sheets. View from the river with dedication lm to Sir Stephen Fox(1627–1716), courtier and statesman who contributed towards the Hospital's foundation. An alternative dedication to Queen Anne with the royal arms 1707–14 is found on BL Maps: *K. top.* 28.4f. In *1724* as nos '17–18', in *1724–9* as '13–14' and in *1720,1740 BI* vol.2 as '60'. Published earlier in *1714–16* vol.3, lii,liii. (*Longford* 4)

53 pl.20 (on banderole upheld by putti) Powis House. H.Terasson fecit. 520 × 565/525 × 575mm. Publication-line cropped by binder, as also in *1724* ('pl.19'), but on the print in BL Maps: *K. top.* 27.10a: 'Sold by Thomas Bowles in St Paul's Church Yard, London 1714'. A rebuilding by Colin Campbell of the French Ambassador's house in Great Ormond Street burned down 1713.

54 pl.21 To the Right Honourable the Commissioners of His Majesties Customs/This Prospect of the Custom House is humbly Presented ... Iohn Harris delin. et sculp. Decber 15th 1714. Sold by Tho: Taylor at ye Golden Lyon in Fleet Street. 420 × 555/465 × 570mm. Listed as 'Douane'. Wren's building of 1669–74, burned down 1718. In *1724* no '20'.

55 (pl.xxi In perpetuam memoriam celeberrimae Urbis flammis prope desolatae, Anno prodigiosi 1666: Columna haec/ ... This famous Column was erected in perpetual remembrance of the dreadful Fire of London ... Guli: Lodge Eboracensis delin: et fecit. P.Tempest exc. Printed and Sold by Henry Overton at the White Horse without Newgate. 565 × 395/610 × 415mm. Only found in *1724*.)

56 (pl.xxii (on swallow-tailed banderole) New Bedlam in More Fields. (bm)Mente Captorum Londinense. Sely fecit. Sold by Henry Overton at ye White Horse without Newgate, London. 390 × 570/415 × 575mm. Thus in *1724* but published earlier in a *1714–16* vol.3, xxxvii.)

57 pl.22–3 (on swallow-tailed banderoles in skies) The West Side of London Bridge – The East-Side of London Bridge. Sutton Nicholls Fecit. Printed for & sold by I.Smith in Exeter Exchange in/ the Strand. 510 × 870/570 × 880mm overall, on two sheets. Two strip views with historical accounts under. In *1724* as 'no

23–4' and in *1724–9* as '11–12'. (*Crace* 7.6; catalogue gives '1710' as date)

58 pl.24 (in sky)The North side of the Royal Exchange as it now is (145 × 260mm) – The Royal Exchange as it was Built before the Fire of London (145 × 195mm) – A View of the Inside of the Royal Exchange as it now is, 1712, describing the walks used/by the Merchants of divers nations. Sold by Thomas Taylor at ye Golden Lyon near ye Horn-Tavern in Fleetstreet London (315 × 555mm). 460 × 555/490 × 560mm overall measurement, including engr of Gresham's statue tr (145 × 60mm). Keyed refs aa – qqq and 'history' in the sky. In *1724* as 'no 25'. (*Crace* 22.48; catalogued as 'Sutton Nicholls sculp.')

59 (pl.1 (on swallow-tailed banderole in sky supported by two angels who also hold trumpets with banners of the City and Mercers' Company arms) The Royall Exchange of London. R. White delint. et sculpsit 1671. 460 × 570/470 × 575mm. With dedication to Gresham College. Publication-line on BL Maps: *K. top.* 24.11a.1: 'London, Printed and are to be Sold by I.Overton at ye White Horse without Newgate'. Found only in *1714–16* vol.2.)

60 pl.27–8 (on banderole in sky supported by seven putti, the central one blowing a trumpet and suspending shields of Royal Stuart arms and City arms surmounted by crests) La Ville de Londres. Prospectus Londinensis. Printed and Sold/by I.Smith/in Exeter Change. 450 × 1160/490 × 1170mm overall, on two sheets. Another caption bc: 'A Prospect of the City of London', flanked by (l) keyed refs 1–35, (r) 36–65. *Crace* 2.76 is numbered 'I' and 'II' and catalogued as 'J.Kip, 1710'. The royal arms are those current from 1707–14. St Paul's Cathedral shown as completed with the exception of the scrolled parapet above the E. apse, St Clement Danes lacks the upper stages added by Gibbs in 1719–20, and the Custom House is Wren's, burned down in 1718. Moored off Bankside and flying the City flag is the 'Folly', a barge adapted as a floating concert room, usually anchored near the Savoy. In *1724* numbered '48–9' and in *1724–9* 'I' and 'II'. Published earlier in *1714–16* vol.2, I and II.

61 (pl.xi-xii (on banderole supported by four putti) The Royal Palace of Hampton Court. 520 × 880/560 × 900mm. Dedication with arms in bm to Charles Spencer, Earl of Sunderland (1674–1722). *1714–15*(V & A) vol.3.)

62 (pl.xxviii-xxix The Royal Palace of Hampton Court. (and in French) Mark Anthony Hauduroy delin: J. Harris sculp. Printed & Sold by Tho.Bowles, Print & Map Seller, next ye Chapter House in St Paul's Church Yard, London. 440 × 655/480 × 665mm. Thus in *1724* but as '41' in *1720,1740 BI* vol.2.)

63 pl.40 The Entrance of Westminster Hall/L'Entrée de la Sale de Westmunster. 40. 225 × 255/240 × 265mm. As '43' in *1724* and *1724–9* but as '40' also in *1714–16* vol.3.

64 pl.41 Prospect of Guild-Hall/Vûe de l'Hôtel de Ville à Londres. 41. 225 × 255/240 × 265mm. This follows seventeenth century engravings in showing a building with crenellated and ogee-domed corner-turrets and a baroque central cupola consisting of a hexagonal stage with sundial, an arcade supported by inverted consoles of the type favoured by Wren and an ogee dome with finial and windvane. This central feature, replacing the Gothic lantern burned in the Great Fire, had disappeared by the early years of the eighteenth century. As '44' in *1724* and *1724–9* but as '41' also in *1714–16* vol.3.

65 pl.42 (on banderole supported by four putti) The Navy Office of London. (bm)To the Right Honourable the Principal Officers & Commissioners of His Majesties Navy/This Prospect ... is humbly presented by ... Tho:Taylor Anno 1714. Sold by Tho:Taylor at the Golden Lyon in Fleet Street. 425 × 590/475 × 600mm. Dedication includes cartouche of arms. As '45' in *1724*.

66 (pl.xxxviii (on pedestal)King Charles I att Charing Cross. 38. 225 × 250/240 × 263mm. The statue by Le Sueur. As '49' in *1724–9* but as '38' also in *1714–16* vol.3.)

67 (pl.xxxix King Charles II att ye entrance of Cornhill. 39. 225 × 250/240 × 263mm. As '49' with the above in *1724–9* but as '39' also in *1714–16* vol.3.)

68 (pl.1i (shows Charles II's statue in the Royal Exchange) P. Vandrebanc Sculp. ex Marmorea Statua G. Gibbons sculpt. Printed, engraved and Sold by/David Mortier at ye Sign of Erasmus's head in ye Strand. 670 × 480mm. Found only in *1714–16* vol.2.)

69 (pl.xxxi A Prospect of the House of Twitenham belonging to ... the Earl of Strafford, Viscount Wentworth ... Plenipotentiary to the States General in 1711. (in work)La Tamise Rivière. 220 × 230/235 × 240mm. Mount Lebanon on the Thames at Twickenham, bought in 1701 by Thomas Wentworth, Earl of Strafford, ambassador at the Hague 1711–14. *1714–15* (V & A)Vol.3.)

Supplement

Supplément du Nouveau Théâtre de la Grande Bretagne; ou description Exacte des Maisons les plus considérables des seigneurs et des gentilhommes de la Grande Bretagne Avec les Plans de plusieurs Villes, Abbayes, & Eglises Cathédrales d'Ecosse, le tout dessiné sur lieux, & gravé en quatre-vingt quatre Planches ... A Londres Chez J.Groenewegen & N. Prévost libraires dans le Strand. MDCCXXVIII.

Folio, 525 × 340mm.   1728

COLLATION Title-page; descriptions and list of plates (8pp); 84 plates, with nos engr tr but without publication-lines.

The plates are drawn by T. Badslade and H.

Winstanley; J.Kip and J.Harris are among the engravers. Twenty of them are an exhaustive record of Audley End House engraved 1676–80. Bound up with this copy is the 'Atlas Anglois', a set of county maps published by J.Smith in 1724 but originally by Mortier in *1714–16* vol.3. The only London plate is:

70 pl.27 (on banderole in sky with arms tc) Howland Great Dock near Deptford. T. Badslade Delin. J. Kip sculp. 335 × 405/345 × 420mm. With a distant view of London. The second wet dock on the Thames, built 1696–7 and named after Elizabeth Howland, only daughter of the family owning the land and wife of the 1st Duke of Bedford's grandson, or possibly after her mother, daughter of Sir Josiah Child of the East India Company. (*Crace* 8.126; catalogue gives 1717 as date)

23 · VAN DER AA'S GALERIE AGREABLE DU MONDE* [c 1715]

Bound up with his 1715 edition of More's *Utopia* (Guildhall, Cock Coll 1.1, no 3) is an extensive catalogue issued by the Leyden publisher and bookseller Pieter van der Aa: *Catalogue des livres, de cartes géographiques, des villes, chateaux &c. de l'univers.* One of his most 'universal' offerings is the *Galerie Agréable du Monde*, in 66 'Tomes' or Parts, depicting Portugal, Spain, France, the Netherlands, Great Britain and Ireland, Asia, Africa and the Americas. Three of these parts, devoted to Great Britain, make up the fourth volume of the BL King's Library set (213.f.6).

La Galerie Agréable du Monde Où l'on voit en un grand nombre de Cartes Tres-Exactes et de belles Tailles-douces, Les principaux Empires, Roïaumes, Républi-ques, Provinces, Villes ... les Antiquitez, les Abbaies, Églises, Académies, Collèges, Bibliothêques, Palais ... les Maisons de Campagne ... Divisée en LXVI Tomes les Estampes aiant été dessinées sur les Lieux, & gravées exactement par les célèbres Luyken, Mulder, Goere'e, Baptist, Stopendaal, & par d'autres Maîtres renomez ... Cette partie comprend le Tome Premier du Grand Bretagne, & d'Irlande (allegorical engraving,50 × 125/52 × 127mm) Le tout mis en ordre & exécuté à Leide, Par Pierre Vander Aa, Marchand Libraire, Imprimeur de l'Université & de la Ville.

Folio, 360 × 260mm.   nd (?1715)

COLLATION Title-page; pp 1–11, description of the United Kingdom; pp 12–14, list of plates (Tome 1: London, Cambridge, Home Counties, etc; Tome 2: Oxford, East Anglia, Midlands and the North; Tome 3: Scotland and Ireland); dedication to George I, in engr frame (1 leaf); 118 plates.

The London illustrations are in the first part of this volume. All but three are from plates originally engraved for a Van der Aa publication of 1707: Beeverell's *Délices de la Grand'Bretagne* (no 20). Originally intended to fit with a centre-fold into this small octavo, they have been adapted by reprinting in twos, threes and fours within a framework designed to suit the pages of a folio 'Gallery'. The folio volumes were published in a limited edition to appeal to collectors and to make further use of the plates for which Van der Aa ransacked his geographical book output of the last decade and, in particular, the *Délices* series of European countries. A notice, 'L'Imprimeur au Lecteur', prefixed to the first volume of all (Portugal and Spain) states:

Le tout est recueilli & représenté par des tailles-douces, exactement de tems en tems gravées par les meilleurs Maîtres dans cette science, à mes propres dépens, ou à ceux de Messieurs Blaeu, Visscher, de Wit, Meurs, Goerée, Halma, Mortier, Allard & d'autres; lesquelles j'ai achetées de leurs Héritiers.... je les ai reduïtes en LXVI Volumes; chaque Empire, Roïaume &c. est precédé d'une Courte Description ... outre le Sommaire couché au dessous de chaque planche ... Je n'ai imprimé que cent exemplaires de cette Galerie du Monde.

As far as the London views are concerned no great skill in draughtsmanship was required of any of the engravers since they are mainly miniaturized versions of plates by Kip, Hollar or the engraver of Morden and Lea's *Prospects* (no 15). References are given to the listing of Beeverell's *Délices* (abbreviated *BEEV*) through which the originals may be identified.

The facing page numbers engraved tr on the plates of the 1707 edition of Beeverell were scraped out for the *Galérie* impressions; for the 1727 Beeverell amended page numbers were engraved in their place, thus creating a third state of the plates. The two engraved frames most generally used are identified in the list as *A* and *B*. Frame *A* consists of beaded framework with decorative cornerpieces and a cornice dividing the two upper views from the lower one in a group of three, the spaces on each side of the lower view being filled with beaded panelling (338 × 414/345 × 428mm). *B* consists of an ornamental frame with blank spaces for four views, two above and two below, allowing room for their plate-marks to clear the framework; there is occasional overprinting of the view plates onto the impression of the framework (335 × 405/345 × 415mm). Plate numbers quoted are from the table of plates; the plates themselves are unnumbered.

1 pl.6 Hampton Court. 121 × 158/130 × 168mm. With views of Fair Lawn and Knowle in Kent. Frame *A*. From *BEEV* 4,871.

2 pl.7 A Prospect of Greenwich Hospitall for Seamen as designed/ and advancing Ao 1699. 121 × 157/127 × 165mm. With views of Audley End and Balms in Middlesex. Frame *A*. From *BEEV* 4,750.

3 pl.7a The House att Chelsey in the County of Middlesex. 121 × 160/130 × 165mm. – The House att Chiswick in the County of Middlesex. 123 × 158/130 × 165mm. With a view of Dawly in Middlesex. Frame *A*. From *BEEV* 4,977d,e. (*Longford* 245)

4 pl.8 (tm) Londini Angliae Regni Metropolis Delineatio Accuratissima. Per Petrum Van der Aa. (on stone bl) A Leide/Chez Pierre Vander Aa. 495 × 577/502 × 584mm. tl a cartouche with ten 'Places of Southwark', tr a banner with 148 other 'Names of Places', br 'London' with the City arms and along the foot of the map a view of a country house. (*Darlington and Howgego* 40 relates this map to one similarly entitled engraved with portraits of King William and Queen Mary and issued by Johannes de Ram.)

5 pl.9 (tc in cartouche terminated by lion masks) Londres/Capitale de l'Angleterre. (bc) a Leide, Chez Pierre vander Aa, Avec Privilege. 205 × 260/350 × 425, view in frame 335 × 415mm. Decorated with swags. Westminster to the Tower viewed from imaginary hill in Southwark. (*Scouloudi* p 74)

6 pl.9a (on banderole with swallow-tailed ends) London. (bl) C. Allard exc. cum Pr. ord. Holl.et Westr. (br) fct. 200 × 255/225 × 285mm, in frame of diced beading. The view is a condensed version of Hollar's long birds-eye view of London from Bankside engraved in 1647 (*Hind* 16). In the table of plates it is referred to as 'Londres, avec, les habits' by way of explanation of two full-lengths of a 'decolletée' lady and a gentleman wearing a plaited wig walking out of the picture and towards the spectator. The costume is not really fancy-dress but the clothes worn by King William and Queen Mary at the time of their accession. Carolus Allard published a number of prints to celebrate this event, all engraved by R. de Hooghe: their reception at St James's, 1688 (*Crace* 12.9), their Coronation, 1689 (*Crace* 14.105) and their portraits with a view of Whitehall (*Crace* 5.128). The illegible credit may be de Hooghe's, half obliterated. Allard also published a broadside on the arrival in England of King William (BM: *Crowle* 4.191).

7 pl.10 La Tour de Londres. 125 × 162/130 × 167mm. –

La Douane, ou Costume House. 121 × 146/133 × 152mm.—Le monument érigé en memoire du grand incendie de Londres. 130 × 158/140 × 165mm. – La Bourse de Londres. 127 × 160/133 × 165mm. Frame *B*. From *BEEV* 4, 802, 808, 809, 811.

8 pl. 11 (tm) The Statue of King Charles II, upon the Royal Exchange. 130 × 165/140 × 170mm. – (tm) The Statue of King Charles II, at the entrance of Cornhill. 133 × 165/140 × 170mm. – Bow Church. 121 × 157/130 × 164mm. – Vue du Guild Hall du Côté du Midi. 127 × 152/135 × 159mm. Frame *B*. The first two subjects are on a larger scale than *BEEV* 4, 812 which groups three statues on one plate and overprints the frame. The other two are from *BEEV* 4, 814 (I,II).

9 pl.12 Vûe de l'Eglise Cathédrale de/S.Paul du côté de l'occident. Avant le feu de 1666. 121 × 154/130 × 165mm. – Vûe du dedans de l'Eglise Paroissiale/de Sainte Foi, Avant le Feu de 1666. 125 × 154/129 × 165mm. – Vûe du dedans de la Nef de l'Eglise/ Cathédrale de S. Paul, Avant le feu de 1666. 123 × 154/130 × 164mm. – Vûe de la partie exterieure/du choeur du côté d'Occident/Avant le feu de 1666. 122 × 153/130 × 163mm. Frame *B*. From *BEEV* 4, 815, 819, 818 (I,II).

10 pl.13 Section du dedans de l'Orient à l'occident de l'Eglise Cathedrale/de S.Paul. 124 × 155/133 × 165mm. – Mercers Chappel. 121 × 157/133 × 160mm. – L'Entrée du Collège Royal des Medecins. 125 × 160/130 × 165mm. – Hôpital de Bethlehem. 121 × 159/127 × 165mm. Frame *B*. From *BEEV* 4, 827, 815(II), 828, 831.

11 pl.14 Temple Barr du Côté du Couchant. 120 × 159/130 × 160mm. – L'Hotel de Sommerset,/ou Sommerset House. 123 × 153/130 × 163mm. – Le Temple. 127 × 160/133 × 165mm. Frame *A*. From *BEEV* 4, 834, 835 (I,II).

12 pl.15 St James Palace and Park. 124 × 155/130 × 165mm. – St James's House. 123 × 155/130 × 165mm. – Partie de White-Hall, qui fait face à la Tamise. 123 × 153/130 × 165mm. – (tm) The Statue of King Charles at Charing Cross in Brass. 133 × 167/142 × 170mm. Frame *B*. The engraving of the statue is on a larger scale than on the triple plate *BEEV* 4, 812 and overprints the frame; the others are from *BEEV* 4, 837 (I,II), 838.

13 pl.16 La Maison appellée Banqueting House. 125 × 163/133 × 167mm. – The Kings Gate, ou Porte Royale/de White-Hall, qui conduit à Westminster. 123 × 153/130 × 165mm. Double frame with trompe l'oeil label 'A Leide/chez Pierre Van der AA' and indented corners; the two views from *BEEV* 4, 839, 840(I).

14 pl.17 Vûe de Westminster-Hall. 123 × 155/130 × 160mm. – Eglise de S.Pierre, ou Abbaye de Westminster. 123 × 155/130 × 169mm. – Partie de Westminster. 123 × 155/130 × 165mm. – Sale de Westminster,/ou Westminster-Hall. 125 × 153/130 × 165mm. Frame *B*. From *BEEV* 4, 840(II), 841, 847, 848.

15 pl.18 Maison de Lambeth,/ou Lambeth House. 125 × 155/130 × 165mm. – Lambeth Palais des Archévêques de Cantorbery. 125 × 155/130 × 165mm. – Eglise de St. Marie dans South Wark. 122 × 158/130 × 165mm. – Chelsey Colledge. 123 × 158/130 × 165mm. Frame B. From *BEEV* 4, 850(I,II), 851, 853. (*Longford* 65)

16 pl.19 Burlington House in Pickadilly. 125 × 157/130 × 165mm. With 'Coacres et Coacresses/dans leurs assemblées/à Londres' and 'Milk-maids of May' in frame A. From *BEEV* 4 (2nd ed), 977c.

24 · CAMPBELL'S VITRUVIUS BRITANNICUS* [1715–25]

Richard Boyle, 3rd Earl of Burlington was seized by a consuming passion for Italian architecture during a grand tour. On his return to England to celebrate his coming of age, in 1715, he was deeply impressed with the work going forward at Wanstead for Sir Richard Child and subscribed to the forthcoming publication of its architect Colen Campbell: a collection of engraved architectural plans and elevations entitled *Vitruvius Britannicus*. It was probably a consequence of these events and of the Earl's ensuing patronage of the style that Palladianism was to become the dominant architectural fashion in Great Britain throughout the century.

Vitruvius Britannicus is not a topographical work, not even to the same extent as its contemporary, the *Britannia Illustrata* (no 22), for it is rarely concerned with the 'genius loci'; rather, as Cambell's introduction makes explicit, it is essentially a work of architectural illustration and propaganda. He deplores the excesses of Italian baroque but accepts with unbounded enthusiasm the 'very great Obligations to those Restorers of Architecture which the Fifteenth and Sixteenth Centuries produced in Italy ... But above all the great Palladio, who has exceeded all that were gone before him and seems to have arrived at a Ne plus ultra of his Art'. In the year of his death, 1729, Campbell published an edition of Palladio's *Five Orders of Architecture*.

Subscribers to the 300 plates of the *Vitruvius* were made up from a good cross-section of the British nobility and gentry and also several architects, including the aged Wren, Vanbrugh, Hawksmoor, John James, and Thomas Archer, besides many engaged in the ancillary trades of bricklayer, stone mason, joiner and plasterer. The lists also include three engravers, William Emmett, Andrew Johnson and John Sturt, the landscape artist and surveyor Thomas Badslade, Sir Hans Sloane and Joseph Addison.

The most imposing items in the second volume are the panoramic twin-plate engravings from drawings acquired from William Emmett of Bromley by Campbell: designs for Whitehall Palace supposedly after Inigo Jones whom he idolized second only to Palladio. This grandiose scheme, never realized, merely serves as a reminder of what might have been accomplished by an English Louis XIV. The majority of the plates in the second and third volumes are plans for fashionable country houses or private palaces such as Wanstead House, Castle Howard and Blenheim. Nevertheless the whole work includes a sufficient number of designs for London houses and public buildings, even though some like Whitehall Palace and the Lincoln's Inn Fields church never got beyond the drawing-board and others were much modified in the execution, to warrant the inclusion of this key architectural work in a book on London illustrators.

Campbell is the draughtsman throughout but in the second and third volumes an engraver's credit appears, that of Henry Hulsbergh of Amsterdam. He settled in London at the turn of the century and seems to have been much sought after by architects. In the King's Library Topographical Collection (BL Maps) are some 20 engravings of London buildings (on a large scale, up to about 75 × 55cm) published between 1711 and 1726 after drawings by Hawksmoor, Gibbs, Flitcroft and John Price. He also engraved some of Wren's rejected elevations and plans of St Paul's Cathedral.

The first volume came out in 1715 and was reissued with the second in 1717. The third, the last by Campbell, was published in 1725 by the author and Joseph Smith of Exeter Exchange, who in the previous year had published a collected edition of the *Nouveau Théâtre* or *Britannia Illustrata* (no 22). The printseller John Bowles also stocked *Vitruvius Britannicus*; in his 1728 catalogue he offers for sale two volumes containing 200 plates and in his 1731 catalogue three volumes with 300 plates 'Price Four Guineas in Boards'.

The three volumes were published in a second edition between 1718 and 1731 and reprinted in the next generation by John Woolfe and James Gandon who added two supplementary volumes (no 45). The title was finally reused for a work of George Richardson's published by the Architectural Library in 1802–8 (no 84).

For a detailed analysis of this work of Campbell's the reader is referred to Howard E. Stutchbury's *The architecture of Colen Campbell*.

Vitruvius Britannicus/or/The British Architect,/Containing/The Plans, Elevations, and Sections/of the Regular Buildings,/both/Publick and Private,/in/Great Britain/ With Variety of New Designs: in 200 large Folio Plates; engraven/by the best Hands: and Drawn either from the Buildings themselves,/or the Original Designs of the Architects:/ In II Volumes/Vol I (II) by Colen Campbell Esqr./ (translation into French follows) Cum Privilegio Regis (rule)/Sold by the Author over against Douglas Coffee-house in St Martins-lane, John Nicholson in/Little Britain, Andrew Bell at the Cross-Keys in Cornhill, W. Taylor in Pater-Noster-Row, Henry/Clements in St Pauls Church-Yard, and Jos. Smith in Exeter-Change. London, MDCCXVII. J.Sturt sculp. (engr 380 × 248mm)
(The vol.2 title-page has been adapted for the reissue of vol.1 by the simple expedient of pasting a slip over one upright of the Roman 'II'.)

The Third Volume of Vitruvius Britannicus: or, the British Architect. containing the Geometrical Plans of the most Considerable Gardens and Plantations: also the Plans Elevations and Sections of the most Regular Buildings not Published in the First and Second Volumes. With Large Views, in Perspective of the most Remarkable Edifices in Great Britain. Engraven by the Best Hands in One Hundred large Folio Plates. By Colen Campbell Esquire, Architect to His Royal Highness the Prince of Wales. (translation into French follows) Tome III. Cum Privilegio Regis, Printed, and sold by the Author, at his House in Middle Scotland-Yard, White-hall; and by Joseph Smith at the Sign of Inigo Jones's Head, near Exeter-Change, in the Strand MDCC.XXV.

Folio, 510 × 345mm.   (1715)1717–25

COLLATION   Vol. 1. Engr title-page; engr calligraphic dedication to George I (1 leaf); introduction (2pp); pp 3–7, explanation and check-list of plates; p 8, royal licence dated 8 April 1715; pp 9–10, list of subscribers; plates numbered 1–100 (extra large plates allotted 2 nos). Vol. 2. Engr title-page, pp 1–6, explanation and checklist of plates; pp 7–8, list of subscribers; plates numbered 1–100 (twin plates allotted 4 nos, extra large plates 2). Vol. 3. Title-page, dedication to George, Prince of Wales (1 leaf); pp 5–6, list of subscribers; pp 7–12, explanation and checklist of plates; plates numbered 1–100 (twin plates allotted 4 nos, extra large plates 2).

The London plates, apart from a birds-eye view of Greenwich Hospital in the third volume, are all plans, elevations or sections with captions below or, if two such are on the same plate, below and above the subjects. French translations of these are usually supplied and each plate includes a scale of feet. Plate numbers are engraved tr. Plate-marks are measured.

VOL. 1

1 pl.3 The plan of St Pauls Church. (and in French) 375 × 255mm.

2 pl.4 The West Prospect of St Pauls Church begun Anno 1672 and finish'd 1710 by/Sr. Christopher Wren Kt. (and in French) Ca: Campbell Delin:. 375 × 250mm. pl.5–7 which follow are of St Peter's, Rome.

3 pl.8 Plan of a new Design of a Church of my Invention for Lincolns Inn Fields. (and in French) 375 × 245mm.

4 pl.9 This new Design (ie elevation) of my Invention for a church in Lincolns inn Fields ... (and in French) Ca. Campbell Inv. et Delin. 375 × 250mm. This and an unsited design in vol. 2 (pl. 27) may have been Campbell's submissions to the Commissioners for the Fifty New Churches. Wren had in the previous century prepared a scheme for the same site and it was upon this, St Paul's Cathedral and St Peter's in Rome that this megalomaniacal scheme, which could never have been realized, was based. 'Done Anno 1712'.

5 pl.12 The section – The plan of ye Banketting house. (and in French) 245 × 375mm.

6 pl.13 The Banquetting House at Whitehall, by Inigo Jones. (and in French) Ca. Campbell delin. 250 × 380mm.

7 pl.14 Plan of ye Second floor. (and in French) – the plan of the first Story of ye King House att Greenwich. 250 × 375mm.

8 pl.15 The elevation of the Queens House to the Park at Greenwich. Invented by Inigo Jones 1639 ... (and in French) Ca. Campbell Delin. 245 × 380mm. Shows six statues above the parapet ranging with the Ionic columns of the loggia.

9 pl.16 The Elevation of the Great Gallery in Somerset House to the River. (and in French) Ca. Campbell Delin. 250 × 378mm. 'This noble arcade was taken from a design of Inigo Jones, but conducted by another hand'.

10 pl.31 The Plan of his Grace the Duke of Kent's Garden Pavilion – The Plan of Burlington House in Pickadilly. (and in French) 240 × 380mm.

11 pl.32 Burlington House in Pickadilly London. 248 × 375mm. Although the plan shows some alterations to the original house within, this elevation towards Piccadilly of the main block has only one minor difference. (in the central bay) from the façade drawn by Knyff before 1704 and engraved by Kip for the *Nouveau Théâtre*, item 11. The Palladian remodelling

by Campbell and the Earl had not yet taken place; it is recorded on pl. 22–5 of vol. 3.

12 pl.34 The Plan of ye Principal Floor of Montague House ... (and in French) 375 × 250mm.

13 pl.35 The prospect of Montague house to the Street London. (and in French) 255 × 380mm. Entrance gate, screen wall and corner pavilions.

14 pl.36 The Elevation of Montague House to the Court in Great Russell Street London.... (and in French) Ca: Campbell Delin. 250 × 378mm. 'The Architecture was conducted by Monsieur Pouget 1678'.

15 pl.39 The plan of Marlborough house St James's. (and in French) 380 × 250mm.

16 pl.40 The Elevation of Marlborough House to St James's Park, Invented by Christopher Wren Esq. 1709.... (and in French, with dedication to Duchess of Marlborough) Ca. Campbell Delin. 255 × 375mm. Statues shown in the niches and in the centre of the parapet a trophy with the Garter surrounding a blank cartouche; neither of these features are present on the *Nouveau Théâtre* plate, item 46, of about 1714.

17 pl.41 The plan of ye first story of Powis house (and in French) – The plan of ye Second Story. (and in French) 250 × 380mm.

18 pl.42 The Elevation of Powis House in Ormond Street London 1714.... (and in French) Ca: Campbell Delin:. 250 × 375mm. Leased by the Marquis of Powis to the French Ambassador, this house had recently been rebuilt after a fire. To secure against further outbreaks the flat roof was designed as a reservoir and fish tank.

19 pl.43 The Plan of Buckingham house in St James's Park. (and in French) 375 × 250mm.

20 pl.44 The Elevation of Buckingham House in St James's Park.... (and in French) Ca: Campbell Delin:. 245 × 375mm. Built by William Winde for John Sheffield, Duke of Buckingham, 1705.

21 pl.49 Plan of the Parlor floor/of Lindsey House – Plan of the principal Story. (and in French) 250 × 375mm.

22 pl.50 The Elevation of Lindsey house in Lincolns inn fields ... (and in French) Ca: Campbell Delin: Inigo Jones Inv:. 250 × 375mm. 'Inigo Jones ... designed it Ao 1640'. Shows urns on the parapet ranging with the Ionic pilasters and a diminutive bust of a queen rising from the break in the pediment of the central window; these have disappeared. 'An instructive study in the rude expression of taste of the 1630's' (Summerson).

23 pl.82–3 General Front of the Royal Hospital at Greenwich. (and in French) 420 × 395mm, large plate.

24 pl.84–5 The General Front of the Royal Hospital at Greenwich ... (and in French) Ca: Campbell Delin:. 655 × 250mm, large plate. The façades to the river front have been completed with their central aedicules but where the Queen's House closes the vista it is here blocked by a third large central dome rising from a colonnade, the scheme for a majestic centrally placed chapel drawn up by Hawksmoor but never adopted.

25 pl.86–7 The Elevation of one of the double Pavillions of the Royal Hospital at Greenwich. (and in French) I. Iones Inven: Ca: Campbell delin:. 375 × 640mm, large plate. The Jones attribution is inexplicable as this shows part of the river front of Hawksmoor's Queen Anne block. The statue of the Queen shown in a niche in the crowning aedicule seems never to have materialized.

26 pl.88–9 The Elevation of one Wing of the Great Court of Greenwich Hospital. (and in French) Ca: Campbell Delin:. 250 × 640mm, large plate. On Vanbrugh's death in 1726 Campbell succeeded to the Surveyorship of the Hospital. In his note on these plates he says: 'The Stile of the Architecture is Great and Noble, executed by Mr Webb from a design of the great Master Inigo Jones'.

VOL. 2

27 pl.2–3 The General Plan of the Principal Story for the Royal Pallace at White-Hall as designed by Inigo Iones: Anno 1639. (and in French) 375 × 455mm.

28 pl.4–7 The Elevation of a Design for the Pallace at White Hall towards the Park, as it was presented to his Majesty King Charles the I by the famous Inigo Jones Anno 1639. (and in French) Ca: Campbell Delin: H. Hulsbergh Sculp:. On twin plates, each 275 × 570mm.

29 pl.8–11 The Elevation of a Design for the Pallace at White-Hall towards the River as it was presented to his Majesty King Charles I by the celebrated Inigo Jones Anno 1639 but interrupted by the Civil Warrs. (and in French) Ca: Campbell Delin. H. Hulsbergh Sculp:. On twin plates, each 275 × 570mm.

30 pl.12–15 The Elevation of a Design for the Pallace at White-Hall, towards Charing-Cross, as it was presented to his Majesty King C: I. by Inigo Iones Anno 1639. (and in French) Ca: Campbell Delin: H. Hulsbergh Sculp:. On twin plates, each 275 × 490mm.

31 pl.16–19 The Section of the Royal Pallace at White-Hall as design'd by the renowned Inigo Iones 1639. Ca: Campbell Delin. H. Hulsbergh Sculp:. On twin plates, each 275 × 580mm.

Of plates 2–19 above (items 27–31) Campbell says in his 'Explanation': 'After much Labour and Expense I have at last procured these excellent Designs of Inigo Jones, for White-hall, from that ingenious Gentleman, William Emmet of Bromley in the County of Kent Esq, from whose Original Drawings the following 5 Plates are publish'd'. His hero-worship of Inigo Jones led him astray since the drawings on which these plates are based are in John Webb's hand, not Jones's. Of all this massive pile, which according to the designs was to occupy most of the space between Whitehall and the river, only the Banqueting House, swamped by the surrounding grandeur, certainly originates with

Jones; nor was his name associated with it until 1658, six years after his death.

32 pl.20 Plan of St Paul Church Covent Garden – The West Front – The Section – The Plan of the Great Piazza Covent Garden. (and in French) 375 × 250mm.

33 pl.21–2 The East Prospect of St Paul Church Covent Garden to the Great Square – The West prospect of Covent Garden. Invented by Inigo Iones 1640. (and in French) Ca: Campbell Delin. H. Hulsbergh Sc:. 375 × 495mm, large plate. 'I have made one single and one double plate of this noble Square, which for the Grandeur of Design is certainly the first in Europe'. The church was completed by about December 1632 and the piazza by 1637.

34 pl.23 Plan of the Royal Exchange. (and in French) London. 250 × 375mm.

35 pl.24–5 The Elevation of the Royal Exchange … (and in French) Ca: Campbell Delin: H. Hulsbergh Sc:. 375 × 500mm, large plate. The plate is dedicated to Sir James Bateman, Lord Mayor in 1716. Campbell says the architecture is not up to Inigo Jones's standard but does not mention Jarman, the architect, by name.

36 pl.26 The Plans, Elevations and Section of Bow-Steeple in Cheapside. Ca: Campbell Delin: H. Hulsbergh Sc:. 377 × 253mm.

37 pl.28 The Elevation of York Stairs to the River, London. Inv: by Inigo Iones 1626. Ca: Campbell Delin: H. Hulsbergh Sculp: 380 × 250mm. 'This Gate was erected by the first Duke of Buckingham Anno 1626 … by Inigo Jones' (Campbell's 'Explanation'). 'The drawing by Webb of the York Water Gate (B.D.IV/8) is dated 1641, and is a measured plan and elevation of the structure erected for the Duke of Buckingham in 1626–7. Jones's participation is unlikely and, at this date, Webb's participation would have been impossible. In the early twenties Jones had been replaced in Buckingham's favour by Sir Balthasar Gerbier (c 1591–1667) to whom may be attributed the design' (RIBA *Burlington-Devonshire Collection* 1, p 46)

VOL. 3

38 pl.3–4 The prospect of the Royall Hospital at Greenwich to the River Thames. Ca: Campbell Delin: H. Hulsbergh Sculp:. 305 × 493/330 × 500mm, large plate. Unlike the other London plates in this work this is a birds-eye view in a border-line; it seems to be an actual prospect of the completed building, like the plate published in the fourth volume of Joseph Smith's *Nouveau Théâtre*, item 48. Architect's drawings of the same subject are listed above, items 23–6.

39 pl.10 The Elevation of General Wade his house in Great Burlington Street/Designed by the Rt Honourable Richard Earl of Burlington and Cork &c. 1723 (with plans). Ca: Campbell delin: H. Hulsbergh Sculp:. 375 × 247mm. Part of the scheme for developing the field behind Burlington House laun-

ched in 1718. The Earl copied the design of a Palladio villa which caused Lord Chesterfield to suggest tartly that 'as the General could not live in it at his ease, he had better take a house over against it and look at it'. It was not demolished until 1923.

40 pl.22 General Plan of Burlington House and Offices in Pickadilly. 380 × 253mm.

41 pl.23–4 Burlington house in Pickadilly London, Erected by the Rt Honourable Richard Boyle, Earl of Burlington and Cork … Designed by Colen Campbell Anno 1717. Ca: Campbell Inv. et Delin: H. Hulsbergh Sculp:. 250 × 505mm, large plate.

42 pl.25 The great Gate at Burlington house in Pickadilly…. Designed by Colen Campbell 1718. H. Hulsbergh Sculp:. (title also in French tl) 245 × 375mm. The original appearance of the house when it was inherited by the Earl in 1715 is given in pl.31–2 of vol. 1 (items 10–11), and Campbell's remodelling of it in the above three plates. In his 'Explanation' he refers obliquely to a predecessor, probably Gibbs: 'the Stables were built by another Architect before I had the Honour of being called to his Lordship's Service, which obliged me to make the offices opposite conformable to these. The Front of the House, the Conjunction from House to the Offices, the great Gate and Street Wall, were all designed & executed by me'. When the Earl returned from Venice at the end of 1719 he found his house transformed to a Palladian palazzo with Venetian windows and a colonnaded forecourt divided from Piccadilly by a rusticated wall and entered by the Great Gate which was later travestied in the satirical print 'Man of Taste'.

43 pl.26 The New Bagnio in the Gardens at Chiswick – erected by the Rt Honble Richard Boyle … in the Year 1717. (elevation and plan) Ca: Campbell Delin: H. Hulsbergh Sculp:. 375 × 245mm. Until he supplanted his predecessor in the modernization of Burlington House it is probable that Campbell was consulted by the Earl on improvements to his Jacobean house in Chiswick and he describes this bagnio as the 'first essay of his Lordship's Happy Invention'.

44 pl.44 Plan of the first (second) Story of the Rolls. 375 × 245mm.

45 pl.45 The West front of the Rolls in Chancery Lane … 1718. Ca: Campbell Inv: et Delin: H. Hulsbergh Sculp:. 250 × 375mm. An official residence with an audience chamber, Campbell's only public building 'built by a Royal Gift from our most gracious sovereign K. George, to Sir Joseph Jekyll, past Master of the Rolls…. All the Ornaments are of Portland Stone'. The commission was no doubt obtained through the good offices of Lord Burlington.

46 pl.48 Elevation of the Right Honourable the/Lord Herbert, his House on Whitehall – Plan of the Principal Story – Plan of the Attick Story. Anno 1724. Ca: Campbell Architectus: H. Hulsbergh Sculp:. 375 × 250mm. Built for the 22 year old Lord Herbert who

obtained a lease of ground in Whitehall Palace occupied until the fire of 1698 by the Queen's apartments. Like Burlington, he had visited Venice and may have collaborated with Campbell in the design of this modest Palladian Villa. 'In the basement is a rustick Arcade, and over it, an Ionick Loggio and Attick. The Gallery of the last Story is most magnificently furnished and gives one of the best Prospects of the Thames'. It was demolished in 1757 to make way for a replacement by Sir William Chambers.

47 pl.56 This new Design of a Bridge over the River Thames at London near Lambeth/is most/humbly Inscribed to the Right Honourable William Pulteney Esqr. Ca: Campbell Inv. et de: H. Hulsbergh Sculp:. 247 × 375mm. A petition for the erection of a bridge across the Thames to supplement London Bridge at Lambeth or Vauxhall was referred to a committee of the House of Commons of which Pulteney, Master of the Rolls and therefore resident in Campbell's newly erected official dwelling, was chairman. At the instance of Lord Burlington, Campbell was invited to submit this design which draws on classical precedents handed down by Palladio. 'The Plan would be no Obstruction to the Navigation of the River. The Bridge was intended to be 770 feet long with 7 Arches'. The scheme was shelved owing to City opposition only to be revived in 1734 under the auspices of Lord Herbert, another of Campbell's patrons, but the Westminster Bridge erected 1738–50 was designed by Charles Labelye, not Campbell.

Supplementary plates, unnumbered and not in check-list (BL:649.b.5)

48 Plan of the Parlour Story and Elevation of Seven New intended Houses on the East Side of Grosvenor Sqr/as Designed by Colen Campbell Esqr 1725. Ca: Campbell Architectus. H. Hulsbergh Sculp:. 250 × 500mm. Not carried out according to this specification.

49 Section of the Back Parlour for Colen Campbell Esqr in Brook Street near Grosvenor Square. 195 × 275mm. Campbell's name is in the Rate Books for no 46, on the N. side of Brook Street, in June 1726.

25 · STOW'S SURVEY [1720]

In Hatton's *New View of London* (1708), on the verso of the title-page, was printed the following advertisement:

In a short time Proposals will be published for Reprinting Mr Stow's large Survey of London improv'd; with very great Additions throughout, and illustrated with about 100 large Copper Cuts, viz. of the City in general, and of several of the Wards thereof: of Westminster, Southwark, and all the Out-Parts of the City as they are now: and also several Ornamental Plates of Churches, and other Public Buildings in Folio.

Note: this Work has been long preparing, the Cutts requiring much Time and Great Expences, but they are now all finished, and may be seen at the Undertakers.

Among the 'undertakers' of Hatton's book were A. Churchill and R. Knaplock who were later concerned in the publication of the 1720 (fifth) edition of Stow's *Survey*. From John Strype's preface to the latter, dated 16 April 1720, it may be deduced that by April 1703 he was already collecting materials for the text of this edition. It was not however until 14 December 1719 that 'proposals' in the *Daily Courant* asserted that 'Above two Thirds of this Book is already Printed' in time for the book to be the first subscribed to by the Society of Antiquaries, on 18 December. On publication it was chosen by the City Fathers for formal presentation to aldermen on their election.

A Survey of the Cities of London and Westminster: containing The Original, Antiquity, Increase, Modern Estate and Government of those Cities. Written at first in the Year MDXCVIII By John Stow, Citizen and Native of London, Since Reprinted and Augmented by the Author: and afterwards by A.M., H.D. and others. Now Lastly, Corrected, Improved, and very much Enlarged and the Survey and History brought down from the Year 1633, (being now Fourscore Years since it was last printed) to the present Time: by John Strype, M.A. a Native also of the said City. Illustrated with Exact Maps of the City and Suburbs and of all the Wards; and likewise of the Out-Parishes of London and Westminster. Together with many other fair Draughts of the more Eminent and Publick Edifices and Monuments. In Six Books.... London: Printed for A. Churchill, J. Knapton, R. Knaplock, J. Walthoe, E. Horne, B. Tooke, D. Midwinter, B. Cowse, R. Robinson, and T. Ward. MDCCXX.

Folio, about 381 × 248mm. 1720

COLLATION Vol. 1. Title-page; dedication to Sir John Fryer Lord Mayor 1720–1 (2pp); pp i–xii, preface and dedicatory epistles; pp i–xxvii, life of Stow; pp xxviii–xlii, bibliography and contents; list of subscribers (2pp); pp 1–308, Survey Book 4; pp 1–208, Book 2; pp 1–285, Book 3. Vol. 2. Title-page; pp 1–120, Survey Book 4; pp 1–459, Book 5; pp 1–93, Book 6; pp 1–143, appendix with half-title; pp 1–26, 2nd appendix; index (25pp).

What a topographical treasure would the first edition of Stow's *Survey* have proved to future ages had it been illustrated with maps and views by competent engravers! The publishers of the fifth edition were clearly determined to remedy this defect for their own period and the 100 engravings mentioned in the 1708 advertisement in Hatton's *New View* as being available for inspection probably included a good proportion of the 70 which they eventually used. The ward maps and some of the parish maps must have been ready by then, since, as Strype explains in his preface, correction and revision had been necessary because these maps were based on 'a careful Survey made of London and Westminster, divers Years ago by Mr Lyborn (possibly William Leybourn, 1626–?1700) and Mr Bloome' (Richard Blome, d 1705). Their titles terminate with the formulas: 'Taken from the last Surveys', 'Corrected from the last Surveys' or 'Taken from the last Surveys with Corrections and Additions' with their final words, 'by Richard Blome', burnished out but in some cases still legible. Indeed in the reissues published with the 1754 Stow (no 37) the still visible name or its vacant space have in some cases been disguised by a stroke or flourish of the burin. A name which might still have been an asset at the time of the advertisement had by 1720 become something of a liability; the maps which had been 'long preparing' in 1708 were by then at least 15 years old. In *Ward maps of the City of London*, which should be consulted for a more detailed description than that given below, Ralph Hyde suggests that the engravers were Sutton Nicholls (fl 1680–1740) or Johannes Kip (1652–1722).

Kip's credit certainly appears on half of the 28 engraved views to which the other half, although anonymous, are similar in style. At the time of their assembly he was the foremost British topographical illustrator having just completed 80 plates of town and country houses for the first volume of Mortier's *Nouveau Théâtre de la Grande Bretagne* (no 22, abbreviated *NTGB*, with item number) of which one dozen were views of buildings in London or its environs. Three of these, or the drawings on which they were based, were copied with only minor alterations for Strype's edition (Book 1, p 64; Book 4, p 105; Book 6, p 4) and four others (Book 1, pp 192, 215; Book 2, p 51; Book 3, p 156) are related to plates by other artists in subsequent volumes of the same collection. The views were not so likely as the maps to date the book since they mostly depict public buildings which altered little over the years, with the one exception of the plate of the Custom

House (Book 2, p 51) showing Wren's building which burned down in 1718. Stow's monument was engraved by John Sturt who specialized in small, decorative frontispieces.

The titles of most of the views are worked on 25mm banderoles tc and those of the maps on cartouches or curtains. Some maps have blank cartouches but vacant spaces are usually filled with lists of references, scale-bars and compass-roses. None of the maps has a credit except that of the parish of St Mary Rotherhithe (Book 6, p 87) revised by John Pullen and engraved by John Harris. Each plate, to ensure correct placing in relation to the text, is engraved tr with the appropriate volume, book and page number, thus: 'VI: B2: p 29'; consequently there are no 'directions to the binder'. Strype's preface, however, speaks of 17 ward maps (ie those in Books 2 and 3 but not the two Tower maps in Book 1), 20 parish maps (in Books 4 and 6) and 'many more Descriptions and delightful Prospects of eminent Places in and about London and Westminster ... to the number of 25' (distributed throughout all Books, except Book 5 which is illustrated only by shields of arms on text pages). Thus the full complement of 70 plates is: 17 ward maps (Books 2 and 3), 20 parish maps (Books 4 and 6), two Tower maps (Book 1), two general maps (Book 1), 28 views of 25 'eminent places' in London, Westminster and Southwark (including three of St Paul's Cathedral), and one engraving of Stow's monument.

1 p xiv The monument of Mr John Stow, now standing in/the Parish Church of St Andrew Undershaft. J. Sturt sculp. 274 × 165mm.

VOL. 1

BOOK 1   (general description of the City)

2 p 1 A New Plan of the City of/London,/Westminster,/ and Southwark. 489 × 660/495 × 686mm. Title in cartouche with allegorical figures and a dedication to Sir George Thorold, Lord Mayor 1719–20. (*Darlington and Howgego* 16)

3 p 1 The City of/London/as in/Q. Elizabeth's Time. 190 × 457/229 × 476mm. Title in cartouche tc. (*Darlington and Howgego* 8, see note)

4 p 14 Ald Gate – Bishops Gate – Moor Gate – Cripple-Gate – Alders Gate – New Gate – Lud Gate – Temple Barr. 210 × 324/216 × 330mm.

5 p 53 (on banderole) London Bridge. 210 × 324/222 × 330mm. Viewed from E.

6 p 54 A Map of the Tower Liberty. 279 × 356/381 × 406mm.

7 p 64 (on banderole) The Tower of London. J. Kip sculp. 203 × 333/213 × 343mm. Similar in all respects to *NTGB* 7.

8 p 64 The Tower/and/St Catherin's/Taken from ye last Survey/with corrections. 279 × 356/381 × 406mm. Title in cartouche with swags. Refs 1–65.

9 p 175 (on banderole) Christ Hospitall. 200 × 324/213 × 337mm.

10 p 176 (on banderole) The Prospect of Bridewell. 203 × 330/210 × 337mm.

11 p 184 (on banderole) St Bartholomew's Hospitall/in Smithfield. 203 × 330/210 × 334mm.

12 p 189 (on banderole) St Thomas. Hospitall/in Southwark. 325 × 205/335 × 213mm.

13 p 192 (on banderole) The Hospitall calld Bedlam. 210 × 337/216 × 343mm. Allied to *NTGB* 56.

14 p 205 (on banderole) The Charter House. J. Kip fecit. 206 × 324/216 × 337mm.

15 p 212 (on banderole) Hoxton Hospitall. 206 × 324/216 × 333mm.

16 p 214 (on banderole) Chelsey Colledge. I. Kip Sculp. 241 × 330/248 × 337mm. Viewed from road. Derived from same source as Beeverell (no 20), item 36. (*Longford* 67)

17 p 215 (on banderole) The Hospital at Greenwich. I. Kip fecit. 241 × 330/248 × 337mm. Viewed from the river. Shows the façades of the King Charles and Queen Anne blocks complete with columns, pediments and attic storeys, all incomplete in the larger but otherwise similar engraving *NTGB* 47.

18 p 219 (inset tc) Morden Colledge. J. Kip Delin: et Sculp:. 203 × 324/216 × 337mm. Blackheath, completed c 1694.

BOOK 2 (13 wards E. of Walbrook)

19 p 3 Portsoken Ward/being part of the Parish of/St Buttolphs Aldgate/taken from the last Survey ... 298 × 178/308 × 184mm. Title in cartouche. Refs 1–80.

20 p 29 Tower Street/Ward/With its Divisions into/Parishes, Taken from/the last Survey ... 292 × 362/298 × 368mm. Title in cartouche. Refs 1–28.

21 p 51 (on banderole) The Custom House. 210 × 318/216 × 330mm. Wren's building burned down in 1718. Not a copy but possibly from a source also used for *NTGB* 54.

22 p 55 Aldgate Ward/with its Divisions into Parishes./Taken from the last Survey ... 302 × 178/308 × 184mm. Title in cartouche. Refs 1–36.

23 p 83 A Mapp of/Lime Street/Ward/Taken from ye last Surveys ... 308 × 175/311 × 178mm. Title in ornamental angle-piece. Refs 1–11.

24 p 90 Bishopsgate Street/Ward/Taken from the last/Survey ... 305 × 178/311 × 190mm. Title in cartouche. Refs 1–71.

25 p 109 Broad Street/Ward/with its divisions into/Parishes taken from/the last Survey ... – Cornhill Ward (*ditto*) 292 × 365/295 × 368mm. First title on curtain, second in cartouche. Refs 1–50.

26 p 135 (inset bc) The Royall Exchange of London. 241 × 286/254 × 292mm. Birds-eye view from Cornhill as in Morden and Lea (no 15), item 8.

27 p 151 Langbourne/Ward/With its Divisions into/Parishes Corrected from/the last Surveys ... – Candlewick/Ward (*ditto*). 292 × 365/298 × 371mm. Titles in cartouches. Refs 1–37.

28 p 165 Billingsgate Ward/and/Bridge Ward Within/With its Division into Parishes,/taken from the last Survey. 305 × 178/311 × 184mm. Title in cartouche. Refs 1–29.

29 p 180 The Monument. 333 × 206/343 × 216mm. Follows closely the Lodge engr. *NTGB* 55.

30 p 191 Walbrook Ward/and/Dowgate Ward/with its Division into Parishes,/taken from the Last Surveys. 308 × 181/314 × 184mm. Title in cartouche. Refs 1–22.

BOOKS 3 (12 wards W. of Walbrook)

31 p 1 Queen Hith Ward/and/Vintry Ward./with their Division into Parishes, taken from/the last Surveys. 305 × 178/311 × 185mm. Title in cartouche. Refs 1–33.

32 p 15 Bread Street Ward/and/Cordwainer Ward/with its Division into Parishes,/taken from the last Survey. 305 × 178/311 × 185mm. Title in cartouche. Refs 1–24.

33 p 25 (inset tc) Bow Church. I. Kip fe. 330 × 203/343 × 216mm.

34 p 26 Cheape Ward/with its Division into Parishes,/taken from the last Survey ... 298 × 356/305 × 368mm. Title in cartouche. Refs 1–12.

35 p 51 (on banderole) The Prospect of Guild Hall. 210 × 324/216 × 330mm. This plate is of particular interest as it seems to be the earliest to have broken with a conspiracy to show the Guildhall as it had been between Wren's post-Fire rebuilding and the late 1680s rather than picture it as it really appeared. Morden and Lea (item 3), Misson de Valbourg (no 19, item 6), Beeverell (item 12) and *NTGB* (item 64) all show a central baroque cupola with sundial on a hexagonal base and a scrolled drum supporting a dome with windvane and the *NTGB* engraving was reissued as late as 1724. The following entry has been found in the Proceedings of the Court of Aldermen: 'It is by this court referred to Mr. Chamberlen ... to give order for takeing downe the Lanthorne upon Guildhall'. It is dated 9 November 1686.

36 p 53 Coleman Street Ward/and/Bashishaw Ward/

Taken from the last Survey ... 349 × 292/356 × 298mm. Title in cartouche. Refs 1–60.

37 p 70 Creplegate Ward/with its Division into Parishes,/taken from the last Survey ... 292 × 349/302 × 359mm. Title in cartouche. Refs 1–160.

38 p 95 Aldersgate Ward/and/St. Martins le Grand/Liberty/Taken from the last/Survey ... 302 × 181/311 × 187mm. Title on curtain. Refs 1–76.

39 p 124 The Wards of/Farington within/and/Baynards Castle/with its Divisions into Parishes/taken from the last Survey ... 292 × 356/298 × 368mm. Title in cartouche. Refs 1–73. In page ref 'B2' engraved in error for 'B3'.

40 p 156 The East End of the Cathedral Church of St Pauls London. J. Kip Sculp. 368 × 292mm pl. mark.

41 p 156 The South Side of the Cathedral Church of St Pauls London. J. Kip Sculp. 368 × 375mm pl. mark.

42 p 156 The Front or West end, of the Cathedral Church of St Pauls London. J. Kip Sculp. 375 × 298mm pl. mark. Although the proportions and details differ these three plates of the Cathedral record the same aspects and general architectural effects as three other views dated 1720. *NTGB* 20, 22, 24.

43 p 231 Farrington Ward/without with its Division into/Parishes, taken from the last/Survey ... 292 × 349/298 × 356mm. Title on curtain. Refs 1–149.

44 p 271 (on banderole) The Temple. 203 × 330/210 × 343mm.

VOL. 2

BOOK 4 (wards in the Borough of Southwark, suburbs of the City and Liberty of the Duchy of Lancaster)

45 p 21 St Olave and/St Mary Magdalens/Bermondsey/Southwark, Taken from ye/last Survey ... 286 × 356/295 × 362mm. Title in cartouche. Refs 1–75.

46 p 27 A Mapp of the/Parishes of/St Saviours Southwark/and/St Georges/Taken from ye last Survey. 289 × 362/298 × 368mm. Title in cartouche. Refs 1–100.

47 p 44 A Map of the Parish of St Mary White Chappel – A Map of the Parish of/St Katherines by the Tower. 273 × 356/276 × 362mm. First title tm, second title br inset. Refs 1–40, 1–27.

48 p 47 The Parish of St John's Wapping – The Parish of St Paul Shadwell. 283 × 362/289 × 368mm. Second title tm. Refs 1–44, 1–24.

49 p 47 A Map of the Parish of St Dunstans Stepney als Stebunheath Divided into Hamlets. 286 × 419/292 × 425mm. Title along tm. Table, with names of streets, etc.

50 p 48 Spittle Fields/and Places Adjacent/Taken from ye last Survey ... 283 × 356/292 × 362mm. Title in cartouche. Refs 1–44.

51 p 50 Shoreditch/Norton Folgate,/and/Crepplegate Without./Taken from ye last Survey ... 283 × 352/292 × 362mm. Title in cartouche. Refs 1–83.

52 p 60 A Map of St Giles's Cripple Gate Without ... 279 × 359/286 × 362mm. Title along tm. Refs 1–71.

53 p 61 Cow Cross/Being St Sepulchers Parish Without/and the/Charter House/Taken from ye last Survey ... 165 × 298/178 × 305mm. Title in cartouche. Refs 1–29.

54 p 63 The Parish of/St James/Clerkenwell/Taken from ye last Survey ... 283 × 356/292 × 368mm. Title in laurel wreath. Refs 1–35.

55 p 69 (in cartouche bl.) The Prospect of/Grays Inn. 200 × 317/213 × 333mm. View to N.

56 p 73 (on banderole) The Prospect of Lincolns Inn. I. Kip fecit. 203 × 327/216 × 337mm. View to N.

57 p 75 A Mapp of the Parish of/St Giles's in the Fields/taken from the last Survey ... 289 × 365/302 × 375mm. Title on curtain. Refs 1–58.

58 p 105 (on banderole) Somerset House. I. Kip Sculp. 206 × 330/216 × 340mm. Shows the floating 'Folly' moored on the S. Bank. Omits the hay barge br but otherwise an exact reduced replica of Kip's plate *NTGB* 6.

59 p 108 A Mapp of the Parishes/of St Clements Dane/St Mary Savoy/with the Rolls Liberty/and Lincolns Inn taken/From the last Survey ... 292 × 349/298 × 362mm. Title in cartouche. Refs 1–61.

BOOK 5 (government and governors, Corporation and trades, laws, orders, customs, militia)

(Illustrated only by shields of arms accompanying the text)

BOOK 6 (City of Westminster)

60 p 4 (on banderole) St James House. I. Kip fecit. 206 × 330/216 × 337mm. The spire of St James, Piccadilly is missing and the distant dome of St Paul's is carelessly sketched in. The building in the foreground bl has a pitched roof and dormer windows whereas in Kip's earlier 12 sheet engraving (*Crace* 2.73) it is shown with a flat roof, as also in Kip's *NTGB* 2.

61 p 5 (on banderole) The Prospect of White-Hall/from the Park of St James. I. Kip scu. 210 × 330/216 × 343mm.

62 p 7 (on banderole) Westminster Abbey. 210 × 324/216 × 337mm. View from N.

63 p 67 A Mapp of the Parish of/St Margarets Westminster/taken from the last Survey ... 292 × 349/298 × 356mm. Title in cartouche. Refs 1–88.

64 p 67 A Mapp of the/Parish of St Martins/in the Fields/taken from ye/last Survey. 356 × 286/362 × 298mm. Title in cartouche. Refs 1–107.

65 p 80 The Parish of/St James's Westminster/taken from the last Survey ... 356 × 292/365 × 298mm. Title in cartouche. Refs 1–47, 1–18.

66 p 85 A/Mapp of the Parish of St Anns./Taken from the last Survey ... 311 × 181/318 × 184mm. Title in cartouche. Refs 1–16. St Anne, Soho.

67 p 85 A Mapp of/St Andrews Holborn/Parish/as well within the Liberty as without/taken from the last Survey. 292 × 324/298 × 330mm. Title in cartouche. Refs 1–114, 1–18.

68 p 87 A Mapp of the/Parish of St Pauls/Covent Garden/taken from the last Survey. 305 × 178/317 × 190mm. Title in cartouche. Refs 1–19.

Appendices to Vol. 2

69 p 83 Lambeth/and/Christ Church/Parish, Southwark/Taken from ye last Survey. 356 × 286/365 × 295mm. Title in cartouche. Refs 1–41.

70 p 87 A Map of the Parish of St Mary Rotherhith, the Survey revis'd & corrected by Ino Pullen. Engrav'd by Ino Harris. 270 × 400/279 × 419mm. Title along tm. Refs 1–21.

26 · OVERTON'S PROSPECTS
[c 1720–30]

The printselling house of Overton, at the White Horse without Newgate, was associated with the earliest reliable views of London. The name of John Overton is to be found in the publication-lines of some of Hollar's later plates and on others, dating from the 1670s, by William Lodge and Robert White. Henry (II), his son, was therefore following a family tradition when in the 1720s he launched a series of 'Prospects', at first confined to London but extended later to the provinces. They were uniform in size and style and intended for binding into a picture book resembling the Morden and Lea album of some 30 years earlier (no 15). It was planned to issue them in twelves with the first of each dozen acting as a title but in the event only the first two title-pages materialized. A glance at their wording suggests a reason: namely that the strain of providing a translation was proving too much for one who was clearly no French scholar.

Throughout his career Henry Overton's name appeared in publication-lines alongside of those of various partners: Thomas Glass and J. Hoole at different stages of the issue of this series and, in later years, the very successful dealers John Bowles and

Robert Sayer. The catalogues put out by the two last named are evidence that the publication of sets of small prints in dozens caught on in the trade.

The plates themselves were unnumbered and apparently neither text nor table of contents accompanied them. When however the 74 items in the series were reissued some time in the 1730s, along with 32 others (engravings of English and Welsh cathedrals and churches by John Harris and Benjamin Cole, originally published as a collection in 1715, and a panorama of Norwich), a numbered table of plates was provided and an engraved general title reading:

Brittannia Illustrata/or/Views of all the Kings Palaces, Several Seats/of the Nobility and Gentry: all/the Cathedrals of England & Wales; with the most considerable/ Publick Buildings and Squares in London and Westminster,/Very neatly Engraved on 107 Copper Plates/Veues/ de tous les Palais royales; des plusieurs Hôtel de la grande & de la petite noblesse; de toutes les/Eglises cathédrales d'Angleterre & de Galle & aussi de toutes les Places & Bâtimens publiques les/plus remarquables dans Londres & Westminster, tres curieusement gravées. Printed & Sold by Hen: Overton & J. Hoole at the White Horse without Newgate London. 185 × 295/200 × 320mm.

The title was borrowed from another publication in which Overton had an interest as early as 1709 and whose separate plates were listed as still available in his 1717 catalogue: *Britannia Illustrata*, alternatively entitled *Nouveau Théâtre de la Grande Bretagne* (no 22). Borrowing was not confined to the title since at least ten of the London plates were derived from these larger plates, published originally about 1707–14, either directly or by way of the illustrations to the 1720 edition of Stow's *Survey* (no 25); this also applies to a number of the engravings of country seats in the Home Counties and provinces. They are reduced in size but their lineaments are faithfully preserved. References to plates from this source are abbreviated in the list as *NTGB* with the relevant item number.

Fourteen other views were based on Kip's engravings for the 1720 edition of Stow and reference is made with the letter *S* followed by Book and facing page number.

A further source was John Bowles's stock of imperial-size views (no 28) published in the 1720s, bound up in 1731, and advertised in his catalogues dated 1728 and 1731 (referred to here as *B 1728* and *B 1731*). The most notable of these, Sutton Nicholls's careful engravings of London squares, were not copied for Overton's *Prospects* but he replaced them with views from other points of the compass which usefully complement the larger ones.

There are no publication-lines except on the title-pages or their substitutes and the only credits are Benjamin Cole's on two views of St Paul's Cathedral (pl. 3 and 14); he was probably the map engraver of that name who turned to architectural subjects and was later responsible for most of the illustrations in the 1756 edition of Maitland's *History of London* (no 38). A Cambridge plate carries the name of J. Clark, the engraver of the title-page of Bowles's *London Described* collection (no 29).

The listing is based on the most complete collection seen, that in the Guildhall Library (A.5.2, no 9). In the GLC History Library is a selection of 30 only of the London plates bound up with the title to the first dozen. The numbering in the later reissue of the plates entitled *Brittannia Illustrata* is given with the abbreviation *OBI*.

1 (engr title in large cartouche bc) Prospects/of the most remarkable places in and about the Citty of/London. Neatly Engraved (rule)/Veues des toutes les endroites que est plus remarquable aussi/bien celles dans le Ville de Londres que d'alentour, Gravé fort/Curieuse-ment./Printed & Sold by Hen: Overton at ye White Horse without Newgate, & Tho: Glass under ye Royal Exchange Cornhill. 163 × 268/170 × 275mm. On *OBI* 36 the title omits the name of the second bookseller; for a later state the date '1739' was substituted. Above the title is a panorama of the City from Southwark, a replica in miniature (110 × 270mm), even to the shipping on the river, of Kip's long view. The only differences are the addition to St Clement Danes of the spire, erected 1719–20, and the removal of the floating folly from off Bankside. *NTGB* 60.

2 The North West view of St Pauls. 150 × 240/170 × 245mm. *OBI* 76.

3 The Inside of the Choir of ye Cathedral Church of St. Paul. London. B. Cole sculp. 145 × 230/170 × 240mm. *OBI* 79. Looking W.

4 The South Sea House in Threadneedle Street. 145 × 230/160 × 240mm. *OBI* 45. Built by James Gould, 1724–5. Simplified, reduced and reversed from the plate listed in *B 1728*.

5 The Custom House. 150 × 242/165 × 245mm. *OBI* 41. The building by Thomas Ripley, 1718, which suc-ceeded Wren's, burned down 1718.

6 The Royal Exchange in Cornhill. 150 × 240/170 × 245mm. *OBI* 42. Statue of Charles II by Grinling Gibbons visible through archway.

7 New Bedlam in Moorfields. 145 × 240/165 × 245mm. *OBI* 37. The standard image, closely following *S* 1,192.

8 Guild Hall, in King Street Cheapside. 150 × 240/170 × 245mm. *OBI* 47. Reduced copy of *S* 3,51.

9 Christ's Hospital in Newgate Street. 153 × 240/170 × 245mm. *OBI* 52. Reduced by closely following *S* 1,175.

10 A Prospect of Greenwich, Deptford, & London, taken from Flamstead hill in Greenwich Park. 143 × 230/165 × 240mm. *OBI* 29.

11 The Church of St Mary L'Bow/in Cheapside – The Monument. 150 × 112, 150 × 112/168 × 245mm. *OBI* 49. Reduced and staffage altered from *S* 3,25 and *S* 2,180.

12 The City Gates: Ald-Gate – Bishops-Gate – Moor-Gate – Cripple-Gate – Alders-Gate – New-Gate – Lud-Gate – Temple-Barr. 150 × 240/165 × 245mm. *OBI* 39. Reduced but follows *S* 1,14.

13 (engr title in large cartouche tc) Prospects/of the most remarkable places in and about the Citty of/London, Neatly Engraved. part ye 2d. (rule)/Veues des toutes les endroites que est plus remarquable aussi/bien celles dans le Ville de Londre que d'alentour, Grave fort Curieusement part L'2de. (bm) A View of Westminster from the River Thames. Printed & Sold by H. Overton & J. Hoole at ye White Horse/without Newgate London. 155 × 265/175 × 275mm. Not in *OBI*. Below the title a replica in miniature, even to the shipping on the river, of Kip's panoramic view from Lambeth with the following additions:
The spire of St Clement Danes, added 1719–20.
The spire of St Mary le Strand, completed 1717, replacing the maypole.
St Anne, Soho spire, added by Talman in 1717.
The new St Martin in the Fields, completed 1726.
St John, Smith Square, completed 1728.
St Giles in the Fields still appears as in Kip's view since Flitcroft's church was not complete until 1734. A reduced copy of *NTGB* 37.

14 The South East Prospect of ye Cathedral Church of St. Paul London. B. Cole sculp. 145 × 230/170 × 240mm. *OBI* 77.

15 The Palace and Park of St James's. 150 × 240/170 × 245mm. *OBI* 5. Looking up the Mall towards the distant City. The dome of St Paul's is better delineated than in the earlier Kip views in *NTGB* and the 1720 Stow but St James, Piccadilly appears to be crowned with the dome originally intended by Wren rather than with the spire actually constructed. In this and all points the plate follows closely *S* 6,4.

16 Lambeth House/in Surry, ye Palace of the Arch Bishop of Canterbury. 150 × 240/165 × 245mm. *OBI* 34. From the river. Shows only the Palace without the more extensive grounds and St Mary's Church shown in the prototype, *NTGB* 8.

17 (tc) A View of the Inside of Westminster Hall. (bm)This was formerly the chief Palace of the Kings of England ... 150 × 232/185 × 250mm. *OBI* 66 with revised lettering: 'A Prospect of Westminster Hall. (1.)The Entrance of the/A. House of Commons /B. The King's Bench (r)The Court of Chancery./D. The Court of Common Pleas/E. The Entrance to ye Exchequer.'

18 A View from the River Thames/of the Parliament House, Westminster Hall, and the Abby. 145 × 232/160 × 240mm. *OBI* 64. Brings up to date a favourite view derived from Hollar's 1647 engraving (*Hind* 86), perhaps via Morden and Lea's *Prospects* (pl. 28).

19 The Admiralty Office at White Hall. 140 × 235/160 × 240mm. *OBI* 59. Built by Thomas Ripley, 1723–6. Reduced in size, foreground eliminated, staffage changed from plate listed in *B 1731*.

20 Buckingham House in St James's Park. 150 × 240/170 × 245mm. *OBI* 16. Reduced and staffage altered from plate listed in *B 1728*, both deriving from *NTGB* 45.

21 Powis House in Ormond Street. 150 × 240/165 × 245mm. *OBI* 17. Reduced but follows closely *NTGB* 53.

22 The Royal Hospital of Chelsey, fronting ye River Thames. 150 × 230/170 × 240mm. *OBI* 31. Reduced in size from the plate listed in *B 1731*. (*Longford* 5).

23 Covent Garden—(l.) 1 Covent Garden Church/2 King Street – (r.) 3 James Street/4 Russell Street. 145 × 233/165 × 240mm. *OBI* 56. N. view, condensed and with distant view eliminated from plate listed in *B 1728*.

24 Tunbridge Wells in the County of Kent. 165 × 215/180 × 225mm. *OBI* 26.

25 The Tower. 145 × 238/165 × 245mm. *OBI* 40. The standard view, from the river, following closely *S* 1,64. This plate is also found adapted as a title-page to the third set of *Prospects*: (bm) 'The Tower of London/ Views of the publick Buildings in and about the City of London. Part 3d. Sold by Hen. Overton without Newgate.'; or, alternatively: 'Sold by C. Dicey & Co in Aldermary/Church Yard.' The latter must be a late state since Cluer Dicey traded from 4 Aldermary Churchyard c 1763.

26 The Inside of St Pauls. 150 × 235/165 × 245mm. *OBI* 80. The nave looking E.

27 The West end of St Paul's – The East end of St Paul's London. 150 × 102,150 × 102/170 × 240mm. *OBI* 78. Much reduced from the two plates found at *S* 3,156.

28 Kings Square in Sohoe.—(l.) A. Merry Andrew Street./B. Thrift Street – (r.) C. Greg Street/D. Sutton Street. 150 × 238/170 × 245mm. *OBI* 71. View to the S.

29 Bloomsbury Square—(l.) AA. Hart Street – (r.) BB.Great Russel Street. 150 × 238/170 × 245mm. *OBI* 69. View to the N.

30 Red Lyon Square—(l.)A. Orange Street/B Lambs Conduit Passage – (r.) C. Princes Street. 150 × 238/165 × 245mm. *OBI* 68. View to the S.

31 Leicester Square—(l.) A. Panton Street – (r.) B. Green Street. 150 × 235/170 × 245mm. *OBI* 72. View to the N.

32 Golden Square—(l.) AA. Iames Street – (r.) BB. Iohn Street. 150 × 240/170 × 245mm. *OBI* 70. View to the E.

33 Hannover Square—(l.) A. Princes Street/B. Hannover Street – (r.) C. Tenderall Street/D Brooks Street. 150 × 238/170 × 245mm. *OBI* 67. View to the N. The latest of these squares, built up 1717–18.

34 Charterhouse Square—(l.) A. Charterhouse Street – (r.) B. Carthusian Street. 148 × 238/165 × 245mm. *OBI* 73. View to the E.

35 The Charter House. 153 × 243/170 × 245mm. *OBI* 53. Following, with minor alterations, *S* 1,205.

36 The South=West Prospect of St Mary's Church in ye Strand, London. 223 × 153/245 × 160mm. *OBI* 55. Reduced in size, surrounding buildings omitted and staffage altered, but follows in the main the plate listed in *B 1728*.

37 Somerset House in the Strand. 150 × 243/170 × 250mm. *OBI* 54. Follows closely *S* 4,105.

38 The King's Gate at White Hall/leading to Westminster II The Entrance of Westminster Hall. 145 × 115,145 × 115/165 × 240mm. *OBI* 65. These compare with Morden and Lea's *Prospects*, pl. 26-7 which show a flat arch under King's Gate here replaced by a round one.

39 The Statue of King Charles the 1st at Charing Cross, London. 150 × 240/170 × 250mm. *OBI* 57. Reduced, but follows the plate listed in *B 1728*.

40 The Inside of Guildhall near Cheapside/London. 138 × 225/165 × 240mm. *OBI* 48.

41 The late Duke of Marlborough's House in St James's Park. 145 × 235/165 × 250mm. *OBI* 58. The Duke died in 1722. This follows the plate listed in *B 1728*.

42 The Inside of the Royal Exchange London. 150 × 235/165 × 243mm. *OBI* 43. View to the N. Lettering in work: 'The North Entrance – The South Entrance'.

43 The Royal Hospital of Chelsea. 150 × 235/165 × 240mm. *OBI* 32. Birds-eye view from the road side (item 22 above is from the river). Staffage apart, closely follows *S* 1,214. (*Longford* 68)

44 The Royal Hospital of Greenwich. 150 × 240/165 × 245mm. *OBI* 30. Adds flanking blocks but otherwise, on a reduced scale, closely follows *S* 1,215.

45 Mountague House in Great Russel Street, Houlburn. 150 × 240/170 × 243mm. *OBI* 15. Rear elevation. Following closely, on a reduced scale, *NTGB* 49.

46 The Navy Office in Cruched Friers, London. 145 × 230/170 × 243mm. *OBI* 38. Follows, on a reduced scale, *NTGB* 65.

47 St Bartholomew's Hospital in West Smithfield. 145 × 238/165 × 243mm. *OBI* 51. Shows Gibbs's gateway of 1702; the quadrangle was begun in 1730. Follows *S* 1,184.

48 Mr Guy's Hospital for Incurables, in the Borough of Southwark. 143 × 230/165 × 238mm. *OBI* 35. Built by Thomas Dance, 1722–5. Staffage altered and background added to plate listed in *B 1728*.

49 The Royal Palace of St James's. 145 × 230/165 × 243mm. *OBI* 4. Façade from the Park.

50 Morden College on Black-heath, in the County of Kent. 148 × 225/165 × 234mm. *OBI* 33.

51 Fair Lawn in the County of Kent, the Seat of the Rt Honble Lord Barnard. 145 × 230/160 × 240mm. *OBI* 12.

52 The Seat of the Honble Sr Gregory Page, Barronet, on Black Heath in Kent. 145 × 228/165 × 238mm. *OBI* 19. Built by John James, 1721.

53 Wanstead House in Essex, ye Seat of ye Rt Honble Ld Viscount Castlemain. 143 × 230/163 × 240mm. *OBI* 18. Built by Colen Campbell, 1715.

54 The Bank of England, in ye Poultry. 150 × 237/167 × 245mm. *OBI* 46. Shows Grocers' Hall; the purpose-built Bank was not erected by George Sampson until 1732-4.

55 Stocks Market in Cornhill. 142 × 230/160 × 235mm. *OBI* 44. Reduced, with sky cut and staffage simplified, from the plate listed in *B 1728*.

56 Westminster Abby. 148 × 235/170 × 240mm. *OBI* 63. From the N. Follows closely *S* 6,7.

57 The Royal Banqueting House at Whitehall. 145 × 225/165 × 240mm. *OBI* 60.

58 A Prospect of Whitehall, from St James's Park. 145 × 238/165 × 240mm. *OBI* 61. Shows Horse Guards and 'Holbein' Gate. On reduced scale, follows *S* 6,5.

59 A View of Whitehall from the River Thames. 141 × 226/160 × 235mm. *OBI* 62.

60 The College of Physicians in Warwick Lane, London. 148 × 232/165 × 243mm. *OBI* 50.

61 Blenheim House near Woodstock, the seat of the late Duke of Marlborough. Printed & Sold by H. Overton/ at the White Horse without/Newgate London. 145 × 240/162 × 242. The presence of a publication-line suggests that this was intended as a title-page for the last dozen plates. Shows main façade, reduced and reversed from upper portion of plate listed in *B 1731*.

62 Long Leate in Wiltshire, the seat of ... Ld. Weymouth. 145 × 230/165 × 240mm. *OBI* 10.

63 Hatfield House, the seat of ... Lord Salisbury. 140 × 240/165 × 245mm. *OBI* 8.

64 Althrop, the seat of ... the Earl of Sunderland. 150 × 230/165 × 240mm. *OBI* 13.

65 Burleigh House, the seat of ... the Earl of Exeter. 135 × 230/165 × 241mm. *OBI* 9.

66 Stanstead ... the seat of the ... Earl of Scarborough. 145 × 230/160 × 238mm. *OBI* 14. In Sussex, birds-eye view.

67 Hamsted Marshall ... Berkshire, the seat of ... Lord Craven. 155 × 228/170 × 235mm. *OBI* 11. Burned in 1718 and rebuilt by Gibbs, 1739. This birds-eye follows the plate in *NTGB* vol.1.

68 Westwood ... Worcestershire, the seat of ... Sir J. Pakington. 150 × 230/168 × 240mm. *OBI* 20.

69 Kings College Chapel in Cambridge. 143 × 233/165 × 245mm. *OBI* 23.

70 Great St Mary's Church in Oxford. 145 × 225/170 × 238mm. *OBI* 22.

71 The Front of the Publick Theatre in Oxford. 148 × 222/170 × 238mm. *OBI* 21.

72 The Royal Chapel of St George in Windsor Castle. 145 × 235/165 × 245mm. *OBI* 25.

73 The New Building at Cambridge in Perspective. J. Clark sc. 1724. 142 × 235/170 × 245mm. *OBI* 24. ie the Royal Library and Senate House built by Gibbs, 1722–30.

74 Edystone Light House,/near Plymouth, Devonshire, 90 Feet high. 148 × 230/165 × 240mm. *OBI* 27.

The first three plates in Overton's *Brittannia Illustrata* were not issued with the above *Prospects*. They are as follows:

75 *OBI* 1 The Royal Palace of Windsor Castle. 143 × 235/163 × 255mm.

76 *OBI* 2 The Royal Palace of Hampton Court. 140 × 240/165 × 245mm.

77 *OBI* 3 The Royal Palace of Kingsington. 135 × 230/158 × 235mm.

27 · DART'S WESTMONASTERIUM [c 1723]

John Dart, who died in 1730, was a failed attorney turned antiquary and, for the last two years of his life, perpetual curate of Yateley in Hampshire. In 1721 he published a pompous poem, 'Westminster Abbey', of which the following address to Dr Atterbury, Bishop of Rochester and Dean of Westminster from 1713, is a fair specimen:

O Thou! by Pious Anna's Favour grac'd
With holy Lawn, and o'er this Temple plac'd.
By whose indulgent Favour warm'd, with Fire

I meditate the Song, and strike the Lyre.
O Thou! for ever Reverenc'd, ever lov'd,
Accept this solemn Verse, you once approv'd.

It is likewise prefixed to the first edition of his *Westmonasterium* which was published between 1723, the date according to the title-page of his 'survey', and 1727 when George, Prince of Wales, to whom it is dedicated, ascended the throne as George II. He also wrote in 1726 a history of Canterbury Cathedral. *Westmonasterium* was at first published by its chief engraver, James Cole, and a combination of two booksellers and four printsellers including Joseph Smith, who specialized in fine illustrated folios such as *Nouveau Théâtre de la Grande Bretagne* (no 22) and *Vitruvius Britannicus* (no 24), and the Bowles brothers. It is listed in John Bowles's 1728 catalogue and again in 1731 as 'Two Vol. Folio Price 3l 3s in Sheets' and only the Bowles brothers' names remain in the imprint of the second edition published in 1742; the catalogue price of this was also three guineas for two volumes. The text of both editions is identical, consisting of the poem, three Books of the 'History' and 'Lives of the Abbats', the 'History' being chiefly taken up with a 'View of the Monuments', a transcription of the epitaphs with some translations from the Latin and brief comments on the commemorated. These transcriptions were Cole's cue for producing engravings of all the monuments referred to by the author which are the great attraction of this book. For the second edition Bowles commissioned other engravers to provide a dozen plates of monuments installed between 1725 and 1740, of which half were sculpted by Michael Rysbrack, and these were incorporated in a revised list indexing the monuments.

Dart's subscribers were, for the most part, the noble or gentle relatives or descendants of the deceased together with the clergy, university dons and librarians, City merchants, country gentlemen and booksellers. However the following had a professional interest in the production of the work: the architects Colen Campbell, J. Leoni, Simon Schynvoet and John Talman; Edward Strong, master mason, and Robert Taylor the mason and monument carver; the painters Sir James Thornhill and John Dowling; Richard Archer and Andrew Johannot, paper makers; with engravers forming the largest category, namely Bernard Baron, John Clark, Benjamin Cole of London and Benjamin Cole of Oxford, Claude Du Bosc, John Faber, Sutton Nicholls, John Pine, William Toms and Gerard and John Van der Gucht, father and son.

Westmonasterium/or/The History and Antiquities/of/the Abbey Church/of/St Peters Westminster/containing,/an Account of its ancient and modern Building, Endowments, Chapels, Altars/Reliques, Customs, Privileges, Forms of Government &c. with ye Copies/of ancient Saxon Charters &c. and other Writings relating to it./Together with a particular History of the Lives of the Abbats,/collected from ancient MSS of that Convent and/Historians; & the Lives of the Deans to this time./(swelled rule)—and also—/A Survey of the Church and Cloysters, taken in the Year 1723; with the/ Monuments there which, with several Prospects of ye Church & other/remarkable things, are curiously Engraven by the best Hands (rule)/In 2 Vol./(rule) By/Mr John Dart (thin and thick rule) To which is added/ Westminster Abbey,/ A/Poem,/ By the same Author/ (rule) Vol. I (II) (rule) London: Printed & Sold by James Cole Engraver in Hatton Garden, Joseph Smith Print Seller in Exeter Exchange, Tho. Bowles/Print Seller in St Paul's Church Yard, Jer. Batley Book Seller in Paternoster Row, Tho. Taylor Print Seller in Fleet Street—/John Bowles Print Seller over against Stocks-Market, and by Andrew Johnstone in Round Court in ye Strand. (engr title-page, 345 × 200mm pl. mark)

Folio, 390 × 250mm. (Large Paper 520 × 350mm)

c 1723

COLLATION   Vol. 1. Engr title-page; dedication to George Augustus, Prince of Wales (2pp); preface (2pp); pp i–iv, list of subscribers; pp i–xlii, Westminster Abbey, a poem; pp 1–195, The History Books 1 and 2; errata (1 leaf). Vol. 2. Engr title-page; list of subscribers (1 leaf); pp 1–146, The History continued; index of persons buried in the church (4pp); pp 1–24, The History Book 3; pp i–xliv, Lives of the Abbats; pp i–xvi, appendix.

(second edition) Engr title-page amended. In place of 'taken in the Year 1723' reads 'King Henry 7th's Chappel' and the imprint revised to read: 'Printed for T. Bowles next the Chapter House in St Paul's Church Yard and J. Bowles at the Black Horse in Cornhill 1742'.

Folio, 395 × 245mm.   1742

COLLATION   As for first edition but between the title-page and dedication in vol. 1 is a revised list of 'Monuments that are engrav'd in the Two Volumes'. Twelve supplementary plates are added to the original engravings.

The permanent interest of this book lies in its illustrations of the funeral monuments as they appeared before being subjected to the damage, defacements and depredations of eight more generations of vandals, souvenir-hunters, barbarous organizers of state occasions and restorers. A comparison of the plates on pp 106 and 156 with photographs of the tombs of John of Eltham and the bronze parclose of Henry VII's tomb are ample demonstration of the value of this evidence. All the plates in the first edition, with only one or two exceptions, are the work of James Cole, and although one suspects that in deference to the contemporary liking for symmetry some of his engravings probably 'restored' broken crockets or cresting, decapitated 'weepers' and angels or missing limbs his plates of the monuments are as fine and complete a record as anyone could desire. What could be more expressive than the engraving (p 110) of Nicholas Stone's noble Roman memorial to the Earl of Clare's 18 year old son or the mighty allegory by Scheemakers and Delvaux (p 162) commemorating John Sheffield, Duke of Buckingham, or more overwhelming than the great mausoleum (p 187) erected to Henry Carey, Lord Hunsdon in Elizabethan times? Cole abstracts the monuments from their surroundings so that they are presented as architectural and sculptural entities with a wholeness, clarity and wealth of detail that photography could never achieve. Notable also are the engraved head and tailpieces, particularly a miniature roundel of the Abbey set in a symbolic trophy and a grisly 'Gothick' tailpiece of a Roman soldier turning tail at the sight of a putrid cadaver. Among the subscribers to the work is Peter le Neve, Norroy King of Arms, and this is not surprising because, quite apart from the plates of subscribers' armorial bearings, even the smallest or most detailed shields on monuments are so carefully engraved that all the charges are quite distinct. If the Abbey is ever burned down or demolished by enemy or terrorist action, or exported stone by stone to the United States, future generations will be as grateful to this illustrator as we are to Hollar for recording so carefully the monuments in old St Paul's before the holocaust.

Cole must have been highly regarded as an architectural engraver since, with Henry Hulsbergh and P. Fourdrinier, he was employed by William Kent to engrave Flitcroft's designs for the sumptuous *Designs of Inigo Jones*. He also engraved portraits and book-plates and the booksellers kept him busy with such work as 'Two Hundred Historys Curiously engraved from Designs of ye best Masters' to illustrate the historical books of the Bible. His name is also to be found on the engraved title-page of vol. 3 of Joseph Smith's *Nouveau Théâtre de la Grande Bretagne*.

The only other credits on the first edition illustrations are those of John Dowling as draughtsman of some of the monuments, of John Faber the mezzotint engraver who contributed the author's portrait and of James Schynvoet, the Dutch artist responsible for the attractive frontispiece to vol. 2, an interior view of Henry VII's chapel. The dozen supplementary plates in the second edition were executed by those popular mid-century book illustrators, François Gravelot and his pupil Charles Grignion, and by the topographical engravers John Harris and Nathaniel Parr.

Monuments are usually set off by a dark background of cross-hatching, at right angles, usually unshaded. Their page numbers are engraved or entered in MS tr and they have tc, in parenthesis, the number allotted to each on the plan and its topographical index. Most separately printed plates have captions in bm but they are here supplied in brackets for those identifiable only by their inscriptions or by reference to the text. The credit 'J.Cole' is engraved br in the margin unless otherwise stated. Vol. 1 plates in the 1742 edition have engraved, besides the page numbers tr, references bl in three alphabetical sequences, which are noted in brackets after the descriptions.

VOL. 1

1 front. Ita erit Consummatione Seculi ... (in work bl)J.Cole Londini sculp. 310 × 229/356 × 245mm. After Michelangelo's 'Last Judgement'.

2 dedication-page. (Royal Hanoverian arms with label. 77 × 153/80 × 160mm. – Initial 'A' showing the author presenting his book to the Prince of Wales. 35 × 39/38 × 40mm.)

3 following preface (Plates of subscribers' arms, each with 42 shields and numbered tr up to IX. 320 × 185/345 × 205mm. Without credits.)

4 facing p i Mr John Dart. I. Faber fect. 260 × 215/310 × 220mm. Mezzotint portrait.

5 p i (Headpiece, allegory of Death, Time and History. 82 × 168/85 × 175mm. – Initial 'H' showing the author making a presentation to the Bishop of Rochester. 45 × 40/50 × 45mm.)

6 p xlii (Tailpiece, miniature N. view of Westminster Abbey in roundel set in a trophy of regalia, musical instruments and symbols of mortality. 60 × 100/65 × 115mm.)

7 p 1 (Headpiece, second allegory of Time and History grouped round a monument in the Abbey with a

draughtsman at work. 78 × 163/85 × 175mm. – Initial 'T' with classical ruins. 40 × 45/45 × 50mm.)

8 facing p 4 Sebert or Segebert, King of the East Saxons & Ethelgoda his Queen. 305 × 195/345 × 203mm. (I)

9 p 34. (Tailpiece of a Roman soldier turning tail at the sight of a putrefying cadaver in a tomb. 65 × 90/73 × 100mm.)

10 p 35 (Headpiece and initial as item 5 above)

11 facing p 62 Richard the IId./From an Antient Painting in the Choir of the Church of Westminster. 312 × 165/340 × 203mm. No credit. (K)

12 p 67 The North Prospect of the Abbey-Church of St Peter's Westminster. 310 × 447/335 × 455mm. The staffage is contemporary but Cole based this plate on Hollar's in *Monasticon Anglicanum* (no 6, item 2); consequently the Galilee Porch removed some 60 years previously is shown. The author explains (p 58) that the N. porch was under repair so that the view was 'taken from a curious Draught … it being impossible to take a new Draught while the Scaffolding remain'd'. (L)

13 p 68 The Inside Prospect of the Church of St Peter's Westminster. 370 × 310/420 × 315mm. Looking down the nave from the W. door. (M)

14 pp 69–70 (tl inside border-line) The Ichnography or Plan/of the Abbey-Church of St. Peter's Westminster. 275 × 410/285 × 420mm. Without credit. On pp 71–2 'The Names of the Monuments figur'd in the Ichnography, or Plan' subdivides the Abbey into its chapels, aisles, etc, allocating each portion a letter of the alphabet, A-S. Tombs, monuments, wall-plaques and slabs in each portion are enumerated with numbers running I-XI, 1–145. Locations are marked on the plan by means of these letters and numbers. (N)

A In the South Cross leading to ye Chapels

15 p 74 (Edmund Spencer) 310 × 195/345 × 205mm. pl. I. (0)

16 p 75 (Headpiece as item 7 above – Initial 'I' with Abbey interior. 45 × 40/50 × 45mm.)

17 p 77 (Thomas Shadwell) 305 × 195/345 × 205mm. pl.II. (P)

18 p 78 (Samuel Butler) 298 × 197/345 × 203mm. pl.III. (Q)

19 p 80 (Michael Drayton) 305 × 197/345 × 203mm. pl.IIII. (R)

20 p 81 (Charles St Denis, Duc de St Evremond) 298 × 197/345 × 203mm. pl.V. (S)

21 p 84 Mr. John Philips. 305 × 195/345 × 205mm. pl.VI. (T)

22 p 85 (Geoffrey Chaucer) 305 × 197/345 × 205mm. pl.VII. (V)

23 p 88 (Abraham Cowley) 303 × 193/340 × 205mm. pl.VIII. (W)

24 p 91 (John Dryden) I. Dowling delin. J.Cole sculp. 303 × 200/343 × 215mm. pl.IX. (X)

25 p 92 (Dr. Richard Busby) J. Dowling delin. J.Cole sculp. 303 × 195/343 × 205mm. pl.X. (Y)

26 p 95 (Robert South) I. Dowling delin: J. Cole sculp. 300 × 200/350 × 205mm. pl. XI. (Z)

B In the Chapel of St Benedict

27 p 98 Hic jacet dominus Simon de Langham – (Lionel Cranfield, Earl of Middlesex) 140 × 200, 160 × 200/345 × 205mm. pl. 1–2. (a)

28 p 101 (George Sprat – William Bill, Dean of Westminster) 200 × 195, 100 × 195/345 × 205mm. pl. 5–6. (b)

29 p 102 Frances Countess of Hertford. 310 × 197/343 × 205mm. pl. 3. (c)

30 p 105 (Gabriel Goodman, Dean of Westminster) 305 × 197/345 × 205mm. pl. 4. (d)

C In the Chapel of St. Edmund

31 p 106 John of Eltham, Earl of Cornwall. 310 × 197/349 × 205mm. Tomb chest, with 'weepers' complete, protected by triple-gabled crocketed canopy with pinnacles intact. pl.7. (e)

32 p 109 (William of Windsor & Blanche of the Tower, Edward II's children – Francis, Duchess of Suffolk) 137 × 200, 163 × 200/345 × 205mm. pl. 8–9. (f)

33 p 110 (Francis Holles, third son of the Earl of Clare – Elizabeth, youngest daughter of Lord John Russell) 311 × 195/345 × 205mm. pl.10–11. (g)

34 p 113 (Lady Jane Seymour – Lady Katherine Knollys) 311 × 197/345 × 205mm. pl. 12–13. (h)

35 p 114 To the Memory of Iohn Lord Russel. 305 × 197/349 × 203mm. pl.14. (i)

36 p 117 Sr Bernard Brocas Kt. – William de Valence Earl of Pembroke. 187 × 195, 107 × 195/345 × 205mm. pl.15–16. (k)

37 p 120 (Sir Richard Pecksal) 300 × 200/343 × 203mm. pl.17. (l)

38 p 123 (Edward Talbot, 8th Earl of Shrewsbury) 315 × 197/343 × 203mm. pl. 18. (m)

39 p 124 (brass to Eleanor de Bohun, Duchess of Gloucester) 305 × 190/349 × 203mm. pl. 19. (n)

40 p 127 (brass to Robert de Walby, Archbishop of York) 308 × 195/345 × 205mm. pl. 20. (o)

D In the Chapel of St. Nicholas

41 p 130 (Lady Jane Clifford – Lady Cecil) 298 × 190/343 × 203mm. pl. 21–2. (p)

42 p 131 The Lady Anne Dutchess of Somerset. 310 × 195/345 × 205mm. pl. 23. (q)

43 p 132 (Lady Elizabeth Fane) 310 × 193/349 × 203mm. pl. 24. (r)

44 p 135 Mildred Lady Burleigh and her daughter Anne

Countess of Oxford. 312 × 195/320 × 203mm. pl. 25. (s)

45 p 138 Winifred, Marchioness of Winchester. 290 × 193/343 × 203mm. pl.26. (t)

46 p 141 (William Dudley, Bishop of Durham – Sir George Villiers) 170 × 195,137 × 195/345 × 205mm. pl.27–8. (v)

47 p 142 (Lady Elizabeth Manners – Nicholas Bagenall – Anne Sophia Harlay) 120 × 195,170 × 195/345 × 203mm. pl.29–31. (w)

48 p 143 (Thomas Sprat) 310 × 195/343 × 203mm. pl.32. (x)

49 p 146 Philippa Filia et Cohaeres Johannis Dmni. Mohun de Dunster, Uxor Edwardi Ducis/Eboracensis, Moritur Anno Dom. 1474. 310 × 200/343 × 203mm. pl.33 (y)

E Chapel of Henry VIIth

50 p 149 (Margaret Countess of Richmond – Margaret Countess of Lennox) 130 × 200,168 × 200/340 × 205mm. pl. 34–5. (z)

51 p 152 (Mary Queen of Scots) 298 × 197/343 × 203mm. pl.36. (a)

52 p 153 The Royal Vault – (Effigies of)King Charles ye IId., Dutchess of Richmond, General Monk/Restorer of King Charles II. 115 × 190,147 × 197/343 × 203mm. pl.37–40. (b)

53 p 156 The Tomb of Henry the Seventh. 187 × 307/216 × 318mm. Without credit. pl. 41. (d)

54 p 156 The sacellum or Chapel of Brass surrounding the Tomb of Henry the Seventh. 200 × 305/203 × 311mm. Without pl. no. The niches, now depleted, still contain all their statues. (c)

55 p 159 Lewis Stuart Duke of Richmond. 307 × 195/343 × 210mm. pl. 42. (e)

56 p 162 John Sheffyld late Duke of Buckingham. 310 × 197/345 × 205mm. pl. XLII. (f)

57 p 165 George Villiers Duke of Buckingham. 318 × 195/343 × 203mm. pl. 43. (g)

58 p 168 (Sophia, daughter of James I – King Edward V and Richard Duke of York – Mary, daughter of James I) 305 × 195/347 × 205mm. pl. 44, 46, 45. (h)

59 p 171 (Queen Elizabeth I) 290 × 195/343 × 203mm. pl. 47. (i)

60 p 172 (Sir George Savile, Marquis of Halifax) 302 × 195/343 × 203mm. pl. 48. (k)

61 p 173 (Charles Montague, 1st Earl of Halifax) 302 × 195/343 × 203mm. pl. 49. (l)

F In the Chapel of St Paul

62 p 176 Sr. John Puckering Knight. 317 × 197/343 × 203mm. pl. 50. (m)

63 p 177 (Sir James Fullerton) – This Tomb was erected to ye Memory of Sr. Giles Dawbeney. 185 × 197,120 × 197/350 × 205mm. pl. 51–2. (n)

64 p 178 (Sir Thomas Bromley) 305 × 197/345 × 205mm. pl. 53. (o)

65 p 179 (Dudley Carleton, Viscount Dorchester) 305 × 195/343 × 203mm. pl.54. (p)

66 p 180 Frances Countess of Sussex. 310 × 197/349 × 203mm. pl. 55. (q)

67 p 182 (Francis, Lord Cottington) 305 × 193/349 × 200mm. The figure of Lord Cottington here shown lying on a marble table at the foot of his wife's memorial; it has been later raised several feet and lies on the sarcophagus above. pl.56. (r)

68 p 183 Lodowick Robsert Lord Bourchier and his Lady. 305 × 195/350 × 203mm. pl. LVII. (s)

G In the Chapel of St. Erasmus (ie St John Baptist)

69 p 184 (Mrs Mary Kendall) 305 × 193/345 × 203mm. pl.57. (t)

70 p 185 This Monument was erected to the memory of Colonel Edward Popham and his Lady ... 308 × 200/350 × 205mm. pl.58. (v)

71 p 186 (Thomas Cary) – Thomas Cecill Comes Exeter, Baro de Burleigh ... 153 × 195, 138 × 195/345 × 205mm. pl. 59–60. (w)

72 p 187 (Henry Carey, Lord Hunsdon.) 310 × 200/349 × 203mm. pl. 61. (x)

73 p 190 Thomas Ruthall Bishop of Durham – William de Colchester, Abbot of Westminster. 185 × 195,110 × 195/340 × 205mm. pl. 62–3. (y)

74 p 191 George Flaccet, Abbot of Westminster. 305 × 195/345 × 205mm. Abbot Fascet. pl. 64. (z)

H In Islip's Chapel

75 p 193 John Islip Abbot of Westminster. 305 × 195/325 × 203mm. pl. 66. (&)

76 p 194 Christopher Hatton Knt. 308 × 195/349 × 203mm. pl. 66. (last plate)

VOL. 2

77 front. A Prospect of the inside of King Henry the VIIth Chapel. J. Schijnvoet, ad vivum fec. 360 × 305/425 × 320mm. No separate credit for engraver.

78 following list of subscribers (Plates of subscribers' arms, each with 42 shields and numbered tr 'Vol.2.p.I' and 'p.II')

79 p 1 (Headpiece as item 7 above – Initial 'A' as item 2 above)

I Chapel of St John the Evangelist

80 p 3 Sr. George Holles. 310 × 193/343 × 205mm. Sculpted by Nicholas Stone. cf with item 33 above. pl. 68.

81 p 4 Edmond Kirton Abbat – John Eastney Abbat – Sr.

Francis Vere Kt. 80 × 197, 80 × 197, 133 × 197/343 × 205mm. pl.71, 67, 69.

K Chapel of St Michael

82 p 5 The late Dutches of Somerset. 310 × 193/343 × 203mm. pl. 70.

L Chapel of St Andrew

83 p 8 Sr. Francis Norris Kt. 325 × 200/343 × 203mm. Abbot Kirton's brass (item 81) is also in this chapel. pl. 72.

M The Area that leads to the Chapel or on the North-side of the Choir

84 p 9 Aveline Wife to Edmund Crouchback. 307 × 197/315 × 205mm. This tomb is not shown but a wall monument to Dean Brian Duppa fixed to the back of it in the N. ambulatory where is also Abbot Estney's slab (item 81). pl. 73

85 p 12 Aymer de Valance Earl of Pembroke. 297 × 197/345 × 210mm. pl. 74.

86 p 13 Edmund Crouchback Earl of Lancaster,/Son to Henry IIId. 310 × 200/347 × 210mm. The angels above the canopy which have disappeared are shown here intact. pl. 75

87 p 16 The Lady Jane Crewe. 300 × 197/345 × 205mm. In N. ambulatory. pl. 76

88 p 17 Esther de la Tour de Governet – Sr. Thomas Ingram Kt. 310 × 197/348 × 205mm. Only a floor slab now commemorates Esther, wife of Lord Eland, in the N. ambulatory; her monument is in the undercroft. pl. 77–8

89 p 20 (Memorial to Sir Robert Aiton) – Children of Henry ye III. 180 × 197, 130 × 197/350 × 203mm. pl. 79–80

N Chapel of St Edward the Confessor

90 p 23 The Shrine of St. Edward. 310 × 195/348 × 205mm. pl. 81

91 p 24 A Prospect of Edward the Confessor's Chapel. 167 × 335/203 × 343mm. The frieze is shown in much better condition than at present. Unnumbered pl.

92 p 27 Margaret Daughter to King Edward IV – The Lady Elizabeth Daughter to King Henry VII. 133 × 200, 155 × 200/349 × 203mm. pl. 83, 82.

93 p 30 Queen Eleanor – Edward ye 1st King of England. 123 × 195, 180 × 195/345 × 205mm. pl. 86, 84

94 p 33 King Henry the IIId. 318 × 197/345 × 208mm. pl. 85.

95 p 38 A Prospect of Henry the 5th Chapel. 305 × 190/347 × 205mm. No credit. Unnumbered pl.

96 p 38 King Henry the Vth. – Queen Philippa Wife to King Edward ye IIId. 150 × 200, 150 × 200/349 × 210mm. Henry V's head restored by the engraver. pl. 87–8.

97 p 43 King Edward the IIId. – King Richard the IId. and his Queen. 145 × 200, 140 × 200/345 × 210mm. pl. 90–1.

98 p 46 Thomas of Woodstock Duke of Gloucester – John Waltham, Bishop of Salisbury. Each 150 × 200/347 × 210mm. Brasses in the Confessor's Chapel. pl. 89, 92.

99 p 57 In Capella Sti. Edmundi Abb: Westmonasteriensis. 325 × 197/345 × 205mm. Obelisk to Nicholas Monck, Bishop of Hereford, in St Edmunds Chapel. Monck died in 1723. Unnumbered pl.

100 p 61 (Matthew Prior). 310 × 200/350 × 210mm. Monument in Poets Corner by Gibbs, Rysbrack and Coysevox. Prior died in 1721. Unnumbered pl.

O The South Cross (ie Poets Corner)

101 p 61 (Ben Jonson) 310 × 197/345 × 205mm. pl. 93.

102 p 63 William Outram D.D. 310 × 197/345 × 203mm. pl. 94.

103 p 64 Isaac Barrow D.D. 310 × 200/347 × 210mm. pl. 95.

104 p 67 Thomas Triplett/D.D. – William Cambden/Esqr. 310 × 197/345 × 207mm. pl. 96, 98.

105 p 68 Isaac Casaubon. 303 × 200/345 × 210mm. pl. 97.

P The South Aisle (of the nave)

106 p 73 The Countess of Annandale. 310 × 197/345 × 207mm. pl. 99.

107 p 74 (Prebendary Thomas Knipe) – William Thynne Esqr. 310 × 197/350 × 205mm. pl. 100, 105.

108 p 75 (Thomas Richardson) 270 × 197/340 × 205mm. pl. 101.

109 p 76 (Elizabeth and Judith Freke) J. Dowling delin. J. Cole sculp. 305 × 200/325 × 210mm. pl. 102.

110 p 77 The Lady Grace Gethin … 310 × 197/345 × 205mm. pl. 103.

111 p 80 (Sir Cloudesley Shovell) J. Dowling delin. J. Cole sculp. 305 × 200/350 × 210mm. Sculpted by Grinling Gibbons. pl. 104.

112 p 81 Thomas Owen Esqr. 310 × 197/347 × 205mm. pl. 106.

113 p 82 (George Stepney) 302 × 200/347 × 205mm. pl. 107.

114 p 85 Thomas Thynne Esqr. J. Dowling delin. J. Cole sculp. 303 × 200/341 × 210mm. Sculpted by Arnold Quellin. pl. 108.

115 p 86 Admiral (George) Churchill. J. Dowling delin. J. Cole sculp. 305 × 200/340 × 205mm. pl. 109.

116 p 87 (Sir Palmes Fairborne) J. Dowling delin. J. Cole sculp. 300 × 197/330 × 205mm. pl. 110.

117 p 90 Major Richard Creed. 310 × 195/345 × 205mm. pl. 111.

118 p 91 Sr. Charles Harbord Kt. & Clement Cottrell Esq. 310 × 200/345 × 210mm. pl. 112.

119 p 92 (Sidney, Earl Godolphin) 310 × 197/350 × 205mm. pl. CXII.

120 p 92 Anne/Filding – Henry Wharton/A.M. – Carolo & Anne/Harsnet. 310 × 197/345 × 205mm. pl. 113, 116, 115.

121 p 93 John Smith Esqr. 305 × 197/345 × 210mm. pl. 114.

Q In the North Isle (of the nave)

122 p 97 (Penelope Needham) J. Dowling delin. J. Cole sculp. 300 × 197/340 × 210mm. pl. 118.

123 p 100 Sr. Lumley/Robinson Bart. – Jane/Stotevill – Heneage/Twysden Esqr. 310 × 200/345 × 205mm. pl. 117, 124, 120.

124 p 101 Coll James Bringfield. 302 × 200/350 × 210mm. pl. 121.

125 p 102 (Robert Killigrew) 305 × 195/340 × 205mm. pl. 122.

126 p 103 (Mrs Mary Beaufoy) 310 × 197/345 × 205mm. pl. 123.

127 p 106 Thomas Mansell & Willm. Morgan Esqr. 310 × 197/345 × 205mm. pl. 125.

128 p 107 Robert & Richard/Cholmondley – Thomas/ Lord Teviot – Edward de Carteret/Gent. 310 × 200/350 × 205mm. pl. 126, 131, 130.

129 p 108 (Vice Admiral John Baker) 305 × 197/345 × 205mm. pl. 127.

130 p 109 (Admiral Priestman) 305 × 197/340 × 208mm. pl. 128.

131 p 112 (Philip Carteret) 310 × 197/345 × 210mm. pl. 129.

132 p 113 (Robert Constable, Viscount Dunbar) J. Dowling delin. J. Cole sculp. 305 × 200/350 × 205mm. pl. 132.

133 p 114 Charles Williams/Esq. – Peter Heylin/D.D. – Sr. Thomas Duppa/Kt. 310 × 195/345 × 205mm. pl. 134, 133, 135.

134 p 117 Richard Le Neve Esqr. 308 × 195/345 × 200mm. pl. 136.

135 p 118 John Blow Doctr. in Musick. 303 × 200/350 × 210mm. pl. 138.

R The North-Cross

136 p 119 (Henry Purcell) – Sr. Thomas Heskett. 310 × 200/348 × 205mm. pl. 137, 139.

137 p 120 Sr. Gilbert Lort Bart. 310 × 197/348 × 205mm. pl. 140.

138 p 123 (William Cavendish, Duke of Newcastle). J. Dowling delin. J. Cole sculp. 300 × 197/345 × 205mm. pl. 151 (ie 141).

139 p 124 John Holles Duke of Newcastle. 330 × 197/345 × 207mm. pl. 142.

140 (Tailpiece as item 9 above)

141 p i of 'Lives of the Abbats' (Headpiece as item 5 above – Initial 'A' with allegorical figures and the Ten Commandments. 40 × 45/45 × 50mm.)

S The Cloisters

142 p xii (Tombs in the cloisters) Said to be that of Laurentius Abbat – Gislebert Crispinus Abbat – William de Humez Abbat. 100 × 200, 95 × 200, 95 × 200/345 × 210mm.

143 Book 3, p 1 (Headpiece as item 7 above – Initial 'I' set against Abbey interior. 47 × 43/50 × 45mm.)

144 p 24 (Tailpiece as item 6 above)

Supplementary plates following p 124 of vol. 2 in the 2nd ed

145 p 125 (Isaac Newton) H. Gravelot delin. C. Grignion sculp. 305 × 192/355 × 205mm. 1731.

146 p 126 (James, Lord Stanhope) H. Gravelot delin. N. Parr sculp. 305 × 192/355 × 210mm. 1733. These two monuments in the nave, l. and r. of the doorway of the pulpitum, designed by Kent, sculpted by Rysbrack.

147 p 127 (Sir Thomas Hardy, Knt) H. Gravelot delin. Grignion sculp. 305 × 190/355 × 198mm. 1732. By Sir Henry Cheere.

148 p 128 (Sir Godfrey Kneller, Knt) H. Gravelot delin. Nathl. Parr sculp. 305 × 190/355 × 210mm. 1730. By Rysbrack.

149 p 129 (James Craggs) J. Harris delin et sculpt. 315 × 195/355 × 205mm. 1725. By Guelfi.

150 p 130 (William Shakespeare) Gul. Kent inv. H. Gravelot delin. 310 × 190/355 × 205mm. 1740. Designed by Kent, sculpted by Scheemakers.

151 p 131 (Milton) H. Gravelot delin. Nathl. Parr sculp. 305 × 190/355 × 210mm. 1737. By Rysbrack.

152 p 132 (John Gay) H. Gravelot delin. Nathl. Parr sculp. 305 × 192/355 × 210mm. 1732. By Rysbrack.

153 p 133 (Rev J.E. Grabe) H. Gravelot del. J. Mynde sculp. 310 × 192/355 × 210mm. 1711. By Francis Bird.

154 p 134 (Hugh Chamberlaine) Petrus Sheemakers & Laur. Delvaux fecerunt. H. Gravelot delin. Grignion sculp. 345 × 192/355 × 210mm. 1728.

155 p 135 (Dr. John Woodward) H. Gravelot delin. Nathl. Parr sculp. 305 × 190/355 × 210mm. c 1730. By Scheemakers.

156 p 136 (Richard Kane) N. Parr sculp. 305 × 190/355 × 205mm. 1736. By Rysbrack.

28 · BOWLES'S BRITISH VIEWS
[1723–4]

John Bowles, born at the turn of the century, followed in his elder brother Thomas's footsteps and in due course became one of the most successful of the London print publishers and sellers. Early in his career, probably in 1723–4, he launched a series of inexpensive popular prints under the title of *British Views* which he described in his catalogues as 'Small Sets of Prints, Cheap and very Saleable'. They came out in three sets and each plate in the second and third sets consisted of a view (about 14 × 21.5cm) with the name of the subject on a banderole and, as the only text, about 200 words engraved in the bottom margin giving 'a particular Account of the Building, its Foundations, and other Remarks worthy of notice'. The first set, however, did not follow this pattern; in competition with his rival, Henry Overton, Bowles offered 36 cathedrals crammed on to nine small plates (about 17 × 23cm). These carried only the names of the churches and were obtainable at the bargain price of one shilling the lot. The second and third series, each consisting of two dozen plates, a plate to a view, were available at 2s 6d the set. They were printed either two to a folio page or singly on oblong paper measuring about 25 × 33cm from copper plates of about 14–18 × 23cm. Overton's *Prospects* (no 26, abbreviated *OP*), which were certainly Bowles's inspiration, used slightly broader plates (about 15–17 × 24cm) printed on larger paper (about 22.5 × 35cm) and with only a caption beneath each view.

With one exception ('Christ's Collegiate Church at Manchester') the small engravings of cathedrals in Set 1 are all copies reduced from the plates engraved by John Harris and Benjamin Cole for Henry Overton's collection, published in 1715 and later issued as a tail to his other Prospects in *Britannia Illustra* (no 22), entitled *Views of all the Cathedral Churches of England and Wales*. Each plate includes the publication-line 'John Bowles Excudit' but there are no credits or letters or numbers indicating order.

All three series have title-pages in uncertain French as well as English but this first set, perhaps in deference to the ecclesiastical content and echoing the third, ecclesiastical, volume of *Nouveau Théâtre de la Grand Bretagne* (ie *Britannia Illustrata*), adds a Latin title also.

The various editions of the three sets can roughly be dated from the addresses in the imprints, the earliest probably being those issued with the royal warrant ('Cum Previllegio Regis') 'Printed and Sold by John Bowles Print and Map Seller at Mercers Hall in Cheapside'. This is the case with those bound together in BM Prints 172*a.28 of which Set 1 has an inked-in date in a contemporary hand, '1723'. In connection with the imprint 'over against Stocks Market' the printed date '1724' is found in the copy of Set 2 in BL Maps 29.a.21 and also in BM Prints 172*b.5 in which the plates have been printed two to a folio page to range with plates from Bowles's *London Described* (no 29, probably issued in 1725) with which they share a binding. The 'Pocket Map' for 1725 included in this issue of *London Described* (*Darlington and Howgego* 72) advertises *British Views* and is published by Bowles 'at his Shop over against Stocks Market and at his Warehouse at Mercer's Hall'. After this 'Stocks Market' disappears from his imprint to be replaced from about 1730 by 'ye Black Horse in Cornhill' (*Darlington and Howgego* 41), which is found as the imprint of the three sets of *British Views* in the Guildhall Library (A.3.5.no 19.) Mercers' Hall persisted in imprints, however, for at least another year and it was from here that Bowles's 1731 catalogue was published.

The plates themselves survived into the next century and were used to supply the 'pennantizers' with extra-illustrations. Robert Wilkinson, Bowles's business successor, issued 22 from the first set and six from the third in about 1810 along with eight 'Perspective Views' and two other London views. Entitled *Several Prospects* (no 105), they were accompanied by tabulated page references to the 1754 Stow (no 37), to Pennant's *London* (no 67) and to works by Maitland (no 38) and Malcolm (no 83) indicating where each plate might be inserted. This has a fictitious imprint 'Published by John Bowles, 31 Cornhill'.

1 (engr title in heraldic frame) Prospects/of all the Cathedral & Collegiate Churches of England & Wales/(swelled rule)neatly Engraved/(swelled rule) Veues de toutes les Eglises/Cathedrales et Collegiats/ d'Angleterre et de Galle,/(swelled rule) proprement

Gravee (swelled rule)/Cum Previllegio Regis. /London, Printed & Sold by/John Bowles/Print and Map=Seller at/Mercers Hall in Cheapside. 178 × 225/190 × 248mm. Title within a double frame enclosing shields with the arms of 24 episcopates and two archbishoprics, with tc a blank shield with the legend 'Ecclesiae/Cathedrales/Angliae/et/Walliae'. Engr round inner frame tr: 'British Views No. 1'. Later ed with address 'att the/Black Horse in Cornhill'.

2 The Cathedral Church of St Asaph. – The Cathedral Church of Bangor – The Cathedral Church of Bath – The Cathedral Church of Bristol. Each 78 × 115 in 172 × 235/180 × 245mm.

3 The Cathedral Church of Canterbury, Metropolitan of England – The Cathedral Church of Carlisle – The Cathedral Church of Chester – The Cathedral Church of St Peter's in Chichester. Each 78 × 115 in 168 × 230/175 × 243mm.

4 The Cathedral Church of St David – The Cathedral Church of Durham – The Cathedral Church of Ely – The Cathedral Church of Exeter. Each 78 × 115 in 170 × 230/178 × 240mm.

5 The North West Prospect of ye Cathedral Church of St Pauls – The Inside of ye Choir of ye Cathedral Church of St Paul's, London – The North Prospect of the Cathedral Church of Rochester – The Cathedral Church of Wells. Each 78 × 115 in 172 × 232/185 × 245mm. The views of St Paul's are derived from *OP* 2 and 3.

6 The Cathedral Church of St Peters Glocester – The Cathedral Church of Hereford – The Cathedral Church of Landaff – The Cathedral Church of St Mary Lincoln. Each 78 × 115 in 172 × 230/180 × 240mm.

7 The Cathedral Church of Litchfield – The Cathedral Church of Norwich – The Cathedral Church of Oxford – The Cathedral Church of Peterborough. Each 78 × 115 in 172 × 230/185 × 245mm.

8 The South West Prospect of Salisbury Cathedral – The Cathedral Church of Winchester – The Cathedral Church of Worcester – The South Prospect of ye Cathedral of St Peter in York. Each 78 × 115 in 172 × 232/183 × 243mm.

9 The Collegiate Church of St Peter's Westminster – The Collegiate Church of St George at Windsor – Christ's Collegiate Church at Manchester – The Collegiate Church of Southwell in Nottinghamshire. Each 78 × 115 in 172 × 230/185 × 245mm. The first two are derived from *OP* 56 and 72; the Manchester view is not found in that work.

The order of the second set, which consists of views of London public buildings, is indicated by a lower-case letter engraved in the br corner. All have the 'Particular account' in the bm but none has either credit or, with the exception of the engraved title, publication-line. Twelve of the plates are copied from Overton's *Prospects* and one from the 1720 edition of Stow (no 25, abbreviated *S*) but the image copied tends to be restricted laterally to suit the narrower plates. The finest impressions are those issued with the title-page dated 1724.

10 pl. a (engr title in architectural framework) Several Prospects/of/the most noted Publick Buildings, in and about the/City of London/with a short Historical Account relating to the same/(swelled rule) Plusieurs Veues/des Bâtiments Public les plus Considérable/tant au dedans/qu'a l'entours de la Ville de Londres./Avec les Remarques Historiques fort Succinctes qui les regardent./London/Printed and Sold by/John Bowles/ Print and Map-seller over/against Stocks Market/ 1724. 167 × 218/183 × 255mm. Title framed by a panel with an architectural setting of Doric columns and: tc City arms and regalia; tl and tr trophies; to l. 'TheMonu/ment', to r. 'Bow Church', both in cartouches supported by Atlantes; bc putti with cannon and a cartouche. No mention of 'British Views no. 2' on this title but the plates appear seriatim under this head in Bowles's 1731 catalogue. There are alternative imprints, undated, one 'Cum Privilegio Regis' and the address 'Mercers Hall' and the other 'at the Black Horse, Cornhill'.

11 pl. b (in sky) The Royal Palace of St James's. (in work) The Terass Walk – St James's Park. (bm) This House was antiently an Hospital ... 167 × 205/183 × 234mm.

12 pl. c (on swallow-tailed banderole in sky) The Royal Banqueting House at White Hall. (bm) This Stately Building ... 168 × 210/186 × 230mm.

13 pl. d (on swallow-tailed banderole in sky) The Cathedral Church of/St Peters Westminster. (bm) Here formerly stood the Temple of Apollo ... 170 × 214/183 × 232mm. Staffage altered, otherwise follows *OP* 56.

14 pl. e (on scroll tc) The Inside of St Peters.(bm) The Inside of this Magnificent Pile ... 170 × 212/180 × 228mm. Nave, looking E.

15 pl. f (on swallow-tailed banderole in sky) The North West Prospect of The Cathedral Church of St Paul. (bm) This Church was first built by Ethelred ... 170 × 210/175 × 218mm. Follows closely, even to staffage, *OP* 2.

16 pl. g The South East Prospect of the Inside of the Cathedral Church of St. Paul. (on scroll tr) The Body of this Church is divided into 3 Ambulatorys ... 170 × 212/173 × 218mm.

17 pl. h (on swallow-tailed banderole in sky) Guild Hall. (bm) This is an Antient handsome Structure ... 170 × 215/180 × 230mm. Follows *OP* 8.

18 pl. i (on scroll tc) Inside of Guildhall. (bm) This Hall is very Spacious and Stately ... 175 × 215/185 ×

235mm. Follows closely, even to staffage, *OP* 40.

19 pl. k (on swallow-tailed banderole in sky) The Royal Exchange. (bm) This Building was first Erected by Sr Tho: Gresham ... 170 × 214/187 × 223mm. Follows closely *OP* 6.

20 pl. l (on swallow-tailed banderole in sky) The Inside of the Royal Exchange. (in work) The North Entrance – The South Entrance. (bm) The Quadrangle is 144 foot long ... 170 × 214/190 × 227mm. Follows *OP* 42.

21 pl. m (on swallow-tailed banderole in sky) Justice Hall in the Old Baily. (in work) The Bail Dock (bm) In this Hall the Ld Mayor, Recorder, Aldermen &c do sit and try Malefactors ... 168 × 210/185 × 240mm.

22 pl. n (on swallow-tailed banderole in sky) The Charterhouse. (in work) the Wilderness – the Terass Walk – the Bowling Green – Part of the Square (bm) The Hospital was antiently a Monastery of Carthusians ... 167 × 210/185 × 230mm. Follows *OP* 35.

23 pl. o (on swallow-tailed banderole in sky) St Paul's School. (in work) The Headmasters House – The School – the Sub-master House. (bm) This school was built & endowed by Dr John Colet ... 174 × 214/190 × 233mm. Façade.

24 pl. p (on swallow-tailed banderole in sky) College of Physicians. (bm) This Colledge belongs to the Society of Physicians ... 170 × 214/185 × 235mm. Warwick Lane, the courtyard.

25 pl. q (on swallow-tailed banderole in sky) St Bartholomew's Hospital. (in work) Little St Bar-/tholomew – Smithfield. (bm) The Hospital is Erected for poor, sick, Wounded and Diseased Persons ... 170 × 214/185 × 235mm. Birds-eye.

26 pl. r (on swallow-tailed banderole in sky) Christs Hospital. (in work) Christ Church. (bm) The Hospital formerly a House of Grey Friars ... 170 × 214/185 × 235mm. Although compressed, follows closely *OP* 9.

27 pl. s (on swallow-tailed banderole in sky) St Thomas's Hospital. (bm) This Hospital was first founded in 1213 ... 170 × 214/185 × 235mm. Birds-eye, with less staffage and surrounding buildings, but follows *S* 1, 189.

28 pl. t (on swallow-tailed banderole in sky) Bethlem Hospital (in work) Moore Fields. (bm) This Hospital was first founded in the year 1246 ... 170 × 210/185 × 228mm. Follows *OP* 7.

29 pl. v (on swallow-tailed banderole in sky) Aske's Hospital. (bm) This Hospital was built by the Company of Haberdashers ... 170 × 210/187 × 228mm. In Hoxton, built by Robert Hooke, 1690–3.

30 pl. w (on swallow-tailed banderole in sky) Navy Office. (bm) This is a Neat pritty Building ... B.Cole sc. 170 × 210/188 × 238mm. Follows *OP* 46.

31 pl. x (on swallow-tailed banderole in sky) Custom House. (bm) The Custom House for the Port of London ... 170 × 213/187 × 238mm. Follows *OP* 5.

32 pl. y (on swallow-tailed banderole in sky) London Bridge. (in work tr) A. The Water Mills/B. The Draw Bridge/C. The Sterlins as they appear at low water/D. the Arches. (bm) At this place a Ferry was formerly kept ... 167 × 214/172 × 234mm.

33 pl. z (on swallow-tailed banderole in sky) The Tower of London. (in work) Traitors Bridge. (bm) The Tower was antiently a Royal Palace ... 170 × 214/180 × 233mm. Follows *OP* 25.

The third set, whose order is likewise established by 24 lower-case letters br, includes public buildings, palaces and country houses. Most of the plates, but not all, have the 'Particular account' engraved in bm and two ('i' and 'z') have a credit, 'Parr sculp.' (Nathaniel Parr who later engraved London views by Canaletto for Henry Overton and Robert Sayer). With the exception of the engraved title none has a publication-line. Nineteen views, including the two title-page panoramas, are copied from Overton's *Prospects* and six are reduced from *Nouveau Théâtre* (*NTGB*), whose alternative title *Britannia Illustrata* has also been borrowed for the occasion.

34 pl. a (engr title in cartouche between two long views) Britannia Illustrata/Several Prospects/of the Royal Palaces & Publick Buildings of England, also ye Views of some of ye most considerable/seats and gardens belonging to the Nobility and Gentry, with short Remarks relating to them/Very neatly Engraved/Les Veues/Des Palais du Roy, et d'autres Publiques Batimens de l'Angleterre et des diverses Maisons et Jardins les plus/considerables des Seigneurs et des Gentilhommes avec des Remarques Historiques fort succinctes qui les regardent. (tr) British Views No. 3 (as a border round the title is a ribbon with the imprint) Printed for and Sold by John Bowles, Print and Map-Seller at Mercers Hall in Cheapside. Cum Privillegio Regis. 178 × 229/184 × 235mm. Also with the imprint 'Printed for and Sold by John Bowles at ye Black Horse in Cornhill London'. The two long views (each about 65 × 230mm) are each identified tc in the sky, the upper as 'Westminster' and the lower as 'London'. They are slightly abbreviated versions of the two title-page views *OP* 13 and 1.

35 pl. b (two long views) A View from the River Thames of the Parliament House, Westminster Hall and Westminster Abby. (in sky above buildings)Parliament House – Westminster Hall – Westminster Abby. – A View of Whitehall from the River Thames. 76 × 229, 89 × 229/184 × 235mm. Central portions extracted, varying staffage and sky from *OP* 18 and 59.

36 pl. c (on swallow-tailed banderole in sky) The Royal Palace of Kingsington. (bm) The Palace was purchased by K:William III ... 140 × 229/184 × 241mm. Follows closely *OP* 77.

37 pl. d (on swallow-tailed banderole in sky) The Royal Palace of Hampton Court. (bm) Hampton Court with its Park ... 140 × 235/184 × 241mm. Follows closely *OP* 76.

38 pl. e (on swallow-tailed banderole in sky) The Royal Palace of Windsor Castle. (bm) The Scituation of this charming Castle ... 152 × 229/184 × 241mm. Closely follows *OP* 75.

39 pl. f The Front of the Charity School in the City of Liverpool ... 171 × 235/190 × 248mm.

40 pl. g (tm) A View of the Inside of Westminster Hall. (bm) This was formerly the chief Palace of the Kings of England ... 152 × 229/184 × 241mm. Same plate as *OP* 17.

41 pl. h (on swallow-tailed banderole in sky) Lambeth House. (bm) Lambeth House. 143 × 235/180 × 245. Follows closely *OP* 16.

42 pl. i The Chapter House/It is a fair House belonging to St Pauls Church. Parr sculp. 165 × 235/184 × 248mm. Much reduced, with altered staffage, from *NTGB* 27.

43 pl. k (on swallow-tailed banderole in sky) Hatfield House. (bm) Hatfield House. An antient and noble Palace. 140 × 229/184 × 241mm. Derived originally from *NTGB* vol. 1, pl. 24 by James Collins but probably by way of *OP* 63.

44 pl. l Stainborough/In the County of York ... 159 × 222/178 × 235mm. This subject, but not this view, in *NTGB* vol. 4.

45 pl. m (tm) The General Front, and the South Front of Houghton in Norfolk ... 159 × 222/190 × 229mm.

46 pl. n Longleate in Wiltshire ... 146 × 222/184 × 241mm. Derived from *NTGB* vol. 1 probably by way of *OP* 62.

47 pl. o Ragley ... Warwick. 159 × 222/178 × 235mm. After *NTGB* vol. 1, pl. 71.

48 pl. p Fairlawn ... Kent. 159 × 222/184 × 241mm. Derived from *NTGB* vol. 1, pl. 49 probably by way of *OP* 51.

49 pl. q Chatsworth in Devonshire ... 159 × 235/184 × 241mm. Follows *NTGB* vol. 1, pl. 17.

50 pl. r New Park/at Richmond in Surry ... 159 × 235/184 × 248mm. Follows *NTGB* vol. 1, pl. 33.

51 pl. s (two long views) Wanstead in Essex – Magnificent Palace of Sr Gregory Page ... Black Heath. 95 × 222, 70 × 222/178 × 235mm. Central portions of *OP* 53, 52.

52 pl. t (on swallow-tailed banderole in sky) Blenheim House. 184 × 235/190 × 241mm. With insets, tl of the E. front and tr of the bridge in the park. Façade only from *OP* 61.

53 pl. u (tm) The Prospects of Stonehenge from the West and from the North. 76 × 222, 76 × 222/184 × 235mm.

54 pl. w (on swallow-tailed banderole in sky tl) Edystone Light House. 140 × 229/184 × 241mm. Follows closely *OP* 74.

55 pl. x A View of the Observatory in Greenwich Park belonging to the King's Professor of Astronimy (!) – A View of Greenwich, Deptford and London, taken from Flamsteade Hill in Greenwich Park. 76 × 229, 83 × 229/178 × 241mm. Two strip views, the first much reduced from *NTGB* 51 and the second copied from the central portion of *OP* 10.

56 pl. y The Royal Hospital at Greenwich. 152 × 210/184 × 229mm. Apart from enlarged domes and centres with aedicules added to the King Charles and Queen Anne blocks, together with abbreviation and elimination of two buildings to the W., this follows *OP* 44.

57 pl. z Chelsey Colledge. Parr sculp. 159 × 222/184 × 235mm. From the road. Altered staffage apart, closely follows *OP* 43. (*Longford* 66)

---

29 · LONDON DESCRIBED [1731]

London Described; or Perspective Views and Elevations of Noted Buildings, in one folio volume, was offered for sale in the *Catalogue of Maps, Prints, Copy-Books &c, from off Copper-Plates* issued by John Bowles in 1753 from the Black Horse in Cornhill. The title-page for this now extremely rare collection was engraved in 1731 but most of the component prints were in circulation earlier, certainly by 1725, the date of a map bound up with the BM Print Room collection (172*.b.5). Forty of them are listed in Bowles's 1728 catalogue and these are repeated, plus an extra eight, in his 1731 catalogue. The most complete collection seen is that in the Guildhall Library (STORE 410.8) which consists of the engraved title of 1731, the map dated 1727 and 45 views and architectural plates of which two, of Blenheim Palace and the Eddystone Lighthouse, have nothing to do with London.

Two plates announced by the 1728 catalogue, of East India House and Bridgewater Square, are no longer offered in 1731 and, since they are bound in neither volume nor found loose in print collections, it may be that they were never actually produced. Of the six views of St Paul's Cathedral and a plan listed in the earlier catalogues only a view from the S.W.

and a composite broadsheet showing the old and new buildings seem to have survived.

Just as Johannes Kip's name is associated with the volumes of *Nouveau Théâtre* (no 22), even though he did not engrave all the plates, so *London Decribed*, with which others were also involved, owes a great deal to one engraver, Sutton Nicholls. It gathered between its covers many of the best of his topographical plates, those pleasurable mementoes of early eighteenth century urbanity which are his birds-eye views of the squares. His year of birth is uncertain but he was at work by 1683 illustrating Philip Ayres's *Emblems of Love in Four Languages* published by Henry Overton with whose firm he was to continue his association, engraving for them maps and views until at least 1739. A greeting card which he designed and worked in 1695 for the parishioners of Shoreditch (*Crowle* Pennant 8.281) is proof that he was not above doing jobbing work and he occasionally engraved small portraits one of which, a medallion of the late Queen, was printed and sold on the ice during the Thames Frost Fair of January 1716 (*Crace* Frost Fairs 29). He was also engaged in serious cartographical undertakings in connection with Lea's reissue of Saxton's maps in 1687 and the 1695 edition of Camden's *Britannia*.

Having adapted his technique to the working of large areas of copper he next turned his attention to panoramic views of a London which was still rising from the burned-out sites of the Great Fire. These, although they are crude and hasty in draughtsmanship and ignore the rules of perspective, are useful in that they pay particular attention to the extant domes, towers and steeples and thus provide a rough index to the progress Wren was making in rebuilding the churches. His East and West 'Prospects', each on two sheets, were published by Overton (*Crace* 2.79–80) and both William Knight and James Walker published 'General Prospects' from the Temple to the Tower, each on three sheets (*Crace* 2,77–8). These were equipped with abundant references in the lower margin keyed to numerals worked above the buildings and they appear to date from the first decade of the century, before the emergence of many later landmarks. The anonymous 'South Prospect' bound in the BM Collection (item 48) is also undoubtedly his work but he made little attempt to bring the scene up to date even when it was published again from John Bowles's Cornhill address in 1732 (*Crace* 2.86).

His other large-scale London prints are: a two-sheet view of the Tower of London which he himself published from the Golden Ball in St Paul's Churchyard (BL Maps: *K. top* 24.23c2) and, on one sheet, from Aldersgate Street near the Half Moon Tavern (*Crace* 8.45); an engraving of the Cavendish estate planned for Lord Harley in 1719 by John Prince (*Crace* Maps 14.20); a 'Prospect of Charterhouse' dedicated to the Governors and published by Overton and Hoole in 1720 (*Crace* 26.11); a 'Prospect of Greenwich from Flamstead Hill' published by Overton in 1724 (*Crace* 36.20). His best and topographically most accurate work, however, is undoubtedly the uniform series of London squares in which he has refined his usual broad and generalizing method to produce a faithful, detailed record of the more plutocratic urban domestic architecture of his day. Their popularity as individual ornaments accounts for the rarity of this work as a whole and for the defoliation of numerous copies of the 1754 edition of Stow (no 37) in which they were later reissued.

The extent to which the family of Bowles dominated the London print market may be judged from the fact that at the time this collection was being got together Thomas Bowles had been trading in St Paul's Churchyard since 1712, where he remained 'next to the Chapter House' for the rest of his long career. His younger brother, John, having retained his original premises at Mercers' Hall as a warehouse, had opened another establishment nearby in the Stocks Market. Between them they had three London addresses. Thomas's name appears in some of the publication-lines of *London Described* because he was originally, like his brother, a map and printseller and publisher. But by 1725 he had also emerged as an engraver and it is in this role that his name is to be found on some of the plates. In the ensuing years he combined the three activities, his separate engravings being published sometimes by himself but more usually by his brother or the Overtons or Robert Sayer; most frequently all three feature in the publicaton-lines. An example of his book work is to be found in Seymour's *Survey of London* (1734, no 30) in which six of the few illustrations were engraved by him, though conveniently based on illustrations in the 1720 edition of Stow (no 25). His output was at its peak in the 1750s, particularly during the period of 1751–3 for which London print collections contain dozens of views for which he did the drawing and engraving himself or which he engraved after contemporaries such as Canaletto and John Maurer. Sayer & Bennett's 1775 catalogue advertises a series of 46 numbered 'Perspective Views' of London and seven of Ranelagh and Vauxhall Gardens of which Bowles was responsible for at least half but they seem not to have been offered as a bound collection at the time and it was not until 1880 that R.H. Laurie, into whose hands some of the well-worn plates had fallen, published an album, *Views of the City of London* (no 91), which includes a number of them.

A near contemporary of *London Described* was Joseph Smith's augmented edition of *Nouveau Théâtre* into which were ingathered engravings made during a period stretching from the reign of Charles II to that of George II. On this work Bowles's artists quite often relied for their delineation of a building or view but the only form of acknowledgment was a tacit one in the credits of Nicholls plates which merely read 'sculp' instead of the ususal formula 'delin. et sculp.' Ten of his prints are certainly drawn from this source, abbreviated in this list as *NTGB* with an item number; seven others as surely derive from illustrations to the 1720 edition of Stow, abbreviated *S* with Book and facing page numbers. The rest, it may be assumed, were drawn 'ad vivum' and engraved by Nicholls or Thomas Bowles with the exception of two plates by H. Terasson and one by Sturt.

Appended to the 47 listed plates found in the Guildhall Library collection, inclusive of the engraved title-page, are four additional engravings from the BM Print Room copy (172*. b.5). This folio, which contains Bowles's popular series of small *British Views* Part 2 (no 28), printed two to a page, as well as the large prints under consideration, has no printed or engraved title; only the manuscript heading referred to both by Upcott and the *Dictionary of National Biography* article on Nicholls: 'Prospects of the Most Considerable Buildings about London (1725)'.

Prior to 1731, when the Guildhall title-page was engraved, John Bowles had apparently given up the Stocks Market address which appears in most of the publication-lines. Of the four plates which were not reissued in 1731 one has no publication-line, two name the Stocks Market and the remaining one is an intruder. On the other hand of 12 items in the Guildhall but not in the earlier collection nos 4–6 have no publication-lines, nos 1, 7–8, 15, 27, 38, 47 have Mercers' Hall, and nos 31 and 46 are published by Thomas Bowles from St Paul's Churchyard. Common to both collections are four items (nos 34, 41–3) whose lines give both addresses and, in the Guildhall 1731 folio, five (10–12, 17, 21) on which the publisher bothered to substitute the Mercers Hall address for a deleted Stocks Market.

The publication-lines and credits are sometimes engraved in the bm but more often in the work bc and bl or br where they tend to merge with foreground cross-hatchings and etched lines. The two most commonly found are abbreviated thus in the list:

(line A) 'London/Sold by Iohn Bowles Print & Map Seller over against Stocks Market.'

(line B) 'London/Sold by John Bowles Print and Mapseller at Mercers Hall in Cheapside.'

Other lines are transcribed in full. Prints listed in the Bowles 1728 catalogue are marked *B* 1728, those only in the 1731 catalogue *B* 1731. Details of later states of a number of the plates may be found in the listing of the 1754 edition of Stow.

1 (engr title) London Described/(between swelled rules) or/the most noted Regular Buildings both Publick and Private/with the Views of several Squares in the Liberties of/London & Westminster/Exhibited in divers Elevations & Perspective Views,/Engraved after Drawings exactly made from ye Buildings/By an able Artist/(flourish)To which are added the Prospects of the/Royal Palaces of England, of Chelsea Hospital,/ Greenwich Hospital, Blenheim (!) House/and of the famous Light House built on the Edystone Rock &c./Londres Décrit ou Representé/(between swelled rules) ou/les plus fameux Edifices Reguliers tant/ Publics que Particuliers,/avec les Veües des divers Quarrés dans les Libertés de/Londre et Westminster./ Representés en plusieurs Elevations et Perspectives/ Gravées d'après les Dessins exactement tirés des Edifices/par une habile Artiste (flourish)/Auxquels sont ajoutés les Perspectives des/Palais Royaux d'Angleterre, des Invalides de Chelsea/de l'hôpital de Greenwich, du Chateau de Blenheim, et/du fameux Fanal bâti sur le Roc d'Edystone./ London/Printed for Thos Bowles in St Paul's Church Yard and Ion Bowles at Mercers Hall in Cheapside. J. Clark sculp. 1731. 373 × 232/385 × 242mm.

2 (composite print) (caption of first strip on scroll tl) A Plan of/London/as in Q. Elizabeth's Days (175 × 445mm) – (other captions on banderoles in sky) (second strip) Old Buildings near ye Temple Gate in Fleet str (75 × 100mm) – Baynards Castle (75 × 105mm) – West View of Old St Paul's (75 × 65mm) –

Cheapside and the Cross as before the Fire 1666 (75 × 185mm) – Inside of the Royal Exchange/as before the Fire (75 × 95mm) – (third strip) The South Prospect of London/as it appeared when it lay in Ruins after the Dreadfull Fire in 1666 (105 × 550mm). Thos. Bowles sculp. (publication-line with a description on scroll tr) London/Sold by John Bowles/over against Stocks=/Market. 360 × 555/375 × 565mm. With panels of text tl and tr. BM Prints copy adds to publication-line: '& at Mercers/hall in Cheapside.' The 'Old Buildings near ye Temple Gate' show the house with Prince Henry's Room. The 'South Prospect' is reduced from Hollar (*Hind* 19). *Darlington and Howgego* (8) date the plan on the first strip 1723; it is offered as a separate item in *B* 1728 and again in *B* 1753, price 6d. It was copied, less the central cartouche and scrolls l. and r., from *S* 1, 1.

3 (in cartouche bc) A Pocket Map/of the Cities of/London, Westminster./and Southwark/with the Addition of the/new Buildings to this/Present Year/1727. Tho: Bowles sculp. (on scroll bl) London 1727/Sold by John Bowles Print & Mapseller at/Mercers Hall in Cheapside./Where may be had Several/Prospects of the most noted Publick Buildings/in and about the City of/London with a short historical account relating to the same. 365 × 560/378 × 575mm. The dates in the BM Prints copy are '1725' and the publication-line: 'Sold by John Bowles at his/Shop over against Stocksmarkt/and at his Warehouse at/Mercers Hall in Cheapside ...' The advertisement is for Bowles's series of *British Views*. (*Darlington and Howgego* 72)

4 The Royal Palace of St James. This House was formerly an Hospital ... (in work) St James's Palace – Marlborough House – Buckingham House – The Canall –The Decoy. 265 × 445/300 × 460mm. With traces of an inscription, possibly another caption, burnished out in top 30mm. *B* 1728. Based on a larger engraving, which views from S. of Rosamond's Pond the whole extent of the Park from Buckingham House to Charing Cross, *NTGB* 39.

5 The Royal Palace of Kensington Joyns to high Park, and was purchased for the Earl of Nottingham ... 263 × 450/295 × 460mm. *B* 1728. Viewed from S.E. with pedimented wall in foreground. Traces of burnished-out inscription in tm. Based on the larger *NTGB* 41.

6 The Royal Palace of Hampton Court with its Park and Gardens ... 265 × 450/285 × 460mm. *B* 1728. View from E. Top of copper plate above work has been cut off. Based on the larger *NTGB* 61.

7 The Royal Palace of Windsor Castle. The Scituation of this charming Castle ... London, Sold by John Bowles at Mercers Hall in Cheapside. 265 × 445/285 × 460mm. *B* 1728. View from the N. Top of copper plate above work has been cut off. Based on the larger *NTGB* 44.

8 (composite plate) (along tm of each scene) A prospect of the Inside of the Collegiate Church of St Peter in Westminster,/from The Quire to the East End ... – The Inthronization of their Majesties/A View of the West End of the Choir ... – A Perspective of Westminster Abbey from the High Altar to the West End/Shewing/The manner of his Majesties Crowning ... – A Prospect of Westminster Hall shewing how the King and/Queen ... did sit at Dinner ... the whole taken from Sandford. Tho. Bowles sculp. Sold by Thos. Bowles in St Pauls Church yard & John Bowles at Mercer's Hall in Cheapside. Each 235–90 × 232–40/590 × 490mm. *B* 1728. Based on the large plates in Sandford's *History of the Coronation* (no 16), items 3, 5, 4, 7.

9 (ten Gates in black borders with captions and descriptions in bm of each) Ald-Gate – Bishops Gate – Moore-Gate – Cripple-Gate – Alders-Gate – New-Gate – Lud-Gate – Temple Bar – Kings-Gate – The Gate. (bm) Sutton Nicholls sculp. (line A) Each 130–64 × 90, 320 × 455/340 × 465mm. Each with compass-rose. *B* 1731. The 'King's Gate' was demolished for road widening in 1723.

10 (on swallow-tailed banderole in sky) Hañover Square (in work) Hamstead – Highgate – Tiborn Road – Prince Street – Hannover Street – Great George Street. Sutton Nicholls delin. et sculp. (line B) 325 × 455/340 × 460mm. With compass-rose. *B* 1728. View to the N. The square was built 1717–18. (BM Prints line A)

11 (on swallow-tailed banderole in sky) Golden Square (in work) John Street – James Street. (bm) Sutton Nicholls delin. & sculp. (line B) 320 × 450/345 × 465mm. With compass-rose. Looking N. *B* 1728. (BM Prints line A)

12 (on swallow-tailed banderole in sky) St James's Square (in work) St James's Church – York Street – King Street – Charles Street. Sutton Nicholls delin. et sculp. (line B) 325 × 455/340 × 460mm. With compass-rose. Looking N. and a couple boating on a central round pond. *B* 1728. But BM Prints (line A) shows centre enclosed in rough railings with a gardener's hut to the r.

13 (on swallow-tailed banderole in sky) Buckingham House in St James's Park. Sutton Nicholls sculp. (line A) 325 × 455/345 × 465mm. *B* 1728. Slightly reduced and with staffage altered but from *NTGB* 45.

14 (on swallow-tailed banderole in sky) Marlborough House/in St James's Park. Sutton Nicholls sculp. (line A) 315 × 440/330 × 450mm. *B* 1728. Closer view and adds a trophy with blank cartouche tc. of parapet, and statues to the empty niches, but follows *NTGB* 46.

15 (on banderole in sky) The Admiralty Office. (bm) Tho. Bowles delin. et sculp. London/Printed and Sold by John Bowles Print & Map-Seller at Mercers Hall in Cheapside. 325 × 455/344 × 470mm. *B* 1731. Coach in forecourt which is surrounded by a low wall and another entering the gates. Built by Thomas Ripley, 1723–6.

16 (on swallow-tailed banderole in sky) The Brass Statue of King Charles ye 1st at Charring Cross. (bm) Sutton Nicholls delin. et sculp. (on plinth of statue line A) 325 ×, 450/345 × 465mm. *B* 1728. Looking W. towards Cockspur Street; sedan chairs are parked around the monument. 'The Mews' indicated in work to r.

17 (on swallow-tailed banderole in sky) Sohoe or Kings Square. (in work) Hamstead – Highgate – Rawbone Place – Tiborn Road – Charles Street – Denmark Street – Sutton Street – Frith Street – Greek Street. Sutton Nicholls sculp. (line B) 320 × 455/340 × 465mm. *B* 1728. View to N. (BM Prints line A)

18 (on swallow-tailed banderole in sky) Mountague House/In Great Russell Street. Sutton Nicholls del. et sculp. (line A) 320 × 445/335 × 455mm. *B* 1728. View of S. façade and front courtyard.

19 (on swallow-tailed banderole in sky) Red Lyon Square (in work) Hamsted – Highgate – Islington – North Street – Drake Str. – Orange Str. – Lambs Conduit Passage – Princess Str. – Fishers Street – Grays Inn Passage. Sutton Nicholls delin. et sculp. (line A) 325 × 455/345 × 460mm. With compass-rose. *B* 1728.

20 (on swallow-tailed banderoles) Powis House/In Ormond Street. Sutton Nicholls sculp. London/Printed and Sold by John Bowles, Print and Mapseller over against/Stocks Market. 330 × 455/345 × 465mm. *B* 1728. Reduced and with alterations to staffage and flanking buildings, otherwise follows *NTGB* 53.

21 (on swallow-tailed banderole in sky) Southampton House or Bloomsbury Square. (in work) Hamsted – Highgate – Islington – Southampton Row – Great Russell Street – Allington Row – Seymour Row – Vernon Street. Sutton Nicholls/delin. et sculp. (line B) 320 × 450/345 × 460mm. With compass-rose. View to N. *B* 1728. (BM Prints line A)

22 (on swallow-tailed banderole in sky) Grays Inn (in work) Hampstead – Highgate – Bedford Row – Coney Court – Grays Inn Lane. Sutton Nicholls sculp. (line A) 325 × 455/350 × 475mm. *B* 1728. Adds a small, detached two-storey house near the gate into Jockey's Fields and the buildings in Bedford Mews, but otherwise deriving from the birds-eye view *S* 4, 69.

23 (on swallow-tailed banderole in sky) Furnivals Inn in Holbourn (in work) Holbourn. Sutton Nicholls delin. et sculp. (line A) 325 × 455/345 × 470mm. *B* 1728.

24 (on swallow-tailed banderole in sky) Lincolns Inn New Square (in work) Searles Gate – A Passage into Chancery Lane – A Passage into Searles Street. Sutton Nicholls del & scul. (line A) 325 × 460/345 × 470mm. With compass-rose. View to the S. *B* 1728. (Kip's view in *S* 4, 73 is to the N.)

25 (on swallow-tailed banderole in sky) Newcastle House/in Lincolns Inn Fields (bm) Sutton Nicholls delin. et sculp. (line A) 435 × 330/455 × 340mm. *B* 1728. Built for the Marquis of Powis by Winde,

1684–9, refitted for the Duke of Newcastle, 1715–17.

26 (on swallow-tailed banderole in sky) Covent Garden. (in work) St Anns – St Giles – James Street – King Street – Russel Street – Henrietta Street. Sutton Nicholls sculp. (line A) 330 × 450/345 × 460mm. *B* 1728.

27 (on banderole in sky) The House of Tho: Archer Esq. in Covent Garden. (bm) London Printed and Sold by John Bowles at Mercers Hall in Cheapside. 330 × 460/345 × 470mm. *B* 1731. Thomas Archer the architect (c1668–1743) built this house in 1716–17 for Admiral Russell, the Earl of Orford who died in 1727 and left it to his niece. On her death soon after it was left to her two married daughters, one of whom was Archer's nephew's wife; they cast lots for it and it was assigned in May 1729 to Archer's nephew and his wife.

28 (on swallow-tailed banderole in sky) St Mary le Strand. (bm) Sutton Nicholls sculp. 440 × 330/465 × 345mm. *B* 1728. Reduced and with different staffage and showing actual rather than ideal architectural neighbours, otherwise follows *NTGB* 32.

29 (on swallow-tailed banderole in sky) Bridewell. Sutton Nicholls delin. et sculp. Sold by John Bowles Print & Mapseller over against Stocks Market. 325 × 455/345 × 470mm. *B* 1728. Varies staffage but otherwise follows closely Kip's *S* 1, 176.

30 (composite plate, captions in work) (first strip) The North View of St Paul's Church as before the Fire of London – The South View of St Paul's Church when/the Spire was Standing – The South View of St Paul's Church as before the Fire (73 × 460mm) – (second strip) The West End of St Paules – The Ichnographie of the parochiall Church of St Faith (170 × 60mm) – (bm) The East End of St Pauls – The North Side of St Paul's Church – The West Front of St Pauls. I. Simon fecit (150 × 335mm) – The East End of St Pauls – The Prospect of the Orientall Part of the Church/ … of St Pauls in London/as before the Fire of London (155 × 60mm) – (third strip) The Prospect of the Parochial Church of St Faith … – The Planographie of the Cathedral/Church of St Paules/as before the Fire of London – The Interior Prospect of the Body of the Cathedrall Church of St Pauls from West to the quire – The Prospect of the Quire of St Pauls Cathedrall (75 × 460mm) – (fourth strip) The Quire as it is at present (65 × 70mm) – (on swallow-tailed banderole) A Prospect of London, as before the Fire (in work) Southworke. D. Loggan fec (65 × 310mm) – The Inside as it now is (65 × 73mm). Printed & Sold by John Bowles at Mercer's Hall London. 392 × 460mm. *B* 1731. This plate, with much burnishing out and re-engraving, survived from 1658 when it was first printed for Daniel King as a broadside urging the restoration of the Cathedral's decaying fabric ('D.King delin et Excudit Ao 1658. D.Loggan fecit.' 385 × 460mm). This was sold by John Overton (BL: *K. top.* 23.33b) and apparently fell into the hands of Thomas Bowles who burnished out Edward Ben-

lowe's lament for the Cathedral's then ruinous condition, engraved in King's cursive script on the centre of the plate, and replaced them with three views of new St Paul's by J.Simon on strip 2. On strip 3 Benlowes's portrait with its dedication and scriptural quotation were removed to make way for the keyed refs to the 'Prospect' while the original refs bl and br to the 'Prospect' were replaced by interiors of new St Paul's. The lettering was brought up to date by the addition, where necessary, of 'as before the Fire of London' and of Bowles's characteristic banderole on the 'Prospect'. Incomplete burnishing has, however, left traces of the original lettering, especially on the upper half of the plate. On r. of tm in Bowles's issue is the letter 'y' and in some copies (eg BL: *K. top* 23.33d) 'vol.14 page 400'. The BM Prints copy has the publication-line 'Printed and Sold by John Bowles over against Stocks-Market London', some variant letterings and the date 1724 in the 'history' under the second strip. The pre-Fire views are all copied from Hollar plates, the 'Prospect' being based on that in Howell's *Londinopolis* (no 7). (*Hind* 17, *Scouloudi* pp 56–8)

31 The South West Prospect of St Paul's Cathedral-Veüe de l'Eglise Cathedral de St Paul du coste de Sud West. H. Terasson fecit. Printed & Sold by Thos Bowles next to the Chapter House in St Paul's Church Yard. 415 × 575/450 × 585mm. *B* 1728.

32 Statue of Her Majesty ... Erected at the West End of St Paul's Anno 1713. Sold by Tho. Bowles in St Paul's Churchyard, London. 635 × 525mm pl. mark. *B* 1731 names engraver, Terasson. Queen Anne by the sculptor Francis Bird.

33 (on swallow-tailed banderole in sky) Charterhouse Square. (in work) Bow Church – St Annes – Great St Bartholomew – St Pauls – Carthusian Street – Charterhouse Str. – Charterhouse Lane. Sutton Nicholls delin. et sculp. (line A) 325 × 458/345 × 470mm. With compass-rose. Looking S. *B* 1728.

34 (on swallow-tailed banderole in sky) The West Prospect of the Church of and Steeple of St Mary le Bow in Cheapside (lm on scroll) St Mary Bow was the first Church in the City builded on Arches of Stone ... London/Sold by John Bowles opposite to Stocks Market & at Mercers Hall in Cheapside. 380 × 325/425 × 335mm. *B* 1731.

35 (on swallow-tailed banderole in sky) Bow Church. (in work) Bow Lane – Cheapside. Sutton Nicholls sculp. (line A) 448 × 340/470 × 350mm. *B* 1728. Apart from trees planted to W. of church and some rebuilding E. of Bow Lane follows Kip's *S* 3, 25.

36 (on swallow-tailed banderole in sky) The Statue of King Charles ye 2d at Stocks Market. (in work) St Christophers – Threadneedle Str. – Princes Str. – Cornhill. Sutton Nicholls delin. et sculp. (line A) 325 × 460/350 × 470mm. *B* 1728. View looking E.

37 (on swallow-tailed banderole in sky) The General Post Office. Sutton Nicholls delin. et sculp. (line A) 330 × 460/345 × 470mm. *B* 1728. In Lombard Street.

38 (on banderole in sky) The South Sea House in Bishopsgate Street. Bowles sculp. (line B) 325 × 455/350 × 470mm. *B* 1728. Built by James Gould, 1724–5.

39 (on swallow-tailed banderole in sky) Devonshire Square. Sutton Nicholls del. et sculp. (line A) 317 × 444/343 × 457mm. *B* 1728. Part of a development commenced about 1680 by Nicholas Barbon on the site of a Cavendish property known as Fisher's Folly situated E. of Bishopsgate Street and opposite to where Liverpool Street Station now stands. In appearance it was not unlike a smaller version of New Square, Lincoln's Inn, according to the view.

40 (on swallow-tailed banderole between scrolls tl and tr carrying description) The Monument. (in work) Fish Street Hill. Sutton Nicholls sculp. (line A) 445 × 333/465 × 345mm. *B* 1728. tr 'dd'. Amends and extends sideways *S* 2, 180.

41 (on swallow-tailed banderole) A Representation of the Carved Work on the West Side of/the Pedestal of the Monument of London. (bm) London/Sold by John Bowles, opposite to Stocks Market & at Mercers Hall in Cheapside. 450 × 435/530 × 450mm. With explanation and refs A–P. *B* 1728.

42 (in sky between cartouche with dedication to the Master and Wardens and an achievement of their arms) Fishmongers Hall/near/London Bridge. (bm) The Fishmongers were at first two severall companies ... Sold by John Bowles, opposite to Stocks Market & at Mercers Hall in Cheapside. 305 × 410/335 × 420mm. View from river. *B* 1728.

43 (on swallow-tailed banderole in sky) Guys Hospital for Incurables. (bm) London/Printed and Sold by John Bowles Printseller over against Stocks Market & att Mercers Hall in Cheapside. 322 × 450/340 × 465mm. *B* 1728. The central block, built by Thomas Dance, 1722–25. This was probably the first engraving, issued also as a composite plate (460 × 650mm), surrounded by eight small supplementary views by Thomas Bowles, four each of the exterior and interior (BL Maps: *K. top.* 27.57b).

44 (on swallow-tailed banderole in sky) The Royall Hospital at Chelsey. (bm) Sutton Nicholls sculp. (line A) 325 × 450/345 × 465mm. *B* 1728. Reduced in size and cut short at each side, otherwise follows *NTGB* 52. (*Longford 5*)

45 (on swallow-tailed banderole in sky) The Royal Hospital at Greenwich. (bm) Sutton Nicholls delin. & sculp. (line A) 325 × 445/340 × 455mm. *B* 1728. The flanking blocks have been built and the river façade is complete with its aedicules and attics, as also in *S* 1, 215.

46 (tc) The Front of Blenheim House/towards the Gardens (and in French) – View of the Bridge of Blenheim (and in French) – The Park front of

Blenheim (and in French) – Plan of the Vaults in Blenheim House (and in French) – Plan of the Principal Floor (and in French). H. Terasson delin. et Fecit. Published & Sold by Tho. Bowles next ye Chapter House in/St Pauls Church Yard. 460 × 600mm. With keyed refs. *B* 1731.

47 (in cartouche flanked by clouds with cherub-heads representing the winds) A Prospect and Section of the/Lighthouse on the Eddystone/Rock ... /the lights put therein ye 28th July 1708. J. Sturt sculp. (tm line B) 540 × 400/600 × 420mm. *B* 1731.

Additional plates bound in BM Prints collection

48 (on banderole in sky between r. City arms with supporters, crest and motto and l. Westminster arms in cartouche supported by two putti) The South Prospect of London and Westminster. (line A) Two sheets, 490 × 585, 490 × 580mm, overall 490 × 1165/505 × 1190mm. (bm) refs 1–118. (tl) descriptive scroll in English with the publication-line and an advertisement for the *Prospects* (*British Views*) and other London engr. (tr) scroll with French description. *B* 1728.

49 (on swallow-tailed banderole in sky) Leicester Square. Sutton Nicholls del. et sculp. (line A) 325 × 450/345 × 460mm. *B* 1728. View to the N. and Leicester House. *Crace* 18.14 (line B) adds a dark shadow on S. side of the square.

50 (on swallow-tailed banderole in sky) The Temple. (bm) Sutton Nicholls del. et sculp. 320 × 450/345 × 465mm. Birds-eye view from the river. *B* 1728. Enlarges but follows, even to the staffage, *S* 3, 271.

51 The Elevation or Prospect of the West End of the Steeple of St Bridget/alias Brides in Fleetstreet London shewing the inside and outside Thereof/being 235 feet high.   Sr. Chr. Wren Kt. Architect. Mr. Sam Foulks Mason. Sold by Joseph Smith at ye/Picture Shop in Exeter/Exchange in the Strand. 570 × 430/610 × 435mm. Elevation, ground plan, section. *Crace* 19.100 catalogue entry with date '1680'. An intruder, presumably, from *NTGB*. *NTGB* 36.

30 · 'SEYMOUR'S' SURVEY [1734–5]

Thirteen years after the publication of Strype's edition of Stow (no 25) another refurbishing of this invaluable Elizabethan *Survey* was launched. It was issued in Parts by J. Read from 1733 to 1735 under the pseudonym 'Robert Seymour' and was illus-trated with copper plates and woodcuts. Upcott describes it as a 'motley performance', a pun on the actual name of the man who wrote it, one John Mottley, a minor dramatist who in 1739 was to publish under another pseudonym *Joe Miller's Jests*. The issue of this work in folio Parts has been analysed in R.M. Wiles's *Serial publications in England before 1750* upon which this account is based.

Each Part, consisting of a signed fascicule of four sheets, was issued on a Saturday, price 6d. No 1 came out on 28 April 1733 (advertised in the *Daily Journal*, 19 April) and No 15 on 4 August (*Daily Advertiser*, 3 August). If weekly issues were maintained the fifty-fourth and final Part of the first volume would have been published by May 1734. By the last Saturday of October 1734 the second volume had reached its No 22 (*St James's Evening Post*, 24 October) so that its fifty-seventh and final Part must have been published and the work completed by June of 1735.

The unrevised sheets of Mottley's book were reissued in 1753 with new title-pages and with dedications to the Lord Mayor substituted for those to George II. The work was now said to be by 'a Gentleman of the Inner Temple'. Sections on the newly completed Westminster Bridge and Mansion House were announced, a promise apparently unfulfilled. The new title-page was aimed at antiquarians since it specifically mentions the long account of the antiquities of Westminster Abbey and drags in Sir William Dugdale's name.

A Survey of the Cities of London and Westminster, Borough of Southwark, And Parts Adjacent.... By Robert Seymour Esq: The Whole being an Improvement of Mr Stow's, and other Surveys, by adding whatever Alterations have happened in the said Cities &c. to the present Year ... Illustrated with several Copper Plates. Vol. I (II). London: Printed for J. Read in White-Fryars, Fleet-Street. MDCC,XXX,IV (M,DCC,XXXV).

Folio, about 395 × 254mm.   1734–5

COLLATION Vol. 1. Title-page; dedication to the monarch (2pp); pp 1–822, Survey. Vol. 2. Title-page; dedication to the Prime Minister, list of subscribers (2pp); pp 1–236, 257–869, Survey continued; pp 870–99, appendix. pp 901–18, index. (Text complete despite irregularity in pagination.)

The History and Survey of the Cities of London and Westminster, Borough of Southwark, And Parts Adja-cent.... In which is introduced Sir William Dugdale's

History of St Pauls Cathedral from its Foundations: Beautified with various Prospects of the Old Fabrick which was destroyed by the Fire of London, 1666. As also the Figures of the Tombs and Monuments therein as they stood in September, 1641, with their Epitaphs neatly imitated, which were defaced in the Grand Rebellion, with an Account of the Foundation and Structure of the New Church till finished: To which is prefixed the Effigies of Sir William Dugdale. Dedicated to Sir Crisp Gascoigne Knt. By a Gentleman of the Inner Temple. ('Vol.II' here in vol. 2) London: Printed for M. Cooper at the Globe in Paternoster-Row; W. Reeve, Fleet-Street and C. Sympson, at the Bible in Chancery Lane. MDCCLIII.

Folio, about 405 × 260mm.   1753

COLLATION Collates as first edition. New title-pages are substituted and in vol. 2 is a dedication to Sir Crisp Gascoigne (Lord Mayor 1752–3).

More parsimoniously illustrated than Strype's Stow of 1720, the earlier edition of this book contains only eight separate plates, of which seven relate to the text of vol. 1, a headpiece consisting of a long view and a map. The remaining illustrations are woodcuts or plates printed with the text, ten being of architectural subjects and 71 of shields of arms. The views, engraved by Thomas Bowles and Thomas Gardner, are all based on plates published in Strype's 1720 Stow but may be distinguished by the banderoles for the captions which are of the swallow-tailed, narrow (5mm) variety much favoured by the Bowles brothers. Modifications have been introduced in the following: Bethlehem Hospital shows a new wing; a clock added for symmetry by Kip to the N.W. tower of St Paul's Cathedral has been more truthfully left out; the Guildhall plate shows improvement of the architectural proportions and details and the costumes have been advanced from the age of Queen Anne to that of George II. References to this source in the list are abbreviated to S followed by Book and page number.

These plates were not transferred bodily to the 1753 edition where they seem to make only haphazard appearances. In an attempt to make good the deficiency and perhaps to vie with the new richly embellished editions of Strype's Stow and Maitland's *History* (no 33) then on the stocks the publishers bound into the two volumes 25 surviving plates from Sir William Dugdale's *History of St Paul's* (no 8). Unfortunately these worthies of old St Paul's, some of which bear Hollar's illustrious credit, were by now ghosts of their former selves,

worn out in the service of two editions of Dugdale and still carrying the page references (tr and tl) to the 1716 edition of *The History of St Paul's* in which they were last printed. These references are quoted in the list with the abbreviation *D* and those plates attributed by A.M. Hind to Hollar are identified by the number given them in his *Wenceslaus Hollar and his views of London and Windsor*.

VOL. 1 (1734)

1 p 3   (headpiece, a view of the City from the South Bank) 112 × 215/120 × 228mm.

2 p 3   (in panel tl) A Map of/London, Westminster/and Southwark./With ye New Buildings to ye Year 1733. 255 × 475/260 × 480mm. (*Darlington and Howgego* 78)

3 pp 15–21 (inset with text, seven City Gates) Woodcuts. About 80–90 × 70mm.

4 p 45   (on banderole) London Bridge. Tho. Gardner sc. 195 × 320/215 × 340mm. Slight variations in sky, water, staffage; otherwise as S 1, 53.

5 p 56   (on banderole) The Tower of London. Tho. Gardner sculp. 194 × 324/210 × 340mm. Variations from Kip: fewer and differently placed cannon barrels on wharf, different staffage, water more agitated and a number of skiffs moored at steps to W.; otherwise follows S 1, 64.

6 p 186   (on banderole) Bethlam Hospital. Thos. Bowles sculp. 205 × 335/210 × 337mm. Adds an extension to the pavilion on the l., curved re-entrant walls flanking the main gateway, the near side to the railed walk in the foreground and different staffage; otherwise follows S 1, 192.

7 p 401   (on banderole) The Royall Exchange. T. Bowles sculp. 248 × 315/260 × 323mm. Foreground now paved and staffage added in front colonnade and portico. Courtyard pavement is shown as chequered and the sky much modified; otherwise as S 2, 135.

8 p 450   (tc) The Monument. T. Bowles sculp. 325 × 203/340 × 205mm. From the same viewpoint but cutting off one bay from houses on each side, dragons on pedestal given forked tails and a pavement with posts added in front; otherwise as S 2, 180.

9 p 542   (on banderole) Guild Hall. T. Bowles sculp. 218 × 340/224 × 350mm. The Corinthian capitals of the colonnade on the l. and the transoms of the window-openings above are more carefully drawn, a wider-angled view is shown, a paved pathway added to the cobbled courtyard which is staffed with people in contemporary costume; clearly an on-site revision of S 3, 51.

10 p 651   (tc) The Front or West end of St Pauls. T. Bowles sculp. 350 × 292mm pl. mark. Kip's view shows a clock in the N.W. tower to balance that in the S.W., both pointing to 12 o'clock, but Bowles has

corrected this error, engraving a blank dial on the N.W. He has also eliminated some of the statues from the parapet; otherwise follows *S* 3, 156.

11 p 651 (inset with text the pre-Fire W. front) Woodcut. 65 × 60mm.

12 p 706 Allhallows Breadstreet. G. Druce delin. T. Bowles sculp. 200 × 190/215 × 200mm, on text page.

13 p 796 (inset with text) Temple Bar. Woodcut. 80 × 75mm.

VOL. 2 (1734)

14 pp 337–60 (inset in text, arms of 12 principal Livery Companies) Woodcuts. About 76 × 76mm.

15 pp 360–407 (inset in text, arms of 59 other Companies) Woodcuts. About 45 × 35mm.

16 p 497 (on banderole) Westminster Abbey. T. Bowles sculp. 205 × 330/215 × 340mm. From the same viewpoint but detail altered, especially the front of the N. transept. A more pronounced ogee arch to the N. entrance to which railings and a paved access-path have been added; otherwise follows *S* 6, 7.

VOL. 1 (1753, additional or alternative plates)

17 front. Gulielmus Dugdale/Aetatis 50. A.MDCLVI. Wen. Hollar delin. et sculp. 218 × 168/235 × 170mm. The portrait or 'Effigies' promised on the title-page. *D* front.

18 p 116 (in panel tc) Capella Thomae Kempe London Ep:. 225 × 250/235 × 260mm. *D* 40. (*Hind* 47)

19 p 181 (in panel tc) Clausura circa Altare/S.Erkenwaldi. W. Hollar fecit 1657. 235 × 170/238 × 175mm. *D* 114. (*Hind* 67)

20 p 241 (tl) In superiori parte Chori prope Altare. 275 × 180mm pl. mark. *D* 60. (*Hind* 49)

21 p 520 (tc) Inter Orientalem partem Ecclesiae et alam australem. 275 × 210mm pl. mark. *D* 82.

22 p 552 (in panel tl) Henricus de Wengham. W. Hollar delin: et sculp. 200 × 270/205 × 275mm. *D* 80. (*Hind* 55)

23 p 553 (tl) In australi Insula a latere Chori. W. Hollar fecit. 260 × 187mm pl. mark. *D* 78. (*Hind* 54)

24 p 608 (in panel tc) In fornice aquilonalis muri ex opposito Chori. 192 × 254/195 × 260mm. Badly reworked Hollar plate. *D* 94. (*Hind* 59)

25 p 645 (tc) In Australi ala/a latere Chori. W. Hollar fecit. 320 × 160mm pl. mark. *D* 74. (*Hind* 52)

26 p 689 (tc) In australi ala ex adverso Chori. W. Hollar fec. 277 × 190mm pl. mark. *D* 72. (*Hind* 51)

27 p 721 (in panel tc) Thomas Heneage Eques Auratus … 285 × 190mm pl. mark. *D* 110.

28 p 748 (tc) Tumulus Henrici de Lacie/Comitis Lincolniae. W. Hollar delin: et sculp:. 275 × 185mm pl. mark. *D* 84. (*Hind* 56)

29 p 769 (tc) Inter alam aquilonalem et Chorum,/

Tumulus Rogeri Cognom: Nigri … W. Hollar fecit. 227 × 170/234 × 173mm. *D* 86. (*Hind* 57)

VOL. 2 (1753, additional or alternative plates)

30 p 229 (tc) Monumentum Septentrionali/Muro Chori affixum. 282 × 185mm pl. mark. *D* 96.

31 p 289 (tc) In Pariete Aquilonali/ex opposito Chori. W. Hollar delin: et sculp:. 303 × 165mm pl. mark. *D* 96. (*Hind* 60)

32 p 348 (in panel tc) In aquilonali muro ex adverso Chori. W. Hollar delin: et sculp:. 168 × 230/173 × 235mm. *D* 100. (*Hind* 61)

33 p 369 (in panel tc) Ecclesiae Parochialis S. Fidis/Prospectus Interior. W. Hollar delin: et sculp:. 187 × 330/200 × 334mm. *D* 117. (*Hind* 33)

34 p 384 (centre)Tumulus Radulphi de Hengham … W. Hollar delin: et sculp. 283 × 194mm pl. mark. *D* 102. (*Hind* 62)

35 p 461 (tc) Tumulus Simonis Burley Militis. W. Hollar delineavit et sculpsit. 283 × 193mm pl. mark. *D* 104. (*Hind* 63)

36 p 512 (tc) In ala boreali: ex adverso Chori. 275 × 160mm pl. mark. *D* 106. (*Hind* 64)·

37 p 581 (tc) Tumulus Iohannis Wolley Eq. Aur:. 266 × 183mm pl. mark. *D* 108. (*Hind* 65)

38 p 753 (in panel tc) Domus Capitularis Sti Pauli a/Meridie Prospectus. W. Hollar delineavit et sculpsit. 195 × 290/200 × 292mm. *D* 128. (*Hind* 34)

39 p 805 (in panel tc) Partis exterioris Chori, ab Occidente/prospectus. W. Hollar delineavit et sculp:. 215 × 320/236 × 325mm. *D* 146. (*Hind* 44)

40 p 825 (along top) Areae Ecclesiae Cathedralis Sti Pauli Ichnographia. Iohn Harris sculp. 230 × 345mm pl. mark. A copy of Hollar's plate. *D* 161. (*Hind* 36)

41 p 860 Orientalis Partis Eccl: Cath: S: Pauli Prospectus Interior. W. Hollar fecit. 290 × 210/305 × 216mm. *D* 148. (*Hind* 46).

31 · VERTUE'S HEADS OF THE KINGS* [1736]

George Vertue, a pupil of Michael Van der Gucht, was later set to work in Sir Godfrey Kneller's academy and soon made his reputation as an engraver of portraits which were much in demand for book frontispieces. In 1717 he became a member of the Society of Antiquaries and was appointed its official engraver. It was therefore natural when the brothers Knapton were preparing their folio edition of Tindal's translation of the French *History of England* by Rapin de Thoyras (4 vols, 1732–47) that they should turn to him for advice on its illustration. Under his supervision 42 portraits and 22 plates of sepulchral monuments were engraved between 1734 and 1736 and were bound in as illustrations, with Vertue's explanatory notes prefixed to the first volume. His Westminster Abbey monuments illustrate the first two volumes.

For customers who preferred engravings to history the publishers decided to make up the eighteenth century equivalent of a 'coffee table' book containing only the plates with Vertue's notes. In their catalogue the Knaptons offer the first two volumes of Rapin in folio complete with 'Heads and Monuments on 77 Folio Copper Plates' but the plates are also available separately, 42 'Heads' at 14s and the 'Monuments' as follows: 'This Sett of Monuments of the Kings &c. in nineteen Half-Sheets and three Whole-Sheet Plates, may be had at 7s. N.B. Gentlemen who have Mr. Rapin's History bound up without the Prints, may have the Heads and Monuments to go with the History sewed up in Paste-boards or bound'. Of these we are only concerned here with the 11 Westminster Abbey plates. The majority of them are drawn by the French artist François Gravelot who was to become a much sought after book illustrator with fine frontispieces and interpretative illustrations to his credit, of which the most famous are perhaps his plates for Theobald's edition of Shakespeare (1740). This work for Knapton, however, was no doubt one of his first commissions on arriving in England in 1732–3 at the invitation of Claude du Bosc, the Parisian engraver who undertook the engraving of five of the plates listed below. Later in his career Gravelot was again associated with Vertue in *Heads of Illustrious Persons of Great Britain* (1743–51); in this series he surrounded Houbraken's portraits with elaborate decoration in wash and Vertue engraved their joint effort. In *Heads of the Kings* there are outstanding examples of his genius for designing elegant rococo frameworks; in particular the two suitably pompous settings for his drawings of Henry VII's tomb and its parclose. He later returned to the Abbey and drew some of the more recent monuments to supplement, in the second

(1742) edition of Dart's *Westmonasterium* (no 27), James Coles's original plates.

Although only the separate plates of Westminster monuments are itemized below it is worth mentioning that under Vertue's 'Head' of Henry III he has engraved a tiny N. view of that monarch's beloved Abbey (55 × 95mm) with a miniature inset of the heart of his great building, the shrine of Edward the Confessor.

The Heads of the Kings of England, proper for Mr Rapin's History, Translated by N. Tindal, M.A. viz. Egbert First Monarch … And all the succeeding Kings and Sovereign Queens, to the Revolution; with some of the most illustrious Princes of the Royal Family. Collected, Drawn, and Engraven, with ornaments and Decorations, By George Vertue. To which are added, the Heads of Mr Rapin and N. Tindal, M.A. and an Account of the several Heads, of the Antiquities that have been followed, and of the Pictures copied for engraving them. Also Twenty-two Plates of the Monuments of the Kings of England, with their Epitaphs, and Inscriptions, and a brief Historical Account of Them. London: Printed for James, John and Paul Knapton, at the Crown in Ludgate Street. MDCCXXXVI.

Folio, 520 × 350mm.   1736

COLLATION Title-page; dedication to Frederick, Prince of Wales (1 leaf); pp 5–8, The Heads; pp 9–12, The Monuments; 42 portrait plates and 22 engravings of monuments, with transcripts of their epitaphs and decorative frames including heraldic cartouches, trophies, torches, lamps, S-scrolls, helms, cornucopia, etc.

Vertue and his artists are clearly dependent for their images of the actual Westminster Abbey monuments on the plates which Hollar and Gaywood engraved to illustrate Sandford's *Genealogical History* (no 12) in 1677. The relevant page reference to this book is therefore given after each description, with the abbreviation *S*.

The Monuments in Westminster Abbey

1 (1) (on banderole divided by cartouche along bm) The Monument of King Edward the Confessor (along bm) In Westminster Abbey. G.Vertue Sct. 350 × 220/365 × 230mm. From a drawing by William Talman made in 1713.

2 (6) The Monument of King Henry III, in Westminster Abbey. Gravelot f. J.V. Schley sculp. 1735. 350 × 225/365 × 230mm. *S* 92.

3 (7) The Monument in Westminster Abbey of K. Edward I. G. Vertue sc. 350 × 220/365 × 230mm. *S* 137.

4 (10) The Monument of King Edward III/in Westmins-

ter Abbey. Gravelot del. C. Du Bosc fecit. 350 × 220/370 × 225mm. *S* 176.

5 (11) The Monument of King Richard II/& Ann his Queen in Westminster Abbey. Gravelot del. Cl. du Bosc fecit. 350 × 220/370 × 230mm. *S* 203.

6 (13) The Monument in Westminster Abbey of K. Henry V. Gravelot del. G. Vertue sculp. 350 × 218/370 × 225mm. Screen, gates, gallery. *S* 281.

7 (14) The Monument of King Henry V in Westminster Abbey. P. Yver sculpsit 1735. 352 × 220/360 × 230mm. Tomb chest and effigy with head restored by the engraver. *S* 282.

8 (16) (on banderole in work along tm) The Monument of King Edward and his Brother Richard (bm) in Westminster Abbey. G. Vertue sct. 347 × 215/365 × 225mm. *S* 403.

9 (17) A Stately Monument in Memory of K: Henry VII. and his Queen, curiously wrought, made of Copper and gilt with Gold; erected in his Magnificent and Royal Chappel in Westminster Abbey. (in work) Pietro Torrigiano Sculptore Fiorentino fecit 1519. Gravelot d. Geo: Vertue Londini Sculpsit 1735. 345 × 348/365 × 460mm. The parclose screen round the tomb chest. *S* 442.

10 (18) The Monument of King Henry VII in Westminster Abbey. Gravelot del. Cl. Du Bosc fecit. 345 × 438/380 × 455mm. Tomb chest and effigies. *S* 443.

11 (19) (on banderole in work along tm) The Monument of King Edward VI (bm) This Monumt (of Brass) was erected in the Chapple of K. Henry VII. at Westminster, at the Head of/His Monument, and destroy'd in the time of the Civil Wars. G. Vertue sculp. 350 × 220/370 × 230mm. *S* 471.

12 (20) The Monument of Mary Queen of Scots in Westminster Abbey. Gravelot del. Cl. Du Bosc fecit.355 × 220/380 × 230mm. *S* 506.

13 (21) The Monument of Queen Elizabeth in Westminster Abbey. Gravelot del. Cl. Du Bosc fecit. 355 × 215/375 × 225mm. *S* 493.

32 · WEST AND TOMS'S ANCIENT CHURCHES [1736–9]

This excellent series of large engravings of pre-Fire churches is a pioneer in this field of antiquarian illustration and an indispensable record of the appearance of London churches mostly now vanished without trace or demolished and rebuilt. It is the joint work of Robert West and William Henry Toms, an engraver to whom John Boydell, the future print publisher and Lord Mayor of London, was to be bound as an apprentice in 1741. During their years of partnership from 1735 to 1739 West and Toms produced together not only the 26 etched plates here described but also four smaller ones to illustrate Maitland's *History of London* (no 33) published in 1739. Later Toms turned to another artist, J.B. Chatelain, for London views; he engraved five of his drawings of Hampstead Heath and three of Highgate in 1745 (*Crace* 36.83, 104) and two of St James's Park, published by Robert Sayer in 1752 (BL Maps: *K. top.* 26.7c,k).

To begin with the artist and engraver themselves published their views by subscription, in two series of a dozen each with the intention that they should be bound with their two title-pages to form an oblong folio volume. Following each title is a list of subscribers which includes the following: Thomas Bowles, Nathaniel Buck, James Cole, H. Gravelot (all engravers); George Dance, James Gibbs, James Leoni, Isaac Ware (architects); John Pine, John Tinney (printsellers); William Maitland, the historian of London and antiquary and—perhaps from family loyalty—Lieutenants Peter and Philip Toms.

The earliest plates of the series, those of St Leonard, Shoreditch, from drawings of 1734–5, were omitted from the collection until a selection of the plates (items 1,3,5,7,9,11,13,15,17–18,19,21,23 and St Leonard's) was later issued by Robert Sayer. They are listed in the 1775 Sayer & Bennett catalogue as *Fourteen Perspective Views of antient Churches and other Buildings, all now standing in London, which escaped the great fire.* 'Each print is 12 inches wide by 11, price 10s 6d. the set'. These were still extant in 1880 when R.H. Laurie issued his collection *Views of the City of London* (no 191) consisting of 71 plates from the stocks of Robert Sayer, Bowles & Carver and of Laurie & Whittle. Both these reissues are noted below.

Each engraving is surrounded by a single or double black border-line with the caption above, along tm and below; bl the name and title of the notable to whom 'This Plate is Humbly Inscribed by the Proprietors Robert West and Willm. Henry Toms'; bc the arms of the dedicatee; br a history of the church and sometimes of its patron saint. Otherwise no text accompanies the plates.

Credits and publication-lines are, with one exception, uniform for each series: Ser 1, 'R. West Delin. 1736. W.H. Toms sculpt. Publish'd March 16, 1736'; Ser 2, 'R. West Delin. 1737. W.H. Toms sculpt. Publish'd March 18, 1739' (with the exception of pl. 7 which West drew in 1736). In the Sayer reissues the above publication-lines are burnished out and replaced by 'Printed for Robt Sayer in Fleetstreet', a line retained in the Laurie collection third state, where serial numbers running from '47' to '60' are engraved tr on each plate.

SER 1

Perspective Views of all the Ancient Churches, and other Buildings, In the Cities of London, and Westminster, and Parts adjacent within the Bills of Mortality. Drawn by Robert West, and Engraved by William Henry Toms. Part 1. Containing Twelve Parish Churches within the City of London, being all that are now standing, which escaped the Fire in 1666, Viz.

Alhallows Barking.	St. Helen.
Alhallows Staining.	St. Katherine Coleman.
Alhallows London-Wall.	St. Katherine Cree-Church.
St. Alphage.	St. Martin Outwich.
St. Andrew Under-Shaft.	St. Olave Hart-Street.
St. Ethelburgh.	St. Peter le Poor.

London: Printed for the Proprietors, Robert West, at the Blue Spike in Compton-Street Soho, Painter; and William Henry Toms, in Union Court, opposite to St. Andrew's Church, in Holbourn, Engraver; and Published, March 16, 1736.

Oblong folio, 356 × 470mm.   1736

1 pl.1 The South-East Prospect of the Church of Alhallows Barking. 235 × 300/280 × 312mm. Reissued by Sayer. '53' in the third state.

2 pl.2 The South-West Prospect of the Church of Alhallows Staining. 235 × 300/280 × 314mm. Demolished except for tower 1870.

3 pl.3 The South-East Prospect of the Church of Alhallows London Wall. 235 × 302/285 × 315mm. Reissued by Sayer. '47' in the third state.

4 pl.4 The South Prospect of the Church of St Alphage. 237 × 307/285 × 318mm.

5 pl.5 The North-West Prospect of the Church of St Andrew Undershaft. 238 × 305/285 × 315mm. Reissued by Sayer. '50' in the third state.

6 pl.6 The West Prospect of the Church of St Ethelburga. 238 × 300/285 × 312mm.

7 pl.7 The South-West Prospect of the Church of St. Helen. 232 × 300/280 × 314mm. Reissued by Sayer. '60' in the third state.

8 pl.8 The South Prospect of the Church of St Katherine Coleman. 235 × 300/280 × 314mm. Rebuilt at about this time, demolished 1926.

9 pl.9 The South-West Prospect of the Church of St Katherine Creechurch. 236 × 305/285 × 318mm. Reissued by Sayer. '54' in the third state.

10 pl.10 The North-East Prospect of the Church of St Martin Outwich. 240 × 308/285 × 320mm. Rebuilt 1796, demolished 1874.

11 pl.11 The North-East Prospect of the Church of St Olave Hart-Street. 235 × 302/281 × 314mm. Reissued by Sayer. '52' in the third state.

12 pl.12 The South-East Prospect of the Church of St Peter le Poor. 242 × 310/288 × 324mm. Rebuilt 1792, demolished 1907.

SER 2

Perspective Views of all the Ancient Churches, and other Buildings, in the Cities of London, and Westminster, and Parts adjacent, within the Bills of Mortality. Drawn by Robert West, and Engraved by William Henry Toms. Part II Containing Twelve Ancient Churches and Chapels within the Liberty of London, &c. viz.

St. Bartholomew the Great.	St. Olave in Southwark.
	St. Saviour in Southwark.
St. Bartholomew the Less.	St. Sepulchre.
St. Botolph without Aldersgate.	The Temple Church.
	The Chapel Royal in the Tower.
St. Botolph without Aldgate.	K. Henry VII's Chapel at Westminster.
St. Dunstan in the West.	
St. Giles without Cripplegate.	

London: Printed for the Proprietors, Robert West in Compton Street, Soho, Painter: and William Henry Toms in Union Court, near Hatton-Garden, Holborn, Engraver: and Publish'd March 18, 1739.

Oblong folio, 356 × 470mm.   1739

13 pl.1 The West Prospect of the Church of St Bartholomew the Great. 235 × 300/280 × 310mm. Reissued by Sayer. '51' in the third state.

14 pl.2 The South-West Prospect of the Church of St Bartholomew the Less. 233 × 298/280 × 314mm.

15 pl.3 The North-East Prospect of the Church of St Botolph without Aldersgate. 235 × 305/280 × 314mm. Reissued by Sayer. '49' in the third state.

16 pl.4 The North-West Prospect of the Church of St Botolph without Aldgate. 230 × 305/280 × 312mm.

17 pl.5 The South-East Prospect of the Church of St Dunstan in the West. 232 × 304/280 × 310mm. Reissued by Sayer. In the third state no '58' and Sayer's publication-line replaced by 'London, published by R.H. Laurie, No 53 Fleet Street'.

18 pl.6 The South-West Prospect of the Church of St Giles without Cripplegate. 232 × 305/280 × 310mm. Reissued by Sayer. '56' in the third state.

19 pl.7 The South Prospect of the Church of St Olave in Southwark. 235 × 300/280 × 310mm. 'R. West Delin.

1736'. Reissued by Sayer. '57' in the third state. The 'history' states 'this was the last Church in or about London, that was remarkable for having 4 Isles and 3 rows of Pillars: towards the close of ye year 1736 ye whole N. row with ye roofs of ye 2 northern Isles suddenly fell down, since which ye Steeple, with ye rest of ye Church was entirely demolished, & is now (in 1738) rebuilding'. The rebuilding was by Flitcroft but his church was demolished 1926–8.

20 pl.8 The South Prospect of the Church of St Saviour in Southwark. 230 × 305/280 × 314mm.

21 pl.9 The South Prospect of the Church of St Sepulchre. 232 × 305/280 × 312mm. Reissued by Sayer. '59' in the third state.

22 pl.10 The South-East Prospect of the Temple Church. 230 × 302/280 × 312mm.

23 pl.11 The South-East Prospect of the Chapel Royal of St Peter in the Tower. 235 × 308/280 × 315mm. Reissued by Sayer. '48' in the third state.

24 pl.12 The South-East Prospect of King Henry the VII's Chapel at Westminster. 232 × 306/280 × 310mm.

Supplementary plates(not in bound collection)

25 The East Prospect of the Church of St Leonard Shoreditch. R.West delin. 1735. W.H. Toms sculp. 220 × 292/265 × 300mm. Reissued by Sayer. '55' in the third state. The 'history' below states that the church shown was declared by surveyors to be ruinous in 1734 and pulled down in 1736. George Dance the elder built the present structure, 1736–40, and Toms made a large engraving of this also, published in 1742 (BL Maps: *K. top.* 23.23.1e).

26 The South West Prospect of the Church of St Leonard Shoreditch. R. West delin. 1734. W.H. Toms sculpt. 220 × 292/265 × 300mm.

33 · MAITLAND'S HISTORY OF LONDON [1739]

William Maitland, a Scottish merchant from Brechin, having acquired wealth in trade with Europe settled in London to his antiquarian pursuits and the writing of history and was elected FRS in 1733 and FSA in 1735. Richard Gough in his *British Topography* expressed a poor opinion of his scholarship, describing him as self-conceited and credulous, but his chief work, *The History of London*, was a popular success and ran through several editions. He announced its first publication in the *London Daily Post and General Advertiser* of 26 April 1737 and his 'Proposals for Printing by Subscription' are dated 3 May. He promised folio Numbers of six sheets to be delivered fortnightly at subscribers' addresses. The whole work was to run to 200 sheets, or 800 pages of letterpress and 'a Variety of Copper Plates'. The author himself was collecting subscriptions 'At the Dial opposite the Old Jury in the Poultry' and quoted 'Two Guineas the Small Paper, and Four Guineas the Royal, or Large Paper' or 1s and 2s per Number respectively. By 12 May 1738 23 Numbers had been delivered (*Daily Post*, 18 May 1738). The printer was Samuel Richardson, better known as a novelist, who put himself down for five copies and praised the work in his edition of Defoe's *Tour thro' Great Britain* (3rd ed, 1742, vol. 2, p 84). The title-page of the complete work, which includes a list of subscribers, is dated 1739.

The History of London, from its foundation by the Romans, to the present time.... With the several accounts of Westminster, Middlesex, Southwark and other parts within The Bill of Mortality. In Nine Books. The Whole Illustrated with a Variety of Fine Cuts. With a Compleat Index. By William Maitland, F.R.S., London, Printed by Samuel Richardson, in Salisbury Court near Fleet-street, MDCCXXXIX.

Folio, 457 × 279mm.   1739

COLLATION Title-page; dedication to the monarch (2pp); pp v–viii, preface dated 26 March 1739; list of subscribers (7pp); pp 1–800, The History; index, errata (14pp).

Chief responsibility for the illustrations rests with William Henry Toms who engraved 21 of the 24 separate plates, four of them in association with Robert West, the partnership which also produced *Perspective Views of Ancient Churches* (no 32). The balance consists of three historical maps showing the town in 1560, 1642–3 and 1666. There is no map of contemporary London and Maitland says in his preface that this was because none suitable was available at the time. Inset with the text are an allegorical engraved headpiece by L.P. Boitard, eight small views of the City Gates engraved by T. Bowles (with his credit on the first) and a series of woodcuts of City Company arms. The selection of views corresponds to that for the 1720 Stow (no 25), the exceptions being plates of St Bride's Church and of five buildings erected since that date. There are fresh views of St Paul's Cathedral, the City Gates and two buildings in course of alteration: St Bartholomew's Hospital and Westminster Abbey. Where, as in most cases, the subjects coincide Toms has clearly based his engraving on the Kip image in the 1720 Stow. In the list this source is abbreviated as *S*, followed by Book and page number. What Toms did not copy are the caption banderoles characteristic of Kip's plates: captions appear in bm and the Maitland page number is engraved tr as a guide to the binder since there is no list of plates.

1 front. (on banderole between Tudor royal arms and City arms) A View of London about the year 1560. (along bm) Reduced … from a large Print in the Collection of Sr Hans Sloane Bart. anno 1738. 252 × 464/310 × 470mm. Refs A–Z, a–z,1–47. For the origins of this map see *Darlington and Howgego* pp 17–19 and Stephen Marks, *The map of sixteenth century London,* pp 18–20.

2 p 1 (allegorical headpiece) C. Frederick, Armiger Inv. Boitard sculp. 60 × 162/70 × 175mm.

3 pp 15–22 (engr on text pages) Ald-Gate. T. Bowles fecit – Bishops-Gate – Moore-Gate – Cripple-gate – Alders-Gate – New-Gate – Lud-Gate – Bridge-Gate. Each about 115 × 85mm.

4 p 33 London Bridge. Toms sc. 197 × 321/210 × 334mm. Slight alterations to sky and staffage; otherwise as *S* 1,53.

5 p 238 A Plan of the City and Suburbs of London as fortified by Order of Parliament in the Year 1642 & 1643. G. Vertue sc. 1738. 195 × 340/222 × 355mm. Explanation of forts on scrolls on each side.

6 p 293 A Plan of the City and Liberties of London after the Dreadful Conflagration in the Year 1666/The blank Part whereof represents the Ruins and Extent of the Fire & the Perspective that left standing. E. Bowen sculp. 203 × 331/230 × 342mm. Refs (tr) A–Z, a–o and (bl) 1–100 to churches. Based on a Hollar plan (*Hind* 11). (*Darlington and Howgego* 19)

7 p 395 St Brigit alias St Brides-Church. Toms sculp. 333 × 210/360 × 226mm.

8 p 433 Guild Hall. Toms sc. 205 × 324/225 × 210mm. Sky altered, architectural detail improved with the central bay heightened, the pinnacles redrawn and details of colonnade brought out; also staffage updated; otherwise as *S* 3,51.

9 p 440 The Monument. W.H. Toms sculpt. 328 × 205/348 × 210mm. The house on the left has an extra bay; sky, shops and staffage slightly altered; otherwise as *S* 2,180.

10 p 452 Bow Church. W.H. Toms sculpt. 325 × 200/350 × 212mm. The houses to right of the church rebuilt; sky and shop fronts altered, staffage up to date; otherwise as *S* 3,25.

11 p 460 The Lord Mayor's House. G. Dance Architect. Toms sculp. 220 × 290mm pl. mark. With a scale of feet. This must have been based on the architect's elevation since the foundation stone was laid only in October 1739. It shows the Mansion House without the unfortunate afterthought, the second attic popularly known as 'The Mare's Nest'.

12 p 466 The Royal Exchange. Toms sculp. 223 × 287/240 × 300mm. Foreground with title on panel omitted and the sky and internal arcade altered; otherwise as *S* 2,135.

13 p 483 The West Prospect of St Paul's Cathedral. Toms sculp. 428 × 365/454 × 390mm. Independent of Kip's engraving.

14 p 493 The Tower of London. Toms sc. 205 × 321/224 × 340mm. Sky is altered and less staffage on quay; otherwise follows closely *S* 1,64.

(pp 598–617 Woodcut arms of the City Companies printed with text)

15 p 622 A Perspective View of the Bank of England. R. West delin. Toms sculp. 335 × 212/360 × 225mm. George Sampson's nucleus, completed 1734. (*Bank of England* 11)

16 p 660 Bethlehem Hospital. Toms sculp. 195 × 381/215 × 390mm. Wings added l. and r. beyond the terminal pavilions, central tower redrawn and staffage modernized. *S* 1,192.

17 p 661 Bridewell. Toms sculp. 200 × 324/225 × 340mm. Hatching added to blank sky and small architectural details altered, eg the oriel window l. of centre. Staffage reduced from *S* 1,176.

18 p 661 The Charter-House Hospital. Toms sculp. 202 × 318/224 × 330mm. More trees planted and an extra fence added in the foreground; staffage added to rear; otherwise as *S* 1,205.

19 p 662 Christ's Hospital. Toms sc. 207 × 320/225 × 330mm. The steeple has been redrawn and given greater prominence (192mm as against 165mm tall); staffage has been renewed and drying-lines added to foreground; otherwise as *S* 1,175.

20 p 667 Guys Hospital. R. West delin. 1738. W.H. Toms sculp. 198 × 362/228 × 373mm. Built 1722–5.

21 p 675 A Perspective View of St Bartholomew's Hospital. Jacobo Gibbs Architecto. R. West delin. Toms sculp. 212 × 315/230 × 327mm. Gibbs started work on the Great Quadrangle in 1730.

22 p 676 St George's Hospital. Toms sculp. 200 × 328/225 × 333mm. Lanesborough House, converted by Isaac Ware, 1733.

23 p 678 St Thomas's Hospital. Toms sc. 312 × 202/333 × 222mm. Shows considerable rebuilding in fore and

rear courts where extra storeys are added; staffage renewed; otherwise as *S* 1,189.

24 p 686 A Perspective View of the Collegiate Church of St. Peter Westminster with the Towers & Spire as Design'd by Sr Christopher Wren. Toms sculp. 410 × 320/445 × 340mm. The W. towers were designed by Hawksmoor in 1734 and completed by John James, c 1745.

25 p 371 The South West Prospect of the Church of St Martin in the Fields. Jacobo Gibbs Archto. R. West delin. 1738. W.H. Toms sculp. 410 × 320/445 × 340mm. Gibbs completed the rebuilding in 1726.

26 p 738 St James's Palace and Parts adjacent. Toms sc. 190 × 327/210 × 340mm. The outline of the dome of St Paul's has been improved and new church steeples (St Martin in the Fields, St Giles in the Fields) added; foreground staffage and statues are altered; otherwise as *S* 6,4.

34 · VITRUVIUS BRITTANICUS VOLUME THE FOURTH* [1739]

A pendant to Colen Campbell's *Vitruvius Britannicus* (no 24) which really has more affinity to *Nouveau Théâtre de la Grande Bretagne* (no 22) was published in 1739 for J. Badeslade and John Rocque the cartographer and mapseller. It consists of an engraved title, a dedication and descriptions followed by large plates, numbered 1–113, drawn by Rocque, T. Badeslade and the architect John Price and engraved by Vivarez, Chatelain, G. Van der Gucht, H. Hulsbergh, Thomas Bowles, John Harris, R. Parr and P. Fourdrinier. Four royal palaces and 37 country houses are surveyed in considerable detail, including their gardens.

Few of the original copies survive but it was fortunately included in the reduced facsimile of all volumes bearing this title, introduced by John Harris and published by Benjamin Blom (New York, 1967–70).

Here are listed the few plates of buildings erected, or intended for erection, in London and its environs, including one of the Navy Office in Seething Lane which was earlier published in the fourth volume of *Nouveau Théâtre de la Grande Bretagne*.

(*Title-page* pl. 1)

Folio, about 510 × 345mm.   1739

COLLATION Title-page; pp 1–4, dedication to Frederick, Prince of Wales; pp 5–12, description of the plates; 113 plates.

1 (engr title) Vitruvius Brittanicus,/Volume the Fourth./Being a/Collection of/Plans, Elevations, and Perspective Views,/of the/Royal Palaces,/Noblemen, and Gentlemens Seats,/in/Great Britain,/Not Exhibited in any Collection of this nature hitherto published./(rule) Design'd by/J. Badeslade and J. Rocque, &c./And Engraven by the Best Hands./ (rule and miniature engraving) The Royal Palace of Richmond in Surrey (rule) London/Printed for, and Sold by John Wilcox in the Strand, George Foster at the White/Horse in St Paul's Church Yard, and Henry Chappelle in Grosvenor Street./ (rule)/ MDCCXXXIX.

2 pl.2–3 (tm) Veue du Palais de Kensington du Côté de l'Orient. J. Rocque delineavit. Vivaret sculpt. Sold at the Canister & Sugar Loaf in Great/Windmill Street St James, London. Published ... 1736. 254 × 460/285 × 519mm.

3 pl.4–5 (in cartouche br, dedicated to the Prince of Wales) This Plan of ye Royal/Palace and Gardens of/Hampton Court. Sold at the Canister & Sugar Loaf in Great/Windmill Street St James, London. Published ... 1736. 405 × 530/431 × 550mm. Refs 1–20.

4 pl.6–7 (tm) Veue de la Maison Royale de Richmond du Côté du Midi à 3 Lieues de Londres 1736. Chatelain sculp. Sold at the Canister & Sugar Loaf in Great/Windmill Street St James, London. 405 × 534/440 × 550mm. Shows chiefly the garden.

5 pl.8–9 (tm) Veue de la Maison Royale de Richmond du Côté de la Tamise à 3 Lieues de Londres. Chatelain sculp. Londini. Sold at the Canister & Sugar Loaf in Great/Windmill Street St James, London. Published ... 1736. 402 × 533/438 × 555mm.

6 pl.9–10 (in cartouche tr) Plan of the House Gardens Park & Hermitage of their/Majesty's at Richmond & the Prince of Wales at Kew. Gravé par J. Rocque 1736. 430 × 580/435 × 585mm.

7 pl.28–9 The Elevation of a New House Intended for His Grace ye Duke of Chandos in Mary-Bone Fields. J. Price Inven: & Del. H. Hulsbergh sculp. 375 × 600/386 × 615mm. Designed by John Price in 1720 for erection in Cavendish Square but never built.

8 pl.82–3 (in cartouche tl) Plan du Jardin & Vue des Maisons de Chiswick sur la/Tamise à deux Lieues de Londres. J. Rocque del. et sculp. Sold at the Canister & Sugar Loaf in Great/Windmill Street St James, London. Published ... 1736. 590 × 758/595 × 770mm. A series of small views of Cassina, etc surrounds a plan of the garden.

9 pl.112–13 (on banderole supported by four putti) The Navy Office London. (bm) To the Right Honourable the Principal Officers & Commissioners of His Majesties Navy/This Prospect ... is humbly presented by ... Tho. Taylor Anno 1714. 425 × 590/475 × 595mm. *Nouveau Théâtre*, item 65.

35 · HISTORY AND PRESENT STATE OF THE BRITISH ISLANDS [1743]

This anonymous two-volume survey of Great Britain (in Guildhall Library, S 9.14/2, and a copy noted in the US *National Union Catalogue*), although self-contained, has printed bl on the first pages of each volume 'Vol.XIV' and 'Vol.XV' respectively and the plates in the first volume are referred to 'vol.14'. The preface starts: 'Having given a Description of the several Kingdoms and States of the Continent of Europe ...', so they clearly belong to a sequence of volumes covering Europe or the world. No such work, published around 1743, is identifiable from library catalogues examined but everything points to these being survivors from an anonymous adaptation of a multi-volume history by Thomas Salmon of which publication commenced in about 1725. Lowndes gives particulars of this *Modern History or Present State of all the Nations* and, following Watt, says that it was abridged, continued and published under various fictitious names. Apparently it was also published in Numbers, since the *Gentleman's Magazine* for July 1731 announces publication of No 82, which was Part 3 of 'Vol.XIV' and was concerned with Great Britain. The US *National Union Catalogue* enters a 32 volume set of 1725–9 from various publishers and later editions, quoted by Watt (1739) and in the British Library (1744–6), have a title closely relating to that of the work under discussion:

Modern History or Present State of all Nations, describing their respective Situations, Persons, Habits, Buildings, Manners, Laws and Customs, Religion and Policy; Arts and Sciences; Trades, Manufactures and Husbandry; Plants, Animals and Minerals; illustrated with Cuts and Maps accurately drawn, according to the geographical parts of this work by Hermann Moll.

The History and present state of the British islands; Describing their respective situations, Buildings, Customs, Arts and Sciences, Manufactures, Husbandry, Plants, Animals, Minerals, Forests, Rivers, Fisheries &c. and more particularly of the County of Middlesex, and City of London showing the Antient as well as Present state of that Metropolis, and Remarks on the several great trading Companies, and on their foreign Trade to all parts of the World. Adorn'd with Maps and Cuts. In Two Volumes. vol. I (Vol. II) London: Printed for Jacob Robinson at the Golden Lyon in Ludgate Street, MDCCXLIII.

Octavo, 185 × 120mm.   1743

COLLATION Vol. 1. Title-page; pp 1–466, History; index (14pp). Vol. 2. Title-page; pp 1–148, History continued; index (12pp).

There are no directions to the binder but the three maps by Hermann Moll and the Bowles broadside that illustrate vol.1 have page references; they all appear to date from about 1731. Five plates from Bowles's *British Views* (no 28) are used to illustrate vol.2 without indication of where they should be placed; these date back to 1723–4 and are abbreviated *BV*.

VOL. 1

1 p 1 A General Map of/Great Britain and Ireland.... 1731 ... by H.Moll ... (tl)Page: 1 vol.XIV. 200 × 255/210 × 270mm.

2 p 6 A map/of ye South part of/Great Britain.... by Hermann Moll ... (tl)Page 6. vol.XIV. 275 × 300/280 × 305mm. Dedicated to Frederick, Prince of Wales.

3 p 198 Middlesex/by/H.Moll/Geographer. 222 × 305mm. With small engravings on each side of the map: (l.) 'Stone found on digging the foundation of Part of Ludgate' (73 × 25mm) – 'Roman Pavement found near London Stone' (60 × 25mm) – 'Kinsington' (birds-eye view of the Palace, 30 × 28mm) – (r.) 'The Monument' (145 × 28mm) – 'Hampton Court' (birds-eye, 30 × 28mm). (tl) '(19) P.198. vol. 14'.

(p 316 Woodcut in text: plan of various stations of traders in the Royal Exchange)

4 p 400 (composite plate, captions in work) (first strip) The North View of St Paul's Church as before the Fire of London – The South View of St Paul's Church when/the Spire was Standing – The South View of St Paul's Church as before the Fire (73 × 460mm) – (second strip) The West End of St Paules – The Ichnographie of the parochiall Church of St Faith (170 × 60mm) – (bm) The East End of St Pauls – The North Side of St Paul's Church – The West Front of St Pauls. I.Simon fecit. (150 × 335mm) – The East End of St

Pauls – The Prospect of the Orientall Part of the Church/ ... of St Pauls in London/as before the Fire of London (155 × 60mm) (third strip) The Prospect of the Parochial Church of St Faith ... – The Planographie of the Cathedral/Church of St Paules/as before the Fire of London – The Interior Prospect of the Body of the Cathedrall Church of St Pauls from West to the quire – The Prospect of the Quire of St Pauls Cathedrall (75 × 460mm) (fourth strip) The Quire as it is at present (65 × 70mm) (on swallow-tailed banderole) A Prospect of London, as before the Fire (in work) Southworke. D.Loggan fec. (65 × 310mm) – The Inside as it now is (65 × 73mm). (tr) vol.14. page 400 'y'. Printed and sold by John Bowles at Mercers Hall, London. 385 × 460/406mm. *London Described* (no 29), item 30.

VOL. 2

5 p 35 (on swallow-tailed banderole in sky) Guild Hall. (bm) This is an Antient handsome Structure ... (br)'h'. 168 × 215/171 × 222mm. *BV* 17.

6 p 77 (on swallow-tailed banderole in sky) The Cathedral Church of/St Peters Westminster. (bm)Here formerly stood the Temple of Apollo ... (br)'d'. 170 × 210/171 × 216mm. *BV* 13.

7 p 89 (tm)A View of the Inside of Westminster Hall. (bm) This was formerly the chief Palace of the Kings of England ... (br) 'g'. 146 × 229/184 × 241mm. *BV* 40.

8 p 104 (on swallow-tailed banderole in sky)The Royal Banqueting House at White Hall. (bm)This Stately Building ... (br)'c'. 165 × 205/175 × 220mm. *BV* 12.

9 p 107 (in sky) The Royal Palace of St James's. (in work)The Terass Walk – St James's Park. (bm)This House was antiently an Hospital ... (br)'b' (tr, partly burnished out)'Vol.15 pl ...' 165 × 197/171 × 210mm. *BV* 11.

36 · VETUSTA MONUMENTA* [1747–1835]

George Vertue was born in the parish of St Martin in the Fields. Testifying to his affection for the old building and his love of antiquity are the two views and plan of the original parish church he engraved before demolition started in September 1721 to make way for Gibbs's grander and more fashionable edifice. He had been apprenticed first to a French heraldic engraver and then to Michael Van der Gucht but started working independently in 1709, being employed by Sir Godfrey Kneller to engrave some portraits. In 1717 he joined the revived Society of Antiquaries and became its official engraver, contributing regular plates to the series *Vetusta Monumenta* until 1755, when he became too ill to carry out his duties. The Society, in view of the valuable contribution he had made to the graphic side of their publications, accepted his resignation with the greatest reluctance and he died in July of the following year. After an interregnum and another, short-lived, appointment a worthy successor was found in James Basire senior.

Vertue's antiquarian and engraving activities went much beyond his official duties. In the minutes of the Society it is recorded that on 14 December 1720:

W. Stukeley proposed to the President that the Society should take drawings of all the Old Edifices in London that have not yet been well done and have them inserted from time to time in Mr. Strype's Stow's Annalls belonging to the Society which was agreed to. It was likewise added that Every Member be desired to buy all good Prints of such public Buildings Monuments and the like that happen in his way at as reasonable a price as he can which shall be repay'd by the Treasurer out of the Society's money.

The book was duly interleaved to accommodate the prints but the inserted pages remained blank. On 7 February 1722, however, 'Mr. Vertue brought the Remaining parcell of the Original Groundplots of the City of London made after the ffire and from which Hollar made his print', and two years later he dedicated his engraving of them to the Society. Art historians are indebted to Vertue for the earliest catalogue and description of Hollar's etchings, published in 1745, and for the 40 notebooks on English painters and engravers which Horace Walpole acquired from his widow and used as a basis for his *Anecdotes on Painting* (1762–71).

Some of Vertue's engravings were still being published in 1789, in the second volume of *Vetusta Monumenta*, but by this time the majority of the plates are credited to James Basire, who had been elected as engraver to the Society on 8 March 1759. He was the son of an engraver of maps and book illustrations and himself became a gifted engraver, in line, of portraits and historical paintings. It was to his studio in Great Queen Street that the 14 year old William Blake went to serve his apprenticeship in 1771 and from which he was sent out to make drawings in Westminster Abbey and other churches for the engravings in Gough's *Sepulchral Monuments*. But by the time the fourth volume of *Vetusta Monumenta* appeared in 1815 son had succeeded to father as engraver to the Society and it is to James Basire junior that the credits in this and the fifth volume (1835) refer.

An important annexe to these illustrations must also be recorded. In 1770 the Society decided to commission historical engravings on so large a scale that Basire had to use his powers of persuasion to induce Whatmans to manufacture specially a paper suitable for printing them; it measured 2 feet 7 inches by 4 feet 5 inches and was given the name of 'Antiquarian'. While these large engravings were being printed off, in 1776, Vertue's widow sold to the Society some of the major plates which her husband had published on his own account. The Society reprinted these for their members and they are sometimes to be found bound in an elephant folio with the 'Antiquarian' prints but without title or contents list. A list of its publications, dated 22 April 1845, details these under the heading 'Prints Engraved by Vertue, now the property of the Society of Antiquaries' at prices varying from 2s to 10s each. The listing below consists of London subjects to be found in both *Vetusta Monumenta* and the outsize series.

Vetusta Monumenta: Quae ad Rerum Britannicarum Memoriam Conservandam Societas Antiquariorum Londini Sumptu Suo Edenda Curavit. Volumen Primum (etc) Londini: Anno Domini MDCCXLVII (etc).

Folio, 540 × 365mm. Vols 1-2, 4-5: 1747–89, 1815–35

COLLATION Vol. 1. Title-page; list of 70 plates (2pp). (No text relevant to the London plates.) Vol. 2. Title-page; list of 55 plates (1 leaf). (Only texts relevant to London plates are an account of Greenwich Palace, 2pp and 2 plates, Sir Josef Ayloffe's 'An Account of some Ancient Monuments in Westminster Abby', 15pp and 7 plates, published 23 April 1780, and 'St. Bartholomew's Priory', 8pp and 2 plates.) Vol. 4. Title-page; list of 52 plates (1 leaf). (Only texts relevant to London plates are 'The Death and funeral of Abbot Islip of Westminster', 3pp and 5 plates, published 23 April 1808, and 'The Tower of London', 2pp and 14 plates, published 1 January 1815.) Vol. 5. Title-page; list of 69 plates (1 leaf). (Only texts relevant to London plates are William Capon's 'Notes and Remarks to accompany his Plan of the ancient Palace of Westminster', 7pp and 1 plate, read on 23 December 1824, and George Gwilt's 'Observations on the Church of St. Mary le Bow', 5pp and 5 plates, read on 12 June 1828.)

Plates were published on an average two or three a year. Plate numbers given are taken from the contents lists to each volume but they are sometimes engraved on the plates tr. The publication formula 'Sumptibus Societatis Antiquariae Londinensis' is abbreviated below to 'SSAL'.

VOL. 1

1 Vas Marmoreum/Sacro Baptismati Dicatum Acroterio Deaurato Coronatum/in Ecclesia Divi Iacobi Westmonasterii./Opus Grinlini Gibbons Aere jam perenniori sculpsit Georgius Vertue 1718. Car. Woodfield delin. Ex Collectione S.G. 410 × 260/450 × 280mm. This was apparently Vertue's first London engraving for the Society, to the publication of which a number of the members subscribed 5s in 1717. The drawing of the St James, Piccadilly font (carved by Gibbons in 1684) from which it was engraved was in the collection of Samuel Gale, a founder member. pl. 3.

2 Richardus II. Rex Angliae/Ex Tabula in Choro D.Petri Westmonast; Soc. Londini Rei Antiquariae Studiosa in Aere incidi Curavit A.D. MDCCXVIII. Giosep. Grisoni delin. Ex Coll. I.Talman Ar. Vertue sculp. 490 × 250/535 × 265mm. This painting, removed later from the choir to the Jerusalem Chamber and now displayed beneath the S. tower of the nave is thought to be of fourteenth century English origin. John Talman, who commissioned the unreliable drawing from which Vertue made this engraving for a 20 guinea fee, was the first Director of the Society and as such responsible for publishing prints of antiquarian subjects. pl.4.

3 Mausoleum Sive Feretrum Sti Edvardi Confessoris Regis Angliae.... uti hodie in Ecclesia Westmonasteriensi conspicitur. I. Talman designavit. G. Vertue sculp. SSAL MDCCXXIV. 600 × 425/640 × 445mm. pl.16.

4 (above Gate) The Gate at Whitehall/Said to be Design'd by Hans Holbein. G. Vertue d. et sculp. SSAL 1725. 410 × 260/423 × 270mm. Horsemen passing beneath. The Gate was demolished in 1759. pl. 17.

5 (above Gate) King Street Gate Westminster/demolish'd Anno 1723. G. Vertue d. et sculp. SSAL 1725. 380 × 255/390 × 265mm. Coach passing beneath. pl. 18.

6 A Plan of King Street Gate – A Plan of Whitehall Gate. SSAL 1725. 370 × 195mm. pl. 19 (misnumbered '17').

7 (tm) A True and Exact Draught of the Tower Liberties, survey'd in the Year 1597 by Gulielmus Haiward and J. Gascoyne. SSAL MDCCXLII. 390 × 530/415 × 550mm. (tl) royal arms above a curtain with 'The Description of the/Tower of London ...' (tr, in cartouche) 'A note of the Boundaries of ye Liberties of the Tower'. Refs A-Y, AB-AI. pl.63.

VOL. 2

8 (rococo cartouche tc) Londinium Redivivum/Presented by me to his Majesty,/a Week after the Conflagration,/together with a Discourse now/in the Paper Office. J.E. – Another Projection. J.E. SSAL 1748. 240 × 350, 225 × 350/475 × 360mm. Refs to upper plan 1–38, etc. Evelyn's *Diary*, 13 Sept 1666: 'I presented his Majestie with a survey of the ruines, and a Plot for a new Citty, with a discourse on it'. pl.1.

9 (in cartouche above) A Plan of London/Containing twenty-five Churches only reserved on their old Foundations, with all the principal Streets almost in the same … Described by I. Evelyn Esq. F.R.S. – A Plan of the City of London after the great Fire in … 1666 according to the design and proposal of Sr Christopher Wren for rebuilding it. SSAL 1748. 470 × 350/480 × 360mm. Refs to Evelyn plan 1-82. The Wren plan was earlier engraved by Hulsbergh and published in 1721 (BL Maps: *K. top.* 20.19.3). pl.2.

10 (on banderole in sky) A View of the Savoy/from the River Thames. Drawn with the plan of the Place by G.V. in 1736: and published at the Expence of the Antiquary Society of London, 1750. 290 × 440/320 × 460mm. Refs A–G and a 'history' on the label fixed to the wall in foreground. pl.5.

11 (tm) The Savoy Hospital in the Strand – The Chapel of the Hospital. G. Vertue delin. et sculp. SSAL 1753. Published … Nov. 29, 1753. 180 × 130,180 × 145, 190 × 310/455 × 340mm. Three views. pl.12.

12 (on banderole above) A Plan of the Ground and Buildings in the Strand/called the Savoy, taken in the Year 1736. G. Vertue delin. et sculp. SSAL 1754. Published … June 20, 1754. 460 × 340/480 × 350mm. Measured drawing. pl.14.

Greenwich Palace

13 A View of the Antient Royal Palace called Placentia, in East Greenwich. J. Basire sculpsit. Published … April 23rd 1767. SSAL. 320 × 490/330 × 495mm. 'Engraven from a Drawing in the Possession of Dr. Ducarel'. pl.25.

14 The Great East-Window of the Parish Church of St Margaret in Westminster … Basire sculp. SSAL MDCCLXVIII. 495 × 345/560 × 380mm. Engraving with arched top. pl.26.

An Account of some Ancient Monuments in Westminster Abby
(All plates credited 'J. Basire del. et sc. SSAL April 23, 1780'.)

15 The front of the Monument of Aveline first wife of Edmund Crouchback/Earl of Lancaster, on the North Side of the Altar. 465 × 295/485 × 310mm. pl.29.

16 The figure of Aveline, Countess of Lancaster, cumbent on her Monument. 465 × 290/480 × 310mm. pl.30.

17 (Details of the canopy of the Countess of Lancaster's tomb) 455 × 290/480 × 310mm. Details A-D. pl. 31.

18 The North Front of the Monument of King Sebert, on the South Side of the/Altar in Westminster Abby. 465 × 295/480 × 310mm. pl.32.

19 The figures supposed to be those of King Sebert (1) and King Henry III(2)/as painted on the North front of the Monument of King Sebert in Westminster Abby. 465 × 300/480 × 310mm. pl.33.

20 Heads & Ornaments on the North Side of the Monument of King Sebert, in Westminster Abby. 460 × 295/485 × 310mm. Details 1–11. pl.34.

21 The Monument of Ann of Cleves, Fourth Wife of King Henry VIII on the South Side of the Altar in Westminster Abby. 295 × 465/320 × 485mm. pl.35.

St. Bartholomew's Priory

22 The Monument of Raherus, Founder & First Prior of St Bartholomew's Priory & Hospital,/in the Year 1123, as it now remains in the Priory Church near Smithfield. J. Carter fecit. J. Basire sc. SSAL Published … 23 April 1784. 440 × 290/455 × 300mm. pl.36 The lapse of time between pl.35 and 36 was occasioned by the expense and disturbance of installing the Society in its official Somerset House appartments in 1780–1.

23 Specimens of Architecture in the Priory Church of St. Bartholomew near Smithfield. J. Carter fecit. J. Basire sc. SSAL Published … 23 April 1784. 440 × 285/460 × 305mm. John Carter was appointed the Society's draughtsman in the previous month.

VOL. 4

The Death and funeral of Abbot Islip of Westminster
(All plates credited 'James Basire sculp.' with publication-line 'Published by the Society of Antiquaries, 23 April 1808'.)

24 (Miniature portrait in architectural framework) Engraved after an original drawing on a Roll of Vellum, representing the Death, Funeral &c. of John Islip Abbot of Westminster, who died Anno 1532, in the possession of the Society of Antiquaries. 410 × 310/490 × 360mm. Actually the Islip Roll was lent to the Society in 1791; these drawings were made for engraving by James Basire junior but the Roll was not restored to its owners until 1906. pl.16.

25 (Islip's death bed, with attendant saints) 410 × 320/490 × 360mm. pl.17.

26 (Islip's catafalque with mourners and heraldic banners set before the High Altar in Westminster Abbey) 415 × 320/490 × 360mm. The funeral took place on 16 May 1532. pl.18.

27 (St Erasmus's Chapel, with Islip's tomb) 445 × 330/490 × 360mm. pl.19.

28 (Miniature of the coronation in the Abbey of Henry VIII) 290 × 285/360 × 360mm. pl.20.

The Tower of London
(All plates credited 'Js Basire sculp.' with publication-line 'Published by the Society of Antiquaries of London, January 1st, 1815'.)

29 Plan of the Tower of London/from a Drawing made between 1681 and 1689 by Order of Ld Dartmouth, Mar Genl of the Ordnance. 275 × 355/360 × 540mm. Refs A-Z, a-r. A birds-eye map-view. pl.39.

30 (tr) Plan/of the/Tower of London/from a Drawing/made in the year/MDCCXXVI. C.Lempriere delt. 1726. 310 × 410/370 × 540mm. pl.40.

31 Three Views of the Tower of London taken from a drawing made by order of Lord Dartmouth, Master Genral of the Ordnance, between the years 1681 and 1689. Each 112 × 270/480 × 330mm. N. view – S. view – N.E. view. pl.41.

32 South Elevation of the White Tower in the Tower of London. F. Nash delin. 440 × 340/500 × 365mm. pl.42.

33 Plan of the Upper Story of the White Tower. F. Nash delin. 470 × 350/540 × 370mm. pl. 43.

34 Section of the White Tower, from North to South. F. Nash delin. 475 × 345/540 × 370mm. pl. 44.

35 Section of the White Tower, from East to West. F. Nash delin. 445 × 345/500 × 365mm. pl. 45.

36 West side of the room marked 'A' in the Plan of the upper Story – East side of the same room. F. Nash delin. 315 × 480/360 × 535mm. pl. 46.

37 View of the Great Room on the upper story of the White-Tower. F.Nash delin. 408 × 330/525 × 370mm. pl.47.

38 Plan of the Chapel in the White-Tower. F. Nash delin. 505 × 340/540 × 370mm. pl.48.

39 Transverse Section of the Chapel in the White-Tower. F. Nash delin. 450 × 330/490 × 370mm. pl. 49.

40 Longitudinal Section of the Chapel in the White-Tower. F.Nash delin. 325 × 495/365 × 540mm. pl. 50.

41 Plan of the Cells under the Chapel of the White-Tower. F.Nash delin. 455 × 320/510 × 365mm. pl. 51.

42 Plan, Section & Perspective View of a Room at the S.W. Angle of the Watergate of the Tower. F. Nash delin. 450 × 240/490 × 305mm. pl. 52.

VOL. 5

Plans, elevations and sections of the Temple Church
(Measured drawings, seven plates, all with credits 'F. Nash del. J. Basire sculp.' and publication-line 'Published by the Society of Antiquaries of London, April 23rd 1818'.)

43 Plan of the Temple Church. 310 × 490/370 × 525mm. pl. 19.

44 Specimen of the internal Architecture of the Circular part of the Temple Church. 480 × 335/525 × 365mm. pl. 20.

45 Elevation of the East end of the Temple Church. 320 × 480/365 × 530mm. pl. 21.

46 Section of the Temple Church from East to West. 270 × 470/325 × 530mm. pl. 22.

47 The great Western Entrance to the Temple Church. 485 × 340/540 × 365mm. Elevation and plan. pl. 23.

48 One of the Windows of the Temple Church. 470 × 315/530 × 365mm. Elevation and plan of triple lancet. pl. 24.

49 Plans, Elevations and Sections of the Bases, Capitals and Mouldings of the Temple Church. 465 × 325/530 × 355mm. pl. 25.

Notes and Remarks by the late Mr William Capon

50 (br) Plan of the ancient/Palace of Westminster/by the late/Mr William Capon/measured and drawn between 1793 and 1823. Engraved by James Basire. Published ... 23rd April 1828. 490 × 660/540 × 700mm. Refs A. The Hall, B. The Cloister, C. Small Chapel, D. Under croft of St. Stephen's. pl. 47.

Observations on the Church of St. Mary le Bow

51 (bl) Tower of St Mary le Bow/said to have been erected upon a Roman causeway/vide Parentalia P.265 – (bc)Plan of the Crypt/under/the Church of St Mary le Bow. G. Gwilt Del. Js Basire sculp. Published ... 23rd April 1835. 305 × 425/365 × 485mm. Two plans. pl. 61.

52 Section of St Mary le Bow Cheapside with the remains of the ancient crypt erected in the reign/of William the Conqueror. G.Gwilt Del. Js. Basire sculp. Published ... 23rd April 1835. 465 × 695/535 × 710mm. pl. 62.

53 View of the Operations upon removing the ground of the Crypt at Bow Church/from a sketch taken by F. Nash Jany 1818. Drawn by J.H. Nixon under the direction of G. Gwilt. Engraved by J. Basire. Published ... 23rd April 1835. 355 × 290/490 × 360mm. pl. 63.

54 Crypt in Bow Church from the North Side near the East end of the Nave. G. Gwilt del. Js Basire sculp. Published ... 23rd April 1835. 300 × 340/410 × 370mm. pl. 64.

55 Crypt in Bow Church from the West end of the South Aisle or Corridor. G. Gwilt Del. Js Basire sculp. Published ... 23rd April 1835. 280 × 320/405 × 360mm. pl.65.

The 12 outsize plates of London subjects in chronological order of their first publication

56 The View of the Charity Children in the Strand upon the VII of July, MDCCXIII, being the day appointed by her late Majesty Queen Anne, for a Publick Thanksgiving for the Peace; when both Houses of Parliament made a solemn procession to the Cathedral of St. Paul ... Geo. Vertue delin et sculpsit 1715. 375 × 1255/380 × 1260mm. N. side of the Strand, looking towards the opening of Catherine Street, with Exeter

Exchange on the extreme l. and the Strand maypole on the r.; this 1713 view is the last sight of the latter since in the following year its site was relinquished for the foundations of St Mary le Strand. The print further describes the occasion: 'Near IV thousand Charity Children being new cloathed ... during the whole processing which lasted near three Hours, they sung & repeated the Hymns, which were prepared upon the expectation of her Majesty's Royal Presence'. Above the buildings are draperies and the obverse and reverse of a Queen Anne medal.

57 (on banderole) An Exact Surveigh of the Streets, Lanes, and Churches, Comprehendd within the Ruins of the City of London first described in Six/Plats, 10 December, 1666 ... & reduced into one intire plat by Iohn Leake. (views, etc along top) Old Buildings near the Temple Gate Fleetstreet (63 × 98mm) – Baynards Castle (63 × 98mm) – The Old South View of St Pauls church (63 × 98mm) – The West View of St Pauls (63 × 57mm) – Cheapside and the Cross taken before the Fire 1666 (63 × 175mm) – The South Front of Guild Hall (63 × 80mm) – The Royal Exchange London/As Built by Sr Thomas Gresham. (courtyard) (63 × 100mm) – A Plan of the City of London and Westminster (93 × 185mm). Refs B–V. 530 × 1280/535 × 1290mm. Dedicated by Vertue to the Society, 1723. (*Darlington and Howgego* 21a)

58 (tm) The South Prospect of St Martin's Church in the Liberty of Westminster. (on scroll) Plan of the Church Drawn/Engraved & thus described by G. Vertue. 230 × 318/240 × 332mm.

59 (tm) The West Prospect of St Martin's Church in the Fields, Westminster. (on scroll, a dedication to Browne Willis, Esq) George Vertue a native of the said Parish. 230 × 318/240 × 330mm.

60 (on banderole) The Plan of St Martin's Church before it/was pull'd down Ao 1730. 235 × 360/240 × 365mm. Details in three panels on l. The date must be an error for 1720 as the new church was completed by 1726.

61 (above horizon, between Tudor royal arms within the Garter and City arms belaurelled) Civitas Londinum Ano Dni circiter MDLX. 345 × 475mm. Each of 4 sheets joined laterally. The N. portion of the birds-eye view that follows (item 62).

62 (in oblong cartouche bl) Londinum Antiqua/This Plan shows the ancient extent of the famous Cities/of London and Westminster as it was near the/beginning of the Reign of Queen Elisabeth. Vertue Soc. Antiq. London. excudit 1737. 345 × 475mm each of 4 sheets, joined laterally. This S. portion together with its N. counterpart (item 61) assembles into a birds-eye view measuring some 700 × 1900mm. The pewter plates from which it was printed are still with the Society. Their relation to other sixteenth century maps of London and Vertue's alterations are explored by Stephen Marks in *The map of sixteenth century London*. (*Darlington and Howgego* 8a).

63 (on banderole tc) Survey & Ground Plot of the Royal Palace of Whitehall/with the Lodgings & Apartments belonging to their Majesties/Ao Do 1680. Survey'd by John Fisher. (br) Drawn & Publish'd by G. Vertue, Ano Dom. 1747. 530 × 705/550 × 720mm. Subsidiary plans of York Place and Whitehall tl and tr. Rococo panels lc and rc with refs A–Z (Gothic) and A–Z (Roman) and refs 1–65 below. With cartouche tc arms of Hubert de Burgh, Walter Grey, Cardinal Wolsey and Henry VIII, with supporters and Garter.

64 (in cartouche tc) The Inside Perspective View of/the Under Chappel of St Thomas/within London Bridge from/the West to the East End, the Foundation/was laid in ye Reign of K.Hen 2d Ao 1176 ... – (on banderole) The Inside South View of the Under Chappel from East to West (on banderole bc) Represents the Manner and form of this rare Piece of Ancient Architecture/thus Drawn and transmitted to Posterity by G.V. Antiquary 1744. Published and sold by G. Vertue in Brownlow Street, Drury Lane. 1747. 277 × 470/235 × 480mm. Measured drawing.

65 (tm) A View of the West Front of the Chappel dedicated to St. Thomas on London Bridge; also the Inside View from West to East of the said Chappel as it was first built, Ano 1209 – (elevation and plan) London Bridge as it was first built Ano 1209. Drawn, Engrav'd & Publish'd by G. Vertue in Brownlow Street, Drury Lane, 1748. 520 × 470/542 × 490mm. Below is engraved the history of the bridge, set in an emblematic architectural frame headed by the City arms and regalia and maritime emblems.

66 (cartouche bl) Lincoln's Inn/Chappel/Being erected at the Expence of/the Honble Gentlemen of the Inn/from a Plan of Mr Inigo Jones/Surveyor of His Majesties Works and Buildings Ao Dni MDCXXIII. Drawn, Engraved and Sold by G. Vertue 1751. 280 × 405, 235 × 405/540 × 420mm. S. elevation and 'ambulatory' or undercroft of the Chapel. Refs A-B.

67 The Procession of King Edward VI/from the Tower of London to Westminster, Feb XIX, MDXLVII, previous to his Coronation./Engraved from a coeval painting at Cowdray in Sussex, the Seat of Lord Viscount Montagu. Drawn from the original by S.H. Grimm. Engraved by James Basire. SSAL 1787. 555 × 1280/625 × 1300mm on 'Antiquarian' paper. John Carter, the official Society draughtsman, was much offended because Grimm, rather than himself, was sent to Cowdray to prepare for this important engraving. With it goes an 'Historical and Descriptive Account':

The buildings represented in the line of the procession, which more immediately attract our attention, are the Tower of London, Bow Church, the Great Conduit, the Cross, the Little Conduit, and Goldsmith's Row in Cheapside, the church of St Paul's in its then state, with its high spire, Ludgate and Temple Bar, Charing-cross, and the Palace at Westminster. The view from the gate on Tower-hill to Cheapside is fore-shortened, or almost entirely concealed; and the parts beyond Temple-Bar, all the way to Westminster, are contracted so as to enable the painter to exhibit the whole distance to the spectator.

37 · STOW'S SURVEY [1754]

Strype, Stow's editor, died in 1737 but his edition of the *Survey* (no 25) was still in demand. The prospectus for a sixth edition, dated 2 March 1754, stated: 'This is the Book presented by the City to every Alderman, at his Election, ever since it was published in the Year 1720'. It had now been 'brought down to the present time by Careful Hands' and was to be published in weekly Parts consisting of three sheets of letterpress and one copper plate 'finely engraved', all stitched in a strong wrapper at 6d per Part. Only one publisher, J. Knapton, was common to the fifth and sixth editions although a 1754 'J. Ward' may have been connected with 1720 'T. Ward'.

It is claimed that the ward and parish maps are the result of a 'careful Survey lately taken' and the squares, Inns of Court, noblemen's houses and churches are 'almost all of them upon whole Sheet Plates, and measure about 17 inches by 13 feet. Subscribers' names are to be printed and Part 1 is offered free of charge. Part 3 is announced for publication on 2 March (a Saturday) and is to contain a broad sheet print of the Lord Mayor's Mansion House. Weekly issues must have fallen into arrears since Part 126 was not published until 12 June 1757 according to the *Public Advertiser* of that date. Nevertheless the plates issued with Parts 129 and 136 are still dated 1756.

The directions to the binder list the plates in the order in which they are to be arranged in the two bound volumes but refer also to a different numeration: that of the 136 weekly Parts in which the text was issued. It was these Part numbers that were engraved on the plates, usually br. The numbers thus appearing on the 132 plates are 1–129 and 134–6, so presumably Parts 130–3 consisted of text without plates. The text was issued sequentially

and was not necessarily illustrated by the plate that accompanied each Part.

It must have been quite a job for the publishers to keep this stream of illustrative material flowing and, although perhaps a few maps and views were specially commissioned, they largely depended on three tributaries of pre-existing work. A little under half consisted of nearly all the plates made for the fifth edition with minor alterations to the ward and parish maps, the burnishing out of the original references to volume, Book and page numbers and the addition of Part numbers and an appropriate publication-line. The rest was drawn chiefly from two other sources: the current stock-in-trade of the printseller John Bowles and the architectural plates engraved by Benjamin Cole for the second edition of Maitland's *History of London* (no 38) which was coming out also in Parts, between 1754 and 1756.

The following is an inventory of their borrowings and additional material:

Stow (5th ed)
64 of the 70 plates issued including 23 of the views which may be attributed to Kip. Kip's plates of the Monument and Bow Church were replaced by those of Sutton Nicholls (pl.43 and 48, Parts 1 and 10), his three views of St Paul's Cathedral by Thomas Bowles's (pl.57–9, Parts 7–9). The 1720 City plan was replaced by R.W. Seal's 1756 plan (pl.1, Part 136).

John Bowles's stock
32 plates made up of 22 advertised in his catalogues of 1728 and 1731 and mostly bound up in his folio of 1731, *London Described* (no 29); these are chiefly the work of Sutton Nicholls with the specified measurements of 13 × 17 inches. To these were added 10 'Perspective Views' about 8½ × 15½ inches (216 × 394mm) engraved by T. Bowles, Fourdrinier, Maurer, J.S. Müller and Truchy and listed in his 1753 catalogue as Series 50, nos 5, 7, 19, 24, 37–9, 42 and Series 51, nos 1, 7.

Maitland's History
23 architectural plates, mostly without staffage, of parish churches, hospitals, Company halls, etc.

Addenda
13 assorted plates, comprising:
8 additional parish maps issued with Parts 80–7.
3 additional views, one of the exterior of St Martin in

the Fields, measuring 13 × 17 inches, another of Merchant Taylors' School and the third an interior of St Stephen, Walbrook (pl.110, 47,45,Parts 2,129 and 134).
2 plans by R.W. Seale (pl. 1,71, Parts 135–6).

Part numbers afford some insight into the publisher's strategy to attract and hold subscribers by the promise of the engraving which embellished each instalment of text. With the first 27, for instance, they received selections from Bowles's stock including attractive Sutton Nicholls birds-eye views of squares; other plates from this source were not introduced until Parts 100–2,123–4 and 128. Once the work was safely launched the old refurbished fifth edition plates were gradually introduced, to be bound eventually in their original context. By the time the Parts had reached the 70 mark these sources were drying up and so eight new parish maps were provided with Parts 80–7. Moreover the architecture so far illustrated was beginning to have an antiquarian look since most of the views were between 25 and 35 years old and in the interval there had been much building activity, not least as a result of the Act of 1711 for building 50 new churches. To make good this deficiency the publisher set an anonymous engraver to copying a selection of the plates then appearing with the second edition of Maitland's *History of London*. These near facsimiles, mainly of new churches, were distributed with Parts 54,99,103–13,115–17,119–22,125–7. With the two architectural plates of unknown origin and the two maps by Seale this completes the quota of 132 plates.

There have been passing references to alterations made to the Bowles plates for this reissue—in Hugh Phillips's *Mid-Georgian London*, p 6 and *Survey of London* vol. 33 (1966), p 60—but no special study of their first and later states. In every case an attempt was made to burnish out the Bowles imprint engraved in the lower part of the work, replacing it with cross-hatching or burin strokes to merge with the foreground. In its stead a Stow publication-line was engraved along the bm. The credits were left standing and most of the plates are otherwise unaltered, though showing signs of wear. The staffage and the outmoded fashions of costume and carriages, which were left intact, must in 1754 have given the views an old-world appearance. But in a number of cases the plates, particularly those of

squares, were re-engraved to show recent changes of layout. A round pond, apparently used for boating, appeared in St James's Square (pl. 113). In Leicester Square (pl. 115) the gardens were replanned and an equestrian statue placed in the middle. The railings round the gardens of Golden Square (pl. 121) and Soho Square (pl. 116) were altered to accommodate lamps at the corners and over the entrance gates, no doubt in conformity with the Lighting Acts of 1736 and 1738. An attempt was made at showing a Palladian alteration to the N.W. corner of Soho Square and considerable alterations to the forecourt of Newcastle House (pl. 93) in Lincoln's Inn Fields are recorded. A deterioration from the original formal layout of the gardens in Bloomsbury Square (pl. 96), Hanover Square (pl. 120) and Golden Square is observable. The trophy and cartouche encircled by the Garter which originally was shown above the centre of Marlborough House (pl. 124) is eliminated, perhaps after its removal by the third Duke when he succeeded to the title in 1733. The architect Thomas Archer's nephew's promotion to the Upper House was signified by an amendment to the banderole above the roof of his Covent Garden dwelling (pl. 118). Prints depicting buildings and developments of recent years were also provided: The Mansion House (pl. 46), Kent's Horse Guards (pl. 105) and Westminster Bridge (pl. 108).

The larger body of more recent architecture, however, consists of a selection from the 100 or so plates contributed by Benjamin Cole to the second edition of Maitland's *History*. At first sight it might seem that the same plates had been used for both publications with a Part number substituted for the 'B. Cole' credit. A closer inspection reveals that these are facsimile engravings, probably made from the published prints. There are significant differences in the measurements of the border-lines of the copies which are between 3mm to 20mm shorter than the originals (eg pl. 85, 'St Leonard Shoreditch', 353 × 195mm as against 355 × 198mm, and pl. 82, 'Christ Church Spittlefields', 315 × 230mm as against 335 × 240mm). Church towers are similarly curtailed by about 5mm to 8mm. The wording of the captions is retained but they are engraved in differing scripts. The facsimiles were sometimes over-etched with consequent darkening of shadows and blurring of detail as may be seen from a comparison of 'St Andrew Holborn' (pl. 63) with Cole's original. Architectural 'minutiae' such as urns and cherub keystones (pl. 73, 'St George's Southwark', and pl. 95, 'St Giles in the Fields') and ironwork (pl. 63, 'St Andrew Holborn') are divergent. Some details have been overlooked or deliberately omitted: a swag is missing from above the N. entrance of St Magnus (pl. 40), the building to the S. of St George, Hanover Square (pl. 119) has been eliminated and figures have been perfunctorily copied, and some wholly suppressed, from the only plate to include staffage (pl. 23, 'The Foundling Hospital'). The twin-subject plate showing Goldsmiths' Hall and Ironmongers' Hall (pl. 55) was assembled from two separate plates in the original in which each had a different companion. Finally, a few of the illustrations present a mirror image of their originals. St Michael, Cornhill (pl. 37) thus seems to be viewed from a different point of the compass with its wind-vanes reversed. The shadow of St George's Hospital (pl. 21) is cast on the opposite side. The hands of the clock of St Mary, Islington (pl. 132) point to 11.20 instead of 1.40 while the figures on the clock-faces at St George, Southwark (pl. 73) and St Giles in the Fields (pl. 95) actually run anti-clockwise. These vagaries suggest either that the prints used as models were copied onto copper plates for etching without making the usual adjustments to counteract the reversal of the image when printed or that the originals were laid down as transparencies on the plates as a guide to the engraver, some face downwards and some face upwards.

A Survey of the Cities of London and Westminster And the Borough of Southwark Containing The Original, Antiquity, Increase, present State and Government of those Cities Written at first in the Year 1698 (vol. 2 title corrects '1598'). By John Stow Citizen and Native of London. Corrected, improved and very much Enlarged in the Year 1720 By John Strype M.A., A Native also of the Said City. The Survey and History brought down to the present time by Careful Hands. Illustrated with exact Maps of the City and Suburbs, and of all the Wards; and likewise of the Out-Parishes of London and Westminster, and the Country ten miles round London. Together with many fair Draughts of the most Eminent Buildings.... In Two Volumes. Vol. I (II). The Sixth Edition. London; Printed for W.Innys and J.Richardson, J. and P.Knapton, S.Birt, R.Ware, T. and T.Longman, W.Meadows, J.Clarke, H.Whitridge, D.Browne, E.Wicksteed, J.Ward and C.Bathurst (vol.2: 'and H.S.Cox'). MDCCLIV.

Folio, about 380 × 240mm.   1754–6

COLLATION   Vol. 1. Title-page; contents (8pp); pp i–xx, life of Stow; pp 1–758, Survey Books 1–3. Vol. 2. Title-page; pp 1–671, Survey Books 4–6; pp 672–838, appendices; indices to vols 1–2, directions to binder (14pp).

The 'Directions to the Binder' state 'The Number of the plates is 132, which are ranged in this list according to the Pages where they are to be inserted'. The list below preserves this order and also refers to the page numbers. The number of the weekly Part with which each print was published, usually engraved br, is given before the dimensions. Following the dimensions there are notes on the state in which prints were issued, building dates when significant and references to the three sources quoted in the prefatory note, as follows: Stow (1720) abbreviated *S* with Book and page numbers; Bowles plates abbreviated according to the catalogue in which they are first listed as *B* 1728, *B* 1731 or *B* 1753 (for those previously collected there is an additional reference to *London Described*, abbreviated with the item number); Maitland's *History* abbreviated *M* with page reference.

VOL. 1

1 front. A New and Exact Plan of the Cities of London and Westminster, and Borough of Southwark, with the Additional Buildings to the Year 1756. R.W. Seale sculp. Pt 136. 318 × 686/343 × 711mm. (*Darlington and Howgego* 104)

2 p xi The monument of Mr John Stow ... J. Sturt sculp. Pt 35. 279 × 165mm pl.mark. *S* 1,xiv.

3 p 1 The City of/London/as in/Queen Elizabeth's Time. 1754. Pt 98. 190 × 457/229 × 476mm. *S* 1,1. (*Darlington and Howgego* 8, see note)

4 p 15 Ald Gate – Bishops Gate – Moor Gate – Cripple-Gate – Alders-Gate – New Gate – Lud Gate – Temple Barr. 1755. Pt 94. 210 × 324/216 × 330mm. *S* 1,14.

5 p 57 London Bridge. Pt 30. 210 × 324/222 × 330mm. *S* 1,53.

6 p 69 The Tower of London. 1754. Pt 29. 203 × 333/213 × 343mm. Without Kip's credit. *S* 1,64.

7 p 69 A Map of the Tower Liberty. 1754. Pt 38. 279 × 356/381 × 406mm. *S* 1,54.

8 p 69 The Tower and St Catherin's/Taken from ye last Survey ... 1754. Pt 37. 279 × 356/381 × 406mm. *S* 1,64.

9 p 200 Christs Hospital. 1755. Pt 69. 200 × 324/213 × 337mm. *S* 1,175.

10 p 206 St Bartholomew's Hospitall. Pt 93. 203 × 330/210 × 337mm. *S* 1,184.

11 p 210 The East Prospect/The South Prospect of St

Bartholomews Hospital. Pt 122. 349 × 229/368 × 235mm. With a plan. Gibbs's quadrangle, 1730. *M* 983.

12 p 212 St Thomas Hospitall/in Southwark. 1755. Pt 89. 324 × 210/330 × 216mm. *S* 1,189.

13 p 215 The Prospect of Bridewell. 1755. Pt 90. 203 × 330/210 × 337mm. *S* 1,176.

14 p 216 The Hospitall called Bedlam. 1754. Pt 31. 210 × 337/216 × 343mm. *S* 1,192.

15 p 231 The Charter House. 1755. Pt 67. 206 × 324/216 × 337mm. Without Kip's credit. *S* 1,205.

16 p 237 Hoxton Hospitall. 1754. Pt 28. 206 × 324/216 × 333mm. *S* 1,212.

17 p 238 Chelsea Colledge. 1756. Pt 114. 241 × 330/248 × 337mm. *S* 1,214. (*Longford* 67)

18 p 238 The Inside View of the Rotunda in Ranelagh Gardens/with the company at Breakfast. (and in French) Bowles delin. et sculp. 1754. Pt 27. 254 × 381/292 × 394mm. Built 1742. *B* 1753. (*Longford* 340)

19 p 239 The Hospital at Greenwich. 1755. Pt 72. 241 × 330/248 × 337mm. Without Kip's credit. *S* 1,215.

20 p 243 Morden Colledge. 1755. Pt 70. 203 × 324/216 × 337mm. Without Kip's credit *S* 1,219.

21 p 257 St George's Hospital. Pt 118. 197 × 324/222 × 333mm. Building converted to a hospital 1733. *M* 1302.

22 p 261 St Luke's, London, and Bencrafts Hospitals. Pt 127. 343 × 232/365 × 236mm. St Luke's Hospital, Old Street, instituted 1751; London Hospital, Whitechapel Road, built 1752–7, Boulton Mainwaring surveyor; Bancroft's Almshouses, Mile End Road, 1729–35. *M* 1289, 1312.

23 p 266 A View of the Foundling Hospital. Pt 116. 181 × 318/210 × 330mm. Built 1742–52. A perfunctory copy, especially as regards staffage. *M* 1293.

24 p 274 (on swallow-tailed banderole in sky) Guys Hospital for Incurables. Pt 100. 324 × 438/330 × 445mm. Publication-line burnished out. *B* 1728. *LD* 43.

25 p 355 Portsoken Ward ... taken from the last Survey. 1754. Pt 32. 298 × 178/308 × 184mm. *S* 2,3.

26 p 369 The Parish Church of St Botolph without Aldgate. 1744/5. Pt 111. 381 × 229/400 × 235mm. Built by George Dance senior, 1741. *M* 1079.

27 p 371 Tower Street Ward ... taken from the last Survey. 1754. Pt 33. 292 × 362/298 × 368mm. Binder's reference for 1720 ed still stands. Spire has been added to St Dunstan in the East. *S* 2,29.

28 p 387 The Custom House. 1755. Pt 88. 210 × 318/261 × 330mm. *S* 2,51.

29 p 390 Aldgate Ward ... taken from the last Survey. 1754. Pt 36. 302 × 175/311 × 178mm. Engraved flourish in cartouche obliterates suppressed credit. *S* 2,55.

30 p 415 A Mapp of Lime Street Ward.... 1754. Pt 34. 308 × 175/311 × 178mm. Additions in Herb Market area and swelled rule added to cartouche. *S* 2,83.

31 p 421 Bishopsgate Street Ward taken from the last Survey. 1754. Pt 39. 305 × 178/311 × 190mm. *S* 2,90.

32 p 421 The North East Prospect of the Parish Church of St Botolph without Bishopsgate. Pt 117. 343 × 233/368 × 244mm. Rebuilt by James Gould and George Dance senior, 1727. *M* 1084.

33 p 436 (on swallow-tailed banderole in sky) Devonshire Square. Sutton Nicholls del. et sc. Publish'd 1754 for Stow's Survey. Pt 21. 320 × 454/343 × 457mm. Publication-line burnished out. *B* 1728. *LD* 39.

34 p 437 Broad Street Ward ... Cornhill Ward ... taken from the last Survey. 1754. Pt 40. 292 × 365/298 × 371mm. With numerous alterations. *S* 2,109.

35 p 446 (on banderole in sky) The South Sea House in Bishopsgate Street. Bowles sculp. Publish'd according to Act of Parliament 1754 for Stowe's Survey. Pt 4. 324 × 445/343 × 457mm. Publication-line burnished out. *B* 1728. LD 38.

36 p 462 The Royall Exchange of London. 1755. Pt 68. 241 × 286/254 × 292mm. *S* 2,135.

37 p 468 The West Prospect of the Parish Church of St Michael Cornhill. Pt 103. 337 × 212/362 × 230mm. *M* 1147.

38 p 475 Langborne Ward ... Candlewick Ward ... from the last Surveys. 1754. Pt 41. 292 × 365/298 × 371mm. Ironmongers' Hall added. *S* 2,151.

39 p 486 Billingsgate Ward and Bridge Ward Within ... taken from the last Survey. 1754. Pt 42. 305 × 178/311 × 184mm. *S* 2,165.

40 p 494 The North West Prospect of the Parish Church of St Magnus the Martyr, the North East End of London Bridge. Pt 119. 349 × 229/368 × 235mm. Omits swag over N. entrance. *M* 1124.

41 p 497 The North-West Prospect of the Parish Church of St Bennet Gracechurch. Pt 124. 343 × 229/375 × 235mm. Listed as Pt 125 in directions to binder. *M* 1072.

42 p 498 (on banderole in sky) Fishmongers Hall. Sutton Nicholls delin. et sculp. Pt 102. 324 × 419/337 × 445mm. *B* 1753.

43 p 500 (on swallow-tailed banderole between inscribed scrolls) The Monument. Pt 1. 432 × 330/451 × 343mm. Publication line burnished out. *B* 1728. *LD* 40.

44 p 510 Walbrook Ward and Dowgate Ward ... from the last Surveys. 1754. Pt 43. 308 × 181/314 × 184mm. Mansion House replaces Stocks Market. Swelled rule added under title. *S* 2,191.

45 p 514 The Inside of the Parish Church of St Stephen Wallbrook. Pack sculp. Pt 134. 292 × 394/305 × 406mm. With engraved ornamental frame.

46 p 517 The Lord Mayor's Mansion House/shewing the

Front of the House and the West Side. (and in French) Wale delint. Fourdrinier sculp. Publish'd ... Decr. 21 1754. Pt 3. 235 × 393/260 × 406mm. Built by George Dance senior, 1739–52. *B* 1753.

47 p 524 Scholae Mercatorum Scissorum Lond. facies orientalis. J. Mynde sc. Stowe's Survey ed. 1756. vol. 1 page 189. Pt 129. 190 × 305/241 × 317mm. Page ref amended in directions to binder.

48 p 542 (on swallow-tailed banderole in sky) Bow Church. Sutton Nicholls sculp. Publish'd ... 1754 for Stow's Survey. Pt 10. 457 × 337/469 × 343mm. Publication-line burnished out. *B* 1728. *LD* 35.

49 p 546 Cheape Ward ... taken from the last Survey. 1754. Pt 46. 298 × 356/305 × 368mm. Buildings added round Honey Lane Market. Swelled rule added under title. *S* 3,26.

50 p 558 (on banderole) The Prospect of Guild Hall. 1755. Pt 71. 210 × 324/216 × 330mm. *S* 3,51.

51 p 569 Coleman Street Ward and Bashishaw Ward taken from the last Survey. 1754. Pt 47. 349 × 292/356 × 298mm. *S* 3,53.

52 p 582 Creplegate Ward ... taken from the last Survey. 1755. Pt 48. 292 × 349/302 × 359mm. Area round St Giles slightly altered. *S* 3,70.

53 p 585 The North East Prospect of the Parish Church of St Alphage near Sion College. Pt 125. 337 × 233/368 × 235mm. The title of the original 'St Albans Wood Street' changed in error. As Pt 126 in directions to binder. *M* 1050.

54 p 601 Aldersgate Ward and St Martins le Grand Liberty taken from the last Survey. 1755. Pt 50. 302 × 181/311 × 187mm. Swelled rule added under title. *S* 3,95.

55 p 604 Goldsmiths Hall in Foster Lane – Ironmongers Hall in Fenchurch Street London. Pt 121. 337 × 222/368 × 235mm. Goldsmiths' Hall built 1748, Ironmongers' Hall built 1748–50. *M* 763,848.

56 p 623 The Wards of Farington within and Baynards Castle ... taken from the last Survey. 1755. Pt 51. 292 × 356/298 × 368mm. Stalls added in Newgate Market area. Swelled rule added under title. *S* 3,124.

57 p 650 The North West Prospect of St Pauls Cathedral in London. (and in French) Bowles fecit. Publish'd ... 1754 for Stow's Survey. Pt 7. 260 × 406/298 × 419mm. *B* 1753.

58 p 650 The Inside of St Paul's Cathedral from the West End to the Choir. (and in French) Publish'd for Stow's Survey 1754. Pt 8. 260 × 413/292 × 419mm. *B* 1753.

59 p 650 The Choir of St Paul's Cathedral. (and in French) Pt 9. 260 × 406/292 × 419mm. *B* 1753.

60 p 686 Bread Street Ward and Cordwainer's Ward ... taken from the last Survey. 1754. Pt 45. 305 × 178/311 × 185mm. Swelled rule added under title. *S* 3,15.

61 p 692 Queen Hith Ward and Vintry Ward ... taken from the last Surveys. 1754. Pt 44. 305 × 178/311 ×

185mm. Swelled rule added under title. *S* 3,1.

62 p 711 Farrington Ward without ... taken from the last Survey. 1755. Pt 52. 292 × 349/298 × 356mm. Fleet Market shown in lieu of Canal. Swelled rule added under title. *S* 3,231.

63 p 725 The North Prospect of St Andrew's Church in Holborn. Pt 115. 308 × 194/340 × 208mm. *M* 1059.

64 p 728 A Mapp of St Andrews Holborn Parish. 1755. Pt 53. 292 × 324/298 × 330mm. Adds the name 'Powis House', a chapel near Little Ormond Street and a swelled rule under title. *S* 6,85.

65 p 729 (on swallow-tailed banderole in sky) Furnivals Inn in Holbourn. Sutton Nicholls delin. et sculp. Publish'd ... 1754 for Stowe's Survey. Pt 13. 318 × 451/343 × 457mm. Publication-line burnished out. *B* 1728. *LD* 23.

66 p 730 The Prospect of Gray's Inn. 1755. Pt 97. 200 × 317/213 × 337mm. *S* 4,69.

67 p 731 (on two swallow-tailed banderoles) Powis House/in Ormond Street. Sutton Nicholls sculp. Published ... 1754 for Stows Survey. Pt 11. 330 × 451/343 × 457mm. Publication-line burnished out. *B* 1728. *LD* 20.

68 p 739 St Bridget, alias St Bride's Church. Pt 120. 337 × 210/356 × 229mm. *M* 1086.

69 p 744 The Temple. Publish'd ... 1755 for Stow's Survey. Pt 54. 203 × 330/210 × 343mm. *S* 3,271.

70 p 757 The Surgeon's Theatre in the Old Bailey. Pt 105. 191 × 330/203 × 343mm. Built by George Dance senior, 1745. *M* 991.

VOL. 2

71 front. A New Mapp of the countries Ten Miles round the Cities of London & Westminster & Borough of Southwark. R.W. Seale sculp. Pt 135. 210 × 292/229 × 305mm.

72 p 12 A Mapp of the Parishes of St Saviours Southwark and St Georges. 1755. Pt 56. 289 × 362/298 × 368mm. *S* 4,27.

73 p 18 The North West Prospect of the Parish Church of St George in Southwark. Pt 107. 337 × 229/368 × 237mm. Figures on clock face run anti-clockwise. Built by John Price, 1734–6. *M* 1382.

74 p 21 A Map of the Parishes of St Olave and St Thomas Southwark. Publish'd ... 1755 for Stow's Survey. Pt 84. 279 × 349/292 × 356mm. Title along tm. Refs 1–63.

75 p 22 St Olave and St Mary Magdalens Bermondsey ... Taken from ye last Survey. 1755. Pt 55. 286 × 356/295 × 362mm. *S* 4,21.

76 p 26 A Map of the Parish of St Mary Magdalen Bermondsey. Publish'd ... 1755 for Stow's Survey. Pt 82. 286 × 349/292 × 356mm. Refs 1–40, A–Q.

77 p 37 St Mary White Chapel/and St John, Wapping, Parish/Taken from ye last Survey With Corrections and Additions. (in cartouche tr) Publish'd ... 1755 for

Stow's Survey. Pt 83. 352 × 284/360 × 295mm. Refs 1–75.

78 p 37 The Parish of St John's Wapping – The Parish of St Paul Shadwell. 1755. Pt 58. 283 × 363/289 × 368mm. *S* 4,47.

79 p 44 A Map of the Parish of St Mary White Chappel – A Map of the Parish of St Katherines by the Tower. 1755. Pt 57. 273 × 356/276 × 362mm. *S* 4,44.

80 p 46 An Actuall Survey of the/Parish of St Dunstans Stepney/alias Stebunheath … Publish'd … 1755 for Stows Survey. Pt 85. 343 × 279/356 × 292mm. Title in cartouche. Refs 1–112.

81 p 46 A Map of the Parish of St Dunstans Stepney als Stebunheath … 1755. Pt 59. 286 × 419/292 × 425mm. *S* 4,47.

82 p 47 The North West Prospect of Christ Church in Spittlefields. Pt 113. 315 × 229/340 × 233mm. Built by Hawksmoor, 1723–9. *M* 1350.

83 p 48 Spittlefields … Taken from ye last Survey. 1755. Pt 60. 283 × 356/292 × 362mm. Swelled rule added under title. *S* 4,48.

84 p 50 Shoreditch, Norton Folgate, and Crepplegate Without Taken from ye last Survey. 1755. Pt 61. 283 × 352/292 × 362mm. St Luke's Workhouse in Old Street added. *S* 4,50.

85 p 50 The South West Prospect of the Church of St Leonard Shoreditch. Pt 108. 353 × 195/375 × 205mm. Built by George Dance senior, 1736–40. *M* 1366.

86 p 50 South West View of the Parish Church of St Luke in Old Street. Pt 104. 356 × 218/375 × 223mm. Erroneously attributed to George Dance senior and John James, 1727–33. *M* 1368.

87 p 58 A Map of St Giles's Cripple Gate Without. 1755. Pt 49. 279 × 359/286 × 362mm. St Luke's Workhouse in Old Street added. Flourish added after title. *S* 4,60.

88 p 59 Cow Cross Being St Sepulchers Parish Without and the Charterhouse Taken from ye last Survey. 1755. Pt 62. 165 × 298/178 × 305mm. 'Porter's Block' added near Cow Cross. *S* 4,61.

89 p 60 (on swallow-tailed banderole in sky) Charterhouse Square. Sutton Nicholls delin. et sculp. For Stowes Survey. Pt 124. 330 × 445/349 × 457mm. Publication-line burnished out. *B* 1728. *LD* 33.

90 p 61 A Map of St Sepulchers without Charterhouse Liberty and Clarken Well Parish. Publish'd 1755 for Stow's Survey. Pt 86. 279 × 362/305 × 381mm. Title along tm.

91 p 62 The Parish of St James Clerkenwell Taken from ye last Survey. 1755. Pt 63. 283 × 356/292 × 368mm. Additional ref '36', Red Lion Street and Cold Bath Fields Buildings. *S* 4,63.

92 p 71 The Prospect of Lincolns Inn. 1755. Pt 96. 203 × 317/216 × 337mm. Without Kip's credit. *S* 4,73.

93 p 72 (on swallow-tailed banderole in sky) Newcastle House/in Lincolns Inn Fields. Sutton Nicholls delin. et sculp. Publish'd … 1754 for Stowes Survey. Pt 15. 432 × 324/457 × 337mm. Publication-line burnished out. Rusticated wall with balustrade and ball ornaments and two gates to front court substituted for wrought-iron grilles, two round-headed arches and a flight of steps. *B* 1728. *LD* 25.

94 p 76 A Mapp of the Parish of St Giles's in the Fields. 1755. Pt 64. 289 × 365/302 × 375mm. Swelled rule added under title. 'Bason' of water added to centre of Lincolns Inn Fields, diagonal and cross paths to Bloomsbury Square; also Seven Dials is identified. *S* 4,75.

95 p 78 The North West View of St Giles Church in the Fields. Pt 106. 305 × 191/325 × 203mm. Clock-face reversed, showing 10 instead of 2 o'clock. Built by Henry Flitcroft, 1731–4. *M* 1362.

96 p 83 (on swallow-tailed banderole in sky) South-ampton or Bloomsbury Square. Sutton Nicholls delin. et sculp. Published 1754 for Stowe's Survey. Pt 18. 324 × 445/343 × 457mm. Publication-line burnished out. Cruciform, railed paths in the centre replaced by a converging pattern of diagonals. *B* 1728. *LD* 21.

97 p 84 The Parish Church of St Mary le Bone in Middlesex – A Prospect of the Parish Church of St George in Bloomsbury. Pt 110. 349 × 210/376 × 220mm. St George's built by Hawksmoor, 1720–30. *M* 1360.

98 p 84 (on swallow-tailed banderole in sky) Mountague House/In Great Russell Street. Sutton Nicholls del. & sculp. For Stowe's Survey. Pt 123. 324 × 445/337 × 457mm. Publication-line partly burnished out. *B* 1728. *LD* 18.

99 p 103 (on swallow-tailed banderole in sky) St Mary le Strand. Sutton Nicholls sculp. Pt 101. 445 × 337/457 × 343mm. *B* 1728. *LD* 28.

100 p 107 Somerset House. Publish'd 1755 for Stow's Survey. Pt 66. 206 × 330/216 × 340mm. Without Kip's credit. *S* 4,105.

101 p 108 St Clements Danes in the Strand. (tl)Pt 99. 337 × 210/370 × 213mm. Caption changed. *M* 1335.

102 p 112 A Mapp of the Parishes of St Clements Dane, St Mary Savoy with the Rolls Liberty and Lincolns Inn. Pt 65. 292 × 349/298 × 362mm. Swelled rule added under title. *S* 4,108.

103 p 579 A Perspective View of Whitehall. (and in French) J. Maurer delin et sculp. Publish'd … 1754 for Stowe's Survey. Pt 24. 210 × 406/267 × 432mm. *B* 1753.

104 p 579 The Prospect of Whitehall. 1755. Pt 91. 210 × 330/216 × 343mm. Without Kip's credit. *S* 6,5.

105 p 579 A Perspective View of Ye Parade in St James's Park/the Treasury, the New Buildings for the Horse Guards … (and in French) J. Maurer delin. et sculp. Publish'd … 1754 for Stowe's Survey. Pt 5. 210 × 406/254 × 419mm. Horse Guards built to Kent's

design after his death by John Vardy and William Robinson, 1750–8. *B* 1753.

106 p 581 Westminster Abbey. 1755. Pt 95. 210 × 324/216 × 337mm. Hawksmoor's W. towers, completed c 1745, added. *S* 6,7.

107 p 641 A Mapp of the Parish of St Margarets Westminster. 1755. Pt 73. 292 × 349/298 × 356mm. Flourish added under title. Neither Westminster Bridge nor the Abbey towers added. *S* 6,67.

108 p 641 A View of Westminster Bridge from Lambeth. (and in French) J. Maurer Delint. P. Fourdrinier sculpt. Pulished 1754 for Stowe's Survey. Pt 17. 216 × 394/254 × 406mm. Refs 1–5. *B* 1753.

109 p 645 A Mapp of the Parish of St Martins in the Fields. 1755. Pt 74. 356 × 286/362 × 298mm. Swelled rule added under the title. *S* 6,67.

110 p 647 (on banderole) St Martins Church. Pt 2. 445 × 330/457 × 343mm. Viewed from S.W. With plan.

111 p 652 St James House. 1755. Pt 92. 206 × 330/216 × 337mm. *S* 6,4.

112 p 655 The Parish of St James's Westminster taken from the last Survey. 1755. Pt 75. 356 × 292/365 × 298mm. Flourish added under title. A round pond has been added in St James's Square and Carnaby Market is identified. *S* 6,80.

113 p 655 (on swallow-tailed banderole in sky) St James's Square. Sutton Nicholls delin et sculp. Publish'd ... 1754 for Stowe's Survey. Pt 12. 318 × 457/343 × 470mm. Publication-line burnished out. In the centre a round pond and fountain with a boating couple; the garden is surrounded by octagonal railings with obelisks at the angles. In its original state this showed a centre of open ground shut off only by a rectangle of rough rails and with a gardener's hut rc. *B* 1728. *LD* 12.

114 p 659 A Mapp of the Parish of St Anns. 1755. Pt 76. 311 × 181/318 × 184mm. Flourish added under title. *S* 6,85.

115 p 660 (on swallow-tailed banderole in sky) Leicester Square. Sutton Nicholls del. et sculp. Publish'd ... 1754 for Stowe's Survey. Pt 16. 324 × 445/343 × 457mm. Publication-line burnished out. This plate is amended from its second state in which quadripartite lawns around a central tree are planted out with trees within rectangular railings with obelisks at the gates and corners. Now the trees have gone and the centrepiece is an equestrian statue of George I which came from Canons and was installed by Frederick, Prince of Wales to vex his father George II. It was unveiled in November 1748. Railings round the lawn are now octagonal. *B* 1728. *LD* 49.

116 p 661 (on swallow-tailed banderole in sky) Sohoe or Kings Square. Sutton Nicholls sculp. Published ... 1754 for Stowes Survey. Pt 26. 318 × 445/337 × 457mm. Publication-line burnished out. Central garden altered in layout and the gate posts of the railings

replaced by arched metal lampholders, the corner-posts by lampstands. Also recorded are the 1745–8 alterations to the house in the N.W. corner, no 7, mentioned in *Survey of London* vol. 33, p 60. *B* 1728. *LD* 17.

117 p 661 A Mapp of the Parish of St Pauls Covent Garden. 1755. Pt 77. 305 × 178/317 × 190mm. Flourish added under title. Broad Court is identified. *S* 6,87.

118 p 667 (on banderole in sky) The House of Lord Archer in Covent Garden. Publish'd 1754 for Stowe's Survey. Pt 6. 324 × 457/349 × 463mm. Publication-line burnished out. Caption altered from 'The House of Thomas Archer Esq.' on his elevation to the peerage in 1747. See *Survey of London* vol. 36, pp 166–7. *B* 1731. *LD* 27.

119 p 667 The North West Prospect of the Parish Church of St George Hanover Square. Pt 112. 354 × 227/375 × 240mm. Building to the S. eliminated, shadow of porch altered. Built by John James, 1712–25. *M* 1336.

120 p 667 (on swallow-tailed banderole in sky) Hanover Square. Sutton Nicholls delin. et sculp. Publish'd ... 1754 for Stowes Survey. Pt 19. 324 × 457/343 × 470mm. Publication-line burnished out. Rectangular lawn now segmented by converging paths; iron railings, posts and gates replaced by wooden posts and rails. *B* 1728. *LD* 10.

121 p 668 (on swallow-tailed banderole in sky) Golden Square. Sutton Nicholls delin. et sculp. Published ... 1754 for Stowes Survey. Pt 25. 324 × 457/337 × 470mm. Publication-line burnished out. The centre, formerly shown as occupied by four segmental lawns adorned with trees, surrounding a central clump within rectangular railings and gates of iron, is now shown with a round lawn and central statue with octagonal railings and lampstands. The statue is of George II by Van der Nost the elder and was acquired from the Canons sale and erected in March 1753. *B* 1728. *LD* 11.

122 p 668 (on banderole) Grovenor Square. Published ... for Stow's Survey 1754. Pt 14. 318 × 445/343 × 457mm. The square was formed 1725–35. *B* 1731.

123 p 670 (on swallow-tailed banderole in sky) Buckingham House in St James's Park. Sutton Nicholls sculp. Published ... 1754 for Stowe's Survey. Pt 22. 324 × 445/343 × 457mm. Publication-line burnished out. Forecourt basin and fountain eliminated. *B* 1728. *LD* 13.

124 p 670 (on swallow-tailed banderole in sky) Marlborough House/In St James's Park. Sutton Nicholls sculp. Published ... 1754 for Stowes Survey. Pt 23. 318 × 432/337 × 445mm. Publication-line burnished out. Trophy with Garter and blank cartouche removed from centre of parapet. *B* 1728. *LD* 14.

125 p 723 The Royal Palace of Kensington. (and in French) Maurer del. Truchy sculp. Publish'd ... 1754

for Stowe's Survey. Pt 20. 229 × 394/254 × 419mm. *B* 1753.

126 p 744 A Mapp of the Parishes of Lambeth and Christ Church. Publish'd 1755 for Stow's Survey. Pt 87. 280 × 360/286 × 363mm.

127 p 744 Lambeth and Christ Church Parish, South-wark, Taken from ye last Survey. 1755. Pt 78. 356 × 286/365 × 295mm. *S*,Appendix 83.

128 p 744 A General Prospect of Vaux Hall Gardens (and in French) Shewing at one View the disposition of the whole Gardens. Wale delint. J.S. Muller sculp. Pt 128. 267 × 387/292 × 406mm. *B* 1753.

129 p 748 Redriffe and Part of/St Mary Magdalens Parish/Southwark,/Taken from ye last Survey with/ Corrections. Publish'd ... 1755 for Stow's Survey. Pt 81. 175 × 300/184 × 307mm. Title in cartouche tc. Refs 1–34.

130 p 764 St Pauls/Parish/Shadwell/Taken from ye last Survey/With Corrections. Publish'd ... 1755 for Stows Survey. Pt 80. 173 × 300/181 × 307mm. Title in laurel wreath tr. Refs 1–28.

131 p 784 A Map of the Parish of St Mary Rotherhith. Publish'd ... 1755 for Stows Survey. Pt 79. 270 × 400/279 × 419mm. *S*,Appendix 87.

132 p 805 The North West Prospect of the Parish Church of St Mary at Islington. Pt 109. 356 × 215/375 × 224mm. Clock-face reversed, showing 11.20 instead of 1.40. Designed by Launcelot Dowbiggin, 1751–4. *M* 1370.

38 · MAITLAND'S HISTORY OF LONDON [1756]

Fifteen years after the publication of Maitland's own edition of his *History* (no 33) it was announced that a second edition was to be published in weekly Numbers of which the first appeared on Saturday, 29 December 1753, with the promise of 30 altogether by the end of July 1754. Publication of this revision was undertaken by a conger of booksellers headed by that same Thomas Osborne whom Dr Johnson in 1742 had beaten down with a folio. Completion of 60 Numbers, forming the first volume, was announced in the *Public Advertiser*, 4 March 1755. The title-pages of the two bound volumes are dated 1756 and the last plate was issued

in February of that year; Maitland, who died the year after, had increased the text by 600 pages.

In competition, perhaps, with the 1754 Stow (no 37) the illustrations were also much augmented: 120 plates are promised in the title 'by the best Hands' and two extra were actually issued. Twenty-one of these, mostly engravings by W.H. Toms, were those used in the author's edition. The remainder were engraved by Benjamin Cole either from the buildings themselves, from architect's designs or models or from the series published 20 years previously by Robert West and W.H. Toms, *Perspective Views of all the Ancient Churches* (no 32); it is noteworthy that the names of Maitland and of the engravers James Cole and Thomas Bowles are on the subscription-list for this publication.

The subjects of Cole's plates supplemented the traditional views of the Tower, Guildhall and other historic sites and were a new departure in that they featured recently erected buildings, with a preponderance of churches. Plates of no fewer than 79 churches and chapels were added to the three which appeared in the 1739 edition and Cole introduced 26 more of these and eight more public buildings as ornaments on the 17 ward maps.

In 1760 Osborne reissued the work in a third edition, retaining the same illustrations (except the headpiece). There were now 'Directions to the Bookbinder' with the plates misleadingly numbered 1–147 (less nos 131–9 which are left out)—misleading because this is really a name index to the plates which, with the addition of an interior of St Stephen, Walbrook, now numbered 123. Since Cole had produced so many architectural plates for a predominantly historical narrative the publisher thought some explanatory text was called for. In notes grouped under the headings Churches, Palaces, Bridges, Gates, Public Buildings and Maps each subject is described, some with considerable architectural detail. The actual names of the architects, however, with the exception of Inigo Jones, are taboo even when the works of such masters as Wren, Hawksmoor or Gibbs are discussed. This peculiarity of London guides of the period seems especially incongruous in a work introduced in these terms:

The purpose of this work is, to give an history of the Publick Buildings in the metropolis: representing them in elegant figures and accompanying these by an illustration of two kinds: the first for general use; containing with their history whatsoever concerning them is worth the attention of the curious; the other destined to the service of the practical architect; proposing them to him as models, and acquainting him what, in their several structures, he should imitate, and what to avoid.

These notes came in the form of a 112 page supplement bound at the back of the first volume with its own title, *English Architecture or the Publick Buildings of London and Westminster*.

This supplement, misnamed since it did not stray beyond the limits of London and its suburbs, was no doubt available separately, both to those who already possessed the text of the 1756 edition and to a professional clientele which, it was hoped, would appreciate the plates grouped according to building type with a descriptive text. That Londoners in general were becoming more interested in the aesthetics of their surroundings is suggested by the publication in that same year of the first Number of Dodsley's *London and its Environs* (no 41), illustrated with 80 small plates (and with a gazetteer equally innocent of architects' names). To ensure correct arrangement in *English Architecture* the 123 plates were engraved with a serial number tl, although a few escaped the graver and were numbered in MS; plates with the engraved number are certainly in a second state and belonged to this collection or later editions of Maitland.

In 1769 S. Bladon of Paternoster Row (in conjunction with J. Wilkie, T. Lowndes and G. Kearsley who later published the *Copper-plate Magazine*) reissued the text of Maitland's second edition with 'Directions' and plates as in 1760. Although the text of *English Architecture* was not included the plates were in their second state with engraved numerals. These booksellers then engaged the Rev John Entick, a schoolmaster who in 1766 had published his four-volume history of London (no 44) to bring Maitland's text up to date. They issued a prospectus which said that Maitland's book was 'presented at the City's Expence to every new Alderman' and announced that the first weekly Number of the new edition, continued down to 1771, would be published on Saturday, 23 February 1771, price sixpence. When complete the two bound volumes costing £3 10s would be 'embellished with One Hundred and Twenty Three Folio Copper-Plates, which cost upwards of Eight Hundred Pounds Drawing and Engraving'.

The completed volumes were prefaced by long-winded title-pages dated 1772 including this puff for the illustrations: 'Exactly drawn and curiously engraved on One Hundred and Thirty Copper-Plates, by the Best Hands and on so large a Scale, that each Plate could not be sold separate for less than One Shilling'. The 123 plates of the prospectus which are said to have cost so much are none other than the originals in their second (numbered) state. To these were added nine specially engraved extras, numbered 122–30, bringing the total up to 132; these were bound before the 'Directions to the Bookbinder' which makes no mention of them, being unrevised from the previous edition. The text consists of Maitland's second edition, the *English Architecture* supplement and Entick's 'continuation' of 148 pages; the last two with their own, undated title-pages.

Finally, in 1775, two of Bladon's partners reissued the second edition text with Entick's 'continuation' and the plates as in 1772, but without *English Architecture*. For the ten-mile circuit map, originally the second edition frontispiece, they substitute a new 20-mile circuit map numbered '131' in continuation of the 1772 extra plates.

The History of London from its foundation to the present time ... including The Several Parishes in Westminster, Middlesex, Southwark &c within the Bills of Mortality. By William Maitland, F.R.S. and Others. With a Complete Set of the Churches, Palaces, Publick Buildings, Hospitals, Bridges, &c, within and adjacent to this great Metropolis: The Plans of London, exhibiting its Appearance before the Fire: in its Ruins after that Conflagration in 1666; and as it is now rebuilt and extended: and a Map of all the Villages and Country within ten Miles Circumference: Exactly drawn and curiously engraved on One Hundred and Twenty Copper-Plates by the best Hands, and on so large a Scale, that each Plate could not be sold separate for less than one Shilling.... Vol. I. By the King's Authority. London: Printed for T. Osborne and J. Shipton, in Gray's-Inn; and J. Hodges, near London-Bridge, MDCCLVI.
(title of vol. 2 reset) The History and Survey of London from its foundation to the present time. Vol. II. Containing the political history of London. With an accurate survey of the several Wards, Liberties, Precincts, &c. An account of the several Parishes and Churches ... The whole illustrated with one Hundred and Twenty-one Copper-Plates ... MDCCLVI.

Folio, 413 × 260mm. 1756

COLLATION Vol. 1. Title-page; pp iii-iv, contents; pp 3–712, The History. Vol. 2. Title-page; dedication to

Slingsby Bethell (Lord Mayor 1755–6), contents of vol. 2 (4pp); pp 713–1392, The History continued; pp 1387–91 (bis), appendix; list of subscribers (6pp); pp 1393–410, index.

There are 122 plates, more than promised on either title-page: 21 of the 24 first edition plates (18 of these are by Toms, with his credit burnished out from seven, and three are historical maps); one composite plate made up from the eight small Bowles engravings of City Gates printed separately with text in 1739; 17 ward maps by Benjamin Cole, based on the Blome maps used in the 1720 edition of Stow (no 25; further details of these are to be found in Ralph Hyde's *Ward maps of the City of London*, where there is also information on Cole); one parish map by Cole; two general maps by Cole (country ten miles around, Westminster and the Duchy of Lancaster); four plans (Evelyn's for rebuilding London, Cole's plans for rebuilding the three bridges); 76 architectural plates by Cole (79 churches and chapels and 38 public buildings).

Benjamin Cole (fl 1700–67), of a well-known family of engravers, was at first chiefly engaged on producing maps and trade-cards. His first architectural venture seems to have been a series of small, clumsy engravings of English and Welsh cathedrals which he and John Harris published in 1715 and which subsequently were incorporated in Overton's *Prospects* (no. 26). For the same publisher he engraved in 1725 *Views of the Several Parts of the Palace or Castle of Versailles* and in 1736 he illustrated, with W.H. Toms, Hawksmoor's pamphlet *A short historical account of London Bridge*. His architectural plates, except when they are copied from some other engraver, are notable for their lack of staffage or background work aping, without his professional drawing skill, Colen Campbell's austere *Vitruvius Britannicus* (no 24) elevations.

The Inns of Court and squares so attractively illustrated in the contemporary 1754 Stow are absentees from this series of plates.

All plates, unless there is a statement to the contrary, have the credit 'B. Cole sc.' or 'B. Cole sculp.' in work br. Numbers on plates for publication in their second state with *English Architecture*, engraved or in MS tl, are quoted with the abbreviation EA after the dimensions. The letter *M* followed by a page number indicates the position of a plate in the 1739 edition. Plates based on West and Toms's *Perspective Views* are identified by *WT*.

VOL. 1

1 front. Ald-Gate – Bishop's-Gate – Moore-Gate – Cripple-Gate – Aldersgate – New-Gate – Lud-Gate – The Bridge-Gate. 230 × 360/245 × 370mm. EA 63. Composite plate from 8 small engr published in 1739 on separate pages. 'T.Bowles' credit on Ald-Gate. *M* 15–22.

2 viii (Allegorical headpiece) C. Frederick, Armiger Inv. Boitard sculp. 60 × 162/70 × 175mm. *M* 1.

3 p 43 London Bridge. Toms sc. 197 × 321/210 × 334mm. EA 59, with credit burnished out. *M* 33.

4 p 146 The Tower of London. Toms sc. 203 × 330/224 × 340mm. EA 64, with credit burnished out. *M* 493.

5 p 252 (on banderole between Tudor royal arms and City arms) A View of London about the year 1560. (along bm)Reduced ... from a large Print in the Collection of Sr Hans Sloane Bart. anno 1738. 252 × 464/310 × 470mm. EA 99. Refs A–Z, a-z, 1–47. *M* front. (*Darlington and Howgego* 8)

6 p 369 A Plan of the City and Suburbs of London as fortified by Order of Parliament in the Year 1642 & 1643. G. Vertue 1738. 195 × 340/222 × 355mm. EA 100. Explanation of forts on scrolls on each side. *M* 238.

7 p 432 (along tm) A Plan of the City and Liberties of London after the Dreadful Conflagration in the Year 1666/The Blank Part whereof represents the Ruins and Extent of the Fire & the Perspective that left standing. 203 × 331/230 × 342mm. EA101. Credit 'E. Bowen' burnished out. Refs (tr) A–Z, a-o, (bl) to churches 1–100. Based on the Hollar plan (*Hind* 11). *M* 293. (*Darlington and Howgego* 19)

8 p 447 London Restored or Sir John Evelyn's Plan for Rebuilding that Antient Metropolis after the Fire in 1666. Sir J. Evelyn delin. B. Cole sculp. 192 × 340/210 × 352mm. EA 102. Views of Holy Trinity, Minories (tl) and Rolls Chapel (tr). Refs. 1–38 and symbols bl and br. cf with larger engraving (475 × 360mm), 1748, in *Vetusta Monumenta* (no 36), item 8.

VOL. 2

9 front. (tm) A New Map of the Countries Ten Miles round the Cities of London & Westminster & Borough of Southwark. 247 × 290/255 × 302mm. EA 122. (*Darlington and Howgego* 105)

10 p 761 (tl) Aldersgate Ward/with its Divisions into/ Precincts and Parishes/And the Liberty of St Martins/ le Grand, according to a/New Survey. 232 × 377/245 × 386mm. EA 106. Insets of St Anne and St Agnes, Gresham Street and St Botolph, Aldersgate, 'built 1754'. (*Hyde* 3)

11 p 763 Goldsmiths' Hall, in Foster Lane – Stationers

Hall, near Paternoster Row. 360 × 230/377 × 240mm. EA 98. Goldsmiths' Hall built 1748.

12 p 776 (tl) The City of London/Lying-in Hospital/for Married Women/At Shaftesbury House in/Aldersgate Street/Instituted March 30 1750. 337 × 231/375 × 235mm. EA 88.

13 p 776 (tl) Aldgate Ward/with its Divisions into/Precincts & Parishes/according to a/New Survey. 233 × 360/242 × 365mm. EA 105. Insets of St James, Duke's Place and St Katherine Coleman, Fenchurch Street. (*Hyde* 9).

14 p 790 (bl) Billingsgate Ward/and/Bridge Ward Within/with their Divisions into/Parishes/According to a new Survey. 240 × 362/247 × 370mm. EA 107. Insets of St Mary at Hill and St Botolph (ie St George), Botolph Lane. (*Hyde* 14).

15 p 793 (tc) Bishops-Gate Ward/within and without/According to a/New Survey. 1754. 232 × 365/240 × 372mm. EA 108. Insets of St Ethelburga and St Helen, both Bishopsgate Street. (*Hyde* 20)

16 p 823 (bc) Breadstreet Ward/and/Cordwainers Ward/with their Divisions into/Parishes/According to a New Survey. 1755. 230 × 358/235 × 368mm. EA 117. Insets of St Matthew, Friday Street and St Mildred, Bread Street. (*Hyde* 23)

17 p 828 These Plans of London Bridge, exclusive of the Houses: No 1, As it may be amended by reducing the sterlings. No 2, As it may be altered by reducing the arches, are most humbly presented unto ... Sir Richard Hoare Lord Mayor ... by Charles Labelye Esqre 1746. 210 × 380/230 × 387mm. EA 60.

18 p 834 The Monument. W.H. Toms sculpt. 328 × 205/348 × 210mm. EA 71, with credit burnished out. *M* 440.

19 p 838 (bc) Broad Street/Ward/Divided into Parishes according to/A New Survey – Cornhill/Ward/Divided into Parishes/according to/A New Survey. 352 × 470/375 × 490mm. EA 110. Insets of St Christopher le Stock, St Bartholomew by the Exchange and St Benet Fink. (*Hyde* 28)

20 p 846 A Perspective View of the Bank of England. 335 × 212/360 × 225mm. EA 73. Anon, with West and Toms credits burnished out. *M* 622. (*Bank of England* 11)

21 p 848 Ironmongers' Hall in Fenchurch Street London – The South Sea House in Threadneedle Street. 368 × 240/387 × 250mm. EA 96. Ironmongers' Hall rebuilt 1748–50, South Sea House erected 1724–5.

22 p 857 The College of Arms or Heralds' Office. 220 × 327/235 × 337mm. EA 94

23 p 880 (bc)Cheap Ward/with/its Divisions into/Parishes/according/to a New Survey. 1755. 360 × 480/376 × 490mm. EA 118. Insets of Guildhall Chapel, St Mildred (Poultry), Grocers' Hall and Blackwell Hall. (*Hyde* 38)

24 p 882 A View of the Guildhall of the City of London. (tc)Engraved for the History of London (tr)No 2. 205 × 324/225 × 335mm. EA 74. Toms credit burnished out, staffage brought up to date; three carriages in the forecourt but only one in first state. *M* 433.

25 p 892 (rc) The Wards of/Coleman Street/and/Bassishaw/Taken from the last Survey/with corrections and amendments. 1754. 355 × 240/366 × 251mm. EA 109. Insets of St Michael Bassishaw and St Stephen, Coleman Street. (*Hyde* 42)

26 p 898 The Royal Exchange. 223 × 287/240 × 300mm. EA 72. Anon, with Toms credit burnished out and Grinling Gibbons's statue of Charles II now shown inside main entrance. *M* 466.

27 p 904 (br)Cripplegate Ward/with/its Divisions into/Parishes/According to a New Survey. 1755. 353 × 240/368 × 248mm. EA 111. Inset of St Luke's Hospital. (*Hyde* 48)

28 p 922 (bc) Baynards Castle Ward/and/Faringdon Ward within/with their Divisions into/Parishes/according to a new/Survey. 1755. 352 × 460/368 × 470mm. EA 119. Insets of St Benet, Paul's Wharf, St Martin, Ludgate and St Andrew by the Wardrobe. (*Hyde* 33)

29 p 932 Merchant Taylors School – St Paul's School. 356 × 235/381 × 241mm. EA 92.

30 p 960 (tl) Farringdon Ward/without/with its divisions into/Parishes/according to a new/Survey. 1755. 360 × 465/380 × 475mm. EA 121. Insets of Temple Bar and N. gate of Bridewell. (*Hyde* 55)

31 p 967 The South East Prospect of the Temple Church. 190 × 320/210 × 331mm. EA 51. But for a blank sky and the wall to the l. extended to fill the broader plate corresponds to *WT* 2,10.

32 p 979 Bridewell. 203 × 325/225 × 340mm. EA 80. Anon, with Toms credit burnished out. *M* 661.

33 p 983 The South Prospect of St Bartholomew's Hospital – The General Plan of the new Building – The East Prospect of St Bartholomew's Hospital. 356 × 241/375 × 250mm. EA 84. Cole's engr which shows Gibbs's work, started in 1730, replaces the Toms plate. *M* 675.

34 p 991 The Surgeon's Theatre in the Old Bailey. 198 × 342/213 × 350mm. EA 95. Built by George Dance senior, 1745.

35 p 995 (tc)Langborn Ward/and/Candlewick Ward/with their Divisions into/Parishes/according to a New Survey. 1755. 356 × 463/368 × 470mm. EA 120. Insets of 'Allhallows Staining' (ie St Olave, Hart Street), St Clement, Eastcheap and St Mary 'Woolnorth'. (*Hyde* 58)

36 p 999 (tc) A New and Correct/Plan/of/Limestreet Ward/with its/Divisions into Parishes/according to a New Survey. 1755. 225 × 362/241 × 368mm. EA 112. Inset of front of Leadenhall Market. (*Hyde* 60)

37 p 1006 (bl)Portsoken/Ward/with its Divisions/into Parishes/According to a New/Survey. 1755. 362 × 225/381 × 235mm. EA 114. (*Hyde* 63)

38 p 1024 (bc)Queen-Hith Ward/and/Vintry Ward/with their Divisions/into Parishes/according to a/New Survey. 1755. 227 × 365/245 × 377mm. EA 113. Inset of St Michael, Queenhithe. (*Hyde* 66)

39 p 1026 The North West Prospect of the Danes Church in Wellclose Square – The South West Prospect of the Sweeds Church in Princes Square Ratcliff highway. 362 × 235/381 × 241mm. EA 40.

40 p 1031 (tl)Tower Street/Ward/with their Divisons/into Parishes/according to a/New Survey. 368 × 232/375 × 241mm. EA 116. Insets of East India House and entrance of Westminster Hall. (*Hyde* 70)

41 p 1033 The Custom House. 205 × 322/220 × 338mm. EA 66. Anon. This plate seems to derive directly from the 1720 ed of Stow (*S* 2,51) although new end-pavilions and a rusticated centre are added and buildings on each side seem to be screened by hoardings. Rebuilt by Thomas Ripley, c 1722.

42 p 1041 Fishmongers Hall near London Bridge – Vintners Hall in Thames Street. 350 × 230/375 × 245mm. EA 97

43 p 1046 (bc) Walbrook Ward/and/Dowgate Ward/with their Divisions into/Parishes/according to a New/Survey. 227 × 357/240 × 372mm. EA 115. Insets of St Stephen and St Michael Royal. Inscribed to Alderman Bethell, etc, 1755. (*Hyde* 73)

44 p 1046 The Mansion House for the Reception of the Lord Mayor of the City of London for the time Being. 228 × 308/245 × 370mm. EA 75. The 'Mare's Nest' has been added since the Toms plate (*M* 460) so a new Cole plate has been substituted.

45 p 1050 The North West Prospect of the Parish Church of St Alban in Wood Street. 345 × 240/370 × 250mm. EA 23.

46 p 1053 The North West Prospect of the Parish Church of All-hallows in Bread Street – The East Prospect of the Parish Church of St Michael in Wood Street. 229 × 368/241 × 381mm. EA 41.

47 p 1054 The Parish Church of Allhallows the Great in Thames Street – The French Hospital near Old Street. 355 × 241/381 × 248mm. EA 54. The French Hospital was in Bath Street running N. from Old Street.

48 p 1059 The North Prospect of St Andrew's Church in Holborn/1754. 315 × 200/333 × 210mm. EA 29.

49 p 1062 The North West Prospect of the Parish Church of St Andrew Undershaft in Leadenhall Street – A Perspective View of the Parish Church of St John the Evangelist in Westminster. 381 × 229/394 × 238mm. EA 22. The St Andrew's view is much cruder but derives from *WT* 1,5.

50 p 1066 The North West Prospect of the Parish Church of St Anthony in Budge Row. 343 × 216/368 × 229mm. EA 20. ie St Antholin's.

51 p 1069 The West Prospect of the Church of St Bartholomew the Great – The Southwest Prospect of the Church of St Bartholomew the Less. 311 × 203/330 × 216mm. EA 48. Reduced copies, eliminating staffage. *WT* 2, 1-2.

52 p 1072 The North West Prospect of the Parish Church of St Bennet Grace Church. 343 × 241/368 × 250mm. EA 25.

53 p 1079 The Parish Church of St Botolph without Aldgate built AD. 1740 4/5. J. Smith delin. 388 × 230/408 × 240mm. EA 28. Built by George Dance senior.

54 p 1084 The North East Prospect of the Parish Church of St Botolph without Bishopsgate. 356 × 241/375 × 248mm. EA 14. Rebuilt by James Gould and George Dance senior, 1727–9.

55 p 1086 St Brigit alias St Brides-Church. Toms sculp. 333 × 210/360 × 226mm. EA 8, with credit 'B. Cole' substituted. *M* 395.

56 p 1093 The Parish Church of/St Dunstan's in the East – The Parish Church of/St James at Garlick hith. 229 × 362/241 × 368mm. EA 44.

57 p 1094 The South East Prospect of the Church of St Dunstan in the West. 205 × 360/225 × 377mm. EA 27. Buildings added each side to fill broader plate but follows closely, even to the contemporary staffage, *WT* 2,5.

58 p 1101 The South East Prospect of the Chapel Royal of St Peter in the Tower – The West Prospect of the Parish Church of St Giles Cripplegate. 356 × 241/381 × 248mm. EA 45. Follows closely, even to staffage and work in sky, *WT* 2,11 and 6.

59 p 1116 The South west Prospect of the Parish Church of St Catherine Cree, in Leadenhall Street. 203 × 343/229 × 349mm. EA 21. Differing in detail, eg the pediment over the entrance, the bell turret and buildings to the r., but same viewpoint as *WT* 1,9.

60 p 1124 The North-West Prospect of the Parish Church of St Magnus the Martyr, the North East End of London Bridge. 360 × 238/375 × 245mm. EA 16.

61 p 1126 The West prospect of the Parish Church of St Olave in the Old Jewry – The South East prospect of the Parish Church of St Margaret Lothbury. 229 × 356/241 × 368mm. EA 47.

62 p 1128 The Parish Church of St Mary/Aldermary in Bow Lane – The Parish Church of St Margaret/Pattens in little Tower Street. 241 × 365/248 × 368mm. EA 52.

63 p 1133 The South East Prospect of the Parish Church of/St Mary Abchurch in Abchurch Lane – The North East Prospect of the Parish Church of/St. Martin Outwich in Threadneedle Street. 235 × 365/241 × 375mm. EA 33.

64 p 1134 The East prospect of the Parish Church of St Mary Aldermanbury – The East prospect of the Parish Church of Alhallows in London Wall. 229 × 362/241 × 368mm. EA 46.

65 p 1137 Bow Church. W.H. Toms sculp. 325 × 200/350 × 212mm. EA 13, with credit burnished out. *M* 452.

66 p 1141 The South East Prospect of the Parish Church of St Mary Magdalen in Old Fish Street – The South East Prospect of the Parish Church of St Lawrence Jewry. 235 × 362/241 × 381mm. EA 37.

67 p 1147 The West Prospect of the Parish Church of St Michael Cornhill. 355 × 220/375 × 232mm. EA 53.

68 p 1162 The West Prospect of St Paul's Cathedral. (tr) Plate I. No 1. Toms sculp. 428 × 365/454 × 390mm. EA 2, with credit burnished out. *M* 483.

69 p 1175 St Vedast alias Foster Lane – Alhallows Barking – St Peters in Cornhill. 222 × 368/241 × 381mm. EA 39.

70 p 1177 The North East prospect of St Olives Church Hart Street – The South East prospect of St Peter's le Poor in Broad Street. 349 × 235/368 × 241mm. EA 32. St Olave's is viewed from the N. and *WT* 1,11 is from a more easterly viewpoint. St Peter's from same viewpoint as *WT* 1,12.

71 p 1178 The South Prospect of the Church of St Sepulchre. 224 × 315/228 × 324mm. EA 49. Blank sky, otherwise follows *WT* 2,9.

72 p 1183 The Parish Church of St Swithin in Cannon Street – The Parish Church of St Edmund the King/in/Lombard Street (finished 1690) – The Parish Church of St Nicholas Coleabby, Old Fish Street. 216 × 362/241 × 368mm. EA 38.

(p 1193 Ancient seal of City, with letterpress)

(pp 1242–58 Arms of City Companies: wood-engravings with text. *M* 598–617.)

73 p 1263 The Treasury in St James's Park – The Admiralty near Whitehall. 349 × 235/362 × 241mm. EA 70. Kent's Treasury Building built 1734–6, Ripley's Admiralty built 1723–6, before the Adam screen of 1759–61.

74 p 1281 A View of the House of Peers/… at the end of the Session 1755. 343 × 229/362 × 235mm. EA 67. Interior.

75 p 1288 The East Prospect of Haberdashers Alms Houses at Hoxton. 222 × 362/241 × 375mm. EA 85.

76 p 1289 Fishmongers Alms-houses at Newington Butts, Surry – Bancrofts Alms-houses in Bow Road. 356 × 235/381 × 241mm. EA 86.

77 p 1290 Bethlehem Hospital. Toms sculp. 195 × 381/215 × 390mm. EA 81, with credit burnished out. *M* 660.

78 p 1291 The Charter-House Hospital. Toms sc. 202 × 320/225 × 330mm. EA 79, with credit burnished out. *M* 661.

79 p 1292 Christ's Hospital. Toms sc. 207 × 320/225 × 330mm. EA 91, with credit burnished out. *M* 662.

80 p 1293 A View of the Foundling Hospital. 188 × 322/208 × 330mm. EA 89. Built 1742–52.

81 p 1302 St George's Hospital. Toms sc. 200 × 328/225 × 333mm. EA 90, with credit burnished out. *M* 676.

82 p 1305 Guys Hospital. R. West Delin. W.H. Toms sculp. 198 × 362/228 × 373mm. EA 82, with credit 'B.Cole sculp.' substituted. Lamp posts, railings and gate posts added to the front courtyard. *M* 667.

83 p 1312 The College of Physicians in Warwick Lane – The London Hospital in Whitechapel Road – St John the Baptists in the Savoy. 358 × 230/378 × 244mm. EA 76. London Hospital built 1752.

84 p 1322 St Thomas's Hospital. 312 × 202/333 × 222mm. EA 83. Anon, with Toms credit burnished out. *M* 678.

85 p 1326 The fore front of the Royal Hospital at Chelsea – The back front of the Royal Hospital at Chelsea. 191 × 330/216 × 356mm. EA 78. (*Longford* 7)

86 p 1327 (in rococo cartouche) A/New and Accurate Plan/of the/City of Westminster/The Dutchy of Lancaster/and Places Adjacent. 262 × 229/375 × 235mm. EA 103.

87 p 1328 The East Prospect of the Abby of St Peter & of the Parish Church of St Margaret/Westminster. 280 × 410/318 × 419mm. EA 1. W. towers completed by John James, c 1745. This supersedes the fanciful view in the 1st ed (*M* 686) by Toms, and is copied from an engraving by J. June after J. Maurer (*Crowle* 2.153).

88 p 1335 South West View of the Parish Church of St Clement's Danes in the Strand. 342 × 215/368 × 225mm. EA 19.

89 p 1336 The North West Prospect of the Parish church of St George Hanover Square. 358 × 231/390 × 245mm. EA 7. Built 1712–25.

90 p 1337 The South Prospect of St James's Westminster – The North Prospect of St Anne's Westminster. 352 × 242/370 × 248mm. EA 17.

91 p 1340 A View of the House of Commons. 349 × 229/368 × 235mm. EA 68. Interior.

92 p 1342 The East Front of the Horse and Foot Guards at Whitehall. 190 × 323/210 × 332mm. EA 65. Built to William Kent's designs by John Vardy and W. Robinson, 1750–8.

93 p 1343 The Royal Banqueting House at White Hall – The Navy Office in Broad Street. 348 × 230/365 × 240mm. EA 69. The Navy Office was in Seething Lane, the Navy Pay Office was in Broad Street.

94 p 1343 A Perspective View of St Martin's Church. 312 × 198/333 × 210mm. EA 4. Reduced from the West and Toms engraving (*M* 731).

95 p 1345 Trinity Alms houses in Mile End Road – Ironmongers Alms Houses in Kingsland Road – His Majesty's Stables in the Mews. 356 × 241/375 × 248mm. EA 87.

96 p 1345 St James's Palace and Parts Adjacent. 190 × 328/210 × 340mm. EA 55. Anon, with Toms credit burnished out. *M* 738.

97 p 1345 The South West Prospect of St Mary's Church in the Strand. 308 × 198/328 × 208mm. EA 5.

98 p 1346 The North East Prospect of the Parish Church of St George in Queen Square, near Holborn – The North East Prospect of the Parish Church of St Paul in Covent Garden. 368 × 241/381 × 249mm. EA 3. St George the Martyr was built in 1706 and bought by the Fifty New Church Commissioners in 1723 as a parish church.

99 p 1346 The South prospect of Somerset House in the Strand. 225 × 357/245 × 372mm. EA 57.

100 p 1348 The South East Prospect of Westminster Bridge. 362 × 559/406 × 573mm. EA 61. Refs A-R.

101 p 1348 A Front View of the Royal Palace of Kensington. 216 × 356/241 × 381mm. EA 56.

102 p 1350 The North West Prospect of Christ Church in Spittlefields. 318 × 240/338 × 252mm. EA 10. Built 1723–9; the engraving appears to have been made from a model.

103 p 1350 (in cartouche) A/New and Accurate Survey/of the Parishes/of St Andrew Holbourn, without the Freedom/St George Queen Square, St James Clerkenwell/St Luke Old Street, St Mary Islington/And/The Charterhouse Liberty. 230 × 360/240 × 375mm. EA 104. The only parish map in the collection.

104 p 1353 A South West Prospect of St Dunstan's Church at Stepney. 1755. 225 × 362/241 × 390mm. EA 24. Above building on l.: 'Durham Row'. Work in the sky and in the foreground suggest a copy from a West and Toms engraving so far untraced.

105 p 1360 The Parish Church of St Mary le Bone in Middlesex – A Prospect of the Parish Church of St George in Bloomsbury. 360 × 212/378 × 225mm. EA 6. St George's built 1720–30.

106 p 1361 The Parish Church of St George in Ratcliff highway – The Parish Church of St Ann at Limehouse. 229 × 368/241 × 373mm. EA 30. St George's built 1715–23, St Anne's built 1712–24. The St Anne's engraving is a travesty of Hawksmoor's architecture.

107 p 1362 The North West View of St Giles's Church in the Fields. 310 × 195/330 × 208mm. EA 9. The engraving appears to have been made from the wooden model, still preserved. Rebuilt by Henry Flitcroft, 1731–4.

108 p 1363 The Southwest prospect of the Parish Church of St James's Clerkenwell – The Southwest prospect of the Parish Church of St Matthew at Bethnal Green. 349 × 235/368 × 241mm. EA 31. St Matthew's built by George Dance senior, 1740–6.

109 p 1365 The Parish Church of St John at Hackney – The Parish Church of St Thomas in Southwark. 362 × 229/381 × 236mm. EA 35. St John's rebuilt c 1730.

110 p 1366 The South West Prospect of the Church of St Leonard Shoreditch. 356 × 203/375 × 222mm. EA 11. Built by George Dance senior, 1736–40.

111 p 1368 South West View of the Parish Church of St Luke in Old Street. 358 × 216/375 × 222mm. EA 18. Built 1727–35.

112 p 1370 The North East Prospect of the Parish Church of St Mary at Islington. 356 × 216/381 × 229mm. EA 15. Built 1751–4.

113 p 1373 The North West Prospect of the Parish Church of St Mary White Chapple. 210 × 362/229 × 368mm. EA 26.

114 p 1379 The South West Prospect of the Parish Church of St Pauls at Shadwel – The South East Prospect of the Parish Church of St Johns at Wapping. 362 × 241/381 × 250mm. EA 34. St John's built 1734–5.

115 p 1382 The North West Prospect of the Parish Church of St George in Southwark. 349 × 229/375 × 240mm. EA 12. Built 1734–5.

116 p 1383 The Parish Church of St John in Southwark – The Parish Church of St Mary in Rotherhithe. 235 × 355/241 × 381mm. EA 42. St John Horsleydown built 1732, St Mary's built c 1714 (tower 1739).

117 p 1384 The South East Prospect of Christ Church in Surry – The South East Prospect of the Parish Church/of St Mary at Lambeth. 362 × 235/368 × 241mm. EA 43. Christ Church, Blackfriars Road built 1738.

118 p 1386 The Arch Bishop of Canterbury's Palace at Lambeth. 216 × 356/241 × 368mm. EA 58.

119 p 1387 The Parish Church of St Mary Magdalen Bermondsey – The Parish Church of St Mary Newington Butts. 356 × 235/381 × 241mm. EA 36. St Mary, Newington rebuilt 1721.

120 p 1389 The Excise Office – The Parish Church of St Olave, Southwark. 356 × 235/381 × 241mm. EA 93. St Olave, Tooley Street rebuilt by Flitcroft, 1728.

121 p 1390 The South Prospect of the Church of St Saviour in Southwark. 210 × 310/230 × 324mm. EA 50.

122 p 1390 A perspective View of the Royal Hospital at Greenwich. 332 × 515/373 × 522mm. EA 77.

123 p 1391 To the Rt Honble Slingsby Bethell ... Lord Mayor ... these Designs for Building a Bridge with Stone to Cross the River Thames from Blackfryers ... is ... inscribed by ... Edward Oakley. Edwd Oakley Archit. Inven. et Delin. Publish'd Feb. 1756. 317 × 398/325 × 400mm. EA 62. Bethell was Lord Mayor 1755–6.

The History and Survey of London from its foundation to the present time In two volumes.... Illustrated with One Hundred and Twenty-Three Copper-Plates, exhibiting the plans of the Wards in London, of the City of Westminster and Parishes adjacent; and Views of the whole City at different Times, and of all the Churches, Palaces, Bridges, Halls, Hospitals &c, and a Map of the Country ten Miles round this great City. The Third Edition To which is now first added A Succinct Review of their History and a Candid Examination of their Defects also an additional Plate of ... St Stephen's Walbroke ... By William Maitland, F.R.S. and others. Vol. I (II). By the King's Authority, London, Printed for T. Osborne, in Gray's Inn. MDCCLX.

Folio, 415 × 260mm.   1760

COLLATION Vol. 1. Title-page; dedication to Sir Slingsby Bethell (Lord Mayor 1755–6); list of subscribers (8pp); pp iii–viii, contents; pp 3–712, The History; subtitle; pp 1–112, English Architecture. Vol. 2. Title-page; contents of vol. 2 (2pp); pp 713–1392, The History continued; pp 1387–91 (bis), appendix; pp 1393–410, index; directions to binder (2pp).

The text is as the 1756 edition with the exception of the 112 supplementary pages in vol. 1 with a title:

English Architecture: or, The Publick Buildings of London and Westminster, with Plans of the Streets and Squares, represented In One Hundred and Twenty-three Folio Plates; with a succinct Review of their History, and a candid Examination of their Perfections and Defects. London, Printed for T. Osborne in Gray's Inn.

The 123 plates mentioned are identical with those in the 1756 edition with the exception of the engraved headpiece on p viii which is replaced by a printer's ornament. An extra plate, however, which is mentioned in the general title, fronts the *English Architecture* title-page:

124 front. Saint Stephen Wallbrook. 190 × 311/216 × 324mm. EA 123. Interior.

The History of London from its foundation to the present time ... By William Maitland, F.R.S. and Continued to the Year 1772 by the Rev. John Entick, M.A. Illustrated with a Complete Set of the Churches, Palaces, Publick Buildings, Hospitals, Bridges &c. within and adjacent to this great Metropolis. The Plans of London exhibiting its Appearance before the Fire; in its Ruins after that Conflagration in 1666: and as it is now rebuilt and extended. With a large Map of all the Villages and Country within ten Miles Circumference. Exactly drawn and curiously engraved on One Hundred and Thirty Copper-Plates, by the Best Hands and on so large a Scale, that each Plate could not be sold separate for less than One Shilling.... In Two Volumes. Vol. I (II). By the King's Authority. London, Printed for J. Wilkie, in St Paul's Churchyard: T. Lowndes in Fleet-Street; G. Kearsly, in Ludgate-Street; and S. Bladon in Pater-Noster-Row. MDCCLXXII (vol. 2 nd; title-page not repeated for vol. 3).

Folio, 420 × 255mm.   1772

COLLATION Vols 1 and 2 unillustrated but otherwise as in 1756 ed. Vol. 3. Title-page for English Architecture (undated); preface (2pp); pp 1–112, English

Architecture; index, directions to binder (4pp); half-title, A Continuation of the History and Survey ... to the present time; pp 3–148, Entick's continuation.

The text of the first two volumes corresponds with that of the 1756 edition. The third volume has no general title-page: it consists of the 112 pages of *English Architecture* with its original title-page and 148 pages of Entick's 'Continuation of the History and Survey' with an undated title. The Plates are all gathered in vol. 3; the prospectus promises 123, the title-page 130, but finally 132 were actually issued. They consist of 123 plates issued with the third edition in 1760 but in their second state, numbered as for *English Architecture* and with a substitute for the 'Map of the Countries Ten Miles Round', together with 9 plates of recently erected buildings as a supplement, of which the first two are numbered repetitively '122' and '123'.

125 ('122') Black Friers Bridge – South Front of the Small Pox Hospital in Cold Bath Fields – The Small Pox Hospital near Pancras where the patients are prepared for inoculation – West Front of the Small Pox Hospital in Cold Bath Fields. Publish'd ... May 29, 1771. 100 × 380, 97 × 380/235 × 390mm. Robert Mylne's Blackfriars Bridge, built 1760–9.

126 ('123') Magdalen Hospital in St George's Fields – Westminster lying-in Hospital near Westminster Bridge. Published ... June 20th, 1771. 210 × 375/235 × 390mm. Work on the Magdalen Hospital began 1772. Lying-in Hospital built 1760–7, demolished c 1820.

127 (124) The Bank of England – New Newgate. Publish'd ... August 1st 1771. 240 × 403mm pl. mark. Sir Robert Taylor's additions to the Bank, 1766–83; George Dance junior's Newgate Prison, 1770–8. (*Bank of England* 21)

128 (125) West Front of the New Excise Office in London. W. Robinson Architecto. T. Robinson delint. Septr 7th, 1771. 235 × 380mm pl. mark. Built 1770–5.

129 (126) The Buildings called Adelphi. Ben Green del. et sculp. 205 × 380/235 × 400mm. By the Adam brothers, 1768–72.

130 (127) The City of London Lying-in Hospital. Mylne Architect. J. Roberts sculpt. 245 × 400mm pl. mark. Built 1770–3 in the City Road, demolished c 1903.

131 (128) New River Office – Front of Newgate. Publish'd ... March 6th, 1772. 235 × 405mm pl. mark. New River Office by R. Mylne, 1770; George Dance junior's Newgate Prison, 1770–8.

132 (129) The Circus and Obelisk in St George's Fields ... Febry 20, 1770. 243 × 405/250 × 420mm. Plan and elevation of development begun 1768.

133 (130) Front of the Sessions House in the Old Bailey March 31, 1772. 243 × 405/250 × 420mm. Destroyed in Gordon Riots, 1780.

134 (131) An Accurate Map of the Countries Twenty Miles round London. Drawn from Surveys Describing the Cities, Boroughs, Market Towns, Churches, Seats, Roads, Distances. 330 × 368/343 × 381mm. Substituting for item 9 above. (*Darlington and Howgego* 155)

The 'Directions to the Bookbinder for Placing the Copper Plates' from the third edition, retained in Entick's edition, is now quite irrelevant as the plates are no longer distributed through the text. The same publishers issued Maitland's 1756 text in two other forms. In 1769 it appeared without the *English Architecture* supplement but with the 123 plates in their second (numbered) state but arranged as in the 1760 (third) edition with a title similar to that of the 1772 edition. A 1775 reissue has Entick's 'continuation' with the nine supplementary plates appended to the second of its two volumes; the text of *English Architecture* is excluded, the original 122 plates are bound up as in the 1756 edition and the 1772 title-page is reprinted with an amended date.

39 · BELLIN'S ESSAI GEOGRAPHIQUE* [1757]

This work by Jacques Nicholas Bellin, a French naval engineer and member of our Royal Society, was intended to supplement the Navy Department charts issued to navigators with a description of the country on whose harbours and ports they were dependent for shelter, fresh water and revictualling and to act generally as a guide to the coastal towns of Great Britain. In fact it was very much the sort of compilation that our Naval Intelligence Divison produced on other countries at the time of the Second World War. The first edition (1757) included no fewer than 40 maps, plans and views of towns and harbours but these were reduced to 16 in the 1759 edition.

The four small London plates are decorative rather than topographical in intent and two of them were in 1759 promoted from their original roles as headpieces to being printed as separate, tipped-in illustrations. One of these, a miniature map of London, is an early work of P.P. Choffard and consequently much more decorative than useful.

Essai géographique sur les Isles Britanniques, Première Partie, contenant une description de l'Angleterre de l'Ecosse et de l'Irlande, Et les Détails particuliers des Provinces qui les composent; avec les Itinéraires pour l'Intérieur du Pays. (Seconde Partie, contenant Le Portuland ou Routier des Côtes d'Angleterre, d'Ecosse et d'Irlande: Avec le Détail particulier des Ports, Rades, Mouillages, & dangers que les Navigateurs doivent connoître.) Pour joindre à la Carte de ces Isles, en cinq grands Feuilles Par M. Bellin, Ingénieur de la Marine … A Paris Chez Nyon, Libraire, Quai des Augustins, à l'Occasion. MD.CC.LIX.

Duodecimo, 160 × 95mm.   1759

COLLATION   Vol. 1. Title-page; pp v–viii, Avertissement, contents; pp 1–315, Essai géographique. Vol. 2. Title-page; pp 1–346, Essai géographique continued; pp 347–8, contents of vol. 2, directions to binder.

VOL. 1

1 p 25 Veue de Westminster ver le Sud Est. Js. de Cruce sculp. 1756. 57 × 140/65 × 143. Birds-eye view from Somerset House to beyond Westminster Bridge. On p 5 in 1757 quarto ed, as headpiece.

2 p 27 (at the head of an elaborate rococo cartouche, cornucopia, wreaths, festoons, shell, etc) Plan de/ Londres. P.P. Choffard s. 1756. 55–150 × 80–110/155 × 115mm. (*Darlington and Howgego* 104)

VOL. 2

3 p 145 Veue de Londres vers le Sud Est. 55 × 135/63 × 140mm. Tower, old London Bridge, St Paul's Cathedral, viewed from the Pool of London. On p 1 in 1757 quarto ed, as headpiece.

1757 quarto ed only

4 p 394 (tailpiece in cartouche with architectural design and foliage) Deptford. Cruce sculp. 50–75 × 75–100/ 89 × 115mm.

40 · MARTIN'S NATURAL HISTORY OF ENGLAND* [1759]

Benjamin Martin (1704–82) a Chichester schoolmaster, became a self-appointed itinerant lecturer on natural history, mathematics, philology and philosophy. He was also an instrument maker with an interest in astronomy and a zeal to disseminate knowledge cheaply through the printed word as well as by word of mouth. The *Natural History of England* first appeared as Part II of his *General Magazine* published by W. Owen of Fleet Street at 6d monthly from 1755 to 1763. A precursor of our contemporary part-issue 'Books of Knowledge', each monthly Number consisted of six octavo half-sheets, paginated and signed in five separate, concurrent series so that the leaves could be sorted out and eventually bound up into 13 volumes on five distinct subjects with over 200 illustrations.

The Natural History of England; or, a Description of each particular County, in regard to the curious productions of Nature and Art. Illustrated by a Map of each County, and Sculptures of Natural curiosities. Vol. I containing: I. Cornwall, II. Devonshire,... X. Middlesex,... By Benjamin Martin: London: Printed and sold by W. Owen, Temple Bar, and by the Author, at his House in Fleet-Street. MDCCLIX.

Octavo, 222 × 152mm. 1759

COLLATION Title-page; pp ii–iv, dedication to the Prince of Wales; pp 1–410, Natural History; index (8pp).

1 p 207 (on cartouche tl) Middlesex/Divided into its/Hundreds/containing the Cities of/London/and/ Westminster,/Market Towns &c/By Eman. Bowen Geogr./to His Majesty. (along bm) Engraved for the General Magazine of Arts and Science for W. Owen at Temple Bar 1757. 175 × 195/180 × 200mm.

2 p 217 (in panel tr) The/Ichnography/of the Cities of/London/and Westminster/and the Borough of/ Southwark. (along bm) Engraved for the General Magazine of Arts and Science for W. Owen at Temple Bar 1757. 205 × 410/225 × 420mm. Extends W. to Hyde Park, E. to Bethnal Green, N. to Sadler's Wells, S. to Lambeth Palace. (*Darlington and Howgego* 108)

3 p 259 The Front or West-End of St Pauls. 205 × 115mm pl. mark. Reduced from Kip's engraving in Stow (1720, no 25) 1, 156.

4 p 263 A View of St Paul's Cathedral before its Spire was destroy'd by Lightning. 190 × 205mm. Based on p 133 in Dugdale's *St Paul's* (no 8).

5 p 293 A View of Westminster Abby from the North West. 170 × 195/185 × 210mm. With staffage and W. towers.

Robert Dodsley in his youth was a footman, a literate Joseph Andrews, whose published accounts of his servitude and pious exhortations to his fellow servants attracted influential patrons. In 1735, his thirty-second year, a play of his, 'The Toy-shop', was well received at Covent Garden and he was able, with the assistance of the poet Pope and other well-wishers, to open a bookseller's shop at the Tully's Head in Pall Mall. He established a flourishing business and was partnered in due course by his younger brother James. He published works by Pope, Young, Akenside and Johnson, brought out a 12 volume *Select Collection of Old Plays* in 1744, was associated with the publication of Johnson's *Dictionary* in 1755 and launched the perennial *Annual Register* in 1758. He also found time to pursue his career as a poet, dramatist and literary editor, writing and publishing numerous plays, songs and masques and editing collections of plays and poems. The theory that this anonymous *London and its Environs* was compiled by Dodsley in person is the more credible considering that he had in 1759 handed over the running of the business to his brother, presumably to devote himself to his literary interests. The preface points out that this is the first London guide to include the surrounding country seats; this inclusion enabled the editor to solicit from their noble and gentle owners the descriptions and lists of Old Masters and pieces of sculpture which are transcribed in the text, a form of flattery which brought him to their notice and no doubt sold a number of copies of the book. Unfortunately his curiosity did not extend to the architects of the buildings, who are rarely mentioned. The work was available in sixpenny Numbers, or as a whole, and the first Number was advertised in the *Public Advertiser* for 3 November 1760 as having been published on 1 November.

London and its Environs Described containing An Account of whatever is most remarkable for Grandeur, Elegance, Curiosity or Use, In the City and in the Country Twenty Miles round it. Comprehending also Whatever is most material in the History and Antiquities of this great

Metropolis. Decorated and illustrated with a great Number of Views in Perspective, engraved from original Drawings, taken on purpose for this Work. Together with a Plan of London, A Map of the Environs, and several other useful Cuts. (In Six Volumes) Vol. I (etc) London: Printed for R. and J. Dodsley in Pall-Mall. M DCC LXI.

Octavo, about 200 × 125mm.   1761

COLLATION Vol. 1. Title-page; dedication to the Prince of Wales; preface (8pp); pp 1–344, London and its Environs AB to BRE. Vol. 2. Title-page; pp 1–352, BRE to FUR. Vol. 3. Title-page; pp 1–328, GAB to LOM. Vol. 4. Title-page; pp 1–355, LON to MON. Vol. 5. Title-page; pp 1–348, MON to SIN.Vol. 6. Title-page; pp 1–372, SION to ZOAR; pp 373–6, directions to the binder for vols 1–6.

The quality and number of the illustrations make this an unsurpassed guide to the appearance of mid-eighteenth century London, almost—though not quite—on a par with the 1741 pocket guide to Rome by Fausto Amidei which numbers among its small plates six of Piranesi's first published etchings. Dodsley took trouble over the look of his publications and states with some justification in the preface that 'the prints with which the whole is decorated, are all engraved by the best hands, after original drawings which were taken on purpose for this work'. All the designs are by Samuel Wale whom he had already employed to produce frontispieces for Cooper's *Letters Concerning Taste* (1755) and *Epistles to the Great* (1757), engraved by Grignion, and he must have valued his talents highly since he entrusted him with the ornamentation of his own favourite project, the *Select Fables of Esop* printed by Baskerville and also published with a 1761 imprint. Wale's chief concern was with book illustrations and his output of these was stupendous. Hammelmann lists over 100 different publications containing almost 1,000 of his designs which appeared between 1744 and the end of the century among which are Pope's *Works* (9 vols, 1751), a number of *Oxford Almanacks* for the 1750s and 1760s, Walton's *Compleat Angler* (1760) and the first illustrated *Clarissa Harlowe* (8 vols, 1768). In later years he accepted numerous commissions from Cooke and Hogg, the 'Paternoster Row Number' publishers, contributing plates to the books on London issued under the names of Chamberlain (no 48), Harrison (no 57) and Thornton (no 61) and to various popular histories of England; his many energetic designs are the chief attractions of

Cooke's *Tyburn Chronicle* (4 vols, 1768) and *Newgate Calendar* (5 vols, 1773).

Wale is thought to have been a drawing pupil of Francis Hayman, possibly at the St Martin's Lane Academy. He was an established artist when he contributed to the newly erected Foundling Hospital three small roundels in oils depicting St Thomas's Hospital, Greenwich Hospital and Christ's Hospital which still decorate the courtroom. His usual media, however, were the pen and wash and water-colour of the drawings which he showed at the Spring Gardens exhibitions of the Society of Artists between 1760 and 1767. He was one of the foundation members of the Royal Academy in 1768 and their first Professor of Perspective. His was a frugal, bachelor existence and he shared a house in Leicester Fields with the architect John Gwynn, a lifelong friend. No doubt the profusion of commissions from publishers brought him less reward than they did to his engravers who were paid according to the time spent on preparing the copper plate. One guinea was probably the usual payment for the design for an octavo illustration.

The present volumes contain two maps, three plans and 76 plates of views. All but four anonymous views are credited bl 'S. Wale delin.' or 'S. Wale del.' so this information is not repeated in the list; these also carry credits br for the eight engravers. Forty were engraved either by Benjamin Green or J. Green. These were probably brothers and each of them occasionally added 'Oxon.' to his name in the credits; both engraved headpieces to the *Oxford Almanacks*, some of which in the 1750s and 1760s were designed by Wale. Benjamin was drawing-master at Christ's Hospital and, like Wale, was a member of the Society of Artists, exhibiting from 1765 to 1774. Eight plates (5,60,65–6,68–9,73,77) are by Edward Rooker who had engraved larger London views after Canaletto in 1750–1 and in 1755 a section of St Paul's Cathedral from a drawing by Wale and John Gwynn. Eight others (1, 3, 4, 12, 14, 25, 52, 57) were by one of the foremost book engravers, Charles Grignion, who had carried out plates after Gravelot, Hayman and Hogarth and whose name, from now on, often appeared with Wale's on book illustrations. The remaining 12 views were distributed, four apiece, to four more engravers, all reputable: W. Elliott (35,64,70–1), François Vivares (the park scenes, 43,58–9,81), both exhibitors at the Society of Artists in the 1760s;

J. Fougeron (29, 47–8, 67) and J. Taylor (23, 39, 61, 74), possibly the younger brother of Isaac Taylor who engraved many Wale book illustrations between 1762 and 1777.

The whole collection of plates, which contains but one interior view (68), provides an architectural symposium both of the oldest central London buildings like Westminster Hall and of the new, like Spencer House which was still in course of erection on Green Park; and, in addition, of notable Home Counties country seats and their grounds, including innovations as recent as 'Athenian' Stuart's Belvedere House at Erith. Most of the views in this copper plate 'London in Miniature' are necessarily devoid of that sense of teeming life conveyed by the refinement of detail available to the next century's engravers on steel, such as those who worked on Elmes and Shepherd's similarly entitled survey, *London and its Environs in the Nineteenth Century* (1829, no 154). Nevertheless the architectural forms are firmly and convincingly drawn and shown in their setting, natural or otherwise, and their scale is nearly always established by the inclusion of adequate staffage; Rooker's plates are particularly successful in filling a confined space with telling and well-proportioned detail. On pl. 10 Wale himself is shown, sitting on the lawn, back to the viewer, beneath a parasol, sketching Belvedere House.

VOL. 1 (AB to BRE)

1 front. (allegory with St Paul's and the City churches as background – Britannia holds up a map before an angel in an annunciatory pose while a City merchant, holding his day book and purse, looks on – putti with surveying instruments) C. Grignion sc. 80 × 140/110 × 180mm.

2 p 1 The Abby Church of St Peter's, Westminster. J. Green sc. Oxon. 80 × 140/110 × 180mm. W. front and St Margaret's Church.

3 p 51 Monument of Shakespeare. C. Grignion sc. 140 × 80/180 × 110mm.

4 p 75 Capt. Cornwall's Monument. C. Grignion sc. 140 × 82/180 × 110mm.

5 p 113 Henry the Seventh's Chapel. E. Rooker sc. 83 × 140/120 × 180mm. Exterior from E.

6 p 134 Admiralty. J. Green sc. Oxon. 84 × 180/120 × 190mm. The courtyard is fronted by a brick wall; Robert Adam's colonnaded screen was erected in 1760. The guide criticizes the main portico of the building for the 'immoderate height and ill shape of the columns' but does not name the architect, Ripley.

7 p 234 The Bank. J. Green sc. Oxon. 142 × 83/190 ×

110mm. With the tower of St Christopher le Stocks, demolished 1781. (*Bank of England* 12)

8 p 244 Banquetting House. J. Green sc. Oxon. 80 × 145/120 × 190mm.

9 p 260 St Bartholomew's Hospital. B. Green sculp. 85 × 140/120 × 190mm. Courtyard.

10 p 271 Belvedere House. B. Green sculp. 85 × 140/115 × 190mm. Built near Erith, Kent by James Stuart for Sir Sampson Gideon who collected Old Masters, here catalogued. The artist is seen in foreground sketching.

11 p 297 Bethlem – London Bridge. B. Green sculp. 35 × 140, 40 × 140/120 × 190mm.

12 p 298 Figures on Bethlem Gate. C. Grignion sc. 82 × 140/115 × 190mm. Cibber's 'Madness' and 'Melancholy'.

13 p 314 Sr Gregory Pages Seat. B. Green sc. Oxon. 80 × 140/115 × 190mm. Wricklemarsh, Blackheath by John James, 1721.

14 p 330 Bedford House. C. Grignion sculp. 80 × 140/115 × 190mm. N. of Bloomsbury Square. Old Masters catalogued.

VOL. 2 (BRE to FUR)

15 front. The Environs, or Countries Twenty Miles round London, drawn from Accurate Surveys by Thomas Kitchin, Geographer. Printed for and sold by R & I Dodsley in Pall Mall. 473 × 545/490 × 555mm. Scale somewhat less than 1″ to 2 miles, border and county boundaries tinted by hand. (*Darlington and Howgego* 119)

16 p 17 Entrance to the British Museum, from Rusel Street – Garden Front. J. Green sc. Oxon. 45 × 140, 40 × 140/115 × 190mm. Second view shows Hawksmoor's St George's Church.

17 p 32 (British Museum) No. 1, First State Story – No. 2, Second State Story. R. Benning sculp. 165 × 140, 60 × 140/285 × 180mm. Ground-plans.

18 p 57 Burlington House. B. Green sculp. 83 × 140/115 × 190mm.

19 p 71 Cashiobury – Moor Park. 41 × 140, 37 × 140/120 × 190mm. Hertfordshire seats of the Earl of Essex and Lord Anson. No credits.

20 p 105 North Front of Chelsea Hospital – South Front of the same. J. Green sc. Oxon. Each 40 × 140/115 × 190mm. (*Longford* 71, 20)

21 p 110 Ld. Egremont's – Chesterfield House. B. Green sculp. 65 × 83, 60 × 83/190 × 115mm. Egremont House, Piccadilly, now no 94, the Naval and Military Club, by Andrew Brettingham, begun 1756; Chesterfield House, S. Audley Street by Isaac Ware, 1748–9.

22 p 114 Chiswick House. B. Green sculp. Oxon. 83 × 140/115 × 190mm. From S.E. Description of house and grounds and catalogue of pictures and statues.

23 p 135 Christ's-Church Hospital. J. Taylor sc. 83 ×

142/115 × 190mm. Mathematical School and Christ Church W. side.

24 p 139 Claremont. B. Green sculp. 82 × 140/120 × 190mm. Seat of the Duke of Newcastle at Esher. By Vanbrugh, 1715–20; demolished c 1763.

25 p 165 Entrance to the House of Lords – House of Commons. C. Grignion sculp. Each 80 × 70/115 × 190mm. St Stephen's Hall from the E.

26 p 194 Covent Garden. 82 × 140/120 × 190mm. From S. No credits.

27 p 213 Custom House. B. Green sculp. Oxon. 83 × 140/120 × 190mm. Thomas Ripley's building, 1718.

28 p 225 Devonshire House. B. Green sculp. 83 × 140/115 × 190mm. The Duke's Piccadilly house, by William Kent, 1734–5. Catalogue of Old Masters in text.

29 p 253 St Dunstan in the East. J. Fougeron sculp. 140 × 83/190 × 115mm. Tower from the S.

30 p 263 East India House. B. Green sculp. 82 × 140/115 × 190mm. By T. Jacobsen, 1729.

31 p 277 Esher Place. B. Green sc. Oxon. 83 × 142/115 × 190mm. Altered by William Kent, c 1730, for the Hon Henry Pelham.

32 p 280 Eaton College. J. Green sc. Oxon. 83 × 140/115 × 190mm.

33 p 312 Foots Cray Place. B. Green sc. Oxon. 83 × 140/115 × 190mm. 'The seat of Bouchier Cleeve, Esq; and was built by himself after a design of Palladio'. Attributed to Isaac Ware, c 1754. Catalogue of Old Masters in text.

34 p 327 South East View of the Foundling Hospital – Front of the Same. 35 × 140, 45 × 140/115 × 190mm. Built by T. Jacobsen, 1742–52.

VOL. 3 (GAB to LOM)

35 p 5 Bloomsbury Church. Elliot sculp. 142 × 83/180 × 115mm. Portico and steeple from S.E. Severely criticized but Hawksmoor unmentioned.

36 p 58 Gray's Inn. B. Green sculp. 80 × 140/115 × 190mm. Chapel and Hall from N.

37 p 65 Mr. Spencer's. B. Green sculp. 85 × 140/115 × 190mm. Lord Spencer's house facing Green Park, by John Vardy and others, 1756–65.

38 p 69 Greenwich Hospital. B. Green sculp. 80 × 140/115 × 190mm. From the Isle of Dogs.

39 p 76 Gresham College. J. Taylor sculp. 83 × 143/115 × 190mm. Courtyard with cloister, Bishopsgate Street.

40 p 100 Guild Hall. B. Green sc. Oxon. 83 × 143/115 × 190mm.

41 p 110 Gunnersbury. B. Green sculp. 83 × 140/115 × 190mm. House near Ealing purchased in 1761 for Princess Amelia, daughter of George II.

42 p 112 Guy's Hospital. B. Green sc. Oxon. 83 × 140/115 × 190mm. Front courtyard.

43 p 132 Cascade at Ham Farm. F. Vivares sculp. 83 × 140/115 × 190mm. Grounds of the seat of the Earl of Portmore at Weybridge.

44 p 162 Hampton Court from the Garden. J. Green sc. Oxon. 80 × 140/115 × 190mm.

45 p 215 St James's Palace, view'd from Pall Mall – The Same from the Park. J. Green sc. Oxon. 42 × 143, 35 × 143/115 × 190mm.

46 p 266 Kensington Palace. B. Green sculp. 83 × 140/115 × 190mm. From the S.E.

47 p 291 Lambeth Palace. J. Fougeron sculp. 83 × 140/115 × 190mm. From the river.

48 p 309 Lincoln's Inn. J. Fougeron sculp. 81 × 140/115 × 190mm. New Square with central obelisk and water-basin.

VOL. 4 (LON to MON)

49 front. (in compartment br) A New and Correct Plan of London,/Westminster and Southwark,/with several Additional Improvements/Not in any former Survey. London, Engraved and Printed for R. and J. Dodsley in Pall-Mall. 345 × 640/365 × 660mm. 6″ to 1 mile. (*Darlington and Howgego* 118)

50 p 160 The Centre of the West Side of Lincoln's Inn Fields,/late the Duke of Ancaster's by Inigo Jones – Shaftesbury House, now the Lying in Hospital,/by Inigo Jones. Each 63 × 83/190 × 115mm.

51 p 244 The Mansion House. B. Green sculp. 81 × 140/115 × 190mm. By George Dance senior, 1739–52. Says of the top excrescence: 'Nor can it ever be viewed to advantage unless ... the heavy load at the top should be taken off'.

52 p 262 Marlborough House. C. Grignion sculp. 80 × 140/115 × 190mm.

53 p 288 Bow Steeple. J. Green sc. 143 × 80/195 × 115mm.

54 p 323 Part of the Meuse and/St Martin's Church. B. Green sculp. 140 × 83/190 × 115mm.

VOL. 5 (MON to SIN)

55 p 1 Monument. J. Green sc. Oxon. 142 × 83/195 × 115mm.

56 p 53 Northumberland House & Charing Cross. J. Green sc. Oxon. 82 × 140/115 × 190mm.

57 p 59 South View of Northumberland House. C. Grignion sculp. 82 × 140/115 × 190mm. Pen and wash drawing (80 × 140mm) in Museum of London.

58 p 60 View from the Terrace at Oatland. F. Vivares sculp. 83 × 140/115 × 190mm. Earl of Lincoln's seat near Weybridge.

59 p 101 A Scene in the Gardens of Pains Hill. F. Vivares sculp. 85 × 140/115 × 190mm. Seat of Hon Charles Hamilton, near Cobham, Surrey.

60 p 139 St Paul's. E. Rooker sculp. 79 × 140/115 × 190mm. S.W. view of Cathedral.

61 p 193 College of Physicians. J. Taylor sc. 83 × 140/115 × 190mm. N.W. corner of Warwick Lane, the courtyard.

62 p 244 View of Ranelagh. B. Green sc. Oxon. 83 × 140/115 × 190mm. (*Longford* 320)

63 p 280 Front of the Royal Exchange. J. Green sc. Oxon. 83 × 140/115 × 190mm.

VOL. 6 (SION to ZOAR)

64 p 7 Sion House view'd from Richmond Gardens. Elliot sculp. 80 × 138/110 × 190mm.

65 p 14 Sion House view'd from opposite Isleworth Church. E. Rooker sculp. 83 × 140/115 × 190mm.

66 p 43 Somerset House. E. Rooker sculp. 83 × 140/115 × 190mm. From river.

67 p 50 South Sea House. J. Fougeron sculp. 80 × 142/115 × 190mm. N.W. corner of Threadneedle Street. Built by James Gould, 1724–5. Pen and wash drawing (80 × 145mm) in Museum of London.

68 p 66 (on banderole) St Stephen Walbrook. E. Rooker sculp. 93 × 83, 43 × 83/190 × 115mm. Interior, putti displaying section and plan below.

69 p 114 Entrance into the Temple & Temple Bar – York Stairs. E. Rooker sc. 83 × 88, 83 × 48/115 × 190mm. Second view, York Watergate.

70 p 129 St Thomas's Hospital. Elliott sculp. 78 × 140/115 × 190mm. Courtyard.

71 p 148 The Tower. Elliot sculp. 76 × 140/115 × 190mm. From the river.

72 p 196 The Treasury & Horse Guards. 81 × 140/115 × 190mm. No credits.

73 p 216 View at the Entrance into Vaux Hall. E. Rooker sc. 85 × 140/115 × 190mm.

74 p 247 Wansted, the Seat of the Earl of Tilney. J. Taylor sc. 80 × 140/115 × 190mm. 'The house was built by the late Earl of Tilney and designed by Col. Campbell, and is certainly one of the noblest houses not only near London, but in the kingdom'. By Colin Campbell, 1715.

75 p 288 Westminster Bridge. – Walton Bridge. B. Green sc. Oxon. 45 × 140, 37 × 140/115 × 190mm. Charles Labelye's Westminster Bridge in use from November 1750, William Etheridge's wooden bridge built across the Thames at Walton, 1748–50.

76 p 296 Westminster Hall. J. Green sc. Oxon. 83 × 143/115 × 190mm. N. view. Pen and wash drawing (80 × 145mm) on pink paper in Westminster Public Library, reverse of the engraving.

77 p 315 A Gate belonging to the Old Palace of White Hall. E. Rooker sc. 83 × 144/115 × 190mm. 'Holbein' Gate and Banqueting Hall from S.

78 p 326 Windsor Castle. B. Green sculp. 83 × 140/115 × 190mm. From Windsor Great Park.

79 p 353 (in compartment tl) A Plan of/Windsor Castle/shewing alphabetically at one View/the several Appartments in the/Royal Palace/as shewn to ye Publick and sundry other/Appartments/belonging to the Officers of State &c. &c./1760. R. Benning sculp. 217 × 360/227 × 367mm. Refs A–W,1–5,a–z, etc.

80 p 353 (ditto) No. 1. First State Story – No. 2. Second State Story. R. Benning sculp. 170 × 140, 70 × 140/285 × 180mm. These plans accompany a detailed account of the Castle and its contents.

81 p 361 A Scene in Wooburn Farm. F. Vivares sculp. 82 × 140/115 × 190mm. 'The seat of the late Philip Southcote, Esq ... 'Tis what the French call a "Ferme ornée" '. Near Chertsey, designed for Southcote by William Kent.

---

42 · ENGLAND ILLUSTRATED*
[1764]

The publishers R. and J. Dodsley followed up their successful *London and its Environs Described* (No 41) with a two-volume descriptive guide to all England, illustrated with maps by Thomas Kitchen, panoramic views of cities engraved by I. Ryland and head and tailpieces to chapters arranged in alphabetical order of counties. These last were drawn by B. Ralph and engraved by Ryland or by three of the engravers concerned with the earlier Dodsley work: B. Green, C. Grignion and E. Rooker.

England illustrated: or, a compendium of the Natural History, Geography, Topography and Antiquities Ecclesiastical and Civil of England and Wales with Maps of the several Counties, and Engravings of many Remains of Antiquities, remarkable Buildings and principal Towns. Vol. 2 London: Printed for R. & J. Dodsley, in Pall Mall. MDCCLXIV.

Quarto, about 287 × 220mm.   1764

COLLATION Vol. 2. Title-page; contents (2pp); pp 1–490, England Illustrated: Middlesex to Yorkshire, Wales, Isle of Man.

The preface to vol. 1 modestly declares that 'the cuts are ornaments not wholly without use' and 'the maps are useful illustrations executed with an elegance which renders them in some degree ornamental'. The three London views are in vol. 2, printed with the letterpress of 'Middlesex' (head and tailpieces) and 'Surrey' (headpiece). The page references engraved on them are wrong. Illustrations are unlisted. The draughtsman was possibly the landscape painter Benjamin Ralph, and the engraver John Ryland, engraver, printer and print-seller of Old Bailey.

1 p 1 Westminster Abbey/P.31. B. Ralph del. I. Ryland sculp. 85 × 128/105 × 146mm. Headpiece. W. towers and St Margaret's Church.

2 p 79 St Paul's/P.15. B. Ralph del. I. Ryland sculp. Roundel, 105/130 × 123mm. Tailpiece. Cathedral from S.W.

3 p 274 Lambeth Palace/P.54. B. Ralph del. J. Ryland sculp. 85 × 125/110 × 146mm. Headpiece. From the river.

---

43 · REEVES'S NEW HISTORY OF LONDON [1764]

The Rev George Reeves, clearly a pedagogue, says in his introduction that no publications hitherto 'have attempted an epitome of the history and description of London, Westminster and the out parts, for the amusement and improvement of youth, and as a guide to persons coming up from the country or from abroad.... The present work is executed by way of dialogue'. Examples of the mind-blowing dullness of his catechetical method are:

Q. What is remarkable of Mr Craggs's monument?
A. That it was one of the first in the abbey that was represented in a standing posture.
Q. For what particular use was the marine society formed?
A. For furnishing the fleet with boys for the sea, who in a short time became useful mariners.

The first-named publisher, George Kearsley, issued John Wilkes's *North Briton* and had in the previous year been arrested for issuing the notorious no 45.

Both editions of Reeves's book appeared in 1764, the second being identical except that a folding map was added.

A New history of London, from its Foundation to the Present Year, containing Among many other interesting Particulars,

I. A curious account of the foundation, name and extent, of London and Westminster.
II. History of London Bridge.
III. An ample account of the tower of London and its curiosities, together with the prices paid for seeing them.
IV. History of the cathedral church of St Paul, and its curiosities.
V. An account of the dreadful fire of London, and the Monument.
VI. History of Westminster Abbey, with a circumstantial description of the tombs, monuments, and other curiosities to be seen there;
with the stated prices for seeing them.
VII. An account of the city of Westminster, and its bridge.
VIII. The public halls and buildings of the cities of London and Westminster.
IX. The churches of London and Westminster, remarkable for their architecture.
X. The hospitals and other public charities.
XI. The civil government of London, courts of justice, &c.
XII. An account of the palaces, remarkable houses, prisons, societies, companies, &c &c &c.

Being a useful companion for strangers and foreigners, desirous of being acquainted with the curiosities of the great metropolis. By the Rev. George Reeves M.A. Embellish'd with Eight elegant Copper Plates. Printed for G. Kearsley, W. Griffin, J. Payne, W. Nicoll and J. Johnson 1764. (Price 2s 6d Bound).
(The second edition title-page reads: 'A New history of London from its Foundation to the Present Year *By Question and Answer*' and, before the imprint: 'and a Plan of London, with the New Buildings to the present Year. The Second Edition'. Otherwise it is identical with the first.)

Duodecimo, 164 × 100mm.   1764

COLLATION   Title-page; introduction (2pp); pp i–iv, contents, pp 1–208, History.

Kearsley's *Copper-plate Magazine*, which ran from 1774 to 1778, contained fine engravings by Grignion, W. Walker, M.A. Rooker and others. For this History, however, he employed James Hulett, a line-engraver who had previously worked for Robert Sayer on plates after Canaletto (*Constable* 730), to relieve the tedium of the catechism with eight plates copied from views in two other current London books: *London and its Environs Described* (no 41) and Maitland's *History* (no 38). These are referred to in the list respectively as *LED* and *M*. 'The proprietors have been at a great expence in illustrating the whole with elegant copper-plates', the introduction says grandly. Each plate has the opposite page number engraved tr.

1 p 8 The Tower. 77 × 143/98 × 160mm. From the river. *M* 143.

2 p 17 St Paul's Church. J. Hulett sculp. 83 × 140/98 × 160mm. Cathedral from S.W. *LED* 5,139.

3 p 21 The Monument. 142 × 77/160 × 95mm. Reduced from *M* 834.

4 p 24 The Abby Church of St Peter's Westminster. J. Hulett sculp. 83 × 140/98 × 160mm. With St Margaret's Church, from W. *LED* 1,1.

5 p 62 King Henry the Seventh's Chapel. J. Hulett sculp. 83 × 140/98 × 158mm. Exterior from E. *LED* 1,113.

6 p 71 Westminster Hall. 78 × 140/98 × 160mm. *LED* 6,296.

7 p 87 Bethlem Hospital. J. Hulett sculp. 83 × 140/98 × 155mm. From the S. Reduced from *M* 1290.

8 p 193 Guild Hall. 78 × 140/98 × 160mm. Reduced from *M* 882.

9 2nd ed only, front. (in compartment tr) A Map of/London, Westminster/And Southwark/With ye New Buildings to ye Year 1764. (tc) Engraved for Reeves's History of London. 245 × 495/265 × 510mm. (*Darlington and Howgego* 125)

44 · ENTICK'S HISTORY AND SURVEY OF LONDON [1766]

John Entick, the reverend author, whose belligerent features set off by wig and bands are enshrined in the frontispiece to vol. 1, was a resident of St Dunstan, Stepney and worked for some 50 years as a tutor, schoolmaster and polygrapher. In addition to the present work he published other histories, dictionaries, grammars and theological treatises, commencing in 1728 with a Latin primer and ending in 1774 with a four-volume *Present State of the British Empire*. Five years after the publicaton of this *History and Survey of London* he was commissioned by the publisher S. Bladon to bring up to date Maitland's *History* (No 38) and his 'continuation' to the year 1772 appeared in subsequent editions. He also did much proof correction for his publisher, Edward Dilly, a friend of Dr Johnson's; it was his firm that later published Boswell's *Life* of the Doctor.

A New and Accurate History and Survey of London, Westminster, Southwark, and Places Adjacent; Containing whatever is most worthy of Notice In their Ancient and Present State: In which are Described ... The several Wards, Liberties, Precincts, Districts, Parishes, Churches, Religious and Charitable Foundations, and other Public Edifices: Particularly the Curiosities of the Tower of London, St Paul's Cathedral, Westminster Abbey, the Royal Exchange, Sir Hans Sloan's Museum &c.... Illustrated with A Variety of Heads, Views, Plans, and Maps, neatly Engraved. Vol. 1 (2–4) By the Rev. John Entick, M.A. London: Printed for Edward and Charles Dilly, in the Poultry, near the Mansion-House. MDCCLXVI.

Octavo, about 205 × 120mm.   1766

COLLATION   Vol. 1. Title-page; dedication to Lord Mayor, etc (1 leaf); pp 1–2, introduction; pp 3–500, History. Vol. 2. Title-page; pp 3–516, History continued. Vol. 3. Title-page; pp 3–292, History continued; pp 293–464, Survey. Vol. 4. Title-page; pp 3–449, Survey continued; index, directions to binder for vols 1–4 (15pp).

These volumes are illustrated by nine portraits of City Fathers engraved by A. Benoist and C. Grignion, one general map issued by Carington Bowles and 30 topographical plates engraved by Thomas Simpson, water-colourist, engraver, drawing-master and printseller who, worked at different times in the City and in Clerkenwell and who exhibited between 1765 and 1778 at the Society of Artists. Only pl. 8 is all his own work; all the rest have an additional credit 'S. Wale delin.'

According to Upcott (vol. 2, p 638), 'The plates of the Buildings in this volume are worked from the same coppers retouched, as are given in *London and its Environs Described* (no 41) produced by Dodsley in the year 1761'. For three reasons, taken together, this is unacceptable: (1) Throughout the plate-marks are invariably smaller in the Simpson versions and the work areas frequently; (2) The wording of the captions is identical but they have been newly engraved, as have the Wale credits; (3) The views on two plates (24 and 40) have been reversed, as also the staffage and sky on pl. 21 and 38.

Clearly Simpson copied, quite mechanically, a selection of the engravings published with Dodsley's volumes. His work stands in the same relation to the original engravings of Wales's drawings as W.H.

Toms's in Maitland's *History* of 1739 (No 33) to the engravers of Stow's *Survey* of 1720 (No 25). Later, in 1770, the same publishers, E. and C. Dilly, commissioned Wale and Simpson to design the frontispieces for their six-volume edition of Plutarch's *Lives*.

All the topographical plates, unless otherwise stated, bear the credits 'S. Wale delin.' and 'T. Simpson Sc.', 'sculp.' or 'sculpt.' Volume and page number references to the original plates in *London and its Environs Described* are given after each description with the abbreviation *LED*.

VOL. 1

1 front. (above frame) The Revd. John Entick, M.A. Burgess fecit. Benoist sculp. 166 × 93/180 × 115mm. In oval frame, 112 × 93mm. Below an allegorical group: Britannia with spear and cap of liberty and an angel writing in a book 'Pax data Victis' with London and the Thames as a background.

2 p 291 Sir William Wallworth/From an Original Statue in/Fishmongers Hall. C. Grignion sculp. In oval frame, 112 × 87/167 × 109mm.

VOL. 2

3 front. Henry Fitzalwine, Knight.... /from an Original Painting at Drapers Hall. Grignion sculp. 123 × 100/180 × 115mm.

4 p 55 Sr Thomas Gresham. Benoist sculp. In oval frame, 90 × 83/115 × 97mm.

5 p 268 Monument. 80 × 138/110 × 178mm. *LED* 5,1.

6 p 464 The Mansion House. 80 × 138/110 × 178mm. *LED* 4,244.

VOL. 3

7 front. Sr. Richd Wittington,/from an Original Painting at Mercers Hall. Benoist sculp. In oval frame, 90 × 83/118 × 97mm.

8 p 38 Westminster Bridge – Black Friars Bridge. T. Simpson del. et sculp. 32 × 140,42 × 140/110 × 170mm. Mylne's Blackfriars Bridge was still under construction; it was opened to the public November 1769.

9 p 95 Sr Robert Ladbrooke. Benoist sculp. In oval frame, 90 × 80/115 × 98mm.

10 p 138 Bethlem – London Bridge. 42 × 138,38 × 138/100 × 180mm. *LED* 1,297.

11 p 141 Sr. John Bernard. Benoist sculp. In oval frame, 90 × 80/118 × 100mm.

12 p 196 St Paul's. 78 × 140/110 × 178mm. From S.W. *LED* 5,139.

13 p 217 William Beckford, Esqr. Benoist sculp. In oval frame, 92 × 83/115 × 100mm.

14 p 293 The/London Guide/or/A Pocket Plan/of the/

Cities of London/& Westminster,/and Borough of/Southwark;/with the New Buildings &c/to the present year:/Printed for Carington Bowles, Map & Printseller;/in St. Paul's Church Yard, London. 270 × 568/275 × 600mm. Scale 4½″ to 1 mile. Title in compartment bc with tables of the fares of watermen & hackney coaches. (*Darlington and Howgego* 141)

15 p 397 Gresham College. 80 × 140/115 × 178mm. *LED* 3,76.

VOL. 4

16 front. The Right Honble George Nelson, Esqr./Lord Mayor of London. Burgess delin. Benoist sculp. 150 × 92/185 × 115mm. In oval frame, 105 × 90mm. Portrait of Lord Mayor for 1765, with trophy of City attributes below.

17 p 58 Guild Hall. 80 × 142/105 × 180mm. *LED* 3,100.

18 p 92 Bow Steeple. 140 × 80/175 × 110mm. *LED* 4,288.

19 p 99 Front of the Royal Exchange. 80 × 137/110 × 180mm. *LED* 5,280.

20 p 184 College of Physicians. 80 × 138/115 × 178mm. *LED* 5,192.

21 p 253 St Bartholomew's Hospital. 80 × 140/110 × 178mm. Staffage and sky reversed from *LED* 1,260.

22 p 302 East India House. 80 × 139/110 × 180mm. *LED* 2,263.

23 p 336 The Tower. 75 × 139/110 × 180mm. *LED* 6,148.

24 p 360 (on banderole tc) St. Stephen Walbrook. 92 × 80,42 × 80/176 × 110mm. Interior; below, putti displaying plan and section. Reversed from *LED* 6,66.

25 p 395 Lambeth Palace. 80 × 140/115 × 178mm. *LED* 3,291.

26 p 404 Somerset House. 80 × 143/110 × 178mm. *LED* 6,43.

27 p 408 Banquetting House. 78 × 143/110 × 178mm. *LED* 1,244.

28 p 411 The Abby Church of St Peter's, Westminster. 78 × 140/110 × 178mm. *LED* 1,1.

29 p 420 Westminster Hall. 81 × 142/110 × 175mm. *LED* 6,297.

30 p 421 Entrance of the House of Lords,/with the Office of Ordinance – House of Commons. Each 78 × 69/110 × 175mm. *LED* 2,165.

31 p 422 Admiralty. 82 × 140/110 × 178mm. Copied without modification, to show the Adam screen-wall erected 1760, from *LED* 1,134.

32 p 423 St James's Palace, view'd from Pall Mall – The Same from the Park. 40 × 140,35 × 140/110 × 178mm. *LED* 3,215.

33 p 427 Entrance of the British Museum from Russel Street – Garden Front. Each 40 × 140/110 × 175mm. *LED* 2,17.

34 p 442 Kensington Palace. 80 × 140/110 × 180mm. *LED* 3,266.

35 p 442 North Front of Chelsea Hospital – South Front of the Same. Each 39 × 138/115 × 179mm. *LED* 2,105. (*Longford* 71,20)

36 p 442 View of Ranelagh. 80 × 140/115 × 176mm. *LED* 5,244. (*Longford* 320)

37 p 442 View at the Entrance into Vauxhall. 80 × 138/115 × 176mm. *LED* 6,216.

38 p 442 Greenwich Hospital. 78 × 138/110 × 180mm. Twin-masted ship eliminated to reveal central domes; other craft on river and the sky reversed in copying from *LED* 3,69.

39 p 442 Sir Gregory Page's Seat. 80 × 140/110 × 180mm. *LED* 1,314.

40 p 442 Wansted, the Seat of the Earl of Tilney. 80 × 140/110 × 180mm. Reversed from *LED* 6,247.

---

45 · GANDON AND WOOLFE'S VITRUVIUS BRITANNICUS* [1767–71]

Colen Campbell's *Vitruvius Britannicus* of 1715–25 (no 24) heralded a long procession of books on architecture and building which served both as an advertisement for the architect authors and as pattern books for builders and craftsmen but they were mostly devoted to the work of individual practitioners such as Inigo Jones, William Kent, James Gibbs and Isaac Ware. The only book which set out to survey the London architectural scene as such was an anonymous *Critical Review of the Public Buildings of London* (1734) which was unillustrated and also sternly dismissive of any departures from what Summerson has defined as the triad of loyalties: to Vitruvius, to Palladio himself and to Inigo Jones. It was not until 1767 that a general, illustrated review of current architectural practice was again available. This was compiled by James Gandon, a pupil of William Chambers and designer of public buildings for Dublin (most notably the Custom House), and John Woolfe, an employee of the Board of Works. Together with a second volume which appeared in 1771 it illustrated specimens of the work of most leading practitioners of the day. To stress the continuity of 'the great tradition' it was published as vols 4 and 5 of *Vitruvius Britannicus* with reissues of Campbell's original three-volume book.

Subscribers numbered several architects, including Robert Adam, John Carr, Kenton Couse, George Dance, Henry Flitcroft, Richard Jupp junior, James Payne, William Robinson, John Taylor, James Stuart, Nicholas Revett and John Wood, besides a number of craftsmen: carpenters, bricklayers, paviours and masons. Robert Sayer the printseller and Richard Dalton the Royal Librarian each subscribed for three copies; 'Capability' Brown, the gardener, took one.

The London plates show buildings by John James, William Kent, Matthew Brettingham senior, John Vardy, George Dance senior and Isaac Ware. They are drawn by one or other of the editors and engraved by M. Darly who specialized in etching architectural design and ornament and by Anthony Walker.

Virtuvius Britannicus,/or/the British Architect;/containing/plans, elevations and sections;/of the regular buildings both/public and private,/in/Great Britain./Comprised in one hundred folio plates, engrav'd/by the best hands; taken from the buildings,/or original designs/by Woolfe and Gandon architects./Vol: IV (V) (the title is repeated in a French translation after an ornamental rule)/ MDCCLXVII (MDCCLXXI). (engr, 380 × 263mm)

Folio, 520 × 360mm.   1767–71

COLLATION   Vol. 4. Engr title-page; engr calligraphic dedication to George III (1 leaf); pp 1–2, introduction; pp 3–10, explanation of plates; pp 11–12, list of subscribers; pl. 3–98. Vol. 5. Engr title-page; engr dedication to Queen Charlotte (1 leaf); list of subscribers (2pp); pp 3–10, explanation of plates; pl. 3–100.

In their style the engravings follow those in the first three volumes. Plate numbers are tr, scale of feet and captions in English and French bc, credits for the architect bl, for the draughtsman bc, and for the engraver br.

VOL. 4

1 pl. 5 Elevation of His Royal Highness the Duke of York's Palace in Pall Mall. Brettingham Archt. J. Woolfe delin. M. Darly sc. 265 × 380mm.

2 pl. 6 The Principal Floor – Plan of the Ground Floor of His Royal/Highness the Duke of Yorks Palace in/Pall Mall. Brickingham Archt. J. Woolfe del. Darly Sculp. 380 × 253mm.

3 pl. 7 Section of His Royal Highness the Duke of York's Palace in Pall Mall. Brettingham Archt. Woolfe delt. M. Darly sculpt. 265 × 380mm. No 86 Pall Mall, built 1760–7, now demolished. 'From the principal apartments on the South, an agreeable and

pleasing prospect over St James's Park and the county of Surry'.

4 pl. 19 General Plan of his Grace the Duke of Devonshire's in Piccadilly. W. Kent Archt. J. Woolfe del. M. Darly sc. 250 × 378mm.

5 pl. 20 Elevation of his Grace the Duke of Devonshire's in Piccadilly – Plan of ... W. Kent Archt. J. Woolfe del. T. Müller sc. 250 × 380mm. Built for the 3rd Duke, 1734–5; demolished 1924–5.

6 pl. 37 Principal Floor – Plan of the Ground Floor of ye Rt Honble the Earl Spencer's. J. Vardy Archt. Gandon delt. M. Darly sc. 380 × 253mm.

7 pl. 38 Front to the Street of the Rt Honble Earl Spencer's. J. Vardy Archt. J. Gandon del. M. Darly sculp. 263 × 405mm.

8 pl. 39–40 Front to St James's Park of the Rt Honble/Earl Spencer's. J. Vardy Archt. Gandon delt. M. Darly sc. 265 × 515mm. Built 1756–65; still stands overlooking Green Park.

9 pl. 41 Plan of the principal Floor of the Mansion House of the Lord Mayor of London. G. Dance Archt. J. Woolfe del. M. Darly sculp. 405 × 250mm.

10 pl. 42 Elevation of the Mansion House/of the Lord Mayor of London. G. Dance Archt. J. Woolfe del. M. Darly sculp. 260 × 375mm.

11 pl. 43–4 Section of the Mansion House of the Lord Mayor of London. G. Dance Archt. J. Woolfe del. M. Darly sculp. 255 × 515mm. Built by George Dance senior, 1739–52.

12 pl. 59 General Plan of the Seat of Sir Gregory Page Bart. in Kent. J. James Archt. A. Walker sculp. 395 × 450mm.

13 pl. 60 Principal Floor of the Seat/of Sr Gregory Page – Attic Floor. J. James Archt. M. Darly sc. 380 × 250mm.

14 pl. 61 Front to the South of Sir Gregory Pages. J. James Archt. A. Walker sculp. 250 × 375mm.

15 pl. 62–3 Elevation of the Flank of Sir Gregory Page Bart. J. James Archt. T. Müller sc. 255 × 605mm.

16 pl. 64 Section of Sir Gregory Page's Bart. House at Black Heath. J. James Arch. M. Darly sc. 250 × 380mm. Wricklemarsh, Blackheath; the side elevation resembles that of Beckenham Place Park into which its colonnade, removed on demolition in 1789, was clumsily incorporated. Built by John James, 1721.

17 pl. 67 Plan of the Ground Floor of the Rt Honble the Earl of Chesterfield's House in May Fair. I. Ware Arch. J. Woolfe del. M. Darly sc. 250 × 380mm.

18 pl. 68–9 Elevation of the Rt Honble the Earl of Chesterfield's House in South Audley Street May Fair. I. Ware Arch. J. Woolfe del. M. Darly sc. 255 × 483mm. Built for the 4th Earl, 1748–9.

VOL. 5

19 pl. 3 Plan of the Ground Floor of the Horse Guards at Whitehall. W. Kent Archt. J. Woolfe del. T. White sculpt. 250 × 380mm.

20 pl. 4 Plan of the Principal Floor of the Horse Guards. W. Kent Archt. J. Woolfe delt. T. White sculpt. 260 × 375mm.

21 pl. 5–6 East Front of the Horse Guards at Whitehall. Kent Archt. T. White sc. 255 × 575mm.

22 pl. 7–8 West Front of the Horse Guards at Whitehall. W. Kent Archt. T. White sc. 250 × 620mm. Built after Kent's death by John Vardy and William Robinson as joint Clerks of Works, 1750–8.

23 pl. 9 Plan of the principal Floor of Shelburn House, Berkeley Square. R. Adam Archt. J. Gandon delt. T. White sculpt. 395 × 267mm. No doubt based on a larger plan engraved by White (585 × 457mm) in BM (*Crace* Maps 10.57). Built for the Earl of Bute, 1765–7; sold by him before completion to Lord Shelburne, subsequently to the Marquis of Lansdowne; in 1926 it was the home of Gordon Selfridge.

24 pl. 10 Front of Shelburn House. R. Adam Archt. J. Gandon delt. T. White sculpt. 250 × 400mm.

46 · DESCRIPTION OF ENGLAND AND WALES* [1769–70]

Newbery and Carnan, the publishers of these ten volumes, were chiefly notable for selling children's books but this work is intended for adults: a county by county survey, in alphabetical order of the counties. The illustrations are line-engravings without credits or publication-lines; there is no listing but each plate has, tr or tl, reference to the volume and page number opposite which it should be bound. Subjects are mainly provincial but two views of central London bring it into the ambit of this work. The engravings are in appearance and size similar to those in Dodsley's *London and its Environs* (no 41).

A Description of England and Wales containing a particular Account of each County, with its Antiquities, Curiosities ... Cities, Towns, Palaces, Seats ... Embellished with two hundred and forty Copper Plates, of Palaces, Castles, Cathedrals ... Abbeys, Monasteries and other Religious Houses. Vol. VI (IX) London: Printed for Newbery and Carnan, No 65 the North Side of St. Paul's Church-Yard. M DCC LXIX (M DCC LXX).

Duodecimo, 170 × 100mm.   1769, 1770

COLLATION Vol. 6. Title-page; pp 3–288, Lincoln-shire to Norfolk (pp 21–207, Middlesex). Vol. 9. Title-page; pp 3–288, Suffolk to Wiltshire (pp 38–130, Surrey).

VOL. 6

1 p 36 A View of Hampton Court in the County of Middlesex from the Garden. 72 × 138/90 × 160mm.

2 p 45 (tm) The South West View of Sion House in the County of Middlesex. 75 × 140/90 × 165mm.

3 p 107 (tm) The South View of the Tower of London. 72 × 140/95 × 165mm. The river in the foreground.

VOL. 9

4 p 66 The North West View of Lambeth Palace, in the County of Surrey. 70 × 135/95 × 160mm.

47 · BOYDELL'S COLLECTION OF VIEWS* [1770]

Shropshire-born John Boydell (1719–1804) was trained as a land surveyor, his father's profession, which when he approached his majority he abandoned. He went to London to study art at the St Martin's Lane Academy and was apprenticed in 1741 to W.H. Toms the engraver who, a few years earlier, had published with Robert West 26 *Perspective Views* of ancient London churches (no 32) and was later to be engaged on illustrating Maitland's *History of London* (no 38). In after years he was inclined to blame his comparative lack of skill on the shortcomings of his master but he certainly made up in enterprise for whatever he may have lacked in inspiration or expertise. He began by copying the work of the celebrated French engraver Le Bas and publishing small landscapes which, for lack of other outlets, he sold through the Westminster toy shops at sixpence a set. He then graduated to larger topographical views of Derbyshire, Wales, London, Oxford and Blenheim which sold for a shilling each, sea pieces after Van der Velde and Charles Brooking and landscapes after Gainsborough, Salvator Rosa and Ostade. His earliest place of business appears to have been the Globe near Durham Yard in the Strand but by 1751 he was publishing from 90 Cheapside, having progressed

from half a shop to a whole house, and he traded there until his death.

In about 1767, recognizing his own limitations, he turned from engraving to being a printseller and publisher of the work of other artists. He displays a becoming modesty in this advertisement to his retrospective collection dated September 1790, by which time he had made a fortune in what he had helped to make a flourishing trade:

The Prints that form the following Volume were never before collected all together. The Engraver has now collected them, more to show the Improvement of the Art in this Country, since the Period of their Publication, than from any Idea of their own Merits. He is very sensible, that he began to learn the Art of Engraving too late in life, to arrive at great Perfection, being within a few months of Twenty-one Years of Age, when he put himself Apprentice to the Art, and that too, to a Master who had himself never arisen to any great Degree of Perfection. Indeed, at that Period (about fifty Years ago) there were no Engravers of any Eminence in this Country.

To the Lovers of the Fine Arts, this Volume may be an object of some Curiosity, as it was from the Profits of these Prints, that the Engraver of them was first enabled to hold out encouragement to young Artists in this Line, and thereby, he flatters himself, has somewhat contributed to bring the Art of Engraving to that wonderful State of Perfection in England, which at present gives its Artists so decided a Superiority over all the rest of Europe.

Boydell's claim was justified in that at least some of the plates in the volume had never before been collected but the London ones, with which we are concerned, had in fact already been published in a bound volume (in the Guildhall Library: Store 267.3) soon after he set up his printselling business.

A Collection of One Hundred Views in England and Wales Publish'd by John Boydell, Engraver, in Cheapside, London, 1770. Price Three Pounds Three Shillings, half bound. (and in French)

Folio, 515 × 360mm.   1770

COLLATION 1 leaf, printed recto with title and list of plates and verso with the continuation of the list; 100 plates.

This earlier collection contained eight London plates published over the same period as the others (1750–6) but which were not Boydell's own work and were therefore omitted from his 1790 personal retrospect, reducing the London total from 47 to 39. So, as indicated in the list, the engraved numbers on the plates after pl. 26 were adjusted in the later issue to allow for the omission of non-Boydell pl. 27–8, 30, 39.

A Collection of Views in England and Wales drawn and engraved by John Boydell. To which are added, engraved by the same hand, some miscellaneous subjects after various masters. Sold by John and Josiah Boydell, No 90, Cheapside and at the Shakespeare Gallery, Pall Mall, London, 1790.

Folio, 560 × 420mm.   1790

COLLATION Title-page; catalogue of prints and advertisement dated September 1790 (1 leaf); plates.

The British Library copy (744.g.10) is inscribed in these terms:

Aldn Boydell's Respectful Compliments to Miss Banks, desires her acceptance of a Collection of Prints, the Author does not claim any merit in the Execution of them, but presumes it may be thought worthy of remark that it is the only Book that had the Honour of making a Lord Mayor of London. Cheapside, May 29th, 1792.

This collected edition of 100 plates, mostly drawn and all engraved by himself, was available at five guineas in sheets or, bound in calf, at six guineas. A later issue with the advertisement now dated 'Jan. 1794' (BM: Prints, 172*b.1), adds to the basic 100 his first efforts at engraving dating from his apprenticeship in 1741 up to 1746 and brings the total to 152 plates. This expanded collection is advertised in Boydell's 1803 *Alphabetical Catalogue*: 'In One Volume: Imperial Folio Sewed £5. 5. 0.' This subdivides the London views into 'Views on the Thames, Drawn on the Spot', 'Below London Bridge' and 'Views in London' for items 1–8, 9–21 and 22–39 respectively and gives dimensions for items 1–35 of 17½″ × 10¾″ or 10½″; individual plates are priced at a shilling. Oblong London views of this size and price were particularly popular when these were originally engraved (1750–5) and were also issued by the firms of Bowles and of Sayer after paintings by Canaletto and Joli or drawings by Maurer, Chatelain, Rigaud and Wale engraved by Grignion, I.S. Müller, Thomas Bowles, F. Vivarez and others (see nos 191 and 193). Boydell's collection, although wholly engraved and mostly drawn by himself, compares quite favourably with these other series in which the publishers employed a number of engravers, some of them quite eminent. They are certainly firmly drawn, cleanly engraved, and have reasonable topographical accuracy and, where appropriate, add staffage.

The subjects are chiefly drawn from Westminster and the Thames-side suburbs and residences rather than from the City which by that time had been sufficiently limned in older prints available from Overton, Bowles and Sayer. Later in the century the publishers of London histories, such as Harrison (no 57) and Thornton (no 61), took their cue from Boydell. Both these have their illustrations rounded off with a number of Thames-side surburban views.

All 39 Boydell plates carry his credit br or bl in one of the following forms: 'J. (Jno, or John) Boydell Del. et Sculp.' or 'Boydell Del. et Sculp.' Serial numbers are engraved on plates br. In general a version of the following publication-line, with or without a date, may be assumed unless there is a statement to the contrary: 'Publish'd according to Act of Parliament (and Sold) by J. (or John) Boydell (Engraver) at the Unicorn the Corner of Queen Street Cheapside. (Price 1s.)' Any dates given are quoted in the list and other variations of the publication-line are transcribed in full.

1 A View up the Thames between Richmond and Isleworth. 240 × 415/265 × 425mm.

2 A View of Sunbury, up the River Thames. 240 × 417/265 × 425mm.

3 A View of Sheperton.... 1752. 240 × 405/265 × 420mm.

4 A View of Putney, took of Fulham Bridge. 238 × 405/260 × 420mm.

5 A View of Chelsea Water Works. London 1752. 235 × 410/263 × 425mm. (*Longford* 642)

6 A View taken near Battersea Church looking towards Chelsea. London 1752. 240 × 413/265 × 430mm. (*Longford* 251)

7 A View taken from Mr Smith's House at Battersea looking up the Thames. 1752. 238 × 410/263 × 425mm.

8 A View of Hammersmith looking down the Thames. London 1752. 235 × 408/260 × 420mm.

9 A View of Erith looking up the Thames. Publish'd according to Act of Parliament by Jno Boydell at the Globe near Durham Yard in the Strand 1750. Price 1s. 240 × 418/263 × 425mm.

10 A View taken near the Store House, at Deptford. Publish'd according to Act of Parliament by J. Boydell Engraver 1750. Price 1s. 240 × 415/260 × 430mm.

11 A View of Blackwall, looking towards Greenwich. Publish'd according to Act of Parliament by J. Boydell Engraver 1750. Price 1s. 240 × 412/265 × 425mm.

12 A View of Woolwich. Publish'd according to Act of

Parliament by J. Boydell Engraver 1750. 240 × 415/262 × 430mm.

13 A View of London Bridge taken near St Olaves Stairs. Publish'd according to Act of Parliament by J. Boydell, Engraver at the Globe near Durham Yard in the Strand 1751. Price 1s. 240 × 420/265 × 435mm. Shows the houses on the bridge later removed as the result of an Act of Parliament passed in 1756.

14 A View taken near Limehouse Bridge, looking down the Thames. Publish'd according to Act of Parliament by J. Boydell Engraver 1751. Price 1s. 240 × 415/260 × 430mm.

15 A View of the Tower taken upon the Thames. Publish'd according to Act of Parliament by J. Boydell Engraver 1751. 240 × 420/265 × 433mm. From the E.

16 A View of Greenwich Hospital. Publish'd according to Act of Parliament by J. Boydell Engraver 1751. 240 × 425/260 × 430mm. River front from N.E.

17 Greenwich Hospital. 1753. 230 × 410/255 × 425mm. River front from N.

18 A View of Purfleet in the County of Essex. (and in French) 1752. 235 × 408/255 × 420mm.

19 A View of Lord Duncannon's House in the County of Kent. (and in French) 1752. 235 × 405/255 × 420mm.

20 A View of Northfleet in the County of Kent. (and in French) 1752. 230 × 405/255 × 420mm.

21 A View of Gravesend in the County of Kent. (and in French) 1752. 230 × 400/255 × 410mm.

22 A View of London taken off the Thames near York Buildings. (and in French) 240 × 420/260 × 430mm. From the S.

23 A View of Westminster Bridge. (and in French, both captions with a description) 1753. 230 × 410/255 × 420mm. Looking N.E.

24 A View of London taken off Lambeth Church. (and in French) London 1752. 238 × 420/260 × 430mm.

25 A View of Mortlake up the Thames. (and in French) 1753. 240 × 403/260 × 410mm.

26 A View taken off Wandsworth Hill looking towards Fulham. (and in French) 1753. 230 × 405/255 × 415mm.

27 A View of Sion House, looking towards Kew. (and in French) 1753. 235 × 408/260 × 420. Also numbered 29.

28 A View near Twickenham (and in French)/Barnaby Backwell Esqr. 1753. 230 × 403/255 × 410mm. A riverside residence. Also numbered 31.

29 A View of Governour Pitts House at Twickenham. (and in French) 1753. 235 × 412/260 × 425mm. Also numbered 32. The riverside Orleans House, occupied by George Morton Pitt, formerly Governor of Fort St George.

30 A View of the Earl of Radnor's House at Twickenham. (and in French) 1754. 230 × 400/255 ×

410mm. Also numbered 33. Riverside house in would-be Gothic style, midway between Pope's Villa and Strawberry Hill.

31 A View on Twickenham Common. (and in French) Lord Kingston's – Green Esqr. 1753. 230 × 405/250 × 412mm. Also numbered 34.

32 A View of New Palace Yard Westminster. (and in French) 235 × 418/260 × 430mm. Also numbered 35.

33 A View of Privy Garden Westminster. (and in French) 1751. 235 × 410/260 × 430mm. Looking S. Also numbered 36.

34 A View of the Parade in St James's Park. (and in French) Publish'd ... March 13th 1753. 235 × 410/260 × 420mm. Also numbered 37. The Horse Guards Parade. Cupola shown, probably only just completed.

35 A View of the Treasury & Canal in St James's Park. (and in French) Boydell delin. Smith sculp. 1755. 230 × 405/255 × 420mm. Also numbered 38.

36 (in rococo proscenium, caption on banderole bc) St Stephen Walbrook. Thos Boydell Delin. Jno Boydell Sculp. Publish'd according to Act of Parliament by J. Boydell Engraver at the Globe near Durham Yard in the Strand London. 1750. Price 1s. 248 × 340/275 × 363mm. Interior. Also numbered 41.

37 (on banderole above draped proscenium arch) The Temple Church. Thomas Boydell Delin. 1750. L. Boydell Sculp. Publish'd according to Act of Parliament by J. Boydell at the Globe near Durham Yard in the Strand 1750. Price 1s. 253 × 345/265 × 360mm. Interior looking towards altar; description in lm. Also numbered 42.

38 (interior view in rococo proscenium arch with draperies, caption lm) St Martin's in the Fields. Thos Boydell Delin. Jno Boydell sculp. Ja. Gibbs Archt. Publish'd according to Act of Parliament by J. Boydell Engraver 1751. Price 1s. 278 × 420/300 × 430mm. Also numbered 43.

39 (interior view in rococo proscenium arch with draperies, caption lm) St Clement's Danes. Thos Boydell Delin. Jno Boydell Sculp. Publish'd according to Act of Parliament 1751 by Jno Boydell Engraver at the Globe near Durham Yard in the Strand. Price 1s. 280 × 410/300 × 440mm. Also numbered 44.

Extra plates in 1770 collection (not engraved by Boydell)

40 pl. 27 A View of the Rt Honble the Earl of Burlington's House/at Chiswick, and part of the Town. (and in French) Pr Brookes delin. Ino Fougeron Sculp. London: Printed for J. Boydell Engraver at the Unicorn the corner of Queen Street Cheapside. Publish'd ... May 31st 1750. 248 × 445/280 × 457mm.

41 pl. 28 A View of Sion House and the Parts adjacent,/ Taken from the River next the Royal Gardens at Richmond. (and in French) P. Brookes delin. P. Benazech sculp ... January the 24th 1750. London:

Printed for J. Boydell Engraver at the Unicorn the corner of Queen Street Cheapside. 245 × 438/270 × 455mm.

42 pl. 30 A View of Richmond, taken near Twickenham. (and in French) Collert Delin. et sculp. Sold by J. Boydell Engraver at the Unicorn the Corner of Queen Street Cheapside 1753. 230 × 410/255 × 422mm. Also found with Boydell's credit as both artist and engraver. (*Gascoigne* 9)

43 pl. 39 A View of Stocks Market. (and in French) Nichols Pinxt. Fletcher sculp. Publish'd according to Act of Parliament by J. Boydell at the Unicorn the Corner of Queen Street Cheapside 1753. 305 × 445/318 × 450mm. A larger version was published in 1752 (BL Maps: *K. top.* 22.21b).

44 pl. 40 A View of the Fountain in the Temple. (and in French) Nichols Pinxt. Fletcher sculp. Publish'd according to Act of Parliament 1753 by J. Boydell at the Unicorn the Corner of Queen Street Cheapside. 292 × 445/303 × 445mm. A larger version was published in 1752 (BL Maps: *K. top.* 25.18c). The original oil painting by Joseph Nichols is owned by the Middle Temple.

45–6 pl. 45–6 A View of London as it was in the Year 1647. (on sheet 2 in French) R. Benning del. et sculp. Sold by J. Boydell at the Unicorn in Cheapside London 1756. Each sheet 263 × 480/310 × 490mm. Refs 1–34 on sheet 1 and 1–20 on sheet 2. Copy of Hollar's long birds-eye view (*Scouloudi* p 67).

47 pl. 47 The Hospital of Bethlehem. (and in French) 250 × 365/280 × 370mm. Without credits or publication-line, but engr by Fletcher according to Boydell's *Alphabetical Catalogue*.

48 · CHAMBERLAIN'S NEW AND COMPLEAT HISTORY AND SURVEY [1770]

A prospectus issued by the bookseller John Cooke announces:

By the Royal Licence and Authority of His Majesty King George the IIId.... on Saturday the 10th of March, 1770, will be published (Price Six-Pence) Elegantly printed on a New Letter and Fine Paper, adorned with a curious Frontispiece designed by Wale, and engraved by Grignion; also a beautiful View of the Mansion-House and Guildhall, Number I (to be continued Weekly) of a New and Compleat History and Survey of the Cities of London and Westminster ... Three sheets of the Work and a curious Copper-Plate, or two Sheets and two Copper-Plates shall be delivered Weekly.

The subscriber is promised that the work will be completed in 60 Numbers at sixpence each, any extras to be delivered gratis, and will be 'Embellished and illustrated with a great Number of curious Copper-Plates, from original drawings made on purpose for this work by the celebrated Wale, and engraved by Grignion and other very eminent Artists'. In fact the publication had already been running for over a year, since the *Gazetteer & Daily Advertiser* of 21 January 1769 had announced that the first Number was published on the previous day.

Samuel Wale had been designing illustrations for books and magazines, of which many were engraved by Charles Grignion, for 25 years. The plates credited to them in this work are distinguished from the rest by rococo frames, their subjects being historical or topical. The quality of the topographical illustrations varies from the competent to the totally inept and, although he had previously drawn the 80 topographical plates for Dodsley's *London and its Environs Described* (no 41), there is no cause to associate Wale with them. One plate (item 33) is credited to T. Malton and the prentice hand of the creator of the *Picturesque Tour through London and Westminster* (no 72) may be discerned in the broad stretch of cloud-banked sky that sets off Sampson's Bank of England façade with its one completed wing of Sir Robert Taylor's extension.

This is the first of four topographical books (nos 48, 52, 57, 60) to be issued from the 'Shakespeare's Head'. John Cooke, publisher of the *Lady's Magazine,* is said to have amassed a fortune by issuing works in weekly Numbers, of which the most profitable was an illustrated *Universal Family Bible or Christian's Divine Library* (1773–4). This was put out as the work of the Rev Henry Southwell, LLD, who received a fee for the use of his name while the impecunious Robert Sanders, with a wife and five children to feed, actually compiled the book. Sanders also wrote for Cooke *The Complete English Traveller* (no 52) under the pseudonym 'Nathaniel Spencer' and this was later reissued as *The Modern Universal British Traveller* (no 60) under three pseudonyms, English, Welsh and Scottish.

A New and Compleat History and Survey of the Cities of London and Westminster, the Borough of Southwark, and Parts adjacent from the Earliest Accounts, to the

Beginning of the Year 1770.... By a Society of Gentlemen: Revised, Corrected and Improved, by Henry Chamberlain of Hatton-Garden, Esq ... London: Printed for J. Cooke, at Shakespear's-Head No 17, Pater-Noster-Row.

Folio, about 360 × 235mm.   nd

COLLATION Title-page; dedication to Samuel Turner, Lord Mayor, dated 16 January 1769, royal licence dated 19 December 1768 (addressed to John Cooke with no mention of the author of the book), list of subscribers (6pp); pp 7–682, New and Compleat History; appendix to 1770, index, directions to binder (10pp).

The topographical and historical plates and maps are mostly without credits. Pictures are in ruled frames unless the characteristic rococo or beaded frames are specified. All plates, except the frontispieces and headpiece, are superscribed with the title 'Engraved for Chamberlain's History of London'. They are unnumbered and unpaged and include from one to eight separate subjects. Dimensions given are those of the subjects (exclusive of frames and titles) and of the plate-marks.

1 front. Sir Christopher Wren presenting to/King Chares IId his plan/for rebuilding the City. Wale Delin. Grignion Sculp. 152 × 102/254 × 165mm. Rococo.

1a alternative front. His Majesty King George III Granting/his Royal Licence for the Publication of this Work. Wale Delin. Grignion Sculp. 160 × 100/250 × 160mm. Rococo.

2 p 4 (headpiece) The Genius of London. 60 × 153/75 × 170mm.

3 p 10 View of the City Gates as they Appeared before they were Pulled Down. 155 × 275/170 × 290mm. (Cripplegate 75 × 66mm, Ludgate 75 × 75mm, Moorgate 75 × 70mm, Newgate 75 × 68mm, Aldersgate 80 × 68mm, Bishopsgate 80 × 75mm, Bridge Gate 80 × 68mm.)

4 p 25 Bishops and Citizens Swearing Fealty to/William the Conqueror. Wale del. Grignion sculp. 155 × 100/250 × 170mm. Rococo.

5 p 41 Henry Fitzalwine Knt – Sir William Walworth. Jas Record sculp. 135 × 235/185 × 275mm. Double portrait.

6 p 81 Ceremony of the Champion's Challenge/at the Coronation. Wale del. Grignion sculp. 165 × 100/250 × 160mm. Rococo.

7 p 85 Richard II Appeases the Rebels on the death of Wat Tyler. Wale del. Grignion sculp. 155 × 100/250 × 160mm. Rococo.

8 p 89 View of the Tower from the River Thames – View of the Custom House. Each 120 × 170/270 × 180mm. Beaded.

9 p 106 Blood and his Accomplices/Escaping after stealing the Crown from the Tower. Wale del. Grignion sculp. 160 × 103/250 × 160mm. Rococo.

10 p 113 Dr Shaw/Preaching at St Paul's Cross. 165 × 100/255 × 163mm. Rococo.

11 p 114 A Representation of an Ancient/Tournament. Wale del. Grignion sculp. 155 × 100/250 × 160mm. Rococo.

12 p 118 Manner of Burning the Martyrs in Smithfield. Wale del. Grignion sculp. 158 × 98/250 × 160mm. Rococo.

13 p 138 The Abbey Church of St Peter Westminster – The Admiralty Office. Each 90 × 150/275 × 190mm. Beaded. Abbey seen from W.

14 p 138 View of the Inside of Westminster Abby – View of the Inside of St Paul's Cathedral. Each 100 × 150/270 × 190mm. Beaded. The E. ends.

15 p 142 The Chapel of King Henry VII in Westminster Abbey – The front veiw of Westminster Hall. Each 93 × 150/270 × 190mm. Beaded.

16 p 207 View of an Ancient Shooting-match between the/Citizens of London. 153 × 106/250 × 160mm. Rococo.

17 p 228 Habit of the Lady Mayoress of London in 1640 – Habit of a Merchant's Wife of London in 1640. Each 180 × 130/205 × 280mm.

18 p 229 Habit of the Lord Mayor of London in 1640 – Habit of a Merchant of London in 1640. Each 180 × 135/205 × 280mm.

19 p 251 View of the manner of burying the dead Bodies/at Holy-well mount during the dreadful Plague in 1665. Wale delin. Grignion sculp. 150 × 100/250 × 160mm. Rococo.

20 p 253 View of St Bennets Grace Church/Fenchurch Street – View of the Monument/Fish Street Hill – View of St Magnus Church/London Bridge. Each 143 × 75/185 × 270mm. Beaded.

21 p 253 View of Part of London as it appeared in the Dreadful Fire in 1666. 165 × 104/240 × 160mm. Rococo.

22 p 256 Sr Christopher Wren's Plan for Rebuilding the City. 170 × 270/200 × 295mm.

23 p 275 View of St Paul's Cathedral – View of St Paul's School. T. White sculp. Each 95 × 148/275 × 185mm. Beaded. Cathedral from S.W.

24 p 301 View of Westminster Bridge – View of Black-fryer's Bridge – View of London Bridge. Each 60 × 160/270 × 180mm.

25 p 305 The Mansion House – The Guildhall of London. Each 90 × 145/270 × 183mm. Beaded. Façades.

26 p 307 View of the Foundling Hospital Lambs Conduit Fields – View of the Small-Pox Hospital near St Pancrass. Each 90 × 150/270 × 190mm. Beaded.

27 p 341 View of the British Museum – View of Bedford

House. A. Smith sculpt. Each 90 × 155/270 × 185mm. Beaded.

28 p 364 View of the Temporary Bridge of London/on Fire in the Night of April 11th 1758. Wale delin. Grignion sculp. 165 × 108/254 × 159mm. Rococo.

29 p 375 The Ceremony of Laying the first Stone of Black Friars Bridge/by the Lord Mayor & Aldermen ... Wale delint. C. Grignion sculp. 160 × 100/250 × 160mm. 31 October 1760. Rococo.

30 p 436 (tm) A New and Correct Plan of London Westminster and Southwark with the Additional Buildings to the Year 1770. 280 × 500/305 × 525mm. Engraved by J. Flyn. (*Darlington and Howgego* 149)

31 p 449 St Annes & Agnes Aldersgate – St Botolph Aldersgate – St Martin Outwick Threadneedle Street – St Olave's Old Jewry – St Bartholomew the Great – St Bartholomew the Less. In pairs, 70 × 75, 85 × 75, 75 × 75/275 × 178mm.

32 p 462 View of St Botolph's Church/Bishopsgate Street – View of Christ Church/Spittlefields – View of St Leonard's Church/Shoreditch. Each 160 × 85/185 × 275mm.

33 p 473 St Christopher's Church, The Bank of England & St Bartholomew's Church/Threadneedle Street. T. Malton delin. Adam Smith sculp. 145 × 240/190 × 275mm. Beaded. (*Bank of England* 17)

34 p 475 View of the South Sea House – View of the East India House. A. Smith sculpt. Each 90 × 155/270 × 190mm. Beaded.

35 p 486 View of St Mildred's Church/in the Poultry – View of St Michael's/Church Cornhill – View of St Peter's Cornhill. 143 × 85, 143 × 75, 143 × 85/185 × 275mm.

36 p 487 View of Grocer's Hall – View of Goldsmith's Hall. T. White sculpt. Each 90 × 145/250 × 180mm. Beaded.

37 p 496 St Mary Aldermary Church/Bow Lane – View of St Mary le Bow/Cheapside – View of St Mildred's Church/Bread Street. 157 × 85, 157 × 80, 157 × 85/185 × 270mm.

38 p 498 View of the Royal Exchange – Gresham College as it appeared before it was taken down to Build an Excise Office. Each 93 × 150/270 × 185mm. The courtyard of Gresham College which was replaced by the Excise Office built to the design of William Robinson, 1769.

39 p 502 St Mary Aldermanbury – St Lawrence Jewry Cateaton Street – St Michael's Wood Street – St Giles's Cripplegate – St Stephen's Coleman Street – St Margaret's Lothbury. Each 85 × 85/206 × 280mm.

40 p 516 View of Christ's-Church Hospital – View of St Bartholomew's Hospital. A. Smith sculpt. Each 90 × 150/270 × 185mm. Beaded.

41 p 535 View of St Andrew's Church Holborn – View of St Sepulchre's Church Snow Hill. Each 95 × 145/270 × 185mm. Beaded.

42 p 537 View of Surgeon's Hall, Old Bailey – View of College of Physicians Warwick Lane. Each 90 × 145/275 × 190mm. Beaded. College courtyard.

43 p 540 View of St Edmond the King/Lombard Street – View of Allhallows/Lombard Street – View of St Mary Woolnorth/Lombard Street. 143 × 80, 143 × 80, 143 × 85/180 × 260mm.

44 p 546 St Trinity Minories – St Andrew Undershaft Leadenhall Street – St Margaret Pattens Little Tower Street – St Mary Abchurch Abchurch Lane – St Clements Eastcheap – Allhallows Staining Crutchard Fryers. Each 80 × 85/210 × 280mm. Allhallows Staining is in Mark Lane; St Olave, Hart Street is shown.

45 p 557 St James's Garlick Hith – St Nicholas Coleabby Old Fish Street – St Mary Magdalen Old Fish Street – St Swithin's Cannon Street – St Matthew's Friday Street – St Michael's College Hill. Each 85 × 70/290 × 180mm.

46 p 558 St Stephen's Wallbrook – Allhallows the Great Thames Street – St Michael's Queenhythe – St Mary at Hill near Billingsgate – St Botolph's in Botolph Lane – The Chappel in the Tower. Each 83 × 85/210 × 280mm. The chapel is St Peter ad Vincula.

47 p 562 View of St Olave's Church/Southwark – View of St George's/Southwark – View of Christ's Church/Surry. 140 × 80, 140 × 70, 140 × 80/185 × 270mm.

48 p 563 St John's Church Southwark – St Mary Magdalen's/Church Bermondsey Street – St Mary's Church Rotherhith. Each 160 × 85/195 × 275mm.

49 p 566 View of St Thomas's Hospital in Southwark – View of Guy's Hospital in Southwark. Each 93 × 150/275 × 185mm. Beaded. Interior court of St Thomas's, exterior court of Guy's.

50 p 576 View of Greenwich Hospital – View of Chelsea Hospital. T. White sculp. Each 95 × 150/275 × 185mm. Beaded. Both viewed from river. (*Longford* 15)

51 p 577 View of London from Greenwich Park. 195 × 300/225 × 325mm.

52 p 585 View of the Royal Stables & part of St Martin's Church – View of St George's Church Bloomsbury. A. Smith sculpt. Each 142 × 108/190 × 270mm. Beaded.

53 p 585 View of St Paul's Church/Covent Garden – View of St Mary le Strand – View of St Clement's Church/Strand. 145 × 85, 145 × 80, 145 × 80/185 × 270mm.

54 p 588 View of the Treasury & Horse Guards – View of the Banqueting House. Each 90 × 145/270 × 185mm. Beaded.

55 p 590 St John the Evangelist, Westminster – St Bennets Pauls Wharf – St Martin's Ludgate – St Bride's Fleet Street – St Dunstan's in Fleet Street. 65

× 65, 65 × 65; 85 × 65, 85 × 65; 85 × 135/270 × 160mm.

56 p 591 View of the House of Commons from the/River Thames – View of the Office of Ordnance with the Entrance of the/House of Lords. A. Smith del. et sculp. Each 140 × 110/190 × 270mm. Beaded.

57 p 596 View of St James's Palace – View of Kensington Palace. Each 90 × 145/270 × 185mm. Beaded.

58 p 597 The Hospital of St George at Hyde Park corner – The South View of the Middlesex Hospital near Oxford Road. T. White sulp. Each 95 × 150/270 × 180mm. Beaded.

59 p 601 St Giles in the Fields – St George's Hanover Square – St James's Westminster – St Anne's Westminster – St George's Queen Square – Temple Bar. 85 × 75, 85 × 75; 75 × 75, 75 × 75; 75 × 75, 75 × 75/275 × 180mm.

60 p 601 View of Lincoln's Inn – View of Gray's Inn. Each 95 × 150/270 × 190mm. Beaded. New Square, Lincoln's Inn; Gray's Inn from N.

61 p 605 View of St Luke's Hospital in Upper Moorfields – View of Bethlem Hospital. Each 95 × 150/275 × 190mm. Beaded.

62 p 608 View of Ironmongers' Alms-Houses Kingsland Road – Trinity Alms-Houses Mile End Road. Each 90 × 150/280 × 190mm. Beaded.

63 p 609 St Mary's Whitechappel – St Paul's Shadwel – St Anne's Limehouse – St George's Ratcliff highway – St Dunstan's Stepney – St John's Wapping. Each 85 × 85/210 × 280mm.

64 p 617 General View of Ranelagh Gardens – View of Vaux-Hall Gardens. A. Smith sculp. Each 90 × 153/270 × 190mm. Beaded. (*Longford* 320)

65 p 620 View of Part of the Town of Fulham and the Bridge View of ye Arch-Bishop's Palace & St Mary's Church Lambeth. Each 90 × 150/265 × 185mm. Beaded.

66 p 620 View of the Parish Church of Stoke Newington – View of the Church of St John at Hackney – View of the Church of St Mathew at Bethnal Green. Each 78 × 143/270 × 180mm.

67 p 623 View of St Mary's Church/Islington – View of St James's Church/Clerkenwell – View of St Luke's Church/Old Street. 143 × 75, 143 × 90, 143 × 80/190 × 275mm.

68 p 632 (tm) A New and Correct Map of the Countries Twenty Miles Round London. By Thos. Bowen. 323 × 370/345 × 385mm. Three miles to an inch. (*Darlington and Howgego* 147)

49 · CURIOSITIES OF LONDON AND WESTMINSTER [1771]

This miniature book, a bijou guide in four volumes to the sights of London, was compiled by David Henry and first published by Francis Newbery, nephew to John Newbery famed for the tiny volumes in his 'Juvenile Library' bound in flowered and gilt Dutch paper. He is to be distinguished from John's son, also confusingly called Francis, who was something of a dilettante, being enriched by the quack medicine side of his father's business and who, with his publishing partner, Carnan, had moved shop to 65 St Paul's Churchyard.

Francis the nephew operated from 20 Ludgate Street, alias 20 St Paul's Churchyard, and maintained his uncle's literary connection since he published the first edition of *The Vicar of Wakefield* in 1766 and of *She Stoops to Conquer* in 1773 and ran the *Gentleman's Magazine* from the year of John's death, 1767, to that of his own in 1780. Thenceforward his widow, Elizabeth, succeeded to the business and for 20 years ran it with the help of two managers, Badcock and John Harris. Finally, in 1801, Harris took over and started publishing under his own name.

The earliest complete set of *The Curiosities of London* seen is that of 1771 (although volumes dated 1770 are cited by Roscoe) when it was sold at 2s the set of four volumes or 6d each volume bound and gilt. Subsequently individual volumes were reprinted as required so that each volume of a set might be of a different date. The BL set, for instance, consists of a 1786 vol. 1, a 1783 vol. 2, a 1784 vol. 3 and a 1782 vol. 4; the Guildhall Library has 1786 and 1798 editions of vol. 2 besides a complete set dated 1771. According to Roscoe the work was again, and finally, reprinted as a whole in 1799.

John Harris retained the title but issued it in two volumes of different format and with fresh plates in 1805 (no 91).

Each volume is illustrated by half a dozen small, anonymous engravings, all but four (items 14, 18, 20, 24) being reduced and simplified versions of Dodsley's plates in his six-volume *London and its*

Environs Described (no 41), referred to in the list as *LED*.

The Curiosities of London and Westminster described in four Volumes embellished with elegant copper plates. Volume I, Containing a Description of

The Tower of London	St Luke's Hospital
The Monument	The Magdalen House
London Bridge	Gresham College
The Custom House	Sion College
The Royal Exchange	and
Bethlem Hospital	The South Sea-House

London: Printed for F. Newbery (after 1780 'E. Newbery'), at the Corner of St Paul's Church-Yard 1771. Price Six-pence.

Sextodecimo, 100 × 63mm.   1771, etc

COLLATION   Title-page; pp 3–126, Curiosities; Newbery catalogue (2 pp).

1 front. The Tower of London. 50 × 80mm. *LED* 6, 148.

2 p 59 The Monument. 85 × 50mm. *LED* 5, 1.

3 p 69 London Bridge. 50 × 80mm. *LED* 1, 297(b).

4 p 80 The Custom House. 52 × 82mm. *LED* 2, 213.

5 p 86 The Royal Exchange. 52 × 82mm. *LED* 5, 280.

6 p 90 Bethlem Hospital. 50 × 80mm. *LED* 1, 297(a).

The Curiosities of London and Westminster described in four Volumes embellished with elegant copper plates. Volume II, Containing a Description of

Guildhall	The East India House
Guildhall Chapel	St Stephen Walbrook
The Bank of England	St Mary le Bow
St Thomas's Hospital	Bridewell Hospital
The Mansion House	Christ's Hospital and
Foundling Hospital	London Stone

London: Printed for F. Newbery (after 1780 'E. Newbery'), at the Corner of St Paul's Church-Yard 1771. Price Six-pence.

Sextodecimo, 100 × 63mm.   1771, etc

COLLATION   Title-page; pp 1–125 (pp 3–127 in later eds), Curiosities.

7 front. Guild-Hall. 50 × 75mm. p 3 in later eds. *LED* 3, 100.

   (pp 11–12 Woodcuts of 'Gog' and 'Magog'. pp 12–13 in later eds.)

8 p 42 The Bank. 75 × 50mm. p 44 in later eds. *LED* 1, 234.

9 p 51 St Thomas's Hospital. 45 × 77/60 × 83mm. p 53 in later eds. *LED* 6, 129.

10 p 61 The Mansion House. 45 × 77/60 × 83mm. p 63 in later eds. *LED* 4, 244.

11 p 67 Foundling Hospital. 50 × 77mm. p 69 in later eds. *LED* 2, 327.

12 p 93 East India House. 47 × 77mm. p 95 in later eds. *LED* 2, 263.

The Curiosities of London and Westminster described in four Volumes embellished with elegant copper plates. Volume III, Containing a Description of

St. Paul's Cathedral	St Bartholomew's
Black Friars Bridge	Hospital
The British Museum	Northumberland house
The Temple	Charing Cross, and
Temple Bar	Lincolns Inn

London: Printed for F. Newbery (after 1780 'E. Newbery'), at the Corner of St Paul's Church-Yard 1771. Price Six-pence.

Sextodecimo, 100 × 63mm.   1771, etc

COLLATION   Title-page; pp 3–126, Curiosities.

13 front. St. Paul's Cathedral. 50 × 83mm. *LED* 5, 139.

14 p 55 Black Fryers Bridge. 50 × 83mm. Opened November 1769.

15 p 67 The British Museum. 50 × 83mm. p 67 in later eds. *LED* 2, 17(b).

16 p 100 Temple Bar. 50 × 82/60 × 90mm. *LED* 6, 114(a).

17 p 102 St Bartholomew's Hospital. 50 × 84mm. *LED* 1, 260.

18 p 107 Northumberland House. 50 × 82/55 × 90mm.

The Curiosities of London and Westminster described in four volumes embellished with elegant copper plates. Volume IV, Containing a Description of

Westminster-Abby	Buckingham House, or
Westminster-Bridge	the Queen's Palace
Westminster-Hall	The Banqueting House
The House of Lords	The Horse Guards and
The H. of Commons	The Admiralty Office

London: Printed for F. Newbery (after 1780 'E. Newbery'), at the Corner of St Paul's Church-Yard 1771. Price Six-pence.

Sextodecimo, 100 × 63mm.   1771, etc

COLLATION   Title-page; pp 1–125 (pp 3–125 in later eds), Curiosities.

19 front. Westminster-Abby. 50 × 85mm. *LED* 1, 1.

20 p 93 Westminster-Bridge. 50 × 85mm.

21 p 103 The House of Lords. 80 × 55mm. p 104 in later edds. *LED* 2, 165(a).

22 p 109 The House of Commons. 80 × 53mm. *LED* 2, 165(b).

23 p 118 White Hall. 52 × 85mm. p 120 in later eds. *LED* 1, 244.

24 p 125 Horse Guards. 50 × 85mm.

50 · GROSE'S ANTIQUITIES OF ENGLAND AND WALES* [1773–87]

More reputable than the 'Paternoster Row Numbers', although available in the same form, was this work by Francis Grose, an FSA and exhibitor at the Royal Academy of tinted drawings. His first edition was issued in 14 vols folio from 1773 to 1776, with supplements in 1777 and 1787. A paginated preface with appendix contained general observations on the antiquities but thenceforward the work was made up from single unnumbered, unsigned and unpaginated sheets; each with an engraving of a particular object, building or map accompanied by a commentary written by Grose or a fellow antiquary. These were to be bound up in alphabetical order of the counties of England followed by Wales and the offshore islands and each volume was supplied with an engraved title-page and an index-checklist of subjects. In 1783 the second (quarto) edition started to come out and ran until an eighth and supplementary volume, dated 1787. This edition, according to an advertisement in the *Daily Universal Register* of 1 January 1785, might be purchased either in volume form or in Numbers 'delivered weekly, once a fortnight or monthly'. It followed the same arrangement as the folio edition but it was paginated, albeit somewhat erratically, with the engravings on separate plates facing the printed descriptions instead of being set on the same pages as the letterpress. This makes for quicker reference so the London plates have been listed as bound in the quarto edition with divergences from the folio issues individually noted.

(engr title) The/Antiquities/of/England and Wales/ by Francis Grose Esq. F.A.S./Vol. 2(3, Suppl 1-2) (oval vignette with picturesque landscape engraved by S. Sparrow) London: Printed for S. Hooper, No. 25 Ludgate Hill MD CC LXXIV (etc).

Folio, about 318 × 235mm.   1774–5, 1777–87

COLLATION   Vol. 2. Engr title-page; preface, description of frontispiece (4pp); Isle of Wight to Northampton (unpaginated and unsigned leaves, items 2–6). Vol. 3. Engr title-page; To the Public (4pp); Northumberland to Sussex (unpaginated and unsigned leaves, items 8–11). Suppl. 1. Engr title-page; pp i–iv, To the Public dated 13 September 1777; advertisement (2pp); postscript (2pp); county index to Suppl. 1 (4pp); Dorsetshire to Staffordshire (unpaginated and unsigned leaves, items 1, 7, 13–15). Suppl. 2. Engr title-page; county index (3pp); Suffolk to Yorkshire, Wales, offshore islands (unpaginated and unsigned leaves, item 12); pp 1–35 (and 4pp), addenda to preface; pp 1–8, general index, directions to binder.

The Antiquities of England and Wales: being a Collection of Views of the Most remarkable Ruins and ancient Buildings, Accurately drawn on the spot. To each View is added An Historical Account of its Situation, when and by whom built ... Collected from the Best Authorities by Francis Grose, Esq. F.A.S. Vol. I. The Second Edition, corrected and enlarged. London: Printed by C. Clarke for S. Hooper, No 212, High Holborn, opposite Southampton Street, Bloomsbury Square, M.DCC. LXXXIII. (Only vol. 1 has a printed title-page. Those for vols 2–8 are engraved plates modified from the folio ed.)

Quarto, about 260 × 175mm.   1783–7

COLLATION   Vol. 3. Engr title-page; county index (2pp); pp 1–168, Kent to Monmouthshire. Vol. 5. Engr title-page; county index (2pp); pp 1–95, Shropshire to Sussex. Vol. 8. Engr title-page; pp 1–4, county index; pp i–iv, To the Public dated 13 September 1787; pp 1–163, supplement; pp 165–217 (ie 172), general index, directions to binder.

Most of the drawings for the illustrations were Grose's own, the London subjects being engraved by R.B. Godfrey, James Newton, Record and S. Sparrow. Some, in water-colour or wash, often reduced in size from larger originals (of which three are in the BM) for engraving, are in the library of the Society of Antiquaries and are described by J.H. Hopkins, the Librarian, in *The Antiquarian Journal* vol. 56 (1976), pp 253–5. The original folio issues afford a well-balanced combination of Caslon letterpress and topographical etching, each sheet being a pleasing object complete in itself but throughout the second edition plates are bound in separately in the conventional way. Thus the second edition plates have captions of their own while the folio edition plates are identified by the letterpress headings. Perhaps the design of the latter was suggested by John Bowles's popular *British Views* (no 28), in which however both the views and descriptions were engraved on the same plate.

VOL. 3

1 front. The New Temple, London. Jas Newton sculp. Pub. 12 Jany 1785 by S. Hooper. 205 × 133/225 × 150mm. Folio ed suppl. 1. Society of Antiquaries,

123

wash drawing (212 × 138mm). Interior of the Round 'drawn 1784'.

2 p 130 Christ's Hospital, London. Pl. 1. Record sculp. Pub. 21 Octr 1784 by S. Hooper. 105 × 150/120 × 175mm. Folio ed: 'S. Hooper Exct. Record sculp March 24th 1776'. The N. cloister.

3 p 132 Christ's Hospital, London Pl. 2 Record sculp. Pub. 21 Octr 1784 by S. Hooper. 100 × 147/115 × 158mm. Folio ed: 'Hooper Exh. Record sculp. May 30, 1776'. Mathematical School and Christ Church.

4 p 133 Ely House, London. Pl. 1. R. Godfrey Sc. Pub. 20 Octr 1784 by S. Hooper. 105 × 150/115 × 165mm. Folio ed: 'R. Godfrey Sc. May 16 1772'. Society of Antiquaries, wash drawing (102 × 148mm). N. side of Great Hall, St Andrew's Chapel and cloister.

5 p 134 Ely House. Printed for S. Hooper. 230 × 170/260 × 205mm. Folio ed: '20th Jany 1776'. Society of Antiquaries, pen and ink drawing (230 × 135mm). A plan.

6 p 137 Ely House, London. Pl. 2. Dent Sculp. Pub. 26 Octr 1784 by S. Hooper. 105 × 150/125 × 168mm. Folio ed: 'Dent Sculp. Publish'd by S. Hooper No 25 Ludgate Hill'. Society of Antiquaries, wash drawing (104 × 150mm). Courtyard, colonnade and S. side of Great Hall.

7 p 140 White Tower, or Tower of London. Jas. Newton Sc. Pub. 12 Novr 1784 by S. Hooper. 112 × 162/140 × 190mm. Folio ed. suppl. 1. Society of Antiquaries, water-colour (112 × 162mm). N.W. aspect, 'view drawn 1784'.

VOL. 5

8 p 81 Bermondsey Abbey, Surry. Godfrey Sc. (stippled) Pub. 20 May 1785, by S. Hooper. 105 × 155/120 × 170mm. Folio ed: 'The Abbey of Bermondsey, Surry/Plate I. Godfrey Sc. Feb. 2 1772', with credit and date stippled.

9 p 96 Lambeth Palace, Surrey. Pl. 1. Pub. 10 Septr 1784 by S. Hooper. 108 × 160/120 × 165mm. Folio ed: 'Sparrow sculp. April 4 1773'. The Great Gate, 'drawn 1773'.

10 p 96 Lambeth Palace, Surrey Pl. 2. Sparrow Sculp. Pub. 10 Septr 1784 by S. Hooper. 105 × 150/120 × 165mm. Folio ed: 'Sparrow Sculp. Decr. 15, 1773'. The E. and part of the N. front of the Palace with Lambeth Church, from the kitchen garden.

11 p 105 Lambeth Palace, Surrey Pl. 3. Godfrey Sc. (stippled). Pub. 10 Septr 1784 by S. Hooper. 103 × 153/108 × 165mm. Folio ed: 'Godfrey Sc. May 2, 1778'. The N. side of the Palace from the bowling green.

12 (cartouche) Plan/of/Lambeth/Palace/1750. (bm) From an original in the Possession of Mr. Singleton of Lambeth. J. Reeves del. Cook sculp. 210 × 170/245 × 183mm. Folio ed suppl. 2.

VOL. 8

13 p 110 Savoy Church, London. Sparrow Sc. Published June 26, 1787 by S. Hooper. 110 × 155/130 × 165mm. Folio ed suppl. 1. Society of Antiquaries, water-colour (108 × 155mm). The E. side showing the refectory window.

14 p 112 Savoy Church, London. Pl. 2. Sparrow Sc. Published July 14 1787 by S. Hooper. 108 × 155/125 × 170mm. Folio ed suppl. 1. Society of Antiquaries, water-colour (112 × 155mm). The refectory window from another angle. The building in a state of dilapidation after a fire.

15 p 114 A Gateway called King John's Castle, Oldford Middlesex. J. Newton direxit. Pub. July 9, 1787 by S. Hooper. 105 × 150/135 × 180mm. Folio ed suppl. 1. Society of Antiquaries, water-colour (108 × 185mm).

51 · NOORTHOUCK'S NEW HISTORY [1773]

John Noorthouck, a bookseller's son and liveryman of the Company of Stationers, lived for most of his life in Barnard's Inn, Holborn. He earned his living as a proof corrector and indexer but was moved to write this history because, in his own words, Maitland (no 38) and his continuator John Entick (no 44) amplified Stow (no 37) with 'abundance of frivolous particulars; and have destroyed the connexion and unity of the whole ... Maitland's *Survey of London* being thus rendered bulky, expensive, tediously prolix ... unnecessarily swelled to two bulky volumes in folio'. His aim was a 'work more extensive in its object, yet to be comprehended in a more convenient size'.

A New History of London including Westminster and Southwark. To which is added a General Survey of the Whole; describing the Public Buildings, Late Improvements, &c. Illustrated with Copper-Plates. By John Noorthouck. (engraving by Longmate of the arms of the City, Westminster and Southwark, 55 × 135mm) London, Printed for R. Baldwin, No. 47, Pater-noster Row. MDCCLXXIII.

Quarto, about 275 × 215mm.   1773

COLLATION Title-page; dedication to Lord Mayor, etc (1 leaf); pp i–viii, preface dated from 'Bernard's Inn' 28 March 1773; contents (4pp); pp 1–772, History; pp

773–902, appendix, addenda; index, errata, directions to binder (42pp).

Presumably the bookseller, Robert Baldwin, publisher of the *London Magazine* from 1746 to 1784, collected the illustrations for which Noorthouck is somewhat apologetic. Speaking of the plates he says 'one or two of them have indeed fallen short of what the author had a just right to expect; but there are several of them that do credit to the names of the engravers'. In fact 17 consist of ward maps, probably by Thomas Bowen, all but two of which were engraved for publication in Baldwin's magazine between April 1766 and July 1772 (marked *LM*). A detailed account of substitutions in aldermen's arms and the added book title are given by Hyde. Besides these there are the two customary general maps of London and environs, the latter by Thomas Kitchin, facsimiles of two seventeenth century plans and four armorial plates by the specialist engraver Barak Longmate, who also features on the title-page.

Among the views are 16 small engravings, two or three to a plate, by Joseph Collyer, Isaac Taylor senior and Benjamin Green. Ten of these are derived from Wale's drawings for Dodsley's *'London and its Environs Described* (no 41, *LED*) on which Benjamin with his putative brother John Green had been employed. Collyer later gained a reputation for engraved portraits, was elected an Associate of the Royal Academy and appointed engraver to Queen Charlotte. Taylor became a well-known book illustrator and his work was admired by Bewick whom he befriended during his brief and unhappy experience of London life. These engravers also supplied ten larger views, some of which require folded insets, bringing the total number of plates to 42. Each is inscribed, tc or bc, '(Engraved for) Noorthouck's History of London', and in some cases the date 1772 is added although plate 23 is marked 1773.

1 p 225 A Plan of the City and Liberties of London, showing the Extent of the Dreadful Conflagration in the Year 1666. 1772. 205 × 330/230 × 345mm. Refs (bl) 1–100 and (tr) A–Z, a–o. (*Darlington and Howgego* 19b)

2 p 232 Sir Christopher Wren's Plan for Rebuilding the City of London after the Great Fire in 1666 – Mr. John Evelyn's Plan for Rebuilding the City of London after the Great Fire in 1666. 155 × 293, 140 × 293/375 × 310mm. Refs l. 1–38, etc.

3 p 521 (tm) A New Plan of London, Westminster and Southwark Engraved for Noorthouck's History of London, 1772. Ashby sculp. 405 × 685/430 × 710mm. Open spaces tinted green, City boundary red. (*Darlington and Howgego* 157)

4 p 543 (tm) Views of the several Gates of London, which, Temple Bar and Newgate excepted, were taken down in ye Years 1760 & 1761/with the elegant Gothic Gate at White Hall built by K. Henry VIII in 1532, which was taken down about ye same time. B. Green sculp. 225 × 405mm. (Newgate 90 × 70mm, Aldgate 65 × 75mm, Moorgate 75 × 55mm, Bishopsgate 70 × 70mm, Cripplegate 75 × 70mm, Bridge Gate 80 × 65mm, Temple Bar 80 × 65mm, Whitehall Gate 70 × 50mm, Ludgate 75 × 65mm, Aldersgate 85 × 70mm.)

5 p 543 (cartouche bc) Aldersgate Ward/with its Divisions into/Precincts and Parishes/and the Liberty of St Martin's le Grand, According/to a New Survey. 1772. 180 × 235/195 × 250mm. Views bl of St Anne and St Agnes, Gresham Street and br of St Botolph, Aldersgate, rebuilt 1754. *LM* April 1766.

6 p 545 (cartouche bc) Aldgate Ward/with its Divisions into/Precincts and Parishes,/according to a/New Survey. 1772. 172 × 235/190 × 245mm. Views bl of St James, Duke's Place and br of St Catherine Coleman. *LM* August 1766.

7 p 549 (cartouche rc) The Wards of/Coleman Street/and Bassishaw/Taken from the latest Survey/with Corrections and Amendments. 1772. 224 × 170/240 × 190mm. Views br of St Stephen, Coleman Street and tl of St Michael Bassishaw. *LM* February 1767.

8 p 551 (cartouche tr) A New and Accurate Plan of/Billingsgate Ward,/and Bridge Ward Within/Divided into Parishes, from/a late Survey. 1772. 172 × 233/185 × 250mm. Views tr of St Mary at Hill and br of St Botolph, Botolph Lane.

9 p 554 (cartouche bl) Bishops Gate Ward/Within and Without/According to a/New Survey. 1772. 175 × 230/190 × 250mm. Views bl of St Ethelburga and br of St Helen, both Bishopsgate Street. *LM* November 1767.

10 p 558 (cartouche bc) Breadstreet Ward/and/Cordwainers Ward/with their Divisions into/Parishes/according to a new Survey. 1772. 170 × 230/190 × 250mm. Views bl of St Matthew, Friday Street and br of St Mildred, Bread Street. *LM* October 1766.

11 p 561 London Bridge with the Houses on it – London Bridge as re-edified – Blackfriars Bridge – Westminster Bridge. T. White sculpt. 230 × 395/255 × 415mm.

12 p 562 St Mary le Bow Cheapside – The Monument on Fish Street Hill – St Brides Church Fleet Street. 147 × 60, 147 × 72, 147 × 58/175 × 225mm. The Monument from *LED* 5, front.

13 p 566 (cartouche lc) Broad Street/& Cornhill Wards,/Divided into/Parishes,/according to a/New Survey.

125

1772. 180 × 230/190 × 245mm. Views tl of St Christopher le Stocks, rc of St Bartholomew by the Exchange and br of St Benet Fink. *LM* December 1768.

14 p 567 Front View of the Bank of England in Threadneedle Street, including St Christophers Church, and/the Tower of St Bartholomews, behind the Royal Exchange. J. Collyer sculp. 1773. 140 × 190/170 × 220mm. Similar view to Malton's in Chamberlain's *New and Compleat History* (no 48), p 473. (*Bank of England* 16).

15 p 576 (cartouche tc) Candlewick and/Langborn Wards./With their Divisions into/Parishes according to a New Survey. 1772. 180 × 240/190 × 245mm. Views tl of All Hallows, Lombard Street, tr of 'Allhallows Staining Crutched Friars' (ie St Olave, Hart Street; All Hallows Staining is correctly delineated on the map, W. of Mark Lane), bl of St Clement, Eastcheap and br of St Mary Woolnoth. *LM* December 1768.

16 p 579 (cartouche tl) Baynards Castle Ward/and/Faringdon Ward Within/With their Divisions into/Parishes, according to a/New Survey. 185 × 240/190 × 250mm. Views bl of St Martin, Ludgate, tr of St Benet, Paul's Wharf and br of St Andrew by the Wardrobe. *LM* August 1767.

17 p 587 (cartouche lc) Cheap Ward/with its Divisions into/Parishes/According to a/New Survey. 1772. 170 × 230/188 × 245mm. Views tl of Guildhall Chapel, tr of Grocers' Hall, bl of St Mildred, Poultry and br of Blackwell Hall. *LM* January 1769.

18 p 588 Guildhall – The Mansion House. Each 85 × 150/240 × 170mm. *LED* 3, 100 and 4, 244.

19 p 601 Front of the Royal Exchange (and plan). 85 × 147,75 × 85/240 × 170mm. *LED* 5,286.

20 p 606 (cartouche bl) Cripplegate/Ward/Divided into its/Parishes/from a late Survey. 1772. 170 × 225/180 × 240mm. View br of St Alban, Wood Street. *LM* August 1771.

21 p 612 (cartouche bl) A New and/Accurate Plan of/Walbrook/and Dowgate Wards/divided into Parishes/from a late Survey. 1772. 175 × 235/188 × 250mm. Views bc of St Stephen, Walbrook and br of St Michael, College Hill.

22 p 629 Cathedral Church of St Paul, London. I. Taylor sculp. 140 × 175/163 × 190mm. From N.W.

23 p 639 (cartouche br) Farringdon Ward/Without/with its Division into/Parishes/from a late/Survey. 1773. 165 × 220/185 × 235mm. *LM* July 1772.

24 p 662 (cartouche tr) Limestreet/Ward/Divided into/Parishes/According to a late/Survey. 1772. 165 × 220/180 × 235mm. View tl of front of Leadenhall. *LM* November 1771.

25 p 663 (cartouche tr) Portsoken/Ward,/with its Divisions into/Parishes from a late Survey. 1772. 167 ×

223/185 × 240mm. View bl of St Botolph, Aldgate. *LM* May 1771.

26 p 666 (cartouche bc) Queen Hith/and/Vintry Wards/Divided into/Parishes/from a late/survey. Thos. Bowen sculpt. 1772. 165 × 220/180 × 235mm. View bl of St Michael, Queenhithe. *LM* July 1771.

27 p 668 (cartouche tr) Tower Street/Ward/Divided into its/Parishes/Accoding to a late Survey. 1772. 170 × 225/185 × 238mm.

28 p 668 Custom House – West Front of the Excise Office in London. 105 × 195, 62 × 190/228 × 214mm. Custom House from *LED* 3,212.

29 p 675 A View of the Inside of the Church of St Stephens Walbrook/Built after the Design of Sir Christopher Wren. White sculp. 1772. 160 × 245/200 × 260mm. From standard mid-eighteenth century E. view, less staffage; bc miniature plan and section. 30 × 50mm.

30 p 692 Westminster Hall – Lambeth Palace. J. Collyer sculp. 85 × 145, 80 × 140/220 × 165mm. *LED* 6,297 and 3,291.

31 p 707 The Abbey Church of St Peter's Westminster. Ben. Green delin. & sculp. 142 × 204/172 × 225mm. View from W. cf with *LED* 1,1.

32 p 718 A View of St James's Palace from Pall-Mall – The Same from the Park. J. Collyer sculp. – Somerset House View'd from the River. J. Collyer sculp. 40 × 142, 35 × 142, 82 × 140/210 × 175mm. *LED* 3,214 and 5,43.

33 p 719 A Perspective View of the Queen's Palace, formerly Buckingham House in St James's Park. J. Collyer del. et sculpt. 1772. 138 × 193/170 × 220mm.

34 p 721 Banquetting House White-Hall. B. Green sculp. – The Treasury in St James's Park. B. Green delin. & sculp. Each 80 × 144/225 × 170mm. Banqueting Hall copied from *LED* 1,244.

35 p 722 A View of the Buildings for the Horse Guards from the Parade in St James's Park. J. Collyer sculp. – The Admiralty. J. Collyer sculp. Each 82 × 140/220 × 165mm. Robert Adam's Admiralty screen wall, built in 1760, is shown and described in the text as 'a piazza of neat columns with a stone arched gateway in the center'. cf with *LED* 1,134.

36 p 727 The New Buildings called the Adelphi viewed from the River. Isc Taylor sculp. 1772. 165 × 280/190 × 300mm. Published in the year in which the Adelphi was completed.

37 p 762 A North-west View of the Tower of London. I. Taylor sculp. 1772. 160 × 268/185 × 285mm. Reduced from a Maurer engraving published by Bowles c 1753 (230 × 380mm); the mariners and hucksters in the foreground are faithfully copied but the once-fashionable citizens and their coach are omitted.

38 p 772 (tm) A Map of the Country Thirty Miles round London Drawn and Engraved from Accurate Surveys

by Thos Kitchin, Hydrographer to His Majesty. 465 × 520/500 × 530mm. County boundaries tinted. (*Darlington and Howgego* 110)

39–42 p 888 (tm) Arms of the City Companies (pl. 1–3) – Arms of Trading Companies, Hospitals, Inns of Court, Societies &c. (pl. 1–4) B. Longmate sculpsit. Each 214 × 170/240 × 190mm.

52 · 'SPENCER'S' COMPLETE ENGLISH TRAVELLER* [1773]

The royal licence made out to John Cooke and dated 7 May 1772 refers to his petition in which he asserted that he had employed Nathaniel Spencer to write this book and claimed that he had also been 'at great Expence in procuring Drawings, and employing the most ingenious Artists to engrave elegant Copper Plates for the said Work'.

As in his previous topographical venture, Chamberlain's *New and Compleat History* (no 48), it is possible to reconstruct the original issue of the book in sixpenny weekly Numbers from the small Arabic numerals printed bl. There were 60 altogether, each consisting of 12 pages of text and one plate. Title-pages exist dated both 1771 and 1773 so publication probably spanned these years. Numbers 23–8, paginated 266–325, included the chapter on Middlesex.

Although the author was actually the tetchy booksellers' hack Robert Sanders, a self-styled LLD with accommodation addresses at coffee-houses such as the New England, St Paul's and New Slaughter's, Cooke seems to have had no qualms about incorporating the name of a fictitious writer in his plea for royal patronage.

The Complete English Traveller: or, a New Survey and Description of England and Wales containing a full Account of Whatever is Curious and Entertaining ... By Nathaniel Spencer, Esq. London: Printed for J. Cooke, at Shakespear's-Head in Pater-Noster-Row, MDCCLXXIII.

Folio, about 370 × 240mm.   1771 or 1773

COLLATION   Title-page; pp i–iv, royal licence, list of subscribers (4pp); pp 1–696, Complete English Traveller; index, directions to binder (12pp).

Of the 60 plates only six illustrate London and its environs. Each has the book title engraved in copperplate script tm, reading 'Engraved for the Complete English Traveller', although two of them had already appeared in Chamberlain's *New and Compleat History* (abbreviated *C*). They are numbered only in the binder's directions.

1 p 100 Perspective View of the Castle or Royal Palace, at Windsor in Berkshire. 153 × 270/175 × 290mm. No 6.

2 p 132 Perspective View of the Archbishop's Palace with St Mary's Church Lambeth. 155 × 270/175 × 290mm. No 32.

3 p 275 View of London from Greenwich Park. 185 × 300/215 × 325mm. No 42. *C* 577.

4 p 298 The Ceremony of Laying the first Stone of Black Friars Bridge/by the Lord Mayor & Aldermen of the City of London. Wale delin. C. Grignion sculp. 160 × 100/250 × 160mm. No 26. *C* 375.

5 p 307 Perspective View of St Paul's Cathedral London, also of Westminster Abbey and St Margaret's Church. Each 160 × 180/188 × 385mm. No 55.

6 p 317 Perspective View of the Royal Palace, and Gardens at Hampton Court. 150 × 270/175 × 290mm. No 10.

53 · BEAUTIES OF NATURE AND ART* [1774–5]

The second edition of this miniature travel library was published in 13 volumes by a Paternoster Row bookseller, George Robinson, trading from the Addison's Head from 1764 to his demise.

The Beauties of Nature and Art Displayed, in a Tour through the World ... Illustrated and embellished with Copper Plates. The Second Edition, greatly improved. Vol. 1 (etc) London: Printed for G. Robinson, in Pater-Noster-Row, 1774 (etc).

Duodecimo, about 140 × 85mm.   1774–5

COLLATION   Title-page; pp v-xii, preface; pp 1-216, Beauties (Part 1, of Europe).

The nine line-engravings of London views are to be found in section 5 (pp 111–216), 'Particular Descriptions of the most remarkable Public Buildings ... in Great Britain'. All but pl. 2 are derived from two related sources, both published in 1764: *London and its Environs Described* (No 41, *LED*) and Reeves's *New History* (No 43, *RE*). The publisher of the first edition, which appeared in 1763–4 (in 14 vols 18mo), was John Payne, a Paternoster Row Bookseller who later followed the local trend by issuing books in Numbers. He also had a hand in publishing the Reeves work and frugally reused five of its plates. Of these pl. 4, 7 and 9 below are in the original state, even to the Reeves page number, pl. 3 has lost its credit and page number and pl. 5 has lost its page number. Pl. 1 has been reduced from Reeves and pl. 6 and 8 from *London and its Environs*. Although none of the plates in this volume bears the name of the Reeves illustrator, James Hulett, his credit appears in other volumes of the series.

1 p 111 St Pauls. 57 × 110/65 × 120mm. Cathedral from the S.W. Reduced from *RE* 17.

2 p 125 St Paul's – Westminster Abbey. 78 × 95,85 × 98/180 × 125mm. Cathedral from N.W., Abbey from W.

3 p 126 King Henry the Seventh's Chapel. 83 × 140/98 × 150mm. Credit and page no removed from *RE* 62.

4 p 126 Westminster Hall. (tr 'Page 71') 78 × 140/90 × 160mm. *RE* 71.

5 p 170 The Tower. 78 × 140/95 × 155mm. Page no removed from *RE* 8.

6 p 187 Greenwich Hospital. 55 × 110/70 × 120mm. From river. Reduced from *LED* 3, 69.

7 p 193 Guild Hall. (tr 'Page 193') 75 × 140/95 × 160mm. *RE* 193.

8 p 211 A View of the entrance into Vauxhall Gardens. 58 × 110/75 × 120mm. Reduced from *LED* 6, 216.

9 p 213 The Monument. (tr 'Page 21') 140 × 77/160 × 90mm. *RE* 21.

54 · BUCKS'S ANTIQUITIES* [1774]

It was under this general title that Robert Sayer collected into three volumes the engravings of Samuel and Nathaniel Buck, including the famous panoramic view showing London by the Thames at mid-century. Samuel Buck's first object was an antiquarian one: in the tradition of Hollar and Dugdale he set out to record by means of pen and ink sketches the abbeys, priories and castles remaining in every English county, some of which were unlikely to survive for the admiration of a further generation. He started his search for these at an early age and from 1720 he was able to engrave from his drawings. By May 1726 he was ready to publish his first collection of 'XXIV perspective Views of the Ruins of ye most noted Abbeys & Castles in the County of York' with the following comment:

The kind reception the Author has been favoured with in this his first Attempt encouraging him to proceed he purposes annually to oblige Lovers of Perspective & Antiquity with a Collection of XXIV Views of the most remarkable Ruins of Abbeys and Castles now remaining in one or two Counties, till the whole be gone thro'.

The second batch of 24 views, in Lincoln and Nottingham, followed in May of the ensuing year, after which he was assisted by his brother Nathaniel and future plates were credited 'Saml & Nathl Buck delin. et sculpt.' In the summer months the brothers would go sketching in the shires and then engrave from their drawings while wintering in London. By next spring would emerge a further set of 24 plates and so on, without fail, annually; at first from the suitable sign of the Golden Buck in Warwick Street, then, from 1731, Great Russell Street, Bloomsbury and, from 1735, 1 Garden Court, Middle Temple. By March 1739 the whole of England had been surveyed in no fewer than 344 views. Another 84 views despatched Wales, and the whole series was concluded by April 1742. Not all the buildings depicted were 'remarkable ruins'; some were fully inhabited country houses and the twelfth Collection, issued in March 1737, includes three London plates, two of the Tower of London and one of Lambeth Palace.

Not content with putting on record particular antiquities in the counties they visited, in 1728 the brothers started publication of a series of prospects, perspective views or panoramas of their principal towns and cities, which came to an end only in 1753. It is to this activity that we owe prospects of Greenwich and Deptford of 1739 and the grand London panorama published ten years later.

In 1774 Sayer thus introduced his republication of both the Buck series:

The following Plates were the Production of above Thirty-two Years Labour attended with great Difficulties and Expenses, not only in the Engraving but in visiting the Spots at such remove Distances and in making the Drawings from the mouldering Remains of tottering Ruins. The encouragement that attended this Undertaking of Messrs Bucks seldom waits on merit for a more respectable list of subscribers is rarely seen than favoured their first publication (sold in separate numbers for above Forty-eight Pounds); the Design of which was to rescue from the irresistible hand of Time, and convey to Futurity those venerable Piles of ancient Grandeur, crumbling to dust and hastening to their final dissolution; many of which are now no more; having been since intirely demolished for modern Structures, or perished by time or accident.

He bound the 428 'venerable remains' plates into two volumes, expunged the 24 numerals engraved bl on the plates in each annual batch and renumbered them tr in a single sequence. Each volume was equipped with an historical account of the sites additional to the information engraved bm on each plate, a list of plates and a title-page. An index-map to the sites was also provided. A third binding contained prospects of 73 towns engraved on 83 plates; of these one each was allotted to Deptford and Greenwich and five made up the long view of London and Westminster. The whole work was priced in Sayer's catalogue at 'Eighteen Guineas in Sheets, or Twenty Guineas elegantly bound'.

Buck's Antiquities: or Venerable remains of above four hundred castles, monasteries, palaces &c &c in England and Wales. With near One Hundred Views of Cities and Chief Towns. By Messrs. Samuel and Nathaniel Buck, Who were employed upwards of Thirty-two Years in the Undertaking. In Three Volumes. Vol. I and II. consist of Castles, Monasteries, Palaces &c. Vol. III of Cities and Chief Towns. London, Printed by D. Bond, at St. John's Gate, and sold by Robert Sayer, Map and Printer Seller in Fleet Street. MDCCLXXIV

Buck's Perspective Views of near One Hundred Cities and Chief Towns, in England and Wales: with historical accounts on their Antiquity, Foundation, Situation, Castles, Churches, remarkable Buildings, Trade, Manufactures, Curiosities, Fair and Market-Days, &c &c. By Messrs. Samuel and Nathaniel Buck, who were employed upwards of Thirty-two Years in the Undertaking. Volume the Third. London, Printed by D. Bond at St. John's Gate, and Sold by Robert Sayer, Map and Printseller in Fleet Street. MDCCLXXIV.

Folio, vols 1 and 2 445 × 280mm, vol. 3 440 × 445mm.   1774

COLLATION   Vol. 1. Title-page; preface (1 leaf); pp v-viii, introduction; pp 9–24, Historical Account (Bedfordshire to Northumberland); list of plates in vol. 1, nos 1–224 (1 leaf). Vol. 2. Title-page; pp 2–17, Historical Account (Nottinghamshire to Yorkshire and Wales); p 18, list of plates in vol. 2, nos 225–428. Vol. 3. Title-page; preface and list of plates (2pp); pp 5–22, Historical Account of Perspective Views of Cities and Chief Towns; pl. 1–83 (Bath to York).

Views of the Tower and of Lambeth Palace were favourite components of sets of London engravings and both had featured in Hollar's 1647 'Prospects' (no 5), at the turn of the century in *Nouveau Théâtre de la Grande Bretagne* (no 22) and some 20 years later in Overton's *Prospects* (no 26). The foreground of the river with its passing craft, the long, varied frontages and the eventful skylines made attractive pictures and the buildings themselves were of symbolic significance to the life of the capital and the nation. They were therefore obvious choices for the Bucks to make when selecting London plates for their twelfth collection of venerable architecture, published in 1737. The *Nouveau Théâtre* and Overton also included engravings of Greenwich Hospital and the Bucks followed suit, in their parallel series of town perspectives, with panoramic river views both of Greenwich and of Deptford, published in 1739. These were originally joined together in one long waterfront view, being as it were a trial run for the great London panorama completed ten years later.

September 1748 saw the publication of six of their perspective views of towns in Wales, after which the Bucks turned their attention to the most remarkable single work of their career, mentioned in an advertisement of 5 October 1749: 'This day is published by S. and N. Buck five views of London and one of Portsmouth, which complete the collection of cities, sea ports, and capital towns. To be delivered to their subscribers at their chambers No. 1 Garden Court, Middle Temple'. It is only necessary to compare their five-plate London panorama with those of some of its post-Fire predecessors to realize how skilled the Bucks had become, both in outline-drawing and perspective. The most notable seventeenth century example in this genre is that published in 1682 as an ornament to Ogilby and Morgan's map, *London Actually Survey'd* which was, in the words of Ralph Hyde (in the 1977 facsimile), 'the first engraved panorama of London from the Thames that attempted to show

129

every Thames-side building, significant and insignificant'. Next in succession are the two long prospects, of London and Westminster, in the *Nouveau Théâtre de la Grande Bretagne*, engraved by J. Kip and published between 1714 and 1716. These are excellent of their kind and an invaluable witness to the appearance of Augustan London with its fanfare of new church steeples by Wren, attaining a trumphant climax in the dome of his just completed Cathedral. During the reign of George I a number of other riverside prospects were engraved for the printsellers William Knight, James Walker, John Bowles and Henry Overton, but their execution was largely monopolized by Sutton Nicholls who, in spite of the verisimilitude of his birds-eye views of the London squares (in *London Described*, no 29), yet contrived to turn the river front into a graceless procession of grotesquely drawn church spires, all in one plane without regard to recession or their relative locations.

The most noticeable difference between the Bucks's version of the water front and that of their predecessors is that they contented themselves with depicting what could actually be seen from five specific points on the South Bank. The Morgan and Kip panoramas followed the example of Hollar's pre-Fire engraving, purporting to be a birds-eye view over the City and Westminster from the tower of St Mary Overy by London Bridge. They imagined they had taken up fictitiously elevated positions on the South Bank which would enable them to cast an eye over the whole of the built-up area of the capital to the suburbs beyond of Kensington, Hampstead and Highgate, picking out on the way, and enlarging, the outlines of any buildings of note. The sweep of the Bucks's view is almost identically that of the two Kip panoramas joined, that is to say from Peterborough House on Millbank (eliminating Lambeth, already depicted in their 1737 collection) to the Tower. Yet it is almost twice as long (400cm as against 228cm) and treats all the waterfront buildings with equal care, whatever their social standing. While Kip's view, when compared with Morgan's, demonstrates the final stages of the creation of Wren's City skyline, it is the changes in Westminster that are most obvious in Bucks's: the uprearing of Thomas Archer's St John, Smith Square, completed in 1728, and Labelye's Westminster Bridge which, along with Hawksmoor's twin Abbey towers, was completed just in time to be shown by the artist, free

of scaffolding. The 'Folly', a floating houseboat of ill repute, moored across river from St Paul's Cathedral in Kip's view, has vanished from the Bucks's since by that time it had been moved to Stansgate Stairs on the far, and invisible, side of Westminster Bridge.

Fortunately the 13 foot scroll, Samuel Buck's drawing in pen and ink with delicate wash shading, from which the long view was engraved, is preserved in the British Museum and it is possible to see how the engraver has adhered quite faithfully to every detail of the architecture and river craft. His only marked divergence from the artist is in the occupants of these barges, wherries and sailing boats. Crew, fishermen, boatmen and passengers are, in the drawing, suitably clad and justly proportioned to the vessels they occupy but in the print they are redrawn and reduced to a pigmy size, especially disproportionate in the foreground. Also, perhaps with Canaletto paintings in mind, the engraver has peopled the vacant stonemason's yard at the foot of Westminster Bridge with workmen. There are two other minor amendments in the print: firstly, a rather obscure passage in the drawing to the west of Somerset House, which shows only two extra bays, is amended (at ref 30) to five bays as it appears on Kip's view but in the revision the fountain before the house itself has been lost; secondly (at ref 51) the handsome brick house to the east of the Fleet Canal, which by this time had degenerated into the warehouse of Sir John Delane & Co, has, in the drawing, its colonnaded penthouse roof stacked with an overspill of timber from Howell's wharf next door; this had been cleared by the time the Bucks came to engrave this section of the view.

Impressions of later states of the engravings are found in which passages have been burnished out to admit of the insertion of such innovations as Blackfriars Bridge (1769) and the Adelphi (1772).

VOL. 1

1 pl 182 (tm) The South View of the Tower of London. Saml & Nathl Buck delin: & sculp: Publish't according to Act of Parliament March 25th 1737. 145 × 350/195 × 370mm. Arms of John, Earl of Leicester to whom the plate is dedicated bm. pl. 22 in the 12th Collection.

2 pl. 183 (tm) The West View of the Tower of London. Saml & Nathl Buck delin: & sculp: Publish't according to Act of Parliament March 25th 1737. 145 × 350/190 × 370mm. Historical descriptions bm. pl. 23 in the 12th Collection.

3 pl. 281 (tm) The North-West View of Lambeth Palace, in the County of Surry. Saml & Nathl Buck del: & sculp: Publish't according to Act of Parliament March 25th 1737. 145 × 350/195 × 370mm. Historical description and dedication to John (Potter), nominated Archbishop of Canterbury February 1737 bm. pl. 18 in the 12th Collection.

VOL. 3

4 pl. 19 (tm) The North-West Prospect of Deptford in the County of Kent. Saml & Nathl Buck delin: et sculp: Publish'd according to Act of Parliament March 26 1739. Garden Court, No 1 Middle Temple London. 240 × 780/310 × 820mm. Description and refs 1–10 bm. One of a group of Kentish views in the collected Prospects for 1739.

5 pl. 29 (tm) The North West Prospect of Greenwich, in the County of Kent. Saml & Nathl Buck delin: et sculp: Publish'd according to Act of Parliament March 26 1739. Garden Court, No 1 Middle Temple London. 245 × 780/130 × 820mm. Description and refs 1–15 bm. In first collection of Prospects joined onto item 4 above.

Long View of London

6 pl. 41 1, The New Bridge/at Westminster.... 11, Part of ye Treasury. This Drawing, taken (from Mr. Scheve's Sugar House, opposite to York House) & Engraved by S. & N. Buck is Publish'd according to Act of Parliamt. Sep. 11th 1749, No 1, Garden Court, Middle Temple London. 280 × 795/315 × 820mm.

7 pl. 42 12, Part of the Treasury.... 30, Part of Somerset/House. This Drawing, taken (from Mr. Watson's Summer House, opposite to Somerset House) & Engraved by S. & N. Buck is Publish'd according to Act of Parliamt. Sep. 11th 1749, No. 1, Garden Court, Middle Temple London. 280 × 800/315 × 820mm.

8 pl. 43 31, Somerset House.... 48, Bridewel. This Drawing, taken (from Mr. Everard's Summer-House opposite to St. Bride's Church) and Engraved by S. and N. Buck, is Published according to Act of Parliamt. Septr. 11th 1749, Garden-Court No 1, Middle Temple, London. 280 × 800/315 × 820mm.

9 pl. 44 49, Fleet Ditch.... 82, St. Michael's,/Bassingshaw. This Drawing, taken (from the West part of the Leads of St. Mary Overy's Church in Southwark) and Engraved by S. & N. Buck is Publish'd according to Act of Parliamt. Sep. 11th 1749, No 1, Garden Court, Middle Temple London. 280 × 800/315 × 820mm.

10 pl. 45 83, Old Street Church.... 90, Mansion House. 1, St. Swithin's ... 40, London Bridge. This Drawing taken (from the West part of the Leads of St. Mary Overy's Church in Southwark) and Engrav'd by S. & N. Buck is Published according to Act of Parliamt. Septr. 11th, 1749, No. 1, Garden Court, Middle Temple, London. 280 × 800/315 × 820mm.

55 · CURIOSITIES, NATURAL AND ARTIFICIAL* [1774–5]

This six-volume compendium on the British Isles, first published by Richard Snagg, bookseller of 29 Paternoster Row, is described disdainfully by Richard Gough as being 'in 60 numbers 1775, Folio—a catchpenny publication' (*Topography* 1, pp 57–8). The whole work contains some 60 plates while the first volume, which is concerned with London, Westminster, Southwark and the Home Counties, boasts a frontispiece and eight views. The imprint is undated but the title-page must have been issued before Snagg left his Paternoster Row premises in about 1775: the text refers to the purchase in 1772 for the British Museum of Sir William Hamilton's collection of Greek and Roman antiquities and among the plates is one of James Wyatt's Oxford Street Pantheon, completed that year, so a date of 1774–5 may be assumed. In 1775, after his removal to 129 Fleet Street, he reissued the first 200 pages of the text, bound up with four of the plates and two added maps, under the title:

A Description of the County of Middlesex; containing a Circumstantial Account of its Public Buildings, Seats of the Nobility and Gentry, Places of Resort and Entertainment, Curiosities of Nature and Art, (including those of London and Westminster) &c. &c. The Whole forming a Complete Guide to those who may Visit the Metropolis, or make a tour through the County. Illustrated with Copper-Plates. London: Printed for R. Snagg, No 129 Fleet Street, MDCCLXXV.

The complete work was republished in 1777 by Messrs Fielding & Walker under yet another title:

Britannica Curiosa: or, A Description of the most remarkable curiosities of ... Britain ... In Six Volumes. The Second Edition. Illustrated with Fifty-Nine Copper Plates. Vol. I (-VI). London: Printed for Fielding and Walker, No. 20, Paternoster-Row. MDCCLXXVII.

The plates, which are quite respectable small line-engravings, are uncredited, unnumbered and unlisted and have no publication-lines. Captions are in copperplate script.

The Curiosities, Natural and Artificial, of the Island of Great Britain containing a full and accurate Description of Whatever is remarkable and worthy of Notice in the

Works of Nature and Art, in the Several Counties, Cities, Towns, Villages, &c. of England, Wales and Scotland, the Principal Seats of the Nobility and Gentry, Public Buildings, Places of Resort and Entertainment, &c. Carefully and faithfully Displayed. Vol. I. London: Printed for the Proprietor; and Sold by R. Snagg, No 29 Pater-noster-Row, and by all the Booksellers and News-Carriers in Great Britain.

Octavo, 210 × 130mm.   c1774

COLLATION Title-page; pp iii–iv, introduction; pp 1–400, Curiosities.

1 front. The Polite Arts Presenting their Productions/to Britania. 142 × 90/178 × 105mm.

2 p 39 (on banderole above) St Stephen Walbrook. 95 × 85,50 × 85/180 × 105mm. Interior, looking E. – Section and plan, supported by two putti. (At the same place in *Description*.)

3 p 48 The Choir of St Pauls Cathedral. 90 × 153/105 × 170mm. From E. end.

4 p 68 Adelphi Buildings. 88 × 153/105 × 180mm. 'This surprising work was begun in June 1768 and is not yet entirely completed', says the text. It was built between 1768 and 1772. (At the same place in *Description*.)

5 p 109 The Pantheon. 87 × 153/105 × 175mm. James Wyatt's masterpiece, on the S. side of Oxford Street, opened as a theatre and public promenade in January 1772. This interior view looks into the rotunda. (At the same place in *Description*.)

6 p 189 Hampton Court. 85 × 150/105 × 175mm. The first quadrangle. (At the same place in *Description*.)

7 p 278 Wanstead House in Essex. 80 × 150/110 × 178mm.

8 p 341 Greenwich Hospital. 85 × 153/105 × 175mm. From river.

9 p 348 West-Gate Canterbury. 85 × 150/105 × 175mm.

Maps additionally bound with Description:

10 front. (in cartouche tl) Middlesex/Divided into Hundreds &c … /By Eman. Bowen … /& Thos. Bowen … Printed for Thomas Kitchin at No 59 Holborn Hill, London. 230 × 325mm.

11 (tm) The London Guide, or Pocket Plan of the Cities of London, Westminster, & Borough of Southwark, with the New Buildings, &c to the Present Year 1775. London, Printed for Robert Sayer Map & Printseller at No 53 in Fleet Street. Price 6d. 265 × 510/270 × 520mm. Thames and City boundaries colour washed. (*Darlington and Howgego* 164)

56 · GROSE'S ANTIQUARIAN REPERTORY* [1775–84]

In its first edition this work was issued anonymously and only in its second was it posthumously associated with the antiquary Francis Grose. Indeed it ran contemporaneously, and apparently in competition, with his major undertaking, *The Antiquities of England and Wales* (no 50). It was first issued in 48 Numbers of 24 pages each, accompanied by one or two plates. Batches of 12 Numbers were paginated and signed throughout and, when equipped with a title-page and index, made up a volume. One of the three booksellers concerned was John Sewell who published in his *European Magazine* from 1782 to 1802 some 60 London illustrations.

The introduction states: 'this Collection is meant as a Repository for fugitive pieces, respecting the History and Antiquities of this country'.

The second edition in four volumes was published 1807–9 by Edward Jeffery, a bookseller with a shop opposite Carlton House in Pall Mall. In his 'Advertisement' prefixed to the first volume he says both that it is quite natural to publish again a popular work which is much in demand and becoming rare and also that, as a result of many years trading in secondhand books and of moving in a circle of antiquarian collectors, he has acquired a number of tracts suitable to supplement those published in the first edition. He is therefore rearranging the old materials in a more logical sequence and amplifying them with the new.

The Antiquarian Repertory: a Miscellany, Intended to Preserve and Illustrate Several Valuable Remains of Old Times. Adorned with Elegant Sculptures. Vol. I (III) London: Printed for the Proprietors, and Sold by Francis Blyth, No 87 Cornhill (J. Sewell, No 32 Cornhill) and T. Evans, No. 54 Paternoster Row. 1775 (1780).

Small folio, about 265 × 210mm.   1775, 1780

COLLATION Vol. 1. Title-page; pp iii–viii, introduction; pp 1–286, Repertory; index (2pp). Vol. 3. Title-page; pp 1–276, Repertory continued; index (6pp); directions to binder (1 leaf).

With reference to the illustrations the 'Advertisement' says 'care shall be taken to admit only such Views as may be depended on, and have never before been published and which, at the same time as they please the eye, shall represent some remains of Antiquity, some capital Mansion, or striking Prospect'. There are six London plates in vol. 1, two after originals by Thomas Sandby and one after a Hollar drawing, all engraved by Richard Godfrey; vol. 3 has one engraved by Edmund Scot.

In the second edition six of these plates are reused; the slight variation in measurements is attributable to their having been printed on wove paper in their later appearance. The Hollar view is retained but newly engraved by H.R. Cook and there is an additional double-page aquatint of a Griffier painting of the Great Fire which is contributed by William Birch, the enamel painter, who was also responsible for a charming series of small views entitled *Délices de la Grande Bretagne* (no 69) and was an exhibitor at the Royal Academy from 1781 to 1794. R.B. Godfrey, who drew and engraved views and antiquities, was Grose's associate and had contributed to his *Antiquities of England and Wales* (no 50).

VOL. 1

1 p 18 The Temporary Bridge at Blackfriars/Engraved from an Original Drawing. R. Godfrey del. et sculp. Published Feby 1st, 1775. 143 × 210/180 × 225mm. No. 1. 2nd ed vol. 1 (1807), p 380. 142 × 210/183 × 225mm.

2 p 25 Ely House/Engraved from an Original Drawing. R. Godfrey del. et sculp. March 1, 1775. 145 × 205/180 × 225mm. No. 2. 2nd ed vol. 1 (1807), p 387. 145 × 208/183 × 230mm.

3 p 42 Westminster Abbey/Engraved from an Original Drawing. T. Sandby del. R. Godfrey sc. March 1, 1775. 146 × 210/185 × 230mm. No. 2. 2nd ed vol. 1 (1807), p 375. 145 × 212/185 × 230mm.

4 p 86 Whitehall/Engraved from an Original Drawing. T. Sandby del. R. Godfrey sculp. July 1, 1775. 143 × 212/180 × 223mm. No. 4. 2nd ed vol. 1 (1807), p 372. 142 × 206/185 × 228mm. 'Holbein' Gate and Banqueting Hall from S. The Gate was demolished in 1759. There are two versions of Sandby's drawing in the Royal Collection, one dated 1743 (*Oppé* 165-6), and other versions in the BM and Guildhall Library.

5 p 197 A view of St James's Palace and Westminster Abbey/From the Village of Charing. Hollar delin. Godfrey sculp. Published Feby 1, 1776 by F. Blyth, No 87 Cornhill. 153 × 240/185 × 253mm. No 9. Keyed refs: '1. St James's Palace. 2. A Public House at the Village of Charing. 3. Westminster Abbey. 4. Westminster Hall. 5. A Wall belonging to the Palace now Pall-Mall. 6. Fields now St James's Park. 7. A Conduit supposed standing where St James's Square now is.'

This engraving is copied in Harrison's *History* (no 57, p 528) and its derivatives. Large water-colour copies seem to have been popular with collectors (*Crace* 11.23, 190 × 406mm; BL Maps: *K. top.* 21.63, 305 × 470mm; *Crowle* 4.159, 279 × 514mm) but the surviving Hollar original in the Royal Collection (*Oppé* 370) is modest in size (100 × 301mm). The easternmost section of the engraving, which shows a tree and a public house, is absent from the drawing and omitted from its five keyed refs, the other omission being 'Fields now St James's Park'

6 p 282 View of Old London from Blackheath. Wyck del. Godfrey sc. Publish'd July 1st, 1776 by F. Blyth, No 87 Cornhill. 120 × 257/157 × 265mm. No 12. 2nd ed vol. 3 (1808), p 181. 119 × 255/154 × 265mm. Grose states: 'This drawing was made by Thomas Wyck, who died Anno 1682.... It was communicated by Paul Sandby Esq. in whose possession it now is'. Thomas Wyck (c 1616–77), a Netherlandish landscape painter, visited London during the 1660s and painted and sketched the scene before, during and after the Great Fire. His son Jan (1652–1700) followed his father's profession and settled permanently in England and to him are attributed two distant views of London from Greenwich Park, an oil painting of about 1680 and a large wash drawing of about 1686 in the BM. His drawing of London and Southwark during the Frost Fair of 1683–4, also in the BM, was likewise the source of later engravings.

VOL. 3

7 p 125 A View from Constitution Hill/Anno 1735. J.H. del. Edmd Scot sc. 1776. 138 × 203/175 × 220mm. No 5. 2nd ed vol. 2 (1808), p 181 in later state 'Published 1st June, 1779 by Richd Godfrey, No 120 Long Acre'. 138 × 202/170 × 220mm. 'Drawn on the spot by the late ingenious Mr Hackell'. Shows Buckingham House before it became a royal residence and Westminster Abbey with only one of its W. towers completed.

The Antiquarian Repertory, a Miscellaneous Assemblage of Topography, History, Biography, Customs, and Manners Intended to Illustrate and Preserve Several Valuable Remains of Old Times. Chiefly compiled by, or under the direction of Francis Grose Esq. F.R. and A.S., Thomas Astle Esq. F.R. & A.S. and other Eminent Antiquaries. Adorned with Numerous Views, Portraits, and Monuments. A New Edition ... In Four Volumes. Vol. 1 (2–3) London: Printed and Published for Edward Jeffery, No 11 Pall-Mall. Likewise Sold by Messrs Faulder & Son, New Bond Street: Longman, Hurst, Rees & Orme, Paternoster Row: Cuthell and Martin, Middle-Row, Holborn; W.J. and J. Richardson, and J. Aspern, Cornhill, 1807 (1808).

Quarto, about 285 × 240mm.   1807, 1808, 1808

COLLATION Vol. 1. Title-page; publisher's dedication dated 1 November 1806 (1 leaf); pp v-xvii, advertisement; p xviii, directions to binder; pp xix–xxii, contents; pp 1–391, Repertory. Vol. 2. Title-page; publisher's dedication dated 20 December 1807 (1 leaf); pp v–viii, advertisement; directions to binder (2pp); contents (4pp); pp 1–432, Repertory continued. Vol. 3. Title-page, publisher's dedication dated 20 December 1807 (1 leaf); pp v–vi, advertisement; pp i–vi, contents; pp vii–viii, directions to binder; pp 1–446, Repertory continued.

VOL. 1

8 p 371 A View of St James's Palace and Westminster Abbey/From the Village of Charing. Hollar delin. H.R. Cook sculpt. Published Sepr 29, 1806, by Edwd Jeffery, Pall Mall. 150 × 235/210 × 265mm. Replaces pl. 5 above.

Vol. 1 also contains four of the plates from the original edition, vol. 1: pl. 1, p 380; pl. 2, p 387; pl. 3, p 375; pl. 4, p 372.

VOL. 2

9 p 150 The Great Fire of London in the Year 1666/From the Original in the Possession of/Robert Golden Esq. Painted by Old Griffier at the time of the Fire. The Scene is the Original Ludgate taken at the instant of Time when the Walls of the Goal/adjoining it fell and exhibited to the View Old St Pauls Church just taking Fire and Old Bow Church in the Background. Vide Pennant's London. Engraved and Published by W. Birch, Enamel Painter, No. 2 Macclesfield Street, Soho. Decr 1st, 1792. 245 × 337/280 × 390mm. This aquatint must originally have been issued for extra-illustrators of Pennant's *London* (no 67) of which editions appeared in 1790 and 1791. (*Hayes* 48)

Vol. 2 also reissues pl.7 from the original vol. 3, but in a later state. Vol. 3 re-issues pl.6 from the original vol. 2.

57 · HARRISON'S HISTORY OF LONDON [1775]

Only five years after the publication of Chamberlain's *London* (no 48) John Cooke embarked upon another history in weekly Parts, this time ascribed to one Walter Harrison. Seventy Numbers were issued in all of which 40 consisted of 12 pages of text and 30 of eight, as indicated by the small Arabic numerals, printed bl in Cooke's normal fashion. Either one or two plates were issued with each Number. Title-pages are found dated both 1775 and 1776; in the former case the ensuing dedication is dated 16 December 1775; in the latter the day of the month is left standing but the year omitted. The plate (68) issued with No 32 is dated 1776, No 67 contains an account of the events of 22 March 1777 and with No 69 was issued a map of London dated 1777, so it would appear that the work was completed in the spring of that year.

A New and Universal History, Description and Survey of the Cities of London and Westminster, the Borough of Southwark, and their Adjacent Parts ... to the extent of twenty miles round, comprizing a circle of near one hundred and fifty miles.... by Walter Harrison, Esq. Enriched with upwards of One Hundred elegant copper-plate Engravings, exhibiting architect(u)ral, perspective antique, and rural views of churches, chapels, palaces, gates, antiquities, ruins, hospitals, bridges, and other buildings, public and private; delightful landscapes, beautiful prospects, and captivating situations; besides plans, maps, surveys, &c. London: Printed for J. Cooke, at Shakespeare's Head, in Pater-Noster Row, MDCCLXXV.

Folio, about 375 × 235mm.   1775 or 1776

COLLATION Title-page; dedication to Lord Mayor, etc dated 16 December 1775 (2pp); pp 5–697, New and Universal History; pp 698–720, addenda, index, directions to binder.

Illustrations are lavish, with 192 subjects and four maps and plans, engraved on 102 plates. All, with the exception of the front. and pl. 64, are inscribed 'Engraved for Harrison's History of London' (tm, or occasionally bm) and most lack credits. Directions to the binder indicate with which Number each was issued and the page facing with which they are to be bound. In the list below the Numbers are quoted after the sizes.

Three plates (63, 66, 68) are derived from Noorthouck's *New History* (no 51) and two (97, 101) from Spencer's *Complete English Traveller* (no 52) but the majority were originally engraved for Cooke's earlier publication, Chamberlain's *New and Compleat History* (no 48), abbreviated *C* together with page reference. The beaded frames surrounding many of the Chamberlain topographical plates were now obliterated (except on pl. 28, 46, 52, 72) and the vacant spaces filled with extensions to the view, particularly conspicuous on pl. 9, 29, 34, 43, 48, 65 and 82. Furthermore the charming scrolled rococo frames which at first set off the rather stagy Wale historical prints were, with the exception of pl. 6 and 10, now replaced either with a stodgy, moulded frame ornamented with a scalloped centrepiece and labels or by wreathed baguettes. In the list all framework is excluded from the interior measurements.

Among plates probably specially commissioned for this work are four more of Wale's historical subjects, two of them engraved by William Walker who also worked for John Boydell and for George Kearsley's two publications the *Copper-plate Magazine* (1774–8) and Paul Sandby's *Select Views of England* (1778). A number of additional suburban and Thames-side views seem all to have been drawn by J. Oliphant and engraved by John Royce. They may have been suggested by Boydell's riverside views published between 1750 and 1753 and J.B. Chatelain's *Views in the Vicinity of London* of about the same date. The more carefully composed plates are reminiscent of Richard Wilson paintings such as 'The Thames near Marble Hill' exhibited in 1762.

1 front. Time and History presenting to Britannia the antient/progressive and present state of London, the Capital/of the British Empire. 190 × 112/300 × 200mm. No 1. Moulded. Allegorical figures with S.W. view of St Paul's Cathedral in background.

2 p 17 Bishops and Citizens swearing Fealty to/William the Conqueror. 163 × 110/250 × 170mm. No 10. Moulded. *C* 25.

3 p 23 London Bridge as it appeared before the houses were pulled down – The Bridge in its present state with the Water Works, as viewed from the City Shore. Each 80 × 295/200 × 315mm. No 5. The houses had been removed by 1763.

4 p 26 Henry Fitzalwine Knt/First Lord Mayor of London – Sir William Walworth/Lord Mayor of London. Jas. Record sculp. 135 × 235/185 × 275mm. No 26. Double portrait. *C* 41.

5 p 70 Edward the Black Prince making his public Entry/with the King of France his Prisoner. 160 × 102/245 × 163mm. No 37. Moulded.

6 p 75 Sir John Dimmock Performing the/Ceremony of the Champion's Challenge/at the Coronation of Richard 2 in Westminster Hall. S. Wale del. C. Grignion sculp. 165 × 100/250 × 160mm. No 65. Rococo. *C* 81.

7 p 78 The Burning of St John's Monastery/near Smithfield by Wat Tyler's Rabble. S. Wale delin. W. Walker sculp. 165 × 100/252 × 160mm. No 52. Rococo.

8 p 79 Richard II Appeases the Rebels/on the Death of Wat Tyler in Smithfield. 155 × 100/250 × 160mm. No 19. Moulded. *C* 85.

9 p 82 View of the Tower from the River Thames – View of the Custom House. Each 110 × 160/270 × 180mm. No 44. *C* 89.

10 p 92 Blood and his Accomplices/Escaping after stealing the Crown from the Tower. Wale del. Grignion sculp. 160 × 103/250 × 160mm. No 68. Rococo. *C* 106.

11 p 100 A Representation of an Ancient/Tournament. 160 × 100/250 × 162mm. No 23. Wreathed baguettes. *C* 114.

12 p 123 Doctor Shaw/Preaching at St Paul's Cross. 165 × 100/255 × 163mm. No 33. Wreathed baguettes. *C* 113.

13 p 130 View of the Inside of Westminster Abbey – View of the Inside of St Paul's Cathedral. 109 × 157, 105 × 157/270 × 190mm. No 21. Both looking E. *C* 138.

14 p 130 The Abbey Church of St Peter Westminster – The Admiralty Office. Each 102 × 150/275 × 190mm. No 15. Abbey W. front. Admiralty staffage re-engraved from *C* 138.

15 p 132 The Chapel of King Henry VII in Westminster Abbey – The front view of Westminster Hall. Each 105 × 150/270 × 190mm. No 6. Henry VII Chapel exterior from E. *C* 142.

16 p 199 View of St Thomas's Hospital in Southwark – View of Guy's Hospital in Southwark. Each 109 × 166/278 × 190mm. No 70. Guy's staffage re-engraved. *C* 566.

17 p 200 View of Christ's-Church Hospital – View of St. Bartholomew's Hospital. Each 102 × 165/270 × 190mm. No 41. Courtyard of St Bartholomew's. *C* 516.

18 p 207 Manner of Burning the Martyrs in Smithfield. 152 × 100/250 × 165mm. No 29. Moulded. *C* 118.

19 p 213 View of the Royal Exchange – Gresham College as it appeared before it was taken Down to Build an Excise Office. Each 105 × 162/270 × 185mm. No 61. *C* 498.

20 p 217 Representation of a grand Shooting Match by/the London Archers in the Year 1583. 162 × 110/250 × 160mm. No 16. Moulded. *C* 207.

21 p 244 Habit of the Lord Mayor of London in 1640 – Habit of a Merchant of London about 1640. 204 × 280mm pl. mark. No 9. *C* 229.

22 p 244 Habit of a Lady Mayoress of London in 1640 – Habit of a Merchant's Wife of London about 1640. 205 × 285mm pl. mark. No 12. *C* 228.

23 p 253 A Plan of the City and Environs of London as fortified by Order of Parliament in the Years 1642 & 1643. 185 × 310/205 × 320mm. No 49. From George Vertue's engraving of 1738 (no 33, item 5). Refs (l.) 1–11 (r.) 12–23.

24 p 273 Part of Cheapside, with the Cross, &c as they appeared in 1660. 138 × 225/160 × 245mm. No 46. Topographical details based on Puget de la Serre's *Histoire* (no 3), pl. 9.

25 p 278 View of the manner of burying the dead Bodies/At Holy-Well mount during the dreadful Plague in 1665. 150 × 100/250 × 162. No 27. Wreathed baguettes. *C* 251.

26 p 280 A View of London as it appeared/before the dreadful-Fire in 1666. 144 × 280/190 × 290mm. No 1. Refs (bl) 1–12, (br) 13–26. From Hollar's front. (*Hind* 17) to Howell's *Londinopolis* (1657, no 7). (*Scouloudi* p 58)

27 p 281 View of Part of London as it appeared in the Dreadful Fire in 1666. 165 × 105/245 × 165mm. No 42. Wreathed baguettes. *C* 253.

28 p 282 View of St Bennets Grace Church/Fenchurch Street – View of the Monument/Fish Street Hill – View of St Magnus Church/London Bridge. Each 143 × 75/185 × 270mm. No 39. Beaded. *C* 253.

29 p 286 Sr. Christopher Wren's Plan for Rebuilding the City of London after the dreadful Conflagration in 1666. 170 × 270/200 × 290mm. No 24. *C* 256.

30 p 287 Sir John Evelyn's Plan for Rebuilding the City of London after the Great Fire in 1666. 150 × 285/170 × 300mm. No 36. Refs l. 1–38 +.

31 p 303 The Bishops Loyd, Ken, Turner, Lake, White, and Trelawny,/presenting their petition to James II. April 27th 1688. Wale delin. Grignion sculpt. 180 × 112/308 × 200mm. No 2. Moulded.

32 p 313 St Christopher's Church, The Bank of England & St Bartholomew's Church/Threadneedle Street. 160 × 255/190 × 270mm. No 25. *C* 473. (*Bank of England* 17)

33 p 324 North view of Old St Paul's Church after the Spire was destroyed by Lightning – South view of the Same after the Spire was destroyed by Lightning – South view of the Same when the Spire was standing. 70 × 160, 65 × 160, 110 × 160/285 × 175mm. No 8. After Hollar. Dugdale's *St Paul's* (no 8), items 37,36,34.

34 p 324 View of St Paul's Cathedral – View of St Paul's School. Each 105 × 162/275 × 190mm. No 36. *C* 275.

35 p 361 The Mansion House – The Guildhall of London. 100 × 160, 100 × 157/275 × 185mm. No 27. *C* 305.

36 p 362 View of the Foundling Hospital Lambs Conduit Fields – View of the Small-Pox Hospital near St Pancrass. Each 100 × 164/270 × 190mm. No 28. *C* 307.

37 p 395 View of the British Museum – View of Bedford House. 105 × 165, 100 × 165/270 × 190. No 18. *C* 341.

38 p 410 View of the Temporary Bridge of London/on Fire in the Night of April 11th 1758. 163 × 110/250 × 163mm. No 13. Moulded. *C* 364.

39 p 419 (lm) A New and Complete Plan of London, Westminster and Southwark with the Additional Buildings to the Year 1777. 255 × 490/280 × 505mm. No 69. (*Darlington and Howgego* 169)

40 p 426 (tm) The City Gates as they appeared before they were pulled down. Each about 70–80 × 70/203 ×

350mm. No 11. Moorgate, Aldgate, Bishopsgate, Cripplegate/Ludgate, Newgate, Aldersgate and Bridge Gate.

41 p 427 St Annes & Agnes Aldersgate – St Botolph's Aldersgate/St Martin Outwick Threadneedle Street – St Olave's Old Jewry/St Bartholomew the Great – St Bartholomew the Less. 70 × 75, 85 × 75, 75 × 75/272 × 178mm. No 47. *C* 449.

(pp 427–54 Wood-engravings of arms of City Companies printed with text)

42 p 437 View of St Botolph's Church/Bishopsgate Street – View of Christ Church/Spittlefields – View of St Leonard's Church/Shoreditch. Each 160 × 85/185 × 275mm. No 51. *C* 462.

43 p 445 View of the South Sea House – View of the East India House. Each 100 × 167/270 × 190mm. No 35. *C* 475.

44 p 448 Baynard's Castle. 150 × 255/172 × 278mm. No 47. (tr) 'face Page 448'.

45 p 453 View of St Mildred's Church/in the Poultry – View of St Michael's/Church Cornhill – View of St Peter's Cornhill. 145 × 87/145 × 75, 145 × 87/190 × 280mm. No 67. Some re-engraving on view of St Michael's bl. *C* 486.

46 p 453 View of Grocer's Hall – View of Goldsmith's Hall. T. White sculpt. Each 90 × 145/250 × 180mm. No 51. Beaded. *C* 487.

47 p 456 View of Guild Hall Chapel – West View of Blackwell Hall. Each 158 × 105/190 × 270mm. No 59.

48 p 459 View of St Luke's Hospital in Upper Moore-fields – View of Bethlem Hospital. Each 105 × 163/275 × 190mm. No 64. *C* 605

49 p 460 View of St Mary Aldermary Church/Bow Lane – View of St Mary le Bow/Cheapside – View of St Mildred's Church/Bread Street. 160 × 85, 160 × 80, 160 × 85/185 × 270mm. No 63. *C* 496.

50 p 468 St Mary Aldermanbury – St Lawrence Jewry Cateaton Street – St Michael's Wood Street/ St Giles' Cripplegate – St Stephen's Coleman Street – St Margaret's Lothbury. Each 85 × 85/205 × 278mm. No 21. *C* 502.

51 p 477 St John the Evangelist Westminster – St Bennets Pauls Wharf/ St Martin's Ludgate – St Bride's Fleet Street/ St Dunstan's in Fleet Street. 65 × 65, 85 × 65, 85 × 135/270 × 160mm. No 60. *C* 590.

52 p 481 View of St Andrew's Church Holborn – View of St Sepulchre's Church Snow hill. Each 95 × 145/270 × 185mm. No 65. Beaded. *C* 535.

53 p 483 View of Surgeons Hall Old Bailey – View of New Sessions House Old Bailey. 100 × 160, 100 × 165/275 × 190mm. No 54. Sessions House is substituted for College of Physicians. *C* 537.

54 p 485 View of St Edmond the King/Lombard Street – View of Alhallows/Lombard Street – View of St Mary Woolnorth/Lombard Street. 145 × 80, 145 × 80, 145

× 85/183 × 265mm. No 61. *C* 540.

55 p 489 St Trinity Minories – St Andrew Undershaft Leadenhall St – St Margaret Pattens Little Tower Street/ St Mary Abchurch Abchurch Lane – St Clements Eastcheap – Alhallow's Staining Crutchard Fryers. Each 80 × 85/215 × 275mm. No 45. St Olave, Hart Street is shown in lieu of All Hallows Staining; this error in Chamberlain has its origin in the Candlewick Ward map published in the *London Magazine* for December 1768. cf with Noorthouck p 576. *C* 546.

56 p 495 St James's Garlick Hith – St Nicholas Coleabby Old Fish Street/ St Mary Magdalen Old Fish Street – St Swithin's Cannon Street/ St Mathew's Friday Street – St Michael's College Hill. Each 85 × 70/285 × 180mm. No 57. *C* 557.

57 p 496 St Stephen's Walbrook – Alhallows the Great Thames Street – St Michaels Queenhythe/ St Mary at Hill near Billingsgate – St Botolph's in Botolph Lane – The Chappel in the Tower. Each 83 × 85/210 × 280mm. No 49. The Tower Chapel is St Peter's. *C* 558.

58 p 497 Jack Cade Declaring himself Lord of the City of London. Wale del. Walker sculp. 168 × 104/250 × 163mm. No 48. Rococo.

59 p 506 St John's Church Southwark – St Mary Magdalen's/Church Bermondsey Street – St Mary's Church Rotherhith. Each 160 × 85/195 × 275mm. No 43. *C* 563.

60 p 509 View of St Olave's Church/Southwark – View of St George's/Southwark – View of Christ's Church/ Surry. 143 × 93, 143 × 73, 143 × 80/190 × 270mm. No 53. *C* 562.

61 p 518 View of the House of Commons from the/River Thames – View of the Office of Ordnance with the Entrance of the/House of Lords. Each 155 × 115/190 × 270mm. No 30. *C* 591.

62 p 524 View of St Pauls Church/Covent Garden – View of St Mary le Strand – View of St Clements Church/Strand. 145 × 85, 145 × 80, 145 × 80/185 × 270mm. No 55. *C* 585.

63 p 525 The Adelphi Buildings. 155 × 270/180 × 288mm. No 4. Standard flying from St Martin's, new staffage; otherwise as plate published in 1772. Noorthouck p 727.

64 p 528 (tm) An Ancient View of St James's, Westminster-Abby, & Hall, &c. from the Village of Charing now Charing Cross. 149 × 273/188 × 290mm. No 31. Refs (bl) 1–3, (br) 4–7. This plate lacks book title and is identical with that published on 1 February 1776 by Francis Grose in his *Antiquarian Repertory* (no 56), p 197.

65 p 529 View of the Treasury & Horse Guards – View of the Banqueting House. Each 105 × 167/275 × 185mm. No 12. *C* 588.

66 p 530 The Queen's Palace in St James's Park. 155 × 265/185 × 290mm. No 7. Shows Buckingham Palace from the same viewpoint as Collyer's view in Noorthouck, p 719 and on the same scale but with an additional 17mm in height and 35mm to l. and r. Staffage differs and the tree in the foreground is omitted, though its shadow remains.

67 p 530 The Hospital of St George at Hyde Park corner – The South east View of the Middlesex Hospital near Oxford Road. 105 × 170, 110 × 170/265 × 180mm. No 33. *C* 597.

68 p 531 St James's Palace from Pall Mall – The Same from the Park – Somerset House & Stairs,/As they appeared before they were pulled down in 1776. 50 × 160, 43 × 160, 100 × 160/260 × 190mm. No 32. Old Somerset House demolished 1775. Original extended by 10mm l. and r. Noorthouck p 718.

69 p 533 Front of Drury-Lane-Theatre – Pantheon in Oxford-Road. Each 155 × 109/190 × 250mm. No 69. Drury Lane as refronted by Robert Adam, 1775–6; James Wyatt's Pantheon, 1770–2.

70 p 536 St Giles's in the Fields – St George's Hanover Square/ St James's Westminster – St Anne's Westminster/ St George's Queen Square – Temple Bar. 85 × 78, 75 × 75, 75 × 75/273 × 178mm. No 59. *C* 601.

71 p 537 View of the Royal Stables & part of St Martins Church – View of St Georges Church Bloomsbury. 160 × 115, 160 × 113/190 × 270mm. No 41. *C* 585.

72 p 545 View of Ironmongers Alms-Houses Kingsland Road – View of Trinity Alms-Houses Mile End Road. 90 × 150/280 × 190mm. No 66. Beaded. *C* 608.

73 p 547 View of the Parish Church of Stoke Newington – View of the Church of St John at Hackney – View of the Church of St Mathew at Bethnal Green. Each 78 × 143/270 × 180mm. No 63. *C* 620.

74 p 548 St Mary's Whitechappel – St Paul's Shadwel – St Ann's Limehouse/ St George's Ratcliff highway – St Dunstan's Stepney – St John's Wapping. Each 85 × 85/210 × 280 mm. No 24. *C* 609.

75 p 555 View of Acton from the South West. Royce sc. 150 × 270/178 × 285mm. No 17. Stylized 'feather duster' trees seem to mark out Oliphant and Royce views of the suburbs.

76 p 557 View of Camberwell from the Grove. 150 × 270/173 × 286. No 22.

77 p 558 View of Chelsea from Battersea Church Yard. 150 × 275/173 × 290. No 9. (*Longford* 261)

78 p 559 View of Chiswick from the River. 153 × 273/180 × 290mm. No 15.

79 p 560 View of Clapham from the Common. 152 × 263/178 × 285mm. No 30. The most attractive of this set.

80 p 560 A View of Deptford. 150 × 270/180 × 290mm. No 62.

81 p 560 Dulwich College, J. Oliphant delin. 153 × 275/175 × 288mm. No 3.

82 p 563 View of Greenwich Hospital – View of Chelsea

Hospital. 103 × 165, 105 × 165/270 × 180mm. No 18. *C* 576. (*Longford* 16)

83 p 563 View of Greenwich from Deptford. 150 × 275/185 × 297mm. No 70.

84 p 564 View of Hackney. 150 × 265/180 × 280mm. No 53.

85 p 564 A View of Hammersmith from Chiswick. J. Oliphant delin. Royce sc. 148 × 270/178 × 285mm. No 6.

86 p 564 View of Hampstead from Primrose Hill. Royce sc. 153 × 270/176 × 285mm. No 43.

87 p 566 View of St Mary's Church/Islington – View of St James's Church/Clerkenwell – View of St Luke's Church/Old Street. 143 × 75, 143 × 90, 143 × 80/190 × 273mm. No 55. *C* 623.

88 p 567 View of Isleworth from Richmond Gardens. Royce sc. 150 × 265/180 × 280mm. No 14.

89 p 569 View of Kew from the North. 155 × 275/180 × 295mm. No 50.

90 p 570 View of Mortlake from the River. 150 × 270/180 × 290mm. No 45.

91 p 572 View of Putney & Fulham from Mr Vanneck's. 153 × 275/177 × 290mm. No 40.

92 p 572 View of Richmond from the River. Royce sc. 153 × 270/177 × 278. No 20. (*Gascoigne* 16)

93 p 575 View of Twickenham from the River. 155 × 272/175 × 288m. No 34.

94 p 576 View of Wandsworth from Mr Van Necks. J. Oliphant delin. 150 × 270/178 × 288mm. No 3.

95 p 577 View of Wansted House, on Epping Forest; the Seat of the Earl of Tilney. 165 × 290/195 × 310mm. No 56.

96 p 578 (tm) A New and Correct Map of the Countries Twenty Miles Round London. By Thos. Bowen. 321 × 368/345 × 390. No. 67. *C* 632.

97 p 584 Perspective View of the Castle, or Royal Palace, at Windsor in Berkshire. 153 × 268/175 × 290mm. No 57. Also in Spencer's *Complete English Traveller* (no 52), p 100.

98 p 592 View of Chertsey. 155 × 270/190 × 295mm. No 68.

99 p 593 View of Westminster Bridge – View of Black-Fryer's Bridge – View of Walton Bridge. Each 60 × 160/270 × 185mm. No 70. Robert Mylne's Blackfriars Bridge completed 1769.

100 p 593 View of Hampton Court from the River. 155 × 275/182 × 292mm. No 38.

101 p 594 Perspective View of the Royal Palace, and Gardens, at Hampton Court. 152 × 265/175 × 290mm. No 58. A copy apparently of an engraving c 1750. Also in Spencer's *Complete English Traveller*, p 317.

102 p 632 The Ceremony of Laying the first Stone of

Black Friars Bridge/by the Lord Mayor & Aldermen of the City of London. 158 × 100/250 × 160mm. Moulded. *C* 375.

---

58 · ROOKER'S VIEWS [1777]

Edward Rooker was a skilful architectural engraver and worked on plates for several famous works including Sir W. Chambers's *Civil Architecture*, James Stuart's *Antiquities of Athens* and Robert Adam's *Ruins of the Palace of Diocletian*. His large etchings often call to mind Piranesi who clearly influenced his style. It is no accident that one of the 'Six Views of London', originally published in December 1766 and showing Robert Mylne's Blackfriars Bridge with the centerings still in place, as in July of that year, was a subject which Piranesi had treated at an earlier stage of construction in August 1764, although he only published in the same year as Rooker. These views embody his best work although he also engraved landscapes after William Pars, Richard Wilson and others. His skills were rewarded with a pittance of three shillings a day but he successfully 'moonlighted' at the Drury Lane Theatre in the role of the talented harlequin Ned Rooker.

The views were originally his own publication but John Boydell reissued them in a numbered series in January 1777 and added a seventh view of similar dimensions showing the Admiralty. The set of six was still on offer at £1 10s in Boydell's 1803 catalogue. They are loosely referred to as being based on drawings by Paul and Thomas Sandby but this applies to only four of them. The Blackfriars Bridge view was his own work and two others were drawn by his brilliant artist son Michael, dubbed Michael Angelo at the St Martin's Lane school where he was taught by Paul Sandby—a nickname which stuck to him for the rest of his life. He was elected ARA in 1770 and exhibited many drawings but also followed his father's profession, engraving for Kearsley's *Copper-plate Magazine* and for several of the *Oxford Almanacks*. Failing eyesight caused him to turn, like his father, to the theatre for a living, and as chief scene-painter at George Colman's Haymarket Theatre he was billed as 'Signor Rookerini'.

Only the Covent Garden Piazza view is based on a drawing of the elder Sandby, but this was a favourite subject of his as two tinted drawings and a pen and ink sketch in the British Museum bear witness (*Crowle* 6.24–6).

The publication-line of the reissue reads: 'Published Jany 1st 1777 by John Boydell', but Boydell also published the views on a reduced scale (about 160 × 225mm) with a publication date 1 February 1777.

1 A view of St. James's Gate from Cleveland Row. P. Sandby delin. Edwd. Rooker sculp. Publish'd ... by Edwd. Rooker, Decr 31, 1766. 375 × 525/405 × 545mm. (BL Maps: *K. top.* 26.2e)

2 Part of the Bridge at Blackfriars/as it was in July 1766. Edwd. Rooker delin. et sculp. Publish'd by Edward Rooker, December the 31, 1766. 375 × 530/390 × 535mm. Robert Mylne's bridge, built between 1760 and 1769. (BL Maps: *K. top.* 22.38d)

3 The Horse Guards. M.A. Rooker delin. Edwd Rooker sculp. Publish'd Feby 20th 1768 by Edwd Rooker, in Queens Court, Queen Street, Lincolns Inn Fields. 375 × 525/410 × 550mm. (BL Maps: *K. top.* 25.4a)

4 Scotland Yard with part of the Banqueting-House. P. Sandby delin. Edwd Rooker sculp. Publish'd ... by Edwd Rooker Decr 31. 1766. 375 × 525/405 × 545mm. A water-colour sketch of this subject in the Guildhall Library (160 × 220mm) was perhaps made for Boydell's reduced engraving. (BL Maps: *K. top.* 22.20)

5 The West Front of St Paul's Covent Garden. P. Sandby delin. Edwd. Rooker. sculp. Publish'd ... by Edwd Rooker, Decr 31. 1766. 365 × 520/405 × 555mm. A child's funeral is about to take place, with the mourners dressed in white. (BL Maps: *K. top.* 24.1a)

6 Covent Garden Piazza. T. Sandby delin. Edwd Rooker sculp. Publish'd ... Feby 20 1768 by Edwd Rooker, Queens Court, Queens Street, Lincolns Inn Fields. 372 × 525/400 × 550mm. (BL Maps: *K. top.* 22.28d)

(7) The Admiralty entrance from Whitehall. M.A. Rooker del. Edwd Rooker sculp. Published Jany 1st 1777 by John Boydell. 380 × 530mm, pl. mark cropped. (Guildhall Library)

59 · KEARSLEY'S VIRTUOSI'S MUSEUM* [1778–80]

George Kearsley was the publisher of John Wilkes's notorious *North Briton* but he also issued, from 1774 to 1778, a series of engravings entitled *The Copperplate Magazine, or Monthly Treasure, for the Admirers of the Imitative Arts.* This brought him into contact with a group of artists, including Paul Sandby, M.A. Rooker and Benjamin Green, and a number of engravers such as James Fittler, Charles Grignion, Peter Mazell, Daniel Lerpiniere, Thomas Medland, William Walker and William Watts. After the magazine was discontinued he stayed in fine art publishing and employed some of these on engraving the drawings of Paul Sandby and one or two other artists, over a period of three years, for *The Virtuosi's Museum*. Its 36 Parts each consisted of three plates and a leaf of text with descriptions on both sides; it was advertised: 'The Virtuosi's Museum: Proof Impressions of complete sets or any odd numbers of the Work, may be had of G. Kearsley, near Serjeant's Inn, Fleet Street; J. Walker at Charing Cross; Messrs. Almon & Debrett in Piccadilly; R. Faulder in New Bond Street; T. Sewell in Cornhill.—Numbers supplied weekly or monthly'. For the bound set, which made an oblong folio of about 220 × 290mm, a list of the plates by Numbers (which were engraved on them tr) was issued, also an index to their subjects, an engraved, calligraphic title and a leaf of prefatory matter in which the publisher reasoned:

If intellectual delight affords greater satisfaction to the rational mind than sensual pleasures; a plan calculated to draw off the attention of youth from the improper pursuit of the latter to the virtuous gratifications of the former, will not want the aid of a long prefatory address, or of servile solicitations in its favour.

That such is the laudable design of the present undertaking, no one can entertain a doubt, who reflects that the student, as well as the admirer of the ingenious art of sculpture, will be supplied with elegant engravings from the designs of one of the first artists of this kingdom at the very moderate price of One Shilling for each plate, instead of the usual demand of, from 2s 6d to 5s made for landscapes of inferior merit.

Few of the engravings are of London scenes since

most are concerned with that favourite eighteenth century topic of 'gentlemen's seats'. There are, however, three which, though not particularly urban, do depict London and were drawn in the aftermath of the Gordon Riots when, for reasons of public safety, troops were stationed in the parks and in open spaces near London. These temporary camps, which lasted from June to August 1780, with their military paraphernalia and drilling and manoeuvres of the soldiers became a popular spectacle which Sandby, who lived in St George's Row opposite Hyde Park, was well placed to observe. In the next year he exhibited at the Royal Academy three views of the Hyde Park camp, two of that in St James's Park and one each of the Museum Garden and Blackheath. In the Royal Collection at Windsor are 11 of these drawings (*Oppé* 169–79) and there are two in the British Museum, of St James's Park and Blackheath. Sandby himself produced four aquatints, full size, and two sets of smaller ones (about 215 × 290mm), some of which are to be found in the Crace Collection (9, 80–85).

The publication-line reads: 'Published as the Act directs by G. Kearsley at No 46, in Fleet Street (date)'.

1 (engr title) The/Virtuosi's Museum/Containing/Select Views,/in England, Scotland and Ireland;/ Drawn by P. Sandby Esqr. R.A./London./ Printed for G. Kearsley, at No 46, near Serjeant's Inn, Fleet Street/1778. Shepherd sc. 150 × 210mm pl. mark.

2 pl.67 The Royal Foundery, Woolwich. P. Sandby, R.A. Pinxt. J. Fittler sculp. Decr. 1, 1779. 132 × 180/170 × 215mm. Sandby was chief drawing-master at the Royal Military Academy, Woolwich from 1768 to 1797.

3 pl.94 View of the Encampment in Hyde Park, from Marshal Sax's Tent. P. Sandby R.A. Pinxt. F. Chesham sculpt. Septr. 1, 1780. 132 × 180/160 × 205mm. Aquatint. (BL Maps: *K. top.* 26.6c)

4 pl.99 View of the Encampment in the Museum Garden, August 5th, 1780. P. Sandby Pinxt. R.A. James Fittler sculp. Octr. 1, 1780. 130 × 180/170 × 210mm. N. of Montague House. Aquatint. (BL Maps: *K. top.* 24.17b)

5 pl.103 View of the late Encampment in St James's Park, August 1780. P. Sandby R.A. Pinxt. James Fittler sculpt. Decr. 1, 1780. 130 × 180/170 × 210mm. Aquatint. (*Crace*12.60)

60 · 'BURLINGTON'S' MODERN UNIVERSAL BRITISH TRAVELLER* [1779]

An early instance of the use of the word 'ghost' as applied to undercover authorship is to be found in the review of this book in the *Gentleman's Magazine* for April 1779: 'This respectable trio of an Englishman, a Welshman and a Scotchman, a Squier, a Gentleman and a Graduate, come to us in such questionable shape, so much like ghosts or men of straw, that if we speak to them they cannot answer'. Nevertheless the reviewer makes no bones about criticizing adversely the recently published folio, a cumulation of 80 of those sixpeny Numbers in which John Cooke published the weekly output of his Grub Street hacks. These consisted of eight or 12 pages of text numbered bl, with one or two plates. The triple pseudonym probably conceals the identity of that same Robert Sanders whose earlier labours, disguised as the work of 'Nathaniel Spencer', were published in 1773 (no 52). London with its environs are covered in pp 1–72 (Kent and Surrey) and pp 258–346 (Middlesex).

The Modern Universal British Traveller; or, A New, Complete and Accurate Tour through England, Wales, Scotland ... being the result of an actual and late general survey of the whole kingdom and including various Maps ... A Collection of Landscapes, Views &c that make an admirable groupe of elegant copper plate prints, A Complete Road Book ... The Articles relating to England by Charles Burlington, Esq. Such as relate to Wales by David Llewellyn Rees, Gent. and the description of Scotland by Alexander Murray, M.A. London: Printed for J. Cooke, No 17, at Shakespeare's head, Pater-noster Row; MDCCLXXIX.

Folio, about 370 × 230mm.   1779

COLLATION Title-page; pp iii–iv, preface; pp v–vi, introduction; pp 1–836, The Modern Universal British Traveller; index, directions to binder, list of subscribers (20pp).

Once again Cooke drew on existing plates in stock from a previous publication, namely Harrison's *New and Universal History* (No 57, abbreviated *H*) and Spencer's *Complete English Traveller* (abbreviated *S*). These, with the exception of pl. 8 which has no book title, had substituted for their original title

'Engraved for the Modern Universal British Traveller'. Similarly headed are nine additional London and 'campagna' views in a style not unlike those commissioned for Harrison, making 19 out of a total of 108 plates issued in ones or twos with each of the 80 Numbers. They include a view of Sunbury by White, probably the T. White who also worked on Chamberlain's *New and Compleat History* (no 48), and one of David Garrick's riverside home by Taylor, perhaps the illustrator of Noorthouck's *New History* (no 51).

1 p 23 View of Greenwich from Deptford. 150 × 270/190 × 295mm. No 72. *H* 563.

2 p 24 A View of Deptford. 150 × 270/180 × 290mm. No 56. *H* 560.

3 p 57 Perspective View of the Arch-Bishop's Palace, with St Mary's Church Lambeth. 157 × 270/180 × 288mm. No 40. *S* 132.

4 p 66 View of Richmond from the River. 155 × 275/180 × 285mm. No 53. *H* 572. (*Gascoigne* 17)

5 p 259 View of London from One Tree Hill in Greenwich Park. 160 × 270/190 × 300mm. No 37.

6 p 284 Perspective View of St Paul's Cathedral London, also of Westminster Abbey and St Margaret's Church. Each 160 × 180/188 × 385mm. No 78. St Paul's from N.W., the Abbey from W. *S* 307.

7 p 292 View of the Stairs at York Buildings in the Strand with the Water Works & a distant prospect of Westminster Bridge &c. 160 × 266/180 × 300mm. No 25.

8 p 293 (tm) An Ancient View of St James's, Westminster Abby, & Hall &c from the Village now Charing Cross. 150 × 270/190 × 290mm. No 31. *H* 528.

9 p 329 View of Putney & Fulham from Mr. Vanneck's. 150 × 280/180 × 295mm. No 64. *H* 572.

10 p 330 The Duke of Devonshire's Seat at Chiswick as seen from the Garden. 165 × 270/180 × 300mm. No 15. Grotto and waterfall r. foreground, gardener wheeling water-cart.

11 p 330 View of the back part of the Cassina and Serpentine River in Chiswick Gardens. 165 × 270/185 × 300mm. No 33.

12 p 331 View of Isleworth from Richmond Gardens. 150 × 267/180 × 280mm. No 60. *H* 567.

13 p 331 View of Twickenham from the River. 155 × 272/175 × 285mm. No 36. *H* 575.

14 p 332 A View of the Seat of David Garrick Esqr at Hampton, with a prospect of the Temple of Shakespeare in the Garden. Taylor delin et sculp. 160 × 268/180 × 294mm. No 2.

15 p 334 View of the Seat of Lord Hawke at Sunbury in Middlesex. Dodd delin. White sculp. 160 × 265/180 × 285mm. No 18.

16 p 335 A View of the Church of St Pancrass in the County of Middlesex. 160 × 270/185 × 300mm. No 6.

17 p 336 Hornsey Church in the County of Middlesex with the adjacent country. 158 × 275/190 × 305mm. No 30.

18 p 336 View of the Seat of Joseph Mellish Esqr near Enfield in Middlesex. 165 × 270/185 × 300mm. No 74.

19 p 337 View of Hackney. 150 × 265/180 × 280mm. No 68. *H* 564.

61 · THORNTON'S HISTORY OF LONDON [1784]

Alexander Hogg was John Cooke's journeyman but from about 1778 he set up on his own at the King's Arms, 16 Paternoster Row, near to his former master at no 17. He also adopted Cooke's publishing technique of issuing works serially in the much advertised weekly Paternoster Row Numbers and eventually took over some of his surplus stock. In a catalogue of 25 of his publications he offers them all either in sixpenny Numbers or bound. The first book listed is Thornton's *London*, 'to be completed in only Sixty Numbers, in large Folio, Price 6d each, or the overplus punctually delivered gratis—the whole making a very handsome volume in Folio, Prices £1. 16s. neatly bound in calf and lettered'. There was in fact no 'overplus', the book being completed in 60 Numbers each consisting of eight or 12 pages of text and one or two plates, as indicated by small Arabic numerals printed periodically bl in the text. Plates issued with Numbers 1–11 have dated publication-lines running from 12 June to 24 August 1784; the following plates are undated but, provided issues were punctual, the work should have been ready for the binder by early August 1785. The name of the Lord Mayor for that year appears in the list published with the final Number. The binder is instructed to insert a list of subscribers at the end of the volume but no copies seen include this.

The New, Complete, and Universal History, Description,

and Survey of The Cities of London and Westminster, The Borough of Southwark, And the Parts adjacent including not only all the Parishes within the Bills of Mortality, but likewise the Towns, Villages, Palaces, Seats, and Country, To the Extent of above Twenty Miles round: with all the late Improvements and Alterations.... The great Number (upwards of One Hundred) of Copper-plates with which the Work will be Embellished in a superior Stile, exhibit architectural, perspective, antique and rural Views &c of the Churches, Chapels, Palaces, Gates, Antiquities, Ruins, Hospitals, Bridges, Landscapes, beautiful Prospects, Seats; Plans, Maps, Surveys &c. &c. executed by Messrs. Page, Peltro, Wale, Dod, Thornton, Pollard, Lodge, Royce, Roberts, Wooding, Carey, Hogg, Taylor, Rennoldson, Conder, Noble, Bonner, Golder, Morris, Grainger, Myers, Smith, Sparrow, Clowes &c.... By a Society of Gentlemen. The Whole Revised, Corrected, and Improved, By William Thornton Esq. Assisted by George Smith L.L.D., the Rev. Alex. Townsend, M.A. and other Gentlemen. London: Printed for Alex. Hogg at the Kings Arms, No 16, Pater-noster-Row, and sold by all Booksellers in Great Britain, Ireland, France, America, East & West Indies, &c. MDCCLXXXIV

Folio, about 390 × 250mm.   1784

COLLATION   Title-page; pp iii–iv, preface, dedication to the Lord Mayor, etc; pp 5–524, History; pp 525–32, contents, addenda, directions to binder.

About half of the 106 plates which comprise the illustrations carry a title in the upper margin, 'Engraved for Thornton's New & Complete History & Survey of London & Westminster &c.', and the publication-line 'London, Published by Alexr Hogg at the Kings Arms No 16 Paternoster Row.' A date is added to this on pl. 1, 6, 9, 15–16, 25, 27, 35–6, 43, 46, 51, 60–1, 68, 79–80, 84, 87, 99. Seven ward maps bear a title but no publication-line. Forty seven other plates have a publication-line but are untitled: pl. 5, 8–11, 14, 19, 22–4, 26, 30–5, 38, 45–6, 49, 54, 64, 66, 70–8, 82–100, 102–6. Two of them, pl. 4 and 12, both printed from pairs of small copper plates, have neither title nor publication-line to associate them with the book.

That an excellent 'rapport' must have been maintained between Cooke and his former journeyman can be adduced from a comparison of this book with Harrison's *New and Universal History* (no 57), published nine years before. Of the 206 topographical or architectural subjects on 68 of the plates issued with Thornton no fewer than 142 are derived from Harrison illustrations. Of the 40 historical and antiquarian subjects on 26 Thornton plates 19 are copied from Harrison, as are four of the 12 maps and

plans. Pl. 72, 84 and 95 derive from another Cooke publication, *The Modern Universal British Traveller* of 1779 (no 60). The remaining maps, all of wards, derive from Noorthouck's *New History* (no 51). These derivations are indicated in the list by, respectively, *H, MUBT* and *N*, followed by the facing page number.

To enhance the value of his plates (if not to disguise their recent origins) Hogg commissioned the copyist engravers to add decorative borders which in fact amount to ornate, engraved frames. These, as an important distinguishing feature, are described below. Pl. 35, for instance, combines the subjects from two Harrison plates (*H* 362,395) and decorates them with festoons and urns. Pl. 76 reproduces *H* 528 but frames it in flower garlands. Pl. 97 is embellished with motives suggested by the two views of the Thames: running water and fishing nets, a notion developed by Tombleson 50 years later for his steel-engravings of the Thames (no 178). Hogg's advertisement, by which he hoped no doubt to attract subscribers from among print collectors, asserts that the plates 'exceed in value those sold in the Print Shops at 3s. each' and are by 'the most renowned artists in the United Kingdom'. This is hardly substantiated by the 24 names of artists and engravers which appear on the title-page. Those which most frequently reappear as credits on the plates, although sometimes only in later states, are in descending order: Royce, Wale, Taylor, Page, Wooding, Goldar, Rennoldson and Peltro, all merely competent craftsmen except for Wale whose topographical and historical drawings for books dominated the period and Taylor, probably Isaac the younger or James of an established family of book illustration engravers. Benoist, Downes, Grignion, Hamilton, Hawkins and G. Walker, although not mentioned on the title-page, were also involved. Grignion was a skilled engraver and William Hamilton a decorative painter and designer of engravings. Later states of some of the plates were issued with Walpoole's *New British Traveller* (no 62) and Dalton's revision of it, as well as Boswell's *Antiquities of England and Wales* (no 63), and of others with the reissue of Thornton noted at the end of this entry.

1 front. This Most Superb Frontispiece/Emblematically represents London, Westminster and the Borough of Southwark ... Neptune pours out his Treasure at the feet/of London &c whilst the Author is penning an

Entire New History, Description and Survey of the ancient places. Mercury is seen flying abroad with Proposals of the Work.... Hamilton delin. Page sculp. Published ... June 12, 1784. 210 × 140/325 × 215mm. No 1. Moulded frame with urns and pendants of husks broken into tc by clouds and two putti supporting shields of the City, Westminster and Southwark arms.

2 p 5 A New & Correct Plan of the Cities of London and Westminster, with the Borough of Southwark &c. Including all the Improvements & Alterations to the present Year. 300 × 525/323 × 540mm. No 60. Later state 'Royce sc.', no 1, p 381. (*Darlington and Howgego* 179)

3 p 17 Bishops and Citizens of London/swearing Fealty to/William the Conqueror – The Revd. Dr Shaw Preaching at/St. Paul's Cross, London. 155 × 95, 155 × 100/240 × 312mm. No 18. Moulded frames with scallops tc, captions on trompe-l'oeil labels pinned bc. Copied from *H* 17,123.

4 p 25 Henry Fitzalwine Knight/Noble by Birth ... Lord Mayor of London/from an Original Painting at Drapers Hall – Sir William Wallworth/from the Original Statue in Fishmongers Hall. C. Grignion sculp. 125 × 100/180 × 125; oval 105 × 85/165 × 110mm. No 25. No title or publication-line. Copied from *H* 26.

5 p 54 Edward the Black Prince (eldest son of Edward III) conducting/the King of France his Prisoner through the City of London, 1356. Wale delin. Noble sculp. 175 × 117/340 × 210mm. No 33. Moulded frame with festoons, scrolls, trophies and urns. Copied from *H* 70.

6 p 60 The Burning of St John's Monastry near Smithfield by Wat Tyler's Mob – Blood & his Accomplices making their/Escape after Stealing the Crown from/the Tower of London. Published ... June 26, 1784. 157 × 100, 157 × 105/233 × 320mm. No 3. Later state undated, no 13. Moulded frames with scallops tc, captions on trompe-l'oeil labels pinned bc. Both copied, the first in reverse, from *H* 78, 92.

7 p 63 View of the Tower of London – View of the Custom House, London – View of the Royal Exchange, London. Each 95 × 160/370 × 240mm. No 19. Moulded frame with swags and flower sprays, lyre tc, mask bc. Copied from *H* 82, 213.

8 p 70 Various Weapons & Implements of War, which have been employed against the/English by different Enemies: Now deposited in the Tower of London. Drawn by Hamilton. Engraved by G. Walker. 247 × 165/325 × 220mm. No 27. Later state no 48. Moulded frame with chained gorgon mask tc.

9–11 p 74 A New Collection of English Coins from/Egbert to Hardicanute (Edward the Confessor to Richard II, Henry IV to George III) Accurately taken from the originals. Drawn by Hamilton, Engraved by Thornton (Pollard, Thornton). Each 255 × 170/315 ×

220mm. Nos 48–50. Moulded frames, pendants of oak leaves, urns tc pouring out coins.

12 p 78 Sr. Richard Whittington/from an Original Painting at/Mercers Hall – Sr. Thomas Gresham. Benoist sculp. Ovals, each 90 × 80mm/115 × 100mm. No 52. No title or publication-line.

13 p 84 Jack Cade in Cannon Street/declaring himself Lord of the City of London – Richard II appeases the Rebels/on the death of Wat Tyler in/West Smithfield, London. 155 × 95, 155 × 100/240 × 310mm. No 21. Moulded frames with scallops tc, captions on trompe-l'oeil labels pinned bc. Copied from *H* 497,79.

14 p 94 Edward V & the Duke of York his Brother smothered in the Tower of London/by Tyrrel & his accomplices, which assassination was ordered by the Duke of Gloucester/their Uncle afterward Richard III. S. Wale delin. J.G. Wooding sculp. 175 × 114/300 × 200mm. No 35. Later state no 47. Moulded frame with festoons, scrolls, trophies and urns.

15 p 97 Inside View of Westminster Abbey – Inside View of St Paul's Church – Inside View of St Stephen's Church, Wallbrook. Royce sculp. Published ... July 10, 1784. Each 97 × 153/350 × 220mm. No 5. Later state undated, no 2. Framed by moulded uprights with leaf pattern. First two subjects based on *H* 130.

16 p 146 Lord Cromwell presenting a New Translation/of the Bible to Henry VIII at London, in the year 1538 ... – The Bishops of St Asaph, Chester, Bath, Wells, Ely, Rochester & Peterborough ... presenting their petition ... to James II, at St James's April 27, 1688. Wale delin. Roberts sculp. Published ... June 19, 1784. Each 155 × 100/240 × 375mm. No 2. Frame ornamented with trophies, serpents, chains; torches and masks tc. Second subject copied from *H* 303.

17 p 147 View of St Bartholomew's Hospital near West Smithfield – View of St Thomas's Hospital in the Borough of Southwark – View of Guy's Hospital, St Thomas's Street, Southwark. Each 85 × 175/360 × 240mm. No 17. First two views, showing inner courtyards, copied from *H* 199–200.

18 p 166 A Representation of/a grand Shooting Match by the/London Archers in the Year/1583 – A Representation of an Antient Tournament formerly practised/by the Inhabitants of London &c. 158 × 95, 158 × 100/230 × 350mm. No 15. Moulded frames with scallops tc, captions on trompe-l'oeil labels pinned bc. Copied, the first in reverse, from *H* 217,100.

19 p 173 The Seizing of Guy Fawkes who was going to blow up/the Parliament House in the reign of James the first 1606. Wale delin. Thornton sculp. 180 × 120/340 × 230mm. No 47. Moulded frame, scrolls, trophies, festoons and urns.

20 p 184 Habit of the Lord Mayor/of London in the Year 1640 – Habit of the Lady Mayoress/of London in the Year 1640 – Habit of a Merchant of/London in the Year 1640 – Habit of a Merchant's Wife/of London in

the Year 1640. Ovals, each 112 × 70/345 × 225mm. No 15. Moulded frame, pendant leaves with studs. Reduced from two plates, *H* 244.

21 p 192 A Plan of the City and Environs of London, as fortified by Order of Parliament in the Year 1642 and 1643. 180 × 315/218 × 340mm. No 42. Later state 'Downs sc.', no 30. 'An Explanation/of the several Forts' (l.) 1–11, (r.) 12–23. Copied from *H* 253.

22 p 202 The Execution of King Charles the First/before the Banqueting House Whitehall January 30, 1648–9. Sir G. Kneller pinx. Thornton sculp. 160 × 245/210 × 310mm. No 28. Moulded frame, scrolls, studs, pendants and acanthus leaves.

23 p 203 The Dissolution of the Long Parliament, 1653/ by Oliver Cromwell in order to introduce Triennial Elections. Wale delin. Goldar sculp. 180 × 120/310 × 205mm. No 32. Moulded frame, scrolls, trophies, festoons and urns.

24 p 212 The Manner of Burying the Dead at Holy Well Mount near London/during the dreadful Plague in the reign of Charles II 1665.... 180 × 120/240 × 230. No 31. Moulded frame with husks and ribbons, scrolled urn tc. Copied, in reverse, from *H* 278.

25 p 213 An Elegant & Correct View of London, as it appeared before the Dreadful Fire in the Year 1666. Peltro sculpt. Published ... June 12th 1784. 170 × 280/240 × 350mm. No 1. Refs 1–26. Copied from *H* 280. (*Scouloudi*, pp 58–9)

26 p 213 Part of London as it appeared during the Dreadful Fire/in the reign of Charles IId 1666. Wale delin. Taylor sculp. 175 × 110/305 × 210mm. No 34. Moulded frame with scrolls and acanthus leaves; garlanded urn tc. Copied from *H* 281.

27 p 217 Sir Christopher Wren presenting/to King Charles IId his Plan for Rebuilding/the City of London, after the Great Fire in 1666 – View of the Temporary Bridge of London/as it appeared on Fire in the Night of April 11, 1758. Wale delin. Myers sculp. Published ... July 31st 1784. Each 155 × 102/240 × 365mm. No 8. Later state undated, no 10. Moulded double frame, pendants of oak leaves and scrolls. The Bridge view, in reverse, copied from *H* 410.

28 p 218 Sir John Evelyn's Plan for Rebuilding the City of London after the Great Fire in the Year 1666. 135 × 285/180 × 350mm. No 41. Later state 'Downes sc.', no 22. On l. refs 1–38. Copied, with slight alteration, from *H* 287.

29 p 218 Sir Christopher Wren's Plan for Rebuilding the City of London after the Great Fire in the Year 1666. 155 × 295/205 × 320mm. No 43. Later state 'Downes sc.', no 10. Copied from *H* 286.

30 p 235 The Bill of Rights ratified at the Revolution by King William, and Queen Mary, previous to their Coronation. Wale delin. Carey sculp. 185 × 120/305 × 210mm. No 37. Frame with urns, trophies, garlands, scrolls and pendants.

31 p 238 View of the Bank of England, with the New Wing, built where St Christopher's/Church formerly stood, also of St Bartholomew's Church, Threadneedle Street. 142 × 238/205 × 305mm. No 38. Later state 'Peltro sc.', no 21. Moulded frame with scrolls and husks. Based on earlier view, substituting Sir Robert Taylor's N. wing for the Church (demolished 1781), *H* 313. (*Bank of England* 22)

32 p 246 View of St Paul's Cathedral London. 135 × 220/180 × 255mm. No 27. Moulded frame. From N.W.

33 p 246 North View of Old St Paul's Church after the Spire was destroy'd by Lightning – South View of Old St Paul's Church after the Spire was destroy'd by Lightning – South View of Old St Paul's Church when the Spire was standing. 74 × 160, 70 × 160, 110 × 160/340 × 222mm. No 46. Later state unframed, 'Royce sc.', no 24, p 247. Frame with studs, leaves and berries. Copied from *H* 324.

34 p 284 A View of the manner of Beheading the Rebel Lords on Tower Hill/London, in the Reign of George II. Dodd delin. Goldar sculp. 180 × 120/350 × 215mm. No 30. Moulded frame, festoons and pendants of husks; urn tc, cartouche bc.

35 p 300 The British Museum in Great Russell Street – The Foundling Hospital in Lamb's Conduit Fields/ – Bedford House in Bloomsbury Square – The Small-Pox Hospital near St Pancrass. J.G. Wooding sculpt. Published ... July 3, 1784. 90 × 160, 90 × 160, 95 × 160, 95 × 160/240 × 370mm. No 4. Later state undated, no 6. Moulded frame, urns and festoons of husks. Reduced copies, in reverse, from *H* 362, 395.

36 p 324 The Ceremony of Laying the first Stone of/Blackfriars Bridge by the Lord Mayor/ & Aldermen of the City of London – The Ceremony of Performing the Champion's/Challenge, at the Coronation in/ Westminster Hall. Wale delin. Hawkins sculpt. Published ... July 17th 1784. 155 × 100, 155 × 95/240 × 320mm. No 6. Moulded frames with scallops tc, captions on trompe-l'oeil labels pinned bc. Copied, in reverse, from *H* 632, 75.

37 p 325 Sr Robert Ladbroke – George Nelson Esq – William Beckford Esq. – Sir John Bernard. Each 130 × 95/360 × 245mm. No 11. Later state undated, no 44. Four portraits in ovals; moulded frame with City arms tc, City trophy bc.

38 p 381 A General View of London, the Capital of England Taken from an eminence near Islington. Page scu. 162 × 260/210 × 285mm. No 29. Later state no 46, p 483.

39 p 388 (plans framed and divided by C-scrolls, cartouche bl) Plan of/Aldgate Ward/with its Divisions into/Precincts & Parishes,/from a New Survey – (tr) Plan of/Lime Street Ward/Divided into Parishes,/from a New Survey – (br) Plan of/Queen Hith/and Vintry Wards/Divided into Parishes,/from a New Survey.

Royce sculp. 320 × 200/345 × 217mm. No 20. Copied from *N* 545,662,666. (*Hyde* 11)

40 p 389 The Jewish manner of Holding up the Law in the sight of the People, at Duke's Place, London. 145 × 240/190 × 285mm. No 26. Later state 'Scott sc.', no 39. Moulded frame.

41 p 391 (in cartouche tl) Plan of/Billingsgate/Ward and Bridge/Ward Within/Divided into Parishes/from a New Survey – (br) Plan of Farringdon Ward/Without/Divided into Parishes/from a New Survey. 285 × 175/340 × 220mm. No 54. Later state 'Royce sc.', no 33, retains title. Wreathed frame. Faringdon section copied from *N* 639. (*Hyde* 17)

42 p 391 St Margaret Pattens, Little Tower Street – St Andrew Undershaft Leadenhall Street/ – St Clements, Eastcheap – St Trinity Minories/ – St Mary Abchurch Abchurch Lane – Allhallows Staining Crutched Fryers. 85 × 85, 85 × 80; 85 × 85, 85 × 80; 85 × 85, 85 × 80/365 × 240mm. No 21. Later state 'Taylor sc.', no 23, p 389. Moulded frame decorated with scrolls and husks, beading between subjects. Individually copied from *H* 489.

43 p 392 Views of the City Gates as they appeared before they were pulled down, together with the Old Gate at Whitehall & Templebar: Bishopsgate – Cripplegate – Ludgate – Newgate – Moorgate/ – Aldgate – Bridge-gate – Aldersgate – Templebar – Whitehallgate. J.G. Wooding sculp. Published ... July 10, 1784. 183 × 335/240 × 365mm. No 5. Later state undated, no 17, p 382. Thin frame festooned and garlanded, swags and husks below.

44 p 392 (on tablets, etc) Plan of /Aldersgate/Ward./Divided into Parishes/From a New Survey – (br) Plan of/Bishopsgate Ward/Within & Without./Divided into Parishes/From a New Survey – (l.) Plan of/Bread Street/ & Cordwainers,/Ward S./Divided into Parishes/From a New Survey. 320 × 200/340 × 215mm. No 58. Later state 'Royce sc.', no 42. Beaded frames. (*Hyde* 5)

45 p 393 St Botolph, Bishopsgate Street – St Leonards, Shoreditch/ – Christ's Spitalfields – St Bennet's, Grace Church Street/ – The Monument on Fish Street Hill – St Magnus, London Bridge. 90 × 80, 90 × 85; 85 × 80, 85 × 85; 85 × 80, 85 × 85/350 × 233mm. No 57. Later state 'Grainger sc.', no 43. Reduced copies from *H* 437,282.

46 p 395 (captions above each) View of London Bridge as it appeared before the Houses were Pulled Down – View of London Bridge in its Present State with the Waterworks as viewed from the City Shore – View of Blackfriars Bridge – View of Westminster Bridge. Published ... August 24th, 1784. Each 55 × 295/240 × 370mm. No 10. Later state undated, no 25. London Bridge views modified from *H* 23.

47 p 396 (on tablets, br) Plan of/Broad Street/& Cornhill Wards./Divided into Parishes/from a New Survey – (tr) Plan of/Walbrook & Downgate/Wards/Divided

into Parishes from a New Survey. Royce sculp. 310 × 188/355 × 220mm. No 12. Later state no 8. Beaded frame. Largely copied from *N* 566, 612. (*Hyde* 30)

48 p 398 The Arms of the City Companies together with those of the Trading Companies, Hospitals, Inns of Court, Societies, &c. Plate II. Page sc. 210 × 340/240 × 365mm. No 19.

49 p 398 The South Sea House, in Threadneedle Street – The East India House in Leadenhall Street – The Mansion House of London. 90 × 175, 90 × 175, 85 × 175/365 × 238mm. No. 53. Later state 'Taylor sc.', no 16. Copied, with extension, from *H* 445,361.

50 p 400 (tablets, tl) Plan of/Baynards Castle/Ward, & Faringdon/Ward, Within./Divided into Parishes/From a New Survey – (br) Plan of/Candlewick and/Langborn Wards/Divided into Parishes,/from a New Survey. 300 × 180/340 × 225mm. No 50. Later state 'Royce sc.', no 18. Frame with studs and husks. Copied from *N* 579,576. (*Hyde* 35)

51 p 404 An Antient View of part of Cheapside, with the Cross, &c./as they appeared in the Year 1660 – An exact view of Baynards Castle, formerly/built by Wm Baynard. Published ... August 14th 1784. 138 × 214, 135 × 214/365 × 240mm. No 11. Later state 'Wooding sc.', undated, less frame and with captions re-engraved, no 32. Moulded frame wreathed with husks and decorated with lamps and studs; bearded mask tc. Copied from *H* 273,448.

52 p 404 The Arms of the City Companies together with those of the Trading Companies, Hospitals, Inns of Court, Societies, &c. Plate I. Page sc. 210 × 340/240 × 355mm. No 16.

53 p 404 (on tablets, tr) Plan of/Cheap Ward/Divided into Parishes/from a New Survey – (tl) Plan of/Tower Street Ward/Divided into Parishes/from a New Survey. 350 × 180/342 × 210mm. No 36. Later state 'Royce sc.', no 40, p 391 or 431. Frame with dart ornament. Copied from *N* 587,668. (*Hyde* 40)

54 p 404 St Mildred's, Bread Street – St Mary's, Aldermanbury/ – St Mary le Bow, Cheapside – St Mildred's, Poultry/ – St Michael's, Cornhill – St Peter's, Cornhill. 80 × 80, 80 × 80; 77 × 80, 77 × 80; 80 × 80, 80 × 80/375 × 230mm. No 59. Later state 'Rennoldson sc.', no 26, p 411. Framed in scrollwork, City arms tc, City trophy bc. Second caption should be 'St Mary Aldermary'. Reduced from *H* 460,453.

55 p 405 View of the Guild Hall of London – View of Grocers Hall in the Poultry – View of Goldsmiths Hall Foster Lane. 90 × 150, 85 × 150, 85 × 150/370 × 240mm. No 13. Later state no 14, p 387. Moulded frame, garlanded and festooned; mask and lyre tc. Reduced from *H* 361,453.

56 p 406 View of Guild-Hall Chapel – West View of Blackwell Hall – View of Gresham College as it appeared before it was taken down to/Build a new Excise office. Published ... August 7th, 1784. 148 × 80, 148 × 80, 105 × 162/365 × 240mm. No 9. Later

state undated, no 7. Moulded frame, City arms tc, City trophy bc. Copied from *H* 456,213.

57 p 407 (on tablets, tl) Plan of/Coleman Street/and/ Bassishaw Wards/Divided into Parishes/from a New Survey – (tr) Plan of/Portsoken/Ward/Divided into Parishes/from a New Survey – (lc) Plan of Cripplegate Ward/Divided into Parishes/from a New Survey. 305 × 190/340 × 225mm. No 52. Later state 'Royce sc.', no 27. Frame decorated with studs and husks. First section copied from *N* 549. (*Hyde* 44)

58 p 412 St Albans, Wood Street – St James's Dukes Place/ – St Ethelburga, within Bishopsgate – St Catherine, Coleman Street/ – Great St Helens Bishopsgate Street – St Michael Bassishaw, Basinghall Street. 85 × 80, 85 × 77; 85 × 80, 85 × 77; 85 × 80, 85 × 77/370 × 240mm. No 24. Later state 'Bonner sculpsit', no 41. Moulded frame, wreathed bust tc. St Catherine's was in Fenchurch Street.

59 p 413 St Mary, Aldermanbury – St Lawrence Jewry, Cateaton Street/ – St Michael, Wood Street – St Giles's Cripplegate/ – St Stephens, Coleman Street – St Margarets, Lothbury. Each 85 × 87/370 × 250mm. No 18. Moulded frame, side-pieces with laurel wreaths and husks; beaded partitions. Copied from *H* 468.

60 p 416 Allhallows the Great Thames Street – St Stephens, Walbrook/ – The Chapel in the Tower – St Michaels, Queenhythe/ – St Botolphs, Botolph Lane – St Mary at Hill, near Billingsgate. Taylor sculp. Published ... July 31st, 1784. 87 × 82, 87 × 85; 87 × 82, 87 × 85; 85 × 82, 85 × 85/365 × 235mm. No 8. Later state undated, no 9, p 316. Moulded frame with wreaths, urns and swags; beading between subjects. Individually copied from *H* 496.

61 p 418 St Mathew's, Friday Street – St Michael's, College Hill/ – St Swithin's, Cannon Street – St Mary Magdalen, Old Fish Street/ – St Nicholas Coleabby, Old Fish Street – St James's Garlick Hith. Publish'd ... June 26, 1784. 87 × 83, 87 × 85; 87 × 83, 87 × 85; 87 × 83, 87 × 85/350 × 240mm. No 3. Later state 'Taylor sc.', undated, no 15. Moulded side-pieces and base, with scrolls, wreaths, urns and swags. Individually copied from *H* 495.

62 p 425 St Bartholomew the Great, Cloth Fair – St Bartholomew the Less, near the Hospital/ – St Botolph's Aldersgate Street – St Martin Outwick Threadneedle Street/ – St Ann & St Agnes, St Ann's Lane – St Olives Old Jewry. Each 90 × 85/360 × 240mm. No 20. Frames with laurel wreaths and garlands, beaded partitions. Copied from *H* 427.

63 p 425 View of the New Sessions House, Old Bailey – View of Surgeons Hall, Old Bailey – View of New Hicks Hall, Clerkenwell Green. 100 × 165, 100 × 165, 105 × 165/360 × 240mm. No 14. Framed by wreaths, shields and husks. The last subject is Middlesex County Sessions House by Thomas Rogers, 1779–82. First two copied from *H* 483.

64 p 440 St Olive's Southwark – St George's Southwark/ –

Christ's Church, Surrey – St Mary's, Rotherhithe/ – St Mary Magdalens, Bermondsey – St John's Southwark. 78 × 78, 78 × 78; 82 × 78, 82 × 78; 82 × 78, 82 × 78/375 × 230mm. No 51. Later state 'Rennoldson sc.', no 31. Moulded frame with corner studs, City Arms tc, City Trophy bc. Reduced from *H* 509,506.

65 p 444 View of Lambeth Palace in Surrey – View of Westminster Abbey & St Margarets Church adjoining. Each 130 × 170/355 × 240mm. No 17. Moulded frame with husks and wreaths.

66 p 447 View of the City of Westminster &c/ taken near the Landing Place at Lambeth Palace – View of Windsor in Berkshire, taken to the/Westward from the opposite Shore of the River Thames. Each 130 × 175/350 × 230mm. No 32. Later state 'Lodge sc.', no 48. Side-pieces with scrolls, wreaths and husks.

67 p 448 View of Westmnister (sic) Hall – View of St George's Church/Bloomsbury – General View of Covent Garden Market/London. Each 158 × 95/230 × 350mm. No 14. Framed in swags, studs and plant shoots. First two subjects copied from *H* 132,537.

68 p 449 The Entrance of the House of Lords, with/the late Office of Ordnance, adjoining – View of the Royal Stables, and part of/the church of St Martins in the Fields – View of the House of Commons from/the River Thames. Published ... August 7th, 1784. 157 × 95, 157 × 97, 157 × 95/230 × 358mm. No 9. Later state undated, no 3, p 450. Frame with festoons and studs, scallop tc. *H* 518,537.

69 p 452 St John the Evangelist, Westminster – St Bennet, Paul's Wharf/ – St Martin, Ludgate – St Bride, Fleet Street/ – St Andrew, Holbourn – St Sepulchre, Snow Hill. 80 × 80, 80 × 80; 85 × 80, 85 × 80; 82 × 80, 82 × 80/375 × 235mm. No 13. Later state no 5. Framed in scrolls and floral pendants, City arms tc, City trophy bc. Adapted from *H* 477, 481.

70 p 454 St Paul's, Covent Garden – St Mary, le Strand/ – St Clement's Strand – St Mary Woolnorth, Lombard Street/ – St Edmund the King, Lombard Street – Allhallows, Lombard Street. 87 × 80, 87 × 80; 87 × 80, 87 × 80; 84 × 80, 84 × 80/370 × 230mm. No 54. Later state 'Rennoldson sc.', no 29. Moulded frame with corner studs, City arms tc, City trophy bc. Copied from *H* 524,485.

71 p 455 The New Buildings in the Strand, called the Adelphi, viewed from the River Thames. 160 × 273/240 × 390mm. No 56. Later state 'Carey sc.', no 37. Copied, with additional staffage, omitting pendant on St Martin in the Fields, from *H* 525.

72 p 455 View of the Stairs at York Buildings, London, with the Water Works,/and a distant Prospect of Westminster Bridge. 153 × 257/177 × 273mm. No 23. Later state 'Taylor sc.', no 38. Side and angle-pieces with husks, studs, wreaths and scrolls. Copied from *MUBT* 292.

73 p 458 View of the Banqueting House, White Hall – View of the Royal Palace & Garden at Hampton

Court – View of the Treasury & Horse Guards in St James's Park. Each 95 × 175/360 × 240mm. No 47. Frame with studs only. Copied, Hampton Court reduced, from *H* 529,594.

74 p 459 View of St James's Palace, from Pall Mall – View of St James's Palace, from the Park – View of the Queens Palace, formerly Buckingham House,/in St James's Park. 87 × 175, 87 × 175, 90 × 175/360 × 240mm. No 55. Later state 'Taylor sc.', no 19. Copied from *H* 531,530.

75 p 459 View of St George's Hospital at Hyde Park Corner – View of the Middlesex Hospital near Oxford Street – View of Christ's Hospital & Church, near Newgate Street. Each 90 × 170/353 × 240mm. No 40. Later state 'Taylor sc.', no 36. Copied from *H* 530,200.

76 p 459 An Antient View of St James's, Westminster Abbey & Hall &c. from the Village of Charing, now Charing Cross. 153 × 285/225 × 350mm. No 22. Later state 'Myers sc.', no 45, p 460. Refs 1–7. Frame garlanded with flowers, with studs and a scallop tc. Copied from *H* 528.

77 p 460 St James's, Westminster – St George's, Hanover Square/ – St Giles's in the Fields – St Ann's Westminster/ – St George's Queen Square – St Dunstan's, Fleet Street. Each 90 × 85/360 × 230mm. No 58. Later state 'Taylor sc.', no 35, p 461. First five copied from *H* 536.

78 p 461 The Pantheon in Oxford Street – The Front of Drury Lane Theatre. Each 155 × 110/220 × 340mm. No 39. Later state 'Royce sc.', no 28. Frames with foliage. Copied, in reverse, from *H* 533.

79 p 464 View of Grays Inn, near Holbourn – View of Lincoln's Inn, Chancery Lane – View of Northumberland House & Charing Cross. Taylor sculp. Published ... June 20th 1784. Each 87 × 175/353 × 235mm. No 7. Later state undated, no 11. Framed in wreaths, palms and ovals.

80 p 468 View of St Luke's Hospital, Upper Moorefields – View of Bethlem Hospital, Moorefields – View of St Paul's School, London. Peltro sculpt. Published ... July 17th, 1784. Each 95 × 183/353 × 240mm. No 6. Later state undated, no 12. Frame with beads and studs. Copied from *H* 459,324.

81 p 469 View of Ironmongers Alms Houses, Kingsland Road – View of the New Excise Office, Old Broad Street, London – View of Trinity Alms Houses, Mile End Road. 90 × 150, 85 × 190, 92 × 150/357 × 225mm. No 12. Later state no 4. Broken frame decorated with leaves, berries, studs and swags. Almshouses copied from *H* 545.

82 p 477 View of Chelsea in Middlesex/taken near Battersea Church Yard – View of the River Thames &c near Northfleet in Kent. Each 130 × 170/355 × 240mm. No 40. Later state 'Goldar sc.', unlisted. Moulded side-pieces with palms and wreaths. Chelsea copied from *H* 558. (*Longford* 261)

83 p 478 View of Chiswick in Middlesex – View of Acton, in Middlesex. Each 125 × 180/345 × 240mm. No 23. Moulded frame with urns and ball ornaments, garlands below. Reduced from *H* 559,555.

84 p 478 View of the back part of the/Cassina and Serpentine River, in/Chiswick Gardens. Carey sculp. Published ... April 10, 1784. 165 × 265/230 × 355mm. No 26. Frame of studs and ivy tendrils. Copied from *MUBT* 330.

85 p 479 View of Gunnersbury House, near Ealing in Middlesex,/the Seat of Princess Amelia – View of Wanstead House, on Epping Forest in Essex/the Seat of the Earl of Tilney – A Representation of the Capital Figures of Bethlem/Hospital Gate, London. Each 95 × 165/350 × 245mm. No 31 Moulded frame with beads, scallop tc. Wanstead House reduced from *H* 577.

86 p 479 View of Dulwich College in Surrey – View of Camberwell from the Grove. Each 130 × 175/360 × 235mm. No 30. Moulded side-pieces, wreaths and husks. Adapted from *H* 560,557.

87 p 480 View of the Bishop of London's Seat, at/Fulham in Middlesex – View of Lord Stormont's House/near Wandsworth in Surry. Published ... May 22, 1784. Each 130 × 170/345 × 230mm. No 28. Side-pieces with husks, wreaths and studs.

88 p 480 View of the Duke of Chandos's Seat at/Southgate in Middlesex – View of Waltham Abbey Church in Essex. Each 120 × 160/360 × 235mm. No 34. Framed with studs and pendants of leaves, wreath tc.

89 p 480 View of Greenwich in Kent – View of Deptford in Kent. Each 130 × 170/360 × 235mm. No 29. Moulded side-pieces with husks, studs, scrolls, and wreaths. Adapted from *H* 563, 560.

90 p 480 View of Greenwich Hospital – View of the Admiralty Office – View of Chelsea Hospital. 90 × 170, 90 × 155, 90 × 170/375 × 240mm. No 25. Moulded frame with corner studs. Adapted from *H* 563,130. (*Longford* 16)

91 p 483 St Mary's Islington – St James's, Clerkenwell/ – St Luke's Old Street – The Church of Stoke Newington/ – St John's Hackney – St Matthews, Bethnal Green. 85 × 85, 85 × 83; 87 × 85, 87 × 83; 87 × 87, 87 × 83/350 × 230mm. No 52. Later state 'Grainger sc.', no 34, p 481. Reduced from *H* 566,547.

92 p 484 View of Sion House between Brentford & Isleworth in Middlesex/the Seat of His Grace the Duke of Northumberland – View of Cane Wood the Superb Villa of the Earl of Mansfield/near Highgate in Middlesex. 133 × 175, 133 × 180/350 × 240mm. No 42. Side-pieces with studs, wreaths, husks and palms; divided by scrolls, urn in centre.

93 p 485 View of Kensington Palace – View of Ranelaugh Gardens near Chelsea – View of Vaux-Hall Gardens. Each 85 × 175/350 × 240mm. No 43. Side-pieces with husks, studs, wreaths and palms. (*Longford* 321)

94 p 485 View of the Town and Bridge of Kew,/in Surrey – View of Roehampton in Surrey. Each 125 × 170/340 × 230mm. No 22. Side-pieces with wreaths, husks, scrolls. Kew view copied from *H* 569.

95 p 486 View of the Church of St Pancras, in Middlesex – View of Hornsey-Church in Middlesex/With the Adjacent Country. Each 130 × 175/350 × 235mm. No 25. Framed in wreaths, husks and scrolls. First subject copied from *MUBT* 335.

96 p 486 View of Mortlake in Surrey, from the River Thames – View of Hammersmith in Middlesex/taken from Chiswick. 135 × 175, 130 × 175/355 × 235mm. No 38. Moulded side-pieces with wreaths. Reduced from *H* 570,564.

97 p 487 A View from Richmond Hill,/down the River Thames – A View from One Tree Hill in Greenwich Park. Each 130 × 175/345 × 235mm. No 35. Later state 'Carey sc.', unlisted. Frame with rushing stream tc, swags of fishing net and vine leaves.

98 p 487 View of Putney and Fulham the former in Surry and the latter in Middlesex – View of Hackney in Middlesex. Each 130 × 170/365 × 240mm. No 44. Moulded side-pieces with husks and wreaths. Reduced from *H* 572,564.

99 p 489 View of Twickenham in Middlesex – View of Isleworth, in Middlesex,/from the opposite Shore in Richmond Gardens. Published ... May 22, 1784. Each 130 × 175/350 × 240mm. No 24. Frames with studs and pendant leaves. Isleworth view copied from *H* 567.

100 p 490 View of Wandsworth in Surrey from Mr Vannecks – View of Clapham in Surrey, from the Common. Each 130 × 172/350 × 240mm. No 33. Moulded side-pieces with wreaths and husks. Reduced from *H* 576,560.

101 p 491 (tm) A New and Correct Map of the Countries upwards of Twenty Miles Round London: Drawn from Modern Surveys & Engraved for Thornton's History of London, &c. Downes sculp. 320 × 360/345 × 385mm. No 37. Later state no 20, p 475. 3 miles to 1 inch. Apparently Thomas Bowen's, as *H* 578. (*Darlington and Howgego* 178)

102 p 502 View of Hampton Court, from the opposite Shore/of the River Thames – View of Chertsey in Surrey. Each 123 × 175/345 × 235mm. No 44. Later state 'Roberts sc.', unlisted. Moulded side-pieces with palms and wreaths. Copied from *H* 593,592.

103 p 502 View of the Seat of Admiral Keppel at Bagshot in Surrey – View of the Seat of David Garrick Esqr nr. Hampton/with the Temple of Shakespeare. 115 × 170, 110 × 170/365 × 235mm. No 45. Later state: 'the late David Garrick', 'Page sc.', unlisted. Frame with pendants of husks and flowers, garlanded mask tc. Garrick died in 1779. Copied from *MUBT* 332.

104 p 506 View of Addington Place the Seat of/Jas Trecothic Esq. near Croydon in Surrey – View of the Royal Circus near/the Obelisk in St George's Fields, Surry. Each 125 × 170/340 × 225mm. No 41. Moulded frame with festoons and scrolls, laurel wreath tc. The St George's Fields obelisk was erected 1771.

105 p 507 View of Gravesend in Kent – View of Woolwich in Kent. Each 130 × 180/350 × 235mm. No 36. Moulded frame, side-pieces with wreaths of bays.

106 p 520 The Devastations occasioned by the Rioters of London Firing the New Goal of Newgate/and burning Mr. Akerman's Furniture &c. June 6, 1780. Hamilton delin. Thornton sculp. 155 × 255/220 × 315mm. No 39. Frame with studs and leaf pendants, scallop tc.

Thornton's *History* was undersubscribed as Hogg still had sheets for disposal 12 years after its original publication and reissued it with an appendix of recent events and a list of Lord Mayors updated to 1796. To give it a new lease of life he went so far as to discard the alleged author of the work and to attribute it on a new, undated title-page to one Richard Skinner. He also commissioned Grignion to engrave for it a fresh allegorical frontispiece.

A New and Complete History and Description of the Cities of London, Westminster the Borough of Southwark, and parts adjacent, containing the whole histories of London, Westminster, Southwark, &c ... from the very earliest intelligence to the year 1796 ... By Richard Skinner Esquire ... Embellish'd with several Hundred Elegant Engravings by eminent Artists ... Printed for Alex. Hogg, in Paternoster row and sold by all the Booksellers ...

Folio, about 390 × 250mm.   1796

COLLATION Title-page; pp iii-iv, preface; pp 5-538, History (including an appendix on pp 523–8, events of 1783–93); pp 525–32 (bis), contents, list of Lord Mayors, etc, directions to binder; list of subscribers (4pp).

Disregarding the extravagant claim of the title-page the binder is directed to insert only 51 of the plates issued with the 1784 edition, mostly in their original positions. In the listing above these are recorded as 'later states'. Publication-lines were retained minus the dates but the title, which included Thornton's name, was removed from all plates except for pl. 2, 41 and 101, all maps. Pl. 33 and 51 lost their ornamental frames. Engravers' credits were added to many plates which had appeared anonymously. Plates reissued were: 1–2, 6, 8, 14–15, 21, 27–9, 31, 33, 35, 37–8, 40–7, 49–51, 53–8, 60–1, 64, 66, 68–72, 74–81, 91, 101, and the frontispiece added:

107 front. The Principal Figure seated on the Banks of the Thames represents London Crowning/Industry

who is introducing Plenty, while Royalty is joining hands with Loyalty. Drawn by Riley. Engraved by Grignion. Published ... Feby 21st 1795. 210 × 140/325 × 215mm. Moulded frame, City arms tc.

A hybrid edition (in the London Library) is in all respects similar to Skinner but has the original title-page and frontispiece and four unlisted plates (82,97,102–3, in later states, with engravers added) bound at the end.

62 · WALPOOLE'S NEW BRITISH TRAVELLER* [1784]

When Thornton's *London* (no 61) was still coming out Hogg embarked on another 'Paternoster Row Numbers' publication, a survey, this time, of the whole of Great Britain with suitably named collaborators for each of its component nations. It was thus advertised:

No. 1. To be completed in only Sixty Numbers, in large Folio, Price 6d each, or the Overplus punctually delivered gratis of Walpoole's New British Traveller ... Now publishing in Weekly Numbers, one or two of which may be had at a Time the Whole making a very large handsome Volume in Folio Price £1. 16s bound.

The title-page and plates are undated but there is a reference in No 25 (p 233) to 'The New-Fire-Office incorporated this present year 1784' and there is a puff for 'Thornton's *History* (now publishing in weekly numbers)' in the text of No 24 (p 227). Like the Thornton work it was issued in 60 Numbers, each of ten to 12 pages of text and one or more plates. The terms of the advertisement, appended to the British Library copy (10348.l.3), which offer the alternative of a bound volume, suggest that the weekly Numbers were not necessarily received hot from the press but that an 'easy terms' subscription might begin whenever it suited the customer.

The New British Traveller: or a Complete Modern Universal Display of Great Britain and Ireland ... being really the Result of An actual and late General Survey, accurately made by a Society of Gentlemen ... and

including a valuable collection of landscapes, views, county-maps, &c which make an admirable and inimitable group of elegant copper-plate prints.... drawn with critical Exactness by the most capital Painters and Designers of England, Scotland and Ireland, namely Hamilton, Carter, Griffith, O'Neal, Dodd, Metz &c. and engraved by the following ingenious artists, viz. Thornton, Pollard, Lodge, Page, Roberts, Royce, Taylor, Carey, Rennoldson, Wooding, Kitchen, Conder, Hawkins, Walker, Flyn, Simpson, Grainger, Hogg, Myers, Smith, Clowes and others ... The whole published under the immediate inspection of George Augustus Walpoole Esq Assisted ... by David Wynne Evans, F.R.S.... Alexander Burnet, L.L.D.... Robert Conway, A.M.... Embellished with upwards of One Hundred and Fifty large, grand and superb Views ... Printed for Alex. Hogg, at the Kings-Arms, No 16 Paternoster Row.

Folio, about 385 × 245mm.   (1784)

COLLATION   Title-page; pp iii-iv, preface; pp v-vi, introduction; pp 7–520, New British Traveller, directions to binder (p 520); list of subscribers (4pp); catalogue (2pp).

An allegorical frontispiece designed by Hamilton and engraved by Thornton and 112 illustrative plates were issued with the 60 Numbers. All but two of the 28 plates of London and its environs were also published with Thornton (abbreviated in the list as *T* with facing page number). One of the two exceptions was partly derived from Cooke's publication *The Modern Universal British Traveller* (No 60, abbreviated *MUBT*). They carry no book title but all have the publication-line 'Published by Alexr Hogg at the King's Arms, No 16 Paternoster Row'.

In the British Library copy the Thornton plates appear in their original state but in that of the Guildhall Library some credits are added and this suggests that, in spite of a similar title-page, this is intermediate between the original issue and the Dalton reissue noted below. The team of artists and engravers mentioned on the title-page is substantially that of the Thornton title-page.

1 p 21 View of Gravesend in Kent – View of Woolwich in Kent. Each 130 × 180/350 × 235mm. No 24. Later state 'Carey sc.', Dalton no 49. Moulded frame, side-pieces with wreaths of bays. *T* 507.

2 p 23 View of Greenwich in Kent – View of Deptford in Kent. Each 130 × 170/360 × 235mm. No 18. Later state 'Taylor sc.', Dalton no 21. Moulded side-pieces with husks, studs, scrolls and wreaths. *T* 480.

3 p 53 View of Lambeth Palace in Surrey – View of Westminster Abbey & St Margarets Church adjoining. Each 130 × 170/355 × 240mm. No 48. Later state

'Carey sc.', frame deleted. Moulded frame with husks and wreaths. *T* 444.

4 p 55 View of Dulwich College in Surrey – View of Camberwell from the Grove. Each 130 × 175/360 × 235mm. No 19. Later state 'Lodge sc.', Dalton no 18. Moulded side-pieces, wreaths and husks. *T* 479.

5 p 56 View of Addington Place the Seat of/Jas Trecothic Esq. near Croydon in Surrey – View of the Royal Circus near/the Obelisk in St George's Fields, Surry. Each 125 × 170/340 × 225mm. No 35. Later state 'Wooding sc.', Dalton no 30. Moulded frame with festoons and scrolls, laurel wreath tc. *T* 506.

6 p 59 View of the Seat of Admiral Keppel at Bagshot in Surrey – View of the Seat of the late David Garrick Esqr nr. Hampton/with the Temple of Shakespeare. 115 × 170, 110 × 170/365 × 235mm. No 51. Later state 'Page sc.'; Dalton no 14 lacks credit. Frame with pendants of husks and flowers, garlanded mask tc. *T* 502.

7 p 61 A View from Richmond Hill,/down the River Thames – A View from One Tree Hill in Greenwich Park. Each 130 × 175/345 × 235mm. No 24. Later state 'Carey sc'. Frame with rushing stream tc, swags of fishing net and vine leaves. *T* 487. (*Gascoigne* 20)

8 p 61 View of Richmond in Surrey/from the River Thames – View of Richmond in Yorkshire. Each 120 × 160/350 × 220mm. No 56. Later state 'Carey sc.', Dalton no 27. Moulded frame, festoons of bays, scrolls, wreath with sunburst tc. First view reduced from *MUBT* 66. (*Gascoigne* 21)

9 p 62 View of the Town and Bridge of Kew,/in Surrey – View of Roehampton in Surrey. Each 125 × 170/340 × 230mm. No 16. Later state 'Taylor sc.', Dalton no 20. Side-pieces with wreaths, husks and scrolls. *T* 485.

10 p 62 View of Mortlake in Surrey, from the River Thames – View of Hammersmith in Middlesex/taken from Chiswick. 135 × 175, 130 × 175/355 × 235mm. No 26. Later state 'Lodge sc.', Dalton no 41. Moulded side-pieces with wreaths. *T* 486.

11 p 62 View of Wandsworth in Surrey from Mr Vannecks – View of Clapham in Surrey, from the Common. Each 130 × 172/350 × 240mm. No 27. Later state 'Roberts sculp', Dalton no 37. Moulded side-pieces with wreaths and husks. *T* 490.

12 p 227 A General View of London, the Capital of England Taken from an eminence near Islington. Page scu. 162 × 260/210 × 285mm. No 54. *T* 381.

13 p 247 View of St Paul's Cathedral London. 135 × 220/180 × 255mm. No 52. Later state 'Barclay sc.', Dalton no 43. Moulded frame. *T* 246.

14 p 254 View of the Stairs at York Buildings, London, with the Water Works,/and a distant Prospect of Westminster Bridge. 153 × 257/177 × 273mm. No 47. Later state 'Taylor scu.' Side and angle-pieces with husks, studs, wreaths and scrolls. *T* 455.

15 p 281 View of the Bishop of London's Seat, at/Fulham in Middle-sex – View of Lord Stormont's House/near Wandsworth in Surrey. Published ... May 22, 1784. Each 130 × 170/345 × 230mm. No 9. Later state undated, 'Taylor sc.', Dalton no 34 Side-pieces with husks, wreaths and studs. *T* 480.

16 p 281 View of Putney and Fulham the former in Surry and the latter in Middlesex – View of Hackney in Middlesex. Each 130 × 170/365 × 240mm. No 29. Later state with studs, swags and branches added to blank upper and lower portions of frame; Dalton no 42. Moulded side-pieces with husks and wreaths. *T* 487.

17 p 281 View of Kensington Palace – View of Ranelaugh Gardens near Chelsea – View of Vaux-Hall Gardens. Each 85 × 175/350 × 240mm. No 42. Later state 'Carey sc.', Dalton no 36. Side-pieces with husks, studs, wreaths and palms. *T* 485. (*Longford* 321)

18 p 281 View of Chelsea in Middlesex/taken near Battersea Church Yard – View of the River Thames &c near Northfleet in Kent. Each 130 × 170/355 × 240mm. no 36. Moulded side-pieces with palms and wreaths. *T* 477. (*Longford* 261)

19 p 282 View of the back part of the/Cassina and Serpentine River, in/Chiswick Gardens. Carey sculp. 165 × 265/230 × 355mm. No 3. Later state without credit, Dalton no 40. Frame of studs and ivy tendrils. *T* 478.

20 p 282 View of Chiswick in Middlesex – View of Acton, in Middlesex. Each 125 × 180/345 × 240mm. No 13. Later state 'Peltro sc.', Dalton no 25. Moulded frame with urn and ball ornaments, garlands below. *T* 478.

21 p 282 View of Gunnersbury House, near Ealing in Middlesex,/the Seat of Princess Amelia – View of Wanstead House, on Epping Forest in Essex/the Seat of the Earl of Tilney – A Representation of the Capital Figures of Bethlem/Hospital Gate, London. Each 95 × 165/350 × 245mm. No 23. Later state 'Peltro sc.' Moulded frame with beads, scallop tc. *T* 479.

22 p 282 View of Sion House between Brentford & Isleworth in Middlesex/the Seat of His Grace the Duke of Northumberland – View of Cane Wood the Superb Villa of the Earl of Mansfield/near Highgate in Middlesex. 133 × 175, 133 × 180/350 × 240mm. No 37. Later state credit 'Roberts sc.' added under each subject and frame deleted. Side-pieces with studs, wreaths, husks and palms; divided by scrolls, urn in centre. *T* 484.

23 p 283 View of Hampton Court, from the opposite Shore/of the River Thames – View of Chertsey in Surrey. Each 123 × 175/345 × 235mm. No 27. Moulded side-pieces with palms and wreaths. *T* 502.

24 p 283 View of Twickenham in Middlesex – View of Isleworth, in Middlesex,/from the opposite Shore in Richmond Gardens. Each 130 × 175/350 × 240mm. No 9. Later state 'Engr. by Mr Peltro', Dalton no 50. Frames with studs and pendant leaves. *T* 489.

25 p 286 View of the Church of St Pancrass, in Middlesex – View of Hornsey-Church in Middlesex/With the Adjacent Country. Each 130 × 175/350 × 235mm. No 16. Later state 'Lodge sc.', Dalton no 22. Framed in wreaths, husks and scrolls. *T* 486.

26 p 286 View of the Duke of Chandos's Seat at/Southgate in Middlesex – View of Waltham Abbey Church in Essex. Each 120 × 160/360 × 235mm. No 20. Later state 'Roberts sc.', Dalton no 17. Framed with studs and pendants of leaves, wreath tc. *T* 480.

27 p 286 View of Hampstead in Middlesex/taken from the footway in Pond Street – View of Highgate in Middlesex,/taken from Upper Holloway. Each 125 × 170/345 × 220mm. No 22. Frame with studs and pendant leaves.

28 p 452 View of the City of Westminster &c/taken near the Landing Place at Lambeth Palace – View of Windsor in Berkshire, taken to the/Westward from the opposite Shore of the River Thames. Each 130 × 175/350 × 230mm. No 21. Later state 'Lodge sc.' Side-pieces with scrolls, wreaths and husks. *T* 447.

As with the Thornton work Hogg decided to give a second lease of life to existing sheets and plates. The complete text of Walpoole was reissued some ten years after its first appearance with only a few minor alterations and resettings but with a brand new author, named as William Dalton. One of the emendations was to omit the reference on p 233 to the New Fire Office 'incorporated in this present year 1784'; one of the oldest insurance companies, the Phoenix, was substituted. The slightly varied title-page is undated but the frontispiece is dated 22 November 1794. The text was portioned out in 50 instead of 60 Numbers, each accompanied by one or two plates.

The New and Complete English Traveller ... written and compiled from the best authorities, by a Society of Gentlemen.... revised by William Hugh Dalton, Esq.... Enriched and embellished with a ... frontispiece, designed by Riley, and near One Hundred large, grand and superb Views. London: Printed for Alex. Hogg, No 16 Paternoster Row.

Folio, about 380 × 245mm.   (1794)

COLLATION Title-page; pp iii-iv, preface; pp v-vi, introduction; pp 7–520, New and Complete English Traveller, directions to binder (p 520); index (4pp); list of subscribers (4pp).

The pretentious titled allegorical frontispiece is drawn by Riley and engraved by Scott. Of a total of 70 plates 21 are of London views, 18 of them being Walpoole plates (1–2,4–6,8–11,13,15–17, 19–20,24–

6) bound usually facing the same text pages and bearing Hogg's publication-line but no book-title. These are all in their later state with the engraver's credit added, as specified in the above list. The three other plates are as follows:

29 p 24 A View of Greenwich Reach taken from Mr Wells's Dock. Engraved by Mr Graham. 150 × 275/185 × 290mm. No 6.

30 p 24 Greenwich Hospital – Admiralty Office – Chelsea Hospital. Page sc. 90 × 170, 90 × 155, 90 × 170/375 × 240mm. No 44. Moulded frame with corner studs. Later state with credit added. *T* 480. (*Longford* 16(1))

31 p 62 View of the New Bridge at Richmond in Surrey. 165 × 255/200 × 280mm. No 5. Framed with swags and pendants of bays. The stone bridge shown was built 1774–7. (*Gascoigne* 33)

The Guildhall copy of Walpoole looks as if it had been issued between 1783 and the above reprint. It includes the 28 original London plates but of these 11 (1,3, 6–7, 13–15, 21–2, 24, 28) are in the later state with the engravers' credits. The list of illustrators on the title-page has also been slightly amended: Wooding is omitted, Eastgate substituted for Hogg and Smyth substituted for Smith.

63 · BOSWELL'S ANTIQUITIES OF ENGLAND AND WALES* [1786]

From 1773 to 1787 Francis Grose, draughtsman and antiquary, was bringing out his four folio volumes of *The Antiquities of England and Wales* (No 50) in which each engraved plate was accompanied by a short description. This no doubt inspired Hogg to produce a similar work which would enable him to make further use of the plates which had already served in Thornton's *New, Complete, and Universal History* (no 61) and other of his 'Paternoster Row Numbers'. Boswell's *Antiquities* was issued in exactly 100 Numbers of from two to eight pages each. Most were unpaginated, without signatures and only fitfully numbered, so that when the volume was finally assembled the binder had, as best he could, to collate the text pages with the plates listed in the index according to the sequence of the

Numbers. A further confusion was introduced by issuing plates with Numbers whose text made no reference to their subjects and listing them in the index check-list under this erroneous Number with a cross-reference to the correct one. The title-page is undated but there is a frontispiece dated 25 November 1786.

Historical descriptions of New and Elegant Picturesque Views of the Antiquities of England and Wales: Being a Grand Copper-plate Repository of Elegance, Taste, and Entertainment containing a New and Complete Collection of Superb Views of all the most remarkable Ruins and Antient Buildings ... Accompanied by Elegant Letterpress descriptions of the several Places Delineated ... The Whole Forming An Admirable Groupe of Elegant and Delightful Copperplate Prints ... Cheaper than any yet extant ... (than any work of the kind hitherto Published ...) Published under the inspection of Henry Boswell, Esq. F.A.R.S. (By Henry Boswell Esq. F.A.S., Assisted by many Antiquarians ...) Assisted by Robert Hamilton, L.L.D. and other ingenious Gentlemen ... Printed for Alex. Hogg, at the King's Arms, No 16, Paternoster-Row ...

Folio, about 380 × 240mm.   (1786)

COLLATION Title-page (with variant wording); pp iii-iv, preface, signed by H. Boswell; list of subscribers (4pp); pp 1–42 (Nos 16–25, 27), A General History of Antient Castles; other Nos, unpaginated and mostly unnumbered; list of plates (referring them to the Nos with which they were published) (4pp).

The allegorical frontispiece, 'History recording Antiquities', drawn by I. Hamilton and engraved by Noble, is dated but the county maps by Thomas Kitchin and the views carry neither dates nor a book-title. Most of the illustrations consist of two views, sometimes printed together from individual plates, but those issued with the later Numbers crowd up to six small subjects to a plate. The preface claims that all views will be 'engraved by the first Artists with utmost Accuracy' and 'will be published in a detached or promiscuous Way, just as finished by the respective Artists'. This may have been true for some of the subjects: with No 8, for instance, was issued an attractive engraving by T.F. Burney and W. and J. Walker of the iron bridge built over the Severn at Coalbrookdale in 1779. But is is not true of the 17 London subjects which are mainly either copies or plates from Thornton stock. Of the 20 or so engravers employed on the collection as a whole most were also engaged on Thornton; two of them, Record and Sparrow, were also heavily engaged on

Grose's similarly titled volumes (refs below are to the 1783–7 ed, abbreviated G, with vol. and page no). Most Thornton plates are in their later state; they are shown as T.

This was not quite Hogg's final fling with the Thornton plates since he reused five of the historical subjects (5, 22, 26, 34, 106) as illustrations to Edward Barnard's History of England (c 1793).

Publication-lines read: 'Published by Alexr Hogg No 16 Paternoster Row.'

1 No 16 Various Weapons & Implements of War, which have been employed against the/English by different Enemies: Now deposited in the Tower of London. Drawn by Hamilton. Engraved by G. Walker. 247 × 165/325 × 220mm. Moulded frame with chained gorgon mask tc. T 70.

2 No 17 (tm) An Elevation, Plan and History of the Royal Exchange of London. J. Donowell Delin. A. Walker sculp. 320 × 230/330 × 235mm. Originally published 1761. No publication-line. (Crace 22.59)

3 No 23 Lambeth Palace in Surrey. Plate 1 – Plate 2. Ellis direxit. 130 × 180, 130 × 183/350 × 220mm. Credit under each plate. cf with G 5,96.

4 No 24 A New Collection of English Coins ... Accurately taken from the originals from Egbert to Hardicanute. 255 × 170/315 × 220mm. Moulded frame, pendants of oak leaves, urn tc pouring out coins. T 74.

5 No 26 Views of the City Gates as they appeared before they were pulled down, together with the Old Gate at Whitehall & Templebar: Bishopsgate – Cripplegate – Ludgate – Newgate – Moorgate/ – Aldgate – Bridgegate – Aldersgate – Templebar – Whitehallgate. J.G. Wooding sculp. 183 × 335/240 × 365mm. Thin frame festooned and garlanded, swags and husks below. Undated issue. T 392.

6 No 29 North View of Old St Paul's Church after the Spire was destroy'd by Lightning – South View of Old St Paul's Church after the Spire was destroy'd by Lightning – South View of Old St Paul's Church when the Spire was standing. 75 × 160, 70 × 160, 110 × 160/340 × 222mm. With frame deleted. T 246.

7 No 30 (captions above each) View of London Bridge as it appeared before the Houses were Pulled Down – View of London Bridge in its Present State with the Waterworks as viewed from the City Shore – View of Blackfriars Bridge – View of Westminster Bridge. Each 55 × 295/240 × 370mm. T 395.

8–9 Nos 40, 45 A New Collection of English Coins from Edward the Confessor to Richard III (Henry IV to George III). Drawn by Hamilton. Engraved by Thornton. Each 255 × 170/315 × 220mm. Moulded frames, pendants of oak leaves, urns tc pouring out coins. T 74.

10 No 52 An Antient View of part of Cheapside, with the Cross, &c./ as they appeared in the Year 1660 – An exact view of Baynards Castle, formerly/built by Wm Baynard. 138 × 214, 135 × 214/365 × 240mm. Less frame, with 'Wooding sculp' added to each view, later state of *T* 404.

11 No 54 View of Lambeth Palace in Surrey – View of Westminster Abbey & St Margarets Church adjoining. Taylor sculpt. Each 130 × 170/355 × 240mm. Less frame, with credits added to each view, later state of *T* 444.

12 No 63 St Paul's. S. Wale delt. T. Simpson sculpt. 95 × 157/120 × 175mm. S.W. view, with a plate of Oxford Cathedral. cf with Entick's *New and Accurate History and Survey* (no 44) 3, 196.

13 No 84 An Antient View of St James's, Westminster Abbey & Hall &c. from the Village of Charing, now Charing Cross. 153 × 285/225 × 350mm. Refs 1–7. Frame garlanded with flowers, with studs and a scallop tc. *T* 459.

14 No 86 The CharterHouse. 113 × 198/130 × 202mm. Birds-eye view with features labelled thus: 'The Kitchen Garden', 'The Wilderness', 'The Terrass Walk', 'The Bowling Green', 'Part of the Square'. cf with Bowles's *British Views* (1724, no 28), item 22.

15 No 90 St John's Gate in Clerkenwell, Middlesex. Plate 1 – Plate 2. Peltro sculpt. Each 125 × 183/355 × 220. Viewed from E. and W. Credit under each plate.

16 No 98 Royal Palace at Hampton Court – Ely House, London. Each 80 × 100/220 × 350mm. Two of six small subjects. cf Ely House with *G* 3,137.

17 No 99 Bermondsey Abbey in Surrey. 78 × 98/220 × 355mm. One of six small subjects. cf with *G* 5,81.

64 · CARTER'S VIEWS OF ANCIENT BUILDINGS* [1786–93]

John Carter, the son of a Piccadilly marble carver, and a self-taught draughtsman, left school early to work as designer in his father's business. In his sixteenth year, on his father's death in 1764, he obtained work in a surveyor's office and was in due course employed by the publisher Newbery to illustrate the *Builder's Magazine*. His skill came to the notice of the Society of Antiquaries which appointed him as official draughtsman in 1795. Although they had experienced considerable diffi-

culties with him over their commissioning drawings also from Grimm and Schnebbelie, they received him as a Fellow. His major published work is *The Ancient Architecture of England* (2 vols, folio, 1795–1814) in which engravings of specimens are grouped chronologically. He was a pioneer in architectural history and vigorously campaigned over many years in the *Gentleman's Magazine* against the wanton destruction or insensitive restoration of Gothic buildings. These half dozen sextodecimo volumes of *Views of Ancient Buildings* are made up of miniature etchings, chiefly of abbeys, cathedrals, churches and castles. Each volume was published at five shillings sewed and is introduced by a catalogue of the architectural plates it actually contains together with details of his relevant unpublished drawings, as explained in his introduction:

The following views of ancient buildings in England sketch'd in different towns, and engraved by me, commencing 1764 and continued to 1777, forming Vol.l, are what I had the inclination or conveniencey to collect while on the spot. I must observe that I have copied other subjects of antiquity besides views, which will not be introduced engraved here as foreign to the work; but I have placed them in the succession they were taken into my port-folios' forming 'A collection of sketches of every kind of subject relating to the antiquities of this kingdom ...' which I shall set down with the description of the views.

The first volume has an etched title-page decorated with Gothic architecture but the other volumes only half-titles, seemingly in manuscript. The catalogues are printed in letterpress. Vols 3 and 6 contain no London plates.

(*Title-page* pl. 1)

Sextodecimo, 112 × 80mm.   1786,1786,1789–91

COLLATION Vol. 1. Title-page; pp 1–2, index, introduction; pp 3–12, notes on plates; pl. 1–20. Vol. 2. Half-title (MS); p 13, index; pp 14–32, notes on plates; pl. 21–38. Vol. 4. Half-title (MS); p 53, index; pp 54–64, notes on plates; pl. 59–73. Vol. 5. Half-title (MS); p 65, index; pp 66–82, notes on plates; pl. 79–98.

In 1824, seven years after Carter's death, the Pall Mall publisher Jeffery reissued the etchings in four 16mo volumes with an explanatory printed text. He collected all London illustrations together in vol. 3.

Specimens of Gothic Architecture and Ancient Buildings in England; comprised in one hundred and twenty views drawn and engraved by John Carter, F.S.A.... In four volumes. Vol III. London: Printed for Edward Jeffery and Son, Pall Mall ... MDCCCXXIV.

Sextodecimo, 115 × 90mm.   1824

COLLATION   Vol. 1. Title-page; pp v-vii, Account of the Works of Mr Carter; pp ix-xvi, list of plates ('London and its environs' pp xiii-xiv); pp 1–132, Specimens. Vol. 3. Title-page; pp 1–151, Specimens continued.

The 119 small etchings are numbered throughout tr in Roman numerals. Captions, publication-lines and the dates of the original drawings are etched on the plates in Carter's handwriting. Plate-marks have been trimmed off. Only the 18 London subjects, in vols 1,2,4 and 5 are described below. They were republished in 1824 in a sequence numbered 61 to 78. These later state numbers and their facing page numbers are given at the end of each description.

VOL. 1 (with publication-line 'Engrav'd & Pub'd Jany 1786 by J. Carter, Wood St. Westr.')

1 pl.1 (etched title, framed by Gothic arch) Views/of/ Ancient Buildings/in England/Drawn in different Towns and Engrav'd/by John Carter/commencing 1764/Vol.1. (lm) View of the remains of the Gateway and part of the west end of the Abbey, Westminster. Drawn 1785. Engrav'd ... 75 × 65mm. The gateway was taken down in 1776. 1824 ed less title,pl.69,p 55.

2 pl.3 View of the Chapel of St John Baptist ... Abbey of Westminster. Drawn 1766. Engrav'd ... 75 × 62mm. 1824 ed pl. 73,p 69.

3 pl.18 General north east view of Ely palace, Holborn. Drawn 1776. Engrav'd ... 60 × 80mm. 1824 ed pl.64, p 10.

4 pl.19 View in the Undercroft of the chapel of Ely palace, Holborn. Drawn 1776. Engrav'd ... 75 × 62mm. 1824 ed pl. 65, p 16.

5 pl.20 East view behind the altar of St Mary Overy's, Borough Southwark. Drawn 1776. Engrav'd ... 75 × 62mm. 1824 ed pl.77, p 79.

VOL. 2 (with publication-line 'Engrav'd & Pubd April 1st 1786 by J. Carter, Wood St. Westr.')

6 pl.22 North west View of Edward the Confessor's chapel, in Westminster Abbey. Sketch'd 1777. Engrav'd ... 60 × 83mm. 1824 ed pl.75, p 74.

7 pl.23 View in the east Cloister of Westminster Abbey. Sketch'd 1779. Engrav'd ... 75 × 63mm. 1824 ed pl.71,p 61.

8 pl.24 West view in the circular part of the Temple church Fleet street. Sketch'd 1779. Engrav'd ... 75 × 63mm. 1824 ed pl.63,p 8.

9 pl.25 View in the avenue leading into Westminster Hall from Old Palace Yard. Sketch'd 1780. Engrav'd ... 77 × 62mm. 1824 ed pl.74,p 71.

10 pl.37 View of the remains of the South transept of St Bartholomew's the Great Smithfield. Sketch'd 1781. Engrav'd ... 75 × 60mm. 1824 ed pl.61,p 1.

VOL. 4. (with publication-line 'Engrav'd & Pubd Jany 1, 1789 by J. Carter Hamilton St. Hyde Park Corner')

11 pl.59 North view in the inside of an ancient building under/a house adjoining the pump at Aldgate. Sketch'd 1784. Engrav'd ... 73 × 62mm. A vaulted undercroft. 1824 ed pl.66,p 23.

12 pl.60 View of the Tomb of Edward III & the entrance into/Henry VII chapel, in Westminster Abbey. Sketch'd 1784. Engrav'd ... 75 × 60mm. 1824 ed pl.72,p 64.

13 pl.61 View in the nave of Westminster Abbey, during the/Commemoration of Handel. Sketch'd 1784. Engrav'd ... 78 × 63mm. 1824 ed pl.68,p 51.

VOL. 5 (with publication-line 'Engrav'd & Pubd Jany 1st 1791 by J. Carter Hamilton St. Hyde Park Corner')

14 pl.94 South view of Westminster Abbey, taken from Deans Yard. Sketch'd 1785. Engrav'd ... 60 × 80mm. 1824 ed pl.67,p 26.

15 pl.95 View of the Jerusalem Chamber on the south side of the towers of Westminster Abbey. Sketch'd 1785. Engrav'd ... 75 × 62mm. 1824 ed pl.70,p 59.

16 pl.96.1,2 Two Views of the remains of the Bishop of Winchester's Palace, near St Mary Overies Church Southwark: (I) fronting the Thames (II) in the courtyard at the back of do. Sketch'd 1785. Engrav'd ... Each 57 × 40mm. 1824 ed pl.78,p 81.

17 pl.97 North view of the Gate of Bermondsey Monastery, in the Borough, Southwark. Sketch'd 1785. Engrav'd ... 57 × 82mm. 1824 ed pl.76,p 77.

18 pl.98 North-east view of Leaden-hall London. Sketch'd 1785. Engrav'd ... 57 × 82mm. 1824 ed pl.62,p 4.

65 · DE SERRES DE LA TOUR'S LONDRES ET SES ENVIRONS [1788]

This two-volume French equivalent of Dodsley's six-volume *London and its Environs Described* (no 41) was published in Paris anonymously, first in 1788 'Avec Approbation & Privilège du Roi' and in a second edition, without benefit of royalty, in 1790. The first volume contains a general narrative account of inner London while the second, arranged like the Dodsley work in the form of a gazetteer, deals with the suburbs and villages within a 25 mile circuit of the capital, with some notes on the chief provincial cities. The initials on the title-page are accepted as indicating the authorship of (Monsieur) Alphonse de Serres de La Tour.

Londres et ses environs, ou guide des voyageurs, curieux et amateurs dans cette partie de l'Angleterre Qui fait connôitre tout ce qui peut interesser & exciter la curiosité des Voyageurs, des Curieux & des Amateurs de tous les états ... On y a joint les Vues des principaux Edifices & Maisons Royales, & une Carte, gravés en taille-douce. Ouvrage fait à Londres par M.D.S.L. Tome Premier. Londres, Soutwarck & Westminster (Tome Second. Environs de Londres; Notice des Villes commerçantes). A Paris, Chez Buisson, Libraire, Hôtel de Mesgrigny, rue des Poitevins, No. 13. 1788. Avec Approbation & Privilège du Roi (Seconde édition ... A Paris, Chez Buisson, libraire, rue Haute-feuille, no. 20. 1790).

Duodecimo, 160 × 95mm to 170 × 98mm. 1788,1790

COLLATION Vol. 1. Title-page; Avis du Libraire (2pp); pp 1–367, Londres; pp 368–72, contents. Vol. 2. Title-page; pp 1–323, Environs de Londres; contents, royal licence (5pp).

The nine plates fold and are therefore larger and more handsome than those usually found in a duodecimo volume. They are of stock architectural subjects but seem not to be associated with any British prints of the period. Most view the buildings at an unusually oblique angle and include engraved skies and much architectural detail. There is also carefully added staffage, costumed rather in the 1750s than the 1780s. Unfortunately they have no credits or publication-lines. They do, however, include a volume reference tl and a page reference tr and an instruction from the publisher: 'Il faut mettre la Carte Géographique en face de la première page du Tome II. Toutes les autres Planches seront placées aux indications qu'elles portent'.

VOL. 1

1 p 51 L'Abbaye de Westminster. 203 × 225/260 × 260mm. From N.W.

2 p 114 La Cathédrale de St. Paul. 240 × 265/270 × 300mm. From N.W.

3 p 133 L'Hôtel du Lord Maire de Londres. 185 × 198/230 × 215mm. From N.W.

4 p 140 La Bourse Royale. 200 × 208/240 × 230mm. From S.E.

5 p 299 Le Couvent Jardin. 120 × 310/150 × 335mm. N. view of the Covent Garden 'piazzas'.

VOL. 2

6 p 1 (tl) Carte/des Royaumes/d'Angleterre, d'Ecosse/ et d'Irlande/d'après les dernières Observations. 335 × 228/350 × 245mm.

7 p 54 L'Hôpital Royal des Invalides à Chelsea. 125 × 305/150 × 330mm. From the river. (*Longford* 8)

8 p 106 L'Hôpital de Greenwich du côté de la rivière. 130 × 330/155 × 345mm.

9 p 128 Le Palais Royal de Hampton Court. 135 × 235/155 × 245mm.

10 p 249 Le Palais Royal de Windsor Castle. 135 × 312/160 × 330mm. From the river.

66 · DECREMPS'S LE PARISIEN A LONDRES [1789]

This book, published from Amsterdam in the year of the French Revolution, is by Henri Decremps, born in 1746 and educated at Toulouse. He afterwards made for Paris but as the city did not come up to his expectations he armed himself with a stout stick, a water bottle and a writing case and set out on a prolonged walking tour. In his journeying he visited Germany, Holland and England, keeping a travel diary of anything he found worthy of note. During his stay in London he learned English and started giving lessons in astronomy but his revolutionary fervour came to the notice of the authorities and he was forced to quit the country in 1793. He then specialized in the occult.

Le Parisien a Londres, ou avis aux Français qui vont en Angleterre, contenant le parallèle des deux plus grandes villes de l'Europe, avec six planches et le plan de Londres. Par M.Decremps (epigraph) Première Partie (Seconde Partie). Amsterdam, et se trouve a Paris, Chez Maradan, Libraire, rue des Noyers, No. 33, 1789.

Duodecimo, 160 × 100mm. 1789

COLLATION Pt 1. Title-page; half-title; pp 1–12, preface; pp 13–215, Le Parisien; pp 215–16, contents. Pt 2. Title-page; half-title; pp 1–168, Le Parisien continued; pp 169–70, contents.

The illustrations consist of small line-engravings, crude generalizations of views in current prints. They are unnumbered and without credits or publication-lines.

PART 1

1 p 44 (tl) Plan/de Londres/Contenant/Les Rues et les Places/Principales. 320 × 445/335 × 455mm. (*Darlington and Howgego* 148)

2 p 128 La Cathédrale de St Paul 75 × 135/95 × 158mm. N.W. view.

3 p 214 L'Hôpital de Greenwich du côté de la rivière. 75 × 135/95 × 160mm.

4 p 214 Le Palais Royal de Windsor Castle. 75 × 138/95 × 160mm. View from river.

PART 2

5 p 129 Le Pont de Westminster. 75 × 135/95 × 160mm.

6 p 166 L'hôpital Royal des Invalides, à Chelsea. 75 × 135/90 × 160mm. View from river. (*Longford* 8(1))

7 p 166 La Bourse Royale. 75 × 135/95 × 160mm.

---

67 · PENNANT'S LONDON [1790]

Thomas Pennant (1726–98) of Downing in Flintshire is more noted as a naturalist and a traveller than as an historian. His zoological works won the respect of Cuvier and Buffon, he corresponded with Linnaeus, and his *Tour in Scotland* (1769) was praised by Dr Johnson. In all his writings he expressed himself clearly and well, however, and when after some 20 years of regular visits to London, with perambulations notebook in hand, he produced an account or history of London much more palatable then the usual antiquarian stodge it was an immediate success and ran into several editions. In his dual role as a writer of books on natural history and travel he was very much concerned with the quality of the engravings illustrating them; towards the end of his career he reckoned that no fewer than 802 had been prepared under his supervision. To ensure authenticity he encouraged and took with him on his tours a self-taught Welsh water-colourist, Moses Griffith, whose job it was to make sketches of the scenery for reproduction by engravers.

In this book the plates by Griffith, John Carter and Peter Mazell are few and, in the light of the author's special interest in the subject, somewhat disappointing. Nonetheless it is a landmark in the history of London illustration simply because it became a magnet attracting to itself hundreds of water-colours and thousands of prints and even whole volumes of engravings, such as those of J.T. Smith (nos 70 and 98) and J.P. Malcolm (no 82), as illustrative material and set a fashion which continued for three decades. It was the progenitor of innumerable interleavings, ranging from those glorified Regency scrapbooks in one or two volumes which quite often still appear in the sale-room to the more splendid diversions of the wealthy such as the 14 volume Crowle Pennant in the British Museum which is an art collection in its own right, the Soane six-volume Pennant acquired by the architect after its compiler, the banker Henry Fauntleroy, had been hanged for forgery, and a twentieth century progeny in the British Museum 'Marx' Pennant whose 12 sumptuous volumes include water-colours from Pennant's own collection.

For Pennant was himself an avid collector of prints and drawings and a rabid grangerizer. In his *History of the Parishes of Whiteford and Holywell* (1896) he confesses: 'My own labours might fill an ordinary book-room; many of them receive considerable value from the smaller drawings and prints with which they are illustrated on the margins, as well as by the larger intermixed with the leaves'.

His magpie instinct is described by Eiluned Rees and G. Walter ('The Library of Thomas Pennant', *The Library* ser 5, vol.25, 1970):

A typical entry in the Sotheby Catalogue (of the chief portion of the ... library formed at Downing Flintshire, by ... Thomas Pennant, 1913) reads: 'British Topography. 4000 engravings in 11 portfolios'. Pennant, it seems, collected prints with all the ardour he put into book collection. Much of this activity was directed towards his hobby of grangerizing books, and the introduction to the Christie sale catalogue of 1938 makes a fair comment in stating 'it would appear that he hoped in his declining years, to out-grangerize even the Reverend Mr. Granger.

In 1819, when the fever of pennantizing was at its height, Richard Triphook, a bookseller of 23 Old Bond Street, issued a little prospectus charmingly printed by Charles Whittingham for what he described as 'A splendid and unique illustration of Pennant's London'. Beginning with a patriotic tribute to the capital, he continues:

Of such a city it must be interesting to trace the progress of its advancement ... and this can only be done by means of Maps, Plans and Prints ... A vast collection of these is hereby announced which may be regarded as a *library* of topographical and antiquarian information ... and is now offered to the *public* as the most comprehensive and valuable *Illustration of London* ever yet collected, and arranged ... The work when bound will constitute *twenty-four volumes in atlas folio*; but as the whole is in loose sheets and classed in appropriate folios, the possessor may please himself in making any arrangement he may choose. Although the illustrations are so very numerous, amounting to more than *three thousand prints and drawings*, the work is susceptible of great additions. Hence the purchaser has the option of either binding it in its present state, or augmenting its embellishments to almost any extent. In general terms it may be said to consist of maps, plans, portraits, views, armorial bearings, fragments of antiquity &c....

The topographical prints comprehend, Inigo Jones's Series illustrative of Whitehall:- Hollar's View of Old St Paul's:- Dart's Monuments of Westminster Abbey:- Pyne's Tapestry of the House of Lords:- Smith's Etchings of London and Westminster:- Britton's Henry the Seventh's Chapel, Temple Church and Hall:- Malton's Views:- Daniel's Panoramic Views of London, the Docks and Bridges ...

The Topographical and Antiquarian Gallery, is also accompanied by its appropriate Catalogue Raisonnée; each calculated to elucidate the other, impart knowledge and afford amusement to the possessor. The justly celebrated copy of *Pennant's Illustrated London* presented by Mr. Crowle to the British Museum, has immortalized his name, and rendered it noted in the annals of illustrated topography: but the work, now announced for sale, is admitted by many persons of acknowledged taste and judgement to be every way superior to that admired collection.

Sotheby's catalogue of a sale on 25 February 1822 describes a 'valuable and choice collection of prints and drawings, illustrative of Pennant's History of London, the property of a gentleman, collected at considerable expence and with the utmost care and assiduity'. This was perhaps the property of one of Mr Triphook's customers who stayed the course for only half of the 24 'atlas folios'. It included a copy of the fourth edition text of 1805 'interlined wherever there are Prints of the Persons or Places mentioned', 12 portfolios lettered 'Pennant's London Illustrated' and 463 lots of topographical prints and portraits. Using the original book as a subject index (or 'catalogue raisonnée') was decidedly a cheaper and less time-consuming method for the collector than grangerizing page by page.

Pennant's text was first published by Robert Faulder in 1790, to be followed in the next year by another quarto edition with the title altered from *Of London* to *Some Account of London*. Also in 1791 was published in Dublin a so-called third edition in octavo but Faulder's own third edition came out in quarto in 1793, and was extra-illustrated by Charles Crowle into the famous 14 volume set with specially printed title-pages, *Some Account of London, by Pennant. Illustrated with Portraits, Views, Plans &c &c &c. MDCCCI*. The posthumous fourth edition appeared in 1805, a quarto with some copies printed on Large Paper, and provided the standard text for many pennantizers, including Fauntleroy. From now on this virus was so active that, to give booksellers an excuse for selling their customers any print that could conceivably be associated with Pennant's text, it was thought worthwhile in 1814 to publish separately a 62 page index:

A copious Index to Pennant's Account of London, arranged in strict alphabetical order: containing the names of every person and place mentioned in that popular work, with references to every circumstance of importance. By Thomas Downes. London, Printed for Taylor and Hessey, 93 Fleet Street, 1814.

Compiled from the fourth edition, it is often found as an adjunct to that text, interleaved, extra-illustrated and bound up into several volumes, each with its own printed title-page. Hard on its heels came a 45 page index, issued in conjunction with an unillustrated and slightly modified reprint of the 1805 text:

The History and Antiquites of London. By Thomas Pennant Esq. A New Edition. With an Appendix and Index. London: Printed for Edward Jeffery, No 11 Pall Mall; By B. McMillan, Bow Street, Covent Garden. 1814.

Quarto, 285 × 225mm. 1814

COLLATION Title-page; advertisement (1 leaf); preface to the 1st ed (1 leaf); pp 1–336, History of London; pp 337–81, index.

This text is also to be found with alternative title-pages. One has the imprint above but reads:

Mr Pennant's History of London, Westminster and Southwark, illustrated with portraits, views, historical prints, medals &c together with an Appendix and Index. Vol.I (II).

Another, also issued for the extra-illustrator, but with no imprint or volume number, reads as follows:

Some Account of London, Westminster, and Southwark: Illustrated with portraits, views, historical prints, medals,

&c. together with an Appendix and Index. By Pennant. Vol. ( ) London, Printed for the Illustrator.

The 'advertisement' contains the following 'apologia':

The quarto edition of Mr. Pennant's History of London being entirely out of print, and the folio extremely rare, I was induced by accidentally seeing an octavo edition printing at Mr M'Millan's to agree with the Publisher of that edition to over-run the work, and print on my own account twenty-five copies in folio and one hundred and seventy-five copies in quarto, and to make an Index and Appendix on an extensive scale, containing much valuable amusing matter omitted by the original author. This edition is printed without any Illustrations or prints whatever: but titles are printed for the purchasers who choose to amuse themselves in the pursuit of illustrating; and an assortment of portraits, views, medals and historical prints, may be had, together or separate at the Publishers No 11 Pall Mall. Oct. 10, 1814.

Yet another plain reprint, with an 1826 watermark, survives in the Society of Antiquaries Library in the form of two extra-illustrated volumes:

Some Account of London, Westminster and Southwark: illustrated with numerous views of houses, monuments, statues and other curious remains & antiquities; historical prints, and portraits of kings, queens, princes, nobility, statesmen, and remarkable characters together with an appendix and index. By Pennant. Vol. ( ) London, Printed for the Illustrator.

Quarto, 300 × 240mm.   nd

COLLATION Title-page; pp 1–424, Some Account of London; pp 425–33, appendix; pp 435–42, index.

No doubt other reprints survive from this age of printselling euphoria: neutral texts, free from prefabricated plates; a virgin field for the creative extra-illustrator or for the less ambitious with their 'do-it-yourself' kits from the booksellers.

The following editions were published with illustrations:

(engr title only) Of/London (trophy described below)/London./Printed for Robt. Faulder, No. 42, New Bond Street./MDCCXC.

Quarto, 240 × 190mm.   1790

COLLATION Title-page; pp iii–vi, advertisement dated 1 March 1790; directions to binder (1 leaf); pp 1–428, Of London; pp 429–39, appendix; index (8pp).

(engr title) Some Account/of/London;/Second edition (trophy as in 1st ed)/London. Printed for Robt. Faulder, No. 42, New Bond Street./MDCCXCI.

Quarto, 230 × 185mm.   1791

COLLATION Title-page; pp iii-vi, advertisement; directions to binder (1 leaf); pp 1–468, Some Account of London; pp 469–79, appendix; index (9pp).

(engr title) Some Account/of/London:/Third edition (trophy as in 1st ed)/London./Printed for Robt. Faulder, No. 42, New Bond Street./MDCCXCIII.

Quarto, 240 × 190mm.   1793

COLLATION Title-page; pp iii-vi, advertisement; directions to binder (1 leaf); pp 1–492, Some Account of London; pp 493–502, appendix; index (9pp).

Some Account of London: By Thomas Pennant, Esq. The Fourth edition/with considerable additions. Printed for Robert Faulder, New Bond Street by R. Taylor and Co. 38, Shoe Lane, Fleet Street, 1805.
(engr title) Some Account/of/London;/Fourth edition (trophy as in 1st ed)/London./Printed for Robt. Faulder, No. 42, New Bond Street./MDCCCV.

Quarto, 290 × 230mm. (Large Paper 525 × 365mm)
                                                       1805

COLLATION Title-page; engr title; pp v-viii, itinerary; pp1–635, Some Account of London; pp 639–48, appendix; pp 649–60, index.

An engraved title-page and 12 plates in the first edition are arranged to face the pages designated in the check-list which also notes that items 6–10 and 13 were drawn and etched by John Carter. A map and two further plates by Peter Mazell were added in the second edition and the map and one of the extra plates also accompanies Pennant's *Additions and Corrections to the First Edition* (54pp) published by Faulder in 1791. All 16 were reused in the third and fourth editions, placed to fit the reset texts.

1 (engr title) Of/London (trophy of City regalia and cap of Liberty, 'Domine Dirige Nos') P. Mazell fecit. London./Printed for Robt. Faulder, No 42 New Bond Street./(date). 90 × 120/190 × 160mm.

2 front. Sir Henry Lee, Knt. M. Griffith del. Basire sc. 185 × 155/225 × 170mm.

3 p 98 (Robert Dudley, Earl of Leicester, armed for the Tilt-yard) 265 × 195 pl. mark. No caption and no credits; title from check-list.

4 p 100 (Cabinet of Charles I and part of Old Whitehall) 100 × 210/130 × 230mm. No caption and no credits; title from check-list. Actually St James's Palace gatehouse and the 'German Chapel'.

5 p 103 Old Horse Guards. P. Mazell del. et sculpt. 128 × 190/160 × 220mm. From an oil painting by Hendrick Danckerts, 37" × 67½". (*Burlington Fine Arts Club Catalogue* 1919, 96)

6 p 136 Savoy Hospital. 136. 110 × 140/130 × 163mm.

7 p 191 Ruins of Clerkenwell Church. 100 × 140/130 × 168mm.

8 p 193 St Iohns Gate. 193. 140 × 118/170 × 140mm.

9 p 218 King Charles Ist Porter & Dwarf – Boar in East Cheap. 93 × 70,65 × 110/183 × 128mm. Inn signs.

10 p 219 Sculpture in Pannier Alley. 150 × 93/170 × 108mm.

11 p 221 (Aldersgate and part of the Walls and Towers on each side, taken from a very antient Drawing in the archives of St Bartholomew's; communicated by Dr. Combe) 130 × 405mm pl. mark. No caption and no credits; title from check-list.

12 p 389 Sir Richard Clough Knt. M. Griffith del. Basire sc. 190 × 140/235 × 180mm.

13 p 416 Hall in Crosbie Place. 140 × 120/170 × 140mm. (*Longford* 422)

Extra plates in 2nd ed, republished in 3rd and 4th eds

14 front. Charles the 1st/From an Original Bronze by Bernini/From a Picture by Vandyke. Peter Mazell del. & sculp. 230 × 170mm pl. mark.

15 p 1 (along tm) London and Westminster in the Reign of Queen Elizabeth Anno Dom. 1563. (lm) Londinum Antiqua … Aggas. Neele sculpt No 356 Strand. 195 × 540/215 × 555mm. Refs A-K. After Vertue (no 36), item 62.

16 p 324 (lm) A View of Part of London as it appeared in the Great Fire of 1666/From an original Painting in Painter Stainers Hall. Peter Mazell del. & sculp. 108 × 350/150 × 325mm.

Before describing the fifth edition in octavo two others, both published in 1791, should be mentioned. A German translation by J.H. Wiedmann, *Beschreibung von London*, published in Nuremberg, is illustrated only by a reduced copy of the title-page trophy and by copies of items 9 and 10 between pp 344–5. The other, an octavo published in Dublin, has a distinctly piratical air since all the plates have been re-etched in reduced format by Irish artists. They have been inserted in appropriate places in the reset text and page numbers have been engraved on items 4, 6–7, 9, 13–14.

(*Title-page* pl. 1)

Octavo, 240 × 145mm.   1791

COLLATION Title-page; list of subscribers (8pp); pp iii-iv, advertisement; directions to binder (1 leaf); pp 1–468, Some Account of London; pp 469–79, appendix; index (8pp).

1 (engr title) Some Account/of/London/by Thomas

Pennant (trophy of City regalia) H. Brocas sc./Third Edition./Dublin/Printed for John Archer/1791. 100 × 125/200 × 130mm.

2 front. Charles the 1st/From an Original Bronze by Bernini/From a Picture by Vandyke. H. Brocas sculp. 230 × 135mm pl. mark.

3 p 1 (along tm) London and Westminster in the Reign of Queen Elizabeth, Anno Dom. 1563. (lm) Londinum Antiqua … Aggas. C. Henecy sculp. 190 × 525/220 × 550mm.

4 p 104 Robert Dudley/Earl of Leicester/Armed for the Tiltyard. Page 104. 180 × 115/210 × 130mm.

5 p 104 Sir Hy Lee Knt. H. Brocas sculp. 160 × 120/235 × 140mm.

6 p 106 The Cabinet Room of Charles 1st and part of old Whitehall. Esdall sculp. Page 106. 105 × 190/125 × 215mm.

7 p 110 View of the Old Horse Guards. Esdall sculp. Page 110. 103 × 188/143 × 220mm.

8 p 146 Savoy Hospital. Etch'd by H. Brocas. 98 × 135/130 × 170mm.

9 p 209 St John's Gate. 193. 135 × 115/170 × 130. The copier has absent-mindedly inserted the page number on the original.

10 p 210 Ruins of Clerkenwell Church. Etch'd by H. Brocas. 100 × 133/120 × 170mm.

11 p 235 King Charles 1st Porter and Dwarf – Boar in East Cheap. Etch'd by H. Brocas. 90 × 65,60 × 105/170 × 110mm.

12 p 236 Sculpture in Pannier Alley. Etch'd by H.B. 145 × 90/170 × 110mm.

13 p 237 Aldersgate/And part of the Wall Towers on each side/Engraved from a very Ancient Drawing in the Archives of St Bartholomew's. Page 237. 140 × 230mm pl. mark.

14 p 324 A View of part of London as it appeared in the Great Fire of 1666/From an original Painting in Painter Stainers Hall. Esdall sculp. Page 134. 105 × 210/130 × 230mm.

15 p 423 Sir Richard Clough Knt. H. Brocas sculp. 160 × 115/235 × 145mm.

16 p 449 Hall in Crosbie Place. Etch'd by H. Brocas. 135 × 112/170 × 125mm. (*Longford* 422(1))

The foregoing and Faulder's fifth edition were published in octavo format for reading purposes rather than extra-illustration. So also were the abridgements: by John Wallis in the form of a guidebook with a few illustrations of its own in 1790 and 1795 and, unillustrated, in 1810 and 1814 (no 68), and *The Antiquities of London* printed for J. Coxhead between 1813 and 1818 (no 111) with numerous engravings. The plates in the fifth edition are simply reduced copies of the originals.

Some Account of London: by Thomas Pennant, Esq. The Fifth Edition, with considerable additions. London: Printed for J. Faulder; F.C. and J. Rivington; Wilkie and Robinson; J. Nunn; J. Richardson; Longman and Co.; Cadell and Davies; J. Mawman; J. and A. Arch; R. Baldwin; White, Cochrane, and Co.; J. Booth; and B. Crosby and Co. 1813

Octavo, 210 × 127mm. (also royal octavo)   1813

COLLATION Title-page; engr title-page; pp v-viii, itinerary; pp 1–635, Some Account of London; pp 637–48, appendix; pp 649–60, index.

1 (engr title) Some Account/of/London/Fifth Edition. (rule)/(trophy of City regalia)/London/Printed for J. Faulder, White Cochrane & Co., Longman, Hurst, Rees, Orme & Brown, Cadell & Davies, J. Walker/J. Nunn; J. Booth; R. Baldwin; Wilkie and Robinson; J. Richardson; J. & A. Arch; F.C. & J. Rivington; B. & R. Crosby &c./1813.

2 (tm) London and Westminster in the Reign of Queen Elizabeth, Anno Domini 1563. (bm) Londinum Antiqua. 197 × 533mm. Refs A-K.

3 p 126 Charles the 1st. 110 × 80mm. From the Bernini bust.

4 p 137 Sir Henry Lee Knt. M. Griffith del. C. Heath direxit. 102 × 83mm.

5 p 139 (Robert Dudley, Earl of Leicester, armed for the Tilt-Yard) 140 × 89mm Vignetted.

6 p 143 (Cabinet of Charles I and part of Old Whitehall) 102 × 165mm.

7 p 148 The Old Horse Guards. 102 × 165mm.

8 p 199 Savoy Hospital. 136. 83 × 114mm. Number refers to 1st ed.

9 p 287 St John's Gate. 114 × 95mm.

10 p 289 Ruins of Clerkenwell Church. 102 × 140mm.

11 p 324 King Charles 1st Porter & Dwarf – Boar in East Cheap. 76 × 51, 51 × 83mm.

12 p 325 Sculpture in Pannier Alley. 127 × 76mm.

13 p 327 (Aldersgate and part of the Wall and Towers on each side) 25 × 197mm.

14 p 453 A View of London as it appeared in the Great Fire of 1666/From an original Painting in Painter Stainers Hall. Peter Mazell del. & sculp. 108 × 298/152 × 324mm.

15 p 578 Sir Richard Clough Knt. M. Griffith del. C. Heath direxit. 101 × 70mm.

16 p 612 Hall in Crosby Place. 114 × 95mm. (*Longford* 422(2))

68 · WALLIS'S LONDON [1790]

The impact of Thomas Pennant's *Of London* (no 67) upon later works of description is exemplified in the very year of its publication, when John Wallis, purveyor of prints, children's books, toys and jigsaw puzzles of the Yorick's Head, 16 Ludgate Hill, published an abridgement, rearranging the material in two sections: a brief history followed by a tour with information on the famous buildings seen 'en route'—a general pattern followed by editors of London guidebooks, although with increasing complexity and sophistication, for the next half-century or more. Consonant with the gist of the original text this was illustrated not with a current map or views but with four plates of an antiquarian nature. Three further editions appeared, the second in 1795 resembling the first, and two more, published by Sherwood, Neely & Jones and now entitled *London: being a complete guide to the British capital*, were based on Pennant's fourth edition; but the 1810 edition is unillustrated and the 1814 equipped with only a map.

London: or, an abridgement of the celebrated Mr Pennant's Description of the British Capital, and its Environs. Containing an … account of the most memorable Revolutions in Politics, Historical Events … with Critical Observations on the Public Buildings … and Four capital Plates. By Mr. John Wallis. London: Printed for the Editor, and sold by W. Bentley, No. 22, Fetter Lane, MDCCXC. (Second Edition. London: Printed for H.D. Symonds, No 20 Paternoster Row 1795. Price three shillings, sewed.)

Duodecimo, 180 × 110mm, 167 × 100mm.

1790,1795

COLLATION Title-page; preface (2pp); pp 13–223, London; pp 224–8, addenda.

1 front. (tc in sky) An exact Section of St. Paul's. 170 × 235mm. Section from N. Engraving without borderline; dimensions of the building engr bm.

2 p 24 A View of Lambeth House from the River Thames/Taken at the Revolution. 118 × 240/135 × 242mm. Caption in copperplate script.

3 p 44 A view of Westminster Hall and the Abby in St James's Parke/Taken in 1670. 108 × 253/135 × 260mm. Detail of Westminster Palace, St. Margaret's and Westminster Abbey, probably copied from one of

the many illustrations after Hollar's drawing in the Royal Collection such as Godfrey's in *The Antiquarian Repertory* published in 1776 (no 50), item 5.

4 p 182 Ichnographic Plan of St. Paul's Cathedral. 145 × 290mm. No border-line. 1795 ed p 19.

69 · BIRCH'S DELICES DE LA GRANDE BRETAGNE* [1791]

William Birch, born in Warwick in 1755, took up residence in Hampstead and painted enamels which he exhibited at the Royal Academy in 1781 and 1782 and for which he received a Society of Arts medal in 1785. He was also an etcher of landscape paintings and liberally stippled his work to give it an atmospheric quality, present in the aquatint medium which was then starting to be used for this type of reproduction. Stipple also enabled him to introduce minute detail to which he was accustomed in his trade of enamel painting. The effects he was aiming at (and often obtained) are not unlike the delicate work produced by steel-engravers of the next generation, such as Charles Heath (no 147). He conceived the idea of etching plates of a uniform size after topographical paintings by well-known artists of the day and of eventually publishing them as a 'beautiful Britain' album with brief descriptions of each.

Thirty six were assembled based on work by RAs and others. The former included Gainsborough and Reynolds, Richard Wilson, John Opie, William Hodges, Benjamin West and Philip de Loutherbourg and among non-academicians were Abraham Pether, Philip Reinagle and Rowlandson. The name of Joseph Farington, of whom four paintings were included, is most widely known through his published diaries and aquatint versions of his work, more especially from those executed by J.C. Stadler for Boydell's *History of the River Thames* (no 75). Birch published the volume in 1791, at three guineas in boards or proofs five guineas, with a list of some 250 subscribers, including members of the royal family, dukes, the fifth Earl of Chesterfield, Charles Greville, Horace Walpole, William Beckford and

the Rev Mr Cracherode. Among professional subscribers were the architects Robert Adam and James Wyatt, John Bacon the sculptor and his fellow artists Cosway, Farington, Fuseli, Reynolds, Sandby, Stubbs and Benjamin West. Booksellers and printsellers included his agents, Dilly (24 copies) and Edwards (12 copies), and also Faden, Faulder, Manson, Simco and Wilkinson.

The French title, rather unsuitable to so English a book, was borrowed from the illustrated work by Beeverell published at Leyden in 1707 (no 20).

From his engraving of a painting by Griffier showing the Fire of London, issued with Grose's *Antiquarian Repertory* (no 56, item 9), it appears that Birch had moved by December 1792 to 2 Macclesfield Street, Soho. In 1794 he emigrated to America, painted a portrait of George Washington and died in Philadelphia in 1834.

Délices de La Grande Bretagne. Engraved and Published by William Birch, Enamel Painter, Hampstead-Heath. Sold by Edwards. Pall-Mall; and Dilly, in the Poultry, 1791.

Oblong folio, 205 × 280mm.   1791

COLLATION Title-page; leaves ii-x, British Landscape (an introduction, printed on recto only); contents, list of subscribers (6pp); descriptions (36 leaves printed on recto only and interleaved with 36 plates).

Each stippled view is surrounded by a double frame of etched lines and has a caption in voided italic capitals beneath, followed by credits in copperplate and a publication-line. In the case of nine of the plates published between 1 July and 1 December 1788 and 17 between 1 February and December 1789 this reads: 'Published (date) by Wm. Birch, Hampstead Heath, & sold by T. Thornton Southampton Street, Covt. Garden.', but for those between 1 February and 1 June 1790: 'Published (date) by W. Birch Hampstead Heath.'

Both plates and check-list are unnumbered. A leaf of rice-paper is bound in with each plate to prevent offset.

Details of the views of London and its environs follow, in check-list order.

1 (pl.1) View from Sir Joshua Reynolds's House Richmond Hill./Painted by himself & Engraved by Wm. Birch, Enamel Painter. Published July 1, 1788 by Wm. Birch, Hampstead Heath & sold by T. Thornton, Southampton Strt. Covt. Garden. 83 × 108/154 × 180mm. 'The size of the picture is 3 feet wide by 2 feet

4 inches high, and in Sir Joshua Reynolds's possession'. (*Gascoigne* 23)

2 (pl.4) A View in Kew Gardens,/ Painted by Richard Wilson, R.A. and engraved by W. Birch, Enamel Painter. Publish'd Feby 1 1789 by Wm. Birch Hampstead Heath and sold by T. Thornton, Southampton Strt. Covt. Garden. 88 × 125/160 × 183mm. 'The picture ... measures two feet five inches by one foot seven, and is in the possession of Mr. Opie'.

3 (pl.6) A Meadow Scene at Hampstead, Middlesex./ Painted by W. Robson & engraved by W. Birch, Enamel Painter. Published Feby 1, 1790 by W. Birch, Hampstead Heath. 90 × 130/153 × 178mm.

4 (pl.15) The Garden Front of Kenwood the Seat of the Earl of Mansfied./Painted and engraved by W. Birch, Enamel Painter. Published June 1, 1789 by Wm. Birch, Hampstead Heath, & sold by T. Thornton, Southampton Strt. Covent Garden. 100 × 128/150 × 175mm. 'This picture ... has been favoured by the approbation of Mr. Adams, who has displayed his usual skill in the architecture of the house'.

5 (pl.22) Strawberry Hill/Seat of the Honorable Horace Walpole./Painted by J.C. Barrow, and engraved by W. Birch Enamel Painter. Publish'd Apr. 1, 1790 by Wm. Birch, Hampstead Heath, 102 × 138/150 × 180mm. Joseph Charles Barrow was an RA exhibitor 1789–1802.

6 (pl.23) A View from Mr. Cosway's Breakfast-Room Pall Mall,/with the portrait of Mrs. Cosway./The Landscape Painted by Wm. Hodges, R.A. and the Portrait by Rd. Cosway R.A./& engraved by W. Birch, Enamel Painter. Published Feby. 1, 1789 by Wm. Birch, Hampstead Heath, & sold by T. Thornton, Southampton Strt. Covt. Garden. 88 × 128/150 × 175mm. 'The size of the picture is three feet ten inches wide, by two feet eight high; was painted in the year 1787, and is in Mr. Cosway's possession'. This view from a 'picture window' in Schomberg House surveys Westminster Hall, St Margaret's, the Abbey and St John, Smith Square, with the Mall in the middle distance. The foreground is occupied by the charming Mrs Cosway; no wonder the Prince of Wales was in the habit of creeping in through a private door from Carlton House to the miniaturist's Sunday evening receptions!

7 (pl.24) A View of the Thames, from Rotherhithe Stairs,/during the Frost in 1789./Painted by G:Samuel, & engraved by W: Birch, Enamel Painter. Publish'd Augt. 1789 by Wm. Birch, Hampstead Heath & sold by T. Thornton, Southampton Strt. Covt. Garden. 96 × 135/150 × 175mm. 'The size of the picture is two feet three inches, by one foot eight inches high'. George Samuel was an RA exhibitor 1786–1823.

8 (pl.27) Golders Green,/near Hendon, Middlesex,/ Painted by J. Russel, R.A. & engraved by W. Birch, Enamel Painter. Published Augt. 1, 1789, by Wm. Birch, Hampstead Heath, & sold by T. Thornton Southampton Street, Covent Garden. 87 × 127/150 × 175mm. 'Mr. Russel has been very happy in giving much effect to this picture in crayons, which is rather an unusual subject for that species of painting ... The size of the picture two feet wide, by one foot and a half high'.

70 · SMITH'S ANTIQUITIES OF LONDON [1791 (–1800)]

John Thomas Smith's father Nathaniel, a printseller at the sign of Rembrandt's Head in May's Buildings, St Martin's Lane had in his youth been apprenticed to the sculptor Roubillac while Joseph Nollekens, a fellow pupil at the Strand drawing school he attended, was apprenticed to the equally eminent Peter Scheemakers. When Nollekens set up on his own he employed Nathaniel as an assistant sculptor and in due course the 12 year old John Thomas was also placed in the Nollekens studio but after three years he abandoned sculpture and went to J.K. Sherwin, the mezzotinter, to learn engraving. By 1784 he found that he could make a living from topographical drawings which he made of Windsor and of London for his patron J.C. Crowle, a keen collector who was later to set the fashion for extra-illustrating copies of Pennant's *Of London* (no 67).

In 1790, when his work was first published, he was settled in Edmonton as a drawing-master and in the following year he embarked on a project which made use of his combined skills as draughtsman and etcher, the *Antiquities of London*. He intended to encourage the new breed of extra-illustrators by supplying them with readily obtainable antiquarian plates and to profit from the drawings he had on hand by selling etchings through his father's print shop. To this end his engraved captions nearly all include page references to the current edition of Pennant, and some to a variety of other works, including Maitland's *History* (no 38), Stow's *Survey* (no 37), Gough's edition of Camden's *Britannia* and Noorthouck's *New History of London* (no 51). That he intended also to build up a self-contained collection is evident from the engraved title-page, issued in January 1791 at the very outset of the series which was not completed until October 1800 when the sales had been transferred from his father's shop to the Pall Mall bookseller John Manson. In marketing his subsequent topographical works he continued catering for both types of purchaser and although they were issued as illustrated texts he never ignored the sales potential of the plates on their own to be used for the illustration of different texts.

Thus few extra-illustrated Pennants are without plates engraved either for this work, for the *Antiquities of Westminster* (1804–8, no 98) or for the *Ancient Topography of London* (1810–15, no 115). The year after the completion of the last named Smith was appointed Keeper of the Prints and Drawings in the British Museum and so found himself in charge of the famous copy of Pennant expanded, with the aid of some 50 of his own water-colours and prints, to 14 volumes and bequested by his former patron J.C. Crowle in 1811. He managed to combine his museum responsibilities with a continuing literary output: *Vagabondiana*, illustrated by his own etchings, came out in 1817 and in 1828 a cantankerous but perceptive biography of his former master, *Nollekens and his Times*. He died in harness in 1833 and left behind him enough material for three posthumous publications.

Most of the plates are a carefully etched record of 'antiquarian' architecture: Gothic gateways and Tudor timbered houses, many seemingly on the point of collapse, and a number of subjects included simply for their quaintness or some local tradition attaching to them. This was clearly his favourite vein since it also runs through the *Antiquities of Westminster* and forms the main theme of *Ancient Topography of London*. Monotony is held at bay, however, by a number of plates in other styles, such as the delicately sketched 'Bayswater Conduit' (item 76), the charming, stippled view of Lambeth Palace from Westminster (item 7) or the atmospheric aquatinted etching of 'Rosamond's Pond' in St James's Park (item 23). A few severely architectural plates of post-Fire buildings hark back to the style of Overton's *Prospects* (no 26) and Benjamin Cole's work for Maitland's *History*, for instance Monmouth House (item 24) and Cleveland House (item 26).

Of a total of 96, 55 plates were published between 11 January 1791 and June 1794 with a publication-line which is uniform, apart from the abbreviation used for 'published' and the inclusion or otherwise of 'No. 18' before 'Great Mays Buildings'. Where only the date is quoted this line may be assumed: 'Pub. (or 'Pubd.') (date) by N. Smith, (No. 18) Great (or 'Gt') Mays Buildings St. Martins Lane.'

Nine further plates (items 8, 13, 16, 41, 48, 73, 95–7), published either on 1 August 1791 or in May or June 1795, are issued from the 'Rembrandt's Head', an alternative for 'No 18'. Ten plates (19, 27, 40, 60, 63, 66–8, 76, 85), published on 10 August 1798, and one (26) published on 26 June 1799, name both father and son: 'Published (date) by N. Smith, Rembrandt's Head, Gt Mays Buildings, St Martin's Lane & I.T. Smith, (No.) 40, Frith Street, Soho.'

The remaining 21 plates (6, 12, 30–1, 34, 36, 39, 42, 50–1, 53–8, 61, 77, 83, 86, 92) were all published between 1 May and 1 October 1800 by one of the booksellers whose names appear on the title-page: 'Published (date) by John Manson (No. 6) Pall Mall.' No plates were issued in either 1796 or 1797.

Complete sets of the prints in their first state are bound in chronological order of issue, unnumbered and without a check-list so that those published on the same date are found in variable sequence. It is for this reason and because it juxtaposes views of the same subject that this listing follows the order of the check-list appended to the later issue in the Guildhall Library (A.5.2, no 27). This must have been put together some time after 1805 as it refers each print to the relevant page of the Pennant fourth edition of that date (abbreviated here as *P*). Where plates in their original state bore a page reference to one of the first three editions of Pennant these have been burnished out in the reissue. Smith also occasionally amends a caption, most noticeably that of Rosamond's Pond (item 23). Apparently all the plates are based on the engraver's own drawings with the exception of the two Christ's Hospital soft-ground etchings by a fellow drawing-master, Benjamin Green (items 44–5), the Lambeth Palace view after Marlow (item 7) and some adaptations of prints by Hollar and others (items 22–4, 27, 29, 49, 74–5, 91).

1a (engr title) Antiquities of London/and environs./ Engraved & Publish'd by J.T. Smith Dedicated to/Sir James Winter Lake, Bart. F.S.A./Containing many Curious/Houses, Monuments & Statues/never before Publish'd, and also from/original drawings/Communicated by several Members of the/Antiquarian Society/ with Remarks & References to the much admired Works of/Mr. Pennant/Stowe, Weaver, Camden, Maitland etc. (rule) London. Pub'd by J. Sewell, Cornhill, R. Faulder, New Bond Street, T. Simco, Great/Queen Street, J. Manson, Dukes Court, St Martin's Lane. Messrs Molteno and/Colnaghi Pall Mall, J.T. Smith, Engraver, Edmonton & Nath. Smith, Antient/Printseller, No 18 Great Mays Buildings, St Martins Lane/Published Jan 18, 1791 According to Act of Parliament. 225 × 180mm pl. mark.

1b (alternative engr title) Antiquities of London/and its Environs: by/John Thomas Smith:/Dedicated to/Sir James Winter Lake, Bart. F.S.A./Containing views of/Houses, Monuments, Statues,/and other curious remains of Antiquity:/engraved from the original subjects and from/original Drawings,/Communicated by several Members of the/Society of Antiquaries:/ With Remarks & References to the Historical Works of/Pennant, Lysons,/Stow, Weaver, Camden, Maitland &c. (swelled rule)/First volume containing 64 Plates. Price £2 2s 0. in Boards./London/Pubd. by T. Sewell, Cornhill, R. Faulder, New Bond Street, T. Simco,/Great Queen Street, J. Manson, Dukes Court, St Martin's Lane, Messrs. Molteno and/Colnaghi, Pall Mall, J.T. Smith, Engraver, Edmonton & Nath. Smith, Antient/Printseller, No. 18 Great Mays Buildings, St Martin's Lane./ Published Jan 18, 1791 According to Act of Parliament. 225 × 180mm pl. mark.

2 London Stone/in Cannon Street ... See Pennant P.4, Maitland P.16, Camden P.371 & Shakespeare's Henry 6, Act 4, Scene 6. Pub. Jany 11 1791. 168 × 133/230 × 180mm. P 3.

3 Part of/London Wall/In the Church-Yard of St Giles Cripplegate.... See Strype's Stow p 10 & Pennants London p 7. Pubd. May 10, 1792. 148 × 165/225 × 175mm. P 6.

4 A Front View of the Watch Tower/Discovered on Ludgate Hill May 1, 1792 ... See Pennants London 3d. Editn. P.199. Published Jany 7, 1793. 180 × 155/228 × 175mm. P 7.

5 London Wall/The fire on Ludgate Hill, May 1, 1792 disclosed this venerable piece of antiquity—See Pennant's London. Pubd. May 10 1792. 175 × 145/225 × 175mm. P 7.

6 Venerable Remains of London-Wall,/in the Church-yard of/St Giles, Cripplegate./ See Stowe, Camden, Howel, Maitland, and Pennant's London 3d. Edit: Published, Septr. 29th 1800, by John Manson, No. 6 Pall Mall. 170 × 150/225 × 175mm. Pennant ed burnished out in later state. P 8.

7 The Archiepiscopal Palace of Lambeth,/From a Picture by Marlow, in the Possession of/Captain Webb ... /Mr. Pennant having given an excellent Account of Lambeth Palace, I will/only add a list of the Archbishops ... Pubd. May 19, 1792. 110 × 150/225 × 178mm. Stipple. P 15.

8 Lollards Prison/Situated on the North Side of Lambeth Palace.... See Dr Ducarels History of Lambeth, No 27 Bibliotheca Britannica, in which a Plan of the Prison is given. Publish'd by J. Nichols, Fleet Street, Printer to the Society of Antiquaries. See Pennant's London, Page 19. Publish'd Augt. 1, 1791 by N. Smith, Rembrandt's Head, Gt. Mays Buildings St Martins Lane. 130 × 170/225 × 175mm. P 17.

9 Pedlar & his Dog./Saint Mary Lambeth.... see Maitland V 2 Page 1387 Bibliotheca Topographica Britannica No. 39 P.30. Pubd. 11 Jan 1791. 180 × 150/230 × 180mm. P 21.

10 St Mary Lambeth/on the North side of the Chancel, is this monument ... Near to this Lyeth Interred the Body of Robert Scott Esqr ... Pubd. 2 April 1791. 160 × 130/230 × 175mm. P 22.

11 The Monument of the Tradescants in the/Church Yard of St Mary Lambeth, with their Portraits, Copied from Hollers Print. See Mr. Lysons Surry p 280, Dr Ducarel's Appx. to the History of Lambeth & Mr. Pennant's London 3 editn. P 28. Publish'd July 15 1793. 200 × 165/225 × 175mm. Pennant ed and page no burnished out in later state. P 23.

12 South Remains of Winchester House/Southwark. Published Septr 29th 1800 by John Manson, Pall Mall. 160 × 130/225 × 175mm. P 40.

13 St Saviours Surthwark/This figure of a Knight Templar .../This Monument ... in memory of Old Overie, father of/Mary Overie ... See Pennant pages 49 & 50, 3d Edit: Pubd. May 30, 1795 by N. Smith, Rembrandts Head, Gt Mays Buildings, St Martins Lane. Each 175 × 55/220 × 175mm. P 41.

14 In St Mary Overies or/St Saviours Southwark. See Pennant's London. Pub. Jan 11, 1791. 170 × 130/225 × 175mm. Wall tablet to William Emerson. P 42.

15 The Gate of the Ancient Abbey, of St. Saviours Bermondsey./Bermondsey Priory was founded 1082 ... See Goughs Camden, page 9 & 27, Strypes Stow, p. 25, Pennant, p. 56, 3d Edit: & Lyson's Surrey, p. 547. Pub. 1 April 1794. 160 × 150/225 × 175mm. P 46.

16 A Specimen of Ancient Buildings./These Houses are Situated on the West side of King Street, Westminster ... Pubd Aug 1, 1791 by N. Smith, Rembrandts Head Gt Mays Buildings St Martins Lane. 145 × 160/225 × 175mm. Caption revised in later state: 'Old houses situate ...' P 50.

17 Camden's monument/Poets Corner, Westminster Abbey. Pubd Aug 1, 1791. 187 × 110/225 × 175mm. Aquatint. P 58.

18 Richard II/From an Original Picture which formerly hung in the Choir of St Peter's Westminster, was in/1744 taken down ... & convey'd to the Jerusalem Chamber, where it now is.... See ... Walpole's Anecdotes, vol. 1, p 41, Strypes Stow, Book VI p 585, Granger, vol. 1, p 15 & Pennant's London, p. 70. Pubd. Octr. 28 1791. 170 × 95/225 × 175mm. Pennant page no burnished out in later state. P 61.

19 Van Duns Almshouses in Petty France, with his Mural monument on the North side of St Margarets Church Westminster. Published Aug 10 1798 by N. Smith, Rembrandt's Head, Gt Mays Buildings, St Martins Lane: & I.T. Smith, No. 40, Frith Street, Soho. 195 × 155/230 × 180mm. *P* 70.

20 James 1st/Taken from a Bronze larger than life over the principal entrance/in Whitehall. Publish'd Jany 1, 1793. 160 × 145/230 × 175mm. *P*. 88.

21 King James the Second/in Privy Gardens … See the Honble Horace Walpole's Anecdotes on Painting &c. vol. 3, p 152 & Mr Pennant's London, p. 108. Pubd. May 13, 1791. 190 × 170/230 × 175mm. Aquatint, Pennant page no burnished out in later state. Grinling Gibbons's statue now outside National Gallery. *P* 92.

22 Old Charing Cross/Copied from a Print … found in a … genealogy published 1602 relative to the Stuart family … See Pennant's London, p. 107. Pubd. May 10, 1792. 175 × 120/225 × 175mm. Pennant page no burnished out in later state. *P* 93.

23 Rosamond's Pond/The South West Corner of Saint James's Park was enriched with this romantic/scene. … This spot was often the receptacle of many unhappy Persons who in the stillness of Evening/Plung'd themselves into Eternity. The Drawing from which this was Engraved was made in 1758. The Pond/was filled up 1770. see Ralph's Critical Review, p 37 & London in Miniature, p 181. Pubd. Augt. 1 1791. 115 × 160/230 × 175mm. In the reissue Smith revised the second sentence of the caption to read: 'but its melancholy/secluded situation, seems to have tempted more persons (especially/young women) to suicide by drowning, than any other place about town …' *P* 95.

24 Monmouth House, Soho Square./Built by the unfortunate Duke of Monmouth … and was taken down/ 1773, and on the site, Bateman's Buildings now stand. Pub. Jan 11, 1791. 187 × 147/240 × 180mm. Attributed to the architect Thomas Archer. *P* 106.

25 St Ann Westminster…. see Frederic's Memoirs of Corsica, Biogral. Dict. V.12 p 148. Moreri last ed. Gent. Mag. & Pennant's London. Pubd. April 2, 1791. 160 × 135/225 × 175mm. Aquatint, showing the monument to Theodore, King of Corsica. *P* 107.

26 Cleveland House/by St James's…. as it/appeared in the original structure in May 1795, since which it has been altered by its present/owner, the Duke of Bridgwater … Publish'd June 26th 1799 by N. Smith, Rembrandt's Head, Gt Mays Buildings, St Martins Lane and I.T. Smith, No 40 Frith Street, Soho. 155 × 170/225 × 175mm. View with miniature plan below showing Berkshire House on whose site Cleveland House was built. Alterations undertaken by James Lewis, 1797. *P* 111.

27 Clarendon House/This view was copied from a rare print in the choice collection of Thomas Allen Esq…. The above section was taken from a map of London … in the possession of John Charles Crowle Esqr. See Clarendon p. 512 and Pennants London 3 edit. Publish'd Aug 10 1798 by N. Smith, Rembrandt's Head, Gt. Mays Buildings, St Martins Lane and I.T. Smith, No 40 Frith Street, Soho. 135 × 160/225 × 170mm. *P* 113.

28 Savoy Prison/Part of the ancient Palace of the Savoy, now used as a Military Prison. See Pennants London 3rd Editn. Publish'd Jany 1 1793. 190 × 170/225 × 175mm. Pennant ed burnished out in later state. *P* 125.

29 Savoy/As it was about the Year 1650, from a very scarce Etching by W. Hollar – As it is at present 1792. … See Strype's Stow & Pennant's London. Pubd. May 10 1792. Each 55 × 90/225 × 175mm. Hollar original 60 × 87mm. *P* 126. (*Hind* 84)

30 Lady Arabella Countess Dowager of Nottingham's/ monument, in the Church of St Mary le Savoy. Publish'd Oct 1, 1800 by John Manson, Pall Mall. 160 × 130/225 × 175mm. *P* 126.

31 An Antient Monument/in the Chancel of St Mary le Savoy. Publish'd Oct 1, 1800 by John Manson, Pall Mall. 160 × 130/225 × 175mm. *P* 126.

32 A Monument/with the old Vestry Door in/St Mary le Savoy. Pub. Jan 11, 1791. 190 × 145/225 × 175mm. Monument of Alicia Steward, died 1572. *P* 127.

33 William Earl of Craven/From a Picture in Craven Buildings … see Granger vol 3, p 210, Pennant p. ( ) Pubd April 2, 1791. 190 × 160/230 × 180mm. *P* 134.

34 Craven House,/Craven Buildings/Drury Lane. See Pennant 3d Edit. Publish'd Septr 29th 1800 by John Manson, No 6 Pall Mall. 150 × 165/225 × 180mm. Pennant ed burnished out in later state. *P* 134.

35 The Old Theatre Drury Lane/This Front which stood in Bridges Street … See Pennant's London. Publish'd June 1 1794. 170 × 125/225 × 175mm. Henry Holland's new Drury Lane had been opened on 12 March 1794. The original theatre had been refronted by Robert Adam, 1775–6. *P* 135.

36 An Antient Monument/of a Bishop/ … in the Temple Church. See Stow, Maitland, and Pennant's London 3d edit. Published Septr 29th 1800 by John Manson, Pall Mall. 120 × 150/225 × 175mm. *P* 140.

37 On the North Wall in the Temple Church. See Strype's Stow p 745 & Pennant's Lond. 3 Edit. p 166. Publish'd May 1 1794. 210 × 170/230 × 180mm. Monument of Richard Martin, Recorder of London, 1618. *P* 140.

38 Plowden's Monument/on the Nave Wall in the Temple Church. In Strype's Stow p 747 vol. 1 & Pennant's London. p. 168 3 Edit. Publish'd June 4, 1794. 205 × 170/225 × 175mm. *P* 140.

39 Lincoln's-Inn Gate/Chancery Lane. See Pennant 3d. Editn. Pubd. June 1st 1800 by John Manson, Pall Mall. 170 × 140/225 × 175mm. *P* 147.

40 The Monument of/Frances Dutchess Dudley/ … in the North Aisle of/St Giles in the Fields. Pennants London 3 Edit. Publish'd Aug 10, 1798 by N. Smith,

Rembrandt's Head, Gt. Mays Buildings, St Martins Lane: and I.T. Smith, No. 40, Frith Street, Soho. 150 × 140/225 × 180mm. *P* 151.

41 The Tombs of Richard Pendrell and George Chapman/in the Church-yard of St Giles in the fields/See Strype's Stow p 80 2 vol. Walpole ... p 269 2 vol: Granger's Biographic History of England p 199, 4 vol. and Pennants London p 180 3d Edit. Pubd. June 16 1795 by N. Smith, Rembrandt's Head, Gt Mays Buildings, St Martins Lane. 225 × 175 pl. mark. *P* 151.

42 Staple's-Inn/Holborn. See Stowe's London, Maitlands London, Weever's Monument, Camden's Britannia & Pennant's London 3rd Edit. Publish'd Septr. 29th 1800 by John Manson, No 6 Pall Mall. 145 × 145/230 × 180mm. Pennant ed burnished out in later state. *P* 158.

43 The Principal Gate of the Priory of St. Bartholomew, Smithfield.... see Strypes Stow Book 3d. Page 714 & Pennants London 3 Editn. P. 199. Publish'd Jany. 1, 1793. 165 × 125/225 × 175mm. Pennant ed and page no burnished out in later state. *P* 167.

44 The West Front of the Mathematical School, Christs Hospital 1775. Benj. Green del & sculp. See Pennants London 3rd Edition. London, Publish'd Jany 1, 1793. Oval, 130 × 153/150 × 174mm. Soft-ground etching. *P* 169.

45 Part of Christs Hospital taken from the Stewards Office 1765. Benjamin Green sculpt. London, Pubd. Jany 1, 1793 ... A view of the Library Founded in 1429 by Richard Whittington. See Pennants London. Oval, 120 × 150/145 × 175mm. Soft ground-etching. *P* 172.

46 Mrs Salmons/Fleet Street. Publish'd June 26 1793. 175 × 145/225 × 180mm. Waxworks exhibition on the N. side of Fleet Street, which moved in 1795 across the way to the house known as 'Prince Henry's Room' next to Inner Temple Gate. *P* 185.

47 Entrance to Mr. Holden's family vault/... St Brides Churchyard. Pub. May 14, 1795 by N. Smith Rembrandts Head, Gt Mays Buildings. 165 × 125/225 × 175mm. *P* 188.

48 These engravings are made from the whole length but mutilated figures of King Lud and his two sons ... Pubd. June 15 1795 by N. Smith Rembrandts Head, Gt Mays Buildings, St Martins Lane. 225 × 175 pl. mark. At St Dunstan in the West. *P* 200.

49 Newgate.... see Elstracks print of Whittington, Stow p. 18, Howell's London, Camden p 311, Maitland, p 18, Noorthucks London p 615, London in Miniature p 218, Ralph's critical Review, p 12 & Pennant's London p 217. Pubd. April 3, 1791. 185 × 135/230 × 180mm. Pennant page no burnished out in later state. Shows the Gate rebuilt 1672 and demolished 1767. *P* 202.

50 Prince Rupert's House/Beech Lane, Barbican. See Pennant's London. London: Pubd. May 1st 1800, by John Manson, Pall Mall. 170 × 145/225 × 175mm. *P* 209.

51 The Queen's Nursery/Golden Lane, Barbican ... See Pennant's London 3d Edit. London: Pubd. May 1st 1800, by John Manson, Pall Mall. 160 × 130/230 × 175mm. *P* 210.

52 Speed's Monument/In the Chancel of St Giles Cripplegate ... see Granger V.2 p 320 & Pennant's London, p 227. Pubd Augt 1, 1791. 130 × 150/230 × 175mm. *P* 211.

53 Barber Surgeon's-Hall/Monkwell Street. See Pennant's 3d. Edit. Published Septr. 29th 1800, by John Manson, No. 6 Pall Mall. 160 × 130/230 × 175mm. *P* 211.

54 Barber Surgeon's Hall/from the Church Yard of St Giles,/Cripplegate. See Stowe, Maitland and Pennant's London 3d Edit. Published Septr. 29th 1800, by John Manson, No. 6 Pall Mall. 155 × 125/225 × 175mm. *P* 212.

55 Sion College/This College is seated over against London Wall, near Cripplegate ... See Strype's Stowe & Pennants London 3 Edit. Publish'd July 20, 1800 by John Manson. 160 × 140/225 × 175mm. Pennant ed burnished out in later state. *P* 215.

56 The Kitchen belonging to/Leathersellers Hall/Demolished 1799. Published Sept 11, 1800 by John Manson, Pall Mall. 165–200 × 140–80/225 × 185mm. *P* 227.

57 The principal or Street entrance to/Leathersellers Hall,/Demolished 1799. Published Sept 11, 1800 by John Manson, Pall Mall. 155–210 × 115–70/225 × 175mm. *P* 227.

58 Remains of a crypt part of the antient priory of Black Nuns/adjoining St Helens Church in Bishopgate Street/... demolish'd in the year 1799. Publish'd July 20, 1800 by John Manson, Pall Mall. 145–90 × 120–65/225 × 175mm. *P* 227.

59 A Curious Pump/in the yard belonging to the Company of Leather Sellers, opposite their Hall. Pubd May 2, 1791. 195 × 160/230 × 180mm. Caption of later issue reads: '... belonging to Leather sellers hall, near Bishopsgate Street'. *P* 228.

60 Old Houses in the Butcher Row/The right hand corner house ... which stood on the east side of St. Clement's lane near Clement's Inn .../was taken down 30 March 1798/ ... Pub. Aug 10, 1798 by N. Smith, Rembrandt's Head, Gt Mays Buildings, St Martins Lane, & I.T. Smith, 40 Frith Street, Soho. 185 × 170/225 × 175mm. *P* 228.

61 White Hart/Bishopsgate Street ... Pubd June 2d 1800 by John Manson, Pall Mall. 160 × 130/225 × 175mm. *P* 229.

62 Duke's Place/The South & Principal Gate of the Ancient Monastery, or Priory of the Holy Trinity ... see Pennant's London 3 Edn. Publish'd Jany 1, 1793. 165 × 150/225 × 175mm. Pennant ed burnished out in later state and caption altered to read: 'The south gates, being now the principal remains of Dukes Place'. *P* 230.

63 Lord Darcie's Monument ... St Botolphs church, Aldgate. Publish'd Aug 10, 1798 by N. Smith, Rembrandt's Head, Gt Mays Buildings, St Martins Lane, & I.T. Smith, 40 Frith Street, Soho. 175 × 125/225 × 175mm. *P* 231.

64 Robert Dow's Monument St Botolph's Aldgate. See Pennant's London last Edition. Publish'd Jany 1, 1793. 140 × 120/225 × 175mm. *P* 231.

65 St Botolph's Bishopsgate without/In the Church Yard this Monument was/Erected to the memory of Coya Shawsware, a Persian Merchant ... buried the 10 of August 1626.... See Strype's Stowe p 424 & Pennants London 2nd Edition, p 206. Pubd. May 10, 1792. 135 × 160/220 × 175mm. Pennant ed and page no burnished out in later state. *P* 232.

66 The Old Fountain in the Minories/(taken down 1793) was formerly an Inn ... Published Aug 10, 1798 by N. Smith, Rembrandt's Head, Gt. Mays Buildings, St Martins Lane & I.T. Smith, 40 Frith Street, Soho. 160 × 130/225 × 175mm. *P* 234.

67 South View of the Bloody Tower. Publish'd Aug 10, 1798 by N. Smith, Rembrandt's Head, Gt Mays Buildings, St Martins Lane & I.T. Smith, No. 40, Frith Street, Soho. 175 × 150/225 × 178mm. Tower of London, gateway only. *P* 243.

68 North, or inside, view of Traitors Gate/being the principal entrance of the Tower of London. Publish'd Aug 10, 1798 by N. Smith, Rembrandt's Head, Gt Mays Buildings, St Martins Lane & I.T. Smith, No. 40, Frith Street, Soho. 195 × 180/230 × 190mm. *P* 243.

69 An Old House which is now standing on Little Tower Hill/This House was erected about the time of Henry VIII ... London Pubd. May 20, 1792. 160 × 130/225 × 175mm. *P* 248.

70 A Curious Gate at Stepney. ... by Tradition called King John's Gate. Pub. Jan 11, 1791. 125 × 190/180 × 230mm. 'King John's Gate', Stepney. *P* 268.

71 Pye Corner Smithfield/The Fire of London 1666 began in Pudding Lane and ended at Pye Corner, Smithfield Where this boy/was put up as a memorial. (in work on boy's statue) This Boy/is/in Memory Put up for/the late Fire of/London/Occasioned by the/Sin of Gluttony/1666. Pub. Jan 11, 1791. 185 × 150/225 × 175mm. Caption of later state reads: '... began in Pudding Lane and ended At an old house at Pye Corner'. Aquatint. *P* 287.

72 Guy Earl of Warwick/From a Basso Relievo in Warwick Lane ... See Speed's Britannia, p 53. Dugdale's Warwickshire, Stow Book 3rd p 193, Camden p 286, 602 & 614, Echhard's History of England, p 36, Maitland p 400 & Pennant's London, p 324. Pubd. April 3rd. 1791. 155 × 135/230 × 175mm. Aquatint. Pennant page no burnished out in later state. *P* 312.

73 Gerards Hall/In Basing lane, Bread Street, Cheapside. See Strype's Stow vol. 1 p. 690 Noorthoucks

London p. 559 and Pennants London 3d edit. p. 409. Pub. May 14, 1795 by N. Smith Rembrandts Head, Gt Mays Buildings, St Martins Lane. 180 × 160/225 × 175mm. *P* 339.

74 Cheapside Cross/Copied from the original Print of the Procession of Mary de Medici on a visit to her Daughter Henrietta Maria.... See Strype's Stow p 553 & 554 & Pennants London. Pubd. May 10 1792. 185 × 168/275 × 175mm. Copied from De la Serre's *Histoire de l'entrée de la Reyne Mère* (no 3), item 9. *P* 349.

75 Cheapside Cross./The 2d. of May 1643 The Cross in Cheapside was pull'd down ... See Pennants London 3d. Editn. Page 481 & 482. Pubd. Apr. 10 1793. 125 × 150/225 × 175mm. Etching in sepia ink with aquatint frame, etched portion 70 × 90mm. Copied from part of a Hollar etching (71 × 92mm) illustrating John Vicars's *A Sight of the Transactions of these latter yeares* (1646, no 4). The long inscription etched around the Cross in the original is here added to the caption in lm. *P* 349. (*Hind* 31)

76 The Conduit, near Bayswater,/in the parish of Paddington, stands in a meadow,/opposite the north side of Kensington Garden ... Stowe, Howell, Pennant's Lond. 3 edit. and Lysons Midd. p 331. Pub. Aug 10, 1798 by N. Smith, Rembrandt's Head, Gt Mays Buildings, St Martins Lane & I.T. Smith, 40, Frith Street, Soho. 160 × 170/225 × 180mm. Delicately etched with Rembrandtesque tree in foreground. *P* 352.

77 Guild-hall Chapel. See Pennants 3d Edit. Published June 4, 1800 by John Manson, Pall Mall. 185 × 145/230 × 175mm. *P* 362.

78 In the Ambulatory belonging to Mercers Chapel ... See Pennant 3rd Editn. p 439. Publish'd July 15 1793. 195 × 168/325 × 180mm. The tomb of Richard Fishborne, died 1625. Pennant ed burnished out in later state. *P* 364.

79 Sir Thomas Gresham/Founder of the Royal Exchange/ and Gresham College. See Pennants London 3rd Editn. P 446, 470, 475, & 477. Publish'd June 10, 1793. 140 × 110/225 × 175mm. *P* 369.

80 In the Church of St Catherine Cree/Lyeth the Body of Sir Nicholas Throckmorton, Knt. See Mr. Lysons Surry P 132 & 133, Strype's Stow, Book 2, P 397 and Pennant's London, 3d edit. P 451. Publish'd June 10, 1793. 155 × 160/225 × 175mm. *P* 373.

81 Stowe's Monument/In the North Aisle of St Andrews Undershaft ... See Strype's Stow, p 14, Maitland, p 1062, Grangier, p 269 & Pennant p 397 & 404. Pubd. Augt 1 1791. 190 × 80/225 × 175mm. *P* 375.

82 John Stowe, Historian & Antiquary/(from his monument in the Church of St Andrew, Undershaft) ... See Granger P 269 & Pennants London p 397. Pubd May 10 1792. 148 × 148/225 × 175mm. Stipple. Pennant page no burnished out in later state. *P* 375.

83 Winchester House,/in Winchester Street,/London

Wall. See Stowe, Maitland and Pennants 3d Edit. Published Septr. 29th 1800, by John Manson, No 6 Pall Mall. 170 × 173/225 × 175mm. *P* 381.

84 Sir Paul Pinders, Lodge in Half Moon Alley,/near his mansion house in Bishopsgate Street ... Pub. Jan 11, 1791. 195 × 145/230 × 180mm. *P* 391.

85 Sir Paul Pindar's Monument/near the Communion table/St Botolph's Bishopsgate. Publish'd Aug 10, 1798 by N. Smith, Rembrandts Head, Gt Mays Buildings, St Martin's Lane & I.T. Smith, 40 Frith Street, Soho. 155 × 110/230 × 180mm. *P* 392.

86 Building at the entrance of Little St. Helen's,/lately a Dissenting Meeting house; demolished in 1799./ Published Sept. 11, 1800 by John Manson Pall Mall. 190 × 160/225 × 175mm. *P* 392.

87 Bancrofts Monument/in the Church of St Helen Bishopsgate Street ... See Strype Stow p. 278, Maitland, p 1289, Pennants London p 476 3d Ed. & Gough's Camden p 30. 2 vol. Publish'd May 20, 1794. 145 × 165/225 × 175mm. Pennant ed and page no burnished out in later state. *P* 394.

88 Sir John Crosby's Monument/in the Church of St Helen Bishopsgate Street. See Strype's Stow p 431 & 435. Maitlands London p 300, Pennant's Lond. 3 Edit p 473 and 476 and Gough's Camden p. 51 vol. 2. Publish'd June 1 1794. 195 × 160/225 × 175mm. *P* 394.

Smith's Views which do not come into Pennant

89 A Basso Relievo of a Gardiner/Against Mr. Holylands Stables Gardiners Lane ... Pubd April 23 1791. 155 × 140/225 × 175mm. Dated 1670 in brickwork.

90 Wood Street Compter/on the east side of Wood Street ... Publish'd Jany 1, 1793. 155 × 160/225 × 175mm. Removed to Giltspur Street in 1791.

91 Bruce Castle, Tottenham, Middlesex. Wolridge pinxit 1686. See Gough's Camden Page 29. Publish'd May 1 1794. 135 × 165/225 × 175mm.

92 The Old Manor House, Hackney ... See Lyson's Environs of London. Publish'd July 20, 1800 by John Manson, Pall Mall. 175 × 160/225 × 175mm.

93 St Pancras in the Fields/On the South Side of the Chancel is this Monument/Samuel Cooper Miniature Painter was born in London in the Year 1609 ... Pubd Augt 1 1791 150 × 95/225 × 175mm. Caption re-engraved in later state: 'Monument of Cooper/the celebrated miniature painter, on the South Side of the Chancel in the Church of/St Pancras in the Fields.'

94 Sir Edward Wynter's Monument/on the South Wall in Battersea Church ... See Strype's Stow p. 740 & Lyson's Survey p. 33. Publish'd May 1 1794. 175 × 140/225 × 175mm.

95 Rectorial House, Newington Butts/(from the South East).... Vide Lysons Surrey p 394 and Gents Magazine Supplt for 1794. Pubd. June 15, 1795 by N. Smith Rembrandt's Head, Gt Mays Buildings, St Martins Lane. 155 × 170/230 × 175mm.

96 Wm Woolletts Tomb/in the Churchyard of St Pancras Middx ... See Strutt's Dictionary of Engravers page 427 2d Vol. and Lyson's Middlesex. Pub May 14, 1795 by N. Smith Rembrandts Head, Gt Mays Buildings, St Martin's Lane. 140 × 110/225 × 175mm.

97 Wm Hogarth's Tomb/In Chiswick Church-yard Middx.... See Walpole ... and River Thames page 136 2 vol. Pubd June 9, 1795 by N. Smith Rembrandts Head Gt Mays Buildings, St Martins Lane. 190 × 170/225 × 175mm. The second ref is to a wood-engraving in Samuel Ireland's *Picturesque Views of the River Thames* (no 71) vol. 2.

71 · IRELAND'S PICTURESQUE VIEWS OF THE THAMES [1792]

Ten years before this book was published the Rev William Gilpin's *Observations on the River Wye*, illustrated with aquatints engraved from sketches he had made on his journey, demonstrated a new mode of travel. It suggested to the reader that instead of conforming with the usual unimaginative, eighteenth century practice of getting across country as quickly and safely as horse or vehicle would permit he should actually look around him, even pause before certain set-piece views which were calculated to give aesthetic pleasure amounting to exaltation. With his *Observations Chiefly Relating to Picturesque Beauty* (1786) he supplied a keyword which crystallized a fashion lasting well into the next century so that, in 1807, Southey (in *Letters from England*) could write:

Within the last thirty years a taste for the picturesque has sprung up;—and a course of summer travelling is now looked upon to be essential as ever a course of spring physic was in old times. While one of the flocks of fashion migrates to the sea-coast, another flies off to the mountains of Wales, to the lakes in the northern provinces, or to Scotland; some to mineralogize, some to botanize, some take views of the country,—all to study the picturesque, a new science for which a new language has been formed and for which the English have discovered a new sense in themselves, which assuredly was not possessed by their fathers.

By 1809 the cult of the Picturesque was so general that William Combe's satire on the reverend schoolmaster and his sketching holidays, 'Dr Syntax's' adventures, illustrated by Rowlandson in

Ackermann's *Poetical Magazine*, took the country by storm. Such ridicule did nothing to stem the fashionable tide, since Ackermann himself, when he later published a series of picture books on rivers, deemed it wise to associate them with the favourite catchword; as witness the *Picturesque Tour of the River Thames* (no 157).

Samuel Ireland, both artist and author of this book, began life in Spitalfields as a weaver but early turned to dealing in prints, acquiring skills both as a draughtsman and engraver; he was awarded a Society of Arts medal in 1760 and submitted a view of Oxford to the Royal Academy in 1784. He made a living etching plates after the Old Masters and Hogarth, engraved portraits, exhibited water-colour drawings of architecture and became an avid, though none too scrupulous, collector of books and pictures. In 1790 he dedicated to Francis Grose a two-volume *Picturesque Tour through Holland, Brabant and Part of France*, illustrated with sketches which he claimed were made 'on the spot'; these were engraved in aquatint by Cornelis Apostool, an Amsterdam painter, engraver and dilettante. His next book, the *Picturesque Views on the Thames*, was also illustrated with his own drawings engraved by Apostool, who by now had settled in London, where he was to spend the years 1791–4 before returning to Holland and eventually becoming director of the Royal Museum in Amsterdam. This was the first of a sequence of four *Picturesque View* books on English rivers, and one on the Inns of Court (no 81), all illustrated with his drawings.

Picturesque Views on the River Thames, from its Source in Gloucestershire to the Nore with Observations on the Public Buildings and other Works of Art in its vicinity. In two volumes. By Samuel Ireland, Author of A Picturesque Tour through Holland, Brabant and Part of France. Vol. I (II). London: Published by T. and J. Egerton, Whitehall. MDCCXCII.

Picturesque Views on the River Thames, from its Source in Gloucestershire to the Nore with Observations on the Public Buildings and other Works of Art in its vicinity. In two volumes. By Samuel Ireland, Author of A Tour through Holland, Brabant &c., Picturesque Views of the Rivers Medway, Avon and Wye: of Graphic Illustrations of Hogarth, and of Picturesque Views of the Inns of Court, &c.&c. Vol. I (II). London; Printed by C. Clarke, Northumberland Court, Strand. Published by T. Egerton, Whitehall. MDCCCI (MDCCCII).

Octavo, 225 × 155mm. (Large Paper 340 × 240mm) 1792, 2nd ed 1801–2

COLLATION Vol. 1. Half-title; title-page; pp v–viii, dedication to Earl Harcourt dated from Norfolk Street, 12 January 1792; pp ix–xiv, preface; pp xv–xvi, list of prints; pp 1–209, Picturesque Views; errata (1 leaf). Vol. 2. Half-title; title-page; pp vii–viii, list of prints; pp 1–258, Picturesque Views continued; errata (1 leaf).

Ireland, in his preface, says:

(The views) are all from the pencil of the author; (except the view of Strawberry-hill, which is from a drawing given to him seven or eight years ago, by his late valuable friend Francis Grose); the principal part of them was taken in the summer of 1790, the other, from sketches made several years since, when the idea of the work first suggested itself in consequence of frequent excursions on this noble river. The engravings are executed by the same artist who was engaged on the former work.

The last remark refers to Apostool whose pleasing aquatint plates were printed in sepia, although copies of both editions survive in which they have been quite skilfully coloured by hand. The drawings on which they are based cannot now stand comparison with those later executed for aquatint engraving by Malton, Farington and Pugin, who were much superior draughtsmen, but at the time of their first publication the soft tones and translucent fluidity of the new medium must have made a welcome change from the formality of the line-engravings in which such subjects had hitherto been depicted. The plates in the first edition are printed on laid paper, although the text is on Whatman wove, but both in the second edition are on wove. Twenty pretty wood-engravings are printed as ornaments in the text.

The plates are unnumbered but listed with the pages they face. Plate-marks are cropped by the binder and work measurements are fairly uniform. Captions are in italic and, apart from the engraved title, there are no credits nor, in the first edition, publication-lines. In the second 'Pub. for S. Ireland May 1, 1799' is to be found on all plates except items 1–2, 4–5, 12, 14, 19–20, 30–1, 37–8, 48, 51, 54 and 56. In the second edition one unlisted plate (item 37a) is bound in, showing Thomas Sandby's short-lived Staines Bridge, opened in March 1797.

VOL. 1

1 (engr title) Picturesque Views/on the/River Thames/ with Observations on the/Works of Art/in its Vicinity/ by/Saml Ireland/Vol.I. C. Apostool f. S.I. invt. London, June 1, 1791. Published by T. & I. Egerton, Whitehall. 185 × 135mm. Vignetted aquatint showing

Thomas Banks's statue of 'Thames' at the entrance to Somerset House, a fisherman with his nets and a river foreground.

2 p 1 Course of River Thames from its source to Maidenhead Bridge. 150 × 225mm. Map, line-engraved.

3 p 1 Thames-head, bridge &c. 110 × 165mm.

4 p 9 Entrance to the Tunnell, leading to Sapperton Hill, Glocestershire. 110 × 165mm.

5 p 23 Eisey-Bridge, Wiltshire. 110 × 165mm.

6 p 26 Kempsford Church &c Glocestershire. 110 × 165mm.

7 p 33 St John's, and the adjoining bridge, across the new cut, near Lechlade, Glocestershire. 110 × 165mm.

8 p 39 Radcote-bridge, Farringdon-hill etc. 110 × 165mm.

9 p 47 New-bridge. 110 × 165mm. 'Oxfordshire' added in 2nd ed.

10 p 48 Stanton Harcourt, Oxfordshire. 110 × 165mm.

11 p 55 Ensham-Bridge, Oxon. 110 × 167mm.

12 p 61 Blenheim Castle. 110 × 165mm.

13 p 71 Remains of Henry the 2ds Palace, as it stood in Woodstock-park in 1714. 110 × 165mm.

14 p 85 Godstow-bridge & remains of the Nunnery. 110 × 165mm.

15 p 89 Magdalen College and Bridge, Oxford. 110 × 165mm.

16 p 113 Christ Church College & South Bridge Oxford. 110 × 165mm.

17 p 115 View of Ifley, near Oxford. 110 × 165mm.

18 p 119 Earl Harcourt's, at Nuneham Courtenay, Oxon. 110 × 165mm.

19 p 131 View at Abingdon Berks. 110 × 165mm.

20 p 138 Culham-bridge, near Abingdon. 110 × 165mm.

21 p 140 Clifton, Oxfordshire. 110 × 167mm.

22 p 143 Shillingford bridge, Berks. 110 × 167mm.

23 p 147 Wallingford bridge &c. 110 × 165mm.

24 p 153 Goreing Oxfordshire. 110 × 165mm.

25 p 159 Caversham-bridge, Oxfordshire. 110 × 165mm.

26 p 169 Sunning-bridge &c Berks. 110 × 165mm.

27 p 179 Henley-bridge, Oxon. 110 × 165mm.

28 p 195 Marlow bridge &c. 112 × 167mm.

29 p 206 Cliefden spring Berks. 110 × 165mm.

VOL. 2

30 (engr title, as for vol. 1, but 'Vol. II')

31 p 1 Course of the River Thames from Maidenhead Bridge to the Nore. 150 × 225mm. Map, line-engraved.

32 p 1 Maidenhead Bridge, Cliefden-Woods, &c. 111 × 165mm.

33 p 8 Windsor Castle. 111 × 165mm.

34 p 16 Herne's Oak, Windsor Park. 111 × 116mm.

35 p 35 Eton College. 111 × 166mm.

36 p 43 South East View of Datchet bridge. 110 × 165mm.

37 p 53 East view of Staines-bridge. 110 × 165mm.

37a New Staines Bridge. 112 × 180mm.

38 p 56 Chertsey bridge &c. 112 × 165mm.

39 p 73 Walton-bridge, Surry. 110 × 165mm.

40 p 81 Hampton Court-bridge &c. 110 × 165mm.

41 p 91 Kingston Surry. 110 × 165mm.

42 p 94 Strawberry hill. 112 × 165mm.

43 p 107 Richmond-bridge. 111 × 166mm. (*Gascoigne* 25)

44 p 127 Kew bridge &c from Strand on the green. 110 × 165mm.

45 p 140 Putney-bridge & Church. 110 × 165mm.

46 p 147 Chelsea. 110 × 165mm. (*Longford* 150)

47 p 155 Chelsea College & Ranelagh-house. 110 × 168mm. (*Longford* 21)

48 p 163 Lambeth Palace &c. 110 × 166mm.

49 p 169 Westminster-bridge Abbey &c. 110 × 168mm. From S. Bank.

50 p 185 Somerset Place. 110 × 165mm. Somerset House.

51 p 187 Design for a bridge near Somerset place by Thos. Sandby Esq. R.A. 110 × 165mm. With covered walks for pedestrians, triumphal arches and domed 'tempiettos'; never executed, but exhibited at the RA, 1781.

52 p 199 Black-friars-bridge &c. 110 × 165mm. From W.

53 p 221 London-bridge &c. 110 × 165mm.

54 p 232 Tower of London. 110 × 165mm. Pool of London with ships.

55 p 239 Greenwich Hospital. 110 × 165mm.

56 p 253 Tilbury Fort. 110 × 165mm.

72 · MALTON'S PICTURESQUE TOUR [1792]

Thomas Malton junior was the son of an architectural draughtsman and writer on perspective who exhibited drawings at the Incorporated Society of

Artists and at the Royal Academy. Malton the younger was placed with the architect James Gandon and admitted to the Royal Academy Schools as an architectural student in 1773, where he was awarded a silver medal in the following year and in 1782 a gold for a theatre design. He was a constant Academy exhibitor, chiefly of views of London streets and buildings, very carefully drawn in Indian ink and tinted; with staffage of elongated, mainly fashionable figures added, it is believed, by Francis Wheatley. He also designed scenery for Covent Garden Theatre and was noted for his drawing-school where the young Turner and Girtin were made to undergo a rigorous course of drawing in perpective and were taught strict accuracy in architectural detail and the art of representing buildings in a convincing way. In a contribution to the 1974 exhibition catalogue *Turner 1775–1851* Andrew Wilton remarks:

The sense of scale which lends such impact to, say, the interior of Ely Cathedral was something which he might have learnt from Thomas Malton, whose aquatints of London buildings display a highly dramatic use of steep perspective in order to achieve grandeur. The low viewpoint and plunging perspective of many architectural views by both Turner and Girtin seem to derive from Malton's example.

An instance of Turner's capacity to convey interior space is his water-colour drawing of Westminster Abbey, dated 1796 (BM: 1958–7–12–402), which may be related to the Abbey interiors Malton had engraved three years earlier for the *Picturesque Tour* (pl.8–10). In 1795 Turner drew York House Watergate (*Turner in the British Museum* 8) from almost the same viewpoint as that adopted by Malton for his pl.28, engraved the same year. Moreover three Girtin water-colours in the British Museum, stylistically dated to 1795, relate to a set of larger London aquatints by Malton of subjects to be included in the *Picturesque Tour* but published some five to ten years earlier and this suggests that copying his drawings was an exercise customarily imposed on his pupils by Malton.

The *Picturesque Tour* is remarkable, if not unique, in that the 100 large plates of which it is composed were all engraved and aquatinted by the artist in person. The secret of the aquatint process, rediscovered in France in 1768 by Le Prince, had crossed the Channel with Charles Greville and in 1774 was passed on to Paul Sandby, who dubbed it

'aquatinta' and applied it to his 24 *Views in Wales* and four *Views of Warwick Castle* published in the three succeeding years. Malton's project was on an altogether larger scale as it was not only the first considerable collection of London topography and architecture engraved in aquatint but also the first large British assembly of such engravings on any topic.

As indicated, it was not indeed his earliest attempt at publishing such a collection. Between May 1781 and June 1787 he had drawn, and aquatinted in grey, a dozen large plates (about 330 × 480/360 × 510mm) of the London scene, a series in all but name. These usually have to be sought individually for they are dispersed by locality in such collections as the Crace, BL Maps (*K. top.* vols 22–6) and the BM 'Marx' Pennant (where they are coloured); a set, however, was sold at Sotheby's in 1947 (Boney Sale, 7–9 October). As precursors of the *Picturesque Tour* it seems appropriate to describe them here, indicating their relationship to the more extensive collection by the abbreviation *PT* and a plate number:

T. Malton delint. & fecit. Publish'd (date) and Sold by T. Malton, No. 8, Carlisle Street, Soho.

A The Royal Academy. May 21st 1781. *PT* 36.

B The Banqueting House. May 21st 1781. *PT* 15.

C The Bank. Octr 1, 1781. *PT* 63, but a much broader view of the S. front, including the tower of St Christopher le Stocks demolished in 1782. (*Bank of England* 20)

D The Royal Exchange. Octr 1, 1781. *PT* 68, published in 1798, but even the staffage is the same. The Girtin water-colour (340 × 390mm) is a similar composition but with different staffage (BM: 1878–12–28–32).

E New Palace Yard. May 28, 1782. *PT* 3. BL Maps: *K. top.* 22.15c is an unsigned water-colour of this subject, about 330 × 480mm.

F Old Palace Yard from Margaret Street. May 28, 1782. *PT* 4.

G The Mansion House. Feby 27, 1783. *PT* 62 of 1798, with similar staffage. The Girtin water-colour (360 × 345mm) shows the portico in the same perspective but allows a broader vista (BM: 1878–12–28–24).

H King Street, Guildhall. Feby 27, 1783. *PT* 58, published in 1798, shows the renewal by George Dance, in 1788–9, of the S. front and the colonnade to the W. of the façade has been replaced by an ordinary brick wall. cf with drawing *Crace* 21.79.

T. Malton fecit. Publish'd (date) by T. Malton, No 6 Conduit Street, Hanover Square.

I St George's Hanover Square. Feby 21, 1787. *PT* 33 similar, but different staffage. The Girtin watercolour (360 × 345mm) uses the same perspective but extends the view to the l. (BM: 1878–12–28–25).

J St Paul's Covent Garden. Feby 21, 1787. *PT* 33 similar, but includes the arcade to the r. of Lord Archer's house and eliminates the objects hanging from the penthouse roof in the foreground.

K Charing Cross. June 4, 1787. *PT* 19 similar, but a chimney is truncated to show off to better advantage the statue of Charles I.

L A View of St Dunstan's Fleet Street. June 4, 1787. *PT* 47 of 1797, with alterations to the staffage and the printseller's shop against the E. wall of the church now in the hands of a silversmith. A version of the larger aquatint lent by Lord Aldenham to the Burlington Fine Arts Club Exhibition of 1919 was described as a 'watercolour on etched outline'.

Surviving water-colours and drawings of other *Picturesque Tour* subjects suggest that Malton's first designs may all have been of this size and were scaled down for aquatinting.

The following proposals were issued in March 1791:

Dedicated (by permission) to his Royal Highness the Prince of Wales. Proposals for publishing, by subscription, A Picturesque Tour through the Cities of London and Westminster, illustrated with the most interesting scenes of all that adorns and dignifies the Metropolis: accurately delineated from the most striking points of view, and executed in aquatinta by T. Malton.

This Work will be completed in Twenty-Four Numbers, making Two Volumes, of the same Superb Quarto Size as Boydell's Shakespeare; each Number to contain Four Views, the Size Twelve Inches by Eight. The Letter-Press will be executed with the utmost Elegance, from an entire new Type by Caslon, Letter-Founder to His Majesty, and printed on a beautiful Vellum Wove Paper.

Price to Subscribers Twelve Shillings each Number, to be paid on delivery; and as no Proof will be sold, Subscribers may depend they will be scrupulously delivered in the Order they are subscribed for.

The First Number will be published by Midsummer next, and a succeeding Number every Three Months till completed. A List of the Subscribers will be printed, and the Price advanced to Non-Subscribers.

A great Number of the finished Drawings, and Specimens of the Engravings, to be seen at Mr Malton's, No 81, Great Tichfield Street where the Names of Subscribers are received.

Subscriptions were in fact received from the King's Library and the Royal Family, the Duke of Norfolk, Lord Melbourne, William Beckford, John Townly and Josiah Wedgwood of Etruria. Fellow architects S.P. Cockerell, Dance, Hakewill, Nash, Soane, Vulliamy and James Wyatt subscribed, and so did fellow artists Benjamin West, PRA, Thomas Lawrence, Nollekens and Richard Westall. The trade was represented by Alderman Boydell, Ackermann, Colnaghi, Molteno and Faden.

The work got off to a slow start, only seven Numbers being published from 1792 to 1795 and thenceforward three or, as promised by the prospectus, four per annum. The first four plates were published on 3 June 1792 and the last on 1 March 1801, a span of nine years in lieu of the six scheduled for completion of the book which apparently ended with an unscheduled twenty-fifth Number. There were no printed title-pages but those engraved for both parts of the work are dated 21 August 1792; both usually carry the address 103 Long Acre, whither Malton moved in 1792, but copies of the first exist with the 81 Titchfield Street address, from which the proposals were issued in 1791.

(*Title-pages* pl. 0,00)

Folio, 410–25 × 310–25mm.   1792

COLLATION Vol. 1. Title-page; engr dedication to the Prince of Wales dated 30 June 1792, with vignette of feathered badge and royal supporters (engr 130 × 230mm, 1 leaf); pp i–ii, list of subscribers; pp iii–iv, introduction; p 1–60, Picturesque Tour. Vol. 2. Title-page; pp 61–112, Picturesque Tour continued, colophon (T. Bensley, Printer, Bolt Ct. Fleet Street, London).

Martin Hardie (*Water-colour painting in Britain* vol. 1.) judges that Malton at his best was:

an accomplished draughtsman, using hard, precise outlines with rigid and mathematical accuracy. The underpainting in a neutral tint gives well-observed indications of light and shade, knitting the different passages together, but the colour is slight and merely gives diversity without suggestion of atmosphere or depth. He does not possess Girtin's power of realising a building, but he does give a faithful portrait of it, without any of that artificial picturesqueness, which for example is at times to be found in Samuel Prout's drawings.

Malton's text does not contain very much in the way of aesthetic criticism but his architectural priorities may be judged from the proportion of plates he devotes to specific buildings: nine to St Paul's Cathedral, seven each to the Abbey and Somerset House, four each to the Adelphi and

Royal Exchange and three to the Bank of England.

The Guildhall Library has an interesting binding of half the plates in outline-etching only, before aquatinting. The British Museum has copies of 37 of the plates in this state, only coloured by hand to serve as a model for the preparation of the aquatint. Reference is made to these outlines, of which 36 are distributed throughout the Crowle Pennant. Original drawings for pl.36 are in the Victoria and Albert Museum and for pl.42 and 52 in the British Museum; all three are larger than the plates derived from them. According to Abbey (204) coloured copies were issued after completion of the Numbers and 'only for one or two special clients'; surely an underestimate. In the Mayson Beeton Collection (Dept of Environment) is a copy with pairs of each plate, coloured and uncoloured, bound together.

The plates in the first volume are numbered tr or tl, thus: 'No. 8', but as the plate-marks have been cropped throughout the book the numbers, which are at the extreme edge, are often gathered into the binding or cut off. After the second title-page the numbers have been centered below the publication-line and are consequently visible. The arrangement of plates, with the exception of pl. 13,20 and 64, roughly follows the chronological order of their publication and, although there are no binder's instructions, each of them is usually bound in approximately the same position in relation to the text. In early issues watermarks appear only in the second half of the work: 'J. WHATMAN 1794'. There are no credits but publication-lines throughout read simply: 'Publish'd (date) by T. Malton'.

VOL. 1

0 (engr title) A/Picturesque Tour/Through the Cities of/London and Westminster,/illustrated/With the most interesting Views, accurately delineated/And executed in Aquatinta/by/Thomas Malton/London. Published Augt. 21st. 1792 /By Thos Malton No. 81 Titchfield Street, Portland Place. Tomkins Scr. Ashby Sculp.

1 p 3 Westminster Bridge. June 30. 1792. 215 × 305mm. From Surrey side. (*Crowle* 3.280)

2 p 4 View on Westminster Bridge. June 30. 1792. 215 × 305mm. (*Crowle* 3.281)

3 p 5 New Palace Yard. June 30. 1792. 215 × 305mm. No 5 of larger views. (*Crowle* 3.158)

4 p 6 View in Margaret Street. June 30. 1792. 215 × 305mm. No 6 of larger views. (*Crowle* 3.159, 258)

5 p 9 Old Palace Yard. Jan 31. 1793. 215 × 302mm.

6 p 10 Deans Yard. Jan. 30. 1793. 217 × 310mm.

7 p 11 North West View of Westminster Abbey. Jan 31. 1793. 215 × 305mm. Water-colour (215 × 305mm) in Museum of London.

8 p 12 Westminster Abbey from the West Entrance. July 30th 1793. 305 × 230mm. (*Crowle* 2.160)

9 p 14 Transept of Westminster Abbey. Aug. 1st 1793. 305 × 230mm. (*Crowle* 2.159)

10 p 10 Part of the Sachristary leading to the Chapel of Henry VII. July 30. 1793. 305 × 230mm. Thus probably in 1st state; later amended to 'Sacristary'. Water-colour (602 × 451mm) in Museum of London. (*Crowle* 2.161)

11 p 18 Henry VII Chapel. Aug. 21st 1793. 305 × 230mm. Publisher unnamed. Parclose of tomb. (*Crowle* 3.18)

12 p 22 North Front of Westminster Abbey. Jan 30. 1793. 215 × 310mm. Publisher unnamed.

13 p 26 Melbourne House, White-Hall. Jan 18th 1797. 218 × 308mm. Portico and domed entrance hall built by Henry Holland, 1787.

14 p 27 Privy Garden. Octr. 30 1794. 215 × 305mm. Whitehall.

15 p 27 White Hall. Octr. 30 1794. 215 × 305mm. No 2 of larger views.

16 p 27 The Horse Guards. Septr. 30th 1794. 215 × 315mm. From Whitehall.

17 p 28 The Parade. Septr. 30th 1794. 215 × 302mm. Horse Guards. (*Crowle* 4.79)

18 p 30 The Admiralty. Feb 25. 1795. 220 × 308mm. (*Crowle* 4.105)

19 p 32 Charing Cross. Feb 25. 1795. 215 × 312mm. No 11 of larger views. (*Crowle* 4.139)

20 p 32 Cockspur Street. Jan 18th 1797. 215 × 305mm. (*Crowle* 4.153)

21 p 33 The Mews. Decr 30th 1794. 302 × 228mm. Outline-etching coloured as aquatint model in BM (1871–12–9–996).

22 p 33 Inside of the Mews. Decr 30th 1794. 302 × 228mm.

23 p 35 St. Martins in the Fields. May 30th 1795. 230 × 302mm. Interior, looking E.

24 p 35 North Front of St. Martins Church. May 16 1795. 305 × 225mm. Pencil, pen and ink drawing (477 × 355mm) in Guildhall Library.

25 p 35 South West View of St. Martins Church. May 16 1795. 305 × 225mm.

26 p 36 Northumberland House. May 30th 1795. 305 × 230mm.

27 p 38 View from Scotland Yard. Decr 15th 1795. 212 × 312mm. On river, looking N.E.

28 p 39 Watergate, York Buildings. Decr 15th 1795. 212 × 302mm. A pencil and water-colour sketch of this

same view (300 × 421mm), by J.M.W. Turner, dated 1795, is in the BM (T.B.XXVII-W).

29 p 41 The Adelphi. June 15 1796. 215 × 305mm. On river, looking S.W. (*Crowle* 5.270)

30 p 42 John Street, Adelphi. Decr 21st 1795. 307 × 230mm. Pencil, pen and ink drawing (460 × 355mm) in Westminster Public Library. (*Crowle* 5.271)

31 p 42 The Adelphi Terrace. Decr 21st 1795. 305 × 230mm.

32 p 43 Adam Street, Adelphi. March 15th 1796. 305 × 230mm. Pencil, pen and ink drawing (450 × 350mm) in Westminster Public Library. (*Crowle* 5.272)

33 p 46 St. Paul's Covent Garden. March 15th 1796. 215 × 305mm. Misnumbered '32'. No 10 of larger views. Water-colour at the Whitworth Gallery, Manchester. (*Crowle* 6.29)

34 p 46 Covent Garden. March 15th 1796. 302 × 230mm. From the end of King Street. Pencil, pen and ink drawing (475 × 355mm) in Westminster Public Library. (*Crowle* 6.31)

35 p 47 Piazza, Covent Garden. March 15th 1796. 215 × 305mm. Of this plate the *Beauties of England and Wales* (no 104; vol. 10, 3b, p 280) says: ' "A great and regular design," says Mr. Malton, "When once carried into execution, ought to be considered as public property. One tasteless occupier of a part of the Piazza has rebuilt the superstructure without the pilasters, the cornice or the dressings of the windows". Mr. Malton, however, in his *Picturesque Tour* has, in honour of the architect, represented the whole as it was executed by him'. (*Crowle* 6.30)

36 p 49 St. Mary's Church and Somerset House in the Strand. Novr 5th 1796. 215 × 307mm. No 1 of larger views. An original drawing (330 × 480mm) in the V & A (1725–1871).

37 p 49 Vestibule, Somerset Place. Novr 5th 1796. 305 × 235mm.

38 p 49 Great Court, Somerset Place. Nov 5th 1796. 218 × 308mm.

39 p 50 North Side of the Great Court, Somerset Place. Novr 5th 1796. 215 × 305mm.

40 p 50 Part of Somerset Place. June 15 1796. 302 × 230mm. The Doric gateway.

41 p 50 Somerset Terrace. June 15 1796. 302 × 225mm.

42 p 51 Somerset Place. June 15 1796. 215 × 302mm. General view from river. Water-colour (300 × 440mm), from same direction but closer, in BM (*Crace* 6.226).

43 p 52 South Front of St. Mary's Church, Strand. Decr. 10th 1796. 308 × 230mm.

44 p 53 Temple Bar. Decr. 10th 1796. 215 × 304mm. From the W. (*Crowle* 6.162)

45 p 56 Inner Temple Court. Decr. 10th 1796. 302 × 225mm. Shows a house built over the Temple Church porch and a bookshop beneath. (*Crowle* 6.189)

46 p 56 Ancient Church of the Knights Templars. Decr. 10th 1796. 305 × 230mm. Interior, the 'round'. (*Crowle* 6.190)

47 p 58 St. Dunstan's Fleet Street. Jan. 18th 1797. 215 × 305mm. No 12 of larger views.

48 p 59 Black Friars Bridge. Jan. 18th 1797. 215 × 305mm. From the W.

VOL. 2

00 (engr title) A/Picturesque Tour/Through the Cities of/London and Westminster,/illustrated/With the most interesting Views, accurately delineated/And executed in Aquatinta/by/Thomas Malton/London. Published Augt. 21st 1792/By Thos. Malton No. 103 Long Acre./Vol. II. Tomkins Scr. Ashby Sculp.

49 p 62 St. Paul's from Ludgate Hill. Augst. 21st. 1797. 350 × 228mm. (*Crowle* 11.91)

50 p 62 West Front of St. Pauls. Jany. 1st. 1798. 318 × 240mm. From S.W.

51 p 63 South Front of St. Pauls. Jany. 1st 1798. 320 × 235mm. With St Martin, Ludgate. Water-colour (602 × 445mm) in Guildhall Art Gallery. (*Crowle* 11.92)

52 p 67 St. Paul's Cathedral from the West Entrance. Augst. 21st 1797. 310 × 228mm. This view, drawn in Indian ink, partly tinted with water-colour, is in the BM; the original is much larger (610 × 475mm) and includes different staffage. (*Crowle* 11.93)

53 p 68 St. Paul's Cathedral. May 22 1798. 248 × 352mm. View down the nave from under the dome. '103 Long Acre' added to publication-line.

54 p 69 Transept of St. Paul's from the North Entrance. Septr. 29th 1797. 305 × 228mm. (*Crowle* 11.94)

55 p 70 The North Front of St. Pauls. May 22 1798. 265 × 355mm.

56 p 71 St. Paul's from Cheapside. Sepr. 29th 1797. 305 × 228mm.

57 p 72 Bow Steeple Cheapside. Jany 1st 1798. 302 × 228mm. Looking E.

58 p73 St. Lawrence's Church & Guild-Hall. Novr. 5th 1798. 218 × 310mm. Sometimes misnumbered '88'. From S.E.

59 p 75 The Mansion House from the Poultry. Novr. 5th 1798. 218 × 308mm.

60 p 75 West Front of the Mansion House. Jany 1st 1798. 300 × 228mm. Water-colour (458 × 353mm) in Museum of London.

61 p 76 St. Stephen's Walbrook. Decr. 15 1798. 318 × 232mm. Interior. (*Crowle* 11.206)

62 p 76 The Mansion House from Cornhill. Decr. 15 1798. 218 × 305mm. No 7 of larger views.

63 p 76 South Front of the Bank. Novr. 5th 1798. 218 × 305mm. (*Crowle* 12.104; *Bank of England* 33–4)

64 p 77 Lothbury Court, Bank. March 1 1801. 215 × 305mm. (*Crowle* 12.105; *Bank of England* 125)

65 p 77 North Front of the Bank. July 31st 1797. 300 × 225mm. (*Crowle* 12.106; *Bank of England* 52)

66 p 78 Arcade of the North Front of the Royal Exchange. July 31st 1797. 305 × 228mm. Includes church of St Christopher le Stocks, demolished in 1781 to make way for the Bank of England. (*Bank of England* 18–19)

67 p 78 The Royal Exchange. Decr. 15 1798. 210 × 300mm. Quadrangle.

68 p 79 South Front of the Royal Exchange. Novr. 5th 1798. 215 × 310mm. No 4 of larger views.

69 p 79 North Front of the Royal Exchange. Decr. 15 1798. 218 × 305mm.

70 p 80 St. Bennet's Fink, Threadneedle Street. Septr. 29th. 1797. 305 × 225mm.

71 p 80 St. Peter le Poor, Broad Street. Septr. 29th 1797. 303 × 223mm.

72 p 80 London Wall. March 31st 1798. 305 × 230mm. With All Hallows Church, built by George Dance junior, 1765.

73 p 81 The East India House. Nov. 30 1799. 215 × 302mm. Designed by Richard Jupp, 1796; completed by Henry Holland, 1800. Misnumbered '33'.

74 p 81 The Monument. March 31st 1798. 305 × 230mm.

75 p 83 London Bridge. May 29th 1799. 215 × 305mm. From the S.W. (*Crowle* 10.40)

76 p 85 The Custom House. May 29th 1799. 215 × 302mm. From the river. (*Crowle* 9.239)

77 p 86 The Tower. May 22nd 1799. 215 × 305mm. From the river. (*Crowle* 9.87)

78 p 87 The Great Court of the Tower. May 22nd 1799. 215 × 305mm. (*Crowle* 9.105)

79 p 89 North Front of Greenwich Hospital. Septr. 2nd 1799. 215 × 305mm.

80 p 89 The Great Court of Greenwich Hospital. Sepr. 2d 1799. 213 × 305mm.

81 p 89 North Front of the Chapel and Hall of Greenwich Hospital. Sepr 2d. 1799. 305 × 228mm.

82 p 91 The Trinity House. Septr. 2d 1799. 215 × 305mm. Built on Tower Hill by Samuel Wyatt, 1793–5.

83 p 93 St. Bartholomew the Greater. May 15th 1800. 305 × 230mm. Interior. Water-colour (460 × 355mm) in Museum of London. (*Crowle* 7.157)

84 p 95 The Sessions House for the County of Middlesex. Novr. 30 1799. 215 × 305mm. On Clerkenwell Green. Built by Thomas Rogers, 1779–82.

85 p 95 Newgate. Novr. 30 1799. 215 × 305mm. Built 1770–8, demolished 1902.

86 p 96 St. George's Bloomsbury. Nov. 30 1799. 300 × 227mm. (*Crowle* 7.80)

87 p 99 Fitzroy Square. May 15th 1800. 217 × 308mm. Built by Robert Adam, 1790–1800.

88 p 100 Portland Place. May 15th 1800. 215 × 308mm. Built by Robert Adam, c 1776–80.

89 p 101 Cavendish Square. July 28 1800. 215 × 305mm.

90 p 102 Hanover Square. July 28 1800. 220 × 308mm.

91 p 103 Grosvenor Square. July 28 1800. 215 × 315mm.

92 p 106 St. George's Hanover Square. July 28 1800. 215 × 305mm. No 9 of larger views. Water-colour (328 × 480mm) in Museum of London.

93 p 106 Uxbridge House. May 15th 1800. 310 × 230mm. Built in Burlington Gardens for the Duke of Queensberry, reconstructed in 1792 by J. Vardy and J. Bonomi as Uxbridge House and became Bank of England Western Branch. Water-colour (320 × 430mm) in Museum of London. (*Bank of England* 212)

94 p 107 St. James's Street, Novr 15 1800. 215 × 302mm. Looking S., with Brooks's Club built by Henry Holland, 1776–8.

95 p 107 Hyde Park Corner. Decr 15 1800. 215 × 315mm. To the r. Apsley House, as designed by Robert Adam for Lord Bathurst, c 1775.

96 p 108 Spencer House. Novr 29 1800. 215 × 305mm. Green Park.

97 p 109 The Queen's Palace. Decr 15 1800. 215 × 308mm.

98 p 109 Chelsea Hospital. Novr 15 1800. 218 × 305mm. (*Longford* 81)

99 p 112 Carlton House. Novr 29 1800. 212 × 302mm. As altered by Henry Holland for the Prince of Wales, 1783–5; demolished 1827–8.

100 p 112 North West View of St Pauls. March 1 1801. 255 × 360mm.

---

73 · PRINCIPAL BUILDINGS IN LONDON [1792–4]

Samuel William Fores, printseller, engraver, book-seller and stationer, set up business in the Strand in 1770 but by 1785 he had moved to 3 Piccadilly, or the 'Caracature Warehouse' as it came to be known because of the large number of prints imitating Gillray and Rowlandson that filled its window, of which Hazlitt said: 'I should suppose there is more drollery and unction in the caricatures in Fores' shop-window than in all the masks of Italy, without exception' (*Sketches and Essays*, 1839, pp 55–6).

Selections of these prints were hired out in portfolios, by the evening, to amuse drawing-room company. In the year of the French Revolution Fores also published from this address a timely *New Guide for Foreigners, to London and Westminster* and soon after this set of views, intended also, no doubt, as souvenirs for foreign visitors.

No text or title-page accompanies them but each of the six plates has below the general caption 'Principal Buildings in London' with a plate number. Four subjects are line-engraved on each plate, with plate-marks varying from 375 × 270mm to 390 × 280mm and each view is in the form of a small roundel of 95mm enclosed in a frame of 175 × 125mm with its caption in the lower segment of the circle and its publication-line at the base of each frame: 'Pub'd (date) by S.W. Fores No 3 Piccadilly'.

The engravings are naively colour-washed, largely in pale blues and pinks with a uniform dove grey for the frames. With the sincerest form of flattery, starting in the succeeding year, Charles Taylor published 24 similar views in *The Temple of Taste* (no 135).

1 Horse Guards from the Park – Buckingham House – Carleton House – Melbourne House. May 21 1792.

2 Mansion House – Foundling Hospital – Admiralty – Royal Exchange. May 21 1792.

3 St Paul's – Somerset Place – Adelphi – Guild Hall. July 2 1792.

4 Lansdown House – Banqueting House/Whitehall – Burlington House – The Bank. Decr. 21 1792. (*Bank of England* 30)

5 Westminster/Bridge – Westminster/Hall – Newgate – Bartholomew/Hospital. Feby 15 1794.

6 Westminster Abbey – India House – The King's Mews – Excise Office. May 1st 1794.

---

74 · THANE'S VIEWS OF ARUNDEL HOUSE [1792]

John Thane, printseller and publisher, dealt in Old Master prints of which he amassed a considerable collection, sold by auction after his death in 1818. Among these were catalogued a few of Hollar's etchings but none of his London views, panoramas or plans which had been in great demand for the extra-illustration of Pennant's *Of London* (no 67), first published in 1790. The three Hollar etchings of Arundel House must certainly have passed through his hands but were rare enough to make it worth his while to commission facsimile engravings of them for publication in a slim quarto two years after Pennant's book. There is no suspicion of forgery since Hollar's characteristic signature was not copied but what is strange is that there is no mention of so illustrious an artist either on Thane's title-page or in his brief introduction to the plates. On the other hand the credits for Adam A. Bierling are copied but transferred from br to bl.

(*Title-page* pl. 1)

Quarto, 355 × 285mm.   1792

COLLATION   Engr title-page; introduction (1 leaf); 3 plates.

1 (engr title) Views of/Arundel House/in the/Strand MDCXLVI – View of London from the Top of Arundel House (75 × 130mm). London/Published by J. Thane, Rupert Street, Haymarket/1792. 230 × 150/262 × 188mm. Hollar's view (*Hind* 81) reproduced inset, eliminating from the sky the caption 'London from ye top of Arundell House' and Hollar's name from the credit.

2 Thomas Howard, Earl of Arundel &c./From Originals by Van Dyck./The Seal & Autograph of the Earl of Arundel & his Son Lord Maltravers, written at Arundel House/From the Original in possession of John Thane. Oval portraits, each 90 × 70/195 × 165mm.

3 The Ground-Plot of Arundel House & Gardens/ … Publish'd March 1, 1792, by J. Thane, Rupert Street, Haymarket. 170 × 190/200 × 205mm.

4a North View of Arundel House in London 1646. Adam A. Bierling delin: London, Pub. by J. Thane, Rupert Street, Haymarket, 1792. 75 × 190mm on pl. with 4b. (*Hind* 82: 'Aula Domus Arrundelianae Londini, Septentrionem versus', 83 × 194mm)

4b South View of Arundel House in London 1646. Adam A. Bierling delin: London, Pub. by J. Thane, Rupert Street, Haymarket, 1792. 75 × 190/200 × 205mm. (*Hind* 83: 'Aula Domus Arrundelianae Meridiem versus', 81 × 194mm)

75 · BOYDELL'S HISTORY OF THE THAMES [1794–6]

Alderman Boydell, the prosperous printseller, who was elected Lord Mayor in 1790, had built up his fortune on the sale of cheap topographical prints engraved by himself. To celebrate his mayoralty he issued a retrospective collection of these line-engravings which includes 30 pleasant views of the Thames from Sunbury to Gravesend, measuring about 240 × 420mm and originally published between 1750 and 1753 at 1s each. Although he was now an entrepreneur and exporter of prints on a large scale he may have had in mind the pleasant sketching trips of his younger days when, in 1792, he decided to publish yet another 'Boydell's Thames', depicting the river in 76 plates from its source to its estuary.

This time, however, he commissioned the drawings from a successful landscape painter, Joseph Farington, a pupil of Richard Wilson who had gained great influence in the councils of the Royal Academy. Twenty years previously the young Farington had been sent by Boydell up to Houghton Hall to draw the paintings for his *Collection of Prints after the most capital Paintings in England* (2 vols, 1782) and in the interval he had engaged himself elsewhere for the two topographical series *Views of the Lakes in Cumberland and Westmorland* (1789) and *Views of Cities and Towns in England* (1790–2), respectively engraved and published by William Byrne.

In spite of the trade recession, and loss of an export market resulting from recent events in France, Boydell had it in mind to extend the scope of the work beyond the Thames and, in the *Gentleman's Magazine* of January 1792, published this advertisement:

Dedicated by Permission to His Majesty—Mr. Alderman Boydell, and Mr. Josiah Boydell, propose to publish by subscription, The Picturesque Views and Scenery of the Thames and Severn, the Forth and the Clyde, from their Sources to the Sea. Drawn by J. Farington, R.A. and intended to illustrate an original History of those Rivers, including all that adorns, dignifies or enriches them and their Vicinities whether of Art of Nature.

This Work will be completed in Five Volumes of the same superb Quarto size as the Shakespeare, and printed on a beautiful Wove Paper. The Letter Press will be executed in the utmost elegance by Mr. Bulmer and Co. with Types by Mr. Martin.

The Literary Part, the Proprietors have every Reason to expect, will contribute its full share towards the completion of their Object; which is to render this Work the first of its Kind that has been published, at any Time, or in any Country.

Each Volume will contain at least Forty Plates, engraved in Aquatints by Mr. Stadler &c. from accurate drawings made by Mr. Farington, of the most beautiful and interesting Parts of the River it records with about Three Hundred pages of Letterpress; and a map, describing the Course of the River.

Subscriptions will be received for the whole Work, or the History of either River, by Messrs Boydell, Shakespeare Gallery, Pall Mall, at No 90, Cheapside and at Mr. Farington's, Upper Charlotte Street, Rathbone-place. The Price to Subscribers will be Five Guineas each Volume; Two Guineas and a half to be paid at the time of subscribing and the Remainder on the Delivery.

The materials for the whole of the Work are almost entirely completed. The History of the Thames and the Forth, which will be first offered to the Publick, are in such a state of Preparation, that the Former will be ready for Delivery very early in the Year 1793, and the latter will shortly follow. The Histories of the Severn and the Clyde are also in great Forwardness, and will be ready for Publication, as it is hoped, in the Spring of the year 1794....

Although the printer and the type-caster are mentioned by name the prospectus is silent on the identity of the author of the 'Literary Part', William Combe, who was later to perform a similar service for several of Ackermann's illustrated publications.

In the event the Severn, Forth and Clyde were abandoned but *The Thames* proved a great success. It is advertised in the Boydell catalogue of December 1810 as 'Uniform in size with the Shakespeare and Milton, 10 guineas in boards. The same Work, with the plates printed in bistre, 10 guineas'. Surprisingly, sets with plates coloured in imitation of the original drawings cost no more than the monochrome edition. Sets exist watermarked as late as 1815 and, according to Tooley, the work was reissued in 1831–4. The two volumes were offered by Bohn, in his 1841 catalogue, at £3 13s 6d bound in calf or £5 5s in red morocco. Sets which include the general title-page 'An History of the Principal Rivers', followed by a dedication to George III, are likely to be of the first printing since these were omitted from the binding when the larger project was cancelled.

An History of the Principal Rivers of Great Britain. Vol. I (II). London: Printed by W. Bulmer and Co., Shakespeare Printing-Office for John and Josiah Boydell; from the Types of W. Martin. 1794 (1796).

An History of the River Thames. Vol. I. (II). London: Printed by W. Bulmer and Co. for John and Josiah Boydell. 1794 (1796).

Folio, 415 × 315mm.   1794–6

COLLATION   Vol. 1. General title-page; dedication to George III (1 leaf); History of the River Thames title-page; dedication to Horace Walpole (1 leaf); pp ix–xiv, preface; contents (1 leaf); list of plates (1 leaf); pp 1–312, History. Vol. 2. General title-page; History of Thames title-page; contents (1 leaf); list of plates (1 leaf); pp 1–294, History continued.

The medium chosen for reproducing the drawings was not the superlatively finished line-engraving of the Woollett school, generally associated with Boydell and his versions of Old Master oil-paintings, but a combination of line-etching and aquatint. This was well suited to Farington's water-colours which were first drawn in diluted brown or black ink, then washed over with a silver-grey tint to convey light and shade, and finished with thin, slight washes of pale colours. Though not great art, they are pleasing examples of the topographical work of the period: panoramic views with valleys and rolling hills receding to blue horizons, in composition and colouring not unlike Rowlandson's rural landscapes.

Also they are executed with an eye to the reproduction process which, literally, recreated them since it involved making a plate, firmly etched, for printing the outlines in grey or sepia and aquatinting in shades of grey, for tone, and blue also, on occasion, for skies. This reduced the area to be covered by the colourists who could concentrate on applying wash within the printed outlines in the reticent shades prescribed, of green, ochre, gamboge, pink, blue and mauve. Blue-printed aquatint skies may be observed on items 4,29–31,33,37,39–40,53,55,62–4,67, 69 and 76.

For Joseph Stadler, the German engraver employed to carry out the whole of the work, this was an opportunity to demonstrate his interpretative skill and to make a début in the growth industry of colour-plate books. This was to bear fruit in the following century when he was constantly employed by his compatriot, Rudolf Ackermann, both in book illustration and in the engraving of large, decora-

tive, aquatinted pictures. The publication of this work coincides with that of another early aquatint book on London, Malton's *Picturesque Tour* (no 72), but its rural subjects, elaborately presented, surrounded by frames aquatinted or colour-washed, and the highly professional engraving, brought it the greater popularity.

Captions are engraved in hatched italic capitals, bc, within the tinted bands of the frames. Credits are uniformly 'J. Farington R.A. delt. J.C. Stadler sculpt.' Pubication-lines read: 'Pub. (Pubd., Publish'd, date) by J. & J. Boydell, Shakespeare Gally. Pall Mall & (No. 90) Cheapside (London)'. The date throughout vol. 1 is 'June 1, 1793' but in vol. 2 it is also both 'June 1, 1795' and 'June 1, 1796' and is therefore quoted. The dimensions given are those of the views themselves and those of the aquatint frames, excluding the outer rules; plate-marks have been cropped by the binder. Plates are unnumbered.

0   front. Tamesis. J. Parker sculpt./from an original/by/ The Honble M. Damer./Publish'd … Jan. 1. 1796. J. Girtin sculpt. Oval, 180 × 130mm. Line-engr of mask of Father Thames. In later eds opposite p 255.

00 p 1 (l.) The Course/of the/River Thames from its Source/to the/Sea/Engraved for Boydell's Rivers./By/ John Cooke/of/Hendon. Publish'd June 1, 1795. 2sh. Each 310 × 595mm. The source to Barnes – Barnes to the estuary.

VOL. 1 (aquatint plates, Thames Head to Hampton Court)

1   p 2 Thames Head. 190 × 298,202 × 310mm.

2   p 4 Bridge in Kemble Meadow. 190 × 298,205 × 313mm.

3   p 6 Ewen Mill. 190 × 300,203 × 310mm.

4   p 34 Cirencester. 193 × 300,208 × 315mm.

5   p 38 Cricklade. 190 × 300,205 × 315mm.

6   p 48 Junction of the Thames and Canal near Lechlade. 194 × 298,208 × 315mm.

7   p 52 Buscot Park. 185 × 300,205 × 315mm.

8   p 66 Stanton Harcourt. 190 × 300,205 × 315mm.

9   p 76 Langley Ware. 190 × 300,205 × 312mm.

10 p 86 Blenheim. 185 × 300,202 × 315mm. Bridge over lake on r.

11 p 88 Blenheim. 190 × 298,205 × 315mm. Bridge over lake on l.

12 p 90 View at Blenheim. 190 × 298,205 × 315mm.

13 p 118 Oxford. 200 × 303,218 × 318mm.

14 p 120 View of High-Street, in Oxford. 200 × 305,215 × 318mm.

70 p 266 Gravesend. June 1, 1795. 198 × 300,215 × 318mm.

71 p 270 Penshurst. June 1, 1795. 190 × 300,205 × 315mm.

72 p 274 Tunbridge Castle. June 1, 1795. 190 × 300,208 × 315mm.

73 p 276 Maidstone, June 1, 1795. 192 × 300,210 × 315mm.

74 p 284 Rochester Bridge and Castle. June 1, 1795. 195 × 302,215 × 320mm.

75 p 286 Rochester and Chatham. June 1, 1795. 305 × 525,328 × 545mm.

76 p 290 View from Upnor towards Sheerness. June 1, 1795. 198 × 300,212 × 320mm.

76 · COLNAGHI'S SELECT VIEWS [1795–1800]

On 1 April 1795 Colnaghi & Co of 132 Pall Mall published a first batch of four views of Westminster and a second batch on 1 April of the following year. All but one were etched by Thomas Medland, topographical painter and engraver working in line and aquatint who was to be appointed drawing-master at the East India Company's newly founded Haileybury College. He had contributed plates to the *Copper-plate Magazine* and to many books including Farington's *Views of the Lakes* (1789) and Stothard's *Robinson Crusoe* (1790) and became an occasional water-colour exhibitor at the Royal Academy up to 1822. The draughtsman of these eight views is credited as 'Miller' and may perhaps be identified with James Miller, four of whose water-colours of London subjects are in the Victoria and Albert Museum and who exhibited views of London, Richmond and Chatham from 1773 to 1791 at the Incorporated Society of Artists and from 1781 to 1788 at the Royal Academy. There are also seven 'J. Miller' drawings in the Crace Collection, of which three are the originals for these Colnaghi views, and Binyon states that he was working about 1781–1814 but that there is insufficient data to identify him with any one of several artists of the same name exhibiting about 1800. In any event they are charming and carefully drawn views and

Medland has managed to transfer some of the luminosity of aquatint to his etched plates.

In 1800 the eight plates were reissued (the publishers being now styled Colnaghi, Sala & Co, of 23 Cockspur Street) along with nine further views, mostly of the City of London. Miller drew three of these but his engraver was now William Watts who, under the auspices of Edward Rooker, had like Medland contributed to the *Copper-plate Magazine*, engraved country seats after Paul Sandby from whom he received his art training, and published a set of his own Scottish views (1791–4). Artists' and engravers' credits have been omitted from five of the extra plates.

Proofs before letters of the first issues are to be found with the publication-line and credits lightly etched in just below the work and a plate-mark of 235 × 295mm, but after the lettering was added this was reduced to 215 × 285mm and the space in the lm was filled with a caption in voided capitals, the publisher's dedication to appropriate nobility with their achievement of arms and his publication-line. In sets the plates are usually to be found in this last state, each with a numbered sheet of descriptive text and with the plate-marks cropped by the binder. Exceptionally the British Museum (Prints and Drawings: 172.b.4) has a Large Paper folio containing pl.1–8 lettered and pl.11–14 before letters with text pages numbered I–XII.

Publication-lines are denoted by the following key letters:

(a) 'London, Pubd (date) by Colnaghi & Co. No 132 Pall Mall.'

(b) 'London, Pubd (date) by Colnaghi Sala & Co. No 23 Cockspur Street, opposite Great Suffolk Street, Charing Cross.'

Select Views in London and Westminster. London: Published by Colnaghi and Co. (No. 132), Pall Mall.

Oblong quarto, 210 × 280mm. (Large Paper 265 × 370mm)   (1795–1800)

COLLATION   Title-page; pl.1–17 (I–VIII in 1796 ed), each with facing page of descriptive text.

1 Horse Guards. /Dedicated ... /To His Royal Highness the Duke of York./Commander in Chief of the British Forces. Miller delt. Medland sculpt. (a) April 1, 1795. 135 × 190mm.

2 Charing Cross. /Dedicated ... /to his Grace the Duke

of Northumberland. Miller delt. Medland sculpt. (a) April 1, 1795. 135 × 185mm.

3 York House. /Dedicated ... to the Right Honble Lord Viscount Melbourne. Miller delt. Medland sculpt. (a) April 1, 1795. 130 × 190mm. Afterwards called Melbourne House and now Dover House, Whitehall.

4 Westminster Hall. /Dedicated ... to the Right Honble Lord Loughborough/High Chancellor of England. Miller delt. Aquafortis by Angus, finish'd by Testolini. (a) April 1, 1795. 130 × 185mm. Miller's original water-colour is in BM (*Crace* 15.75).

5 Old Palace Yard./ Humbly Dedicated/to the Right Honble William Pitt. Miller delt. Medland sculpt. (a) April 1, 1796. 135 × 190mm.

6 Westminster Abbey. /Humbly Dedicated/to the Right Honble Lady A. Polworth. Miller delt. Medland sculpt. (a) April 1, 1796. 135 × 185mm. N.W. view.

7 Whitehall./ Humbly Dedicated/to the Right Honble the Earl of Warwick. Miller delt. Medland sculpt. (a) April 1, 1796. 135 × 190mm. Original water-colour, 'Whitehall, looking towards Charing Cross 1796', in BM (*Crace* 16.32).

8 The Admiralty. /Humbly Dedicated to the Right Honble Earl Spenser. Miller delt. Medland sculpt. (a) April 1, 1796, 130 × 187mm.

9 West Front of Westminster Abbey. (b) April 15, 1800. 220 × 160mm. No credits.

10 Interior of Westminster Abbey. (b) April 15, 1800. 220 × 157mm. No Credits.

11 The East India House. /Dedicated by permission,/To the Honble East India Company. Watts delt et sculpt. (b) April 15,1800. 130 × 185mm.

12 Temple Bar. /Dedicated to the/Promoters & Supporters of the Actual Improvement. Miller delt. Watts sculp. (b) April 15,1800. 135 × 185mm. Original water-colour, 'Temple Bar and Entrance to the Temple,1800', in BM (*Crace* 19.16).

13 The Custom House. /Dedicated ... to the Honble the Board of Commissioners of His Majesty's Customs. Miller delt. Watts sculpt. (b) April 15, 1800. 135 × 185mm.

14 Newgate. /Dedicated ... to the Rt Honble the Lord Mayor, Aldermen and Recorder. Miller delt. Medland sculpt. (b) April 15, 1800. 132 × 183mm.

15 St Pauls from Cheapside. (b) April 15, 1800. 135 × 182mm. No credits.

16 View in Fleet Street. (b) April 15, 1800. 132 × 185mm. No credits but given by the *Crace* catalogue (19.42) to Miller and Watts.

17 Portland Place. (b) April 15, 1800. 133 × 185mm. No credits. View to N.E.

77 · FAULDER'S ILLUSTRATIONS TO MR PENNANT [c 1796]

Robert Faulder, of 42 New Bond Street, was the publisher of the first five editions of Thomas Pennant's *Of London* (no 67) and these plates were brought together to enable purchasers of the third edition (1793) to extra-illustrate their copies. Although hardly relevant, Daniel Lysons's *Environs of London* (4 vols, 1792–6), just completed, was also mentioned on the title-page since it was providing almost as much of a spur to the current extra-illustrating mania as was Pennant's work itself. Associated with Faulder in this publication were T.J. Hookham, bookseller and stationer, and James Carpenter, bookseller, of 14 and 15 Old Bond Street. During this decade both Faulder and Hookham were appointed booksellers to the King.

The collection consists of 22 views (including the title-page) and 12 miscellaneous portraits. An index is provided which refers the collector to the page in the Pennant third edition relevant to each plate, so that the binder can interleave them correctly, although the plates themselves are not numbered; only the view of Nonsuch and the portrait of the miniature painter J. Meyer are referred to Lysons.

With two exceptions the portraits are all line or stipple-engravings of recent date whose subjects can be related to one or other of the texts. Of the views 19 are genuine antiques, namely the line-engravings made a whole century earlier for Robert Morden and Philip Lea's *Prospect of London* (no 15). Unfortunately, however, the publishers were not content to have the copper plates reprinted on suitable contemporary paper but attempted artificial 'aging' of the paper to make it appear as though the views were in the original impression. This clumsy faking was carried out by superimposing another plate coated with yellow pigment or varnish —a transparent piece of deception, especially when the two plate-marks are not in register.

Reference to Morden and Lea is made by the abbreviation *ML*, together with item number.

1 (engr title) Illustrations/to/Mr. Pennant and Mr. Lysons'/History/of/London, Westminster,/and its/environs./(engraved view) 'Nonsuch Palace'. London:/

Sold by Faulder, and Hookham and Carpenter, New Bond Street. (Price Eighteen Shillings Sewed)

2 (on banderole) The Hospitall of Bethlehem. 132 × 187/137 × 195mm. Pennant p 265. *ML 6.*

3 (in sky) Bow Church. 135 × 190/140 × 195mm. Pennant p 420. *ML 2.*

4 (in sky) The Statue of King Charles I/at Charing Cross in Brass. 130 × 190/140 × 195mm. Pennant p 112. *ML 23.*

5 (in sky) The Statue of King Charles II/at the/Entrance of Cornhill. 130 × 192/140 × 200mm. Pennant p 448. *ML 5.*

6 (on banderole) The Custom House. John Dunstall fecit. 130 × 195/140 × 215mm. Pennant p 330. *ML 10.*

7 Robert Devereux Earl of Essex Ano Domo 1643. 140 × 117/170 × 127mm. Pennant p 163.

8 Falstaff.... Jno Flaxman del. Wm. Flaxman sculpt. Published March 19, 1788 by Wm Flaxman, No 7 Dukes Court, St Martins Lane. 140/200 × 172mm, Stipple. Pennant p 344.

9 Henric FitzAlwine Kt. 125 × 105/140 × 110mm. Pennant p 467.

10 The Globe on the Banke Side Where Shakespere acted. From the long Antwerp view of London in the Pepysian Library. 80 × 80/170 × 90mm, Vignette. Pennant p 60. Detail of Hollar's 1647 birds-eye long view from Bankside, drawn and etched in London and Antwerp (*Hind* 16).

11 (on banderole) Guild-Hall. 135 × 195/140 × 200mm. Pennant p 427. *ML 3.*

12 (Hogarth) 120 × 100/215 × 160mm. Stipple, proof before letters. Pennant p 201.

13 (Holbein) Holbein pinx. Engr. by B. Reading. 115 × 105/150 × 135mm. Pennant p 228.

14 (on banderole) Lambeth House. 128 × 192/135 × 200mm. Pennant p 18. *ML 13.*

15 William Laud, Archbp. of Canterbury. 168 × 105/180 × 115mm. Pennant p 24.

16 Sir Peter Lely ... Published by Edward Jeffery, Pall Mall, 1793. 115 × 100/150 × 118mm. Line. Pennant p 428.

17 (Crude miniature line engraving of the City from South Bank in the seventeenth century, probably originally a head or tailpiece) 38 × 102/40 × 110mm. Pennant p 350.

18 (on banderole) St Marie Ouers in/South Wark. 130 × 192/135 × 195mm. Pennant p 46. *ML 12.*

19 (in sky) Mercer's Chappel. 130 × 190/140 × 200mm. Pennant p 439. *ML 4.*

20 J. Meyer, Encaustic and Miniature Painter to the King. Dr. by P. Falconet. Reading sculp. 130 × 110/150 × 185mm, Stipple. Lysons.

21 (on banderole) The M/ON/UMENT. 135 × 195/140 × 200mm. Description in bm. Pennant p 346. *ML 7.*

22 Matthaeus Parker Archiepiscopus Cantuariensis. Printed for John Wyat at the Rose in St. Pauls Church-Yard. Geo. Vertue sculp. 245 × 150/220 × 160mm. Pennant p 21.

23 (on banderole) St Paul's Covent Garden. Covent Garden. Iohn Seller Excudit. 132 × 190/140 × 190mm. Pennant p 149. *ML 21.*

24 (tc in sky) The Cathedral Church of St Paul as it was before ye Fire of London. 132 × 190/142 × 195mm. Pennant p 378. *ML 14.*

25 (tc in sky) The Royall Exchange of/London. 135 × 180/140 × 190mm. Pennant p 446. *ML 8.*

26 John Selden. W. Birch sculp. Published July 1, 1789 by Jeffery, Pall Mall. 55 × 45/105 × 55mm. Stipple oval. Pennant p 168.

27 (on banderole) Somerset House. 130 × 193/140 × 195mm. Pennant p 154. *ML 22.*

28 (on banderole) The Tower of London. 130 × 192/135 × 195mm. Pennant p 290. *ML 11.*

29 (on banderole) Part of Westminster. 133 × 198/135 × 200mm. Pennant p 84. *ML 28.*

30 (tc in sky) The Entrance of Westminster Hall. 135 × 195/145 × 200mm. Pennant p 88. *ML 27.*

31 (on banderole) Westminster Hall. 130 × 190/135 × 195mm. Pennant p 88. Palace Yard, etc. *ML 29.*

32 (on banderole) Whitehall. 132 × 190/140 × 200mm. Pennant p 105. *ML 24.*

33 Richard Whittington. B. Elstrack sculpsit. 178 × 108/182 × 112mm. Pennant p 358.

34 Dr James Usher. John Dunstall sc. 152 × 113/160 × 122mm. Pennant p 111.

78 · DAGATY AND ROWLANDSON'S VIEWS OF LONDON [1797–8]

Not long after his removal to 101 Strand Ackermann started publishing a series of views of the various 'entrances into London', marked by barriers across the road and lodges or huts for the servants of the Turnpike Trusts established by local Acts of Parliament, whose business it was to collect tolls for road maintenance from the passing traffic. Their presence resulted in the eighteenth century equivalent of a modern traffic jam and so they were ideal sites for an artist to record the variety of coaches, carriages, drays, delivery vans, country carts, riders on horseback, street traders, milkmaids, suburban pedestrians and driven flocks and herds while they were being held up on their way into, or out of, central London. The first two plates, published in August and September 1797, were drawn, engraved and aquatinted by one Dagaty (possibly Edouard, of the French family of painters and engravers Gautier d'Agoty), but in the following year his place as draughtsman was taken by Rowlandson and the engraving was carried out by H.J. Schütz. These four additional plates, published a decade earlier than those of the *Microcosm of London* (no 99), are a delightful foretaste of the human interest which Rowlandson's genius could instil into the London street scene of the 1790s, so much more staidly recorded by Malton (no 72), and the complete set is a valuable contribution to the history of London transport at the turn of the century. Fortunately Ackermann was then employing Schütz, a very competent engraver from Frankfurt, who saw to the aquatinting of the plates, having just completed for him the engraving of eight London views by Mannskirsch (no 110).

No general title-page to the set seems to have been printed; perhaps they would have been issued in an album or portfolio had not the series been brought to an end before Rowlandson could finish sketching the turnpike roads. Like Mannskirsch's *Parks and Gardens* they were republished by Ackermann in 1813.

1 Views of London, No. 1./ Entrance of Piccadilly or Hyde Park Corner Turnpike, with a view of St George's Hospital. Dagaty Delin & Sculpt. Publish'd August 1, 1797 by R. Ackermann, 101 Strand. 310 × 420/350 × 450mm.

2 Views of London, No. 2./Entrance of St Georges Road or the Obelisk Turnpike with a view of the Royal Circus. Dagaty Delin et Sculpt. Publish'd Sepr 1, 1797 .by R. Ackermann, 101 Strand. 310 × 420/360 × 455mm.

3 Views of London, No. 3./Entrance of Tottenham Court Road Turnpike with a View of St James's Chapel. Rowlandson Delin. Schutz Sculpt. London Publish'd April 1, 1798 at Ackermann's Gallery, No 101 Strand. 315 × 410/360 × 455mm.

4 Views of London, No. 4./ Entrance of Oxford Street or Tyburn Turnpike, with a View of Park Lane. Rowlandson Delin. Schutz Sculp. London Publish'd April 1, 1798 at Ackermann's Gallery, No 101 Strand. 305 × 405/360 × 455mm.

5 Views of London, No. 5./ Entranec (sic) from Mile End or White Chaple Turnpike. Rowlandson Delin. Schutz sculp. London, Pub. June 1, 1798, at Ackermann's Gallery, No 101 Strand. 305 × 410/360 × 465mm.

6 Views of London, No. 6./ Entrance from Hackney and Cambridge Heath Turnpike with a distant View of St Pauls. Rowlandson Delin. Schutz sculp. London, Pub. June 1, 1798. 300 × 400/360 × 460mm.

---

79 · ELLIS'S SAINT LEONARD SHOREDITCH [1798]

This juvenile work by a future British Museum Keeper of Printed Books, compiled while he was still an assistant at the Bodleian Library, was his introduction to the Society of Antiquaries to which he was elected as a Fellow in 1807 and as Secretary in 1813.

The History and Antiquities of the parish of Saint Leonard Shoreditch, and Liberty of Norton Folgate, in the suburbs of London. By Henry Ellis, Fellow of St. John's College, Oxford. London: Printed by and for J. Nichols, Printer to the Society of Antiquaries: and sold by all the Booksellers, in London, Oxford, Cambridge &c. MDCCXCVIII. (Price Sixteen Shillings in Boards)

Quarto, 270 × 210mm.   1798

COLLATION Title-page; dedication to Richard Gough dated 6 October 1798 (2pp); pp 1–354 (pp 242–52 bis), The History; pp 355–66, addenda; pp 367–70, index, directions to binder.

The illustrations consist of a hastily assembled assortment of copper plate engravings. Two of them, by Benjamin Cole, had served over 40 years before in Maitland's *History* (no 38), and a clumsily drawn and stiffly engraved view from the W., described in the directions as 'New Church 1798', is also to be found independently with the credit 'J.P. 1797'. Some plates from drawings of the old church were contributed by James Basire junior, the official engraver to the Society. Each is numbered and given a page reference tr, besides being listed in the 'Directions'. There are no publication-lines.

1 front. St Leonard Shoreditch Old Church/Taken in 1694. F. Cary sculp. 1795. 185 × 153/260 × 195mm.

2 p 9 The South West Prospect of the Church of St Leonard Shoreditch. B. Cole sculp. 1740. 355 × 205/375 × 225mm. Maitland 8, 1366, but without the date which is that of the completion of George Dance's church.

3 p 11 Shoreditch Church, N.W. 175 × 123/210 × 130mm. Also found with credit 'J.P. 1797'.

4 p 51 Shoreditch Church – Monument of Sir Thomas Leigh – In the East window of the Chantry/Chapel in the North Aisle. 163 × 215/190 × 230mm. Outline engr.

5 p 51 (tm) Monument at Shoreditch, Four Ladies of the Rutland Family. 170 × 120/260 × 180mm.

6 p 52 The Tomb of Sr John Elrington 1481, on the North side of the Altar in St Leonard's Church Shoreditch, 1735. Basire sc. 210 × 380/230 × 390mm.

7 p 136 The East Prospect of Haberdashers Alms Houses at Hoxton. B. Cole sculp. 220 × 365/250 × 375mm. As in Maitland 6, 1288.

8 p 193 (Five Coats in the Library of Richard Gough Esq. at Enfield, with the Lovel Arms, &c from the Gatehouse at Lincolns Inn. Basire sc.) 240 × 200mm. Details.

80 · CABINET OF THE ARTS*
[1799]

Sixteen small engravings after drawings by J.M.W. Turner appeared in the 1794–6 issues of three of Harrison & Co.'s periodicals, *The Pocket Magazine, The Ladies' Pocket Magazine* and *The Pocket Print Magazine*. Among them were two London views, of Chelsea Hospital and the Tower of London, engraved by J.S. Storer and T. Tagg, which survived for reprinting in the job lot of etched plates entitled *The Cabinet of Arts*. This miscellany includes oval portraits and various book illustrations, frontispieces and title-pages in line and stipple, together with 19 small topographical etchings, of which four represent London buildings and two views in the environs. There is no text and the title-page is the only preamble to this odd assortment: on it appears a string of artists' names, but not Turner's, who is relegated to the '&c'. For this he was no doubt grateful, both because the engravers employed by Harrison (and by John Walker of the *Copper-plate Magazine* for whom he was also working at this

period) could scarcely do justice to his originals and because these particular plates had abominably deteriorated by the time they were reprinted in the *Cabinet*, having already served their turn in the three magazines. An indication that edition after edition was being printed off them is to be found in the British Library copy (140.i.25) in which some of the tissues protecting the plates are watermarked '1803'.

The Cabinet of the Arts. A series of engravings by English artists, from original designs, by Stothard, Burney, Harding, Corbould, Van Assen, Potter, Cosway, Paul Sandby, Mather Brown, Catton, &c. London. M.DCC.XCIX. Price Five Guineas Bound. (with an allegorical stipple in the style of Corbould, printed in bistre, 110 × 150mm) London, Published by Castildine & Dunn, Copper-Plate Printers, No 9 Bagnio Court, Newgate Street, February 3, 1796.

Small quarto, 225 × 150mm.   1799

The credits remain but the titles of the periodicals in which the plates originated have been burnished out.

1 The Admiralty. Van Assen del. Rothwell sculpt. 63 × 100/90 × 135mm. pl.1. From *Pocket Magazine* 11, June 1795, p 389.

2 The Bank. Van Assen del. Rothwell sculpt. 65 × 105/90 × 140mm. pl.2. From *Pocket Magazine* 13, August 1795, p 115. (*Bank of England* 48)

3 Chelsea Hospital. Turner del. Storer sculpt. 67 × 113/90 × 138mm. pl.4. River view. From *Pocket Magazine* 7, February 1795, p 109. (*Longford* 22)

4 The Tower of London. W. Turner del. T. Tagg sc. 68 × 110/90 × 147mm. From *Pocket Magazine* 5, December 1794, p 329.

5 View from Woolwich Warren. Paul Sandby Esq. R.A. delt. T. Tagg sculpt. 67 × 112/98 × 150mm. From *Pocket Magazine* 2, September 1794, p 113.

6 Windsor. W. Turner del. Rothwell sculp. 67 × 112/80 × 125mm. From *Pocket Magazine* 22, May 1796, p 329.

81 · IRELAND'S PICTURESQUE VIEWS OF THE INNS OF COURT
[1800]

Samuel Ireland, who is perhaps best known as the father of the perpetrator of Shakespeare forgeries, William Henry Ireland, started life as a Spitalfields

184

weaver but turned to the sale of prints and drawings and then taught himself to draw and engrave, winning a Society of Arts medal in 1760. He issued his most substantial work, *Graphic Illustrations of Hogarth*, in 1794, but in 1790 had ventured into the realms of the Picturesque with a two-volume tour of France, Holland and Brabant containing aquatints of his own drawings, and with *Picturesque Views on the River Thames* (No 71) in 1792 and on the Medway in 1793, similarly illustrated. The *Inns of Court* was his swan-song. In its preface he says: 'As a painful illness has for several months severely afflicted the author, and greatly retarded his pursuits, he cherishes the hope, that candor will excuse the inaccuracies which may frequently occur'; and there is an editorial announcement that he had died 'on the Day in which the last Sheet of this Work went to the Press'.

His text was handsomely printed by C. Clarke in the Strand and published both on Large Paper as a quarto and as an octavo. The sepia aquatints which he engraved from his own drawings are notable for a quality of innocence and positively limpid cleanliness, far from realistic, even from his own account of squalid and mouldering quarters such as Lyons Inn, belonging to the Inner Temple but situated among the foetid slums of Holywell and Wych Street which later gave place to Aldwych. The book is described by Abbey (207):

Picturesque Views, with An Historical Account of the Inns of Court, in London and Westminster. By Samuel Ireland, Author of A Tour through Holland, Brabant, &c. of Picturesque Views on the River Thames, Medway, Avon and Wye, and of Graphic Illustrations of Hogarth, &c. &c. London: Printed by C. Clarke, Northumberland-Court, Strand; and published by R. Faulder, New Bond-Street, and J. Egerton, Whitehall. 1800.

Quarto, 333 × 230mm; octavo, 245 × 175mm. 1800

COLLATION Half-title; title-page; dedication to Lord Loughborough dated June 1800 (1 leaf); pp vii–xii, preface; notice of author's death (1 leaf); pp xv–xvi, list of prints; pp 1–254, Picturesque Views; errata (1 leaf).

The plates themselves are unnumbered and all carry the credit 'S. Ireland delt.' and the publication-line 'Pub. for S, Ireland March 31 1800'.

1 p 1 Middle Temple Gate &c. 125 × 165/220 × 315mm.
2 p 9 Temple Church. 133 × 170/225 × 310mm.
3 p 19 Inner Temple. 130 × 180/220 × 315mm.
4 p 69 Clements Inn. 127 × 175/210 × 310mm.
5 p 75 Clifford's Inn. 125 × 165/220 × 310mm.
6 p 81 Lions Inn. 125 × 170/220 × 305mm.
7 p 83 North frt. of Temple Hall. 127 × 173/220 × 315mm.
8 p 85 S.W. View of Middle Temple Hall. 130 × 170/220 × 305mm.
9 p 103 New Inn. 115 × 160/225 × 310mm.
10 p 107 Lincolns Inn gate. 127 × 180/220 × 290mm.
11 p 111 Lincolns Inn Hall & Chapel. 130 × 180/220 × 290mm.
12 p 125 Stone Buildings Lincolns Inn. 120 × 175/220 × 310mm.
13 p 163 Furnivals Inn. 127 × 162/220 × 295mm.
14 p 167 Garden front of Furnivals Inn. 127 × 172/220 × 315mm.
15 p 173 Grays Inn. 127 × 175/225 × 315mm.
16 p 185 Staple Inn. 125 × 162/225 × 310mm.
17 p 191 Barnards Inn. 123 × 167/220 × 310mm.
18 p 195 Serjeants Inn, Chancery Lane. 127 × 172/225 × 300mm.
19 p 199 Rolls Chapel, &c. 127 × 160/225 × 310mm. Shows also the house of the Master of the Rolls.
20 p 209 Guildhall &c. 122 × 168/225 × 310mm.
21 p 227 Westminster Hall. 123 × 165/225 × 315mm.

82 · MALCOLM'S VIEWS WITHIN TWELVE MILES ROUND LONDON* [1800]

J.P. Malcolm's chief contribution to London topography is his *Anecdotes of the Manners and Customs of London* (no 100) but this pre-dates it by eight years, being a by-product of Daniel Lysons's *Environs of London* (4 vols, 1792–6) which was becoming almost as popular an object of grangerizing as Pennant's *Of London* (no 67). He was already at the time a contributor of topographical and antiquarian illustrations to the *Gentleman's Magazine* and had been engaged by his printer, John Nichols, to supply the engravings for his life work, *The History and Antiquities of Leicester* (1795–1815). Each of the 75 plates of views and antiquities in London and the Home Counties is referred by the index to the appropriate volume and page in Lysons and these references are occasionally engraved on the plates themselves, which are otherwise unnumbered. The collection was published at £3. A dozen plates of places near the centre of London are here listed.

Views within twelve miles round London drawn and engraved by James Peller Malcolm. As almost all the Subjects are particularly noticed and described by Mr Lysons in his Environs of London, it is hoped they will form a proper Appendage to that Work, for which Purpose, an Index to the Prints is added from his Pages. To those who do not possess the Environs of London, the Index will prove so much of a Description, as to make it a pleasing independent Work, tending to preserve the perishable Forms of many a Building whose Fate has been pronounced, and whose Remembrance shall only be had from this and similar Works (epigraph) Vol. I. London, Printed by John Nichols, Red Lion Passage, Fleet Street:/And Sold by Mr. Wilkie, Pater-noster Row; Mr. Simco, Warwick Street, Golden Square; and J.P. Malcolm, No 22, Somers Place, East. 1800.

Quarto, 273 × 216mm.   1800

COLLATION   Title-page; pp iv-vi, index; 75 plates.

The 'Vol. I' on the title-page is explained by the note printed after the Index: 'J.P. Malcolm begs leave to inform his Purchasers, that a Second Volume of Prints, on the Plan, Numbers and Price, of the above, is intended if a sufficient Number of Names are sent to Mr. Wilkie'.

1 Somerset Place/1650. CB pinx. Malcolm sculp. Publish'd Decr 1, 1797 by J.P. Malcolm, Middlesex St, Somers Town. 115 × 185/127 × 197mm. Vol. 1, p 112. This and item 2 'taken from one picture at Dulwich College by C.B. or Charles Beale about 1650', according to the text; actually by Cornelys Bol, a Dutch painter.

2 Westminster 1650. CB pinx. Malcolm sculp. Publish'd Decr 1, 1797 by J.P. Malcolm, Middlesex St, Somers Town. 113 × 185/128 × 190mm. Vol. 1, p 112. This and item 1 'taken from one picture at Dulwich College by C.B. or Charles Beale about 1650', according to the text; actually by Cornelys Bol, a Dutch painter.

3 Bishop of Rochester's Ancient Palace Lambeth. Malcolm del. et sculp. Pubd. Mar 1 1798 by J.P. Malcolm, 34 Chalton Street, Somers Town. 146 × 102/152 × 115mm. Vol. 1, p 276. Subsequently Carlisle House, at this time an academy for young gentlemen; demolished 1827.

4 Remains of Aldgate, Bethnal Green. Malcolm. Publish'd Mar 1, 1800 by Malcolm, Somers Place. 115 × 165/127 × 178mm. Vol. 2, p 32.

5 Sir Hans Sloane's Tomb/Chelsea. Malcolm del. et sculp. Publish'd by J.P. Malcolm, No 10 Middlesex Str, Somers Town. 132 × 185/150 × 205mm. 'Vol. II p. 111'. View of churchyard and river. (*Longford* 158)

6 Lindsey House Chelsea. Malcolm. Publish'd May 1, 1800 by J.P. Malcolm, 22 Somers Place. 102 × 152/120 × 165mm. Vol. 2, p 130. (*Longford* 234)

7 The Reed Moat Field/Islington. Malcolm del. et sculp. Publish'd Decr 1, 1796 by J.P. Malcolm, No 2 Evesham's Buildings, Somers Town. 121 × 203/140 × 215mm. Vol. 3, p 126.

8 View of Islington from White Conduit House. 89 × 178/115 × 190mm. Vol. 3, p 163. Without credit or publication-line. St James, Clerkenwell visible on both Islington views.

9 Perry's Dock Blackwall. 76 × 127/89 × 133mm. Without credit or publication-line. Vol. 3, p 469.

10 The Duke of Norfolk's Alms House Greenwich. Malcolm del. et sculp. 1796. Publish'd Decr 1, 1796 by J.P. Malcolm No 2 Evesham Buildings Sommers Town. 120 × 203/140 × 216mm. Vol. 4, p 463.

11 Lord Spencer's, St James Park. Malcolm sc. Schnebbelie del. Publish'd Jan 11, 1798 by J.P. Malcolm, 34 Chalton Street, Somers Town. 102 × 160/115 × 165mm. No ref to Lysons.

12 St John's Chapel in the White Tower, London. Malcolm del. et sculp. Pubd. March 7, 1799 by J.P. Malcolm 34 Chalton Street, Somers Town. 140 × 197/150 × 205mm. No ref to Lysons.

---

83 · MALCOLM'S LONDINIUM REDIVIVUM* [1802–7]

Malcolm's preoccupation with the research for this work and the writing of the text of its four volumes must have detracted from his usual interest in illustration since the plates are a job lot of antiquarian sketches and views, some of which had already been used in a different context by his printer, John Nichols, and of which many were to make further appearances. Six were drawn from Malcolm's earlier publication, *Views within twelve miles round London* (no 82, abbreviated *VWTM* with item number), and three of St Katherine by the Tower come from *Bibliotheca Topographica Britannica* no 5, published in 1782 by John Nichols as Printer to the Society of Antiquaries, abbreviated

BTB with plate number. Each volume includes a check-list of plates so those without topographical significance are omitted from the list below.

Londinium Redivivum;/or,/an Ancient History and Modern description/of/London./Compiled from Parochial Records, Archives of various Foundations,/the Harleian MSS and other authentic sources (ornament)/By/James Peller Malcolm./Volume I (II–IV). (rule) /London: Printed by John Nichols & Son, Red Lion Passage, Fleet Street/and sold by F. & C. Rivington, St Paul's Church Yard, T. Payne, Mews Gate; /G. Wilkie, Paternoster Row & J. White, Fleet Street./ 1803 (1807).

Quarto, 265 × 210mm   1803–7

COLLATION   Vol. 1. Engr title-page (1803); printed title-page, with the same wording (1802); pp i-iii, advertisement dated Somers Town, 7 June 1802; p iv, list of 10 plates; contents (2pp); pp 5–436, Londinium Redivivum; pp 437–9, addenda; pp 440–52, indices. Vol. 2. Engr title-page (1803); pp iii-vii, advertisement dated March 1805; pp ix-x, contents; pp 5–596, Londinium Redivivum continued; pp 597–611, index, list of 8 plates. Vol. 3. Engr title-page (1803); pp iii-viii, advertisement dated March 1805; p ix, contents; pp 5–572, Londinium Redivivum continued; pp 573–87, index, list of 17 plates. Vol. 4. Engr title-page, amended (adding 'F.S.A.' to Malcolm's name and with the imprint 'Printed for John Nichols & Son, Red Lion Passage, Fleet Street/& Sold by Longman, Rees, Hurst, & Orme, Paternoster Row, 1807'); pp iii-v, advertisement; p vi, contents; pp 1–640, Londinium Redivivum continued; pp 641–54, index, list of 11 plates.

VOL. 1

1 p 89 (Specimens of the mosaic pavement in King Edward the Confessor's Chapel, Westminster Abbey, etc.) Malcolm del. et sc. Publish'd Jan 1, 1802 by J.P. Malcolm, 52 Chalton St. Somers Town. 220 × 150mm pl. mark.

2 p 155 Altar in the Chapel of St Blase, at Westminster Abbey. J.P. Malcolm sc. 200 × 160/215 × 180mm.

3 p 282 The Crypt of the Church of Holy Trinity at Aldgate … Publish'd Nov. 1, 1801 by J.P. Malcolm, 52 Chalton St., Somers Town. 120 × 165mm pl. mark. Remains of the priory in the parish of St Katherine Cree.

4 p 291 St Bartholomew's South Transept. 110 × 165/125 × 170mm.

5 p 293 St Bartholomews. Malcolm. 185 × 220/205 × 255mm. Interior of St Bartholomew the Great, looking E.

6 p 303 St Bartholomew Parva. Publish'd May 1, 1802 by Malcolm, Somers Town. 130 × 160/150 × 175mm. Rebuilt by George Dance junior, 1793.

VOL. 2

7 p 228 Bangor House, London. Publish'd Feb 1, 1805 by J.P. Malcolm, Somers Town. 150 × 95/165 × 110mm.

8 p 230 Ely Chapel. Malcolm del. et sc. Publish'd Jan 1 1805 by J.P. Malcolm in Somers Town. 170 × 115/185 × 125mm.

9 p 317 Monument of Francis Beaumont at the Charterhouse … and of William Lambe at Lambe's Chapel … 135 × 230 pl. mark. The chapel of the ancient hermitage of Cripplegate was bought by William Lambe in 1543 and left to the Clothworkers' Company. It was rebuilt in Wood Street Square, St Pancras in 1825 and finally demolished in 1872.

10 p 496 Sir Hans Sloane's Tomb/Chelsea. Malcolm del. et sculp. Publish'd by J.P. Malcolm, No 10 Middlesex Str., Somers Town. 132 × 185/150 × 205mm. View of churchyard and river. *VWTM* 5. (*Longford*, 158)

11 p 532 Remains of Aldgate, Bethnal Green. Malcolm. Publish'd Mar 1, 1800 by Malcolm, Somers Place. 115 × 165/125 × 178mm. *VWTM* 4.

12 p 573 Gothick altarpiece in the Collegiate Church of St. Katharine … B.T. Pouncy delin. et sculpt. Published by I. Nichols … Decr. 1, 1779. 140 × 215/175 × 240mm. *BTB* pl.XV.

13 p 574 Ichnography of the Collegiate Church of/St Katharine. B.T. Pouncy delin. et sculpt., 1779. 240 × 175mm pl. mark. *BTB* pl. VI.

14 p 577 North East View of the Collegiate Church of St Katharine. B.T. Pouncy del. et fct. London, Published by I. Nichols … Decr. 1, 1779. 130 × 175/155 × 190mm. *BTB* pl. V.

VOL. 3

15 p 61 Dr. Donne—East End of the North Crypt of St Paul's/dedicated to St Faith. Malcolm. Publish'd Jan. 1, 1805 by J.P. Malcolm, Somers Town. 160 × 200mm pl. mark. Donne's shrouded effigy.

16 p 191 St Paul's School & Dean Colet's House. Publish'd Jan 1, 1805 by J.P. Malcolm, Somers Town. 82 × 110,85 × 102/185 × 125mm.

17 p 212 Sir W. Weston. Schnebbelie del. 1787. 205 × 138mm pl. mark. Monument in St James, Clerkenwell.

18 p 271 St Giles Cripplegate & London Wall. Malcolm del. et sc. Publish'd Oct 1, 1801 by J.P. Malcolm, 52 Chalton Street, Somers Town. 155 × 98/175 × 110mm.

19 p 366 Part of cloisters of Christ's Hospital. 110 × 140/125 × 150mm.

20 p 456 (Portrait of Queen Elizabeth from painted glass in St Dunstan's in the West) Published May 1, 1800 by J.P. Malcolm, Somers Place. 108 × 70/180 × 95mm.

21 p 553 Inside of St Helen's. Malcolm del. et sc.

Publish'd Dec 1, 1801 by J.P. Malcolm, 52 Chalton St., Somers Town. 120 × 150/140 × 160mm.

22 p 554 (Grate for the nuns in St Helen's Church &c) Publish'd Oct. 10, 1800 by J.P. Malcolm, Somers Place. 150 × 200mm pl. mark.

23 p 555 St Helen's. Malcolm del. et sc. Publish'd Nov. 1, 1801 by J.P. Malcolm, 52 Chalton St., Somers Town. 110 × 178/125 × 185mm. Exterior.

24 p 563 Leather-seller's Hall. Malcolm del. et sc. Publish'd Mar. 1 1799 by J.P. Malcolm, 34 Chalton St., Somers Town. 175 × 240/190 × 260mm. Interior towards screens.

25 p 565 Crosby Hall. Malcolm del. et sc. Published Jan. 1, 1805 by J.P. Malcolm. 230 × 170/245 × 190mm. (*Longford* 450)

VOL. 4

26 p 1 Remains of the Holy Trinity Aldgate, destroyed ca. 1803. 90 × 108/100 × 120mm. The Priory in the parish of St Katherine Cree.

27 p 26 (along tm) Finsbury-Fields/North. (bl) To his/affect. friends ... and all other lovers of/Archerie ... Will. Hole. (tl arms of the Goldsmiths' Company) 210 × 128/225 × 145mm. A plan of the Butts.

28 p 247 Earl Spencer's, St James's Park. Malcolm sc. Publish'd Jan. 16, 1798 by J.P. Malcolm, 34 Chalton St., Somers Town. 102 × 135/115 × 140mm. cf with *VWTM* 11.

29 p 289 Somerset Place/1650. CB pinx. Malcolm sculp. Publish'd Dec. 1, 1797 by J.P. Malcolm, Middlesex St., Somers Town. 115 × 190/130 × 200mm. 'Pl. 1, p. 80'. This and item 30 'taken from one picture at Dulwich College by C.B. or Charles Beale about 1650', according to the text; actually by Cornelys Bol, a Dutch painter. *VWTM* 1.

30 p 303 Westminster 1650. CB pinx. Malcolm sculp. Publish'd Decr 1, 1797 by J.P. Malcolm, Middlesex St., Somers Town. 110 × 185/128 × 192mm. This and item 29 'taken from one picture at Dulwich College by C.B. or Charles Beale about 1650', according to the text; actually by Cornelys Bol, a Dutch painter, *VWTM* 2.

31 p 331 A Perspective View of Lord Clarendon's House ... G. Hart fec. Cook sc. 130 × 190mm pl. mark. (tr) 'Gent. Mag. April 1789 Pl II, p. 685'.

32 p 335 Trinity Chapel. Engr. by J. Swaine. 115 × 175mm pl. mark. (tr) 'Gent. Mag. June 1804 Pl. I. p. 497'. In Conduit Street.

33 p 515 Death of Whittington. 90 × 80/140 × 110mm. From MS belonging to Mercers' Company.

34 p 628 (The Tower of London from the MS of the Poems of Charles, Duke of Orleans in the British Museum) J. Basire sc. Published by I. Nichols & Son, 23rd April, 1803. 190 × 160mm pl. mark.

35 p 629 St John's Chapel in the White Tower, London.

Malcolm del. et sculp. Pubd. March 7, 1799 by J.P. Malcolm 34 Chalton Street, Somers Town. 140 × 197/150 × 205mm. *VWTM* 12.

84 · RICHARDSON'S NEW VITRUVIUS BRITANNICUS [1802–8]

'It is now near one hundred years since the first volume of *Vitruvius Britannicus* was published by Campbell (no 24) and thirty years have elapsed since the last volume of that work was published by Woolfe and Gandon (no 45), it was therefore deemed expedient to enlarge the continuation ... as well for our own use as for the advantage of ingenious foreigners, who are anxious to know the superior taste and elegance of an English mansion'. This work is thus introduced by George Richardson, a specialist in designing architectural decoration after the antique who was engaged with the Adam brothers on interior decoration. His *Book of Ceilings* (1774) was dedicated to Lord Scarsdale. He produced and published numerous collections of designs illustrated, like the present volumes, with aquatinted drawings executed by himself or his son. The eight London plates are printed in grey tones and numbered in Roman numerals tr, two numbers being allotted to larger plates. Captions are along tm.

The New Vitruvius Britannicus: consisting of Plans and Elevations of Modern Buildings, public and private, erected in Great Britain by the most celebrated architects engraved on LXXII plates (Vol. 2: 'on LXX plates'), from original drawings. (Volume II) By George Richardson, Architect (and in French) London: printed by W. Bulmer and Co. Cleveland-Row, for the author; and sold by J. Taylor, at the Architectural Library, High Holborn. MDCCCII (Vol. 2: 'Printed by T. Bensley, Bolt Court, Fleet Street ... MDCCCVIII').

Folio, 550 × 370mm.   1802–8

COLLATION   Vol. 1. Title-page; pp iii-iv, introduction (in English and French); contents of both vols (2pp); list of subscribers (2pp); pl. 1–72; pp 1–20, explanation of plates. Vol. 2. Title-page; pl. 1–70; pp 1–10, explanation of plates.

1 pl. 22 Plans of the Trinity House, erected on Great Tower Hill, London/S. Wyatt Archt. London, June 30th 1798. Engraved & Published by G. Richardson. 435 × 265mm.

2 pl. 23 South Front of the Trinity House, erected on Great Tower Hill, London/S. Wyatt Archt. London, June 30th 1798. Engraved & Published by G. Richardson. 265 × 435mm. Built by Samuel Wyatt 1793–5.

3 pl. 34 Plans of the Session-House/for the/County of Middlesex./London./Thos. Rogers Archt. London, March 30th 1799. Engraved & Published by George Richardson. 265 × 450mm.

4 pl. 35 Principal Elevation of the Session-House for the County of Middlesex, London./Thos. Rogers Archt/ London, March 30th 1799. Engraved & Published by George Richardson. 295 × 450mm.

VOL. 2

5 pl. 5 The Principal Front of the Hall of the Worshipful Company of Grocers, in the City of London, erected in the year 1800/Thomas Leverton, Archt. London, Nov. 10th 1802. Engraved & Published by George Richardson. 280 × 455mm.

6 pl. 6 The Principal Story and Front towards the Garden of the Hall of the Worshipful Company of Grocers, London/erected in the Year 1800/Thomas Leverton, Archt. London, Nov. 10th 1802. Engraved & Published by George Richardson. 455 × 305mm. Built 1798–1802, rebuilt 1889 and again after 1965.

7 pl. 39–40 Principal Floor of the Royal Military Asylum at Chelsea in the County of Middlesex/John Sanders Archt. London Dec. 22d 1804. Engraved & Published by George Richardson. 370 × 630mm.

8 pl. 41–2 Elevation of the Royal Military Asylum at Chelsea in the County of Middlesex/John Sanders Archt. London Dec. 22d 1804. Engraved & Published by George Richardson. 205 × 690mm. Built 1801–3, later Duke of York's Headquarters, King's Road. (*Longford* 691)

85 · PICTURE OF LONDON
[1802, etc]

Richard Phillips, the radical bookseller, gaoled in 1793 for selling copies of Paine's *Rights of Man*, in 1797 set up in St Paul's Churchyard as a book and periodical publisher and in 1802 launched *The Picture of London*, a guidebook which he continued to issue annually until 1810. Another edition appeared in 1812 but by this time, in contrast to his success in the City where he had been elected Sheriff in 1807 and received a knighthood, his bookselling business was foundering and he was forced to sell off his copyrights, including the guidebook which subsequently appeared under the imprint of Longman & Co. The new owners pursued the same policy of annual publication without much change in content until they engaged John Britton to revise, for a fee of 100 guineas, the now very out of date text originally compiled by an aged antiquary called John Feltham. It was then renamed *The Original Picture of London* (no 151) to distinguish it from possible spurious imitations, such as the *New Picture of London* of Tegg and Castleman (no 86) and that of Samuel Leigh (no 167).

The Picture of London, for 1802 (etc); being a correct guide to all the curiosities, amusements, exhibitions, public establishments, and remarkable objects, in and near London; with a collection of appropriate tables for the use of strangers, foreigners, and all persons who are not intimately acquainted with the British Metropolis. London: Printed by W. Lewis, Paternoster-Row; for R. Phillips, 71, St. Paul's Church-Yard/sold also by J. Ginger, 169 Piccadilly, by all Booksellers, And at the Bars of the principal Inns and Coffee-houses. (Price 5s. bound in Red)

Duodecimo, 135 × 185mm.   1802, etc

COLLATION Title-page; pp 3–4, preface; pp v–xii, index; pp 1–420, Picture of London.

In the 1802 edition Phillips, in addition to maps of central London and the environs, included four views. These were increased by four in 1803 but when he published the 1805 edition he had decided to hive off the pictorial element into a work of format more suitable to topographical plates, his *Modern London* (no 89):

The great approbation bestowed on this work has induced the proprietor to print an enlarged and extended edition, under the title of Modern London, in one elegant volume quarto, illustrated with sixty beautiful copper-plates, at once the most splendid work in the English language, and worthy of the great City which it describes. No 6, New Bridge-street, January 1805.

Thenceforward, until the 1820 edition for which Longmans commissioned numerous small engravings by Greig, the *Picture of London* was rarely illustrated with more than the two maps, a frontispiece and occasional plans of theatres or recent developments, although between 1813 and 1815 embellishment with about 20 poor woodcuts was attempted. Few of the small and unskilled line-engravings published in the earlier editions have either credits or publication-lines.

1803

1 front. Part of London from Primrose Hill. 62 × 113mm.

2 p 30   The new West India Dock and Warehouses in the/Isle of Dogs. 60 × 115mm.

3 p 36   Blackfryars Bridge & St. Pauls. 60 × 110mm. Recaptioned 'Black Friars Bridge' in 1802.

4 p 44   Westminster Bridge, Abbey & Hall. 60 × 110mm. Recaptioned 'Westminster Bridge' in 1802.

5 p 130   London and the Thames from Greenwich. 60 × 110mm. Recaptioned 'London from the Royal Observatory Greenwich' in 1802.

6 p 254   London Bridge and the Monument. 60 × 110mm. Recaptioned 'London Bridge' in 1802.

7 p 256   The intended Iron Bridge in place of the/present London Bridge. 62 × 115mm. Single span, designed by Thomas Telford and James Douglas for the Select Committee on the Improvement of the Port of London, c 1800.

1806

8 front. London from the Royal Observatory Greenwich. London, Publish'd March 28, 1806 by Richard Phillips, No. 6 New Bridge Street, Blackfriars. 96 × 172mm. This frontispiece appears again and again between 1807 and 1817 with the publication-line suitably updated.

1808

9 front. The House of Commons. E. Pugh Del. J. Fittler Sc. 120 × 180mm. Interior.

10 p 77   The New Opening at Westminster. Pub. May 1, 1808 by R. Phillips, 6 Bridge St. 105 × 175mm. Westminster Hall, St Margaret's Church and the Abbey.

---

86 · TEGG AND CASTLEMAN'S NEW PICTURE OF LONDON [1803]

Thomas Tegg, after serving as assistant to the Quaker booksellers J. and A. Arch, in 1800 set up on his own in St John Street, Clerkenwell. Spurred on by the success in 1802 of Richard Phillips's

Picture of London (no 85), the very next year he ventured into guidebook publishing with the *New Picture of London* by one H.J. Sarrett. It was priced at 3s 6d as against 5s for Phillips's book and must have had some success since in the first year it ran into two editions, the first with a preface dated 4 June and the second 4 July 1803; and moreover a 1s abridgement was issued by another publisher, B. Crosby. Unfortunately he was unable to build on this success because he was cheated of money by a friend and, in order to repair his fortunes, was obliged to tour the country as a roving book auctioneer. By this means he paid his outstanding debts and in 1805 set up shop again, at 111 Cheapside, where he quickly established a publisher's list of bestselling sixpenny abridgements of popular works, song-books and the like and also dealt in publishers' remainders. The *New Picture* was republished just once more in 1814. He became a highly respected figure in the City and by the year of his death had issued some 4,000 publications.

Tegg and Castleman's New Picture of London for 1803–4, or A Guide through this Immense Metropolis, On a Plan hitherto unattempted: containing Comprehensive Descriptions of the Publick Edifices, Collections of Curiosities, and Places of Entertainment ... By H.J. Sarrett: Author of Koenigsmark; the History of Man &c. &c. London: Printed for Tegg and Castleman, No. 122 St. John Street, West-Smithfield; T. Brown, Edinburgh; and M. Keene, Dublin.

Duodecimo, 150 × 90mm.   1803

COLLATION   Title-page; pp iii–iv, preface dated 4 June 1802; pp 1–242, New Picture of London; pp 243–50, index.

——The Second Edition. London: Printed for Tegg and Castleman, No. 23, Warwick Square, Paternoster Row. (Provincial agents also)

Duodecimo, 145 × 90mm.   1803

COLLATION   Title page; pp iii–iv, preface dated 4 July 1803; pp 1–243, New Picture of London; pp 244–50, index.

To compete with Phillips's book, Tegg inserted into his a handful of line-engravings and a map. Apart from the view of his own shop, 'The Eccentric Book Warehouse', it is hard to guess why he chose these particular subjects. The same plates were used in both editions but, by the time the second was issued, the map had been amended for Crosby's abridgement and redated September 1803. The 1814 revival, following the example of the 1813 edition of Phillips's *Picture*, was illustrated with odd-shaped wood-engravings only. Publication-lines on the line-engravings read: 'Published June 1st 1803 by Tegg & Co.'

1 front. (tm) View of Skinner Street from Fleet Market. 75 × 125mm.

2 p i (tm) The Eccentric Book Warehouse, St Johns Street. Vaughn del. Page sct. 75 × 130mm.

3 p 1 (tr) A Plan of/London/Westminster,/and/Southwark. Barlow sculp. 160 × 275mm. 2nd ed: (tm) 'Engraved for Crosby's View of London', (bm) 'Published by B. Crosby & Co. Stationers Court, Sept: 1803'. (*Darlington and Howgego* 230)

4 p 165 Grosvenor Gate Park Lane. Craig del. Taylor sc. 72 × 123mm. 2nd ed p 66.

5 p 238 Montague House Portman Square. 75 × 123mm. 2nd ed p 165.

87 · ENGLAND DELINEATED* [1804]

The Temple of Muses in Finsbury Square, a celebrated London bookshop, was opened by James Lackington in 1793. By 1804 his third cousin, George Lackington, was managing a shop famous for its large stock and notorious for its cut prices; also it occasionally issued picture-books, such as this, under its own imprint. By 1809 it had become so permanent a part of the London scene that it featured among the aquatint illustrations in the very first issue of the *Repository of the Arts* (see no 117), the publication of a rival bookseller, Rudolph Ackermann.

(engr title) England/Delineated/In Two Volumes/Vol. I (II). Suffield sc. Fleet Street (vignette of ruins with an allegory of Time) W. Angus sculp./London/Printed for Lackington Allen & Co./Temple of the Muses, Finsbury Square/1804. 130 × 190/235 × 140mm.

Octavo, 240 × 143mm.   1804

COLLATION   Vol. 1. Engr title-page; half-title; pp i–ii, advertisement; contents (1 leaf); pp 1–148, England Delineated. Vol. 2. Engr title-page; half-title; contents (1 leaf); pp 1–148, England Delineated continued.

There are 74 plates per volume, each accompanied by two pages of text but without either plate numbers or publication-lines. Among them are only four London views; two bear the credit of 'Metcalf' (probably R. Metcalf, the official engraver of plans to the Surveyor's Office in the Guildhall, who worked hard by Finsbury Square at 127 Bunhill Row) and a third that of James Basire (probably the junior of that name). Their old-fashioned look results from three having been copied from a similar publication of 1764, Dodsley's *England Illustrated* (no 42, abbreviated *EI*).

VOL. 1

1 p 111 Westminster Abbey (from West). Metcalf sct. 83 × 128/108 × 148mm. *EI* 2,1.

2 p 113 South and West of St Stephen's Chapel Westminster restored 1800. Js. Basire sc. 108 × 155/125 × 190mm.

3 p 115 St Pauls. Metcalf sct. 90 × 90/120 × 120mm. The Cathedral from the N.W. Adapted from the roundel in *EI* 2,79.

VOL. 2

4 p 37 Lambeth Palace. 80 × 125/115 × 145mm. *EI* 2,274.

88 · HERBERT'S ANTIQUITIES OF THE INNS OF COURT [1804]

This is one of the earliest published works of William Herbert, antiquarian and topographer and friend of E.W. Brayley. It is a much more serious history than that of Samuel Ireland (no 81), written purely as an accompaniment to his aquatints four years earlier. Herbert was particularly interested in Lambeth, where he lived, and in 1806 published a history of the Palace. In the next decade he was associated with the printseller Wilkinson in *Londina Illustrata* (no 131) and started to publish on his own account a work in Numbers entitled *London before the Great Fire* (no 120). His most notable historical book is the *History of the Twelve Great Livery Companies* (2 vols, 1836–7) written some years after he had been elected Librarian of the Guildhall Library in 1828. The *Antiquities of the Inns of Court* appeared in a 'de luxe' edition in quarto and an ordinary octavo edition.

Antiquities of the Inns of Court and Chancery: containing historical and descriptive sketches relating to their original foundation, customs, ceremonies, buildings, government &c &c. with A Concise History of the English Law. By W. Herbert. Embellished with twenty-four plates. London: Printed for Vernor & Hood, Poultry: J. Storer and J. Greig, Chapel street, Pentonville, 1804.

Quarto, 270 × 210mm; octavo, 235 × 145mm. 1804

COLLATION   Title-page; dedication to Lord Eldon (1 leaf); pp vii-viii, advertisement; pp ix-xii, contents; pp 1–377, Antiquities; index (7pp); directions to binder (1 leaf).

This book is illustrated more exhaustively and with more realism than Ireland's and the etched copper plates, although they bear no credits, are certainly the work of James Storer and John Greig. Their names occur, with those of the publishers Vernor & Hood, both in the imprint and in the publication-lines of each separate plate. It was published in the same year as the first of a two-volume *Select Views of London* (no 90), issued in Numbers and also published by Vernor and Hood with engravings by Storer and Greig. As the text of the last named is attributed to Herbert it would appear that there was some reciprocal arrangement for the engravers to illustrate Herbert's text while he wrote descriptions to publish with their batches of plates. Each plate carries the same dated publication-line: 'London, Published May 15, 1804 by Vernor & Hood, Poultry, J. Storer & J. Greig, Chapel Street, Pentonville'. These plates and those from the *Select Views* were later combined and reissued by Vernor & Hood without text under the title *London Illustrated or A Series of Plates to illustrate the History of London and Westminster*.

1 front. Interior of the Temple Hall. 145 × 100/200 × 155mm. Middle Temple.

2 p 182 The Temple Church/(from the Cloisters). 103 × 152/150 × 203mm.

3 p 192 Inner Temple Hall/(from the Kings Bench Walk). 100 × 152/150 × 200mm.

4 p 211 Middle Temple Hall/(from the N.E.). 146 × 102/200 × 150mm.

5 p 243 S.W. View of the/Middle-Temple Hall. 100 × 152/150 × 200mm.

6 p 259 Inside of the Temple Church. 148 × 102/200 × 150mm.

7 p 272 Cliffords Inn. 98 × 150/155 × 200mm.

8 p 276 Lyons Inn. 100 × 150/155 × 200mm. Between Holywell Street and Wych Street, an appendage of the Inner Temple.

9 p 278 Clement's Inn. 100 × 150/150 × 195mm.

10 p 282 New Inn. 95 × 150/150 × 200mm. 'contiguous to Clements Inn on the W.'

11 p 286 Lincolns Inn Great Square. 100 × 150/160 × 205mm. ie 'New Square'.

12 p 296 Lincolns Inn Hall and Chapel. 98 × 150/150 × 200mm.

13 p 299 Interior of Lincoln's Inn Chapel. 100 × 150/150 × 200mm.

14 p 301 The Stone Buildings/(from the Garden, Lincolns Inn). 95 × 150/150 × 200mm.

15 p 324 Furnival's Inn/(Holborn). 100 × 150/150 × 200mm.

16 p 327 Furnival's Inn/(from the Inner Square). 100 × 150/150 × 200mm.

17 p 328 Interior of/Furnival's Inn Hall. 145 × 100/205 × 150mm.

18 p 329 Gray's Inn Hall & Chapel/(from the Great Square). 100 × 148/140 × 195mm.

19 p 339 Gray's Inn Gardens. 100 × 150/150 × 200mm.

20 p 340 Interior of Gray's Inn Hall. 147 × 98/200 × 153mm.

21 p 347 Staple's Inn/(Holborn). 100 × 150/155 × 210mm.

22 p 349 Bernard's Inn. 150 × 100/200 × 150mm. ie Barnard's Inn which appertained to Gray's Inn but on the S. side of Holborn.

23 p 352 Serjeant's Inn/(Chancery Lane). 150 × 100/200 × 150mm.

24 p 356 Serjeant's Inn/(Fleet street). 150 × 98/202 × 105mm.

---

89 · PHILLIPS'S MODERN LONDON [1804]

Richard Phillips, a bookseller of radical views, was imprisoned for 18 months in 1793 for selling copies of Tom Paine's *Rights of Man* but by 1797 he was settled in premises in St Paul's Churchyard and publishing the *Monthly Magazine* and the *Antiquary's Magazine*. He also published textbooks, manuals and guidebooks written by himself, his *Picture of London* (no 85) becoming a bestseller and a new edition coming out almost annually. He prefaced the 1805 edition with this self-satisfied puff:

The great approbation bestowed on this work has induced the proprietor to print an enlarged and extended edition, under the title MODERN LONDON, in one elegant volume, quarto, illustrated with sixty beautiful copper-plates, at once the most splendid work in the English language, and worthy of the great City which it describes. No. 6, New Bridge-street, January, 1805.

Prosperity and the move to New Bridge Street, Blackfriars spelled a break with the past; he was elected a City Sheriff in 1807 and knighted the year after. *Modern London* is an outsize guidebook combined with a sort of 'anatomy' of the contemporary town and descriptions of the individual topographical plates and of the 'London Cries' with their familiar street settings. A catalogue bound with the 1807 *Picture* amends the earlier notice and describes the new work as 'one large elegant volume 4to embellished with 54 copper plates thirty-one of which are coloured. £3. 3s. boards'.

Modern London being the History and Present State of the British Metropolis. Illustrated with numerous copper plates. London: Printed for Richard Phillips, No 71, St Paul's Church-Yard By C. Mercier and Co. Northumberland-court, Strand. 1804.

Quarto, 260 × 200mm. (Large Paper 425 × 260mm)   1804

COLLATION Title-page; pp iii–vi, advertisement; pp vii–viii, contents; pp 1–474, Modern London; pp 475–501, description of plates; description of plates of 'itinerant traders' (31 leaves interleaved with plates); pp 537–64, appendix; pp 565–71, index; pp 572–3, lists of plates. (Errors in pagination are noted by Upcott.)

All but two of the topographical plates were drawn by Edward Pugh, a miniature painter, architectural draughtsman and aquatint engraver who exhibited at the Royal Academy from 1793 and died in 1813. Most are etched in a mechanical, uninspired fashion but the originals must take some of the blame for this lifelessness since the views of St Paul's and Westminster Abbey, drawn by Samuel Rawle, are decidedly the most impressive. The engraving was entrusted to Rawle, one of the Cookes, John Pass, Thomas Reeve, Richard Rhodes, James Fittler, James Newton, J.P. Thompson, Isaac Taylor the pedagogue, J.G. Walker and Edward Edwards—certainly more competent engravers than the anonymous hacks usually employed on guidebook illustration. The chief attraction of the book lies in the 31 Cries of London, each in an identified setting, and hand coloured. They were drawn by William Marshall Craig, a fashionable miniature painter who exhibited at the Royal Academy from 1788 to 1827 and was appointed painter in water-colours to Queen Charlotte. There is only one engraver's credit, that of Edward Edwards, but the uniformity of the etchings suggests that they were all by one hand.

All plates have Phillips's publication-line bm or tm with dates in 1804 ranging from March to September, quoted in the descriptions: 'Published (date) by Richard Phillips, 71 St. Paul's Church Yard'. They are unnumbered, except in the checklist. The 'itinerant traders' usually have their plate-marks cropped but the subjects uniformly measure 98 × 68mm and the engraved frames 133 × 100mm.

1 front. The Cities of London & Westminster/accurately copied from the Table of the Camera Obscura in the Royal Observatory at Greenwich. Pugh del. Cooke sculp. Augt 11, 1804. 160 × 365/205 × 400mm.

2 p 105 (tm) A Plan of London with its modern improvements. S.J. Neele sculpt, 352 Strand. Published Augt 12th 1804 by Richd Phillips, St Paul's Church Yard. 225 × 575/250 × 590mm. (*Darlington and Howgego* 229(2))

3 p 169 The West India Docks in the Isle of Dogs, with Greenwich Hospital in the foreground./Drawn in the Camera Obscura of the Royal Observatory. Pugh delin. Reeve sculpt. Augt 11, 1804. 130 × 185/185 × 255mm. The first section of the dock had been opened in August 1802.

4 p 176 Greenwich Park, with the Royal Observatory, on Easter Monday. Pugh delt. Pass sculpt. April 20, 1804. 125 × 183/175 × 238mm.

5 p 233 The Court of King's Bench, Westminster. E. Pugh del. J.G. Walker sc. Augt 11, 1804. 130 × 185/165 × 230mm.

6 p 256 The Promenade in St James's Park. Pugh delt. Edwards sculp. March 20, 1804. 128 × 182/183 × 255mm.

7 p 262 The Entrance to Hyde Park on a Sunday. Pugh delt. Pass sculp. Augt 11, 1804. 125 × 183/185 × 235mm.

8 p 264 The Admiralty, the War Office, & the Treasury. Pugh delin. Pass sculp. Augt 11, 1804. 125 × 183/185 × 235mm. Shows the telegraph arms on the Admiralty roof, a new-fangled French invention.

9 p 265 Westminster from Lambeth. Pugh del. Rawle sc. Augt 11, 1804. 130 × 185/180 × 235mm.

10 p 267 The Houses of Parliament, with the Royal Processions. Pugh delin. Thompson sculp. April 20, 1804. 128 × 185/187 × 240mm.

11 p 268 The King on his Throne in the House of Lords. E. Pugh Del. J. Fittler sc. Augt 11, 1804. 128 × 183/170 × 210mm.

12 p 270 The House of Commons. E. Pugh Del. J. Fittler sc. Augt 11, 1804. 130 × 185/170 × 205mm.

13 p 297 The Rotunda in the Bank of England. Pugh delt. Edwards sculp. March 20, 1804. 185 × 128/245 × 190mm. Built by Soane, 1794–5. (*Bank of England* 168)

14 p 304 The Bank, Bank Buildings, Royal Exchange & Cornhill. Pugh delt. Reeve sculp. Augt 11, 1804. 125 × 185/175 × 245mm. (*Bank of England* 37)

15 p 306 The Royal Exchange. E. Pugh del. J.G. Walker sc. Augt 11, 1804. 130 × 187/170 × 230mm. Inner courtyard, merchants consulting.

16 p 308 St Paul's Cathedral, with Lord Mayor's Show on the Water. Pugh delt. Newton sculp. Augt 11, 1804. 130 × 185/185 × 245mm.

17 p 363 St Paul's Cathedral. Rawle delt. Reeve scpt. Sept 1, 1804. 135 × 190/190 × 253mm. W. front with a portion of Tijou railing, removed in 1886, still surrounding Queen Anne's statue and the steps.

18 p 368 The annual meeting of the Charity Children/in St Paul's Cathedral. E. Pugh D.J. Fittler sc. Augt 11, 1804. 185 × 130/230 × 155mm.

19 p 376 Westminster Abbey. Drawn & Engraved by S. Rawle. Augt 14, 1804. 135 × 193/195 × 260mm. View from N.

20 p 406 The Society of Arts distributing its premiums. Pugh del. Engraved by Isaac Taylor. Augt 11, 1804. 130 × 185/175 × 215mm.

21 p 451 Drury Lane Theatre/from the Stage during the performance. Pugh delint. Engraved by Isaac Taylor. Aug. 11, 1804. 125 × 180/180 × 220mm. Henry Holland's building, opened 1794.

22 p 452 The Royal Family at Covent Garden Theatre. E. Pugh Del. J. Fittler Sc. Augt 11, 1804. 130 × 183/180 × 210mm. Henry Holland's rebuilding, opened 1792.

23 p 456 Vauxhall/on a Gala Night. Pugh del. Rhodes sc. June 11, 1804. 130 × 185/180 × 245mm.

24 Stratford Place—Baking or Boiling Apples! Craig del. Augt 25, 1804.

25 Tabarts Juvenile Library (Bond St.)—Band Boxes! Craig del. April 25, 1804.

26 Whitfields Tabernacle—Baskets! Craig del. April 25, 1804.

27 Smithfield—Bellows to Mend! Craig del. Augst 25, 1804.

28 Portman Square—Brick Dust! Craig del. April 25, 1804.

29 Theatre Drury Lane—Buy a Bill of Play! Craig del. Augt 25, 1805.

30 Bethlem Hospital—Cat's & Dog's Meat! Craig del. April 25, 1804.

31 Soho Square—Chairs to Mend! Craig del. Augst 25, 1804.

32 St James's Place—Cherries! Craig del. Augst 25, 1804.

33 Charing Cross—Door Mats! Craig del. Augst 25, 1804.

34 New Church Strand—Dust O! Drawn by Craig. Etched by Edwards. April 25, 1804. St Mary le Strand.

35 Newgate—Green Hasteds! Craig del. Augst 25, 1804. ie 'Hastens', peas.

36 Shoreditch Church—Hair Brooms! Craig del. April 25, 1804.

37 St Martins Church—Hot Loaves! Craig del. April 25, 1804. St Martin in the Fields.

38 Pantheon—Hot Special Gingerbread! Craig del. April 25, 1804.

39 Whitehall—Knives to Grind! Craig del. Augst 25, 1804.

40 Temple Bar—Lavender! Craig del. April 25, 1804.

41 Billingsgate—Mackerel! Craig del. Augst 25, 1804.

42 Mansion House—Matches! Augst 25, 1804. No credits.

43 Cavendish Square—Milk Below! Craig del. Augst 25, 1804.

44 Middlesex Hospital—New Potatoes! Craig del. April 25, 1804.

45 Fitzroy Square—Old Clothes! April 25, 1804. No credits.

46 Blackfryars Bridge—A Poor Sweep, Sir! Craig del. April 25, 1804.

47 Portland Place—Rabbits! Craig del. Augst 25, 1804.

48 Russell Square—Rhubard! Craig del. April 25, 1804.

49 St Giles's Church—Sand O! Craig del. Aug 7, 1804. St Giles in the Fields.

50 Hyde Park Corner—A Showman. July 7, 1804. No credits.

51 Somerset House—Slippers! Augst 25, 1804. No credits.

52 Foundling Hospital—Sweep Soot O! April 25, 1804. No credits.

53 Covent Garden—Strawberries! Craig del. Augst 25, 1804.

54 Hanover Square—Water Cresses! Craig del. April 25, 1804.

90 · STORER AND GREIG'S SELECT VIEWS [1804]

At the turn of the century James Storer was engraving from paintings and drawings by notable British topographical artists for the better class of illustrated periodical, such as the *Copper-plate Magazine* and the *Monthly Register*. In the former the work was shared out between himself, the skilful John Walker and John Greig, with whom he was destined to be closely associated. Greig was his sole fellow engraver for Herbert's *Antiquities of the Inns of Court* (no 88), for these *Select Views*, for the long-running *Antiquarian and Topographical Cabinet* (no 118) and for albums of literary landscapes illustrating Cowper, Bloomfield and Burns. The first two of these are published by Vernor & Hood, to whose major topographical series *The Beauties of England and Wales* (no 104) Storer also contributed some plates.

As with the *Beauties*, Vernor & Hood offered these *Select Views* to the public in monthly Numbers:

Select Views of London and its Environs. To be continued monthly. On the First of January, 1804, will be published, Elegantly printed in Demy Quarto, on a beautiful Vellum Paper, carefully Hotpressed, Price 5s. Number 1 of Select Views of London and its Environs; containing a Collection of Highly-Finished Engravings, From Original Paintings and Drawings, accompanied by Copious Letter-press Descriptions of such objects in the Metropolis and the surrounding Country As are most remarkable for Antiquity, Architectural Grandeur, or Picturesque Beauty. No. I. Will contain 16 pages of Letter-Press, and the following Plates, Executed in the very best Style, by Messrs STORER and GREIG.

1. The Abbey Church, St Albans, Herts, from the S.E. Shepherd
2. St Michael's Church ditto Shepherd
3. View of the Royal Hospital, Greenwich Nash
4. Distant view of Windsor Castle, from the Park Turner, R.A.

Conditions

I. A number of this work shall be published regularly on the first day of every month. Price 5s.
II. Each number shall contain from 12 to 16 pages of Letter-Press and every *Three* numbers, upon an average,

Eight Engravings, exclusive of a Vignette, containing some miscellaneous object of curiosity. In the course of publication will be given numerous *interior views*, engraved in a superior style of excellence.
III. To accommodate the curious, a few copies will be printed on extra fine super-royal paper, with the first impressions of the plates, worked in the manner of proofs. Price 7s 6d. each number.
IV. Engraved Title Pages, including elegant Vignettes, will be given gratis, at the conclusion of each Volume. J. Swan, printer, Angel-street.

An 'Advertisement' gives more specific information on the illustrations than does the prospectus:

The engravings will be executed, with the greatest care, by Messrs Storer and Greig, from *original paintings* and *drawings*, actually taken for the work, by artists of professional eminence, and upon a scale which will admit of making out the architectural parts of buildings with the utmost precision....

In apportioning the letter-press to the different plates, contained in each number, the importance of the object described will invariably form a criterion with regard to length ... It will frequently happen that the *entire* letter-press of a number, perhaps more, will be devoted to *one* plate ... The work, when bound in volumes, will form not merely a collection of engravings, but an interesting body of topography....

Interiors of buildings, from the labour necessary to be bestowed upon them, and their consequent great expence, are nearly strangers in topographical collections: arrangements have been made for the frequent introduction of such subjects: this will considerably enhance the charges of the publication, but we have no doubt it will extend its sale....

London: published by Vernor and Hood, Poultry; J. Storer and J. Greig, Chapel Street, Pentonville.

In the *Monthly Literary Advertiser* of September 1805 20 Numbers with 60 plates were advertised at £4 5s or imperial quarto in boards at £7 10s.

The text, attributed to William Herbert of the *Inns of Court*, was issued unpaginated ('in order', say the directions, 'that the purchaser might be left at liberty to arrange the subjects treated of in a manner most agreeable to himself') but, after the first 32 pages, it was signed in pairs of leaves: vol. 1 from 'G' to '4B', vol. 2 from 'B' to 'NN'. Each volume opens with a two-page 'Subjects treated ... with a list of plates which illustrate them'; this list is numbered but not in the order in which the subjects were eventually bound up which, in spite of the above advice, is fairly consistent. These numbers are quoted after each description of a plate and after each group of plates is a note of the relevant text. A copy of the book in the Royal Library, specially made up in or after 1822, contains some of the separate plates and vignettes in triplicate (without letters, with letters, on India paper with letters) and some in duplicate.

Select views of London and its Environs: containing a Collection of Highly Finished Engravings, from Original Paintings and Drawings, accompanied by Copious Letter-Press Descriptions of such objects in the Metropolis and Surrounding Country as are most remarkable for Antiquity, Architectural Grandeur, or Picturesque Beauty. Volume I (II). (vignette, different in each vol.) London: Published by Vernor and Hood, Poultry; J. Storer and J. Greig, Chapel Street, Pentonville. 1804(1805). Printed by S. Gosnell, Little Queen Street.

Folio, 350 × 270mm. (Large Paper)   1804–5

COLLATION   Vol. 1. Title-page; lists of subjects and plates (3pp); 32pp unsigned, followed by pairs of leaves signed G–4B. Vol. 2. Title-page; lists of subjects and plates (2pp); letterpress in pairs of leaves signed B–NN2.

An undated reissue, without text, of all 74 of the separate plates and the vignettes, together with 24 from Herbert's *Inns of Court*, was later published by Vernor, Hood & Sharp, the name under which the firm traded between 1806 and 1812. Two newly worded titles are decorated with vignettes from the original title-pages and are aimed to attract the growing number of extra-illustrators—successfully, since these plates are to be found dispersed among the pages of most extra-illustrated copies of Pennant (no 67). The uncaptioned vignettes, printed on the text pages of the original, are now printed without letterpress but with added captions. These are recorded in the descriptions below.

London Illustrated:/or/A Series of Plates/to/illustrate the History of/London and Westminster. (vignette as described under item 41) Published by Vernor, Hood & Sharp, Poultry.

Pennant's Account of London Illustrated. (vignette as described under item 1)

The list of draughtsmen, of which Storer is one, contains many of the names which feature in the contemporary *Beauties of England and Wales* including, as it does, George Arnald, George Shepherd, Frederick Nash and T. Whichelo. There is also a Turner view of Windsor (item 6) and some drawings of the environs by the 21 year old Samuel Prout and by John Powell. Plates in the first volume are dated between January and December 1804, those in the second between January and September

1805. The publication-line for the plates is uniform: 'London: Publish'd (date) by Vernor & Hood, Poultry, J. Storer & J. Greig, Chapel Street, Pentonville.', and for the vignettes: 'Publ. (date)'.

VOL. 1

1 (title-page vignette) London from Bankside. Drawn & Engraved by Jas. Storer. 75 × 140/335 × 240mm.

2 S.E. View of the Abbey Church/St Albans Herts. Engraved by J. Storer from a Drawing by G. Shepperd ... Jany 1, 1804. 127 × 182/225 × 310mm. (No 1,1)

3 Interior of the Abbey Church/St Albans. Engraved by J. Storer from a Drawing by F. Nash ... Novr 1, 1804. 190 × 140/320 × 230mm. (No 1,2)

4 (St Michael's Church/St Albans/Hertfordshire) G. Shepherd del. J. Greig sculp. Publ. Jany 1, 1804. 110 × 140/350 × 230mm. Caption only appears on reissue. (No 1,3)

(20pp unsigned text)

5 The Hall of Greenwich Hospital/Kent. Engraved by J. Storer from a Drawing by F. Nash ... Jany 1, 1804. 135 × 185/225 × 310mm. (No 11,1)

(10pp unsigned text)

6 Windsor from the Forest/Berks. Drawn by J. Greig from a Drawing by Wm Turner R.A.... Jany 2, 1804. 185 × 135/330 × 230mm. The Royal Academy *Turner 1775–1851* exhibition catalogue notes that the Petworth House 'Windsor Castle' (80) was the first of a number of pictures showing places in and around Windsor and was based on a water-colour in a sketchbook Turner was using from 1804 to 1805. (No 22) (Rawlinson, *Engraved work of J.M.W. Turner* 72)

(2pp unsigned text)

7 Waltham Abbey/Essex. Engraved by J. Greig from a Drawing by G. Arnald ... Jany 2, 1804. 130 × 185/225 × 310mm. Gateway. (No 19,3)

8 N.E. View of Waltham Abbey Church/Essex. Drawn and Engraved by J. Greig ... July 1, 1804. 135 × 193/235 × 320mm. (No 19,1)

9 Interior of Waltham Abbey Church/Essex. Engraved by J. Greig from a Drawing by F. Nash ... Dec 1, 1804. 195 × 140/320 × 235mm. (No 19,2)

(16pp text, sigs G–K)

10 London from Greenwich/Kent. Engrav'd by J. Greig from a Painting by G. Arnald ... Feby 1, 1804. 127 × 188/230 × 320mm. (No 13,1)

(2pp unsigned text)

11 S.E. View of Stepney Church/Middlesex. Engraved by J. Storer from a Drawing by G. Shepperd ... Feby 1, 1804. 130 × 190/225 × 320mm. (No 17,1)

12 (Antiquities at Stepney Church/Middlesex.) Drawn & Engraved by J. Storer and J. Greig. Publ. March 1,

1804. 90 × 160/330 × 230mm. Caption added to this vignette only in the reissue. (No 17,2)

(12pp text, sigs L–N)

13 Westminster Hall. Engrav'd by J. Greig from a Drawing by F. Nash … March 1, 1804. 130 × 187/230 × 330mm. Exterior from the N. with Abbey in background, stormy sky. (No 21,1)

14 The Painted Chamber,/Westminster. Engrav'd by J. Greig from a Drawing by T. Whichillo … April 1, 1804. 130 × 185/230 × 330mm. (No 21,2)

(12pp text, sigs O–Q)

15 West View of St Paul's Cathedral,/London. Engrav'd by J. Storer from a Drawing by F. Nash … March 1, 1804. 192 × 135/318 × 230mm. (No 14)

(26pp text, sigs R–Z)

16 Chingford Church/Essex. Engraved by J. Storer from a Drawing by G. Sheppard … April 1, 1804. 133 × 185/230 × 320mm. (No 7)

(4pp text, sig AA)

17 S.W. View of the Remains of Eltham Palace/Kent. Drawn & Engrav'd by J. Greig … June 1, 1804. 137 × 190/230 × 330mm. (No 10,1)

18 Interior of the Hall of Eltham Palace/Kent. Engraved by J. Storer after a Drawing by Baynes … May 1, 1804. 190 × 135/320 × 235mm. (No 10,2)

19 (vignette) John of Eltham's Tomb. Whichelo del. Greig sculp. Publ. May 1st, 1804. 140 × 145/340 × 240mm. Westminster Abbey. (No 10,3)

(10pp text, sigs BB–CC)

20 London from the Thames, S.W. of Blackfriars Bridge. Engraved by J. Greig from a Drawing by Lady Arden … May 1, 1804. 132 × 190/230 × 330mm. (No 13,2)

(2pp text, sig DD)

21 Crosby Hall/London. Engraved by J. Greig after a Drawing by Whichello … May 1, 1804. 185 × 130/330 × 230mm. Exterior. (No 9,1) (Longford 424)

22 Interior of Crosby Hall. Engraved by J. Storer after a Drawing by F. Nash … Octr 1, 1804. 182 × 130/320 × 225mm. (No 9,2) (Longford 442)

23 (Gateway &c in Crosby Square/London) Whichelo del. Storer sculp. 120 × 165/320 × 230mm. Caption added to vignette in reissue. (No 9,3)

(12pp text, sigs EE–FF)

24 Christ's Hospital (from the Cloisters)/London. Drawn and Engrav'd by J. Storer … June 1, 1804. 140 × 195/230 × 330mm. (No 8)

(21pp text, sigs HH–MM)

25 The Old Bridge at Stratford le Bow/Middlesex. Drawn & Engrav'd by J. Storer … July 1, 1804. 132 × 193/245 × 330mm. (No 4)

(8pp text, sigs NN–OO)

26 St Andrew Undershaft,/Leadenhall Street. Engraved by J. Greig from a Drawing by J. Wichello … August 1, 1804. 193 × 135/330 × 235mm. (No 2,1)

27 (vignette) Stow's Monument. Whichelo del. Storer sc. 150 × 130/330 × 230mm. No publication-line. (No 2,2)

(8pp text, sigs PP–QQ)

28 Part of Lambeth Palace/from the/Bishops Walk. Engrav'd by J. Greig from a Drawing by J. Wichello … Octr 1, 1804. 195 × 135/330 × 230mm. (No 12,2)

29 The Lollard's Tower, Lambeth Palace/Surry. Engrav'd by J. Greig after a Drawing by T. Whichello … April 1, 1804. 188 × 130/325 × 230mm. (No 12,3)

30 Interior of the Hall of Lambeth Palace. Engrav'd by J. Greig after a Drawing by T. Whichillo … Novr 1, 1804. 180 × 130/330 × 230mm. (No 12,4)

31 Lambeth Palace from the Garden. Engrav'd by J. Greig from a Drawing by T. Wichillo … August 1, 1804. 133 × 195/230 × 330mm. (No 12,1)

(56pp text, sigs RR–3G)

32 Temple Bar from Butcher Row/London. Engrav'd by J. Storer after a Drawing by E. Dayes in June 1796 … Septr 1, 1804. 190 × 132/330 × 225mm. (No 18)

(2pp text, sig 3H)

33 Remains of Cannonbury/Islington. Drawn & Engrav'd by J. Storer … Septr 1, 1804. 132 × 195/230 × 340 mm. Canonbury Tower. (No 5)

(8pp text, sigs 3I–3K)

34 The Charter House/London. Drawn & Engrav'd by J. Storer … August 1, 1804. 135 × 192/230 × 340mm. From the garden. (No 6,2)

35 The Charter House/from the/Square. Drawn & Engrav'd by J. Greig … Septr 1, 1804. 137 × 195/230 × 335mm. (No 6,1)

(18pp text, sigs 3L–3O)

36 Barking: Essex. Engrav'd by J. Storer from a Drawing by S. Prout … Novr 1, 1804. 133 × 187/225 × 330mm. (No 3,1)

37 (Bell Fire Gate/Barking/Essex) J. Greig del et sculp. 140 × 140/325 × 230mm. No publication-line. Caption added to vignette in reissue. (No 3,2)

(17pp text, sigs 3P–3T)

38 Sadlers Wells. Drawn and Engraved by J. Greig after a Sketch by S. Prout … Novr 1, 1804. 135 × 190/230 × 325mm. (No 16)

(2pp unsigned text)

39 The Royal College of Physicians/London. Engraved by J. Storer from a Drawing by Whichelo … Decr 1st 1804. 185 × 130/310 × 230mm. (No 15)

(10pp text, sigs 3U–3Y)

40 Westminster (from Lambeth). Engraved by J. Greig from a Drawing by F. Wichello … Decr 1, 1804. 132 × 195/240 × 340mm. (No 20)

(13pp text, sigs 3Z–4B)

41 (title-page vignette of a distant view of the City and Cathedral from Millbank) J. Greig del. et sculp. 80 × 145/335 × 240mm. No caption.

42 St Saviours,/Southwark. Drawn by F. Nash. Engraved by J. Storer ... Jan 1, 1805. 138 × 187/240 × 330mm. The N. front. (No 12,1)

43 (vignette with caption over) The Tomb of/Bishop Andrews/in the Church of St Mary Overies/Southwark. J. Greig fecit ... June 1st 1805. 130 × 150/330 × 240mm. (No 12,2)

(16pp text, sigs B–E)

44 Remains of St Bartholomew's Priory/West Smithfield. Drawn & Engrav'd by J. Greig ... Jany 1, 1805. 187 × 135/340 × 240mm. (No 3,3)

45 Eastern Cloister of St Bartholomew's Priory. Drawn and Etched by J. Greig ... Feby 1, 1805. 180 × 153/330 × 235mm. (No 3,6)

46 (vignettes) Eastern side of the Cloister of St Bartholomew's Priory – Vaulted Passage, part of ... St Bartholomew's Priory. Etch'd by J. Storer ... Jany 1, 1805. 120 × 150,110 × 150/330 × 240mm. (No 3, 4–5)

47 Interior of the Church of St Bartholomew the Great. Engraved by J. Greig from a Drawing by F. Nash ... March 1, 1805. 180 × 125/330 × 240mm. (No 3,1)

48 (Tomb of Prior Rahere/Church of St Bartholomew the Great/London.) Drawn by F. Nash. Engraved by J. Storer. 130 × 130/330 × 240mm. (No 3,2)

(24pp text, sigs F–L)

49 Chelsea Hospital. Engraved by J. Storer from a Drawing by S. Prout ... Feb 1, 1805. 135 × 190/240 × 325mm. (No 5) (Longford 28)

(8pp text, sigs M–N)

50 The Admiralty and Horse Guards/Westminster. Engraved by J. Storer from a Drawing by F. Nash ... March 1, 1805. 132 × 190/245 × 330mm. From the Parade. (No 2)

(2pp text, sig O)

51 Marks Hall/Essex. Engrav'd by J. Greig from a Drawing by S. Prout ... Apr 1, 1805 ... 130 × 185/240 × 330mm. (No 11)

(2pp unsigned text)

52 Stoke Church/Bucks. Engraved by J. Storer from a Drawing by J.Powell ... Apr 1, 1805. 130 × 185/240 × 330mm. (No 14)

(6pp, sigs P–Q)

53 Sion House/Middlesex. Engrav'd by J. Greig from a Drawing by J. Powell ... Septr 1, 1805. 130 × 185/240 × 325mm. (No 13)

(16pp text, sigs R–U)

54 Westminster Abbey/(N. Choir Aisle). Drawn by F. Nash. Engrav'd by J. Storer ... May 1, 1805. 190 × 130/325 × 240mm. (No 1,1)

55 (vignettes) Entrance to the Chapel of St Erasmus, Westminster – The Abbot's Tomb within the Chapel. Etch'd by J. Storer ... Sepr 1, 1805. 120 × 90,130 × 150/240 × 330mm. (No 1, 3–4)

56 (vignettes) The Chantry and Tomb of Henry 5th/Westminster Abbey ... Sepr 1, 1805. 140 × 120,120 × 120/245 × 330mm. No credits. (No 1,5)

57 (Shrine of Edward the Confessor/Westminster Abbey). Wichelo del. J. Greig sculp. 140 × 140/330 × 240mm. Caption added to this vignette in the reissue. (No 1,6)

58 Poet's Corner, Westminster Abbey. Engrav'd by Storer from a Drawing by Wichelo ... Septr 1, 1805. 185 × 130/330 × 240mm. (No 1,2)

59 (vignette) Entrance to Henry VIIth Chapel Westminster. Whichelo del. Storer sculp. 120 × 130/330 × 240mm. (No 1,7)

60 (vignettes) The Jerusalem Chamber, Westminster – Entrance to the Cloisters from the Deans Yard. 150 × 110,150 × 112/245 × 330mm. No credits or publication-lines. (No 1, 8–9)

61 (vignette) Entrance to the Chapter House Westminster. Engraved by J. Storer. 160 × 125/320 × 240mm. (No 1,10)

(44pp text, sigs X–HH)

62 Burnham Abbey/Bucks. Drawn by J. Powell. Engraved by J. Storer ... May 1, 1805. 130 × 183/240 × 330mm. Not included in 'List of Subjects'.

63 (vignette) (Burnham Abbey/Bucks) Engraved by J. Greig. Drawn by J. Powell. 100 × 130/320 × 230mm. Not included in 'List of Subjects'.

(4pp text, sig II)

64 Eton College/Bucks. Drawn by I. Powell. Engraved by Jas Storer ... July 1st 1805. 130 × 185/250 × 330mm. (No 6)

65 (vignette) The chapel of Eton College. J. Powell del. J. Storer sculp. 95 × 140/325 × 240mm. Not included in 'List of Subjects'.

(4pp text, sig KK)

66 Hampstead/Middlesex. Drawn & Engrav'd by J. Greig ... June 1st, 1805. 135 × 195/240 × 320mm. (No 8,2)

67 Highgate Church. Drawn & Etch'd by J. Greig – Hampstead Church. Drawn & Etch'd by J. Storer ... June 1, 1805. Each 155 × 110/240 × 330mm. (No 8, 3–4)

68 Kentish Town and Highgate from the South/Middlesex. Drawn & Engrav'd by J. Storer ... June 1, 1805. 130 × 185/240 × 330mm. (No 8,1)

(2pp unsigned text)

69 Bray, Berks. Engrav'd by Greig from a Drawing by Powell ... Sept 1, 1805. 132 × 185/245 × 330mm. (No 4)

(2pp text, sig LL)

70 Great Marlow/Bucks. Engraved by J. Greig from a Drawing by T. Powell ... July 1st, 1805. 137 × 195/245 × 330mm. (No 10)

(2pp unsigned text)

71 Maidenhead/Berks. Drawn by S. Powell. Engraved by J. Storer ... Sepr 1, 1805. 135 × 185/245 × 330mm. (No 9)

(2pp text, sig MM)

72 View from Richmond Hill/Surry. Engraved by J. Storer from a Drawing by J. Powell ... Augt 1, 1805. 133 × 183/250 × 330mm. Not included in 'List of Subjects'. (*Gascoigne* 41)

(2pp unsigned text)

73 (vignettes) Remains of Winchester Palace – A window/in the Hall of Winchester Palace, Southwark. Etch'd by J. Storer ... June 1, 1805. (No 16)

(2pp text, sig NN)

74 Interior of the Royal Exchange/London. Engrav'd by J. Greig from a Drawing by Elms ... Sept 1, 1805. 135 × 187/235 × 330mm. Perhaps the work of the architect James Elmes who entered the Royal Academy Schools and won a Silver Medal in 1805; later the author of *Metropolitan Improvements* (no 154). (No 7)

91 · CURIOSITIES OF LONDON AND WESTMINSTER [1805]

John Harris, the publisher of this guidebook, was apprenticed to the bookseller Thomas Evans (whose periodical articles provoked Goldsmith to assault) and was subsequently an assistant to John Murray and then to Francis Newbery. On the death of the latter in 1780 he became manager to the widowed Elizabeth Newbery and took over her business when she retired at the end of the century. Shortly after doing so he revived the bestselling title of *Curiosities of London and Westminster* (no 49) which the firm had been selling for 30 years in four volumes of miniature format. He reduced the number of volumes to two and considerably increased their size. He also discarded the by now very old-fashioned plates, reduced from views originally engraved about 1760, and then replaced them with a

dozen poorly drawn anonymous views in the current style. These copper engravings carry the publication-line 'Published July 15, 1805 by J. Harris, corner of St Paul's Church Yard, London', although the title-page is undated. There is neither check-list nor numbering.

Curiosities of London and Westminster described. In Two Volumes, vol. I (II), Containing a description of ... London: Printed for J. Harris (successor to E. Newbery), Corner of St Paul's Churchyard.

Sextodecimo, 135 × 80mm. c 1805

COLLATION Vol. 1. Title-page; pp 3–4, preface; pp 5–8, introduction; pp 9–198, Curiosities of London, Vol. 2. Title-page; pp 3–213, Curiosities of London continued.

VOL. 1

1 front. The Tower. 63 × 95mm.

2 p 52 The Monument. Published July 25, 1805 ... 95 × 63mm.

3 p 73 The Royal Exchange. 83 × 62mm.

4 p 109 Guild-Hall. 65 × 95mm.

5 p 135 The Mansion House. 60 × 90mm.

6 p 148 East India House. 60 × 75mm.

VOL. 2

7 front. St Paul's. 60 × 95mm.

8 p 48 Black Friars Bridge. 60 × 98mm.

9 p 71 Somerset House. 60 × 75mm. View from Strand.

10 p 106 Westminster Abbey. 95 × 62mm. W. front.

11 p 208 The Horse Guards. 63 × 95mm.

12 p 212 The London Docks. 60 × 100mm. First dock opened 30 January 1805.

92 · DANIELL'S SIX VIEWS OF THE METROPOLIS [1805]

William Daniell accompanied his uncle Thomas to India in 1784 and remained there as his assistant from the age of 15 to the age of 25. Together they published locally views of Calcutta and, on their return to England, the famous book *Oriental Scenery* (1795–1808). From 1795 William exhibited topographical paintings of both India and Great Britain at the Royal Academy. The Academy

Professor of Architecture from 1798 was George Dance junior, a busy architect and a man of some influence who in 1768 had succeeded his father as the City's Clerk of the Works. He became Daniell's patron and commissioned him to paint in oils and make an official aquatint of his grandiose scheme for improving the Port of London, submitted to a Select Committee but never realized. The painting, measuring 3 × 6 feet, and the engraving, which was published in November 1800 at about one third of the size, both turn into an alluring eastward riverscape the architect's design for twin London Bridges with alternate drawbridges to allow for the passage of ships, a new Custom House and Legal Quay and two vast hemicycles at the bridge's head and foot, forming piazzas for the Monument to the north and for a 'proposed Naval Trophy' to the south. From this beginning sprang a magnificent series of birds-eye views in aquatint of the new docks then being excavated to relieve congestion in the Pool. These were unnumbered but some of the following may sometimes be found sharing a contemporary binding or portfolio with the *Six Views*:

A View of London, with the Improvements of its Port,/submitted to the Select Committee of the ... House of Commons, by Mr. Dance ... Published ... for William Daniell ... August 15th, 1802. 405 × 780/490 × 860mm.

B An Elevated View of the New Docks & Warehouses now constructing on the Isle of Dogs near Limehouse for ... Shipping in the West India Trade ... Drawn & Engraved by Wm Daniell & Published by him Octr 15, 1802. 400 × 780/490 × 860mm.

C An Elevated View of the New Dock in Wapping.... Drawn and Engraved by William Daniell & Published by him Jany 1 1803. 405 × 780/480 × 855mm.

D Brunswick Dock on the Thames at Blackwall.... opened for the reception of Shipping on the 20th of Novr. 1790. Drawn & Engraved by William Daniell & Published by him Octr 20 1803. 400 × 775/480 × 850mm.

E A View of the Commercial Docks at Rotherhithe. Drawn & Engraved by William Daniell & Published by him, 1813. 405 × 780/480 × 855mm.

F A View of the East India Docks.... Drawn, Engraved & Published Octr 1st 1808 by William Daniell. 405 × 780/490 × 855mm.

G A View of the London Dock.... Drawn, Engraved & Published by William Daniell ... Octr 1st, 1808. 405 × 780/490 × 855mm.

Engraved on each dock view is quite a lengthy caption with an historical note but there is no separate title-page or dedication, nor any printed text. The river, the basins, the dock buildings, the forests of masts, the distant houses and churches and the broad skies are all discreetly washed over in subdued colours.

The *Six Views* are similarly coloured, only the title-page, which takes the form of a dedication to Daniell's patron, being printed as a vignette in monochrome aquatint. Like the dock views they are accompanied by no text but, unlike them, they lack descriptive captions. Two plates were published in each of June and August 1804 and two more in January 1805, which is also the date of the dedication. The charge for the set was £10 10s. Plate numbers in voided capitals and Roman numerals are centered in the lower margins and are followed by the publication-line: 'Drawn, Engraved and published by William Daniell,/No. 9 Cleveland Street, Fitzory Square, London (date).'

0 To/George Dance Esquire RA/Architect to the/City of London. &c./These Six Views of the Metropolis/of the British Empire/are Respectfully Dedicated by William Daniell/London January 1st 1805. 280 × 370/540 × 715mm. Uncoloured aquatint, the dedication carved on a monument in the foreground, accompanied by a broken Corinthian capital amid wooded countryside on the S. Bank; the City viewed across the river.

1 London,/from Greenwich Park./Plate I/...August 1, 1804. 405 × 655/470 × 720mm. The view is from One Tree Hill. An original water-colour is in the BM (*Crace* 36.42).

2 London./Plate II./...August 1, 1804. 400 × 650/470 × 715mm. Birds-eye view of the Tower and Pool of London looking W. An original water-colour is in the BM (*Crace* 8.68).

3 London./Plate III./...June 1, 1804. 405 × 660/475 × 720mm. S.E. view, from Tooley Street, of London Bridge and adjacent portions of the N.bank, including old Fishmongers' Hall.

4 London./Plate IV./...June 1, 1804. 400 × 655/475 × 720mm. Blackfriars Bridge, St. Paul's and the City from Bankside.

5 London./Plate V./... Jany. 1, 1805. 400 × 645/470 × 715mm. The unembanked Somerset House viewed from the opposite shore; Drury Lane on the skyline.

6 London./Plate VI./...Jany. 1, 1805. 405 × 650/475 × 710mm. Westminster Bridge and Abbey, from Somerset House Terrace.

This work was originally issued over a period of five years in 149 Numbers of about 24 pages each, for binding into six volumes. One hundred and fifty copper plate engravings accompanied the Numbers and each volume was equipped both with a printed and an engraved title.

A discursive history of London to the year 1800 fills the first volume, published in 1805, and was brought up to 1810 in the addenda (Nos 146–8) which completed the text of the sixth. Vols 2–4 blend topography, antiquities, local history and architecture with guidebook information. The title-pages promise to impart all this in the form of a perambulation and indeed 'Perambulation I' is to be found in vol. 2 (p 99), to be followed by 'Second Route' (p 361) and 'Route III' (p 452); 'Routes' 5–9 are contained in vol. 3 and 10–11 in vol. 4. Each volume is separately indexed so it is hard to track down any particular topic, but descriptions of central London, our concern here, are concentrated in the first four volumes; vols 5–6, headed 'Circuit of London', are concerned with the environs: Kent, Surrey, Berkshire, Hertfordshire and Essex.

At the end of the last volume there is a notice:

A New Edition is now in the Press and considerable Progress made in the Printing. Such of the Plates as have been in any Manner injured by the Number of Impressions taken off, are restored to their Original Perfection, others have been newly engraved and where any Alteration or Emendation could be made, it has not been omitted.

In fact the individual numbers were apparently reprinted as and when they went out of print, a practice which is common to many works published in this form and which makes it impossible to compile a standard description. The protean nature of the book is exemplified in a Guildhall Library set (SL.71) in which nearly all the plates have second-state publication-lines but the text is found thus:

Vol. 1 Title-page with the undated imprint of the later of the second-state publishers, James Robins, but only the first four of 26 Numbers have been reset.

Vol.2 Title-page with the undated imprint of the earlier of the second-state publishers, Joseph Robins & Sons. Nos 34 and 37–45 have been reset.

Vol.3 Title-page with the imprint of the original publisher, dated 1806, but Nos 51–60 have been reset. Updating of the text is indicated by a reference on p 316 to July 1813.

Vol.4 Title-page with the imprint of the original publisher, dated 1807, but after p 288 a section of repeated pagination has been corrected so that the plates now appear opposite higher page numbers.

A 'List of Embellishments' appended to the first edition enumerates 150 copper plate engravings, including views, maps, portraits and costume plates but not the engraved titles or numerous woodcuts. It arranges them approximately in chronological order of publication but indicates exactly where they are to be bound. The list numbers, which do not appear on the plates themselves, are transcribed in the descriptions below.

In the later edition the check-list marshals the plates in their binding order. Original publication-lines have generally been burnished out and undated ones, for either of the two publishers who succeeded Stratford, have been substituted. In all editions the credits usually take this form: 'Drawn by ... & Engraved by ... for Dr Hughson's Description of London'. The publication-lines, referred to in the descriptions by their key letters, are:

(a) 'Published by J. Stratford, 112 Holborn Hill (date).'
(b) 'Published by Joseph Robins, 57 Tooley Street.'
(c) 'Published by Joseph Robins & Sons, 57 Tooley Street.'

or a selection of elements from:

(d) 'Published by J. Robins & Co., Albion Press, Ivy Lane, Paternoster Row, London.'

James Stratford traded from 1789 to 1816 as printer, bookseller and stationer at 112 Holborn Hill. Joseph Robins published from Tooley Street, alone from 1800 to 1812 and under an imprint including his sons from 1813 to 1837. James Robins makes his first appearance in the directories in 1819 as 'Robins & Co., printer & publisher of 11 Ivy Lane, Newgate', where he continued until 1832. Stratford's last, dated publication-line (in vol.6) is in October 1810, so it may be assumed that those engravings with (b) or (c) substituted were reissued after that date and those with (d) after 1819. This latter assumption is supported by the text of the first volume, reissued, which carries the history up to the death of Queen Caroline on 7 August 1821, also by the only dated James Robins plate (item 66), of 5 July 1823.

J. Dugdale's *New British Traveller* (no 130; vol.4, 1820, p 791) advertises '*Hughson's London*' reissued 'in 30 Parts price 2s 6d each, embellished with views of Parochial churches, neatly engraved on wood in addition to 150 Copper Plate Engravings— a superior edition on fine wove paper, with additional embellishments, price 5s each part'.

'Hughson' is a pseudonym, the author's real name being David Pugh.

London; being an accurate History and Description of the British Metropolis and its Neighbourhood to Thirty Miles extent From an actual Perambulation. By David Hughson, LL.D. Vol. I (II–IV) (epigraph) London: Printed by W. Stratford, Crown-Court, Temple-Bar, for J. Stratford, No. 112, Holborn-Hill; and sold by all other booksellers. 1805 (etc).
(Later, undated title-pages are found with imprints 'London: Printed and Published by Joseph Robins and Sons, 57 Tooley Street, Southwark ...' or: 'London: J. Robins and Co., Albion Press, Ivy Lane, Paternoster Row.')

Octavo, 205 × 130mm. (Large Paper 260 × 210mm)
1805–9

COLLATION Vol. 1 (1805). Title-page; dedication to George III (2pp); pp v-viii, preface; pp 9–652 (Nos 1–27), London; pp i-xvi, index. (Later undated eds of vol. 1 collate: Title-page; pp 9–680 (Nos 1–27, 145–6), London; pp i-xvi, index. The 2 extra Nos bring the History to 7 August 1821. The Robins eds of vols 2–4 collate as the Stratford ed.) Vol. 2 (1805). Title-page; pp 3–540 (Nos 27–50), London; pp i-xvi, index. Vol. 3 (1806). Title-page; pp 3–640 (Nos 50–76), London; pp i-viii (No 149), index. Vol. 4 (1807). Title-page; pp 3–579 (Nos 77–101), London; pp i-viii (No 149), index.

The uninspired but agreeable topographical plates engraved on copper are mostly the work of Ambrose William Warren, son of the engraver Charles Warren and, later on, a contributor to the annuals. The chief artists are Robert Blemmel Schnebbelie, who was practically monopolized by the printseller Robert Wilkinson and provided many drawings for publication in his *Londina Illustrata* (no 131), and Edward Gyfford, a reput-

able architectural draughtsman. Among other engravers employed were William Woolnoth and John Roffe, who both specialized in engraving architectural subjects for booksellers, and J.S. Storer, the busiest antiquarian, architectural and topographical draughtsman and etcher of the first two decades of the century, with a prodigious output of illustrations to his credit.

The attractive engraved titles, of which there are half a dozen, consist of miniature turnpike views, framed and captioned and supported by varying numbers of putti and allegorical females, all set against delightful cloudy stippled backgrounds. They are the work of members of the Corbould family, well known both as landscape and miniature painters and for their book illustrations, and engraved by H.R. Cook, E. Mackenzie and James Hopwood junior who specialized in the use of stipple.

Four of the plates in the first volume, which lack publication-lines, are identifiable with those used by the publisher John Cooke in 1775 to illustrate Harrison's *London* (no 57), and two more are obviously copied from the same source. Attention is drawn to these by the abbreviation *H* followed by the page number.

Printed within the text pages is a large number of diminutive wood-engravings of churches, uncredited and in a homely style, but quite adequate to the needs of perambulating church spotters of the day. On 11 pages bound together into vol. 4 are 52 woodcuts of coats of arms, chiefly of Livery Companies.

The list below describes:

1 Copper plate engravings in vols 1–4 issued initially by James Stratford and later by Joseph or by James Robins.

2 Substitute engraved titles and additional plates included only in later issues of those volumes.

VOL. 1 (also undated ed with imprint 'London: J. Robins and Co., Albion Press, Ivy Lane, Paternoster Row')

1 (engr half-title) London/and its Neighbourhood/to Thirty Miles Extent/Vol. 1 (inset miniature) Entrance to London by Hyde Park Corner. R. Corbould delint. H.R. Cook sculp. Published by (a) Oct. 26, 1805. 28 × 48/215 × 125mm. Used for vol.3 of the later ed, with publication-line 'London:/James Robins & Co., Ivy Lane, Paternoster Row'.

2 front. Emblematical representation of Commerce and

Plenty presenting the City of London with the Riches of the/Four Quarters of the World. R. Corbould del. C. Warren sculp. Published by (a) Apr. 27, 1805; and (c). 120 × 190mm. No 1. Vignetted.

3 p iii George III. Chapman sculp./... from a drawing by R. Corbould. Published by (a) April 27, 1805; and (c). 140 × 88mm.

4 p 140 (tr) Plan/of/London/in the Reign of/Queen Elizabeth. Published by (a) and by (c) (undated). 200 × 500/215 × 510mm. No 148. From St James's Park, W., to Stepney, E. Faces p 141 in later ed.

5 p 175 Old Cheapside with the Cross. Engraved by A.W. Warren ... Published by (a) Augt. 16, 1806; and (d). 100 × 165/120 × 195mm. No 60. Faces p 225 in vol. 3 of later ed. Derived from *H* 273.

6 p 182 A Plan of the City and Environs of London as fortified by order of Parliament in the Years 1642 & 1643. 185 × 310/200 × 320mm. No 133. Refs (l.) 1–11, (r.) 12–23. Faces p 183 in later ed. *H* 253.

7 p 220 A View of London as it appeared/before the dreadful Fire in 1666. 145 × 280/185 × 290mm. No 131. Refs (lm and l.) 1–12, (r.) 13–26. Faces p 218 in later ed. *H* 280.

8 p 245 A Plan of the City of London, after the Great Fire ... according to the design & proposal of Sir Christopher Wren, Kt. for rebuilding it. 170 × 265/195 × 290mm. No 136. Derived from *H* 286.

9 p 248 Sir John Evelyn's Plan for Rebuilding the City of London after the Great Fire in 1666. 137 × 285/165 × 300mm. No 134. Refs l. 1–38, etc. *H* 287.

10 p 451 (tm) The City Gates as they appeared before they were pulled down: Moor gate – Aldgate – Bishopsgate – Cripplegate/Ludgate – New gate – Aldersgate – Bridge gate. 70 × 50,65 × 70,65 × 68,70 × 70; 80 × 65,85 × 65,80 × 63,80 × 65/200 × 305mm. No 130. *H* 426.

VOL. 2. (also undated ed with imprint 'London: Printed and Published by Joseph Robins and Sons, 57 Tooley Street, Southwark; and sold by all other booksellers')

11 (engr half-title) London/and its Neighbourhood/to Thirty Miles Extent/Vol.2. (inset miniature) Entrance to London by Oxford Street. R. Corbould delint. H.R. Cook sculp. Published by (a) Oct. 18, 1806. 25 × 40/210 × 125mm. Used for vol. 6 of the later ed with publication-line 'London:/James Robins & co., Ivy Lane, Paternoster Row.'

12 p 99 (tr) London/extending from the Head of the Paddington Canal West/to the West India Docks East with the proposed Improvements between/the Royal Exchange and Finsbury Square. Drawn & Engraved by J. Russell. Published by (a) Octr. 6, 1806 and (d). 225 × 530/330 × 550mm. No 67. Refs 1–128, a-z, etc to churches, principal buildings and squares. The later, undated issue is bound in front of vol. 2, omits the 'Improvements' from the title and indicates proposed

line of Regent Street. (*Darlington and Howgego* 240, 267)

13 p 147 East India House. Drawn by Schnebbelie. Engraved by Woolnoth.... Published by (a) August 3rd 1805; and (d). 98 × 165/120 × 195mm. No 15. Faces p 156 in later ed. Built by Richard Jupp and completed by Henry Holland in 1800.

14 p 169 Stow – Gresham. Engraved by A.W. Warren.... Published by (a) Decr. 10, 1808; and (c). Each 100 × 80/125 × 190mm. No 121. Two portraits.

15 p 213 Trinity House, Tower Hill. Drawn & Engraved by A. Warren.... Published by (a) Octr. 12, 1805; and (c). 95 × 165/120 × 190mm. No 25.

16 p 225 Traitors Gate, Tower of London. Storer delin et sculp.... Published by (a) Augst 2, 1806; and (d). 165 × 100/200 × 120mm. No 58.

17 p 317 London Bridge/in the year 1757. Engraved by Warren from a Picture by Scott.... Published by (a) Oct. 3, 1807; and (d). 95 × 165/120 × 195mm. No 95. Faces p 316 in later ed. Based on the Guildhall Art Gallery Samuel Scott 'Old London Bridge c. 1747' (22 × 48 inches) or some identical painting.

18 p 320 Fish Street Hill. Drawn by Gyfford & Engrav'd by Roffe.... Published by (a) Octr. 10th, 1807; and (d). 165 × 95/195 × 120mm. No 96. Looking N.; St Magnus, the Monument and St Bennet Gracechurch.

19 p 397 Specimen of Antient Building, Bishopsgate Street. Drawn & Engraved by Storer & Greig.... Published by (a) Septr 6, 1806; and (d). 165 × 98/200 × 120mm. No 63. 'Sir Paul Pindar's House'.

20 p 509 Interior of St Stephen's Walbrook. Drawn by Gyfford & engraved by Storer & Greig.... Published by (a) March 14, 1807; and (d). 165 × 95/200 × 115mm. No 80. The V & A has a Gyfford drawing of this subject (175 × 122mm).

21 p 513 Mansion House. Drawn by Schnebbelie & Engraved by Wolnoth.... Published by (a) Aug 24, 1805; and (d). 100 × 168/120 × 195mm. No 18.

22 p 515 Egyptian Hall, Mansion House. Engraved by Warren from a Drawing by Schnebbelie.... Published by (a) Novr. 8, 1806; and (d). 150 × 98/185 × 120mm. No 69.

VOL. 3

23 (engr half-title) London/and its Neighbourhood/to Thirty Miles Extent/Vol. III. (inset miniature) Entrance to London at Mile End. Corbould delin. E. Mackenzie sculp. Published by (a) May 20, 1809. 25 × 50/215 × 125mm. The Tower of London in a stippled, vignetted backdrop. Used for vol. 5 of the later ed with the publication-line 'London:/James Robins & Co., Ivy Lane, Paternoster Row'.

24 p 31 Figures in front of Bethlem Hospital. Engraved by C. Warren.... Published by (a) Decr 10th, 1808; and (d). 95 × 165/120 × 195mm. No 122. As front. in later ed.

25 p 96 Bank of England/Taken by Permission from a Drawing in Possession of J. Soane Esqr. Engraved by Warren.... Published by (a) Jany 3rd 1807; and (d). 100 × 160/115 × 190mm. No 77. The Soane screen wall from Princes Street, with Tivoli corner. (*Bank of England* 53)

26 p 97 Bank of England. Drawn by Shnebbelie and Engraved by A. Warren.... Published by (a) May 11th 1805; and (c). 95 × 165/120 × 185mm. No 3. Faces p 31 in later ed. Sampson and Taylor S. front, looking towards Mansion House. (*Bank of England* 36)

27 p 103 New Three Per Cent Office, Bank of England. Engraved by Roffe from a Drawing presented by J. Soane Esqr.... Published by (a) Sept 10th, 1808; and (d). 93 × 165/120 × 190mm. No 115. Interior of Consols Office, built 1797. (*Bank of England* 181)

28 p 245 Guildhall. Engraved by Hay from a Drawing by Gyfford.... Published by (a) July 20, 1807; and (d). 160 × 95/195 × 120mm. No 87.

29 p 260 Monument to the Memory of Alderman Beckford/In Guildhall. Grainger sc. Published by (a) (undated); and (c). 145 × 95/190 × 120mm. No 125.

30 p 261 (on tablet) Monument in Guildhall to the Memory of the/Earl of Chatham. Engraved by Grainger. Published by (a) (undated); and (d). 165 × 95/195 × 120mm. No 109.

31 p 505 St Paul's Cathedral./From the South East. Engd by Warren from a Drawing by Gyfford.... Published by (a) May 6, 1808; and (d). 165 × 100/190 × 115mm. No 107. Faces p 512 in later ed.

32 p 529 Interior of St Paul's Cathedral. Published by (a) April 15, 1809; and (d). 95 × 160/120 × 190mm. No 132. Nave, looking E.

33 p 608 Great Hall, Charter House. Drawn by Schnebbelie & Engraved by A. Warren.... Published by (a) Oct. 19, 1808; and (c). 97 × 165/125 × 190 mm. No 26. A Schnebbelie water-colour of this subject (120 × 165mm) is in the BM (*Crace* 26.17).

34 p 622 Specimen of Antient Building, Fleet Street. Drawn by Schnebbelie. Engraved by Warren.... Published by (a) Jany 17, 1807; and (c). 100 × 165/120 × 190mm. No 76. In vol. 4 of later ed, facing p 130. 'Prince Henry's Room' and waxworks. A Schnebbelie drawing of this subject (127 × 165mm) is in the BM (*Crace* 19.29).

VOL. 4

35 (engr half-title) London/and its Neighbourhood/to Thirty Miles Extent/By David Hughson LL.D./In Six Volumes/Vol. IV. (inset miniature) Entrance to London by the Obelisk. H. Corbould delint. Hopwood sculpt. Published by (a) Aug. 18th 1810. 30 × 50/215 × 130mm. Used for vol. 1 of the later ed with publication-line 'London: James Robins & Co., Ivy Lane/Paternoster Row'.

36 p 18 Myddleton – Wren. Warren sc. Published by (a)

Jany 24, 1809; and (c). Each 80 × 65/120 × 190mm. No 123. Two portraits.

37 p 183 Somerset House. Engraved by Warren from a Drawing by Varley.... Published by (a) Octr 4, 1806; and (d). 95 × 160/120 × 192mm. No 66. From river, looking S.W.

38 p 194 Drury Lane Theatre. Engraved by Ellis from a Drawing by Schnebbelie.... Published by (a) May 25, 1805; and (c). 150 × 95/190 × 115mm. No 5. Faces p 191 in later ed, with this addition to the caption: 'Destroyed by Fire 24th Feb 1809'.

39 p 200 Savoy Chapel and Palace. Drawn by Schnebbelie & Engraved by Warren.... Published by (a) July 11th 1807; and (d). 95 × 160/120 × 190mm. No 89.

40 p 233 Scotland Yard. Engraved by Warren from a Painting by Rooker.... Published by (a) Jany 1st, 1808; and (d). 100 × 157/120 × 190mm. No 100. Based on Edward Rooker's large engraving of 1766, after Paul Sandby (no 58, item 4).

41 p 245 Westminster. Engraved by Warren from a drawing by Hassell.... Published by (a) Octr 15th, 1808; and (d). 92 × 158/122 × 188mm. No 117. The Hall and Bridge from Lambeth.

42 p 250 Westminster Hall. Engraved by Taylor from a Drawing by Shnebbelie.... Published by (a) Novr 22, 1805; and (c). 100 × 165/120 × 190mm. No 31. View from N.

43 p 268 Westminster Abbey. Drawn by Schnebbelie & Engraved by A. Warren.... Published by (a) June 8th, 1805; and (c). 163 × 95/185 × 120mm. No 7. W. front from Tothill Street.

44 p 270 Interior of Westminster Abbey.... Published by (a) April 22nd 1809; and (d). 100 × 160/120 × 190mm. Faces p 271 in later ed. No 126. Nave, looking E.

45 p 317 Carlton House. Drawn by H. Brown & Engraved by J. Jones.... Published by (a) Novr. 26th 1808; and (d). 95 × 160/115 × 180mm. No 135. Faces p 334 in later ed.

46 p 319 (tm) An Ancient View of St James's, Westminster-Abby, & Hall &c from the Village of Charing now Charing Cross. (lm) Engraved by Permission from/the Antiquarian Repertory (no 56). 147 × 260/187 × 290mm. No 129. Refs 1–7. In vol. 1 of the later ed, facing p 141.

47 p 351 Lansdowne House, Berkeley Square. Drawn by Schnebbelie & Engraved by Sparrow.... Published by (a) May 14th, 1808; and (d). 100 × 165/120 × 190mm. No 108. Faces p 367 in later ed.

48 p 354 Entrance to London by Oxford Street. Drawn by Gyfford & Engraved by W. Hawkins.... Published by (a) Augt. 22, 1807; and (d). 95 × 160/120 × 190mm. No 93. Faces p 371 in later ed.

49 p 388 British Museum. Drawn by Schnebbelie & Engraved by A. Warren.... Published by (a) Augst 31, 1805; and (c). 95 × 165/120 × 190mm. No 19. Courtyard. Faces p 404 in later ed.

50 p 419 Entrance to London at Shoreditch Church. Drawn by Schnebbelie & Engraved by Hay.... Published by (a) May 24, 1810; and (d). 100 × 162/120 × 190mm. No 143. Faces p 435 in later ed.

51 p 428 Aldgate House/Bethnall Green. Drawn by Schnebbelie & Engraved by Warren.... Published by (a) Jany 15th, 1808; and (d). 155 × 95/190 × 120mm. No 101. Faces p 444 in later ed.

52 p 448 London Docks, Wapping. Drawn by Schnebbelie & Engraved by W. Hawkins.... Published by (a) Aug. 17, 1805; and (c). 97 × 165/120 × 195mm. No 17. Faces p 464 in later ed.

53 p 451 London, from Chatham Place, Blackfriars. Engraved by R. Roffe from a Drawing by Schnebbelie.... Published by (a) Jany 14th, 1809; and (d). 92 × 165/120 × 195mm. No 124. Faces p 466 in later ed with caption corrected to 'Southwark, from Chatham Place'.

54 p 459 Bermondsey Priory. Drawn by Schnebbelie & Engraved by Warren.... Published by (a) July 27, 1805; and (d). 95 × 165/120 × 190mm. No 14. Faces p 476 in later ed. The gatehouse demolished in 1807 for road development; the later ed adds to the caption 'as it formerly stood'.

55 p 498 Southwark/Towards St Margaret's Hill. Drawn by Gyfford & Engraved by Busby.... Published by (a) April 18, 1807; and (d). 160 × 95/190 × 120mm. No 82. Faces p 507 in later ed. Shows Church of St George the Martyr.

56 p 504 Entrance to London by the Obelisk in the Surry Road. Drawn by Schnebbelie & Engraved by Sparrow.... Published by (a) and (d). 100 × 160/120 × 185mm. No 144. Faces p 520 in later ed.

57 p 563 Ancient English Dresses: An Oliverian of 1640 – An English Gentleman of 1700. Engraved by Warren. ... Published by (a) Nov. 21, 1807. 95 × 75,95 × 80/125 × 195mm. No 97. Faces p 568 in later ed.

58 p 563 Costume of London 1640: A Nobleman – A Lady. Warren sc. Published by (a) Feby 6, 1808; and (d). 93 × 77,95 × 77/125 × 190mm. No 102. Faces p 564 in later ed.

59 p 581 Dresses of Eminent Citizens in 1640: A Merchant – A Merchant's Wife. Warren sc. Published by (a) Augst 15, 1807; and (d). Each 97 × 77/125 × 190mm. No 92. Thus paginated in the check-list but bound at the end of the vol.

60 p 582 Dresses of Eminent Citizens in 1640: Lady Mayoress – Lord Mayor. Published by (a) May 23, 1807; and (d). Each 97 × 77/125 × 190mm. No 85. Thus paginated in the check-list but bound at the end of the vol.

James Robins's ed of vols 1–4: extra plates and engr titles
VOL. 2

61 (engr half-title) Circuit/of/London/by David Hughson LL.D./Vol. 2 (inset miniature) Entrance to London from Islington. Drawn by Corbould. Engraved by Hopwood. London, James Robins & Co., Ivy Lane/ Paternoster Row. 25 × 40/205 × 120mm. Used for vol. 5 of the 1st ed with publication-line (a).

VOL. 3

62 front. Southwark Bridge. Drawn & Engraved by J. Shury.... Published by (d). 95 × 165/120 × 190mm. The bridge was opened 24 March 1819.

VOL. 4

63 (engr half-title) London/Westminster/and Southwark/ By D. Hughson LL.D./Vol.IV./ (inset miniature) Entrance to London at Shoreditch. H. Corbould del. J. Hopwood sculp. London/James Robins & Co., Ivy Lane, Paternoster Row. 25 × 40/205 × 120mm. Used for vol. 6 of the 1st ed with publication-line (a).

64 front. The Thames Tunnel. Published by (d). 150 × 100/210 × 120mm. Work commenced on the tunnel in January 1825.

65 p 26 The Temple Church. Storer & Greig sculp. Published by James Robins & Co., Ivy Lane, Paternoster Row. 102 × 150/125 × 185mm. cf with Herbert's *Antiquities* (no 88), item 2.

66 p 28 Interior of the Temple Church. Published by (d) July 5, 1823. 150 × 100/200 × 125mm. The only dated plate with (d) publication-line. cf with Herbert's *Antiquities*, item 6.

67 p 42 Serjeant's Inn, Fleet Street. Storer & Greig sculp. Published by James Robins & Co., Ivy Lane, Paternoster Row. 147 × 97/200 × 125mm. cf with Herbert's *Antiquities*, item 24.

68 p 122 Stone Buildings , Lincoln's Inn. Engraved by J. Storer & J. Greig.... Published by (d). 100 × 147/125 × 200mm. cf with Herbert's *Antiquities*, item 14.

69 p 124 Lincoln's Inn Hall & Chapel. 100 × 150/125 × 200mm. Without credits or publication-line. cf with Herbert's *Antiquities*, item 12.

70 p 416 Grays Inn Gardens. 98 × 150/125 × 195mm. Without credits or publication-line. cf with Herbert's *Antiquities*, item 19.

---

94 · A VISIT TO LONDON [1805]

This follows the usual pattern of juvenile guides to London. An imaginary provincial Mr Sandby, living 'in a small village about 80 miles from London', decides to initiate his family into the delights of the capital city and so removes thence his wife and two elder children, George and Maria. Once there they are subjected to a course of paternal lectures on the history and 'raison d'être' of the notable buildings of the City and Westminster. This was no doubt a book used in the schoolroom and the drabness of the text is relieved only by half a dozen line-engravings in each of the first four editions examined. These are without credits but occasionally have publication-lines. The publishers revised the text and reillustrated the book for Queen Victoria's reign (no 187).

A Visit to London, containing a Description of the Principal Curiosities in the British Metropolis. By S.W. author of The Visit to a Farm-House and The Puzzle for a Curious Girl. With six copper plates. London: Printed by J. Adlard, Duke Street, Smithfield for Tabart and Co. at the Juvenile and School Library, No. 157 New Bond Street; and to be had of all booksellers. 1805.

Duodecimo, 140 × 85mm. 1805

COLLATION Title-page; pp i–ii, preface; pp 1–192, An Excursion to London.

—1808
Duodecimo, 140 × 85mm. 1808

COLLATION Title-page; preface, contents (2pp); pp 1–188, An Excursion to London.

—A New Edition, with Additions and Improvements, London: Printed by and for W. Darton, Jun. 58 Holborn Hill; and to be had of all Booksellers, Price Half-a-Crown. 1813.

Duodecimo, 235 × 85mm. 1813

COLLATION Title-page; preface, contents (2pp); pp 1–212, An Excursion to London.

—With copper plates. A New Edition, with Additions and Improvements by T.H. London: William Darton, 58 Holborn Hill. Price Half-a-Crown. 1820.

Duodecimo, 140 × 85mm. 1820

COLLATION Title-page; preface, contents (2pp); pp 1–212 (text reset), An Excursion to London.

1805 (with publication-line 'Published by Tabart & Co. 157 New Bond Street')

1 front. London from Camberwell, (on the South). 60 × 110mm. Thus 1808 and 1813; 1820 p 7.

2 p 48 Blackfryars Bridge & St. Paul's Church. 60 × 110mm. 1808 also.

3 p 84 The Menagerie in the Tower. London Publish'd Jan. 1805 by Tabart & Co. 65 × 110mm. 1808 also.

4 p 104 Westminster Bridge, Hall & Abbey. 63 × 110mm. From N.E. Thus 1808; 1813 p 109, 'Published

Octr 9th 1813 by William Darton, Holborn Hill'; 1820 p 101.

5 p 138 London Bridge & the Monument. 60 × 110mm. 1808 also; 1813 p 85; 1820 p 125.

6 p 156 The Juvenile Library. Jan. 1805. 65 × 110mm. Uninteresting interior view of Tabart's shop. Suppressed after 1808.

1813 (alternative plates, with publication-line 'Published Octr 9th 1813 by William Darton, Holborn Hill')

7 p 134 London and the River Thames, from Greenwich. 62 × 108mm. 1820 front.

8 p 157 The West India Docks, from the South West. 90 × 150/120 × 160mm. 1820 p 143.

9 p 168 The New Docks in the Isle of Dogs. 63 × 115mm. 1820 p 145.

1820 (alternative plate, no publication-line)

10 p 1 London from Primrose Hill. 65 × 112mm.

95 · HERBERT AND BRAYLEY'S LAMBETH PALACE [1806]

The years 1804–6 were particularly fruitful for the antiquarian William Herbert since he then produced *Antiquities of the Inns of Court* (no 88), the text of Storer and Greig's *Select Views of London* (no 90) and, with his friend Edward Brayley, this history of Lambeth Palace which was not half a mile from his own home near Marsh Gate. He was always ready to meet the requirements of the extra-illustrators and was later concerned with the publication of series such as *London Before the Great Fire* (no 120) solely with their needs in view. *Lambeth Palace* was issued in two editions, one on extra large paper intended specifically for extra-illustrators in which the integral plates are so diverse and ill-organized that, without a list, it is difficult to distinguish them from the embellishments.

A Concise Account, Historical and Descriptive, of Lambeth Palace. London: Printed by S. Gosnell, Little Queen Street, for E.W. Brayley, Wilderness Row, Goswell Street and W. Herbert, Globe Place, Lambeth. 1806.

Folio, 465 × 285mm. (Large Paper 495 × 315mm)
1806

COLLATION   Title-page; dedication (1 leaf); pp iii-iv, advertisement dated 2 April 1806; pp 1–87, Concise Account.

'The publishers', says the advertisement, 'can speak with confidence of the plates, every drawing for which was made under the direction of W. Herbert, and by him in company with the artist compared on the spot, and the engravings in their progress watched with similar attention'. There are three sorts of plate: stipple-engravings of portraits in oils or stained glass, coloured in body colour, one with the engraver's credit 'W. Maddocks'; architectural details drawn by T. Whichelo and engraved by J. and R. Roffe; and views of the interior and exterior drawn by Frederick Nash and engraved by R. Roffe, B. Howlett and W. Wise. Nash was the son of a Lambeth builder who from 1801 studied at the Royal Academy and was a pupil of Thomas Malton junior. With T. Whichelo he had contributed to the earlier Herbert and Brayley publications *Select Views of London* and *Beauties of England and Wales* (no 104) as well as the present work. John and Richard Roffe were regularly employed on Brayley and Britton topographical books for three decades. William Wise and Bartholomew Howlett were later extensive contributors to Wilkinson's *Londina Illustra* (no 131).

The plates are unnumbered and there are no directions to the binder or check-list. Ten were published on 1 May 1805 and one each in January, February and March and five in April 1806; two are undated. The publication-line throughout reads: 'London; Published for W. Herbert, Globe Place; & E.W. Brayley, Wilderness Row, (date)'.

1 (engr title) Lambeth Palace/Illustrated/by a/Series of Views/Representing its most/Interesting Antiquities/in/Buildings, Portraits,/Stained Glass,/&c./ (vignette) Lambeth Palace from Westminster Bridge. Whichelo delint. W. & G. Cooke sculpt./London: Published for W. Herbert, Globe Place; & E.W. Brayley, Wilderness Row; 1st May 1805. 90 × 185/285 × 230mm.

2 front. Queen Catherine Parr. Feby 15, 1806. 100 × 85/280 × 220mm.

3 p 1 The Court Yard with the Gateway &c., Lambeth Palace. Nash del. Wise sculp. March 1, 1806. 183 × 225/230 × 290mm.

4 p 20 The Library, Lambeth Palace. Engraved by R. Roffe from a Drawing by F. Nash. May 1st, 1805. 160 × 223/230 × 300mm.

5 p 25 Archbishop Chicheley. Engraved by R. Roffe from the Painted Glass in the Library of Lambeth Palace. May 1, 1805. 230 × 165/285 × 220mm.

6 p 26 Specimens of Stained Glass in the Library & Stewards Parlour Lambeth Palace. Wichelo delt. Rolfe sculpt. Jany 1, 1806. 230 × 170/290 × 220mm.

7 p 32 Interior of the Guard Room, Lambeth Palace. Engraved by J. Roffe, from a drawing by F. Nash. May 1, 1805. 222 × 152/290 × 230mm.

8 p 40 Archbishop Arundel. April 1, 1806. 120 × 95/250 × 195mm.

9 p 42 Archbishop Chicheley. May 1, 1805. 125 × 88/190 × 125mm. From an oil painting.

10 p 47 Cardinal Pole. Engraved by Maddocks from a Painting at Lambeth Palace. May 1, 1805. 140 × 105/285 × 230mm.

11 p 49 Interior of the Chapel, Lambeth Palace. F. Nash del. B. Howlett sculp. April 1, 1806. 240 × 170/290 × 230mm.

12 p 50 Specimens of the ornamental Carvings, &c in the Chapel, Lambeth Palace. Engraved by J. Roffe from a Drawing by Wichelo. 230 × 195/290 × 230mm.

13 p 53 Architectural Parts of Lambeth Palace. Engraved by J. Roffe from a Drawing by Wichelo. May 1, 1805. 250 × 195/280 × 220mm. Includes the tomb of Archbishop Parker.

14 p 55 Interior of the Post Room in the Lollards Tower, Lambeth Palace. F. Nash del: B. Howlett sculpt. April 1, 1806. 155 × 225/230 × 290mm.

15 p 56 Carvings on the Ceiling of the Post Room, Lambeth Palace. Engraved by J. Roffe from a Drawing by Wichelo. 230 × 170/290 × 230mm.

16 p 59 Architectural Parts of Lambeth. Wichelo del. R. Roffe sc. April 1st 1806. 240 × 180/280 × 220mm. Lollard's Tower.

17 p 61 The Cloisters, with parts of the Guard Room & Chapel, Lambeth Palace. Engraved by R. Roffe from a drawing by T. Wichelo. May 1, 1805. 155 × 225/220 × 290mm.

18 p 62 Ancient Crypt beneath the Chapel, Lambeth Palace. Engraved by J. Roffe from a drawing by Wichelo. May 1, 1805. 155 × 225/220 × 290mm.

19 p 63 Interior of the Great Hall, Lambeth Palace. Drawn by F. Nash. Engraved by D. Smith. Apl. 2, 1806. 195 × 180/285 × 230mm.

20 p 69 Architectural Parts of Lambeth Palace. Engraved by Roffe from a Drawing by Wichelo. May 1st, 1805. 175 × 240/230 × 285mm. The entrance gateway, etc.

96 · LAMBERT'S HISTORY AND SURVEY OF LONDON [1806]

The credentials of this author as a London historian are hardly convincing as they are displayed on the title-page and this four-volume work is now mainly of interest for the modest but generally adequate illustrations which are of the type then appearing in the monthly magazines such as the *Gentleman's Magazine* and *European Magazine*.

The History and Survey of London and its environs from the earliest period to the present time. In Four Volumes. By B. Lambert, editor of Bertholet's Chemical Statics ... vol. I (II–IV). London, Printed for T. Hughes, No 1, Stationers' Court, and M. Jones, No 1, Paternoster-Row; By Dewick and Clarke, Aldersgate-Street. 1806.

Octavo, 205 × 120mm.   1806

COLLATION   Vol. 1. Title-page; advertisement dated 1 May 1806, dedication (4pp); pp 1–560, History and Survey. Vol. 2. Title-page; pp 1–557, History and Survey continued. Vol. 3. Title-page; pp 1–536, History and Survey continued. Vol. 4. Title-page; pp 1–544, History and Survey continued; pp i–xlvi, index, directions to binder.

The illustrations consist of three plans, seven portraits in stipple and topographical plates mostly credited to T. Prattent as draughtsman. Prattent also contributed plates to the *European Magazine* and *Gentleman's Magazine* in the 1790s and ran an engraving, printing and printselling business at 46 Cloth Fair from 1793 to 1800. He engraved one plate himself but the rest were farmed out to Andrew Birrell, H.R. Cook, E. and J. Shirt, W. Poole and others. Each plate bears in the centre of the bm, just below the work, a version of the credit-line '(Drawn &) (Designed &) Engraved for Lambert's History of London.' and below the copperplate caption one or other of the publication-lines:

(a) 'Published by T. Hughes (No. 1) Stationers Court (date).'

(b) 'Published by M. Jones (No. 1) Paternoster Row (date).'

The plate numbers in brackets are not engraved on them but assigned in the check-list.

VOL. 1

1 front. Richard Clark Esq./Chamberlain of London. M. Brown pinxt. K. Mackenzie sculp. (a) April, 1806. 175 × 100/200 × 125mm. (55) Stipple.

2 p 71. Fitzalwine/First Lord Mayor. H.R. Cook sculp. (b) March 1, 1805. 150 × 90/185 × 115mm. (11) Stipple.

3 p 274 Sir Wm. Walworth. Cook sc. (a) July 6, 1806. 148 × 90/180 × 120mm. (26) Stipple.

4 p 332 Sr. Richd. Whittington. Cook sc. (a) June 8, 1805. 148 × 90/175 × 120mm. (21) Stipple.

VOL. 2

5 front. Plan of the City of London in the time of Queen Elizabeth. 110 × 185/120 × 200mm. (45) (tr, with City arms) 'London'. Copied from Norden's plan of 1593.

6 p 89 View of Part of London as it appeared in the Great Fire, 1666. Prattent del. Owen sc. Designed and Engraved ... from an Original Picture in Painter-Stainers' Hall. (a) Novr 1805. 90 × 158/123 × 175mm. (46)

7 p 131 The Bank. Poole del. et sc. (a) Jany 1806. 93 × 150/120 × 190mm. (49) (*Bank of England* 38)

8 p 145 The Mansion House. Prattent del. Birrell sc. (b) May 18, 1805. 90 × 145/120 × 198mm. (18)

9 p 151 Remains of the Cloysters of Bartholomew the Great Priory. Prattent del. J. Simpkins sc. (a) Oct. 1805. 130 × 95/190 × 120mm. (39)

10 p 259 Hicks Hall, Clerkenwell. Prattent del. Poole sc. (a) Septr 1805. 98 × 145/125 × 200mm. (37)

11 p 365 Ald-gate – Bishops-gate. (b) May 10, 1805. 112 × 170mm pl. mark. (17)

12 p 367 Moore Gate – Cripple Gate. (a) June 15, 1805. 115 × 170mm pl. mark. (23)

13 p 370 Aldersgate – Newgate. (a) Oct. 1805. 115 × 170mm pl. mark. (40)

14 p 371 Newgate. Prattent del. Birrell sc. (a) Aug 10, 1805. 85 × 145/125 × 200mm. (34) George Dance junior's prison building.

15 p 374 Lud-Gate – Bridge-Gate. Pub. by M. Jones 1805. 120 × 190mm. (4) Stipple.

16 p 385 Custom House. Prattent del. Owen sc. Published by T. Hughes, Feby 1806. 87 × 145/110 × 188mm. (52) Thomas Ripley's building, destroyed by fire 12 February 1814.

17 p 388 Whittington's House: Hart Street, Crutched Friars. Prattent del. Birrel sc. (b) April 12, 1805. 90 × 150/125 × 195mm. (13)

18 p 393 Remains of St Michaels Chapel, Aldgate. Prattent del. Owen sc. (a) July 5, 1805. 90 × 145/125 × 190mm. (25)

19 p 404 The East India House in its former state. Pub. by M. Jones. 1805. 90 × 145/125 × 200mm. (5) Demolished c 1796.

20 p 404 The East India House. Prattent del. Shirt sc. (b) April 27th 1805. 90 × 150/125 × 200mm. (15) Designed by Richard Jupp and Henry Holland, 1800.

21 p 408 House once Sr Paul Pindar's, Bishopsgate Street. Prattent del. Owen sc. (a) Aug 24, 1805. 140 × 88/180 × 120mm. (29)

22 p 409 Crosby House, Bishopsgate Street. Prattent del. E. Shirt sc. (a) Aug 17, 1805. 95 × 150/125 × 200mm. (31) (*Longford* 430)

23 p 468 The Monument. Drawn & Engraved by W. Poole. (a) Nov. 1805. 150 × 90/190 × 120mm. (42)

24 p 519 Mercers Hall Poultry. Prattent del. Birrell sc. (a) Octr 1805. 147 × 95/200 × 125mm. (38)

25 p 521 Guildhall. Prattent del. E. Shirt sc. (b) April 30th 1805. 90 × 143/125 × 200mm. (12)

26 p 539 Figures over the Gateway of Bethlehem Hospital. Birrell sc. (a) Nov 1805. 95 × 160/125 × 200mm. (43) Copy of the engraving from Stothard's drawing made for *An Historical Account of Bethlem Hospital* (1783).

VOL. 3

27 front. Plan of the City of Westminster in the Time of Queen Elizabeth. Woodthorpe sc. (a) Septr 1805. 110 × 195/125 × 205mm. (33) (tr, on strapwork cartouche) 'Westminster'. Copied from Norden's plan of 1593.

28 p 4 General Monks House, Hanover Square, Grub Street. Prattent del. Birrell sc. (b) March 13th, 1805. 90 × 145/125 × 190mm. (10)

29 p 11 Shaftsbury House, Aldersgate Street. Prattent del. J. Simpkins sc. (a) Feby, 1806. 90 × 145/125 × 175mm. (53)

30 p 39 St Pauls. J. Shirt sc. Published by T. Hughes, Jany 1, 1806. 95 × 150/125 × 200mm. (54) From S.W.

31 p 47 The West View of St Paul's Cathedral/before the Fire of London. 93 × 140/125 × 200mm. (8) No credits or publication-line. Based on Dugdale's *St Paul's* (no 8), item 38.

32 p 137 A Bird's Eye View of the Royal Exchange. Prattent del. Birrel sc. (b) April 19th 1805. 100 × 135/125 × 193mm. (14) Based on Morden and Lea's *Prospects* (no 15), item 8.

33 p 139 Bangor House Shoe Lane. Prattent del. Shirt sc. (a) July 27th, 1805. 145 × 90/200 × 120mm. (28)

34 p 139 Ely Place in its former state. (a) Octr 1805. 95 × 150/120 × 200mm. (36)

35 p 144 Giltspur Street, Compter. Prattent del. Owen sc. (a) Aug 3, 1805. 88 × 142/125 × 175mm. (30) Designed by George Dance junior, 1787.

36 p 146 Principal Gate of St Bartholomews Hospital. Prattent del. Owen sc. (a) July 1805. 140 × 90/190 × 125mm. (27)

37 p 192 London Bridge before and since the Houses were pulled down. Prattent del. Birrell sc. (a) Decr 1805. 90 × 160/125 × 200mm. (48)

38 p 199 Westminster Bridge – Blackfriars Bridge. Prattent del. Owen sc. (a) Jany, 1806. 40 × 145,42 × 145/125 × 170mm. (50)

39 p 375 Abbey Church of St Peter, Westminster. Pub. by M. Jones. 1805. 90 × 145/125 × 200mm. (7) No credits. Viewed from W.

40 p 431 Temple Bar. Busby del. et sc. (a) Decr 1805. 80 × 130/125 × 200mm. (47)

41 p 438 New Court House, Westminster. Poole sc. (a) Decr 1805. 90 × 150/125 × 200mm. (44) Built by S.P. Cockerell, 1805, and unfinished when Poole made this drawing. It is shown with pedimented portico and lantern and wind-vane above the octagon in *Metropolitan Improvements* (no 154), item 96, where it is described as Westminster Guildhall.

42 p 440 Westminster Hall. Green del. Owen sc. (a) Sept 7th 1805. 90 × 148/125 × 180mm. (1) Another version of this was also in circulation, engr by H.R. Cook, 90 × 148/125 × 210mm.

43 p 446 Somerset House. W. Poole del. et sc. (a) Aug 30, 1805. 92 × 150/125 × 200mm. (32) The Strand front.

44 p 452 The Painted Chamber Westminster. Prattent del et sc. (b) March 8th, 1805. 90 × 145/125 × 205mm. (9)

45 p 490 A Gate belonging to the Old Palace of Whitehall. Shirt sc. (b) May 24, 1805. 90 × 140/125 × 200mm. (19) Looking N. Apparently adapted from Godfrey's engr of Thomas Sandby's drawing to get the 'Holbein' Gate and the Banqueting Hall into a narrow compass. The Gate was demolished in 1759. Grose's *Antiquarian Repertory* (no 56), item 4.

46 p 495 St James's Palace. Birrell del et sc. London, Published by T. Hughes. Jany, 1806. 100 × 150/125 × 200mm. (51) From the gatehouse looking E.

VOL. 4

47 front. (tm) Plan of the Cities of London and Westminster with the Borough of Southwark, exhibiting all the New Buildings to the present year MDCCCVI. Neele sculp. 352 Strand. (a) April 21st, 1806. 330 × 710/370 × 720mm. (56) (bm) Alphabetical list of '340 Principal Streets'. (*Darlington and Howgego* 236)

48 p 45 Oliver Cromwell's House, Clerkenwell Close. A. Birrell sculp. 90 × 148/125 × 200mm. (2) No credit-line or publication-line.

49 p 46 St John's Gate. Prattent del. E. Shirt sc. (a) June 20, 1805. 90 × 145/125 × 195mm. (22)

50 p 55 Charter House Great Hall. Prattent del. Owen sc. (a) Octr 1805. 95 × 145/125 × 175mm. (41)

51 p 90 The Tower. W. Poole del. et sc. (a) Septr 13th, 1805. 108 × 180/130 × 200mm. (35) From Tower Hill, to the N.W.

52 p 125 The Trinity House, Tower Hill. Prattent del. Birele sc. (a) June 28, 1805. 90 × 145/125 × 200mm. (24)

53 p 146 Lambeth Palace. Pub. by M. Jones, 1805. 90 ×
145/130 × 200mm. (3) No credit-line. Viewed from the
river.

54 p 379 William Caxton. Hopwood sc. (b) May 3, 1805.
150 × 90/180 × 110mm. (16) Stipple portrait.

55 p 380 Sir Thomas Gresham. Mackenzie sculp. (b)
1805. 150 × 90/170 × 112mm. (6) Stipple portrait.

56 p 387 Sir Hugh Middleton. Freeman sc. (b) June 1,
1805. 150 × 90/180 × 120mm. (20) Stipple portrait.

97 · BRITTON'S ARCHITECTURAL ANTIQUITIES* [1807–14]

John Britton, born near Chippenham, Wiltshire in 1771, the son of a small farmer, maltster and village shopkeeper, was apprenticed to his uncle, a tavern-keeper of Clerkenwell, and once in London became friendly with Edward Brayley. Their antiquarian and topographical interests brought them together, as also their collaboration in the *Beauties of England and Wales* (no 104). This was projected by its publishers as a topographical collection of pictures-que views of general appeal and they therefore discouraged Britton from turning it into a repository of his own antiquarian and architectural interests. Consequently he planned another publication, to run simultaneously, which would give him the opportunity of airing his views on these topics in a series of essays on specific ancient buildings and would enable him to publish plates of measured, architectural drawings for a more specialized clien-tèle:

On June the 24th, 1805, will be published, the First Part of a new work, entitled, The Architectural Antiquities of Great Britain, displayed in a series of Select Engravings, representing the most beautiful, curious and interesting Ancient Edifices of this Country; with an historical and descriptive account of each subject. By John Britton. London: Published by Longman, Hurst, Rees, and Orme, Paternoster-Row; J. Taylor, Architectural Library, 59, High Holborn; and the Author, 21, Wilderness Row, Goswell Street, Where Specimens of the work may be seen.

The four-page prospectus further defined Britton's objectives:

It is a fact justly regretted, that many fine English Buildings are entirely obliterated, and others of singular beauty are *daily* falling a prey to the slow but sure dilapidations of time, and the reprehensible neglect, or destructive hand of man. To preserve correct delinea-tions, and accurate accounts of those that remain to dignify and ornament the country, is the decided object of this work ... the leading feature of which will be *near views* of such buildings as are distinguished for their antiquity, curiosity or elegance. Each of these will be drawn and engraved with scrupulous accuracy, and the most interest-ing will be further illustrated by enlarged representations of particular parts and ornaments.

His subscription terms were outlined as follows:

To avoid the inconvenience and objection that attend works published in Numbers, this will come out in PARTS, one of which will appear every three months.

Each Part will contain six, seven, or eight engravings, with letterpress descriptions of each subject. Four of the plates will be engraved in the *best style* from highly finished drawings; and the others will be principally illustrative details of the former, and executed in a style to correspond with the respective subjects.

It will be printed on Quarto paper, at 10s 6d. each Part which will range with Rees' New Cyclopaedia, the Archaeologia, Lysons' Environs of London, &c. A few copies will be worked off on a superfine Royal Paper, with the *First Impressions of the Plates,* at 16s. each Part.... The First Part will be published on the 24th day of June 1805, and the following parts in regular quarterly succession.

This publication programme was adhered to and completion of the first five Parts was announced in the *Monthly Literary Advertiser* for July 1806; these formed the first 'Half Volume', costing £2 12s 6d or, on Large Paper, £4. The ninth Part was announced in the July 1807 issue as also was the now completed vol. 1, containing 61 engravings at the price of £4 4s or £6 8s on Large Paper. By March 1810 19 Parts had been published and the fortieth and final Part came out in May 1814, the tenth year of issue. Longman's list for that year, which announced the publication of the completed vol. 4, also offered vol. 3 at '£5. 5. 0 medium 4to, boards; £8., large 4to, boards'. In 1827 Britton added a fifth, sup-plementary volume subtitled 'A chronological his-tory and graphic illustrations of Christian Architecture in England' with further views and details of abbeys, cathedrals and churches—all, however, outside London. The joint publisher with Longman, J. Taylor of the Architectural Library, had a list which included many illustrated books written by and intended for architects and builders, such as Sir William Chambers's *Designs for Chinese Buildings* and Richardson's *New Vitruvius Britannicus* (no 84).

The essays in the first volume of *Architectural Antiquities*, describing severally King's College Chapel, Windsor and further abbeys, churches and crosses and Colchester Castle, were separately paginated, but continuous pagination was used for those in the second (Henry VII Chapel, Westminster, Windsor Castle and select churches and country houses); it was also used in the third (St George's Chapel, Windsor and further abbeys, churches and castles) and the fourth (more priories, churches, castles and Crosby Hall). These volumes were praised in the *Quarterly Review* as 'the most beautiful work of this kind that had ever till then appeared'. Nevertheless the five volumes (published at £31 10s) were still available as late as 1847, in half-morocco at £12 12s.

The Architectural Antiquities of Great Britain, represented and illustrated in a series of views, elevations, plans, sections, and details of various ancient English edifices: with historical and descriptive accounts of each. By John Britton, F.S.A. Vol. I (II, IV). London: Printed for Longman, Hurst, Rees and Orme, Paternoster Row; J. Taylor, Architectural Library, 59 High Holborn; and the author. 1807 (1809, 1814).

Quarto, 325 × 240mm.   1807–9, 1814

COLLATION Vol. 1. Engr general title-page; title-page; dedication to the Marquis of Stafford dated 21 March 1807 (1 leaf); pp i–ii, prefatory advertisement; separately paginated Parts; pp 1–6, index, list of plates. Vol. 2. Title-page; engr half-title; pp iii–iv, dedication to Thomas Hope dated September 1809; pp i–ii, introduction; pp 1–114, descriptions; pp 1–6, index, list of plates. Vol. 4. Title-page; engr half-title; pp iii–iv, dedication to the Marquis of Lansdowne dated July 1814; pp iii–viii, preface; pp 1–196, descriptions; pp 1–10, indices, list of plates.

Of the artists employed, Frederick Mackenzie, Frederick Nash, J.R. Thompson and Gyfford also contributed drawings to the *Beauties of England and Wales*. Mackenzie and Nash were both established water-colour painters and Academicians, the former a pupil of the architect John Repton and specializing in Gothic, the latter appointed as draughtsman to the Society of Antiquaries in 1807. J.R. Thompson, an architectural draughtsman who in 1830 was to exhibit at the Royal Academy a design for the new London Bridge (now in the British Museum), became adviser and assistant to

Britton for his several architectural publications. Items 4 and 22 are by J.L. Bond, an accomplished architectural draughtsman and a Royal Academy gold medallist. Other architects who contributed plates, but not of London subjects, were Joseph Gandy and James Elmes.

Among the engravers who interpreted their drawings were some who also made plates for the *Beauties*: F.R. Hay, J. Lee, the Roffes, William Woolnoth and, notably, John Le Keux whose name was to appear on illustrations in Britton's books for 30 years or more. Indeed Britton, who was himself an amateur artist, seems to have had the ability to attract and retain the loyalty of both the artists and engravers on whom the success of his work so much depended.

Architectural Antiquities marks a transition in the history of topographical illustration. Items 2 (the Temple church) and 25 (Holland House), both engraved by William Woolnoth, are in the same idiom of romantic topography as his plates for the *Beauties of England and Wales* and Hughson's *London* (no 93), the idiom to which Storer and Greig adhered in their *Select Views* (no 90) and *Antiquarian and Topographical Cabinet* (no 118). But Britton's other associates were evolving a sparer, more technical style of architectural illustration in which the engraver was only required to reduce in scale the architect's measured drawings, as here in the 19 plates of Henry VII's Chapel and the five of Crosby Hall. Crosby Hall, before its final degradation, was also to be the subject of measured drawings by Frederick Nash for *Londina Illustrata* (no 131, items 79–80), and in 1807 J.T. Smith measured, drew and engraved similar plates of St Stephen's Chapel before the rebuilders got to work on it for the *Antiquities of Westminster* (no 98, items 48–9).

On 1 December 1812 the *European Magazine* published some acrimonious correspondence about the façade of the architect Soane's house in Lincoln's Inn Fields in which it was abused as 'a palpable eyesore destroying the uniformity of the row'; this was illustrated with a rectilinear outline-etching with the minimum of shading—as austere in style as the building itself. Such austerity culminated in *Illustrations of the Public Buildings of London* (no 146) compiled by Britton and Augustus Pugin in which the succinct firmness of outline is emphasized by the toughness of the steel in which it is etched, enabling the draughtsman's line to be attenuated in proportion to the reduction in scale from the original drawing. Britton was moving with the times, influenced no doubt by his younger colleagues Bond, Thompson and Le Keux.

Each volume is equipped with an index of plates. Plate numbers start afresh with each Part. Publication-lines read as follows:

(a) 'London; Published (date) by Longman, Hurst, Rees & Orme, Paternoster Row, J. Taylor, High Holborn (and J. Britton, Tavistock Place (or) and the Author).'

(b) 'London; Published (date) by Longman & Co., Paternoster Row (and J. Taylor, High Holborn).'

VOL. 1

1 (engr title) The/Architectural Antiquities/of/Great Britain/by John Britton, F.S.A./Vol. I/Part of the Screen in Edward the Confessor's Chapel: Westminster Abbey Church. Engraved by John Smith from a drawing by P. Gyfford. (a) April 1, 1807. 205 × 150/305 × 240mm. With 1 leaf of text (Part I).

Essay towards an history of Temples and Round Churches (Part III, 23pp)

2 p 13 Circular Part of/the Temple Church, London.... Engraved by Wm. Woolnoth from a Drawing by F. Nash. (a) Decr. 25, 1805. 195 × 140/300 × 230mm. pl.2.

3 p 16 Doorway to the/Temple Church/London.... Engraved by S. Sparrow from a Drawing by J.C. Smith. (a) April 1, 1807. 145 × 200/240 × 305mm. pl.3.

4 p 16 Plan of/The Temple Church/London. Engraved by John Roffe from a drawing by J.L. Bond. (a) Decr. 25, 1805. 230 × 155/310 × 230mm. pl.1.

VOL. 2

An essay towards an history and description of King Henry the Seventh's Chapel at Westminster (Parts IX–XV, pp 9–51)

5 p 9 (tm) The Ground Plan &c of Henry VIIth's Chapel, shewing the groining of the roof. Engraved by John Roffe from a drawing and measurements made by F. Mackenzie. (a) Jany 1, 1808. 260 × 150/280 × 220mm. pl.1.

6 p 10 Henry VIIth's Chapel/Plan of the Western end of the South aile. Engraved by John Roffe from a drawing and measurements made by F. Mackenzie. (a) Octr. 1, 1807. 205 × 160/290 × 200m. pl.2.

7 p 11 Henry VIIth's Chapel/Groining of the East end of the roof. Engraved by Richard Roffe from a drawing and measurements made by F. Mackenzie. (a) Octr. 1, 1807. 170 × 230/280 × 220mm. pl.3.

8 p 12 Henry VIIth's Chapel/Groining of part of the roof near the East End. Engraved by S. Barenger from a drawing and measurements made by F. Mackenzie. (a) Octr. 1, 1807. 125 × 220/170 × 286mm. pl.4.

9 p 13 Henry VIIth's Chapel/(Interior, looking West with Tomb &c.) Engraved by John Le Keux from a Drawing by F. Mackenzie. (a) Octr. 1,1807. 210 × 150/300 × 220mm. pl.5.

10 p 14 Henry VIIth's Chapel/A Pendant of the Roof &c. Engraved by J. Sparrow from a Drawing by F. Mackenzie. (a) Octr. 1, 1807. 180 × 135/300 × 240mm. pl.6.

11 p 15 Henry VIIth's Chapel/View & Plan of the lower window &c. at the Eastern end. Engrav'd by J. Roffe from a drawing by Thompson. (a) Jany 1, 1808. 245 × 170/290 × 200mm. pl.7.

12 p 16 Henry VIIth's Chapel/(Flying Buttresses, &c). Engraved by John Smith from a Drawing by F. Mackenzie. (a) Octr. 1, 1807. 200 × 135/305 × 240mm. pl.8.

13 p 16 Henry VIIth's Chapel/(shows Window of upper tier at E. end & exterior facing). Engrav'd by John Roffe from a drawing by Thompson. (a) Jany 1, 1808. 215 × 190/285 × 200mm. pl.9.

14 p 17 Buttress & Turret/in the S.E. angle of/Henry VIIth's Chapel. Etch'd by R. Roffe from a drawing by Thornwaite. (a) Jany 1, 1808. 220 × 170/285 × 210mm. pl.10.

15 p 20 Henry VIIth's Chapel/Elevation of the Eastern End.... Engrav'd by Richard Roffe from a drawing by Thornwaite. (a) Jany 1, 1808. 180 × 212/220 × 280mm. pl.11.

16 p 21 Henry VIIth's Chapel/View in the North Aile. ...Engrav'd by S. Sparrow from a drawing by J.C. Smith. (a) May 1, 1808. 205 × 145/305 × 220mm. pl.12.

17 p 24 Henry VIIth's Chapel/The Great Metal Gates of Entrance.... Engrav'd by John Smith from a drawing by Jas. R. Thompson. (a) Jany 1, 1806. 145 × 200/235 × 305mm. pl.13.

18 p 25 Henry VIIth's Chapel/View from the N.E. Engraved by John Smith from a Drawing by J.R. Thompson. (a) May 1, 1808. 150 × 205/230 × 305mm. pl.14.

19 p 44 Henry VIIth's Chapel/Architectural details. Engrav'd by J. Roffe from drawings by J.R. Thompson. (a) May 1, 1808. 160 × 230/210 × 290mm. pl.15.

20 p 45 Henry VIIth's Chapel/Interior View of a Window &c in the S. Aisle. Engraved by F.R. Hay from a drawing by F. Mackenzie. (a) May 1, 1808. 200 × 150/275 × 210mm. pl.16.

21 p 47 Henry VIIth's Chapel/The Western Window, with Plan. Engraved by J. Roffe from a drawing by J.R. Thompson. (a) May 1, 1808. 220 × 152/290 × 200mm. pl.17.

22 p 48 Henry VIIth's Chapel/Elevation &c of part of South side with the Screens restored. Engrav'd by Richd Roffe from drawings by J.L. Bond. (a) May 1, 1808. 225 × 140/295 × 230mm. pl.18.

23 p 50 Henry VIIth's Chapel/Elevation of N.side of the Porch. Engrav'd by J. Lee from a drawing by F. Mackenzie of the sketches by J.R. Thompson. (a) May 1, 1808. 200 × 155/305 × 240mm. pl.19.

An essay towards a history and description of ...
Domestic, or Civil Architecture in England (Parts
XVI–XVIII, pp 53–114)

24 p 85 An Old House,/at Islington/Middlesex. Etch'd by John Smith from a Drawing by J.R. Thompson. (a) July 1, 1808. 200 × 155/310 × 230mm.

25 p 102 Holland House/the Seat of Lord Holland/ Middlesex. Engraved by W. Woolnoth from a drawing by J.C. Smith. (a) July 1, 1808. 140 × 200/230 × 280mm.

VOL. 4

Some Account of Crosby Hall (Part XL, pp 185–8)

26 p 187 Ground Plan Of/Crosby Hall London. J. Palmer del. J. Roffe sc. (b) Dec. 1, 1813. 190 × 240/210 × 298mm. pl.1.

27 p 188 Crosby Hall./London. J. Palmer del. J. Roffe sc. (b) Sep.1, 1813. 155 × 220/220 × 300mm. Section of Great Hall. pl.2.

28 p 188 Crosby Hall./London. J. Palmer del. J. Roffe sc. (b) Dec. 1,1813. 160 × 220/215 × 300mm. Elevation of E.Side of Great Hall. pl.3.

29 p 188 Architectural details of/Crosby Hall./London. Engraved by H.Le Keux. Drawn by J.Palmer from Sketches by J.A. Repton. (b) Jan. 1, 1814. 220 × 170/290 × 225mm. pl.4.

30 p 188 Elevation of Bay Window; West Side/Crosby Hall./London. Engraved by H.Le Keux. Drawn by J.Palmer from Sketches by J.A. Repton. (b) May 1,1814. 210 × 170/285 × 220mm. pl.5. (*Longford* 697)

98 · SMITH'S ANTIQUITIES OF WESTMINSTER [1807]

The career of John Thomas Smith has been outlined in connection with his first collection of London topography, *Antiquities of London and Environs* (no 70). This book on Westminster is his masterpiece and is unlike his earlier work on a number of counts. It is limited to a more restricted area, it is accompanied by a substantial text, other artists and engravers have participated, several reproductive processes have been employed and, finally, some of the plates have been coloured by hand. Moreover it is our main source of information for the appearance of the Palace of Westminster, which fortunately it depicts in great detail, before the fire of 1834 and also of the Abbey precincts before the clearance of the winding alleys and sinister rookeries reflected in the names of Thieving Lane and Little Sanctuary. In addition there are illustrations of buildings in the Strand and Covent Garden and distant views of Westminster. The Abbey itself is not shown in detail because, as explained in the advertisement, Smith's author, J.S. Hawkins, had it in mind to write its history for which Smith was to supply the pictures.

The advertisement also tells how this whole project nearly foundered on his own prickly temperament and the ill-nature of Hawkins who, at a late stage, being vexed by Smith's pencilled suggestions for amending the proofs, adding fulsome dedications, withdrew from the partnership and totally disowned the work. As a result the title-page is a cancel, omitting the original statement that Hawkins was responsible for the 'literary part' and poor Smith was reduced to enumerating all those portions of the text (a substantial part) written by Hawkins and stating that he accepted full responsibility for the remainder.

The work originated with the discoveries made in August 1800 during the enlargement of the House of Commons (then in St Stephen's Chapel) to accommodate the extra MPs elected as a result of the Act of Union with Ireland. When the wainscoting was torn down fourteenth century wall paintings, sculpture and stained glass were revealed. Smith heard of it and applied for permission to make copies which was granted on condition that he made himself scarce every morning by 9 am, when workmen would carry on demolishing the wall which he had been sketching. In spite of these restrictions he managed in six weeks to record all the ornaments and to match their colouring on site. Hawkins heard this story from Smith's father Nathaniel, the St Martin's Lane printseller, and forthwith agreed with the son that he would write an account of the 'find' to be published alongside the prints made from his drawings. Meanwhile the Society of Antiquaries, of which he was a cantankerous Fellow, had engaged the painter Robert Smirke to record the remains by 'tracings' on their behalf. It would indeed have been something of a scoop if Hawkins's account with Smith's plates could have been published soon after the discovery but Smith was as much a perfectionist in the production of the illustrations as he was in the amendment of dedications and text and the eventual title-page bore the date of 9 June 1807.

A progress report was published in John Feltham's *Picture of London for 1805* (pp 274–5):

John Thomas Smith, Newman-street, Oxford-street: In the prints comprising the History of the Antiquities of London Mr. Smith marked himself for industrious enquiry, good choice of subjects, and accurate representations of what he professed to delineate. He has for some time been employed in a work for which he is peculiarly qualified, and for which he has a large number of most respectable subscribers. It will be recollected, that when the alterations were made in the House of Commons, in Sept. 1800, a number of paintings which were many ages concealed from the public eye, were discovered on the walls. In making the repairs, these very curious specimens of the picturesque taste and talent of our ancestors were necessarily destroyed; but, previously to this, Mr. Smith (and he only) had permission to attend and copy them. To this he was very attentive, and has made most accurate copies of these valuable remains. About 17 finished engravings, in the manner of the originals, will be shortly published, in one volume quarto. This work will contain an account and explanation of the paintings, and other ornaments and decorations, including also a variety of original particulars, as to the History of Westminster and the Palace, and other buildings there—including the history of painting and gothic architecture, by John Sidney Hawkins, Esq., F.A.S. a gentleman whose qualifications for a work of this description are so well known, that it is not necessary to enumerate them in this article.

The drawings from the original pictures, which are in view at Mr. Smith's house in Newman-street, have so intimate a connection with the early state of the arts of painting, sculpture, and architecture, in this country, that they must occasionally be extremely curious and interesting to all those whose enquiries are directed to such subjects.

The list of subscribers when the book finally appeared (in blue paper boards at six guineas) was indeed respectable, headed by the King, the Prince of Wales and the Royal Dukes with some 400 other names including the Archbishop of Canterbury, a good cross-section of the nobility and clergy, numerous MPs and FASs and Oxford and Cambridge libraries. It also included John Constable, John Flaxman, Benjamin West, PRA and Thomas Daniell; as well as Thomas Hope, John Britton,

Charles Townley, William Wilberforce and Samuel Rogers.

Antiquities of Westminster; The Old Palace; St Stephen's Chapel, (Now the House of Commons) &c. &c. Containing Two Hundred and Forty-Six Engravings of Topographical Objects, of which one hundred and twenty-two no longer remain. By John Thomas Smith. This work contains copies of manuscripts which throw new and unexpected light on the ancient history of the Arts in England. London: Printed by T. Bensley, Bolt Court, for J.T. Smith, 31, Castle Street East, Oxford Street, and sold by R. Ryan, 353, Oxford Street, near the Pantheon; and J. Manson, 10, Gerrard Street, Soho. June 9, 1807.

Quarto, 335 × 275mm.   1807

COLLATION Half-title; title-page; dedication to George III (1 leaf); advertisement dated 9 June 1807 (2pp); pp iii–xv, preface by J.S. Hawkins; (pp 1–16, J.T. Smith's Vindication); list of (38) plates (1 leaf); pp 1–272, Antiquities; pp 273–6, list of subscribers.

An additional, engraved title-page (300 × 245mm) was issued with the additional plates in 1809:

Sixty-Two/Additional Plates,/to/Smith's/Antiquities/of/Westminster,/Most respectfully dedicated/to/the/King,/(by His Majesty's Gracious Permission.)/ (arms of Westminster)/London./Published as the Act Directs by J.T. Smith, No. 4, Polygon, Somer's Town./ (rule) Six Guineas. (300 × 245mm pl. mark)

Thirty years later J.B. Nichols, the printer-antiquary, issued a reprint. This was called for because the old Palace of Westminster had been gutted by fire in October 1834 and a nostalgic interest attached to a visual record of this now vanished complex of buildings accreted around Edward III's St Stephen's Chapel and Richard II's great Hall; besides which Charles Barry in the previous year had won the prize for his Gothic design of the new Palace and work on the river front foundations was already under way.

The Antiquities of Westminster; The Old Palace; St Stephen's Chapel, &c.&c.&c. Illustrated by Three Hundred and Thirty Engravings of Topographical Subjects, of which the greater part no longer exist. Drawn on the spot, or collected from scarce drawings or paintings, by John Thomas Smith. A New Edition, With Additional Illustrations, and an Index. London: J.B. Nichols and Son, 25, Parliament Street, 1837.

Quarto, 310 × 240mm.   1837

COLLATION Title-page; advertisement dated 9 June 1807 (2pp); pp iii–xv, preface; pp xvii–xix, list of 122 (including 22 additional) plates; pp 1–272, Antiquities; pp 277–8 (sic), index.

Plates on the binder's check-list and included in the first issue (items 1–38) are dated between 1 January 1804 and 25 April 1807 and all, except item 15, are published from 36 Newman Street. By April 1807 Smith had removed to 31 Castle Street East, which address appears on item 15 and on 46 of the supplementary plates published between 10 September 1807 (item 44) and the end of 1808. The remaining 16 plates which bring the total to 100 were published between 9 January and 1 August 1809 (items 91 and 50); these and the engraved title-page were issued from 4 Polygon, Somers Town.

The pictorial value of the volume as originally published lay in the beautifully coloured and gilded line-engravings or aquatints of the paintings, glass and sculpture revealed by the St Stephen's Chapel demolitions and it is with these that the text is mainly concerned. It carried an announcement that Smith was engaged on engraving ten additional plates 'which may be had of him, No. 31, Castle Street East, Oxford Street, Price £1. 1s.'

Bound up with some issues is Smith's 16 page counterblast to a pamphlet which Hawkins published to refute the charge of unreasonable touchiness made against him in Smith's advertisement:

Mr. John Thomas Smith's Vindication being an answer to a Pamphlet written and published by John Sidney Hawkins Esq. F.A.S. concerning Mr. J.T.S.'s conduct to Mr. H. in relation to the *Antiquities of Westminster*. N.B. To be bound up with the work, immediately after the Advertisement.

It is of less interest for its polemics than for the note appended: 'Since the above "Vindication" was written, and a portion of it printed, a dreadful conflagration in the warehouse of Mr. Bensley has rendered useless four hundred remaining copies of Mr. Smith's *Antiquities of Westminster* and has destroyed Five thousand six hundred prints (two thousand elaborately coloured)'.

To recoup this serious financial blow the engraver decided to increase the number of additional plates for sale from ten, as announced, to 62. To ensure a commercial success by catering for the Pennant collectors, a market of growing importance, he included no fewer than 36 facsimiles or copies: 13 of unpublished plans or extracts from antique maps and 23 copies of historic drawings, paintings or

prints by Knyff, Canaletto, Sandby, Samuel Scott, Visscher, Hollar, Vertue, Spilbergh, June and Gravelot. The set, without text, was priced at £6 6s.

In due course a 'de luxe' edition of the plates alone was announced by the architectural publisher John Booth:

Just published £10.10s. in Bds or £11.11s. Half Bound, Russia backs and corners, *Smith's Topographical Illustrations of Westminster*. Only a few copies printed on large Imperial Paper, beautifully Coloured and Gilt, of the Plates to *Smith's* Antiquities.

J. Booth begs leave to inform Topographical Collectors, that he has, at very great expence, rendered these Plates perfectly acceptable to their Libraries by printing them upon Imperial Paper, of the same size as the grand works of the Antiquarian Society, and the large paper copies of Pennant &c. &c.

It is indeed a sumptuous elephant folio containing 98 of the plates carefully printed and with colouring added as in the first issue. The following printed title is prefixed:

The Antiquities of Westminster: The Old Palace, St Stephen's Chapel, now the House of Commons, &c.&c.&c. illustrated by Three Hundred and Ten Engravings of Topographical Subjects, of which the greater part no longer exist. Drawn on the spot, or collected from scarce drawings or paintings, By John Thomas Smith ... London: Sold by John Booth, Duke Street, Portland Place. 1816.

Folio, 560 × 420mm.   1816

A post-1819 binding, without title-page, of all the plates, bar item 13, on Large Paper (610 × 480mm) is in the Royal Library.

A great many of the plates are of Smith's own drawing or etching or both, but he was no hack illustrator and delighted in technical innovation. Apart from woodcut ornaments, books tended to be illustrated in one medium only: line, line and etching (with perhaps a mezzotint portrait as frontispiece), or aquatint. Into this volume, however, Smith introduced variety by using line, etching (including one engraving stated to be 'on iron', item 6), mezzotint (item 11), aquatint, woodcut and even a lithograph (item 13). This last named is generally accepted as the first lithograph in use as a book illustration but as the text (p 50) explains, after the first 300 impressions the printer neglected to keep the stone damp overnight, the image was impaired and the picture had to be remade as an etching.

He also shared the work with other artists and

engravers so that the collection is attractive not only in its diversity of medium but likewise for the variety of talent employed. George Arnald, ARA supplied a number of delightful general views giving prominence to the river (items 16,89,91,93,95) and among the aquatint engravers are J. Jeakes, F.C. Lewis, and W.M. Fellows to whom 15 of the plates (items 57–65,68,80,83,91,93,98) are credited. Samuel Rawle, the hard-working topographical engraver, was responsible for three (items 4,92,97) while Richard Sawyer and John Brock supplied competent facsimiles of seventeenth and eighteenth century drawings, engravings and plans for the supplement.

Among the earliest subscribers was J.C. Crowle and, with the requirements of similar extra-illustrators in mind, the following booksellers and printsellers:

Mr. Ackerman, Printseller	6
Mr. Alderman Boydell	6
Mr. Clarke, Bookseller	6
Mr. Colnaghi, Printseller	6
Mr. Faulder, Bookseller	3
Mr. Hatchard, Bookseller	2
Mr. Manson, Book & Printseller	20
Mr. Edward Orme, Printseller	6
Mr. Payne, Bookseller	12
Mr. Richardson, Printseller	6
Mr. Ryan, Bookseller	20
Mr. Simco, Book & Printseller	2
Mr. Taylor, Architectural Library	5
Mr. White, Bookseller	12
Mr. Wilkinson, Printseller	2

Of these Colnaghi, Faulder, Manson and Simco had already been associated with Smith in the publication of *Antiquities of London* and the names of Manson and Ryan appear on the title-page of this work.

The Nichols reprint of 1837 incorporates the original 100 plates, including even the battered lithograph, but no colour has been added to the 'specimens' of painting, sculpture and glass from St Stephen's Chapel. As an inadequate compensation he has increased the list by 22 extras; a rag-bag of engravings which blend neither with the text nor with the original illustrations. For this purpose he borrowed five plates from the *Gentleman's Magazine* of which he was proprietor, two from his own firm's collection of views illustrating Pennant (published 1815), five from a similar small set of Frederick Nash's views (1805–10), two from J.P.

Malcolm's *Views within twelve miles round London* (no 82) which had been printed by his father in 1800, three from *Modern London* (no 89) published by Richard Phillips in 1804 and one from Bowles's *British Views* (no 28).

In transcribing the lettering from the first 100 plates certain omissions have been made in the interest of brevity:

When no credit is transcribed 'Drawn & Etched by J.T. Smith' should be assumed.

When no publication-line is transcribed from items 1–38 the original line should be assumed. It reads: 'London, Published as the Act directs 1st January 1804, by John Thomas Smith, No. 36, Newman Street, Oxford Street'.

When no publication-line is transcribed from items 39–100 it should be assumed to read 'London, Published as the Act directs (date) by John Thomas Smith, No. 31, Castle Street East, Oxford Street', only the date being supplied.

The Somers Town address used from the beginning of 1809 is transcribed in full where it occurs.

Unless otherwise stated the plates have no original colouring.

The numbering of the first 38 plates follows their order in the binder's check-list. The supplementary plates are numbered arbitrarily as in J.R. Abbey's copy (*Scenery of Great Britain and Ireland* 210). The complete Royal Library copy, however, arranges the supplementary plates according to a printed list which precedes them and which includes two final 'extras' of Westminster Abbey by John Coney. The numbering is noted here below. Particulars of the six woodcuts by William and John Berryman, printed with the text, are inserted in their appropriate places, in parentheses and unnumbered. Nichols's 1837 check-list distributes each plate in relation to a text page; his 22 extras are therefore arranged in the order specified.

1 p 5 Duke de Sully's House in the Strand – Durham House Strand – Guard Room Scotland Yard – Part of the Old Palace of Whitehall from the Water. 108 × 88,108 × 88,105 × 88,105 × 88/350 × 255mm. Durham House 'Drawn by Nathaniel Smith 1790 & etched by J.T. Smith'. The Duc de Sully's house was in Butcher Row.

(p 14 Charing Cross in disrepair. 90 × 80mm.)

(p 19 Duke of Richmond's house, Whitehall. 70 × 60mm.)

2 p 21 Whitehall Gateway with additions, as intended to have been erected at Windsor. Drawn by T. Sandby Esq. R.A. Engraven by J. Jeakes. 185 × 162/305 × 250mm. Aquatint from a drawing 'in the possession of Mr. John Manson, bookseller'.

3 p 23 Busts originally placed in the gateway of Whitehall. Drawn by J.T. Smith. Etched by Isaac Mills. 80 × 70,70 × 80,70 × 65/320 × 250mm.

4 p 24 View in St James's Park, looking towards Whitehall/From a Drawing ... – View of the same/From a Picture ... Engraven by S. Rawle. Published ... 1st June 1804 by John Thomas Smith, Newman Street, Oxford Street. Each 93 × 245/270 × 308. The first is a distant view along Birdcage Walk, the second from the Horse Guards.

5 p 28 (four-centred arch with 'ER 1602' centred on Tudor rose and sunburst, 15 × 55mm) – Water Gate New Palace Yard, seen from the River – Entrance from New Palace Yard to the Speakers Court Yard – The Speaker's Court Yard from the South West. – The Speaker's Court Yard from the South East. Published ... 1st March 1804 by John Thomas Smith, No. 36 Newman Street, Oxford Street.

6 p 29 Ceiling of the Star Chamber. Engraven by J.T. Smith. Published ... 20 January 1805, by John Thomas Smith, No. 36, Newman Street, Oxford Street. 120 × 195/160 × 220mm. 'engraved on iron'.

7 p 30 Buildings on the South side of New Palace Yard. Drawn & Etched by J. Bryant, Landscape Painter. Published ... 1st January 1805 by John Thomas Smith, No. 36, Newman Street, Oxford Street. 230 × 305/255 × 320mm. Pencil, pen and ink sketch (193 × 275mm) in Westminster Public Library.

8 p 34 Old Palace Yard, from the South, from a Drawing in the possession of Thomas Allen ... Aquatinted by F.C. Lewis, Drawn by Cannaletti, Etched by J.T. Smith – North West View of the Tower, now the Parliament Office – South West View of the Tower, now the Parliament Office. Published ... 1st January 1805 by John Thomas Smith, No 36, Newman Street, Oxford Street. 140 × 220,115 × 102,115 × 102/310 × 260mm. All three show the 'Jewel Tower', the first view being aquatinted not, as stated, after 'Cannaletti' but after a drawing by Leonard Knyff now in the BM (*Croft-Murray* p 398). The two smaller views are drawn and etched, as usual, by Smith.

(p 37 Two round arches with dog-tooth ornament at the S. end of the Court of Requests, 1800. 170 × 147mm.)

9 p 38 Plan of the Palace of Westminster/From a Drawing in the possession of Mr. Simco, Bookseller. Engraven by Sawyer Junr. 250 × 315 pl. mark. With scale of feet.

10 p 39 Views of the four sides of a Cellar under the old House of Lords: North - West - South - East. – East end of the Princes Chamber – South side of the Princes Chamber. Published ... 1st July 1804 by John Thomas Smith, No. 36 Newman Street, Oxford Street. 30 × 70,27 × 194,30 × 70,27 × 195; 108 × 88,108 × 88/320 × 250mm.

11 p 41 A Doorway in one of the cellars under the old House of Lords. 175 × 143/200 × 145mm. Engraved by J.T. Smith in mezzotint.

12 p 45 Belt or Girth round Westminster Hall – N.E. View of the Bell Tower of St Stephen's Chapel – Inside View of the same Bell Tower – E. View of Westminster Hall from one of the/uppermost Rooms at the Speaker's. – S.E. View of the same Bell Tower, taken from the/House of Commons – Internal View of the S. door of the Chapel/under St Stephen's – Central door at the E.end of the Painted Chamber – East end of Painted Chamber – North side of Painted Chamber. Published ... October 10, 1805, by John Thomas Smith, No. 36 Newman Street, Oxford Street. 5 × 22,60 × 60,60 × 55,60 × 60; 60 × 60, 60 × 55, 60 × 60; 113 × 93,113 × 93/320 × 250mm.

(p 45 Terra Cotta scroll ornament in cellar under House of Lords. 65 × 55mm.)

13 p 48 (Inside of the Painted Chamber as it was in the Year 1800) 190 × 160mm. No credits or publication-line. This is the earliest lithograph used as a book illustration. After 300 copies had been printed the stone was spoiled by negligence and the following etching was substituted.

14 p 50 Inside of the Painted Chamber as it was in the Year 1800 before the old tapestry/was removed. Published ... 19 November 1806, by John Thomas Smith, No. 36, Newman Street, Oxford Street. 208 × 165/230 × 175mm. Adds two artists, one sketching, to the empty lithographic interior.

15 p 125 Plan of part of Westminster as it was in the time of Richard the second. (in oval) Foundation Plan/of the/Ancient Palace/of Westminster/Measured, Drawn, & Engraved/by/I.T.Smith. Published ... 25 April 1807, by John Thomas Smith, No. 31, Castle Street, East, Oxford Street. 215 × 260/255 × 318mm. With scale of feet and refs A–Z.

16 p 144 View of Westminster from the East. Painted by G. Arnald (signed '1803'). Aquatinted by Frederick Christian Lewis, and afterwards etched and finished by J.T. Smith. Published ... 7 August, 1806 by John Thomas Smith, No. 36 Newman Street, Oxford Street. 182 × 230/265 × 315mm. The Palace and Abbey seen from the Lambeth end of Westminster Bridge.

17 p 145 North East View of the House of Commons, from a Drawing by Thomas Sandby ... in the possession of Paul Sandby – East View of Westminster from the water, from a Drawing ... Published ... 1st January, 1805 by John Thomas Smith, No. 36, Newman Street, Oxford Street. 177 × 214, 95 × 240/320 × 250mm.

18 p 146 South side of the House of Commons, from the roof of the Painted Chamber. Drawn & Etched by G. Arnald, Topographical Landscape Painter. Published

... 1st January 1805, by John Thomas Smith, No. 36, Newman Street, Oxford Street. 215 × 290/250 × 318mm.

(p 147 Exterior view of the upper part of the House of Commons. Copied from the frontispiece to the second volume of Nelson's *Impartial Collections*. 175 × 95mm.)

19 p 150 North West entrance of the Vestibule to the House of Commons. Drawn by J.T. Smith. Engraven by W.J. White. 160 × 120, capitals each 40 × 40/310 × 255mm.

20 p 153 North East corner of St Stephens Chapel – South East corner of the same Chapel. – Part of the South side of the same Chapel. Drawn & Engraven by J.T. Smith. Published ... 10, July 1806, by John Thomas Smith, No. 36, Newman Street, Oxford Street. 115 × 105, 115 × 105, 150 × 220/320 × 255mm. With scale of feet.

21 p 155 Geometrical Construction of the Freeze and Battlements in the House of Commons. Drawn & Engraven by J.T. Smith. Published ... 1st January 1805 by John Thomas Smith, No. 36, Newman Street, Oxford Street. Each 90 × 150/290 × 250mm.

22 p 157 Sculpture and Painted Glass from St. Stephen's Chapel. Drawn & Engraven by J.T. Smith. 280 × 240mm pl.mark. With added body colour.

23 p 232 Specimens of Stained Glass from St. Stephen's Chapel. Drawn & Engraven by J.T. Smith. 290 × 240mm pl. mark. With added body colour. Sprays of foliage.

24 p 232 Specimens of Stained Glass from St. Stephen's Chapel. Drawn & Engraven by J.T. Smith. 285 × 240mm pl. mark. With added body colour. Heraldic lions, fleur-de-lys, tabernacle-work and ornamental borders.

25 p 233 Specimens of Stained Glass from St. Stephen's Chapel. Drawn & Engraven by J.T. Smith. 280 × 230mm pl. mark. Body colour added. Heads and hands and folds of garments.

26 p 234 Grotesque Paintings on the Frieze in St. Stephen's Chapel. Drawn & Engraven by J.T. Smith. 280 × 230mm pl. mark. Aquatinted and printed in brown ink. Blank shields with grotesque supporters.

27 p 235 Grotesque Paintings on the Frieze in St. Stephen's Chapel. Drawn & Engraven by J.T. Smith. 275 × 233mm pl. mark. Aquatinted and printed in brown ink. Six blank shields with grotesque supporters.

28 p 237 Armorial Bearings from St. Stephen's Chapel. /Plate 1. Drawn & Engraven by J.T. Smith. 288 × 240mm pl. mark. With added body colour and gilt. 17 aquatinted shields of the family of Edward III.

29 p 241 Armorial Bearings from St. Stephen's Chapel./ Plate 2. Drawn & Engraven by J.T. Smith. 290 × 235mm pl. mark. With added body colour and gilt. 18 etched shields of fourteenth century noblemen's arms.

30 p 242 Specimens of Sculpture from St. Stephen's Chapel/Plate 1. Drawn & Engraven by J.T. Smith. 275 × 235mm pl. mark. With body colour added. Stiff-leaf corbels, pinnacles, friezes, mouldings, etc.

31 p 242 Specimens of Sculpture from St. Stephen's Chapel./Plate 2. Drawn by J.T. Smith. Engraven by W.J. White. Published ... 1st June 1804 by John Thomas Smith, No. 36, Newman Street, Oxford Street. 310 × 260mm pl. mark. Shafts, corbels, mouldings, friezes, etc.

32 p 244 Specimens of Painting from St. Stephen's Chapel. Drawn & Engraven by J.T. Smith. 210 × 160/320 × 260mm. With added body colour. Wall paintings of two knights, 'Mercure' and 'Eustace'.

33 p 248 Specimen of Painting from St. Stephen's Chapel. Drawn & Engraven by J.T. Smith. 160 × 75/285 × 240mm. Aquatinted, with body colour. An angel appearing to a shepherd.

34 p 249 Specimens of Painting from St. Stephen's Chapel. Drawn & Engraven by J.T. Smith. 173 × 123/290 × 240mm. Aquatinted, printed in brown ink with added body colour and gilt. The adoration of the shepherds.

35 p 250 Specimen of Painting from St. Stephen's Chapel. Drawn & Engraven by J.T. Smith. 150 × 110/285 × 245mm. Aquatinted, with added body colour. Female and male figures with doves, the 'Purification'.

36 p 250 Specimen of Painting from St. Stephen's Chapel. Drawn & Engraven by J.T. Smith. 200 × 123/280 × 250mm. Aquatinted, with body colour. A young king, crowned and bearing a reliquary and sceptre.

37 p 251 Cotton Garden Westminster. 225 × 180/310 × 260mm. Being used as a mason's yard during the demolition. J.T. Smith's ink and wash drawing (215 × 175mm) is in Westminster Public Library.

38 p 252 No. 1, Oak Door discovered in the Speaker's state/Dining Room – No. 2, Cornice of the front of the/Vicars Houses towards the Water – Nos 3–6, Tiles in the Vicars houses – No. 7, Internal View of a Doorway/to one of the Vicars houses – No. 8, Mural Monument in the Cloister, Published ... 7 August, 1806 by John Thomas Smith, No. 36 Newman Street, Oxford Street. 120 × 75, 70 × 40; tiles each 30 × 30; 70 × 40, 75 × 75/330 × 270mm.

(p 269 King Edward III commissioning Hugh de St Albans, John Athelard and Benedict Nightingale to collect painters for St. Stephen's Chapel. From a drawing by T. Stothard. 130 × 120mm.)

Additional plates

(These are usually found bound up at the end of the volume in haphazard order but the order adopted here is that of the Abbey catalogue. The Royal Library, however, owns a copy in which these plates are preceded not only by the supplementary title-page but also by a leaf printed on both sides, 'List of Plates forming the

Supplement to Smith's Antiquities of Westminster, the Old Palace and St Stephen's Chapel', on which the plates are numbered and dated and which includes two extras by John Coney of Westminster Abbey, not in the Abbey catalogue. These supplementary numbers are quoted at the end of each entry.)

39 Plan of part of the City of Westminster copied from Radulphus Aggas's Map, taken in the reign of Queen Elizabeth 1578. Decr. 26 1807. 180 × 257/210 × 265mm. Refs (l.), A–D, (r.) E–H. No credits. (Suppl. no 2)

40 Plan of Westminster; from Norden's Survey, taken in the reign of Queen Elizabeth 1593. Etched by Sawyer jr. February 20th 1808. 150 × 235/200 × 260mm. (Suppl. no 1)

41 This Plan ... /shows the Streets, Courts, Alleys & Yards, as they appeared before the erection of Parliament Street, Bridge Street, &c ... Plan taken between 1734 & 1748. Novr. 10, 1807. 180 × 265/220 × 275mm. No credits. Original plan was owned by Westminster Bridge Commissioners. (Suppl. no 61)

42 This Plan ... /shows the Streets, Courts/Alleys and Yards as they appeared before the erection of Great George Street ... Taken between 1734 & 1748. Octr 1st 1807. 215 × 278/240 × 290mm. No credits. Original plan was owned by Westminster Bridge Commissioners. (Suppl. no 59)

43 This Plan ... /exhibits the buildings from the Admiralty to Charing Cross, as they appeared before the approach to Westminster was widened ... Taken between 1734 & 1748 ... September 18 1807. 205 × 280/240 × 290mm. No credits. Original plan was owned by Westminster Bridge Commissioners. (Suppl. no 58)

44 This plan ... exhibits the site of the buildings which once covered the South-/ern half of Deans Yard with the situation of the two Gate-Houses ... /Taken between 1734 & 1748 ... Septr. 10th 1807. 150 × 255/170 × 265mm. No credits. Original plan was owned by Westminster Bridge Commissioners. (Suppl. no 47)

45 Plan of Duck Island in St James's Park ... 1734. Septr. 10th 1807. 250 × 220/290 × 235mm. No credits. Refs A–H. (Suppl. no 33)

46 Plan of Peterborough House, lately the residence of the Earl of Grosvenor, with the Gardens &c. belonging thereto, together/with the grounds adjacent, as they appeared between the years 1734 & 1748. Oct. 12 1807. 250 × 210/275 × 215mm. No credits. (Suppl. no 60)

47 The Village of Charing, &c: from Radulphus Aggas's Map taken in the reign of Queen Elizabeth 1578. Feby 24th 1808. 175 × 255/200 × 265mm. No credits. (Suppl. no 3)

48 A geometrical view of St Stephens Chapel as it appeared before the alterations in 1806 & after Mr Sandby's View, which was taken about 1755. Measured, Drawn & Engraven by I.T. Smith. Decr. 10 1807. 285 × 180mm pl. mark. With scale of feet. (Suppl. no 28)

49 A geometrical view of the East end of St. Stephen's Chapel,/composed from as many original parts as could be derived from/the views given in this work, & from late discoveries.... Measured, Drawn & Ingraven by I.T. Smith. 10th Decr. 1807. 285 × 180mm pl. mark (Suppl. no 27)

50 House of Commons,/as it appeared in 1741./Drawn by Gravelot: Engraved by W.J. White: Published as the Act directs 1st Augt. 1809, by John Thomas Smith, No. 4, Polygon, Somers Town. 265 × 223/330 × 270mm. (Suppl. no 29)

51 Part of the East-side of the House of Lords:/(the Council Chamber of our early Kings)/... Drawn by J.T. Smith Octr. 10 1807: Engraved by W. Fellows. 10 March 1808. 230 × 180/265 × 200mm. With aquatint. (Suppl. no 23)

52 North East Views of the Old House of Lords the Princes Chamber with the Bishops Robing Room &c: taken from the ruins of Mr Blackerby's house Octor. 12 1807 – South East views of the Princes Chamber and the old House of Lords, taken May 10 1809. Published as the Act directs June 28 1809, by John Thomas Smith, No. 4, Polygon, Somers Town. 190 × 235,100 × 235/330 × 250mm. (Suppl. no 26)

53 South East View of the Princes Chamber taken Octor. 10th 1807. Published as the Act directs June 5th 1809, by John Thomas Smith, No. 4, Polygon, Somers Town. 150 × 240/180 × 250mm. (Suppl. no 25)

54 Views of the East side of the House of Lords: the East end of the Princes Chamber taken Octr 8 1807 from an upper window in the house of Edwd Hussey Delaval/Esq. at the S.E. corner of Cotton Gardens. 5 Nov. 1807. 155 × 245/175 × 255mm. (Suppl. no 24)

55 (View of the Abbey and Parliament drawn by J.C. Keirinx) London the 27 of Mar. An. 1625 – (in sky) Civitatis Westmonasteriensis pars. (above buildings) Parliament House, the Hall, the Abby. W. Hollar ('W H' in monogram) fecit 1647 – (in sky along tm) Sala Regalis cum Curia West-monasterij vulgo Westminster Hall. W. Hollar ('W H' in monogram) fecit 1647. Etch'd by Richd. Sawyer. Published as the Act directs June 1 1809, by John Thomas Smith, No. 4, Polygon, Somers Town. 95 × 255, 90 × 255, 100 × 255/330 × 270mm. The two Hollar views are reduced facsimiles of Hollar's 'Prospects' (no 5), items 5–6. (Suppl. no 6)

56 The North-West View of Westminster Hall, &c./drawn at the bow window of the King's Arms Tavern in New Palace Yard, by Thomas Sandby Esqr ... before the removal of the decayed battlements, and of the coffee-houses which concealed the sculptured decorations ... Engraved by Thos. Hall. April 26 1808. 175 × 245/235 × 290mm. The original oil painting is at

the House of Commons and there is a water-colour version (327 × 483mm) at the Museum of London. Aquatint. (Suppl. no 20)

57 The South West View of Little Dean's Yard, taken from an upper window at the Revd Mr Douglas's. ... Drawn by J.T. Smith April 9th 1808: Engraved by W.M. Fellows. 10 May 1808. 205 × 250/250 × 275mm. Aquatint. (Suppl. no 48)

58 The Entrance to Westminster-School. Drawn by J.T. Smith April 23d. 1808: Engraved by W.M. Fellows. 2 May 1808. 220 × 187/250 × 195mm. Aquatint. (Suppl. no 50)

59 (tm) The Water Front of the Buildings on the Eastern Side of New Palace Yard. Drawn by J.T. Smith April 17 1808: Engraved by W.M. Fellows. May 14 1808. 180 × 250/210 × 270mm. Aquatint. (Suppl. no 22)

60 (tm) Buildings on the Eastern Side of New Palace Yard. Drawn by J.T. Smith April 15 1808: Engraved by W.M. Fellows. May 10 1808. 180 × 250/205 × 265mm. Aquatint. (Suppl. no 21)

61 South East View of the entrances to the Little Sanctuary & to Thieving Lane, from King Street, which are about to be pulled down.... Drawn by J.T. Smith Octr 12 1807: Engraved by W.M. Fellows. 14 April 1808. 220 × 175/265 × 205mm. Aquatint. (Suppl. no 52)

62 North East View of the entrance to Thieving Lane, from King Street: taken after the houses at the corner were pulled down.... Drawn by J.T. Smith Novr 30 1807: Engraved by W.M. Fellows. 14 April 1808. 215 × 185/265 × 210mm. Aquatint. (Suppl. no 53)

63 A View of the Little Sanctuary, from the West End.... Drawn by J.T. Smith: Engraved by W.M. Fellows: March 21st 1808. 220 × 180/250 × 200mm. Aquatint. The Museum of London owns a water-colour (280 × 190mm) entitled 'Little Sanctuary Westminster. Old London 1800', signed 'Ma' which differs only slightly from this engraving. (Suppl. no 51)

64 View of the Southern extremity of Thieving Lane (of late years called Bow Street) through which the Felons were conveyed to the Gate-house, which stood at the Eastern end of Tothill Street. The inhabitants are of the lowest order, & aggravate, by their numbers, that nuisance which the filthiness of their persons & the narrowness of the avenues had already created. Drawn by J.T. Smith Dec 15 1807. Engraved by W.M. Fellows. March 28 1808. 220 × 178/255 × 200mm. Aquatint. (Suppl. no 54)

65 A View of Broken Cross, formerly so called, situate at the Southern extremity of Thieving Lane (alias Bow Street) & partly overhanging old Long Ditch, which now forms Princes Street.... Drawn by J.T. Smith April 1st 1808. Engraved by W.M. Fellows. June 1st 1808. 190 × 220/210 × 235mm. Aquatint. (Suppl. no 55)

66 Entrance to the College Hall &c. Drawn by J.T. Smith

Octor. 15 1808. Published as the Act directs June 26 1809, by John Thomas Smith, No. 4, Polygon, Somers Town. 165 × 225/195 × 245mm. Aquatint. (Suppl. no 49)

67 Part of the Church of St. Margaret, Westminster./ From a rare print by Brook, prefixed to Warner's edition of the book of Common Prayer. John Brock Sculpsit. 19 Decr. 1808. 230 × 190/320 × 230mm. (Suppl. no 46)

68 South-West View of the Old Horse-Guards./Engraved from a Drawing by Canaletti. Engraved by W.M. Fellows. Published as the Act directs 1 Feby 1809, by John Thomas Smith, No. 4, Polygon, Somers Town. 195 × 285/245 × 294. Before 1749; from a pen and wash drawing (346 × 688mm) in the BM (Suppl. no 32) (*Constable* 734)

69 King Street Gate Westminster/Demolished Anno 1723./Reduced from a print drawn & engraved by G. Vertue & published by the Society of Antiquaries, 1725. Engraved by John Brock. Aug 27 1808. 213 × 156/270 × 210mm. From *Vetusta Monumenta* (no 36), item 5. (Suppl. no 36)

70 A reduced copy of Fisher's Ground Plan of the Royal Palace of Whitehall taken in the reign of Charles 2d 1680. Novr. 30 1807. 180 × 280/210 × 285mm. From *Vetusta Monumenta*, item 63: 'A Survey & Ground Plot of the Royal Palace of Whitehall ... Survey'd by John Fisher. Drawn & Publish'd by G. Vertue Ano Dom. 1747.' Refs 1–58. (Suppl. no 31)

71 The Royal Palace of Whitehall from the Water. Engraven by Sawyer Junr. Sept 10 1807. 170 × 250/225 × 275mm. 'Communicated by J.C. Crowle'. The original pen and brown ink drawing over black lead (336 × 488mm), by L. Knyff, passed to the BM with the Crowle Pennant. (Suppl. no 30) (*Croft-Murray* pp 397–8)

72 Whitehall Gate,/Said to be designed by Hans Holbein./Reduced from a print drawn & engraved by G. Vertue & published by the Society of Antiquaries, 1725. Engraved by John Brock. Augt 31 1808. 200 × 140/270 × 210mm. From *Vetusta Monumenta*, item 4. (Suppl. no 35)

73 Statue of King James II in Privy Garden Whitehall. J. Mills Delint. et Sculpt. Published as the Act directs June 28 1809, by John Thomas Smith, No. 4, Polygon, Somers Town. 325 × 205mm pl. mark (Suppl. no 62)

74 These copies are from portions of an extremely rare print by Visscher ... taken early in the reign of King James I ... (facsimile signature) C.J. Visscher Delineavit. Etched by Richd. Sawyer. Published as the Act directs June 3d 1809, by John Thomas Smith, No. 4, Polygon, Somers Town. 258 × 203/300 × 235mm. Westminster and Strand sections of Visscher's panorama (Suppl. no 7)

75 Veüe et Perspective du Palais du Roy d'Angleterre a Londres qui sapelle Whitehall. Silvestre sculp. Israel ex. cum privil. Regis/Taken from a rare print in the

superb collection of Alexander Hendras Sutherland Esq. Israel Silvestre/Born 1621 Died 1691. Etched by Sawyer Junr. 10 Decr. 1808. 120 × 240/210 × 290mm. Facsimile of sparse etched original (*Crace* 16.2). (Suppl. no 34)

76 North View of the City of Westminster (taken in Sept 1807) from the roof of the Banqueting-House, Whitehall. ... gives a full display of the improvements made about 1752, by the erection of Parliament Street. Published as the Act directs Jany 25 1809, by John Thomas Smith, No. 4, Polygon, Somers Town. 220 × 290/255 × 295mm. Etching, with stipple. (Suppl. no 16)

77 (tm) The South Prospect of the Old Church of St Martin in the Fields pulled down in 1721. ... (bm) The West prospect of the same Church. George Vertue delin. John Brock sculp. Sept. 13 1808. 115 × 160, 120 × 160/265 × 210mm. From *Vetusta Monumenta*, items 58–9. (Suppl. no 45)

78 The Front of Northumberland House, next the Strand./Copied by Sawyer Junr. from a large Print. Engraved by J. June & Published by T. Jeffries Feby 24th 1752. Daniel Garrett Archt. Published as the Act directs Jany 15 1809, by John Thomas Smith, No. 4, Polygon, Somers Town. 235 × 300mm pl. mark. The original on two sheets, overall 495 × 724mm (BL Maps: *K. top.* 27.9b). (Suppl. no 42)

79 The Savoy, from the River Thames/Reduced from a view taken by G. Vertue in 1736 & published by the Society of Antiquaries in 1750. Sawyer Jun. sculp. Decr. 12 1808. 185 × 260/210 × 270mm. Refs A–F. From *Vetusta Monumenta*, item 10. (Suppl. no 38)

80 View of the Savoy, Somerset House and the Water-entrance to Cuper's Garden.... Painted by Samuel Scott. Engraved by W.M. Fellows. 15 Septr. 1808. 190 × 270/255 × 305mm. Aquatint. (Suppl. no 37)

81 The Southern Front of Somerset House, with its extensive Gardens &c. Drawn by L. Knyff about 1720. Engraved by Sawyer Junr. April 1st 1808. 165 × 240/190 × 255mm. The original engraving by J. Kip of Knyff's river view of Somerset House was probably made before 1705 for *Nouveau Théâtre de la Grande Bretagne* (no 22), item 6. (Suppl. no 39)

82 Internal View of Somerset House Reduced from a large print drawn, etched & published by W. Moss in 1777. 14 Octr. 1808. 108 × 225/210 × 270mm. The original (438 × 641mm) was also aquatinted by F. Jukes (*Crace* 17.105). (Suppl. no 41)

83 The North Front of Somerset House. Reduced from a large print drawn, etched & published by W. Moss in 1777. Engraved by W.M. Fellows. Augt. 11 1808. 175 × 228/218 × 240mm. The original (438 × 660mm) was also aquatinted by F. Jukes (*Crace* 17.104). (Suppl. no 40)

84 Parts of the Strand and Covent Garden, as they appeared in the reign of Queen Elizabeth./Copied from Aggas's Map Published 1578. Published as the Act directs June 29 1809, by John Thomas Smith, No. 4, Polygon, Somers Town. 185 × 260/205 × 265mm. An enlargement. (Suppl. no 4)

85 Plan of Bedford House, Covent Garden, &c taken about 1690./From a Drawing in the possession of/John Charles Crowle Esq. F.A.S. Published as the Act directs 30 May 1809, by John Thomas Smith, No. 4, Polygon, Somers Town. 208 × 290/245 × 315mm. (Suppl. no 56)

86 A Perfect Description of the Firework in Covent Garden that was performed at the Charge of the Gentry and other inha/bitants of that Parish for ye joyfull returan of His Matie from his Conquest in Ireland Sept. 10 1690. B. Lens fecit. Sold by B. Lens between Bridewell Bridge and Fleet Bridge in Black fryers. Published as the Act directs 30 May 1809, by John Thomas Smith, No. 4, Polygon, Somers Town. 180 × 260/255 × 287mm. Original, mezzotint 241 × 343mm (*Crace* 18.54). (Suppl. no 57)

87 Plan of Arundel and Essex Houses./Copied from Ogilby & Morgan's twenty-sheet plan of London ... Augt. 20 1808. 255 × 290/255 × 305mm. (Suppl. no 8)

88 (in sky) Aula Domus Arrundelianae Londini Septentrionem versus. Adam A. Bierling delin. W Hollar fecit 1646. – (in sky) London from ye top of Arundell House. W. Hollar fecit. – (in sky) Aula Domus Arrundelianae Londini, Meridiem versus. Adam A. Bierling delin. WHollar fecit 1646. These views are copied by Richd. Sawyer, from very rare etchings ... Septr. 20th 1808. 80 × 190, 80 × 133, 78 × 90/300 × 255mm. Facsimiles of originals, 82 × 194,87 × 137, 82 × 194mm (*Hind* 82,81,83). (Suppl. no 5)

89 View of part of Westminster, taken from the Reservoir in the Green Park. Painted by G. Arnold 1807. Etched by Isaac Mills. Augt. 1 1808. 177 × 290/205 × 300mm. (Suppl. no 15)

90 A pictoresque View of St. James's Park taken from the Mall, in front of St. James's Palace. Novr. 1 1807. 160 × 220/175 × 230mm. (Suppl. no 18)

91 View of Westminster, taken from Lambeth Stairs. Painted by G. Arnold 1808. Engraved by W.M. Fellows. Published as the Act directs 9 Jany 1809, by John Thomas Smith, No 4, Polygon, Somers Town. 190 × 260/265 × 330mm. Aquatint. (Suppl. no 12)

92 A South View of Westminster, from the Surrey side of the Thames, near the Nine Elms, Battersea.... Robert Freebairn Pinxt. S. Rawle sculpt. March 25 1808. 190 × 250/245 × 305mm. Etching. (Suppl. no 11)

93 A View of Westminster, taken from Tothill-Fields. Painted by G. Arnold 1807. Engraved by W.M. Fellows. Septr. 20 1808. 190 × 250/245 × 300mm. Aquatint. (Suppl. no 13)

94 A View of the Grounds on the South of Westminster, including the Timber-yard on Mill-Bank, with Tothill Fields in the Distance. Drawn by J.T. Smith. Engraved by T. Hall. March 1 1808. 153 × 215/175 × 228mm. Aquatint. (Suppl. no 19)

95 A View of Westminster, taken from Mill-Bank. Painted by G. Arnald 1807. Engraved by John Hall. Sept 20 1808. 190 × 250/237 × 290mm. Aquatint. (Suppl. no 14)

96 A South-View of Westminster, from Mill-bank; where the King's Scholars-Pond Sewer empties itself into the Thames. Drawn by J.T. Smith. Engraved by T. Hall. March 1st 1808. 173 × 253/210 × 263mm. Aquatint. (Suppl. no 17)

97 A View of Westminster, taken from the garden of Old Somerset House.... Drawn in 1754 by Thos. Sandby Esq. Engraven by S. Rawle. 11 Jan. 1808. 130 × 272/150 × 280mm. A pencil, pen, water-colour and gouache drawing of this subject (295 × 365mm), by Paul and Thomas Sandby, passed into the Royal Collection in about 1812 (Oppé 161) but, says Oppé, 'The subject, obviously deriving from Canaletto, directly or through engravings, was constantly repeated by either or both of the brothers'. The BM has a vast panoramic view (18¼ × 75¾ inches) of the same subject, attributed to Thomas Sandby, which it acquired in 1811 with the Crowle Pennant (Binyon vol. 4, p 29). (Suppl. no 10)

98 View of Westminster, taken upon the Thames at the period of the building of the Bridge. Painted by Canaletti. Engraved by W.M. Fellows. Published as the Act directs 11 Jany 1809, by John Thomas Smith, No. 4, Polygon, Somers Town. 195 × 290/250 × 310mm. 'From a Picture in the Collection of the Honble Percy Wyndham' now untraceable (Constable 437). The three arches on the Lambeth side are yet unbuilt; according to the architect it was passable by July 1746. (Suppl. no 9)

99 Burlington House, Piccadilly/as it appeared about 1720. L. Knyff delin. Richd. Sawyer sculp. Published as the Act directs June 1 1809, by John Thomas Smith, No. 4, Polygon, Somers Town. 190 × 275/240 × 295mm. Engraved by J. Kip before 1704 and included in the first volume of Nouveau Théâtre de la Grande, Bretagne, item 11. (Suppl. no 43)

100 The South, or principal front of Albemarle House (originally called Clarendon House) ... J. Spilbergh delin. W. Skillman sculp. Engraved by R. Sawyer, Jun 1808. May 30th 1808. 215 × 295/270 × 330mm. Based on Skillman's original engraving (508 × 698mm; Crace 10.113). (Suppl. no 44)

100a King Henry the VIIth Chapel – St Peters Coll. Ch. Westminster. Drawn by J. Coney, Engraved by T. Dale for the Architectural Series of London Churches. Published by J. Booth, March 1, 1819. 165 × 245/270 × 330mm. Includes ground plan. See Architectura Ecclesiastica Londini (no 129), item 108. (Suppl. no 63)

100b Interior View of St Peters/looking from the railing of the Altar to the Great Western Entrance. Drawn & Etched by J. Coney for the Architectural Series of London Churches. Published by J. Booth, Feb 20, 1819. 225 × 165/310 × 210mm. See Architectura Ecclesiastica Londini, item 109. (Suppl. no 64)

Nichols's 1837 ed (supplementary plates)

101 p 5 Old Hungerford Market. (tr) Gent. Mag. Aug. 1832 Pl. II p. 113. 115 × 185/160 × 230mm. Originally published in F. Nash's Twelve Views of the Antiquities of London (1805–10). (Upcott p 890)

102 p 6 Plan of Denmark House, 1706. No. 1. Longmate sc. 81 Margaret St. Cavenh.Sq. 230 × 230mm.

103 p 6 Plan of Denmark House, 1706. No. 2. Longmate sc. 190 × 245mm. Two plans engr by Barak Longmate junior for Nichols's One Hundred and Twenty Views and Portraits to illustrate the Fourth Edition of Pennant's Account of London (1815). (Upcott p 839)

104 p 6 Westminster 1650. Malcolm sc. Published Dec. 1, 1797 by J.P. Malcolm, Middlesex St, Somers Town. 110 × 185/130 × 195mm.

105 p 6 Somerset Palace in 1650. C.B. pinx. Malcolm sc. (tr) Pl. 1 p. 80. 115 × 190/130 × 200mm. This and item 104 were engraved by Malcolm from a single painting at Dulwich College by Cornelys Bol and were originally published in his Views within twelve miles round London, items 2,1.

106 p 19 Part of the Palace of White-hall built by Cardinal Wolsey – Restored – as it appeared 1815 – as it appears 1816. J. Carter del. J. Basire sc. (tr)Gent. Mag. Dec 1811, Pl.1, p. 489. 205 × 120/225 × 145mm.

107 p 19 A View from the River Thames of the Parliament House, Westminster Hall, and Westminster Abby – A View of Whitehall. (br) 'b'. 165 × 230/180 × 245mm. From Bowles's British Views, item 35.

108 p 20 (An elevation of the Banqueting House) 225 × 305mm pl. mark.

109 p 26 The Admiralty, the War Office & the Treasury. Pugh delin. Pass sculp. Published Augt 11, 1804 by Richard Phillips ... 125 × 185/190 × 235mm. See Phillips's Modern London (no 89), item 8.

110 p 38 Westminster Abbey. Drawn & Engraved by S. Rawle. Published Augt 14, 1804 by Richard Phillips ... 130 × 190/210 × 270mm. See Phillips's Modern London, item 19.

111 p 38 The North east view of the Old Dormitory in 1758. J.B.sc. – North east view of the remains of part of the Crypt of the Old Dormitory. (tr) Gent. Mag. Sept. 1815, Pl.1, p. 201. 200 × 110/230 × 140mm.

112 p 38 The South View of the Abbey & Dormitory in Westminster. W. Courtenay delint. 1758. 155 × 270/190 × 275mm. As BL Maps: K. top. 24.4h.

113 p 38 The Crypt under Westminster Abbey. Drawn & Etched by Nash. Published March 1, 1810 by H. Setchel & Son, King St, Covent Garden. 115 × 185/160 × 225mm. Originally published in F. Nash's Twelve Views of the Antiquities of London. (Upcott p 890)

114 p 38 W. View of the Jerusalem Chamber. Published Sept. 1, 1805 by Jordan & Maxwell. 120 × 185/145 × 230 mm.

115 p 38 N. Side of the Jerusalem Chamber, Westminster. 120 × 185/145 × 230mm.

116 p 38 Interior of the Jerusalem Chamber, N.W. 120 × 175/155 × 230mm.

117 p 38 Interior of the Jerusalem Chamber, S.E. 120 × 175/155 × 230mm. Although these four views have the line 'Published Septr 1, 1805 by Jordan & Maxwell' they originate with F. Nash's *Twelve Views of the Antiquities of London*. (*Upcott* p 890)

118 p 39 Exterior & Interior Views of the Prince's Chamber & Old House of Lords, Westminster. (tr) Gent. Mag. Dec. 1823, Pl.1, p. 489. 50 × 100, 60 × 80,65 × 80/230 × 155mm. By E. Blore, FSA.

119 p 39 The Houses of Parliament, with the Royal Procession. Pugh delin. Thompson sculp. 125 × 190/190 × 241mm. 'As in 1804'. See Phillips's *Modern London*, item 10.

120 p 147 The Speaker's House, from Westr. Bridge. Levens sculp. Published by A. Beugo, Printseller, No. 38 Maiden Lane, Covent Garden, Nov. 12, 1810. 130 × 178/170 × 220mm. 'As altered by Mr. Wyatt in 1807'. As BL Maps: *K. top. 27.14*.

121 p 156 Vestiges of Sculpture ... Painting/in St Stephen's Chapel, Westminster/after the Fire of October, 1834. R.W. Billings sc. (tr) Gent. Mag. Vol. V. Jan. 1836. 160 × 90/230 × 140mm.

122 p 258 Wall of the Gatehouse remaining in 1836. Hollins del. et sc. – The Gatehouse, Westminster/looking towards Tothill Street. Each 75 × 78/178 × 120mm.

99 · ACKERMANN'S MICROCOSM OF LONDON [1808]

Rudolph Ackermann, son of a Stolberg coach-builder, first migrated to Paris as pupil to the carriage-designer Carossi and then, having acquired the necessary skills, to London where he was soon providing all the fashionable coach-makers with designs, including state coaches for the Lord Lieutenant of Ireland and the Lord Mayor of Dublin. He married an English wife and set up, first at 96 Strand and then in 1796 at 101 Strand, a drawing-school and print shop, with a sideline in fancy goods. These activities brought him into contact with Thomas Rowlandson who was then at the height of his powers. His delightful 'Vauxhall Gardens' exhibited at the Royal Academy in 1784 had been brilliantly aquatinted by Jukes in the following year and since then Rowlandson had been turning out many other tinted drawings of London scenes and types, besides the innumerable caricatures which created a furore at the London printsellers. Consequently Ackermann's first venture into book publishing was in 1799, with the patriotic and seasonally militaristic volume *The Loyal Volunteers of London and Environs* containing 87 aquatint plates, coloured and gilded by hand after drawings by Rowlandson of the gloriously accoutred members of infantry and cavalry corps.

Some eight years later, years which had been filled with a wide range of business activity, including the design of Lord Nelson's hearse in 1805, Ackermann thought of commissioning a set of aquatint plates of London's architecture and social life which would enable him to make use of Rowlandson's immense talents in peopling the scenes on a scale and in a style never yet seen in topographical book illustration. He evidently felt that Rowlandson would be wasted on the quantity of scrupulous architectural draughtsmanship which would be expected of such a work and was inspired with the idea of getting him to work in tandem with the French émigré Augustus Pugin, who had been trained in John Nash's office where he made a series of drawings of ancient buildings as models on which to base current developments, and who was at this time a candidate for the associateship of the Old Water-Colour Society. The text, which turned out more historical than aesthetic, was entrusted to another artist, William Henry Pyne, whose earlier series *Microcosm, or a Picturesque Delineation of the Arts* (1803–6) may have suggested the title for this new work. After the first two volumes Pyne relinquished the task to Ackermann's 'author extraordinary', William Combe.

In his introduction to the first volume the publisher anticipates that the whole work will comprise four volumes, each made up of six monthly Numbers of some text and four plates, or a total of some 200 pages with 24 plates and a frontispiece. In fact even this first volume is made up of eight Numbers (dated January to August 1808) and 232 pages of text.

223

Introducing the second volume, however, he says he now plans a total of three, not four, volumes, 'although the number of plates is the same and the letter-press, both in importance and quantity, more than was originally proposed'. A price rise is announced:

The proprietor ... was anxious to render this work to the public at as moderate a price as possible, and therefore proposed the subscriptions at only *seven shillings per number* but he had not then sufficiently calculated the expence of so considerable an undertaking ... He was at length obliged to raise the subscriptions to ten shillings and sixpence per Number to those who became subscribers after the publication of the first volume.

Ackermann nevertheless congratulates himself on 'the manner in which he performed his engagement to near one thousand of his old subscribers'. This second volume also consisted of eight Numbers published from September 1808 to April 1809, or 32 plates and 239 text pages. On its completion a prospectus was issued: 'Of this Magnificent Work, Sixteen Numbers, forming two Volumes have already appeared. Each Number contains Four Coloured Views ... with appropriate descriptions, occupying from twenty-four to thirty pages of letter-press, printed on large quarto elephant paper, and hot-pressed ... The Microcosm will be completed in 24 Numbers at 10s 6d each'.

A slip in No 17 announced that the work would be extended to 26 Numbers and ten Numbers, published from May 1809 to February 1810, made up the last volume with its 280 text pages and 40 plates. Finally the complete work was advertised as 'Three Volumes, large Elephant Quarto, Price Thirteen Guineas in Boards'.

The 1808 reference to 'near one thousand old subscribers' has sometimes been taken to mean that the edition was limited to that number but this seems unlikely since the work still had 15 months to run and in which to accumulate fresh subscriptions. Also Tooley estimates that plates were being reprinted as late as 1836. Indeed as late as May 1847 Nattali of Covent Garden was offering the three volumes, in the *Monthly Literary Advertiser*, at £3 15s ('published at £15.15s').

Microcosm of London. R. Ackermann's Repository of Arts, No. 101 Strand. Vol. I (II–III). (woodcut title on circular frame surmounted by the royal arms against an architectural setting of St Paul's Cathedral, Westminster Abbey and a window onto Thames shipping) T. Bensley, Printer, Bolt Court, Fleet Street, London.

Quarto, 340–60 × 275–90mm.   nd

COLLATION   Vol. 1. Half-title ('The Microcosm of London; or, London in Miniature'); woodcut title-page; engr dedication to the Prince of Wales ('Thos. Tomkins script Robt Ashby sculpt') with allegorical stipple headpiece ('E.F. Burney del. Tho. Williamson sculp') (1 leaf); pp i-iv, introduction; contents (1 leaf); pp 3–231, Microcosm. Vol. 2. Half-title; woodcut title-page; engr dedication with varied headpiece (1 leaf); pp iii-vi, introduction; contents (1 leaf); pp 1–239, Microcosm continued. Vol. 3. Half-title; woodcut title-page; engr dedication with varied headpiece (1 leaf); pp iii-iv, introduction; contents (1 leaf); pp 1–280, Microcosm continued; index, errata (6pp).

In his prefatory remarks on the illustrations the publisher takes a justifiable pride in his achievement:

The great objection that men fond of the fine arts have hitherto made to engravings on architectural subjects has been that the buildings and figures have almost invariably been designed by the same artists. In consequence of this, the figures have been generally neglected, or are of a very inferior cast, and totally unconnected with the other part of the print ... The architectural part of the subjects that are contained in this work, will be delineated, with the utmost precision and care, by Mr. Pugin, whose uncommon accuracy and elegant taste have been displayed in his former productions. With respect to the figures, they are from the pencil of Mr. Rowlandson, with whose professional talents the public are already so well acquainted, that it is not necessary to expatiate on them here.

In general, with the possible exception of Malton's *Picturesque Tour* (no 72), the staffage of topographical book illustrations, when there was any, was much inferior to the rest of the composition and Ackermann was certainly setting a new standard by engaging two specialist artists and getting them to work harmoniously together. He was also extremely lucky in that Rowlandson, who was the senior and much the more famous of the two, should have been so ready to fall in with Pugin's ideas and to accept without demur his architectural settings. An interesting account of their co-operation, adapted from Desmond Coke's in *Confessions of an incurable collector* (1926), is given by Carl Zigrosser in the *Print Collector's Quarterly* (XXXIV 2, April 1937, pp 145–72). Coke possessed Pugin's own copy of the *Microcosm* which contained, in addition to the published text:

24 pen and ink or water-colour sketches by Pugin or Rowlandson.

97 detailed perspective pencil sketches for the plates, by Rowlandson and Pugin.

104 black and white proofs before colouring, some before letters.

107 coloured impressions, some of which may have been used by colourists as models.

From these it is apparent that, when the two artists had agreed on the viewpoint for a subject, Pugin would make a careful architectural pencil sketch in perspective to the scale of the intended illustration. To this Rowlandson would add appropriate figures, not necessarily in his caricature vein; his sketches for pl. 6, 'Christie's Auction Room', and pl. 56, 'Mounting the Guard', may be seen in the British Museum. Sometimes Pugin would make two drawings from different angles for Rowlandson's consideration and some of the drawings that passed between them are annotated with polite suggestions for adjustments in the light source or in the stature or costume of one of the figures.

When both were satisfied a studio assistant, having made a pencil tracing of the perspective drawing, placed it face down on the copper which had been laid with an etching ground and transferred the image by running the two through the press. The lines were then traced with an etching needle, Rowlandson almost certainly doing his part of the drawing and Pugin probably his. When the plate had been bitten a proof was printed on drawing paper for Rowlandson to indicate with ink washes which portions were to be treated by one of Ackermann's team of four skilled aquatint engravers. After the plate had been lettered the artists would colour-wash the copy or copies to be used as models by the colourists. Some of these may have been promising art students like the youthful Turner and Girtin, who had once tinted engravings for Dayes and John Raphael Smith, but Ackermann must also have retained a permanent staff of professional colourists to judge by the high quality of the work on nearly all the plates of the *Microcosm*, which even on the most conservative estimate must have numbered well over 100,000, while simultaneously work was proceeding on numerous other plates for *The Repository of Arts* (from 1809) and *Costume of the Swedish Army* (1808).

The lion's share of the aquatinting fell to J. Bluck,

a draughtsman and Royal Academy exhibitor since 1791, who was responsible for 55 of the plates. Joseph Stadler, a German who had worked in England since 1780 and engraved 30 of Farington's drawings for Boydell's *Thames* (no 75), undertook 29, and the balance was divided equally between John Hill, who later migrated to North America, and Thomas Sutherland (repeatedly mis-engraved 'Sunderland'). The calligrapher Thomas Tomkins and line-engraver Robert Ashby, who had worked together on the elaborate title-pages to Malton's *Picturesque Tour*, were employed on the dedication for which E.F. Burney drew the three stippled headpieces.

Abbey (214) records a book published in Leipzig in 1812, *Die Haupstadt GrossBritanniens*, with copies of 20 *Microcosm* plates (3,7,15,21,38,45–6, 49,52,56,59,63,65,74,76,80,85,93–4,97) engraved by Hüllmann, C. Schule and Heinrich Muller.

The 96 plates in the first 24 Numbers of this well-organized collection were issued alphabetically by subject and are numbered and bound up in this sequence. The monthly batches of four plates are thus bound in strict chronological sequence also, with the exception of pl. 71, 86, 91 and 92 which have strayed from their companions. The 'extra' plates, 97–104, are dated January and February 1810, with the exception of the last plate, a laggard from the previous November. Reference should be made to Tooley for a thorough study of collectors' 'points' on watermarks and details establishing early states of plates.

The bl credit throughout is 'Rowlandson & Pugin delt. et sculpt.' with the appropriate aquatint engraver br. Publication-lines always read: 'London Pub. (date) at R. Ackermann's Repository of Arts 101 Strand.', except that pl. 1–3 have 'Pubd'.

VOL. 1

1 p 9 Drawing from Life at the Royal Academy,/ (Somerset House). Harraden Aquatin. (later state: 'Bluck Aquat.') Jany 1, 1808. 195 × 260/235 × 285mm.

2 p 10 Exhibition Room, Somerset House. Hill Aquatin. 1 Jany, 1808. 195 × 260/235 × 285mm.

3 p 16 Board Room of the Admiralty. Hill Aquatin. 1 Jany, 1808. 195 × 255/235 × 285mm.

4 p 23 Astley's Amphitheatre. Hill Aquat. Jany 1, 1808. 195 × 263/240 × 295mm. Near Westminster Bridge, on Surrey side.

5 p 25 Dining Hall, Asylum. Hill Aquat. Feb 1 1808. 198 × 260/242 × 300mm. Lambeth.

6 p 32 Christie's Auction Room. J. Bluck Aquat. Feb 1 1808. 198 × 263/243 × 298mm. A pen and watercolour Rowlandson sketch for this, (203 × 285mm) is in the BM.

7 p 40 The Great Hall,/Bank of England. Hill Aquat. Feb 1 1808. 195 × 260/233 × 275mm. (*Bank of England* 202)

8 p 52 Bartholomew Fair. J. Bluck Aquat. Feb 1 1808. 190 × 260/240 × 290mm. Night scene.

9 p 63 Billingsgate Market. J. Bluck Aquat. 1 March 1808. 200 × 260/234 × 280mm.

10 p 69 The Hall, Blue Coat School. Hill aquat. 1 March 1808. 200 × 260/235 × 285mm. Christ's Hospital.

11 p 82 Bow Street Office. Hill aquat. 1 March 1808. 200 × 258/235 × 275mm. Interior.

12 p 92 Pass-Room, Bridewell. Hill aquat. 1 March 1808. 200 × 260/235 × 280mm. Interior. Water-colour (190 × 280mm) is in the Paul Mellon Collection.

13 p 98 British Institution,/(Pall Mall). J. Bluck aquat. 1 April 1808. 195 × 258/230 × 275mm. Interior.

14 p 101 The Hall and Stair Case,/British Museum. J. Bluck aquat. 1st April 1808. 255 × 197/280 × 238mm.

15 p 107 The Hall Carlton House. J. Bluck Aquat. 1 April 1808. 195 × 258/235 × 285mm.

16 p 114 The Roman Catholic Chapel,/(Lincoln's Inn Fields). J. Bluck aquat. 1st April 1808. 200 × 258/238 × 285mm. Interior. Former Sardinian Embassy Chapel rebuilt after destruction in Gordon Riots, 1780.

17 p 119 Coal Exchange. Hill Aquat. 1 May 1808. 185 × 255/225 × 275mm. Interior. Established at 93 Lower Thames Street, 1807, replaced 1847.

18 p 123 Royal Cock Pit. Bluck Aquat. 1 May 1808. 195 × 262/238 × 280mm. Interior. Off Whitehall.

19 p 126 Water-Engine,/Cold-Bath-Fields Prison. J. Bluck Aquat. May 1 1808. 255 × 188/285 × 235mm. 'House of Correction', Clerkenwell, opened 1794. (*Bank of England* 228)

20 p 134 The College of Physicians. Bluck aquat. 1 May 1808. 198 × 258/235 × 285mm. In Warwick Lane, the Hall.

21 p 191 House of Commons. J. Bluck Aquat. 1st June 1808. 193 × 255/238 × 285mm. Interior.

22 p 193 Court of Chancery,/Lincoln's Inn Hall. J.C. Stadler Aquat. 1st June 1808. 195 × 260/230 × 275mm. Interior.

23 p 203 Court of Common Pleas,/Westminster Hall. J.C. Stadler Aquat. 1st June 1808. 195 × 258/233 × 278mm. Interior.

24 p 205 Court of Kings Bench,/Westminster Hall. J. Bluck Aquat. 195 × 258/230 × 278mm. Interior

25 p 207 Court of Exchequer,/Westminster Hall. J.C. Stadler Aquat. July 1 1808. 200 × 262/240 × 285mm. Interior.

26 p 209 Covent Garden Market/Westminster Election. Bluck Aquat. 1 July 1808. 198 × 260/230 × 278mm. Hustings outside St Paul's Church.

27 p 212 Covent Garden Theatre. J. Bluck Aquat. 1 July 1808. 198 × 260/230 × 278mm. Henry Holland's reconstruction, burned down September 1808.

28 p 217 Custom House,/from the River Thames. J. Bluck Aquat. 1 Augt 1808. 195 × 258/230 × 280mm. pl. misnumbered '29'.

29 p 218 The Long Room,/Custom House. J.C. Stadler aquat. 1 July 1808. 200 × 260/230 × 280mm. pl. misnumbered '28'.

30 p 223 Debating Society,/Piccadilly. J.C. Stadler sculpt. Augt 1 1808. 200 × 260/230 × 275. No 22 Piccadilly, the 'Athenian Lyceum', interior. pl. misnumbered '29'.

31 p 224 Doctors Commons. Stadler Aquat. 1 Augt 1808. 200 × 262/230 × 280mm. Interior. Knightrider Street.

32 p 228 Drury Lane Theatre. Bluck Aquat. 1 Augt. 1808. 200 × 260/230 × 280mm. Henry Holland's rebuilding, burned down February 1809.

VOL. 2

33 p 13 Corn Exchange,/Mark Lane. J. Bluck Aquat. 1st Sept. 1808. 198 × 260/230 × 280mm. Built by George Dance senior, 1747–50.

34 p 25 Exhibition of Water Coloured Drawings,/Old Bond Street. Stadler Aquat. 1st Septr. 1808. 200 × 260/235 × 280mm. At the Society of Painters in Water-Colour.

35 p 36 Fire in London. J. Bluck Aquat. 1st Septr. 1808. 200 × 260/230 × 280mm. At the Albion Mills, Blackfriars, 3 March 1791.

36 p 44 Fleet Prison. Stadler Aquat. 1st Septr. 1808. 195 × 255/230 × 280mm. The exercise yard.

37 p 61 Foundling Hospital,/The Chapel. J. Bluck Aquat. 1st Octr. 1808. 192 × 255/230 × 280mm. Interior.

38 p 79 Freemasons Hall,/Great Queen Street. Stadler Aquat. 1st Octr. 1808. 198 × 257/235 × 275mm.

39 p 94 Great Subscription Room at Brooks's,/St James's Street. Bluck Aquat. (later state: 'Stadler Aquat.') 1st Oct 1808. 195 × 260/230 × 280mm. Built by Henry Holland, 1776–8.

40 p 103 Guildhall. J. Bluck Aquat. 1st Octr. 1808. 198 × 260/235 × 280mm. Interior, with flat ceiling in panels.

41 p 116 Common Council Chamber, Guildhall. J. Bluck aquat. 1st Novr. 1808. 255 × 198/275 × 235mm. pl. misnumbered '42'.

42 p 124 Guildhall/Examination of a Bankrupt before his Creditors Court of King's Bench. J. Bluck aquat. 1st Novr. 1808. 200 × 255/230 × 280mm.

227

83 p 172 Tattersall's,/Horse Repository. Sunderland aquat. Septr. 1st 1809. 200 × 260/240 × 275mm. Near Hyde Park Corner.

84 p 174 Temple Church. Bluck aqua. Septr. 1st 1809. 250 × 200/280 × 235mm. Interior, the 'Round'.

85 p 185 View of the Tower. Sunderland aquat. Octr. 1st 1809. 190 × 260/235 × 275mm. Numbered 'Plate 85 Second'.

86 p 188 Horse Armoury,/Tower. Sunderland aquat. Novr. 1st 1809. 200 × 260/240 × 280mm. pl. misnumbered '101'.

87 p 197 Board of Trade. Sunderland aquat. Octr. 1st 1809. 198 × 255/240 × 270mm. Treasury Building, Whitehall. Interior. pl. misnumbered '86'.

88 p 201 Trinity House. Sutherland aquat. Octr. 1st 1809. 200 × 262/240 × 270mm. Interior, Court Room. pl. misnumbered '87'.

89 p 204 Vauxhall Garden. J. Bluck aquat. Octr. 1st 1809 (tm). 255 × 200/280 × 235mm. The orchestra stand. pl. misnumbered '88'.

90 p 208 St. Stephen's,/Walbrook. Bluck aquat. Novr. 1st 1809. 190 × 255/230 × 272mm. Interior.

91 p 217 Watch House,/St Mary le Bone. J. Bluck aquat. Sept. 1st 1809. 195 × 260/250 × 275mm.

92 p 218 West India Docks. Bluck aquat. Jany 1 1810. 198 × 258/240 × 275mm.

93 p 229 Westminster Abbey. Bluck aquat. Decr. 1st 1809. 260 × 195/280 × 235mm. Interior, N. transept.

94 p 235 Westminster Hall. J. Bluck aquat. Decr. 1st 1809. 260 × 195/280 × 240mm. Interior.

95 p 239 Whitehall. J. Bluck aquat. Decr. 1st 1809. 188 × 250/245 × 270mm. Interior of Banqueting Hall, adapted as a chapel.

96 p 242 Workhouse,/St James's Parish. Sunderland aquat. Decr. 1st 1809. 192 × 258/240 × 270mm. Poland Street. Interior.

97 p 246 Greenwich Hospital,/The Painted Hall. Bluck aquat. Jan 1 1810. 200 × 260/240 × 280mm. Interior.

98 p 252 Chelsea Hospital. J. Bluck aquat. Jany 1st 1810. 198 × 258/235 × 278mm. Interior, dining hall. (*Longford* 94)

99 p 256 Military College, Chelsea. Sunderland aquat. Jany 1 1810. 200 × 258/240 × 280mm. Interior, Royal Military Asylum. (*Longford* 400)

100 p 263 New Covent Garden Theatre. Bluck aquat. Jan 1 1810. 198 × 255/240 × 280mm. Interior of Robert Smirke's building of 1809–10, replacing Holland's burnt-out theatre shown on pl. 27.

101 p 267 South Sea House,/Dividend Hall. Sutherland aquat. Feb 1 1810 (tm). 200 × 263/225 × 280mm. Threadneedle Street. Interior. pl. misnumbered '102'.

102 p 269 Excise Office, Broad Street. Sutherland aquat. Feb 1 1810 (tm). 198 × 260/240 × 285mm. Interior. pl. misnumbered '103'.

103 p 278 View of Westminster Hall and Bridge. J. Bluck aquat. Feb 1 1810. 202 × 262/235 × 280mm. pl. misnumbered '104'.

104 p 279 A View of London from the Thames,/taken opposite the Adelphi. J. Bluck aquat. Novr. 1st 1809. 190 × 262/230 × 275mm. pl. misnumbered '89'.

---

100 · MALCOLM'S ANECDOTES OF THE MANNERS AND CUSTOMS OF LONDON [1808]

On the death of James Peller Malcolm in April 1815 an appeal on behalf of his widow and his mother was printed for his publishers, Longmans & Co and Nichols, Son & Bentley. A long illness had reduced him to a state verging on destitution after a lifetime of insufficiently profitable antiquarian writing, drawing and the making of etchings which included contributions to the *Gentleman's Magazine* from 1792 to 1814. Born in Philadelphia, his artistic leanings at school persuaded his mother to raise the money necessary to send him to England as a student at the Royal Academy of which a fellow countryman, Benjamin West, was then a prominent member. His talents, however, proved too mediocre for a painting career and he had to try to make a living by other means. He produced antiquarian and topographical illustrations for works of local history and himself wrote books on history and antiquities with London as his chief theme and, as a result, was elected a Fellow of the Society of Antiquaries. The *Anecdotes*, published in April 1808 at £2 2s in boards, is a discursive social history dealing at large with topics such as theatrical performances, pleasure gardens, sports, places of worship and period costume; it relies to a great extent on newspaper reports and magazine articles and is altogether a much less serious piece of historical writing than his first work, *Londinium Redivivum* (no 83). A second edition in two volumes octavo was published in 1810; its text follows that of the first, omitting only a section on churches and their contents and a summary retrospective to Roman times.

Anecdotes of the Manners and Customs of London during the eighteenth century; including the charities, depravities, dresses and amusements of the citizens of London, during the period with A Review of the State of Society in 1807, to which is added, A sketch of the domestic and ecclesiastical architecture, and of the various improvements in the Metropolis. Illustrated by Fifty Engravings by James Peller Malcolm, F.S.A.... London: Printed for Longman, Hurst, Rees, and Orme, Paternoster Row. 1808.

Quarto, 260 × 203mm.   1808

COLLATION Title-page; pp iii–iv, contents, list of plates; pp 1–2, introduction; pp 3–490, Anecdotes; pp 1–8, index.

Anecdotes of the Manners and Customs of London during the eighteenth century; including the charities, depravities, dresses, and amusements, of the citizens of London, during that period; with A Review of the State of Society in 1807. To which is added, a sketch of the domestic architecture, and of the various improvements in the Metropolis. Illustrated by forty-five engravings. By James Peller Malcolm, F.S.A.... The Second Edition. Volume I (II). London: Printed for Longman, Hurst, Rees, and Orme, Paternoster Row. 1810.

Octavo, 210 × 130mm.   1810

COLLATION Vol. 1. Title-page; pp iii–iv, contents, list of plates; pp v–xxix, preface dated May 1809; half-title; pp 1–432, Anecdotes. Vol. 2. Title-page; pp iii–iv, contents, list of plates; pp 1–423, Anecdotes continued; pp 425–43, index.

With the exception of the costume plates it is vain to seek in the text an explanation of the illustrations bound up with it. They illustrate not the *Anecdotes* but some London buildings at the turn of the century. As topographical plates, however, they do have value for although they are not brilliantly executed they depict several London subjects not often shown and some buildings, like the two sides of Fitzroy Square, in pristine condition as erected. Most are picturesquely vignetted and Malcolm stresses the 'rus in urbe' aspects of the London scene, as in the view of Westminster Abbey seen across a vast stretch of water framed in leafy branches with a cow contentedly occupying the foreground (pl. 47). Plates are listed in the order of

the British Library quarto (577.h.8) since the check-list only allocates a handful to specific page numbers. They are reused, with the exception of five of church furnishings, in the octavo edition and the octavo pages opposite which they occur are noted at the end of each entry. Most of the plates in both editions are inserted in batches rather in the fashion of twentieth century books, but without the consequent irritation of having to refer to them from the text since neither (apart from the costume plates) has any bearing on the other. Malcolm was much pained by a reviewer who insinuated that he had relied on his memory for the costumes without reference to contemporary prints; in his preface to the octavo edition he lists his visual sources, mainly Hogarth engravings. Each plate, unless otherwise stated, has engraved in the work the credit 'Malcolm del. et sc.' and his name also appears in the publication-lines.

1 p 12 The Foundling Hospital. Publish'd Jan 1, 1808 by J.P. Malcolm. 90 × 165/111 × 177mm. Vignette. Farmyard in foreground. (vol. 1, p 15)

2 p 29 The centre of Bancrofts Almshouses, Publish'd Nov 1, 1807 by J.P. Malcolm. 90 × 130/105 × 140mm. Vignette. (vol. 1, p 47)

3 p 29 The Small Pox Hospital. Publish'd Nov 1, 1807 by J.P. Malcolm. 90 × 125/110 × 140mm. Vignette. A general hospital at Hyde Park Corner, the predecessor of St George's. (vol. 1, p 48)

Twelve costume etchings tinted with water-colour washes between pp 425–6 in quarto ed and vol. 2, pp 312–13 in octavo ed

4 Dress 1690–1715. Publish'd Jany 1, 1808 by J.P. Malcolm. 138 × 105mm pl. mark.

5 Dress 1721. Publish'd by J.P. Malcolm. 138 × 105mm pl. mark.

6 Dress 1735: Servant—Common Life. Publish'd Jan 1808 by J.P. Malcolm. 138 × 105mm pl. mark.

7 Dress 1738. Publish'd July 1, 1807 by J.P. Malcolm. 138 × 105mm pl. mark.

8 Dress 1745. Publish'd July 1, 1807 by J.P. Malcolm. 105 × 138mm pl. mark.

9 Dress 1752. Publish'd July 1, 1807 by J.P. Malcolm. 138 × 105mm pl. mark.

10 Dress 1766. Publish'd Nov 1, 1807 by J.P. Malcolm. 138 × 105mm pl. mark.

11 Dress circa 1770, 1773. Publish'd Jan 1, 1808 by J.P. Malcolm. 138 × 105mm pl. mark.

12 Dress 1779. Publish'd Nov 1 1808 by J.P. Malcolm. 138 × 105mm pl. mark.

13 Dress circa 1785. Publish'd June 1, 1807 by J.P. Malcolm. 138 × 105mm pl. mark..

14 Dress 1797. Publish'd Nov 1, 1808 by J.P. Malcolm. 138 × 105mm pl. mark.

15 Dress 1807. Publish'd Nov 1, 1807 by J.P. Malcolm. 138 × 105mm pl. mark.

16 p 453 The Palace of Croydon. 85 × 148/98 × 160mm. No credit or publication-line. (vol. 2, p 364)

17 p 453 Brick Gate near Bromley. 85 × 140/98 × 150mm. No credit or publication-line. (vol. 2, p 364)

18 p 454 Part of the Priory of the Holy Trinity Aldgate. Publish'd Nov 1, 1807 by J.P. Malcolm. 120 × 95/140 × 105mm. (vol. 2, p 366)

19 p 454 The South West Corner of Smithfield. Publish'd Nov 1, 1807 by J.P. Malcolm. 120 × 95/140 × 108mm. Vignette. Tower of St Sepulchre prominent. (vol. 2, p 366)

20 p 454 Chancery Lane. Publish'd Jan 1, 1808 by J.P. Malcolm. 103 × 165/115 × 175mm. (vol. 2, p 366)

21 p 454 The S.E. corner of Guildhall. 125 × 92/138 × 100mm. Credit 'Malcolm'. No publication-line. (vol. 2, p 366)

22 p 454 In Goswell Street/Antient inconvenience, contrasted with modern convenience – Erected in or before the reign of Queen Eliz. – Erected about 1800. 95 × 130/105 × 138mm. No publication-line. (vol. 2, p 366)

23 p 454 The Minced Pie house. 90 × 142/105 × 160mm. No credit or publication-line. On Maze Hill, Greenwich, designed by Sir John Vanbrugh; demolished 1911. (vol. 2, p 404)

24 p 454 Meux's Brewhouse built about 1796. Publish'd Jan 1, 1808 by J.P. Malcolm. 90 × 165/110 × 178mm. Vignette. 'There is a cask now building at Messrs Meux and Company's brewery, Liquorpond Street, Gray's Inn Lane, the size of which exceeds all credibility being designed to hold 20,000 barrels of porter' (*Times,* April 1795). (vol. 2, p 404)

25 p 454 The South Side of Fitzroy Square. Publish'd Novr 1, 1807 by J.P. Malcolm. 95 × 130/110 × 140mm. Built by Robert Adam, 1790–1800. (vol. 2, p 404)

26 p 454 The late Lord Barrymore's house Piccadilly. Publish'd Dec 1, 1807 by J.P. Malcolm. 80 × 120/110 × 140mm. No 105, built by Michael Novosielski. (vol. 2, p 404)

27 p 454 The West end of Upper Brook Street. Publish'd Nov 1, 1807 by J.P. Malcolm. 90 × 130/105 × 140mm. View through Hyde Park railings. (vol. 2, p 404)

28 p 454 Devonshire House. Publish'd Jan 1808 by J.P. Malcolm. 90 × 125/105 × 140mm. From Green Park. Built by William Kent for the 3rd Duke, 1734–5; demolished 1924–5. (vol. 2, p 404)

29 p 454 The west side of Cavendish Square. Publish'd Jan 1808 by J.P. Malcolm. 90 × 132/110 × 142mm.

Behind the screen wall is Harcourt House, built by Thomas Archer for Lord Bingley, 1722; demolished 1906. (vol. 2, p 404)

30 p 454 The Duke of Manchester's. Publish'd Nov 1, 1807 by J.P. Malcolm. 90 × 125/115 × 140mm. Vignette. Hertford House, Manchester Square, as built 1776. (vol. 2, p 404)

31 p 454 The East Side of Fitzroy Square. Publish'd Nov 1, 1807 by J.P. Malcolm. 95 × 130/110 × 140mm. Vignette. Built by Robert Adam, 1790–1800. (vol. 2, p 404)

32 p 454 In Hanover Square. 85 × 125/105 × 140mm. Vignette. No credit or publication-line. No 12, Lord Harewood's house. (vol. 2, p 404)

33 p 454 Entrance to Hyde Park from Park Lane. Publish'd July 1, 1807 by J.P. Malcolm. 90 × 125/105 × 140mm. Vignette. (vol. 2, p 404)

34 p 454 Langley House. 88 × 144/105 × 148mm. No credit or publication-line. Langley Park, Beckenham, Kent, showing the addition by Joseph Bonomi, 1790. (vol. 2, p 404)

35 p 454 Mansion at Twickenham. 90 × 145/110 × 155mm. Credit 'Malcolm scu.' No publication-line. (vol. 2, p 404)

36 p 471 Westminster Abbey. Published Jan 1808 by J.P. Malcolm. 90 × 130/105 × 140mm. From S. with St John, Smith Square. Pencil drawing (105 × 120mm) in Westminster Public Library. (vol. 2, p 404)

37 p 471 Westminster Abbey. Publish'd Jan 1, 1808. 100 × 130/105 × 140mm. E. end, from the river. (vol. 2, p 404)

38 p 471 The Altar of Westminster Abbey. Publish'd Novr 1, 1808 by J.P. Malcolm. 178 × 140mm pl. mark.

39 p 471 The Altar of St Andrew Undershaft. Publish'd Jan 1, 1808 by J.P. Malcolm. 140 × 108mm pl. mark.

40 p 471 The Altar of St Mary Aldermanbury/the last supper by Old Franks. Publish'd July 1, 1807 by J.P. Malcolm. 178 × 140mm pl. mark.

41 p 471 The Altar of St Margaret Westminster. Publish'd Nov 1807 by J.P. Malcolm. 127 × 165/140 × 178mm.

42 p 471 Section of the Pulpit at St Margaret's Westr. 140 × 178mm pl. mark.

43 p 478 West end of Upper Grosvenor Street. Publish'd Jan 1, 1808 by J.P. Malcolm. 95 × 130/105 × 143mm. Vignette. Rural foreground with musket shooting practice; vista terminated by St George, Hanover Square. (vol. 2, p 404)

44 p 478 The old Magazine Hyde Park. Publish'd Nov 1, 1807 by J.P. Malcolm. 85 × 130/110 × 140mm. Vignette. (vol. 2, p 366)

45 p 478 Part of Westminster Bridge. Publish'd Jan 1, 1808. 95 × 125/105 × 140mm. From Lambeth. (vol. 2, p 404)

46 p 478 Westminster from Millbank. Publish'd Nov 1,

1807 by J.P. Malcolm. 85 × 130/105 × 140mm. Vignette. St Paul's Cathedral in distance. (vol. 2, p 404)

47 p 478 View in Hyde Park. Publish'd Jan 1, 1808 by J.P. Malcolm. 100 × 165/105 × 180mm. Vignette. Looking across the canal in St James's Park towards the W. towers of the Abbey. (vol. 2, p 366)

48 p 478 The entrance of great/Portland street. Publish'd Jan 1, 1808 by J.P. Malcolm. 50 × 145/95 × 165mm. Vignette. (vol. 2, p 366)

49 p 478 View in Park Lane. Publish'd Jan 1, 1808 by J.P. Malcolm. 90 × 125/110 × 140mm. Vignette. (vol. 2, p 404)

50 p 478 View in Privy garden. Publish'd Nov 1 1807 by J.P. Malcolm. 90 × 125/105 × 138mm. Vignette. With Sir John Vanbrugh's 'Goose Pie House' on l., looking through the gateway of Fife House towards a distant view of St Paul's Cathedral. The porter's lodge and the part of the stables flanking the gateway were demolished in 1809. An unusual Whitehall view. (vol. 2, p 366)

101 · VIEWS OF THE PRINCIPAL BUILDINGS IN LONDON [c 1808]

Richard Marshall and Cluer Dicey were mapsellers and partners in a business in Aldermary Church Yard. In 1765 they published a large and extensive map of London which was redated and reissued several time and, from 1782, with the imprint of John Marshall & Co of 4 Aldermary Church Yard. John Marshall sold maps, small books and prints and in 1800 published a set of 15 miniature etched views of London mounted on thin cardboard the size of a playing-card. The anonymous engraver was a quite confident draughtsman but the coarseness of the line and the simplicity of the colour-washing are reminiscent of wood-engravings for chap-books. In 1808 Marshall moved to 140 Fleet Street, where he specialized in the sale of books for children, and from there reissued the set of view-cards together with two paperbound, nicely printed little volumes in which they are described: a child's miniature replica of papa's books and prints. The title-pages are undated but the imprints give both the new and old addresses which suggests that they were printed

soon after the removal. The 15 views are also found on a single broadsheet, without text.

Views of the principal buildings in London: with an account of the curiosities they contain. Volume I (II) London: Printed and sold by John Marshall, 140, Fleet Street, from Aldermary Church-Yard.

Duodecimo, 115 × 90mm. (1808)

COLLATION   Vol. 1. Title-page; pp 1–60, Views. Vol. 2. Title-page; pp 1–47, Views continued; 15 plates.

The cards measure about 92 × 124mm, the engraved surface about 40 × 90mm within a plate-mark (when visible) of about 90 × 120mm. Publication-line throughout is 'Pub. Sep.27 1800 by I. Marshall No 4 Aldermary Chh Yd, London.'

1 The Tower of London. (From the river)
2 Westminster Bridge. (From the Surrey side)
3 Westminster Abbey. (From the W.)
4 The Royal Exchange. (From the S.)
5 St Paul's Church. (Cathedral from N.W.)
6 Guildhall.
7 The India House.
8 The Mansion House.
9 The Custom House. (From the river)
10 The Admiralty.
11 The British Museum. (Montague House)
12 St James's Palace.
13 The Bank of England.
14 Chelsea Hospital. (From the river)
15 Greenwich Hospital. (From the river)

102 · MRS WAKEFIELD'S PERAMBULATIONS [1809]

Mrs Priscilla Wakefield, the Quaker wife of a City merchant who lived at Tottenham, was both author and philanthropist for she was one of the first people to encourage the establishment of savings banks for the poor and also wrote books, including several for the instruction and edification of children. Her aim was to impart information painlessly in the form of dialogue, catechism or exchange of letters. In this particular book the medicine of historical and topographical fact is administered with a thinly spread fictional jam, of letters exchanged between a Swiss residing in London, his nephews Philip and Eugenius, over on a visit, and the children of the Middleton family who are country dwellers. In fact the first ten letters are an attempt to disguise an indigestible narrative history of England; only from the eleventh onwards do the correspondents regale each other with descriptions of London sights.

The book was announced as being published 'With Eight Engraved Views of the Principal public Buildings & a Plan of London. Price 6s. 6d. Boards'. Although its publishers, Harvey & Darton, were famous for their juvenile literature they were much more sparing of illustrations than the rival firm of John Harris whose *A Visit to Uncle William in Town* (no 145) was published soon after the second edition of Mrs Wakefield's book. It must immediately have had a warmer reception in the schoolroom since it more or less reversed the proportion of picture to instruction.

Perambulations in London and its Environs comprehending an Historical Sketch of the Ancient State and Progress of the British Metropolis; a concise Description of its Present State, Notices of Eminent Persons, and a short account of the Surrounding Villages. In Letters. Designed for Young Persons. By Priscilla Wakefield. London: Printed and Sold by Darton and Harvey, No 55 Gracechurch-Street. 1809.

Duodecimo, 170 × 100mm.   1809

COLLATION   Title-page; pp iii–iv, introduction; pp 1–510, Perambulations; index (17pp).

—Second Edition, improved. London: Printed for Darton, Harvey and Darton, No 55 Gracechurch-Street. 1814.

Duodecimo, 170 × 100mm.   1814

COLLATION   Title-page; pp iii–iv, introduction; pp 1–510, Perambulations; index (17pp).

Both editions are illustrated with four plates, each having on it two small views engraved on copper, and the second edition substitutes a frontispiece for the map in the first. There are no credits or publication-lines but the plates are numbered and the page of the text they are to face is marked on them. The first edition has also a reference from the second of each pair of views to the appropriate page of text. Owing to the revision of the second edition

text the page numbers on two of the plates were amended. Plate-marks were cropped by the binder.

0 front. (tm) London, Westminster, Southwark, and the New Docks Eastward, 1809. Engraved for P. Wakefield's Perambulations. Published ... October 21st 1809 by Wm Darton & Jos. Harvey, Gracechurch Street, London. 160 × 380/170 × 390mm. (*Darlington and Howgego* 247)

1 p 124 Guildhall – Mansion House, vide page 127. Each 56 × 76mm. 2nd ed. p 122.

2 p 133 Royal Exchange – St Pauls Cathedral, vide page 169. Each 58 × 76mm. 2nd ed also p 133. Shows courtyard of Royal Exchange and N.W. view of St Paul's.

3 p 198 The Monument – The Tower of London, vide page 211. Each 58 × 78mm. Not used in 2nd ed.

4 p 277 Westminster Abbey – The House of Lords. 58 × 77, 57 × 75mm. 2nd ed p 280. W. front of the Abbey.

2nd ed only

00 front. A View of the Monument/from Gracechurch Street, vide p. 197. 130 × 75mm.

5 p 139 India House – Tower of London. Each 58 × 76mm.

103 · BARJAUD AND LANDON'S DESCRIPTION DE LONDRES [1810]

C.P. Landon, artist, man of letters and publisher, was also the translator of Stuart and Revett's *Antiquities of Athens* (1762) and author of a two-volume description of Paris to which this work forms a sequel. Jean-Baptiste Barjaud, born in 1785, was called to the Parisian bar, distinguished himself in the French army at the Battle of Bautzen, was decorated by Napoleon, published epic poems on Charlemagne and Homer, somewhat incongruously (unless he saw it as a work of military intelligence) collaborated in the present book, and was mortally wounded in 1813 at the Battle of Leipzig.

Description de Londres et de ses édifices, avec un précis historique et des observations sur le caractère de leur architecture, et sur les principaux objets d'art et de curiosité qu'ils renferment: Par J-B Barjaud, et C.P. Landon, Peintre, ancien Pensionnaire de l'Académie de

France à Rome, Correspondant de l'Institut royal de Hollande; Ouvrage faisant suite à la Description de Paris et de ses édifices, orné de 42 planches de vues pittoresques, gravées et ombrées en taille douce avec un Plan de Londres, et les Portraits des Artistes les plus célèbres qui ont contribué à l'embellissement de cette ville. A Paris, Chez C.P. Landon, peintre, éditeur-propriétaire, Rue de l'Université, No 19. 1810.

Octavo, 210 × 130mm.   1810

COLLATION Half-title; title-page; pp v–viii, Avis de l'Editeur; pp 1–235, Description de Londres; pp 237–9, contents; pp 1–4, Indication des chiffres et des lettres du plan de Londres.

The illustrations consist of a map, eight unnumbered portraits of London notables (borrowed from a History of England with which Landon was concerned) and 42 small, numbered London views bearing the credit 'Baugean'. Jean-Jérôme Baugean was a painter-engraver, a native of Marseilles, who on establishing himelf in Paris was nominated a 'graveur du Roi' and, like Barjaud, became involved in the Napoleonic drama since his most celebrated picture was of Napoleon boarding the Bellérophon. There is, however, nothing heroic about his contribution to this book since all the views, save pl. 29 and 40, are copied slavishly from two English sources: the ten year old *Select Views in London and Westminster* (no 76) published by Colnaghi, abbreviated *SVL*, and the 50 year old Dodsley *London and its Environs Described* (no 41), abbreviated *LED*. The publisher's note makes a virtue of plagiarism and, in the same breath, condemns English architecture for its impurity:

Les monuments de Londres n'étant pas, en général, remarquables par la regularité et la sévérité du style, par la noblesse et la pureté de l'architecture, il nous a paru plus convenable d'en presenter des vues perspectives, que des plans et des élévations géométrales.... Nous avons taché de n'en presenter aucun qui ne rendit parfaitement l'effet et le caractère particulier de chaque édifice, en un mot, nous avons voulu qu'ils misent sous les yeux des lecteurs, l'édifice même avec tous les accessoires qui peuvent l'accompagner. Les objets qui environnent un monument le font souvent sortir d'avantage.

The plates have been cropped, removing platemarks of views, to fit the small octavo format. Page numbers are engraved tl and plate numbers tr. There are no publication-lines.

0 front. Plan/de Londres/Westminster/et Southwark. (tr) Gravé par Moisy, Place St Michel No 129. 170 × 273/200 × 300mm. Hyde Park, W. to Stepney, E. –

Pentonville, N. to Kennington, S. (*Darlington and Howgego* 251)

(p 20 Middleton. 92 × 60/180 × 115mm. 'Hist. d'Angleterre'.)

1 p 45 Eglise de St; Paul/St Paul's Cathedral. 80 × 140mm. Adds staffage to *LED* 5,139.

(p 57 Wren. Kneller pinxt. Landon descrt. 90 × 52/155 × 100mm. 'Hist. D'Angleterre'.)

2 p 59 Eglise de Bloomsbury/Bloomsbury Church See St George's Bloomsbury. 140 × 80/145 × 82mm. Modifies staffage of *LED* 3,5.

3 p 61 Eglise de Ste Marie des arcs/St Mary le Bow. 145 × 82mm. Adds staffage to *LED* 4,288.

4 p 63 Eglise de St Martin./St Martin's Church and part of the mews King's. 138 × 82mm. Modernizes staffage on *LED* 4,323.

5 p 65 Eglise de St Dunstan à l'est/St Dunstan's Church in the east. 140 × 80mm. *LED* 2,253.

6 p 69 Abbaye de Westminster/Abbey Church of St Peter's Westminster. 85 × 140mm. Adds staffage and alters sky of *LED* 1,1.

7 p 75 Chapelle de Henri VII/Henri the seventh's Chapel. 87 × 140mm. Adds staffage to *LED* 1,113.

8 p 91 Eglise & Hôpital de Christ./Christ's Church and Hospital. 85 × 140mm. Alters staffage on *LED* 2,135.

9 p 93 Hôpital St. Thomas./St Thomas's Hospital. 80 × 140mm. Alters staffage on *LED* 6,129.

10 p 97 Hôpital de St Barthélemi./Bartholomews Hospital. 82 × 140mm. Alters staffage on *LED* 1,260.

11 p 101 Salle de Westminster/Westminster Hall. 87 × 142mm. *LED* 6,296.

12 p 103 L'Amirauté/Admiralty Office. 85 × 137mm. Staffage modified and reduced from *SVL* 10.

13 p 105 La Douane./Custom House. 85 × 135mm. Staffage modified and reduced from *SVL* 13.

14 p 107 Hôtel de la compagnie des Indes/The East India house. 83 × 140mm. With simplified staffage reduced from *SVL* 11.

15 p 109 La Bourse./Royal Exchange. 82 × 140mm. Modernizes staffage on *LED* 5,280.

(p 111 Gresham. 93 × 63mm. 'Hist. D'Angleterre'.)

16 p 113 La Trésorerie/Treasury. 85 × 140mm. Modifies staffage on *LED* 6,196.

17 p 115 Hôtel des Gardes à cheval/Horse Guards. 85 × 137mm. Simplifies staffage and reduces *SVL* 1.

18 p 117 Barrière du Temple/Temple Bar. 87 × 140mm. Reduction, with simplified staffage, of *SVL* 12.

19 p 119 Hôtel de Ville/Guildhall. 80 × 142mm. *LED* 3,100.

20 p 121 Hôtel du Lord Maire/Mansion house. 82 × 140mm. *LED* 4,244.

21 p 123 Prison de Newgate/Newgate. 85 × 135mm. Simplifies staffage on *SVL* 14.

22 p 127 Le Monument./Monument. 140 × 80mm. Modernizes staffage on *LED* 5,1.

23 p 131 La Tour/The Tower. 82 × 140mm. Changes staffage on *LED* 6,148.

24 p 141 Palais Lambeth/Lambeth Palace. 87 × 140mm. Modifies staffage on *LED* 3,291.

25 p 143 Palais de St James/St James's Palace. 80 × 142mm. Modifies staffage and extends sky, narrowed on the half-plate. *LED* 3,215.

26 p 145 Palais de Whitehall/Whitehall Palace. 83 × 140mm. *SVL* 9.

(p 146 Inigo Jones. A.Van dyck pinxt. Landon dirext. 95 × 60/165 × 95mm. 'Hist. D'Angleterre'.)

27 p 149 Salle du Banquet/Banqueting House. 80 × 145mm. Adds staffage to *LED* 1,244.

(p 150 Gibbons. 93 × 57mm. 'Hist. D'Angleterre'.)

28 p 151 Hôtel d'Yorck/Yorck House. 83 × 137mm. Staffage simplified and reduced from *SVL* 3.

29 p 153 Hôtel de Northumberland/Northumberland house. 84 × 140mm.

30 p 155 Hôtel de Sommerset/Sommerset house. 85 × 140mm. Staffage and sky modified from *LED* 6,43.

(p 156 Reynolds. Reynolds pinxt. Landon dirext. 90 × 55/160 × 100mm. 'Hist. D'Angleterre'.)

31 p 159 Place de l'ancien Palais./Old Palace Yard. 85 × 140mm. Staffage simplified from *SVL* 5.

32 p 173 Hôpital de Greenwich/Greenwich Hospital. 85 × 138mm. Alters river craft on *LED* 3,69.

(p 172 Thornhill. 92 × 60mm. 'Hist. D'Angleterre'.)

33 p 179 Hôpital de Chelsea/Chelsea Hospital. 77 × 140mm. Modifies staffage and extends sky, narrowed on half-plate. *LED* 2,105. (*Longford* 17)

34 p 181 Hamptoncourt. 77 × 140mm. *LED* 3,162.

35 p 185 Esher Place. 85 × 140mm. *LED* 2,277.

36 p 187 Claremont. 85 × 140mm. Esher. Alters staffage on *LED* 2,139.

37 p 189 Toots Cray Place. 75 × 140mm. ie Foots-Cray. Plate reversed and staffage altered from *LED* 2,312.

38 p 191 Vanstead. 75 × 140mm. Campbell's Wanstead House. Staffage altered from *LED* 6,247.

39 p 193 Chiswick. 83 × 138mm. Staffage altered from *LED* 2,114.

40 p 197 Maison de campagne de Garrick/David Garrick Seat. 82 × 140mm. At Hampton.

41 p 201 Collège d'Eaton/Eaton College. 77 × 140mm. Staffage altered from *LED* 2,280.

42 p 203 Château de Windsor/Windsor Castle. 80 × 140mm. Staffage altered from *LED* 6,326.

(p 205 Wickham. Houbraken delt. Landon dirext. 95 × 55/170 × 115mm. 'Hist. d'Angleterre'.)

104 · BEAUTIES OF ENGLAND AND WALES* [1810–16]

Beauties of England and Wales. On Wednesday, the 1st of April, 1801, will be published, illustrated with three engravings, Price 2s 6d. or 4s. on Royal Paper, Number 1 of a new work, entitled *The Beauties of England and Wales: or delineations, topographical, historical and descriptive*. Containing a concise, yet satisfactory account of the Cities, Towns, Cathedrals, Castles, Antiquities, Public Edifices and Private Buildings in those parts of the Island of Great Britain.... London: Printed by T. Maiden, Sherbourne Lane. For Vernor & Hood, 31 Poultry; Longmans and Rees, Paternoster Row: J. Cuthell, Holborn: and J. and A. Arch, Gracechurch-Street ... a List of the principal Publications upon the respective Counties will be subjoined to the Conclusion of each Volume.... The Drawings and Engravings will be executed by the most eminent Artists....

Conditions: This Work will be published in Monthly Numbers, Price 2s 6d each. Every Number to contain Five Sheets in Octavo or Eighty Pages of Letter Press printed on a fine wove Demy paper, with an entire new Type ... Every Number will contain Three Engravings, neatly and correctly executed from original Drawings.... Every Six Numbers will form a handsome Volume, which shall be accompanied with a copious Index, and an elegantly engraved Title-Page with an appropriate Vignette. It is presumed the Work will be completed in about Six Volumes.... A few copies, price 4s. each Number, will be printed on a superfine wire-wove Royal Paper, and ornamented with the first Impressions of the Plates worked in the Manner of Proofs.

The prospectus made a serious underestimate in promising only six volumes. This compendium which eventually grew to 25 volumes was the brain-child of two friends, Edward Brayley, an apprentice enameller, and John Britton who was working for a Clerkenwell tavern keeper. The publishers Vernor & Hood had commissioned from Britton the *Beauties of Wiltshire* and, having written it with Brayley's help, he persuaded Hood to take a principal share in a further project which was to embrace no less than the whole of England and Wales. In June 1800 the two friends started tramping the shires, sometimes covering as much as 50 miles a day, and the first Number, a description of Bedfordshire, was published in April 1801 with Berkshire and Buckinghamshire following hard on its heels. The partnership became a regular topographical factory. In 1804 after the first five volumes were completed the authors claimed to have travelled 'over an extent of upwards of 3,500 miles'. Britton attended to bibliographical matters and correspondence and assembled source books and, although their joint names appeared on the title-pages of the first six volumes, the writing was left largely to Brayley. He was under extreme pressure to deliver the substantial monthly instalments promised and sometimes fell into arrears even though, according to Britton, he often wrote for 14 to 16 hours at a stretch with a wet handkerchief tied round his throbbing head.

The *Monthly Literary Advertiser* for December 1808 published the following announcement:

Beauties of England. Vol. 10, No. 1. 2s 6d. royal Paper, 4s. Containing Plates of St Stephen's Walbrook and the Queen's Palace, Buckingham House, Number 1 to be continued Monthly, and completed in one large Volume of London and Middlesex, or a Topographical Account of the Capital and County; being the Tenth volume of the Beauties of England and Wales. By Edward Wedlake Brayley. Printed for Vernor, Hood & Sharpe ...

It also gave details of the availability and prices of the previous nine volumes. By 1816, however, when this one volume had proliferated into five fat sub-volumes on London and its environs both the original publisher and the authors had withdrawn from the work. Hood had died in 1811 and by January 1812 his partners had abandoned the lion's share in the undertaking to John Harris, hitherto only a minor investor. Brayley was having health trouble and apparently got on less well with the new publisher than with Hood. Having completed 18 Numbers of the tenth volume he withdrew in March 1814 without concluding the second London sub-volume. His place was taken by the Rev Joseph Nightingale, a Unitarian minister, but unfortunately, according to the publisher's advertisement dated 12 September 1814, he was given no briefing; he said plaintively: 'Not having any opportunity of conferring with Mr. Brayley, to continue the narrative with the spirit and uniformity of manner and character in which it had been begun, was extremely difficult'.

Signs of the quarrel, like flies in amber, are discernible in the text, between pages 481 and 705 (signatures 2I to 2Y). Unusually each of these sections is dated: 2I to 2N from 9 to 25 June 1813, then a hiatus of six months and 2O to 2Y follow on, dated between 6 January and 24 March 1814, before the dates cease altogether. Harris was publicly

keeping tabs on his author's output. His official explanation was offered in the Address of 1 July 1816:

The completion of the Tenth Volume must be explained by the following brief statement: This Volume consists of 5 pts, and comprises the History of London and Westminster together with that of the County of Middlesex. The 18 first numbers (ending at page 720, of the second Part) were written by Mr. Brayley. It then became desirable to request other assistance, and the task of finishing the topographical account of London and Westminster was undertaken by the Rev. Mr. Nightingale. The Part, containing an account of Middlesex, as a county separate from the metropolis was written by Mr. J. Norris Brewer.

A promised list of subscribers to the whole series was never published but Harris, who had printed 1,000 extra copies in anticipation of increased demand for these volumes, urged subscribers to fill their gaps before he started selling off individual counties to non-subscribers, as he was already doing for the Middlesex volumes:

Note: The above five parts or Volumes of the 'Beauties of England' are published separately under the following title: 'London and Middlesex, or an Historical, Commercial and Descriptive Survey of the Metropolis of Great Britain, including sketches of its environs and a topographical account of the most remarkable places in the above County. Illustrated with Engravings.' The price of the Work in boards: £6. 5s. small paper, or large paper: £10.

When the whole series was complete, in 1818, his prospectus described it in these terms:

'The Beauties of England and Wales' consisting of 25 Parts or Volumes, printed on demy and royal octavo papers, illustrated with upwards of seven hundred copper plate engravings ... the labour of sixteen years.... the whole work, 18 vols, 241 numbers at 2s 6d, small £30. 2. 6., large £48. 4. 0. The portion which comprehends London and Middlesex may be purchased separately.... The Work consists of 5 volumes Octavo (50 Numbers) which are illustrated by upwards of 140 Engravings. The first 3 parts or Volumes comprise an Historical and Topographical account of London, the Fourth Volume contains the History and Description of Westminster. The Fifth Volume is appropriated to A topographical History of the County of Middlesex.

In due course William Sherwood of Paternoster Row and George Cowie of the Poultry, who had both had shares in the publication since 1814, became sole proprietors and announced in their issue of the London and Middlesex volumes: 'These

Volumes form part of that elegant and interesting Work lately completed in Twenty-Five Volumes ... The present Proprietors who have recently purchased the whole remaining Stock and Copy-Right of this Valuable Work, offer it to the Public in separate Counties'.

The Beauties of England and Wales; or, Original Delineations, Topographical, Historical, & Descriptive of each County. Embellished with Engravings. By Edward Wedlake Brayley ... Vol. X. Part I, (II-III, III Continuation, IV) ... London: Printed by W. Wilson, St John's Square, for Vernor, Hood, and Sharpe; Longman, Hurst, Rees, Orme, and Brown; J. Cuthell; J. Harris; J. Cundee; B. Crosby and Co.; and J. and J. Richardson. 1810 (etc).

Octavo, 210 × 135mm. (Large Paper 235 × 155mm)
1810, 1814–15, 1815, 1816

Alternative title:

London and Middlesex: or, an historical, commercial & descriptive Survey of the Metropolis of Great-Britain: including sketches of its environs, and a topographical account of the most remarkable places in the above County. Illustrated with engravings. Vol. III—Part II containing the history and description of the City and Liberty of Westminster. By the Rev. Joseph Nightingale. Printed for J. Harris: Longman & Co.: J. Walker: R. Baldwin: Sherwood & Co: Ja. and J. Cundee: B. and R. Crosby and Co: J. Cuthell: J. & J. Richardson: Cadell and Davies: C. and J. Rivington: and G. Cowie & Co., 1815.

Reissue:

A Topographical and Historical Description of London and Middlesex; containing an account of the Towns, Cathedrals, Castles, Antiquities, Churches, Monuments, Public Edifices, Picturesque Scenery, the Residences of the Nobility and Gentry &c ... By Messrs. Brayley, Brewer and Nightingale. In Five Volumes. Illustrated with One Hundred and Fifty Views of Churches, Castles, Noblemen's and Gentlemen's Seats, &c. Vol. I (etc) London: Printed for Sherwood, Neely and Jones, Paternoster Row; and George Cowie and Co., Poultry.

COLLATION Vol. 1. Title-page; dedication to the Lord Mayor dated September 1810 (1 leaf); author's advertisement (2pp); ('Advertisement by present proprietors' (1 leaf) in the Sherwood, Neely & Jones reissue); pp 1–680, Beauties—Middlesex; bibliography (20pp); indices (46pp). Vol. 2. Title-page (with imprint of alternative 'London and Middlesex' title and date 1814); pp iii–iv, proprietors' advertisement dated 12 September 1814; pp 1–803, Beauties—Middlesex continued; indices (60pp); note on suspension of booklist (1 leaf). Vol. 3. Title-page (with alternative imprint dated 1815 and the Rev Joseph Nightingale as author); advertisement dated 5 July 1815 (2pp); pp 1–756, Beauties—Middlesex con-

tinued; index (24pp). Vol. 4. Title-page (as for vol. 3 but numbered 'Vol. X. Continuation of Part III'); pp v–vii, dedication to the Speaker of the House of Commons dated 28 July 1815 (4pp); pp 9–752, Beauties—Middlesex continued; addenda (6pp); bibliography (16pp); indices (48pp). Vol. 5. Title-page (as for previous vol. but numbered 'Vol. X. Part IV. 1816' and J. Norris Brewer as author); dedication to the Duke of Northumberland dated 7 January 1816 (2pp); pp v–viii, author's preface; pp 1–758, Beauties—Middlesex continued; bibliography (15pp); indices (38pp); addenda (1p); publisher's address dated 1 July 1816 (4pp); directions to binder for vols 1–5 (4pp).

Britton, who exhibited at the Royal Academy, was no mean draughtsman of antiquarian and topographical subjects and himself designed the vignetted title to the first volume of the *Beauties*, dated 1 April 1801. He was therefore well qualified to undertake, in addition to the general editing of Brayley's literary contributions to the work, the direction of the artists and engravers who supplied the illustrative plates. A letter dated 24 August 1817, published in the final (and 'Introductory') volume of the series, shows that the took the responsibility seriously:

We sought a new style of *embellishment*; in which accuracy of representation should be combined with picturesque effect: in which the young draftsman and engraver, should have an opportunity of displaying their respective talents, and vie with each other in the career of fame.—A new era in topographical literature, as you will readily admit, has been created since the commencement of this century—for, before the *Beauties of England* appeared, the generality of county histories and antiquarian works were rather disfigured than adorned by their embellishments. Hollar, Loggan, and Burghers, have bequeathed us many interesting views of buildings, monuments, stained glass, &c.: but many of the works, even of these artists, are very inaccurate; and from the obvious reason, that the engravers were not sufficiently remunerated for their skill and time. The old bird's-eye views, by Kip, Knyff, &c. and the Views by S. and N. Buck, are highly useful and interesting; but this class of embellishment is at present 'out of fashion'. The 'cuts' as they are sometimes called, contained in Grose's 'Antiquities', and those copied from them, are only tolerable in the very infancy of literature and art, and may be regarded as approaching to caricatures in topography.

He chooses to ignore the 'higher spots' of the previous century such a Boydell's *Views* (no 47), Malton's *Picturesque Tour* (no 72) and Miller's *Select Views* (no 76) but he is entitled to proclaim an efflorescence of sound topographical and architectural draughtsmanship in the first decade of the nineteenth century and of engravers on copper with a technique adequate to the requirements of the new school. Undoubtedly many of these must have cut their teeth on work commissioned for the *Beauties* and have been beholden to Britton for their first earnings.

The chief artist, after John Harris took over publication, was John Preston Neale, born in 1780, who was a friend of the water-colourist John Varley who contributed a drawing of the Tower of London (item 51). Neale, a Post Office clerk, had insect drawings exhibited at the Royal Academy in 1797–1803; thereafter he took up topographical painting and drawing and became a skilful delineator of Gothic architecture. His illustrations for Brayley's *Westminster Abbey* (no 123) in particular evince the qualities sought by Britton: 'accuracy of representation combined with picturesque effect'. The suburban and riverside views in the *Beauties* give him ample scope for his picturesque vein. Two other young artists were Frederick Nash, a pupil of Thomas Malton, who also was a specialist in depicting Westminster Abbey, who was appointed architectural draughtsman to the Society of Antiquaries and who supplied Henry Fauntleroy with water-colours to extra-illustrate his copy of Pennant (no 67), and Frederick Mackenzie, also steeped in Gothic, who contributed to Ackermann's *Westminster Abbey* (no 108), *Londina Illustrata* (no 131) and Britton's *Architectural Antiquities* (no 97). Certainly four and possibly seven of the drawings were provided by George Shepherd, the founder of a family of London illustrators; he was somewhat older, probably approaching his fortieth year. Like Nash he had been employed by Henry Fauntleroy, and some 70 of his London water-colours are in the Crace Collection.

Among Britton's youthful engravers are: two of James Basire senior's former apprentices, George Cooke, who later engraved plates for Turner's *Picturesque Views*, and John Le Keux who gained a reputation as an engraver in the medieval style of architecture; John Pye and William Radclyffe, also engravers after Turner who held the latter in high esteem; John Burnet and John and Elizabeth of the Byrne family of engravers and painters; and youngest of all, R. Sands, and Robert Wallis who became a successful engraver on steel and who contributed to *Metropolitan Improvements* (no 154), Heath's *Picturesque Annuals* and the Keep-

sakes. The older school of engraving is represented by William Angus, Samuel Rawle and John Greig.

The 148 plates and five engraved titles supplied with vol. 10 were all worked between September 1805 and July 1816; the largest number (62) being published in 1815 when not a month went by without several being issued. The credits usually read: 'Engraved by … from a Drawing by … for the Beauties of England and Wales'. Only two of the plates (items 109 and 152) carry the original publication-line 'London, Published by Vernor & Hood, Poultry'. In 1806 the firm acquired another partner; thus, until January 1812 when John Harris took over the chief responsibility for the series, the line reads: (a) 'London, Published by Vernor, Hood & Sharpe, Poultry (date)', and thenceforward: (b) 'London, Published by John Harris, St Pauls Church Yard (date)'. The list abbreviates to (a) and (b). As long as Brayley was still engaged in the work engravers added to some plates 'E.W.B.dxt' (ie direxit).

PART 1

1 (engr title) The/Beauties/of/England and Wales;/or/ Delineations/Topographical Historical/and/Descriptive./Vol.X.Part 1. (vignette) Tower Gateway. J.P. Neale del. Sands sculp. London:Published by John Harris, St Pauls Church Yard. March 1,1815. 120 × 120/200 × 125mm.

2 p 63 London Bridge. Engraved by Hay from a Drawing by G. Arnald, A.R.A.… Published by (a)Augt. 1, 1811. 100 × 145/125 × 178mm.

PART 2

3 (engr title) The/Beauties/of/England and Wales;/or/ Delineations/Topographical Historical/and/Descriptive./Vol.X. Part II. (vignette) Temple Bar. J.P. Neale del. R. Sands sculp. London, Published by John Harris, St Paul's Church Yard Jan.3, 1816. 110 × 110/210 × 125mm.

4 p 277 Interior of St Pauls. Engraved by Hobson, from a Drawing by J.P. Neale … Published by (b)July 1, 1816. 148 × 100/190 × 125mm. View to E. end.

5 p 309 St Paul's Cathedral/(West Front)/London. Engraved by J. Burnet from a Drawing by F. Nash … E.W.B. dxt. Published by (a) April 1, 1809. 158 × 110/190 × 125mm.

6 p 310 St Pauls/The View taken from Bank side. Engraved by Radclyffe from a Drawing by J.P. Neale/… Published by (b)Sepr. 1, 1815. 102 × 150/125 × 190mm.

7 p 321 St Paul's School/London. Engraved by Owen, from a Drawing by J.P. Neale … Published by (b)May 1, 1814. 103 × 153/125 × 205mm.

8 p 346 Mercers Hall/Cheapside – Haberdashers Hall,/ Maiden Lane. Engraved by W. Angus ... Published by (a) Augt. 1, 1811. Each 105 × 75/120 × 200mm.

9 p 355 Grocers Hall – Fishmongers Hall. Engraved by Sands. Published by (a) June 23, 1811. Each 70 × 100/250 × 175mm.

10 p 368 Goldsmiths Hall. Engraved by W. Angus ... Published by (a) June 1, 1811. 105 × 155/125 × 200mm.

11 p 373 Salters Hall – Skinners Hall. Engrav'd by Angus ... Published by (a) Augt. 1, 1811. Each 105 × 80/125 × 205mm.

12 p 377 Guild Hall, London – Merchant Taylors Hall/London. Engraved by Angus. Published by (a) July 1, 1811. Each 105 × 75/125 × 205mm.

13 p 382 Merchant Taylors' School/Suffolk Lane/London. Drawn and Engraved by Sheppard ... Published by (b) Oct 1, 1815. 105 × 140/125 × 180mm.

14 p 390 Ironmonger's Hall/Fenchurch Street – Draper's Hall,/Throgmorton Street. Engraved by Sands from a Drawing by White ... Published by (b) March 1st 1812. Each 70 × 95/190 × 115mm.

15 p 399 Cloth Worker's Hall/Mincing Lane – Vintner's Hall/Thames Street. Engraved by Angus from a Drawing by Wilson. Published by (b)Jany 1, 1812. Each 70 × 95/210 × 115mm.

16 p 450 Interior of/Guildhall/London. Engraved by Lewis from a Drawing by J.P. Neale ... Published by (b) May 1, 1816. 150 × 105/190 × 120mm.

17 p 469 Guildhall Chapel/London. Engraved by H. Hobson from a Drawing by J.P. Neale ... Published by (b) July 1, 1815. 148 × 100/205 × 120mm.

18 p 472 The Mansion House/London. Engrav'd by J. Burnet from a Drawing by J.R. Thompson ... E.W.B. dxt. Published by (a) Jan 1, 1810. 160 × 105/205 × 115mm.

19 p 478 Royal Exchange/Looking South westward./ London. Engrav'd by W. Angus from a Drawing by J.R. Thompson ... E.W.B. dxt. Published by (a) March 1, 1809. 150 × 100/210 × 120mm.

20 p 490 Interior of/The Royal Exchange. Engraved by Wallis from a Drawing by J.P. Neale ... Published by (b) Feb. 1. 1816. 100 × 155/120 × 200mm.

21 p 557 Bank of England/South Front. Engraved by Stewart from a Drawing by J.P. Neale ... Published by (b) April 1, 1814. 105 × 155/125 × 200mm. Text criticizes Sir Robert Taylor's meretricious style in his additions to the 'original and admirable plan' of George Sampson. (*Bank of England* 41)

22 p 562 Rotunda/Bank of England. Engraved by Matthews from a Drawing by J.P. Neale ... Published by (b) March 1, 1816. 155 × 100/200 × 115mm. (*Bank of England* 169)

23 p 565 Lothbury Court: Bank New Buildings/London. Engrav'd by J. Burnet from a drawing by J.R.

Thompson ... E.W.B. dxt. Published by (a) Decr 1, 1809. 115 × 160/125 × 210mm. (*Bank of England* 127)

24 p 568 The Bank/North Front, from Lothbury/London. Engraved by Stewart & Burnet from a Drawing by J.R. Thompson ... E.W.B. dxt. Published by (a) Jany 2, 1809. 100 × 158/120 × 210mm. (*Bank of England* 54)

25 p 583 The East-India House,/London. Engraved by W. Angus from a Drawing by J.R. Thompson ... Published by (a) March 1st 1810. 105 × 157/115 × 200mm.

PART 3

26 (engr title) The/Beauties/of/England and Wales;/or/ Delineations/Topographical Historical/and/Descriptive./Vol. X. Part III. (vignette) Westminster Hall. J.P. Neale del. R. Sands sc. London, Published by John Harris, St. Paul's Church Yard, Dec. 1, 1815. 115 × 125/225 × 140mm.

27 p 108 Chinese Pagoda & Bridge, in St James's Park/Middlesex, as it appeared the 1st Augt 1814. Engraved by Rawle from a Drawing by J.P. Neale ... Published by (b) Nov. 1, 1814. 100 × 155/130 × 200mm.

28 p 109 Temple of Concord in the Green Park/ Middlesex/as it appeared Aug 1, 1814. Engraved by Sands from a Drawing by J.P. Neale ... Published by (b) Dec. 1, 1814. 100 × 155/135 × 205mm.

29 p 136 The New Mint/on Tower Hill. Engraved by T.L. Busby from a drawing by G. Stockdale ... Published by (b) June 1, 1813. 105 × 157/140 × 230mm.

30 p 138 Interior of St Catherines Church. Engraved by C. Pye from a Drawing by J.P. Neale ... Published by (b) Mar. 1, 1815. 150 × 100/215 × 135mm. St Katherine by the Tower.

31 p 145 The Entrance to the/London Docks/Engraved by Matthews, from a drawing by J.P. Neale ... Published by (b) July 1, 1815. 103 × 152/135 × 200mm. Original drawing (140 × 203mm) in BM (*Crace* 8.89).

32 p 179 Shoreditch Church. Engraved by Matthews from a drawing by J.P. Neale ... Published by (b) May 1, 1816. 153 × 102/200 × 150mm. St Leonard, Shoreditch in a completely rural setting.

33 p 186 Bethlehem Hospital/(as it appeared in June, 1811)/London. Engraved by R. Watkins from a Drawing by G. Arnald ... E.W.B. dxt. Published by (a) Augt 1, 1811. 98 × 145/135 × 230mm. The Moorfields building in decay; its removal to St George's Fields had been sanctioned by Act of Parliament in the previous year.

34 p 187 St Luke's Hospital/Old Street Road. Engraved by Sands from a Drawing by Shepherd ... Published by (b) July 1, 1815. 92 × 147/135 × 225mm. Built by George Dance junior, 1782–7. (*Bank of England* 219)

35 p 225 The Dutch Church/Austin Friars/London.

Engraved by Wallis from a drawing by J.P. Neale ... Published by (b) June 1, 1815. 100 × 150/135 × 205mm.

36 p 235 The Auction Mart/London. Engraved by J. Shury from a Drawing by J.P. Neale ... Published by (b) Aug 1. 1815. 95 × 146/135 × 220mm. Designed by John Walters, 1808–9.

37 p 250 Stow's Monument/St. Andrew Undershaft/ Leadenhall Street/London. Engraved by C. Pye from a Drawing by J.P. Neale ... Published by (b) Apr.1, 1815. 110 × 105/205 × 130mm.

38 p 271 St Stephen's Walbrook/London. Engraved by J. Byrne from a drawing by Edd Gyfford ... E.W.B. dxt. Published by (a) Decr 1st, 1808. 165 × 107/205 × 135mm. An interior by Gyfford also, engraved by Storer and Greig, in the previous year, for Hughson's *London* (no 93), item 20.

39 p 348 Hall of the Brotherhood of the Holy Trinity/In St Botolph's Parish, Aldersgate/as remaining in February, 1790/London. Engraved by R. Roffe, from a Drawing by W. Capon ... E.W.B. dxt. Published by (a) Feby 1, 1809. 145 × 110/215 × 135mm. Interior.

40 p 361 Bow Church/Cheapside London. Engraved by Shury from a Drawing by J.P. Neale ... Published by (b) April 1, 1815. 152 × 100/210 × 135mm.

41 p 407 Interior of the Priory Church of St Bartholomew/ (looking West)/West Smithfield/London. Engrav'd by J. Burnet, from a drawing by the late T. Malton, R.A. ... E.W.B. dxt. Published by (a) April 1, 1809. 145 × 108/210 × 135mm.

42 p 449 Bartholomews Hospital/London. Engrav'd by Sands, from a drawing by J.P. Neale ... Published by (b) October 1, 1815. 98 × 148/155 × 230mm.

43 p 504 Old Porch, Charter House. Engraved by Owen, from a drawing by J.P. Neale ... Published by (b) May 1, 1815. 100 × 152/143 × 200mm.

44 p 561 The Charter House/Interior of the Great Hall. Engraved by J. Lewis from a Drawing by J.P. Neale ... Published by (b) June 1, 1815. 152 × 100/190 × 145mm.

45 p 587 St John's Gate/Clerkenwell. Engrav'd by Matthews from a drawing by J.P. Neale ... Published by (b) April 1, 1815. 100 × 150/140 × 200mm.

46 p 634 Blackfryar's Bridge, St Paul's Cathedral &c./ From the Surrey Side of the River Thames/London. Engraved by J. Le Keux from a Drawing by F. Mackenzie ... E.W.B. dxt. Published by (a) Feb 1, 1810. 105 × 150/140 × 210mm.

47 p 638 Interior of/the Heralds College. Engraved by Lewis from a drawing by J.P. Neale ... Published by (b) Dec. 1. 1815. 150 × 102/190 × 135mm.

48 p 641 New Iron Bridge/Over the Thames from Queen Street. Engraved by H. Hobson from a drawing by J.P. Neale ... Published by (b) June 1, 1815. 98 × 145/135 × 190mm. Southwark Bridge, opened 24 March 1819.

49 p 647 View on Fish Street Hill/Including the Monument, St Magnus's Church etc./London. Engrav'd by J. Le Keux, from a Drawing by J.R. Thompson ... E.W.B. dxt. Published by (a) Nov 1. 1809. 175 × 105/210 × 130mm.

50 p 651 New Custom House/London Engraved by Elizth Byrne from a Drawing by J.P. Neale ... Published by (b) July 1, 1816. 100 × 147/140 × 200mm. Built by David Laing, 1813–17.

51 p 653 View of the Tower of London. Engraved by W. Angus from a drawing by Varley ... Published by (a) Decr 1st 1811. 102 × 157/140 × 200mm.

52 p 655 The Tower of London/From the Hill. Engraved by Busby from a Drawing by J.P. Neale ... Published by (b) June 1, 1814. 100 × 150/140 × 190mm.

53 p 656 The Chapel in the Tower: now called the Record Office/London. Engraved by J. Lee from a Drawing by F. Nash ... E.W.B. dxt. Published by (a) March 1, 1809. 147 × 102/170 × 130mm. St John's Chapel.

54 p 668 Trinity House/Tower Hill,/London. Engrav'd by W. Angus from a drawing by Shepherd ... Published by (a) April 1, 1811. 105 × 160/140 × 200mm.

55 p 694 St Dunstans in the East. Engraved by Hobson, from a drawing by J.P. Neale ... Published by (b) Oct. 1. 1815. 150 × 100/205 × 140mm.

56 p 715 View of/St Brides Church/taken from the River Thames. Engraved by Matthews from a Drawing by J.P. Neale ... Published by (b) Oct 1. 1815. 152 × 100/205 × 135mm.

57 p 752 Chapel, Ely Place. Engraved by Wallis from a Drawing by J.P. Neale ... Published by (b) Aug.1.1815. 153 × 100/205 × 140mm. Original water-colour of the E. end exterior in BM (*Crace* 27.105).

PART 3 (Continuation)

58 (engr title) The/Beauties/of/England and Wales;/or/ Delineations/Topographical Historical/and/Descriptive./Vol.X. Part IV. (vignette) The Tomb of Henry the Third,/Westminster Abbey. Drawn by J.P. Neale, Engraved by J. Lewis. London, Published by John Harris, St Pauls Church Yard, July 1, 1815. 110 × 125/190 × 130mm.

59 p 9 Westminster Abbey/with the New Improvements. Engraved by Busby from a drawing by Wichelo ... Published by (b) Feb 1, 1814. 100 × 150/125 × 200mm.

60 p 33 The Coronation Chair of the English Sovereigns/ With the Shield and Sword of State of Edward the Third/Westminster Abbey. Engrav'd by J. Roffe ... Published by (a) Feb. 1, 1810. 147 × 115/200 × 125mm.

61 p 96 Entrance to the South Aisle/Westminster Abbey. Engraved by Sands from a Drawing by J.P. Neale ... Published by (b) April 1, 1816. 145 × 95/185 × 120mm.

62 p 98 Interior of/Westminster Abbey./Poets Corner.

Engraved by Lewis from a Drawing by J.P. Neale … Published by (b) Octr 1 1815. 153 × 102/190 × 125mm.

63 p 145 Westminster Abbey/North Porch, with part of Henry the 7th Chapel. Engraved by H. Hobson from a Drawing by J.P. Neale … Published by (b) Nov 1, 1815. 100 × 153/125 × 200mm.

64 p 146 Westminster Abbey,/(Western Tower.) Engraved by T. Matthews from a Drawing by J.P. Neale … Published by (b) Dec. 1, 1815. 155 × 103/200 × 125mm.

65 p 150 View in the Cloisters/(Showing the Entrance to the Chapter House &c.)/Westminster Abbey. Engraved by R. Roffe from a Drawing by J.R. Thompson … E.W.B. dxt. Published for (a) Octr 1, 1809. 150 × 105/205 × 125mm.

66 p 153 Westminster/Shewing the Abbey, Hall, Bridge &c/From the opposite side of the Thames. Engrav'd by J. Pye from a Drawing by W. Anderson … E.W.B. dxt. Published by (a) Augt 1, 1809. 102 × 150/120 × 200mm. Anderson's painting (500 × 650mm), signed and dated 1807, was sold at Christie's (Camperdown sale) on 27 May 1921.

67 p 169 The Savoy/London. Engraved by J. Lewis from a Drawing by J.P. Neale … Published by (b) April 1, 1815. 150 × 100/200 × 120mm.

68 p 174 Interior of the Savoy Chapel,/Westminster. Engrav'd by J. Byrne from a drawing by F. Nash … E.W.B. dxt. Published by (a) Aug 1 1809. 150 × 110/200 × 120mm.

69 p 198 View in the Strand/(Including the North Front of Somerset House, and the Church of St Mary-le-Strand)/Westminster. Engrav'd by H. Le Keux from a Drawing by G. Shepherd … E.W.B. dxt. Published by (a) July 1, 1810. 100 × 145/115 × 205mm.

70 p 209 Somerset House/From the Thames/Westminster. Engraved by J. Le Keux from a Drawing by F. Mackenzie … E.W.B. dxt. Published by (a) Decr 1, 1810. 100 × 150/125 × 200mm.

71 p 213 Old Somerset House – The Savoy, London. Engraved by White … Published by (a) May 1st, 1811. Each 52 × 150/125 × 205mm.

72 p 246 Strand Bridge/London. Engraved by I. Lewis from a Drawing by J.P. Neale … Published by (b) Feb 1 1816. 105 × 155/130 × 190mm. 'The Strand Bridge which is becoming a most commanding object on both sides of the water' (p 247). Rennie's Waterloo Bridge erected 1811–17.

73 p 248 St Martin's Church/Westminster. Engrav'd by T. Bonnor from a Drawing by J.R. Thompson … Published by (a) April 1, 1810. 160 × 105/200 × 125mm. From S.W.

74 p 272 Northumberland House/London. Engraved by J. Shury from a Drawing by J.P. Neale … Published by (b) March 1, 1816. 105 × 155/125 × 200mm.

75 p 278 St Paul's Church./Covent Garden. Engraved by

Lewis from a Drawing by J.P. Neale … Published by (b) May 1, 1816. 103 × 155/125 × 200mm.

76 p 280 Drury Lane Theatre/Westminster/Burnt down in 1809. Engraved by W.J. White from a drawing by J. Capon … Published by (a) June 1, 1811. 102 × 165/125 × 205mm.

77 p 285 New Drury Lane Theatre, Engraved by Busby from a drawing by Wichelo … Published by (b) Septr 1, 1813. 100 × 150/125 × 200mm. Built by Benjamin Wyatt, 1811–12.

78 p 288 Covent Garden Theatre/(Erected in the Year 1809)/Wetminster. Engraved by J. Le Keux from a drawing by Mackenzie … E.W.B. dxt. Published by (a) Jan. 1. 1810. 104 × 153/125 × 180mm. Robert Smirke's building.

79 p 296 St James's Palace/(North west view)/Westminster. Engraved by Stewart and Burnet from a Drawing by J. Burnet … E.W.B. dxt. Published by (a) Feb 1 1809. 105 × 152/120 × 200mm.

80 p 340 Carlton House/Pall Mall. Engraved by J. Pye … Published by (a) July 1, 1810. 102 × 170/120 × 200mm.

81 p 368 The Horse Guards, Treasury &c/(With the Piece of Turkish Ordnance taken by British Troops in Egypt)/Westminster. Engraved by G. Cooke from a Drawing by J.R. Thompson … E.W.B. dxt. Published by (a) Jany 1, 1810. 100 × 150/125 × 200mm.

82 p 369 The Treasury. Engraved by Woolnoth from a Drawing by J.P. Neale … Published by (b) Jun 1 1814. 102 × 155/120 × 200mm.

83 p 376 View in Parliament Street/(Shewing Whitehall, the Treasury &c)/Westminster. Engraved by R. Roffe from a Drawing by G. Shepherd … E.W.B. dxt. Published by (a) Sep 1. 1810. 110 × 162/125 × 205mm.

84 p 517 Westminster Hall/East Entrance. Engraved by Wallis from a Drawing by J.P. Neale … Published for (b) July 1815. 150 × 100/200 × 125mm.

85 p 518 The House of Lords & Commons. Engraved by Miss Byrne from a Drawing by J.P. Neale … Published by (b) Aug. 1 1815. 100 × 150/115 × 200mm.

86 p 522 The lower/Lobby, House of Commons. Engraved by Sands from a Drawing by J.P. Neale … Published by (b) Sepr 1, 1815. 142 × 88/200 × 110mm.

87 p 522 The Speaker's House/Westminster/(River front). Engraved by W. Radclyffe from a Drawing by J.P. Neale … Published by (b) July, 1815. 105 × 150/120 × 205mm.

88 p 523 Interior of/The House of Commons Engraved by Wallis, from a Drawing by J.P. Neale … Published by (b) Nov 1, 1815. 100 × 153/125 × 200mm.

89 p 599 St George's Church/Hanover Square/Westminster. Engraved by J. Le Keux from a Drawing by F. Mackenzie … E.W.B. dxt. Published by (a) July 1, 1810. 155 × 100/200 × 125mm. View from N.W.

90 p 621 Buckingham House,/(The Palace of Her Majesty Queen Charlotte)/St James Park. Drawn &

Engrav'd by J. Burnett ... E.W.B. dxt. Published by (a) Feb 1 1810. 105 × 155/125 × 205mm. Snow scene with skating on the canal. A water-colour in the BM (200 × 300mm), by Copley Fielding, is based on Burnett's drawing but adds to it Queen Charlotte's carriage with the Household Cavalry.

91 p 621 The Queen's Palace/(From the Green Park with the Guard House at Story's Gate &c)/Middlesex. Engraved by R. Roffe from a Painting by Geo. Arnald ... E.W.B. dxt. Published by (a) Decr 1, 1808. 102 × 150/125 × 200mm.

92 p 638 Earl Spencers House/Green Park. Engraved by Miss E. Byrne from a Drawing by J.P. Neale ... Published by (b) March 1, 1815. 100 × 153/125 × 200mm.

93 p 643 Bullock's Museum/Piccadilly. Engraved by R. Sands from a Drawing by J.P. Neale ... Published by (b) Jan 1, 1816. 100 × 142/125 × 200mm.

94 p 672 Lansdown House/Westminster/The Residence of the Most Noble the Marquess of Lansdown. Engraved by Shury from a Drawing by J.P. Neale ... Published by (b) Oct 1, 1815. 100 × 152/120 × 200mm.

95 p 691 Door Way to the Temple Church/London. Engraved by Shury from a Drawing by J.P. Neale ... Published by (b) June 1, 1815. 95 × 145/120 × 200mm.

96 p 692 Interior of/The Temple Church. Engraved by Sands from a Drawing by J.P. Neale ... Published by (b) Jan 1, 1816. 140 × 95/200 × 120mm.

97 p 706 The Surgeons New Theatre/Lincolns Inn Fields. Engraved by Busby from a Drawing by Wichello ... Published by (b) Feb 1, 1814. 150 × 100/120 × 210mm. Described as 'one of the most elegant structures in the metropolis'. Built by George Dance junior and James Lewis, 1806–13.

98 p 709 British Museum. Engraved by Sands from a Drawing by Sheppard... Published by (b) April 1, 1815. 95 × 150/120 × 200mm. Montague House.

99 p 720 The Foundling Hospital. Engraved by Elizth Byrne from a Drawing by J.P. Neale ... Published by (b) June 1, 1816. 100 × 150/120 × 200mm.

100 p 734 North Side of/Cavendish Square/London. Engraved by Woolnoth from a Drawing by J.P. Neale. Published by (b) Nov. 1, 1814. 100 × 150/125 × 200mm.

PART 4

101 (engr title) The/Beauties/of/England and Wales;/or/Delineations/Topographical, Historical/and/Descriptive/Vol.X.P.II. (vignette) A Small Fishing Wier,/on the Thames near Sunbury/Middlesex. G. Arnald A.R.A. pinx. J. Pye sculpt. London, Published by Vernor, Hood & Sharpe, Poultry. July 1, 1811. 75 × 100/195 × 135mm. 'P.II' engraved in error for 'Part IV'.

102 p 59 Chelsea/Middlesex. Engraved by Miss I. Byrne from a Drawing by J.P. Neale ... Published by (b)

March 1, 1815. 100 × 150/125 × 200mm. (*Longford* 145)

103 p 71 Chelsea Hospital/Middlesex. Engraved by Woolnoth from a Drawing by J.P. Neale after a Sketch by G. Moss ... Published by (b) Jan. 1, 1815. 100 × 150/125 × 200mm. (*Longford* 37)

104 p 99 Fulham Bridge & Church/Middlesex. Engraved by J. Pye from a Drawing by W.P. Sherlock ... Published by (b) Sepr 1 1812. 105 × 150/125 × 200mm.

105 p 115 Brandenburgh House & Theatre/Middlesex. Engraved by Lewis from a Drawing by J.P. Neale ... Published by (b) July 1815. 100 × 150/125 × 190mm.

106 p 130 Kensington Palace/Middlesex. Engraved by J. Lewis from a Drawing by J.P. Neale ... Published by (b) Feb 1, 1815. 100 × 150/125 × 190mm.

107 p 136 Holland House/Middlesex. Engraved by Woolnoth from a Drawing by J.P. Neale ... Published by (b) March 1, 1815. 102 × 155/140 × 205mm.

108 p 171 St Pancras Church./Middlesex. Engraved by C. Pye from a Drawing by J.P. Neale ... Published by (b) July 1, 1815. 95 × 145/125 × 200mm. Old church.

109 p 178 Caen Wood/Middlesex. Drawn & Engraved by J. Greig ... Published by (a) Dec 1, 1805. 102 × 155/130 × 200mm.

110 p 201 Child's Hill House,/Hampstead,Middlesex. Engraved by C. Pote from a Drawing by J.P. Neale ... Published by (b) Jan 1, 1813. 90 × 140/125 × 195mm.

111 p 210 Hornsey,/Middlesex. Engraved by J. Greig from a Drawing by J. Clennell ... Published by (a) Novr 1st 1811. 100 × 152/125 × 205mm.

112 p 215 Highgate/Middlesex. Engraved by Shury from a Drawing by J.P. Neale ... Published by (b) Mar 1, 1814. 155 × 103/210 × 125mm.

113 p 222 Highgate Archway/Middlesex. Engraved by Hobson from a Drawing by J.P. Neale ... Published by (b) Nov 1, 1814. 100 × 150/130 × 190mm. Opened 'for passengers and carriages' 21 August 1813.

114 p 265 Hackney Church/Middlesex. Engraved by Hay ... Published by (b) June 1, 1812. 100 × 150/125 × 205mm. In course of erection by James Spiller; the spire is still unbuilt.

115 p 293 Stepney Church/Middlesex. Engraved by Hobson from a Drawing by J.P. Neale ... Published by (b) Feb 1, 1815. 100 × 150/130 × 200mm.

116 p 306 West India Docks. Engraved by Matthews from a Drawing by J.P. Neale ... Published by (b) Aug 1, 1815. 103 × 150/130 × 205mm.

117 p 313 Chiswick/Middlesex. Engraved by J. Lewis from a Drawing by J.P. Neale ... Published by (b) Aug 1, 1815. 100 × 150/130 × 190mm.

118 p 315 Chiswick House/Middlesex/the Seat of His Grace the Duke of Devonshire. Engraved by C. Pye from a Drawing by J.P. Neale ... Published by (b) Feb. 1, 1815. 95 × 145/130 × 205mm.

119 p 336 Castle Hill Lodge,/Middlesex/The Seat of His Royal Highness the Duke of Kent. Engraved by C. Pye from a Drawing by J.P. Neale after a Sketch by W.G. Moss ... Published by (b) Apr. 1 1814. 103 × 155/130 × 210mm. In Ealing, formerly lived in by Mrs Fitzherbert.

120 p 353 Twyford Abbey,/Middlesex.... Engraved by Wallis from a Drawing by J.P. Neale ... Published by (b) Sepr 1, 1815. 100 × 152/125 × 200mm.

121 p 355 Finchley Church,/Middlesex. Engraved by Miss Byrne from a Drawing by J.P. Neale ... Published by (b) Aug 1, 1815. 100 × 150/125 × 205mm.

122 p 359 Isleworth,/Middlesex. Engraved by I. Lewis from a Drawing by J.P. Neale ... Published by (b) Nov. 1, 1815. 97 × 150/125 × 200mm.

123 p 361 Sion House/(Seat of the Duke of Northumberland)/Middlesex. Engraved by Wm. Cooke ... Published by (a) May 1, 1806. 95 × 150/125 × 200mm.

124 p 384 Twickenham,/Middlesex. Engraved by J. Lewis from a Drawing by J.P. Neale ... Published by (b) Dec 1, 1814. 100 × 150/130 × 190mm.

125 p 388 Marble Hall,... /Middlesex. Engraved by Matthews from a Drawing by J.P. Neale ... Published by (b) Oct 1, 1815. 105 × 150/125 × 205mm.

126 p 392 Pope's House,Twickenham/Middlesex. Drawn and Engraved by W. Cooke ... Published by (a) Feb 1, 1807. 100 × 148/125 × 200mm.

127 p 397 Strawberry Hill/the Seat of Countess Dowager Waldegrave/Middlesex. Engraved by W. Radclyffe from a Drawing by J.P. Neale ... Published by (b) Nov 1, 1815. 100 × 150/125 × 190mm.

128 p 432 Whitton/Middlesex.... Engraved by Woolnoth from a Drawing by J.P. Neale ... Published by (b) Feb 1, 1816. 100 × 150/125 × 200mm.

129 p 436 Osterley House,/Middlesex./The Seat of the Earl of Jersey. Engraved by S. Rawle from a Drawing by J.P. Neale ... Published by (b) Jan 1, 1815. 102 × 157/130 × 200mm.

130 p 444 Spring Grove,/Middlesex/the Seat of the Right Honble Sir Joseph Banks Bart. Engraved by R. Sands from a Drawing by J.P. Neale ... Published by (b) Dec 1, 1815. 97 × 145/125 × 210mm.

131 p 457 The Entrance to/Hampton Court Palace,/Middlesex. Engraved by Woolnoth from a Drawing by J.P. Neale ... Published by (b) Jan 1, 1815. 100 × 150/130 × 205mm. The W. front.

132 p 460 Hampton Court Palace. Engraved by T. Matthews from a Drawing by J.P. Neale ... Published by (b) Nov 1, 1815. 100 × 152/130 × 210mm. From the river.

133 p 463 Hampton Court Palace/Middlesex. Engraved by Shury from a Drawing by J.P. Neale ... Published by (b) Dec 1, 1814. 100 × 152/130 × 210mm.

134 p 483 Hampton House/The Seat of Mr. Garrick. Engraved by W. Radclyffe from a Drawing by J.P. Neale ... Published by (b) Dec 1, 1815. 100 × 150/130 × 190mm.

135 p 491 Sunbury Place,/Middlesex,/Seat of the Honble Percy Windham. Engraved by Hay from a Drawing by G. Arnald, A.R.A.... Published by (a) June 1, 1811. 100 × 145/120 × 180mm.

136 p 504 Staines Church,/Middlesex. Engraved by Lewis from a Drawing by J.P. Neale ... Published by (b) Nov 1, 1815. 105 × 150/125 × 200mm

137 p 507 Staines Bridge./Middlesex. Engraved by Woolnoth from a Drawing by J.P. Neale ... Published by (b) Apr 1 1814. 105 × 158/130 × 200mm.

138 p 539 Delaford Park,/... near Uxbridge. Engraved by Cooke from a Painting by G. Arnald, A.R.A.... E.W.B. dxt. Published by (a) Septr 1, 1811. 97 × 152/130 × 205mm.

139 p 571 Harefield Place,/Middlesex. Engrav'd by J. Greig, from a Drawing by G. Shepherd ... Published by (a) Septr 1, 1811. 103 × 150/125 × 200mm.

140 p 619 Harlington Church Porch,/Middlesex.... Engraved by J. Pye from a Drawing by L. Francia ... Published by (b) Feby 1st 1812. 135 × 100/210 × 125mm.

141 p 630 Stanmore House/... Middlesex. Engraved by T. Mathews from a Drawing by J.P. Neale ... Published by (b) June 1, 1815. 100 × 150/130 × 200mm.

142 p 643 Canons.... Engraved by Woolnoth from a Drawing by J.P. Neale ... Published by (b) July 1, 1815. 103 × 155/130 × 200mm. Stanmore; built by a cabinet-maker on the site of and with materials from the Duke of Chandos's palace.

143 p 650 Harrow on the Hill,/Middlesex. Engraved by S. Rawle from a Drawing by J.P. Neale ... Published by (b) Dec 1 1814. 102 × 155/130 × 205mm.

144 p 678 Bentley Priory ... /Middlesex. Engraved by Matthews from a Drawing by J.P. Neale ... Published by (b) May 1, 1815. 100 × 150/130 × 200mm.

145 p 690 Hendon Church,/Middlesex. Engraved by T. Bonnor from a Drawing by J.P. Neale ... Published by (b) Novr 1, 1815. 100 × 155/130 × 200mm.

146 p 698 Bruce Castle,/Tottenham. Engraved by H. Hobson from a Drawing by J.P. Neale ... Published by (b) Dec 1, 1815. 100 × 150/125 × 200mm.

147 p 700 Tottenham Church,/Middlesex. Engraved by T. Bonnor from a Drawing by J.P. Neale ... Published by (b) June 1, 1815. 100 × 155/130 × 205mm.

148 p 707 Wyer Hall,Edmonton,/Middlesex. Engraved by J. Hawkesworth from a Drawing by T.W.L. Stockdale ... Published by (b) Feby 1st 1812. 100 × 150/130 × 205mm.

149 p 709 Arnos Grove/... Middlesex. Engraved by Lewis from a Drawing by J.P. Neale ... Published by (b) Apr 1, 1816. 103 × 150/130 × 210mm.

150 p 734 Trent House,/Middlesex.... Engraved by H.

Hobson from a Drawing by J.P. Neale ... Published by (b) July 1, 1815. 100 × 150/130 × 200mm.

151 p 736 Enfield Church,/Middlesex. Engraved by Hawksworth from a Drawing by Stockdale ... Published by (b) Feb 1, 1813. 100 × 150/125 × 200mm.

152 p 750 Wrotham Park/ ... Middlesex. Drawn & Engraved by W. & G. Cooke ... Published by (a) Sept 1, 1805. 100 × 148/130 × 210mm.

153 p 752 South Mimms Church,/Middlesex. Engraved by Elizth Byrne from a Drawing by J.P. Neale ... Published by (b) June 1, 1815. 102 × 150/130 × 200mm

---

105 · SEVERAL PROSPECTS OF THE MOST NOTED PUBLIC BUILDINGS [c 1810]

In the British Library (Maps 29.b.49) is a folio (325 × 255mm) of London prints published after 1807—according to a pencilled note in 1810. It has a printed introductory leaf consisting of a list of the 38 plates with a title above: 'This day are published, price £1. 1. 0, Several Prospects of the most noted public buildings in and about the City of London, with a short historical account relating to the same. London: Published by John Bowles, 31 Cornhill'.

There is no other text and the 'historical account' takes the form of short descriptions engraved bm on most of the plates. The contents list refers each plate to an appropriate page in four standard histories of London: Stow in the 1754 edition (no 37), Maitland (no 38) in the 1772 edition, Pennant (no 67) in the fourth quarto edition of 1805 and J.P. Malcolm's *Londinium Redivivum* published in four volumes from 1802 to 1807 (no 83). The imprint is a clumsy anachronism since John Bowles died in 1779 and his business passed into the hands of Robert Wilkinson, trading from 58 Cornhill. Moreover on the abolition of hanging signs in 1762 Bowles's place of business, the Black Horse in Cornhill, became no 13, not no 31. The archaic imprint was intended to appeal to ingenuous collectors who might be induced to buy the collection to extra-illustrate any one of the four books with the help of the list of references. These,

taken with the wove paper used, clearly indicate the non-contemporaneity of the impressions.

Most of the plates are drawn from Bowles's *British Views* (no 28), having already served for about 90 years. Of the 24 of the second series only two are missing: 'a' (the title) and 'v' ('Aske's Hospital'), and there are six from the second series, totalling 28. To these are added eight from more recent series of small Bowles plates and two final views whose engravers were active only after Bowles's death. This collection must surely be the enterprise of Robert Wilkinson who had already by this time started issuing facsimiles of old prints in his series *Londina Illustrata* (no 131) which was to appeal to the same public of antiquarians and grangerizers.

Page references to the 1805 edition of Pennant are transcribed below. Dimensions of the *British Views* plates, give or take a few millimetres to allow for the more spongy wove paper and the trimming of worn copper plates, may be assumed to be the same as for the earlier impressions. References to the items in the listing of these are included with the abbreviation *BV*.

1 pl. a (engr title in cartouche between two long views) Britannia Illustrata/Several Prospects/of the Royal Palaces & Publick Buildings of England, also ye Views of some of ye most considerable/seats and gardens belonging to the Nobility and Gentry.... (tr) British Views No. 3. Printed for and Sold by John Bowles ... (with two long views, each about 65 × 230mm, identified in sky: 'Westminster' and 'London'). Pennant p 1. *BV* 34.

2 pl.b A View from the River Thames of the Parliament House, Westminster Hall and Westminster Abby – A View of Whitehall from the River Thames. Pennant p 71. *BV* 35.

3 pl.g (tm) A View of the Inside of Westminster Hall. Pennant p 72. *BV* 40.

4 pl.d (on swallow-tailed banderole in sky) The Cathedral Church of/St Peters Westminster. Pennant p 51. *BV* 13.

5 pl.e (on scroll tc) The Inside of St Peters. Pennant p 52. *BV* 14.

6 pl.c (on swallow-tailed banderole in sky) The Royal Banqueting House at White Hall. Pennant p 87. *BV* 12.

7 pl.b (in sky) The Royal Palace of St James's. Pennant p 94. *BV* 11.

8 pl.1 (bm) The Royal Palace of St James's next the Park. (and in French) Printed for John Bowles in Cornhil. 180 × 240/205 × 253mm. Series title along

tm: 'Perspective Views of the four Royal Palaces and of celebrated Edifices in London, 1'. Pennant p 95.

9 pl.6 A View of Somerset House with St Marys Church/in the Strand London. (and in French) Printed for John Bowles in Cornhil. 182 × 240/205 × 253mm. Pennant p 128.

10 pl.5 A View of Northumberland-House & Charing Cross. (and in French) Printed for John Bowles in Cornhill. 180 × 240/205 × 253mm. Pennant p 118.

11 pl.f (on swallow-tailed banderole in sky) The North West Prospect of the Cathedral Church of St Paul. Pennant p 333. *BV* 15.

12 pl.g The South East Prospect of the Inside of the Cathedral Church of St.Paul. Pennant p 334. *BV* 16.

13 pl.i The Chapter House/It is a fair House belonging to St Pauls Church. Parr sculp. Pennant p 316. *BV* 42.

14 pl.h (on swallow-tailed banderole in sky) Guild Hall. Pennant p 354. *BV* 17.

15 pl.i (on scroll tc) Inside of Guildhall. Pennant p 355. *BV* 18.

16 pl.9 Ironmongers Hall, with a view of Fenchurch Street. (and in French) Printed for John Bowles in Cornhil. 185 × 243/205 × 253mm. Pennant p 401.

17 pl.m (on swallow-tailed banderole in sky) Justice Hall in the Old Baily. Pennant p 201. *BV* 21.

18 pl.k (on swallow-tailed banderole in sky) The Royal Exchange. Pennant p 369. *BV* 19.

19 pl.l (on swallow-tailed banderole in sky) The Inside of the Royal Exchange. Pennant p 370. *BV* 20.

20 pl.8 The Inside View of the Royal Exchange at London. (and in French) Printed for John Bowles in Cornhil. 185 × 245/205 × 255mm. Pennant p 371.

21 pl.z (on swallow-tailed banderole in sky) The Tower of London. Pennant p 248. *BV* 33.

22 pl.10 The Monument of London in remembrance of/the dreadful fire in 1666—its height is 202 feet. (and in French) Printed for John Bowles in Cornhil. 180 × 245/205 × 253mm. Pennant p 287.

23 pl.y (on swallow-tailed banderole in sky) London Bridge. Pennant p 280. *BV* 32.

24 pl.x (on swallow-tailed banderole in sky) Custom House. Pennant p 274. *BV* 31.

25 pl.11 A View of the Custom House & Part of the Tower. (and in French) Printed for John Bowles in Cornhil. 180 × 240/205 × 252mm. Pennant p 275.

26 pl.w (on swallow-tailed banderole in sky) Navy Office. Pennant p 237. *BV* 30.

27 pl.n (on swallow-tailed banderole in sky) The Charterhouse. Pennant p 175. *BV* 22.

28 pl.o (on swallow-tailed banderole in sky) St Paul's School. Pennant p 320. *BV* 23.

29 pl.p (on swallow-tailed banderole in sky) College of Physicians. Pennant p 309. *BV* 24.

30 pl.q (on swallow-tailed banderole in sky) St Bartholomew's Hospital. Pennant p 168. *BV* 25.

31 pl.r (on swallow-tailed banderole in sky) Christs Hospital. Pennant p 166. *BV* 26.

32 pl.s (on swallow-tailed banderole in sky) St Thomas's Hospital. Pennant p 42. *BV* 27.

33 pl.t (on swallow-tailed banderole in sky) Bethlem Hospital. Pennant p 220. *BV* 28.

34 pl.12 The Hospital of Bethlehem. (and in French) Printed for John Bowles in Cornhil. 180 × 240/205 × 253mm. Pennant p 221.

35 pl.z Chelsey Colledge. Parr sculp. Pennant p 18. *BV* 57. (*Longford* 66)

36 pl.y The Royal Hospital at Greenwich. Pennant p 272. *BV* 56.

37 Bermondsey Abbey in Surrey. Hawkins sculpt. 133 × 187/237 × 177mm. Pennant p 46.

38 Ely House, in London. Royce sculpt. 187 × 130/230 × 180mm. Pennant p 60.

---

106 · COOKE AND OWEN'S THAMES [1811]

Samuel Owen's first water-colour exhibit at the Royal Academy in 1794 was catalogued as 'A Sea View' and he continued to paint the sea and shipping for the Royal Academy. Between 1808 and 1810 he sent a large number of maritime subjects to the Associated Artists in Water-Colours. It is not therefore surprising that his illustrations of the Thames are often wind-swept, with choppy waters and masts at angles worthy of Turner at his stormiest. His engraver in these volumes, William Bernard Cooke, was becoming something of a specialist in etching Thames scenery and later, when he engraved for *Views in Sussex* (1816–20) and *Picturesque Views on the Southern Coast* (1814–26), fell under the beneficent spell of Turner. Before this he contributed Thames views, drawn and engraved by himself, to John Britton's *Beauties of England and Wales* (no 104) which was still in course of publication by Vernor, Hood & Sharpe, who were now also publishing his own collection.

The anonymous text was by the journalist William Combe who also had provided a text to accompany the Boydells's *Thames* illustrated by Farington (no

75). It is unpaginated but the pages have occasionally, bc, Arabic figures from 1 to 51, representing the issue of successive Numbers. Each portion of the text, ranging from one leaf with verso blank to ten or more pages, describes a plate or group of plates, with which it was presumably issued, so that it is possible to work out the chronological sequence of the Numbers, which ran from May 1809 to April 1811 and cost 4s 6d each octavo or 7s 6d quarto:

1–4,17	May 1809	26–8	April 1810
5–8	June 1809	29–32	June 1810
9–11	July 1809	33–35	August 1810
12–16	September 1809	36–38	November 1810
18–19	November 1809	41	December 1810
20,22	December 1809	39–40,	February and
21,23–5	February 1810	42–51	April 1811

In June 1811 the complete work was advertised at £3 3s octavo of £5 5s quarto with proofs of the plates.

The Thames: or Graphic Illustrations of Seats, Villas, Public Buildings and Picturesque Scenery, on the Banks of that Noble River. (epigraph) The Engravings executed by William Bernard Cooke from Original Drawings by Samuel Owen, Esq. Vol.I (II) London: Printed for Vernor, Hood and Sharpe, 31 Poultry: and W.B. Cooke, 12, York Place, Pentonville by William Bell and Co., at the Union Office, St John's Square, 1811.

Octavo, 295 × 230mm.   1811

COLLATION   Vol. 1. Title-page; list of plates (2pp); introduction (6pp); descriptive letterpress (77 unpaginated leaves, some with verso blank). Vol. 2. Title-page; list of plates (2pp); descriptive letterpress (79 unpaginated leaves, some with verso blank); A New Table shewing the Distances (1 leaf); index, directions to binder, errata (6pp).

Cooke engraved on copper 82 of Samuel Owen's drawings in the two years during which the Numbers were issued and, considering the pressure under which he must have worked, these etchings are remarkably good. He excels in reproducing Owen's turbulent water in the foreground, although the more distant view is sometimes rather summary and the skies are often engraved to a formula, not unlike Hollar's in the seventeenth century. Strangely enough Cooke suffers most by a comparison with his later self: for his subsequent *Views on the Thames* (no 139) he engraved for a second time 38 of the Owen drawings, but in a decidedly different spirit, for by then he had undergone the influences of Turner and Peter de Wint.

The plates themselves are unnumbered and so are the lists of their subjects, prefixed to each volume. Captions are engraved in italics, mostly br. Most credits read: 'Drawn by S. Owen Esq. Engraved by W. Cooke.' There are alternative publication-lines:

(a) '(London,) Published (date) by Vernor, Hood & Sharpe, Poultry, & W. Cooke, 2 Clarence Place, Pentonville.' (up to July 1810)
(b) '(London,) Published (date) by Vernor, Hood & Sharpe, Poultry, & W. Cooke, 12 York Place, Pentonville.' (from August 1810)

VOL. 1 (The Source to Marble Hill Cottage, Richmond)

1 Source of the Thames. April 1, 1811. 115 × 195/160 × 240mm.

2 Thames Head, taken from the Bridge. Decr 1, 1810. 110 × 190/155 × 240mm.

3 Cricklade, taken near Eisey Chapel. 112 × 192/153 × 240mm. nd.

4 Inglesham Lock. April 1, 1811. 115 × 190/155 × 240mm. With the Thames and Severn Canal.

5 Radcot Wier. Feby 1, 1811. 115 × 195/155 × 240mm.

6 Oxford, taken from Ifley. 115 × 195/155 × 240mm. nd.

7 Nuneham Courtenay, Earl Harcourt. Dec.1, 1810. 115 × 195/155 × 240mm.

8 Nuneham Courtenay Bridge, and Cottage. Feb.1, 1811. 115 × 195/155 × 240mm.

9 Abingdon. April 1,1811. 115 × 195/158 × 240mm.

10 The junction of the Thames and the Isis. Augt 1, 1810. 115 × 192/155 × 230mm.

11 The Grotto House, Basildon Park. Decr 1, 1810. 113 × 190/155 × 240mm.

12 Basildon Park, and Combe Lodge. Decr 1, 1810. 115 × 200/155 × 240mm.

13 Purley Hall, Mr. Storer. Feb. 1, 1811. 115 × 192/155 × 240mm. 'The Seat of the late Anthony Storer, Esq.'

14 Shiplake Lock and Paper Mill. Dec. 1,1810. 115 × 198/155 × 240mm. 'With Wargrave House, the Seat of Joseph Hill Esq.'

15 Park Place, Henley. Feb. 1, 1811. 115 × 200/155 × 240mm. 'The Seat of the Earl of Malmesbury'.

16 Henley. Feb.1,1811. 115 × 192/155 × 238mm.

17 Fawley Court. Feb.1,1810. 115 × 190/155 × 240mm. 'Seen from Henley Bridge, the Seat of Strickland Freeman Esq.'

18 Culham Court. Dec. 1, 1809. 115 × 175/153 × 240mm. 'Near Henley, the Seat of the Honble Frederick West'.

19 Medmenham Abbey. Engraved by S. Middiman. Dec. 1, 1809. 115 × 190/155 × 240mm.

20 Temple House, Owen William Esq. Engraved by

Geo. Cooke. Feb. 1, 1810. 117 × 190/155 × 240mm. 'Between Henley and Marlow'.

21 Harleyford House. Augt 1, 1810. 115 × 192/155 × 238mm. 'The Seat of Sir William Clayton Bart.'

22 Bisham Abbey. April 1, 1810. 115 × 173/155 × 240mm. 'The Seat of George Vansittart, Esq.'

23 Great Marlow. Dec. 1, 1809. 115 × 190/155 × 240mm.

24 Cookham Church. Feb. 1, 1810. 115 × 188/155 × 240mm.

25 Taplow House. Feb. 1, 1810. 115 × 190/155 × 240mm.

26 Maidenhead Bridge. Decr 1, 1810. 115 × 175/155 × 248mm.

27 Monkey Island. Nov. 1, 1809. 160 × 115/238 × 155mm.

28 The Willows. June 1, 1810. 113 × 188/155 × 240mm. 'Seat of the late Townley Ward Esq.'

29 Windsor. Feb.1, 1810. 115 × 158/155 × 238mm.

30 Windsor Castle, taken near the Lock. Feb. 1, 1810. 115 × 190/155 × 240mm.

31 Eton Bridge. June 1, 1809. 110 × 190/150 × 240mm.

32 Old Houses at Eton. June 1, 1809. 110 × 170/150 × 240mm. 'Near Eaton Bridge'.

33 Eton College. May 1, 1809. 112 × 188/155 × 250mm.

34 Beaumont Lodge, Lord Ashbrooke. Novr 1, 1810. 113 × 195/155 × 240mm. 'Old Windsor'.

35 Staines Bridge. Augt 1, 1810. 110 × 172/150 × 240mm.

36 Oatlands, from Shepperton Priory. Nov. 1, 1810. 115 × 193/155 × 240mm.

37 Walton Bridge. Novr 1, 1810. 113 × 190/155 × 240mm.

38 Garrick's House at Hampton. June 1, 1809. 112 × 172/150 × 240mm.

39 Hampton Court. Nov. 1, 1810. 115 × 188/155 × 245mm.

40 Lady Sullivan's Villa. Sept. 1, 1809. 110 × 172/150 × 235mm. 'Thames Ditton'.

41 Kingston. Sept. 1, 1809. 115 × 188/155 × 235mm.

42 Strawberry Hill. July 1, 1809. 155 × 115/240 × 150mm. 'The Seat of the Honble Mrs Damer'.

43 Lady Howe's Villa. Sept. 1, 1809. 110 × 170/150 × 225mm. 'Twickenham'.

44 Twickenham. May 1, 1809. 112 × 190/152 × 253mm.

45 Richmond Hill, from Twickenham. Augt 1, 1810. 114 × 188/150 × 240mm. (*Gascoigne* 541)

46 Marble Hill Cottage, near Richmond. Nov. 1, 1809. 115 × 190/150 × 240mm.

VOL. 2 (Richmond Hill to Sheerness)

47 The Thames from Richmond Hill. Nov. 1, 1810. 110 × 188/150 × 240mm. (*Gascoigne* 542)

48 The Duke of Buccleuch's Villa. Sept. 1, 1809. 112 × 170/150 × 235mm. At Richmond. (*Gascoigne* 543)

49 Richmond Bridge. June 1, 1809. 110 × 190/155 × 255mm. (*Gascoigne* 544)

50 Mr. Keene's, Richmond, late Sir Charles Asgill's. July 1, 1809. 112 × 170/150 × 240mm. (*Gascoigne* 546)

51 The Observatory, Richmond Gardens. Dec. 1, 1809. 160 × 115/240 × 152mm.

52 Keppel House, Isleworth. April 1, 1810. 110 × 173/155 × 240mm.

53 Sion House, the Seat of the Duke of Northumberland. July, 1, 1810. 115 × 193/155 × 240mm.

54 Brandenburg House, near Chiswick, the Seat of the Margravine of Anspach. May 1, 1809. 112 × 170/155 × 250mm.

55 Fulham. Dec. 1, 1809. 115 × 190/155 × 240mm.

56 Battersea. July 1, 1809. 112 × 188/150 × 240mm. Built of timber, under the direction of Henry Holland, 1771–2; demolished 1881. (*Longford* 259)

57 Chelsea Hospital. July 1, 1809. 115 × 190/150 × 240mm. (*Longford* 31)

58 Randall's Mill, Nine Elms. Novr 1, 1809. 155 × 113/245 × 155mm.

59 Randall's Mill, Nine Elms. May 1, 1809. 110 × 172/158 × 240m.

60 Lambeth Palace. April 1, 1810. 115 × 190/155 × 245mm.

61 Westminster Abbey. June 1, 1809. 110 × 172/160 × 240mm. From Lambeth.

62 London & Blackfriar's Bridge, from Hungerford. April 1, 1811. 115 × 195/155 × 240mm.

63 Somerset House. Augt 1, 1810. 112 × 190/153 × 240mm.

64 London Bridge. May 1, 1809. 110 × 170/155 × 250mm. From the E.

65 Custom House. April 1, 1810. 115 × 190/155 × 245mm.

66 Tower of London. Sept. 1, 1809. 115 × 190/150 × 240mm.

67 West India Docks. April 1, 1811. 115 × 195/155 × 240mm. Credits 'S. Owen Delt. W. Cooke fecit 1811'.

68 Deptford. June 1, 1810. 115 × 190/155 × 240mm.

69 Greenwich. Nov. 1, 1809. 112 × 190/153 × 240mm.

70 Mast House, Blackwall. Sept. 1, 1809. 112 × 188/150 × 235mm.

71 Shooters Hill, from Woolwich Reach. April 1, 1810. 112 × 192/150 × 238mm.

72 Woolwich. July 1, 1809. 108 × 173/150 × 240mm.

73 Erith, with Belvidere. Nov. 1, 1809. 114 × 188/155 × 238mm.

74 Purfleet. Augt 1, 1810. 115 × 190/155 × 240mm.

75 Ingries, at Greenhithe, William Havlock Esq. Novr 1, 1810. 115 × 190/155 × 240mm.

76 Northfleet. May 1, 1809. 110 × 190/150 × 240mm.

77 Lime Kilns, Northfleet. Feb. 1, 1810. 113 × 190/155 × 240mm.

78 Gravesend. April 1, 1811. 115 × 193/155 × 240mm.

79 Tilbury Fort. May 1, 1809. 110 × 193/150 × 240mm.

80 Gateway to Tilbury Fort. April 1, 1810. 155 × 110/240 × 145mm.

81 Hadleigh Castle, Essex. Sept. 1, 1809. 115 × 190/150 × 235mm.

82 Leigh, taken near Southend. June 1, 1810. 115 × 190/160 × 240mm.

83 Southend. April 1, 1810. 115 × 193/155 × 238mm.

84 Sheerness. June 1, 1810. 115 × 190/155 × 240mm.

107 · HUNTER'S HISTORY OF LONDON [1811]

Henry Hunter, a Perthshire divine, came to London in 1771 as minister to a Scots congregation at London Wall. He published lectures and sermons and, like many others of his cloth at that period, eked out a living by providing booksellers with translations and literary hack work. Such was his *History of London* of which Numbers first appeared in 1796 but which was unfinished at his death in 1802. John Stockdale, the topographical publisher whose premises in Piccadilly were described as a 'fashionable lounging place', then engaged other hacks to complete the work. But it was available in its entirety only by 1811, with all but two of the plates originally published between 1796 and 1799.

The History of London and its Environs: containing an Account of the Origin of the City;... its Rise and Progress to its Present State of Commercial Greatness: including an historical record of every important and interesting public event ... to the present period: also, a description of its antiquities, public buildings and establishments ... likewise An Account of all the Towns, Villages and Country, within twenty-five miles of London. By the late Rev. Henry Hunter, D.D. and other gentlemen. Embellished with Maps, Plans and Views. In Two Volumes. Vol.

I (II). London: Printed for John Stockdale, Piccadilly by S. Gosnell, Little Queen-Street, Holborn 1811.

Quarto, 290 × 240mm.   1811

COLLATION Vol. 1. Title-page; pp v–x, list of subscribers; list of plates (1 leaf); pp xiii–xix, preface; pp xxi–xxxii, contents; pp 1–924, History of London. Vol. 2. Title-page; pp iii–viii, contents; list of plates (1 leaf); pp 1–811, Description of the Country around London; index to vol. 2 (7pp).

Stockdale published in the same year, 1811, what seemed to be a new title by a different author, John Aikin, the literary physician, writer and editor of many books on subjects ranging from the classics to natural history. It is, however, identical with 'Hunter's' second volume both in text and illustrations, save for a preface dated 4 June 1811, a reset heading to the list of plates and this novel title-page:

The History of the Environs of London, containing an historical and topographical account of every thing that is interesting and curious, within twenty-five miles of the Metropolis. By John Aikin M.D. and other gentlemen. Embellished with Maps, Plans, and Views. London: Printed for John Stockdale, Piccadilly, 1811.

Stockdale was fortunate in persuading an able artist to assist the sales of his jejune compilation in the person of Edward Dayes. This capable draughtsman and charming water-colourist in the tinted drawing manner had made a name for himself by his large views of London squares, the fashionable parade in St James's Park, the interior of St Paul's during the thanksgiving service on St George's day 1789 and the trial of Warren Hastings in the previous year: all of them transmuted into popular aquatint engravings by Pollard, Jukes, Dodd and others. He exhibited landscapes, architecture and figure subjects at the Royal Academy from 1786 to 1804 and his style and technique were much admired and, for a time, closely imitated by his pupil Thomas Girtin and the youthful Turner. All the illustrations, save the maps, were drawn by him and transferred to copper by such competent engravers as Philip Audinet, James Neagle (who also made a large engraving of Dayes's drawing of the procession to the St George's day service) and the ubiquitous James Storer. Thirty of the original views, maps and plans were published between 6 August 1796 and 11 March 1799 and two further views and a map were added in 1810.

One illustration of an earlier date deserves special

mention because, although it is adumbrated in the single word 'London' in the list of plates in vol. 1, it is rarely to be found in its place opposite p 881. It is a long view of London from the steeple of St Mary, Islington, the work of a Dutch artist from Haarlem who migrated to England as a minister of religion; he is named in the list of subscribers as the Rev J. Swertner. A map has sometimes been substituted for this most interesting and unusual panorama. Among the subscribers are also the names of some book and printsellers, including Carrington Bowles, Simco and Vernor, Hood & Sharpe. Thomas Pennant's name is also there and it is quite usual to find nearly all the plates from this book illustrating grangerized copies of his work on London.

Unless otherwise stated (where the date occurs at the end) the publication-line throughout is 'Published (date) by I. (or J.) Stockdale(,) Piccadilly'.

VOL. 1

1 p 3 View of Temple Bar. E. Dayes del. Neagle sculp. Published Feby 23d 1799 ... 175 × 155/220 × 185mm. Looking E.

2 p 232 View of Somerset House. E. Dayes delt. G. Murray sculp. Pub. Feb 24, 1797 ... 155 × 242/195 × 270mm. From the river.

3 p 498 View of St James's Palace. E. Dayes delt. Neagle sculpt. Publish'd March 11th 1799 ... 175 × 155/220 × 180mm. Gatehouse.

4 p 502 View of the Pest Houses at Tothill Fields. E. Dayes delt. C. Pye sculp. Published Aug. 6 1796 ... 153 × 180/185 × 205mm.

5 p 504 (tm) Plan of the City of London before the Fire/Anno Domini 1666. Neele sculpt. 352 Strand. Published ... 1796. 200 × 240/220 × 250mm. Refs. A–Z,a–z,1–21. (*Darlington and Howgego* 15a)

6 p 505 (tm) London/after the Fire Anno Domini 1666. Neele sculpt. 352 Strand. Published ... 1796. 220 × 265/225 × 280mm. Adapted from Hollar's plan (*Hind* 10).

7 p 512 View of the Monument. Dayes delt. Audinet sculp. Publish'd Nov 1, 1796 ... 230 × 170/285 × 210mm. Looking down Fish Street Hill towards St Magnus and the Bridge.

8 p 592 View of the New Church Strand. E. Dayes delt. P. Audinet sculp. Pubd. August 1st, 1810 by John Stockdale, Piccadilly. 185 × 155/260 × 195mm. St Mary le Strand.

9 p 593 View of Buckingham House. E. Dayes delt. W. Knight sculpt. Published March 5th 1799 ... 155 × 240/200 × 270mm.

10 p 667 View of Westminster Bridge. E. Dayes delt. T.

Tagg sculpt. Pub. Feb. 10 1797 ... 155 × 240/205 × 273mm.

11 p 702 View of Blackfriars Bridge. Dayes delt. Tagg sculpt. London. Pub. Oct 5 1796 ... 150 × 240/195 × 270mm.

12 p 858 (Plan of the Wet Docks) S.I. Neale sculp. Strand. Published Decr 3d 1810 ... 175 × 253/220 × 270mm.

13 p 881 A View of the Cities of London and Westminster with the Suburbs and Circumjacent Country/showing the steeples of all the Churches and as many of the Public Buildings as are seen from the gallery of the Steeple of Islington which town appears in the foreground. Delineated, etched and done in Aquatinto by John Swertner. Published July 1st 1789 by John Swertner, No. 10 Nevils Court, Fetter Lane, London. 290 × 723/330 × 735mm. This was equipped with a separate 'Key' in a long strip 95 × 723/127 × 735mm intended for framing below the panorama; this is bound in as a frontispiece to the Guildhall Library copy of vol. 1. As a separate aquatint in BL Maps: *K. top.* 21.56 and *Crace* 32.154–5. Published in facsimile by the London Topographical Society, 1980.
(As an alternative, here or as frontispiece to vol. 1, may be found the following map: 'A New Plan of London, XXIX Miles in Circumference. Engraved by S.J. Neele. Printed Jany 2nd 1797 by J. Stockdale.' Four sheets, each 508 × 736mm. (*Darlington and Howgego* 213))

VOL. 2

14 p 1 (tl) A/Map/of/Middlesex. Published ... 1798. 390 × 510/410 × 530mm.

15 p 1 A New Map of the Country Round London. Engraved by S.J. Neele. Published October 5th 1796 ... Four sheets, each 380 × 457mm. (*Darlington and Howgego* 210)

16 p 8 (tl) A/Map/of/Surrey. Published ... 1798. 390 × 480/410 × 490mm.

17 p 12 (br) A/Map/of/Kent. J. Neele sculp. Strand. Publish'd March 1st 1797 ... 340 × 500/360 × 510mm.

18 p 20 (br) A/Map/of/Essex. S. Neele sculpt Strand. Published March 1st 1797 ... 415 × 520/435 × 530mm.

19 p 26 (tl) A/Map/of/Hartfordshire. Published September 20th 1798 ... 385 × 490/420 × 510mm.

20 p 30 (l.) Map/of the/River Thames. Engraved by S.I. Neele. 352 Strand. Published ... Octr 5th 1796. 850 × 230/830 × 250mm.

21 p 41 View of the Queens Walk/in the Green Park. E. Dayes delt. Storer sculpt. Pub. April 15, 1797 ... 175 × 260/215 × 275mm. Looking from the reservoir and fountain bordering on Piccadilly towards Spencer House.

22 p 44 View of London Bridge. E. Dayes delt. J. Dadley sculpt. Pub. Oct. 10 1798 ... 155 × 240/200 × 278mm.

23 p 46 View of the Tower. E. Dayes delt. P. Audinet

sculpt. Pub. Jan. 1, 1797 ... 155 × 240/200 × 275mm. From river.

24 p 56 Map of the Canals. Neele sculpt 352 Strand. Pubd Oct. 10th 1796 ... 215 × 265/230 × 280mm. (*Darlington and Howgego* 209)

25 p 67 View of Chelsea Hospital. E. Dayes delt. T. Tagg sculpt. Pub. Feb 10 1797 ... 165 × 240/210 × 270mm. From river. (*Longford* 24)

26 p 70 View of Hyde Park Corner. Dayes delt. Hall sculpt. Pubd. August 1st 1810 ... 150 × 177/230 × 255mm. Sepia aquatint view of the turnpike.

27 p 72 View of the Conduit at Bayswater. Dayes delt. Sparrow sculp. Published Oct. 5, 1796 ... 178 × 153/215 × 175mm.

28 p 86 View of London/from Highgate. E. Dayes delt. W. Knight sculpt. London. Pub. Nov. 6 1797 ... 175 × 265/215 × 285mm.

29 p 87 View of Friern House/the Seat of John Bacon Esqr. E. Dayes delt. W. Knight sculp. London. Pub. Nov. 6 1797 ... 175 × 260/210 × 270mm. At Barnet.

30 p 122 View of London/from Camberwell. E. Dayes delt. W. Knight sculp. Published March 31 1797 ... 180 × 265/210 × 290mm.

31 p 129 View of Mount Ararat/the Seat of Edward Clarke Esq. Dayes delt. W. Angus sculp. Pub. Dec 2, 1797 ... 177 × 265/220 × 280mm. At Wimbledon.

32 p 150 View of Guildford. Dayes delt. W. Knight sculp. Published July 25, 1798 ... 180 × 265/225 × 285mm.

33 p 158 View of Greenwich Hospital. E. Dayes delt. P. Audinet sculpt. Pub. Feb 1, 1798 ... 155 × 250/202 × 280mm. From river.

34 p 160 View of London from Greenwich Park. E. Dayes delt. W. Knight sculpt. London, Published March 2d 1799 ... 180 × 267/220 × 285mm.

35 p 427 View of Fairlop Oak. Dayes delt. Owen sculpt. Publish'd Oct 5 1796 ... 167 × 240/210 × 270mm. At Barking Side, Essex.

36 p 435 View of Claybury Hall/the Seat of James Hatch Esq. Dayes delt. W. Knight sculp. Published Jan: 25 1797 ... 153 × 245/190 × 275mm. Near Woodford, Essex.

108 · ACKERMANN'S WESTMINSTER ABBEY [1812]

The year after the completion of the *Microcosm of London* (no 99) the publisher Ackermann embarked upon another London book with a text by William Combe, joint author of the previous work, and illustrated in part by A.C. Pugin whose architectural drawings were so largely responsible for its success:

Proposals for publishing by Subscription, in Sixteen monthly Numbers, (each containing Four beautiful coloured Plates, and about 30 Pages of Letter-Press) forming two volumes ... Westminster Abbey and its Monuments, illustrated by sixty-six highly finished and coloured plates representing exterior and interior views ...

The first Number was published on the 1st of May, 1811; and to be succeeded by a Number every Month ... Subscriptions are received by R. Ackermann, at the Repository of Arts, 101 Strand ... Price, Fifteen Shillings each Number.

The general and decided approbation with which the Public has been pleased to honour the Microcosm of London ... has encouraged me to offer to its attention another publication, which will contain a complete history and copious description, illustrated by numerous engravings, of Westminter Abbey and its Monuments.

The first four plates were issued, as stated, on 1 May 1811 but the work eventually extended beyond the 16 Numbers promised: apparently to 20, as the last batch of engravings is dated 1 December 1812. In each of the intervening months publication of an average of four plates and 30 text pages was steadily maintained, giving a final total of 83 plates (including the portrait, plan and engraved title) and 606 pages. Plates are labelled (with slight discrepancies) 1–63, and also 'A' to 'I' and 'L' to 'U'. As those identified by letters are mostly dated in the second half of 1812 it may be they that were extra to the programme announced in the prospectus.

Although I have seen no set as issued in Numbers, stray wrappers have survived. They are unusually handsome, being decorated by a drawing credited to F. Mackenzie and etched by S. Mitan of the tomb of Aymer de Valance. Lettering inscribed beneath the cusped and crocketed arch and on the plinth reads: 'Westminster/Abbey/and the/Monuments/Forming a Companion and Continuation/of the Microcosm of London./Published at R. Ackermann's/Repository of Arts 101 Strand./In Sixteen Monthly Numbers. (br) No. (stamped in)'. The engraver has forgotten to reverse the numerous 'N's that occur, which gives the inscription a looking-glass appearance.

In his publication list for June 1813 Ackermann advertised the completed work: 'Westminster

Abbey. Illustrated by 82 highly finished and coloured plates. Printed on Elephant Quarto Paper in 2 volumes, price £15 in Boards'.

Upcott, in 1818, notes that there are copies of the work on Large Paper and that he has seen one at the publisher's printed on vellum with the original drawings inserted and sumptuously bound by Hering. This was no doubt the copy destined for the Prince Regent's brother, the Duke of Sussex, which came onto the market in 1926. The price asked was more than the Abbey could afford so George V intervened and the book came to the Dean and Chapter as a gift from the Royal Family; it is now permanently on display in the Abbey.

The subscribers' list includes a number of trade names, such as Boydell, Colnaghi, Lackington, Longman, Molteno and Henry Setchel, connoisseur Thomas Hope, architects George Repton and Philip Wyatt and, from Ackermann's close associates, Combe, Pugin and Rowlandson. As late as May 1847 Nattali of Covent Garden, in the *Monthly Literary Advertiser*, offered the book ('published at £16. 16s.') for £4 4s.

The History of the Abbey Church of St. Peter's Westminster, Its Antiquities and Monuments. In Two Volumes. Vol. I (II). London: Printed for R. Ackermann, 101, Strand, by L. Harrison and J.C. Leigh, 373 Strand. M.DCCC.XII.

Quarto, 345 × 275mm.   1812

COLLATION   Vol. 1. Half-title; title-page; dedication to Dean Vincent (1 leaf); pp vii–xiii, list of subscribers; pp xv–xviii, introduction; list of plates in both vols (2pp); pp 1–292, The History; pp 293–330, appendix; index (6pp). Vol. 2. Half-title; title-page; pp 1–275 (204–5 bis), The History continued; index (4pp).

Although the *Microcosm* itself illustrated few Gothic subjects the continuity of *Westminster Abbey* with its predecessor was to some extent guaranteed by the artists and engravers employed on both publications. A.C. Pugin made 17 drawings for the new work. J. Bluck, who was responsible for very nearly half of the *Microcosm* plates, engraved 49 of the aquatints while Thomas Sutherland, who contributed 18 aquatints to the earlier work, engraved 15 for this. Otherwise the artist most extensively involved, and who must have spent hundreds of hours sketching inside the Abbey, was Frederick Mackenzie, the architectural draughtsman who was closely associated with John Britton and a contribu-

tor to his *Architectural Antiquities* (no 97) and *Beauties of England and wales* (no 104); 33 of the plates, some including extra architectural details, were based on his drawings.

Others with lesser involvement were George Shepherd and Thomas Uwins (five plates each), who had both drawn for Ackermann's *Repository*, and William Johnstone White (eight plates) who had engraved for J.T. Smith's *Antiquities of Westminster* (no 98). The engraver F.C. Lewis (five plates), known for his aquatints after Girtin, had also contributed to *Antiquities of Westminster*, while Hamble (six plates), S. Mitan and Bluck were among Ackermann's regular engravers.

The unique subject of this sequel had an appeal obviously more limited than the great variety of the *Microcosm* and, in contrast to the feverish human activity added by Rowlandson to the earlier work, only a few well-behaved people are allowed to intrude upon the sublimity of the architectural scene. Nevertheless it is a book which should be highly rated both as an exhaustive pictorial record of the Abbey and for its individual architectural plates, beautifully composed and aquatinted with the addition of discreet colour just sufficient to suggest the cloistered intimacy of sunlight filtered by lofty windows onto fretted stone, wood and metal. Even the tombs, monuments and wall-plaques are separately numbered and identified by keyed references in the bm or tm of each plate and by means of the text: nos 1–307 (with slight discrepancies) with various alphabets in the Abbey itself and nos 1–13 in the cloisters. Architectural details are referred to the text by letters of the alphabet.

The main captions are in voided capitals bm. The plate numbers or plate letters are engraved tr but do not govern their arrangement which is established by the list preceding the text of the first volume. Publication-lines read throughout: 'Publish'd (date) for R. Ackermann's Westmr. Abbey at 101(,) Strand London.'

VOL. I

1 front. Plan of Westminster Abbey.... Decr. 1 1812. 250 × 295mm. pl.1. Uncoloured line-engraving.

2 (to face dedication) William Vincent D.D. Dean of Westminster. Painted by Wm. Owen, R.A. Engraved by Henry Meyer.... Feby 4, 1812. 235 × 188/305 × 250mm. Aquatint and stipple, uncoloured.

3 p 1 West Front/of Westminster Abbey. A. Pugin delt.

J. Bluck sculpt.... Augt 1 1811. 255 × 200/300 × 240mm. pl.2.

VOL. 2

4 front. Aymer de Valance Earl of Pembroke. A Pugin delt. S. Mitan sculp. 298 × 210/320 × 235mm. Serves as an engr title, with lettering below the arch and on the plinth as follows: 'Westminster/Abbey/and its/Monuments/–/Forming a Companion and Continuation/of the Microcosm of London./Published at R. Ackermann's/Repository of Arts 101 Strand./In Sixteen Monthly Numbers.' This etching of a thirteenth century tomb, with the credit 'F. Mackenzie' instead of 'A. Pugin' and uncoloured, was used for the pictorial wrappers of the Numbers as evident from the abbreviated 'No.' on the paving br.

5 p 1 North East View/of Westminster Abbey. F. Mackenzie delt. J. Bluck sculpt.... Octr 1, 1811. 210 × 275/235 × 300mm. pl.3.

6 p 6 Henry Seventh Chapel/Shewing two renovated Pinacles. A. Pugin delt. J. Bluck sculp.... May 1, 1811. 260 × 185/295 × 235mm. pl.4.

7 p 6 Fragments & Parts of the Exterior of Henry the Seventh Chapel/Westminster Abbey. F. Mackenzie delt. T. Sutherland sculp.... Octr 1, 1811. 197 × 270/240 × 300mm. pl.12.

8 p 9 Interior View of Westminster Abbey,/from the West Gate. F. Mackenzie delt. J. Bluck sculp.... June 1, 1811. 270 × 195/300 × 235mm. pl.5.

9 p 14 Interior View of Westminster Abbey./Looking towards the West Entrance. F. Mackenzie delt. J. Bluck sculp.... July 1, 1811. 267 × 198/300 × 240mm. pl.6.

10 p 14 West Windows./Westminster Abbey, J. White delt. J. Hamble sculp.... 1 July, 1812. 258 × 200/298 × 235mm. pl. C.

11 p 15 The Choir/Westminster Abbey. F. Mackenzie delt. J. Bluck sculp.... Novr 1, 1811. 270 × 200/300 × 240mm. pl.7.

12 p 18 Mosaic Pavement/Before the Altar, Westminster Abbey. White delt. et sculp.... 1 June, 1812. 200 × 223/235 × 295mm. pl.A.

13 p 24 North Window. W.J. White delt. F.C. Lewis sculp.... 1 April, 1812. 267 × 220/300 × 235mm. pl.D.

14 p 28 Fragments of Ceilings &c. &c. &c. F. Mackenzie delt. T. Sutherland sculp.... 1 Feb. 1812. 283 × 183/295 × 235mm. pl.15.

15 p 28 Fragments, Parts, Windows, Pillars &c. &c./Westminster Abbey. A. Pugin delt. T. Sutherland sculp.... 1 Decr 1811. 200 × 260/235 × 295mm. pl.14.

16 p 28 Fragments & Arches/in Westminster Abbey. A. Pugin delt. T. Sutherland sc.... Augt 1, 1811. 200 × 267/250 × 300mm. pl.11.

17 p 28 Fragments, Windows, Doors, &c./Westminster Abbey. A. Pugin delt. T. Sutherland Aquat.... Novr 1, 1811. 205 × 280/240 × 300mm. pl.13.

18 p 28 West Entrance/Turning to the right—Westminster Abbey. H. Villiers delt. J. Bluck sculp.... Decr 1, 1811. 195 × 267/240 × 300mm. pl.16. Monuments: 1 Captain James Cornwall, 2 Rt. Honble James Craggs, 3 Henry Wharton, 4 Wm. Congreve, 5 John Friend, M.D.

19 p 33 2nd & 3rd Window, South Aisle/Westminster Abbey. H. Villiers delt. J. Bluck sculp....: 1 Jany 1812. 270 × 195/300 × 235mm. pl.17. Monuments: 6 Admiral Tyrell, 7 Ld. Vist. Howe, 8 Sir L. Robinson Br., 9 Dr. Thos. Sprat, 10 Dr. Js. Wilcocks, 11 Dr. Z. Pearce, 12 Mrs. K. Bovey, 13 Dr. I. Thomas.

20 p 37 4th & 5th Window, South Aisle. A. Pugin delt. F.C. Lewis sculp.... 1 March, 1812. 270 × 195/300 × 235mm. pl.18. Monuments: 14 General Fleming, 15 General Wade, 16 Mrs. Ann Fielding, 17 John Smith, 18 Mrs. Harsnet, 19 Col. Davis, 20 Robt. Cannon.

21 p 40 6th & 7th Window/South Aisle. A. Pugin delt. J. Bluck sculpt.... 1 April, 1812. 273 × 203/295 × 235mm. pl.19. Monuments: 21 Sir I. Chardin Bart., 22 Major André,—Tablet on the Right Mrs. B. Radley—23 Sir P. Fairborne, 27 Sir C. Harbord & C. Cottrell, 28 Diana Temple.

22 p 45 Entrance into the Choir./West Entrance. T. Uwins delt. J. Bluck sculp.... March 1, 1812. 132 × 196,132 × 196/290 × 235mm. pl.20. Monuments: 29 Sir Isaac Newton, 30 Earl of Stanhope, 31 Sir Thos. Hardy, 32 John Conduitt Esqr.

23 p 50 8th & 9th Window,/South Aisle. G. Shepherd delt. F.C. Lewis sculpt.... 1 May, 1812. 265 × 207/295 × 235mm. pl.21. Monuments: 33 John Methuen Esqr., 34 Thos. Knipe, 35 G. Stepney Esq., 36 Dr. Is. Watts, 37 Martin Folkes, 38 Sir R. Bingham, 39 Major R. Creed, 40 G. Churchill Esqr., 41 Capt. Wm. Julius, 42 Genl. Strode.

24 p 58 10th Window & Entrance to the Cloister,/North (sic)Aisle. Thomson delt. J. Bluck sculp.... 1 July, 1812. 192 × 263/235 × 295mm. pl.22. Monuments: 43 Rear Adml. John Harrison, 45 Mrs. Ann Wemyss, 44 Sophia Fairholm, 46 Wm. Dalrymple, 47 Sir J. Burland Knt., 48 Sir Cloudesly Shovell, 49 Wm. Wragg Esqr.

25 p 63 South Aisle. G. Shepherd delt. T. Sutherland sculp.... Feb 1, 1812. 270 × 215/300 × 235mm. pl.23. Monuments: 50 Thos. Thynn Esqr., 51 Thos. Owen Esq., 52 Dame Grace Gethin, 53 Eliz. & Judith Freke, 54 Sir Thos. Richardson, 55 Genl. de Paoli, 56 Jas. Kendall Esqar., 57 Wm. Thynne Esqr.

26 p 66 West Side of Poets Corner. H. Villiers delt. J. Bluck sculp.... June 1, 1811. 198 × 268/240 × 300mm. pl.24. Monuments: 58 Stepn. Hales D.D., 59 Ed. Wetenhall M.D., 60 Sr. J. Pringle Bart., 61 Sr. Robt. Taylor Knt., 62 J. Ernest Grabbe, 63 David Garrick, 64 Wm. Outram D.D., 65 Isc. Barrow D.D.,

66 Thos. Triplett D.D., 67 Sr. Richd. Coke, 68 Isc. Casaubon, 69 Wm. Camden.

27 p 74 West Side of Poets Corner. H. Villiers delt. J. Bluck sculp.... Augt 1, 1811. 198 × 270/235 × 290mm. pl.25. Monuments: 70 Mrs. My. Hope, 71 Major Genl.Sr. A. Campbell, 72 G.F. Handel, 73 Rt.Hon. J.S. Mackenzie, 74 Sr. E. Atkyns, 75 Eliz. Dowr. Barons. Lechmere, 76 Wm. Anne Villettes, 77 Richard Busby D.D., 78 Bishop Duppa, 79 Mrs. Christn. Ker, 80 Robt. South D.D., 81 Sr.Js. Adols. Oughton.

28 p 89 Entrance into Poets Corner/Westminster Abbey. A. Pugin delt. J. Bluck Aquat.... Novr 1, 1811. 257 × 202/300 × 240mm. pl.26. Monuments: 82 John Dryden, 83 Martha Birch, 84 A. Cowley, 85 I. Roberts, 86 G. Chaucer, 87 I. Phillips, 88 B. Booth, 89 M. Drayton, 90 Ben Johnson, 91 S. Butler, 92 E. Spencer, 93 I. Milton, 94 Gray, 95 C. Anstey.

29 p 98 Poets Corner/Westminster Abbey. J. White delt. J. Bluck sculp.... 1 Sept, 1812. 285 × 222/300 × 245mm. pl.F. Monuments: 96 Thos. Shadwell, 97 Willm. Mason, 98 Mattw. Prior, 99 St. Evremond, 100 John Phillips—Abm. Cowley, A John Milton.

30 p 103 South View of Poets Corner. Pugin & H. Villiers delt. Bluck sculp.... May 1, 1811. 195 × 255/235 × 300mm. pl.27. Monuments: 101 Mrs. Prichard, 102 Shakespeare, 103 Thomson, 104 Rowe, 105 Gay, 106 Goldsmith, 107 Duke of Argyle, 108 Addison.

31 p 108 North View, across the Transept/from Poets Corner—Westminster Abbey. F. Mackenzie delt. J. Bluck sculp.... Sept 1, 1811. 270 × 195/300 × 240mm. pl.9.

32 p 109 Chapel of St. Benedict. F. Mackenzie delt. J. Bluck sculp.... July 1, 1811. 270 × 198/305 × 240mm. pl.28. Monuments: 107 T. Counts. of Hertford, 108 Dr. Gabriel Goodman, 109 George Sprat, 110 Archbp. Langham, 111 Earl and Counts. of Middlesex, 112 Dr. Wm. Bill.

33 p 112 East View of St. Edmunds Chapel. A. Pugin delt. J. Bluck sculp.... Sept 1, 1811. 200 × 265/240 × 300mm. pl.29. Monuments: 113 Countess of Stafford, 114 Earl of Stafford, 115 Nicholas Monck, 116 Dutchess of Suffolk, 117 Francis Hollis, 118 Lady K. Knollys, 119 Lady Jane Seymour, 120 Lady E. Russell, 121 Lord John Russell, 122 John of Eltham second Son of King Edward the Second, 123 Two children of Edward the Third.

34 p 116 West View of St. Edmunds Chapel. A. Pugin delt. J. Bluck sculp.... June 1, 1811. 197 × 255/235 × 290mm. pl.30. Monuments: 125 Sr. Barnard Brocas, 126 Sir Richard Pecksall, 127 Ed. 8th Earl of Shrewsbury, 128 Earl of Pembroke, 129 Ed. Lord Herbert, 130 Sr. Humphrey Bourchier, 131 Robt. de Waldeby, 132 Dutchess of Gloucester, 133 The Counts. of Stafford, 134 Henry Ferne.

35 p 119 St. Nicholas Chapel/Westminster Abbey. F. Mackenzie delt. J. Bluck sculp.... 1 Jany 1812. 260 × 195/300 × 235mm. pl.31. Monuments: 135 Lady Jane Clifford, 136 Anne Duchess of Somerset, 137 Sr. George & Lady Fane, 138 Lady Burleigh, 139 Lady Cecil, 140 Sr. Humphrey Staley, 141 Baron Carew, 142 Nicholas Bagenall.

36 p 121 West View of St. Nicholas Chapel. A. Pugin delt. J. Bluck sculp.... 1 July 1812. 267 × 202/300 × 250mm. pl.32. Monuments: 143 Sir George Villiers, 144 Wm. de Dudley, 145 Anna Sophia Harley, 146 The Marchs. of Winchester, 147 Lady Ross, 148 The Duchs. of Northumberland, 149 Phillipa, Daughter of Lord Mohun.

37 p 124 South East Area/Westminster Abbey. F. Mackenzie delt. J. Bluck sculp.... Jany 1, 1812. 195 × 270/240 × 300mm. pl.33. Monuments: 153 King Sebert, 154 Richard Tufton, 155 Sir Robt. Aiton, 156 Grave Stone of the Earl of Middlesex, 157 Children of Henry III and Edward I, 158 Sir Thos. Ingram.

38 p 128 Interior of King Sebert's Monument. Pugin & Mackenzie delt. J. Bluck sculp.... 1 Feby 1812. 205 × 275/240 × 300mm. pl.B.

39 p 134 Porch of Henry 7th Chapel. Thompson delt. J. Bluck sculp.... 1 Novr 1812. 200 × 260/250 × 295mm. pl. Q.

40 p 134 Henry the Seventh Chapel/Westminster Abbey. F. Mackenzie delt. J. Bluck sculp.... Octr. 1, 1811. 270 × 198/300 × 240mm. pl.8. Interior looking E.

41 p 134 Fragments of Henry the Seventh Chapel. Mackenzie delt. Sutherland sculp.... July 1, 1811. 197 × 270/240 × 300mm. pl.10. Lettered A–N.

42 p 136 Henry Seventh Monument:/Henry Seventh Chapel. ('162') Mackenzie delt. Bluck sculp.... May 1, 1811. 197 × 270/230 × 295mm. pl.35.

43 p 138 Interior of Henry the Seventh's Monument. ('162')/– Remaining Figures on the Screen of Henry the Seventh's Monument. F. Mackenzie delt. J. Bluck sculp.... 1 June 1812. 135 × 200,120 × 200/300 × 232mm. pl.H.

44 p 152 Lewis Stuart, Duke of Richmond/Henry the Seventh's Chapel. T. Uwins delt. J. Bluck sculp.... 1 Octr. 1812. 268 × 198/300 × 240mm. pl.36. Monument 163.

45 p 153 Henry 7th Chapel. T. Uwins delt. J. Bluck sculp.... 1 Decr 1812. 260 × 210/300 × 240mm. pl.R. Monument: 164 John Sheffield, Duke of Buckingham. A King's Scholar is seated in the choir stalls.

46 p 155 George Villiers, Duke of Buckingham. Mackenzie delt. Bluck & Hopwood sculp.... 1 Augt 1812. 275 × 200/300 × 245mm. pl.37.

47 p 157 East End of South Aisle. F. Mackenzie delt. J. Bluck sculp.... Octr. 1 1811. 270 × 198/300 × 240mm. pl.38. Monuments: 166 Lady Walpole, 167 Duke of Albemarle, 168 Countess of Richmond.

48 p 159 (Monuments) 169 Queen Elizabeth – 170 Mary Queen of Scots. Mackenzie delt. Sutherland Aquat.... May 1 1811. 195 × 132,195 × 134/235 × 295mm. pl.39.

49 p 163 North Aisle,/Henry 7th Chapel. Thompson delt. Sutherland sculp.... 1 Novr. 1812. 192 × 132,192 × 134/250 × 285mm. pl.40. Monuments: 171 Mary, Third Daughter of James 1, 172 Sophia, Fourth Daughter of James I, 173 Edward 5th and his Brothers, 174 Sir George Savile, 175 C.H. Montague.

50 p 170 West Side of the Chapel of St. Paul. Mackenzie delt. Bluck sculp.... Augt 1 1811. 270 × 198/295 × 233mm. pl.41. Monuments: 177 Sr. John Puckering Knt., 178 Sr. Js. Fullerton Knt., 179, Sir Thos. Bromley Knt.

51 p 172 East Side of the Chapel of St.Paul/from an elevated situation. F. Mackenzie delt. J. Bluck Aquat.... July 1, 1811. 205 × 270/235 × 295mm. pl.40. Monuments: 180 Lord Dudley Carleton Viscount of Dorchester, 181 Frances Countess of Sussex, 182 Lady Anne Cottington, 183 Francis Lord Cottington, 184 Lewis Robert Lord Bourchier & his Lady, 185 Sir Giles Dawbeney & his Lady, 186 Lieut.General Sr. Hy. Belasyse.

52 p 176 West Side of St. Erasmus Chapel. A. Pugin delt. J. Bluck sculp.... March 1, 1812. 268 × 208/295 × 235mm. pl.43. Monuments: 186 George Fascet, 187 Mary Kendal, 188 Thos. Vaughan, 189 Ed. Popham.

53 p 179 East Side of St. Erasmus's Chapel. F. Mackenzie delt. J. Bluck sculp.... Feby 1 1812. 263 × 192/292 × 233mm. pl.44. Monuments: 190 Thos. Carey, 191 Hugh de Bohun, 192 Henry Carey, 193 Thos. Cecil Earl of Exeter, 194 William of Colchester, 195 Thos. Ruthall.

54 p 183 Islip Chapel. F. Mackenzie delt. J. Bluck sculp.... 1 Decr 1812. 218 × 270/260 × 300mm. pl.U. Monument: 196 Sir C. Hatton.

55 The Skreen of Abbot Islip's Chapel & the Entrance to the Chapel of St. Erasmus. F. Mackenzie delt. J. Bluck sculp.... 1 Decr. 1812. 210 × 265/250 × 298mm. pl.P. Monuments: A Wm. Barnard, Bishop of Derry, B Juliana Crewe, C Lady Jane Crewe.

56 p 187 Chapel of St. Andrew./ – Chapel of St. John the Evangelist. A. Pugin delt. J. Bluck sculp.... 1 Novr 1812. 198 × 134,198 × 147/250 × 310mm. pl.45. Monuments: Earl & Countess of Mountrath, 197 Admiral Totty, 198 Countess of Kerry, A Lord & Lady Norris from the North Side, 199 Sir Geo. Pocock, 200 Sir Geo. Holles, 201 Sir Francis Vere, B Captn Cooke.

57 p 193 Chapel of St. John the Evangelist. Mackenzie delt. Lewis sculp.... 1 Decr 1812. 230 × 272/250 × 300mm. pl.46. Monuments: 202 The Earl and Counts. of Montrath, 203 Susa. Jane Davidson, 204 Lord & Lady Norris, 205 Dutchess of Somerset, 206 Lady Nightingale.

58 p 194 North Area. T. Uwins delt. J. Bluck sculp.... 1 Septr. 1812. 265 × 197/300 × 250mm. pl.47. Monuments: 207 General Wolfe, 208 Lt. Genl. Villettes, 209 Genl. Stuart, 210 B.J. Forbes and R.G. Forbes, 211 R. Kempenfelt, A Sir J.A. Oughton, B Bishop Duppa.

59 p 196 North East Area. F. Mackenzie delt. J. Bluck sculp.... 1 Augt 1812. 268 × 200/300 × 250mm. pl.N. Monuments: 212 K. Henry the 3rd, A Lady Anne Cottington, B Lord Bourchier, C Henry the 5th.

60 p 198 North Aisle. H. Villiers delt. Bluck sculp.... June 1 1811. 265 × 198/295 × 230mm. pl.49. Monuments: 213 Admiral Holmes, 214 Wm. Pulteney Earl of Bath, 215 Lord Ligonier, 216 Captain Edward Cooke.

61 p 200 (Monument) 218 Edmund Crouchback. A Part of the Screen of Edd. the Confesor. F. Mackenzie delt. T. Sutherland sculpt.... Septr 1, 1811. 275 × 195/300 × 240mm. pl.50.

62 p 201 (Monuments) 119 Queen Phillipa – 120 Queen Eleanor. F. Mackenzie delt. T. Sutherland sculpt.... 1 June 1812. 122 × 195,125 × 195/290 × 230mm. pl.51.

63 p 202 Edward the Confessor's Chapel. F. Mackenzie delt. J. Bluck sculp.... 1 Novr. 1812. 142 × 210,105 × 210/295 × 250mm. pl.L. Monuments: 221 De la Tour Gouvernett, 222 Edward 1st Longshanks, 223 Elizh. Tudor, 224 Margaret, A John Waltham Bishop of Salisbury.

64 p 204* Richard the Second – Edward the Third. F. Mackenzie delt. J. Bluck sculp.... 1st Decr 1811. 140 × 180, 150 × 180/300 × 230mm. pl.34.

65 p 207 The Screen of Edward the Confessor. F. Mackenzie delt. G. Lewis sculpt.... March 1 1812. 195 × 267/240 × 300mm. pl.53.

66 p 207 Edward the Confessor's Monument/Edward the Confessor's Chapel. A. Pugin delt. J. Bluck sculp.... May 1 1812. 268 × 205/298 × 238mm. pl.M. Monument: A Henry the Third.

67 p 208 Henry the Fifth Chapel. F. Mackenzie delt. J. Bluck sculp.... June 1 1811. 265 × 195/295 × 230mm. pl.52. Monument 226.

68 p 210 Screen over the Chantry of Henry the Vth. F. Mackenzie delt. Bluck sculp.... 1 July 1812. 205 × 260/250 × 300mm. pl.O.

69 p 211 East Windows. W.J. White delt. F.C. Lewis sculp.... May 1 1812. 208 × 260/235 × 295mm. pl.E.

70 p 213 Aveline, First Wife of Edmund Crouchback, Earl of Lancaster/on the North Side of the Altar in Westminster Abbey. F. Mackenzie delt. J. Bluck sculp.... 1 April 1812. 210 × 253/235 × 275mm. pl.G.

71 p 218 North Cross. A. Pugin delt. J. Hamble sculp.... 1 Sepr. 1812. 195 × 270/250 × 300mm. pl.54. Monuments: 229 Sir Peter Warren, 230 Hannah Vincent, 231 Adl. Storr, 232 Sir Gilbert Lort, 233 Grace Scott, A Clement Saunders Esq., 248 Percy Kirk Esq., 249 Ld. Beauclerk, 250 John Warren D.D., 251 Sir John Balchen Knt., 252 Genl. Guest.

72 p 220 North Entrance/Westminster Abbey. Mackenzie & H. Villiers delt. Bluck & Williamson sculp.... Nov 1 1811. 200 × 263/240 × 300mm. pl.55. Monuments: 234 Capts. Manners, Blair & Bayne, 235 Earl of Chatham, 236 Sr. Chas. Wager, 237 Adml. Vernon, 238 John Holles, Duke of Newcastle, 239 Duke & Dutchs. of Newcastle.

73 p 221 Lord Chatham. H. Villiers delt. Williamson & Sutherland sculp.... 1 Septr 1812. 280 × 200/300 × 255mm. pl.I.

74 p 221 (Monuments) Duke of Argyle – 240 Lord Mansfield. H. Villiers delt. Williamson & Sutherland sculp.... 1 Decr 1811. 200 × 130,200 × 130/240 × 300mm. pl.56.

75 p 226 North Transept. A. Pugin delt. Hamble sculp.... 1 Novr 1812. 255 × 210/300 × 255mm. pl.57. Monuments: 241 Adml. Charles Watson, 242 Sir Willm. Sanderson, 243 Earl of Halifax, 244 Sir Clifford Wintringham, 245 Jonas Hanway, 246 Genl. Hope, 247 Sir Eyre Coote.

76 p 237 (Wall tablets) 253 Richd. Kane, 254 Dr. Saml. Bradford, 255 Dr. Hugh Boulter, 256 Philip de Saumarez Esqr, 257 John Blow, 258 Wm. Croft, 259 Temple West Esq, 260 Richd. Le Neve Esq., 261 Sir Edmund Prideaux, 262 Chs. Williams, 263 Dr. Peter Heylin, 264 Lord Dunbar. G. Shepherd delt. Josh. Hamble sculp.... 1 June 1812. 212 × 260/245 × 300mm. pl.58.

77 p 241 North Aisle. G. Shepherd delt. T. Sutherland sculp.... 1 Aug 1812. 265 × 215/300 × 250mm. pl.59. Monuments: 268 Sir Thos. Duppa, 269 Dame Elizh. Carteret, 270 Dr. S. Arnold, 271 Almericus De Courcy, 272 H. Purcell Esqr., 273 Hugh Chamberlen, 274 Sir Thos. Heskett, 275 Dame Mary James.

78 p 245 4th & 5th Windows/North Aisle. G. Shepherd delt. F.C. Lewis sculp.... 1 May 1812. 260 × 215/300 × 240mm. pl.60. Monuments: 275 Thos. Livingston, 276 Ed. De Cartert, 277 Philip Carteret, 278 Jas Stewart Denham Bart, 279 Henry Priestman, 280 John Baker Esqr.

79 p 247 6th,7th & 8th Windows, North Aisle. W.J. White del. J. Hamble sculp.... 1 Octr 1812. 230 × 295/260 × 300mm. pl.61. Monuments: 281 R. Mead, 282 Rt. and Rd. Cholmondeley, 283 Ed. Mansell, 284 G. Thornburgh, 285 Ed. Herbert, 286 Ann Whytell, 287 Gideon Loten, 288 Thos. Mansell and Wm. Morgan, 289 Jane Hill, 290 Mary Beaufoy, 291 Josiah and John Twysden, 292 Thos. Banks, 293 Wm. Levintz, 294 Robt. Killigrew, 295 Js. Bringfield, 296 H. Twisden.

80 p 254 9th,10th & 11th Windows, North Aisle. J. White delt. J. Bluck sculp.... Octr. 1 1812. 200 × 262/250 × 295mm. pl.62. Monuments: 297 Capts. Hervey & Hutt, 298 Fred Lake, 299 Jno. Woodward, 300 Martha Price, 301 Anne Counts. of Clanricard, 302 James Egerton, 304 Genl. Lawrence, 305 Penelope Egerton, 306 Sir Godfrey Kneller, 307 Wm. Horneck Esqr.

81 p 256 Capt. Montague ('303') West Entrance – Addison, Poets Corner. T. Uwins delt. Hopwood & Hamble sculp.... Augt 1812. 200 × 130,200 × 130/250 × 300mm. pl.63. Monuments: A Handel, B Lechmore, C Hales, D Outram.

82 p 260 South East Angle of the Cloisters. Thompson delt. Hamble sculp.... 1 Decr 1812. 200 × 265/245 × 295mm. pl.T.

83 p 263 Monuments/in the Cloister. J. White delt. T. Sutherland sculp.... 1 Octr 1812. 212 × 270/250 × 300mm. pl.S. Monuments: 1 Rebecca Broughton, 2 Daniel Pulteney, 3 James Mason, 4 Mary Peters 1668, 5 Anne Winchcombe, 6 George Walsh Esq. 1747, 7 Edwd Tufnel Archt, 8 Ann Palmer, 9 Wm. Woollet Engr., 10 Revd. James Field, 11 Christr. Chapman & Daughter, 12 Elizh. Abrahal, 13 Bonnell Thornton.

109 · ANCIENT RELIQUES*
[1812–13]

The *Antiquarian and Topographical Cabinet* (no 118), completed in 1811, introduced the public to the idea of topographical illustrations in miniature which seemed at the time a novelty but were really in continuation of the tradition of Hollar's little etched views from Islington and J.B. Chatelain's charming mid-century views of suburban churches. It must have scored a success since the group of booksellers who had published it immediately looked round for a successor and brought out the two-volume *Ancient Reliques* in 1812–13. Once again Storer and Greig were brought in as engravers although only Storer contributed to the London views, included in the second volume and listed below. The *Cabinet* formula was followed in that unnumbered plates were issued with unpaginated letterpress and that a check-list of the views was incorporated in each volume.

Ancient Reliques; or, Delineations of Monastic, Castellated, & Domestic Architecture, and other interesting subjects; with Historical and Descriptive Sketches. (epigraph) Volume II. London: Published for the Proprietors by W. Clarke, New Bond Street; J. Carpenter, Old Bond Street; C. Chapple, Pall Mall; J.M. Richardson, Cornhill;

and Sherwood, Neely, and Jones, Paternoster Row. 1813.
Coe, Printer, 10 Little Carter Lane, London.

Duodecimo, 160 × 90mm.   1813

COLLATION   Half-title; title-page; index (2pp); list of
plates (2pp); sigs A-I, Ancient Reliques.

1 sig C The Manor House, Canonbury Middlesex.
Engraved & Published by J. Storer from a drawing by
H. Gastineau. Augt 1 1812. 100 × 75/150 × 90mm.

2 sig F The Hall of Christ's Hospital. Drawn by
Whichelo. Engd. by Woolnoth. Published Novr 1,
1812. 75 × 105/90 × 150mm.

3 sig F Part of the Grey Friars Monastery, or Christ's
Hospital London. Drawn by Whichelo. Engd. by
Lambert. Published Novr 1, 1812. 73 × 105/95 ×
150mm.

4 sig F The Writing School &c Christs Hospital. Drawn
& Engd. by J. Lambert. Published Novr. 1, 1812. 72 ×
105/95 × 150mm.

(6pp of text)

5 sig F Physicians College of London. Drawn &
Engraved by S. Tyrrell. Publish'd Nov. 1, 1812. 105 ×
70/150 × 90mm.

(2pp of text)

6 sig F St Bartholomew's Hospital London. Drawn &
Engrav'd by H. Summons. Publish'd Dec. 1, 1812. 70
× 100/90 × 150mm.

(2pp of text)

7 sig G The Temple Hall, London. Drawn & Engd. by
S. Tyrrell. Published Dec. 1, 1812. 70 × 100/90 ×
150mm. The Middle Temple.

8 sig G Entrance to the Temple Church, London.
Drawn & Engd. by S. Tyrrell. Published Dec. 1, 1812.
70 × 100/90 × 150mm.

9 sig G Part of the Temple Church, London. Drawn &
Engd. by. S. Tyrrell. Published Dec. 1, 1812. 70 ×
100/90 × 150mm.

(2pp of text)

110 · MANNSKIRSCH'S VIEWS OF
PARKS AND GARDENS [1813]

The Abbey catalogue (216) records a reissue of
these views, bound in an album without text or
title-page but with a title on the front board:

*Coloured Views of Parks and Gardens by Manns-
kirsch* (Ackermann, 1813). These aquatints bear
the credits 'F.I. Mannskirsch Delin.' and 'H. Schutz
sculp.' and the publication-line 'London, Published
Mar 1 1813 at Ackermann's Gallery, No 96, Strand';
they are individually numbered 1 to 8. In an earlier
issue, on paper watermarked '1794', publication-
lines dated January and March 1798 are found with
either of Ackermann's addresses, 96 or 101 Strand,
and there is also an intermediate issue dated 'Augst
1st, 1809'.

Franz Josef Mannskirsch, son of a Cologne artist,
was born at Ehrenbreitstein and practised in
Cologne as a landscape and portrait painter. In 1793
he came to London and from 1797 was employed by
Ackermann, whose address he used until 1803. He
exhibited paintings at the Royal Academy and was
also a lithographer and engraver, producing four
plates in the chalk manner of views in South Wales
and a drawing-book for Ackermann's containing
groups of staffage suitable for incorporating picturesquely into landscapes. He eventually returned
to the Continent and in 1822 obtained a teaching
post in the art school in Danzig. Heinrich Josef
Schüz, or Schütz, who was both draughtsman and
aquatint engraver, came from Frankfurt-am-Main
and worked for Ackermann between 1792 and 1797,
engraving for him not only Mannskirsch's *Parks* but
also the more famous plates of London turnpikes
from drawings by Rowlandson and Dagaty (no 78).

1 A distant Front View of the Palace in Kensington
Gardens. 310 × 420/365 × 440mm.

2 A Side View of the Palace in Kensington Gardens. 310
× 420/360 × 440mm.

3 A View in St. James's Park of the Horse Guards & St.
Pauls/ Taken from Buckingham House. 320 × 420/360
× 440mm.

4 A View in St. James's Park of Buckingham House/
Taken from the Parade. 320 × 420/370 × 440mm.

5 A View in the Gardens of Hampton Court Palace/
Taken from the Bridge over the Canal. Feb. 1 1813.
315 × 420/365 × 445mm.

6 A View of Hampton Court Palace/Taken in the
Gardens. 310 × 420/360 × 440mm.

7 A View in Kew Gardens of the Alhambra & Pagoda.
310 × 415/360 × 440mm.

8 A View in Kew Gardens of the Queen's Lodge/Taken
from the Temple of Victory. 315 × 420/365 × 440mm.

111 · PENNANT'S HISTORY AND ANTIQUITIES OF LONDON [1813]

This is a very slightly modified text of Thomas Pennant's book entitled *Of London* or *Some Account of London* (no 67) and was published by J. Coxhead with this new title in the same year as Faulder's fifth (octavo) edition of the original text which retained the old title. It is not included with the other editions because although like them it is illustrated Coxhead did not, or could not, use existing plates made for the quarto or two octavo editions and had to seek elsewhere some ready-made substitutes. He found them in Lambert's *History and Survey of London* (no 96) issued seven years previously. His printer was B. McMillan who made use of the same modifications in text and title for an unillustrated quarto published by the Pall Mall bookseller Edward Jeffery in 1814 and also issued with an 'open' title-page reverting to the original title, but dateless and without imprint other than 'Printed for the Illustrator'.

Wishing to make further use of the plates he had purchased Coxhead did not scruple further to tamper with text and title which now became *The Antiquities of London*; this made further use of the Lambert plates and bound them opposite descriptive gobbets anthologized from Pennant, Maitland's *History* (no 38) and Malcolm's *Londinium Redivivum* (no 83) and was published in 1814 in boards at 15 shillings. A further edition in 1818 was launched with the claim that 2000 copies had been sold in 20 months.

The History and Antiquities of London. By Thomas Pennant, Esq. A New Edition in two volumes, illustrated with forty-one plates. Vol. I (II). London: Printed for J. Coxhead, Holywell-Street, Strand, by B. McMillan, Bow-Street, Covent Garden, 1813.

Octavo, 215 × 135mm.   1813

COLLATION Vol. 1. Title-page; pp iii–vi, Pennant's advertisement to the 1st ed dated from Downing 1 March 1790; pp 1–383, History and Antiquities. Vol. 2. pp 1–289, History and Antiquities continued; pp 291–302, appendix; pp 303–25, index; directions to binder (2pp).

The Antiquities of London: comprising views and historical descriptions of its principal buildings; also anecdotes of eminent persons connected therewith, chiefly from the works of Thomas Pennant, Esq. illustrated with fifty-five plates. London: Printed for J. Coxhead, 53 Holywell-Street, Strand; by B. McMillan, Bow-Street, Covent-Garden, 1814. Price Fifteen Shillings, Boards.

Octavo, 205 × 125mm.   1814

COLLATION Title-page; dedication to Benjamin Coxhead of Bermondsey by Joseph Coxhead dated 15 November 1813 (1 leaf); pp 1–98, Antiquities; pp 99–100, index.

The Antiquities of London: comprising views and historical descriptions of its principal buildings; also anecdotes of eminent persons connected therewith, chiefly from the works of Thomas Pennant, Esq. Second Edition Illustrated with fifty plates. London: Printed for J. Coxhead 249, High Holborn, 1818. Price 12s. Boards.

Octavo, 230 × 140mm.   1818

COLLATION Title-page; To the Public (1 leaf); pp 1–102, Antiquities; pp 103–4, index.

When Coxhead took over the plates from Lambert's publishers he left the captions and credits standing but burnished out the credit-lines and publication-lines which he replaced uniformly with 'Published (Pub.) by J. Coxhead, Holywell Street, Strand, Jany 1st, 1813.' The plates themselves were never numbered but the 41 included in the 1813 *History and Antiquities* are assigned by the checklist their correct placings vis-à-vis the text. For the 1814 *Antiquities* 13 more were added bringing the total to 54 and not, as the title-page claims, 55; the text page numbers near which they should be bound are indicated in the list although both in this edition and that of 1818 the plates are sometimes gathered at the end of the text. Their source in Lambert is abbreviated *LAM* followed by volume and page number. Only two Lambert illustrations were rejected, the map frontispiece to vol.4 and the portrait of William Caxton in the same volume.

Plates in The History and Antiquities (1813)

VOL. 1

1 front. Westminster Hall. Green del. Owen sc. 90 × 148/125 × 180mm. 1814 ed p 73. *LAM* 3,440.

2 p 1 Plan of the City of London in the time of Queen Elizabeth. 110 × 185/120 × 200mm. 1814 ed p 1. *LAM* 2,front.

3 p 23 Fitzalwine/First Lord Mayor. H.R. Cook sculp. 150 × 90/185 × 115mm. 1814 ed p 8. *LAM* 1,71.

4 p 29 Lambeth Palace. 90 × 145/130 × 200mm. 1814 ed p 84. *LAM* 4,146.

5 p 87 Plan of the City of Westminster in the Time of Queen Elizabeth. Woodthorpe sc. 110 × 195/125 × 205mm. 1814 ed p 70. *LAM* 3,front.

6 p 89 Abbey Church of St Peter, Westminster. 90 × 145/125 × 200mm. 1814 ed p 71. *LAM* 3,375.

7 p 132 The Painted Chamber Westminster. Prattent del et sc. 90 × 145/125 × 205mm. 1814 ed p 74. *LAM* 3,452.

8 p 142 A Gate belonging to the Old Palace of Whitehall. Shirt sc. 90 × 140/125 × 200mm. 1814 ed p 78. *LAM* 3,490.

9 p 162 St James's Palace. Birrell del. et sc. 100 × 150/125 × 200mm. 1814 ed p 83. *LAM* 3,495.

10 p 215 Somerset House. W. Poole del. et sc. 92 × 150/125 × 200mm. 1814 ed p 69. *LAM* 3,446.

11 p 227 Temple Bar. Busby del. et sc. 80 × 130/125 × 200mm. 1814 ed p 67. *LAM* 3,431.

12 p 263 Ely Place in its former state. 95 × 150/120 × 200mm. 1814 ed p 53. *LAM* 3,139.

13 p 274 Sir Wm. Walworth. Cook sc. 148 × 90/180 × 120mm. 1814 ed p 9. *LAM* 1,274.

14 p 276 Remains of the Cloysters of Bartholomew the Great Priory. Prattent del. J. Simpkins sc. 130 × 95/190 × 120mm. 1814 ed p 49. *LAM* 2,151.

15 p 277 Principal Gate of St Bartholomews Hospital. Prattent del. Owen sc. 140 × 90/190 × 125mm. 1814 ed p 50. *LAM* 3,146.

16 p 289 Charter House Great Hall. Prattent del. Owen sc. 95 × 145/125 × 175mm. 1814 ed p 44. *LAM* 4,55.

17 p 300 St John's Gate. Prattent del. E. Shirt sc. 90 × 145/125 × 195mm. 1814 ed p 45. *LAM* 4,46.

18 p 305 Oliver Cromwell's House, Clerkenwell Close. A. Birrell sculp. 90 × 148/125 × 200mm. 1814 ed p 46. *LAM* 4,45.

19 p 306 Sir Hugh Middleton. Freeman sc. 150 × 90/180 × 120mm. 1814 ed p 48. *LAM* 4,387.

20 p 335 Newgate. Prattent del. Birrell sc. 85 × 145/125 × 200mm. 1814 ed p 51. *LAM* 2,371.

21 p 337 Giltspur Street, Compter. Prattent del. Owen sc. 88 × 142/125 × 175mm. 1814 ed p 52. *LAM* 3,144.

22 p 343 Shaftsbury House, Aldersgate Street. Prattent del. J. Simpkins sc. 90 × 145/125 × 175mm. 1814 ed p 43. *LAM* 3,11.

23 p 367 Figures over the Gateway of Bethlehem Hospital. Birrell sc. 95 × 160/125 × 200mm. 1814 ed p 24; not in 1818 ed. *LAM* 2,539.

24 p 381 House once Sr Paul Pindar's, Bishopsgate Street. Prattent del. Owen sc. 140 × 88/180 × 120mm. 1814 ed p 21. *LAM* 2,408.

VOL. 2

25 front. Remains of St Michaels Chapel, Aldgate. Prattent del. Owen sc. 90 × 145/125 × 190mm. 1814 ed p 16. *LAM* 2,393.

26 p 17 The Tower. W. Poole del. et sc. 108 × 180/130 × 200mm. 1814 ed p 14. *LAM* 4,90.

27 p 64 Custom House. Prattent del. Owen sc. 87 × 145/110 × 188mm. 1814 ed p 17. *LAM* 2,385.

28 p 67 The Trinity House, Tower Hill. Prattent del. Birrele sc. 90 × 145/125 × 200mm. 1814 ed p 95. *LAM* 4,125.

29 p 86 View of Part of London as it appeared in the Great Fire, 1666. Prattent del. Owen sc. 90 × 158/123 × 175mm. 1814 ed p 10. *LAM* 2,89.

30 p 87 The Monument. Drawn & Engraved by W. Poole. 150 × 90/190 × 120mm. 1814 ed p 11; not in 1818 ed. *LAM* 2,468.

31 p 104 Sr. Richd Whittington. Cook sc. 148 × 90/175 × 120mm. 1814 ed p 97. *LAM* 1,332.

32 p 105 Whittington's House: Hart Street, Crutched Friars. Prattent del. Birrel sc. 1814 ed p 96. *LAM* 2,388.

33 p 176 St Pauls. J. Shirt sc. 95 × 150/125 × 200mm. 1814 ed p 37. *LAM* 3,39.

34 p 200 Guildhall. Prattent del. E. Shirt sc. 90 × 143/125 × 200mm. 1814 ed p 32. *LAM* 2,521.

35 p 216 Mercers Hall Poultry. Prattent del. Birrell sc. 147 × 95/200 × 125mm. 1814 ed p 34. *LAM* 2,519.

36 p 222 The Mansion House. Prattent del. Birrell sc. 90 × 145/120 × 198mm. 1814 ed p 31; not in 1818 ed. *LAM* 2,145.

37 p 227 Sir Thos Gresham. Mackenzie sculp. 150 × 90/170 × 112mm. 1814 ed p 28. *LAM* 4,380.

38 p 231 The East India House in its former state. 90 × 145/125 × 200mm. 1814 ed p 96. *LAM* 2,404.

39 p 232 The East India House. Prattent del. Shirt sc. 90 × 150/125 × 200mm. 1814 ed p 96. *LAM* 2,404.

40 p 237 The Bank. Poole del. et sc. 93 × 150/120 × 190mm. 1814 ed p 29. *LAM* 2,131. (*Bank of England* 38)

41 p 262 Crosby House, Bishopsgate Street. Prattent del. E. Shirt sc. 95 × 150/125 × 200mm. 1814 ed p 20. *LAM* 2,409. (*Longford* 430)

Extra plates in The Antiquities but not in The History and Antiquities

42 p 4 Ald-gate – Bishops-gate. 115 × 170mm pl. mark. *LAM* 2,365.

43 p 5 Moore Gate – Cripple Gate. 115 × 170mm pl. mark. *LAM* 2,367.

44 p 6 Aldersgate – Newgate. 115 × 170mm pl. mark. *LAM* 2,370.

45 p 7 Lud-Gate – Bridge-Gate. 120 × 190mm pl. mark. *LAM* 2,374.

46 p 12 London Bridge before and since the Houses were

pulled down. Prattent del. Birrell sc. 90 × 160/125 × 200mm. *LAM* 3,192.

47 p 27 A Bird's Eye View of the Royal Exchange. Prattent del. Birrel sc. 100 × 135/125 × 193mm. *LAM* 3,137.

48 p 33 Richard Clark Esq./Chamberlain of London. M. Brown pinxt. K. Mackenzie sculp. 175 × 100/200 × 125mm. *LAM* 1,front.

49 p 35 The West View of St Paul's Cathedral/before the Fire of London. 93 × 140/125 × 200mm. *LAM* 3,47.

50 p 47 Hicks Hall, Clerkenwell. Prattent del. Poole sc. 98 × 145/125 × 200mm. *LAM* 2,259.

51 p 56 Bangor House Shoe Lane. Prattent del. Shirt sc. 145 × 90/200 × 120mm. *LAM* 3,139.

52 p 60 Westminster Bridge – Blackfriars Bridge. Prattent del. Owen sc. 40 × 145,42 × 145/125 × 170mm. *LAM* 3,199.

53 p 77 New Court House, Westminster. Poole sc. 90 × 150/125 × 200mm. Not in 1818 ed. *LAM* 3,438.

54 p 98 General Monks House, Hanover Square, Grub Street. Prattent del. Birrell sc. 90 × 145/125 × 190mm. *LAM* 3,4.

112 · BLAGDON'S HISTORICAL MEMENTO [1814]

The elaborate stage sets in the Parks for the Peace Celebrations of 1814 are a favourite subject for London illustrators and this collection of aquatints, coloured by hand, is the finest memento of the occasion, the parallel series issued (without text or title-page) by Thomas Palser of Lambeth being inferior to them in every respect. Edward Orme the publisher, at whose shop in Bond Street were sold 'books of instruction in every branch of drawing, colours, drawing books, and every requisite used in drawing', also patented a method of treating prints so that they became translucent and could be illuminated from the back, described in *An Essay on Transparent Prints* (1807). He specialized in souvenirs of naval, military and state occasions and in 1806 published a *Graphic History* (no 220) of the life of Nelson showing his funeral with aquatints of the river processions (engraved by J. Clark and H. Merke) and the interment in St Paul's Cathedral

(engraved by Clark and Hamble). As the author of the text, the journalist F.W. Blagdon, puts it:

Mr. Edward Orme has not been inactive in the good cause; he has omitted no opportunity of bringing forward to public admiration by the graphic art, the principal events in which our arms have triumphed both by sea and land; publishing at various periods engravings of those great exploits most calculated to impress the mind with correct ideas of the arduous struggles which have immortalised the British name.

The Nelson engraver, John Heaviside Clark, whom he also employed to draw the Peace Celebrations was the author of a book on landscape painting in water-colour and engraved some of the aquatint illustrations to Howitt's *British Field Sports*, both published by Orme in 1807. He was soon to be generally known as 'Waterloo Clark' because immediately after the battle of that name he was on the spot, making sketches for a set of aquatints, engraved by M. Dubourg and published in 1816, again by Orme. Dubourg, besides engraving panoramic battle scenes, produced several outsize aquatints of bridges: in 1811 from Rennie's designs for the future Waterloo Bridge (BL Maps: *K. top.* 22.40a; 430 × 810mm), in 1819 of J. Walker's Vauxhall Bridge (*Crace* 4.15, 315 × 890mm) and in 1825 of the new London Bridge (*Crace* Supplement 7; 120 × 610mm).

The six aquatints show the parks decorated with temporary bridges, pavilions and pagodas and enlivened with firework displays, balloon ascents and a reconstruction on the Serpentine of the battles between the English and French fleets. They are unnumbered and unlisted and the order in which they are bound varies from copy to copy; that of the British Library (Royal Library, 808.m.7) copy has been adopted. Each bears the credits 'J.H. Clark Del. M. Dubourg Sculpt.' and publication-line 'Published & Sold Augt 12th 1814 by Edwd Orme, Publisher to His Majesty and H.R.H. the Prince Regent, Bond Street (corner of Brook Str.)London'. Captions are in hatched capitals, sub-captions in copperplate.

An Historical Memento representing the Different Scenes of Public Rejoicing, which took place the First of August in St. James's and Hyde Parks, London, in celebration of the Glorious Peace of 1814, and of the Centenary of the Accession of the Illustrious House of Brunswick to the Throne of these Kingdoms. London: Edited, Published, and Sold by Edward Orme, Publisher to His Majesty and His Royal Highness the Prince Regent, Bond Street, corner of Brook-Street. 1814.

Folio, 355 × 270mm.   1814

COLLATION   Half-title; title-page; pp 5–40, Historical Introduction by F.W. Blagdon; pp 41–64, The Grand Jubilee.

1 p 41 The Tower & Preparation of the Fire-Works, with the Balloon/In the Park Augt 1st 1814. 153 × 233/203 × 303mm. Buckingham House in the background, by day.

2 p 42 The Revolving Temple of Concord Illuminated,/ As Erected in the Park in celebration of the glorious Peace of 1814. 153 × 230/200 × 302mm. Westminster Abbey and St Margaret, Westminster in the background, by night.

3 p 44 The Chinese Bridge & Pagoda,/Erected in the Park, in commemoration of the Glorious Peace of 1814. 155 × 230/205 × 305mm. Westminster Abbey in the background, by day.

4 p 53 The View of the Fair in Hyde Park, Augt 1st 1814. 155 × 235/200 × 300mm. With the stone bridge in the foreground, by moonlight.

5 p 55 The Fleet on the Serpentine River,/Commemoration of the Battle of the Nile, Augt 1st, 1814. 155 × 230/203 × 303mm. The 'Naumachia', by day.

6 p 61 The Chinese Bridge Illuminated/On the night of the celebration of the Peace 1814. 153 × 233/200 × 303mm. N.W. view of Westminster Abbey in background.

113 · ANTIQUARIAN ITINERARY* [1815–18]

Three of the five publishers of this seven-volume series of diminutive antiquarian etchings had also been concerned with the publication of two earlier sets in the same popular format, the *Antiquarian and Topographical Cabinet* (no 118) and *Ancient Reliques* (no 109) while a fourth, John Murray, took a share in the practically simultaneous reissue of the *Cabinet*. The itinerant illustrators gave central London a wide birth, with the exception of a single excursion to the cellars of Leadenhall Street, but their activities on the South Bank are worth recording—the more so as they were mostly young

engravers laying the foundations of a career in topographical engraving and London book illustration. For instance J.C. Varrall and Thomas Higham both became notable engravers after Turner and other outstanding artists and William Deeble later contributed steel-engravings to Elmes's *Metropolitan Improvements* (no 154) and Godwin and Britton's *Churches of London* (no 189).

The series follows the familiar part-issues pattern of unpaginated text in signed octavo gatherings to accompany plates grouped around a specific site. Vol. 1, consisting of the first six Numbers, was published in June 1815 at 15s in boards, or on Large Paper at 24s, and No 7, the first of vol. 2, was published in the following month at 2s 6d. Each of the seven volumes ends with an 'Index to the copperplate engravings arranged in counties' and an 'Index to the engravings on wood' and these are cumulated in the last volume. South Bank plates are distributed throughout all volumes except the fifth and seventh. There is a standard publication-line: 'Published for the Proprietors (date), by Wm. Clarke, New Bond Street.' Plate-marks are retained only in the Large Paper edition.

The Antiquarian Itinerary, comprising specimens of Architecture, Monastic, Castellated, and Domestic; With other Vestiges of Antiquity in Great Britain. Accompanied with Descriptions. Vol. I (II–IV, VI–VII). London: Published for the Proprietors, By Wm. Clarke, New Bond Street; J. Murray, Albemarle-Street; S. Bagster, Strand; J.M. Richardson, Cornhill; and Sherwood and Co. Paternoster-Row. 1815 (1816–18).

Octavo, 158 × 95mm. (Large Paper 230 × 135mm)
                                                    1815–18

COLLATION   Vol. 1 (1815). Title-page; address (2pp); descriptions (unpaginated); indices (6pp). Vol. 2 (1816). Title-page; descriptions (unpaginated); indices (5pp). Vol. 3 (1816). Title-page; descriptions (unpaginated); indices of engravings (5pp). Vol. 4 (1816). Half-title; title-page; descriptions (unpaginated); indices (4pp). Vol. 6 (1817). Half-title; title-page; descriptions (unpaginated); indices (3pp). Vol. 7 (1818). Half-title; title-page; descriptions (unpaginated); indices (3pp); general index to engravings in all 7 vols (16pp).

VOL. 1

Bishop of Winchester's Palace, Southwark, Surry

1 Remains of Winchester Palace, Southwark. Drawn & Engraved by J.C. Varrall ... Feb 1 1815. 62 × 88/100 × 150mm.

2 Remains of the Hall, Winchester Palace, Southwark.

Drawn and Engraved by T. Higham ... Feb 1 1815. 65 × 85/100 × 150mm.

(4pp of text)

(Tailpiece of the Winchester Palace window. 35 × 55mm. Woodcut.)

VOL. 2

St Mary Overies, or St Saviour's Southwark

3 W.End, St Mary Overies Church, Southwark. Drawn & Engraved by E.I. Roberts ... Dec. 1, 1815. 60 × 85/100 × 150mm.

(Headpiece of monumental effigy of William Emerson in St Mary Overies Church. 30 × 65mm. Woodcut.)

4 Virgin's Chapel, St Mary Overies Church. Drawn & Engraved by W. Deeble ... Augt. 1, 1815. 90 × 65/150 × 100mm.

5 St Mary Overies Church, Southwark. Engraved by T. Higham from a drawing by William Deeble ... Aug. 1, 1815. 65 × 80/90 × 152mm.

6 Gower's Monument, St Mary Overies Church. Drawn & Engraved by W. Deeble ... Augt. 1, 1815. 90 × 63/150 × 100mm.

7 Effigy of a Knight Templar/N. Transept St Mary Overies. Drawn & Engraved by W. Deeble ... Augt. 1, 1815. 100 × 57/155 × 100mm.

8 St Margaret's Chapel, St Mary Overies Church. Drawn & Engraved by W. Deeble ... Septr 1, 1815. 85 × 63/150 × 100mm.

9 Monumental Stone,/in St Mary Overies Church. Drawn & Engraved by W. Deeble ... July 1, 1815. 100 × 30/150 × 100mm. Cadaver in N.W. corner of the nave.

10 Part of the Priory, St Mary Overies, Southwark. Drawn & Engraved by W. Deeble ... Sept 1, 1815. 60 × 85/100 × 150mm.

(16pp of text)

VOL. 3

11 Antient Crypt, Leadenhall Street. Engraved by I.C. Varrall from a Drawing by G. Sheppard ... Feb 1, 1816. 58 × 82/100 × 155mm.

(2pp of text)

VOL. 4

12 Ancient Gateway, Bermondsey. Engraved by E.I. Roberts from a Drawing by J. Wichelo ... Oct 1, 1816. 80 × 65/150 × 100mm.

2pp of text)

(Tailpiece of Saxon sculptures, Bermondsey. 50 × 60mm. Woodcut.)

VOL. 6

13 Bishop Bonners Palace Lambeth Marsh. Engraved by

J. Greig from a Drawing by Ar, Harrison Esqr.... July 1, 1817. 87 × 60/150 × 100mm. 'Situated in Lambeth Marsh, on the right hand side between the turnpike and the Rev. Rowland Hill's Chapel'.

(2pp of text)

114 · ENCYCLOPAEDIA LONDINENSIS VOL. 13* [1815]

In 1810 the following reissue of a work first launched in 1797 was advertised:

Number 1 of a New Edition of Encyclopaedia Londinensis: or, Universal Dictionary of Arts, Sciences and Literature. By John Wilkes, Esq. of Milland House in the County of Sussex ... In Weekly Numbers, or Complete Volumes, Half-yearly. Sold by J. White in Fleet-Street ... To be completed in Sixteen Volumes. J. Adlard, Printer, Duke Street, Smithfield.

John Wilkes died in the same year and by 1815, when the work reached vol.13, publication had been taken over by G. Jones who issued the following prospectus from his former address:

Books published by Jones (late Wilkes) No 17 Ave Maria Lane, St. Pauls. No. 1 of the Fifth Edition of ... Encyclopaedia Londinensis: a Universal Dictionary of Arts, Sciences and Literature. By John Wilkes Esq. of Milland House ... The first Twelve Volumes may be had complete, or in one or more Numbers ... at the following Prices:

On common Paper, with the Plates plain, Eight-pence each Number
On ditto with the Plates coloured, Fourteen-pence
On Fine Vellum Paper, with the Plates plain, One Shilling
On ditto with the Plates coloured. One Shilling and Sixpence....

The Thirteenth Volume commences with the Article LOGIC ... This is followed by a very ample History of the ancient and present state of LONDON ... embellished with a beautiful Frontispiece; an excellent and correct Map, including the Regent's Park ... together with views of St Paul's ancient and modern; the Chapter-house; the ancient City Gates, the original London Bridge and other Antiquities; besides various modern buildings; as Guildhall, the Bank of England, Surgeon's Hall, the Commercial Hall, Covent Garden Theatre &c &c ...

Printed for G. Jones (late Wilkes,) 17 Ave Maria Lane. Sold also by Sherwood, Neely & Jones.

Of this thirteenth volume, which consists of weekly Nos 883–951, the major part is devoted to a survey and history of London and its index (Nos 887–932 and 950–1 respectively). This very long article is illustrated with 26 topographical and antiquarian, and five armorial plates, all published between November 1813 and March 1815.

John Wilkes was a printer of Winchester who had set up as a London bookseller and stationer at 17 Ave Maria Lane in 1790, became a liveryman of the Stationers' Company, prospered and bought himself a house in the country. His chief undertaking was the *Encyclopaedia Londinensis* and it was in connection with this publication that, in 1808, he was fined £100 for pirating material belonging to a fellow publisher named Roworth.

He had established a connection in the previous century with a competent Pentonville copper plate engraver, John Pass, and it was to him and 'J. Chapman', possibly James Chapman in neighbouring Islington, that most of the plates in this volume were entrusted. To conform with current taste they abandoned the austere architectural elevations which were their usual mode of illustration and filled in the skies with clouds and mechanical ruling, in the manner of Phillips's *Modern London* (no 89) to which Pass also contributed.

Wilkes's 24-volume encyclopaedia was kept in print for many years, being offered for sale in the *Monthly Literary Advertiser* of December 1829 for £59, reduced by 1831 to £48.

Encyclopaedia Londinensis: or, a Universal Dictionary of Arts, Sciences and Literature.... embellished by a most magnificent set of copperplate engravings ... together with A Comprehensive History of London ... compiled, digested, and arranged, By John Wilkes, of Milland House, in the County of Sussex, Esquire assisted by eminent scholars ... Vol. XIII. London, Printed for the Proprietor, by J. Adlard, Duke Street, West Smithfield: sold at the Encyclopaedia Office, Ave Maria Lane, St Pauls ... 1815.

Quarto, 270 × 215mm. 1815

COLLATION Title-page; descr of front. (1 leaf); pp 1–49, Logic to Londinieres; pp 49–616, London; pp 617–853, London (Maryland) to Lytton; pp 854–64, indices for Logic and London, directions to binder.

London views are mostly concentrated in this thirteenth volume, although there are a few others, sometimes found as extra-illustrations, which are drawn from articles in other volumes, eg on Inns of Court. Most plates carry two or more subjects and all are headed tc with the word 'LONDON' and tr with a plate number in Roman numerals. There is usually only one credit per plate but each subject has a caption in copperplate beneath. Publication-lines, which are dated, read:

(a) 'Published by G. Jones, Ave Maria Lane (date)'.
(b) '(London,) Published (as the Act Directs) (date) by G. Jones'.

Plates are placed according to the directions in the list at the end of the volume.

1 front. London. A.D. McQuin delt. J. Chapman sculp. (a) March 14, 1815. 235 × 180mm. The City, allegorically portrayed, with a mural crown and cap of Liberty in one hand and a cornucopia in the other, receives tribute from America, Africa, Asia, etc.

2 p 49 London. (b), Ave Maria Lane, Feby 1815. 230 × 380/265 × 400mm. Map, extending from Serpentine, W. to E. India Docks, E. and Hackney, N. to Walworth, S. (*Darlington and Howgego* 265)

3 p 52 View of St Paul's Church from Fleet Street (epigraph) – View of Westminster Abbey, and St Margaret's/Church, from Westminster Bridge. A.D. McQuin del. J. Chapman sculp. (b) June 18, 1814. Each 135 × 93/180 × 250mm. pl.I.

4 p 102 London Bridge in its original state in 1209 before Houses were built upon it – Part of the South side of the Crypt under St. Thomas's Chapel – Inside View of St. Thomas's Chapel from W. to E./London Bridge. J. Pass sc. (b) Jany 27, 1814. 65 × 228,108 × 108, 108 × 108/200 × 260mm. pl.II. The two chapels copied from George Vertue's views of 1747–8 (no 36).

5 p 103 Aldgate – Aldersgate – Ludgate – Bridgegate/ The four original City Gates. J. Pass sc. (b) Decr 7 1813. Each, vignetted, 105 × 90/260 × 205mm. pl.III.

6 p 105 Bishopsgate – Moorgate – Cripplegate – Newgate/City Gates. J. Pass sc. (b) Decr 24, 1813. Each, vignetted, 105 × 90/260 × 205mm. pl.IV. All these Gates had been removed for road widening during the previous century and were copied by Pass, with picturesque accretions, from the first plate in Maitland's *History* of 1756 (no 38).

7 p 396 Plan of the Survey. Thomson sc. 14 Bury St. Bloomsbury. (a) Novr 9, 1814. 175 × 230/205 × 265mm. pl.V. Illustrating the section 'General Survey of Buildings, Streets and Antiquities' with refs in Roman numerals to the plates and Arabic to the pages. (*Darlington and Howgego* 261)

8 p 401 South West View of Old St. Paul's. Chapman sc.

(b) Oct 8 1814. 185 × 245/205 × 260mm. pl. VI. Copied from Dugdale's *St Paul's* (no 8), item 38.

9 p 403 South-view of the Chapter house of old St. Paul's. I.D. McQuin delt. I. Chapman sc. (b) Septr 3, 1814. 210 × 178/240 × 205mm. pl. VII. Copied from Dugdale's *St Paul's*, item 33.

10 p 416 Panier Alley – Pie Corner – East Cheap – Bennetts-Hill./Antiquities of the 17th Century. J. Pass sc. (b) April 28th, 1814. 123 × 88,123 × 88,80 × 88, 80 × 88/260 × 205mm. pl. VII b. Signs of a cherub, the Fat Boy, the Boar's Head (1660) and the George and Dragon (1667).

11 p 429 Old Jewry – Mincing Lane – Milk Street – Thames Street – Duke's Place – Shoreditch./Fragments of Architecture, ancient & modern. J. Pass sc. (b) June 28, 1814. 48 × 55,75 × 102,45 × 55, 90 × 55, 90 × 100,90 × 53/210 × 265mm. pl. VII b*.

12 p 435 The Custom House burnt down Feby 12 1814 – Commercial Hall, Mincing Lane, now used as a Custom House. J. Pass sc. (b) May 20, 1814. Each 100 × 152/265 × 200mm. pl. VII c. The text gives a timely account of the fire.

13 p 438 The Trinity House on Tower Hill – View of the Tower. J. Pass sc. (b) Dec. 24, 1814. Each 103 × 175/260 × 200mm. pl. VII c*.

14 p 451 The East India House in Leadenhall Street – North Front of Guy's Hospital. J. Pass sculp. Published as the Act Directs March 21st 1815. 100 × 158,102 × 158/260 × 200mm. pl. VII e. View of East India House looking towards St Peter, Cornhill and St Michael, Cornhill.

15 p 464 Back and Front View of the Bank of England. J. Pass sc. (b) June 11, 1814. Each 100 × 170/260 × 200mm. pl. VII f. (*Bank of England* 42)

16 p 471 Guildhall. J. Pass delt & sc. (b) July 23, 1814. 158 × 228/200 × 260mm. pl. VII h. Shows Guildhall Chapel, doomed by an Act of Parliament of 1815 but not demolished until 1822.

17 p 497 Sculpture over the Gate of the Cemetery of St. Stephen's Coleman St. – Curious Font at St. Margaret Lothbury. (a) March 4, 1815. 108 × 183, vignetted; 105 × 50 with four 35 × 60/250 × 200mm. pl. VII i. No credit.

18 p 490 Fragments of Architecture No 3. J. Pass sc. (b) Augt 1, 1814. 260 × 200mm pl. mark. pl. VII l. St John's Gate: 3 keystones to arches, 2 doorways, chimney-piece, panelling, numbered 1–8.

19 p 506 John Bunyan's Meeting-house, Zoar-street, Gravel-lane, Southwark. – Entrance to Montague Close and part of St Saviour's Church Southwark. J. Pass sc. (b) Sepr 19th, 1814. Each 108 × 180/260 × 200mm. pl. VII m. The Meeting House is viewed from a slightly different angle than on pl. 72 of *Londina Illustrata* (no 131) of 1 January 1814.

20 p 510 Elevation of the Strand Bridge from a drawing presented by J. Rennie Esqr. – Pediment of Guy's Hospital – The New Bethlem Hospital. J. Pass sc. (b) October 1, 1814. 42 × 230, 50 × 165, with two details, 30 × 30, 65 × 232/205 × 260mm. pl. VII n. 'The rising Strand Bridge in its embryo shape'; Waterloo Bridge was in course of erection 1811–17. James Lewis's Bethlehem Hospital in Southwark was completed 1815.

21 p 513 Asylum for the Deaf and Dumb – Freemasons Charity for Female Children. J. Pass delt et sculp. (b) Sept 1, 1814. Each 105 × 175/260 × 205mm. pl. VII o. Two Southwark charities.

22 p 521 Surry Chapel – Hill's Almshouse, Gravel-Lane, Southwark. J. Pass sc. (b) Sept 1, 1814. 102 × 175, 105 × 175/265 × 200mm. pl. VII p. The Surrey Chapel was built for the Rev Rowland Hill at the corner of Blackfriars Road and Charlotte Street.

23 p 525 The Royal College of Surgeons in Lincolns Inn Square – View of Covent Garden Theatre from Bow Street. J. Chapman sc. (b) Feby 9, 1814. 100 × 157,98 × 157/255 × 195mm. pl. VII d.

24 p 544 North west View of Westminster Abbey. J. Pass sc. Published as the Act directs Feby 4th 1815. 180 × 237/205 × 265mm. pl. VII q.

25 p 546 Interesting Antiquities in Westminster Abbey/ Drawn on the spot and presented to this work by J. Smith junr. Esqr. Thomson sculp. 14 Bury Street Bloomsbury. (a) Feby 3d 1815. 255 × 205mm pl. mark. pl. VII r. Details.

26 p 568 Chinese Pagoda and Bridge in St James's Park – The Temple of Concord erected for the Celebration of Peace, on the 1st of Augt 1814. J. Pass sc. (b) Novr 10, 1814. 85 × 175,135 × 170/260 × 200mm. pl. VII s.

27–31 (The arms of the City of London and of 93 Livery Companies. No credits. Published between November 1813 and March 1814. pl. VIII–XIII.).

---

115 · SMITH'S ANCIENT TOPOGRAPHY OF LONDON [1815]

After his painful experience of collaborating with an author on the *Antiquities of Westminster* (no 98) J.T. Smith himself supplied the accompanying text when he published a further set of etchings based on his accumulated drawings of London buildings. It is intended merely as a commentary on the plates but is far from solemn, being enlivened with numerous historical, literary and biographical asides—written in fact in the pleasantly discursive style which he later perfected in that minor classic *Nollekens and His Times* (1828).

From this date his interest in London transcends the antiquarianism of his first collection, the *Antiquities of London* (no 70), and he turns for light relief from architectural detail and archaeological record to the living elements of the city as he peoples its streets and houses with the characters he sees about him. Indeed he anticipates T.H. Shepherd (no 154) in showing the human dimension of the metropolitan surroundings: no street door is without its group of children playing or its housewife chaffering with a street trader or its idle servant taking the air. All his perambulating tradesmen, beggars, lamplighters and errand boys look thoroughly at home upon their pavements or in their courtyards.

Commenting on the much-reproduced plate of the fine timbered houses at the corner of Chancery Lane and Fleet Street (item 24) he says (p 50): 'The figures introduced into this plate are all drawn from life', and he goes on to mention by name certain cripples, beggars and freaks, all familiars of the then London scene. Among them is one Anne Siggs, a beggar-woman on crutches who put it about that she was a sister of Mrs Siddons and who must have had an extensive beat since she is shown also walking the streets near Smithfield (item 27). He became fascinated by these 'public characters' as he called them and two years later published a collection entirely devoted to the etched portraits of beggars, *Vagabondiana*. These, and his *The Cries of London* (1839) issued posthumously, may well have inspired the illustrations to Mayhew's *London Labour and the London Poor* (1851), although these latter are wood-engravings based on daguerreotypes and therefore lack the immediacy of etchings based upon the artist's own observation. Even a plate which records two crumbling Gothic arches which had survived in Duke's Place (item 11) is humanized by the lurking presence of an old Jewish rag-picker and an arm from an upper window casting a bone to an endearing mongrel below. In the *Antiquities of London* the same subject is portrayed (item 62) without a sign of human or animal life.

Ancient Topography of London: containing not only Views of Buildings which in many instances no longer exist, and for the most part were never before Published; but Some Account of Places and Customs either unknown, or overlooked by the London Historians. By John Thomas Smith. London: Printed by J. M'Creery, Black-Horse-Court; Published and Sold by the Proprietor, John Thomas Smith, No. 4, Chandos-Street, Covent Garden; Sold likewise by Messrs. John and Arthur Arch, Cornhill; Boydell & Co., Cheapside; Mr. Bagster, Strand; Colnaghi and Co., Cockspur-Street; Messrs. Payne and Foss, Pall-Mall; Mr. Clarke, Bond-Street; Mr. Booth, Duke-Street, Portland Place; Mr. Ryan, Oxford-Street; Mr. Setchel, King-Street, Covent-Garden; and Mr. Upham, Bath. 1815.

Quarto, 350 × 280mm. 1815

COLLATION Title-page; preface (1 leaf); pp 1–21, Sacred Architecture (and 10 plates); pp 22–40, Public Architecture (and 8 plates); pp 41–82, Domestic Architecture (and 14 plates).

The reprint has 'Reprinted 1892' added to the title-page, and the same collation. The plates are excellently preserved but printed on thick card stock, thus distinguishing them from the 1815 impressions which are on a much softer, thick wove paper, usually fox-marked.

The engraved title is dated 24 October 1810 and between that date and September 1814 eight plates were issued annually, each year's issue consisting of an assortment from the three architectural categories, Sacred, Public and Domestic. The chronological sequence of the items is as follows:

Title	24 October 1810	
25	19 November 1810	2 sacred, 2 public, 4 domestic
2,12-13, 20-1,26	29 January 1811	
3	19 February 1811	
4,6,18, 22-4,29	14 January 1812	3 sacred, 1 public, 4 domestic
7	21 January 1812	
8,32	1 May 1813	3 sacred, 2 public, 3 domestic
5,10,31	1 October 1813	
19,27	10 November 1813	
15	21 November 1813	
9,11, 14,16-17, 28,30,33	15 September 1814	2 sacred, 3 public, 3 domestic

Eleven of the 32 etchings are based on drawings made before 1800 which may originally have been intended for the *Antiquities of London* completed in that year but there is a marked change of style from that publication. The etching is bolder, with more dramatic contrasts of light and shade, and extending almost to the edges of the plate; the sky is shaded with light corrugated flicks in place of mechanical parallel ruling. Also the artist seems more consciously to be preserving for posterity the image of the streets of Tudor London at a time when, house by house, it was suffering daily erosion. Born in this century he would have been a great asset to any group of conservationists.

On each plate of the *Antiquities of London*, in their earliest state, is a precise reference to the relevant passage in the third edition of Pennant's *London* (1793; see no 67) from which the page number and edition were subsequently burnished out so that the plate might still serve to extra-illustrate editions yet to come with different page numbering. Smith likewise relied on the Pennant collecting craze to extricate him later on from his financial difficulties resulting from the destruction by fire of a large part of the original edition of *Antiquities of Westminster*. Again in 1815, when this third work was published, he gave no fewer than three broad hints to the extra-illustrators, who were now more numerous than ever: on the engraved title-page the Pennant arms occupy the second largest of the shields displayed in a border of 14 and, during an aside on Smithfield, an entire page (p 55) is taken up with a transcript of the grant of those arms; speaking of the office of Master of the Revels (p 43) he refers to J.C. Crowle as one of the office holders and thence remarks gratuitously: 'Mr. Crowle left his illustrated Pennant's London to the British Museum which he valued at £5,000'.

Whereas the *Antiquities of Westminster* plates were published from three different addresses, two off Oxford Street and one in Somers Town, all those in the present work carry the address of Smith's father's printselling business off St Martin's Lane (from which he also issued his *Antiquities of London*). Therefore in the list only the dates are transcribed from a publication-line which usually reads: 'London Published as the Act Directs (date), By John Thomas Smith No. 18, Great May's Buildings St. Martins Lane.', but for items 9, 11, 14, 16, 19, 26, 30, 33: 'Published (date), By J.T. Smith, No. 18, Gt. May's Buildings, St. Martin's Lane.', and for items 5, 10, 15, 27, 31-2: 'Pubd. (date), By J.T. Smith, No. 18, Gt. Mays Buildings, St. Martin's Lane.'

Credits are invariably 'Drawn and Etched by J.T. Smith' and the caption of each plate starts with the heading of the chapter to which it belongs, ie 'Sacred Architecture', 'Public Architecture' or 'Domestic Architecture'.

1 (engr title) Antient Topography/of/London/Embracing Specimens of/Sacred, Public and Domestic/Architecture,/from the Earliest Period to the Time of the Great Fire/1666./Drawn and Etched by/John Thomas Smith,/intended as an accompaniment to the celebrated works of/Stow, Pennant/and others. Richd. Sawyer sculpt. London Published as the Act directs Octr. 24, 1810, by John Thomas Smith, No. 18, Great May's Buildings,/St. Martin's Lane. 295 × 235/320 × 265mm. In a frame with tc an achievement of the City arms, bc the Pennant shield and crest and l., r., and along bm shields of arms of the 12 major Livery Companies, all with heraldic colours added.

Sacred Architecture

2 p 2 North East view of the back of the original altar of St Bartholomew the Greater./Internal specimen of the/plain Norman style.... Drawn in May 1810. Published ... Jany.29 1811. 265 × 225/285 × 228mm.

3 p 4 West entrance to the vestibule of the Temple Church./External specimen of the/Decorated Norman style. Drawn in June 1810. Published ... Feby. 19 1811. 270 × 255/315 × 275mm.

4 p 6 Part of the vestibule of the Temple Church./Internal specimen of the pointed arch in the reign of Henry IInd ... Drawn in May 1809. Published ... Jany. 14th 1812. 280 × 230/305 × 240mm.

5 p 7 Part of the vestibule of the Temple Church. Drawn in May 1800. Pubd. Octor. 1st 1813. 275 × 225/305 × 240mm. The triforium arcade.

6 p 8 Parts of the North and East walls of the Convent of St. Claire or Minoresses./As they appeared after the late Fire.... The Fire happened Thursday the 23rd March 1797. Drawn in April 1797. Published ... Jany. 14th 1812. 275 × 230/305 × 240mm.

7 p 9 Parts of the South and West Walls of the same Convent. Internal specimen of the reign of Edward 1st 1293. Drawn in April 1797. Published ... Jany. 21st,1812. 282 × 228/305 × 240mm.

8 p 10 Antient parts of the Church of St Dunstan in the East. Drawn in June 1811. Published ... May 1st, 1813. 280 × 230/305 × 240mm.

9 p 12 Leadenhall Chapel. Drawn in May 1812. Published Septr. 15, 1814. 285 × 235/300 × 240mm.

10 p 12 North-East view of parts of the Chapel and Granary of Leadenhall. Drawn in June 1812. Pubd. Octor. 1st. 1813. 278 × 225/295 × 227mm.

(p 14 Wood-engraving of King Edward III commissioning Hugh de St Albans, John Athelard and Benedict Nightingale to collect painters for St

Stephen's Chapel. From a drawing by T. Stothard. Appears on p 269 of Smith's *Antiquities of Westminster* (130 × 120mm).)

11 p 18 The South entrance of Duke's Place. Drawn in August 1790. Published Septr. 15, 1814. 275 × 235/305 × 240mm.

Public Architecture

12 p 22 North view of the cell in the South West tower of the Tower of London./Internal specimen of the Early Pointed style.... Drawn in June 1802. Published ... Jany. 29, 1811. 280 × 235/320 × 240mm.

13 p 22 East entrance to the cell in the South West tower of the Tower of London.... Drawn in June 1802. Published ... Jany. 29 1811. 280 × 230/303 × 225mm.

14 p 24 An arch of London Bridge as it appeared in the Great Frost 1814. Drawn Feby. 5th. 1814. Published Septr. 15, 1814. 280 × 235/300 × 237mm.

15 p 26 Inside view of the watch-tower discovered near Ludgate Hill, May 1. 1792. Drawn in June 1792. Pubd. Nov. 21st. 1813. 285 × 235/305 × 240mm.

16 p 28 Parts of London-Wall and Bethlem Hospital. Drawn in June 1812. Published Septr. 15, 1814. 280 × 237/305 × 238mm.

17 p 32 South-West view of Bethlem Hospital and London Wall. Drawn in August 1814. Published Septr. 15, 1814. 277 × 230/303 × 235mm. Shows a bill sticker adding to a wall covered in posters and graffiti.

18 p 36 (caption indented) A venerable fragment of London Wall, as it stood in the church-yard of St. Giles Cripplegate/in 1793, since which period the battlements have been taken down ... Drawn in April 1793. Published ... Jany. 14th. 1812. 265 × 228/280 × 235mm.

19 p 39 Inside view of the Poultry Compter. Drawn in June 1811. Pubd. Novr. 10th. 1813. 275 × 220/300 × 222mm.

Domestic Architecture

20 p 41 North East view of an old house lately standing in Sweedon's Passage, Grub Street.... Drawn in July 1791. Published ... Jany 29 1811. 278 × 230/305 × 240mm.

21 p 42 South East view of the old house lately standing in Sweedon's Passage, Grub Street/External specimen of the/heavy timber style./... This house was taken down/in March 1805. Drawn in July 1791. Published ... Jany.29 1811. 280 × 235/305 × 240mm.

22 p 44 A magnificent mansion lately standing in Hart Street, Crutched Friars./External specimen of the armorial style./in the latter part of the reign of Henry VIII. /This House was taken down in 1801.... Drawn in May 1792. Published ... Jany. 14. 1812. 270 × 235/305 × 240mm.

23 p 46 An upper apartment of the same magnificent mansion./Internal specimen of the decorated style./in

the latter part of the reign of Henry VIII.... Drawn in May 1792. Published ... Jany. 14 1812. 270 × 235/305 × 240mm.

24 p 48 Houses lately standing on the West corner of Chancery Lane, Fleet Street./External specimen of the gro-/tesque bracketed front and/projecting stories, of the/reign of Edward VI.... These houses were taken down/by the City in May 1799 to widen/Chancery Lane.... Drawn in August 1789. Published ... Jany. 14 1812. 270 × 225/305 × 240mm.

25 p 50 East view of a room on the first floor of Sir Paul Pindar's Bishopsgate Street./Internal specimen of the decorated style in the/latter part of the reign of Elizabeth 1600.... Drawn in June 1810. Published ... Nov.19, 1810. 280 × 225/305 × 230mm.

26 p 52 Houses on the South side of Leadenhall Street. Drawn in July 1796. Published Septr. 15, 1814. 280 × 225/305 × 230mm.

27 p 54 View of part of Duke Street, West Smithfield. Drawn in July 1807. Pubd. Novr. 10th. 1813. 280 × 225/300 × 227mm. Retreating on crutches is the tall figure of 'the malignant Ann Siggs praiseworthy for nothing but her cleanliness, a rare quality in a beggar'.

28 p 56 Old houses lately standing at the South corner of Hosier Lane, Smithfield/ External specimen of the plain gable style. These houses were taken down in Octr. 1809. Drawn in April 1795. Published ... Jany. 29th, 1811. 275 × 223/301 × 225mm.

29 p 61 Houses on the South side of a street called London Wall. External specimen of the/foliated style in the reign/of Charles 1st. Drawn in March 1808. Published ... Jany. 14, 1812. 280 × 230/305 × 240mm.

30 p 64 Houses on the West side of Little Moor-Fields. Drawn in May, 1810. Published Septr. 15, 1814. 295 × 235/303 × 240mm.

31 p 66 South-East view of the porch of an old house in Hanover Court, near Grub Street. Drawn in July 1809. Pubd. October. 1st, 1813. 280 × 228/305 × 240mm. Supposedly inhabited by General Monck.

32 p 67 Houses lately standing on the North side of Long Lane, Smithfield. Drawn in May 1810. Pubd. May 1st, 1813. 280 × 235/305 × 240mm.

33 p 68 Winchester Street, London-Wall. Drawn in May, 1804. Published Septr. 15, 1814. 280 × 230/305 × 240mm.

(Wood-engraving of two round arches with dog-tooth ornament in the Court of Bequests, Palace of Westminster. Originally published on p 37 of Smith's *Antiquities of Westminster* (170 × 147mm).)

116 · ACKERMANN'S HISTORY OF THE COLLEGES* [1816]

This, the fifth of Ackermann's sumptuously illustrated volumes of English topography, followed hard on the heels of his histories of Oxford and Cambridge Universities, each published in 20 monthly Parts from 1813 to 1815. Indeed the *Colleges* was supposed to put in an appearance on 1 September 1815 but in the event its first Number was issued on 1 January following. It contained four plates with a portion of text and each succeeding month in 1816 saw the issue of a similar Number. Publication-lines give the following chronology of plates:

Winchester	10	January–March
Eton	10	March–June
Harrow	5	May–July
Charterhouse	5	July–August
Westminster	4	August–September
Christ's Hospital	5	September–October
Rugby	5	October–November
St Paul's	2	December
Merchant Taylors'	2	December

A pecking order is observable both in the proportions of the plates and of the text: W.H. Pyne was allowed, collectively speaking, 168 pages on Winchester, Eton and Harrow, while William Combe's histories of the six other schools occupies a total of 192, of which the largest share falls to Christ's Hospital.

A thousand copies were printed and were subscribable, according to Tooley, at 12s per Number for the first 500 and 16s per Number for the remainder. Fifty copies were printed on Large Paper at one guinea per Number and 25 with uncoloured India paper proof impressions of the plates. The complete work with its 48 plates was advertised as 'Elephant 4to boards, price £7. 7s., large Paper, £12. 12s.' An 1828 advertisement (on the wrapper of Westall's *Picturesque Tour*, no 157) also offers each school for sale individually; these 'separates' were almost always late issues, says Tooley. A separate imprint, 'L. Harrison, Printer, 373 Strand', is to be found on the last text pages of the portions for Eton, St Paul's, Merchant Taylors', Rugby, Christ's Hospital and Westminster. Nattali of Covent Garden, in the *Monthly Literary Advertiser* for May 1847, offered 'History of the Public Schools' ('published at £7. 4s.') for £2.

The History of the Colleges of Winchester, Eton and Westminster: with the Charter-House, the Schools of St. Paul's, Merchant Taylors, Harrow and Rugby, and the Free-school of Christ's Hospital. London: Printed for and published by R. Ackermann, 101, Strand. L. Harrison, Printer, 373 Strand. MDCCC:XVI.

Royal quarto, 368–420 × 292–340mm.　　　1816

COLLATION　Title-page; pp iii–iv, introduction; list of plates (1 leaf); pp v–vi, list of subscribers; pp 1–56, Winchester; pp 1–72, Eton; pp 1–27, Westminster; pp 1–32, Charterhouse; pp 1–34, St Paul's; pp 1–22, Merchant Taylors'; pp 1–40, Harrow; pp 1–34, Rugby; pp 1–43, Christ's Hospital.

The plates, which are chiefly of interior views, are variegated with illustrations of gowned scholars drawn by T. Uwins, fashion editor of the *Repository of Arts*, and engraved in line and stipple by J. Agar; this pair produced over 30 similar plates for the two *Universities* publications. Topographical draughtsmanship was shared, more or less equally, between Augustus Pugin, who had been responsible for all the *Microcosm* plates (no 99), besides a number of *Westminster Abbey* (no 108) and *Universities* plates, Frederick Mackenzie, who was much involved with *Westminster Abbey* and the *Universities*, and William Westall who had worked on the *Universities*. The engraving was carried out by two of Ackermann's most trusted men, Joseph Stadler and J. Bluck, who had both worked for the *Repository of Arts*, the *Microcosm* and the *Universities*, and by Daniel Havell and W.J. Bennett, who had been brought in for the *Universities*.

Captions are in voided capitals and the unnumbered plates are listed in the sequence of the schools with their facing text pages. Watermarks, where present, are mainly 'J. WHATMAN 1811', although '1812' and '1816' are also found. Tooley notes some as late as 1827 and should be referred to for collector's 'points'. Seventeen of the 48 plates, relating to the London public schools, are listed below. Publication-lines read: 'London, Published (date) at 101 Strand for R. Ackermann's History of (name of school).'

History of Westminster School

1 p 8 Westminster Scholar. T. Uwins delt. J. Agar sculpt. Septr 1, 1816. 195 × 80/300 × 255mm. Vignetted in stipple and line.

2 p 21 Hall of Westminster School. A. Pugin delt. J. Stadler sculpt. Augt 1, 1816. 195 × 255/250 × 300mm.

3 p 22 Westminster School Room. A. Pugin delt. J.C. Stadler sculpt. Augt 1, 1816. 202 × 272/250 × 303mm.

4 p 24 Dormitory of Westminster School. A. Pugin delt. J. Bluck sculpt. Septr 1, 1816. 200 × 260/250 × 300mm.

History of Charterhouse (no imprint, but Abbey notes a 'separate' without title)

5 Charter House/from the Square. W. Westall delt. J.C. Stadler sculpt. July 1, 1816. 192 × 265/255 × 290mm. Original water-colour drawing (182 × 257mm) shown at Agnew's 1975 water-colour exhibition.

6 p 22 Charter House/from the Play Ground. W. Westall delt. W. Bennett sculpt. Augt 1, 1816. 185 × 260/250 × 300mm.

7 p 24 Hall of the Charter House. A. Pugin delt. D. Havell sculpt. Augt 1, 1816. 205 × 265/245 × 300mm.

8 p 25 Dr. Fisher's Apartments/Charter House. A. Pugin delt. J. Stadler sculpt. July 1, 1816. 205 × 285/250 × 300mm.

9 p 31 Charter House School Room. A. Pugin delt. J. Bluck sculpt. Augt 1, 1816. 198 × 260/255 × 300mm.

History of St. Paul's School ('separate' in Guildhall Library with title: 'The History of St. Pauls School. Dedicated to the Masters, Wardens, and Court of Assistants of the Worshipful Company of Mercers. London: Printed for and Published by R. Ackermann, 101 Strand. L. Harrison, Printer, 373 Strand. M.DCCC.XVI.')

10 p 1 St. Paul's School. A. Pugin delt. J. Stadler sculpt. Decr 1, 1816. 188 × 265/250 × 300mm.

11 p 27 The School Room of St. Paul's. F. Mackenzie delt. J. Bluck sculpt. Decr 1, 1816. 210 × 265/250 × 300mm.

History of Merchant Taylors' School ('separate' in Guildhall Library with title: 'The History of Merchant Taylors' School. Dedicated to the Master, Wardens, and Court of Assistants of the Worshipful Company of Merchant Taylors. London: Printed for and Published by R. Ackermann, 101 Strand. L. Harrison, Printer, 373 Strand. M.DCCC.XVI.')

12 p 19 The Merchant Taylors' School Room. A. Pugin delt. J. Stadler sculpt. Decr 1, 1816. 198 × 270/250 × 303mm.

13 p 20 Examination Room of Merchant Taylors' School. F. Mackenzie delt. D. Havell sculpt. Decr 1, 1816. 203 × 265/250 × 300mm.

History of Christ's Hospital

14 p 19 Hall of Christ Hospital. A. Pugin delt. J. Stadler sculpt. Octr 1, 1816. 205 × 263/252 × 300mm.

15 p 23 Writing School, Christ Hospital. F. Mackenzie delt. J. Stadler sculpt. Octr 1, 1816. 202 × 262/250 × 300mm.

16 p 23 Grammar School of Christ Church. A. Pugin delt. J. Stadler sculp. Septr 1, 1816. 205 × 270/250 × 300mm.

17 p 31 Interior of Christ Church. F. Mackenzie delt. D. Havell sculpt. Septr 1, 1816. 205 × 265/250 × 300mm.

18 p 32 A Scholar at Christ Hospital. T. Uwins delt. J. Agar sculpt. Oct.1, 1816. 195 × 100/295 × 250mm. Vignetted in line and stipple.

117 · PAPWORTH'S SELECT VIEWS OF LONDON [1816]

Rudolph Ackermann, the fine art publisher, book and printseller, started trading at 101 Strand on the site of old Worcester House in 1796 and named his establishment, which combined shop, art library and drawing-school, The Repository of the Arts. From here, on 2 January 1809, he launched a monthly periodical entitled *The Repository of Arts, Literature, Commerce, Manufactures, Fashions and Politics*. In March Frederic Shoberl was appointed editor and continued in that capacity until publication ceased some 20 years later, by which time it had run through three series, 40 volumes and 240 monthly Parts. Its aim was to provide, at 3s 6d per issue, a more attractive and fashion-conscious version of the long-established *Gentleman's Magazine* and *European Magazine* which would publish notices of current art exhibitions and books, reviews and fashion pages, with literary contributions by William Combe and others.

Its undoubted success, which quickly gained it some 3000 subscribers, must surely be attributed to an abundance of illustrations superior in quality and charm to those of its rivals, which were embellished chiefly with explanatory figures in line, staid views, portraits on copper or blurred woodcuts. Ackermann, on the other hand, introduced every form of engraving available: line, stipple, aquatint, wood and, eventually, lithographic. Moreover he made use of the team of colourists employed on publications such as *The Microcosm of London* (no 99) to apply colour washes both to the aquatint and etched views and to the elegant fashion plates in line—with the latter even including small patterns of the materials used in the garments shown.

Among Ackermann's contributors was John Papworth, the architect responsible for the design of his showroom at 101 Strand. The son of an Office of Works stuccoist, his talents were observed by Sir William Chambers. By the age of 18 he had already learned to draw in perspective, served an apprenticeship to a builder and picked up the rudiments of interior design during a year spent with a well-known firm of furnishers and decorators. He started showing his drawings at the Royal Academy in 1791 and was soon in command of a busy practice, specializing in remodelling houses, laying out gardens and designing furniture and trophies. It was for his design of a Waterloo trophy that his friends acclaimed him a second Michelangelo and led him to adopt Buonarroti as his second name.

Before this, however, he had been writing a regular series of architectural notes for the *Repository* illustrated by coloured aquatints, and in 1816 Ackermann decided to reprint in volume form those that described aspects of contemporary London; the book was issued in paper boards labelled on the spine 'Ackermann's Select Views of London. 76 Plates. £3. 13. 6d.'

Select Views of London; with historical and descriptive sketches of some of the most interesting of its Public Buildings. Compiled and arranged by John B. Papworth. Architect, Author of an Essay on the Dry Rot, &c &c. London: Printed for R. Ackermann, 101, Strand, by J. Diggens, St. Ann's Lane. 1816.

Octavo, 265 × 185mm.   1816

COLLATION Title-page; introduction (4pp); contents (2pp), pp 1–159, Select Views.

Introducing the reprint Papworth speaks of 'the patronage which a portion of this Work received when it was laid before the Public as "Views of London" in the *Repository of Arts*, and which induced a republication in the present form encreased by several new Plates: those which had previously appeared having been under the hands of the Engraver for improvement and higher finish'. The claim of an increase of 'several new plates' is not

borne out by a comparison with the illustrations published in the 14 volumes of the *Repository of Arts* (first series) and the second volume of the second series; only pl.51, 'The Guildhall', is additional. Conversely nine London plates which had appeared in the *Repository* to date were not reissued: vol. 1, pl. 2, 7, 12, 17, 22; vol. 2, pl. 10; vol. 9, pl. 28. They were all showroom interiors of firms selling furniture, pottery, china, glass, drapery and books, by way of advertisement, the first and last being of Ackermann's own establishment; in addition vol. 6, pl. 25, 'An old house at Newington', and vol. 7, pl. 24, 'Southwark Bridge', did not reappear. Thus the original quota of 84 was reduced to 76 plates, wholly aquatinted or line-engraved with aquatinted skies, coloured by hand in pale, transparent washes, as in the *Repository*.

The views are classified in two 'Divisions': the first depicting the places of worship, residence and entertainment of fashionable society and the second the temples of the financial and mercantile City. Of particular topographical interest is the set of views of West End squares, not published systematically on this modest scale since Overton's *Prospects* (no 26) of nearly 100 years earlier. *Select Views* anticipates the compilation of another architect, James Elmes's *Metropolitan Improvements* (no 154), in its illustration of the work of contemporaries (items 27–8, 31, 36, 63, 65, 72) and topically records the ephemeral structures which appeared in the parks to celebrate the Peace of 1814.

Only two plates retain their original publication-lines (items 7 and 8) and these are the only ones with credits. It should be noted, however, that John Phillips, who has made a close study of drawings and etchings by the Shepherd family (*Shepherd's London*, 1976), has established that Thomas Hosmer Shepherd's earliest work was for the *Repository* and that he and his father George contributed no fewer than 35 of the London views; moreover it would appear that Thomas Hosmer himself etched the plates. Locations are given for their drawings for this work in the British Museum, Guildhall Library, Greater London Council and Westminster Public Library.

In the list that follows the caption lettering as it appears in *Select Views*, engraved in voided capitals, has been transcribed and the page opposite which each plate is bound has been noted. After the dimensions are added the dates from the burnished out *Repository* publication-lines and also the volume and plate number which were engraved tr on each view in the *Repository of Arts* (abbreviated *RA*).

Western Division

1 p 1 St. James's Palace. 120 × 190/150 × 250mm. 1 June, 1812. *RA* 7,37.

2 p 6 Carleton House. 117 × 195/150 × 250mm. June 1st, 1809. *RA* 1,27.

3 p 6 Carlton House. 130 × 315/250 × 345mm. Octr 1, 1811. There is a set of this plate in three states, in outline, with aquatint, and coloured, in Westminster Public Library. *RA* 6,19.

4 p 8 The Staircase/at Carlton House. 200 × 252/242 × 305mm. 1 Jany 1812. *RA* 7,1.

5 p 10 The Conservatory at Carlton House. 193 × 255/250 × 300mm. Sepr 1, 1811. *RA* 6,13.

6 p 12 Warwick House/the residence of Her Royal Highness Princess Charlotte of Wales. 175 × 125/255 × 150mm. Dec 1, 1811. *RA* 6,33.

7 p 13 View of the Bridge & Pagoda/St James's Park,/Erected for the Grand Jubilee/In Celebration of the Peace:/Under the Direction of Sir Wm. Congreve Bart./1st Aug. 1814. A. Pugin delt. J.R. Hamble aquat. London Pub. Octr 1st, 1814 at R. Ackermann's, 101 Strand. 180 × 263/250 × 300mm. *RA* 12.

8 p 13 View of the Temple of Concord/in the Green Park/Erected for the Grand Jubilee,/In Celebration of the Peace,/Under the Direction of Sir Wm. Congreve, Bart./1st Aug. 1814. A. Pugin del. J.C. Stadler aqua. 185 × 270/243 × 295mm. Novr 1, 1814. *RA* 12,22.

9 p 16 The Bason/in the Green Park, St. James's. 110 × 185/160 × 250mm. Octr 1, 1810. With view of Spencer House and the Abbey. *RA* 4,22.

10 p 18 St. Stephen's Chapel & Speaker's House./From Westminster Bridge. 120 × 190/150 × 255mm. Sep.1, 1815. Pencil drawing (120 × 189mm), in BM (*Crace* 4.71). *RA* 14,15.

11 p 21 Westminster Abbey & St. Margaret's. 105 × 178/160 × 245mm. 1810. *RA* 3.

12 p 24 St. John's Church/Westminster,/from the river. 125 × 190/160 × 250mm. Decr 1, 1815. *RA* 14.

13 p 25 St. Martin's/in the Fields. 185 × 125/250 × 150mm. 1815. *RA* 13,6.

14 p 30 St. Clement Danes. 180 × 125/250 × 150mm. Feby 1, 1814. Preliminary sketch (172 × 91mm) and detailed drawing (182 × 124mm) in GLC. *RA* 11,8.

15 p 34 St. James's Square. 118 × 190/160 × 250mm. 1812. Pencil drawing (117 × 191mm), signed 'Shepherd', in Guildhall Library. *RA* 8,9.

16 p 36 North Side of Grosvenor Square. 120 × 190/150 × 250mm. 1 Novr 1813. *RA* 10,31.

17 p 38 Berkeley Square. 120 × 190/150 × 250mm. 1Septr 1813. S. and E. sides. *RA* 10,15.

18 p 39 Lansdowne House, Berkeley Square. 115 × 175/150 × 250mm. May 1, 1811. *RA* 5,28.

19 p 41 Portman Square./North Side. 118 × 190/150 × 250mm. 1813. *RA* 10,9.

20 p 43 Manchester Square/North Side. 120 × 192/150 × 250mm. 1 July 1813. *RA* 10,3.

21 p 45 Cavendish Square, North Side. 125 × 195/150 × 250mm. March 1, 1813. *RA* 9,20.

22 p 47 George Street, Hanover Sqre. 165 × 115/250 × 150mm. 1 Novr 1812. *RA* 8,29.

23 p 49 Soho Square. 115 × 187/150 × 250mm. 1 Octr 1812. S.W. view; cows and sheep in foreground. *RA* 8,29.

24 Leicester Square from Leicester Place. 120 × 175/150 × 250mm. 1812. *RA* 7,2.

25 p 55 Lincolns Inn Fields/coming in from Gt. Queen Street. 110 × 170/150 × 240mm. Novr 1, 1810. *RA* 4,28.

26 p 56 Queen Square. 123 × 200/150 × 250mm. 1 Sepr 1812. Looking S. *RA* 8,16.

27 p 58 New Drury Lane Theatre. 120 × 200/150 × 250mm. 1 Novr. 1812. Built by Benjamin Wyatt, opened 10 October 1812. *RA* 8,31.

28 p 61 Theatre Royal, Covent Garden/from Bow Street, 105 × 180/150 × 250mm. Octr 1st 1809. Robert Smirke's building, opened 10 September 1809. *RA* 2,22.

29 p 68 Saloon to the Private Boxes/Covent Garden Theatre. 115 × 175/160 × 250mm. Feb 1, 1810. *RA* 2,12.

30 p 70 Montague House—now the British Museum. 120 × 185/155 × 235mm. 1813. From Great Russell Street. *RA* 10.

31 p 73 British Museum./New Building. 145 × 110/240 × 148mm. April 1, 1810. Line-engraving of Rooms VII and IX of the gallery for the Townley marbles, built by George Saunders, 1804–5; demolished 1851. *RA* 3,23.

32 p 82 Somerset House and the New Church Strand,/ taken from the Morning Post Office. 115 × 193/150 × 232mm. July 1809. *RA* 2,2.

33 p 84 The Hall at the Royal Academy/Sommerset House. 115 × 170/150 × 240mm. May 1, 1810. Line-engraving. *RA* 3,29.

34 p 86 Russell Institution/Great Coram Street. 120 × 198/150 × 250mm. Novr 1, 1811. *RA* 6,26.

35 p 88 The Pantheon. 130 × 190/155 × 240mm. 1814. Oxford Street. *RA* 11,3.

36 p 89 Bullock's Museum/Piccadilly. 120 × 193/150 × 250mm. Augt 1, 1815. Designed by P.F. Robinson, 1811–12; demolished 1904. *RA* 14.

37 p 89 Bullock's Museum./22, Piccadilly. 115 × 170/150

× 245mm. June 1, 1810. Line-engraving of interior. *RA* 3,35.

38 p 91 The Banqueting House. 130 × 200/150 × 250mm. Sepr 1, 1816. *RA* (2nd ser)2,9.

39 p 91 Whitehall Chapel. 110 × 170/150 × 235mm. July 1, 1811. Interior of Banqueting House, with captured French standards to l. *RA* 6,2.

40 p 96 Whitehall Yard/(from the Street opposite the Horse Guards). 125 × 180/150 × 250mm. (1 January 1811) *RA* 4,2.

41 p 97 A View of Whitehall & the Horse Guards. 115 × 180/150 × 240mm. June 1, 1811. Looking N. *RA* 5,34.

42 p 98 Charing Cross/looking up the Strand. 165 × 120/240 × 150mm. Feby 1, 1811. Shows Northumberland House, etc. *RA* 5,8.

43 p 101 Buckingham Stairs Water Gate, from the River. 130 × 180/150 × 250mm. 1 Dec. 1814. Boats moored among the reeds. *RA* 12.

44 p 103 Royal Menagerie, Exeter Change, Strand. 128 × 205/150 × 250mm. 1 July 1812. Captioned 'Polito's Royal Menagerie'. *RA* 8,2.

45 p 104 Portland Place. 128 × 198/150 × 250mm. 1 April 1815. Looking N. T.H. Shepherd's water-colour (128 × 198mm) is in the Ashbridge Collection, Westminster Public Library. *RA* 13,20.

46 p 106 Oxford Street/& Entrance into Stratford Place. 125 × 195/150 × 245mm. 1 March, 1815. Looking W. towards Tyburn. Pencil and water-colour drawing (126 × 195mm) in BM (*Crace* 29.95). *RA* 13,11.

47 p 106 Tyburn Turnpike. 120 × 195/150 × 250mm. Jany 1813. Looking E. down Oxford Street. *RA* 9,3.

48 p 108 View of Piccadilly,/from Hyde Park Corner Turnpike. 100 × 170/150 × 240mm. July 1, 1810. *RA* 4,2.

49 p 110 Tottenham Court Road Turnpike & St James's Chapel. 123 × 198/150 × 250mm. March 1, 1812. Hampstead Road Chapel, built by Thomas Hardwick, 1791–2. *RA* 7,16.

Eastern Division

50 p 111 View of Cornhill, Lombard Street & Mansion House. 110 × 170/145 × 240mm. Sept 1. 1810. *RA* 4,16.

51 p 112 Guildhall. 135 × 198/155 × 250mm. Dance's façade and chapel of St Mary Magdalen. Pencil drawing (139 × 196mm), dated 1813, in Guildhall Library.

52 p 115 South View of the Bank. 105 × 178/135 × 210mm. Nov. 1st 1809. Looking towards Mansion House. *RA* 2,29. (*Bank of England* 39–40)

53 p 115 Bank of England./From Lothbury. 110 × 185/150 × 245mm. Sepr 1st 1809. As 'Bank of England/from Cateaton Street. Pugin delt. S. Mittan sculp.', *RA* 2,16. (*Bank of England* 56)

54 p 116 Interior View of the Bank. 165 × 113/245 ×

150mm. Sepr 1, 1811. The 'Bullion Yard'. *RA* 6,14. (*Bank of England* 129–30)

55 p 117 Royal Exchange. 195 × 125/250 × 150mm. 1 Decr 1812. View towards Cheapside. *RA* 8,40.

56 p 119 A North View of the India House,/Leadenhall Street. 105 × 180/160 × 245mm. March 1, 1810. *RA* 3,15.

57 p 121 St. Paul's Cathedral/West Front. 132 × 190/150 × 248mm. April 1st, 1814. Pencil drawing (134 × 189mm) and pen, ink and water-colour drawing (135 × 190mm), both 'T.H. Shepherd 1814', in Guildhall Library. *RA* 11.

58 p 125 St. Stephen's Church/Walbrook. 185 × 130/250 × 150mm. 1 March, 1814. Drawing with water-colour (185 × 132mm), 'T.H. Shepherd 1814', in GLC. *RA* 11,14.

59 p 127 Christ Church—Spitalfields. 190 × 135/250 × 150mm. 1 Novr 1815. *RA* 14,25.

60 p 128 St. Leonard Shoreditch. 200 × 130/250 × 150mm. 1 May, 1814. The spire from N.W. *RA* 11,28.

61 p 130 View of St. Dunstan's Church, Fleet Street. 165 × 120/250 × 150mm. Feby 1, 1812. Looking towards Temple Bar. *RA* 7,8.

62 p 134 Town Hall,/Southwark. 125 × 193/150 × 253mm. June 1, 1815. Pencil drawing (124 × 192mm) in Guildhall Library. *RA* 13.

63 p 135 The Hall of the Auction Mart. 120 × 200/150 × 250mm. Aug 1, 1811. Building at N. end of Bartholomew Lane, completed January 1810. *RA* 6,8.

64 p 135 Auction Mart Coffee Rooms. 128 × 162/150 × 250mm. 1811. Line-engraving only. *RA* 6,20.

65 p 137 The London Commercial Sale Rooms,/Mark Lane. 125 × 185/150 × 250mm. May 1st 1813. Commenced building June 1811. Pencil and water-colour drawing (125 × 188mm), 'G. Shepherd 1813', in Guildhall Library. *RA* 9,34.

66 p 139 Cheapside. 123 × 195/150 × 250mm. 1813. Looking W. *RA* 9,44.

67 p 141 Mercer's Hall. 195 × 123/250 × 150mm. July 1, 1815. Pencil drawing (185 × 120mm) in Guildhall Library. *RA* 14,2.

68 p 142 Ironmonger Hall. 115 × 175/150 × 235mm. March 1, 1811. *RA* 4,15.

69 p 143 Bridge Street/Blackfriars. 123 × 193/150 × 250mm. 1 May, 1812. Looking N. towards obelisk. *RA* 7,30.

70 p 144 Blackfriars Bridge,/from the Strand Bridge. 120 × 190/150 × 250mm. 1 Octr 1815. ie from Waterloo Bridge in course of erection. Pencil drawing (120 × 190mm) in Guildhall Library. *RA* 14,19.

71 p 146 View of London Bridge. 120 × 205/150 × 250mm. *RA* 12,1.

72 p 149 The New Custom House. 123 × 230/150 ×

255mm. July 1, 1816. Built by David Laing, 1813–17. *RA* (2nd ser) 2,3.

73 p 153 The Monument. 210 × 105/250 × 150mm. 1 April, 1812. London Bridge beyond. *RA* 7,23.

74 p 154 Lunatic Hospital of St. Luke's. 125 × 200/150 × 245mm. 1 Jan 1815. Built by George Dance junior, 1782–7. *RA* 13,1. (*Bank of England* 218)

75 p 155 The Old Bailey. 180 × 125/250 × 150mm. 1 June 1814. *RA* 11,34.

76 Cold Bath Fields Prison. 123 × 203/150 × 250mm. 1 Augt 1814. Pencil and water-colour drawing (123 × 201mm), 'T.H. Shepherd 1814', in BM (*Crace* 32.36). *RA* 12,7.

118 · ANTIQUARIAN AND TOPOGRAPHICAL CABINET* [1817–19]

Publication of the first issue of this work was announced in the *Monthly Literary Advertiser* for December 1806:

Antiquarian Cabinet, No. 1, foolscap 8vo. 2s 6d.

The First Number, containing Eight highly finished Engravings, with appropriate Letter Press Descriptions ... This work will be published in regular Monthly Numbers.... Every Six Numbers to make a Volume, in which will be given an engraved Vignette Title-page and Tailpiece, so that each Volume shall contain Fifty Plates....

Some Copies in demy Octavo will be printed on beautiful paper, at 4s. each Number

The complete work, bound, made up ten volumes running from 1807 to 1811. James Storer and John Greig engraved for it a collection of small-scale etchings, about half the size of those they made for their own *Select Views* (no 90) of 1804–5, and proportionately refined in their execution. Each separate plate is accompanied by two pages of explanatory letterpress. These are unpaginated and are awkwardly referred to from the index by the printer's signatures; there is also a list of plates grouped by county. London illustrations are confined to vols 1, 3, 6–7, 9 and 10 in this first issue.

The year after its completion the same group of booksellers embarked upon another similar, but less

extensive collection, entitled *Ancient Reliques* (no 109), with which Storer and Greig were also connected. In 1817 one of this group, Messrs Sherwood, Neely & Jones, issued this announcement:

This day is published, printed in Royal 8vo, containing 10 beautiful engravings, price 2s 6d No V (to be continued Monthly) of an entirely new and improved edition of the Antiquarian and Topographical Cabinet ... Each Number, price 2s 6d. will comprise Ten Plates printed upon the same page with the Historical Descriptions; each plate forming a head-piece in the manner of Grose's Antiquities. This arrangement will obviate the inconvenience of continually turning the book to view the subjects, as in the first edition.... The whole Work will be comprised in Six Volumes, containing 100 Plates each, with a Vignette Title and Tail-piece.

Not only did the publishers reissue the original plates in this miniaturized Grose format (see no 50) but also threw in etchings from their *Ancient Reliques*, setting out their intentions in the preface:

The design of this work is to comprise in miniature an Assemblage of Views, &c. interesting to the Antiquary, the Topographer, and the Admirer of picturesque Scenery. The *venerable* Cathedral, the *ancient* Castle, the *ruined* Abbey, the *baronial* Mansion, the *modern* Palace, the Druidical Cromlech, or *Logan Stone*, the *sculptured* Font, the *elegant* Cross, the *picturesque* View; in short, whatever scene may be supposed either interesting in itself, or from association with interesting objects, *that* subject will be included among the other decorations.

Each volume will comprise One Hundred Plates, accompanied with two Vignettes, and a List of all the Subjects it contains. At the close of the work a general Index will be given, and the Plates being arranged in Counties alphabetically, no difficulty will occur in finding any subject, although for obvious reasons the work is not paged.

The Antiquarian and Topographical Cabinet: containing a series of elegant views of the most interesting objects of curiosity in Great Britain. Accompanied with letter-press description. Vol. I (II–X). London: Published for the Proprietors by W. Clarke, New Bond Street; J. Carpenter, Old Bond Street; and A.D. Symonds, Paternoster Row (also, in later vols: 'C. Chapple, Pall Mall; J.M. Richardson, Cornhill, and Sherwood, Neeley and Jones, Paternoster Row'). 1807 (1808–11). Coe, Printer, 10 Little Carter Lane, London.

The Antiquarian and Topographical Cabinet: containing a series of elegant views of the most interesting objects of curiosity in Great Britain. Vol. I (II–VI) (vignette and epigraph) London: Published for the Proprietor By J. Murray, Nornaville and Fell, A. Molteno, C. Chapple, Taylor and Hessey, J.M. Richardson, and Sherwood,

Neely, and Jones. ('A Molteno' dropped from imprint after vol.3) 1817 (1818–19). Coe, Printer, Little Carter Lane, St Paul's.

Octavo, 240 × 145mm. 1817–19

COLLATION Vol. 1 (1817). Title-page; preface (1 leaf); 130 plates with letterpress; list of plates (1 leaf). Vol. 2 (1817); Title-page; 134 plates with letterpress; list of plates (1 leaf). Vol. 3 (1818). Title-page; 126 plates with letterpress; list of plates (1 leaf). Vol. 4 (1818). Title-page; 144 plates with letterpress; list of plates (1 leaf). Vol. 5 (1818). Title-page; 139 plates with letterpress; list of plates (1 leaf). Vol. 6 (1819). Title-page; county index to the subjects in vols 1–6 (4pp); 146 plates with letterpress; list of plates (1 leaf).

The plates, now in their second state, were cut down for printing as headpieces to the letterpress, causing publication-line and caption, and sometimes the credits, to disappear. In neither state were they numbered but numbers were assigned to them in the check-lists at the close of each volume and these are used in the listing below. The descriptions of the plates are arranged in the order in which they are bound in the 1817–19 edition, but details are transcribed from the 1807–11 edition and from the *Ancient Reliques* plates before their lettering had been removed. Reference to these is made by means of the abbreviations *ATC* and *AR* followed by the relevant volume number and letterpress signature. the *ATC* publication-lines read: 'Published for the Proprietors by W. Clarke, New Bond Street (and J. Carpenter, Old Bond Street) (date).' Only London plates are listed.

VOL. 1

1 pl.10 Guildhall Chapel ... April 1, 1810. 85 × 60/110 × 90mm. *ATC* 7,F5.

2 pl.74 Tower of London. Engrav'd by J. Storer ... from a Drawing by J. Greig ... Mar 1, 1808. 60 × 85/100 × 150mm. The White Tower. *ATC* 3,E2.

3 pl.75 Part of the Tower of London. Drawn & Engraved by J. Storer ... Jan 1, 1810. 90 × 60/120 × 100mm. The Bloody Tower. *ATC* 7,C11.

VOL. 2

4 pl.9 London Stone ... Feb 1, 1807. 85 × 60/115 × 110mm. *ATC* 1,D13.

5 pl.40 St Augustine's Church, London. Engraved by J. Greig ... from a Drawing by Wm Deeble ... May 1, 1811. 60 × 87/80 × 140mm. Austin Friars. *ATC* 9,G2.

6 pl.41 Priory Gate, Clerkenwell. Engraved by J. Storer from a drawing by H. Gastineau ... June 1, 1811. 85 × 58/115 × 100mm. *ATC* 10.

7 pl.42 (Monumental Effigy of Dr. Donne/St Paul's Cathedral) 95 × 74/110 × 90mm.

VOL. 3

8 pl.32 (Remains of an ancient Crypt in St Martins-le-Grand) 80 × 72/108 × 100mm.

9 pl.44 Ruins of the Convent of Nuns, Minories, London. Engraved by J. Storer ... from a Drawing by J. Cranch ... May 1, 1810. 60 × 85/80 × 140mm. 'Abbey of Nuns, St Botolph Aldgate'. *ATC* 7,G2.

10 pl.45 The Chapel of the White Tower. Drawn & Engraved by J. Storer ... April 1, 1807. 88 × 60/110 × 93mm. St John's Chapel, Tower of London. *ATC* 1,F7.

11 pl.55 The Manor House, Canonbury, Middlesex. Engraved & Published by J. Storer from a drawing by H. Gastineau ... Augt 1, 1812. 100 × 72/110 × 100mm. *AR* 2,B.

12 pl.57a Part of the Temple Church, London. Drawn & Engd. by S. Tyrrell ... Dec 1, 1812. 72 × 100/90 × 140mm. *AR* 2,G.

13 pl.57b Entrance to the Temple Church, London. Drawn & Engd. by S. Tyrrell ... Dec. 1, 1812. 70 × 100/92 × 145mm. *AR* 2,G.

14 pl.62 The Temple Hall, London. Drawn & Engd. by S. Tyrrell ... Dec. 1, 1812. 70 × 100/90 × 140mm. Middle Temple. *AR* 2,G.

15 pl.70 Ancient Gateway, Southwark. Engrav'd by J. Storer ... from a Drawing by G. Herron ... Jan 1, 1810. 60 × 85/80 × 140mm. 'Remains of the Monastery of St Mary Overee'. *ATC* 7,C9.

VOL. 4

16 pl.14 Gerard's Hall, London. Drawn and Engrav'd by J. Greig ... March 1, 1811. 60 × 90/100 × 155mm. *ATC* 9, E4.

17 pl.54a Part of the Grey Friars Monastery or Christs Hospital London. Drawn by T. Whichelo. Engd. by J. Lambert. Published Nov 1, 1812. 72 × 102/90 × 145mm. *AR* 2,F.

18 pl.54b The Writing School &c. Christ's Hospital. Drawn & Engd. by J. Lambert. Published Nov 1, 1812. 70 × 102/90 × 140mm. *AR* 2,F.

19 pl.54c The Hall of Christ's Hospital. Drawn by Whichelo. Engd. by Woolnoth. 75 × 100/98 × 145mm. *AR* 2,F.

VOL. 5

20 pl.19 St Bartholomew's Hospital, London. Drawn & Engd. by H. Summons. Published Dec. 1, 1812. 70 × 100/90 × 140mm. *AR* 2,F.

21 pl.99 Physicians College London. Drawn & Engraved by S. Tyrrell. Published Nov 1, 1812. 100 × 70/110 × 100mm. *AR* 2,F.

22 pl.41 (Nelson's Tomb under the Crypt of St Paul's Cathedral) 75 × 85/110 × 140mm.

23 pl.73a Westminster Hall. Engraved by J. Greig ... from a Drawing by Wm. Deeble ... Sept 1, 1809. 62 × 85/82 × 140mm. *ATC* 6,E7.

24 pl.73b Entrance to Westminster Hall. Engraved by J. Greig ... from a Drawing by Wm. Deeble ... Sept 1, 1809. 63 × 88/80 × 140mm. *ATC* 6,E7.

25 pl.73c Part of Westminster Hall. Engraved by J. Greig ... from a Drawing by Wm. Deeble ... Sept 1, 1809. 85 × 60/105 × 95mm. *ATC* 6,E7.

VOL. 3 (1808 only, at C7)

26 C7 Sutton's Tomb, Charter House, London. Engraved by J. Storer ... from a Drawing by T. Whichelo ... Jan 1, 1808. 100 × 65/150 × 110mm.

119 · CRAPELET'S SOUVENIRS DE LONDRES [1817]

The Imprimerie Crapelet was founded by Charles Crapelet who arrived in Paris from Bassigny in 1774 to serve his apprenticeship in printing and who died there in 1809. According to the Bibliothèque Nationale catalogue the text of this book, which takes the form of informative letters to friends, was written by Georges-A. Crapelet. The illustrations, by Jean-Jérôme Baugean, and the map of London were originally published in the *Description de Londres* of 1810 by Barjaud and Landon (no 103). Their page and plate numbers have been burnished out. The original issue is referred to with the abbreviation *BL* followed by the page number.

Souvenirs de Londres en 1814 et 1816; suivis de l'histoire et de la description de cette ville dans son état actuel; Avec 12 Planches et un Plan de Londres. A Paris, De l'Imprimerie de Crapelet, M.DCCC.XVII.

Octavo, 205 × 110mm.   1817

COLLATION   Half-title; title-page; pp v–vi, Avertissement; pp 1–270, Souvenirs de Londres; pp 271–7, contents; pp 279–81, map refs; directions to binder (1 leaf).

1 p 29 Abbaye de Westminster/Abbey Church of St Peter's Westminster. 85 × 140mm. *BL* 69.

2 p 32 Chapelle de Henry VII/Henri the seventh's Chapel. 87 × 140mm. *BL* 75.

3 p 34 Hôtel de Sommerset/Sommerset house. 85 × 140mm. *BL* 155.

4 p 38 Hôtel de Lord Maire/Mansion House. 82 × 140mm. *BL* 121.

5 p 39 Eglise de St. Paul/St Paul's Cathedral. 80 × 140mm. *BL* 45.

6 p 66 Maison de campagne de Garrick/David Garrick Seat. 82 × 140mm. *BL* 197.

7 p 69 Palais de St James/St James's Palace. 80 × 142mm. *BL* 143.

8 p 80 Château de Windsor/Windsor Castle. 80 × 140mm. *BL* 203.

9 p 119 Hôpital de Greenwich/Greenwich Hospital. 85 × 138mm. *BL* 173.

10 p 127 (ie p 202) Le Monument./Monument. 140 × 80mm. *BL* 127.

11 p 154 La Bourse./Royal Exchange. 82 × 140mm. *BL* 109.

12 p 247 Hôtel de la compagnie des Indes/The East India house. 83 × 140mm. *BL* 107.

13 p 281 (tr) Plan/de Londres/Westminster/et Southwark. Gravé par Moisy, Place St Michel No 129. 170 × 273/200 × 300mm. *BL* front.

120 · HERBERT'S LONDON BEFORE THE GREAT FIRE [1817–18]

That long-running series of London illustrations, *Londina Illustrata* (no 131), which was not published in its entirety until 1834, was started in 1808 by William Herbert, antiquary and close friend of another keen London topographer, Edward Wedlake Brayley. After its first Number it was taken in hand by the printseller Robert Wilkinson, who continued to issue annual batches of prints and text but modified Herbert's original intention, which was to build up a collection of engraved copies of old prints, drawings and paintings of the metropolis. In 1818, however, no Numbers were issued and this was perhaps because Herbert had started publishing a new series on the principles which he had intended should govern *Londina Illustrata*. The new work was promoted by an undated prospectus:

Interesting Topographical Work Just Published (to be continued Periodically), Nos 1 and 2 of London before the Great Fire: or, a Series of Engravings (with historical and topographical accounts) illustrative of the Early State, Buildings, Monuments, and Antiquities of the Metropolis' ... will, as its title imports, be exclusively devoted to Accounts or Representations of the State and Appearance of the Metropolis and its Environs as they formerly existed ... a picture of the Antient London, consisting of General Views, Plans &c of London and its suburbs; prospects of public places, remarkable buildings &c. taken at various periods before the Fire of 1666.

1. The City, its Walls, Gates, Fortresses &c.
2. The Thames, its Banks and Bridges.
3. Streets, Public Places, Monuments &c.
4. Royal Palaces.
5. Mansions of Nobility.
6. Churches and Convents.
7. Public buildings generally.
8. Miscellaneous Objects of Antiquity.

Advertisement: This work will be published in Numbers on papers of the following sizes, and prices, viz. on Vellum Royal 4to, 8s; on Vellum Elephant 4to, 10s 6d; and on Vellum Colombier 4to, 16s each: each Number to consist of Four Plates ... The prints ... will be accompanied by Letter Press ... with numerous vignettes cut in wood. Every sixth Number will conclude a Part and Five Parts or Six will complete the work which will contain upwards of 150 Plates ... Two elegant Volumes. *These prints, which will be found particularly suited to illustrate various popular topographical works, especially *Mr Pennant's Account of London*; may also be had singly, price 2s each on small paper.

London: Published by J.R. Harrison (late of the Firm of Boydell & Co.) Removed to No 78 Cornhill: And sold by W. Herbert, 7, Mead Place, Westminster Bridge Road.

This grandiose scheme for a rival to *Londina Illustrata* came to grief in its second year (1818) whereas the original series resumed publication in January 1819 and flourished until the death of Robert Wilkinson in 1825.

Herbert, who became Librarian of the Guildhall Library in 1828, deposited a set of proofs (A 4.5, no 6) there and, in a manuscript annotation dated 22 August 1831, obligingly described the demise of the series:

The 1st Part of this work was published by me in 1817 ... intended to be confined to the illustrations of the Metropolis at that Period ... Mr Harrison of the late firm of Boydell & Co, Printsellers ... having seen the First Part, was anxious to have a share, and agreed to continue to work in partnership. The plan was enlarged and parts 1

and 2 were published by that house. Before the 3rd Part could be got ready a dispute took place between the Executors of Alderman Boydell and it ended in transferring the house, stock in trade, and whole business to Hurst and Robinson. This change put a total stop to the work which had a number of most respectable subscribers, and bade fair to increase in public favor, and it has ever since laid dormant.

The present copy is made up from the author's own proofs and contains the whole preparation of Part III, viz. the Printer's Proof-sheets of the Letter-press inlaid ... a great deal of very curious matter relative to Winchester House, Southwark, and the Bankside ... It has proof impressions of 4 interesting plates, which were intended to accompany this part together with a wood vignette of the ruins of Winchester House.

Neither of these plates nor a particle of the letter-press of this Part III have ever been published, and probably never will.

Josiah Harrison, a relative of Josiah Boydell's, had been his partner since 1807, but on Boydell's death in 1817 the stock was put up for sale and fetched £40,000 in the following year. The two Numbers of *London before the Great Fire* were acquired by Wilkinson who must have had difficulty in disposing of them since when it was the turn in 1825 of his stock to be sold by auction over 500 copies fell to a bid of £23.

The British Library copy (Cup.1247.ccc.7) of the first two Numbers is in the 'Elephant Quarto' edition, complete with woodcut wrappers with the title in an ornamental border:

London/before the Great Fire;/or,a/Series of Engravings,/(with historical and topographical accounts)/illustrative of the/Early State, Buildings, Monuments,/and Antiquities/of the Metropolis/(thin and thick rule) London:/ Published by (in MS: 'J.R. Harrison 78 Cornhill late of the Firm of') Messrs Boydell and Co. Cheapside (rule)/1818. (in MS: 'And sold by W. Herbert 7 Mead Place, Westmr Bridge Street.')

Quarto, 342 × 280mm.   1818

The Guildhall Library, in addition to Herbert's annotated proof set, has a copy of the first Number with its wrapper, in a form not mentioned in the prospectus: 'Large Paper. No. 1. Price £1.1.0 with Proof Prints'; this measures 440 × 300mm.

The plates are reproductions of, mostly unidentified, sixteenth and seventeenth century views, the only debts acknowledged being to Hollar and Visscher. As in *Londina Illustrata* each view is accompanied by a vignette showing another aspect of the same subject. Two of the plates are credited to

274

Bartholomew Howlett, one of Wilkinson's chief engravers.

There are three varieties of publication-line. On those proof copies which have been lettered:

(a) 'Published for Proprietors by William Herbert, Penlington Place, London, 1817.'

On plates published by Josiah Harrison:

(b) 'London, Published (date) by Boydell & Co. No 90 Cheapside.'

(c) 'London, Published by Messrs Boydell & Co. Cheapside (date).'

NO I

1 pl.1 A View of the South Front of Baynard's Castle, London.... /as it appeared about the year 1640 – Ruins of Baynards Castle after the Fire of 1666. (b) Jany 1818. 125 × 200,45 × 80/210 × 270mm.

(4pp of text with woodcut vignette)

2 pl.2 Bridewell Palace/with the entrance to the Fleet River As they appeared ... 1660 – The Thames Front ... An. 1540. (b) Jany 1818. 145 × 255,60 × 80/215 × 280mm.

(4pp of text with woodcut vignette, 'W. Hughes sc.')

3 pl.3 The Strand/in its Antient State Anno 1547/with the Strand Cross, Covent Garden &c./and the procession of Edward the Sixth/to his coronation – The Strand/and its neighbourhood anno 1700/looking from Arundel House. (b) Jany 1818. Each 158 × 115/230 × 280mm. Another detail of the Cowdray coronation procession is in *Londina Illustrata*, pl. 119. See also *Vetusta Monumenta* (no 36), item 67.

(2pp of text)

4 pl.4 (tm) North West Suburbs of London:– (lm) The Parish of St Giles in the Fields, London – A View/of part of the Northwest Suburbs/of London ... 1570 – The Seal of the Antient Hospital of St Giles. (b) Jany 1818. 162 × 270, etc/215 × 290mm. 'Ralph Aggas partly and partly parish documents'.

(2pp of text)

NO II

5 pl.1 A South East View of London/before the destruction of St Paul's Steeple by Fire A.D.1560.... from a painting in the possession of Mr. John Grove of Richmond, engraved in 1754 ... but the plate was afterwards mislaid.... Engraved by B. Howlett from the Print dedicated to the Earl of Hardwicke. (c) Septr 2, 1818. 180 × 295, etc/250 × 310mm. Copy of BL Maps: *K. top.* 21.58: 'To the Right Honble Philip Earl of Hardwicke ... This South East View of the City of London. Engraved from a very Ancient Picture—is humbly inscribed by ... J. Grove. J. Wood sculp. Publish'd 18th Novr 1754'. 330 × 545/345 × 560mm. A View from St Olave's stairs.

6 pl.2 Bankside, Southwark in 1648, with a view of Holland's Leaguer, and of the Ancient Stews or licensed Brothels there ... B. Howlett sc. (c) Septr 2, 1818. 158 × 250/235 × 280mm. With vignetted map of Bankside. A woodcut of this notorious brothel, reproduced from Nicholas Goodman's tract, was published in 1822 as pl.153 of *Londina Illustrata*.

(14pp of text with woodcut vignettes of Globe and Bear Garden)

7 (pl.2a View of Globe Theatre) Wise sc. 130 × 190/35 × 250mm. Proof before letters.

8 pl.3 Cornhill London/As it appeared about the year 1630 – The Carrefourre with St Peter's ... 1599 (c) October 15th, 1818. 165 × 240,40 × 60/230 × 280mm. cf with *Londina Illustrata*, item 6.

(2pp of text)

9 pl.4 A View of Cold Harbour in Thames Street, London./As it appeared about the year 1600. – Remains of Cold Harbour in the Year 1665. (c) October 15th 1818. 135 × 215/215 × 280mm. The vignette is inspired by Hollar's 'True and Exact Prospect before the Fire' (*Hind* 19).

(2pp of text)

NO III (unpublished)

10 pl.1 A South East View/of Winchester House Bankside, London/as it appeared about the year 1647 ... – The Hall of Winchester House &c from a scarce view 1619. 137 × 230,40 × 70/230 × 280mm. The upper view 'from Hollar's large six sheet view of London'.

(2pp of text)

11 pl.2 Lambeth Marsh/as it appeared about the year 1670 ... Etched by I. Barnett 1820 – One of the antient inns of Lambeth ... 165 × 255,45 × 80/235 × 290mm.

(2pp of text)

12 pl.3 Lambeth Church and Palace/as they appeared about ... 1670 – Lambeth Palace before rebuilding of the Hall/Engraved from Hollar. 160 × 255,40 × 80/230 × 290mm.

(2pp of text)

13 pl.4 A View of the Old Boro' Market Southwark ... /in ... 1616. Engraved from the view of London by Vischer. 152 × 260,60 × 90/225 × 290mm. With a vignette of Nonesuch House on London Bridge.

(4pp of text)

121 · HUGHSON'S WALKS THROUGH LONDON [1817]

David Pugh, alias Hughson, was clearly not going to be outdone by Pennant and Lysons, two other resolute foot-sloggers, when he added to the title-pages of his five-volume description of London (no 93) 'from an actual perambulation'. Twelve years later he was again on the march to gather material for *Walks through London*. John Murray's prospectus for the work announced that it was to be illustrated with 96 engravings on copper and 24 on wood and might be subscribed on the following conditions:

1. This work will be comprised in Twelve Monthly Numbers, which may be bound together or in Two Volumes.

2. Each Number will contain 8 highly-finished Engravings on Copper and Two or more on Wood, and Thirty-six pages of letterpress ... in Foolscap Octavo, price 2s 6d or in Demy Octavo with Proof Impressions of the Plates, price 4s per Number.

** One Hundred Copies, and no more, will be printed in Royal 8vo with India Paper Proofs of the Plates, price 10s 6d each number ... The whole will be ready for delivery April 1st, 1817.

The completed work did indeed include the number of illustrations promised but publication in Numbers must have got off to a slow start because after the first two batches of eight plates output was increased and as many as 24 bear the terminal date of 1 April 1817:

1816	September	8
	October	8
	November	9
	December	11
1817	January	12
	February	8
	March	16
	April	24
		96

To judge by the 'Table of References' to the general map, bound in the first volume, the original scheme was to describe the capital in 12 chapters, each covering a perambulation, with perhaps a thirteenth for the eastern suburbs. Every perambulation was to be based on a separate plan preceding it and ornamented with a vignette of some building which characterized the neighbourhood and there were also to be plates of notable buildings on the route. However the gazetteer itself was misleading since it referred the reader to 'Walks' but the numbers given actually refer to a map-grid. Eleven 'Walks' were issued, as intended, each with its separate, numbered plan, but then the scheme went adrift and a marathon 'Walk 12' runs from p 163 to p 234; it surveys the Strand and Westminster areas outlined on the twelfth and thirteenth plans and is illustrated with two dozen plates. Then follows a misnumbered 'Walk 11' which extends from p 235 to p 278 and comments on the areas shown on the five plans for 'Walks' 14 to 18, ie N. and S. of Oxford Street, E. of Tottenham Court Road, E. of Bishopsgate and Bankside. Perversely, these plans are all directed to be bound in with the text of the 'Walks' headed 'Southwark, Walk 1 and Walk 2' and 'Environs of London, Walks 1 to 5', which have illustrations but no area plans.

The book is rounded off with a 20 page architectural history and includes 'improvements' which were then impending such as Nash's Regent Street, already adumbrated on two of the plans.

Walks through London, including Westminster and the Borough of Southwark, with the Surrounding Suburbs; describing every thing worthy of observation in the Public Buildings, Places of Entertainment, Exhibitions, Commercial and Literary Institutions, &c. down to the present period: Forming a complete Guide to the British Metropolis. By David Hughson, L.L.D. London: Printed for Sherwood, Neely, and Jones, Paternoster-Row; Murray, Albemarle Street; Clarke, New Bond-Street; Lindsell, Wigmore-Street; Chapple, Pall-Mall; Colnaghi, Cockspur-Street; Walker, Strand; Taylor and Hessey, Fleet Street; J.M. Richardson, Cornhill; Cowie and Co. Poultry; Blackwood, Princes-Street, Edinburgh; Brash and Reid, Glasgow; and M. Keene, and J. Cumming, Dublin. 1817.

Octavo, 223 × 140mm.   1817

COLLATION   Title-page; preface (2pp); directions to binder (4pp); table of map refs (4pp); pp 1–368, Walks; list of woodcuts (1 leaf); index, addenda, corrigenda (6pp).
(Or in 2 vols, each with appropriate title-page, the second starting at p 163.)

Duodecimo, 160 × 100mm.   1817

COLLATION Title-page; preface (2pp); list of wood-cuts (1 leaf); directions to binder (4pp); table of map refs (4pp); pp 1–414, Walks; index, addenda, corrigenda (6pp).

(Or in 2 vols, each with appropriate title-page, the second starting at p 183.)

The refinement of the vignettes and the small-scale, well-proportioned copper plates look forward to the delicacy of detail which, at the end of the decade following, became a commonplace among engravers on steel. The three principal artist engravers, J. Greig, T. Higham and W. Wallis, were themselves later to produce plates in this more durable medium to illustrate Elmes's *Metropolitan Improvements* (no 154) and *London and its Environs* (no 161) while J.C. Varrall contributed steel-engravings to Trotter's *Select Illustrated Topography* (no 190). Other artists involved were E.J. Roberts, W. Morland and C.J.M. Whichelo, some of whose work is in the Crace Collection and who contributed drawings which were engraved on copper for a number of the topographical works of the period, such as the *Beauties of England and Wales* (no 104), *Londina Illustra* (no 131) and the Storer and Greig *Select Views* (no 90). It is noteworthy that some of T. Higham's drawings, such as pl.33 ('Entrance to St Bartholomew's Hospital'), pl.69 ('St George's Hanover Square') and pl.75 ('Sessions House, Clerkenwell'), include that staffage of citizens and their dogs and horses which is so pleasing a feature of the two Shepherd books to which he contributed.

The 96 unnumbered plates and the map are arranged according to the binder's directions while the 24 woodcuts (unlisted below), chiefly of Gothic architectural detail, are printed with text. The views, other than those on the plans, are surrounded by a ruled frame beneath which the credit reads: 'Drawn and Engraved by ... for the Walks through London.' Most of the plans include a compass-rose. Below the captions, engraved in swash lettering, is engraved the publication-line 'Published by W. Clarke New Bond Street (date).' The plate listed to appear opposite p 176 in the 'Directions', of Somerset House, is not included in any copy seen, but an unlisted plate, 'Fitzroy Square', is sometimes to be found facing p 252. Plates in the duodecimo edition are trimmed almost down to the plate-marks and appear, because of the resetting of the text, opposite different pages, as indicated; also a different map is substituted for the original.

VOL. 1

1 front. (tr) London,/and its/Environs. (tl, scale, 3¼" to the mile) 230 × 540/250 × 570mm. Extending from Hyde Park to West India Dock, Pentonville Road to Lambeth Palace. (*Darlington and Howgego* 270)

(alternative front. in duodecimo ed) (tr) A Plan of/London,/Westminster/and/Southwark. Pubd July 18th 1814 by Sherwood, Neely & Jones, Paternoster Row. 170 × 275/190 × 310mm. Extent as above. (*Darlington and Howgego* 243b)

2 p 3 Walk 1st (plan centered on the Tower of London) – The New Custom House. Drawn & Engraved by J. Greig ... Published ... Septr. 1, 1816. 25 × 70/147 × 90mm. View vignetted. Custom House rebuilt by David Laing, 1813–17.

3 p 4 The Royal Exchange from Cornhill. Drawn and Engraved by W. Wallis ... Published ... April 1, 1817. 90 × 60/150 × 100mm.

4 p 6 St Michael's Church, Cornhill. Drawn & Engraved by T. Higham ... Published ... Novr. 1, 1816. 90 × 70/150 × 100mm. From churchyard.

5 p 7 The East India House. Drawn & Engraved by J. Greig ... Published ... Sepr. 1, 1816. 65 × 92/90 × 145mm.

6 p 11 Ironmongers Hall. Drawn & Engraved by J. Greig ... Published ... Sepr. 1, 1816. 65 × 92/90 × 145mm. 12mo ed p 13.

7 p 14 The Mint. Drawn & Engraved by I. Varrall ... Published ... Sepr. 1, 1816. 62 × 92/90 × 145mm. 12mo ed p 16.

8 p 17 The Trinity House. Drawn & Engraved by W. Wallis ... Published ... Sepr. 1, 1816. 65 × 92/90 × 145mm. 12mo ed p 19.

9 p 19 The Tower of London. Drawn & Engraved by I.C. Varrall ... Published ... Septr. 1, 1816. 60 × 92/90 × 145mm. From the river. 12mo ed p 20.

10 p 25 St Dunstan's, in the East. Drawn & Engraved by J. Greig ... Published ... Sepr. 1, 1816. 92 × 62/145 × 90mm. 12mo ed p 28.

11 p 28 London Bridge. Drawn & Engraved by W. Wallis ... Published ... Mar. 1, 1817. 60 × 92/100 × 150mm. 12mo ed p 32.

12 p 30 The Monument. Drawn and Engraved by J. Greig ... Published ... January 1, 1817. 92 × 62/145 × 90mm. 12mo ed p 34.

13 p 36 Walk, 2nd (plan centered on Bishopsgate Street) – Crosby Hall. Drawn & Engraved by J. Greig ... Published ... Oct. 1, 1816. 60 × 45/145 × 90mm. View vignetted. 12mo ed p 41. (*Longford* 422)

14 p 45 Finsbury Square. Engraved by J. Greig from a Sketch by W. Morland ... Published ... April 1, 1817. 67 × 93/100 × 150mm. 12mo ed p 51.

15 p 47 The Excise Office. Drawn & Engraved by T. Higham ... Published ... Dec. 1, 1816. 72 × 85/100 × 150mm. 12mo ed p 53. In Broad Street.

16 p 48 Walk 3d. (centered on Lombard Street) – The Mansion House. Drawn & Engraved by J. Greig ... Published ... Novr. 1, 1816. 60 × 70/145 × 90mm. 12 mo ed p 54. View vignetted.

17 p 50 Fishmongers Hall. Engraved by J. Greig from a Drawing by F.W.L. Stockdale ... Published ... Feby 1, 1817. 68 × 82/100 × 150mm. 12mo ed p 56.

18 p 58 Walk 4th. (plan centered on Lothbury) – The Bank from Lothbury. Drawn & Engraved by J. Greig ... Published ... Novr. 1, 1816. 40 × 70/145 × 90mm. 12mo ed p 65. View vignetted. (*Bank of England* 57)

19 p 61 The Auction Mart, Bartholomew Lane. Drawn & Engraved by T. Higham ... Published ... Apr. 1, 1817. 63 × 85/100 × 150mm. 12mo ed p 69.

20 p 64 The London Institution. Engraved by W. Wallis from a drawing by W. Morland ... Published ... Mar. 1, 1817. 63 × 90/100 × 150mm. 12mo ed p 72. Finsbury Circus, built by William Brooks, 1815–19.

21 p 69 Walk 5th. (plan centered on Watling Street) – St Mary le Bow, Cheapside. Drawn & Engraved by J. Greig ... Published ... Dec. 1, 1816. 60 × 37/147 × 100mm. 12mo ed p 78. View vignetted.

22 p 71 Skinners Hall. Drawn & Engraved by J. Greig ... Published ... Jan. 1, 1817. 70 × 85/100 × 150mm. 12mo ed p 80. Façade designed by Wiliam Jupp, 1808.

23 p 78 Walk 6th. (plan centered on London Wall) – Goldsmiths Hall. Drawn & Engraved by J. Greig ... Published ... Dec. 1, 1816. 40 × 65/145 × 90mm. 12mo ed p 87. View vignetted.

24 p 79 St Lawrence's Church, King Street, Cheapside. Drawn & Engraved by J. Greig ... Published ... Jan. 1, 1817. 65 × 80/100 × 150mm. 12mo ed p 88. St Lawrence Jewry from S.E.

25 p 80 Guildhall. Drawn & Engraved by J. Greig ... Published ... Apr. 1, 1817. 87 × 67/150 × 100mm. 12mo ed p 89.

26 p 82 Blackwell Hall, King Street. Drawn & Engraved by T. Higham ... Published ... Feby 1, 1817. 65 × 90/100 × 150mm. 12mo ed p 92.

27 p 84 Sion College, London Wall. Drawn & Engraved by E.I. Roberts ... Published ... Jan. 1, 1817. 90 × 65/150 × 100mm. 12mo ed p 94.

28 p 91 Walk 7 (plan centered on Old Fish Street) – St Pauls School. Drawn & Engraved by J. Greig ... Published ... Jan. 1, 1817. 55 × 80/145 × 90mm. 12mo ed p 103. View vignetted.

29 p 95 Walk 8th. (plan centered on Newgate Street) – Physicians College. Drawn & Engraved by J. Greig ... Published ... Jan. 1, 1817. 60 × 50/145 × 90mm. 12mo ed p 106. View vignetted.

30 p 97 St Pauls Cathedral. Drawn & Engraved by I.C. Varrall ... Published ... October 1, 1816. 93 × 72/150 × 90mm. 12mo ed p 107.

31 p 107 Part of the Ancient Buildings, Christ's Hospital. Engraved by E.I. Roberts from a Drawing by I. Whichelo ... Published ... Novr. 1, 1816. 90 × 62/150 × 100mm. 12mo ed p 122.

32 p 108 Christ's Hospital. Drawn & Engraved by I. Greig ... Published ... April 1, 1817. 60 × 90/100 × 150mm. 12mo ed p 121. The 'New grammar school' built by the surveyor, James Lewis, 1793.

33 p 112 Entrance to St Bartholomews Hospital from Smithfield. Drawn & Engraved by T. Higham ... Published ... Novr. 1, 1816. 90 × 60/150 × 100mm. 12mo ed p 125.

34 p 115 Part of the Charter House. Drawn & Engraved by J. Greig ... Published ... Octr. 1, 1816. 63 × 93/100 × 150mm. 12mo ed p 130.

35 p 117 The Chapel of the Charter House. Drawn & Engraved by T. Higham ... Published ... Apr. 1, 1817. 65 × 93/100 × 150mm. 12mo ed p 131.

36 p 129 Walk 9th. (plan centered on Temple and Bridewell) – Middle Temple Hall. Drawn & Engraved by J. Greig ... Published ... Jan. 1, 1817. 75 × 55/145 × 90mm. 12mo ed p 145. View vignetted.

37 p 133 Interior of the Temple Church. Drawn & Engraved by E.I. Roberts... Published ... October 1, 1816. 92 × 62/150 × 100mm. 12mo ed p 149.

38 p 134 Entrance to the Temple Church. Engraved by E.I. Roberts from a Drawing by J. Turner ... Published ... November 1, 1816. 82 × 67/150 × 100mm. 12mo ed p 150.

39 p 140 Serjeants Inn, Fleet Street. Drawn & Engraved by W. Wallis ... Published ... Feb. 1, 1817. 97 × 62/150 × 100mm. 12mo ed p 157.

40 p 141 St Brides Church, Fleet Street. Engraved by I.C. Varrall from a Sketch by W. Morland ... Published ... March 1, 1817. 92 × 64/150 × 100mm. 12mo ed p 159.

41 p 144 Walk 10th. (plan centered on Hatton Garden) – Furnivals Inn, Interior. Drawn & Engraved by J. Greig ... Published ... Mar. 1, 1817. 55 × 75/145 × 90mm. 12mo ed p 162. View vignetted. Courtyard.

42 p 149 Furnivals Inn, Holborn. Engraved by T. Higham from a Drawing by I. Jones ... Published ... April 1, 1817. 60 × 88/100 × 150mm. 12mo ed p 166.

43 p 151 Walk 11th. (plan centered round Fetter Lane) – Staples Inn, Holborn. Drawn & Engraved by J. Greig ... Published ... Mar. 1, 1817. 55 × 70/145 × 88mm. 12mo ed p 170. View vignetted.

44 p 161 Serjeants Inn, Chancery Lane. Drawn & Engraved by J. Greig ... Published ... Jan 1, 1817. 93 × 60/150 × 90mm. 12mo ed p 181.

45 Temple Bar. Drawn & Engraved by W. Wallis ... Published ... October 1, 1816. 85 × 65/150 × 100mm. 12mo ed p 181.

73 p 260 St Georges Church, Bloomsbury. Engraved by W. Wallis from a Drawing by W. Morland ... Published ... Apr. 1, 1817. 95 × 67/150 × 100mm. 12mo ed p 291.

74 p 260 The Foundling Hospital. Drawn and Engraved by W. Wallis ... Published ... Decr. 1, 1816. 63 × 92/100 × 150mm. 12mo ed p 292.

75 p 264 The Sessions House, Clerkenwell Green. Drawn & Engraved by T. Higham ... Published ... Decr. 1, 1816. 60 × 90/90 × 145mm. 12mo ed p 297.

76 p 269 St Luke's Hospital, Old Street Road. Drawn & Engraved by T. Higham ... Published ... Apr. 1, 1817. 60 × 88/100 × 150mm. 12mo ed p 302. (*Bank of England* 222)

77 p 273 Christ Church, Spitalfields. Engraved by T. Higham from a Drawing by I. Jones ... Published ... Feb. 1, 1817. 98 × 65/148 × 90mm. 12mo ed p 307.

78 p 277 The Shipping Entrance, London Docks. Drawn & Engraved by I.C. Varrall ... Published ... January 1, 1817. 63 × 90/100 × 150mm. 12mo ed p 312.

79 p 279 Walk 14th. (plan centered on Old Bond Street) – Pulteney Hotel. Drawn and Engrav'd by I. Greig ... Published ... Apr. 1, 1817. 30 × 40/145 × 90mm. 12mo ed p 313. The plan has the proposed new Regent Street pecked in. The vignetted view is of Pulteney Hotel, 105 Piccadilly, formerly Lord Barrymore's house, refurbished to house the Emperor of Russia for the celebrations in June 1814; handy for the fireworks across the way in the park (see item 64).

80 p 287 Bishop Andrews Tomb St Mary Overies. Drawn and Engraved by J. Greig ... Published ... Mar. 1, 1817. 85 × 65/153 × 100mm. 12mo ed p 323.

81 p 291 Walk 15th. (plan centered on Wimpole Street) – Cavendish Square. Engraved by J. Greig from a Sketch by W. Morland ... Published ... Apr. 1, 1817. 25 × 50/145 × 90mm. 12mo ed p 328. Pecked lines on the plan show the projected Regent Street. Vignetted view to N. of Cavendish Square.

82 p 293 Christ Church Blackfriars. Engraved by J. Greig from a Drawing by I. Whichelo ... Published ... Mar. 1, 1817. 90 × 63/150 × 100mm. 12mo ed p 330.

83 p 296 The New Bethlem, St George's Fields. Drawn & Engraved by I.C. Varrall ... Published ... Dec. 1, 1816. 60 × 90/90 × 145mm. 12mo ed p 334. Built by James Lewis, 1812–15.

84 p 299 The Deaf and Dumb Asylum, Kent Road. Drawn and Engraved by I.C. Varrall ... Published ... Novr. 1, 1816. 65 × 92/100 × 152mm. 12mo ed p 336.

85 p 300 Walk 16th. (plan centered on High Holborn and Gray's Inn Road) – British Museum. Drawn & Engraved by J. Greig ... Published ... Apr. 1, 1817. 15 × 25/145 × 90mm. 12mo ed p 337. View vignetted. Montague House from the E.

86 p 300 The Entrance to the Archbishop of Canterbury's Palace, Lambeth. Drawn & Engraved by I. Varrall ... Published ... Decr. 1, 1816. 63 × 90/100 × 150mm. 12mo ed p 337.

87 p 301 Lambeth Pallace. Engraved by T. Higham from a Drawing by I. Jones ... Published ... April 1, 1817. 60 × 98/100 × 150mm. 12mo ed p 338. Romantic view from the river prophetic of many steel-engravings.

88 p 301 The Cloisters, Lambeth Palace. Drawn & Engraved by J. Greig ... Published ... Mar. 1, 1817. 62 × 90/100 × 150mm. 12mo ed p 339.

89 p 303 Vauxhall Bridge and Penitentiary, Millbank. Drawn & Engraved by I.C. Varrall ... Published ... Apr. 1, 1817. 52 × 105/100 × 150mm. 12mo ed p 340. Vauxhall Bridge was opened in July 1816; the Penitentiary was begun by John Harvey in 1813 and completed by Robert Smirke in 1816.

90 p 309 London from Greenwich Park. Drawn & Engraved by I.C. Varrall ... Published ... Sepr. 1, 1816. 63 × 92/88 × 145mm. 12mo ed p 347.

91 p 313 Walk 17th. (plan centered on City Road and Old Street) – St. Leonards, Shoreditch. Drawn & Engraved by I. Greig ... Published ... Apr. 1, 1817. 45 × 35/145 × 88mm. 12mo ed p 352. View vignetted.

92 p 331 Walk 18th. (plan centered on Blackfriars Road) – Blackfriars/Bridge. Drawn & Engraved by J. Greig ... Published ... April 1, 1817. 20 × 45/145 × 90mm. 12mo ed p 360. View vignetted. Southwark Road and Waterloo Road indicated on the plan by pecked lines.

93 p 333 Stepney Church. Drawn & Engraved by W. Wallis ... Published ... October 1, 1816. 65 × 90/90 × 145mm. 12mo ed p 374.

94 p 334 West India Import Dock. Drawn and Engraved by I.C. Varrall ... Published ... April 1, 1817. 62 × 92/100 × 150mm. 12mo ed p 376.

95 p 338 Kensington Palace. Drawn and Engraved by I.C. Varrall ... Published ... Oct. 1, 1816. 62 × 90/90 × 145mm. 12mo ed p 380. From Round Pond.

96 p 341 Chelsea Hospital from the banks of the Thames. Drawn and Engraved by W. Wallis ... Published ... November 1, 1816. 65 × 90/100 × 150mm. 12mo ed p 383. (*Longford* 29)

97 p 350 Mary le bone, New Church. Engraved by I. Greig from a Sketch by W. Morland ... Published ... April 1, 1817. 65 × 95/100 × 150mm. Built by Thomas Hardwick junior; consecrated 1817.

122 · DUGDALE'S MONASTICON ANGLICANUM* [1817–30]

The three volumes of Sir William Dugdale's *Monasticon Anglicanum* were first published in, respectively, 1655, 1661 and 1673 (no 6) and reissued in abridgement with supplements by John Stevens between 1718 and 1723. Almost a century elapsed before a new edition was undertaken: by the Rev Bulkeley Bandinel, Keeper of the Bodleian Library, to be published in 54 Parts, of which the first appeared on 1 June 1813. On completion of Part 4 two other editors came to his assistance, John Caley of the Augmentation Office and Henry Ellis, Keeper of Manuscripts at the British Museum, who soon became chief editor and transcribed much additional manuscript material. Seventeen years went by before all the Parts had been issued but by 1830 they were ready with their plates for binding, nominally into six magnificent folios but actually into eight, since the sixth volume was so extensive as to require division by the binder into three separate portions. In April 1846 the eight volumes were offered by James Bohn for £31 10s (as against an original price of £141 15s) and in May 1849 T.G. March of 116 Jermyn Street started reissuing them in monthly Parts. Details are here given of the first and sixth volumes, in which London illustrations feature.

Monasticon Anglicanum: a History of the Abbies and other Monasteries, Hospitals, Fries and Cathedral and Collegiate Churches, with their Dependencies in England and Wales ... Originally published in Latin by Sir William Dugdale Kt ... A New Edition, enriched with a large accession of Materials ... by John Caley, Keeper of the Records in the Augmentation Office, Henry Ellis, Keeper of Manuscripts in the British Museum and the Rev. Bulkeley Bandinel, Keeper of the Bodleian Library Oxford. Volume the First (Sixth). London: Printed for Longman, Hurst, Rees, Orme & Brown; Lackington, Hughes, Harding, Mavor & Jones; and Joseph Harding, 1817 (Printed for Joseph Harding; Harding and Lepard; and Longman, Rees, Orme, Brown and Green, 1830).

Folio, 470 × 320mm.   1817–30

COLLATION   Vol. 1. Half-title; engr title by Finden after Hollar; title-page; pp i–v, preface; p vi, general contents; pp vii–x, list of subscribers; pp xi–xvi, list of

plates; directions to binder, analytical contents (3pp); list of monasteries (1 leaf); pp i–xviii, preface; pp xix–li, introductory material; pp 1–642, Monasticon Anglicanum. Vol. 6 i. Half-title; engr title; title-page; pp v–xliii, analytical contents; half-title; pp iii–xii, The Carthusian Order; pp 1–604, Monasticon Anglicanum continued. Vol. 6 ii. Half-title; engr title; title-page; pp v–xvi, list of monasteries; half-title; pp 606–945, Monasticon Anglicanum continued; pp i–xcix, The Gilbertine Order; pp 947–1154, Monasticon Anglicanum continued. Vol. 6 iii. Half-title; engr title; title-page; pp v–xv, list of monasteries; pp 1159–630, Monasticon Anglicanum continued; pp 1633–62, appendix, corrections; pp 1665–870, general index.

A careful facsimile of Hollar's beautiful title-page was made by the engraver William Finden, who did likewise for all the plates in a new edition of Dugdale's *St Paul's* (no 125) but others were also employed on copying work and some of it, as for instance the three views of St John of Jerusalem, fell much below Finden's standard. No views of St Paul's Cathedral were included since Dugdale's work, specifically on the old Cathedral, was also being brought out in a new edition by Ellis, but strangely no facsimiles were made of the *Monasticon* plates by Hollar of St Katherine by the Tower or St George's Chapel, Windsor. The crowning glory of this edition however are the fine plates of cathedral and monastery interiors and exteriors which were both drawn and etched by John Coney. He was trained as an architect but soon turned away from that profession to make drawings of Gothic buildings which were exhibited at the Royal Academy. From 1810 he was engaged on drawing for John Booth's *Architectura Ecclesiastica Londini* (no 129) to which he contributed about half the views. That Harding the publisher considered himself lucky in obtaining his collaboration as chief illustrator is evident from the preface:

Among the Embellishments which the New Edition of the Monasticon presents the chief of the Prints by Hollar have been re-engraved.... King's Prints have been rejected as altogether worthless. The larger proportion of the Plates, it will be found, have been engraved in a better style of Art, from Drawings made exclusively for this work by Mr. John Coney, an artist whose execution possesses the freedom and delicacy of Piranesi without his occasional obscurity and coarseness.

This sumptuous new *Monasticon*, when complete, contained 246 views (exclusive of wood-engravings printed with the letterpress) provided, it was claimed, at a cost of 6000 guineas.

All the plates listed below recur, with their publication-lines burnished out, in the Middlesex section of vol. 1 of a posthumous collection of Coney's work:

Ecclesiastical Edifices of the Olden Times. A Series of Etchings with ground-plans and facsimiles of Hollar's views of the Cathedral and Conventual Churches, Monasteries, Abbeys, Priories, and other ecclesiastical edifices of England and Wales. By John Coney. In two volumes. London, James Bohn, 12 King William Street, Strand. MDCCCXLII.

VOL. 1 (p 264, Westminster Abbey plates with publication-line 'London, published by Longman & Co. & Lackington & Co. & Joseph Harding')

1 The Ichnography of the Church of Westminster A.D. 1682. 255 × 365mm. No credits, but copied from 1655 ed 1, p 54.

2 Westminster Abby, West View. After Hollar. Engraved by J. Lee. Published June 1, 1813. 265 × 188/370 × 255mm. 1655 ed 1, p 60.

3 Abbey Church of Westminster /King Henry the Seventh's Chapel. Drawn & Engraved by John Coney. Published March 25, 1822. 305 × 410/350 × 440mm. Exterior.

4 Westminster Abby./Chapel of King Edward the Confessor. 1817. Drawn & Engraved by John Coney. Published May 1818. 302 × 410/350 × 440mm. A larger drawing by Coney of the same subject is in the V & A (P.72–1917). It measures 558 × 470mm and is dated 1814.

VOL. 6 i (with publication-line 'London, Published (date) by Longman & Co, Lackington & Co. & Joseph Harding')

5 p 169 Priory Church of St. Saviour Southwark. Drawn & Engraved by John Coney. Published Decr 24 1819. 300 × 205/360 × 260mm. Interior, nave.

6 p 291 Priory of St Bartholomew London. 1818. Drawn & Engraved by John Coney. Published March 1, 1819. 205 × 300/260 × 360mm. Interior, looking W. from near Rahere's tomb.

VOL. 6 ii

7 p 799 South Gate of the House of Hospitallers of St John of Jerusalem – Remains of the Western Front of the Chapel of the House of Hospitallers of St John of Jerusalem – House of the Hospitallers of St John of Jerusalem Clerkenwell, taken from the South East. After Hollar. London: Published May 1, 1830 by Harding & Co. Pall Mall. 102 × 175,100 × 175,125 × 370/310 × 420mm. Poor copy, without credit, of 1661 ed 2, p 504.

8 p 817 The Temple Church, London, 1817. Drawn & Engraved by John Coney. London, Pubd July 1, 1818 by Longman & Co, Lackington & Co. and Joseph

Harding. 295 × 200/360 × 260mm. Interior of the 'Round'.

VOL. 6 iii

9 p 1594 Austin Friars Monastery, Middlesex. Drawn & Engraved by John Coney. London, Pubd. Septr 1, 1828 by Longman & Co., Harding Triphook & Lepard and Joseph Harding. 208 × 310/245 × 345mm. Exterior from N.W.

123 · BRAYLEY'S WESTMINSTER ABBEY [1818–23]

That this work is usually known as 'Neale's Westminster Abbey' is a tribute to the superb quality of the illustrations for which J.P. Neale was responsible and which were nearly all based on his original drawings. For indeed the text by E.W. Brayley is far from negligible and has been eulogized by Francis Bond, a more recent Abbey historian: 'The standard work on Westminster Abbey ... It incorporates the information on preceding writers and to it all books on Westminster published since are but supplementary'.

The printed list of subscribers numbers about 350, headed by George IV, the Emperor of Russia and the Kings of France and Prussia, and including numerous peers and bishops. Booksellers and printsellers also rallied round as the names of James Booth, William Clarke, Colnaghi, Charles Heath, Lackington, Molteno, Simco and Josiah Taylor bear witness, and the architectural profession is represented by John Soane, Jeffery Wyatt, James Elmes and James Lewis. William Capon, John Coney, J.S. Cotman, B.R. Haydon and John Varley are among the artists having no immediate connection with the work, and John Hawkins and Sir Thomas Phillipps among the collectors.

Subscribers marked with an asterisk in the list died before the publication was complete. The Parts were issued at irregular intervals from November 1816 and were available either in royal quarto at 16s, imperial quarto at 24s or 25 copies with proofs at £2 12s 6d. Publication-lines from 1 November 1816 to April 1823 are to be found on the plates, which came out each year in the following quantities:

1816	5	1820	5
1817	15	1821	10
1818	10	1822	4
1819	9	1823	3

The dates of the Whatman watermarks in the text of the first volume are 1814 and 1816, with the exception of the preliminaries, dated 1822. Those in the second volume run through chronologically from 1818 to 1822 and in the Henry VII Chapel supplement from 1822 to 1823. This supplement was paginated separately, explains Brayley in his preface, 'to enable subscribers to include it in the first volume and thus to render the thickness of both volumes proportionable'. The 1818 dedication to the Prince Regent had, by the time the second volume was published, to be supplemented by another to the same person, now George IV. Although written by Brayley alone the editorial work has the Britton-Brayley hallmark of attention to detail and thorough indexing, especially of the plates, which are tabled both in the general work and supplement with particulars of artist and engraver, plate number and name of dedicatee; there is also an extensive annotated bibliography and iconography of the Abbey up to the time of going to press. By May 1823 the work was available, complete in two volumes, at ten guineas royal quarto, 15 guineas imperial quarto (or, including India paper proofs, at £34 13s), 20 guineas crown folio and £34 13s Large Paper.

The History and Antiquities of the Abbey Church of St. Peter, Westminster; including Notices and Biographical Memoirs of the Abbots and Deans of that Foundation. Illustrated by John Preston Neale. The whole of the Literary Department by Edward Wedlake Brayley. In Two Volumes. Vol.I (II). London: Published by the Proprietor, J.P. Neale, Bennett-Street, Blackfriars-Road; and Sold by Longman, Hurst, Rees, Orme, and Brown, Paternoster-Row. 1818 (London: Printed for Hurst, Robinson, and Co. 90, Cheapside, and 8, Pall-Mall. 1823). Printed by T. Davison, Lombard-Street, Whitefriars.

Quarto, 295 × 240mm. (Large Paper 370 × 260mm)
1818–23

COLLATION Vol. 1. Title-page; dedication to the Prince Regent dated 17 June 1818; half-title; pp 3–230, History and Antiquities; index, corrigenda (16pp). Vol. 2. Title-page; dedication to George IV dated 15 February 1823 (2pp); list of subscribers (6pp); author's preface dated from Islington, 15 March 1823, list of principal officers of the collegiate establishment (8pp); half-title; pp 3–304, History and Antiquities continued; indices (27pp); bibliography (9pp); list of plates (4pp). Supplementary vol. Half-title ('An Historical and Architectural Account of King Henry the Seventh's Chapel'); pp 3–72, Henry VII Chapel; bibliography, indices, list of plates (10pp).

Concerning the plates, Brayley says in his preface:

In the Architectural Illustration of this splendid Fabric, all preceding publications have been peculiarly deficient; and it was, principally, with a view to supply the admitted want of authentic perspective Representations, and judicious and correct Details, that Mr. Neale was induced to project and undertake the Work, which is now submitted to the World in a complete form.

This remark can scarcely have been relished by one of the subscribers, A.C. Pugin, whose careful drawings had illustrated Ackermann's fine book published ten years earlier (no 108); the slight was echoed in the bibliography where Brayley misdated the work, dismissed its text as second-hand stuff and named the illustrators without a word of praise for them.

The Abbey has in fact been better served than any other historic London building and, most notably, better than St Paul's Cathedral, since it has been extensively illustrated on three distinct occasions: early in the eighteenth century with the line-engravings of Dart's *Westmonasterium* (no 27), in 1812 with Ackermann's admirable aquatints, and here with an impressive set of plates in line and etching. Even as early as the mid-seventeenth century Hollar himself contributed three engravings of its outward appearance to the *Monasticon Anglicanum* (no 6).

Quite early in his career J.P. Neale was Britton's choice as chief illustrator for the London and Middlesex volumes of the *Beauties of England and Wales* (no 104). The text was by Brayley, who was naturally pleased at his success in persuading him to illustrate his maturer and more scholarly work. It seems, going by the dating of the plates, that he spent many busy hours from the end of 1816 to the beginning of 1823 at work in the Abbey where, with his drawing-board, he must have become a familiar figure. All the illustrations were his exclusive work with the exception of a dozen measured drawings by J.R. Thompson, an architectural draughtsman who had earlier assisted Britton with *Architectural*

Antiquities (no 97), and the view of George IV's coronation to which the figures were added by Henry Moses.

The chief engraver was Robert Sands, with 14 plates to his credit. Next in importance were two members of the Roffe family, with 14 plates between them and two Le Keux's with ten. All these had previously worked for the *Beauties* and the Roffes had engraved plates for Brayley's much earlier *Lambeth Palace* (no 95). Of the score or so employed five others were also *Beauties* engravers, namely John and Elizabeth Byrne, brother and sister, William Radclyffe, William Woolnoth and T. Matthews. Matthews also worked for Neale's *Views of the Seats of Noblemen and Gentlemen* which he brought out from 1818 to 1824 simultaneously with this work.

George IVs own copy, in the British Library (206.g.6), has two versions of each plate facing one another, one printed on India paper and the other directly onto the wove stock. Both are in proof state with letters varying from the commercial edition and some of the copies on wove paper are 'pulls' of the outline only, some without letters of any sort and some with scratched-in credits.

Plates are finished with triple-ruled frames. Most are numbered tr in Roman figures; these numbers, which refer to their chronological order of issue, are quoted or, in their absence, supplied in brackets from the check-list. The captions on items 1–51 all begin with a line in large voided capitals, 'WEST-MINSTER ABBEY', those on items 53–62 with 'HENRY THE SEVENTH'S CHAPEL', and then continue in small voided capitals, followed on the more impressive views by an italic dedication to one of the subscribers. In the list only the names of assistant draughtsmen and engravers are quoted since all plates may be assumed to bear the credit 'Drawn by J.P. Neale'. About half the plates carry a credit for the rolling-press printer, 'Printed by Cox and Barnett'.

Publication-lines are denoted by the following letters:

(c) 'London Published (date) by Longman & Co., Paternoster Row & J.P. Neale, Bennett Street, Blackfriars Road.' (November 1816 to March 1817).

(b) 'London Published (date) by J.P. Neale (16) Bennett Street & Longmans & Co., Paternoster Row.' (July 1817 to March 1819)

(a) 'London Published (date) by J.P. Neale 16 Bennett Street, Blackfriars Road & Hurst Robinson & Co. Cheapside.' (October 1819 to April 1823).

VOL. 1

1 (engr title) Westminster Abbey/Vol. 1/by/J.P. Neale./ Monument of Bishop Dudley in St. Nicholas Chapel./ 1483. Engraved by John Le Keux. (b) March 1, 1818. 210 × 170/280 × 225mm. pl. XXVI.

2 front. The North Transept. Engraved by C. Armstrong. (b) March 1, 1818. 228 × 178/280 × 225mm. pl. XXI. Exterior.

VOL. 2

3 (engr title) Westminster Abbey/Vol.II/By J.P. Neale./ An Enriched Canopy over the Entrance to St. Erasmus's Chapel. Engraved by J. Le Keux. (a) July 1, 1821. 220 × 170/280 × 225mm. pl. XLVIII.

4 front. View from Deans Yard. Engraved by J.C. Varrall. (a) Oct.1, 1822. 165 × 215/225 × 280mm. pl.XLI.

5 p 1 Ground Plan, shewing the groining of the roof, the situation of the principal monuments &c. &c. Drawn by J.P. Neale, architectural admeasurements by J.R. Thompson. Engraved by J. Roffe. (a) July 1, 1820. 220 × 178/250 × 280mm. pl.LX.

6 p 7 Elevation of Three Exterior Compartments of the North Side. Architectural Admeasurement by J.R. Thompson. Engraved by J. Roffe. (b) March 1, 1818. 248 × 173/285 × 220mm. pl.XXII.

7 p 8 Elevation of the North Side. Architectural Admeasurements by J.R. Thompson. Engraved by J. Roffe. (b) June 1, 1818. 158 × 240/220 × 280mm. pl.XXVIII.

8 p 12 View from Poets Corner Looking across the Choir. Engraved by Henry Le Keux. (b) July 1, 1818. 227 × 168/285 × 225mm. pl.XXX.

9 p 16 Elevation & Section of the South Transept/ (Eastern Side). Architectural Admeasurements by J.R. Thompson. Engraved by J. Roffe. (b) March 1, 1819. 160 × 213/220 × 285mm. pl.XXXIII.

10 p 18 Section of the South Side. Architectural Admeasurements by J.R. Thompson. Engraved by J. Roffe. (a) Oct.1, 1819. 150 × 238/225 × 280mm. pl.XLV.

11 p 19 Section and Elevation of the Nave and Western Towers. Architectural Admeasurements by J.R. Thompson. Engraved by J. Roffe. (b) Novr. 1, 1817. 230 × 180/280 × 220mm. pl.XVII.

12 p 24 Capitals and Bases. Etched by J. Carter. (a) July 1, 1822. 175 × 240/220 × 285mm. pl.LXI.

13 p 24 The West End of the Nave/shewing the monument of the Right Honble Wm. Pitt, &c. &c. Engraved by J.C. Varrall. (a) Octr. 1, 1819. 220 × 165/285 × 220mm. pl.XXXVII.

14 p 25 The South Aisle,/shewing the monuments of Camden and Garrick, in Poets Corner. Engraved by J.C. Varrall. (a) July 1, 1820. 215 × 168/285 × 225mm. pl.XXXVI.

15 p 25 View of the North Aisle and Nave. Engraved by J. Lewis. (c) Mar. 1, 1817. 215 × 168/285 × 220mm. pl.IX.

16 p 26 Ancient Shields in the South and North Aisles. Etched by R. Roffe. (b) June 1, 1818. 170 × 245/225 × 280mm. pl.XXVII.

17 p 28 Section of the North Transept. Architectural Admeasurements by J.R. Thompson. Etched by J. Roffe. (c) March 1, 1817. 225 × 165/280 × 220mm. pl.VII.

18 p 30 View of the North Transept and Aisle. Engraved by J. Lewis. (c) Nov. 1, 1816. 218 × 170/275 × 220mm. (pl.IV)

19 p 32 Ornamental Sculpture & Capitals in the Chapel of St. John the Evangelist. Etched by Miss E. Byrne. (b) Novr. 1, 1817. 170 × 242/225 × 285mm. pl.XVI.

20 p 33 View in Poets Corner looking South East. Engraved by T. Matthews. (a) Oct. 1, 1819. 215 × 165/285 × 225mm. pl.XL.

21 p 34 View in Poets Corner looking South. Engraved by R. Sands. (b) Novr. 1, 1817. 215 × 175/285 × 225mm. pl.XVIII.

22 p 37 Sectional Elevation of Three Compartments on the South Side of the Choir./Extending from the Pier of the Great Tower. Architectural Admeasurements by J.R. Thompson. Engraved by J. Roffe. (b) July 1, 1817. 255 × 158/290 × 225mm. pl.XII.

23 p 38 View in the Choir/wth the ceremony of installing the Dean. Etched by R. Sands. Engraved by H. Le Keux. (a) Jany 1st, 1821. 223 × 173/275 × 220mm. pl.XLII.

24 p 46 View in Edward the Confessors Chapel,/shewing the shrine of that Saint, with the monuments of Queen Eleanor, Henry V & Edward III. Engraved by J. Le Keux. (a) Jan. 1, 1821. 165 × 233/225 × 280mm. pl.XXXV.

25 p 48 Historical Entablature on the Screen in Edward the Confessors Chapel. (tc) No.I. Etched by R. Sands. (c) May 1, 1817. 170 × 237/220 × 280mm. pl.VI.

26 p 53 Completion of the Historical Entablature on the Screen in Edward the Confessor's Chapel. (tc) No.2. Etched by R. Sands. (b) July 1, 1817. 170 × 270/220 × 285mm. pl.XI.

27 p 61 View in Edward the Confessors Chapel, shewing Richard the 2ds Monument, the Coronation Chair, &c.&c. Engraved by W. Woolnoth. (b) July 1, 1817. 172 × 215/225 × 280mm. pl.XIII.

28 p 76 King Henry the 3ds. Monument and Queen Eleanor's. Engraved by R. Sands. (b) March 1, 1819. 180 × 215/220 × 280mm. pl.XXXIV.

29 p 79 View in the North Aisle, Shewing Henry the 3ds. Monument, &c. Engraved by J. Le Keux. (b) Novr. 1, 1817. 210 × 168/275 × 225mm. pl.XX.

30 p 83 Part of Henry Vth's Monument & Queen Philippa's. Engraved by John Le Keux. (c) Mar. 1, 1817. 215 × 168/290 × 225mm. pl.X.

31 p 84 View in the North Transept/shewing the monuments of Capts. Manners, Blair & Bayne, the Earl of Chatham, Sir Chas. Wager &c &c. Engraved by W.R. Smith. (a) Oct. 1, 1819. 215 × 172/280 × 225mm. pl.XXXIX.

32 p 93 View of the South Screen &c. of Henry the Vth. Chapel. Engraved by W.R. Smith. (c) Nov. 1, 1816. 220 × 165/290 × 225mm. (pl.V)

33 p 94 Elevation of the North Screen of Henry the Vth.Chapel. Etched by W.D. Taylor. (c) Nov. 1, 1816. 167 × 215/225 × 285mm. (pl.I)

34 p 147 The Tomb of Anne of Cleves; Medallions, Statues & Bosses. Etched by R. Sands. (a) Jan 1, 1821. 220 × 178/280 × 230mm. pl.XLIX.

35 p 151 Archbishop Langham's Monument &c &c. Etched by R. Roffe. (a) July 1, 1820. 170 × 215/225 × 280mm. pl.XLVII.

36 p 153 The Monument of William de Valence Earl of Pembroke./1296. Engraved by C. Armstrong. (b) Novr. 1, 1817. 215 × 170/280 × 225mm. pl.XIX.

37 p 162 View from the Chapel of St. Edmund. Engraved by R. Sands. (b) June 1, 1818. 220 × 172/275 × 225mm. pl.XXIX.

38 p 175 Screen and Entrance to St. Paul's Chapel/with the Monument of/Lodowyck Robsert Lord Bourchier, K.G. Standard Bearer to Henry V. Etched by R. Sands. (c) Nov. 1, 1816. 217 × 172/280 × 225mm. (pl.II)

39 p 184 View in the Chapel of St John the Baptist./ Shewing the Tombs of Bishop Ruthall, Abbot Fascet &c. Engraved by W. Woolnoth. (c) Nov. 1, 1816. (pl.III)

40 p 188 The Screen of Abbot Islip's Chapel. Etched by R. Sands. (b) March 1, 1818. 237 × 190/275 × 225mm. pl.XXIV.

41 p 189 Interior of Abbot Islip's Chapel,/shewing Sir Christopher Hatton's Monument &c. Etched by J. Le Keux. (a) Octr. 1, 1819. 215 × 175/280 × 225mm. pl.XLIV.

42 p 209 Lord Mansfield's Monument, the view looking across the Choir. Engraved by W. Woolnoth. (c) Mar. 1, 1817. 220 × 170/285 × 225mm. pl.VIII.

43 p 270 View from the Vaultings looking West,/shewing the Ceremony of the Coronation of His Majesty King George IIII. Engd. by R. Sands & J. Tingle. Figures etched by H. Moses. (a) Jany. 1, 1823. 220 × 172/275 × 225mm. pl.XXXVIII.

44 p 274 The Monuments of Aveline and Aymer de Valance. Etched by John Le Keux. (a) July 1, 1820. 220 × 180/285 × 230mm. pl.XLIII.

45 p 276 View in the North Aisle looking East, shewing Crouchback's Monument &c. &c. Engraved by W.R. Smith. (b) July 1, 1817. 215 × 168/285 × 225mm. pl.XV.

46 p 281 View in the South Aisle, shewing Seberts Monument &c.&c. Engraved by W. Woolnoth. (b); March 1, 1818. 215 × 172/285 × 230mm. pl.XXV.

47 p 282 Entrance into the South Aisle from the North side of the Cloisters. Engraved by John Scott. (b) March 1, 1818. 170 × 213/230 × 280mm. pl.XXIII.

48 p 283 Door Way into the Nave, from the Western Cloister. Engraved by J. Byrne. (b) July 1, 1817. 215 × 170/280 × 225mm. pl.XIV.

49 p 284 'Section of the Cloisters. – South Cloister/ Entrance from Deans Yard. – East Cloister/Windows &c. – East Cloister/Dado and Entrance to Chapter House and Pix Office. Architectural Admeasurements by J.R. Thompson. Engraved by R. Roffe. (b) March 1, 1819. 165 × 210/225 × 280mm. pl.XXXI.

50 p 284 Section of the Cloisters. – South Cloister – West Cloister – North Cloister. Architectural Admeasurements by J.R. Thompson. Engraved by J. Roffe. (b) March 1, 1819. 160 × 228/225 × 290mm. pl.XXXII.

51 p 285 An Ancient Arch in the East Cloister. Engraved by R. Sands. (a) July 1, 1820. 180 × 212/220 × 270mm. pl.XLVI.

Henry VII Chapel supplement

52 front. Door Way to the Oratory of the North Aisle of Henry the 7th's Chapel. J.P. Neale 1816. 230 × 175/280 × 230mm.

53 p 27 Henry the Seventh's Chapel,/North East View. Outlined by J. Cleghorn. Engraved by R. Roffe. (a) Augt 1, 1822. 223 × 173/285 × 225mm. pl.L.

54 p 30 Henry the Seventh's Chapel,/East End. Engraved by W. Radclyffe. (a) Jany 1, 1821. 165 × 215/230 × 280mm. pl.LI.

55 p 36 Henry the Seventh's Chapel,/Section of the North Side. Architectural Admeasurements by J.R. Thompson. Engraved by J. Roffe. (a) July 1, 1821. 165 × 225/225 × 280mm. pl.LIV.

56 p 40 Henry the Seventh's Chapel,/South-East and South Chapels. Etched by R. Sands. (a) July 1, 1821. 220 × 170/280 × 225mm. pl.LVI.

57 p 42 Henry the Seventh's Chapel,/View looking North West, shewing the Screen of Henry the VIIth Monument. Engraved by J. Roffe. (a) Jany 1, 1823. 227 × 165/280 × 220mm. pl.LIII.

58 p 43 Henry the Seventh's Chapel,/Section of the West End, shewing the Brass Gates, Royal Vault, &c. &c. Architectural Admeasurements by J.R. Thompson. Engraved by John Cleghorn. (a) Jany 1821. 230 × 180/285 × 225mm. pl.LV.

59 p 50 Henry the Seventh's Chapel,/View looking East,/shewing the installation of the Knights of the Bath in 1812. Engraved by H. Le Keux. The Figures by J. Stephanoff and Etched by G. Cooke. (a) April 11, 1823. 220 × 165/280 × 225mm. pl.LII.

60 p 56 Henry the Seventh's Chapel./The Monument of Henry the VIIth and his Queen. – South Side – North Side. Engraved by H. Moses. (a) June 1, 1822. 240 × 173/285 × 230mm. pl.LVIII.

61 p 64 Henry the Seventh's Chapel./The North Aisle/ shewing Queen Elizabeth's Monument &c. Etched by R. Sands. (a) Septr.1, 1822. 222 × 170/280 × 230mm. pl.LVII.

62 p 68 Henry the Seventh's Chapel,/Monuments and Details. The monuments drawn by J.R. Thompson, the details by J.P. Neale. Engraved by J. Carter. (a) July 1, 1821. 175 × 245/230 × 280mm. pl.LIX.

124 · BREWER'S HISTRIONIC TOPOGRAPHY* [1818]

James Norris Brewer, magazine contributor, novelist and topographer, wrote the general introduction to *The Beauties of England and Wales* (no 104), as also the texts of the volumes on Middlesex, Oxfordshire and Warwickshire. He also produced independent architectural and topographical works, such as the *Descriptive and Historical Account of Various Palaces and Public Buildings* (no 137) and *The Picture of England* (1820). The present work, with its 13 views, vignetted title and tailpiece, was to have been part of a larger whole but supposedly attracted too few subscribers to fulfil the hopes expressed in the preface: 'If this specimen should meet with the approbation of those who are inclined to illustrate the History of the Stage, and to preserve a collective memorial of buildings connected with such annals ... future numbers will be published; calculated to form one volume of a moderate size'. The plates, which are drawn and engraved by James Storer and his son Henry, are unnumbered and unlisted; the captions are in voided capitals. The publication-lines, 'for *Cole's Residences of Actors*', are undated.

Histrionic Topography: or, the Birth-places, Residences, and Funeral Monuments of the most Distinguished Actors. Illustrated by Engravings, Executed by Messrs. J.

& H. Storer, and by Historical and Descriptive Notices, written by Mr. J. Norris Brewer ... London: Published by the Proprietors, J. Cole, Lincoln and Sold by J. Barker, Dramatic Repository, Great Russell Street; Baldwin Cradock and Joy; and Sherwood, Neely, and Jones, Paternoster Row. 1818.

Octavo, 210 × 130mm.   1818

COLLATION   Title-page; pp iii–iv, preface; pp 1–37, Histrionic Topography.

1 (engr title) Histrionic topography/or the/Birth-places, Residences,/and/Funeral Monuments/of the most/ Distinguished Actors. (vignette) Shakespeare's Temple/Hampton. Drawn & Engd. by H.S. Storer for Cole's Residences of Actors. 70 × 90/195 × 125mm.

2 front. Garrick's House,/Hampton. Drawn & Engd. by J. Storer. 65 × 90/100 × 150mm. Hampton House where Garrick lived from 1754 till his death in 1779. The Grecian Temple of the title-page was built on the lawn to house Roubillac's statue of Shakespeare.

3 p 5 Garrick's Town House,/ Adelphi. Drawn and Engraved by J. Storer. 90 × 65/155 × 105mm. No 5 in the charmingly pilastered centre before the addition of the top-heavy central pediment. Its situation, facing the Thames, can best be seen in Pastorini's engraving of c 1780 (BL Maps: *K. top.* 22.7b). Garrick was an early Adelphi occupant, in 1771.

4 p 17 Garrick's Monument/Westminster Abbey. Drawn & Engd. by H.S. Storer. 103 × 63/150 × 100mm. Sculpted by Henry Webber, unveiled in May 1797 and described by Charles Lamb as a 'Harlequin figure'.

5 p 25 Shakespeare's Monument,/Westminster Abbey. Drawn & Engd. by J. Storer. 100 × 65/150 × 100mm. 'Placed there in the year 1740, the design was furnished by Kent, and the monument was erected by Scheemakers'.

6 p 27 Davies's House/(author of Dramatic Miscellanies)/ in Russel Street. Drawn & Engraved by J. Storer. 93 × 63/150 × 100mm. No 8 Russell Street, Covent Garden, a house which, after Dr Johnson's death, Boswell could never pass without feelings of 'reverence and regret', for it was here that Thomas Davies, actor turned bookseller, had introduced the one to the other. 'Now occupied as an upholstery warehouse'.

7 p 31 Barton Booth's Monument/Westminster Abbey. Drawn & Engd. by J. Storer. 100 × 65/150 × 100mm. Erected 1772; sculpted by William Tyler, RA.

8 p 35 Residence of the late Mrs Clive/Twickenham. Drawn & Engd. by J. Storer. 65 × 90/100 × 150mm. Little Strawberry Hill in which Kitty Clive, described here as 'the first comic actress of the world', was given permission to live by Horace Walpole until her death in 1785.

125 · DUGDALE'S HISTORY OF ST PAUL'S CATHEDRAL [1818]

On 1 April 1814 a prospectus, including a list of 168 names of subscribers, was published by Lackington, Allen and Longman, Hurst, Rees, Orme & Brown:

In course of the present Month, will be published, Part I of the History of St Paul's Cathedral ... by Sir William Dugdale with additions and a continuation by Henry Ellis, Keeper of Manuscripts in the British Museum.... The *Monasticon Anglicanum* is already in course of publication ... It will contain all the Views with the Monuments of old St Paul's, as engraved by Hollar faithfully copied; together with some additional Plates illustrative of the present Cathedral.

There were to be five Parts, published quarterly, for each of which the first 200 subscribers would pay two guineas and late comers two and a half guineas. A few copies were available on super royal paper with proof impressions of the plates at five guineas per Part.

This 'de luxe' edition, beautifully printed, was intended as a companion to the splendid *Monasticon* (no 122) which had commenced publication in June of the previous year and of which also Henry Ellis had, by this time, become editor-in-chief. His preface is dated 24 July 1818, from which it would seem that on average the Parts were published annually rather than quarterly. Copies of the first edition of 1658 were almost certainly consumed by the Great Fire and there had been no intervening edition since that of 1716, edited by Edward Maynard.

The History of Saint Paul's Cathedral, in London, from its foundation ... by Sir William Dugdale Knt.... with a Continuation and Additions, including the republication of Sir William Dugdale's life from his own Manuscript; by Henry Ellis, F.R.S., Sec. S.A. Keeper of Manuscripts in the British Museum. London: Printed for Lackington, Hughes, Harding, Mavor and Jones, Finsbury Square and Longman, Hurst, Rees, Orme and Brown, Paternoster Row. 1818.

Folio, 475 × 325mm.   1818

COLLATION   Half-title; title-page; pp v–vi, preface; pp vii–xxviii, life of Sir William Dugdale; pp xxix–xxxi, Dugdale's introduction to the 2nd ed; pp 1–284, History of St Paul's Cathedral; pp 285–427, appendix; pp 428–66,

Ceremonials and Processions; pp 467–72, supplement; pp 473–500, index, list of his plates.

In his preface Ellis says of the illustrations:

The whole of Hollar's Plates to the First Edition, have been re-engraved with care and fidelity for the present Work; and a vignette has been added to their number, of the Church in flames in 1666, as it was engraved by Hollar in the title-page of Archbishop Sancroft's Sermon on the Great Fire. The Plates illustrative of the present structure will be found no unimportant accession.

He fails to mention by name the Hollar 're-engraver', William Finden, a young man who, with his brother Edward, had been apprenticed to the engraver James Mitan and was embarking on a career of doing illustrative work for book publishers. These plates are extraordinary examples of facsimile work, the measurements being correct to within a millimetre; had he substituted Hollar's credit for his own and engraved the dedication cartouches and original captions, and had the etchings been printed on laid paper, they would have deceived all but the expert. Prospective subscribers would have had no difficulty in checking the accuracy of these copies since in 1815, acording to Upcott (2, p 705), Robert Wilkinson of 58 Cornhill was offering for sale 'A Collection of Forty-Nine Plates engraved by Hollar, for "Dugdale's Monasticon," and "History of St Paul's Cathedral". Republished from the original Copperplates'. The Findens continued their joint career as book illustrators until the fashion for steel-engravings brought them celebrity for their skill in transforming water-colour drawings into small, brilliantly contrasted black and white vignettes to illustrate books such as *Childe Harold's Pilgrimage* (1841) and Beattie's *Views of Ports and Harbours* (1842). On a larger scale they successfully interpreted two of Turner's water-colours, 'Lake Nemi' and 'Oberwesel', for inclusion in their *Royal Gallery of British Art* (1842).

For Ellis's 'continuation', a history of Wren's Cathedral, Finden etched two of the architect's drawings at All Souls, and John Coney, who was also heavily engaged on the *Monasticon*, drew and etched an exterior and interior as well as plates of Nelson's sarcophagus and Wren's memorial slab. A further 16 plates, drawn by Henry Corbould, who specialized in Greek marbles, and etched in outline by Charles Heath, are devoted to the St Paul's

marble statues, most of them neo-classical memorials to admirals, generals or captains, in pairs, with the name of the sculptor prominent on the plinth.

Unless otherwise stated the credits on the 1658 facsimiles read: 'After Hollar. Engraved by W. Finden', and the originals are referred to by the page of the 1658 edition (no 8) on which they were printed. Publication-lines normally state: 'London, Published by Lackington & Co, & Longman & Co.', and the plates are given their serial numbers in the list at the end of the book.

1 front. Gulielmus Dugdale/Ætatis 50. A.MDCLVI. London, Published Sepr. 1 1817 by Lackington, Hughes, Harding, Mavor and Jones, Finsbury Square and Longman, Hurst, Rees, Orme and Brown, Paternoster Row. 218 × 167mm. 1658 ed front.

2 p 28 Capella Thomae Kempe Lond. in qua tumulus suus quondam exstitit. 220 × 250/235 × 315mm. 1658 ed p 40.

3 p 39 Tumulus Johannis de Bellocampo Militis. 250 × 180/330 × 225mm. 1658 ed p 52.

4 p 45 (above each of 3 brasses) In Choro prope introitum – In medio chori prope Altare – In superiori parte Chori prope Altare. 390 × 230mm. 1658 ed p 60.

5 p 46 Inter Chorum et Alam australem. 285 × 100/320 × 165mm. 1658 ed p 62.

6 p 47 Inter Chorum et alam Australem. Engraved by W. Finden. 328 × 230mm. No Hollar credit. 1658 ed p 64.

7 p 48 Inter Chorum et alam australem. Engraved by W. Finden. 340 × 218mm. No Hollar credit. 1658 ed p 66.

8 p 49 Inter Chorum et alam australem. Engraved by W. Finden. 290 × 215mm. No Hollar credit. 1658 ed p 68.

9 p 50 In Choro ex opposito Monumenti Pembrochiani. Engraved by W. Finden. 325 × 225mm. No Hollar credit. 1658 ed p 70.

10 p 51 In australi Ala ex adverso Chori. 302 × 230mm. 1658 ed p 72.

11 p 52 In Australi ala a latere Chori. April 1, 1814. 330 × 205mm. 1658 ed p 74.

12 p 53 In australi Insula a latere Chori. 278 × 245mm. 1658 ed p 76.

13 p 54 In australi Insula a latere Chori. April 1, 1814. 305 × 230mm. 1658 ed p 78,

14 p 55 (Tombs of Wengham and Fauconberg) April 1, 1814. 200 × 270/230 × 315mm. 1658 ed p 80.

15 p 56 Inter orientalem partem Ecclesiae et Alam australem. Engraved by W. Finden. 305 × 230mm. No Hollar credit. 1658 ed p 82.

16 p 57 Tumulus Roberti de Braybroke Lond: Episcopi/In medio Capellae Beatae Mariae. April 1, 1814. 280 × 230mm. 1658 ed p 84.

288

17 p 58 Inter Alam aquilonalem et Chorum/Tumulus Rogeri cognom. Nigri Londiniensis Episcopi. April 1, 1814. 230 × 170/340 × 215mm. 1658 ed p 86.

18 p 59 Tumulus Gulielmi Comitis Pembrochiae/inter Alam aquilonalem et Chorum. Engraved by W. Finden. 305 × 230mm. No Hollar credit. 1658 ed p 88.

19 p 60 Monumentum Johannis Gandaviensis Ducis Lancastriae et Constantiae Uxoris ejus. 300 × 215mm. 1658 ed p 90.

20 p 64 In Fornice aquilonalis muri ex opposito Chori. 190 × 250/265 × 305mm. 1658 ed p 92.

21 p 65 Monumentum/septentrionali muro Chori affixum. Engraved by W. Finden. 280 × 215mm. 1658 ed p 94.

22 p 66 In Pariete aquilonali ex opposito Chori. 330 × 215mm. 1658 ed p 96.

23 p 67 In aquilonali muro ex adverso chori. April 1, 1814. 165 × 230/215 × 290mm. 1658 ed p 98.

24 p 68 Tumulus Radulphi de Hengham/in aquilonali muro ex adverso Chori. Engraved by W. Finden. 290 × 235mm. No Hollar credit. 1658 ed p 100.

25 p 69 Tumulus Simonis Burley Militis. April 1, 1814. 315 × 260mm. 1658 ed p 102.

26 p 70 In Ala boreali ex adverso Chori. Engraved by W. Finden. 315 × 200mm. No Hollar credit. 1658 ed p 104.

27 p 71 Tumulus Johannis Wolly Eq. Aur./In Capelli Sti Georgii. 272 × 210mm. 1658 ed p 106.

28 p 72 Tumulus Thomae Heneage Eq. aur./in Capella glorios. Virginis Mariae. Engraved by W. Finden. 302 × 225mm. No Hollar credit. 1658 ed p 108.

29 p 73 Alexandri Noelli/Ecclesiae Paulinae Decani/Monumentum. 290 × 210mm. 1658 ed p 110.

30 p 74 Clausura circa Altare S: Erkenwaldi sub Feretro ejusdem. 232 × 170/275 × 210mm. 1658 ed p 112.

31 p 75 Templi Parochialis S. Fidis scil. areae ejusdem Ichnographia. April 1, 1814. 200 × 305mm. 1658 ed p 114.

32 p 75 Ecclesiae Parochialis S. Fidis Prospectus Interior/Fidem haec exhibet Illa Deum. April 1, 1814. 190 × 340/270 × 410mm. 1658 ed p 115.

33 p 87 Domus Capitularis Sti Pauli a Meridie Prospectus. 194 × 288/250 × 340mm. 1658 ed p 127.

34 Ecclesiae Paulinae Prospectus/Qualis olim erat priusquam ejus Pyramis e coelo tacta conflagravit. 315 × 390mm. 1658 ed p 133.

35 p 108 Areae Ecclesiae Cathedralis Sti Pauli Ichnographia. After Hollar 1657. Engraved by W. Finden. 300 × 395mm. 1658 ed p 161.

36 p 108 Ecclesiae Cathedralis S. Pauli a Meridie Prospectus. 302 × 452mm. 1658 ed p 162.

37 p 108 Ecclesiae Cathedralis S. Pauli a Septentrione Prospectus. 277 × 455mm. 1658 ed p 163.

38 p 108 Ecclesiae Cathedralis S. Pauli ab Occidente Prospectus. 210 × 270/250 × 305mm. 1658 ed p 164.

39 p 108 Ecclesiae Cathedralis S. Pauli Orientalis Facies. 270 × 215mm. 1658 ed p 165.

40 p 108 (Another view of the E. end) 190 × 245/265 × 365mm. 1658 ed p 166.

41 p 108 Navis Ecclesiae Cathedralis S. Pauli Prospectus Interior. 272 × 260/340 × 310mm. Reduced from double-page view, 1658 ed p 167.

42 p 108 Partis exterioris Chori ab Occidente prospectus. 218 × 318/278 × 380mm. 1658 ed p 168,

43 p 108 Chori Ecclesiae Cathedralis S. Pauli Prospectus Interior. April 1, 1814. 308 × 220/380 × 275mm. 1658 ed p 169.

44 p 108 Orientalis Partis Eccl. Cath. S. Pauli Prospectus interior. 290 × 212/330 × 252mm. 1658 ed p 170.

p 115: 'The Continuation of the History'

45 p 124 (on banderole) Etiam periere Ruinae. W. Hollar fecit Ao 1666. Engraved by W. Finden. 60 × 100/115 × 160mm. Printed with letterpress. Shows London on fire. Copied from the title-page of Dean Sancroft's sermon on the Great Fire (*Hind* 68).

46 p 130 West Front of an unexecuted Plan for St Paul's Cathedral./From Sir Christr Wren's original design preserved in the Library of All Souls College Oxford. Engraved by W. Finden. 195 × 310/280 × 375mm. Outline etching, measured.

47 p 130 West Front of Sir Christr Wren's Design for St. Paul's Cathedral/with Lucern Windows in the Dome, and other Variations from the present Structure. Engraved by W. Finden. From the original in All Souls College, Oxford. 310 × 225/375 × 290mm. Outline etching, measured.

48 p 180 St Paul's Cathedral South West View. Drawn & Engraved by John Coney. London, Published Septr. 1, 1817 by Lackington, Hughes, Harding, Mavor and Jones, Finsbury Square and Longman, Hurst, Rees, Orme and Brown, Paternoster Row. 290 × 390/353 × 440mm.

49 p 182 Interior of the Dome of St Paul's Cathedral. Drawn & Engraved by John Coney. London, Published Septr. 1, 1817 by Lackington, Hughes, Harding, Mavor and Jones, Finsbury Square and Longman, Hurst, Rees, Orme and Brown, Paternoster Row. 290 × 195/360 × 260mm. Original sepia drawing (298 × 200mm), signed and dated 1817, in V & A.

50 p 184 Ground Plan of St. Paul's Cathedral, 1818. Engraved from actual admeasurement by John Coney. July 1, 1818. 315 × 210/360 × 260mm.

p 199: 'Monuments and Inscriptions in the present Cathedral, A.D. 1816'

51 p 200 Samuel Johnson – Joshua Reynolds – John Howard – Sir William Jones. Drawn by H. Corbould.

Engraved by C. Heath. June 1, 1818. 300 × 200/380 × 260mm.

52 p 202 Capt. G.N. Hardinge – Capt. Richard Rundell Burgess. Drawn by H. Corbould. Engraved by C. Heath. 310 × 200/380 × 260mm.

53 p 203 Capt. R. Willet Miller – Capt. Robert Faulkner. Drawn by H. Corbould. Engraved by C. Heath. 215 × 195/380 × 255mm.

54 p 204 Lord Collingwood – Earl Howe. Drawn by H. Corbould. Engraved by C. Heath. 302 × 195/380 × 255mm.

55 p 205 Sir John Moore – Sir Ralph Abercromby. Drawn by H. Corbould. Engraved by C. Heath. 310 × 195/380 × 255mm.

56 p 206 Capt. John Cooke – Marquis Cornwallis. Drawn by H. Corbould. Engraved by C. Heath. 315 × 195/380 × 255mm.

57 p 206 Generals Mackenzie & Langworth – General Dundas. Drawn by H. Corbould. Engraved by C. Heath. 310 × 200/380 × 255mm.

58 p 207 Generals Craufurd & Mackinnon – Capt. George Blagdon Westcott. Drawn by H. Corbould. Engraved by C. Heath. 310 × 200/380 × 255mm.

59 p 208 Lord Rodney – Captains Moss & Riou. Drawn by H. Corbould. Engraved by C. Heath. 310 × 210/385 × 260mm.

60 p 210 Sir Christopher Wren's Monument/in the Crypt of St. Paul's Cathedral. Drawn & Engraved by John Coney. Published Septr 1, 1817 by Lackington, Hughes, Harding, Mavor and Jones, Finsbury Square and Longman, Hurst, Rees, Orme and Brown, Paternoster Row. 195 × 305/260 × 360mm.

61 p 213 Sarcophagus/under which the body of Lord Nelson is enclosed in the Crypt of St Paul's Cathedral. Drawn & Engraved by John Coney. Published Septr 1 1817 by Lackington, Hughes, Harding, Mavor and Jones, Finsbury Square and Longman, Hurst, Rees, Orme and Brown, Paternoster Row. 280 × 195/350 × 255mm.

62 p 420 (The Daunce of Machabree) After Hollar. Engraved by W. Finden. 145 × 185/155 × 230mm. Printed with letterpress. 1658 ed p 290.

p 469: Supplement

63 p 469 Capt. George Duff – Viscount Nelson. Drawn by H. Corbould. Engraved by C. Heath. 310 × 195/385 × 260mm. The Nelson monument by Flaxman was only just completed in 1818.

64 p 470 Sir Isaac Brock – General Bowes. Drawn by H. Corbould. Engraved by C. Heath. 290 × 165/385 × 260mm.

65 p 470 (Col Sir William) Myers – General Hoghton. Drawn by H. Corbould. Engraved by C. Heath. 255 × 170/385 × 260mm. J. Kendrick's 'Myers', 1816.

66 p 471 General Le Marchant – Sir Samuel Hood. Drawn by H. Corbould. Engraved by C. Heath. 290 × 140/385 × 260mm.

67 p 472 Sir William Ponsonby – Sir Thomas Picton. Drawn by H. Corbould. Engraved by C. Heath. 320 × 200/385 × 260mm.

68 p 472 Generals Gore & Merritt – General Hay. Drawn by H. Corbould. Engraved by C. Heath. 310 × 130/385 × 260mm. The first drawing represents Chantrey's monument to Generals Gore and Skerrett.

69 p 472 General Ross – Colonel Cadogan. Drawn by H. Corbould. Engraved by C. Heath. 275 × 165/385 × 260mm.

---

126 · LEIGH'S NEW PICTURE OF LONDON [1818, etc]

Samuel Leigh, bookseller and publisher, opened a shop in the Strand where he sold, among other publications, a series of guidebooks to European capital cities under the title *A New Picture* … He is best known to topographers for his long aquatinted view of London from the Adelphi in 1824, by M. Clark, and the allied folding 'Panorama of the River Thames from London to Richmond'. He started trading in 1812, the very year in which Longman & Co acquired from Richard Phillips the rights of publishing *The Picture of London* annually. Five or six years later, when he set out to corner for himself a share of the London guidebook market dominated by this entrenched bestseller, he had to provide some enticement to wean away its devotees. To begin with he arranged his information in more distinctive categories, which made his book handier for quick reference purposes. His second objective was to improve on the mere handful of haphazardly chosen views which in the eyes of both Phillips and Longman were sufficient ornament for so utilitarian a compilation. He chose a good moment for publication since in 1818 the price of *The Picture of London* went up from 6s 6d to nine shillings; so that if, for the nine shillings, he was able to offer with his guide the additional inducement of a more extensive collection of views, he could become a strong competitor. He accordingly became a pioneer in the use of thumbnail topographical engravings just large enough to identify the buildings described but small enough for a number to be engraved on a single plate—an innovation which Longman & Co made haste to copy in the next but one edition of their London guide.

In 1820 Leigh was lucky enough to acquire the copyright of 54 engravings of London characters in their street settings, drawn by Rowlandson, which he advertised as follows: 'Rowlandson's Characteristic Sketches of the Lower Orders, intended as a companion to the New Picture of London: consisting of fifty-four plates, neatly coloured. London: printed for Samuel Leigh, 18 Strand. 1820. Price 7s: halfbound'. These little gems of observation, tinted with charming naiveté, are often set against identifiable architectural backgrounds: a vendor of singing birds near St John's Gate, 'distressed sailors' with a building reminiscent of the Admiralty, firemen at work in the vicinity of Christ Church, Newgate, a handsome female ballad singer with a suitable Opera House backcloth, and a humble shoeblack plying his trade before the unmistakably magnificent portico of Christ Church, Spitalfields. Fifteen years earlier Phillips had similarly cheered up the sober topographical engravings of his *Modern London* (no 89) with a coloured set of London street types by W.M. Craig, who lacked however Rowlandson's flair for lively portrayal of the 'lower orders'. From the 1819 edition onwards the *New Picture* was available bound together with the Rowlandson characters in a red full-leather binding with gilt title for 15s—less than the combined price of the separate publications. Alternatively 12s would buy the guidebook with an appendix of 24 of 'Busby's Costumes of the Lower Orders of the Metropolis', also published separately in 1820 by Baldwin, Cradock & Joy in six Numbers. A French version, *Le nouveau tableau de Londres*, at 6s sewed, was announced in *The Literary Gazette* of 18 December 1824.

Leigh's New Picture of London: or, a view of the political, religious, medical, literary, municipal, commercial, and moral state of The British Metropolis. Presenting a brief and luminous guide to the stranger, on all subjects connected with General Information, business, or amusement. Embellished with upwards of One Hundred Elegant Engravings of Royal Palaces and Public Buildings of all Descriptions, in London and its environs; also a correct plan of London. Printed for Samuel Leigh, No 18 Strand. 1818.

Duodecimo, 140 × 90mm. 1818

COLLATION   Title-page; pp iii–vi, preface; pp ix–xv, contents; pp 1–452, New Picture.

(as above, but following 'amusement') Third edition, enlarged. Embellished with numerous engravings of Royal Palaces and Public Buildings of all Descriptions in London and its Vicinity also a correct plan of London and a map of the environs. London: Printed for Samuel Leigh 18, Strand; by W. Clowes, Northumberland-Court. 1819. Price 9s bound. With the Costumes, 12s. with Rowlandson's Characteristic Sketches, 15s.)

Duodecimo, 140 × 90mm. 1819

COLLATION   Title-page; pp iii–vi, preface; pp ii–iii, contents; pp 1–524, New Picture of London; pp 1–36, index to plan, etc.

(as 1818, but following 'amusement') To which is subjoined a Description of the Environs. Embellished with Numerous views, a correct plan of London and a Map of the Environs. New edition, carefully revised. London: Printed for Samuel Leigh, 18 Strand. 1822. Price 9s. bound. With twenty-four Costumes, 12s. bound. With Rowlandson's fifty-four Costumes, 15s. bound.

Duodecimo, 140 × 90mm. 1822

COLLATION   Title-page; pp iii–vi, prefatory address; pp vii–viii, contents; pp 1–472, New Picture of London; pp 473–96, index; pp 1–35, index to plan.

(as 1822, but following 'Strand') and Baldwin, Cradock and Joy Paternoster Row.

With Plan of London and Map of the Environs 6s.
do	do	do and 110 Views &c.	9s.
do	do	do and 24 Costumes.	12s.
do	do	do and Rowlandson's do.	15s.

Duodecimo, 140 × 90mm. 1824–5

COLLATION   Title-page; pp iii–iv, prefatory address; pp v–viii, contents; pp 1–487, New Picture of London; pp 488–512, index; pp 513–20, Leigh's catalogue of books; pp 1–35, index to plan, etc.

The 1818 edition, the earliest seen, is illustrated with half a dozen plates, about the same number as are to be found in the editions to date of *The Picture of London* but with a considerable difference. Sidney Hall of Bury Street, Bloomsbury was engaged by Leigh to engrave an average of 20 small views on five of these plates and on the sixth half a dozen strip views of bridges, in all 109 miniatures plus a folding plan.

This layout was not repeated in the next edition; no doubt large, folding plates proved impractical and became crumpled and torn in a book which received so much use. Thus, in 1819 and 1820, apart from the frontispiece which was one of the former plates, the pages of illustration were halved in size and increased in number to maintain the same quantity of miniature views and two extra plans were added. The process of fission went still further in 1822 and 1823 when the average number of miniatures was reduced to three on a plate equivalent in size to the text pages.

It is clear from the grouping of the views in each edition that these diminutions were not attained by cutting up the original copper plates but involved re-engraving on fresh plates, mostly by purely mechanical copyists, although deliberate alterations in scale are apparent in some of the views carried over to the 1822 and 1824–5 editions. In these editions the following alterations were made:

5 subjects were omitted (items 36, 38, 68, 107, 109). 19 were recaptioned or replaced with more recent views (items 6–7, 18, 47, 56, 62, 84–9, 94–5, 97, 99, 101, 104, 106).
10 new subjects were introduced, of which 8 were recent buildings (items 113–16, 118, 123–5, 128–9).

From 1824–5 the name of the firm of Baldwin, Cradock & Joy appears with Leigh's on the title-pages and in 1830 the joint publishers decided to replace the line-engravings with a similar set of steel-engravings. Details of these are to be found under the *New Picture* for that year (no 167). In 1831 Leigh committed suicide and suceeding editions were published in collaboration with his widow.

The six plates in the 1818 edition are captioned in copperplate script above the top row of views and below the bottom row and carry this combined credit and publication-line: 'Views of Public Edifices (Buildings) in London. Engraved by Sidy Hall, 14 Bury Strt Bloomsbury, London. Published by Samuel Leigh, 18 Strand.' Plate-marks in all editions have been cropped by the binder. The smaller plates of the 1819 edition are identified as 'Public Edifices' and carry the line 'Sidy Hall sculp. London, Published by Samuel Leigh, 18 Strand.' The smallest plates, in the later editions, have no publication-lines or credits.

1818 edition
  front. (pl. 1)
1 Admiralty. 43 × 60mm.
2 Session House Clerkenwell. 43 × 35mm.
3 Westminster Hall. 43 × 35mm.
4 Treasury. 43 × 35mm.
5 Entrance to St James's Palace. 43 × 37mm.
6 Carlton House. 43 × 72mm.
7 Buckingham Palace. 43 × 37mm.
8 Guildhall, Westminster. 43 × 38mm.
9 Giltspur Street Compter. 43 × 35mm.
10 Sessions House Old Bailey. 43 × 37mm.
11 Whitehall. 43 × 55mm.
12 The Tower from Thames Street. 43 × 90mm.
13 Cold Bath Fields Prison/From Gray's Inn Lane. 43 × 50mm.
14 Custom House. 43 × 42mm.
15 Excise Office. 43 × 35mm.
16 The Mint. 43 × 62mm.
17 Newgate. 43 × 37mm.
18 Front of Somerset House. 44 × 43mm.
19 Somerset House from the Thames. 43 × 50mm.
20 Horse Guards from the Park. 43 × 70mm.

  p 127 (pl. 2)
21 St Paul's Cathedral. 90 × 65mm.
22 St Martin in the Fields. 44 × 44mm.
23 St George, Bloomsbury. 44 × 45mm.
24 Christ Church Spitalfields. 43 × 37mm.
25 St Mary le Strand. 43 × 33mm.
26 St Clement Dane. 43 × 33mm.
27 St Paul Covent Garden. 43 × 45mm.
28 St Mary le bone New Church. 43 × 45mm.
29 Shoreditch Church. 43 × 35mm.
30 Bow Ch. Cheapside. 43 × 33mm. Spire only.

31 Pancras Church. 43 × 43mm.
32 St Sepulchre, Skinner Street. 43 × 44mm.
33 St George Hanover Sqre. 43 × 35mm.
34 St Andrew Holborn. 43 × 43mm.
35 Stepney Church. 43 × 45mm.
36 Sweeds Church. 44 × 44mm. Princes Square.
37 Henry 7th's Chapel. 43 × 47mm. E. end.
38 Portland Chapel. 43 × 47mm. St. Paul, Great Portland Street.
39 Westminster Abby. 90 × 65mm.

  p 185 (pl. 3)
40 Temple Bar. 43 × 40mm.

41 Trinity House. 43 × 47mm.

42 The Bank. 43 × 43mm.

43 Mansion House. 43 × 43mm.

44 Foundling Hospital. 43 × 50mm.

45 Monument. 90 × 203mm.

46 British Museum. 43 × 60mm.

47 Surgeon's Hall L.I. Fields. 43 × 42mm. Built by James Lewis, 1806–13.

48 London Institution. 45 × 40mm. Built by William Brooks, 1815–19.

49 St Paul's School. 45 × 45mm. The old building.

50 Bartholomew's Hospital. 43 × 40mm. Entrance gateway.

51 Guildhall. 43 × 50mm.

52 East India House. 43 × 53mm.

53 Royal Exchange. 43 × 53mm.

54 Deaf & Dumb Asylum. 43 × 65mm.

55 Mercers Hall. 43 × 25mm.

56 Shakespere Gallery. 43 × 25mm. In Pall Mall, formerly Boydell the printseller's gallery, now housing the British Institution for Promoting the Fine Arts; built by George Dance junior, 1788.

57 Freemasons Charity-School. 43 × 48mm.

58 City of London Lying in Hospital. 43 × 52mm.

59 New Bethlehem. 43 × 53mm. Southwark. Hospital built by James Lewis, 1812–15.

60 Auction Mart. 43 × 50mm. Opened 1810.

61 St Bride's. 43 × 33mm.

62 Tavistock Chapel. 43 × 37mm. Broad Court, Covent Garden, a Russell proprietary chapel made into the parish church of St John in 1855.

p 273 (pl. 4)

63 Spa Fields Chapel. 43 × 48mm. Formerly the Clerkenwell Pantheon, Exmouth Market.

64 Tabernacle, Moorfields. 43 × 48mm.

65 Surry Chapel. 43 × 47mm. Blackfriars Road.

66 Philanthropic Chapel. 42 × 65mm.

67 Fishmongers Hall. 43 × 47mm.

68 South Sea House. 43 × 47mm.

69 St George's Hospital. 43 × 45mm.

70 Library, Red Cross St. 43 × 33mm. Dr Williams's Library.

71 Charing Cross. 43 × 30mm. Statue of Charles I.

72 St Luke's Hospital. 43 × 50mm.

73 Ironmongers Hall. 43 × 35mm.

74 Christ Church Hospital. 43 × 30mm. ie Christ's Hospital.

75 Marlborough House. 43 × 45mm.

76 Lambeth Palace. 43 × 45mm.

77 Stables, King's Mews. 45 × 65mm.

78 Hyde Park Corner. 44 × 47mm.

79 Adelphi. 44 × 45mm.

80 Albany Piccadilly. 44 × 30mm.

81 Earl Spencer's House. 44 × 37mm. Green Park.

82 Penitentiary. 44 × 50mm. Millbank, completed by Sir Robert Smirke, 1816.

p 303 (pl. 5): 'The Principal Bridges over the River Thames'

83 Westminster Bridge. 23 × 225mm.

84 Waterloo Bridge. 30 × 230mm. Sir John Rennie's bridge, completed 1817.

85 Vauxhall Bridge. 20 × 170mm. Designed by James Walker, opened June 1816.

86 Southwark Bridge. 20 × 170mm. Sir John Rennie's bridge, built 1815–19.

87 Blackfriars Bridge. 35 × 230mm.

88 London Bridge. 34 × 230mm.

p 381 (pl. 6)

89 College of Physicians. 43 × 30mm.

90 Merchant Taylors School. 43 × 38mm.

91 Burlington House. 43 × 40mm.

92 Crosby House. 43 × 35mm. (*Longford* 699)

93 Northumberland House. 43 × 43mm.

94 Chelsea Hospital. 43 × 78mm. (*Longford* 18)

95 Opera House. 43 × 45mm.

96 Covent Garden Theatre. 43 × 55mm.

97 Drury Lane Theatre. 43 × 37mm.

98 Holland House. 43 × 45mm.

99 Bullocks Museum. 43 × 37mm. In the Egyptian Hall, Piccadilly, built 1812.

100 Hampton Court. 44 × 50mm.

101 Frogmore. 44 × 48mm.

102 Oatlands. 44 × 40mm.

103 Windsor Castle. 44 × 50mm.

104 Greenwich Hospital. 44 × 78mm.

105 Kensington Palace. 43 × 45mm.

106 Eton College. 43 × 45mm.

107 St Alban's Abbey. 43 × 38mm.

108 Wanstead House. 43 × 50mm.

109 Independent Academy/Homerton. 43 × 40mm.

p 452 (map)

110 (tm) Leigh's New Plan of London. Engraved by Sidy Hall. London, Published by Samuel Leigh. 430 × 540mm. (*Darlington and Howgego* 274, 1)

1819 ed

front. nos 21–39 (pl. 2, intact).

p 120 nos 8–11,18–20 (pl. 1).

p 156 nos 40–4,51–5 (pl. 3).

p 204 nos 61–5,72–6 (pl. 4).

p 216 nos 1–6, 12–16. (pl. 1).

p 236 nos 7, 17 (pl. 1); 45 (pl. 3); 66,77 (pl. 4); 95,105 (pl. 6).

p 252 nos 67–71, 78–82 (pl. 4).

p 264 nos 84,86,88 (pl. 5).

p 272 nos 83,85,87 (pl. 5).

p 312 nos 46–50, 56–60 (pl. 3).

p 436 nos 96–9, 106–9 (pl. 6).

111 p 452 Leigh's New Map of the Environs of London. Drawn & Engraved by Sidy Hall 14 Bury St. Bloomsby. Published by Samuel Leigh 18 Strand. 205 × 260mm. (*Darlington and Howgego* 278)

112 p 477 Plan of Maze, Hampton Court. 50 × 100mm.

p 504 nos 89–94,100–4 (pl. 6).

p 524 no 110 (map).

1822 and 1824–5 eds

113 front. The Quadrant, Regent Street. 110 × 235mm. Caption in voided capitals.

p 85 nos 55,73,67,17. 1824–5 ed p 85.

p 114 nos 9,13,82. 1824–5 ed p 108.

p 168 no 21. 1824–5 ed p 160.

p 175 no 39. 1824–5 ed p 168.

p 178 nos 22,37. 1824–5 ed p 172.

p 188 nos 33, 25–6, 23. 1824–5 ed p 182.

p 192 nos 28,30–1,61. 1824–5 ed p 186.

114 p 196 St. Lawrence. 50 × 35mm. St. Lawrence Jewry. With nos 24, 27, 29. 1824–5 ed p 190.

p 198 nos 35,32,34. (1824–5, p 192)

115 p 201 Pancras New Church. 50 × 50mm. Built by W.H. Inwood, 1821–2. 1824–5 ed p 197.

116 p 201 Chapel, Waterloo Place. 63 × 63mm. St Philip's Chapel, built by G.S. Repton, 1819–20. 1824–5 ed p 197.

p 202 nos 66, 62 (recaptioned 'Queen's Chapel'), 63. 1824–5 ed p 198.

p 206 nos 65,64. 1824–5 ed p 202.

p 208 nos 5, 7 (recaptioned 'Buckingham House'),6 (recaptioned 'Carlton Palace'). 1824–5 ed p 208.

p 214 nos 105,3,76. 1824–5 ed p 212.

p 224 no 12. 1824–5 ed p 224.

p 229 nos 45,16. 1824–5 ed p 227.

p 234 nos 43,52,42. 1824–5 ed p 232.

p 240 nos 53,60,41. 1824–5 ed p 236.

p 244 nos 14–15,51. 1824–5 ed p 240.

p 248 nos 79,18 (recaptioned 'Somerset House, Strand Front'), 40. 1824–5 ed p 248.

p 250 nos 19,4,71,20. 1824–5 ed p 250.

p 253 nos 1,11,77. 1824–5 ed p 253.

p 256 nos 8,10,2,92,78,80. 1824–5 ed p 254.

p 258 nos 91,75,93,81. 1824–5 ed p 258.

p 266 nos 88, 87, 83. Reduced re-engravings, 10 × 105mm. 1824–5 ed p 266.

p 270 nos 84, 85, 86. Reduced re-engravings, 10 × 105mm. 1824–5 ed p 268.

117 p 273 (tm) Panorama of Remarkable Objects in London. Engraved for Leigh's New Picture of London by Sidy Hall. 210 × 270/240 × 280mm. First appears in 1824–5 ed p 273. (*Darlington and Howgego* 300)

p 296 nos 90,74. 1824–5 ed p 298.

118 p 296 St Paul's School. 50 × 45mm. Built by George Smith, 1823–4. 1824–5 ed p 298.

p 305 nos 44,54. 1824–5 ed p 307.

119 p 310 Greenwich Hospital. 55 × 102mm. cf with no 104. 1824–5 ed p 310.

120 p 312 Chelsea Hospital. 55 × 102mm. cf with no 94. 1824–5 ed p 314. (*Longford* 18)

p 316 nos 59,50,58. 1824–5 ed p 318.

p 324 nos 72,69,57. 1824–5 ed p 324.

121 p 336 Surgeon's Hall, Lincolns Inn Fields. 60 × 55mm. cf with no 47. 1824–5 ed p 336.

122 p 336 College of Physicians (courtyard). 48 × 28mm. cf with no 89. Only in 1822 ed.

123 p 336 Entrance of the College. 45 × 33mm. Only in 1822 ed.

124 p 336 College of Physicians. 33 × 58mm. Built by Robert Smirke, 1824–5. Only in 1824–5 ed.

125 p 336 Union Club House. 48 × 55mm. Trafalgar Square, built by Robert Smirke, 1824–7. Only in 1824–5 ed.

p 349 nos 46,48,70,56 (recaptioned 'British Gallery'), 99 (recaptioned 'Egyptian Hall'). 1824–5 ed p 351.

126 p 412 Opera House. 48 × 60mm. cf with no 95. 1824–5 ed p 422.

127 p 412 Drury Lane Theatre. 58 × 62mm. cf with no 97. 1824–5 ed p 422.

p 414 no 96. 1824–5 ed p 424.

128 p 414 Hay Market Theatre. 60 × 58mm. Built by Nash, 1820–1. 1824–5 ed p 424.

p 428 no 111 (map). 1824–5 ed p 444.

129 p 438 Claremont. 30 × 54mm. 1824–5 ed p 450.

130 p 438 Eton College. 30 × 55. cf with no 106. 1824–5 ed p 450.

131 p 438 Frogmore. 30 × 55mm. cf with no 101. 1824–5 ed p 450.

p 452 nos 98,102,100. 1824–5 ed p 460.

p 468 nos 108,103. 1824–5 ed p 484.

p 520 no 110 (map). Only in 1824–5 ed. (*Darlington and Howgego* 274,3).

127 · LESTER'S ILLUSTRATIONS OF LONDON [1818]

In his foreword the publisher, T. Lester, says that he hopes this work will find acceptance 'in the present day, when a taste for examining and illustrating the History and Antiquities of our Metropolis, is found to prevail among readers of almost every class' and, to enhance its popular appeal, he promises that 'among the engravings will be found a variety of Original Representations, delineated in a chaste and appropriate style'. On the wrapper of the first Part is a prospectus:

Part 1. Price 2s 6d (to be continued Monthly) of Lester's Illustrations of London ...

Conditions: The work will be published regularly in monthly parts; each part containing eight copper-plate engravings, and sixteen pages of letter-press, descriptive of the subjects contained in the part, by which arrangement, each portion of the work will be in itself complete. Every eight parts will form a volume, and an appropriate index will be given. The work will be printed in two sizes, viz, in Foolscap Octavo at 2s 6d per part and in Demy Octavo, with proof impressions of the plates, at 4s. per part.

As the engraved title is abridged the only extended title is to be found on the Part wrappers:

Lester's Illustrations of London containing a Series of Engraved Views and Delineations of Antiquarian, Architectural and other subjects in the Metropolis; with Historical & Topographical Descriptions. To be completed in Twenty Five Parts, forming Three Octavo Volumes, containing Sixty Four Plates in each Volume. London: Published and sold by T. Lester, 14 Finsbury Place, Finsbury Square, and all other Booksellers.

The first three Parts in their original buff and grey wrappers may be seen in the Guildhall Library (Pam 2090). A bound 'Volume 1' seems generally to consist of the first eight Parts and vestiges of a ninth. These were issued in July and September to December 1816, in January and April 1817, in May 1818 (the date of the engraved title, item 57) and in September 1818. It seems therefore likely that the Parts ceased at the eighth, well short of the 25 intended, and that the ninth was never finished and only one out of the three advertised volumes was ever completed.

The small views, careful line-engravings comparable to the contemporary illustrations in Hughson's *Walks through London* (no 121), have captions in copperplate script but no credits, although two surviving drawings are signed 'G. Shepherd'. They are unnumbered and arranged to face their textual references. Neither a list of plates nor the promised index appear to have been published. The publication-lines read: 'Published (date) by T. Lester, Finsbury Place.'

(Title-page as above)

Small octavo, 170 × 95mm; demy octavo, 205 × 130mm. 1818

COLLATION Engr title-page; pp 1–128, Lester's Illustrations of London.

PART 1 (Publication-lines 'July 1, 1816'; text pp 1–16)

1 p 1 Old Gateway, St James's. 63 × 80/105 × 155mm.

2 p 3 Leadenhall Chapel. 65 × 80/105 × 155mm. Water-colour drawing (63 × 80mm), 'G. Shepherd 1815', in the Guildhall Library.

3 p 6 St Ann's Church Limehouse. 65 × 95/105 × 155mm.

4 p 7 Frost Fair on the River Thames. 65 × 97/106 × 150mm. The 1814 fair.

5 p 11 Stow's Monument. 98 × 65/150 × 105mm.

6 p 13 Figure in front of an old Building Golden Lane. 83 × 60/155 × 105mm.

7 p 14 Arms in front of an old Building Golden Lane. 80 × 65/175 × 115mm. Wash drawing (79 × 68mm), 'G. Shepherd 1815', in GLC.

8 p 14 London Stone. 93 × 60/50 × 100mm.

PART 2 (Publication-lines 'Septr 1, 1816'; text pp 17–32)

9 St. Botolph's Church Bishopsgate. 95 × 65/155 × 100mm.

10 p 19 Drury Lane Theatre. 60 × 90/105 × 150mm. 'As re-edified in 1811'.

11 p 20 Ruins of Drury Lane Theatre. 60 × 85/105 × 155mm. 'Burned Feb. 1809'.

12 p 23 Sir Paul Pindar's Lodge. 60 × 55/155 × 100mm.

13 p 23 York Stairs. 57 × 85/100 × 152mm.

14 p 25 Statue of Charles James Fox. 80 × 70/150 × 100mm. Vignetted. 'In Bloomsbury Square'.

15 p 27 Boy at Pye Corner. 85 × 60/155 × 105mm.

16 p 28 Pendrill's tomb. 45 × 105/105 × 155mm. Vignetted. St Giles in the Fields churchyard.

PART 3 (Publication-lines 'Octr 1, 1816'; text pp 33–46)

17 p 33 Sir Paul Pindar's House. 95 × 55/150 × 102mm.

18 p 34 Wesley's Chapel City Road. 63 × 90/100 × 155mm.

19 p 39 Temple Barr. 78 × 56/153 × 100mm.

20 p 41 Pump in Cornhill. 90 × 50/150 × 105mm.

21 p 42 Tomb of Sir Nicholas Throgmorton. 60 × 85/100 × 150mm. In St Katherine Cree Church.

22 p 44 Gateway St Catherine Cree Church. 70 × 60/150 × 105mm. Vignetted.

23 p 45 Mortar, St James's Park. 70 × 85/100 × 155mm. Vignetted.

24 p 47 Figure of Guy Earl of Warwick. 82 × 52/150 × 100mm.

PART 4 (Publication-lines 'Novr 1, 1816'; text pp 47–64)

25 p 49 Shoreditch Church. 85 × 62/150 × 100mm.

26 p 52 Albion Chapel Moorfields. 62 × 90/105 × 150mm.

27 p 55 Ruins of the Savoy Hospital. 60 × 87/105 × 155mm.

28 p 56 Savoy Prison. 65 × 85/105 × 155mm. The courtyard.

29 p 59 Duke of Exeter's Tomb. 65 × 60/150 × 100mm. Vignetted.

30 p 61 Pulpit St Catherines Tower. 60 × 45/150 × 100mm. Vignetted.

31 p 62 Old House Little Moorfields. 85 × 55/155 × 100mm.

32 p 63 Gateway St. Stephens Church Coleman Street. 80 × 65/155 × 100mm. Vignetted.

PART 5 (Publication-lines 'Decr 1, 1816'; text pp 65–80)

33 p 65 St Georges, Hanover Square. 92 × 60/150 × 100mm.

34 p 67 Strand Bridge. 62 × 98/100 × 150mm. ie Waterloo Bridge. 'It is expected it will be open about midsummer next year, 1817'.

35 p 71 Banqueting House, Whitehall. 60 × 85/100 × 150mm.

36 p 75 Statue of King James 2d. 90 × 60/155 × 100mm. Vignetted. By Grinling Gibbons.

37 p 76 Old House, High Street, Southwark. 90 × 50/150 × 100mm.

38 p 78 Entrance to Barber Surgeons' Hall. 96 × 75/150 × 100mm.

39 p 79 Bastion on London Wall. 90 × 60/150 × 100mm.

40 p 80 Speed's Monument. 65 × 70/100 × 150mm. St Giles, Cripplegate.

PART 6 (Publication-lines 'Jany 1, 1817'; text pp 81–96)

41 p 81 St Martins in the Fields. 100 × 58/150 × 100mm.

42 p 84 Covent Garden Theatre. 58 × 95/100 × 153mm. Smirke's building.

43 p 88 Auction Mart. 58 × 75/100 × 150mm.

44 p 91 General Monks House. 85 × 60/155 × 100mm.

45 p 91 Entrance to Mercers Hall. 90 × 55/150 × 102mm.

46 p 93 Fishbornes Monument. 52 × 70/100 × 150mm. Vignetted. In Mercers' Hall.

47 p 93 Statue of King Charles 2d. 100 × 55/150 × 102mm. In Crown Court, off the Borough High Street, Southwark. A caricature of the monarch.

48 p 95 Ancient Egyptian Figure. 90 × 55/150 × 100mm. Vignetted.

PART 7 (Publication-lines 'April 1, 1817'; text pp 97–112)

49 p 97 St. Saviours Southwark. 60 × 90/100 × 150mm.

50 p 100 Gower's Monument. 82 × 58/152 × 102mm. In St Saviour, Southwark.

51 p 101 Effigy of a Knight Templer. 100 × 60/150 × 100mm.

52 p 105 New Custom House. 58 × 92/100 × 150mm. By David Laing, 1813–17. From the river.

53 p 108 Guildhall Chapel. 85 × 60/153 × 103mm.

54 p 110 Gerard's Hall. 90 × 63/152 × 102mm.

55 p 110 Figure at the entrance of Gerard's Hall. 110 × 55/152 × 100mm. Vignetted.

56 p 112 Old House, London Wall. 95 × 58/155 × 103mm.

PART 8 (Publication-lines 'May 1, 1818'; text pp 113–28)

57 p 113 (engr title) Lester's/illustrations/of/London. Gate of the Priory of St. Bartholomew. Published/May 1, 1818 by T. Lester, Finsbury Place. 90 × 62/155 × 105mm.

58 p 114 St Mary le Bow, Cheapside. 100 × 60/155 × 100mm.

59 p 119 The London Institution. 62 × 93/98 × 152mm. By William Brooks, 1815–19.

60 p 120 Dreadful Fire, Corner of Hewit's Court, Strand. 92 × 60/150 × 90mm. 'On Sunday morning March 1, 1818, at 460 Strand'.

61 p 123 Remains of Francis Bancraft Esq. 65 × 90/95 × 150mm.

62 p 125 Tomb of Francis Bancroft Esq. 65 × 90/95 × 150mm.

63 p 127 Porter and Dwarf. 75 × 55/160 × 92. Over Bull's Head Court, Newgate Street.

64 p 128 Bangor House. 90 × 63/150 × 100mm.

PART 9(?) (Publication-lines 'Septr 1, 1818')

65 Old House, Bishopsgate Street. 60 × 90/100 × 150mm.

66 Statue of the Duke of Bedford. 100 × 55/155 × 100mm. Russell Square.

128 · NIGHTINGALE'S HISTORY OF ST SAVIOUR, SOUTHWARK [1818]

This book depicts the church, now known as Southwark Cathedral, shortly before its restoration, first by Gwilt and then by Wallace. It is complemented by Taylor's *Annals* (no 175), which dates from just after those reconstructions. The author is the Unitarian minister who in 1814 took over the compilation of *The Beauties of England and Wales* (no 104) after Brayley had fallen out with the new publisher. He must have been employed by the illustrator W.G. Moss whose name appears in the imprint as the proprietor.

The History and Antiquities of the Parochial Church of St Saviour, Southwark, illustrated by a Series of Engravings, of exterior and interior views, ground plan, and details of that edifice, from drawings, by W.G. Moss. The historical, biographical and descriptive delineations, by the Rev. J. Nightingale. London: Published by the Proprietor, W.G. Moss, Clayton Place, Kennington Road, and sold by Sherwood and Co. Paternoster Row, Hill, High Street, Southwark, and Cox, High Street, Southwark. 1818.

Quarto, 260 × 200mm.   1818

COLLATION   Title-page; pp iii–iv, dedication to the Duke of Cambridge, pp v–vi, preface dated 19 October 1818; pp vii–viii, list of subscribers; half-title; pp 3–94, History and Antiquities; index, list of plates (2pp).

W.G. Moss contributed to the plates in *The Beauties of England and Wales* in 1815 and may thus have come to know Nightingale; three of the engravers he employed were likewise contributors, namely J. Shury, H. Hobson and W.R. Smith. The fourth, Bartholomew Howlett, was soon to become one of Wilkinson's chief engravers for *Londina Illustrata* (no 131). It seems likely that the artist was connected with William Moss, RA, gold medallist and draughtsman of two large views of old Somerset House in 1777, before its demolition to make way for Chambers's building, aquatinted by F. Jukes (BL Maps: *K. top.* 26.4. b,c), perhaps the same person. It is certain that he collaborated with J. Shury again in a view of Waterloo Bridge published as a *Stationers Almanack* for 1821. All the plates are credited 'Drawn by W.G. Moss' and, unless

otherwise stated, 'Engraved (Etched) by J. Shury'. All are also 'Printed by Shury.', save pl. 6, 10, 12 and 16 which are 'Printed by R. & J. Williamson.' and 8 which lacks a printer's name. The publication-lines, which run from July 1817 to October 1818, consist of a variable combination of three of the names in the imprints linked by ampersands (items 1–3, 8–9, 15: b & a; items 4–6, 12–14; 16–17: a & b; items 7, 10: b & c & a; item 11: a):

(a) 'London, Published (date) by W.G. Moss, Clayton Place, Kennington (Road)'.

(b) 'London, published (date) by Sherwood & Co, Paternoster Row'.

(c) 'London, Published (date) by Hill, High Street, Southwark'.

Captions are in voided capitals; the plates are unnumbered, but listed.

1 front. History of St. Saviours Church./St. Saviours Church./Western Entrance. Augt 1818. 215 × 160mm. As with Ackermann's *Westminster Abbey* (no 108) the book title is carved in the stonework.

2 p 1 St. Saviour's Church./Ground Plan shewing the situation of the Tombs. Drawn from actual measurement by S. Barnes. Engraved by W.G. Moss. 1818. 200 × 310/250 × 350mm. Refs A–L.

3 p 42 St Saviour's Church./Monument of John Gower Esqr. July 1817. 180 × 125/240 × 185mm.

4 p 50 St Saviour's Church./View in the North Aisle shewing the entrance to the Virgin Mary's Chapel. Engraved by H. Hobson. July 1817. 175 × 123/230 × 185mm.

5 p 51 St Saviour's Church./The Monument of Richard Humble Esqr. Alderman of London 1616. Novr. 1817. 185 × 130/240 × 190mm.

6 p 53 St Saviour's Church./View of the Nave from the West. Engraved by H. Hobson. Novr. 1817. 180 × 125/230 × 185mm.

7 p 54 St Saviour's Church./View of the Nave from the South Aisle. Feby. 1818. 180 × 125/240 × 182mm.

8 p 57 St Saviour's Church./View of the Choir looking East. Engraved by W.R. Smith. Augst 1818. 180 × 125/260 × 195mm.

9 p 61 St Saviour's Church./Ornamental sculpture on the sofite of the East Window of the Choir: and part of the Cornice over the Altar-piece. Feby 1818. 165 × 225mm.

10 p 62 St Saviour's Church./View of the Choir looking West. Engraved by W.R. Smith. Feby. 1818. 175 × 123/260 × 195mm.

11 p 69 St Saviour's Church./Representation of Two

Bodies found in the Great Vault, Nov 1817. 180 × 130/240 × 180mm.

12 p 71 St Saviour's Church./View from the North Transept. Engraved by H. Hobson. Octr. 1818. 180 × 128/235 × 190mm.

13 p 80 St Saviour's Church./St Mary Magdalen's Chapel. Novr. 1817. 130 × 175/185 × 240mm.

14 p 82 St Saviour's Church./The Virgin Mary's Chapel. July 1817. 125 × 180/185 × 240mm.

15 p 84 St Saviour's Church./Monument of Launcelot Andrews, Bishop of Winchester. Etched by B. Howlett. July 1817. 180 × 125/240 × 180mm.

16 p 90 St Saviour's Church./View from the South. Engraved by B. Howlett. Feby. 1818. 175 × 122/240 × 180mm.

17 p 92 St Saviour's Church./View from the North. Engraved by B. Howlett. Novr. 1817. 175 × 125/245 × 195mm.

129 · ARCHITECTURA ECCLESIASTICA LONDINI [1819]

The initial 20 plates, comprising the first two Numbers, of *Architectura Ecclesiastica* were dated 1 March 1810. The grey paper wrapper in which the first ten were issued reads as follows:

Price 15s. No. 1. (dedication to Lord Mayor, Aldermen, etc) Picturesque Views of the Churches of London from original drawings by W. Pearson ...

Plan and conditions: This Work will contain a View of each Parish Church in the Metropolis, with Two Views of St Paul's and of Westminster Abbey as also some of the remarkable Interiors, with a general Plan of the whole, shewing the relative and particular Situation of each Building, making in the whole Series 120 subjects, which will be completed in Twelve Numbers, of Ten Plates each, equal in size and execution to No. 1 and 2.

Price,	on Quarto Paper, per Number	0.	15.	0
	Large Paper or Royal Folio	1.	1.	0
	First Impressions, or Proofs upon India Paper	2.	2.	0

London: Sold by John Booth, Duke Street, Portland Place; J. Taylor, Architectural Library, Holborn; Sherwood Neely and Jones, Paternoster Row; W. Clarke, Bond Street; J. Richardson, opposite to Royal Exchange; and Setchel and Son, King Street, Covent Garden.

All the booksellers were specialists in topography and it is noteworthy that Josiah Taylor of the Architectural Library, the publisher of Britton's architectural books, shared in this venture. In March 1814 a list issued by John Booth, stationer, bookbinder and circulating library proprietor, advertised the first six Numbers in two Parts each consisting of 30 plates:

Architectura Ecclesiastica Londini, or the Ecclesiastical Architecture of London: Being a series of Views of the Churches in that City, by eminent artists; for a more full illustration of the Topography and History of the Metropolis; and as a suitable accompaniment to *Dugdale's Monasticon*; or the *Vetusta Monumenta* published by the Antiquarian Society. Parts 1 and 2 are now published, containing 60 Plates. Price for Nos 1 and 2, £4. 10s. in Boards. Nos 3 and 4 following will complete the work, and which will shortly appear.... Each engraving will have annexed a concise but well-authenticated account from the earliest record of the foundation, and of the structure ... with the names of the late and present incumbents. Conditions: This work will consist of four parts; each to contain thirty Plates. Per Part:

Price of the Imperial 4to (size of the small ed. of *Dugdale's Monasticon* and of *Britton's large Paper Architectural Antiquities*)	2.	5.	0
Royal folio	3.	3.	0
Royal folio, India paper proofs	6.	6.	0

A few copies, proofs, are printed upon an extra large size, on imperial paper, to accompany ... the largest paper copies of *Pennant*; as also for the *Vetusta Monumenta*.

By 1818 Upcott was able to publish a list of the 90 plates in the first three Parts (or nine Numbers). In January and July 1820 the *Monthly Literary Advertiser* announced publication of the final Numbers, 10 to 12, with 32 plates and of the completed volume, backed in blue leather at £9, royal quarto £12 12s, India paper £25 4s and Large Paper £37 16s.

After the first 20 plates of March 1810 Booth's publication-line replaced Setchel's. The remaining ten plates of the first Part were dated April, May, June and September 1811 and January 1812. All succeeding plates also carried some form of Booth's publication-line. Part 2 (Numbers 4 to 6) bore the dates January, September, October and November 1812, October and November 1813, and January 1814. Part 3 (Numbers 7 to 9) was dated January, February, October and November 1814, with stragglers from October and November 1812. Part 4 (Numbers 10 to 12), comprising 33 plates, was dated July 1816, February 1817, July, September, November and December 1818, and February and March 1819, together with stragglers from May 1811, October 1812 and January 1814—and one after-thought (pl.102, 'St Pancras Middlesex', completed in 1822) dated July 1823. The 'General Plan' promised on the wrapper seems never to have materialized.

On completion of the work a list of the 123 plates was printed, arranging the Cathedral first and then the other churches in alphabetical order of their dedications. They are usually bound in this order, although on the reverse another list is provided, subdividing under the City, Westminster and South-wark. Two differing title-pages were issued, dated 1819 and 1820, and the essay and notes on each plate by Charles Clarke, antiquary and *Gentleman's Magazine* contributor, was supplemented by an article on the Temple Church.

Architectura Ecclesiastica Londini; being a series of views, architectural and topographical of the Cathedral, Collegiate and Parochial Churches, in London, South-wark & Westminster, with the adjoining parishes; the whole illustrative of the Ecclesiastical Architecture of the Metropolis at this period, and of the various topographic-al and historical accounts; consisting of one hundred and twenty-two plates from original drawings By John Coney, George Shepherd &c. To each View is affixed an account of its original foundations, with connected memorabilia, with an introductory essay On Early English Architecture, and descriptional remarks, by Charles Clarke Esq. F.S.A. London: Published by John Booth, Duke Street, Portland Place, 1819.

Architectura Eclesiastica Londini; or graphical survey of the Cathedral, Collegiate and Parochial Churches in London, Southwark and Westminster, with the adjoining parishes; containing also an historical account of their earliest foundation, and other memorabilia, taken from the most authentic records, with descriptional remarks on each structure, prefaced by considerations on The Rise and Progress of Early English Architecture, by Charles Clarke Esq. F.S.A. The whole illustrative of the Ecclesiastical Architecture of the Metropolis at this period, and of the various topographical and historical accounts, consisting of one hundred and twenty-two plates, from original drawings by John Coney, George Shepherd, &c. London: Published by John Booth, Duke Street, Portland Place. 1820.

Quarto, 340 × 265mm (465 × 290mm); folio, 495 × 345mm (535 × 360mm). 1819 (1820)

COLLATION Title-page; dedication to the Bishop of London (1 leaf); pp 1–36, Some Account of the Rise and Progress of Early English Architecture, by Charles Clarke; pp 1–8, Facts and Observations relating to the Temple Church, by Joseph Jekyll, dated February 1811; list of plates, list of churches within the walls and liberties of the City of London (2pp).

Here is the first artistically competent and exhaustive illustration of the golden age of London church building and, as it turned out, the last possible one before the demolitions of the nineteenth and twentieth centuries, the destruction wrought by the second World War and the oversha-dowings, dwarfings and obliterations by office blocks since then. What the steel-engravings in *Metropolitan Improvements* (no 154) did for the new wave of Greek revival churches the larger etchings of the *Architectura Ecclesiastica* did for the baroque and post-baroque church architecture of London. No fewer than 52 Wren churches, apparently still in good fettle, are represented, with four by Hawk-smoor, three by Gibbs and others by Thomas Archer, John James, Flitcroft, the Dances father and son, and several more recent architects. Moreover they are not depicted in the traditional way by an approximate outline quite divorced from its neighbourhood, as in Maitland's *History* (no 38), another book which aimed at completeness, but they stand three-dimensional and four-square in their streets or churchyards, sometimes even ani-mated with staffage of Regency Londoners. Their most likely source of inspiration is the excellent series of line-engravings issued by West and Toms in the first half of the previous century (no 32).

The wrapper title mentions only William Pearson who was employed by Henry Setchel as draughts-man of the first 20 plates of March 1810. He was a water-colourist who had exhibited at the Royal Academy and elsewhere between 1798 and 1809 and whose drawings, in the manner of Girtin, went in for eventful skies, dramatic shadows and strong col-ours, so that his churches appear in full sail through an atmosphere of scudding clouds. He was not so successful however in matters of architectural proportion and detail, and this is perhaps the reason for the survival, in the Crace and Guildhall Library collections, of a number of his drawings clearly intended for the *Architectura* but never engraved. Indeed only two more plates of his were published once John Booth was in control.

He favoured John Coney and George Shepherd, and it is easy to understand a preference for their less rhetorical tinted drawings in the tradition of the Maltons and Sandbys. The series was, after all, an architectural one and their attention to proportion and authentic detail is so close as to perpetuate the enchanting reality of those vanished churches. John Coney, draughtsman and engraver, who drew 57 of the views, was born in the Ratcliff Highway and apprenticed to an architect. He never practised that profession but his earliest studies were of the interior of Westminster Abbey and he first exhibited at the Royal Academy in 1805. As a young artist of 25 he was much beholden to Booth for so important a commission. George Shepherd, the founder of a family of topographical artists, drew 39 of the churches; he became steeped in London architecture since he was contributing simultaneously to *Londina Illustrata* (no 131) and producing endless water-colours for the extra-illustration of Pennant (no 67), such as that of Henry Fauntleroy now in the Soane Museum. A more modest contribution of three drawings was made by another *Londina Illustrata* illustrator, R.B. Schnebbelie. Reference is made to the numerous water-colour drawings for this work in the British Museum and Guildhall Library.

Both Coney and Pearson etched some of their own plates but the chief engravers of the series were: Joseph Skelton, a specialist in topographical and antiquarian subjects who was entrusted with most of the Coney drawings, William Wise, who also worked for *Londina Illustrata* and Hughson's *London* (no 121) and who on this occasion was assigned to George Shepherd's work, Thomas Dale, another *Londina Illustrata* engraver, and Pearson's engraver W. Preston.

What is unusual about the series as a whole, besides the uniformly high quality of the drawing and engraving, is that a large number of the original water-colours have been preserved in the Crace Collection, so that they and the plates derived from them may be examined in the British Museum. Crace catalogue references are given below both to originals and to those drawings which were rejected by the publisher, such as Pearson's St Mary Aldermary (pl.75) set aside in favour of Shepherd's much more convincing version of seventeenth century Gothic.

The plates are captioned in capitals followed by italics giving a short history of the subject and the name of the incumbent. In the 1819 issue they are unnumbered but in 1820 they are numbered (not very consistently) either by an engraved addition or by labels stuck on tr. After the first two Numbers the title 'Architectural Series of London Churches' appears on all Booth's plates with the exception of five issued in November 1813 and January 1814 (pl.44,55–6,61,114–15) where it is altered to 'Ecclesiastical Architecture of London'. Letters standing in for publication-lines are:

(a) 'Published March 1, 1810 by Setchel & Son, 23 King St. Covt. Garden.' (below caption and description)

(b) '(London) Published by J. Booth, Duke Street, Portland Place, (date).' (below caption and description)

(c) 'Drawn by ... Etched by ... for the Architectural Series of London Churches, (Published) by J. Booth (date).' (runs credits, series title and publication-line together)

1 Ground Plan of St Paul's Cathedral, London/showing the Basement Story as also the Groining of the Roofs by Dotted Lines &c. Drawn and engraved from actual measurements by John Coney for the Architectural Series of London Churches. Published by J. Booth Decr. 10th 1818. Plate I. 263 × 185/350 × 270mm. Pt 4.

2 St Paul's London. Drawn and Engraved by John Coney. Published for the Architectural Series of London Churches by J. Booth Decr. 10th 1818. Plate II. 190 × 260/270 × 345mm. Pt 4. Outline etching of exterior.

3 Interior of St Pauls./The view taken from the Northern entrance looking toward the South and West Doors. Drawn by J. Coney. Engraved by J. Skelton. Published by J. Booth Decr. 10th 1818. Plate III. 262 × 190/340 × 270mm. Pt 4. A sepia drawing of this subject (298 × 200mm), by John Coney, dated 1817, in V & A (379–1872).

4 St Albans Wood Strt. Etched by White from a Drawing by Pearson. (a) 210 × 165/345 × 280mm. Pt 1. Built by Wren, 1682–7, 1697–8; gutted 1940. Drawing (210 × 172mm), dated 1810, in BM (*Crace* 21.36).

5 Allhallows Barking. Drawn & Etched by W. Pearson. (a) 170 × 205/285 × 350mm. Pt 1. Unsigned drawing (180 × 200mm) in Guildhall Library.

6 Allhallows Bread Street. Drawn by J. Coney & Etched by J. Skelton. (c) Novr 25, 1814. 220 × 165/345 × 270mm. Pt 3. Built by Wren, 1677–84; demolished 1876. Drawing (215 × 165mm) in BM (*Crace* 20.22).

7 Allhallows the Great. Drawn by J. Coney. Etched by J. Skelton. (b) Jany 1, 1812. 215 × 165/350 × 270mm. Pt 2. Built by Wren, 1677–83; demolished 1894. Drawing (215 × 165mm) in BM (*Crace* 20.26);

alternative by Pearson (215 × 165mm) also in BM (*Crace* 20.28).

8 Allhallows Lombard Street. Drawn by G. Shepherd. Etched by W., Wise. (b) Octr 5, 1812. 225 × 165/345 × 270mm. Pt 2. Built by Wren, 1686–94; demolished 1939.

9 Allhallows London Wall. Etched by Wise from a drawing by W. Pearson. (a) 205 × 170/350 × 270mm. Pt 1. Built by George Dance junior, 1765–7. Drawing (205 × 146mm), dated 1810, in BM (*Crace* 25.85).

10 Allhallows Staining. Etched by W. Preston from a drawing by W. Pearson. (a) 170 × 205/285 × 360mm. Pt 1.

11 St Alphage. Drawn by J. Coney. Etched by J. Skelton (c) Novr 23, 1814. 163 × 215/270 × 345mm. Pt 3. As rebuilt in 1777 with a Venetian window and two pedimented doors. Drawing (165 × 215mm), dated 1812, in BM (*Crace* 25.71).

12 St Andrew Holborn. Drawn by R. Johnson & Etched by S. Jenkins (c) Oct. 10th 1814. 170 × 210/270 × 345mm. Pt 3. Built by Wren, 1684–1704. Drawing (210 × 215mm) in BM (*Crace* 27.95) and another (165 × 205mm) in BM 'Marx' Pennant 9, p 219.

13 St Andrew Undershaft. Drawn by J. Coney & Etched by J. Skelton. (b) Novr. 1812. 233 × 165/350 × 270mm. Pt 2. Alternative drawing (216 × 165mm), by Pearson, in BM (*Crace* 23.71).

14 St Andrews Wardrobe. Etched by J.W. White from a Drawing by Pearson. (a) 213 × 153/345 × 280mm. Pt 1. Built by Wren, 1685–95. Drawing (210 × 153mm), dated 1810, in BM (*Crace* 20.13).

15 St Anne & Agnes. Drawn by J. Coney & Etched by J. Skelton (c) Novr 25, 1814. 165 × 215/270 × 345mm. Pt 3. Built by Wren, 1676–87. Drawing (165 × 215mm), dated 1812, in BM (*Crace* 25.129).

16 St Anne's Limehouse. Etched by W. Wise (c) July 12, 1816. 215 × 165/345 × 270mm. Pt 4. Built by Hawksmoor, 1712–24. Drawing (215 × 165mm), signed by Coney in 1811, in Guildhall Library.

17 St Ann's Westminster. Etched by Preston from a drawing by W. Pearson. (a) 205 × 163/355 × 285mm. Pt 1. Built by Wren, c 1680–6; tower rebuilt by S.P. Cockerell, 1803. Drawing (210 × 140mm), dated 1810, in BM (*Crace* 18.6).

18 St Antholins Watling St. Etched by Preston from a drawing by W. Pearson. (a) 215 × 160/350 × 285mm. Pt 1. Built by Wren, 1678–82, 1688; demolished 1874. Drawing (215 × 160mm), dated 1810, in BM (*Crace* 20.34).

19 St Austin Watling St. Etched by W. Preston from a drawing by W. Pearson. (a) 203 × 160/355 × 285mm. Pt 1. St Augustine's, built by Wren, 1680–9, 1695–8. Drawing (203 × 160mm) in BM (*Crace* 20.36).

20 St Bartholomew the Great. Etched by W. Preston from a drawing by W. Pearson. (a) 165 × 210/285 ×

355mm. Pt 1. Drawing (210 × 230mm), dated 1810, in BM (*Crace* 26.58).

21 Interior of St Bartholomew the Great. Drawn by J. Coney & Etched by J. Skelton (c) Octr 20th 1814. 220 × 177/345 × 270mm. Pt 3.

22 St Bartholomew the Less. Drawn by J. Coney & Etched by S. Jenkins (c) Octr 20th 1814. 170 × 202/265 × 340mm. Pt 3. Rebuilt by George Dance junior, 1793. Drawing (165 × 205mm) in BM (*Crace* 26.62).

23 St Bartholomew Church. Royal Exchange. Drawn by G. Shepherd and Etched by S. Lacy. (b) June 25th, 1811. 218 × 160/340 × 265mm. Pt 1. Built by Wren, 1674–9; demolished 1840–1. Pencil sketch (205 × 156mm) in Guildhall Library.

24 St Bennet Finck. Drawn by G. Shepherd & Etched by J. Wedgwood. (b) April 11th, 1811. 222 × 165/340 × 265mm. Pt 1. Built by Wren, 1681–6; demolished 1842–4. Pencil and water-colour drawing (221 × 164mm), by G. Shepherd, 1810, in Guildhall Library.

25 St Bennet's Gracechurch. Drawn by G. Shepherd and Etched by W. Wise. (b) Novr 3, 1812. 225 × 165/345 × 270mm. Pt 2. Built by Wren, 1681–6; demolished 1867–8.

26 St Bennet (ie St Benedict) Pauls Wharf. Etched by J.W. White from a drawing by W. Pearson (a) 205 × 160/340 × 280mm. Pt 1. Built by Wren, 1677–85. Drawing (205 × 165mm), dated 1810, in BM (*Crace* 20.11).

27 St Botolph Aldgate. Etched by W. Preston from a drawing by Pearson. (a) 210 × 165/355 × 285mm. Pt 1. Built by George Dance senior, 1741–4.

28 St Botolph Aldersgate. Drawn by J. Coney & Etched by J. Skelton (c) Novr 25, 1814. 165 × 215/270 × 345mm. Pt 3. Rebuilt c 1754, 1787–91. Drawing (165 × 215mm), dated 1810, in BM (*Crace* 25.126).

29 St Botolph Bishopsgate. Drawn by J. Coney & Etched by J. Skelton (b) Septr 1, 1812. 218 × 165/345 × 270mm. Pt 2. Rebuilt by James Gould and George Dance senior, 1725–9.

30 St Bride (Brigit). Drawn by G. Shepherd and Etched by W. Wise (c) Octr 10th 1814. 230 × 170/340 × 270mm. Pt 3. Built by Wren, 1670–84, 1701–3. Drawing (190 × 155mm) in BM (*Crace* 19.105).

31 Christ Church. Drawn by G. Shepherd and Etched by W. Wise, (c) Octr 10th 1814. 220 × 168/345 × 265mm. Pt 4. Christchurch, Newgate built by Wren, 1677–91, 1703–4. Drawing (215 × 165mm) in BM (*Crace* 27.35).

32 Christ Church Surry. Etched by Preston from a drawing by W. Pearson. (a) 165 × 205/285 × 355mm. Pt 1. Built 1738 in Blackfriars Road. Drawing (155 × 203mm), dated 1810, in BM (*Crace* 35.1).

33 Christ Church Spitalfields. R.B. Schnebbelie delt. R. Smart sculpt. (b) May 21st 1811. 210 × 165/340 × 265mm. Pt 4. Built by Hawksmoor, 1723–9. A possible

alternative drawing of the subject (215 × 165mm), by G. Shepherd, in BM ('Marx' Pennant 8, p 165).

34 St Clement Danes. Drawn by J. Coney & Etched by J. Skelton (c) Novr 2, 1818. 230 × 168/345 × 270mm. Pt 4. Built by Wren, 1680–2, Gibbs, 1719–20. Drawing (222 × 160mm), '1814', in Guildhall Library.

35 St Clements Eastcheap. Drawn by J. Coney & Etched by J. Skelton. (b) Jany 1, 1812. 165 × 198/270 × 350mm. Pt 2. Built by Wren, 1683–7. Drawing (165 × 215mm) in BM (*Crace* 20.61).

36 St Dionis. Drawn by G. Shepherd and Etched by W. Wise. (b) Octr 11, 1813. 225 × 183/345 × 270mm. Pt 2. Built by Wren, 1670–4, 1684; demolished 1878. Drawing (228 × 182mm) in BM (*Crace* 23.30).

37 St Dunstan's in the East. Drawn by G. Shepherd and Etched by S. Lacy. (b) May 1st, 1811. 230 × 168/340 × 265mm. Pt 2. Built by Wren, 1670–1, 1697–9; destroyed 1941. Drawing (231 × 166mm), '1810', in Guildhall Library.

38 St Dunstan in the West. Drawn by G. Shepherd and Etched by W. Wise (c) Octr 10th 1814. 175 × 230/270 × 345mm. Pt 3.

39 St Dunstans Stepney. Drawn by G. Shepherd & Engraved by T. Dale. (b) Novr 1, 1818. 160 × 230/275 × 345mm. Pt 4. Drawing (184 × 280mm) in BM (*Crace* 33.63) and (152 × 225mm) in Guildhall Library.

40 Interior of St Dunstan's Stepney. Drawn by G. Shepherd and Etched by S. Lacy. (b) Nov 1, 1818. 168 × 228/265 × 342mm. Pt 4.

41 St Edmund the King. Drawn by G. Shepherd and Etched by W. Wise. (b) Octr 11, 1813. 230 × 155/345 × 270mm. Pt 2. Built by Wren, 1670–9, 1706–7. Drawing (235 × 160mm) in BM (*Crace* 23.24).

42 St Ethelburga. Drawn by J. Coney & Etched by J. Skelton. (b) Sepr 1, 1812. 218 × 160/344 × 270mm. Pt 2.

43 St George's Bloomsbury. Drawn by Shepherd & Engraved by W. Wise. (b) Nov 1, 1818. 220 × 175/348 × 270mm. Pt 4. Built by Hawksmoor, 1720–30. Drawing (231 × 189mm), 'G. Shepherd 1811', in Guildhall Library.

44 St George's Botolph. Drawn by J. Coney & Etched by J. Skelton. (b) Feby 15, 1814. 218 × 165/350 × 265mm. Pt 3. Built by Wren, 1671–4; demolished 1903–4.

45 St Georges (in the East) Middlesex. Drawn by J. Coney, Engraved by S. Jenkins (c) Nov 2, 1818. 225 × 165/345 × 270mm. Pt 4. Built by Hawksmoor, 1715–23; gutted 1941. Drawing (215 × 160mm), '1811', in Guildhall Library.

46 St George's Hanover Square. Drawn by J. Coney and Etched by J. Skelton for the Ecclesiastical Architecture of London. (b) Jany 1, 1814. 175 × 215/270 × 345mm. Pt 2. Built by John James, 1712–25.

47 St George the Martyr, Queen Square. Drawn by J. Coney. Etched by J. Coney. (b) Nov 1, 1818. 255 × 170/345 × 270mm. Pt 4. Exterior and interior, built 1706.

48 St George's Southwark. Drawn by G. Shepherd and Etched by J. Skelton. (b) Feby 15, 1814. 218 × 160/340 × 265mm. Pt 3. Built by John Price, 1734–6. Drawing (216 × 160mm) in BM (*Crace* 34.81).

49 St Giles Cripplegate. Etched by Preston and Pearson from a Drawing by W. Pearson. (a) 168 × 205/285 × 355mm. Pt 1. Drawing (165 × 203mm), dated 1813, in BM (*Crace* 25.116).

50 St Giles. G. Shepherd delt. W. Wise sculpt. (b) April 11th 1811. 223 × 163/342 × 265mm. Pt 2. St Giles in the Fields, built by Henry Flitcroft, 1731–4.

51 St Helens Bishopsgate. Etched by White from a Drawing by W. Pearson. (a) 170 × 205/285 × 345mm. Pt 1. Unsigned drawing (170 × 200mm) in Guildhall Library.

52 St James Clerkenwell. Drawn by J. Coney and Etched by J. Skelton (c) Sepr 1 1818. 240 × 173/345 × 270mm. Pt 4. Built by James Carr, 1780–92. Drawing (240 × 178mm), dated 1812, in BM (*Crace* 32.30).

53 St James, Dukes Place. Drawn by J. Coney & Etched by J. Skelton. (b) Nov 1, 1812. 173 × 220/268 × 345mm. Pt 2. Alternative drawing (190 × 198mm), by Pearson, in BM (*Crace* 23.96); pencil drawing (170 × 245mm) and signed water-colour (170 × 215mm) in Guildhall Library.

54 St James Garlick Hithe. Drawn by J. Coney & Etched by J. Skelton. (b) Octr 11 1813. 225 × 165/345 × 270mm. Pt 2. Built by Wren, 1674–87. Pencil drawing (265 × 168mm) and water-colour (220 × 165mm), '1811', in Guildhall Library.

55 St James, Westminster. Drawn by J. Coney and Etched by J. Skelton, for the Ecclesiastical Architecture of London. (b) Jany 1, 1814. 220 × 175/345 × 270mm. Pt 2. Built by Wren, 1682–4.

56 St John the Evangelist. Drawn by J. Coney and Etched by J. Skelton for the Ecclesiastical Architecture of London. (b) Jany 1, 1814. 165 × 235/270 × 345mm. Pt 4. St John, Smith Square built by Thomas Archer, 1714–28. Pencil drawing (170 × 255mm) in Westminster Public Library.

57 St John of Jerusalem Clerkenwell. Drawn by J. Coney and Etched by J. Skelton (c) Sepr 1, 1818. 215 × 160/345 × 270mm. Pt 4.

58 St John Horslydown. Drawn by G. Shepherd and Etched by W. Wise. (b) Jany 25, 1814. 242 × 175/345 × 270mm. Pt 3. Built 1732; bombed 1941. Alternative drawing (215 × 165mm), by Pearson, in BM (*Crace* 34.31).

59 St John Wapping. Drawn by G. Shepherd and Etched by W. Angus (c) Novr 2 1818. 160 × 225/270 × 345mm. Pt 4. Built by Joel Johnson, 1756; gutted in

World War II. Water-colour (160 × 220mm), signed and dated 1817, in Museum of London.

60 St Katharine Coleman Street. Drawn by J. Coney & Etched by J. Skelton. (b) Nov 1, 1812. 165 × 217/275 × 350mm. Pt 2. Built by James Horne, 1739–40; demolished 1926.

61 St Catharine Cree Church. Drawn & Etched by J. Skelton for the Ecclesiastical Architecture of London. (b) Novr 1 1813. 165 × 205/268 × 345mm. Pt 2. Built 1628.

62 St Katherine's Tower. Etched by Preston from a Drawing by W. Pearson. (a) 165 × 205/285 × 355mm. Pt 1. Unsigned drawing (160 × 200mm) in Guildhall Library.

63 St Lawrence Jewry. Drawn by R.B. Schnebbelie, and Etched by J. Wedgwood. (b) May 1, 1811. 163 × 200/270 × 340mm. Pt 1. Built by Wren, 1670–87.

64 St Leonard Shoreditch. Drawn by J. Coney. Etched by W. Jenkins (c) July 4, 1816. 223 × 163/345 × 275mm. Pt 4. Built by George Dance senior, 1736–40. Water-colour (216 × 159mm), dated 1811, in Guildhall Library.

65 St Luke's/Situated on N. of Old Street. Drawn & Etched by J. Coney (c) Dec 1, 1818. 238 × 168/345 × 270mm. Pt 4. Built 1727–33; erroneously attributed to George Dance senior. Alternative drawing (241 × 178mm), by G. Shepherd, in BM (*Crace* 33.10).

66 St Magnus. Drawn by G. Shepherd and Etched by W. Wise. (b) Feby 15 1814. 225 × 160/340 × 265mm. Pt 3. Built by Wren, 1671–87, 1703–6. Drawing (223 × 140mm) in BM (*Crace* 24.2).

67 St Margaret Lothbury. Drawn by J. Coney and Etched by J. Wise (c) 220 × 163/345 × 270mm. Pt 4. Built by Wren, 1686–9,1698–1700. (*Bank of England* 73)

68 St Margaret Pattens. Drawn by J. Coney and Etched by J. Skelton. (b) Feby 15, 1814. 230 × 165/345 × 270mm. Pt 3. Built by Wren 1684–9, 1689–1701. Drawing (215 × 215mm), dated 1812, in BM (*Crace* 20.90).

69 St Margaret's Westminster. Etched by Preston from a drawing by Pearson. (a) 210 × 163/355 × 285mm. Pt 1. Unsigned drawing (205 × 158mm) in Guildhall Library.

70 St Martins in the Fields/(from the Mews). Etched by Preston from a drawing by W. Pearson. (a) 213 × 168/365 × 280mm. Pt 1. Built by Gibbs, 1722–6.

71 St Martins (in the Fields) Westminster. Drawn by J. Coney. Engraved by T. Dale. (c) March 15th 1819. 260 × 195/350 × 270mm. Pt 4. Ground plan in 1m, 35 × 50mm.

72 St Martin Ludgate. Drawn by G. Shepherd & Etched by S. Jenkins (c) Octr 10th 1814. 218 × 158/345 × 265mm. Pt 3. Built by Wren, 1677–87. Drawing (215 × 165mm) in BM (*Crace* 19.126).

73 St Martins Outwich. Drawn by G. Shepherd and Etched by J. Skelton. (b) Augst 12th 1811. 163 × 220/270 × 340mm. Pt 1. Built by S.P. Cockerell, 1796; demolished 1874. Drawing (165 × 205mm) in BM (*Crace* 24.40).

74 St Mary Abchurch. Drawn by J. Coney and Etched by J. Skelton. (b) Jany 1, 1812. 215 × 162/335 × 268mm. Pt 2. Built by Wren, 1681–7. Drawing (215 × 165mm) in BM (*Crace* 20.66).

75 St Mary Aldermary. Drawn by G. Shepherd and Etched by W. Wise. (b) Jany 1, 1812. 223 × 155/345 × 265mm. Pt 1. Built by Wren, 1682, 1701–4. Alternative drawing (228 × 165mm), by Pearson, in BM (*Crace* 20.38).

76 St Mary Aldermanbury. Drawn by G. Shepherd & Etched by J. Skelton (c) Novr 25, 1814. 165 × 220/270 × 345mm. Pt 3. Built by Wren, 1672–87; gutted and exported. Drawings (215 × 215mm), dated 1814, in BM (*Crace* 25.51) and (162 × 216mm), dated 1811, in V & A (D.404–1899).

77 St Mary at Hill. Drawn by J. Coney and Etched by J. Skelton. (b) Jany 25, 1814. 170 × 215/270 × 345mm. Pt 3. Built by Wren, 1670–6. Drawing (165 × 215mm), dated 1812, in BM (*Crace* 20.93).

78 St Mary's Lambeth. Drawn by G. Shepherd. Engraved by S. Jenkins. (c) Dec. 1, 1818. 163 × 240/265 × 340mm. Pt 4. Drawing (160 × 240mm) in Guildhall Library.

79 St Marylebone (New Church). Drawn by J. Coney. Engraved by W. Wise (c) Feby 20, 1817. 210 × 170/350 × 270mm. Pt 4. Built by Thomas Hardwick, 1813–17. Pencil drawing (185 × 145mm) in the Ashbridge Collection, Westminster Public Library.

80 St Mary le Bow. Drawn by G. Shepherd and Etched by W. Wise. (b) Jany 1, 1812. 210 × 155/345 × 270mm. Pt 1. Built by Wren, 1670–83. Drawing (215 × 160mm) in BM (*Crace* 21.21).

81 St Mary le Strand. Drawn by J. Coney. (c) Dec 1, 1818. Engraved by J. Skelton. 218 × 168/345 × 270mm. Pt 4. Built by Gibbs, 1714–17.

82 St Mary Magdalen Knightrider Street. Drawn by G. Shepherd and Etched by J. Skelton. (b) Jany 1 1812. 228 × 160/340 × 265m. Pt 2. Built by Wren, 1683–5; demolished 1887. Alternative drawing (228 × 165mm), by Pearson, in BM (*Crace* 20.8).

83 St Mary Magdalen Bermondsey. Drawn and Etched by W. Pearson. (a) 165 × 210/285 × 355mm. Pt 1. Drawing (165 × 205mm) in BM (*Crace* 34.11).

84 St Mary Rotherhithe. Drawn & Etched by J. Coney (c) Dec 1, 1818. 220 × 170/345 × 275mm. Pt 4. Built 1714, c 1739.

85 St Mary Somerset. Drawn by J. Coney and Etched by J. Skelton. (b) Octr 5, 1812. 210 × 163/345 × 275mm. Pt 3. Built by Wren, 1686–95; demolished (except tower) 1872. Drawing (210 × 165mm) in BM (*Crace* 20.19).

86 St Mary Whitechapel. Drawn by J. Coney. Etched by S. Jenkins (c) July 4th 1816. 170 × 213/265 × 345mm. Pt 4. Drawing (163 × 205mm), '1811', in Guildhall Library.

87 St Mary Woolnoth. Drawn by G. Shepherd & Etched by J. Skelton. (b) Octr 13, 1812. 220 × 173/345 × 275mm. Pt 3. Built by Hawksmoor, 1716–27. Drawing (240 × 165mm), '1811', in BM (*Crace* 23.27).

88 St Matthew Bethnal Green. Drawn by G. Shepherd & Etched by W. Angus (c) Novr 2, 1818. 165 × 225/265 × 335mm. Pt 4. Built by George Dance senior, 1746. Pen and water-colour drawing (162 × 227mm), '1817', in Guildhall Library.

89 St Mathew Friday Street. Drawn by J. Coney & Etched by J. Skelton (c) Octr 10th 1814. 160 × 220/275 × 345mm. Pt 3. Built by Wren, 1681–5; demolished 1881. Drawing (165 × 215mm), dated 1812, in BM (*Crace* 21.41).

90 St Michael Bassishaw. Drawn by J. Coney & Etched by J. Skelton. (b) Septr 1, 1812. 205 × 160/345 × 270mm. Pt 2. Built by Wren, 1676–9; demolished 1899. Drawing (215 × 165mm), dated 1811, in BM (*Crace* 21.88).

91 St Michaels Cornhill. Drawn by G. Shepherd and Etched by W. Wise. (b) May 21st 1811. 220 × 170/340 × 270mm. Pt 1. Built by Wren, 1670–2. Drawings (222 × 165mm) in BM (*Crace* 23.9) and (227 × 165mm), 'Aug 25, 1810', in Guildhall Library.

92 St Michaels Crooked Lane. Drawn by J. Coney and Etched by J. Skelton. (b) Jany 1, 1812. 208 × 165/345 × 275mm. Pt 2. Built by Wren, 1684–8,1698; demolished 1831. Drawing (215 × 165mm) in BM (*Crace* 20.63).

93 St Michael Paternoster Royal. Drawn by J. Coney and Etched by J. Skelton. (b) Novr 3, 1812. 222 × 162/345 × 270mm. Pt 2. Built by Wren, 1686–94,1715–17. Drawing (215 × 165mm) in BM (*Crace* 20.40).

94 St Michael Queen-Hithe. Drawn by W. Coney and Etched by J. Skelton. (b) Novr 3, 1812. 230 × 165/348 × 265mm. Pt 3. Built by Wren, 1676–87; demolished 1876. Drawing (228 × 165mm) in BM (*Crace* 20.16) and alternative drawing (210 × 165mm), by Pearson (*Crace* 20.18).

95 St Michael Wood Street. Drawn by J. Coney & Etched by J. Skelton (c) Novr 25, 1814. 215 × 165/345 × 270mm. Pt 3. Built by Wren, 1670–5; demolished 1894. Drawing (215 × 165mm), dated 1812, in BM (*Crace* 21.38).

96 St Mildred Bread Street. Drawn by J. Coney & Etched by J. Skelton (c) Novr 25, 1814. 212 × 165/345 × 270mm. Pt 3. Built by Wren, 1677–83; destroyed 1941. Drawing (215 × 165mm) in BM (*Crace* 20.24).

97 St Mildred's, Poultry. Drawn by G. Shepherd and Etched by J. Skelton. (b) Novr 25, 1814. 212 × 162/345 × 270mm. Pt 1. Built by Wren, 1670–6; demolished 1872.

98 St Nicholas Cole Abbey. Drawn by W. Coney & Etched by J. Skelton. (b) Octr 13, 1812. 225 × 163/345 × 270mm. Pt 3. Built by Wren, 1671–81. Drawing (228 × 165mm), dated 1811, in BM (*Crace* 20.9).

99 St Olave Hart Street. Etched by Preston from a Drawing by W. Pearson. (a) 163 × 210/280 × 355mm. Pt 1. Unsigned drawing (160 × 205mm) in Guildhall Library.

100 St Olave Old Jewry. Drawn by J. Coney and Etched by W. Wise (c) July 12 1818. 215 × 165/345 × 275mm. Pt 4. Built by Wren, 1670–6; demolished (except tower) 1888. Drawing (215 × 152mm), dated 1812, in BM (*Crace* 21.86).

101 St Olave, Southwark. Drawn by G. Shepherd and Etched by S. Jenkins. (b) Feby 15 1814. 170 × 220/270 × 345mm. Pt 3. St Olave, Tooley Street, from the river; built by Henry Flitcroft, 1738; demolished 1926–8. Water-colour (170 × 215mm) in Museum of London.

102 St Pancras Middlesex. W. & H.W. Inwood Archts. Drawn by G. Shepherd. Engraved by T. Dale. (c) July 1, 1823. 250 × 188/330 × 265mm. Pt 4. Built 1819–22.

103 St Paul's Covent Garden. Etched by Preston from a Drawing by W. Pearson. (a) 163 × 215/285 × 352mm. Pt 1. Built by Inigo Jones, 1633; rebuilt by Thomas Hardwick, 1796.

104 St Paul's Shadwell/This Fabrick which since the finishing of this Plate, has been erased to the ground & now about to be rebuilt from the design of Mr. Walters ... Drawn by J. Shepherd & Engraved by I. Dale (c) Feb 20th 1819. 168 × 230/270 × 345mm. Pt 4. Rebuilt by John Walters, 1820.

105 St Peters Cornhill. Drawn by G. Shepherd and Etched by W. Wise. (b) May 1, 1811. 210 × 165/340 × 265mm. Pt 1. Built by Wren, 1677–87.

106 St Peter's the Poor ... /Rebuilt by Mr. Gibbs, & opened 1793. Drawn by R.B. Schnebbelie and Etched by S. Lacy. (b) May 1st 1811. 210 × 160/345 × 270mm. Pt 1. Actually rebuilt by Jesse Gibson, 1788–92; demolished 1907. Drawing (210 × 160mm) in BM (*Crace* 25.27), and pencil drawing (180 × 130mm) in Guildhall Library.

107 Interior of St Peter ad Vincula, within the Tower. Drawn by J. Coney, Engraved by S. Jenkins (c) Dec 1, 1818. 168 × 228/260 × 340mm. Pt 4. Signed pencil drawing (215 × 370mm) and water-colour (170 × 225mm), dated 1814, in Guildhall Library.

108 King Henry the VIIth Chapel – St Peters Coll. Ch. Westminster. Drawn by J. Coney, Engraved by T. Dale (c) March 1, 1819. 164 × 247/265 × 345mm. Pt 4. A N.E. view of the Abbey with ground plan in lm. 43 × 75mm. Drawing (170 × 245mm), '1811', in Guildhall Library.

109 Interior View of St Peters/looking from the railing of the Altar to the Great Western entrance. Drawn &

Etched by J. Coney (c) Feb 20, 1819. 230 × 165/320 × 208mm. Pt 4. Soft-ground etching.

110 St Saviours, anciently St Mary Overie's Southwark. Drawn by J. Coney and Etched by J. Skelton. (b) Jany 25, 1814. 165 × 214/265 × 345mm. Pt 3. View from S.W.

111 St Saviour—Interior. Drawn by J. Coney and Etched by J. Lacy. (b) Jany 25, 1814. 215 × 177/350 × 275mm. Pt 3.

112 St Sepulchre Snow Hill. Drawn by G. Shepherd & Etched by J. Skelton (c) Octr 10th 1814. 180 × 220/265 × 340mm. Pt 3. Alternative drawing (178 × 216mm), by Coney, in BM (*Crace* 27.75).

113 St Stephens Coleman Street. Drawn by J. Coney and Etched by J. Wise (c) 167 × 218/275 × 345mm. Pt 4. nd. Built by Wren, 1674–6; destroyed 1940. Drawing (165 × 215mm), dated 1812, in BM (*Crace* 25.49).

114 St Stephen Walbrook. Drawn by J. Coney & Etched by J. Skelton for the Ecclesiastical Architecture of London. (b) Novr 1, 1813. 215 × 162/345 × 265mm. Pt 2. Built by Wren, 1672–7, 1717. Drawing (210 × 165mm), dated 1811, in BM (*Crace* 21.91).

115 Interior of St Stephen Walbrook. Drawn by J. Coney & Etched by J. Skelton for the Ecclesiastical Architecture of London. (b) Novr 1, 1813. 195 × 225/265 × 345mm. Pt 2.

116 St Swithin. Drawn by J. Coney & Etched by J. Skelton (b) Novr 1, 1812. 235 × 175/345 × 270mm. Pt 2. Built by Wren, 1677–85; gutted 1940. Drawing (230 × 185mm) in BM (*Crace* 20.50) and alternative drawing (203 × 165mm), by Pearson (*Crace* 20.51).

117 The Temple Church. Drawn by G. Shepherd and Etched by W. Wise. (b) May 25, 1811. 155 × 210/265 × 340mm. Pt 2. View from N. Pencil and water-colour drawing (157 × 222mm) in Guildhall Library.

118 The Temple Church/Southern View with the Master's House. Drawn by G. Shepherd & Etched by J. Skelton. (b) Jany 1, 1812. 160 × 230/270 × 345mm. Pt 2. Pen and water-colour drawing (158 × 229mm), '1811', in Guildhall Library.

119 Interior of the Temple Church No. 1. Drawn by J. Coney and Etched by S. Lacy. (b) Jany 1, 1812. 220 × 180/350 × 270mm. Pt 2. The 'Round'.

120 Interior of the Temple Church No. 2. Drawn by G. Shepherd & Etched by J. Skelton. (b) Jany 1, 1812. 172 × 238/270 × 345mm. Pt 2. The chancel.

121 St Thomas's Southwark. Drawn by G. Shepherd and Etched by W. Wise. (b) Jany 25, 1814. 220 × 170/345 × 270mm. Pt 3. Drawing (213 × 168mm) in BM (*Crace* 34.83).

122 Trinity Church Minories. Drawn by Pearson. Engraved by T. Dale (c) Dec. 1, 1818. 210 × 170/345 × 270mm. Pt 4.

123 St Vedast Foster Lane. Drawn by G. Shepherd & Etched by S. Rawle (c) Octr 10th 1814. 235 × 163/350

× 275mm. Built by Wren, 1695–1700, 1709–12. Alternative drawing (203 × 172mm), by Pearson, in BM (*Crace* 25.150).

---

130 · DUGDALE'S NEW BRITISH TRAVELLER* [1819]

Here is a late example of a frugal publisher making use of plates which had already served their turn in an earlier publication to promote sales of a work offered for subscription by cheap instalments. James Cundee and Joseph Robins, the publishers of *The New British Traveller*, said to be written by one James Dugdale, LL D, did not however draw on their own earlier publications *The Beauties of England and Wales* (no 104) or Hughson's *London* (no 93) for illustrations but on plates engraved in 1804–5 by James Storer and John Greig for Vernor & Hood's *Select Views* (no 90). Plates now showing signs of degradation, especially in their almost blank skies, but originally intended as collectors' pieces and published in monthly Numbers, 'Demy Quarto, on a beautiful Vellum Paper, carefully Hotpressed, Price 5s.', were now reprinted for a less discriminating public:

Dugdale's New British Traveller. Printed in Demy Quarto, on a superfine Wove Paper, with a new and distinct Type, illustrated by Views of Public Buildings, Antiquities, and a complete British Atlas.

This Day is published, (No. 1, Price Eight-Pence) of the New British Traveller; or, Modern Panorama of England and Wales.... This Work will be completed in about 150 Weekly Numbers; price Eight-pence each; neatly stitched.... a new Number will be regularly published every following Saturday. The Numbers will contain, alternately, three and four half sheets of Letter-press; and a Map, or View will be given in every other Number. The Maps will form in the whole a Complete British Atlas, including a large Royal Sheet Map of England and Wales; and the Views will comprise the principal Public Buildings, Gentlemen's Seats, Antiquities &c....

It will also be neatly done up in Parts; each containing Twelve Numbers, price 8s. each. The Work will form, in the whole, four handsome Quarto Volumes ... Albion Press: Printed for J. and J. Cundee, Ivy Lane, Paternoster-Row, London.

The work was eventually extended beyond its prospectus limits to 195 Numbers, each with a text varying from four to 20 pages, or 16 eight-shilling Parts, illustrated by a total of 50 plates and 44 county maps. Publication-lines range from 1814 to 1820, which suggests a five or six-year span and therefore some interruption in the intended weekly frequency. Each volume is separately paginated and signed but the progress of the Numbers is indicated bl on text pages throughout the work, thus: 'vol. 1— No. ( )'.

The New British Traveller, or, modern panorama of England and Wales; Exhibiting at one comprehensive View, an ample, accurate, and popular account, Historical, Topographical, and Statistical ... Forming a complete Survey of South Britain. By James Dugdale, LL.D. Illustrated by a Complete Set of Correct Maps, Views of Public Buildings, Antiquities, &c. &c. Vol. I (IV) London: Printed and published by J. Robins and Co. Albion Press, Ivy Lane, Paternoster Row (vols II–III: 'London: Printed by and for John Cundee, Ivy Lane, Paternoster Row').

(engr title) The New/British Traveller,/or/Modern Panorama/of England and Wales./Vol. I (II–IV) (vignette) London:/Published by J. Robins & Co., Albion Press, Ivy Lane, Paternoster Row/1819.

Quarto, 290 × 200mm.   1819

COLLATION Vol. 1. Title-page; pp 3–4, preface; pp i–liv, introduction; pp 1–628 (Nos 1–45), Bedfordshire to Cumberland; Vol. 2. Title-page; pp 1–606 (Nos 46–88), Derbyshire to Herefordshire. Vol. 3. Title-page; pp 1–736 (Nos 89–140), Hertfordshire to Northumberland. Vol. 4. Title-page; pp 1–764 (Nos 141–95), Nottingham to Yorkshire, Wales, Isle of Wight; pp 765–91, general index, directions to binder.

The illustrations actually issued fell short of the prospectus promises. Thirty eight of the Storer & Greig *Select Views* plates were reissued, abbreviated in the following list as *SG* followed by the item number. To these were added 12 inferior line-engraved plates of places outside London, four subjects to a plate, and the 44 unnumbered county maps, not listed below. The *SG* plates have been thinly disguised by the addition of a ruled frame on all but the vignettes, plate numbers in sequence with the other view plates tr, captions in voided capitals in lieu of copperplate, and revised publication-lines, now reading:

(a) 'Published by J. & J. Cundee, Albion Press, London' (for plates dated 1814).

(b) 'Published by J. Robins & Co., Albion Press, London' (for plates dated 1818 to 1820).

The plates themselves were cut down from about 250 × 330mm to an average 190 × 250mm.

VOL. 1

1 (engr title) Burnham Abbey, Bucks. Drawn by J. Powell. Engraved by J. Greig. (b) 1819. Vignette, 100 × 130mm. *SG* 63.

2 p 68 Bray, Berks. Engrav'd by Greig from a Drawing by Powell. (b) 1818. 132 × 185mm. pl. 34. *SG* 69.

3 p 79 Maidenhead/Berks. Drawn by S. Powell. Engraved by J. Storer. (b) 1818. 135 × 185mm. pl.33. *SG* 71.

4 p 145 Burnham Abbey/Bucks. Drawn by J. Powell. Engraved by J. Storer. (a) 1814. 130 × 183mm. pl.13. *SG* 62.

5 p 161 Great Marlow/Bucks. Engraved by J. Greig from a Drawing by T. Powell. (b) 1818. 137 × 195mm. pl.1. *SG* 70.

6 p 172 Stoke Church/Bucks. Engraved by J. Storer from a Drawing by J. Powell. (b) 1818. 130 × 185mm. pl.32. *SG* 52.

VOL. 2

7 (engr title) The Bell Gate, Barking, Essex. J. Greig del. et sculp. (b) 1819. Vignette, 140 × 140mm. *SG* 37.

8 front. Interior of Waltham Abbey Church/Essex. Engraved by J. Greig from a Drawing by F. Nash. (b) 1819. 195 × 140mm. pl.38. *SG* 9.

9 p 355 Barking: Essex. Engrav'd by J. Storer from a Drawing by S. Prout. (a) 1814. 133 × 187mm. pl.8. *SG* 36.

10 p 365 Chingford Church/Essex. Engraved by J. Storer from a Drawing by G. Sheppard. J. Robins, Ivy Lane. 133 × 185mm. pl.42. nd. *SG* 16.

11 p 393 Marks Hall/Essex. Engrav'd by J. Greig from a Drawing by S. Prout. (b) 1818. 130 × 185mm. (pl.37) *SG* 51.

12 p 407 N.E. View of Waltham Abbey Church/Essex. Drawn and Engraved by J. Greig. (b) 1818. 135 × 193mm. pl.4. *SG* 8.

VOL. 3

13 (engr title) St. Michael's Church, St. Albans, Herts. G. Shepherd del. J. Greig sculp. (b) 1819. Vignette, 110 × 140mm. *SG* 4.

14 front. Interior of the Hall of Eltham Palace/Kent. Engraved by J. Storer after a Drawing by Baynes. (b) 1818. 190 × 135mm. pl.40. *SG* 18.

15 p 15 S.E. View of the Abbey Church./St Albans Herts. Engraved by J. Storer from a Drawing by G. Sheppherd. (a) 1814. 127 × 182. pl.16. *SG* 2.

16 p 16 Interior of the Abbey Church/St Albans, Herts.

Engraved by J. Storer from a Drawing by F. Nash. (b) 1818. 190 × 140mm. pl.36. *SG* 3.

17 p 180 Remains of Eltham Palace/Kent. Drawing engraved by J. Greig. (b) 1820. 137 × 190mm. pl.46. *SG* 17.

18 p 193 The Hall of Greenwich Hospital/Kent. Engraved by J. Storer from a Drawing by F. Nash. (b) 1818. 135 × 185mm. pl.12. *SG* 5.

19 p 195 London from Greenwich/Kent. Engraved by J. Greig from a Painting by G. Arnald. (b) 1818. 130 × 190mm. *SG* 10.

20 p 478 Chelsea Hospital. Engraved by J. Storer from a Drawing by S. Prout. (a) 1814. 135 × 190mm. pl.14. From the river. *SG* 49. (*Longford* 28)

21 p 491 Hampstead/Middlesex. Drawn & Engrav'd by J. Greig. (b) 135 × 195mm. pl.43. nd. *SG* 66.

22 p 505 Remains of Canonbury/Islington. Drawn and Engraved by J. Storer. (a) 1814. 133 × 195m. pl.5. *SG* 33.

23 p 508 Sion House/Middlesex. Engrav'd by J. Greig from a Drawing by J. Powell. (b) 1818. 132 × 182mm. pl.17. *SG* 53.

24 p 512 London. Engraved by J. Greig from a Drawing by the Rt. Hon. Lady Arden. (b) 132 × 190mm. pl.44. nd. From S.W. of Blackfriars Bridge. *SG* 20.

25 p 518 Westminster/from Lambeth. (a) 1814. 132 × 195mm. (pl.35) *SG* 40.

26 p 520 West front of St Paul's Cathedral. Engraved by J. Storer from a Drawing by F. Nash. (a) 1814. 192 × 135mm. pl.3. *SG* 15.

27 p 526 The Charter House/London. Drawn & Engraved by J. Storer. (a) 1814. 135 × 195mm. pl.11. *SG* 34.

28 p 531 The Admiralty and Horse Guards/Westminster. Engraved by J. Storer from a Drawing by F. Nash. (a) 1814. 130 × 190mm. pl.6. *SG* 50.

29 p 533 Interior of the Royal Exchange/London. Engraved by J. Greig from a Drawing by Elms. (a) 1814. 135 × 185mm. pl.10. *SG* 74.

30 p 542 Kentish Town and Highgate/Middlesex. Drawn & Engraved by J. Storer. (b) 1820. 130 × 180mm. pl.49. *SG* 68.

31 p 546 S.E. View of Stepney Church/Middlesex. Engraved by J. Storer from a Drawing by G. Sheppherd. (b) 1818. 130 × 185mm. pl.9. *SG* 11.

32 p 548 Bridge at Stratford le Bow,/Essex. Drawn & Engrav'd by J. Storer. (b) 1820. 132 × 193mm. pl.47. *SG* 25.

VOL. 4

33 (engr title) Bishop Andrew's Tomb, St Mary Overies, Southwark. (b) 1819. 130 × 150mm. Vignette. *SG* 43.

34 front. The Lollards Tower, Lambeth Palace./Surrey.

Engrav'd by J. Greig from a Drawing by J. Wichello. (b) 1820. 188 × 130mm. pl.44. *SG* 29.

35 p 329 Lambeth Palace/from the Bishop's Walk/Surry. Engrav'd by J. Greig from a Drawing by J. Wichello. (b) 1820. 195 × 135mm. pl.44. *SG* 28.

36 p 335 Interior of the Hall of Lambeth Palace/Surry. Engraved by J. Greig from a Drawing by T. Whichello. (b) 1820. 180 × 130mm. pl.45. *SG* 30.

37 p 345 Richmond Hill/Surry. Engraved by J. Storer from a Drawing by J. Powell. (b) 1818. 133 × 183mm. pl.39. *SG* 72.

38 p 347 St. Saviours Church, Southwark,/Surry. Drawn by F. Nash. Engraved by J. Storer. (b) 1820. 138 × 187mm. pl.50. *SG* 42.

131 · LONDINA ILLUSTRATA [1819–34]

William Herbert, antiquary and author of *Antiquities of the Inns of Court* (no 88) and of the text to Storer and Greig's *Select Views of London* (no 90), published in June 1808 from his home at Marsh Gate, Lambeth the first Number of *Londina Illustrata* consisting of four copies of sixteenth and seventeenth century London prints and a drawing. Robert Wilkinson, the printseller, who held a large stock of London views at the disposal of pennantizers, then became associated with the project and placed it on a business footing. By the end of the year a second Number had been issued under their joint imprint: a facsimile of Hollar's 'St John of Jerusalem' engraving and prints of three of his Thames-side drawings. Its pink wrapper gave these particulars to subscribers:

Scarce Topographical Prints. No. II. Price Eight Shillings, (to be continued every two months,) of Londina Illustrata; or, a Collection of Plates, consisting of Engravings from Original Paintings and Drawings, and Fac-simile Copies of Scarce Prints, displaying the State of the Metropolis from the reign of Elizabeth to the Revolution and adapted to illustrate the admired topographical works of Strype, Stowe, Pennant &c &c. with Descriptions, Original and Compiled. London: Printed for and Published by W. Herbert, Marsh Gate, Lambeth; and R. Wilkinson, Map and Printseller, No. 58 Cornhill; and sold by J. Scott, No 442 Strand; Maxwell and Wilson, Skinner Street, Symonds, Paternoster Row; Clarke, New Bond

Street; and the other Principal Booksellers and Printsellers of London. S. Gosnell, Printer, Little Queen Street.

Four more Numbers, containing 15 further plates, came out under the joint imprint but in the seventh, consisting of views of the Bear Garden and the Globe Theatre on Bankside, the prints bore only Wilkinson's publication-line of October 1810. From June 1812 Large Paper copies also were available at 10s 6d per Number.

Although Herbert was no longer overtly concerned with the series he probably continued to advise the publisher and possibly to contribute some of the explanatory text, varying from a single sheet to a number of pages on chosen subjects. For all that the major part of this was ascribed by the *Gentleman's Magazine* obituarist (1826, 1, p 569) to the prolific author and printseller James Caulfield.

The scope of the work was broadened to include drawings 'ad vivum' from extant subjects of topographical, historical and architectural interest, particularly of churches, theatres and charitable institutions. Numbers still consisted of three or four plates and text and the publication schedule of the first 22, containing 84 prints, is recorded by Upcott. As will be seen, the two-monthly interval between issues promised in the advertisement was abandoned and a three-monthly interval was the best that could be achieved. Plate numbers refer to the last and most comprehensive edition:

No
1	1808	(1/6): 41, 86–7, 112 (4 pl.)
2		(30/11, 1/12): 48, 96–8 (4 pl.)
3	1809	(1/1): 14, 119–20 (3 pl.)
4		(3/4–19/5): 2, 88, 121–2 (4 pl.)
5		(13/6): 31, 89, 172, 176 (4 pl.)
6		(11/10): 95, 165, 171, 177 (4 pl.)
7	1810	(11/10): 166–7, 169–70 (4 pl.)
8	1811	(11/2): 10, 109, 130, 193 (4 pl.)
9		(4/6): 92, 174, 12 (3 pl.)
10		(7/8, 8/8): 3, 181, 179 (3 pl.)
11		(7/10): 45, 173, 175, 182 (4 pl.)
12	1812	(1/1–8/5): 46, 99, 118, 168 (4 pl.)
13	1813	(1/1, 10/2): 42, 67, 71, 148 (4 pl.)
14		(1/1): 92, 101, 110 (3 pl.)
15		(11/10): 57, 90, 184, 190 (4 pl.)
16	1813	(1/12), 1814 (1/1): 43, 72, 140, 178 (4 pl.)
17–18	1814	(1/5, 4/6, 5/8): 5–7, 94, 102, 123, 195, 202 (8 pl.)

| 19–20 | 1815 | (2/1, 11/3, 11/4): 15–18, 47, 117, 131, 141 (8 pl.) |
| 21–2 | | (1/12): 11, 53, 58, 159, 185, 192, 196, 198 (8 pl.) |

On 11 October of the two succeeding years, 1816 and 1817, were published respectively 13 and 11 more plates which, with one undated and 18 (including a title-page) published on 1 January 1819, brought the total to the 127 found in the two-volume edition published in that year:

1816	(11/10): 65–6, 74–80, 160, 188, 194, 197 (13 pl.)
1817	(11/10): 24–6, 29–30, 64, 83–4, 145, 199, 203 (11 pl.)
1819	(1/1): 1, 4, 28, 61–2, 69, 81–8, 100, 111, 113, 142, 144, 146–7, 183, 200–1 (18 pl.)
Undated	13 (1 pl.)

This first edition includes a text of 202 (unpaginated) pages and a contents list intended to marry text and plates which simply adds to the unpaginated confusion as it does not include a sufficiently specific description of the plates to act as a check-list. In the *Monthly Literary Advertiser* for May 1820 the plates and text so far issued were priced at quarto £12 in sheets, atlas size 15 guineas, as also proofs of plates without text, or 30 Numbers at 8s or 10s 6d each.

Wilkinson published no plates in 1818, perhaps because Herbert, through another publisher, had just launched a similar publication, *London before the Great Fire* (no 120). This however had been abortive, and from 1820 to 1823 Wilkinson continued *Londina Illustrata*:

1820	(27/9): 49–53, 56, 85, 114–16, 124–5, 128, 180, 189, 191 (16 pl.)
1821	(25/3, 7/8): 19–20, 55, 104, 154, 204 (6 pl.)
1822	(1/1–1/12): 21–2, 54, 73, 103, 105, 126–7, 138, 149, 153, 164, 187, 205–6 (15 pl.)
1823	(1/1): 107, 150, 186 (3 pl.)

These supplementary plates, with their texts, were issued as a continuation volume (vol. 2, i) in 1823 (at £3 5s elephant quarto and £4 10s atlas size in boards, unbound proofs £4 10s the set), although no title-page seems to have been printed or engraved. On Wilkinson's death in 1825 his stock of books, maps, charts, prints and copper plates was sold by auction at Sotheby's (29 September and three following days). Among the items catalogued are the materials, in several forms, for *Londina Illustrata* which were knocked down for £1000 to one Gale (possibly connected with John Gale, engraver and copper plate printer of Crooked Lane). He acquired bound sets of vol. 1 and vol. 2 i (ie of the text and 127 plates issued between June 1808 and January 1819 and of the 40 extra plates issued with text between September 1820 and January 1823), and a selection of Numbers, prints and bundles of letterpress, all on large and small paper of various qualities and some in proof. In addition to these he bought 'Continuation of Londina, with the original Manuscript, unpublished together with the copper plates of the following thirty views' and 'Nine Copper Plates of which only one Proof has been taken'. These, specified in Sotheby's catalogue, comprise the 39 plates and texts intended by Wilkinson to form vol. 2 ii as they carry his publication-line dated January and February 1825 or were given a posthumous publication-line in the comprehensive edition of 1834 containing 206 plates:

1825	(1/1, 1/2): 8–9, 27, 32–40, 44, 58–60, 91, 106, 129, 132–7, 139, 143, 151, 155–8, 163 (33 pl.)
1834	23, 70, 108, 152, 161–2 (6 pl.)

Lowndes, in *The bibliographer's manual* (p 1393), thus summarizes the work:

Londina Illustrata, printed for Robert Wilkinson, 1808–25, elephant 4o. Published in 36 parts at 10s. 6d. each. Large Paper, atlas 4o at £1. 1s. each, forming 2 vols. containing 207 plates. Reduced by H.G. Bohn to £4. 4s. Large Paper, £6. 6s.... with proofs on India Paper, £15. 15s. Colombier Paper, atlas folio. Twelve sets of the plates only struck off at 25 Guineas....

(*Title-pages* pl. 1, 163)

Folio, 336 × 267mm. (Large Paper 410 × 310mm) 1819, (1823), 1834

COLLATION   Vol. 1. Title-page; contents, classifying 202pp of unpaginated and unsigned text with unspecific refs to the plates (4pp), Vol. 1 ('2, Pt 2'). Title-page; list of 40 plates (1 leaf).

The most complete form of the work, issued in 1834 or thereafter, consists of 206 plates with twin check-lists, each of two pages, for pl. 1–108 and pl. 109–206, bound in each of two volumes. Texts included with each plate vary from a short note on one side of a single sheet to an independently paginated essay of from two to 20 or more pages. These 'descriptions' often post-date the publication-lines of the plates and some were extended on reissue, which may be explained by what the encyclopaedia salesmen now describe as a 'policy of continuous revision'. The copy in the Royal Library at Windsor is particularly notable for its amplified text. An attempt to co-ordinate this information was made by printing a two-page index, of small value in the absence of overall pagination. In the list which follows each section of letterpress is collated in conjunction with its plate.

Strangely the only guide to the correct arrangement of the 127 plates in the original issue of 1819 is to be found not in the book itself but on a wrapper of its short-lived rival, Herbert's *London before the Great Fire*. The plate numbers there assigned are included after the measurements, as also are references to the initial 22 Numbers recorded by Upcott.

William Herbert originally conceived *Londina Illustrata* as a series of facsimiles of scarce seventeenth century prints and drawings, selected by himself and mechanically copied in line by craftsmen such as James Stow. Some excellent facsimiles in the first two Numbers retain their usefulness, even in these days of photographic reproduction, but the copying eventually deteriorated into uncritically presented and topographically worthless details enlarged from the long views of Visscher and Hollar, such as those of the Elizabethan Bankside theatres (pl. 166–71) in which the engraver has had to draw on his imagination to supply what was invisible in the small-scale original so as to create a pleasing view.

Fortunately Wilkinson had other ideas, and also a talented team of artists, engravers and surveyors. They were set to work to produce large-scale prints, vignettes and plans of sites and buildings of historical interest which were being put to industrial uses or had otherwise gone down in the world, which were being demolished or had come to light in digging foundations, or which were undergoing restoration, alteration or replacement. Then, as now, stage history held a fascination for the public, so he published, rather than speculative reconstructions of the Globe or Swan, engravings after on-site drawings of Covent Garden Opera House and Drury Lane Theatre, burned down respectively in 1808 and 1809, and seedy suburban theatres on their way out for lack of patronage (pl. 178–203); all were assembled under the sub-title *Theatrum Illustrata*. A rustic charm pervades the large views (pl. 155–6) of the concert-room in Cuper's Pleasure Garden, in use by Messrs Beaufoy as a vinegar factory and, further east, the barn-like structure off Gravel Lane known as Bunyan's Meeting House but full of all the impedimenta of a millwright's shop (pl. 72). Innovations in topographical publishing are the excellent 'neighbourhood plans', commissioned by the publisher and professionally drawn up, which frequently accompany and pinpoint the views. As an alternative vignettes are sometimes added to show another aspect of the building or some architectural details, and the margins are quite often ornamented with carefully engraved heraldic shields, crests and seals relevant to the subject.

Four handsome plates (pl. 113–6) depict the final phase of one of the Inns of Court, Furnival's Inn, which, with its fine hall and quadrangle, must in its heyday have appeared as dignified and harmonious as King's Bench Walk in the Temple or New Square, Lincoln's Inn. These were drawn by R.B. Schnebbelie, talented son of an artist of Swiss descent who became a draughtsman to the Society of Antiquaries. Indeed he was responsible for about one quarter of the total drawings for *Londina Illustrata* and many of the original water-colours, including a number of draughts not accepted for engraving which survive in the Guildhall Library, the British Museum, the Museum of London and the Victoria and Albert Museum. He also drew for other London topographical books such as Hughson's *London* (no 93) and the *Architectura Ecclesiastica Londini* (no 129) but became so immersed in this particular work that when in 1820 he submitted a picture to the Royal Academy he gave as his address Wilkinson's Fenchurch Street print shop.

About half as many drawings were by C.J.M. Whichelo, a water-colourist who first exhibited at the Royal Academy in 1810 and was to make his reputation as a painter of marine subjects, especially coastal and harbour views. For this series however he drew Gothic architectural subjects, including three large views of the Chapel of the Holy Trinity in Leadenhall, a handsome Perpendicular building ruthlessly demolished in 1812 (pl. 134–6), two impressive views of what is now Southwark Cathedral (pl. 42–3), and a double-page panorama of the astonishingly open country around Bermondsey in

1805 as seen from the steeple of St Mary Magdalen Church (pl. 49) of which there is a pen and ink original in the British Museum (*Crace* 34.2). A dozen or so views were contributed by another Gothic specialist, Frederick Nash, a pupil of Thomas Malton the younger and architectural draughtsman to the Society of Antiquaries. He had already published his own *Twelve Views of the Antiquities of London* (Setchel, 1805–10) and his 'penchant' for romantic ruins was amply indulged in the following decade which witnessed more neglect and vandalism of London's architectural heritage than is now conceivable. He depicts, for instance, the roofless and half-demolished south transept of St Bartholomew the Great (pl. 20), the crumbling walls of the nunnery of St Helen, Bishopsgate (pl. 28), and a detailed record of the neighbouring Crosby Hall (pl. 75–80) before its beautiful fifteenth century interior fell prey to local merchants and tradesmen who dismantled it and put it to commercial use. Other illustrators were George and T.H. Shepherd, father and son, who between them supplied drawings for about another dozen of the plates.

T.H. Shepherd's fame as a book illustrator rests chiefly on the views in Elmes's *Metropolitan Improvements* (no 154), of which some were engraved on steel by Thomas Dale. He was already familiar with the London scene through having engraved it on copper for Wilkinson. A considerable proportion of the *Londina Illustrata* plates, particularly those after Schnebbelie but including also some Shepherd designs, are also Dale's work. Some 30 more plates were engraved by William Wise, who was also engaged to etch for the *Architectura Ecclesiastica Londini*, and almost as many by Benjamin Howlett, a Lincolnshire craftsman who had served his apprenticeship with James Heath and specialized in topographical and antiquarian work. James Stow, line-engraver and former apprentice of William Woollett, was chiefly employed in reproducing old prints and it seems probable that some of those without credits were of his copying.

Plates were unnumbered until they were published in the '1834' comprehensive edition, when most of them had their plate numbers added according to the two check-lists. They were either engraved after the publication-line or scratched in br.

Publication-lines vary according to the original date of issue although in one or two cases a more recent line has been substituted in a later issue. They are referred to in the descriptions by the key letters noted below. Possible variants in respect of contractions of 'Robert', etc are inserted in parentheses:

(a) 'Published for Wm Herbert, Marsh Gate, Lambeth (date).' (1 June 1808)

(b) 'Published (date) by Wm Herbert (Lambeth) and Robert (Robt., Rt.) Wilkinson, (Printseller) No 58 Cornhill (London).' (30 November 1808 to 11 October 1809)

(c) 'London, Published (date) by Robt. Wilkinson, No. 58 Cornhill.' (11 October 1810 to 1 December 1815)

(d) 'London, Published (date) by Robert Wilkinson, (No.) 125 Fenchurch Street.' (11 October 1816 to 1 February 1825)

(e) 'Wilkinson's Londina Illustrata 1834.' (after 1 February 1825)

VOL. 1

1 (engr title) Londina Illustrata,/Graphic/And Historic Memorials/of/Monasteries, Churches, Chapels, Schools,/Charitable Foundations,/Palaces, Halls, Courts, Processions,/Places of Early Amusement/and Modern & Present Theatres,/In the Cities and Suburbs of/London & Westminster. (vignette by E. Burney: History simultaneously writing, dictating to a putto and warding off the onslaught of Time, with a background of Charing Cross, London Stone and Gothic tracery) (d) Jany 1819. 120 × 165/325 × 260mm. 1st ed pl. 1.

General Views of London and of the Walls and Streets

2 (on central cartouche in sky supported by heraldic lions and surmounted by the City arms between C-scrolls) London/London the glory of Great Britaines Ile/Behold her Landschip here and tru pourfile. 190 × 310/270 × 345mm. 1st ed pl. 2. No IV. Keyed refs 1–46 bm to nos engraved above landmarks. From Howell's *Londinopolis* (no 7).

(1 leaf of text)

3 The Great Fire of London, 1666./Engraved from an Original Picture in the Possession of Mrs Lawrence of Thames Street, London.... J. Stow sculp. (c) August 7th, 1811. 245 × 400/305 × 430mm. 1st ed pl. 3. No X. Shows Ludgate, St Paul's Cathedral, St Mary le Bow. Original by Jan Griffier the elder (*Hayes* 48). Also reproduced by Grose in his *Antiquarian Repertory* (no 56), item 9.

4 A View of Part of the Antient Remains of London Wall,/now Standing near Postern Row, Tower Hill ... September 1818. Schnebbelie del. Dale sculp. (d) 1 January 1819. 190 × 300,60 × 120/260 × 320mm. 1st ed pl. 4. Includes a plan.

5 West Cheap/as it appeared in the year 1585/From a Drawing, at that Period by R. Treswell. Howlett sculp. (c) 1st May 1814. 265 × 390/305 × 412mm. 1st ed pl. 5. Nos XVII–XVIII. Shows St Michael le Querne, Cheapside.

6 Antient North East View of Cornhill.... the Pump formerly situated at the Intersection of Gracechurch Street, Cornhill, Bishopsgate Street and Leadenhall Street.... (c) 4 June 1814. 180 × 270/240 × 305mm. 1st ed pl. 6. Nos XVII–XVIII. No credits. Pencil and water-colour drawing (181 × 270mm), 'G. Shepherd, 1811', in BM (*Crace* 24.36).

7 Antient North East View of Bishopsgate Street./Exhibiting the North Side of the Church of St Martin Outwich ... (c) 4 June 1814. 172 × 270/200 × 320mm. 1st ed pl. 7. Nos XVII–XVIII. No credits.

(4pp of text)

8 (tm) A Plan of the Fire in Bishopsgate Street, Cornhill and Leadenhall Street ... on the 7 November 1765 ... (d) 1st January 1825. 258 × 230/298 × 250mm.

(6pp of text)

9 N.W. View of the Fair on the River Thames during the Great Frost 1683/4 /from an Original Drawing by Wyke in the British Museum/Taken near the Temple Stairs. J. Stow sculp. (d) 1st January 1825. 185 × 320/250 × 340mm. The Indian ink and black chalk drawing by Jan Wyck in the *Crowle* Pennant (8, 239), measuring 9¼" × 28¼", is inscribed 'Munday February the 4 Ao 1683/4'.

(2pp of text, including iconography and Bibliography)

10 The Strand/preparatory to its improvement in the year 1810./The View takes in the East end of St Clements Church ... Whichelo del. (c) Feby 1, 1811. 152 × 203,90 × 202/305 × 252mm. 1st ed pl. 9. No VIII. With plan showing Alderman Pickett's suggested improvements.

11 South West View of an Antient Structure in Ship Yard Temple Bar/Supposed to have been the residence of Elias Ashmole. Schnebbelie del. (c) 1st Decr 1815. 265 × 217/300 × 250mm. 1st ed pl. 8. Nos XXI–XXIII. Water-colour (293 × 210mm) in Guildhall Library.

(2pp of text)

CHURCHES

St. Paul's Cathedral

12 St Pauls Cross ... as it appeared on Sunday the 26th of March 1620, at which time it was visited by King James the I ... Engraved from an original picture in the possession of the Society of Antiquaries. J. Stow sculp. (c) June 4th 1811. 360 × 270/440 × 300mm. 1st ed pl. 93. No IX.

(2pp of text)

13 (in cartouche tl) Ecclesiae Cathedralis/Sti Pauli/a Meridie Prospectus. W. Hollar delin. et sculp. (d) 205 × 380mm. nd. 1st ed pl. 42. This is either the original plate re-engraved with Wilkinson's publication-line or a perfect forgery. cf with Dugdale's *St Paul's* (no 8), item 36.

(2pp of text)

14 'Paul's Cross and Preaching there' ... From an original Drawing in the Pepysian Library Cambridge. (b) 1 January 1809. 155 × 148/280 × 200mm. 1st ed pl. 93. No III.

(2pp of text; 4pp in Royal Library copy)

St. Alphage London Wall

15 An interior view of the Porch of the Parish Church of St. Alphage,/London Wall ... (c) 2 January, 1815. 233 × 167/340 × 250mm. 1st ed pl. 29. Nos XIX–XX.

16 Specimens of antient architecture/exhibited in the Porch and Belfry of St Alphage, London Wall ... (c) 2 January 1815. 260 × 180/340 × 250mm. 1st ed pl. 30, Nos XIX–XX.

17 North-West View of the interior of St Alphage Church London Wall. Schenebellie Del. Wise sculp. (c) 11th March 1815. 212 × 278/250 × 305mm. 1st ed pl. 31. Nos XIX–XX.

18 The North Front of Sion College London Wall, as it appeared in the year 1800 before it was rebuilt/from an original drawing in the possession of ... Sion College. W. Wise sculp. (c) 11th April, 1815. 230 × 260/250 × 315mm. 1st ed pl. 32. Nos XIX–XX.

(10pp of text)

St. Bartholomew the Great

19 A General Plan of the Church Cloisters &c of the Priory of St Bartholomew the Great. T. Bourne sculp. (d) 25th March 1821. 380 × 310/435 × 345mm.

20 Part of the Choir/With the Remains of the South Transept of the Church of St Bartholomew the Great/in West Smithfield. Nash del. Dale sculp. (d) 25th March, 1821. 280 × 225/315 × 255mm. Water-colour (279 × 225mm), 'copied from a sketch by Nash by R.B. Schnebbelie 1815', in Guildhall Library.

21 Interior of the Choir of/The Priory Church of St Bartholomew the Great, West Smithfield. T.H. Shepherd del. Howlett sculp. (d) 1st March, 1822. 285 × 230/325 × 260mm. Pen and ink and water-colour drawing (285 × 230mm) in Guildhall Library.

22 West View of the Interior of/The Chapel of Saint Bartholomew the Great, West Smithfield. T.H. Shepherd Del. Dale sculp. (d) 1ts (sic) March 1822. 220 × 290/260 × 330mm. Signed pencil and water-colour drawing (225 × 280mm), '1821', in Guildhall Library.

(2pp of text; 6pp in Royal Library copy)

St. Bartholomew the Less

23 Interior of the Church of St Bartholomew the Less

West Smithfield looking towards the Altar – Exterior of the same, South & East sides, from the Cloisters of St Bartholomews Hospital. (e) 1834. 200 × 225,104 × 162/345 × 255mm.

(2pp of text)

St. Helen Within Bishopsgate with the account of Crosby Hall

24 South West View of the Church of St Helen./Bishopsgate Street, London. Schnebbelie del. Wise sculp. (d) 11th October 1817. 215 × 255/260 × 300mm. 1st ed pl. 22. Signed water-colour (235 × 285mm), dated 25 March 1816, in Guildhall Library.

25 South West View of the Interior of the Church of St. Helen, Bishopsgate Street;/Taken during the Repair in 1808—Exhibiting also some of the principal Monuments. F. Nash Del. B. Howlett sculp. (d) 11th October 1817. 278 × 230/325 × 260mm. 1st ed pl. 23. Water-colour (280 × 230mm), by Schnebbelie after Nash, in Guildhall Library.

26 (tr) Plan of the/Nunnery and Church of St. Helen,/Bishopsgate Street, London./Shewing the situations of the Sepulchral Monuments, &c in the Church./Taken after the General Repair in 1808. Gardner Del. (d) 11th October 1817. 300 × 475mm. 1st ed pl. 24.

27 Monument of Sir Andrew Judd, Kt. Sheriff in 1544 and Mayor 1551;/Erected in the Choir of the Church of St. Helen, Bishopsgate Within, London. Fisher del. Stow sculp. (d) 1 January 1825. 255 × 200/320 × 255mm.

(4pp of text)

28 South East View of the Nunnery of St Helen, Bishopsgate Street. Nash del. Springsguth sculp. (d) 1 January, 1819. 238 × 305/270 × 330mm. 1st ed pl. 25.

29 The Crypt of the Antient Nunnery of St. Helen, Bishopsgate Street London;/over which was erected the Hall &c of the Leather Sellers Company. W. Capon del. Wise sculp. (d) 11th October 1817. 148 × 242, etc/250 × 318mm. 1st ed pl. 26.

30 The Crypt of the Nunnery of St. Helen in Bishopsgate Street/from the North ... the upper part of the plate exhibits the Ceiling &c of a fine apartment over the Crypt which was used as the Dining Hall of the Leathersellers' Company ... and which was pulled down by their order in 1799.... W. Capon del. Wise sculp. (d) 11 October 1817. 205 × 240/260 × 320mm. 1st ed pl. 27.

(8pp of text)

31 The Original Antient Steeple of St. Michael in Cornhill, London,/as it appeared previous to its destruction in 1421/From a singularly curious Drawing of the Time ... (b) 13 June 1809. 310 × 180/350 × 255mm. 1st ed pl. 43. No V.

(3pp of text; 8pp in Royal Library copy)

St. Paul Shadwell

32 View of St Paul's, Shadwell, Taken down 1819.

Schnebbelie del. Dale sculp. (d) 1 January 1825. 215 × 270/255 × 325mm.

33 North West View of St Paul's, Shadwell, Taken down 1817. Schnebbelie del. Dale sculp. (d) 1 January 1825. 208 × 250/270 × 335mm.

34 West View of the Interior of St. Paul's, Shadwell, Taken down 1817. Schnebbelie del. Dale sculp. (d) 1 January 1825. 224 × 285/255 × 330mm.

35 (tl) Plan/of the Church of,/St. Paul/Shadwell./Taken Down 1817. (d) 1 January 1825. 325 × 260mm. Refs a–q, A–GG.

36 North West View of St. Paul's, Shadwell, Built 1820. Schnebbelie del. Dale sculp. (d) 1 January 1825. 278 × 200/330 × 258mm. The new church, built 'from the design of the late Mr. John Walters, of Fen-Church Buildings, by Mr. J. Streather', 1820–1. Water-colour (275 × 200mm), '1822', in Guildhall Library.

(8pp of text)

St. Peter upon Cornhill

37 South View of the Church of St. Peter upon Cornhill, London. Whichelo del. Dale sculp. (d) 1 January 1825. 300 × 215/325 × 255mm. Note on similar sketch (270 × 184mm) in Guildhall Library: 'Drawn by Whichelo 1805, copied by Schnebbelie 1816'.

38 Interior of the Church of St. Peter upon Cornhill London. Whichelo del. Dale sculp. (d) 1 January 1825. 295 × 212/325 × 255mm.

39 (tm) A Reduced Fac-simile Copy of the Brass Plate,/in the Church of St. Peter, Upon Cornhill. (d) 1st January 1825. 285 × 237mm. The plate claims that the church was founded by Lucius, AD 179.

40 (tm) In the Church of St. Peter upon Cornhill. C.R. Ryley del. F. Bartilozzi R.A. sculp. (c) 1st January 1798 and (d) 1st January 1825. 150 × 115/285 × 230mm. The Woodmason monument to seven children who perished in a Leadenhall Street fire.

(40a) (tm) Some Account of an Interesting Monument ... 300 × 227mm. ie of the loss of the Woodmason children.

(26pp of text, with the date 1831 on pp 16, 24)

St. Saviour, Southwark

41 St Saviours Church Southwark. W. Hollar delin: et sculp; 1661. (c) June 1, 1808. 170 × 230/245 × 300mm. 1st ed pl. 56, with publication-line (a). No I. Facsimile from Dugdale's *Monasticon* (no 6) 2,940.

(1 leaf of text)

42 North East View of St Saviour's Church, Consistory Court and Chapel of St John. C.J.M. Whichelo del. Joseph Skelton sculp. (c) 10th February, 1813. 200 × 300/270 × 325mm. 1st ed pl. 58, No XIII.

43 The Chapel in the Church of St. Saviour, Southwark./In which are interred the Remains of Dr. Lancelot Andrews ... Schnebbelie del. Dale sculp. (d) 1st

January 1825. 280 × 218/328 × 260mm. Numbered '44' in check-list. Exterior of Lady Chapel.

44 West View of the Choir of St. Saviour's, Southwark, Surry. C.J.M. Whichelo del. (c) 1st January, 1814. 300 × 250/330 × 270mm. Numbered '43' in check-list. 1st ed pl. 59. No XVI.

(4 + 2pp of text, with a note on p 3 about restoration commenced March 1830)

45 Gateway of St Mary's Priory, Southwark. Whichelo del. Stow sculp. – A Plan/of the Church of/St Saviour/site of/Winchester/House &c. (c) 7th October 1811. 200 × 215,80 × 230/320 × 265mm. 1st ed pl. 57. No XI.

46 South View of the Palace of the Bishops of Winchester near St. Saviour's Southwark ... Whichelo del. (c) 1 Jany 1812. 195 × 240/225 × 295mm. 1st ed pl. 60. No XII.

47 North West View of the Hall of Winchester Palace, Southwark,/as it appeared after the fire which happened the 28th of Augt. 1814.... B. Howlett sculp. (c) 11th April, 1815. 210 × 290/270 × 310mm. 1st ed pl. 61. Nos XIX–XX. Includes inset detail of rose window, 65mm.

(included in 4pp of text on St Saviour)

REMAINS OF RELIGIOUS HOUSES AND ANCIENT CHAPELS—MEETING HOUSES

48 (tm) The Monastery of St. John of Jerusalem,/London. (b) 1 Jan. 1809. 238 × 360/320 × 380mm. 1st ed pl. 28. No II. Copied from Dugdale's *Monasticon* 2,504.

(1 leaf of text)

Abbey of St. Saviour, Bermondsey, Surrey

49 A General View of the Remains of Bermondsey Abbey, Surry./As it appeared in the Year 1805 with the adjacent Country taken from the Steeple of the Church of St. Mary Magdalen.... Drawn by C.I.M. Whichello. Engraved by B. Howlett. (d) 27th September 1820. 285 × 450/330 × 435mm.

50 East View of the Gateway of Bermondsey Abbey/near the Church and in the Parish of St Mary Magdalen Surry. F. Nash del. Dale sculp. (d) 27th September, 1820. 210 × 270/260 × 300mm.

51 Inside of the Hall, Bermondsey Abbey. C.J.M. Whichelo del. 1811. Dale sculp. – Outside of the Hall. (d) 27th September 1820. 177 × 188, etc/330 × 255mm.

52 Inside of one of the Rooms under the Hall, Bermondsey Abbey – Section of the Panneling – Saxon Ornament near the Gateway. C.J.M. Whichelo del. 1811. Dale sculp. (d) 27th Septr. 1820. 143 × 228, etc/330 × 255mm.

53 Inside of a Room adjoining those under the Hall, Bermondsey Abbey – Saxon Ornaments in the great

Wall, near the Church Yard ... C.J.M. Whichelo del. 1811. Cook sculp. (d) 27th Septr. 1820. 150 × 230, etc/330 × 250mm.

54 (tr) A Ground Plan/of/Bermondsey Abbey./From an original Drawing taken in 1679 – (vignette tl)The Old Church of St. Mary Magdalen. (40 × 65mm) – (br) A View of the North and West Gates of the Abbey. (70 × 100mm) (d) 1st January, 1822. 270 × 300/280 × 330mm.

55 The Arms and Seals,/of the Prior and Convent of St. Saviour at Bermondsey. (d) 25th March, 1821. 305 × 260mm.

56 (tm) Fac Simile from one of the Books of Indentures for the Foundation of King Henry the Seventh's Chapel/at Westminster, to which the Abbot of Bermondsey was a party ... Drawn & Engraved by B. Howlett. (d) 27th September 1820. 315 × 240mm.

(4pp of text; 10pp in Royal Library copy)

57 South View of London Street, Dockhead., in the Water Side Division of the Parish of St. Mary Magdalen Bermondsey, Surrey./with the Adjacent Plan. Schnebbelie del. Wise sculp. (c) Oct. 11th 1813. 165 × 240,105 × 210/285 × 265mm. 1st ed pl. 10. No XV. Water-colour (184 × 241mm) in Guildhall Library.

Priory of the Holy Trinity, near Aldgate

58 Ruins of Part of the Priory of the Holy Trinity,/called Christ-Church near Aldgate. Schnebbelie Del. W. Taylor sculp. (d) 1st January 1825. 130 × 228,165 × 190/320 × 255mm. With plan and details.

59 Gateway of the Priory of the Holy Trinity,/called Christ-Church, near Aldgate. Schnebbelie Del. Dale Sculp. (d) 1st January, 1825. 235 × 185,60 × 110/325 × 255mm. With plan. Shows demolition in November 1815.

60 (tm) St. Helen's Nunnery./Indenture between Richard the Prior and the Convent of the Holy Trinity within Aldgate/and the Prioress and Nuns of St Helen London. (d) 1st January 1825. 320 × 250mm.

(6pp of text)

College of St. Martin's le Grand

61 View of a Crypt on the Site of the Late College of St Martin's le Grand./Discovered in clearing for the New Post Office. Schnebbelie del. Dale sculp. (d) 1 January 1819. 215 × 252/260 × 320mm. 1st ed pl. 33. Original water-colour (210 × 255mm), '1817', in Guildhall Library.

62 View of the Ruins of Part of the late Church of St. Leonard/and the Steeple of St. Vedast Foster Lane – View of the Crypt on the Site of the late College of St. Martin le Grand: S. East, S. West. Schnebbelie del. Cook sculp. (d) 1 January 1819. 165 × 160,110 × 110, 110 × 105/315 × 260mm. 1st ed pl. 34. Signed

water-colour, (290 × 215mm), '1819', in Guildhall Library.

(2pp of text)

Collegiate Chapel of St. Mary Magdalen and All Saints Guildhall

63 View of the Collegiate Chapel of St. Mary Magdalen and All Saints, Guildhall, London. Schnebbelie del. Wise sculp. (c) 1st Decr. 1815. 270 × 210/300 × 255mm. 1st ed pl. 35. Nos XXI–XXII.

64 Interior of the Antient chapel of St Mary Magdalen, Guildhall;/now the Court of Requests ... G. Jones del. M. Springsguth sculp. (d) 11 October 1817. 180 × 255/260 × 320mm. 1st ed pl. 36.

(2pp of text)

Chapels attached to Hospitals for Lepers

65 Chapel Royal, St. James's Palace,/Formerly belonging to a House of Female Lepers founded by the Citizens of London. Schnebbelie del. Wise sculp. (d) Octr. 11th 1816. 270 × 210/300 × 245mm. 1st ed pl. 37. Pen and ink drawing (230 × 175mm), dated 10 February 1816, in Westminster Public Library.

66 Chapel Great Ilford, Essex,/formerly belonging to the Hospital for Male Lepers ... – Exterior of the Above. Schnebbelie del. Wise sculp. (d) 11th Octr. 1816. 168 × 215, 100 × 185/300 × 235mm. 1st ed pl. 38.

67 The Chapel of the Hospital/for Lepers in Kent Street,/Southwark, called Le Lock ... Whichelo del. (c) 1st January 1813. 228 × 200/325 × 265mm. 1st ed pl. 39. No XIII.

68 West View of the Lock Hospital and its Chapel, Kingsland – Interior of the Chapel. Schnebbelie del. Wise sculp. (c) 1st Decr. 1815. 168 × 290,63 × 115/255 × 310mm. 1st ed pl. 40. Nos XXI–XXII.

(2pp of text)

69 Interior & Front of the Chapel at Knightsbridge/Formerly belonging to the Hospital of Lepers. Schnebbelie del. Howlett sculp. (d) 1st Jany 1819. 160 × 235,105 × 150/320 × 260mm. 1st ed pl. 41.

(2pp of text)

70 Interior of Old Lambe's Chapel, Monkwell Street, looking towards/the Founders Monument & the Masters Seat at the East End. – Exterior of the South Side of the Chapel drawn from the Court of the Alms Houses./This Building was taken down in 1825. (e) 1834. 150 × 215,110 × 155/315 × 260mm.

(8pp of text)

Meeting-Houses

71 View of the late Revd. Charles Skelton's Meeting House adjacent to the site of the Globe/Theatre, Maid Lane, Southwark. G. Shepherd del. Stow sculp. – A Mill erected, some years sinse, on the Basement of the Meeting House. (c) 1st January 1813. 145 × 210,155 ×

130/325 × 265mm. 1st ed pl. 46. No XIII. Signed water-colour (354 × 250mm), '1812', in GLC.

(1 leaf of text)

72 E.S.E. View of John Bunyan's Meeting House, in Zoar Street, Gravel Lane, Southwark, with the Adjacent Plan. (c) 1st January, 1814. 185 × 240,90 × 160/305 × 265mm. 1st ed pl. 47. No XVI.

73 An Interior View of John Bunyan's Meeting House in Zoar Street, Gravel Lane, Southwark in its present state – An Interior View of the School connected with & under a part of the Meeting House. Schnibbelee Del. Dale Sculp. (d) 1 December 1822. 175 × 205,113 × 155/ 330 × 265mm. The Meeting House in use as a millwright's shop.

(1 leaf of text)

PALACES AND MANSIONS

Crosby Hall, Bishopsgate Street

74 Plan and Views of the/Vaults of Crosby Hall,/ Bishopsgate Street. Nash del. Wise sculpt. (d) 11th Octr. 1816. 65 × 78, 78 × 95, 70 × 72/260 × 335mm. 1st ed pl. 13.

75 A South West View of the Principal Quadrangle or Court Yard of Crosby Hall/(restored to its original state). F. Nash Delt. S. Rawle sculpt. (d) 11th Octr 1816. 194 × 245/275 × 320mm. 1st ed pl. 14. (*Longford* 436)

76 North East View of Crosby Hall,/(showing part of the interior of the Great Hall.) F. Nash del. Wise sculpt. (d) 11th Octr. 1816. 185 × 240/275 × 330mm. 1st ed pl. 15. (*Longford* 439)

77 Interior of Crosby Hall./(Looking South). F. Nash del. Wise sculpt. (d) 11th Octr. 1816. 240 × 210/290 × 280mm. 1st ed pl. 16. (*Longford* 454)

78 Interior of Part of Crosby Hall, called the Council Room/Looking East. F. Nash del. Rawle sculpt. (d) 11th Octr. 1816. 240 × 195/305 × 250mm. 1st ed pl. 17. (*Longford* 459)

79 Elevation of Part of the Interior of Crosby Hall./ (called the Council Room.) Nash del. Rawle sculpt. (d) 11th Octr. 1816. 205 × 175/305 × 270mm. 1st ed pl. 18.

80 (br) Ceiling Plan of Crosby Hall/Bishopsgate Street. Nash del. Bourne sculpt. (d) 11th Octr. 1816. 275 × 385mm. 1st ed pl. 19.

81 Specimens of Architecture, in Crosby Hall, Bishopsgate Street. Schnebbelie del. Cook sculp. (d) 1 January 1819. 260 × 135, etc/320 × 270mm. 1st ed pl. 20. Original water-colour in Royal Library.

82 Interior of the Great Bay Window or Recess in the Hall of Crosby Place, Bishopsgate Street/with part of the Vaults and Entrances under the North-Wing/(The Entrance to Crosby Hall & its Crypt from Great St Helens.) Schnebbelie del. Howlett sculp. (d) 1 January, 1819. 200 × 125, 112 × 102, etc/255 × 320mm. 1st ed pl. 21. (*Longford* 456)

Inn of the Priors of Lewes, Tooley Street, Southwark

83 North View of the Oratory of the Ancient Inn/Situated in Tooley Street, Southwark & formerly belonging to the Priors of Lewes, in Sussex/ Taken from Point 'a' in the Plan. Nash del. (d) 11th October 1817. 180 × 220/270 × 338mm. 1st ed pl. 44.

84 (tl) Plan of the Ancient Inn,/Situated in Tooley Street, Southwark,/H. Gardner del. (d) 11th October, 1817. 260 × 310mm. 1st ed pl. 45.

85 A Ground Plan, Elevation & Specimens of the Capitals, Columns &c. of the Crypt under the Inn/in Tooley Street belonging to the Priors of Lewes in Sussex. F. Nash del. Rawle sculp. (d) 27th September, 1820. 255 × 315mm.

(2pp of text)

Palace of Whitehall

86 Veüe et Perspective du Palais du Roy d'Angleterre a Londres qui sappelle Whitehall. Silvestre sculp. Israël ex. cum privil Regis. 98./The Palace of Whitehall. (a) June 1st 1808. 120 × 238/240 × 300mm. 1st ed pl. 62. No I. 'etched by Sylvester about the year 1638; and forms one of a series of views, chiefly of places abroad, published by the same artist, about that period'.

87 The Palace of Whitehall./As it appeared about the Reign of James the second. From an original drawing in the possession of Thomas Griffiths Esq. (a) June 1, 1808. 160 × 220/200 × 315mm. 1st ed pl. 63. No I. The original drawing, ascribed to L. Knyff ('eight times the size of this print'), formerly in the Gardner Collection, is now in Westminster Public Library.

(2pp of text)

88 The Palace of Whitehall.... /From a Drawing by Hollar in the Pepysian Library Cambridge.... The Drawing was made in the early part of the reign of Charles I. (b) May 1st 1809. 142 × 315/190 × 340mm. 1st ed pl. 64. No IV.

89 St James's Palace and part of the City of Westminster/ Taken from the Nth side of Pall Mall/As they appeared about the Year 1660./From an Antient Drawing in the possession of John Towneley ... The Conduit, a conspicuous object in the above view, stood nearly on the site of St James's Square. Holler An. 1660. Etched by Richd Sawyer. (b) June 13th 1809. 113 × 300/210 × 323mm. 1st ed pl. 65. No. V. Refs in the work: '1. Westminster Abby. 2. Westminster Hall. 3. St James's Palace. 4. Pell mall. 5. Conduit.' The original Hollar drawing (100 × 301mm) in the Royal Collection (*Oppé* 370).

(1 leaf of text)

Fawkes-hall or Vauxhall in the County of Surrey

90 A View of the Antient Manor House of/Fawkeshall or Vauxhall,Surrey/Engraved from a drawing in Pen and Ink/in the Possession of Mr. John Simco with a Plan of the Site & its Environs. (c) 11th October 1813. 177 × 283,50 × 115/270 × 310mm. 1st ed pl. 66. No XV.

315

91 Vauxhall Tickets/The Above Tickets of Admission to the Gardens ... are all Struck in Silver after/designs by Mr W. Hogarth ... Engraved from the Original Medallions, by James Stow. (d) 1st January 1825. 325 × 270mm.

(2pp of text; 4pp in Royal Library copy)

Totten hall or Tottenham Court

92 Remains of the Manor House, denominated the Lordship of Toten-Hall; now vulgarly called Tottenham Court, and/occupied by the Adam and Eve Tea House and Gardens. – Plan of the Vicinity. Shepherd Del. Wise sculp. (c) Jan 1st 1813. 180 × 215,120 × 230/320 × 265mm. 1st ed pl. 67. No XIV.

93 An antient Structure, denominated in various Records King John's Palace; lately situated near the New River Company's/Reservoir, Tottenham Court. – Part of the Adam and Eve Coffee Rooms, Hampstead Road, built on the Site of the/Old Manor House of Toten-hall ... J. Carter Del. W. Wise sculp. (c) 4th June 1811. 183 × 215,100 × 130/230 × 265mm. 1st ed pl. 68. No IX.

94 Clarendon House; called also Albemarle House – This structure was erected by Edward Hyde Earl of Clarendon/during the reign of Charles II ... Its Site now forms Grafton Street, Piccadilly. Wise sculp. (c) 4 June 1814. 187 × 260/228 × 290mm. 1st ed pl. 69. Nos XVII–XVIII. From an engraving (508 × 698mm), c 1665, by W. Skilman after Johann Spilberg in BM (*Crace* 10.13).

(2pp of text in Royal Library copy)

95 Somerset House,/In its Original State./With the various Buildings on the Banks of the River Thames, as far as Westminster/From an Antient Painting in Dulwich College./ This View exhibits Somerset House, previous to the alterations made by Inigo Jones ... Adjoining it is the Savoy and immediately behind it, the only view extant of Exeter House.... (b) 11 October 1809. 230 × 405/305 × 440mm. 1st ed pl. 70. No VI. The original is 'London—A view on the Thames' by Cornelys Bol ('IV').

(2pp of text)

96 Suffolk House Charing Cross.... originally called Northampton House ... From a Drawing by Hollar in the Pepysian Library, Cambridge. (b) 1st Decr. 1808. 123 × 223/175 × 265mm. 1st ed pl. 72. No II. Later called Northumberland House. Unsigned pen and ink drawing (54 × 152mm) in Pepys Library (*Catalogue* III, 2972/237a).

97 York House ... York Stairs still remain and are universally admired. From a Drawing by Hollar in the Pepysian Library in Cambridge. (b) Dec. 1, 1808. 125 × 225/195 × 275mm. 1st ed pl. 73. No II. Unsigned pen and ink drawing (54 × 152mm) in Pepys Library (*Catalogue* III, 2972/237b).

98 Durham House – Salisbury House – Worcester House. ... Durham Yard now the Adelphi ... Salisbury and Cecil Streets ... Beauforts Buildings. From a drawing by Hollar in the Pepysian Library, Cambridge. (b) 30th Novr 1808. 122 × 225/197 × 280mm. 1st ed pl. 71. No II. Unsigned pen and ink drawing (33 × 152mm) in Pepys Library (*Catalogue* III, 2972/237c).

(2pp of text; 6pp in Royal Library copy)

Sir Paul Pindar's House, Bishopsgate Street Without

99 View of the Front of Sir Paul Pindar's House on the West side of Bishopsgate Street Without – The Vignette exhibits part of the First Floor Cieling. Shepherd Del. Sawyer sculp. (c) 8, May 1812. 245 × 220,60 × 125/330 × 265mm. 1st ed pl. 74. No XII. Pencil drawing (317 × 215mm), signed by George Shepherd, in Bishopsgate Institute.

100 Sir Paul Pindar's Lodge or Garden House, Half-Moon Alley, Bishopsgate Street. Schnebbelie delt. Dale sculp. (d) 1st January 1819. 168 × 250, etc/260 × 320mm. 1st ed pl. 75. Signed wash drawing (160 × 240mm), '19 Dec. 1817', in Guildhall Library.

(2pp of text)

101 Montague House/(now the British Museum) built about 1680, in its original state,/taken from the Garden with a vignette of the/New Building at the Museum erecd. 1804. (c) 1st January 1813. 180 × 285,50 × 155/250 × 325mm. 1st ed pl. 76. No XIV. The new building is the Townley Gallery, built 1804–8 by the Trustees' architect George Saunders to house the marbles and demolished in 1851. The original house copied from James Simon's engraving for *Nouveau Théâtre de la Grande Bretagne* (no 22), item 49.

(4pp of text; 6pp in Royal Library copy)

102 (tl) A Plan of London House,/Now in the Possession of Mr. Jacob Ilive Decr. 1747./It is situate on the West side of Aldersgate Street, in the Parish of St. Botolph.... (c) August 5th, 1814. 295 × 245/315 × 255mm. 1st ed pl. 77. Nos XVII–XVIII. Jacob Ilive was the son of T. Ilive and was a printer and type-founder. The house was burned down in 1766.

103 North Front of Bedford House, Bloomsbury Square. Howlett sculp. Engraved from the original drawing purchased at the sale in Bedford House now in the possession of the publisher R. Wilkinson. (d) December 1, 1822. 200 × 300/265 × 330mm. Demolished 1800 and replaced by Bedford Place and Montague Street. Water-colour (190 × 300mm), by Schnebbelie, in Museum of London.

(2pp of text)

104 The House of Earl Grosvenor on the Bankside Westminster/Occupied by the present Earl till 1809 when it was taken down, to facilitate the great Improvements making in that neighbourhood. (vignette) Peterborough House 1666. T. Shepherd del. Dale sculp. (d) 25th March, 1821. 200 × 290,40 × 30/250 × 328mm. The note says: 'This part of the estate of Earl Grosvenor ... is now (1822) leased to Mr. John Johnson, who is considerably improving this

quarter of the metropolis, by forming new streets &c. One of the 'improvements' was the Millbank Penitentiary.

(1 leaf of text)

105 The Queen of Bohemia's Palace or Craven House, in Drury Lane; as it appeared in the Year 1800. – View of Part of Craven House in Wych Street. The Site of the Olympic Theatre. Ravenhill del. B. Howlett sc. – Plan/of the/Estate/belonging to ... Lord Craven/In the Parish of St Clement Danes/Shewing the Site of Craven House/Taken in the Year 1788. (d) 1st January 1822. 123 × 194,90 × 140,70 × 150/315 × 250mm.

(2pp of text)

106 A North West View of the House of William Parker Lord Monteagle; In the Parish of St. Saviour's Southwark/ He Died 1 July 1622 at Halingberye Morely in the County of Essex. Schnebbelie Del. (d) 1 January 1825. 220 × 298/265 × 320mm. Water-colour (225 × 300mm), 'sketched 11 Nov. 1815', in Museum of London.

(4pp of text, in which a footnote refers to an 1832 publication)

Oldbourne Hall, Shoe Lane

107 View of Oldbourn-Hall and Ceiling./Situated on the East Side of Shoe Lane, in the Parish of St. Andrew Holborn/In the occupation of Messrs. Pontifex Sons and Wood, Copper and Brass Founders. Banks del. Banks sculp. (d) 1st of January 1823. 156 × 235,120 × 232/315 × 260mm.

108 Carved Fire-Place and Mantle-Piece in the Principal/ Apartment of Oldbourne Hall, Shoe Lane. (e) 1834. 270 × 235/320 × 260mm.

(2pp of text)

VOL. 2 i

COURTS, HALLS AND PUBLIC BUILDINGS

109 Pye Powder Court, Cloth Fair, West Smithfield./This Court is held at a Public House known by the sign of the Hand and Shears, the corner of Middle Street and King Street, as exhibited in the Vignette.... Whichelo Del. (c) Feby 11, 1811. 160 × 215,110 × 150/305 × 255mm. 1st ed pl. 80. No VIII.

(8pp of text)

110 Representation of the Ceremony of presenting the Sheriffs of London/Samuel Birch & William Heygate Esqrs./in the Court of Exchequer, on Michaelmas Day, 1811. G.J.M. Whichelo delt. Stow sculpt. (c) 1st January 1813. 280 × 375/317 × 410mm. 1st ed pl. 81. No XIV.

(7pp of text)

The Royal Exchange

111 Royal Exchange South. (d) 1st of January 1819. 195 × 267/230 × 303mm. (tc) Elizabethan royal arms, Sir Thomas Gresham's below, flanked by cartouches. 1st

ed pl. 82. Original engraving (15½" × 21"), 'Francis Hogenburg 1570', in BM (*Crace* 22.34). See also item 112.

112 Royal Exchange. (a) June 1, 1808. 185 × 240/270 × 315mm. 1st ed pl. 83. No I. Courtyard with staffage and Corinthian column topped by grasshopper in background, off-centre to make way for royal arms tc. *Crace* 22.35 attributes both this and the previous print to Francis Hogenburg without reason given. An acceptable attribution according to Sidney Colvin.

(2pp of text)

Furnival's Inn

113 Furnival's Inn Holborn/Antiently the Mansion of the Lords Furnival. Schnebbelie del. Dale sculp. (d) 1st January 1819. 205 × 300/260 × 323mm. 1st ed pl. 84. Water-colour and pen and ink sketch (215 × 295mm), both dated 29 June 1815, in Guildhall Library.

114 West View of the Interior of Furnivals Inn. Schnebbelie del. Banks sculp. (d) 27th September, 1820. 215 × 275/265 × 320mm. Water-colour (290 × 375mm) in Guildhall Library.

115 North View of the Interior of Furnivals Inn. Schnebbelie del. Dale sculp. (d) 27th September, 1820. 215 × 300/255 × 320mm.

116 Interior of the Hall of Furnivals Inn. Schnebbelie Del. Banks sculp. (d) 27th September 1820. 288 × 240/317 × 280mm. Shows the Hall being dismantled of its panelling in 1818 when it ceased to be an Inn of Court. Signed water-colour (315 × 240mm), dated 1819, in Guildhall Library.

(2pp of text)

117 South View of the Custom House, London. in the reign of Queen Elizabeth./Burnt in the Great Fire of London, 1666. Engraved from a scarce Print dated 1663, by Barthw. Howlett. (c) 11th March 1815. 120 × 200,145 × 215/315 × 235mm. 1st ed pl. 85. Nos XIX–XX. 'South View of the Ruins of the Custom House, London, built by Mr Thomas Ripley, after the former structure, built/in 1668, was destroyed by Fire in the year 1718. This Fabric was also demolished by Fire. 14th February 1814. Fellows del. W. Wise sc.'

(2pp of text)

118 A View of the South Front of the North Side of the Marshalsea Prison, near Blackman Street, Southwark. Taken from No 1 in the Gallery Jan 23, 1773 by I. Lewis, Surveyor and Draughtsman. – Part of the Borough of Southwark,/including the Scite of the Marshalsea Prison. (c) 1 Jany 1812. 142 × 297,75 × 157/245 × 310mm. 1st ed pl. 86. No XII. Refs A–Z, a–yy.

(2pp of text, with reference to an 1814 publication)

119 Cheapside Cross/(as it appeared in the Year 1547.)/ With part of the procession of Edw.VI to his Coronation at Westminster. / From a painting of the time lately at Cowdry in Sussex. (b) Jan 1, 1809. 208 ×

275/260 × 340mm. 1st ed pl. 87. No III. A drawing from the Cowdray painting was made by S.H. Grimm and engr by James Basire for the Society of Antiquaries in 1787 (no 36), item 67.

120 Cheapside Cross, alone/(as it appeared on its erection in 1606.... From an original drawing in the Pepysian Library, Cambridge. (b) Jan. 1 1809. 225 × 160/280 × 195mm. 1st ed pl. 88. No III. Unsigned drawing (229 × 160mm) in Pepys Library (*Catalogue* III/1–2972/82a).

121 A North East View of Cheapside with/the Cross and Conduit/and part of the procession of the Queen Mother Mary de Medicis ... From La Serre's Entrée Royale de la Reyne Mère du Roy 1638. (b) April 3rd 1809. 203 × 280/260 × 330mm. 1st ed pl. 89. No IV. La Serre (no 3), item 9.

122 A Plan of/Part of Cheapside;/Intended to shew the precise sites of the Antient/Cross and Conduit. – (Hollar's etching of the pulling down of Cheapside Cross, 2nd May 1643 and the burning on its site of the 'Book of Sports' on 10th May). (b) May 19th 1809. 117 × 185,120 × 90/275 × 195mm. 1st ed pl. 91. No IV. See *Parliamentary Mercies* (no 4). (*Hind* 31)

123 Charing Cross/Erected by Pietro Cavalini, in Memory of the amiable Queen Eleanor of Castile ... Engraved from a drawing mentioned by Pennant, in the last edition of his London, p. 93, as being in the possession of Dr. Combe: but now in the Crowle Collection, British Museum. (c) 4 June 1814. 270 × 195/370 × 260mm. 1st ed pl. 90. Nos XVII–XVIII. (*Crowle* Pennant 4, 135)

(8pp of text; 22pp in Royal Library copy)

124 East Front of the Queen's Treasury, from the River Thames – West Front of the Queen's Treasury, from Scotland Yard – Part of/White Hall,/Destroyed by Fire/MDCXCVII. Schnebbelie del. Dale sculp. (d) 27th September 1820. 150 × 205,130 × 170,60 × 40,60 × 40/310 × 260mm. Signed drawings (150 × 200 and 130 × 170mm), dated May 1818, in Guildhall Library.

(1 leaf of text)

125 View of the Brewery & Dwelling House belonging to Messrs. Calvert & Co./Erected on the Scite of Cold Harbour. Schnebbelie delt. Howlett fect. (135 × 188/160 × 240mm) – View of Waterman's Hall, Cold Harbour, Upper Thames Street./As it Appeared Anno 1650. G. Shepherd delt. from the Original by Hollar ... B. Howlett fect. (130 × 190/160 × 240mm) (d) 27th September 1820. Water-colours (140 × 190mm) in Museum of London and Guildhall Library.

(2pp of text)

126 The Late Hall of the Worshipful/Company of Salters, & Part of the Meeting./Situate in St. Swithin's Lane, Cannon Street. T.H. Shepherd del. Dale sculp. (d) 1st March 1822. 275 × 220/320 × 260mm.

127 Interior of Salters Hall Meeting.... T.H. Shepherd del. Dale sculp. (d) 14th March 1822. 220 × 275/260 × 320mm. Both demolished c 1821.

(2pp of text)

128 West View of Blackwell Hall, King Street Cheapside – (plan). Schnebbelie Del. 1819. Dale sculp. (d) 27th September 1820. 160 × 240,150 × 240/310 × 250mm. 'Taken down about December, 1819'. The text includes a note on the appointment of William Herbert as Guildhall Librarian in 1828 and says that by October 1834 the Library held a total of nearly 5000 vols. Signed drawings (190 × 285 and 160 × 290mm) in Guildhall Library.

(4pp of text)

129 View of the Town-Hall, St Margarets Hill, Southwark/ Previous to the present erection by the Corporation of London in 1793. Ravenhill Del. Dale sculp. (d) 1st January 1825. 215 × 280/255 × 325mm.

(2pp of text, with mention of April 1834.)

130 S.W. View of Gerrards Hall. – (plan of vaulting). (c) Feby 11, 1811. 1st ed pl. 78. No VIII. 215 × 195, 95 × 198/345 × 260mm. Water-colour (235 × 215mm), by C.J.M. Whichelo, dated 1810, in Museum of London.

131 Remains of the Antient Church of St. Michael, now subterranean, Situated at the Junction of Leadenhall Street,/Aldgate High Street and Fenchurch Street – with a Plan of the groined arches. Shepherd del. Wise sculp. (c) 11th April 1815. 185 × 220,80 × 215, etc/305 × 250mm. 1st ed pl. 79. Nos XIX–XX.

(2pp of text)

132 Vestiges of a Crypt in Leadenhall Street,/Now a Kitchen – Houses on the North Side of Leadenhall Street,/Erected on the Site of those Destroyed by the Extensive Fire of 1765. B. Howlett sculp. (d) 1st January 1825. 147 × 220,85 × 200/135 × 250mm. The lower engraving is a forerunner of Tallis's *London Street Views* of 1838 (see no 186).

(2pp of text)

133 Interior of the Crypt called the Powder Plot Cellar beneath the old Palace of Westminster,/looking towards Charing Cross – Taken down in June 1833. Drawn by W. Capon July 1799. Engraved by G. Dale. (e) 142 × 355/230 × 360mm. nd.

(2pp of text)

Leaden Hall and Chapel. Taken down in 1812

134 N.E. View of the Chapel of the Holy Trinity, Leadenhall,/In the Parish of St. Peter upon Cornhill London. Whichelo Del. Dale sculp. (d) 1 January 1825. 215 × 275/255 × 320mm.

135 S.E. View of the Chapel of the Holy Trinity, Leadenhall ... Whichelo Del. Dale sculp. (d) 1 January 1825. 205 × 275/255 × 330mm.

136 Interior of the Chapel of the Holy Trinity, Leadenhall ... Whichelo Del. Dale sculp. (d) 1 January 1825. 295 × 230/325 × 250mm.

137 View of the Skin-Market in Leadenhall ... Samuel del. Dale sculp. (d) 1 January 1825. 284 × 225/322 × 255mm.

(8pp of text)

138 Ruins discovered at the Corner of Whitcomb Street,/ near Charing Cross, December 1821. Banks del. et sculp. – Plan of the Neighbourhood – Plan of the Ruins. (d) 1st June 1822. 130 × 215,65 × 100, etc/315 × 250mm.

(1 leaf of text)

139 Hungerford Market, near York Buildings, Strand/ Built by Sir Edward Hungerford ... 1682. Schnebbelie del. Maddocks sculp. (d) 1st Feby 1825. 175 × 235, etc/325 × 255mm.

(8pp of text up to the opening of the new Hungerford Market, June 1833)

SCHOOLS

140 A South View of Queen Elizabeth's Free Grammar School in Tooley Street in the Parish of St. Olave, Southwark: with a Plan of the adjacent Neighbourhood. Schnebbelie del. Wise sculp. (c) 1st Decr. 1813. 185 × 245,90 × 160/305 × 260mm. 1st ed pl. 48. No XVI.

(4pp of text)

141 North View of Queen Elizabeth's Free Grammar School, St. Saviour's, Southwark. Schnebbelie del. Howlett sculp. – South View of the same Structure: with Impressions of the Silver Medal, presented by the Corporation of Governors to the best deserving Boy. (c) 11 March 1815. 170 × 235, 100 × 130, etc/310 × 250mm. 1st ed pl. 49. Nos XIX–XX.

(6pp of text)

142 Schools founded by the Revd. Ralph Davenant, Rector of the Parish of St. Mary, Whitechapel.... Schnebbelie del. Howlett sculp. (d) 1 January 1819. 190 × 195, etc/320 × 255mm. Signed pen, ink and wash drawings (210 × 199mm), '6th Oct. 1815', in Guildhall Library.

(2pp of text)

143 Saint Pauls School.... The original building was destroyed by the great Fire in 1666 and rebuilt soon after ... In 1783 it was repaired and beautified, and in 1823 it was taken down for the purpose of erecting a splendid structure on its site. B. Howlet sculp. (d) 1 January 1825. 190 × 290/255 × 325mm.

(16pp of text, including an 1829 ref on p 16)

ALMS HOUSES, HOSPITALS, ETC

144 These Alms Houses Built/and Endowed by/William Meggs Esqr Anno 1658. Repaired improved and further endowed by Benjamin Goodwin ... Anno 1767. – (plan of neighbourhood) Schnebbelie del. Cook sculp. (d) 1st January 1819. 170 × 225,120 × 180/320 × 260mm. 1st ed pl. 51. Whitechapel.

(2pp of text)

145 North West View of the Antient Structure of Merchant-Taylors Hall,/and the Alms-Houses adjoining in Threadneedle Street.... From a Drawing Taken by William Goodman in the Year 1599 now in the possession of the Worshipful Company. (d) 11th October, 1817. 150 × 235/210 × 270mm. 1st ed pl. 52. Pencil and water-colour drawing (153 × 233mm), 'G. Shepherd 1811', in BM (*Crace* 25.12).

146 West Front, or Principal Entrance of the London Workhouse, Bishopsgate Street./ with the Stewards Side, or Internal Part of the same structure. Schnebbelie del. Dale sculp. (d) 1 January 1819. 195 × 200,80 × 130, etc/320 × 260mm. 1st ed pl. 53. Signed water-colours (195 × 198 and 70 × 135mm), dated 8 December 1817, in Guildhall Library.

(2pp of text)

147 Ludgate Prison, with a Plan of the London Workhouse, Sir Paul Pindar's House, Lodge, &c. Schnebbelie del. Cook sc. (d) 1st January 1819. 145 × 220,150 × 220/320 × 250mm. 1st ed pl. 54. Signed water-colour (140 × 215mm), dated 8 December 1817, in Guildhall Library.

Bridewell Hospital Blackfriars

148 N.W. View of the Chapel and Part of the Great Stair-Case leading to the Hall of Bridewell Hospital, London – N.E. View of the Court Room. C.J.M. Whichelo del. 1803. B. Howlett sc. (c) 1st January 1813. 205 × 215,185 × 120/325 × 255mm. 1st ed pl. 55. No XIII. Pencil drawing (311 × 235mm) in Guildhall Library.

149 View of Part of the Quadrangle of Bridewell Hospital,/Comprising the Male Prison, part of the Female Prison and the Great Hall ... T.H. Shepherd Del. T. Dale sculp. (d) 1st February 1822. 220 × 285/275 × 325mm. Signed pencil drawing and water-colour (186 × 276 and 226 × 284mm), dated 1821, in Guildhall Library.

(2pp of text)

150 St. John's House, Hoxton with a Plan of its Environs./Farm-House for City and other Poor kept by Mr Thomas Tipple. Schnebbelie del. Dale sculp. (d) 1st January 1823. 178 × 228, 100 × 175/320 × 260mm.

(1 leaf of text)

151 The Elevation of the Alms-Houses endowed by Sr Andrew Judd Kt./Great St. Helen's Bishopsgate within London. – (plan of neighbourhood) Schnebbelie del. Maddocks sc. (d) 1 January 1825. 250 × 250,40 × 130/325 × 250mm.

(2pp of text, with 1826 ref)

152 West front of the Old Alms Houses Founded by Elizabeth, Viscountess Lumley,/and erected in 1672 in the Pest-House Field Shoreditch. Taken down 1822. (e) 1834. 120 × 240, etc/260 × 315mm. In Shepherd's Walk, City Road.

(2pp of text)

PLACES OF AMUSEMENT

Holland's Leaguer, in the Manor of Paris Garden, Bankside

153 (tm) Holland's Leaguer, or Manor House of Paris Garden – (bl) Part/of the/Parish/of Christ Church/ Surrey/Antiently the Manor of/Paris Garden.... In the Year 1746. (d) December 1st 1822. 130 × 130,120 × 220/320 × 240mm.

(2pp of text)

154 (lc) Parish/of/Christ Church,/Surrey,/Surveyed by H. Gardner, Blackfriars. – (bl) Christ Church built about 1737. (d) 7 Augt. 1821. 315 × 255,80 × 62,/340 × 275mm.

Cuper's Gardens, Lambeth Marsh

155 View in Cuper's Gardens, Lambeth – (tl.) A Plan of/Cupers Gardens/With Part of the Parish of Lambeth,/In the Year 1746/Shewing also the Site of/the Waterloo Bridge Road. – (vignette tr) The New Church of St. John the Evangelist. Ravenhill delt. B. Howlett sculp. 155 × 220, 140 × 220,75 × 50/330 × 255mm.

156 View in Cuper's Gardens, Lambeth/Shewing the Orchestra at the time it was occupied by Messrs. Beaufoy for the British Wine Manufactory. G. Shepherd del. Dale sculp. (d) 1st January 1825. 212 × 310/250 × 330mm. Signed pencil and water-colour drawing (173 × 237mm), dated 1809, in BM (*Crace* 35.50).

157 View of the Feathers Tavern, Cupers-Bridge, Lambeth. De Cort del. B. Howlett sculp. (d) 1st January, 1825. 220 × 305/260 × 330mm. With refs: 'The Sluice', 'Chandlers Shop', 'Distant view of the Strand near Hungerford'.

(6pp of text, including ref to May 1834)

158 South East View of the Grotto now the Goldsmith's Arms/In the parish of St George Southwark. Schnebbelie del. Maddocks sculp. (d) 1 January 1825. 213 × 300/255 × 330mm.

(2pp of text, including ref to 1830)

MISCELLANEOUS OBJECTS OF ANTIQUITY

159 Autograph of Anna Boullen, during Her Imprisonment in the Tower,/Copied from the Original in the Regalia Office. Schnebbelie del. Wise sculp. (c) 1st Decr. 1815. 290 × 220/300 × 240mm. 1st ed pl. 11. Nos XXI–XXII.

(1 leaf of text)

160 The Coffin Plates of the Rebel Lords, who were executed on Tower Hill 1746 & 1747. (d) Octr 11 1816. Each 140 × 100, etc/255 × 320mm. 1st ed pl. 12.

(1 leaf of text)

THE MONUMENT ON FISH STREET HILL

161 Sculpture in Basso-Rilievo, Executed by Caius Gabriel Cibber,/on the Western Front of the Base of the Monument,/in Commemmoration of the Fire of London. (e) 1834. 215 × 205/330 × 255mm.

162 Inscriptions engraven on the base of the Monument, descriptive of the Burning & Rebuilding of London, with the/celebrated Inscription round the plinth of the Column, erased by order of the Common Council Sept. 26, 1831. (e) 1834. 210 × 280/260 × 330mm.

(12pp of text)

VOL. 2 ii

ANCIENT AND MODERN THEATRES

163 (engr title) Theatrum Illustrata/Graphic/and Historic Memorials/Ancient Playhouses. Modern Theatres/ Other Places of Public Amusement/in the/ Cities and Suburbs/of London & Westminster/With Scenic and incidental Illustrations/From the time of Shakspear to the present Period. (d) 1st Jany 1825. (allegorical vignette of Drama) E. Burney Pinx. J. Stow sculp. 100 × 170/325 × 250mm.

164 Clerks-Well/A View of the Pump near Clerks Well, Ray Street in the Parish of Clerkenwell ... as it appeared in 1822/Also a plan of the Site and Vicinity./It was near this Well that the Parish Clerks of London in the year 1409 ... are said to have acted for 8 days successively a Play which 'was matter from the creation of the World' ... Drawn by H. Gardner. Engraved by B. Howlett. (d) 1st May 1822. 280 × 215/320 × 260mm.

(2pp of text)

The Bear Garden, Bankside, Southwark

165 The above curious plan of Bankside/exhibits various particulars, illustrative of its antient state, not elsewhere to be found. (on scroll br) Bankside/with the Bull and Bear Baiting/from an Antient Survey on Vellum/made in the reign of Qu.Elizabeth. (b) or (c) 11 Octr. 1809. 130 × 260/275 × 325mm. 1st ed pl. 94. No VI.

(2pp of text)

166 The Bear Garden. From an enlarged Drawing of an extensive View of London in 1647 ... engraved by Hollar. 130 × 190/300 × 250mm. 1st ed pl. 96. No VII. See item 167.

167 The Bear Garden. From an enlarged Drawing of a very scarce View of London, called 'the Antwerp View', in the Possession of John Dent Esq. 135 × 190/305 × 255mm. 1st ed pl. 95. No VII. It is the previous plate that derives from Hollar's long view, usually known as the 'Antwerp view' (*Hind* 16); this appears to be a detail from Visscher's long view of 1616. See item 168.

The Globe Theatre, Bankside

168 The Globe Theatre/Bankside, Southwark/From a Drawing in the ... Pennant's London;/Bequeathed by the late John Charles Crowle Esqr./To the British Museum. Stow sculp. (c) 8 May 1812. 250 × 170/325 ×

265mm. Apparently based on Visscher's long view. See item 167.

169 The Globe Theatre/on the Bankside/As it appeared in the reign of King James I. Enlarged from an engraved view of London made about the year 1612. (c) Octr. 11th 1810. 130 × 193/310 × 250mm. With plan. 1st ed pl. 98. No VII. Seems to be extracted from Merian's long view which was used to illustrate Gottfried's *Neuwe Archontologia* (no 2).

170 The Globe Theatre. From an enlarged Drawing of an extensive View of London in 1647 ... engraved by Hollar. (c) Octr. 11th 1810. 130 × 190/305 × 255mm. 1st ed pl. 99. No VII. See item 167.

171 The Swan Theatre on the Bankside/as it appeared A.D. 1614. From the Long View of London called 'The Antwerp View'. – (vignette) The Swan about the Year 1620. Wise sc. (b) or (c) 11th Octr. 1809. 130 × 182/200 × 275mm. 1st ed pl. 100. No VI. See item 167.

(4pp of text; 8pp in Royal Library copy)

172 Inside of the Red Bull Playhouse.... near the upper end of St John's Street Clerkenwell ... From Kirkman's Drolls, Published 1672. (b) June 13th 1809. 180 × 122/275 × 195mm. 1st ed pl. 101. No V.

(4pp of text)

173 The Fortune Playhouse, Golden Lane – Site of the Theatre and the/Adjoining Avenues. Shepherd del. 1811. Wise sculp. (c) 7th Oct. 1811. 210 × 220,80 × 215/320 × 265mm. 1st ed pl. 102. No XI. Pencil and water-colour drawing (286 × 191mm), by George Shepherd, in Guildhall Library.

(2pp of text)

174 A South View of the Falcon Tavern, on the Bankside, Southwark; as it appeared in 1805:/celebrated for the daily resort of Shakespeare, and his Dramatic Companions./With a Plan of the Site and its Vicinity. F. Nash del. W. Wise sculp. (c) June 4th 1811. 155 × 205,125 × 230/320 × 265mm. 1st ed pl. 103. No IX.

175 South View of the Theatre Royal, in Portugal Street, Lincolns Inn Fields/Open'd in the year 1714, under the direction of the late John Rich Esqr.... /Now the Salopian China Warehouse. Shepherd Del. Wise sculp. (c) 7th Octr 1811. 220 × 300/260 × 320mm. 1st ed pl. 104. No XI. Water-colour (215 × 295mm) in Guildhall Library.

(2pp of text)

The Duke's Theatre, Dorset Gardens, Fleet Street

176 The Duke's Theatre,/Dorset Garden. From Elkannah Settles Empress of Morocco. (b) 13 June 1809, or (c) 4th June 1813. 200 × 155/310 × 215mm. 1st ed pl. 105. No V.

177 Inside of the Dukes Theatre/in Lincolns Inn Fields/as it appeared in the reign of King Charles II. Richd Sawyer sculpt. (b) 11 October 1809. 95 × 150/300 ×

210mm. 1st ed pl. 106. No VI. A scene from Settle's *Empress of Morocco*.

(4pp of text)

Theatre Royal, Drury Lane

178 Internal View of the Old Theatre Royal Drury Lane, as it appeared in 1792. Capon del. Howlett sculp. – North West View of the Theatre Royal Drury Lane, from Great Russell Street. Whichelo del. Howlett sculp. (c) 1st Jany 1814. 150 × 205,130 × 205/320 × 260mm. 1st ed pl. 107. No XVI.

179 The Theatre Royal, Drury Lane;/Built by the late Henry Holland Esqr. R.A./As it appeared from the North East; Antecedent to its destruction by Fire, on the Night of the 24th February, 1809. With a Plan. W. Capon Del. W. Wise sculp. (c) July 27th 1811. 155 × 203, 95 × 190/300 × 250mm. 1st ed pl. 108. No X.

180 Interior of the late Theatre Royal Drury Lane; Built by Henry Holland Esqr. R.A./... Opened ... 12th March 1794; Destroyed by Fire 24th February 1809. Dale sculp. (d) 27th Septr. 1820. 215 × 275/250 × 302mm.

181 Drury Lane Theatre,/taken from Westminster Bridge during the Conflagration on the Night of 24th February, 1809. Whichelo Del. Wise sculp. – The Ruins of the Theatre from Bridges Street, after the Fire. (c) August 7th 1811. 155 × 200,125 × 170/320 × 270mm. 1st ed pl. 209. No X.

(2pp of text)

Theatre Royal, Covent Garden

182 (tm) Rich's Glory or his Triumphant Entry into Covent-Garden. W.H. le Sculp. (c) 7 Oct. 1811. 170 × 305/215 × 220mm. 1st ed pl. 110. No XI. After a satirical print sometimes attributed to Hogarth.

183 Theatre Royal Covent Garden, as altered previous to the opening on 15th Sep. 1794. Destroyed by Fire Sepr 20th 1808. Engraved from an Original Drawing ... Springsguth sculp. – The Original Entrance from the Piazza to the late Covent Garden Theatre ... (d) 1st Jan. 1819. 190 × 240,100 × 90/325 × 275mm. 1st ed pl. 112.

184 E.N.E. View of Covent Garden Theatre from Bow Street. C.J. Whichet del. Wise sculp. – A Plan of/the Theatres of/Covent Garden & Drury Lane./with the/Adjacent Streets. (c) 11th Oct. 1813. 150 × 220,140 × 200/310 × 265mm. 1st ed pl. 111. No XV.

(2pp of text)

Theatre Royal Haymarket

185 Interior of the Little Theatre, Haymarket. Geo. Jones del. I. Stow sculp. – Front of the Above. (c) 1st Decr. 1815. 145 × 195,120 × 120/310 × 260mm. 1st ed pl. 113. Nos XXI–XXII. 'Built in 1720 by a carpenter, named Potter'; demolished 1820.

(2pp of text)

186 Interior of the New Theatre/Royal Hay Market,/as it

appeared on the Night of its opening 4th July 1821. Schnebbelie del. J. Stow sculp. (d) 1st January 1823. 240 × 220,60 × 110/318 × 260mm. Includes plan.

187 View of the New Theatre Royal Haymarket/Opened July 4th 1821/Shewing also the relative situation of the old theatre previous to its demolition. Schnebbelie del. Dale sculp. (d) 1st June, 1822. 220 × 290/260 × 325mm. Built by John Nash, 1820–1.

(1 leaf of text)

King's Theatre, Haymarket: the Opera House

188 Proscenium of the Opera House. G. Jones del. H. Cook sculp. – Entrance in the Haymarket. (d) 11th Octr. 1816. 170 × 195,110 × 120/360 × 250mm. 1st ed pl. 125.

189 The King's Theatre, Haymarket/This Theatre destroyed by Fire 17th June 1789, rebuilt by Michael Novosielski Esqr. in 1790–1 … /The present Elevation after a design by John Nash Esqr. was completed in 1819. Schnebbelie del. B. Howlett sculp. (d) 27th September, 1820. 195 × 265/250 × 330mm.

(4pp of text, dated 1825)

Theatre in Great Ayliffe Street, Goodman's Fields

190 S.E. View of the Theatre in Ayliff Street Goodmans Fields and its Environs./From a Drawing in the British Museum. Wise sc. – (plan of neighbourhood). (c) Oct. 11, 1813. 150 × 200,120 × 200/305 × 260mm. 1st ed pl. 114. No XV. Drawing, in India ink and water-colour (165 × 254mm), by William Capon, dated 6 October 1801, in BM (*Crace* 33.114). The theatre was burnt down in June 1802.

191 The Painted Celing the performance of William Oram, formerly over the Pit of the Old Theatre in Aliff Street/Goodman's Fields … /From the Original Drawing in the British Museum made by William Capon in 1786…. (d) 27th September 1820. 150 × 250/260 × 300mm.

192 Arena of he Royalty Theatre, Well Street, Wellclose Square: Built by John Palmer Esq. formerly of/the Theatre Royal, Drury Lane – Proscenium. C. Westmacott del. B. Howlett sculp. (c) 1st Decr. 1815. 145 × 202,120 × 140/300 × 265mm. 1st ed pl. 115. Nos XXI–XXII.

(2pp of text)

193 Remains/of/Gibbon's Tennis Court,/as it appeared after the Fire,/17 September, 1809./Used in 1660 as the first Theatre of the/Kings Company of Comedians,/until the erection of the Theatre Royal Drury Lane;/and in 1695, again opened by/Betterton's Company. (d) Feby 11 1811. 145 × 210, etc/305 × 250mm. 1st ed pl. 116. No VIII.

194 Interior of the Olympic Theatre near Drury Lane. Schnebbelie del. H. Cook sculp. – Exterior of the above Theatre. (d) 11th Octr. 1816. 170 × 220,100 × 160/320 × 235mm. 1st ed pl. 117. Signed sepia wash

drawings (180 × 220 and 95 × 150mm), dated 19 and 21 March 1816, in Guildhall Library.

(2pp of text)

195 South West View of Sadler's Wells,/from a Drawing by R.C. Andrews, 1792 – View of the Theatre in its former state. Wise sculp. (c) 4 June 1814. 193 × 280,60 × 160/260 × 320mm. 1st ed pl. 118. Nos XVII–XVIII. (Original painting, *Burlington Fine Arts Club Catalogue* 1919, 67)

(2pp of text)

196 Interior of the Pantheon Theatre – Proscenium. G. Jones del. Wise sculp. (c) 1 December 1815. 145 × 200,105 × 160/310 × 250mm. 1st ed pl. 119. Nos XXI–XXII. In Oxford Street.

(2pp of text)

197 Interior of the Sans Pareil Theatre. G. Jones del. S. Springsguth Junr. sculp. – Entrance in the Strand. (d) 11th Octr. 1816. 125 × 180,110 × 125/295 × 230mm. 1st ed pl. 120. The entrance was opposite the Adelphi in the Strand.

(2pp of text)

198 Arena of Astley's Amphitheatre, Surrey Road. Geo. Jones del. Wise sculp. – Front of the Above. (c) 1st Decr. 1815. 165 × 220,110 × 100/295 × 250mm. 1st ed pl. 121. Nos XXI–XXII.

199 Interior of the Regency Theatre, Tottenham Street, Tottenham Court Road./Built on the Site of the Kings Concert Rooms. Schnebbelie delt. Cook sculpt. – Exterior of the Above Theatre. (d) 11 October 1817. 270 × 220,95 × 145/320 × 260mm. 1st ed pl. 122.

(2pp of text)

Royal Cobourg (Victoria) Theatre, Waterloo Bridge Road

200 Royal Cobourg Theatre, Surry. Schnebbelie del. Dale sculp. (d) 1st January 1819. 195 × 260,45 × 90/250 × 320mm. 1st ed pl. 123. In Waterloo Bridge Road, opened May 1818.

201 Royal Cobourg/Theatre Surry/as first opened 11 May, 1818. Schnebbelie del. Stow sculp. (d) 1, January 1819. 195 × 260, etc/250 × 325mm. 1st ed pl. 124. In lm shield and crests of Prince Leopold of Saxe-Cobourg.

(2pp of text)

202 North East View of/the Surrey Theatre,/formerly/The Royal Circus/near the Obelisk. Great Surrey Street – (plan of neighbourhood) Shepherd del. Wise sculpt. (c) 1st May 1814. 200 × 310,40 × 130/270 × 330mm. 1st ed pl. 126.

(2pp of text, dated 1819)

203 The Proscenium of the English Opera House in the Strand, (Late Lyceum.) – Front Boxes and Gallery. E. Burney Pinxt. J. Stow sct. (d) 11 October 1817. 170 × 165,110 × 90/330 × 255mm. 1st ed pl. 127 and last.

(2pp of text, dated 1819)

204 Theatre in Tankard Street Ipswich where Garrick made his first public appearance, 21st July 1711. Dale sculp. (d) 25th March 1821. 165 × 240/250 × 305mm.

(2pp of text)

205 Elevation of the Theatre Royal, Liverpool./Engraved from the Original Drawing (same size) by Robert Chaffers, taken 12th May 1773 ... by Taylor. 280 × 253/330 × 280mm.

206 (tm) Checks and Tickets of Admission to the Public Theatres and other Places of Amusement.... Engraved by J. Stow. (d) 1st June 1822. 320 × 255mm.

(1 leaf of text)

132 · PYNE'S ROYAL RESIDENCES [1819]

William Henry Pyne, the son of a Holborn leatherseller, was trained as an artist in the drawing-school of Henry Pars and in 1790 started showing tinted landscape drawings at the Royal Academy. He published a work in Parts, from 1803, entitled *Microcosm, or Picturesque Delineation*, for which he drew and etched 1000 small groups of figures, aquatinted by Hill, for use as landscape staffage. He also produced a number of drawing textbooks or copybooks. In 1808 *Costume of Great Britain*, with his own illustrations, was published and in the same year he was engaged by Ackermann to write the text of *Microcosm of London* (no 99), although he had no hand in its famous illustrations. Nevertheless their success must have given him the idea of himself both writing and publishing a similar picture-book of architectural interiors and exteriors and issuing it in Numbers.

The first Number of his *History of the Royal Residences* appeared in June 1816 with plates of apartments in Kensington Palace, Windsor Castle, St James's Palace and Hampton Court. The text was a medley of national and royal history, architectural description, a survey of interior decoration room by room and a detailed account of the oil paintings and other art objects which furnished them.

Three more Numbers were published bi-monthly in 1816 and six Numbers each in 1817 and 1818, also bi-monthly, on the first day of February, April,

June, August, October and December. In 1819 the frequency increased to monthly, with the last of the illustrated Numbers dated 1 September, well ahead of schedule. It is apparent from the brown paper wrappers to Nos 13–24, bound in with the copy *Abbey* 396, that these Numbers, which included a portion of text and four coloured plates, were sold at a guinea each, or twice as much as the *Microcosm* Numbers. But Pyne, unlike Ackermann, was not able to spread his overheads and risks over several similar publications and by the seventeenth Number had run into financial difficulties of which he reminded the Prince Regent in the advertisement published with the other preliminaries in the final Number:

The author of The History of the Royal Residences feels it incumbent to state, that the pledge which was given to his Royal Highness the Prince Regent, that the work should be completed strictly to the letter of the prospectus, he has redeemed to the extent of his abilities, and, happily, to the satisfaction of his patrons: for although an expense of some thousand pounds above the estimate has been incurred, and many unforeseen impediments have been superadded to the arduous difficulties attending its progress, yet it has been brought to a termination nearly twelve months within the period prescribed.

During the last year of publication the name of 'A.Dry' alternated with his own in publication-lines. This association apparently enabled the work itself to be completed but no more was heard of the 'Second Series, of Interior Views of the most magnificent seats of the Nobility and Gentry through Great Britain', a sequel announced by Pyne in the first Number of the *Royal Residences*.

A set of all 25 Numbers in their original wrappers is preserved in the Arents Collection of Books in Parts in the New York Public Library, a great rarity since the wrappings were usually discarded when the wealthy subscribers had the work sumptuously bound in leather. According to the spine labels on a cloth-bound copy (*Abbey* 397) the work with the plates uncoloured was available at 15 guineas the three volumes. The cataloguer surmises that this was a copy remaindered by Messrs Bohn in the 1830s as they specialized in remarketing dead stocks of colour-plate books.

The History of the Royal Residences of Windsor Castle, St James's Palace, Carlton House, Kensington Palace, Hampton Court, Buckingham House, and Frogmore, by W.H. Pyne. Illustrated by one hundred highly finished and coloured engravings, Fac=Similes of original drawings by the most eminent artists. In Three Volumes. Vol. I (II–III). London: Printed for A. Dry, 36 Upper Charlotte Street, Fitzroy Square; and sold by the principal booksellers in the United Kingdom. L. Harrison, Printer, 373 Strand. M.DCCC.XIX.

Quarto, 355–410 × 290–320mm.   1819

COLLATION Vol. 1. Title-page; dedication to the Queen Consort dated June 1817 (1 leaf); advertisement (2pp); half-title; pp 1–188, Windsor Castle; half-title; pp 1–21, Frogmore. Vol. 2. Title-page; dedication to the Prince Regent dated June 1818 (1 leaf); half-title; pp 1–88, Hampton Court; half-title; pp 1–28, Buckingham House; half-title; pp 1–88, Kensington Palace. Vol. 3. Title-page; dedication to the Duke of York dated June 1819 (1 leaf); pp 1–80, St James's Palace; half-title; pp 1–92, Carlton House- pp 1–13, list of portraits in royal collections; directions to binder (2pp).

This set of plates could not hope to equal in popularity Ackermann's *Microcosm* since there could only be a limited public for a series consisting chiefly of well-upholstered palace interiors peopled only by the occasional decorous gentlemen or lady in waiting, or obsequious flunkeys and innumerable oil paintings—a far cry from Rowlandson's Billingsgate fishwives, Covent Garden bully-boys and St James's macaronis. It was issued in approximately the same number of Parts and with the same tally of plates but, because it was intended to appeal to court circles and the wealthy bourgeoisie, at twice the price. Its interest today lies in its careful drawing of vanished or altered interiors and furnishings and objects of art since dispersed, particularly of Buckingham Palace apartments before Nash's alterations of 1825 and Carlton House before its demolition in 1827–8 to make room for Nash's terrace.

While the *Microcosm* stemmed from the collaboration of two artists, the 100 plates of *Royal Residences* were mostly drawn by Charles Wild and James Stephanoff severally, with minor contributions from Richard Cattermole and William Westall and a frontispiece of Windsor Castle by the esteemed topographical painter George Samuel. Charles Wild, with the lion's share of 59 drawings, was a pupil of Thomas Malton. He first exhibited at the Royal Academy in 1803, specializing in drawings of French and English cathedrals, some of which were published as handsome coloured aquatints between 1807 and 1830. He became a member of the Old Water Colour Society in 1812 and its Secretary in 1822. James Stephanoff, with 25 contributions,

was born in England, son of an émigré Russian portrait painter, and trained at the Royal Academy Schools, exhibiting at the Academy and at the Old Water Colour Society over a period of nearly 50 years. This work established him as something of a court artist for he was commissioned, with his brother Francis, to provide the aquatint illustrations to Sir George Nayler's record of George IV's coronation (no 232; begun in 1823, the original paintings preserved in the Victoria and Albert Museum) and was later appointed 'historical painter in water colours' to William IV. Richard Cattermole, who provided nine drawings, was a contributor with his more celebrated younger brother George to John Britton's *Cathedral Antiquities* (from 1814) but later abandoned art, obtained his BD at Cambridge and became vicar of Little Marlow. The remaining half dozen plates were drawn by William Westall, brother of the historical painter Richard Westall, who in the earlier years of the century had an adventurous career, first as official draughtsman to Matthew Flinders's ill-fated voyage of exploration to Australia and then in sketching expeditions to Canton, Bombay and the Mahratta mountains. He also became an Associate to the Old Water Colour Society in 1810 and of the Royal Academy in 1812. In 1816 a number of his views were published in Ackermann's *History of the Colleges* (no 116) and many more, on the Thames and in the environs of London, were engraved in the following decade.

Pyne's chief engraver was Thomas Sutherland (36 plates) who had already proved his worth in the 33 aquatint plates he engraved for Ackermann's *Microcosm* and *Westminster Abbey* (no 108). He also employed three other Ackermann engravers: R.G. Reeve (28 plates), W.J. Bennett, a pupil of Westall's (23 plates), and Daniel Havell, of the family of engravers (11 plates), the remaining two plates being aquatinted by J. Baily.

As in Ackermann publications after the application of aquatint the plates were coloured individually by hand. To save on colourists' time, however, some of the plates showing outdoor views were printed in two colours, brown for foreground and buildings and blue for the sky; with a magnifying glass the blue reticulations can easily be distinguished from the normal greyish or brownish aquatint. The washes, on the whole, are less limpid than those applied to the *Microcosm* plates, body colour being sometimes used to suggest the rich tones of mahogany, gold carving, silk and velvet hangings, deep carpeting and oil paint with which the interiors abound. Captions are engraved in a mixture of copperplate script and voided capitals. The plates themselves are unnumbered but the last volume contains a 'List of Plates Which are to be placed according to their Titles and Pages' and the instruction to the binder that 'the pages of each separate Palace must be observed as the order for binding, and no regard paid to the signatures', leaving no ambiguity either as to correct order or placing.

Three alternative publicaton-lines referred to read:

(a) '(London) Pub. (rarely Pubd.) by W.H. Pyne, 9 Nassau Street, Soho'. (February 1816 to December 1818)

(b) '(London) Pub. (rarely Pubd.) by W.H. Pyne, 36 Upper Charlotte Street, Fitzroy Square'. (February to June and August 1819, except for pl.17)

(c) '(London) Pub. by A. Dry, 36 Upper Charlotte Street, Fitzroy Square'. (December 1818, June to September 1819)

VOL. 1

The History of the Royal Palace of Windsor

1 front. North Front of Windsor Castle. G. Samuel delt. T. Sutherland sculp. (b) Feb. 1. 1819. 160 × 275/270 × 320mm.

2 p 14 Ancient Kitchen/Windsor Castle. Drawn by J.P. Stephanoff. Engraved by W.J. Bennett. (a) Feby 1. 1818. 210 × 272/258 × 320mm.

3 p 35 Ancient Bell Tower/Windsor Castle. R. Cattermole delt. R. Reeve sculpt. (a) Augt 1. 1818. 245 × 210/320 × 260mm.

4 p 83 The Upper Ward/Windsor Castle. C. Wild delt. T. Sutherland sculpt. (b) April 1. 1819. 200 × 252/260 × 320mm.

5 p 87 Staircase/Windsor Castle. C. Wild delt. W.J. Bennett sculpt. (a) April 1. 1818. 200 × 250/280 × 315mm.

6 p 88 Queen's Guard Chamber/Windsor Castle. Drawn by C. Wild. Engraved by T. Sutherland. (a) Feby 1. 1817. 200 × 250/258 × 310mm.

7 p 90 The Queen's Presence Chamber/Windsor Castle. Drawn by C. Wild. Engraved by J. Bennett. (a) April 1. 1817. 203 × 250/275 × 320mm.

8 p 93 Queen's Audience Chamber/Windsor Castle. Drawn by C. Wild. Engraved by W.J. Bennett. (a) Feby 1. 1818. 210 × 250/270 × 320mm.

9 p 99 Ball Room/Windsor Castle. Drawn by C. Wild. Engraved by Sutherland. (a) Feby 1. 1817. 198 × 250/260 × 320mm.

10 p 106 The Queen's Drawing Room Windsor Castle. Drawn by C. Wild. Engraved by T. Sutherland. (a) Aug 1. 1816. 202 × 253/250 × 300mm.

11 p 116 Queen's State Bedchamber/Windsor Castle. J. Stephanoff del. J. Baily sculp. (a) April 1. 1818. 205 × 255/260 × 320mm.

12 p 135 The King's Closet/Windsor Castle. Drawn by C. Wild. Engraved by W.J. Bennett. (a) Oct 1. 1816. 200 × 255/270 × 320mm.

13 p 147 The King's Dressing Room/Windsor Castle. Drawn by C. Wild. Engraved by W.I. Bennett. (a) Oct 1. 1816. 205 × 250/260 × 320mm.

14 p 152 The King's Old State Bed Chamber/Windsor Castle. Drawn by C. Wild. Engraved by T. Sutherland. (a) June 4. 1816. 202 × 253/240 × 300mm.

15 p 155 The King's Drawing Room/Windsor Castle. J. Stephanoff delt. T. Sutherland sculpt. (a) Decr 1. 1817. 190 × 255/255 × 320mm.

16 p 161 Queen Ann's Bed/Windsor Castle. Drawn by C. Wild. Engraved by T. Sutherland. (a) April 1. 1816. 250 × 200/302 × 240mm.

17 p 166 The King's Audience Chamber/Windsor Castle. C. Wild delt. T. Sutherland sculpt. (b) Feb.1. 1818. 205 × 252/255 × 320mm.

18 p 170 King's Presence Chamber/Windsor Castle. J. Stephanoff delt. W.J. Bennett sculpt. (a) April 1 1818. 203 × 250/255 × 315mm.

19 p 172 King's Guard Chamber/Windsor Castle. C. Wild delt. T. Sutherland sculpt. (a) Feby 1. 1818. 200 × 253/260 × 320mm.

20 p 176 St Georges Hall/Windsor Castle. Drawn by C. Wild. Engraved by W.I. Bennett. (a) Dec 1st. 1816. 202 × 253/260 × 322mm.

21 p 179 The Royal Chapel/Windsor Castle. C. Wild delt. T. Sutherland sculpt. (a) June 1. 1818. 205 × 255/260 × 320mm.

22 p 182 Choir of St Georges Chapel/Windsor Castle. C. Wild delt. T. Sutherland sculpt. (a) Dec 1. 1818. 250 × 220/310 × 260mm. Looking E.

23 p 183 St Georges Chapel/from the Altar/Windsor Castle. C. Wild delt. T. Sutherland sculpt. (c) June 1. 1819. 253 × 202/320 × 260mm.

24 p 187 Ancient Staircase/Round Tower/Windsor Castle. J. Stephanoff delt. R. Reeve sculpt. (c) Decr. 1. 1818. 260 × 220/315 × 255mm.

25 p 188 Old Guard Chamber/Round Tower/Windsor Castle. Drawn by James Stephanoff. Engraved by T. Sutherland. (a) Feby 1. 1818. 208 × 250/255 × 320mm.

The History of the Queens House of Frogmore

26 p 1 Frogmore. C. Wild delt. W.J. Bennett sculpt. (c)

59 p 46 Queen Caroline's Drawing Room/Kensington Palace. Drawn by C. Wild. Engraved by T. Sutherland. (a) Aug. 1. 1816. 203 × 250/260 × 302mm.

60 p 53 The Admiral's Gallery/Kensington Palace. J. Stephanoff delt. D. Havell sculpt. (a) April 1. 1817. 200 × 250/270 × 320mm.

61 p 56 Old Dining Room/Kensington Palace. J. Stephanoff delt. T. Sutherland sculpt. (a) Octr. 1. 1818. 195 × 260/250 × 305mm.

62 p 63 The Queen's Closet/Kensington Palace. J. Stephanoff delt. W.J. Bennett sculpt. (a) Decr 1. 1817. 255 × 205/320 × 270mm.

63 p 67 The Queen's Gallery/Kensington Palace. J. Stephanoff delt. T. Sutherland sculpt. (c) Sep. 1. 1819. 193 × 252/255 × 320mm.

64 p 72 The Cupola Room/Kensington Palace. Drawn by R. Cattermole. Engraved by T. Sutherland. (a) April 1. 1817. 205 × 252/260 × 320mm.

65 p 74 The King's Great Drawing Room Kensington Palace. Drawn by C. Wild. Engraved by W.J. Bennett. (a) Feb. 1. 1816. 205 × 250/260 × 320mm.

66 p 78 The King's Gallery/Kensington Palace. Drawn by C. Wild. Engraved by T. Sutherland. (a) Oct 1. 1816. 200 × 253/260 × 320mm.

67 p 83 The Queen's Bed Chamber/Kensington Palace. R. Cattermole delt. W.J. Bennett sculp. (a) Aug. 1. 1818. 205 × 260/258 × 320mm.

68 p 85 The King's Closet/Kensington Palace. J. Stephanoff delt. R. Reeve sculpt. (b) March 1. 1819. 200 × 250/255 × 315mm.

VOL. 3

The History of the Royal Palace of St James's

69 front. St James's Palace. C. Wild delt. R. Reeve sculpt. (c) July 1. 1819. 195 × 258/240 × 305mm. Gatehouse from Pall Mall. Wild's painting of this subject, of the same dimensions, in V & A (AL 8532).

70 p 9 Guard Chamber/St James's. C. Wild delt. R. Reeve sculpt. (a) June 1. 1818. 202 × 252/255 × 315mm.

71 p 10 The King's Presence Chamber/St James's. Drawn by C. Wild. Engraved by T. Sutherland. (a) April 1. 1816. 202 × 250/252 × 300mm.

72 p 15 The Queen's Levee Room/St James's. Drawn by C. Wild. Engraved by W.J. Bennett. (a) Aug 1. 1816. 203 × 255/260 × 320mm.

73 p 33 Old Bed Chamber/St James's/In which was born the son of James II. C. Wild delt. R. Reeve sculpt. (c) Septr 1. 1819. 200 × 252/255 × 320mm.

74 p 39 The German Chapel/St James's Palace. C. Wild delt. Engraved by D.L. Havell. (a) Aug 1. 1816. 255 × 205/300 × 240mm.

75 p 43 Kitchen/St James's Palace. J. Stephanoff delt. W.J. Bennett sculpt. (b) April 1. 1819. 208 × 255/255 × 315mm.

76 The Queen's Library/St James's. C. Wild delt. R. Reeve sculpt. (b) June 1. 1819. 198 × 255/240 × 300mm. Pencil sketch (195 × 245mm) in Westminster Public Library.

The History of the Royal Residence of Carlton House

77 front. Carlton House/South Front. W. Westall A.R.A. delt. R. Reeve sculpt. (b) April 1. 1819. 195 × 255/240 × 300mm. Refaced by Henry Flitcroft, c 1733.

78 p 12 Carlton House/North Front. W. Westall A.R.A. delt. R. Reeve sculpt. (b) April 1. 1819. 202 × 255/255 × 315mm. Henry Holland added the Corinthian portico and Ionic screen and remodelled the interior, 1783–5.

79 p 13 The Hall of Entrance/Carlton House. C. Wild delt. R. Reeve sculpt. (b) March 1. 1819. 202 × 255/255 × 310mm.

80 p 15 The Vestibule/Carlton House. C. Wild delt. R. Reeve sculpt. (b) April 1. 1819. 210 × 255/255 × 310mm.

81 p 16 Grand Stair-case/Carlton House. C. Wild delt. J. Reeve sculpt. (b) 315 × 255/320 × 255mm. nd.

82 p 16 Gallery of the Staircase/Carlton House. C. Wild delt. T. Sutherland sculpt. (b) May 1. 1819. 195 × 250/255 × 310mm.

83 p 17 The West Ante Room/Carlton House. C. Wild delt. R. Reeve sculpt. (b) April 1. 1819. 202 × 253/260 × 320mm.

84 p 20 Crimson Drawing Room/Carlton House. Drawn by C. Wild. Engraved by T. Sutherland. (a) Oct 1. 1816. 205 × 258/260 × 320mm.

85 p 24 The Circular Room/Carlton House. Drawn by C. Wild. Engraved by T. Sutherland. (a) June 1. 1817. 200 × 255/270 × 320mm.

86 p 25 The Throne Room/Carlton House. C. Wild delt. T. Sutherland sculpt. (a) Oct 1. 1818. 205 × 255/250 × 315mm.

87 p 28 Ante Chamber/leading to the Throne Room/Carlton House. Drawn by C. Wild. Engraved by T. Sutherland. (a) Decr 1. 1816. 202 × 255/260 × 320mm.

88 p 31 The Rose Satin Drawing Room/Carlton House. C. Wild delt. D. Havell sculpt. (a) Decr. 1. 1817. 202 × 270/260 × 320mm.

89 p 32 Rose Satin Drawing Room/Second View/Carlton House. C. Wild delt. R. Reeve sculpt. (a) Dec 1. 1818. 202 × 250/255 × 320mm.

90 Ante Room/Carlton House. Drawn by C. Wild. Engraved by T. Sutherland. (a) Oct 1. 1817. 202 × 250/260 × 320mm.

91 p 43 Ante Room/Looking North/Carlton House. C. Wild delt. W.J. Bennett sculpt. (a) Oct 1. 1818. 202 × 250/265 × 310mm.

92 p 45 The Blue Velvet Room/Carlton House. Drawn by C. Wild. Engraved by D. Havell. (a) Oct 1. 1816. 205 × 250/270 × 320mm.

93 p 48 The Blue Velvet Closet/Carlton House. C. Wild delt. R. Reeve sculpt.(a) Aug 1. 1818. 202 × 252/255 × 315mm.

94 p 52 The Lower Vestibule/Carlton House. C. Wild delt. R. Reeve sculpt. (b) April 1. 1819. 195 × 250/260 × 315mm.

95 p 58 The Golden Drawing Room/Carlton House. Drawn by C. Wild. Engraved by T. Sutherland. (a) June 1. 1817. 195 × 255/270 × 320mm. Designed by John Nash, 1813–14.

96 p 60 The Alcove/Golden Drawing Room/Carlton House. C. Wild delt. W.J. Bennett sc. (a) June 1. 1817. 252 × 200/320 × 270mm.

97 p 63 Gothic Drawing Room/Carlton House. Drawn by C. Wild. Engraved by T. Sutherland. (a) Augt 1. 1817. 192 × 262/270 × 318mm. Designed by John Nash, 1813–14.

98 p 80 Dining Room/Carlton House. Drawn by C. Wild. Engraved by T. Sutherland. (a) Octr. 1. 1817. 200 × 255/255 × 320mm. Designed by John Nash, 1813–14.

99 p 84 The Conservatory/Carlton House. C. Wild delt. T. Sutherland sculpt. (a) Aug. 1. 1817. 255 × 205/320 × 268mm. Designed by Thomas Hopper, 1807.

100 p 88 Conservatory/(Second View)/Carlton House. C. Wild delt. R. Reeve sculpt. (b) March 1. 1819. 252 × 202/315 × 265mm.

133 · HAVELL'S VIEWS OF THE PUBLIC BUILDINGS AND BRIDGES [1820–1]

The full ramifications of the remarkable Havell family of artists and engravers have yet to be clarified but the 'Robert and Son' in the imprint of this book were, respectively, son and grandson of Daniel Havell. Robert senior at first worked with his father and later set up an establishment of his own at the Zoological Gallery opposite the Pantheon in Oxford Street, where he published works of art and sold natural history specimens. This father-son partnership produced an attractive album of topographical prints aquatinted from the drawings of the most talented member of the family, William, a cousin who later spent many years in China and India. Although entitled *Series of Picturesque Views of the River Thames* (1812), it contained only views up-river from Windsor. William's father was a drawing-master at Reading and three of his brothers also engaged in artistic careers: Edmund, Frederick James, who specialized in architecture and engraved for *Illustrations of the Public Buildings of London* (no 146) and *Metropolitan Improvements* (no 154), and George, an animal painter and engraver who may possibly be the 'G. Havell, Printer' of the imprint of this book. Robert Havell junior was a landscape painter and engraver and worked as partner in his father's business which produced the illustrations for a number of works of travel and topography such as Audubon's *Birds of America*, Daniell's *Views in India*, Dodswell's *Views in Greece* and Salt's *Views in Africa*. It also published such curiosities as a three-foot 'Aeronautical View of London and the surrounding Country' (*Crace* 36.1) and a 'Geometrical Elevation of the West Front of the Cathedral of St Paul, compared with St Peter's, Rome, the Cathedrals of Salisbury and Norwich, and the Great Pyramid of Egypt' (*Crace* 19.174), both dated 1831.

This *Series of Views of the Public Buildings and Bridges*, which were apparently both drawn and engraved by the Roberts, father and son, and published by them jointly with Colnaghi's, was succeeded in 1823 by a *Series of Picturesque Views of Noblemen's & Gentlemen's Seats* (no 141) in which the drawings were by various well-known names, including William Havell, but the engraving was all carried out by the publishing firm. In 1828 the partnership was dissolved and Robert junior emigrated to America to set up as a painter of landscapes.

Abbey (no 220) copy

Series of Views of the Public Buildings and Bridges in London and its Environs, from drawings taken on the spot by R. Havell, Jun. London: Published by Messrs. Colnaghi and Co., Cockspur Street and R. Havell and Son, Chapel Street, Tottenham Court Road. G. Havell, Printer, Tottenham Court Road.

Oblong folio, 340 × 500mm. (1820–1)

COLLATION Title-page; 12 plates. (Bound up without the three sheets of description found in the Guildhall copy and with a variant tile-page; an earlier watermark, 'J. Whatman 1818', is recorded, the earliest in the Guildhall copy being '1820'.)

Guildhall copy

Series of Views of the Public Buildings and Bridges in London and its environs from drawings taken on the spot by R. Havell, Jun. London: Printed for Rodwell and Martin, 46 New Bond Street. (verso) G. Havell, Printer, Chapel Street, Tottenham Court Road.

Oblong folio, 335 × 475mm.   (1820–1)

COLLATION Title-page; 12 plates; 3 sheets of descriptions, printed on rectos only and watermarked 'J. Whatman 1821'.

This is a rare collection and most of the edition must have been sold in unbound plates: all but two of them are distributed among the portfolios of the Crace Collection and five were still forthcoming to illustrate the 'Marx' Pennant (no 67). Their chief attractions are the delicate aquatint engraving and the water-colour washes varying in intensity from pale greys, and blues for skies, stonework and river to dashes of vivid colour highlighting the staffage of folk, river craft and coaches and the foliage. Daniel was sometimes employed on Ackermann aquatints and the Havells recruited similar, if not the same, colourists as those employed at the famous Repository at 101 Strand; an example of the extra charge for this colouring is the 42s per 100 they asked for tinting plates of Daniell's *Voyage to India*. Robert Havell junior's topographical drawing is tolerable but his figures have the stuffed look of the arrested strollers on a seaside postcard. Indeed the Havells obtained happier results when they were engraving from the work of more talented draughtsmen and were most adept at producing large plates without coarsening the grain. Such were the 1813 'View of Charterhouse' by T. Ward, measuring 305 × 445mm (BL Maps: *K. top.* 25.9b), and the panoramic river view from near Waterloo Bridge by T.S. Roberts published by Boydell in 1817 and measuring 430 × 610mm (BL Maps: *K. top.* 21.57,7).

Captions in English and French are separated by a double vertical rule. The credit 'Drawn & Engraved by Robt Havell & Son' is engraved between the base of each view and the frame-line. The publication-line is invariable apart from the date: 'London, Published (date) by Messrs. Colnaghi & Co. Cockspur Street.' Plate numbers are engraved tr. Measurements are firstly of the view, then of the engraved frame and lastly of the plate-mark. Plates in the Guildhall copy are inlaid in larger paper which ranges with the text sheets.

1 A View of London Bridge and Custom House/with the Margate Steam Yachts. July 6, 1820. 205 × 305,225 × 325/270 × 360mm.

2 A View of London Taken from Greenwich Park. Octr. 1, 1820. 210 × 320,225 × 340/265 × 360mm.

3 A View of Southwark Bridge. July 6, 1820. 200 × 305,225 × 325/265 × 360mm. Built by John Rennie, 1815–19.

4 A View of Blackfriar's Bridge & St. Pauls. August 1 1820. 200 × 305,220 × 325/265 × 360mm.

5 View of Waterloo Bridge. Octr 1, 1820. 200 × 310,220 × 325/265 × 365mm. Built by John Rennie, 1811–17.

6 A View of Westminster Bridge and Lambeth Palace. August 1, 1820. 205 × 312,220 × 330/265 × 360mm.

7 View of the Horse Guards & Melbourne House,/taken from St James's Park. Feby 1, 1821. 202 × 300,223 × 320/270 × 370mm.

8 View of Vauxhall Bridge. Feby 1, 1821. 200 × 305,220 × 320/265 × 360mm. Built to the designs of James Walker, civil engineer, 1811–16.

9 View of Somerset House. June 22, 1821. 200 × 305,220 × 325/265 × 370mm. Incomplete as to the E. and W. wings.

10 View of the Tower of London and the Mint. June 1821. 200 × 328,220 × 348/265 × 385mm.

11 View of Westminster Abbey & St Margaret's Church. nd. 200 × 305,220 × 325/265 × 360mm. From N.W.

12 View of the House of Lords and Commons/From Old Palace Yard. nd. 205 × 305,220 × 320/265 × 365mm.

---

134 · PICTURE OF LONDON [1820]

The earlier history of this guidebook is related in connection with the first edition of 1802 (no 85). Longman & Co, having acquired the copyright in 1812, continued between 1813 and 1819 to churn out annually much the same fare, illustrated only by a frontispiece and a small handful of very slightly variable maps and plans. Because of this 'laisser-faire' policy sales must have declined and in the advertisement prefixed to the 1820 edition they declared: 'Flattered by public encouragement and determined to render this volume in every respect worthy of the favour and preference of the public, the proprietors have embellished this Edition with One Hundred and Twenty Engravings by Greig, representing the principal Buildings, and most striking Public Places in and near the Metropolis'. In 1818 the price had risen from 6s 6d to nine shillings and now the illustrations were being thrown in as an added attraction. In the following year, 1821, the public were given the choice of an illustrated edition at nine shillings or an unillustrated 6s edition.

The Picture of London for 1820; being a Correct Guide to all the Curiosities, Amusements, Exhibitions, Public Establishments, and Remarkable Objects, in and near London. With a Collection of Appropriate Tables, illustrated by Two Large Maps, and embellished with One Hundred and Twenty Views. The Twenty-First Edition. London: Printed for Longman, Hurst, Rees, Orme and Brown, Paternoster-Row; and sold by all Booksellers; and at the Bars of all the principal Inns and Coffeehouses. (Price 9s, Bound).

Duodecimo, 143 × 85mm.   1820

COLLATION Title-page; advertisement (1 leaf); pp v–x, contents; pp 1–430, Picture of London; pp 431–8, map refs, etc.

The miniature views, four to a plate, were certainly inspired by the even smaller thumbnail engravings with which, in 1818, a rival publication, *Leigh's New Picture of London* (no 126), also priced at nine shillings, had been illustrated. John Greig, the maker of the plates, was a well-established engraver who had combined with James Storer in an important series of London views (no 90) and in Herbert's *Inns of Court* (no 88) at the beginning of the century. He contributed to the *Beauties of England and Wales* (no 104) and many other topographical books and periodicals and was also chief engraver to Hughson's *Walks through London* (no 121) which contains vignetted views little larger than these. He depicts in his miniatures all the usual public buildings, churches and bridges but, more originally, also includes Lilliputian panoramas of such places as Grosvenor and Cavendish Squares, Tower Hill and Charterhouse where, in an oblong the size of a letterhead, he somehow contrives a sense of spaciousness.

From p 89 onwards the text describes remarkable buildings, bridges, hospitals, charities, prisons and so on, and the plates are bound as near to their four subjects as possible. The title-page estimate of 120 Greig views is an exaggeration; there are 100 together with an engraved title, frontispiece, plan and maps. None of the Greig plates has a credit or publication-line and the plates are unnumbered and unlisted.

1 (engr title) The/Picture/of/London/1820 (vignette)

Hyde Park Corner, London/Publish'd by Longman, Hurst, Rees, Orme and Brown/Paternoster Row. 40 × 70 mm.

2 front. (tm) The Strand Bridge, finished in 1816. Published Nov. 28 1816 by Longman, Hurst, Rees, Orme and Brown, London. J. Le Keux. 100 × 165mm. With four identifications of landmarks in lm.

3 p 1 (tm) A Panorama of the Curiosities of London. 112 × 215mm. Sketch map of sites, with 43 refs l. and r. A feature of the guidebook since 1813.

4 p 99 Westminster Hall – Courts of Law, Westminster Hall – House of Lords – House of Commons. 53 × 33,53 × 33, 27 × 67,27 × 67mm.

5 p 116 White Hall, Parliament Street – Horse Guards – Admiralty – Treasury. Each 27 × 70mm.

6 p 122 British Museum – St. James's Palace – Lansdown House – Earl Spencer's House. Each 53 × 35mm.

7 p 130 Cavendish Square – Covent Garden Theatre – Grosvenor Square – Waterloo Place. Each 27 × 68mm.

8 p 133 Somerset House – N. Porch Westmr. Abbey – West Towers Westmr. Abbey – St. Paul's Cathedral. Each 55 × 35mm. Strand view of Somerset House, W. front of St Paul's.

9 p 140 The Tower – Auction Mart – Interior of the Bank – The Bank. Each 27 × 68mm. First view from Tower Hill. (*Bank of England* 131,44)

10 p 153 Mansion House – Royal Exchange – Guild Hall – Monument. Each 54 × 33mm.

11 p 173 Entrance to the London Docks – Excise Office – Mint – Trinity House. 53 × 33,53 × 33, 27 × 70,27 × 70mm.

12 p 176 London Institution – Ironmongers Hall – Fishmongers Hall – Goldsmiths Hall. Each 27 × 65mm.

13 p 178 Pagoda, St James's Park – St Paul's Church Covent Garden – Greenwich Hospital – Opera House. Each 27 × 70mm. The pagoda, surmounting the bridge built by Nash over the canal for the 1814 peace celebrations, was nearing its end; he was instructed to design a new iron bridge in 1820.

14 p 180 St. George's Church Bloomsbury – St. George's Church Hanover Square – St. Magnus Church London Bridge – St. Leonards Church Shoreditch. Each 52 × 34mm.

15 p 182 Bow Church – Mary-le-bone Church – The New Church, Strand – St. Martin's Church. Each 53 × 33mm. ie St. Mary le Bow, St Marylebone New Church built by Thomas Hardwick, 1813–17, St Mary le Strand and St Martin in the Fields.

16 p 187 Southwark Bridge – Blackfryars Bridge – London Bridge – Sessions House Clerkenwell. Each 27 × 67mm. Rennie's iron Southwark Bridge, built 1815–19.

17 p 190 Vauxhall Bridge – Westminster Bridge – Waterloo Bridge – Christ's Hospital. Each 27 × 70mm. Vauxhall Bridge opened June 1816, Waterloo Bridge opened June 1817.

18 p 199 Chapel to the Philanthropic – Guy's Hospital – St. Luke's Hospital – Bartholomew Hospital. Each 27 × 68mm.

19 p 208 Magdalen Hospital – Foundling Hospital – New Bethlehem Hospital St. George' Fields – Deaf & Dumb Asylum. Each 27 × 70mm. The Deaf and Dumb Asylum in the Old Kent Road was enlarged in 1819.

20 p 219 Newgate – House of Correction Cold Bath Fields – White Cross Compter – London Hospital. Each 27 × 67mm.

21 p 225 Entrance to the Fleet Prison – Session House Old Bailey – Kings Bench Prison – Chapel to the Charterhouse. 52 × 34, 52 × 34, 27 × 68, 27 × 68mm.

22 p 239 St. Margarets Church & Westmr. Abbey – Somerset House from the Thames – Adelphi – Henry 7th. Chapel. Each 27 × 67mm. The Chapel from the N.

23 p 252 Bullock's Museum – Surgeon's Hall – Drury Lane Theatre – Charing Cross. Each 50 × 32mm. The Museum, in the Egyptian Hall, Piccadilly, was dispersed in 1819. 'Charing Cross' shows the Charles I statue.

24 p 366 Entrance to Westminster School – Temple Bar – Foreign Office – Highgate Archway. Each 52 × 33mm. The first view is the entrance to 'School' or 'Monos'. Archway Road was formally opened in 1813.

25 p 371 Hampton Court Palace – Royal Military Academy, Woolwich – Royal Military Asylum Chelsea – Pultney Hotel. Each 27 × 67mm. (*Longford* 389)

26 p 375 Windsor Castle – Holland House – Eton College – The Cobourg Theatre. Each 26 × 65mm. The Cobourg Theatre, built by Rudolph Cabanel, was opened in May 1818.

27 p 377 Kensington Palace – Royal Artillery Barracks, Woolwich – Chelsea Hospital – Kew Palace. Each 27 × 68mm. (*Longford* 36)

28 p 384 West India Docks – Tower – Custom House – East India House. Each 27 × 70mm. The Tower and the Custom House both seen from the river.

29 p 448 (tr) London/and its/Environs. Published by Longman, Hurst, Rees, Orme & Brown, Paternoster Row, Jany 1st, 1818. 415 × 630mm. Map.

30 p 448 Map of the Environs of London. Neele sculpt 352 Strand. Published Jan. 1815 by Longman, Hurst, Rees, Orme & Brown, Paternoster Row. 185 × 235mm. (*Darlington and Howgego* 275(1), 263(2))

135 · PUBLIC EDIFICES OF THE BRITISH METROPOLIS [1820]

Charles Taylor, one of the two bookseller sons of the engraver Isaac Taylor, was apprenticed to his father and studied with Bartolozzi and therefore naturally gravitated towards the publication of illustrated works, eg Fénelon's *Adventures of Telemachus* (1792) with roundels engraved by himself, John Corbould and William Nutter. In November 1794 he launched a monthly magazine of which each Number was illustrated by two or three plates: one or two of allegorical or classical groups drawn by Samuel Shelley and stipple-engraved by Nutter in the Bartolozzi manner and one line-engraving of a London building:

The Temple of Taste comprising, Elegant, Historical Engravings; also, Views of the Principal Buildings in London; also, a select variety of elegant and amusing subjects with the histories and other connected information at large. By the Best Artists: Designers, and Engravers. London: Printed for C. Taylor, No 10, Holborn, near Castle Street.

The London buildings were discontinued after July 1796 but by then 21 of them had been published. Like the Fénelon illustrations they were all engraved as roundels, about 125mm in diameter in a circular thread-line frame. Two centimetres above the base of the roundel the view is ruled off and in the lower segment are engraved the publication-line and the caption in voided capitals against a hatched background. In the Guildhall Library is a pen and ink sketch of the Royal Mews which follows this formula exactly, even to the precise dimensions, and there is another, of the Banqueting House, Whitehall, in the Victoria and Albert Museum (Dyce Bequest, D.721). Both are signed by Thomas Girtin, the first being apparently rejected and the second engraved.

On the publication of the first Number of *The Temple of Taste* Girtin was still only 19 and had just made his début at the Royal Academy with a water-colour of Ely Cathedral. He had escaped from his onerous apprenticeship with Edward Dayes and was living with his mother and stepfather at 2 St Martin's-le-Grand. To a great extent he was self-trained and until his admission to the Royal Academy as a student late in 1795 he had set himself to copy architectural prints, including the aquatints of the London illustrator Thomas Malton junior, and had sketched out of doors on the shores of the Thames. To get pocket money he tinted prints, alongside the youthful J.M.W. Turner, for the engraver and printseller John Raphael Smith and eventually had drawings accepted for publication in James Walker's highly regarded monthly, the *Copper-plate Magazine*. It is therefore quite within the bounds of probability that at this juncture he would welcome a commission to supply a monthly drawing of London to *The Temple of Taste* and that this was a source of income for him until July 1796. The engraving was probably by Taylor or one of his associates but Girtin's name, unlike that of the well-established Samuel Shelley, was still too obscure to appear as a credit on the prints.

Taylor continued selling the roundels as individual prints long after the magazine had ceased publication and copies survive on large wove paper watermarked '1815' which were in demand as a change from the engraved rectangle in the extra-illustration of Pennant (no 67). In 1820 he decided to collect them in a binding, adding three more plates, a printed title and a description, on both sides of 12 printed sheets, of all 24. In 1825 he dropped the three extra plates, revised the title and reduced the text to 11 sheets.

The diameter of the roundels is 125mm with a plate-mark varying between 190 × 150 and 200 × 160mm. All but the last three plates have the publication-line 'London, Publish'd by C. Taylor, (No. 10) Holborn (date).' The Number of *The Temple of Taste* issue in which each view originally appeared is given with the abbreviation *TT*.

The Public Edifices of the British Metropolis containing (here follows a list of the views in two columns, numbered I–XIII and XIV–XXIV). London: Published by C. Taylor, Hatton Gardens, Sherwood Neely and Jones, Paternoster Row, and Simpkin Marshall, Stationers' Court. 1820.

The Public Edifices of the British Metropolis; with; Historical and Descriptive Accounts of the different Buildings: containing (here follows a list of the views in two columns, numbered I–XI and XII–XXI). London: Published by C. Taylor, 160 Fleet Street; Sherwood, Gilbert and Piper, Paternoster Row; Simpkin, Marshall and Co. Stationers' Court; T. Hughes, Ludgate Hill, and T. Mason, jun. Holborn. 1825.

Folio, 330 × 250mm.   1820, 1825

COLLATION   Title-page; 12 (11 in 1825) sheets printed on both sides with descriptions and interleaved with the plates.

1 Front of St. Paul's, London.... July 1; 1795. *TT* 9.

2 Side View of St. Paul's, London.... Decr 1;1795. From S.W. *TT* 14.

3 Inside of St. Pauls Cathedral.... July 1;1796. Nave, looking E. *TT* 21.

4 Henry VII's Chapel, in Westminster Abby.... 1 April 1795. *TT* 6.

5 West Front of Westminster Abbey.... Augt 1st 1795. *TT* 10.

6 Inside of Westminster Abby.... May 2nd 1796. Nave looking E. *TT* 19.

7 Inside of St. Stephen's Walbrook.... March 1st 1796. *TT* 17.

8 St. George's Church Hanover Square.... Sep.1st 1795. From S. *TT* 11.

9 East Front of St. Paul's Covent Garden.... Dec; 1; 1794. *TT* 2.

10 West Front of St. Martin's Church.... June 1;1795. *TT* 8.

11 The Queen's Palace.... Novr 1;1794. Buckingham House. *TT* 1.

12 Parade Front of the Horse-Guards.... Novr 2; 1795. *TT* 13.

13 Carlton House.... June 1st 1796. *TT* 20.

14 The Banqueting-House, Whitehall.... May 1;1795. *TT* 7.

15 Front of the Royal Academy, Strand.... Feby 2;1795. ie Somerset House. *TT* 4.

16 Front of the Pantheon, Oxford Street.... March 1;1795. *TT* 5.

17 The Bank of England.... Feby 1; 1796. *TT* 16. (*Bank of England* 31)

18 The Royal Exchange.... April 1; 1796. *TT* 18.

19 Black-Fryers Bridge.... Octr 1; 1795. *TT* 12.

20 View of Westminster Bridge.... Jany 1; 1796. *TT* 15.

21 The Monument.... Jany 1;1795. *TT* 3.

22 Front of St Pauls at London. 190 × 125mm pl.mark. 'Geometrical elevation', not in roundel, No publication-line. 1820 collection only.

23 Side Elevation of St Pauls at London. 185 × 250mm pl.mark. 'Geometrical elevation' of S.side, not in roundel. No publication-line. 1820 collection only.

24 Front of St Peters at Rome. 190 × 125mm pl.mark. 'Geometrical elevation', not in roundel. No publication-line. 1820 collection only.

136 · BAYLEY'S HISTORY OF THE TOWER [1821–5]

John Bayley, a Gloucestershire farmer's son, became a junior clerk at the Tower of London Record Office at an early age and by 1819 had attained the rank of chief clerk. In this year also he was elected a Fellow of the Society of Antiquaries and in 1821 he published the first part of his *History of the Tower* whose excellence is his chief claim to fame. The rest of his career at the Tower, as sub-commissioner on the Public Records, was overshadowed by the bad relations with his commissioners: they criticized his editing of the Elizabethan calendars of Chancery Proceedings (1827–32) and the exorbitant rate he charged for this work and extorted from outsiders for searching the records on their behalf. Eventually, in 1834, on the grounds of his long periods of absence, his office was declared vacant. A projected history of London was announced but never published. His *History of the Tower*, however, is a thoroughgoing piece of careful, antiquarian scholarship and is still a standard work on the subject. The quarto edition was advertised in the *Monthly Literary Advertiser*: the first volume in July 1821 at £3 13s 6d boards, or Large Paper with proofs at £7 7s, the second in July 1825 at £3 3s and £5 5s. It was succeeded in 1830 by a popular, slightly abridged, octavo edition.

The History and Antiquities of the Tower of London, with Memoirs of Royal and Distinguished Persons, deduced from Records, State-papers, and Manuscripts and from other original and authentic sources. By John Bayley, Esq., F.S.A. of the Honourable Society of the Inner Temple, and one of His Majesty's sub-commissioners of the Public Records. In two parts. Part I (II). London: Printed for T. Cadell, in the Strand. 1821 (1825). (Printer:) J.M. Creery, Tooks Court, Chancery Lane, London.

Quarto, 375 × 260mm.   1821–5

COLLATION Part 1. Title-page; dedication to George IV (1 leaf); pp vii–x, preface to pt 1 dated 29 May 1821; pp xi–xvi, contents; list of plates, errata (1 leaf); pp 1–272, History; pp i–xxxiv, appendix. Part 2. Title-page; pp v–vi, preface to pt 2; contents, errata (1 leaf); pp 273–671, History continued; pp xxxv–cxxviii, appendix; index (17pp).

The drawings for the 27 numbered plates are divided between a painter and an architect: Frederick Nash, the Lambeth artist and illustrator of *Lambeth Palace* (no 95), a contributor to Britton's publications and to many of the important works illustrative of London published since the beginning of the century; and Edward Blore, also a Britton contributor, future surveyor of Westminster Abbey and architect in charge of works at Windsor Castle and Buckingham Palace. Chief engraver-etcher was John Pye, former employee of James Heath; he also worked for Britton and became something of a specialist in engraving after Turner landscapes. Assisting him were William R. Smith, Robert Sands and John Byrne, all former contributors to Brayley's *Westminster Abbey* (no 123), William Cooke, nephew of George Cooke, and others. The plates are printed on India paper and include a handful of impressive views. The engravings as a whole are a trustworthy record of Tower of London architecture before the 1841 Armoury fire and subsequent demolitions, rebuildings and restorations. On publication the copper plates were destroyed.

Some of the 27 listed plates, which are numbered tr, in Roman numerals, have the publication-line 'London, Published (date) by T. Cadell in the Strand.' In others the line is undated or absent. In addition to this official quota are nine unlisted plates, with the numbers of page they should face engraved tr. Eight of these are without credits.

1 front. View of the Tower of London from the River Thames. Drawn by F. Nash. Engraved by J. Pye.... March 13, 1821. 140 × 215/260 × 370mm. pl.I.

2 p 1 A true and exact draught of the Tower liberties, surveyed in the year 1597, by Gulielmus Hayward and J. Gascoyne. Engraved by H. Matlow. 248 × 340/300 × 380mm. pl.II. Also in *Vetusta Monumenta* (no 36), item 7.

3 p 107 N.E. View of the White Tower. Drawn by F. Nash. Engraved by J. Pye.... Feby 12, 1821. 162 × 215/- × 370mm. pl.III.

4 p 110 Plan of the First Floor of the White Tower. Drawn by F. Nash. J. Barnett sc. 175 × 205mm. No publication-line. pl.IV.

5 p 110 Vaulted room and staircase in the White Tower, Drawn by E. Blore. Engraved by W. Cooke Junr.... March 6, 1821. 170 × 105,170 × 115/220 × 270mm. pl.VI (sic).

6 p 112 Plan of the Second Floor of the White Tower. Drawn by F. Nash. J. Barnett Sc. 175 × 205mm. pl.VI.

7 p 112 Chapel in the White Tower. Drawn by E. Blore. Engraved by William R. Smith.... May 21st, 1821. 230 × 170/365 × 260mm. pl.VII.

8 p 115 Plan of the upper Floor of the White Tower. Drawn by F. Nash. J. Barnett sc. 173 × 205mm. pl.VIII.

9 p 115 Council Chamber in the White Tower. Drawn by F. Nash. Engraved by J. Lee.... March 6, 1821. 210 × 165/280 × 225mm. pl.IX.

10 p 116 Room adjoining the Council Chamber in the White Tower.... May 28, 1821. 103 × 130/125 × 165mm. Unlisted.

11 p 117 View of the Chapel of St. Peter in the Tower. Drawn by F. Nash. Engraved by J. Byrne.... March 6, 1821. 150 × 220/250 × 365mm. pl.X.

12 p 119 Interior of the Chapel of St. Peter in the Tower. Drawn by F. Nash. Engraved by W. Smith.... March 6, 1821. 210 × 165/265 × 250mm. pl.XI.

13 p 122 Tomb of Sir Richard Cholmondeley and Lady Elizabeth his wife, in the Tower Chapel. Drawn by F. Nash. Engraved by R. Sands.... Septr 1, 1823. 170 × 225/250 × 310mm. (pl.XII)

14 p 134 Plan of the First Floor of the Beauchamp Tower. Drawn by F. Nash in 1802. J. Barnett sc. 150 × 210/- × 365mm. No publication-line. pl.XIII.

15 p 134 Vaulted Room in the Bell Tower.... May 28, 1821. 128 × 105/160 × 112mm. Unlisted.

16 p 137 Prison Room in the Beauchamp Tower. Drawn by F. Nash. Engraved by H. Hobson.... March 6, 1821. 155 × 220/- × 360mm. pl.XIII(sic).

17 p 138 Inscriptions of T. Peverel and the Earl of Arundel, in the/Beauchamp Tower. Drawn by F. Nash. Engraved by J. Pye.... March 6, 1821. 210 × 170/- × 370mm. pl.XV.

18 p 147 Inscription of John Dudley, Earl of Warwick. Drawn by F. Nash. Engraved by J. Pye.... March 6, 1821. 205 × 180/- × 370mm. pl.XVI.

19 p 148 Inscriptions of G. Gyfford and others in the Beauchamp Tower. Drawn by F. Nash. Engraved by J. Pye.... May 28, 1821. 225 × 170/- × 365mm. Unlisted.

20 p 149 Inscription of Charles Bailly, in the Beauchamp Tower. Drawn by F. Nash. Engraved by J. Pye.... March 6, 1821. 220 × 175/- × 365mm. pl.XVII.

21 p 154 Inscriptions of Thomas Clarke and others, in the Beauchamp Tower. Drawn by F. Nash. Engraved by W. Cook.... March 6, 1821. 245 × 180/340 × 245mm. pl.XIX.

22 p 161 Inscriptions of Arthur and Edmund Poole in the Beauchamp Tower. Drawn by F. Nash. Engraved by W. Smith.... March 6, 1821. 175 × 240/- × 360mm. pl.XVIII.

23 p 176 Inscription in the Upper Chamber of the/Beauchamp Tower. Drawn by F. Nash. Engraved by J. Pye.... March 6, 1821. 205 × 165/- × 365mm. T. Salmon's inscription. pl.XX.

24 p 180 Interior of the Bowyer Tower. Drawn & Engraved by F. Nash.... March 6, 1821. 198 × 160/- × 365mm. pl.XXI.

25 p 210 Carving by Hugh Draper in the Salt Tower. Drawn by F. Nash. Engraved by W. Smith.... March 6, 1821. 180 × 220mm. pl.XXII.

26 p 258 Saml. Lysons Esqr. V.P.R.S. & F.S.A./Keeper of H.M. Records in the Tower/Engraved by W. Bond from a Miniature by W.J. Newton.... Feb. 1st, 1823. 140 × 105/300 × 220mm. With engraved frame. (pl.XXIII)

27 p 262 Gateway of the Bloody Tower. Drawn & Engraved by F. Nash.... March 6, 1821. 210 × 163mm. pl.XXIII (ie XXIV).

28 p 262 View of the Bloody Tower.... May 28, 1821. 205 × 160mm. Unlisted.

29 p 262 Gateway of the Bloody Tower.... May 28, 1821. 95 × 135mm. Unlisted.

30 p 267 Interior of the Well Tower. Drawn & Engraved by Edw. Blore.... June 1, 1823. 165 × 115/325 × 250mm. pl.XXV.

31 p 267 Interior of the Well Tower.... May 28, 1821. 200 × 165mm. Unlisted.

32 p 268 Gateway under the Cradle Tower. Drawn by E. Blore. Engraved by R. Sands.... Septr. 1, 1823. 165 × 115mm. No pl. no.

33 p 268 Traitor's Tower, or Water Tower.... 95 × 135mm. Unlisted and no publication-line.

34 p 268 View of the By-Ward Tower. Drawn by F. Nash. Engraved by W. Cook.... March 6, 1821. 205 × 165/335 × 240mm. pl.XXVI.

35 p 268 Interior of the By-Ward Tower. Drawn by E. Blore. Engraved by R. Sands.... 195 × 165/285 × 225mm. pl.XXVII.

36 p 269 Martin's Tower.... May 28, 1821. 95 × 130/112 × 155mm. Unlisted.

137 · BREWER'S ACCOUNT OF VARIOUS PALACES* [1821]

J.N. Brewer, novelist and topographer, who wrote the introduction to *The Beauties of England and Wales* (no 104) and contributed to it histories of Oxfordshire and Warwickshire and a part of the 'Middlesex' text, was also the author of *Histrionic*

Topography (no 124) and a number of other historical and topographical works. These 20 essays, which vary in length from eight to 24 pages, were issued in Numbers to accompany engravings of historic European buildings such as the Louvre, the Panthéon, the Escurial, Monte Cavallo and a number of British palaces and houses.

A Descriptive and Historical Account of Various Palaces and Public Buildings, (English and Foreign:) with Biographical Notices of their Founders, and other eminent persons. By James Norris Brewer.... London, Printed by W. Lewis, Finch Lane, for William Gilling, Suffolk Street. 1821.

Quarto, 285 × 220mm.   1821

COLLATION Half-title; title-page; contents ('*To each subject is prefixed an elegant Copper-plate Engraving') (1 leaf); pp vii–viii, preface dated 30 May 1821; 24 unpaginated Numbers (sigs B–2R).

The preface explains that 'The Engravings have been executed by artists of the greatest celebrity and the utmost attention has been paid to exactitude and correctness'. Of the artists' credits on the London views one is 'J. Taylor', another 'Taylor' and the rest 'T. Taylor'. That 'J' should stand for James, the brother of Isaac Taylor senior, might seem impossible in view of the fact that he died in 1797, but it becomes more credible when it is realized that all these plates were engraved almost 20 years before this collection was published. The other Taylor concerned may be James's engraver son. The engraving was carried out by James Basire, S. Porter and James Storer for J. Wyatt of 182 Fleet Street and the plates were published in 1802–3 in his periodical the *Monthly Register*. The first six issues each contained both a European view and one of London or its environs and these were followed by engravings of proposed London 'improvements'. In 1809 some of the views were reissued, without mention of the periodical, by W.H. Wyatt, related presumably to the original publisher, and the Numbers were first published in book form in 1810.

1 No 4 The Tower of London. J. Taylor Delt. Jas Basire sc. Published 1st Augt. 1802 for the Monthly Register. 120 × 200/150 × 230mm. Seen from the entrance near the Byward Tower. With 24pp of text signed FGH.

2 No 5 Somerset House. T. Taylor del. S. Porter sculp. Published by W.H. Wyatt, July 1, 1809. 118 × 200/145 × 228mm. River front with St Paul's in the distance. Originally in the *Monthly Register* for June 1802. With 22pp of text signed I–L.

3 No 9 Kensington Palace. T. Taylor del. J. Storer sculp. Published Octr 1, 1802 for the Monthly Register. 115 × 190/155 × 230mm. With 8pp of text signed O–P.

4 No 12 India House. T. Taylor del. J. Storer sc. London, Published by W.H. Wyatt, 1st August 1809. 115 × 190/150 × 225mm. Originally in the *Monthly Register* for September 1803. With 20pp of text signed S–U.

5 No 14 Windsor Castle. Taylor delt. Engraved by S. Porter & J. Storer. London, Published by W.H. Wyatt, 1st Septr 1809. 120 × 197/150 × 230mm. Originally in the *Monthly Register* for April 1802. With 24pp of text signed Y–2B.

6 No 23 Hampton Court. T. Taylor delt. J. Storer sct. London, Published by W.H. Wyatt, 1st Octr 1809. 115 × 190/150 × 225mm. Originally in the *Monthly Register* for May 1802. With 24pp of text signed 2O–2Q.

138 · MILLER'S VIEWS IN LONDON [c 1821]

Robert Miller specialized in cheap editions, edifying biographies, toy books for children, picture cards, music cards and portraits. His *Catalogue of Books & Fancy Articles*, which dates from after January 1820 (since it advertises an engraving of George IV), lists 'Twenty-six Views of London, consisting of the most remarkable Buildings, with an Historical description of each, and a correct Map of London, Westminster, and Southwark, price 2s 6d. half-bound'. The title-page of this volume is undated but the Old Fish Street address, from which Miller seems to have moved in 1821 to set up as a copper plate and lithographic printer at 14 Paternoster Row, taken together with the catalogue bound at the back of the views and the watermark '1820', visible on some of them, suggest a publication date not later than 1821.

The same plates and title-page were issued with a different publication-line and an imprint which includes the booksellers John Bysh, who was in Paternoster Row from 1818 to 1821, and Messrs Langley and Belch, who were at 173 Borough High Street from 1807 to 1817. If this edition is earlier than Miller's it cannot be much earlier than June

1817 when the Strand Bridge, marked on the map, was opened and, if later, probably not later than 1824 when the first pile of Rennie's London Bridge was driven, since it makes no mention of a reconstruction.

The only general text is the thumbnail description of London printed on the reverse of the map and referring to the census of 1811. Otherwise each view has below its caption an historical note, apparently engraved in ingenious but irregular imitation of letterpress in order to avoid printing each leaf both in relief and intaglio.

Copper plate London views printed at the head of an historical description are first found in sets in Grose's *Antiquities of England and Wales* (no 50) and again some 40 years later in the second edition of Storer and Greig's *Antiquarian and Topographical Cabinet* (no 118), but then on a much more modest scale. In this popular little souvenir book, or 'present from London', they have been revived in a format as miniature as that used for the tiny plates in Newbery's bestselling toy book *The Curiosities of London* (no 49).

The views are vignetted and there are no credits. In the Robert Miller edition, but not in the edition with the alternative imprint, they are numbered bc 1–26. The publication-line, engraved below the note, reads either 'London Published by Robert Miller, 24, Old Fish Street, Doctors Commons.' or, alternatively, 'London Pubd by T. Crabb, 1 Ivy Lane, Paternoster Row & 15 John St. Blackfriars Road.'

(*Title-page* pl. 1)

Duodecimo, 135–40 × 85mm.   c 1821

COLLATION   Title-page; map with letterpress description on verso (1 leaf); 26 plates.

  1 (engr title) Views in London/consisting of the most/ Remarkable Buildings/with an/Historical Description/ of each/ Copper Plate edition. (vignette of City arms and regalia, with background of St Paul's, Monument, London Bridge) London/Published by R. Miller, 24 Old Fish Street Doctors Commons (alternatively: 'Publish'd by Thos. Crabb, 15 John Street, Blackfriars Road./Sold also by R. Hill & Langley & Belch, Borough, C. Penny Wood St., J. Bysh Paternoster Row & all Booksellers'). 60 × 70/120 × 80mm.

  2 (tr) London/Westminster/and Southwark. 70 × 108/80 × 122mm. Map originally published in *Miller's New Miniature Atlas*. (*Darlington and Howgego* 254)

  3 pl.1 Tower of London. 50 × 65/120 × 80mm. Traitor's Gate, White Tower, from river.

  4 pl.2 The Mint. 50 × 60/125 × 85mm.

  5 pl.3 Trinity House. 50 × 60/120 × 80mm.

  6 pl.4 The Customs House. 50 × 65/120 × 80mm. Built by David Laing, 1813–17.

  7 pl.5 The Monument. 50 × 65/123 × 82mm.

  8 pl.6 London Bridge. 45 × 70/123 × 82mm.

  9 pl.7 East India House. 50 × 70/118 × 85mm. Not, as the note says, 'elevated according to the plan of Mr Soane the Architect' but by the East India Company's architect Richard Jupp and Henry Holland; in fact its erection was the cause of a feud between Jupp and the ambitious young Soane.

 10 pl.8 Excise Office. 50 × 65/123 × 80mm.

 11 pl.9 The Bank of England. 45 × 65/123 × 85mm. Soane's 'Tivoli Corner'. (*Bank of England* 58)

 12 pl.10 The Mansion House. 50 × 65/124 × 84mm.

 13 pl.11 Guildhall. 50 × 60/125 × 83mm. The note mentions the 1814 City banquet for the Emperor of Russia, King of Prussia and Prince Regent.

 14 pl.12 St. Paul's Cathedral. 50 × 65/120 × 82mm. From N.W.

 15 pl.13 Temple Bar. 50 × 55/120 × 80mm.

 16 pl.14 Somerset House. 50 × 70/123 × 80mm. From river; shows N. end of 'Strand Bridge'.

 17 pl.15 Savoy Palace and Chapel. 45 × 70/120 × 80mm.

 18 pl.16 Carlton House. 45 × 60/120 × 85mm. Demolished 1827–8.

 19 pl.17 St James's Palace. 50 × 65/120 × 83mm.

 20 pl.18 Queen's Palace. 50 × 70/120 × 80mm. Buckingham House.

 21 pl.19 Admiralty. 45 × 70/120 × 85mm. 'The Admiralty is brilliantly illuminated, and always with the appropriate emblem of an Anchor'. The note also defends against his critics the architect Thomas Ripley, but calls him 'Shipley'.

 22 pl.20 Horse Guards. 50 × 65/120 × 85mm.

 23 pl.21 Whitehall. 45 × 60/125 × 85mm. Banqueting Hall.

 24 pl.22 Westminster Hall. 50 × 65/122 × 85mm. From N.

 25 pl.23 Westminster Abbey. 50 × 65/120 × 80mm. And St Margaret's from W.

 26 pl.24 Lambeth Palace. 50 × 65/120 × 80mm. Gatehouse.

 27 pl.25 St. John's Gate. 50 × 60/123 × 80mm.

 28 pl.26 London Institution. 45 × 65/120 × 80mm. Built by William Brooks, 1815–19.

139 · COOKE'S VIEWS ON THE THAMES [1822]

The anonymous text, illustrated with drawings by Samuel Owen engraved by W.B. Cooke, is slightly revised and amplified from that of William Combe for the 1811 publication *The Thames* (no 106). Some of the leaves of description, which are unpaginated, retain the printed figures of the Numbers in which they were originally issued but have been added to, in order to accommodate new plates. Upcott, in 1818, knew of the forthcoming edition (the publication of the second Number of which had been noted in the *Monthly Literary Advertiser* for February 1815):

A new edition of the work is in course of publication to be completed in Six Parts, each Part containing thirteen Engravings; the letter-press description will appear at the Conclusion as an Octavo volume. It is intended to reengrave several of the plates, to omit some altogether and to substitute new ones of a more interesting description. To be printed in Royal Quarto; also in Imperial Quarto, with Proof impressions, and a small number to be taken off on India paper, first proofs

John Britton, in the introduction to *The Beauties of England and Wales* (no 104), of the same year, gave the work his blessing as a worthy offshoot of his own publication:

'The Thames, with Graphic Illustrations' two Vols 4to and 8vo, produced by Messrs. W. and G. Cooke, and so highly creditable to their professional talents, would probably never have appeared but from the excitement and example of the Beauties of England, for which work, both those excellent Engravers executed some of the early plates. It is a pleasing circumstance to the true lover of topography, to contemplate such eminent literary and graphic publications, and to know that the taste for, and the laudable rivalry displayed in them, have originated in a work, which was as humble and unassuming in its origin, as the authors were in circumstances and pretensions.

Further details appeared in the catalogue of the Quaker publishers John and Arthur Arch:

To be completed in Six Numbers, 4to, price £1. 1s. each, on royal paper £1. 10s. and on India paper £2. 2s. each Number:

Cooke's Thames. A Picturesque Delineation of the beautiful scenery on the banks of the River Thames, from its source to its confluence with the Sea. No. 1 to 4. Engraved by W.B. Cooke and G. Cooke.

A supplement to the former edition, containing the new plates engraved for the present extended and improved work, is publishing at the same time, to be completed in Eight Numbers, price 7s. 6d. each, 8vo and 10s. 6d, 4to.

Finally, the bound collection was sold in royal quarto at £8, imperial quarto with proofs £12 and India paper with proofs £15.

Description to the Plates of Thames Scenery engraved by W.B. Cooke & G. Cooke, from original drawings by Eminent Artists. London, Published by John Murray, Albemarle Street, and W.B. Cooke, 13, Judd Place East, New Road. 1818.

(engr title) Descriptions/of the/Views on the Thames/ engraved by/W.B. Cooke, and G. Cooke./ 'View of Cookham'. Drawn by P. Dewint. Engraved by W.B. Cooke./London./Published by W.B. Cooke, 9 Soho Square. June 1st, 1822.

Octavo, 235 × 155mm; folio, 370 × 260mm.   1818–22

COLLATION   Vol. 1. Title-page; engr title-page (78 × 120/240 × 170mm); introduction (6pp); list of 75 views (excluding pl. 35a) (4pp); unpaginated descriptions of the views of from 1p to 16pp bound up in list order; table of distances (1 leaf); index, errata (8pp). Vol. 2. Folio plates bound in list order with no text or title-page.

Views on the Thames; engraved by W.B. Cooke and George Cooke. London: Published by W.B. Cooke, 9 Soho Square. 1822.

Quarto, 295 × 230mm.   1822

COLLATION   Vol. 1. Title-page; dedication to Sir John Swinburne (1 leaf); list of 75 views (excluding pl. 35a), advertisement for Cooke publications illustrated with engravings (4pp); introduction (6pp); Views on the Thames (67 unpaginated leaves interleaved with 36 plates); table of distances, index, errata (6pp). Vol. 2. Title-page; Views on the Thames continued (72 unpaginated leaves interleaved with 40 plates); table of distances (1 leaf); index (5pp).

The 'de-luxe' edition, with illustrations on India paper, was clearly intended to supplant the older, standard work on Thames scenery, Boydell's *History of the Thames* (no 75), whose aquatinted plates were by now very worn. As in Boydell the illustrations in the quarto edition are split up into two volumes, the first extending from Thames head to Richmond and the second from Richmond to Southend. Also as in Boydell the text is subordinated to the engravings which are mostly the work of a single engraver.

Of the 84 plates based on Samuel Owen's

drawings of the 1811 edition 38 are retained in 1822, all re-engraved and transformed by W.B. Cooke whose style had been romanticized through his work for Turner and his association with Peter de Wint. The etched shades are now blacker, more highlights are introduced, skies are eventful with massing clouds and flights of birds, and the foliage has become less stylized. For comparison the re-engraved plates are referred to their predecessors, with relevant item numbers. Three hitherto unpublished drawings of Owen were added (items 2–3, 53), including one of Billingsgate, the subject of a water-colour (190 × 238mm) in the Victoria and Albert Museum (D.410–1899). On the other hand eight former Owen subjects were given to de Wint (items 5, 8, 10, 14, 26–7, 32–3) whose 14 views, foreshadowing those poetic miniatures shortly to be engraved by Heath (no 147), completely transform the collection. Louis Francia's four contributions (items 39, 56, 61, 69) are evidence of the fascination that Thames river craft, shipbuilding and shipbreaking exercised on a number of artists of the period. Other contributors include artists as accomplished as R. Reinagle (one of whose views shows the opening of Waterloo Bridge in 1817), Luke Clennell, William Havell (who drew Turner's villa at Twickenham) and George Barret junior. The lion's share of the engraving once again fell to W.B. Cooke, although he entrusted 14 of the plates to fellow engravers for Turner's *Picturesque Views*: ten to his brother George and four to J.C. Allen.

The engraver's credit, unless otherwise stated, reads 'Engraved by W.B. Cooke'. Captions are in voided capitals with italic sub-captions. Random numbering of a dozen of the plates between '1' and '98' indicates that this was to be the extent of the collection, ultimately abridged to 75 plates; otherwise plates are unnumbered, as are the lists prefixed to each volume.

One of the plates is undated but publication-lines of the remainder fall between March 1814 and August 1822:

1814 (March, May, October)	24
1815 (July)	13
1817 (January–February)	12
1819 (February)	12
1821 (November, July)	8
1822 (June–August)	5

Extra, unlisted plates are items 14a (June 1822) and

35a (March 1814). The watermark most prevalent on the plates of the folio edition is 'J. WHATMAN 1821' but the dates 1815, 1816, 1818 and 1820 also appear. Alternative publication-lines are:

(a) 'London, Published (date) by W.B. Cooke, 12 York Place, Pentonville.' (1814–17)
(b) 'London, Published (date) by W.B. Cooke, 13 Judd Place East, New Road.' (1819)
(c) 'London, Published (date) by W.B. Cooke, 9 Soho-Square.' (1821–2)

Smaller collections of these Cooke plates are to be found without text or list. One such in the Guildhall Library (A. 4.5, no 23) has a title-page dating from their initial year which includes the names of two other publishers:

The Thames, a picturesque delineation of the most beautiful scenery on the Banks of that River, from its source to its confluence with the sea. Engraved by W.B. Cooke and G. Cooke from original drawings by S. Owen and other Eminent Artists. (epigraph) London: Published by John Murray, Albemarle Street, J. & A. Arch, Cornhill; and W.B. Cooke, York-Place, Pentonville. 1814.

VOL. 1

1 (engr in sky) Source/of the Thames. Drawn by P. Dewint. May 1, 1814. 140 × 130/240 × 160mm. Vignetted. Also found minus the title, as a front.

2 Dudgrove Double lock. Drawn by S. Owen. Octr 1, 1814. 115 × 200/153 × 238mm.

3 Lechlade. Drawn by S. Owen. Engraved by G. Cooke. July 1, 1815. 158 × 198/150 × 240mm.

4 Radcot Wier. Drawn by S. Owen. Octr 1, 1814. 115 × 195/155 × 235mm. 1811 ed item 5.

5 Oxford/taken near Oseney. Drawn by P. Dewint from a Sketch by G. Hollis. July 1, 1822. 145 × 208/162 × 245mm.

6 Wier near Oxford. Drawn by P. Dewint. July 1, 1815. 170 × 140/220 × 153mm. Vignetted.

7 Nuneham Courtenay. Drawn by John Hughes Esq. Feby 1, 1819. 118 × 198/150 × 246mm.

8 Park Place near Henley/Seat of the Earl of Malmesbury. Drawn by P. Dewint. Novr 1, 1821. 150 × 210/185 × 240mm.

9 The Druid's Altar at Park Place, Henley/Seat of the Earl of Malmesbury. Drawn by the late Wm Alexander F.S.A. of the British Museum. Engraved by George Cooke. Jan 1, 1817. 125 × 210/170 × 232mm.

10 Henley. Drawn by P. Dewint. Novr 1, 1821. 112 × 205/170 × 255mm.

11 Temple House. Drawn by S. Owen. Engraved by

Geo. Cooke. March 31, 1814. 112 × 190/150 × 240mm. 1811 ed item 20.

12 Harleyford House/Seat of Sir Wm Clayton Bart. Drawn by S. Owen. Jan 1, 1817. 120 × 190/150 × 210mm. 1811 ed item 21.

13 Great Marlow. Drawn by S. Owen. Oct.1, 1814. 112 × 190/150 × 240mm. 1811 ed item 23.

14 An Osier Island near Cookham. Drawn by P. Dewint. July 1, 1815. 180 × 150/240 × 175mm. Vignetted.

14a View of Cookham. Drawn by P. Dewint. Published by W.B. Cooke, 9 Soho-Square. 75 × 120mm. Vignette. Not listed in this position but as the engraved title to the 1818 octavo 'Description of the Views' where it is bound as a front., engraved with the title and the date 'June 1st, 1822'.

15 Cliefden. Drawn by W. Havell. Oct. 1, 1814. 115 × 203/160 × 240mm.

16 Bray/seen from Maidenhead Bridge. Drawn by P. Dewint. Feby 1, 1819. 168 × 155/218 × 178mm.

17 The Willows/Seat of the late Townley Ward Esq. Drawn by S. Owen. July 1, 1815. 112 × 187/155 × 238mm. 1811 ed item 28.

18 Eton Bridge. Drawn by S. Owen. July 1, 1815. 115 × 190/150 × 235mm. 1811 ed item 31.

19 Old Houses at Eton. Drawn by S. Owen. Feby 1, 1819. 110 × 170/150 × 240mm. 1811 ed item 32.

20 Windsor Castle, Taken near the Lock. Drawn by S. Owen. Jan.1, 1817. 115 × 188/155 × 238mm. 1811 ed item 30.

21 Beaumont Lodge/near Old Windsor. Drawn by S. Owen. Feby 1, 1819. 120 × 195/155 × 238mm. 1811 ed item 34.

22 Stone at Staines/marking the western boundary of the jurisdiction of the City of London on the River Thames. Painted by G. Arnald, A.R.A. Novr 1, 1821. 125 × 215/165 × 250mm.

23 Staines Bridge. Drawn by S. Owen. Oct. 1, 1814. 110 × 170/150 × 240mm. 1811 ed item 35.

24 Oatlands/Seat of H.R.H. Duke of York. Drawn by S. Owen. Jan. 1, 1817. 112 × 192/155 × 240mm. 1811 ed item 36.

25 Walton Bridge. Drawn by S. Owen. Feby 1, 1819. 112 × 192/150 × 238mm. 1811 ed item 37.

26 Garrick's House/at Hampton. Drawn by P. Dewint. Feby 1, 1819. 118 × 200/155 × 225mm.

27 Hampton Court and Bridge. Drawn by P. Dewint. Novr 1, 1821. 105 × 195/140 × 225mm.

28 Lady Sullivan's Villa/Thames Ditton. Drawn by S. Owen. July 1, 1815. 115 × 185/150 × 225mm. 1811 ed item 40.

29 Kingston. Drawn by S. Owen. July 1, 1815. 112 × 188/155 × 225mm. 1811 ed item 41.

30 Strawberry Hill/Seat of the Honble Mrs Damer.

Drawn by S. Owen. Jan. 1, 1817. 160 × 115/212 × 150mm. 1811 ed item 42.

31 Baroness Howe's Villa and Pope's Grotto/(epigraph: 'Stanzas to Pope's Weeping Willow') Drawn by G. Barrett. Engraved by J.C. Allen. Augst 1, 1822. 75 × 115/160 × 218mm.

32 Marble Hill Cottage/near Richmond. Drawn by P. Dewint. Feby 1, 1819. 120 × 195/155 × 240mm.

33 Richmond Hill. Drawn by P. Dewint. Jan. 1, 1817. 125 × 210/155 × 240mm. (*Gascoigne* 547)

34 Sandycombe Lodge, Twickenham/Villa of J.M.W. Turner Esqr. R.A. Drawn by W. Havell. March 31, 1814. 110 × 200/160 × 240mm. 'Pl.56'.

35 Richmond/seen from the Meadows near Isleworth. Drawn by R.R. Reinagle A.R.A. Engraved by J.C. Allen. Feby 1, 1819. 120 × 218/170 × 265mm. (*Gascoigne* 548)

35a Richmond Bridge. Drawn by S. Owen. March 1, 1814. 112 × 190/155 × 255mm. 'Pl.55'. Not bound up in 1818 or included in 'List of Plates'. New lettering, but as 1811 ed item 49. (*Gascoigne* 545)

VOL. 2

36 Villa at Richmond/Residence of Whitshed Keene Esq. Drawn by S. Owen. Octr 1, 1814. 112 × 190/150 × 222mm. 1811 ed item 50. (*Gascoigne* 549)

37 Sion House/Seat of the Duke of Northumberland. Drawn by R.R. Reinagle. Novr 1, 1821. 122 × 215/155 × 250mm.

38 Battersea. W.B. Cooke 1821. July 1, 1821. 115 × 190/150 × 240mm. The Bridge, from S. Owen's drawing. 1811 ed item 56.

39 The Little Belt/Breaking up at Battersea. Drawn by L. Francia. Feby 1, 1819. 180 × 160/210 × 180mm. Vignetted. A naval vessel, broken up 1811. (*Longford* 294)

40 Chelsea Hospital. Drawn by S. Owen. Jan. 1, 1817. 120 × 190/150 × 240mm. 1811 ed item 57. (*Longford* 32)

41 Thames Craft/a Scene from/Millbank. Drawn by P. Dewint. Engraved by J.C. Allen. Feb 1, 1817. 175 × 160/215 × 175mm.

42 Mill (Randall's) at Nine Elms. Drawn by S. Owen. March 1, 1814. 155 × 115/230 × 155mm. 'Pl. 66'. 1811 ed item 58.

43 Lambeth Palace/Taken from the water-steps of the Penitentiary. Drawn by G. Barrett. Etched by G. Cooke. Finished by W.B. Cooke. Augst 1, 1822. 125 × 190/170 × 245mm.

44 Opening of Waterloo Bridge on the 18th of June 1817/as seen from the Corner of Cecil Street in the Strand. Drawn by R.R. Reinagle, A.R.A. Engraved by George Cooke. Augst 1, 1822. 120 × 210/155 × 235mm.

45 The Strand Bridge/New erecting by J. Rennie Esqr.

Drawn by E. Blore. Engraved by George Cooke. March 31, 1814. 125 × 202/155 × 220mm. 'Pl.72'.

46 Works of the Strand Bridge/(taken in the Year 1815). Drawn by Edw. Blore. Engraved by George Cooke. Jan. 1, 1817. 115 × 165/155 × 215mm.

47 Elevation of one of the Arches of the Waterloo Bridge (above). Drawn by the late John Rennie Esqr., Engineer and Architect by whom it was liberally presented to this work. 135 × 225/205 × 265mm. Outline-etching. nd, but 1819 publication-line.

48 Section of one of the Arches of the Waterloo Bridge/with the Centring under it. Drawn by the late John Rennie ... Novr. 1, 1821. 135 × 225/205 × 265mm. Outline-etching.

49 Somerset House. Drawn by S. Owen. March 31, 1814. 110 × 188/155 × 250mm. 'Pl.75'. 1811 ed item 63.

50 London/from Blackfriars Bridge/in the Year 1814. Drawn by L. Clennell. Jan. 1, 1817. 115 × 200/155 × 240mm.

51 Fair on the Thames, Feb. 1814. Drawn by Luke Clennell. Engraved by George Cooke. March 31, 1814. 100 × 195/150 × 235mm. Vignetted.

52 London Bridge. Drawn by S. Owen. Octr 1, 1814. 115 × 182/155 × 240mm. 1811 ed item 64.

53 Billingsgate/the London Fish Market. Drawn by S. Owen. March 31, 1814. 115 × 190/155 × 240mm. 'Pl. 80'.

54 The Custom House/Destroyed by Fire Feby 12th 1814. Drawn by S. Owen. March 31, 1814. 112 × 190/150 × 242mm. 1811 ed item 65.

55 Tower of London. Drawn by S. Owen. July 1, 1815. 115 × 190/150 × 240mm. 1811 ed item 66.

56 Floating Dock at Rotherhithe. Drawn by L. Francia. Engraved by J.C. Allen. July 1, 1815. 140 × 205/160 × 245mm. Sepia wash drawing (140 × 200mm) in Guildhall Library.

57 Deptford. Drawn by S. Owen. Feby 1, 1819. 112 × 190/155 × 240mm. 1811 ed item 68.

58 Greenwich. Drawn by S. Owen. Octobr 1, 1814. 115 × 190/150 × 240mm. 1811 ed item 69.

59 The Thames from Greenwich Park/From a Drawing in the possession of the Duke of Argyll. Drawn by P. Dewint. June 1, 1822. 120 × 222/165 × 250mm.

60 Mast House, Blackwall. Drawn by S. Owen. March 31, 1814. 112 × 188/150 × 235mm. 'Pl.88'. 1811 ed item 70.

61 The Nelson/on the Stocks, building at Woolwich, in the Year 1814. Drawn by L. Francia. July 1, 1815. 125 × 205/160 × 240mm.

62 Launch of the Nelson/at Woolwich, July 4th, 1814. Drawn by L. Clennell. Etched by G. Cooke. Engraved by W.B. Cooke. Octr 1, 1814. 125 × 210/170 × 240mm.

63 Erith and Belvidere. Drawn by S. Owen. Feby 1, 1819. 112 × 190/152 × 240mm. 1811 ed item 73.

64 Purfleet. Drawn by S. Owen. Oct. 1, 1814. 115 × 190/155 × 242mm. 1811 ed item 74.

65 Ingress/at Greenhithe. Drawn by S. Owen. Novr 1, 1821. 115 × 190/155 × 240mm. 1811 ed item 75.

66 Northfleet. Drawn by S. Owen. July 1, 1815. 110 × 190/155 × 240mm. 1811 ed item 76.

67 Lime Kilns at Northfleet. Drawn by S. Owen. Jan. 1, 1817. 110 × 192/155 × 240mm. 1811 ed item 77.

68 Gravesend. Drawn by S. Owen. March 31, 1814. 115 × 192/155 × 240mm. 'Pl. 97'. 1811 ed item 78.

69 Danish Greenlandsman/Breaking up below Gravesend. Drawn by L. Francia. Oct. 1, 1814. 140 × 160/225 × 180mm. Vignetted.

70 Tilbury Fort. Drawn by S. Owen. March 1, 1814. 110 × 192/150 × 240mm. 'Pl. 98'. 1811 ed item 79.

71 Gateway, Tilbury Fort. Drawn by S. Owen. July 1, 1815. 155 × 110/240 × 150mm. 1811 ed item 80.

72 Hadleigh Castle/near Southend. Drawn by S. Owen. Jan. 1, 1817. 118 × 190/150 × 238mm. 1811 ed item 81.

73 Leigh/from near Southend. Drawn by S. Owen. Octr 1, 1814. 110 × 190/155 × 240mm. 1811 ed item 82.

74 The Crow Stone/near Southend/Marking the Eastern Termination of the/jurisdiction of the City of London/on the River Thames. July 1, 1815. 170 × 140/215 × 150mm. Vignetted.

75 Southend. Drawn by S. Owen. Feby 1, 1819. 113 × 195/155 × 240mm. 1811 ed item 83.

140 · HASSELL'S EXCURSIONS OF PLEASURE [1823]

John Hassell, biographer of George Morland and drawing-master, was the author of several books on water-colour drawing and was a pioneer in the use of aquatint engraving for book illustration. His earliest Academy exhibit, in 1789, was a view of Stonehenge and his artistic output thenceforward consisted entirely of topographical water-colours and engravings. As early as 1790 he published a *Tour of the Isle of Wight* illustrated with aquatints washed over by hand, each with a single tint, and the *Picturesque Guide to Bath* of 1793 is enlivened with 16 of his hand-coloured aquatints. In a work published in

Parts in 1813, *Aqua Pictura*, the reproduction in colour of pictures by each of 19 well-known artists is demonstrated, step by step, in four plates: first an etched outline, secondly an aquatint to represent Indian ink or sepia wash, thirdly a plate tinted with a single warm tone, and lastly an aquatint with the addition of the full range of colours of the original.

He was active not only as water-colourist, colour theorist and engraver but also as a publisher and printseller, specializing in small guidebooks illustrated with his own drawings reproduced as miniature aquatints, hand coloured. Most of these were concerned only with places in the Home Counties or farther afield: such were *Picturesque Rides and Walks* (1817–18), 120 views in Bedfordshire, Berkshire, Buckinghamshire, Essex, Hertfordshire, Kent, Middlesex and Surrey 'in 24 parts each containing 5 plates coloured in imitation of Drawings price 2s 6d or large paper, 4s. each', and *Tour of the Grand Junction Canal* (1819). His final essay in this genre, *Excursions of Pleasure*, is however included here since its 24 pretty little tinted plates depict beauty spots strung along the course of the Thames, including all the bridges of central London.

Abbey (no 221) records a set of 12 Numbers in their original wrappers, printed as follows: 'Continued Monthly. Excursions of Pleasure and Sports of the Thames: illustrated in a series of engravings coloured after nature: Accompanied by a Descriptive and Historical Account ... To be completed within Twelve Numbers, price 1s. each. London: Printed for W. Simpkin and R. Marshall, Stationers' Hall Court, Ludgate-street. 1822'. Numbers were indeed published over a year at one shilling each, the wrappers for the first five being dated February 1822 and the publication-lines of Nos 6–12 dated June 1822 to January 1823. Each consisted of a 16 page section of text and a couple of plates not necessarily illustrative of that section, the last comprising the title-page, directions for the plates, 15 pages of the text and the index.

Excursions of Pleasure and Sports on the Thames, illustrated in a series of Engravings in Aqua-Tinta, Coloured after Nature, Accompanied by a descriptive and historical account of every Town, Village, Mansion, and the adjacent country on the banks of that River, the places and periods for enjoying the Sports of Angling, Shooting, Sailing, &c. Also a particular account of all places of Amusement in its Vicinity, and the list of Inns and Taverns, for the Accommodation of Company. By J. Hassell. (epigraph from Pope) London: Printed for W.

Simpkin and R. Marshall, Stationers' Hall Court, Ludgate Street. 1823.

Small octavo, 160 × 100mm.   1823

COLLATION Title-page; list of plates (1 leaf); pp 1–191, Excursions; pp i–iii, index.

These small coloured aquatints have captions bc but no credits. They are set off by a narrow frame of double rules and the plate-marks have been cropped in binding. They are unnumbered and the plates of the first four Numbers were issued without publication-lines. From No 5 these read: 'London. Pubd. (date) by (Messrs.) Simpkin & Marshall.', but they are frequently out of sight, being gathered into the sewing of the binding.

Copies are found with extra-illustrations from other small-plate publications, particularly Hassell's own *Picturesque Rides*, which cover much of the same ground. The latter may be distinguished from the genuine illustrations by the absence of a ruled frame around the work and by publication-lines dated 1816 or 1817.

1 front. Custom House. 65 × 100mm. nd. No 1.

2 p 18 Blackwall. 60 × 98mm. nd. No 4.

3 p 25 Erith Reach. 1 Jany 1823. 60 × 95mm. No 12.

4 p 27 Purfleet. 1st Octr 1822. 63 × 97mm. No 9.

5 p 29 Greenhithe. 1st June 1822. 65 × 97mm. No 5.

6 p 30 Northfleet Kent. 60 × 98mm. nd. No 3.

7 p 32 Gravesend West entrance. 1st June 1822. 63 × 97mm. No 6.

8 p 47 Windsor Bridge. 1 Jany 1823. 60 × 95mm. No 12.

9 p 58 Southwark Bridge. 62 × 95mm. nd. No 2.

10 p 60 Blackfriars Bridge. 1st Septr 1822. 65 × 98mm. No 8.

11 p 62 Waterloo Bridge. 1st June 1822. 65 × 98mm. No 5.

12 p 64 Westminster Bridge. 1st Octr 1822. 63 × 98mm. No 9.

13 p 72 Vauxhall Bridge. 1st Novr 1822. 62 × 98mm. No 10.

14 p 80 Battersea Reach. 1st June 1822. 65 × 95mm. No 6. (*Longford* 253)

15 p 83 Putney. 1 Decr 1822. 63 × 95mm. No 11.

16 p 117 Richmond, Surrey. 65 × 98mm. nd. No 4. (*Gascoigne* 77)

17 p 118 Twickenham reach. 1st Septr 1822. 65 × 98mm. No 7.

18 p 145 London Bridge. 1st Septr 1822. 65 × 100mm. No 7.

19 p 178 Windsor Bucks. 63 × 100mm. nd. No 3. With the Castle.

20 p 179 Eton College Bucks. 62 × 98mm. nd. No 1.

21 p 180 Charter Island. 1st Septr 1822. 65 × 97mm. No 8. ie Runnymede.

22 p 181 Staines-reach. 1st Novr 1822. 63 × 98mm. No 10.

23 p 182 Chertsey Bridge. 1 Decr 1822. 63 × 97mm. No 11.

24 p 184 Oatlands, Surrey. 63 × 97mm. nd. No 2.

---

141 · HAVELL'S NOBLEMEN'S AND GENTLEMEN'S SEATS* [1823]

In 1814 the landscape painter William Havell set out to paint the country seats of the aristocracy for a series of aquatints to be engraved by his relations in the firm of Robert Havell & Son. His sixth view was published in May 1815 and he drew no more, since by the following year he was in China with Lord Amhurst's mission. The series did not however come to a halt since other artists kept it going until a twentieth plate was issued on 1 July 1823. A drawing of Cassiobury was contributed by Turner and others by lesser but highly competent topographical artists such as Copley Fielding, Frederick Mackenzie, Henry Gastineau, Thomas Higham and John Britton. When the complete collection was published by Havell each plate was accompanied by one leaf of printed text, signed 'J.B.' (for John Britton) or 'J.M.M.', with the exception of 'Windsor Castle' and 'Blenheim' which had two leaves apiece. Most of the views were drawn from the Home or from southern counties (see *Tooley* 253).

One which deserves special comment is that of Buckingham House in winter. The original view, sketched from the edge of the frozen lake, was done about 1810 by John Burnet for *The Beauties of England and Wales* (no 104), item 90; he was a pupil of Robert Scott, the landscape engraver, and with his painter brother James Burnet was strongly influenced by the Dutch School. Subsequently Copley Fielding, the water-colourist, copied this sketch and made the most of the contrast between the bleak snow-bound setting, the rosy brick of the house and the wintry jollifications in the foreground. He also added Queen Charlotte's carriage approaching the gates with a mounted escort and some of the skating figures. It was clearly his version (now in the British Museum) which was engraved by the Havells yet, although they acknowledge his intervention in three other views in the series, this plate is simply credited to Burnet. For the sake of comparison details of two other views, in the environs, are given.

The aquatints, unnumbered and unlisted, are printed on thick cartridge paper with Whatman watermarks 1814 to 1816. Each view is surrounded by a tinted frame, whose dimensions are given below second. Publication-lines read: 'London. Published (date) by R. Havell, No 3 Chapel Street, Tottenham Court Road.' Only an engraved title-page was issued, coloured by hand as were the other plates.

(*Title-page* pl. 1)

Folio, 480 × 320mm.   1823

COLLATION 42pp of unpaginated descriptions interleaved with 20 plates.

1 (aquatint title) A Series/of/Picturesque Views/of/Noblemen's & Gentlemen's Seats./With/Historical & Descriptive Accounts/of/Each Subject/Engraved in Aquatinta/By R. Havell & Son. (a series of miniature views and an architectural framework with ogee arch, etc surround the title) References 1: 3: 8: 9: 11: & 15: Buildings & Scenery in Stowe Gardens – 2: The Royal Arms – 4: Mausoleum at Brocklesby/ – 5: Carlton Palace (45 × 95mm) – 10: Grotto at Oatlands – 12: Wilton House &c. Drawn & Etched by H. Shaw. Engraved by R. Havell & Son. London, Published July 1, 1823 by R. Havell, Chapel Strt Tottenham Court Road. 320 × 245/380 × 290mm.

2 Buckingham House, Middlesex a Palace of Her Majesty. Drawn by J. Burnett. Engraved by R. Havell & Son. London. Published June 2, 1817 ... To Mrs Watts Russell of Ilam Hall, an admirer & patron of the Fine Arts, this Plate is inscribed. 200 × 300,220 × 320/280 × 370mm.

3 Holland House, Middlesex, the Seat of the Right Honorable Lord Holland. Drawn by J.C. Smith. Engraved by R. Havell & Son. London. Published June 2, 1817 ... To the Right Honorable Eliza Vassall Lady Holland, a patron and lover of polite literature, this Plate is respectfully inscribed. 200 × 300,220 × 320/280 × 365mm.

4 Chiswick House, Middlesex./The Garden, or North front. Drawn by C. Fielding from a sketch by G.

Cattermole. Engraved by R. Havell & Son. London, Published July 1, 1823 ... To His Grace the Duke of Devonshire, this plate of his elegant villa is respectfully inscribed. 197 × 290,215 × 310/290 × 380mm.

142 · 'S. AND R. PERCY'S' LONDON [1823–4]

Sholto and Reuben Percy were the pseudonyms for Joseph Clinton Robertson, a Fleet Street patent agent and Thomas Byerley, a journalist, who derived their names from their habit of meeting at the Percy Coffee-house in Rathbone Place. They produced collaborative works issued in monthly Parts, most notably *The Percy Anecdotes* (20 vols, 1821–3), a classified series of anecdotes collected from newspapers. They also planned the 'Percy Histories, or interesting Memorials of the Capitals of Europe', but of this only three duodecimo volumes on London were printed, being advertised in June 1824, bound, for 16s.

Though this was sparsely illustrated, with woodcut tailpieces, a frontispiece portrait of George IV, a map and four line-engravings (in vols. 1 and 3), the latter are of especial interest since, together with the title-pages, they are engraved on steel and predate the pioneer illustrated works on London in this medium: Heath's *Views* (no 147) by two years, and *Metropolitan Improvements* (no 154) by five. Moreover two of them were drawn by J.P. Neale, the draughtsman for Brayley's *Westminster Abbey* (no 123), and all were engraved by W. Cooke junior. This presumably is the credit whereby William John Cooke, who had been apprenticed to his uncle George, at first distinguished his work from that of his other engraving uncle, William Bernard Cooke. Publication-lines, dating between 1 April 1823 and May 1824, visible in *Londres et l'Angleterre* (no 150), are here bound in.

(steel engr) London/or/interesting memorials/of its/rise, progress & present state./By/Sholto & Reuben Percy,/Brothers of the Benedictine Monastery,/Mount Benger./Three volumes./Volume 1 (2–3)./London: Printed for T.

Boys, Ludgate Hill./1823 (1824). (A general title, also steel-engraved, reads: 'The Percy Histories...')

Duodecimo, 138 × 80mm.   1823–4

COLLATION Vol. 1. Title-page; series title ('The Percy Histories'); dedication to George IV; pp i–iv, preface, list of illustrations; pp 3–360, London. Vol. 2. Series title; pp 1–360, London continued. Vol. 3. Series title; pp 1–360, London continued; index (8pp).

VOL. 1

1 p 1 A New Map of London, Westminster, Southwark, and their Suburbs. Drawn from actual Survey for the History of London by Sholto & Reuben Percy. Drawn & Engraved by Benjn. Davies, 34 Compton Str. Published Octr. 1, 1823 by T. Boys, 7 Ludgate Hill. 240 × 385mm. (*Darlington and Howgego* 294)

2 p 31 Westminster Abbey & Vicinity. Dr. by J.P. Neale. Engr. on steel by W. Cooke jnr. 70 × 120mm. E. end, and exterior of Henry VII Chapel.

VOL. 3

3 p 15 The Custom House London. Dr. by J. Cartwright. Engr. by W. Cooke jnr. 70 × 120mm. From river.

4 p 269 Somerset House, London. Dr. by T. Barrett. Engr. by W. Cooke junr. 70 × 120mm.

5 p 355 Hanover Terrace Regents Park. J.P. Neale. W. Cooke jnr. 70 × 120mm. Built to the designs of John Nash by J.M. Aitkens, 1822–3.

143 · THE PORT-FOLIO* [1823–4]

Collections of small antiquarian engravings were apparently still in favour in the third decade of the century, since two of the publishers of the second issue of the Storer and Greig *Antiquarian and Topographical Cabinet* (no 118) were prepared to hazard yet another series of precisely the same nature—indeed a sequel, as acknowledged in their preface: 'A Work of this character upon a plan so economical was never attempted until the appearance of the Antiquarian and Topographical Cabinet, of which highly-esteemed collection the Port-Folio may be considered a Second Series'.

Four volumes were published, each with exactly 96 pages of text descriptive of the plates. This however was paginated, enabling the index in each volume to refer to a plate by the number of the page it faced.

The Port-folio; a collection of engravings from Antiquarian, architectural, & topographical subjects, curious works of art, &c &c. with descriptions. Vol. I (II–IV). London: Published by Nornaville & Fell, New Bond Street; and Sherwood, Jones & Co, Paternoster Row, 1823 (1824).

Sextodecimo, 155 × 95mm.   1823–4

COLLATION   Vol. 1 (1823). Engr title; title-page; pp iii–iv, preface; index, list of plates (2pp); pp 1–96, The Port-folio. Vol. 2 (1823). Half-title; title-page; index, list of plates (2pp); pp 1–96, The Port-folio continued. Vol. 3 (1824). Engr half-title; title-page; index, list of plates (2pp); pp 1–96, The Port-folio continued. Vol. 4 (1824). Engr half-title; title-page; index, list of plates (2pp); pp 1–96, The Port-folio continued.

Once again James Storer was called in for the engraving but this time he was partnered by his son Henry Sargent Storer. Central London views were in the first two volumes and a suburban view in each of the others. Credits on these plates are uniformly: 'Drawn & Engraved by J. & H.S. Storer' and the publication-line: 'Pubd. by Sherwood & Co. (date)'.

VOL. 1

1 p 31 Statue/(Gerard's Hall London.) ... Nov. 1, 1822. 110 × 60/150 × 95mm.

2 p 73 Burlington Arcade.... 102 × 68/155 × 95mm. No publication-line.

VOL. 2

3 front. (half-title) Christ's Hospital./(passage to the Hall, &c.) Drawn & Engd by J. & H.S. Storer for the Port-Folio. Pubd. by Sherwood & Co. Augt 1, 1823. 110 × 75/150 × 90mm. Vignetted.

4 p 39 St Pauls/from Aldersgate Street.... June 1, 1823. 82 × 80/150 × 95mm.

5 p 39 St Pauls./from Sermon Lane Doctors Commons. ... June 1, 1823. 105 × 63/150 × 90mm.

6 p 53 Christ's Hospital/(Cloisters & part of the Hall.) ... July 1, 1823. 65 × 105/90 × 150mm.

7 p 53 Christ's Hospital/Ward No. 4.... July 1, 1823. 70 × 100/95 × 150mm.

8 p 53 Christ's Hospital/The Grammer School, Writing School &c.... July 1, 1823. 65 × 110/95 × 150mm.

9 p 53 Christ's Hospital/the Writing School.... July 1, 1823. 67 × 90/95 × 150mm. Interior.

VOL. 3

10 p 43 The Tunnell/Islington.... Decr. 1, 1823. 60 × 110/95 × 150mm. On the Regent's Canal.

VOL. 4

11 p 33 Whittington College/Highgate.... G. Smith Esqr. Architect.... June 1, 1824. 60 × 110/90 × 150mm. Founded on College Hill in the City but removed to Highgate by the Mercers' Company in 1822.

144 · DESCRIPTION OF LONDON [1824]

This attractive pamphlet guide with a brief but quite straightforward descriptive text was intended for William Darton's usual juvenile market. Its illustrations, however, are somewhat more sophisticated than was usual in such books: 12 line-engraved views, two to a plate united by a double-line border with captions above and below. Each plate has the publication-line 'London, William Darton, 58 Holborn Hill, 8mo 28 1824.', presumably standing for 28 August. For sixpence extra they could be had nicely colour-washed. The buff paper wrapper reads as the title-page, with the addition of the prices (1s plain, 1s 6d coloured).

A Description of London, containing a Sketch of its History and Present State, and of all the most celebrated Public Buildings &c. Embellished with Engravings. London: Wiliam Darton, 58 Holborn Hill.

Duodecimo, 170 × 105mm.   (1824)

COLLATION   Title-page; pp 1–36, descriptions.

1 front. St Paul's Cathedral – The Bank of England. Each 70 × 82mm. The Bank's 'Tivoli Corner'.

2 p 12 Westminster Abbey – Westminster Hall. Each 70 × 82mm. Both from the N.

3 p 18 The Horse Guards – White Hall. Each 70 × 82mm. Horse Guards Parade and the Banqueting Hall.

4 p 19 Carlton Palace – Hay Market Theatre. Each 70 × 82mm. Nash's Haymarket, completed in 1821.

5 p 25 Somerset House – Covent Garden Theatre. Each 70 × 82mm. Somerset House from the Strand.

6 p 36 The Royal Exchange – Waterloo Bridge. Each 70 × 82mm. Courtyard of the Royal Exchange.

145 · LONDON SCENES [1824]

John Harris, proprietor of the 'Juvenile Library', was the flourishing successor to the celebrated publisher of children's books Francis Newbery, on whose death he managed the business for widow Newbery and eventually took it over himself. In 1805 he republished one of the Newbery stock items, the miniature *Curiosities of London* (no 49), in competition with a rival in children's literature, John Marshall, whose set of little etched cards, *Views of the Principal Buildings in London* (no 101), came out in 1800. Harris's *Curiosities*, however, with its 400 odd text pages illustrated by only 11 small plates spread over the two volumes, as against 24 in the Newbery edition, must have proved rather arid fare for the nursery.

In 1818 he published a new, more lavishly illustrated child's guide to London in quasi-fictional form entitled *A Visit to Uncle William in Town*. The fiction is that one William Beresford, 'an opulent merchant in the City, and an old batchelor of fifty-seven … one of the most eccentric and benevolent men in the world', sets out for the country to visit his brother-in-law, a widower clergyman. With this relative's consent he collects the five orphaned children, Matilda aged 14, Elizabeth 12, Julia 7, William 15 and Henry 10, packs them into his carriage and takes them back to his house in Guildford Street, Bloomsbury and the care of his housekeeper. Hard facts come in once he has them in his power. He takes them on daily expeditions by conveyance or on foot to see the sights, and they are indeed spared very little, being made to admire such buildings as the County Gaol in Horsemonger Lane, the King's Bench Prison, St Luke's Asylum and the House of Correction in Cold Bath Fields. They are told of the Elgin Marbles but spared a visit to the British Museum; no doubt Bullock's Museum in Piccadilly, as a commercial undertaking, was preferred and the Soho Bazaar (a *Visit to the Bazaar* being available from John Harris's shop), where they are allowed to buy gifts for papa and the housekeeper. Theatres in general were merely pointed out as landmarks but, as a treat, they were taken to an evening performance at

Sadler's Wells. Most of their adventures are illustrated by 66 small views, three to a plate, whose subjects include nearly all of those formerly illustrated for the *Curiosities*.

When a new edition was brought out in 1824 the publisher's introduction quoted a protest from a modern, pleasure-loving child about the former: 'I think there is too little diversity in a book which is professedly designed for the amusement and instruction of children. We have merely an account of *plans* and *buidings* without anything to relieve or enliven the spirits'. In deference to this infant objection he reset the text in order to insert some slightly more frivolous matter, illustrated by six new plates, each with two subjects such as 'Mad Ox on Blackfriars Bridge', 'The Dancing Sweeps' or 'Skating on the Serpentine River' (items 1, 3, 6, 8, 13, 21). The price was 6s 'half bound' or 7s 6d with the plates coloured.

A Visit to Uncle William in Town; or, a Description of the most remarkable Buildings and Curiosities in the British Metropolis. Illustrated with 66 Copper-plate Engravings. London: Printed for J. Harris, Corner of St Paul's Church-Yard. 1818.

Duodecimo, 165 × 100mm. 1818

COLLATION Title-page; pp iii–viii, introduction; pp 1–119, A Visit.

London Scenes, or a Visit to Uncle William in Town: containing a description of the most remarkable Buildings and Curiosities in the British Metropolis. Illustrated by 78 copperplate engravings. 'This is London! how do you like it?'. London: John Harris, corner of St Paul's Church Yard.

Duodecimo, 170 × 105mm. (1824)

COLLATION Title-page; pp iii–vi, introduction; pp vii–x, Description of the Metropolis (verses); pp xi–xvi, index; pp 1–211, London Scenes.

The plates are unnumbered and unlisted and have no credits. Each view however has a reference to the relevant text page. Publication-lines on first edition plates read: 'Publish'd Novr. 20, 1818 by J. Harris, corner of St Pauls', and on those added in the second edition: 'Publish'd Oct 1, 1824 by J. Harris, corner of St. Pauls'. The pages opposite which the plates are bound are quoted below as in the second edition, with the first edition reference following in brackets. Engraved page references to each subject in the text, which have been corrected on the reissued plates, are treated in the same way. First edition views measure uniformly 40 × 68mm; second edition measurements, where different, are quoted in the list. Plate-marks have been cropped.

1 front. Mr. Beresford's Arrival, page 6. – Temple Bar, page 7. Each 58 × 72mm.

2 p 7(8) Temple Bar, page 7(8). – Interior of Temple Church, page 8(9). – Fountain, Temple, page 9(10).

3 p 10 St Dunstan's Church Fleet Street, page 10. – Mad Ox on Blackfriars Bridge, page 15. Each 58 × 72mm.

4 p 15(front.) Black Friars Bridge, page 15 (14). – St. Paul's Church, page 21(19). – St Paul's School, page 30(24). The bridge from the S.W., the Cathedral from the W. A note in the 1824 ed explains that by now this building of St Paul's School had been superseded.

5 p 34(26) Fishmongers Hall, page 34(26). – St Dunstan in the East, page 44(27). – The Monument &c, page 39(28).

6 p 35 The Dancing Sweeps, page 35. – Heroic conduct of Edd. Osborne, page 37. 60 × 72,58 × 72mm. Sir Edward Osborne, Lord Mayor in 1583, apprenticed in his youth to Sir William Hewet, clothworker, rescued his master's little daughter when she fell into the Thames from his house on London Bridge, subsequently married her and succeeded to the business.

7 p 36(27) London Bridge, page 36(30). – The Custom House, page 45(32). – The Trinity House, page 208(33).

8 p 43 London Stone, page 42. – Rag Fair in Rosemary Lane, page 58. Each 57 × 72mm.

9 p 46(34) The Tower, page 46(34). – The Mint, page 57(38). – Interior of St. Catherines, page 61(39).

10 p 62(38) London Docks, page 62 (40). – West India Docks, page 62(40). – Ironmongers Hall, page 68(43).

11 p 79(47) Excise Office, page 79(46). – The Bank, page 81(48). – The Auction Mart, page 83(49).

12 p 84(47) Interior of the Royal Exchange, page 84(50). – The Mansion House, page 86(53). – St Stephens Walbrook, page 88(55). Interior of St Stephen's.

13 p 87 Lord Mayors Day, page 87. – Bartholomew Fair, page 109. Each 55 × 72mm.

14 p 90(57) Interior of Guildhall, page 89(59). – Southwark Bridge, page 97(61). – Christs Hospital, page (62).

15 p 105(63) St Bartholomew's Hospital, page 104(62). – Newgate, page 111(65). – New Surgeons Hall, page 113(67). 'New' Surgeons Hall, built in Lincolns Inn Fields, 1806–13.

16 p 122 (99) Northumberland House, page 122(100). – The Admiralty, page 166(102). – The Horse Guards, page 167(103). Admiralty screen-wall not shown.

17 p 129(99) Covent Garden Theatre, page 128(98). – St Paul's Covent Garden, page 128(98). – Drury Lane Theatre, page 129(99). Shows Smirke's Covent Gar-den Theatre of 1809 and Benjamin Wyatt's Drury Lane of 1811.

18 p 132(63) Foundling Hospital, page 131(69). – British Museum, page 136(72). – Cavendish Square, page 210(73).

19 p 145(77) Bullock's Museum, page 144(76). – St James's Palace, page 146(80). – Carlton House, page 151(82). Bullock's Museum in Egyptian Hall, Piccadilly built in 1812; contents dispersed in 1819.

20 p 152(77) Waterloo Place, page 153(83). – The Opera House, page 153(83). – Kensington Palace, page 157(85).

21 p 158 Skating on the Serpentine River, page 158. – Guy Fawkes in Effigy, page 183. Each 55 × 72mm.

22 p 161(89) Lord Spencer's House, page 161(88). – Buckingham House, page 161(88). – Chinese Bridge, page 163(89). Bridge and pagoda built by Nash in St James's Park in honour of the Allied Sovereigns, 1814.

23 p 164(89) Turkish Ordnance, page 164(91). – The Waterloo Bridge, page 115(93). – Somerset House, page 118(96). The Bridge was opened in June 1817.

24 p 168(103) Whitehall, page 168(103). – The Treasury, page 172(104). – Westminster Abby &c., page 172(105). Whitehall view shows the Banqueting Hall.

25 p 184(103) House of Lords, & Commons, page 184(107). – The Speaker's House, page 187(108). – Westminster Bridge, page 192(109).

26 p 197(115) New Bethlem Hospital, page 197(110). – Philanthropic Chapel, page 196(110). – Magdalen Hospital, page 210(113). The Bethlehem Hospital rebuilt in St George's Fields, Southwark, 1812–15.

27 p 198(115) Kings Bench Prison, page 198(114). – Cobourg Theatre, page 117(95). – Guys Hospital, page 207(116).

28 p 209(57) The London Institution, page 209(56). – St Luke's Hospital, page 209(57). – Interior of the Charter House, page 133(57). The London Institution built in Finsbury Circus, 1815–19.

---

146 · BRITTON AND PUGIN'S ILLUSTRATIONS OF THE PUBLIC BUILDINGS OF LONDON [1825–8]

John Britton, although primarily a topographer and antiquarian, was also a keen critic of architecture and, as early as 1805, started issuing a series that combined two of his three interests, *The Architectu-*

ral Antiquities of Great Britain (no 97) and in 1814 the *Cathedral Antiquities of England*. He thus associated with himself budding architects and architectural draughtsmen and engravers, in particular Augustus Charles Pugin, John Nash's valued assistant, and his many pupils. He edited Pugin's *Specimens of Gothic Architecture* (1821–3) and their names appear together on the title-page of the present work which, although it includes the mandatory accounts of Westminster Abbey and Hall, moves on from Gothic to baroque and thence, with scant attention to the Palladians, to the work of contemporaries. It is, indeed, almost a Regency 'Pevsner'.

The text take the form of short, descriptive, signed essays on the buildings illustrated, mostly written by Britton or his friend Brayley. But practising architects were also involved: Joseph Gwilt whose substantial contribution includes a paper on St Paul's Cathedral delivered to the Architects' and Antiquaries' Club in 1823, J.B. Papworth who had already written similar descriptions of the aquatints in Ackermann's *Select Views of London* (no 117), and Decimus Burton whose note on one of his earliest commissions, a villa in Regent's Park, was published. Detailed accounts of the principal theatres were signed by Charles Dibdin, natural son of the dramatist of that name and actor-manager at Sadler's Wells. A further contributor was W.H. Leeds who reissued the complete work in 1838 with 20 supplementary plates and his own addenda to the original essays.

Progress reports appeared in Ackermann's *Repository of Arts*, such as that for April 1823: 'The first number of "Architectural Illustrations of the Public Buildings of London" will appear on the 1st of April and will contain seven engravings of St Paul's Cathedral, the New Entrance to the House of Lords, the Temple Church, the Custom House, with two sheets of letter-press'. In the *Literary Gazette* of 6 November 1824 it was announced that the ninth Number (Drury Lane and Haymarket Theatres, with seven engravings) was delayed because of a fire at the printer's and that three more Numbers would complete the first volume. By April 1825 the completed first volume was available for review by the *Gentleman's Magazine* and in the following year the December *Repository* announced that the seventeenth Number, containing seven engravings and letterpress, was then available. In January 1828

it gave notice that the whole of the second volume, with 72 engravings, was forthcoming and in March advertised thus: 'Intelligence: completion of "Architectural Illustrations of the Public Buildings of London" edited ... by J. Britton, F.S.A. containing 144 engravings, mostly in outline by Le Keux, Roffe, Gladwin &c. from drawings by A. Pugin in one vol. imperial 8°'. Josiah Taylor's catalogue of architectural publications offered ordinary and 'de luxe' editions: 'In Two vol. Med. 8vo, price £5. 5s; Imp. 8vo, £8. 8s; 4to with Proofs on India paper £14. 14s.'

Meanwhile the *Gentleman's Magazine*, which had merely compared the first volume to Ralph's unillustrated *Review of the Publick Buildings* and Malton's *Picturesque Tour* (no 72), launched into an exhaustive serial appreciation of the essays from August to December 1827 and April to May 1828. Britton's intentions are set out in his preface:

In the design and prosecution of this publication, it was the Editor's hope to render it amusing and instructive, not only to the professional *Architect*, but also to the *Topographer, Antiquary* and *Connoisseur*.... we are persuaded that the aggregate amount of persons and materials employed on building in London and environs, within the year 1824, was considerably greater than in any one year subsequent to that extensive conflagration....

It is notorious that foreigners, in general, as well as country gentlemen, and even the great bulk of Londoners themselves, know very little of the metropolitan edifices. It is equally a fact, that no publication has hitherto appeared calculated to furnish satisfactory information. Such a work, however, is now attempted.

Of the second edition in 1838 Leeds has to say:

One unquestionable improvement upon the first edition is, that instead of the subjects being mixed together without any attempt at arrangement, they are now classified under the respective heads of: I Churches; II Theatres; III Commercial and Civic Buildings; IV Buildings connected with Literature and Art, &c; V Palaces and Private Mansions; VI Bridges.

To coincide with its appearance Weale published a volume supplementary to the first edition of which Leeds says in his preface:

The subjects it contains are those which have been incorporated in the new edition, and which are thus printed separately in order to accommodate the purchasers of the first. By this means they are enabled to possess all the additional plates and the letter-press belonging to them; although not all the fresh matter which has been introduced into the Second Edition consisting of extensive notes and remarks by the present Editor.

The 1838 rearrangement has been indicated in the following list by adding the revised page numbers of the essays to the corresponding numbers of the first edition and its supplement.

Illustrations of the Public Buildings of London: with Historical and Descriptive Accounts of Each Edifice. (epigraph) By J. Britton, F.S.A. &c.—and A. Pugin, Architect. Vol. I (II). London: Printed for J. Taylor, 59 High Holborn: J. Britton, Burton Street; and A. Pugin, Great Russell Street. 1825 (1828).

Octavo, 227 × 140mm. (Large Paper, India paper 295 × 235mm)   1825–8

COLLATION   Vol. 1. Half-title; title-page; dedication to George IV dated New Year's Day 1825 (3pp); contents (1 leaf); pp ix–xvi, preface; pp 1–333, illustrations; pp 334–6, index. Vol. 2. Half-title; title-page; dedication to Prince Leopold of Saxe-Coburg dated 30 November 1827 (1 leaf); contents, tabular view of the bridges (2pp); pp vii–xxii, preface; List of Public Buildings in London, Squares, Parks, &c. (4pp); pp 1–327, illustrations continued; pp 328–80, index.

Illustrations of the Public Buildings of London: with Descriptive Accounts of Each Edifice. Supplement: containing the new subjects and descriptions incorporated in the second edition. By W.H. Leeds. (epigraph) London, John Weale, Architectural Library, 59 High Holborn, 1838.

Octavo, 227 × 140mm.   1838

COLLATION   Title-page; pp iii–xiii, preface; contents (1 leaf); pp 1–134, illustrations; pp 135–6, index.

Illustrations of the Public Buildings of London: with Historical and Descriptive Accounts of Each Edifice. By Pugin and Britton. Second edition, greatly enlarged by W.H. Leeds. In Two Volumes. Vol 1 (2). London: John Weale, Architectural Library, 59 High Holborn, 1838.

Octavo, 245 × 150mm.   1838

COLLATION   Vol. 1. Title-page; dedication to Sydney Smirke (1 leaf); pp v–xviii, preface; pp xix–xx, contents; pp 1–375, illustrations; index (3pp). Vol. 2. Title-page; pp iii–iv, contents; pp 1–401, illustrations continued; pp 403–5, index.

Pevsner's two *London* volumes in the 'Buildings of Britain' series are illustrated by about 130 small photographs while this Regency counterpart feasts the eye with an equivalent number of outline steel-engravings based on drawings by the leading architects and architectural draughtsmen of the period. In the Middlesex volumes of *The Beauties of England and Wales* (no 104) Britton had assumed the duties of picture editor but for this new series he

was ably seconded by Pugin, a seasoned architectural and topographical artist with many London drawings to his credit, aquatinted and published by Ackermann in *Microcosm of London* (1808–10, no 99), the monthly *Repository of Arts* (from 1809), the *History of Westminster Abbey* (1811–12, no 108) and engraved for *Views in Islington and Pentonville* (1819) with a text by Brayley.

But this was something new in illustrated London books, being designed not so much for the collector and framer of hand-coloured prints or the topographer as for the architectural profession and its clientele and those whom Britton calls 'connoisseurs' of architecture. Pugin himself provided a large number of the elevations, plans and sections but he also enrolled pupils from his school of architectural drawing: Francis Arundale, Talbot Bury, J. D'Egville, Benjamin Ferrey, R. Grantham, C.J. Matthews (the comedian) and G.B. Moore, most of whom were in their early twenties, one or two still in their teens. Also among the draughtsmen were young practising architects such as James Pennethorne, a former Pugin pupil, Decimus Burton and Philip Hardwick and two of Britton's constant architectural advisers, Henry Shaw and George Cattermole.

Expert architectural engravers were employed to transfer these drawings to steel plates, most of the work being carried out by John Le Keux, son of a Huguenot pewter manufacturer and pupil of James Basire junior, who had already been associated with Britton in illustrating the *Beauties of England and Wales*, and by George Gladwin. Other copper engravers who adapted their art to this new medium were John Roffe and William Deeble, while among the younger etchers were Henry Adlard, James Carter, Frederick J. Havell, J. Tingle and H. Winkles who opened a school of steel-engraving in Karlsruhe in 1824. It may be noted that E.W. Brayley's essay on Westminster Abbey refers back to his book on the subject (no 123) with which this work has in common the engravers Le Keux, Roffe, Sands and James Carter. Architects of contemporary buildings illustrated must also have been co-opted since a number of the designs are based on drawings of buildings which were still in course of construction. Each building is classified in tm, eg: 'Edifices of London—Palaces'. Credits are conscientiously engraved for architect, draughtsman and engraver. Sometimes the picture editor is mentioned, and even the three plate printers, Cox & Co, McQueen or Barnett & Son, are occasionally indicated br. Apart from the dates in the first edition publication-lines are almost invariable:

(a) 'London, Published (date), by J. Taylor, (59) High Holborn'. (first ed, vols 1-2)
(b) 'John Weale, Architectural Library, 59, High Holborn'. (1838 ed and supplement)

Each volume has a list of subjects indicating how many plates should be bound with each essay with the instruction: 'The Prints to be placed at the beginning or ends of the sheets where they are respectively described'. An erratic attempt has been made to order each group by plate numbers engraved tr.

VOL. 1

1 (engr title, on a shield in a cusped panel, surrounded by six miniature views with two shields, all in a cusped and crested four-centered arch, surmounted by shields with components of the royal arms) Illustrations/of the/Public Buildings/of/London./by/J. Britton, F.S.A./&/A. Pugin, Archt./Vol. 1. 175 × 120/225 × 155mm. The ornaments are keyed thus: '1. Bronze figures by Bacon: Somerset House – 2. Carlton Palace – 3. Statue of King Charles 1st Charing Cross – 4. Monument of London & St Magnus Church – 5. Steeple of Bow Church – 6. Arms of the City of London – 7. Somerset House, Strand front – 8. Arms of the City of Westminster – 9. Parts from Crosby Hall (the architectural frame of the page) – 10. Royal Hanoverian Arms'.

CHURCHES

St Paul's Cathedral by Joseph Gwilt and E.W. Brayley. (pp 1–40*; 1838 ed 1, 1–46)

2 pl.1 St Paul's Cathedral Church/transverse section and plan of vaults. A. Pugin direxit. C.J. Mathews del. G. Gladwin sculp. April 1, 1823. 165 × 100/202 × 150mm.

3 pl.2 St Paul's Cathedral: West Front. A. Pugin direxit. J. D'Egville del. J. Cleghorn sc. June 1, 1823. 160 × 102/200 × 150mm. With plan.

4 pl.III St Paul's Cathedral/Longitudinal Section. A. Pugin direxit. C.J. Mathews del. G. Gladwin sculp. June 1, 1823. 110 × 165/150 × 200mm.

5 pl.IV St Paul's Cathedral Church/Section across the nave looking West. Measured & Drawn by C. Moore. G. Gladwin sculp. 1824. 110 × 170/150 × 200mm.

6 pl.5 S.E. View of St Paul's Cathedral Church. A. Pugin direxit. G. Gladwin sculp. July 1, 1824. 115 × 170/150 × 200mm.

7 pl.VI St Paul's Cathedral Church/View of the interior

taken from the North Transept. A. Pugin direxit. J. Le Keux sc. Nov. 1, 1824. 160 × 110/225 × 140mm.

8 pl.VII St Paul's Cathedral Church/No 1, Section of N. Transept & half of Dome. – No 2, Elevation of S. Transept & half of Dome. Measured & Drawn by A. Pugin. G. Gladwin sculpt. Decr. 1, 1824. 165 × 125/200 × 150mm.

9 pl.VIII St Paul's Cathedral Church/Plan of Dome &c to accompany half elevation & half Section, pl.VII. Measured & Drawn by A. Pugin. G. Gladwin sculpt. Decr. 1, 1824. 168 × 120/200 × 150mm.

St Stephen's Wallbrook by Joseph Gwilt. (pp 33–8; 1838 ed 1, 47–56)

10 pl.1 St Stephen's Church, Wallbrook/Plan & Sections. J. Britton dirext. S. Rayner del. G. Gladwin sculp. June 1, 1823. 170 × 108/205 × 132mm.

11 pl.2 St Stephen's Church, Wallbrook/interior view looking east. J. Britton direxit. G. Cattermole del. J. Le Keux sculp. April 1, 1823. 115 × 160/150 × 200mm.

St Martin in the Fields by Joseph Gwilt. (pp 39–45; 1838 ed 1, 101–9)

12 pl.1 Church of St Martins in the Fields/West front & Section of Tower &c. Gibbs Archt. Thos. Bradberry del. J. Le Keux sculp. April 1, 1823. 175 × 123/200 × 150mm. Pen and ink drawing (210 × 125mm) in Westminster Public Library.

13 pl.II Church of St Martins in the Fields/Elevation of South Side & Section East to West. Gibbs Archt. Thos. Bradberry del. J. Le Keux sculp. April 1, 1823. 115 × 160/150 × 200mm. Pen and ink drawing (120 × 173mm) in Westminster Public Library.

14 pl.III Church of St Martins in the Fields/A,Elevation of East End – B,Section of Do – C,Plan. Jas Gibbs Archt. J. Britton direxit. Bradbury del. J. Le Keux sculp. June 1, 1823. 115 × 160/150 × 200mm. Pen and ink drawing (120 × 175mm) in Westminster Public Library.

PUBLIC BUILDINGS

Custom House by John Britton. (pp 46–54; 1838 ed 2, 1–10)

15 pl.1 Custom House, London./D. Laing Archt 1817. G. Gladwin sculp. April 1, 1823. 105 × 168/132 × 210mm. Section and plans.

16 pl.2 Custom House, London/South or Water Front. D. Laing Archt 1817. C.J. Mathews delt. J. Le Keux sculpt. Augt 1, 1823. 100 × 162/150 × 200mm.

British Museum by J.M. Moffatt. (pp 55–65; 1838 ed 2, 177–89)

17 pl.1 British Museum. Pouget Archt 1678. A. Pugin delt. J. Roffe sculpt. Augt 1, 1823. 160 × 105/200 × 150mm. Elevation and plan. 1838 ed 2, p 185, woodcut plan with texts.

The Diorama. By J.B. Papworth. (pp 66–71; 1838 ed 1, 362–7)

18 Diorama, Park Square, Regents Park. A. Pugin & J. Morgan Archts 1823. R. Grantham del. G. Gladwin sculp. Novr 1, 1823. 168 × 110/200 × 150mm.

King's Theatre Haymarket. By J.B. Papworth. (pp 72–9; 1838 ed 1, 305–11, as 'Italian Opera House')

19 King's Theatre Haymarket/East Front. John Nash & G.S. Repton Archts 1818. A. Pugin del. J. Roffe sculp. June 1, 1823. 110 × 170/150 × 200mm. In 1838 ed as 'Queen's Theatre'.

20 pl.II King's Theatre, Hay Market/Transverse section, shewing the concert room. Noveleski (ie Novosielski) Archt. about 1790. J. Willis del. J. Le Keux sculp. Augt 1, 1823. 95 × 168/150 × 200mm. In 1838 ed as 'Queen's Theatre'.

PRIVATE BUILDINGS

Uxbridge House, Burlington Gardens. By J.B. Papworth. (pp 80–2; 1838 ed 2, 342–4)

21 Uxbridge House, Vardy Archt 1792. C.J. Mathews del. Roffe sculp. April 1, 1823. 168 × 108/200 × 150mm. Elevation and plan.

Remarks on English Villas, By John B. Papworth. (pp 83–8; 1838 ed 2, 350–5)

22 Villa of James Burton Esqr. Marylebone Park. D. Burton del. J. Roffe sculp. Novr 1, 1823. 170 × 105/200 × 150mm. Plan and elevations.

CHURCHES

Parish Church of St Mary Woolnoth, Lombard Street. By Joseph Gwilt. (pp 89–94; 1838 ed 1, 88–94)

23 pl.1 Church of St Mary Woolnoth, Lombard Street/ A, Plan of the Church – B, Section East to West – C, Elevation of West end – D, Elevation of N. side. N. Hawksmoor Archt. J.B. direxit. T. Bradberry delt. J. Le Keux sc. Nov 1, 1823. 110 × 170/150 × 200mm.

24 pl.2 Church of St Mary Woolnoth, Lombard Street/ Interior, looking East. N. Hawkesmoor Archt. J.B. direxit. T. Bradberry delt. J. Le Keux sc. Nov 1, 1823. 155 × 115/230 × 143mm. Shows galleries and box pews in place.

PRIVATE BUILDINGS

Burlington House. By J. Britton. (pp 95–101; 1838 ed 2, 334–41)

25 Burlington House, Piccadilly. Lord Burlington & Colin Campbell Archts 1717. Augt Pugin del. G. Gladwin sculp. Decr 1823. 170 × 100/200 × 150mm. Plans and elevations.

CHAPELS

St Philip's Chapel, Regent Street. By J.B. Papworth. (pp 102–6; 1838 1, pp 155–61)

26 St Philip's Chapel, Regent Street. G.S. Repton archt.

A. Pugin delt. J. Roffe sculp. Novr 1, 1823. 163 × 100/200 × 150mm. Plan and elevation. Pen and ink drawing (160 × 100mm) in Westminster Public Library.

27 pl.2 St Philip's Chapel, Regent Street/Longitudinal section. G. Repton Archt. 1820. A. Pugin del. F.J. Havell sculpt. June 1, 1824. 110 × 170/150 × 200mm. Built 1819–20; demolished 1904.

CHURCHES

St Paul's Covent Garden. By E.W. Brayley. (pp 107–17; 1838 ed 1, 115–25)

28 St Paul's Church, Covent Garden. Inigo Jones Archt 1640. A. Pugin del. T. Bradley sculp. Novr 1, 1823. 165 × 108/200 × 150mm. Elevation, section, plan. 'Longman & Co Paternoster Row' publication-line.

St Bride's Church. By E.W. Brayley. (pp 118–27; 1838 ed 1, 68–78)

29 pl.1 Spire &c of St Brides Church Fleet Street/A, Elevation West front – B, Section – a & b, Plans. S. Rayner delt. J. Le Keux sc. Nov 1, 1823. 178 × 110/200 × 150mm.

30 pl.2 Spire &c of St Brides Church Fleet Street/A, Section – B, Elevation of the East end – C, Longitudinal Section – D, Plan. J.B. direxit. H. Ansted delt. J. Le Keux sc. March 1, 1824. 160 × 110/200 × 150mm.

St Mary's Church, Inner Temple. By E.W. Brayley & J. Britton. (pp 128–44; 1838 ed 2, 200–9)

31 Temple Church/A, Transverse Section – B, Long Section – C, Plan. J. Britton direxit. S. Rayner delt. J. Le Keux sc. Augt 1, 1823. 170 × 112/198 × 150mm.

32 pl.2 Temple Church/Circular part looking East. J. Britton direxit. G. Cattermole del. J. Le Keux sculp. April 1, 1823. 160 × 120/230 × 140mm. Interior view.

33 Temple Church/View looking East. J. Britton direxit. S. Rayner delt. J. Le Keux sc. Augt 1, 1823. 110 × 145/150 × 200mm. Interior view.

Church of St Pancras. By J. Britton & E.W. Brayley. (pp 145–66; 1838 ed 1, 137–54)

34 pl.1 St Pancras Church/C, Plan – B, Longitudinal elevation & – A, Longitudinal Section. W. & H. Inwood Archts 1822. J. Britton direxit. H. Bishop del. J. Le Keux sc. Augt. 1, 1823. 170 × 110/200 × 150mm.

35 pl.2 St Pancras Church/B, Elevation – & A, Section of the East End. W. & H. Inwood Archts. J. Britton direxit. H. Bishop del. J. Le Keux sc. Augt. 1, 1823. 170 × 110/200 × 150mm.

36 pl.3 St Pancras Church/West Front. W. & H. Inwood Archts 1822. J. Britton direxit. H. Bishop del. J. Le Keux sc. April 1, 1823. 170 × 110/200 × 150mm.

Church of St Marylebone. By E.W. Brayley. (pp 167–79; 1838 ed 1, 126–36)

37 St Mary-le-Bone Church/North Front &c. Thos

Hardwicke Archt 1819. J. Pennethorne del. J. Roffe sculpt. July 1, 1823. 170 × 110/200 × 150mm.

Parish Church of St James's Westminster. By Joseph Gwilt. (pp 180–5; 1838 ed 1, 79–85)

38 St James's Church Piccadilly/Plan & Section looking East. Sir Chr. Wren Archt 1683. A. Pugin delt. Jas Carter sculpt. Aug 1, 1824. 170 × 108/225 × 140mm.

PUBLIC BUILDINGS

London Institution. By Charles F. Partington. (pp 186–92; 1838 ed 2, pp 232–7)

39 pl.1 The London Institution, Moorfields/No 1, Elevation of Principal front – 2, Plan of Library on upper story – 3, Plan of Ground Floor. W. Brooks Archt. J.B. dirext. H. Ansted del. J. Le Keux sc. May 1824. 165 × 110/200 × 150mm.

40 pl.2 The London Institution/View of the Library. W. Brooks Archt. J.B. dirext. H. Ansted del. J. Carter sc. Aug 1, 1824. 115 × 160/140 × 225mm.

THEATRES

Theatre Royal Covent Garden (etc.) By C. Dibdin. (pp 193–226; 1838 ed 1, 312–23)

41 pl.1 Covent Garden Theatre/Principal Plan. R. Smirke Archt. G. Wightwick del. J. Le Keux sc. Oct 1, 1824. 168 × 113/200 × 150mm.

42 pl.2 Covent Garden Theatre/Transverse Section C to D. See Plan. R. Smirke Archt. G. Wightwick del. J. Roffe sc. May 1, 1824. 112 × 170/153 × 203mm.

43 pl.3 Covent Garden Theatre/Longitudinal Section a to b on Plan. R. Smirke Archt. G. Wightwick del. J. Le Keux sc. May 1824. 110 × 180/150 × 203mm.

44 pl.4 Covent Garden Theatre/Elevation of Principal front. – B, Section through Saloon & Entrance Hall – C, Transverse Section through Staircase. R. Smirke Archt. G. Wightwick del. H. Winkles sc. May 1824. 115 × 180/153 × 215mm.

45 pl.5 Covent Garden Theatre/Staircase to Boxes. R. Smirke Archt. G. Wightwick del. J. Le Keux sc. May 1824. 170 × 120/200 × 152mm.

46 pl.6 Covent Garden Theatre/View from the Stage. R. Smirke Archt. S. Rayner del. J. Carter sc. January 1825. 115 × 170/145 × 210mm.

Theatre Royal Drury Lane. By C. Dibdin & E.W. Brayley. (pp 227–61; 1838 ed 1, 324–43)

47 pl.2 Drury Lane Theatre/View at the N.W. angle. B. Wyatt Archt. T. Wyatt delt. J. Le Keux sc. Dec 1, 1824. 105 × 190/140 × 225mm.

48 pl.II Drury Lane Theatre/Plan. B. Wyatt Archt. T. Wyatt delt. J. Le Keux sc. Jan. 1825. 195 × 110/225 × 138mm.

49 pl.III Rotunda, Drury Lane Theatre. B. Wyatt Archt. A. Pugin direxit. G.B. Moore del. T. Kearnan sculpt. Septr 1, 1826. 113 × 160/150 × 200mm.

50 pl.IV Drury Lane Theatre/Longitudinal section from East to West. T. Wyatt delt. J. Le Keux sc. Jan. 1825. 105 × 195/135 × 225mm.

51 pl.V Drury Lane Theatre/A, Transverse Section looking to the Stage – B, Section of Rotunda & Stairs to Boxes. T. Wyatt delt. J. Le Keux sc. Jan 1, 1825. 170 × 120/200 × 150mm.

52 pl.VI Drury Lane Theatre/View from the Stage. T. Wyatt delt. J. Le Keux sc. Jan 1825. 110 × 165/150 × 205mm.

Haymarket Theatre. By C. Dibdin. (pp 262–72; 1838 ed 1, 344–7)

53 Theatre Royal Haymarket. J. Nash Archt. 1821. A. Pugin delt. G. Gladwin sculp. Novr 1, 1823. 165 × 105/200 × 150mm. Front and plan.

54 pl.2 Haymarket Theatre/Interior View of the stage. J. Nash Archt. 1821. A. Pugin delt. G. Gladwin sculp. March 1, 1825. 115 × 160/150 × 200mm.

Theatre Royal English Opera House. By C. Dibdin. (pp 273–8; 1838 ed 1, 348–55)

55 English Opera House/View from the stage. S. Beazley Archt. S. Rayner delt. H. Winkles sc. Jan 1 1825. 110 × 175/150 × 200mm. Situated in the Strand, opposite Wellington Street.

Royal Amphitheatre, Westminster Bridge. By C. Dibdin. (pp 279–86; 1838 ed 1, 356–61)

56 Amphitheatre, Westminster Bridge/View of the interior. H. Ansted delt. R. Roffe sc. Dec 1, 1824. 110 × 160/155 × 205mm. Astley's Amphitheatre.

PUBLIC BUILDINGS

Royal Exchange. By E.W. Brayley. (pp 287–97; 1838 ed 1, 242–53)

57 The Royal Exchange/South Elevation. Edw. Jerman Arch. 1667, alter'd by G. Smith Archt. 1820. A. Pugin delt. G. Gladwin sculp. Mar 1, 1824. 115 × 170/150 × 200mm.

58 Royal Exchange/Interior looking S.W. J.B. direxit. E. Arundale del. T. Kearnan sc. 110 × 180/150 × 200mm.

Bethlehem Hospital. By E.W. Brayley. (pp 298–304; 1838 ed 2, 161–7)

59 Bethlehem Hospital/South Front. James Lewis Archt. 1815. P. Hardwick del. J. Le Keux sculp. Decr 1, 1823. 108 × 170/140 × 220mm. Plan and elevation. Built in St George's Fields.

Russell Institution. By John Britton. (pp 305–9; 1838 ed 2, 238–41)

60 Russel Institution, Gt Coram Street. J.B. dirext. G. Cattermole del. J. Le Keux sc. March 1, 1824. 115 × 170/150 × 200mm.

PRIVATE HOUSES

Mansion of Thomas Hope, Duchess Street, Portland

Place. By J. Britton. (pp 310–12; 1838 ed 2, 345–7; no pl. 1)

61 pl.2 Mansion of Thomas Hope Esqr/Flemish Picture Gallery. J.B. dirext. S. Rayner delt. J. Carter sc. Aug 1, 1824. 105 × 160/140 × 225mm.

62 pl.3 Mansion of Thomas Hope Esqr./J.B. direxit. H. Ansted del. J. Carter sc. May 1824. 180 × 105/225 × 138mm. Section and plan. The house was 'originally built by Mr. Adam'.

The House of John Soane Esq. Lincolns Inn Fields. By J. Britton. (pp 313–20; 1838 ed 2, 316–27, as 'Sir J. Soane's House and Museum')

63 pl.1 House of J. Soane Esq. Lincolns Inn Fields/Ante Library. J. Soane R.A. &c Archt. J. Britton dirext. H. Shaw del. J. Le Keux sculp. Novr 1 1823. 115 × 165/150 × 205mm.

64 pl.2 Picture Gallery/in the house of John Soane Esq. Lincolns Inn Fields. J. Soane R.A. &c Archt. Drawn by H. Shaw. J.B. dirext. J. Le Keux sculp. March 1, 1824. 105 × 165/142 × 225mm.

Freemasons Hall. By J. Britton and E.W. Brayley. (pp 321–33; 1838 ed 2, 242–8)

65 Freemasons Hall Great Queen Street. T. Sanby (ie Sandby) Archt. J.B. dirext. Wightwick del. J. Le Keux sc. Aug 1, 1824. 115 × 175/150 × 200mm.

VOL. 2

66 (engr title) Temple Bar/West Front. Sir Christopher Wren Archt. A. Pugin dirext. J. Le Keux sculpt. Jany 1828. (framed by the archway) Edifices of London/ Public Buildings/Vol.II/By/J. Britton, F.S.A. & A. Pugin Archts. 172 × 120/200 × 150mm. Plan and elevation. 1838 ed 2, p 114, title burnished out.

67 Plan of the Cities of London and Westminster with the Borough of Southwark. J.B. direxit. H.A. del. Sidy Hall sculpt. 123 × 205/160 × 230mm. Keyed to the 'List of Public Buildings etc.' at the start of the volume. (*Darlington and Howgego* 318)

Mr Greenhough's Villa. By D. Burton. (pp 1–4; 1838 ed 2, 356–9)

68 pl.I Villa of G.B. Greenhough Esqr Mary-le-Bone Park. D. Burton Arch. 1822 del. G. Gladwin sculpt. May 1, 1824. 170 × 105/202 × 150mm. Elevation, section, plan.

69 pl.II Villa of G.B. Greenhough Esqr. Regent's Park. D. Burton delt., Archt. 1822. H. Winkles sculpt. May 1st 1825. 110 × 175/150 × 203mm. Described as 'Grove House' in *Metropolitan Improvements* (no 154), pp 30–4.

Roman Catholic Chapel Moorfields. By E.W. Brayley. (pp 5–11; 1838 ed 1, 194–9)

70 pl.I Roman Catholic Chapel, Moorfields/a, Plan – b, Section – c, Section of Altar end. J. Newman Archt 1817. Heron delt. J. Le Keux sculpt. May 1, 1825. 115 × 175/150 × 200mm.

71 pl.II Roman Catholic Chapel Moorfields/Interior view, looking West. J. Newman Archt 1817. Heron delt. J. Le Keux sculpt. May 1, 1825. 155 × 120/200 × 150mm. St Mary, Blomfield Street, built 1817–20; demolished 1899.

PUBLIC BUILDINGS

York Stairs Water-Gate. By E.W. Brayley. (pp 12–15; 1838 ed 2, 138–40)

72 York Stairs. Inigo Jones Archt 1686. Augt Pugin delt. Havell sculpt. July 1, 1824. 180 × 110/200 × 145mm. Elevation, plan, section.

Somerset House and Place. By E.W. Brayley. (pp 16–31; 1838 ed 2, 118–37)

73 pl.1 Somerset House/Strand Front. Sir W. Chambers Archt. W. Jenkins delt. G. Gladwin sculpt. May 1, 1824. 110 × 170/150 × 205mm.

74 pl.2 Somerset House/Vestibule, looking to the West. Sir W. Chambers Archt. Pugin delt. G. Gladwin sculpt. Sep 1, 1825. 147 × 120/204 × 150mm.

75 pl.3 Somerset House/View of the Court, looking North. Sir W. Chambers Archt. Pugin delt. G. Gladwin sculpt. Aug 1, 1825. 100 × 175/150 × 200mm.

76 pl.4 Navy Office, Somerset House. Sir W. Chambers Archt. Pugin delt. G. Gladwin sculpt. July 1826. 165 × 130/200 × 150mm. Entrance beneath domed centre.

77 pl.5 Somerset House/River Front. Sir W. Chambers Archt. A. Pugin delt. G. Gladwin sculpt. Augt 1, 1825. 110 × 175/150 × 200mm.

78 Somerset Place/No 1, Ground Floor – No 2, Gateway at O in plan. Sir W. Chambers Archt. A. Pugin delt. H. Adlard sculpt. July 1, 1826. 165 × 107/192 × 145mm. Plan and elevation of E. and W. internal gateways.

Society for the Encouragement of Arts, Manufactures and Commerce. By E.W. Brayley. (pp 32–43; 1838 ed 2, 223–31, as 'Society of Arts')

79 Society for the Encouragement of Arts, Manufactures and Commerce/John Street, Adelphi. A. Pugin dirext. W. Young delt. G. Gladwin sculpt. April 1, 1825. 160 × 120/200 × 150mm.

College of Physicians, Warwick Lane. By E.W. Brayley. (pp 44–53; 1838 ed 2, 95–101, as 'Old College of Physicians')

80 pl.I College of Physicians/Warwick Lane/ A, Elevation – B, Section of the Theatre. Sir Christopher Wren Archt. S. Ware Esqr. Archt. delt. J. Le Keux sculpt. Septr 1, 1825. 175 × 115/250 × 150mm.

81 pl.II College of Physicians/ Ground plan & elevation. S. Ware Esqr Archt. delt. J. Le Keux sculpt. Jan 1, 1826. 183 × 117/200 × 155mm.

PRISONS

Prison of Newgate. By H. Leeds and E.W. Brayley. (pp 54–66; 1838 ed 2, 102–13)

82 Newgate/Ground Plan & Elevation. Geo. Dance Archt. T. Bradberry delt. J. Le Keux sc. Jan 1 1826. 120 × 180/150 × 200mm.

PUBLIC BUILDINGS

Horse Guards, Whitehall. By J.M. Moffatt and W.H. Leeds. (pp 67–71; 1838 ed 2, 145–51)

83 The Horse Guards. W. Kent Archt. A. Pugin delt. J. Cleghorn sculpt. May 1, 1825. 107 × 170/150 × 200mm. W. elevation and plan.

CHURCHES

St Peter-le-Poor, Broad Street. By J.M. Moffat and W.H. Leeds. (pp 72–6; 1838 ed 1, 110–14)

84 pl.2 Church of St Peter le Poor/Broad Street/A, Plan – B, Elevation – C. Section. Sepr 1, 1825. 110 × 185/150 × 200mm. The only plate of this church which was rebuilt by Jesse Gibson, 1788–92.

COMMERCIAL

East India House, Leadenhall Street. By J. Britton and J.M. Moffatt. (pp 77–89; 1838 ed 2, 35–41)

85 East India House/Ground Plan of the Principal Front & Elevation. Jupp Archt. T. Bradberry delt. J. Le Keux sculp. Jan 1, 1826. 115 × 175/150 × 200mm.

PRIVATE

Ashburnham House, Little Deans Yard, Westminster. By J. Britton and C. Atkinson. (pp 90–3; 1838 ed 2, 328–33)

86 pl.I Staircase in a Prebendal House/Deans Yard, Westminster. Inigo Jones Archt. Jos. Gwilt Archt. del. J. Le Keux sc. Aug 1, 1825. 112 × 160/150 × 200mm. Section and plan.

87 pl.II Staircase in a Prebendal House, Westminster. Inigo Jones Archt. Jos Gwilt Archt del. J. Le Keux sc. May 1, 1825. 150 × 120/200 × 150mm.

CHURCHES

Church of St George in the East, near Ratcliffe-Highway. (pp 94–8; 1838 ed 1, 95–100)

88 pl.I Church of St. George in the East/A, Plan of Ground & Gallery floors. – B, Elevation of the South Side. Thos Bradberry delt. J. Le Keux sc. June 1, 1826. 170 × 120/200 × 150mm.

89 pl.II Church of St. George in the East/West Front. Thos Bradberry delt. J. Le Keux sc. June 1, 1826. 170 × 110/200 × 150mm.

90 pl.III Church of St. George in the East/A, Elevation of East End – B, Section of Do. Thos Bradberry delt. J. Le Keux sc. July 1, 1826. 170 × 110/200 × 150mm. Built by Hawksmoor, 1715–23.

All Souls Church, Langham Place. (pp 99–101; 1838 ed 1, 173–5)

91 All Souls Church, Langham Place. John Nash Archt 1824. A. Pugin del. F.J. Havell sculp. April 1825. 170 × 108/200 × 150mm. Plan and elevation.

HALLS

Westminster Hall. By J. Britton. (pp 102–13; 1838 ed 1, 249–58)

92 Westminster Hall. /No 1, Transverse Section – No 2 & 3, Half plans. Built 1397. A. Pugin dirext. J. Willis del. J. Roffe sculpt. June 1826. 170 × 115/213 × 160mm. Black and red ink drawing (170 × 112mm) in Westminster Public Library.

93 pl.2 Westminster Hall./North Front. Built 1397. A. Pugin dirext. J. Willis del. G. Gladwin sculpt. July 1, 1824. 165 × 107/200 × 150mm.

94 Westminster Hall/looking South. A. Pugin direxit. T.T. Bury delt. B. Winkles sculpt. Nov. 1826. 115 × 173/150 × 200mm. Interior. Black and red ink drawing (112 × 170mm) in Westminster Public Library.

PALACES

The Banqueting Hall, and Whitehall Palace. By S. Tymms. (pp 114–19; 1838 ed 2, 141–4, as 'Banqueting-House')

95 Banqueting Room &c. White-Hall. A, Elevation West front – B, Section looking South – C, Plan of principal storys. Inigo Jones Archt. A. Pugin del. B. Winkles sculpt. June 1, 1826. 180 × 110/200 × 150mm.

PUBLIC BUILDINGS

The Mansion House. By J.M. Moffatt. (pp 120–5; 1838 ed 2, 74–81)

96 The Mansion House/No 1, Principal Front – No 2, Plan of the Principal Floor. G. Dance Archt. A. Pugin delt. G. Gladwin sculpt. July 1, 1826. 165 × 120/200 × 150mm.

County Fire Office, &c, Regent Street. By J. Britton. (pp 126–9; 1838 ed 2, 158–60)

97 The County Fire Office. Robt Abraham Archt. 1819. A. Pugin delt. J. Roffe sculpt. Feby 1st, 1825. 170 × 108/200 × 150mm. Elevation and plans.

University Club House, Suffolk Street. By John Britton. (pp 130–4; 1838 ed 2, 254–7)

98 University Club House/Suffolk Street/A,B, Elevation – C, Ground Plan. W. Wilkins & J.P. Gandy Archts. H. Ansted del. B. Bosley sc. Augt 1, 1826. 160 × 108/210 × 140mm. Built 1822–6; demolished 1906.

Church of St Mary-le-Bow, Cheapside. By H.A. (pp 135–44; 1838 ed 1, 57–67)

99 Steeple of Bow Church./No 1, Elevation of North Side – No 2, Section from North to South. Sir Christopher Wren Archt. A. Pugin del. J. Roffe sculpt. July 1, 1826. 170 × 108/200 × 150mm.

CHURCHES

Abbey Church of St. Peter, Westminster. By E.W. Brayley. (pp 145–86; 1838 ed 1, 210–48)

100 pl.1 Westminster Abbey and Henry 7ths Chapel./ North Front. A. Pugin delt. H. Winkles sculpt. Novr 1, 1823. 110 × 165/130 × 185mm.

101 pl.2 Westminster Abbey Church/Ground Plan. A. Pugin delt. J. Roffe sculpt. April 1825. 170 × 110/200 × 140mm.

102 Longitudinal Section from East to West/of/Westminster Abbey Church, &c. A. Pugin delt. from Neale & Brayley's 'History of Westr Abbey'. G. Gladwin sculpt. June 1, 1826. 103 × 173/140 × 200mm.

103 pl.iv Westminster Abbey & Henry 7th Chapel/A,B, Elevation and Section of South Transept. – c. Section of Nave. A. Pugin delt. T. Bradley sculpt. Decr 1823. 110 × 173/140 × 203mm.

104 pl.2 (again) Westminster Abbey Church/the Choir, looking East. A. Pugin delt. J. Le Keux sc. Nov 1, 1824. 160 × 115/203 × 140mm.

105 pl.6 Henry 7ths Chapel, Westminster/Longitudinal section. A. Pugin dirext from Sections made by J.P. Neale. W.W. Law sculpt. March 1827. 110 × 173/140 × 200mm.

106 Henry 7ths Chapel, Westminster/Plan and transverse section looking West. Begun 1502. A. Pugin delt. F.J. Havell sculpt. May 1, 1824. 170 × 105/200 × 140mm.

SCHOOLS

New Hall, Christ's Hospital, Newgate Street. By J. Britton. (pp 187–92; 1838 ed 2, 90–4)

107 Great Hall &c Christ's Hospital. John Shaw Archt. F.S.A., 1826. H. Ansted del. R. Roffe sc. May 1, 1826. 155 × 115/205 × 140mm. Elevation, plan. Built 1825–9; demolished 1902.

PALACES

Carlton Palace. By W.H. Leeds. (pp 193–201; 1838 ed 2, 272–81)

108 Carlton Palace. Holland Archt. A. Pugin delt. Adlard sculpt. Novr 1826. 107 × 170/140 × 205mm. Plans. Demolished 1827–8.

109 Carlton Palace/transverse section. A. Pugin dirext. Measured & drawn by A. Mauduit. G. Gladwin sculpt. Decr 1826. 105 × 175/140 × 200mm.

110 Carlton Palace/Hall. A. Pugin dirext. G. Moore delt. Jas Tingle sculpt. Octr 1826. 115 × 175/140 × 203mm.

111 Carlton Palace/Portico Screen &c. A. Pugin dirext. F. Arundale delt. T. Kearnan sculpt. Septr 1, 1826. 118 × 170/140 × 202mm.

112 pl.5 Carlton Palace,/Great Staircase. A. Pugin delt. J. Tingle sculpt. March 1, 1827. 130 × 175/160 × 200mm.

CHURCHES

All Saints Poplar. (pp 202–4; 1838 ed 1, 176–8)

113 All Saints Church, Poplar/A, West Front – B, S.Side – C, Plan. C. Hollis Archt. 1821. W.W. Law sc. Feby 1, 1827 by J. Britton, Burton Street. 110 × 170/140 × 220mm.

St Luke, Chelsea. By J. Britton. (pp 205–18; 1838 ed 1, 162–72)

114 Church of St Luke, Chelsea./A, Longitudinal Section – B, Elevation of S. Side – C, Plan. Jas Savage Archt. H. Ansted del. R. Tingle sc. June 1, 1826. 155 × 105/200 × 140mm. (*Longford* 703)

115 Church of St Luke, Chelsea./A, East End – Section of do and B, West end. Jas Savage Archt. H. Ansted del. R. Tingle sc. July 1, 1826. 115 × 175/140 × 195mm. (*Longford* 702)

INSTITUTIONS

College of Physicians and Union Club House, Charing Cross. By W.H. Leeds. (pp 219–23; 1838 ed 2, 249–53)

116 pl.I College of Physicians & Union Club House/A, Ground Plan – B, Plan of Library of the College. R. Smirke Archt. H. Ansted del. Deeble sc. Sep 1, 1826. 110 × 168/140 × 200mm. Built 1824–5 and 1824–7.

117 pl.II College of Physicians, & Union Club House/ Elevation of the two Buildings – B, Elevation of Club House – C, Portico of College of Physicians. R. Smirke Archt. H. Ansted del. Deeble sc. Sep 1, 1826. 110 × 173/140 × 200mm.

Terraces and other buildings in the Regents Park. J. Britton & W.H. Leeds. (pp 224–35; 1838 ed 2, 360–8)

118 No. 1, Cornwall Terrace. Decimus Burton Archt 1823 – No. 2, Hanover Terrace. John Nash Archt 1825. A. Pugin delt. F.J. Havell sculpt. May 1826. 110 × 172/140 × 203mm.

PUBLIC BUILDINGS

Privy Council Office and Board of Trade, Parliament Street. By J. Britton. (pp 236–40; 1838 ed 2, 152–7)

119 Council Office, Board of Trade, &c. J. Soane Esq. Archt. 1826. A. Pugin delt. G. Gladwin sculpt. Augt 1, 1827. 110 × 175/140 × 205mm. Elevation and plan.

The Bank of England. By W.H. Leeds. (pp 241–56; 1838 ed 2, 54–73)

120 pl.I Bank of England (front, Threadneedle Street – front, Bartholomew Lane). J. Soane Archt. A. Pugin dirext. H. Adlard sculpt. Jany 1828. 105 × 180/140 × 200mm. (*Bank of England* 88–9)

121 pl.II The Bank of England/from Lothbury Court. J. Soane Archt. A. Pugin dirext. F. Arundale delt. T. Kearnan sculpt. March 1, 1827. 113 × 180/140 × 205mm. (*Bank of England* 132–3)

122 pl.III Bank of England/View of N. & W. Fronts. J. Soane Archt. A. Pugin dirext. F. Arundale delt. W. Deeble sculpt. May 1, 1827. 108 × 178/140 × 200mm. (*Bank of England* 62–3)

Law Courts at Westminster. By J. Britton. (pp 257–66; 1838 ed 1, 259–68)

123 Law Courts at Westminster. Soane Archt. C. Hacker del. J. Roffe sc. Nov. 1, 1827. 130 × 200/150 × 223mm. Demolished 1883. Plan.

124 Court of Chancery, Westminster. J. Soane Archt. 1826. A. Pugin dirext. A. Mauduit del. W. Deeble sculpt. Jany 1, 1827. 118 × 170/150 × 200mm.

125 Court of Kings Bench, Westminster. J. Soane archt. 1826. A. Pugin dirext. G.B. Moore del. W. Deeble sc. Feby 1, 1827. 115 × 170/155 × 203mm.

New entrance for His Majesty to the House of Lords. By J. Britton. (pp 267–70; 1838 ed 1, 269–73)

126 Royal Vestibule, House of Lords. John Soane Esq. F.R.A. Archt. T. Wyatt delt. Bosley sc. Sept 15, 1826. 155 × 110/203 × 140mm.

127 pl.3 The King's Entrance; House of Lords. J. Soane, R.A. &c Archt. 1822. J. Britton dirext. H. Shaw del. R. Sands sculp. Novr 1, 1823. 165 × 113/200 × 155mm.

128 The King's Entrance, House of Lords/Section, North Side. J. Soane, Archt. J. Britton dirext. H. Shaw del. J. Le Keux sculpt. April 1, 1823. 105 × 158/150 × 203mm. All these destroyed by fire in 1834.

EXHIBITIONS

Panoramic Building in Regents Park called the Colosseum. by J.B. and T.H. (pp 271–5; 1838 ed 1, 368–75)

129 Panorama. Regents Park. D. Burton Archt. 1826. W.W. Law sc. Decr 1, 1826. 112 × 178/165 × 220mm. Built 1823–7; demolished 1875.

Hanover Chapel in Regent Street. (pp 276–82; 1838 ed 1, 179–86)

130 Hanover Chapel/E. Elevation, Longitudinal Section and Plan. C.R. Cockerell Archt. 1823. A. Pugin dirext. F. Arundale delt. H. Adlard sculpt. Decr. 1826. 175 × 113/200 × 150mm. Built 1823–5; demolished 1896.

CHURCHES

Temple Bar, Fleet Street, The Tower &c of St Dunstans in the East. By J. Britton. (pp 283–6; 1838 ed 1, 86–7 and 2, 114–17)

131 Tower of the Church/St Dunstan in the East. Sir Chris Wren Archt. Thos Bradberry del. J. Roffe sc. Decr 1, 1826. 172 × 110/202 × 150mm.

PRIVATE BUILDINGS

The Houses of John Nash and John Edwards Esqrs. Regent Street. By J. Britton. (pp 287–9; 1838 ed 2, 348–9)

132 The Houses of John Nash and John Edwards Esqrs. Regent Street. J. Nash Archt. 1823. A. Pugin dirext. C.J. Matthews and J. Roffe sculpt. Jany 1, 1823. 108 × 175/150 × 200mm.

133 Gallery in the house of John Nash Esqr. A. Pugin dirext. E. Arundale delt. T. Kearnan sculpt. Augt 1, 1826. 118 × 168/150 × 205mm.

Belgrave Square, Eaton Square and the Villa of T.R. Kemp. By J. Britton. (pp 290–4; 1838 ed 2, 369–75)

134 View of the East side of Belgrave Square. George Basevi F.S.A. Architect 1827. G.B. Moore delt. J. Le Keux sculpt. Jany 1828. 102 × 178/152 × 202mm. With staffage.

135 Part of Eaton Square/New building by T. & L. Cubitt in the parish of St George Hanover Square. G. Hacker de. from a drawing by Messrs. Cubitt. Gladwin sc. Dec 1827. 92 × 182/140 × 200mm. With staffage.

136 Villa of T.R. Kemp Esqr. M.P., Belgrave Square. H.E. Kendall Archt. 1826. T.W. Atkinson delt. G. Gladwin sculpt. March 1827. 113 × 185/152 × 202mm. Elevation of 24 Belgrave Square. With staffage.

137 Villa of T.R. Kemp Esqr. M.P., Belgrave Square. H.E. Kendall Archt. 1826. T.W. Atkinson delt. G. Gladwin sculpt. March 1827. 104 × 180/150 × 200mm. Plan.

BRIDGES

History and Structure of Bridges, with accounts of those of London, Southwark, Blackfriars, Waterloo and Vauxhall. By John Britton. (pp 295–327; 1838 ed 2, 376–401)

138 View of Old London Bridge/with coffer dams &c preparing for the new bridge, as seen Septr 1826. W.H. Bartlett del. W. Deeble sc. June 1 1827. 110 × 170/152 × 200mm. A view with hatched shading. The foundation stone of the first pier was laid on 15 June 1825.

139 London Bridge./A, New Building – D, Half Plan of do – B, Bridge as now used – C, Half plan of do with Sterlings. J. Rennie Engineer &c. H. Ansted del. G. Gladwin sc. Decr 1, 1827. 110 × 180/150 × 202mm.

140 Southwark Bridge. John Rennie, Engineer, F.R.S. &c. Measured & Drawn by William Knight. Engraved by G. Gladwin. 110 × 173/150 × 200mm.

141 pl.2 Southwark Bridge, London/Section showing the construction of the arches, piers, centering &c. John Rennie Engineer F.R.S. &c. Measured and drawn by Wm Knight. Engraved by G. Gladwin. June 1 1827. 92 × 192/132 × 205mm. Iron bridge, built 1815–19; rebuilt 1920–1.

142 Blackfriars Bridge/No 1, West Elevation and Plan – 2, Elevation and Section of Centre Arch. Robert Mylne Archt 1760. A. Pugin dirext. F. Arundale delt. G. Gladwin sculpt. Jany 1828. 108 × 172/150 × 200mm.

143 Waterloo Bridge./J. Rennie Archt & Engineer. C. Hacker del. from materials by Wm. Knight. J. Roffe sc. Jany 1, 1828. 105 × 183/130 × 205mm. Elevation, plan, arch, section.

144 pl.II Waterloo Bridge/Section, shewing the construc-

tion of the arches, the centering &c. Jn Rennie Archt & Engineer. W. Knight del. 1826. Gladwin sc. Feby 1 1827. 118 × 190/155 × 215mm. Built 1811–17; demolished 1938.

145 pl.I Westminster Bridge/1, Elevation and Plan – 2, Sections of Arches. C. Labelye Archt. Began 1738. Finished 1750. A. Pugin dirext. F. Arundale delt. W.W. Law sculpt. June 1827. 110 × 180/162 × 220mm.

146 pl.2 Westminster Bridge/Elevation & longitudinal section of the centre arch. A. Pugin dirext. F. Arundale delt. G. Gladwin sculpt. June 1827. 170 × 112/200 × 150mm.

Supplement (plates arranged facing specific pages)

147 p 1 St Dunstan's in the West. B. Ferrey del. T. Bury sculp. 103 × 173/140 × 223mm. Built by John Shaw, 1831–3. 1838 ed 1, 187–93.

148 p 20 New Corn Exchange. B. Ferrey del. T. Bury sculp. 175 × 123/200 × 140mm. In Mark Lane. Built by George Smith, 1827–8. 1838 ed 2, 11–22.

149 p 32 Fishmongers Hall. B. Ferrey del. T. Bury sculp. 118 × 170/140 × 200mm. Elevation and plan. Built by Henry Roberts, 1831–3. 1838 ed 2, 23–4.

150 p 33 Post Office. C.J. Richardson del. F. Mansell sculp. 130 × 200/193 × 245mm.

151 p 40 Post Office/Ground Plan. W. Butler del. F. Mansell sculp. 120 × 200/140 × 230mm. St Martin's-Le-Grand, built by Robert Smirke, 1824–9; demolished 1912–13. Article by Sydney Smirke. 1838 ed 2, 82–9.

152 p 41 St Georges Hospital – /East Front –/North Front. W. Wilkins del. J. Hawksworth sc. 125 × 200/140 × 225mm. Hyde Park Corner, built by William Wilkins, 1828–9.

153 p 49 Plan of St Georges Hospital. W. Wilkins del. J. Hawksworth sc. 120 × 215/140 × 225mm. 1838 ed 2, 168–76.

(p 51 Wood-engraved plan of Robert Smirke's British Museum. 115 × 100mm)

154 p 56 National Gallery – /Front Elevation – /Longitudinal Section. W. Wilkins del. J. Hawksworth sculp. 130 × 205/140 × 225mm.

155 p 76 National Gallery/Ground Floor – /Gallery Floor. W. Wilkins del. J. Hawksworth sculp. 130 × 202/140 × 230mm. Plans. Built by William Wilkins, 1834–8. 1838 ed 2, 190–210.

156 p 77 London University/elevation and Plan. B. Ferrey del. T. Bury sculp. 110 × 175/140 × 225mm.

157 p 82 London University/Portico & Section. B. Ferrey del. T. Bury sculp. 115 × 175/140 × 225mm. University College, built by William Wilkins and J.P. Deering, 1827–8. 1838 ed 2, 211–22.

158 p 89 Travellers Club House. T.L. Walker del. T.

Bury sculp. 170 × 105/203 × 140mm. By Charles Barry, 1829–31. 1838 ed 2, 258–71.

(p 100 Wood-engraved plan of Travellers' Club, 140 × 95mm)

159 p 103 Buckingham Palace/Plan of the Ground Story. J. Hakewell del. J. Hawksworth sc. 200 × 265/225 × 275mm.

160 p 122 Buckingham Palace/West or Garden Front. J. Hakewell del. J. Hawksworth sc. 115 × 203/140 × 227mm.

161 p 122 Buckingham Palace/Plan of the Principal Floor. J. Hakewell del. J. Hawksworth sc. 195 × 260/228 × 275mm.

162 p 122 Buckingham Palace/North Wing. J. Hakewell del. J. Hawksworth sc. 200 × 265/230 × 280mm.

163 p 122 Buckingham Palace/East Front. J. Hakewell del. J. Hawksworth sc. 203 × 475/230 × 500mm. Built by John Nash, 1825–30; completed by Edward Blore, 1831–7. 1838 ed 2, 282–304.

164 p 124 Archway, Green Park. B. Ferrey del. T. Bury sculp. 180 × 110/200 × 140mm. Decimus Burton's arch, intended as a N. entrance to the gardens of Buckingham Palace but erected in 1827–8 at the top of Constitution Hill (Hyde Park Corner). 1838 ed 2, 305–15.

147 · HEATH'S VIEWS OF LONDON [1825]

Charles Heath, illegitimate son and pupil of James Heath, the historical engraver to George III, was engraving at the age of six and became as proficient as his father at reproducing in line on large plates the paintings of Old Masters and living Academicians. He also developed a flair for work on a much smaller scale and was employed by publishers to illustrate the popular editions of the English classics which were proliferating at the turn of the century. This talent for miniaturizing came into its own when, some time after 1818, as a consequence of entering into partnership in a banknote printing business with the American Jacob Perkins, he discovered that steel plates could be used instead of copper and that the finest lines could be engraved and held intact on them for long runs without the re-engraving required by more rapidly deteriorating copper plates. The *Views of London* is therefore a pioneer work in a new medium and a landmark in the history of illustration.

The circumscribed brilliance of this new technique was the perfect adjunct to the boudoir daintiness of the little collections of verse and prose, known generically as Annuals, which were then popular as Christmas presents and adorned the drawing-room tables of the upper and middle classes of society. From being a mere publisher's hack Heath now became an entrepreneur: *The Literary Souvenir* was launched in the same year as *Views of London* and was followed by *The Amulet* (from 1826), *The Keepsake* (1827), *Heath's Picturesque Annual* (1832) and *The Book of Beauty* (1833).

No doubt he regarded these seasonal ephemera as money-spinners which would enable him to finance a serious artistic project, a more ambitious sequel to the London views, *Picturesque Views in England and Wales*. J.M.W. Turner undertook to supply no fewer than 120 drawings for this new series and between the years 1826 and 1837 he travelled the country and turned out some of the finest watercolours of his career. Each, on reaching London, was immediately transferred to copper by one of a band of his favoured engravers which included W. Radclyffe, Robert Wallis, W.T. Willmore, W.R. Smith and R. Brandard. From 1827 to 1838 these engravings came out in 24 Parts, accumulated into a first volume made up of the planned 60 plates, and a second which contained only 36—for by this time the publication had ruined Heath. His stock was put up for auction, but to protect his own plates from abuse Turner intervened and bought them together with the unsold stock of prints at the reserve price of £3,000.

This commercial failure may have been partly due to the reversion to copper, chosen as more suitable for engravings fixed at a size of about 160 × 240mm. Steel, so well adapted to Turner's work published in the Annuals or Rogers's *Italy* (1830), favoured by the artist himself in other contexts and with all the appeal of a novel process, might have turned the work into a financial success. Three years later Jones & Co 'struck oil' with *Metropolitan Improvements; or London in the Nineteenth Century* (no 154), covering much the same ground as *Views of London* and, like Heath's series, engraved on steel.

The publisher, Hurst Robinson, by issuing Heath's London engravings appears to have forestalled a rival's intention of publishing a similar set of plates by James C. Allen after drawings by four eminent artists, including Turner and Westall, as announced in Ackermann's *Repository of Arts* for August 1824:

A Work which is to appear in numbers every 4 months has been announced with the title 'Views in London and its Environs' ... in which not only the localities will be faithfully represented, but it will be the endeavour of the artists to depict the character and interest which such scenes borrow from life and its various occupations. The drawings will be made expressly for this work by J.M.W. Turner Esq. R.A., W. Callcott, R.A., F.Nash and W. Westall A.R.A.; and engraved in a highly finished line manner, by J.C. Allen. Each number will contain two engravings.

His own prospectus reads thus:

Views of London

- - -

On the 10th of January, 1825, will be published: No 1, containing five highly-finished engravings of A Series of Picturesque Views in London and its Environs. Engraved by Charles Heath from Drawings by P. Dewint, W. Westall, A.R.A. and F. Mackenzie. London: Printed for Hurst Robinson, and Co, 90, Cheapside, and 8 Pall Mall and R. Jennings, Poultry.

Conditions: This work will comprise the most beautiful and remarkable Scenes on the River Thames, Delineations of the most important Public Buildings, with a variety of miscellaneous Picturesque Views in the British Metropolis and its extensive Environs.

It is intended that it shall consist of Twelve Numbers, each containing Five Engravings with brief appropriate letterpress Descriptions of the Several Views. The Plates will be executed in the most finished line manner by Mr. Charles Heath, from Drawings made expressly for the work; the Picturesque Views by Dewint, the Architectural by Mackenzie and Westall.

In consequence of the advanced state of most of the Engravings, the Publishers can confidently promise that a Number shall appear regularly on the first day of each month, so that the work will be completed within a year.

The Parts will be published in the following sizes, and at the prices annexed:

Imperial 8vo, Price 9s.—Proofs, royal 4to, 14s.
India proofs, royal 4to, £1—A Few copies, before the writing, on India paper, imperial 4to, price £1. 10s.

As with the *Picturesque Views* the work was not completed. It was discontinued after only 45 of the promised 60 plates had been published (although a forty-sixth, a view by Westall of Waterloo Bridge which must have been alternative to de Wint's pl.5, is reported by a private collector). The last Number to appear was the ninth. Consequently the title-page and list of plates which were to be issued with the twelfth Number were apparently never printed. The authority for the title is therefore the prospectus, with the confirmation of a wrapper in which the Numbers were issued where the title appears in an engraved, ornamental frame with City arms and supporters:

Views/of/London/Printed for Hurst, Robinson & Co & R. Jennings/London./ Proofs. Royal 4to. 14s. (No 9)

Quarto, 290 × 230mm.   1825

COLLATION   45 unpaginated leaves of description, printed on recto only, interleaved with 45 plates in a standard, but unlisted, sequence.

Drawings for 23 of the plates were made by Peter de Wint, a near contemporary of Charles Heath's, the son of a Staffordshire physician descended from the Amsterdam merchant family. He was trained by the engraver John Raphael Smith and then studied at the Royal Academy, of which he became a member in 1811. He was already familiar with the requirements of engravers for between 1815 and 1821 he contributed a dozen plates to the set of Thames views delicately engraved and published by W.B. and George Cooke (no 139). This master of English landscape painting in oil and water-colour is interpreted with great sensitivity by Heath, especially in the Wordsworthian calm of his urban riverscapes and the subtle play of light in street scenes such as 'The Auction Mart' (pl.9) and 'The Monument' (pl.26).

William Westall was a younger brother of the historical painter Richard Westall, from whom he received lessons while attending the Royal Academy Schools. At the age of 19 he was appointed official artist to Matthew Flinders's expedition to Australia and was wrecked on a coral reef; his sketches however survived with him and were later engraved in line to illustrate the explorer's *Voyage to Terra Australis* (1814). On his return home he exhibited topographical paintings at the Royal Academy and established a connection with the publishers of books with coloured plates. From 1814 to 1819 he produced 28 views for Ackermann's *Histories of the Universities of Oxford and Cambridge*, 15 for the same publisher's *History of the Colleges* (no 116), six for Pyne's *Royal Residences* (no 132) and, in 1824, all the illustrations for Rodwell and Martin's *Thirty-five Views on the Thames*. To the work at present under discussion his contribution was 15 drawings, chiefly on inland and architectural subjects.

The remaining seven plates are engraved from drawings by Frederick Mackenzie, a skilled presenter of architectural subjects. He also was an Ackermann draughtsman, for aquatints in the *History of Westminster Abbey* (no 108), *History of the Colleges* and *History of the Universities*, and his earlier work had been engraved in line for John Britton's *Architectural Antiquities* (no 97) and *The Beauties of England and Wales* (no 104).

1 London Bridge. Drawn by P. Dewint. 68 × 135/125 × 200mm.

2 Burlington Arcade. Drawn by Mackenzie. 75 × 102/125 × 200mm.

3 View from Richmond Hill. Drawn by P. Dewint. 78 × 125/123 × 200mm. (*Gascoigne* 81)

4 Custom House. Drawn by W. Westall. 75 × 130/125 × 198mm.

5 View of Waterloo Bridge/from the garden of M.A. Taylor Esq. Drawn by P. Dewint. 65 × 125/125 × 198mm.

6 The Quadrant. Drawn by W. Westall. 83 × 126/125 × 198mm. Regent Street.

7 London from Greenwich Hill. Drawn by P. Dewint. 65 × 128/125 × 200mm.

8 The Tower from the River. Drawn by P. Dewint. 78 × 118/125 × 200mm.

9 The Auction Mart, Bank &c. Drawn by P. Dewint. 83 × 95/125 × 195. In Bartholomew Lane, with a view of St Bartholomew by the Exchange and the cupola on the Royal Exchange, completed in 1824. (*Bank of England* 77)

10 Westminster Hall. Drawn by P. Dewint. 65 × 135/128 × 200mm. From Westminster Bridge.

11 Hampton Court. Drawn by P. Dewint. 70 × 132/125 × 200mm.

12 Cornhill, &c. Drawn by Mackenzie. 72 × 108/125 × 200mm. From beneath the Mansion House.

13 Tower Hill. Drawn by P. Dewint. 77 × 130/125 × 200mm.

14 Pool of London. Drawn by P. Dewint. 70 × 133/123 × 200mm.

15 Regents Park, &c./From Primrose Hill. Drawn by W. Westall, A.R.A. 77 × 122/125 × 202mm.

16 Windsor Great Park. Drawn by P. Dewint. 77 × 125/125 × 197mm.

17 View from the Terrace of Somerset House. Drawn by P. Dewint. 62 × 145/123 × 198mm. Looking towards Blackfriars Bridge and the City.

18 Opera House. Drawn by W. Westall. 75 × 128/125 × 200mm. Novosielski and Nash's building, Haymarket.

19 Sussex Place, Regent's Park. Drawn by W. Westall, A.R.A. 73 × 125/125 × 200mm.

20 London Bridge/(second view). Drawn by W. Westall. 75 × 128/125 × 198mm. From S. Bank.

21 Cornwall Terrace. Drawn by W. Westall, A.R.A. 72 × 125/125 × 198mm. Regent's Park.

22 Westminster Bridge. Drawn by P. Dewint. 63 × 148/125 × 190mm. From N.

23 Green Park. Drawn by W. Westall. 75 × 118/125 × 198mm.

24 Entrance to the London Docks. Drawn by P. Dewint. 75 × 130/125 × 200mm.

25 St Pancras New Church. Drawn by Mackenzie. 83 × 120/125 × 195mm.

26 Monument. Drawn by P. Dewint. 125 × 75/200 × 125mm.

27 All Souls Church/(Langham Place). Drawn by W. Westall, A.R.A. 82 × 120/125 × 200mm.

28 Lambeth Palace. Drawn by P. Dewint. 70 × 132/125 × 200mm.

29 The Penitentiary/& Distant View of Westminster Bridge. Drawn by P. Dewint. 63 × 130/125 × 190mm. Millbank Penitentiary.

30 Battersea Bridge/(from Cheyne Walk Chelsea). Drawn by P. Dewint. 70 × 137/125 × 198mm. (*Longford* 263)

31 Richmond Hill/(second view). Drawn by P. Dewint. 80 × 128/125 × 195mm. (*Gascoigne* 82)

32 Waterloo Place Pall Mall. Drawn by W. Westall, A.R.A. 68 × 138/125 × 202mm.

33 Greenwich Hospital. Drawn by P. Dewint. 65 × 138/120 × 200mm. From N. bank.

34 Regent's Canal Basin, City Road. Drawn by P. Dewint. 75 × 128/125 × 200mm.

35 St Pauls/(from Bankside). Drawn by W. Westall, A.R.A. 85 × 120/122 × 200mm.

36 Haymarket. Drawn by W. Westall, A.R.A. 80 × 120/125 × 200mm. With the Haymarket Theatre, 'raised 1822'.

37 Southwark Bridge. Drawn by P. Dewint. 63 × 135/125 × 200mm. From E.

38 Regent Street/(looking towards Carlton Palace). Drawn by W. Westall, A.R.A. 80 × 115/125 × 198mm.

39 Richmond Bridge. Drawn by P. Dewint. 65 × 137/125 × 200mm. (*Gascoigne* 83)

40 Regent Street/(With the Argyle Rooms). Drawn by W. Westall, A.R.A. 82 × 128/125 × 198mm. Looking N. towards All Souls Church.

41 Bow Church. Drawn by Mackenzie. 115 × 83/195 × 125mm. St Mary le Bow, Cheapside.

42 Elgin Gallery. Drawn by Mackenzie. 80 × 120/125 × 200mm. A temporary British Museum gallery; the permanent Elgin Gallery was not opened until 1831.

43 Somerset House & New Church. Drawn by Mackenzie. 77 × 128/125 × 198mm. ie St Mary le Strand.

44 New Buildings, Regents Park. Drawn by W. Westall. 72 × 130/125 × 200mm. The N.W. corner: Sussex Place; Hanover, Cornwall and York Terraces. Sheep and cattle grazing.

45 View from Old Palace Yard. Drawn by Mackenzie. 80 × 240/125 × 202mm.

148 · BRAYLEY'S THEATRES OF LONDON [1826]

The names of one or other of the joint authors of the London volumes of *The Beauties of England and Wales* (no 104) recur on title-pages of books concerned with London architecture or topography over the better part of half a century. While John Britton was editing *Illustrations of the Public Buildings* (no 146) for Josiah Taylor of the Architectural Library, Edward Brayley was writing for the same publisher an account of the theatres of London to accompany a set of aquatinted plates by Daniel Havell. Six of the buildings illustrated are described in both works, for which reason the publisher attached to the *Theatres* check-list the following note: 'Sectional Representations, Ground Plans, and Views exterior and interior of the Theatres marked above with an asterisk are given in the first volume of "Illustrations of the Public Buildings of London" '. Items thus marked were pl.1–5 and 8.

The aquatints, having a more general appeal than the steel-engraved measured drawings and being printed in a much shorter run, have made Brayley's the scarcer and more sought-after of the two books—the more so as minor theatres have tended to be overlooked by topographical editors and artists; the first attempt to depict them systematically having been made ten years earlier in *Londina Illustrata* (no 131).

Historical and Descriptive Accounts of the Theatres of London; by Edward Wedlake Brayley, F.A.S. &c. &c.

Secretary to the Russell Institution. Illustrated with a view of each theatre, elegantly coloured, Drawn and Engraved by the late Daniel Havell. London: Printed for J. Taylor, Architectural Library, High Holborn. M.DCCC.XXVI.

Quarto, 300 × 220mm.   1826

COLLATION Half-title; title-page; dedication to Charles Mathews dated 9 June 1827 (2pp); pp v–vi, preface by E.W. Brayley dated 25 March 1826; list of plates (1 leaf); pp 1–92, London Theatres; pp 1–4, addenda.

The artist who both drew and engraved the plates, Daniel Havell, did not live until 1827 to see them published in book form. He was a senior member of a family very gifted with artistic ability, as witness *Picturesque Views on the River Thames* (1812) for which he and his son Robert engraved in aquatint the water-colour drawings of William Havell, a probable nephew. Father and son between them, or severally, produced a number of other illustrated books, among which were *Views of the Public Buildings and Bridges* (no 133) and *Picturesque Views of Noblemen's & Gentlemen's Seats* (no 141). From 1815 to 1819 Daniel was much taken up with engraving the work of other artists. Ackermann employed him for a dozen of the plates in his *History of the Colleges* (no 116) and Pyne for nine in the *Royal Residences* (no 132). Also for Ackermann he produced five large aquatint plates (about 400 × 500mm) of London views after J. Gendall and T.H. Shepherd (*Crace* 5.114, 8.71, 19.171, 22.22, 22.84) and for T. Clay even larger panoramic views (about 400 × 600mm) after H. Haseler, showing London from three points of view (BL Maps: *K. top.* 21.57). He generally obtained better results when engraving from the work of others than from his own drawings but nevertheless his pictorial record of late Georgian theatreland has proved invaluable to stage historians and the good taste of his colourists often turns the plates into topographical gems (eg Sadler's Wells 'coloured as Night').

In spite of the title-page there are uncoloured copies. Unless otherwise stated plates bear the credit 'Drawn & Engraved by Daniel Havell' and the publication-line 'London, Published by J. Taylor, High Holborn, 1826'. They are numbered tr in Roman numerals and each is bound opposite the first page of its textual description.

1 Theatre Royal, Drury Lane. 112 × 178/155 × 248mm. No credit. Built by Benjamin Wyatt, 1811–12.

2 Theatre Royal, Covent Garden. 112 × 182/155 × 250mm. Built by Robert Smirke, 1809–10.

3 The Opera House. 135 × 210/163 × 250mm. King's Theatre or 'Italian Opera House', rebuilt by Novosielski, 1790–1; remodelled by Nash and G.S. Repton, 1816–18; burned down 1867.

4 New Theatre Royal Haymarket. 125 × 187/162 × 225mm. Built by Nash, 1820–1.

5 Box Entrance to the English Opera House. 182 × 125/225 × 162mm. Also known as Royal Lyceum Theatre. Built by S. Beazley, 1816; burned down 1830.

6 The Pantheon. 112 × 175/155 × 245mm. No credit. Thomas Cundy's 1812 reconstruction of the 'Winter Ranelagh' to serve its original purpose; demolished 1936.

7 Sadler's Wells. 113 × 172/150 × 225mm.

8 Astley's Amphitheatre. 180 × 112/225 × 150mm. Third building of this name erected in Westminster Bridge Road after a conflagration in 1803; burned down 1841.

9 Surry Theatre. 115 × 180/160 × 250mm. Built in the Blackfriars Road by James Donaldson junior to the design of Rudolph Cabanel junior, 1805–6; burned down 1865.

10 East London Theatre. 113 × 180/150 × 225mm. ie the Royalty Theatre, Well Street, Wellclose Square, said to have been built by Cornelius Dixon, 1785–7; burned down 1826.

11 Regency Theatre. 115 × 180/150 × 225mm. Tottenham Street, Tottenham Court Road, 'originally built by old Paschali, father of Mrs. Regina Novosielski, enlarged by James Wyatt'; finally abandoned 1880.

12 The Sans Pareil Theatre. 153 × 110/220 × 150mm. 'nearly opposite Robert Street, Strand'. Built by John Scott, a colour merchant, to publicize his daughter's talents. Opened in 1806; later the Adelphi.

13 The Olympic Theatre. 160 × 118/225 × 150mm. Built by Philip Astley in Drury Lane in the grounds of the former Craven House. Opened 1806; burned down 1849. A nocturnal view.

14 Royal Coburg Theatre. 112 × 178/155 × 225mm. Built in the Waterloo Road by Rudolph Cabanel junior, 1817–18; reconstructed 1924 as the 'Old Vic'.

15 Plan of Covent Garden Theatre. Plan of Drury Lane Theatre. 175 × 200mm. Refs A–U, A–X. No credits and uncoloured.

16 Plan of the Opera House. Plan of the Haymarket Theatre. 175 × 200mm. Refs A–K, A–S. No credits and uncoloured.

149 · COOKE'S VIEWS IN LONDON AND ITS VICINITY [1826–34]

George Cooke, the son of a German immigrant named Guch, was apprenticed in 1795 to James Basire senior, the line-engraver, and on completion of his training was employed with his elder brother, William Bernard, on plates for *The Beauties of England and Wales* (no 104). For his brother's first collection, *The Thames* (no 106), he engraved a view of Temple House, Henley and, for its later edition (no 139), 'The Launch of the Nelson at Woolwich' and a view of the 1814 Frost Fair, both after Luke Clennell, and Reinagle's 'Opening of Waterloo Bridge'. Between 1814 and 1826 he was engaged on 15 plates for his brother's *Picturesque Views on the Southern Coast of England*, based largely on Turner drawings. He also engraved from Turner watercolours, after drawings by James Hakewill, for the *Picturesque Tour of Italy* published in 1820 and illustrations for a number of other foreign travel books and for English county and local histories. He planned a series of reproductions of Callcott's paintings which did not advance beyond a single engraving of Rotterdam but the publication of his son Edward's *Views of Old and New London Bridge* (no 172) was successfully concluded in 1833.

This series of views of London and its environs was, however, his pet project and he persuaded a number of distinguished fellow artists to supplement the contributions by himself and his son. Its first issue, in four-plate Numbers, at 4s octavo and 6s 6d quarto, was available in December 1826 but the series approached completion only in April 1833, when it was announced:

Part XI is just published. Part XII, which will complete the Work in Forty-Eight Plates will be ready in the summer of 1833, and contains Five Plates; with Descriptions of all the views from the Commencement; with Title &c. &c. In PARTS:

Octavo. 5s. 0d Quarto 7s. 6d A few copies on India Paper 10s. 6d

A wrapper of this particular Number reads: 'No. 11. India Proofs, Unlettered, Price Ten Shillings and Sixpence. London and its Vicinity, to the extent of about Twenty Miles, by George Cooke. London. Published by Longman, Rees, Orme, Brown, and Green, Paternoster-Row and G. Cooke (Barnes, Surrey)'. Cooke died in February 1834, having lived to see his ambition fulfilled, as the address to the bound volume, dated October 1834 from Barnes Terrace, puts it: 'The distinguished engraver, whose eminent abilities have long been recognised and fully appreciated, was lost to society and art just as he had completed this the favourite object of his life. His Widow submits, with confidence, this volume to the public'.

Views in London and its Vicinity. Complete in forty-eight plates, engraved on copper by George Cooke, from drawings by Callcott, R.A., Stanfield A.R.A., Prout, Roberts, Stark, Harding, Cotman, Havell &c. &c. after the original sketches made on the spot by Edward W. Cooke. London: Published by Longman and Co. Paternoster Row, J. & A. Arch, Cornhill; Hodgson, Boys and Graves Pall Mall: and Mrs. G. Cooke, Barnes, Surrey.

Quarto, 310 × 250mm. (Large Paper 380 × 275mm)

1834

COLLATION Title-page; address, dated from Barnes Terrace, Surrey October 1834 (1 leaf); pp 1–7, description of pl. 1–48.

In half a dozen of George and Edward Cooke's contribution of a total of 22 drawings they were assisted by A.W. Callcott, Clarkson Stanfield and William Harvey with 'Figures and Effect'. Stanfield, by now famous, also contributed nine of his own drawings of both river and inland subjects while his friend David Roberts drew St Dunstan in the West, just completed to the designs of John Shaw. Callcott's share was two Thames views and one of the demolition of Swallow Street, in 1821, to make way for Regent Street. Samuel Prout's six plates also include four of the Thames, including one of the sinister convict hulk lying off Deptford. J.D. Harding, best known as a lithographer, drew the Hammersmith Suspension Bridge and two other subjects and William Havell, John Sell Cotman and Peter de Wint were each represented by a single plate. Two up-river views, of Kew and Fulham and Putney, were by James Stark.

The chronology of the plates is somewhat erratic. Six are undated, seven dated 1826, 22 dated 1827 and another seven dated 1828. Then there is a gap, until seven more appeared bearing the dates 1832 and 1833. Havell's drawing of Chiswick was finally engraved by Cooke in 1834, just before he died.

The 'India Proofs', published at £6 16s 6d, as stated on the wrapper, are 'unlettered', which seems to mean that they have credits and captions but no publication-lines. In the lesser editions changes are rung on three publication-lines, in Cooke's address of 'Hackney' being replaced by 'Barnes' or 'Barnes Terrace' after his removal there in 1829:

(a) 'London, Published by Longman & Co. Paternoster Row, J. and A. Arch, Cornhill & G. Cooke.'
(b) 'London, Published by Longman & Co., J. & A. Arch & G. Cooke.'
(c) 'London, Pubd by Longman & Co., J. & A. Arch, Carpenter & Sons, & G. Cooke.'

1 London Bridge/from Bankside/As seen in Septr 1826. E.W.C. the Figures and Effect by A.W. Callcott R.A. George Cooke. 1826. (a) 93 × 153/175 × 240mm. (Publication by 'I. & J. Arch'.)

2 The Works of/the New London Bridge taken July 28, 1827. Drawn by E.W. Cooke. the Effect by Cn. Stanfield A.R.A. Engraved by George Cooke 1827. (a) Barnes. 125 × 195/190 × 280mm.

3 Part of the Old and New London Bridges. Drawn July 1, 1832 by E.W. Cooke. Engraved by George Cooke 1833. (b) 130 × 190/180 × 255mm.

4 Billingsgate. Drawn by Augs. W. Callcott R.A. Engraved by George Cooke 1828. (b) Hackney. 168 × 118/280 × 190mm.

5 Ballast Dredger, off the Tower. Drawn by Clarkson Stanfield, 1827. Engraved by George Cooke 1827. (a) Hackney. Printed by S.H. Hawkins. 130 × 180/190 × 280mm.

6 The Tower of London./From the excavations for the St. Katharine's Docks. Drawn by Clarkson Stanfield. Engraved by George Cooke, 1827. (a) Hackney. 110 × 165/190 × 275mm.

7 Stratford, Bow./As seen in Sep. 1826. The Figures & Effect by A.W. Callcott, R.A. Engraved by George Cooke, 1826. (a) Hackney. 88 × 150/190 × 278mm. Alternative caption on India paper ed: 'Bow, Middlesex'.

8 Shoreditch. G. Cooke 1827. (a) Hackney. Printed by S. Hawkins. 95 × 150/190 × 280mm.

9 Tottenham High-Cross. George Cooke 1827. (b) Hackney. 70 × 125/190 × 280mm.

10 Enfield/Middlesex. Drawn by Clarkson Stanfield. Engraved by George Cooke 1827. (b) Hackney, 1828. 108 × 150/190 × 230mm. Pencil drawing (170 × 350mm), 'E.W.C. May 19, 1827', in Guildhall Library.

11 Clock House, St. Albans. Drawn by James Burton Junr. George Cooke 1828. (a) Hackney. 100 × 150/190 × 280mm.

12 Wilsdon Church/Middlesex. Engraved by George Cooke 1828. 75 × 125/155 × 210mm. No publication-line. ie Willesden.

13 Harrow on the Hill. The Schools. George Cooke, 1827. (a) Hackney. 110 × 165/190 × 280mm.

14 Pinner/Middlesex. Engraved by George Cooke. 1828. (b) Hackney. 88 × 155/160 × 230mm.

15 St. Pancras Old Church. George Cooke 1827. (b) 75 × 128/190 × 280mm.

16 The Villa of J. Burton Esqre. Regent's Park. Drawn by J.D. Harding. Figures Drawn by Wm. Harvey. Engraved by George Cooke, 1827. (c) 122 × 178/165 × 240mm.

17 Hanover Terrace. Regents Park. The Figures drawn by William Harvey 1827. Engraved by George Cooke 1827. (c) 112 × 178/165 × 240mm.

18 Hornsey. The Figures and Effect by W. Callcott R.A. George Cooke 1826. (b) Hackney. 72 × 123/190 × 275mm.

19 Canonbury/House/Islington. G. Cooke. 1827. (b) 80 × 140/190 × 280mm. Pencil drawing (135 × 220mm) in Guildhall Library.

20 Sessions House, Clerkenwell Green. Drawn & Engraved by George Cooke 1826. (a) Hackney. 92 × 152/195 × 280mm. Pencil drawing (190 × 320mm), with different staffage, in Guildhall Library.

21 The Post Office & St Pauls/from St Martins le Grand. Drawn by C. Stanfield A.R.A. Engraved by George Cooke 1833. (b) 128 × 198/180 × 255mm.

22 St Dunstan's Church, Fleet Street. Drawn by D. Roberts Oct. from a sketch made in July 1832. Engraved by George Cooke Decr 1832. (b) 140 × 195/190 × 240mm. Shows new tower rising above the Gothic walls of the old church.

23 Exeter Change. George Cooke fect. London. (a) Hackney. 100 × 150/190 × 275mm.

24 Demolition of Swallow Street/Taken in the Autumn of/1821. Drawn by A.W. Callcott, R.A. Engraved by George Cooke. 1827. (a) Hackney. 160 × 120/270 × 190mm.

25 Caxton's House in the Almonry./Westminster. Drawn by S. Prout 1827. Engraved by Geo. Cooke, 1827. (b) 123 × 100/245 × 155mm.

26 Westminster/from Vauxhall. Drawn by S. Prout. Geo. Cooke 1827. 92 × 150/193 × 280mm. No publication-line.

27 Suspension Bridge at Hammersmith/Designed by & executed under the direction of/Wm Tierney Clark Esqre./opened in/1827. Drawn by J.D. Harding. Engraved by George Cooke 1827. (a) Hackney. 105 × 155/190 × 280mm.

28 Chiswick. Drawn by W. Havell. Engraved by George Cooke 1834. (b) 110 × 153/168 × 200mm. Pencil drawing (150 × 205mm), 'April 1827', in Guildhall Library.

29 Kew Bridge from Strand on Green. Drawn by James Stark. Engraved by George Cooke 1832. (a) Barnes Terrace, 1833. 122 × 190/185 × 260mm.

30 Windsor/in 1812. Figures and effect by A.W. Callcott R.A. George Cooke 1826. (a) Hackney. 78 × 130/155 × 255mm.

31 The remaining Tower of Cardinal Wolsey's Palace at Esher. Drawn by W. Havell, 1827. Engraved by George Cooke 1827. (c) 108 × 158/158 × 104mm.

32 Wolsey's Well at Esher/Surrey. Engraved by G. Cooke. (b) 120 × 85/240 × 150mm.

33 Twickenham. Drawn by Clarkson Stanfield. Engraved by George Cooke 1833. (b) 110 × 175/180 × 240mm.

34 Mill on Wimbledon Common. George Cooke fecit. (b) 75 × 125/150 × 225mm.

35 Tooting Church. Drawn by J.D. Harding. George Cooke 1827. (a) Barnes. 93 × 127/190 × 278mm.

36 Remains of Winchester Palace/Southwark. Drawn by John Sell Cotman, 1828. Engraved by George Cooke, 1828. (b) Hackney. 108 × 158/175 × 225mm. In conflict with the 'Cotman' credit, a Guildhall Library pencil drawing (205 × 290mm) reads 'E.W.C. Aug. 21, 1827'.

37 Part of Waterloo Bridge with the Shot Tower &c. Drawn by Clarkson Stanfield A.R.A. Engraved by George Cooke, 1832. (a) Barnes Terrace. 200 × 150/255 × 195mm. Original water-colour (262 × 200mm) in V & A (2983–1876).

38 The Southwark Iron Bridge. Drawn by S. Prout, 1828. Engraved by George Cooke, 1828. (b) Hackney. 108 × 175/180 × 230mm.

39 Blackfriars Bridge. From a drawing by Saml. Prout. Engraved by George Cooke, 1827. (a) Hackney. 85 × 150/192 × 280mm.

40 St Dunstans in the East/from the Custom-House. Drawn by E.W. Cooke. Engraved by George Cooke 1828. (c) 1828. 155 × 110/240 × 165mm. Pencil drawing (300 × 215mm), 'E.W. Cooke, 27 July, 1827', in Guildhall Library.

41 The Diving Bell/Used at the Thames Tunnel after the Irruption of the Water on the 18th of May 1827./Rotherhithe Church in the distance. Drawn by Clarkson Stanfield, A.R.A. Engraved by George Cooke. (a) Barnes Terrace. 150 × 225/190 × 280mm.

42 Commercial Docks. Engraved by Geo. Cooke, 1827. (a) Hackney. 88 × 150/190 × 280mm.

43 Ship Breaking/opposite Wapping. Drawn by Saml. Prout. George Cooke 1826. (a) Hackney. 85 × 130/190 × 275mm.

44 The Thames near Limehouse, called the Lower Pool/Tiers of Colliers Craft &c. Drawn & Etched by E.W. Cooke 1830. Engraved by George Cooke 1832. (a) Barnes Terrace. 120 × 195/190 × 250mm.

45 Prison Ship/at Deptford. Drawn by Saml. Prout. Engraved by George Cooke, 1826. (a) Hackney. 92 × 150/190 × 280mm.

46 Peter-Boats. Fishermen dredging,/at Mill Wall. Isle of Dogs. Drawn by Clarkson Stanfield A.R.A. Engraved by George Cooke 1827. (c) 130 × 178/185 × 250mm.

47 Greenwich. Drawn by Augusts Wall Callcott R.A. 1827. Engraved by George Cooke 1827. (a) Hackney. 107 × 152/190 × 280mm.

48 Greenwich Hospital./1828. Drawn by Clarkson Stanfield, 1828, for G. Cooke's London & vicinity. Engraved by George Cooke 1828. (c) 132 × 182/180 × 230mm. Water-colour (203 × 260mm) in Manchester Art Gallery.

49 Fulham & Putney from the Surrey Shore. Drawn by James Stark. Engraved by George Cooke. 125 × 180/230 × 280mm. No publication-line. Not listed in 'Descriptions'.

50 Richmond Hill. Drawn by P. Dewint. Engraved by Geo Cooke. 102 × 170/170 × 213mm. No publication-line. Not listed in 'Descriptions'.

150 · LONDRES ET L'ANGLETERRE [1826]

This French schoolroom book took over from T. Boys, the Ludgate Hill bookseller, the five plates he had used to illustrate *London or Interesting Memorials* (no 142). That work, however, had a smaller format and the publication-lines of the plates are lost in its binding. Here they are clearly visible, dated between 1 April 1823 and 1 May 1824.

Londres et l'Angleterre, ouvrage élémentaire à l'usage de la jeunesse. Paris. Bossange Frères. 1826. (Imprimé chez Paul Renouard, Rue Garancière, no. 5.)

Duodecimo, 165 × 195mm.   1826

COLLATION Title-page; pp 1–12, introduction; pp 13–348, Londres et l'Angleterre; pp i–xi, indices.

1 front. George IV. Engraved by W.T. Fry. Published, April 1 1823 by T. Boys, 7 Ludgate Hill. Printed by Adlard. 100 × 65mm. Vignetted.

2 p 55 The Custom House, London. Drawn by J. Cartwright. Engraved on steel by Wm Cooke Junr. Published July 1, 1823 by T. Boys, Ludgate-Hill. Printed by H. Adlard. 70 × 120mm.

3 p 131 Somerset House, London. Drawn by T. Barrett. Engraved by Wm. Cooke Junr. Published August 1, 1823 by T. Boys, Ludgate-Hill. Printed by H. Adlard. 70 × 120mm.

4 p 169 Hanover Terrace, Regent's Park. Drawn by J.P. Neale. Engraved by William Cooke Junr. on Steel. Published March 1, 1824 by T. Boys, Ludgate-Hill. Printed by H. Adlard. 70 × 120mm.

5 p 182 Westminster Abbey/& Vicinity. Drawn by J.P. Neale. Engraved on Steel by W. Cooke Junr. Published May 1, 1824 by T. Boys, Ludgate-Hill. Printed by H. Adlard. 70 × 120mm.

151 · BRITTON'S ORIGINAL PICTURE OF LONDON [1826, etc]

The earlier history of this work is to be found under its original title, *The Picture of London* (nos. 85, 134). After trying to refurbish the old text with Greig's views in the 1820 edition Longman & Co issued two more editions (the twenty-second and twenty-third) with various amendments and finally resolved to have the book thoroughly overhauled by the antiquary John Britton for a 100 guinea fee. His revision, with introductory matter dated variously January, November and December 1826, ran into four undated editions with a text which had been stereotyped. It was probably the twenty-eighth and last that was offered for sale in the January 1837 'Catalogue Raisonné' of Britton's books: 'The Original Picture of London. Re-edited with map & views. 1836. 9/-'. The amount of editing, amendment and expansion Britton carried out for his fee says much for his integrity, for at the time of the revision he was also at work on his 14 volume series of *Cathedral Antiquities of England,* on a supplement to the *Architectural Antiquities* (no 97), on the *Public Buildings of London* (no 146), and had only just completed the third volume of *The Beauties of Wiltshire.*

The Original Picture of London Enlarged and Improved: being A Correct Guide for the Stranger, as well as for the inhabitant, to the Metropolis of the British Empire, together with A Description of the Environs. (epigraph) The Twenty-Sixth Edition, Revised and Corrected to the Present Time. London, Printed for Longman, Rees, Orme, Brown and Green, Paternoster Row.

Duodecimo, 140 × 85mm.   1827

COLLATION   Title-page; pp v–vi, contents; pp vii–xii, preface; pp xiii–xlii, introduction, signed 'J.B.', dated December 1826; pp 1–475, Original Picture; pp 476–98, index.

Greig's engravings, four to a plate, made for the 1820 *Picture of London* were retained but with re-engraving, probably at Britton's request, in which the hatching was refined and, in some cases, a view has been burnished out from the plate and a different subject inserted. Some complete new plates were also added showing post-1820 buildings, such as the Haymarket Theatre and St Pancras Church. Two plates of non-conformist chapels, previously overlooked, were inserted. Only the frontispiece, title and maps have anything in the way of credits or publication-lines. Reference is made to the pages in the 1820 edition opposite which some plates first made an appearance.

1 (engr title) The/Original/Picture of London,/Re-edited by/J. Britton F.S.A. &c. (vignette of Constitution Arch and screen, Hyde Park Corner) Higham sc. 50 × 85mm.

2 front. (tc) Waterloo Bridge. London. Published by Longman & Co. Paternoster Row. 100 × 175mm. With five identifications of landmarks in lm. View to the E.

3 p 97 Henry 7th Chapel – West Towers Westr. Abbey – Drury Lane Theatre – Somerset House. 30 × 68, 55 × 32, 55 × 32, 30 × 68mm.

4 p 107 St. George's Church Bloomsbury – St. George's Church Hanover Square – St. Magnus Church London Bridge – St. Leonards Church Shoreditch. Each 52 × 34mm. Re-engraved from 1820 ed p 180.

5 p 109 Bow Church – Mary-le-bone Church – The New Church, Strand – St. Martin's Church. Each 53 × 33mm. Re-engraved from 1820 ed p 182.

6 p 120 Spa Fields Chapel – The Tabernacle Moorfields – Jewin Street Chapel – Wesleyan Chapel City Road. Each 27 × 67mm.

7 p 122 Albion Chapel Moorfields – Surrey Chapel – Tottenham Court Road Chapel – Roman Catholic Chapel Moorfields. Each 27 × 67mm.

8 p 135 Mansion House – Royal Exchange – Guild Hall – Monument. Each 54 × 35mm. Re-engraved from 1820 ed p 153.

9 p 148 South Sea House – Excise Office – The Mint – Trinity House. Each 27 × 70mm. Third and fourth re-engraved from 1820 ed p 173.

10 p 150 London Institution – Ironmongers Hall –

Fishmongers Hall – Goldsmiths Hall. Each 30 × 68mm. Re-engraved from 1820 ed p 176.

11 p 153 Carlton Palace – Pall Mall West – House of Lords – House of Commons. Each 28 × 68mm. Third and fourth re-engraved from 1820 ed p 99.

12 p 156 White Hall, Parliament Street – Horse Guards – Admiralty – Treasury. Each 27 × 70mm. Re-engraved from 1820 ed p 116.

13 p 175 The Tower – Auction Mart – Interior of the Bank – The Bank. Each 27 × 68mm. Re-engraved from 1820 ed p 140.

14 p 183 Hertford College – Harrow School – Sessions House Old Bailey – Chapel to the Charterhouse. 27 × 67, 53 × 35, 53 × 35, 27 × 67mm. The first view is of East India College, near Hertford, built for the Company by W. Wilkins, 1806–9, later called Haileybury. Third and fourth re-engraved from 1820 ed p 225.

15 p 198 Southwark Bridge – Blackfryars Bridge – London Bridge – Sessions House Clerkenwell. Each 27 × 67mm. Re-engraved from 1820 ed p 187.

16 p 201 Vauxhall Bridge – Westminster Bridge – Richmond Bridge – Christ's Hospital. Each 27 × 70mm. Waterloo Bridge replaced by Richmond Bridge, otherwise as 1820 ed p 190.

17 p 228 Newgate – House of Correction Cold Bath Fields – White Cross Compter – London Hospital. Each 27 × 67mm. Re-engraved from 1820 ed p 219.

18 p 238 Islington – Guy's Hospital – St. Luke's Hospital – Bartholomew Hospital. Each 27 × 67mm. Philanthropic Chapel replaced by Islington, otherwise as 1820 ed p 199.

19 p 249 Magdalen Hospital – Foundling Hospital – New Bethlehem Hospital St. George's Fields – Deaf & Dumb Asylum. Each 27 × 70mm. Re-engraved from 1820 ed p 208.

20 p 269 St. Pauls School – Surgeons College – Commercial Sale Rooms – Merchant Taylors School. 55 × 35, 55 × 35, 27 × 65, 27 × 65mm. St Paul's School, George Smith's new building of 1823–4.

21 p 287 British Museum – St. James's Palace – Lansdown House – Earl Spencer's House. Each 53 × 35mm. Re-engraved from 1820 ed p 122.

22 p 319 Lambeth Palace – Buckingham House – Carlton House – Northumberland House. Each 27 × 67mm. Carlton House demolished 1827–8.

23 p 353 Covent Garden Theatre – Somerset House from the Thames – Adelphi – St. Paul's Cathedral. N.E. Each 27 × 68mm. Second and third re-engraved from 1820 ed p 239.

24 p 357 St. Paul's Covent Garden – Opera House – Regent Street – Quadrant. Each 30 × 68mm. The Royal Opera House remodelled by Nash and Repton, 1816–18 and the Regent Street Quadrant by Nash, 1818–20.

25 p 373 Waterloo Place – Haymarket Theatre – Burlington Arcade – Pancrass New Church. 30 × 68, 52 × 30, 52 × 30, 30 × 68mm. Waterloo Place was built from 1815, Nash's Haymarket Theatre, 1820–1, Burlington Arcade, 1816–18 and W. Inwood's St Pancras Church, 1819–22.

26 p 390 Bullocks Museum – Temple Bar – Foreign Office – Highgate Archway. Each 52 × 32mm. Re-engraved from 1820 ed pp 252, 366.

27 p 398 Windsor Castle – Holland House – Eton College – Cobourg Theatre. Each 26 × 65mm. Another view of Eton College Chapel has been substituted, otherwise re-engraved from 1820 ed p 375.

28 p 402 Picture Gallery Dulwich College – Westminster School – Statue in Hyde Park – Pall Mall East. Each 30 × 67mm. The statue is the Achilles of 1822 by Sir Richard Westmacott and two of his sons.

29 p 407 West India Docks – Tower – Custom House – East India House. Each 27 × 70mm. Re-engraved from 1820 ed p 384.

30 p 476 Plan of the Cities of London & Westminster, with the Borough of Southwark. Shewing the Situation of the Public Buildings, Parks, Squares &c. J.B. dirext. H.A. del. Sidy Hall sculpt. 118 × 204mm. (*Darlington and Howgego* 305)

31 p 498 (bl) Map of the/Environs of/London. Neele sculpt. 352 Strand. Published Jan. 1815 by Longman Hurst Rees Orme & Brown, Paternoster Row. 190 × 230mm. (*Darlington and Howgego* 263(2))

---

152 · ALLEN'S HISTORY AND ANTIQUITIES OF LONDON [1827–37]

Thomas Allen, the son of a map engraver, was born in 1803 and fell victim to cholera in 1833. For so short a life his output of topographical works was prodigious, including *The History and Antiquities of the Parish of Lambeth* (1827), a *History of the County of York* (1828–31) in three large volumes and a *History of the Counties of Surrey and Sussex* (1829–30, no 158) in two, both from the publisher I.T. Hinton, and a two-volume *History of the County of Lincoln* published posthumously in 1834. At the same period as the first three works he prepared and issued a guidebook, *The Panorama of London* (no 162), and this *History and Antiquities*.

A fifth volume, with an engraved title borrowed from Partington's *National History* (no 177), was published posthumously by George Virtue in 1837 because, as he explained in the 'Address', it was 'thought that a History of London was not complete without some account of the suburbs', by which was meant Bloomsbury, Chelsea, Kensington, Knightsbridge, Marylebone, Paddington, Regent's Park, St Pancras and northwards to Hackney, Islington and Highgate. At the same time Virtue reissued the first four volumes, the whole being revised by Thomas Wright.

The History and Antiquities of London, Westminster, Southwark, and parts adjacent by Thomas Allen, with engravings. Vol. I (II–IV). London, Cowie and Strange, Paternoster Row and Fetter Lane. MDCCCXXVII (1827–9).

The History and Antiquities of London, Westminster, Southwark, and parts adjacent by Thomas Allen continued to the present time, by Thomas Wright Esq. of Trin.Coll. Cambridge ... Vol. I (II–V). London: Published by George Virtue, 26 Ivy Lane, Paternoster Row. 1837.

Octavo, 208 × 130mm.   1827–37.

COLLATION   Vol. 1. Title-page; (1st ed: dedication, undated (1 leaf)); preface (1st ed dated 1 August 1827) (2pp); pp 1–468, History and Antiquities; indices (16pp). Vol. 2. Title-page; contents, list of engravings (2pp); pp 1–554, History and Antiquities continued; pp 555–89, indices. Vol. 3. Title-page; (1st ed: dedication, undated (1 leaf)); contents, list of engravings (4pp); pp 1–776, History and Antiquities continued; pp 777–88, indices. Vol. 4. Title-page; (1st ed: dedication, undated (1 leaf)); contents, list of engravings (3pp); pp 1–555, History and Antiquities continued; (1st ed: pp 556–62, addenda); pp 557–68 (1st ed pp 563–74), indices. Vol. 5. Title-page; address (2pp); pp 1–496, History and Antiquities continued; pp 497–500, index, list of engravings (no index in 1st ed).

Allen was also draughtsman and engraver and contributed to this work of his some cramped and stilted plates on copper, mostly groups of antiquarian relics or facsimiles of plates from folio and quarto works, such as Wilkinson's *Londina Illustrata* (no 131), reduced to insignificance to fit the modest octavo format. Probably also his are over 100 wooduts of City and Company arms, antiquities, houses, churches, chapels, gates and bridges, not listed here because printed with the text. In his reissue Virtue added to the first four volumes a map, engraved title-pages with vignetted views, some frontispieces and a plate of the opening of the new London Bridge in August 1831; the fifth volume he illustrated summarily with a borrowed title, a frontispiece and four double-view, steel-engraved plates, of which six were borrowed from Whittock's *Modern Picture of London* (no 183), another of his books published the previous year. The matter is further confused by extra-illustrated copies of Allen, treated by some extra-illustrators as a successor to Pennant (no 67).

The plates are unnumbered, although listed. Publication-lines are quoted where they occur. They are sometimes burnished out in the second edition and sometimes replaced by 'G. Virtue, 26 Ivy Lane'.

VOL. 1

1 (engr title) The/History and Antiquities/of/London/ Westminster Southwark/and Parts Adjacent/By Thomas Allen/Vol. I/London:/Cowie & Strange./Paternoster Row & Fetter Lane,/1827.

1a (engr title) A New History/of/London & Westminster./By Thomas Allen/continued to the present time/By Thomas Wright Esq./of Trinity College Cambridge.... (vignette, 70 × 100mm) The New National Gallery/London, Geo: Virtue, 26 Ivy Lane 1836. 2nd ed only.

2 front. London from Blackfriars Bridge. Drawn by Campion. Engraved by J. Rogers. 100 × 163/120 × 200mm. 2nd ed only. From Allen's *Panorama*.

3 p 1 (tm) The New Plan of London, from Actual Survey. (bm) G. Virtue, London. 400 × 555/420 × 560mm. 2nd ed only. (*Darlington and Howgego* 335)

4 p 16 Roman London/From the Best authorities. T. Allen delt et Fect. 92 × 145/110 × 175mm.

5 p 28 Antiquities/Discovered in Lombard Street and Birchin Lane, 1785. T. Allen delt & Fect. 200 × 125mm pl. mark.

6 p 32 Antiquities/Discovered in Ludgate-Hill &c. T. Allen delt. 200 × 125mm pl. mark. 'G. Virtue, 26 Ivy Lane' added in 2nd ed.

7 p 347 Lambeth Church & Palace. N. Whittock. W. Syms. London, Published by Geo. Virtue, 26, Ivy Lane 1836. 95 × 152/130 × 200mm. 2nd ed only.

8 p 438 Plan for Rebuilding the City of London/By Sir C. Wren. Pub. by Cowie & Strange, 1827. 70 × 145/120 × 170mm.

VOL. 2

9 (engr title) The/History and Antiquities/of/London/ Westminster Southwark/and Parts Adjacent/By Thomas Allen/Vol. II/London:/Cowie & Strange./Paternoster Row & Fetter Lane,/1828.

9a (engr title) A New History of/London/Westminster and the Borough/of Southwark/By Thomas Allen

Esqr. (vignette, 75 × 80mm) A View of the Old and New Haymarket Theatres H. Adlard sculp./Vol.II./London:/Published by George Virtue, 26 Ivy Lane/Paternoster Row.

10 p 430 Plan of the River Thames/From the best authorities – London Mark Stone/near Staines Church – Seal of Port of London/found near Queenhithe, 1810. T. Allen delt et Fect. Pub. by Cowie & Strange, 1827. 95 × 168/105 × 175mm.

11 p 466 London Bridge 1600/From a rare printe by Hollar – Plan of London Bridge 1799 – Elevation of New London Bridge – Plan. 200 × 120mm pl. mark.

12 p 487 The New London Bridge/opened 1st August, 1831 by their Majesties King William IV & Queen Adelaide. 75 × 138/105 × 155mm. 2nd ed only.

13 p 515 White Tower/Tower of London – White Tower – Plan of Chapel – Chapel – Council Chamber. 55 × 90,100 × 50,52 × 42,52 × 42/200 × 120mm.

14 p 517 Plan, View and Inscriptions, Beauchamp Tower/Tower of London. 120 × 205mm pl. mark. 1st ed only.

VOL.3

15 (engr title) The/History and Antiquities/of/London/Westminster Southwark/and Parts Adjacent/By Thomas Allen/Vol. III/London:/Cowie & Strange./Paternoster Row & Fetter Lane,/1828.

15a (engr title) A New History of/London/Westminster and the Borough/of Southwark/By Thomas Allen Esqr. (vignette, 80 × 90mm) View of the Exterior of Covent Garden Theatre/Vol. III/London:/Published by George Virtue, 26 Ivy Lane Paternoster Row/1833.

16 p 1 (bm) Plan of the City of London/Divided into Wards./Published by Cowie & Strange, London, 1828. Engraved Expressly for Allen's History of London. 150 × 240/200 × 255mm. (*Darlington and Howgego* 314)

17 p 53 New Post Office/St Martins le Grand – Roman & gothic remains discovered nearby. T.A. Delt. & Dirext. 50 × 95,50 × 93 and 40 × 45/200 × 125mm.

18 p 54 The New Post Office. Neale del. Barber sc. 75 × 130/100 × 162mm. 2nd ed only.

19 p 134 Plan of St Helens Church/Sir J. Crosby's Monument, and the Nun's Grate/Bishopsgate. T.A. delt. et Fect. Pub. by Cowie & Strange, London, 1828. 200 × 125 pl. mark.

20 p 137 Sir J. Caesar's Tomb/St Helen's Church. T. Allen fect. 175 × 100/200 × 120mm.

21 p 152 (on cartouche bc) Typus/Parochiae Divi Martini/vulgo St Martin's Outwich/una cum parte Parochiae Divi Petri in Cornehill in/Civitate Londini/Inventus … per/Gulielmum Goodman/1mo Januarii/Ann 1599. Published by Cowie & Strange 1827. 100 × 160/110 × 170mm. 2nd ed only.

22 p 153 Remains of Crosby Hall/Bishopsgate Street.

Pub. by Cowie & Strange, 1828. 40 × 45, etc/190 × 120mm. (*Longford* 423)

23 p 157 Leathersellers' Hall &c./St Helen's Place./Pub. by Cowie & Strange, 1828. 125 × 205mm pl. mark.

24 p 269 St Paul's Cathedral. On Steel. G. Adcock sculp. Pub. by Cowie & Strange, 1828. N.E. view.

24a p 269 St Paul's Cathedral. Drawn by H. West. Engraved by J. Shury. 100 × 152/130 × 205mm. S.W. view. 2nd ed only.

25 p 275 St Paul's Cathedral 1640. Listed in 1st ed.

26 p 294 Plan of St Paul's Cathedral/1645. Pub. by Cowie & Strange, 1828. 125 × 200mm pl. mark.

27 p 375 Guildhall/1788. T.A. delt. 90 × 70, etc./125 × 200mm. In aquatint. George Dance junior's rebuilding in progress.

28 p 432 Cheapside Cross – Bow Church – Plan of Cheapside – Cross & Standard. Pub. by Cowie & Strange, 1828. 200 × 125mm pl. mark. 2nd ed has Virtue's publication-line.

29 p 439 Ancient Crypt Bow Church/Cheapside. Pub. by Cowie & Strange, London, 1828. 42 × 50, etc/200 × 120mm.

30 p 443 Steeple of St. Michael's Church Cornhill/1421. Pub. by Cowie & Strange, London, 1828. 160 × 60/200 × 120mm. Vignetted.

31 p 559 New Hall of Christ's Hospital. Published by Cowie & Strange, Paternoster Row & Fetter Lane. 55 × 150/120 × 175mm. Vignetted.

32 p 576 Cheapside &c/1585. R. Treswell 1585. T. Allen fect. Pub. by Cowie & Strange, 1828. 95 × 142/125 × 200mm.

33 p 597 Ludgate, St Pauls, and Bow Church/During the Great Fire 1666. From an original painting. Aquatinted by H. Pyall. Pub. by Cowie & Strange, 1827. 90 × 150/125 × 180mm. 2nd ed has Virtue's publication-line. From the same source as *Londina Illustrata*, item 3.

34 p 635 Plan of the Priory of/St Bartholomew the Great/Smithfield. T.A. del. et fect. Pub. by Cowie & Strange, London, 1828. 140 × 100/205 × 120mm.

35 p 770 Great Seal/of the/City of London. T.A. Allen delt et Fecit. 120 × 185mm pl. mark.

VOL. 4

36 (engr title) The/History and Antiquities/of/London/Westminster Southwark/and Parts Adjacent/By Thomas Allen/Vol.IV/London:/Cowie & Strange./Paternoster Row & Fetter Lane,/1828.

36a (engr title) A New History/of/London & Westminster./By Thomas Allen/continued to the present time/By Thomas Wright Esq./of Trinity College Cambridge…. (vignette, 60 × 85mm) View of the Exterior of Drury Lane Theatre/Vol.IV./London:/Published by George Virtue, 26 Ivy Lane/Paternoster Row.

37 front. Guys Hospital. N. Whittock. J. Rogers. 88 × 155/125 × 205mm. 2nd ed only.

38 p 1 (bl) Plan/of the/City of/Westminster,/Divided into/Parishes. Pub. by Cowie & Strange, 1829. Engraved Expressly for Allen's History of London. 160 × 200/185 × 210mm.

39 p 48 Westminster Abbey. G. Adcock sculp. Steel Plate. Pubd. by Cowie. 100 × 150/125 × 200mm.

40 p 60 Historical Frieze/Edward the Confessor's Chapel/Westminster Abbey. 125 × 200mm pl. mark.

41 p 165 Ground Plan of the ancient/Palace of Westminster. T.A. delt et Fect. – Bell Tower of St Stephens – Interior of the Painted Chamber. Pub. by Cowie & Strange, 1827. 62 × 100,60 × 40,60 × 45/180 × 115mm. Refs to plan 1–16.

42 p 208 The Sanctuary church/at/Westminster/From an original Drawing by Dr Stukeley. Pub. by Cowie & Strange, London, 1828. 115 × 200mm pl. mark.

43 p 246 Houses of the nobility in the Strand/1660. Suffolk Ho. – Worcester Ho. – Salisbury Ho. Durham Ho. – York Ho. Pub. by Cowie & Strange, 1828. 125 × 200mm pl. mark. From the same source as *Londina Illustrata*, items 96–8.

44 p 248 Plan of the Village of Charing/By Ralph Aggas/1560 – Charing Cross, 1500 & 1600. Pub. by Cowie & Strange, 1828. 90 × 120, etc/120 × 200mm.

45 p 395 Interior of St Mary's Church/Inner Temple – Exterior of St Mary's Church/Inner Temple T.A. delt. Pub. by Cowie & Strange. 80 × 55,60 × 90/205 × 125mm.

46 p 397 Sepulchral Effigies/Temple Church. Pubd. by Cowie & Strange, 1827. 200 × 120mm pl. mark.

47 p 433 (bl) The/Borough of Southwark/Divided into Parishes. Pub. by Cowie & Strange, London, 1829. Engraved Expressly for Allen's History of London. 160 × 205/190 × 210mm.

48 p 517 Bankside/Southwark/From an ancient survey on vellum made in the reign of Queen Elizabeth in the possession of W. Bray, F.S.A. Pub. by Cowie & Strange, 1827. 85 × 160/110 × 170mm.

VOL. 5

49 (engr title) National/History and Views of London/with its environs/including its Antiquities/Modern Improvements &c./from original drawings/by Eminent Artists/Vol. V./(vignette, 100 × 100mm) Entrance to the Green Park. Drawn by H. West. Engraved by J. Shury./London/1837.

50 front. View of London/from Waterloo Bridge. Drawn by H. West. Engraved by J. Shury. 98 × 165/125 × 205mm.

51 p 191 Fishmongers Hall &c. from New London Bridge – Goldsmith's Hall. Each 60 × 92/205 × 125mm. From *Modern Picture,* items 28,3.

52 p 274 New Westminster Hospital – New St George's

Hospital. Each 60 × 90/210 × 125mm. From *Modern Picture*, items 63,65.

53 p 280 Duke of York's Column – New English Opera House. Each 60 × 90/200 × 125mm. From *Modern Picture,* items 62, 51.

54 p 291 West Strand. Drawn by H. West. – King's College Strand. 50 × 60,58 × 85/200 × 125mm.

153 · BUCKLER'S SIXTY VIEWS OF ENDOWED GRAMMAR SCHOOLS* [1827]

John Chessell Buckler, an architect by profession, was also the son of an architect, John Buckler, who had much less taste for the routine duties of his practice than for drawing perspective views of English cathedrals, abbeys, ancient parish churches and other antique buildings for noble or academic patrons. Among these were Lord Grenville, the Duke of Buckingham, Sir Richard Colt Hoare, Lord Bagot and Dr Routh, President of Magdalen College, Oxford which gave the elder Buckler his first job and later employed him as bailiff of its London properties. He reckoned that during his career he made some 13,000 sketches, many of buildings since altered or removed; included in these are the pen, ink and wash drawings of Oxford colleges, some of which he published as aquatints, and 16 of London palaces and parks made in 1827 for the Crace Collection. The son, John Chessell, was much more active professionally and pursued a successful career as an architect in the Gothic mode, his competition designs for the post-fire Houses of Parliament being adjudged only second to those of Charles Barry. At the same time he cherished a fondness for drawing old buildings, having received lessons in painting from Francis Nicholson as well as from his father. Indeed, in a large collection of sepia wash drawings of Oxford the work of father and son is virtually indistinguishable, apart from the initials of the signature. John Chessell's earliest public work, *Views of Cathedral Churches in England*, contained 22 plates based largely on his father's drawings and he no doubt drew upon his father's sketchbooks when he etched the present collection of views of 55 endowed grammar schools. They are rather more humdrum in their execution than one might expect from so proficient a topographical draughtsman but they do usefully preserve aspects of institutions which have largely been rebuilt, or removed entirely.

Five of the schools are allotted two plates. There are no publication-lines but the credit 'JCB 1823' is to be found on some, concealed in the work br. They are unnumbered but arranged in alphabetical order of the schools with descriptions interleaved, printed on recto only.

Sixty Views of Endowed Grammar Schools from Original Drawings by J.C. Buckler: with letter-press descriptions. London: Printed for Thomas Hurst and Company, 65 St. Paul's Church-Yard. 1827.

Folio, 290 × 215mm.   1827

COLLATION Title-page; list of plates (1 leaf); 59 plates, interleaved with as many descriptions, unpaginated and printed on recto only.

1 Old School at the Charter House. 95 × 140/140 × 170mm.
2 New Grammar School at the Charter House. JCB 1823. 95 × 143/135 × 165mm.
3 Old Quadrangle Christ's Hospital London. 100 × 142/135 × 168mm.
4 Grammar School at Christ's Hospital. 95 × 140/138 × 170mm.
5 Mercers School/College Hill/London. 140 × 95/190 × 120mm.
6 Merchant Tailors' School, Suffolk Lane London. JCB 1823. 95 × 140/130 × 160mm.
7 Cloisters of Merchant Tailors' School. 95 × 140/140 × 175mm.
8 Grammar School at Saint Mary Overies Southwark. 98 × 143/140 × 165mm.
9 Grammar School of St. Olave's Southwark. 95 × 142/140 × 175mm.
10 Westminster College/from Little Deans Yard. 95 × 153/138 × 175mm.

154 · ELMES'S METROPOLITAN IMPROVEMENTS: LONDON IN THE NINETEENTH CENTURY [1827–30]

Two of the most widely-known sets of illustrations of late Georgian London, *Metropolitan Improvements* and its sequel, owe their existence to the coming together of an enterprising publisher, Jones & Co of the Kingsland Road, and the topographical artist Thomas H. Shepherd. The Architectural Library had already tried out the market for steel-engraved plates of contemporary buildings with Britton and Pugin's *Illustrations of the Public Buildings of London* (no 146), and no sooner was that work completed than the first Number of *Metropolitan Improvements* was on offer to subscribers. Although less retrospective in intention the new collection eventually included no fewer than 30 of the same subjects, but with fewer technical trimmings and less austerely, since Shepherd's skies, lighting and animated staffage bring some warmth to bear even on the sternest and purest of Greek revival façades. It was an immediate success and became one of the most generally appreciated topographical series of the century. In the autumn of 1828, by the time the No 27 had been distributed, the now flourishing firm had moved into James Lackington's former premises, the Temple of the Muses in Finsbury Square. Here they consolidated plans for future publications which would enable them to cash in on the exceptional talents and diligence of their 'house artist'. Accretions to the original series are chronicled in the advertisements printed on the buff wrappers into which issues of *Metropolitan Improvements* were stitched.

In No 23 (August 1828) subscriptions were invited to views of Edinburgh, *Modern Athens*, 'in demy Quarto, each Number to contain 4 views ... 4 pages of letter-press, price One Shilling', of which No 1 came out the following January. On 13 September 1828 a work on Dublin and on university cities and seaports was adumbrated but heard of no more. In the next Number the following were 'preparing for the Press and will speedily be published': 'Views of the New Buildings, Modern

Improvements, Picturesque Scenery &c of the Cities of Bath and Bristol ... engraved by Mr. Thomas Shepherd'. The artist had been in Scotland and the West Country accumulating drawings for two of these works in 1827. With No 35, in the spring of 1829, appeared a more specific advertisement for 'Jones's Views of the City of Bath and Bristol with the Counties of Somerset and Gloucester ... with historical and descriptive illustrations by John Britton; in quarto at two shillings for India Proofs'. Not content with just a handful of cities the publisher unveiled with No 29 a grandiose vista, suggesting that Britton and Brayley had been working on him to finance a worthy successor to their *Beauties of England and Wales* (no 104). It was to be called 'Jones's Great Britain Illustrated' and to involve the production of quarto Numbers containing four steel-engravings into an illimitable future. Shepherd, who was now engaged on the *Metropolitan Improvements* sequel, could not be expected immediately to implement these plans and an advertisement in No 30 for 'Jones's Views of the Seats, Mansions, Castles &c. of Noblemen and Gentlemen ... forming part of Jones's Great Britain Illustrated' was for a re-engraving on steel, with new credits and publication-lines, of some of J.P. Neale's second series of etchings which Sherwood Jones & Co, of Paternoster Row, had been publishing since 1824. Moreover J.P. Neale and W.H. Bartlett were engaged to lend a hand with *Bath and Bristol* (1829) and Henry Gastineau to do all the drawing for *Wales Illustrated* and *South Wales Illustrated* (1830). Bartlett and Thomas Allom shared the labour, and a second publisher the risks, of *Devonshire and Cornwall* (1829–32), announced thus in No 38 (July 1829):

Views in Devonshire. Four highly finished line engravings in each Number for One Shilling.... Now Publishing, to be continued Monthly, or oftener ... from original Drawings taken expressly by Thomas Allom and W.H. Bartlett, with historical and topographical descriptions by J. Britton and E.W. Brayley forming part of Fisher's 'Grand National Improvements' and Jones's 'Great Britain Illustrated'.

The final Number of *Metropolitan Improvements*, published in January 1830, included four specimen pages of its London sequel and an 'Address' from the publisher concerning a 'Second Series, to comprise the Earlier Buildings and Antiquities'. But the binder's instructions also included a label for the spine of the completed work which read: 'London in the Nineteenth Century: Vol.2, comprising the Metropolitan Improvements'; thus subscribers were made to feel the necessity of acquiring the first volume since they now possessed the second complete, and then, who knows, perhaps they would collect the whole series of 'Great Britain Illustrated'.

The chance survival in original wrappers of two complete sets of the *Metropolitan Improvements* and one set of its retrospective sequel facilitates an analysis of their publication history, which may be taken as typical of many of the topographical works of this period.

The first monthly Number, which must have been available by June 1827, included, besides the usual four pages of text and four views on two plates, a printed title and an engraved one dated 5 May. Twelve such Numbers, at 1s each for ordinary plates and 2s for India paper proofs, were issued monthly until May 1828, when a new prospectus was printed: 'A fair Specimen is submitted for approbation per the bearer, who will receive, and promptly attend to any orders, and deliver the work as published fortnightly; Nos 1 to 12 comprising Fifty Views being already out'. From May to 1 July Nos 13 to 20 came out at weekly intervals and Nos 21 to 25 at fortnightly intervals from July to September. Another prospectus, probably issued when the publisher was on the move to Finsbury Square, promised only monthly instalments, which were resumed until the ultimate Number (41) came out on 1 January 1830. It was also open to subscribers to opt for less frequent deliveries in 'Parts' made up of five Numbers, at 5s for the ordinary edition; a prospectus of January 1829 announces that No 30 and Part VI 'will be published and ready for delivery about the 27th Instant'.

Those preferring their *Metropolitan Improvements* in a more handy format might subscribe to octavo Numbers, also stitched in buff wrappers, with an extended text and one view per plate instead of two: 'in about 80 weekly Numbers at 6d. or 20 Parts, 2s each, or Proofs on Royal Paper, Numbers 1s. and Parts 4s. each with 160 brilliant engravings on steel'. Thus one might choose to collect either quarto plates on plain or on India paper and in 41 Numbers or in eight Parts, or octavo plates on plain or on India paper and in 80 weekly Numbers or in 20 Parts, a complex pattern of distribution which would daunt all but the most efficiently organized publishing house.

All these various issues were eventually destined for binding and although the paginated half-sheets presented the binder with no problems, the same cannot be said of the plates as will presently appear. Subscriptions might be started at any point in the progress of the work and late entrants be furnished with arrears; this accounts for printed title-pages being found either undated or with dates ranging from 1827 to 1833 and for Numbers in anachronistic wrappers. Thus subscribers who started with the sequel might at the same time acquire the so-called 'Volume 2' with an 1830 printed title and a new engraved title dated 1829, 'Price £2. 2s. or India Paper Proofs £4. 4s., Boards'.

No printed title was supplied with the octavo edition, which was frequently reissued with a stereotyped text and a selection of plates, until its final appearance at mid-century retitled *Views and History of London in the Nineteenth Century*.

James Elmes, the author of the text, was a prolific writer on architecture, the biographer of Wren and a friend of Haydon and Keats. He was Surveyor to the Port of London and also sought private work since he advertises, somewhat unprofessionally, on the wrapper of No 20: 'designs & estimates for new buildings, alterations, repairs &c in any part of the kingdom'. The publishers when they engaged him were intent on giving their series the same sort of architectural 'cachet' which attached to Britton's *Illustrations of Public Buildings*.

Metropolitan Improvements; or London in the Nineteenth Century: displayed in a Series of Engravings of the New Buildings, Improvements, &c. by the most eminent artists, from original drawings, taken from the objects themselves expressly for this work, By Mr. Thos. H. Shepherd: comprising the palaces, parks, new churches, bridges, streets, river scenery, public offices and institutions, gentlemen's seats and mansions, and every other object worthy of notice throughout the metropolis and its environs, with Historical, Topographical and Critical Illustrations, By James Elmes, M.R.I.A. Architect, Author of the Life of Sir Christopher Wren, Lectures on Architecture, Dictionary of the Fine Arts, &c. London: Published by Jones and Co, Acton Place, Kingsland Road (Removed from Acton Place to The Temple of the Muses—Late Lackington's,—Finsbury Square.) and sold by Simpkin Marshall, Stationers' Hall Court; and all book and printsellers. 1827 (1828, 1830, 1831, 1833, nd).—Entered at Stationers' Hall. (on verso) Printed by J. Haddon, Castle Street, Finsbury.

Quarto, 270–80 × 210mm.   1827, etc

COLLATION   Title-page; pp iii–vi, dedication to the King dated 1 July 1827, with wood-engraved headpiece of royal arms; pp 1–172, Metropolitan Improvements; pp i–ii, list of engravings.

Octavo, 210–30 × 140–5mm.   1828, nd

COLLATION   Engr title-page; pp iii–vi, dedication to the King; pp i–xlii, Brief View of the Early History of London; pp 1–316, Metropolitan Improvements; list of 158 separate plates (2pp).

(*Title-page* as above)

Octavo, 210 × 140mm.   (1847 stereotype)

COLLATION   (As above, but with only 43 views, without dedication and, in lieu of the list, a tipped-in slip dated 1 September 1847 reading: 'The historical and descriptive letter-press of the work being the same as that in the large 4to edition of "Metropolitan Improvements" which contains 160 engravings it frequently occurs in this volume that the words "see Engraving" or "see Plate so-and-so" appear: these remarks do not refer to the 8vo Edition which contains under Fifty Engravings, but being printed from the same stereotype plates as the 4to work, these notices cannot be prevented'.)

Views and History of London in the Nineteenth Century, being A Series of Illustrations of the Most Interesting Objects in the British Metropolis and its Vicinity, from original drawings by Mr. Thomas H. Shepherd: with Historical Descriptions from the earliest Periods. London: Published by Thomas Holmes, (successor to Edward Lacey) 76 St Paul's Church Yard.

Octavo, 210 × 140mm.   nd stereotype (?1850)

COLLATION   (As original octavo, but without list or dedication and only 40 views.)

This book and its sequel *London in the Nineteenth Century* are for convenience called 'Shepherd's London', and with good reason since they are more prized for their engravings based on 350 separate drawings by Thomas H. Shepherd than for their texts: in the first volume by Elmes they are chiefly descriptive and in the second anonymous and quite subordinate. It would be difficult to point to any other artist in the history of topographical book illustration who can so consistently combine spontaneity with a likeness so vivid that one is persuaded that one has walked the streets he portrayed. Besides this genius he must have possessed most unusual stamina, for while he was working on this mammoth assignment he was also visiting Edinburgh for *Modern Athens* and the West Country for

Bath and Bristol as well as carrying on with the bread-and-butter job on which he was able to rely from 1809 to 1859: the painting of some 450 water-colours of London scenes for the collector Frederick Crace.

For the steel-engravings he first made a pencil drawing 'in situ' which would then be turned into a sepia wash-drawing on which they were based. Specimens of these survive in the Greater London Council, Guildhall Library, Museum of London and Westminster Public Library print collections and most of the sepia drawings of Edinburgh for *Modern Athens* are preserved as a series in the British Museum Department of Prints and Drawings. The engraved views would then be returned to him for approval and annotation, as may be seen in a set of marked proofs of *Metropolitan Improvements* in the Guildhall Library. As an experienced engraver himself he clearly had a say in the choice of an engraver and exercised some control over the finished article.

Over 40 engravers were employed on the two London series although about half of these were represented by not more than five plates each. The busiest was William Wallis who contributed 35; he was the son of one of Charles Heath's assistants and also contributed miniature engravings to Heath's *Picturesque Annuals* and *Keepsakes*. Thirty three were by James Tingle, who specialized in landscape and architectural line-engraving and aquatint, 26 by Thomas Barber, 22 by W. Watkins and 20 by R. Acon. Seven other engravers produced ten or more plates and 20 of them were simultaneously engaged on other sections of the projected 'Great Britain Illustrated' (*Modern Athens, Bath and Bristol* and *Wales Illustrated*), some on all three series together. Among the less prolific participants were three names prominent in landscape illustration, particularly after Turner—James B. Allen, Thomas Higham and William Radclyffe—and also a member of the talented Havell family. Those bringing up the rear were no doubt mature apprentices, permitted a credit or two by their masters.

The publisher's address printed on the wrappers of some of the issues of *Metropolitan Improvements* gives as its objective 'to depict with justice those truly astonishing and splendid undertakings, which have been for some time past, and still continue in rapid progress throughout the British Metropolis and its Environs; and which must render it, like Athens of old, the admiration of surrounding nations to future ages'. There then follows a list of architects and builders who have 'subscribed to, patronised and bestowed liberal and cheering encomiums on this Work', including Soane, Nash, Smirke, Wyatville, Wilkins and the Inwoods of the 'establishment' and 'high-flyers' among the younger fraternity such as Decimus Burton, G.S. Repton, Basevi and Poynter. Indeed the first half of the volume consists of Elmes's guide to the shining new communal, private and commercial palaces of Regent's Park and Regent's Street, a lavishly illustrated survey of the work of that master who in 1810 'found us all brick' and had, by this time, 'left us all plaster'. The rest consists of views of and comments on all important new buildings, re-fashionings and public works by recent and contemporary architects and engineers. It is as Sir John Summerson remarks (in *Georgian London*):

a useful and nearly complete, guide to the new buildings of George IV's London; for it interprets its title broadly, 'improvements' meaning anything from the formation of Regent Street by John Nash to the erection of the School for the Indigent Blind by a Mr. Tappen. Behind the book is the apprehension that London, within a matter of 15 or 20 years, had taken on a new character.

The illustrations themselves were innovatory since, to display as much as possible of the Nash façades, Shepherd devised a new type of perspective street-scape which was to culminate in the endless panoramic elevations of Tallis's utilitarian *London Street Views* (see 'Street Views' in the introductory History).

With the quarto edition was issued an 'Alphabetical List of the Engravings, with a reference to the description of the subjects'. As two views, whose descriptions did not necessarily fall on the same text page, were engraved on each plate the binder was confronted with a dilemma: was he to place a plate depicting, for instance, All Souls, Langham Place (described on p 97) and St Pancras Church (described on p 166) opposite the first reference or the second? Some chose to bind the plate after the first reference, some after the second, and others abandoned any sort of orderly arrangement and bound them at random. The publisher did nothing to establish a standard collation when, on an 1830 wrapper, he recommended an impossible procedure:

Directions for Binding &c. It is recommended not to blend the letterpress and Engravings but to keep each separate, placing the former at the commencement, and the latter at the end of the volume, with tissue paper between each plate; and instead of binding, merely to put the volume in Boards or Cloth, leaving it uncut, to admit of additions.... For facility of reference, the binder is requested to let the Engravings follow in the same order as per the foregoing Alphabetical List....

Consequently in many copies plates are found grouped together at the end of the text, in no discernible order.

This difficulty did not arise in the octavo edition since the plates had been guillotined, along a line engraved for the purpose, into two separate views and each was bound facing its description, as instructed in the alphabetical list. The stereotyped octavo included no such list and the 40 or so plates illustrating it are variable both as to subject and position.

For lack of any fixed order the plates are listed below as they first appeared in their Numbers, which at least approximates to a chronological order of their issue, and reference is made to the pages opposite which the binder is most likely to have placed them in the quarto edition and the pages opposite which he was instructed to place them in the original octavo.

All views but one have the credit bl 'Drawn by Thos. Shepherd', which is therefore not reproduced, and the engraver's credit 'Engraved by ...' or, '... sculp.', which is. Captions in voided capitals under each view are sometimes followed by a dedication, which is not reproduced. Nearly all the views have one of two publication-lines, variable only as to date:

(a) 'Published (date) by Jones & Co. 3, Acton Place, Kingsland Road, London.'
(b) 'Published (date) by Jones & Co. Temple of the Muses, Finsbury Square, London.'

Only the dimensions of the actual work (which is surrounded by a narrow ruled frame) are given. The plate-marks have been cropped in all copies seen. In general plates are unnumbered, though some copies have plates between 1 and 12 tentatively numbered bl.

The Museum of London accession numbers of 25 of Shepherd's pencil and sepia wash drawings, some pencilled with the name of the engraver to whom they were sent, are quoted with the abbreviation

ML. Unless otherwise stated they are the exact size of the engravings. Items from the Greater London Council collection are cited as GLC.

NO 1 (PART I)

0 (engr title) Metropolitan Improvements;/or/London/in the/Nineteenth Century:/being a/Series of Views,/of the new and most interesting objects,/in the/British Metropolis and its Vicinity:/from Original Drawings by/Mr. Thos H. Shepherd./With/historical, topographical & critical illustrations,/by/James Elmes, M.R.I.A./ (vignette) Sussex Place, Regent's Park. Drawn by Thos H. Shepherd. Engraved by W. Wallis. Published May 5, 1827 by Jones & Co, 3 Acton Place, Kingsland Road. 75 × 110/220 × 145mm. One of the Guildhall Library copies of this book, which lacks a printed title-page, has this engraved title without the line on authorship. There is thus no mention of Elmes.

00 (alternative engr title) Metropolitan Improvements;/or/London/in the/Nineteenth Century:/being a/Series of Views,/of the new and most interesting objects,/in the/British Metropolis and its Vicinity:/from Original Drawings by/Mr. Thos H. Shepherd./With/historical, topographical & critical illustrations,/by/James Elmes, M.R.I.A./Author of the life of Sir Christopher Wren,/Lectures on Architecture &c. (vignette, 90 × 145mm) The King's Palace Pimlico. Drawn by Thos. H. Shepherd. Engraved by J. Allen. London/Published April 11, 1829 by Jones & Co., Temple of the Muses/Finsbury Square. Pencil drawing (84 × 158mm), dated 3 July 1829, in Westminster Public Library.

1 London. Wm. Wallis. (a) March 31, 1827. 85 × 150mm. Quarto ed p 1 or 128; octavo ed p 1. Downstream from Shot Tower.

2 Bank of England. Wm. Tombleson. (a) March 31, 1827. 87 × 153mm. Quarto ed p 1 or 128, octavo ed p 181. (*Bank of England* 82)

3 The Coliseum, Regent's Park. H. Wallis (a) April 21, 1827. 87 × 145mm. Quarto ed p 68 or 35; octavo ed p 68. Built by Decimus Burton for Thomas Hornor, 1823–7.

4 York Gate, Regent's Park & Mary-le-Bone Church. H. Wallis (a) April 21, 1827. 85 × 145mm. Quarto ed p 68 or 35, octavo ed p 35. York Gate built by Nash, 1822, the Church by Thomas Hardwick, 1813–17. Wash drawing (90 × 145mm), dated 1826, in the Ashbridge Collection, Westminster Public Library.

(title-page; pp iii–iv, dedication)

NO 2

5 East Gate, Regent's Park. T. Barber. (a) March 31, 1827. 87 × 148mm. Quarto ed p 23 or 46, octavo ed p 21. Built by Nash, 1822. *ML* A 23060/3, dated 1827.

6 Clarence Terrace, Regent's Park. T. Barber. (a) March 31, 1827. 87 × 150mm. Quarto ed p 23 or 46, octavo ed p 46. Built by Decimus Barton, c 1822. Sepia

wash drawing (86 × 149mm), dated 1826, in West-minster Public Library (St Marylebone).

7 All Soul's Church, Langham Place. Jas. Tingle. (a) March 31, 1827. 150 × 93mm. Quarto ed p 97 or 166, octavo ed p 97. Built by Nash, 1824.

8 St Pancras Church, West Front. Jas. Tingle. (a) May 5, 1827. 150 × 90mm. Quarto ed p 97 or 166, octavo ed p 252. Built by W. and H. Inwood, 1819–22. *ML* A 23070/1.

(pp v–vi, dedication continued; subjects of views in Nos 1–2 (2pp, discarded by binders))

NO 3

9 Hanover Terrace, Regent's Park. W. Wallis. (a) May 5, 1827. 85 × 150mm. Quarto ed p 48 or 30, octavo ed p 48. Built by Nash, 1822–3. *ML* A 23060/1, dated '1826'.

10 Villa in the Regent's Park./The residence of G.B. Greenhough. W. Wallis. (a) May 5, 1827. 85 × 150mm. Quarto ed p 48 or 30, octavo ed p 30. Grove House, built by Decimus Burton, 1822. *ML* A 23068/2.

11 Regent's Quadrant. Thos. Dale. (a) June 16, 1827. 85 × 145mm. Quarto ed p 114 or 58, octavo ed p 139. Built by Nash, 1820–2. *ML* A 23036, a watercolour (130 × 190mm) from the same viewpoint but with different staffage.

12 Macclesfield Bridge, Regent's Park. R. Acon. (a) June 16, 1827. 88 × 145mm. Quarto ed p 114 or 58, octavo ed p 57. Built by James Morgan, 1815–16. *ML* A 23068/1; also a water-colour (243 × 358mm).

(subjects of views in Nos 3–4, with some forthcoming plates, including a projected No 5 (4pp, discarded by binders))

NO 4

13 Southwark Bridge, from Bankside. W. Wallis. (a) July 28, 1827. 87 × 148mm. Quarto ed p 127, octavo ed p 165.

14 Waterloo Bridge. W. Wallis. (a) July 28, 1827. 87 × 148mm. Quarto ed p 127, octavo ed p 158.

15 Statue of Achilles./In Hyde Park. S. Freeman. (a) July 7, 1827. 120 × 105mm. Vignette. Quarto ed p 133, octavo ed p 215.

16 Entrance to the Kings Palace./Hyde Park Corner. J. Cleghorn. (a) July 7, 1827. 95 × 95mm. Vignette. Quarto ed p 133, octavo ed p 217. Designed by Decimus Burton and erected on Constitution Hill, 1827–8.

(pp 1–4)

NO 5

17 Hanover Lodge, Regent's Park. W. Tombleson. (a) Aug. 10, 1827. 90 × 148mm. Quarto ed p 50 or 46, octavo ed p 50. Built by Decimus Burton.

18 Cornwall Terrace, Regent's Park. W. Deeble. (a) Aug. 10, 1827. 85 × 148mm. Quarto ed p 50 or 46, octavo ed p 46. Built by Decimus Burton, c 1821. *ML* A 23068/4.

19 College of the Church Missionary Society, Islington. T. Dale. (a) July 28, 1827. 85 × 148mm. Quarto ed p 145, octavo ed p 236.

20 Highbury College, South West Front. T. Dale. (a) July 28, 1827. 85 × 105mm. Quarto ed p 145, octavo ed p 236. Built by John Davies (fl 1819–65).

(pp 5–8)

NO 6 (PART II)

21 St. Philip's Chapel, Regent Street. Jas. Tingle. (a) Sept.8, 1827. 83 × 145mm. Quarto ed p 167 or 100, octavo ed p 145. Built by G.S. Repton, 1819–20; demolished 1904. Pencil sketch (93 × 153mm), dated 1825, in Westminster Public Library.

22 St George's Chapel, Regent Street. Jas. Tingle. (a) Sept. 8, 1827. 85 × 145mm. Quarto ed p 167 or 100, octavo ed p 99. Built by C.R. Cockerell, 1823.

23 The Limehouse Dock, Regent's Canal. F.J. Havell. (a) Aug. 25, 1827. 87 × 145mm. Quarto ed p 157, octavo ed p 175. Pencil and water-colour drawing (247 × 371mm) in Museum of London; Sepia wash drawing (94 × 147mm) in BM (*Crace* 8.96).

24 The Double Lock, & East Entrance/to the Islington Tunnel, Regent's Canal. F.J. Havell. (a) Aug. 25, 1827. 87 × 145mm. Quarto ed p 157, octavo ed p 172. Pencil and water-colour drawing (242 × 360mm) in Museum of London; sepia wash drawing (88 × 146mm) in BM (*Crace* 30.42).

(pp 9–12)

NO 7

25 The Holme, Regent's Park./The residence of James Burton. J. Henshall. (a) Sept. 15, 1827. 87 × 150mm. Quarto ed p 27 or 79, octavo ed p 27. Built by Decimus Burton, c 1818. Pen and water-colour drawing (95 × 148mm) in Westminster Public Library (St Marylebone).

26 Ulster Terrace, Regent's Park. J. Henshall. (a) Sept. 15, 1827. 85 × 145mm. Quarto ed p 27 or 79, octavo ed p 79. Built by Nash, 1823–6. Sepia wash drawing (87 × 144mm) in Westminster Public Library (St Marylebone).

27 Chapel of Ease, West Hackney. W. Bond. (a) Sept. 22, 1827. 140 × 88mm. Quarto ed p 164 or 163, octavo ed p 250. 'Printed by W. Read'.

28 St John's, Hoxton. W. Bond. (a) Sept. 22, 1827. 143 × 88mm. Quarto ed p 164 or 163, octavo ed p 250. 'Printed by W. Read'. Built by Francis Edwards, 1825–6.

(pp 13–16)

NO 8

29 Part of the East Side of Regent Street. Wm. Wallis. (a)

Sept. 10, 1827. 85 × 148mm. Quarto ed p 114 or 125, octavo ed p 98. Centre with colonnade and 'acroteria', vista with All Souls. Sepia wash drawing (88 × 144mm) in Westminster Public Library.

30 United Service Military Club House, Haymarket Theatre/& Part of the Opera colonade, from Regent Street. Wm. Wallis. (a) Sep. 10, 1827. 88 × 145mm. Quarto ed p 98, 114 or 125, octavo ed p 151. Built by Nash, 1826–8.

31 Villa in Regent's Park,/the residence of John Maberly. T. Barber. (a) May 5, 1827. 85 × 148mm. Quarto ed p 24 or 44, octavo ed p 24.

32 York Terrace, Regent's Park. T. Barber. (a) July 21, 1827. 88 × 150mm. Quarto ed p 24 or 44, octavo ed p 44. Built by Nash, 1822.

(pp 17–20)

NO 9

33 St. Paul's School. Wm. Deeble. (a) Sept. 29, 1827. 87 × 145mm. Quarto ed p 126, octavo ed p 194. Built by George Smith, 1823–4; demolished 1884.

34 The London Institution, Finsbury Circus. Wm. Deeble. (a) Sep. 29, 1827. 87 × 145mm. Quarto ed p 126, octavo ed p 175. Built by William Brooks, 1815–19; demolished 1936.

35 Chapel of Ease,/to Marylebone, Stafford St. New Road. Thos. Dale. (a) Octr. 13, 1827. 140 × 88mm. Quarto ed p 167 or 165, octavo ed p 249. Later, Christ Church, Cosway Street, built by Philip Hardwick, 1825.

36 St. Peter's Church,/Eaton Square, Pimlico. Thos. Dale. (a) Octr. 13, 1827. 140 × 90mm. Quarto ed p 167 or 165, octavo ed p 251. Built by Henry Hakewill, 1824–7.

(pp 21–4)

NO 10

37 The New Bridge, over the Serpentine, Hyde Park. M.S. Barenger. (a) Dec. 1, 1827. 85 × 145mm. Quarto ed p 136 or 137, octavo ed p 213. Built by John Rennie.

38 Richmond Terrace, Whitehall. M.S. Barenger. (a) Dec. 1, 1827. 85 × 148mm. Quarto ed p 136 or 137, octavo ed p 208. Built by Thomas Chawner, 1822–5.

39 New Church, Somers Town. W. Deeble. (a) Dec. 1, 1827. 140 × 90mm. Quarto ed p 163 or 168, octavo ed p 253. Later, St Mary the Virgin, Eversholt Street, built by W. and H. Inwood, 1824–7.

40 New Church, Haggerstone. W. Deeble. (a) Dec. 1, 1827. 140 × 88mm. Quarto ed p 163 or 168, octavo ed p 254. Built by Nash, 1826–7.

(pp 25–8)

NO 11 (PART III)

41 The Royal Hospital of St Katherine, Regent's Park. W. Tombleson. (a) Dec. 8, 1827. 88 × 150mm. Quarto ed p 59 or 65, octavo ed p 59. Chapel built by Ambrose Poynter, 1826. *ML* A 23068/3.

42 Residence of Genl. Sir Herbert Taylor, Bart. Regent's Park/Master of St. Katherine's. W. Tombleson. (a) Dec. 8, 1827. 88 × 147mm. Quarto ed p 59 or 65, octavo ed p 65. Built by Ambrose Poynter, c 1828. *ML* A 23060/2, dated 1827.

43 (along upper edge) Plan of the Regent's Park. J. Cleghorn. (a) July 28, 1827. 200 × 230mm. Quarto ed p 19, octavo ed p 19. Refs l., A–Z.

(pp 29–32)

NO 12

44 Villa in the Regent's Park,/the residence of the Marquis of Hertford. Jas. Tingle. (a) Dec. 15, 1827. 85 × 148mm. Quarto ed p 24 or 23, octavo ed p 51. 'St Dunstan's Lodge', built by Decimus Burton, 1825.

45 Cumberland Terrace, Regent's Park. Jas. Tingle. (a) Dec. 15, 1827. 85 × 147mm. Quarto ed p 24 or 23, octavo ed p 311. Built by Nash, 1826.

46 The Catholic Church, Finsbury. Thos. Barber. (a) Dec. 15, 1827. 93 × 145mm. Quarto ed p 170 or 163, octavo ed p 179. Built by John Newman, 1817–20. *ML* A 23067/4.

47 Finsbury Chapel. Thos. Barber. (a) Dec. 15, 1827. 88 × 143mm. Quarto ed p 170 or 163, octavo ed p 177. Built by William Brooks for a congregation of dissenters from the Albion Chapel (see item 121). *ML* A 23067/2, dated 1828.

(pp 33–6)

NO 13

48 Buildings on the East Side of Regent Street. R. Acon. (a) Jan. 5, 1828. 85 × 148mm. Quarto ed p 114 or 68, octavo ed p 114.

49 Cambridge Terrace and the Coliseum Regent's Park. R. Acon. (a) Jan. 5, 1828. 88 × 148mm. Quarto ed p 114 or 68, octavo ed p 68. Cambridge Terrace built by Nash, 1824, the Colosseum by Decimus Burton, 1823–7.

50 Haberdasher's Alms Houses, Hoxton. John Ralph. (a) Jan. 12, 1828. 85 × 148mm. Quarto ed p 143 or 144, octavo ed p 277. Rebuilt by D.R. Roper, 1825–6.

51 Theatre Royal, Covent Garden. John Ralph. (a) Jan. 12, 1828. 90 × 150mm. Quarto ed p 143 or 144, octavo ed p 196. Built by Robert Smirke, 1809–10. *ML* A 23062/2.

(pp 37–40)

NO 14

52 York House, St James's Park. Robt. Wallis. (a) Feb. 9, 1828. 87 × 148mm. Quarto ed p 122 or 99, octavo ed p 263. Built by Benjamin and Philip Wyatt, 1825, now called Lancaster House. *ML* A 23057, dated 1826.

53 Regent Street from the Circus Piccadilly./Previous to taking down Carlton Palace. Robt. Wallis. (a) Feb. 9,

1828. 88 × 148mm. Quarto ed p 122 or 99, octavo ed p 152. ie 'Lower' Regent Street.

54 St. Luke's Church, Chelsea. S. Lacey. (a) Jan. 31, 1828. 145 × 92mm. Quarto ed p 164 or 165, octavo ed p246. Built by James Savage, 1820–4. (*Longford* 466)

55 St Mark the Evangelist, Pentonville. S. Lacey. (a) Jan. 31, 1828. 145 × 92mm. Quarto ed p 164 or 165, octavo ed p 255. Built by W.C. Milne, 1826–8.

(pp 41–4)

NO 15

56 Lord Grosvenor's Gallery, Park Lane. W. Deeble. (a) Feb. 9, 1828. 88 × 143mm. Quarto ed p 145 or 146, octavo ed p 263. W. wing of his town house 'now in the course of erection from the designs of Mr. Cundy'. *ML* A 23062/1.

57 The Royal College of Surgeons, Lincolns Inn Fields. W. Deeble. (a) Feb. 9, 1828. 90 × 145mm. Quarto ed p 145 or 146, octavo ed p 264. Built by George Dance junior and James Lewis, 1806–13.

58 City Basin, Regent's Canal. F.J. Havell. (a) Jany. 26, 1828. 85 × 148mm. Quarto ed p 157, octavo ed p 175. Pencil and water-colour drawing (241 × 365mm) in Museum of London; sepia wash drawing (90 × 148mm) in BM (*Crace* 30.46).

59 Entrance to the Regent's Canal, Limehouse. F.J. Havell. (a) Jan. 26, 1828. Quarto ed p 157, octavo ed p 172. Pencil and water-colour drawing (246 × 366mm) in Museum of London.

(pp 45–8)

NO 16 (PART IV)

60 Waterloo Place, & Part of Regent Street. W. Tombleson. (a) March 1, 1828. 88 × 148mm. Quarto ed p 121 or 99, octavo ed p 275. Built by Nash, 1815.

61 Regent Street, from the Quadrant. W. Tombleson. (a) March 1, 1828. 88 × 148mm. Quarto ed p 121 or 99, octavo ed p 275.

62 The Quadrant, and Part of Regent Street. Wm. Wallis. (a) Feby. 16, 1828. 85 × 145mm. Quarto ed p 114 or 102, octavo ed p 139. Built by Nash, 1819.

63 Harmonic Institution, Regent Street. Wm. Wallis. (a) Feby. 16, 1828. 85 × 145mm. Quarto ed p 114 or 102, octavo ed p 102. Built by Nash, 1819.

(pp 49–52)

NO 17

64 The New Treasury, Whitehall. M. Fox. (a) Feby. 23, 1828. 88 × 148mm. Quarto ed p 148, octavo ed p 271. Built by John Soane, 1824–7. Sepia wash drawing (88 × 146mm) in GLC.

65 Italian Opera House, Haymarket./From Pall Mall East. M. Fox. (a) Feby. 23, 1828. 88 × 148mm. Quarto ed p 148, octavo ed p 274. Built by M. Novosielski, reconstructed by Nash and G. Repton, 1816–18.

66 Whittington's Alms Houses, Highgate. T. Dale. (a)

March 31, 1827 (sic). 90 × 148mm. Quarto ed p 141 or 142, octavo ed p 277. Built by George Smith, 1822. *ML* A 23054, dated 1826; pencil drawing (129 × 233mm) in GLC.

67 Brewer's Alms Houses, Mile End. Robt. Tingle. (a) Jany. 1, 1828. 88 × 140mm. Quarto ed p 141 or 142, octavo ed p 278. Sepia wash drawing (88 × 142mm) in GLC.

(pp 53–6)

NO 18

68 An Island on the Lake & Part of Cornwall & Clarence Terrace/Regent's Park. W. Tombleson. (a) April 12, 1828. 90 × 155mm. Quarto ed p 19, octavo ed p 275. Both terraces probably built by Decimus Burton, 1821–2.

69 The Coliseum and Part of the Lake Regent's Park. W. Tombleson. (a) April 12, 1828. 90 × 155mm. Quarto ed p 19, octavo ed p 19. The Colosseum built by Decimus Burton, 1823–7.

70 Surry Theatre, Blackfriars Road. Thos. Dale. (a) Feby. 16, 1828. 93 × 145mm. Quarto ed p 134 or 135, octavo ed p 206. Built by Rudolph Cabanel junior. 1805–6; burned down 1865.

71 Theatre Royal, Drury Lane. Thos. Dale. (a) Feby. 16, 1828. 88 × 145mm. Quarto ed p 134 or 135, octavo ed p 201. Built by Benjamin Wyatt, 1811–12.

(pp 57–60)

NO 19

72 The New College of Physicians, Pall Mall East. Thos. Barber. (a) April 26 1828. 90 × 147mm. Quarto ed p 124, octavo ed p 232. Built by Robert Smirke, 1824–5. *ML* A 23059/1, dated 1827.

73 Improvements, Charing Cross. Thos. Barber. (a) April 26 1828. 85 × 148mm. Quarto ed p 124, octavo ed p 315. Sepia wash drawing (94 × 161mm) in Westminster Public Library.

74 The New Church, Regent Square, Sidmouth Street. C. Westwood. (a) April 12, 1828. 140 × 88mm. Quarto ed p 162 or 168, octavo ed p 256. Built by W. and H. Inwood, 1824–6, dedicated to St Peter.

75 The New Church, Camden Town. T. Dale. (a) April 12, 1828. 142 × 90mm. Quarto ed p 162 or 168, octavo ed p 256. Built by W. and H. Inwood, 1822–4, dedicated to All Saints.

(pp 61–4)

NO 20

76 Furnivals Inn, Holborn. J. Henshall. (a) May 17, 1828. 92 × 145mm. Quarto ed p 138 or 139, octavo ed p 209.

77 New Government Mews, Princes' Street, Story's Gate,/Westminster. J. Henshall. (a) May 17, 1828. 95 × 145mm. Quarto ed p 138 or 139, octavo ed p 212. Built by Decimus Burton, 1826. Pen and wash drawing

(90 × 145mm), dated May 1828, in Westminster Public Library.

78 Junction of the Regent's Canal, at Paddington. S. Lacey. (a) May 24, 1828. 90 × 150mm. Quarto ed p 157 or 20, octavo ed p 172. Pencil and water-colour drawing (245 × 374mm) in Museum of London.

79 View in the Regent's Park,/East Gate, a Villa and St. Katherine's Hospital. S. Lacey. (a) May 24, 1828. 90 × 148mm. Quarto ed p 157 or 20, octavo ed p 21. *ML* A 23068/3.

(pp 65–8)

NO 21 (PART V)

80 Asylum for Female Orphans, Westminster. A. McClatchy. (a) June 7, 1828. 85 × 148mm. Quarto ed p 170 or 157, octavo ed p 279.

81 Egyptian Hall, Piccadilly. A. McClatchy. (a) June 7, 1828. 95 × 145mm. Quarto ed p 170 or 157, octavo ed p 301. Built by P.F. Robinson, 1811–12; demolished 1904.

82 Trinity Church, New Road. W. Bond. (a) May 10, 1828. 145 × 90mm. Quarto ed p 81 or 166, octavo ed p 81. Built by John Soane, 1824–8. Sepia wash drawing (145 × 95mm) in the Ashbridge Collection, Westminster Public Library.

83 St Mary's Church, Wyndham Place, & District Rectory to St. Mary-le-Bone. Archer. (a) May 10, 1828. 145 × 90mm. Quarto ed p 81 or 166, octavo ed p 257. Built by Robert Smirke, 1823–4.

(pp 69–72)

NO 22

84 Salters-Hall. W. Wallis (a) Aug. 2, 1828. 90 × 148mm. Quarto ed p 152, octavo ed p 270. Built by Henry Carr, 1823–7. *ML* A 23069/1, dated 7 February 1827; Pencil drawing (112 × 174mm) in Guildhall Library.

85 The Guild-Hall. Robt. Acon. (a) Aug. 2, 1828. 100 × 147mm. Quarto ed p 152, octavo ed p 270. Pencil drawing (100 × 145mm) in Guildhall Library.

86 South Villa, Regent's Park. J. Tingle. (a) April 26 1828. 85 × 147mm. Quarto ed p 24 or 67, octavo ed p 276.

87 Chester Terrace, Regent's Park. H. Melville. (a) April 26, 1828. 85 × 147mm. Quarto ed p 24 or 67, octavo ed p 67. Built by Nash, 1825

(pp 73–6)

NO 23

88 North & West Front of the Bank of England, from Lothbury. W. Wallis. (a) Aug 9, 1828. 85 × 153mm. Quarto ed p 128, octavo ed p 190. Soane's 'Tivoli Corner'. (*Bank of England* 65)

89 East Front of the Bank of England, and New Tower of/Royal Exchange, from St. Bartholomew Lane. W.

Wallis. (a) Aug. 9, 1828. 90 × 150mm. Quarto ed p 128, octavo ed p 189. (*Bank of England* 75)

90 St. Mary le-Bone Chapel, St John's Wood Road. W. Watkins. (a) June 28, 1828. 90 × 143mm. Quarto ed p 165 or 24, octavo ed p 259. St John's Chapel, built by Thomas Hardwick, 1814.

91 Doric Villa, Regent's Park. W. Watkins. (a) June 28, 1828. 90 × 143mm. Quarto ed p 165 or 24, octavo ed p 311. Built by Nash.

(pp 77–80)

NO 24

92 Suspension Bridge, over the Thames at Hammersmith. T. Higham. (a) Aug. 16, 1826. 90 × 150mm. Quarto ed p 147, octavo ed p 268. Erected from designs by W. Tierney Clark, 1824–7.

93 New London Bridge, with the Lord Mayor's Procession passing under/the unfinished arches, Novr. 9, 1827. T. Higham. (a) Aug. 16, 1828. 90 × 145mm. Quarto ed p 147, octavo ed p 267. *ML* A 16160.

94 Villa in the Regent's Park. W. Radclyffe. (a) June 14, 1828. 90 × 140mm. Quarto ed p 24 or 80, octavo ed p 24. 'St John's Lodge', an Ionic temple built for C.A. Tulk, MP by John Raffield, 1818–19. Original drawing in Guildhall Library.

95 St. Andrews Place, Regent's Park. W. Radclyffe. (a) June 14, 1828. 90 × 147mm. Quarto ed p 24 or 80, octavo ed p 80. Built by Nash, 1823–6.

(pp 81–4)

NO 25

96 The Guildhall, Westminster. M. Barrenger. (a) Aug. 9, 1828. 87 × 145mm. Quarto ed p 155, octavo ed p 298. Built by S.P. Cockerell, 1805. Pencil sketch (90 × 143mm), dated 1828, in Westminster Public Library

97 New Buildings Pall-Mall East, and University Club House. M. Barrenger. (a) Aug. 9, 1828. 87 × 147mm. Quarto ed p 155, octavo ed p 299. The club house built by William Wilkins and J.P. Gandy Deering, 1822–6; demolished 1902.

98 New Church, Waterloo Road. J. Cleghorn. (a) July 5, 1828. 143 × 90mm. Quarto ed p 169 or 162, octavo ed p 257. St. John's, built by Francis Bedford, 1823–5.

99 St. Barnabas, King Square. J. Cleghorn. (a) July 5, 1828. 143 × 90mm. Quarto ed p 169 or 162, octavo ed p 259. Built by Thomas Hardwick, 1822–6

(pp 85–8)

NO 26 (PART VI)

100 The New Custom House, from Billingsgate. W. Tombleson. (a) Aug. 30, 1828. 92 × 147mm. Quarto ed p 132 or 158, octavo ed p 265. Built by David Laing, 1813–17 and Robert Smirke, 1825. Pencil sketch (90 × 142mm) in Guildhall Library.

101 The New Post Office, St. Martins le-Grand. W. Tombleson. (a) Aug 30, 1828. 87 × 147mm. Quarto ed

p 132 or 158, octavo ed p 269. Built by Robert Smirke, 1818–29. Pencil and sepia wash drawing (104 × 152mm) in Guildhall Library.

102 New Church, Stepney. W. Deeble. (a) June 21, 1828. 95 × 145mm. Quarto ed p 139 or 140, octavo ed p 260. St. Philip's Chapel, built by John Walters, 1819. *ML* A 23067/3.

103 The New Hall, Christ's Hospital. W. Deeble. (a) June 21, 1828. 95 × 147mm. Quarto ed p 139 or 140, octavo ed p 235. Built by John Shaw, 1825–9.

(pp 89–92)

NO 27

104 Grand Entrance to Hyde Park, Piccadilly. W. Wallis. (b) Sep. 29, 1828. 87 × 150mm. Quarto ed p 138 or 137, octavo ed p 219. Ionic screen by Decimus Burton, c 1825.

105 One of the New Lodges, Hyde Park. W. Wallis. (b) Sep. 29, 1828. 87 × 147mm. Quarto ed p 138 or 137, octavo ed p 219. Designed by Decimus Burton.

106 North West view of the/London Horse & Carriage Repository, Gray's Inn Road. W. Deeble. (b) Oct. 1, 1828. 90 × 150mm. Quarto ed p 142, octavo ed p 283.

107 South East view of the/London Horse & Carriage Repository, Gray's Inn Road. W. Deeble. (b) Oct. 1, 1828. 90 × 147mm. Quarto ed p 142, octavo ed p 283.

(pp 93–6)

NO 28

108 The London University. W. Wallis. (b) Nov 15, 1828. 85 × 155mm. Quarto ed p 125 or 170, octavo ed p 221. University College, built by William Wilkins and J.P. Gandy Deering, 1827–8.

109 Temple of the Muses, Finsbury Square. W. Wallis. (b) Nov. 15, 1828. 95 × 155mm. Quarto ed p 125 or 170, octavo ed p 282. On the façade is a banner advertising 'Metropolitan Improvements'. Square built by George Dance junior, 1777–8. Sepia wash drawing (96 × 154mm) in Guildhall Library.

110 Crockford's Club House, St James's Street. Wm. Tombleson. (b) Oct. 25, 1828. 87 × 147mm. Quarto ed p 140 or 141, octavo ed p 280. Built by Benjamin and Philip Wyatt, 1827.

111 Burlington Arcade, Piccadilly. Wm. Tombleson. (b) Oct. 25, 1828. 92 × 147mm. Quarto ed p 140 or 141, octavo ed p 281. Built by Samuel Ware, 1816–18.

(pp 97–100)

NO 29

112 The New Corn Exchange, Mark Lane. J. Henshall. (b) Nov. 1, 1828. 97 × 147mm. Quarto ed p 146 or 132, octavo ed p 271. Built by George Smith with A.B. Clayton, 1827–8. *ML* A 23069/3.

113 The Custom House, from Thames Street. J. Henshall. (b) Nov. 1, 1828. 95 × 145mm. Quarto ed p 146 or 132, octavo ed p 266. For river view see item 100.

Sepia wash drawing (94 × 147mm) in Guildhall Library.

114 St Paul's Church, Ball's Pond. J.F. Havell. (a) Aug. 16, 1828. 90 × 143mm. Quarto ed p 168 or 169, octavo ed p 260. Built by Charles Barry, 1827–8.

115 The Unitarian Chapel, Finsbury. J.F. Havell. (a) Aug. 16, 1828. 87 × 145mm. Quarto ed p 168 or 169, octavo ed p 260.

(pp 101–4)

NO 30

116 North East Side of Belgrave Square, Pimlico. S. Lacy. (b) Nov. 15, 1828. 87 × 145mm. Quarto ed p 154 or 153, octavo ed p 295. Built by Thomas Cubitt.

117 Belgrave Chapel, and West side of Belgrave Square. S. Lacy. (b) Nov. 15, 1828. 87 × 145mm. Quarto ed p 154 or 153, octavo ed p 294. Built by Robert Smirke, c 1825.

118 The Temple Church, as restored. J. Carter. (a) Aug. 16, 1828. 93 × 147mm. Quarto ed p 131 or 132, octavo ed p 261. Restoration by Robert Smirke, 1827–8.

119 The Russell Institution, Great Coram Street. J. Carter. (a) Aug. 16, 1828. 84 × 147mm. Quarto ed p 131 or 132, octavo ed p 236. Built by James Burton, c 1800.

(pp 105–8)

NO 31 (PART VII)

120 The New Caledonian Asylum. T. Barber. (b) Nov. 22, 1828. 87 × 143mm. Quarto ed p 156 or 170, octavo ed p 300. In Copenhagen Fields, built by George Tappen, 1827–8. *ML* A 23059/3.

121 Albion Chapel, Moorgate. T. Barber. (b) Nov. 22, 1828. 90 × 147mm. Quarto ed p 156 or 170, octavo ed p 261. Built by William Jay, before 1817. Pencil drawing (89 × 145mm) in Guildhall Library.

122 Part of West Side of Regent Street. W. Watkins. (b) Dec. 21, 1828. 87 × 145mm. Quarto ed p 97, octavo ed p 135. Giant Corinthian pilasters and central pediment.

123 Part of West Side of Regent Street./Continued. W. Watkins. (b) Dec. 21, 1828. 87 × 145mm. Quarto ed p 97, octavo ed p 131. Ionic tetrastyle centre.

(pp 109–12)

NO 32

124 The New Opening to St. Martin's Church./From Pall Mall East. H.W. Bond. 90 × 147mm. No publication-line. Quarto ed p 123, octavo ed p 315. Pencil drawing (90 × 147mm) in Westminster Public Library.

125 Suffolk Street, Pall Mall East. H.W. Bond. (b) Jan. 10, 1829. 90 × 147mm. Quarto ed p 123, octavo ed p 297. Built 1821–4.

126 West Side of Langham Place. S. Owen. (b) Sept. 29, 1828. 87 × 147mm. Quarto ed p 94 or 98, octavo ed p 97.

127 Part of East Side of Regent Street. W. Wallis. (b) Sept. 29, 1828. 87 × 147mm. Quarto ed p 94 or 98, octavo ed p 114. Corinthian façade with projecting centre and pavilions; 'No.123' to the r. Sepia wash drawing (90 × 145mm) in Westminster Public Library.

(pp 113–16)

NO 33

128 Royal Exchange, Cornhill. J. Tingle. (b) Jan. 17, 1829. 143 × 93mm. Quarto ed p 149 or 158, octavo ed p 303. New façade and tower built by George Smith, 1820–6; burned down 1838.

129 St. Bride's Avenue, Fleet Street. J. Tingle. (b) Jan. 17, 1829. 143 × 90mm. Quarto ed p 149 or 158, octavo ed p 237. Built by J.B. Papworth, 1823–30.

130 Park Village East, Regent's Park. W. Radcliff. 90 × 153mm. No publication-line. Quarto ed p 20, octavo ed p 297. Canal tow-path and house backs.

131 Park Village East, Regent's Park. W. Radcliff. (b) Jan. 17, 1829. 90 × 155mm. Quarto ed p 20, octavo ed p 297. Street fronts. Built by Nash, 1824–8.

(pp 117–20)

NO 34

132 The Parliament House, from Old Palace Yard./ Westminster. W. Deeble. 90 × 153mm. No publication-line. Quarto ed p 153, octavo ed p 292.

133 The King's Entrance to the House of Lords./from Poets Corner. W. Deeble. (b) Feb. 21, 1829. 93 × 150mm. Quarto ed p 153, octavo ed p 292. Built by John Soane, 1822–4; burned down 1834.

134 Royal York Baths, Regent's Park. W.R. Smith. (a) April 5, 1828. 87 × 145mm. Quarto ed p 44 or 48, octavo ed p 310.

135 Sussex Place, Regent's Park. W.R. Smith. (a) April 5, 1828. 87 × 147mm. Quarto ed p 44 or 48, octavo ed p 48. Built by Nash, c 1822.

(pp 121–4)

NO 35

136 London Ophthalmic Infirmary &c. Finsbury. R. Acon. 90 × 147mm. No publication-line. Quarto ed p 149, octavo ed p 291. View includes Catholic Church (cf with item 46).

137 Asylum for the Indigent Blind, Westminster Road. R. Acon. (b) March 28, 1829. 93 × 150mm. Quarto ed p 149, octavo ed p 291. Built by George Tappen, 1812–14.

138 Part of East Side, Regent Street. M. Barrenger. 90 × 147mm. No publication-line. Quarto ed p 98, octavo ed p 116. The Quadrant curving away to r. *ML* 62.145/3, dated 1828.

139 Part of West Side of Regent Street. M. Barrenger. (b) Feb. 28, 1829. 87 × 143mm. Quarto ed p 98, octavo ed p 135. Second shop from corner 'No.129'. *ML*

62.145/4 (92 × 150mm), dated 1828.

(pp 125–8)

NO 36 (PART VIII)

140 West Gate, Regent's Park. W. Wallis. 90 × 143mm. No publication-line. Quarto ed p 19 or 23, octavo ed p 310. Built by Nash, 1822.

141 The Centre of Cumberland Terrace, Regent's Park. W. Wallis. (b) April 18, 1829. 90 × 143mm. Quarto ed p 19 or 23, octavo ed p 313. Built by Nash, 1826.

142 Trinity Church, Cloudesley Square. J.F. Havel. 93 × 147mm. No publication-line. Quarto ed p 169 or 151, octavo ed p 261. Built by Charles Barry, 1827–8.

145 New National Scotch Church, Sidmouth St. Grays Inn Road. W. Watkins. (b) April 25, 1829. 117 × 157mm. Quarto ed p 169 or 151, octavo ed p 289. Built by William Tite, 1824–7. *ML* A 16160/2, dated 1829.

(pp 129–32)

NO 37

144 East Side of Park Crescent. J. Redaway. 90 × 143mm. No publication-line. Quarto ed p 92 or 80, octavo ed p 92. Built by Nash, 1812; completed 1822.

145 East Side of Park Square, and Diorama,/Regent's Park. W. Watkins. (b) June 6, 1829. 87 × 142mm. Quarto ed p 92 or 80, octavo ed p 88. Diorama built by Jacob Smith, 1823.

146 Licensed Victuallers School, Kennington. H.W. Bond. (a) March 15, 1828. 87 × 147mm. Quarto ed p 157 or 170, octavo ed p 302.

147 London Orphan Asylum, Clapton. H.W. Bond. (a) March 15, 1828. 87 × 146mm. Quarto ed p 157 or 170, octavo ed p 301.

(pp 133–40)

NO 38

148 The New Shot Mill, near Waterloo Bridge. J. Hinchcliff. 92 × 147mm. No publication-line. Quarto ed p 127 or 159, octavo ed p 288. Built by D.R. Roper and A.B. Clayton, 1826.

149 Vauxhall Bridge, from Millbank. James B. Allen. Jones & Co London, July 25, 1829. 100 × 155mm. Quarto ed p 127 or 159, octavo ed p 284. Built by James Walker, civil engineer, 1813–16.

150 New Bethlem Hospital, St George's Fields. J. Tingle. 85 × 145mm. No publication-line. Quarto ed p 151 or 150, octavo ed p 288. Built by James Lewis, 1812–15.

151 Penitentiary, Millbank, Westminster. J. Tingle. (b) July 11, 1829. 95 × 150mm. Completed by Robert Smirke, 1816. Pencil sketch (105 × 183mm), dated 1829, in Westminster Public Library.

(pp 141–8)

NO 39

152 Albany Cottage, Regent's Park. W. Tombleson. 90 × 147mm. No publication-line. Quarto ed p 49 or 160,

379

octavo ed p 49. Built by C.R. Cockerell and Decimus Burton, 1821–3. *ML* A 23060/4, marked to 'Tombleson or Lacey'.

153 Apsley House, Hyde Park Corner. T. Barber. (b) Sept. 26, 1829. 95 × 147mm. Quarto ed p 49 or 160, octavo ed p 300. Built by Robert Adam, c 1775; enlarged and refaced by Benjamin and Philip Wyatt, 1828.

154 Gas Works, Near the Regent's Canal. A. McClatchie. (b) Dec. 14, 1828. 87 × 145mm. Quarto ed p 161, octavo ed p 305. Also issued without publication-line. Sepia wash drawing (90 × 148mm) in BM (*Crace* 31.31).

155 Buildings, Highfield, Camden Road. A. McClatchie. (b) Nov. 1, 1829 (or Dec. 14, 1828). 90 × 145mm. Quarto ed p 161, octavo ed p 114.

(pp 149–56)

NO 40

156 The N.W. Façade of the New Covent Garden Market. W. Watkins. 90 × 147mm. No publication-line. 90 × 147mm. Quarto ed p 160 or 159, octavo ed p 306. Built by Charles Fowler, 1828–30.

157 Auction Mart, St. Bartholomew's Lane. W. Watkins. (b) 1829. 93 × 145mm. Quarto ed p 160 or 159, octavo ed p 300.

158 St John's Church, Holloway. 100 × 150mm. No publication-line. Quarto ed p 169 or 162, octavo ed p 304. Built by Charles Barry, 1827–8. *ML* A 23067/1, dated 1829.

159 The New Library, and Parliament Chambers,/Temple. J. Hinchcliff. (b) Nov. 28, 1829. 97 × 148mm. Quarto ed p 169 or 162, octavo ed p 307. Built by Robert Smirke, 1824–8; destroyed 1941.

(pp 157–64)

NO 41

(pp 165–72; alphabetical list of engravings (2pp); directions to binder, label for spine, advertisement (1 leaf))

155 · BRAYLEY'S LONDINIANA [1828]

Edward Wedlake Brayley's first major topographical work on London was written in collaboration with his friend John Britton and published in 1810 as the 'London and Middlesex' section of *The Beauties of England and Wales* (no 104). Between the publication of this and *Londiniana* he contributed several commentaries to other illustrated London books, including Pugin's *Series of Views in Islington and Pentonville,* published by Ackermann in 1819, Daniel Havell's *Theatres of London* (no 148), published by Josiah Taylor in 1826, and John Preston Neale's views of Westminster Abbey (no 123), of which the second volume was published in 1823 by Hurst, Robinson.

Hurst, Robinson's interest in topographical illustration dated from 1818 when, as a result of a disagreement between the executors of Alderman Boydell, they acquired the stock in trade of that famous printseller and in 1825 they published an early and exquisite example of steel-engraved topography, Charles Heath's *Views of London* (no 147). *Londiniana* came out under the imprint of Thomas Hurst and Edward Chance of 55 St Paul's Churchyard and its appearance was announced prematurely in John Britton's *Original Picture of London* (24th ed, 1826; no 161): 'Early in Spring will be Published in 5 Volumes small 8vo Illustrated by 150 Engravings a new work entitled "Londiniana" '.

In the event only four volumes with 103 engravings appeared (at £2 10s the bound set) and Brayley dated his preface 20 November 1828 from the Russell Institution of which he had been Secretary and Librarian since 1825:

In the general design of this work, diversity of information, and accuracy in the details, have been the leading objects. No particular classification, or arrangement, has been observed, and none was intended. Subjects of antiquarian and historical research, are mingled with the lighter graces of poetry, and the severity of local description is interwoven with sketches of biography and manners, traits of character, and personal anecdote. Let it, however, be recollected that the main feature of this undertaking, is to illustrate the Topography of the Metropolis as it existed in former times; yet still continuing its history to the present day, whenever the place or object noticed appeared deserving of that regard.

Londiniana; or, Reminiscences of the British Metropolis: including Characteristic Sketches, Antiquarian, Topographical, Descriptive, and Literary. By Edward Wedlake Brayley, F.A.S., M.R.S.L. &c &c. (various epigraphs) In Four Volumes. Vol. I (II–IV). London: Hurst, Chance and Co. 1828 (or 1829).

Small octavo, 165 × 100mm.   1828 (1829)

COLLATION Vol. 1 (1828 or 1829). Half-title; title-page; pp v–viii, preface dated 20 November 1828; pp ix–xxii, analytical contents; pp xxiii–xxiv, list of plates; pp

1–304 (pp 65–120 bis), Londiniana. Vol. 2 (1829). Half-title; title-page; pp v–xx, analytical contents, list of plates; pp 1–312 (pp 17–56 bis), Londiniana continued. Vol. 3 (1828 or 1829). Half-title; title-page; pp v–xviii, analytical contents; pp xix–xx, list of plates; pp 1–344, Londiniana continued. Vol. 4 (1828 or 1829). Half-title; title-page; pp v–xviii, analytical contents; pp xix–xx, list of plates; pp 1–320, Londiniana continued; pp 321–54, index.

Of the illustrations the preface has this to say:

The engravings are of a mixed description ... as it was intended that the work should be rendered popular from its cheapness as well as from its character. But that inferiority refers principally to those prints which have been copied from Strype's Stow, and were selected to shew the state of our Metropolis buildings as they existed in the early part of the last century; and it will be found, on comparing them, that the general style of every copy is correspondent with that of the original. The subjects and plans introduced from more finished engravings, or taken from drawings, are executed in a superior manner.

The only engraver named as a copyist is one Fenner of Paternoster Row whose credit appears on items 6, 27–9 and 67 and who may conceivably have reproduced many of the other originals. Those reduced from Strype's 1720 edition of Stow (no 25) are below referred to their source by the abbreviation *S* followed by the numbers of the relevant Book and facing page. Sources on which the engravers have otherwise drawn include the publications of the Society of Antiquaries (*Vetusta Monumenta*, no 36), of which Brayley was a Fellow, a set of three fine views engraved in 1766 by Edward Rooker after drawings by Paul Sandby and a number of plates from more recent uncredited drawings made at the turn of the century. Since these very diminished reproductions were almost certainly engraved on steel it was possible to bring the work out in a large and popular edition with plates which, though somewhat dependent on the use of mechanical ruling for the flat tints of the skies, are quite adequate and well suited to its format.

The captions in voided capitals usually give the dates of each original print and every plate has tl 'Brayley's' and tr 'Londiniana' with a uniform undated publication-line in lm: 'Thos. Hurst, Edwd Chance & Co. London.' They are unnumbered but each volume contains a check-list of them with instructions to the binder. Plate-marks have usually been cropped in the bindery.

VOL. 1

1 front. Civitas Londinum A.D. Circiter, MDLX. 145 ×

395mm. Reduced from Vertue's version of the 'Agas' map published for the Society of Antiquaries. (*Darlington and Howgego* 8a)

2 p 47 Londinium Augusta. 70 × 103mm. Roman London.

3 p 68* Westminster Abbey, from the Dean's Yard. 70 × 98mm.

4 p 76* Westminster Abbey, North Transept. 90 × 67mm. Exterior.

5 p 78* Westminster Abbey, View in the South Aisle. 98 × 70mm.

6 p 89* The Tower and its Liberties/Taken from correct Surveys made in the Reign of Queen Elizabeth. Fenner sc. Paternoster Row. 125 × 187mm. Reduced from Haiward and Gascoyne's 'True and Great Draught' engraved for the Society of Antiquaries and published in *Vetusta Monumenta*.

7 p 109* The Tower, in 1810, with the Enterprize tender. 70 × 100mm.

8 p 89 Guildhall, Guildhall Chapel &c. in 1720. 130 × 180/163 × 200mm. *S* 3,51.

9 p 94 Guildhall and Chapel in 1810. 98 × 67mm. Oblique view.

10 p 101 (tm) Guildhall/ Plan of the Great Hall as fitted up for the Entertainment of His Royal Highness the Prince Regent on the 18th of June 1814. 50 × 125mm. With key to seating.

11 Interior of Guild Hall,/As it appeared at the Royal Entertainment given to the/Prince Regent, (Now George the III,)/and his illustrious visitors,/On Saturday June 18th. 1814. 97 × 68mm.

12 p 121 Hospital of St. John of Jerusalem, about 1640./Eastern Side towards St. John's Street. 85 × 170mm. This and items 13–14 reduced from Hollar's etching published in *Monasticon Anglicanum* (no 6) vol. 2, p 504.

13 p 131 St. John's Hospital, & Chapel (West Side) Clerkenwell. 65 × 105mm. See item 12.

14 p 138 Gate of St. John's Hospital, Clerkenwell. 63 × 120mm. See item 12.

15 p 190 Fish Street Hill, in 1800/Shewing the Monument, St Magnus Church & Old London Bridge. 100 × 70mm.

16 p 194 Gresham College, about 1740. G. Vertue del. 110 × 142mm. Reduced from birds-eye view in John Ward's *Lives of the Professors of Gresham College* (1740).

17 p 203 Design for a Monument for King Henry VI./From a Drawing in the British Museum. 110 × 70mm. 'Bibl. Cottoniana, Augustus II'.

18 p 206 Gateway of Bermondsey Abbey, in 1790. 70 × 95mm. Demolished c 1811.

19 p 209 Westminster Hall, in Term Time; about 1770. 125 × 142mm. 'taken from an engraving by C. Mosley,

after a delineation by Gravelot'. Still available from Laurie & Whittle in 1770 but originally engraved c 1739–40. BL Maps: *K. top.* 24.24g is a 1797 reissue.

20 p 223 Ely Chapel, 1760. 65 × 95mm. ie '1780'. Reduced from Grose's *Antiquities of England and Wales* (no 50) vol. 3, p 133.

21 p 231 Mercer's Hall. 95 × 68mm.

22 p 238 Will Sommers/King Henry the Eight's Jester. 97 × 67mm.

23 p 244 St. Paul's Cross, in the reign of James I./From a large Painting of St. Paul's Cathedral, in the Possession of the/Society of Antiquaries. 103 × 75mm.

24 p 276 Goldsmith's Hall. 68 × 109mm. Demolished for Philip Hardwick's rebuilding in 1829.

25 p 291 Skinners' Hall. 95 × 70mm. 'built about twenty years ago, from designs by the late Mr. Jupp'.

VOL. 2

26 front. London/in 1657. 85 × 315/130 × 347mm. Reduced from Hollar's front. to *Londinopolis* (no 7).

27 p 17* Royal Palace, Whitehall; Eastern or River Front:/As Designed by Inigo Jones. Fenner sc. Paternoster Row. 130 × 270mm.

28 p 44* Royal Palace, Whitehall; Western or Street Front:/As Designed by Inigo Jones. Fenner sc. Paternoster Row. 130 × 270mm. See pp 42–3*: 'Three sets of engravings have been published, but with considerable variations from each other, of the Palace designed by Inigo Jones. The earliest of these consists of views of the fronts in Campbell's "Vitruvius Britannicus," printed in 1717; the next of elevations, plans, sections, &c., amounting to fifty-seven plates, in Kent's first volume of Jones's "Designs," published in 1727; and the last, of large prints of the four fronts, &c. published by Lord Burlington, in 1748 and 1749'. The engravings chosen are from the last-named set, by A. Benoist, E. Rooker, Canot and D.M. Müller junr, published in March 1748 and May 1749, each measuring 580 × 915mm (BL Maps: *K. top.* 26. 5y and 5aa). cf with *Vitruvius Britannicus* (no 24), items 28–9.

29 p 50* Palace of Whitehall, in Charles the Second's Reign: Anno 1680. Fenner sc. Paternoster Row. 147 × 255mm. 'Fisher's Plan', based on Vertue's engraving in *Vetusta Monumenta*, item 63.

30 p 56* Whitehall &c from St James's Park about 1720. 65 × 108mm. *S* 6,5.

31 p 76 Merchant Tailors' Hall. 95 × 70mm.

32 p 91 Westminster Abbey: Chapel of St. Edward the Confessor./Shewing the Shrine, the Coronation Chair, Henry the Fifth's Chapel &c. 77 × 120mm.

33 p 121 Fishmongers' Hall, in June 1827. 67 × 100mm. 'In consequence of the site of the *new* London Bridge having been fixed at a short distance westward from the old Bridge ... the materials of Fishmongers' Hall

were sold by auction in July 1827, and the whole building has been since pulled down'.

34 p 130 Vintners' Hall. 67 × 100mm.

35 p 134 Remains of Sir Paul Pinder's Mansion./Bishopsgate St. 1806. 100 × 70mm.

36 p 137 Lodge of Sir Paul Pinder, about 1760. 103 × 70mm.

37 p 140 Clothworker's Hall. 70 × 100mm.

38 p 145 Christ Church Hospital in 1720. 70 × 95mm. *S* 1,175.

39 p 154 Christ's Hospital, within the Cloisters 1800. 70 × 95mm.

40 p 165 Bridewell Hospital in 1720. 70 × 100mm. *S* 1,176.

41 p 171 Temple Bar from Butcher Row, 1800, looking East. 95 × 67mm.

42 p 181 Church of St. Mary Overie, or St. Saviour Southwark,/about 1660. 70 × 100mm. Reduced from *Monasticon Anglicanum* vol. 2, p 940.

43 p 191 Council Chamber of King Henry VIII. 105 × 70mm. As reproduced in Dibdin's *Typographical Antiquities* vol. 3, from Hall's *Chronicle*.

44 p 198 The Charter House, about 1720. 110 × 70cm. *S* 1,205.

45 p 230 Durham House – Salisbury House – Worcester House/About 1630. 65 × 97mm. From *Londina Illustrata* (no 131), item 98.

46 p 236 Old London Bridge in 1825. 70 × 95mm. From Pool of London.

47 p 272 Tower of London, in Henry the Sixth's Reign. 125 × 100mm. From MS of the poems of Charles, Duke of Orleans (BL MS: 16.F.II).

48 p 274 Suffolk House, about 1630. 68 × 95mm. From *Londina Illustrata*, item 96.

49 p 277 Scotland Yard, Banquetting House, &c. in 1776. 70 × 105mm. Reduced from large engraving by Edward Rooker after Paul Sandby, 1766 (no 58), item 4.

50 p 280 The Font in St James's Church Westminster. G. Vertue del. 105 × 70mm. A poor and very reduced copy of the first item in *Vetusta Monumenta*, engraved by George Vertue in 1718.

51 p 283 Lincoln's Inn, about 1720. 70 × 110mm. *S* 4,73.

52 p 287 Buildings in Clerkenwell Close in 1791./Oliver Cromwell is said to have resided in one of these houses. 70 × 95mm.

53 p 288 Salters' Hall in 1810. 100 × 70mm.

54 p 297 Dean Colet's House, Stepney in 1797. 67 × 95mm. 'From a drawing by the late Mr. John Ireland'.

55 p 301 Gate of St James's Palace, in 1776./From Cleveland Row. 65 × 97mm. Reduced from large engraving by Edward Rooker after Paul Sandby, 1766 (no 58), item 1.

LI – AA

98 p 292 Craven House, Drury Lane, in 1790. 70 × 98mm.

99 p 301 Remains of Prince Rupert's Residence, in 1796./Beech Lane Barbican. 68 × 100mm. 'from a drawing by the late Mr. John Ireland'.

100 p 302 General Post Office, Lombard Street, about 1793. 70 × 98mm. 'The General Post-Office adjoins to the Church of St Mary Woolnoth; but its business will, in the course of a year or two, be altogether removed into the new Post-Office in St Martin's-le-Grand'.

101 p 304 St. Peter's Church, Walworth, Built 1824. 100 × 72mm. 'designed by John Soane ... consecrated on February the 24th 1825'.

102 p 310 The Custom House, about 1720. 68 × 108mm. *S* 2,51.

103 p 314 Old Buildings in Fleet Street, near Chancery Lane, in 1790. 68 × 98mm.

---

156 · ROBSON'S PICTURESQUE VIEWS OF THE ENGLISH CITIES* [1828]

George Fennell Robson is not a name usually associated with London topographical engravings; most of his earlier drawings were of Scottish scenes, in the Highlands especially. He was born at Durham, one of 23 children of a wine merchant, who encouraged him in his youthful enthusiasm for art by sending him to a local drawing-master. He then went to London and by the age of 20 had already exhibited at the Royal Academy and published a print of Durham. In 1810 he began to show landscapes at the Bond Street gallery of what was to become the Old Water Colour Society and, in the same year, he published from 36 Percy Street in Soho a large aquatint view of St Paul's Cathedral and Blackfriars Bridge, engraved by W.J. Bennett (BL Maps: *K. top.* 22.38g; 405 × 595mm). This was apparently his only engraved London view before the three which form part of this collection of views of English cities. He submitted drawings for these to John Britton in 1825, and since no one else would publish the work Britton himself issued the 31 plates worked on steel by a bevy of distinguished engravers. Some, like H. Adlard, J. Le Keux, H.

Matthews, W.D. Taylor and W. Woolnoth, had been associated with Britton before and had engraved on copper for some of his earlier publications; while most of the others were also employed by Jones of the Temple of the Muses on making steel-engravings from T.H. Shepherd's drawings for several topographical publications which were then coming out. The four Numbers in which the work was issued included no letterpress (not even a list) as Britton was anxious to avoid the obligation of legally depositing 11 copies. There was an impression of 750 copies on ordinary paper and 250 on Large Paper and then, in January 1829, the plates were destroyed. The completed work was available in degrees of exclusiveness to suit every taste:

Super royal folio with proofs and etchings	£25	4s
Super royal folio with proofs only	£18	
Super imperial quarto with proofs and etchings	£16	10s
Super imperial quarto proofs	£8	
Super medium quarto	£4	4s

All the alternatives were still available, but at half price or under, when Britton's stock of books was sold off in 1837. A complete check-list of plates is given in Holloway's *Steel engravings in nineteenth century British topographical books* (1977).

0 (wood-engraved title) Picturesque Views/of/the English cities/from drawings/by G.F. Robson./Edited by J. Britton F.S.A. etc./containing/thirty-two engravings/by/Adlard, Barrenger, Barber, Higham, Le Keux, Jeavons, Varrall, Tombleson, Redaway, Taylor, Woolnoth etc. representing ... Border (composed of architectural and sculptural ornaments, etc analogous to cities) designed by J. Britton:-/Drawn by H. Ansted:- Engraved on wood by S. Williams. /London/Published by J. Britton, Burton Street/ 1828. 180 × 120mm.

00 (steel-engr front.) Picturesque/views of the/Cities/of/England/By G.F. Robson ... /London. Published Jany 1, 1828, by J. Britton, Burton Street. Designed by J. Britton, drawn by H. Ansted, effect by P. Williams. Engraved by W. Woolnoth. 225 × 170mm. With an architectural and heraldic design.

1 City of London. /Arch of Waterloo Bridge. G.F. Robson del. W. Tombleson sc. To John Rennie Esq., Architect, Engineer and a patron of the Fine Arts this plate is inscribed by J. Britton. London, Published Decr 25, 1827 by J. Britton, Burton Street. Printed by Hayward. 135 × 230/225 × 302mm.

2 The City of London/ from London Bridge, S.E. /G.F.

Robson del. Jas Redaway sc./To Matthew Wood Esqr
M.P. for the City of London & one of its aldermen who
as Lord Mayor laid a foundation stone on the City side
of Southwark Bridge this plate is inscribed by J.
Britton. London, Published Feby 1, 1828 by J.
Britton, Burton Street. 132 × 213/200 × 290mm.
Shows Southwark Bridge

3 East View of/the City of Westminster/ To the
Honourable Lord George Granville Leveson Gower,
M.P. &c. this plate is inscribed by the Editor. G.F.
Robson del. Matthews sc. Printed by Hayward.
London, Published Jany 1, 1828 by J. Britton, Burton
Street. 132 × 212/240 × 302mm. From the Surrey side
of Westminster Bridge, with a crescent moon in the
sky.

---

157 · WESTALL AND OWEN'S PICTURESQUE TOUR [1828]

Rudolph Ackermann published this collection the
year after his return to 96 The Strand where he had
first opened a print shop in 1795; it was the last book
on British topography to be published by the firm
during his lifetime. The title, derived from Malton's
Picturesque Tour of 1792 (no 72), links it with other
Ackermann 'Picturesque Tours' of rivers, each
illustrated with a similar number of plates: *The
Rhine* (1820), *The Seine* (1821) and *Along the Rivers
Ganges and Jumna* (1824), each advertised on its
wrappers as being still available in 'Elephant 4to, £4.
4s. boards, Ditto Atlas £6 6s.'

Its publication in April was announced in the
February 1828 *Repository of Arts* but it was on 1
May that the first of its six Numbers appeared, with
the following announcement:

Publishing by Subscription, by R. Ackermann, 96 Strand,
'A Picturesque Tour of the River Thames'...
Conditions: 'The Picturesque Tour of the Thames' will be
printed in Elephant Quarto corresponding with the
Picturesque Tours of the Rhine, the Seine and the
Ganges. Each Number will contain Four coloured Views
and from Three to Four Sheets of Descriptive Letter-
press. The Work will be completed in Six Monthly
Numbers, beginning the 1st of May, 1828, price Fourteen
Shillings each Number. A few Copies will be printed on
Large Paper price one Guinea each Number. After the
publication of the Sixth Number the price will be raised to
Non-Subscribers.

The only title-page issued was the engraved one.
An expanded title is printed in an ornamental
border on the wrappers which are identical, but for
the numbers tr, for the first two Numbers. On those
for Nos 4 to 6 Samuel Owen's name is added to
Westall's:

A Picturesque Tour of the River Thames from Oxford to
its Mouth. Illustrated by Twenty-Four Highly Finished
and Coloured Views, a Map and Vignettes. From Original
Drawings made on the spot, By William Westall, A.R.A.
(and Samuel Owen), with illustrations, Historical and
Descriptive. London: Published by R. Ackermann, 96
Strand ... 1828.

Royal Quarto, 305 × 245mm. (Large Paper 400 ×
315mm)   1828

COLLATION   Engr title-page; pp iii–iv, preface; contents, list of plates (2pp); pp 1–169, Picturesque Tour;
index (2pp); colophon ('Printed by L. Harrison, 5 Princes
Street, Soho.')

The tradition of picture-books on the Thames was
started by Samuel Ireland with his *Picturesque
Views on the River Thames* (no 71) published in
1791–2, but Boydell was quick to compete in 1793
with his own two-volume *History of the Thames* (no
75). Both of these, like the present volume, were
illustrated with aquatints and between them they
established a canon of most-favoured views from the
source to the sea. In 1811 William Havell made
drawings of a dozen of these and his cousin, Robert,
aquatinted and published them in the following
year, but they stopped short at Staines. A popular
guidebook, illustrated also with aquatints, but in
miniature, was John Hassell's *Excursions of Pleasure and Sport on the Thames* (no 140), published in
1823. Samuel Owen, Westall's collaborator in the
present volume, had already drawn over 80 Thames
views, which were etched by W.B. Cooke between
1809 and 1811 and many of them were re-engraved
for a second edition published in 1822 as *Views on
the Thames* (nos 106, 139).

The preface to this collection acknowledges only
one of its predecessors:

To the 'History of the Thames', written by the late
William Combe Esq. and published by Messrs. Boydell,
the author acknowledges particular obligation; but while
he attests the copiousness and accuracy of the historical
and descriptive details, he cannot refrain from observing
that a comparison of the coloured engravings in that
work—splendid as it professes to be—with those contained in this volume will furnish striking evidence of the

extraordinary improvements made during the last thirty years in the getting-up, as it is called, of this kind of graphic embellishments.

The colouring is less subdued than Boydell's, and there are more unaquatinted spaces where the interpretation has been left to the colour-washing artist. This gives the plates a greater resemblance to spontaneous water-colour drawings but leads inevitably to a greater disparity between individual copies. There is some blue aquatint printing of skies (eg pl. 3, 8, 18, 22–3) but this is not easily distinguishable since it is blended with colour-washing.

All the plates of the first four Numbers and three from the fifth are from drawings by William Westall, an adventurous topographical artist whose early travels bore fruit in paintings of Australia, China, India and Madeira. On his return home he produced collections of views of Yorkshire and the Lake District and, during 1821–3, *Thirty-Five Views on the Thames* (down as far as Richmond), lithographed by Hüllmandel and issued in five Parts by Rodwell & Martin. He was also responsible for 15 of the plates engraved on steel by Charles Heath in 1825 for his *Views of London* (no 147). Samuel Owen, primarily a marine artist, contributed one drawing to the fifth Number, four to the sixth and also the engraved title and tailpiece of the book.

Thirteen of the plates are the work of the aquatint engraver R.G. Reeve, who was on Ackermann's permanent list having also engraved for the histories of the universities (1814–15) and, more recently, for the *Scenery, Costumes and Architecture of India* (1826). He had also produced colour aquatints for the drawing-books by S. and J. Fuller in 1814 and 1825 and about one third of the illustrations in Pyne's *Royal Residences* (no 132). Five plates are engraved by a young water-colour painter, Charles Bentley, who also worked in aquatint and lithography, and the balance by J. Bailey and J. Feilding.

The plates, which have captions in voided capitals, are numbered only in the list prefixed to the book. Plate-marks have been cropped by the binder and the publication-line is invariable: 'Published 1828 by R. Ackermann, 96 Strand, London.'

0 p 1 (br) Map/of the/River Thames/from Oxford to its Mouth. J. & J. Neele sc. 356 Strand. London Published Sept.24,1828 by R. Ackermann, 96 Strand. 275 × 445/300 × 465mm.

1 (engr title) Picturesque tour of the River Thames; illustrated by twenty-four coloured views, a map and vignettes, from original drawings taken on the spot by William Westall and Samuel Owen. (aquatint vignette, 120 × 170mm) Source of the Thames. S. Owen del. Publish'd 1828 by R. Ackermann, 96 Strand, London.

NO 1

2 p 35 Oxford. W. Westall A.R.A. delt. R.G. Reeve sculpt. 175 × 265mm.

3 p 76 Park Place,/Henley-on-Thames/Seat of Fuller Maitland Esqr., M.P. W. Westall A.R.A. delt. R.G. Reeve sculpt. 177 × 268mm.

4 p 83 Cullum Court/Henley-upon-Thames/ Seat of the Honble Fredk West. W. Westall A.R.A. delt. R.G. Reeve sculpt. 175 × 268mm.

5 p 90 Maidenhead Bridge. W. Westall A.R.A. delt. J. Bailey sculpt. 178 × 268mm.

NO 2

6 p 93 Windsor Castle/from Eton. W. Westall A.R.A. delt. R.G. Reeve sculpt. 180 × 267mm.

7 p 106 Eton College/from the River. W. Westall A.R.A. delt. J. Feilding sculpt. 178 × 265mm.

8 p 110 Beaumont Lodge, Old Windsor/The Seat of Viscount Ashbrooke. W. Westall A.R.A. delt. C. Bentley sculpt. 178 × 265mm.

9 p 112 Staines Bridge. W. Westall A.R.A. delt. C. Bentley sculpt. 177 × 263mm.

NO 3

10 p 117 Hampton House,/The Seat of Thomas Carr Esqre. W. Westall A.R.A. delt. R.G. Reeve sculpt. 180 × 267mm.

11 p 128 Pope's Villa/Twickenham. W. Westall A.R.A. delt. C. Bentley sculp. 180 × 263mm.

12 p 130 Twickenham. W. Westall A.R.A. delt. R.G. Reeve sculpt. 180 × 265mm.

13 p 131 View from Richmond Hill. W. Westall A.R.A. delt. R.G. Reeve sculpt. 180 × 265mm. (*Gascoigne* 89)

NO 4

14 p 133 Richmond. W. Westall A.R.A. delt. R.G. Reeve sculpt. 180 × 265mm. (*Gascoigne* 90)

15 p 134 St Margaret's, Twickenham,/Seat of the Earl of Cassillis. W. Westall A.R.A. delt. C. Bentley sculpt. 180 × 265mm.

16 p 136 Sion House/Seat of His Grace the Duke of Northumberland. W. Westall A.R.A. delt. J. Bailey sculpt. 180 × 265mm.

17 p 139 Suspension Bridge/Hammersmith. W. Westall A.R.A. delt. J. Baily sculpt. 178 × 262mm.

18 p 148 Westminster Bridge. W. Westall A.R.A. delt. R.G. Reeve sculpt. 180 × 263mm. From N.

19 p 150 Waterloo Bridge. W. Westall A.R.A. delt. R.G. Reeve sculpt. 175 × 270mm. From W.

20 p 152 Southwark Bridge. W. Westall A.R.A. delt. C. Bentley sculpt. 173 × 263mm. From W.

21 p 154 The Custom House. S. Owen delt. R.G. Reeve sculpt. 180 × 265mm. From E.

NO 6

22 p 156 Greenwich Hospital. S. Owen delt. R.G. Reeve sculpt. 175 × 267mm.

23 p 161 Gravesend. S. Owen delt. R.G. Reeve sculpt. 177 × 260mm.

24 p 164 Tilbury Fort. S. Owen delt. R.G. Reeve sculpt. 177 × 263mm.

25 p 164 Sheerness. S. Owen delt. R.G. Reeve sculpt. 180 × 263mm.

26 p 169 (tailpiece) The Crow Stone. S. Owen delint. 120 × 150mm. Vignetted.

158 · ALLEN'S HISTORY OF SURREY AND SUSSEX* [1829]

With an imprint of the same date as his *Panorama of London* (no 162) and the fourth volume of his *History and Antiquities of London* (no 152) was another of Thomas Allen's historical and topographical books, the two-volume *History of the Counties of Surrey and Sussex*. Our concern is with the first volume which illustrates Lambeth, Southwark, Bemondsey and some river suburbs; views in the second are of places deeper into Surrey and Sussex, as far afield as Brighton and Hastings. Plate-marks have been cropped to fit them in to the octavo format. There is no printed title-page but the engraved title is dated 1829, with the publisher as I.T. Hinton; this imprint is unaltered in later issues in which some of the publication-lines substitute the name of Edward Lacey, publisher of the second volume. In May 1832 George Virtue reissued the book, complete in 33 Numbers at two shillings each or in four bound volumes.

Besides the octavo volumes there is a quarto edition on India paper with abridged text of 64 pages but with the prints on larger paper which extends beyond the plate-marks. This has a different title with a printed wrapper dated 1830 and an engraved title-page adapted to the new title but still dated 1829:

The Picturesque Beauties of England & Wales: in a series of views, comprising every object of public interest and picturesque character from drawings taken expressly for this work, By N. Whittock & H. Gastineau, Esqrs. and other eminent artists. Engraved on steel by Rogers, Shury, Cooke, Rolls, Winkles, Lambert &c. with topographical, historical, and biographical sketches. By Thomas Allen Esq. author of Surrey and Sussex—To be complete in twenty-four numbers, or in eight parts. London: Isaac Taylor Hinton, Warwick Square, 1830.

(*Title-page* pl. 1)

Octavo, 210 × 135mm.   1829

COLLATION   Vol. 1. Engr title-page; pp i–ii, contents, list of plates; pp 1–484, History of the Counties of Surrey and Sussex.

Most of the drawings are by Nathaniel Whittock; other contributors are J. and N. Fletcher, G.T. Philips and R.L. Wright. Engraving is by J. Rogers, Richard Winkles and J. Shury. The plates are unnumbered. Of the plates listed, all as bound in *Picturesque Beauties*, except items 2 and 3, have the publication-line 'London, Published by I.T. Hinton (4) Warwick Square (date).' The exception has 'Published by E. Lacey, 76 St Pauls London/and Messrs Shepherd & Sutton.' Publication-lines visible in the octavo edition are as listed. Plate-marks are given in brackets as measured in *Picturesque Beauties*.

1 (engr title) History of/the Counties of Surrey and Sussex:/by/Thomas Allen./Illustrated by a Series of Views,/engraved on steel from original drawings/by/Nathaniel Whittock. (vignette) St. Saviours Church Southwark. N. Whittock del. J. Rogers sc. London, I.T. Hinton 4 Warwick Square,/and Holdsworth & Ball, 18, St. Pauls Church Yard, 1829. 105 × 120/(220 × 160)mm.

1a (engr title) Picturesque Beauties/of/England and Wales,/in a/Series of Views,/From Original Drawings/by N. Whittock and H. Gastineau. (vignette) St. Saviours Church,/Southwark. N. Whittock del. J. Rogers sc./London, I.T. Hinton, 4 Warwick Square/& Holdsworth & Ball, 18 St. Pauls Church Yard, 1829. 105 × 120/220 × 160mm. Plate-marks are retained on these India paper versions with a page size about 280 × 230mm.

2 p 273 Guys Hospital. N. Whittock. J. Rogers. 90 × 155/(140 × 210)mm. Hinton publication-line undated.

3 p 285 Ancient Crypt, Southwark. Drawn by N. Whittock. Engraved by J. Shury. Published by Edward Lacey, 76 St Pauls, London, May 1, 1830. 100 × 155/(140 × 230)mm.

4 p 316 Stamford Street. Drawn & Engraved by R.L. Wright. 93 × 153/(140 × 227)mm. Hinton publication-line dated April 1830, or: 'Published by Geo. Virtue, 26 Ivy Lane, 1836.'

5 p 331 Lambeth Church and Palace. N. Whittock. W. Syms. 93 × 150/(190 × 220)mm. Hinton publication-line dated 1829, or burnished out.

6 p 382 General Lying-in Hospital, York Road. Drawn by N. Whittock. Engraved on steel by J. Shury. 100 × 155/(135 × 225)mm. Hinton publication-line dated 1 April 1830, or burnished out. The hospital was built in 1829.

7 p 407 Trinity Church Southwark. N. Whittock del. R. Winkles sc. 98 × 155/(140 × 225)mm. Hinton publication-line dated 1830. Built by Francis Bedford, 1823-4.

8 p 416 St James Bermondsey. Drawn by N. Whittock. Rd. Winkles sc. 150 × 90/(215 × 145)mm. Hinton publication-line dated 1829. Built by James Savage, 1827-9.

9 p 433 Dulwich College. Drawn by N. Whittock. Engraved by J. Rogers. 85 × 150/(140 × 220)mm. Hinton publication-line dated 1829.

10 p 446 Battersea Church. J. Fletcher delt. J. Rogers sc. 95 × 145/(140 × 220)mm. Hinton publication-line dated 1829.

11 p 457 St Anne's Church, Wandsworth. N. Fletcher del. J.R. Winkles sc. 150 × 90/(225 × 145)mm. Hinton publication-line dated 1830, or: 'Publ. by Edward Lacey, 76 St Pauls London.' Built by R. Smirke, 1822.

12 p 462 Putney Bridge. N. Whittock delt. J. Rogers sc. 98 × 150/(135 × 220)mm. Hinton publication-line dated 1829.

13 p 473 Barnes, Surrey. Drawn by G.T. Philips. Engraved by R. Winkles. 95 × 153/(140 × 225)mm. Hinton publication-line dated July 1830, or: 'Published by Edward Lacey, 76 St Pauls London.'

14 p 476 Hammersmith Bridge. J. Fletcher delt. J. Rogers sc. 90 × 150/(140 × 225)mm. Hinton publication-line undated, or burnished out.

159 · BRIEF ACCOUNT OF THE COLOSSEUM [1829]

On the initiative of a surveyor named Thomas Hornor the Colosseum was built to the design of the 23 year old Decimus Burton in the south-east corner of Regent's Park, between 1823 and 1827. In spite of its name it most resembled the Pantheon, being 126 feet in diameter and completed by a hexastyle Doric portico with columns equivalent in size to those of the Parthenon and a dome somewhat wider than that of St Paul's Cathedral. 'It is polygonal on the outside, having 16 faces, each measuring 25 feet in length ... The height of the walls is 64 feet at the outside, 79 feet within and to the sky-light 112 feet'.

Its purpose was to exhibit a panorama of London from St Paul's drawn by Hornor, who 'finished the sketches for its execution in 1824, having constructed scaffolding and a susended house, or large box, above the highest cross of the Cathedral, at a time when a new ball and cross were required, to crown the summit of that edifice'.

Although probably the most prodigious of its kind, because of the size and pretensions of the building and the complicated mechanics of its lighting, stairs and lifts which brought visitors up to viewing level, the conception of a London panorama was by no means a novelty. Already on 10 January 1792 the *Times* carried an advertisement for the exhibition at 28 Castle Street of a panoramic view of London from the roof of Albion Mills at the foot of Blackfriars Bridge, painted in distemper by Robert Barker; this was semi-circular but was later extended to full circle in Barker's purpose-built Panorama in nearby Leicester Square. In 1802 Thomas Girtin's vast circular picture of London, Westminster and the environs, the 'Eidometropolis', was on view in the Great Room in Spring Gardens and panoramas, 'dioramas' and 'cosmoramas' were regular features of the entertainment provided at Vauxhall Gardens throughout the early years of the century.

Having made his gigantic survey from the dizzy heights above St Paul's cross and having built his Colosseum, Hornor had next to seek a painter almost as intrepid as himself:

After the sketches were completed, on several hundred sheets of paper—after the walls of the building were raised, and its roof finished, the original Projector experienced the greatest difficulty in finding artists of talent, and sufficient hardihood to execute his required works. In this dilemma, Mr. E.T. Parris was found not only to be fearless in all situations, but possessing a fertile mind, a considerable knowledge of mechanics, perspective, and also practical execution in painting.... Standing in a basket, supported by two loose poles, and lifted to a great height by ropes, he has painted and finished nearly the whole surface of this immense picture.

Parris, then in his early thirties, was indeed the perfect candidate since he was trained in the Royal Academy Schools and had recently submitted his invention of an apparatus which would permit restorers to reach Thornhill's paintings high up inside the dome of St Paul's safely.

He was at work on the walls of the Colosseum for four years and, by November 1829, when he and his assistants had reached the end of their task, it is said that they had covered 46,000 square feet of canvas. Nothing daunted, Parris went on to assist William Daniell in painting and housing a panorama of Madras, and in due course to win fame as an Academy artist. He was appointed historical painter to Queen Adelaide and commissioned in 1838 by Messrs Hodgson & Graves to paint Queen Victoria's coronation for commemorative engraving so that he received sittings from the young Queen herself and from the principal dignitaries involved.

A permanent record of Robert Barker's panorama of 1792–3 was made by his son in half a dozen engravings attractively aquatinted by Frederick Birnie (*Crace* 3.92). Hornor's souvenir, published on the opening of the Colosseum, is a more functional publication: an oblong quarto containing a summary history of the project by John Britton and eight grey lithographic reproductions by Engelmann, Graf, Coindet & Co of Hornor's sketches, each keyed with references to select buildings. There are no captions, so the descriptions below endeavour to suggest the general direction of each birds-eye viewing by citing a few of the references to objects near and far. The modest price was two shillings.

A Brief Account of the Colosseum, in the Regent's Park, London: comprising a Description of the Buildings. (wood-engr vignette of exterior, 75 × 115mm) The Panoramic View from the Top of St. Paul's Cathedral: The Conservatory &c. Printed for the Proprietors and sold at the Exhibition: and by all Booksellers. 1829. (verso) The Letter-Press by T. Bensley, Crane Court, Fleet-Street.

Oblong quarto, 260 × 390mm. 1829

COLLATION Title-page; pp 1–8, Account of Colosseum; 8 plates.

1 1–2 (S.W. turret of St Paul's – St Andrew's Hill – Blackfriars Bridge – Waterloo Bridge – Shot Tower – Wimbledon) 200 × 295mm. Refs 1–45.

2 2–3 (N.W. turret of St Paul's – Amen Corner – Ludgate Hill – Newgate – Holborn – Bloomsbury – the Colosseum – Grand Junction Reservoir, Bayswater) 195 × 298mm. Refs 1–62.

3 3–4 (Dolley's Chop House – Newgate – Christ's Hospital – Clerkenwell – Battle Bridge – Pentonville – Islington – Highgate Archway) 188 × 310mm. Refs 1–51.

4 4–5 (Paternoster Row – Foster Lane – Aldersgate – Wood Street – Aldgate – Old Street – Shoreditch – Hoxton – Bethnal Green) 195 × 312mm. Refs 1–44.

5 5–6 (St Paul's School – Cheapside – St Mary le Bow – St Matthew, Friday Street – St Lawrence Jewry – Bank of England – Moorfields – Cornhill – London Docks – St George in the East – Stratford, Essex) 188 × 290mm. Refs 1–48.

6 6–7 (St Augustine, Watling Street – St Antholin – St Swithin – the Monument – the Tower – Thames Street – Southwark – Woolwich) 190 × 295mm. Refs 1–32.

7 7–8 (St Mary Magdalen, Old Fish Street – St Nicholas Cole Abbey – St Mary Somerset – Southwark Bridge – Southwark Cathedral – St George, Southwark – bridge on the Surrey Canal, Kent Road – Beckenham Church) 200 × 310mm. Refs 1–18.

8 8–9 (Carter Lane – St Benet, Paul's Wharf – Herald's Office – Doctors' Commons – Bankside – Christchurch, Southwark – Brixton – Streatham – Clapham – Norwood Church) 188 × 310mm. Refs 1–22.

160 · ACKERMANN'S GRAPHIC ILLUSTRATIONS OF THE COLOSSEUM [1829]

This set of five large aquatints was published by Ackermann to coincide with the opening of the Colosseum in Regent's Park, as was the official *Brief Account* (no 159), but the two publications served different purposes. The *Brief Account* gave a verbal description of Decimus Burton's building but its plates were confined to a series of lithographic line reproductions of the London panorama which covered its internal walls. *Graphic Illustrations* was intended as a visual souvenir of the building itself, a suitable presentation perhaps for influential patrons of the establishment; its verbal description of the architecture is limited to some notes on the plates printed on the back wrapper (folio, 430 × 330mm). There is no other text and no title-page. A hand-coloured collotype facsimile edition, with introduction by Ralph Hyde, was issued by Arthur Ackermann Publishing Ltd in 1982. The front wrapper reads:

Graphic Illustrations of the Colosseum, Regent's Park, in Five Plates, from drawings by Gandy, Mackenzie, and other eminent artists. London: Published First of June, by R. Ackermann and Co., Strand; and at the Colosseum, Regent's Park. M.DCCC.XXIX. (verso) London: J. Moyes, Took's Court, Chancery Lane.

The Gandy named on the wrapper is no doubt J.M. Gandy, an architect who specialized in painting capriccios and architectural fantasies and a contributor, earlier in the century, to Britton's *Architectural Antiquities* (no 97). The Piranesi-like staircase to the viewing galleries would have had great appeal for him. The other artist named is Frederick Mackenzie, also a contributor to Britton's book, who was an experienced draughtsman for aquatint work and many of whose drawings for Ackermann were reproduced in the coloured plates of *Westminster Abbey* (no 108) and *History of the Colleges* (no 116). Plates are numbered bl in Roman figures. The publication-line reads: 'Published June, 1829 by R. Ackermann & Co. 96, Strand.'

1 Grand Entrance to the Colosseum,/Regent's Park. 280 × 340mm. Vignetted.
2 South side of the Ground surrounding the Colosseum,/Regent's Park. 218 × 320/290 × 360mm.
3 The Fountain surrounding a marble Statue,/at the Colosseum, Regent's Park. 277 × 335mm. Vignetted.
4 The geometrical Ascent to the Galleries,/in the Colosseum, Regent's Park. 283 × 220/338 × 275mm.
5 Bird's eye View from the Stair-case & the upper part of the Pavilion,/in the Colosseum, Regent's Park. 292 × 220/335 × 275mm.

161 · LONDON AND ITS ENVIRONS IN THE NINETEENTH CENTURY [1829–31]

On the wrapper of No 41, the last Number of *Metropolitan Improvements* (no 154), published on 1 January 1830, Jones thus addressed their subscribers:

The Publishers having as nearly as possible completed the First Series of 'London in the Nineteenth Century', comprising the 'Metropolitan Improvements', within the quantity proposed, beg to remind the Subscribers that there are yet several very important Improvements in progress, which, whenever they can be given, will render the present volume still more complete and valuable: as for instance, the New London Bridge—the New Palace, Pimlico—the Buildings on the site of Carlton Palace—the New Fleet Market, &c....

In the mean time, at the suggestion and in compliance with the wishes of a numerous body of Subscribers, a Second Series, to comprise the Earlier Buildings and Antiquities, has been long announced and in preparation, of which a fair Specimen is now respectfully submitted. This part will embrace a brief General History of the Metropolis from the earliest period ... as well as a description of each particular building and object worthy of notice; so as to present together the only Complete, Historical, Topographical, and Graphic Illustration of the First City in the World, *brought down to the present day*.

In 1828 already, on the wrapper of Part 3 of *Metropolitan Improvements*, the publisher had announced his intention of following it with 'the whole of the other objects worthy of Graphic Illustration, throughout the Metropolis and its Environs ... by the same Artist', in about 60 Numbers.

The sub-title of the original volume was adapted as the title of its sequel, engraved on a title-page dated 1 November 1829 as *London and its Environs in the Nineteenth Century ... Series the First, comprising the Earlier Edifices, Antiquities, &c*. In the final Part, issued in 1832, the directions for binding included a spine label, reading 'London in the Nineteenth Century: vol. 1. comprising the Antiquities in 193 engravings on steel.' Most of its subjects—Gothic and baroque churches, Company halls, prisons and hospitals, the Inns of Court and historic buildings in general—had often been depicted since the turn of the century, albeit engraved on copper, in such works as Phillips's *Modern London* (no 89), Hughson's *London* (no 93), Lambert's *History* (no 96) and *The Beauties of England and Wales* (no 104). So, in spite of the continuing excellences of Shepherd's designs, and of his engravers on steel, the new book had not the fashionable appeal of its up-to-the-minute predecessor. With this in mind the publishers included a 'fair Specimen' in the last Number of the *Improvements* and held over until Part 9, which otherwise consisted of the first five Numbers of the sequel, the last two half-sheets of *Improvements* and its list of engravings. Also, to establish their interdependence, they labelled the two completed series as vols 2 and 1 of *London in the Nineteenth Century*. Moreover they included in the new volume all but one of the 'improvements' omitted from the original (items 23, 173, 190) and, for full measure, issued seven more in the final Part (items 185–9, 191–2).

The publication history of the sequel is less succinct than that of the original volume as only 15 surviving Numbers, in bluish wrappers, have been seen: two, numbered 1 and 2, and 13 numbered 67 to 79, in which the series had run on from Nos 1–41 of *Metropolitan Improvements* to a terminal No 80. A complete set of Parts, however, dated from 1 January 1830 to 1832, has happily survived, in buff wrappers like those of the original work and numbered in continuation of that from 9 to 16. From this it is evident that the second series followed much the same pattern as the first and that instalments were available over a period of about two and a half years, in 40 Numbers or eight Parts. Printing of the text must also have been in instalments since there is reference on p 150 to the opening of London Bridge on 1 August 1831. Although no octavo edition was ever planned the occasional bisected plate may be found bound up with the later stereotyped octavos of *Metropolitan Improvements*.

The name of James Elmes, the author of the original work, does not appear in the sequel and it seems unlikely that he chose the subjects or wrote the descriptive text. Architects' names are conspicuous by their absence. Wren's name hardly occurs although many of his important churches are illustrated and none of the three Hawksmoor churches depicted earns him a mention. Gibbs is nowhere to be found although St Clement Danes and St Bartholomew's Hospital are shown; on the other hand St Martin in the Fields and St Mary le Strand and Flitcroft's St Giles in the Field are quite ignored. Other eighteenth century architects passed over in the text are Archer, James, Kent, Flitcroft, Vardy and the two Dances, although specimens of the work of each of them are illustrated. Ascriptions, in fact, are only to be found for a handful of contemporary buildings omitted from *Metropolitan Improvements*, in the notes which may well have been held over from Elmes's original text. There are three views of buildings on the point of demolition (items 9, 16, 33) and a certain amount of architectural description is included with the topographical notes but not such as would have been beyond the competence of, say, some of the regular engravers.

(*title-page* pl. 1)

Quarto, 270 × 205mm.   1829

COLLATION   Engr title-page; pp 1–160, London in the Nineteenth Century; pp i–iii, list of engravings.

Sixteen of the most favoured engravers were also employed on the *Improvements* views. With the exception of John Greig of the Storer and Greig partnership (no 90) and A. Cruse, each of the remaining 15 contributed only two or three views. Shepherd himself engraved four (items 175–6, 187–8). Each plate was engraved either with two oblong views, or two small upright views and an oblong, or four small upright views. As they were made only for binding into a quarto edition they were treated as collective entities with only one publication-line at the bottom of the page and, occasionally, with only a single set of credits. Each separate view is numbered bl and the numbering reflects in general the order in which they were published in Numbers, ie it is roughly chronological. Plates are not so arranged when bound but each is inserted as near as possible to the pages describing its subjects and to which reference is made from the alphabetical list. This arrangement, although similar to that of the earlier volume, is here more successful since the textual notes are grouped according to the clusters of subjects on each plate. It has therefore been possible to list the plates in the order in which they are most usually bound and to cite the approximate facing page number.

The only credit quoted is the name of the engraver abbreviated from the formula 'Engraved by ...',

'Engd. by ...', or occasionally '... sculp.' The other credit, 'Drawn by Tho. H. Shepherd', appears bl on every view or pair of views. The publication-line is almost invariably 'Jones & Co. Temple of the Muses, Finsbury Square, London (date).' The plate-marks, as with *Metropolitan Improvements*, are mostly cropped at one or more of the edges; occasionally even the publication-line has been cropped.

The Museum of London accession numbers of 56 of Shepherd's pencil and sepia wash drawings are quoted with the abbreviation *ML*. They are the exact size of the engravings. Locations are also given for preparatory pencil and wash sketches in the collections of Guildhall Library, Greater London Council and Westminster Public Library.

0 front. (engr title) London/And its Environs in the/ Nineteenth Century,/Illustrated/By a Series of Views/ From Original Drawings/By Thomas H. Shepherd./ With Historical, Topographical and Critical Notices/ Series the First, comprising the earlier edifices,/ Antiquities, &c. (vignette) Temple Bar, from the Strand. Drawn by Tho. H. Shepherd. Engraved by W. Wallis. London. Published Nov 1, 1829, by Jones & Co. Temple of the Muses. Finsbury Square. 110 × 130/265 × 200mm. Pencil drawing (100 × 140mm) in Guildhall Library.

1 p 37 St. Paul's Cathedral/from the River. J. Tingle. pl.181. 100 × 158mm.

2 Westminster Abbey/West Front. J. Tingle. pl.182. 102 × 155mm. Pencil drawing (105 × 150mm) in Westminster Public Library. nd.

3 p 41 Westminster Abbey, and St Margaret's Church. W. Wallis. pl. 1. 100 × 143mm.

4 Banqueting House, Whitehall. W. Wallis. pl.2. 87 × 145mm. 1829.

5 p 42 Somerset House, Strand. pl.xi, 90 × 145mm.

6 East India House, Leadenhall Street. pl.12. 90 × 145mm. W. Tombleson. Oct 31, 1829.

7 p 44 St James's Palace, Pall Mall. pl.6. 95 × 145mm.

8 p 44 The Old White Hart Tavern, Bishopsgate Street/now pulled down. pl.7. 90 × 143mm. S. Lacey. Pencil drawing (113 × 185mm), dated May 1828, in Guildhall Library. Nov 14, 1829.

9 p 45 British Museum, Great Russel Street. pl.23. 92 × 140mm. The text makes no mention of Smirke's plans for the Museum, begun in 1823; the building shown is Montague House. *ML* A 23065/1.

10 Carpenter's Hall, London Wall. pl.24. 90 × 145mm. W. Henshall. Jan 1, 1830.

11 p 49 Horse Guards, Parliament Street. J. Tingle. pl.38. 95 × 145mm.

12 The Mint, Tower Hill. J. Tingle. pl.39. 90 × 150mm. Feb 20, 1830.

13 p 50 The King's Mews, Charing Cross. J. Tingle. pl.68. 95 × 165mm.

14 The Admiralty, Parliament Street. J. Tingle. pl.69. 100 × 170mm. 1830.

15 p 51 Smithfield Market, from the Barrs. T. Barber. pl.57. 95 × 145mm. *ML* A 23064/1.

16 Hungerford Market, Strand. T. Barber. pl.58. 100 × 145mm. May 14, 1830. *ML* A 23061/2, dated 1830. Charles Fowler started rebuilding Hungerford Market in the following year.

17 p 53 Physicians College, Warwick Lane. pl.54. 108 × 68mm.

18 Whittington's College, College Hill. W. Wallis. pl.55. 108 × 68mm.

19 Herald's College, Bennet's Hill. W. Wallis. pl.56. 108 × 147mm. April 17, 1830.

20 p 58 Haberdasher's Hall, Maiden Lane. pl.59. 95 × 64mm. Pencil drawing (100 × 70mm) and sepia wash drawing (94 × 65mm) in Guildhall Library.

21 Sadler's Hall, Cheapside. W. Watkins. pl.60. 95 × 62mm. Pencil drawing (101 × 68mm) in Guildhall Library.

22 Merchant Taylor's Hall, Threadneedle Street. W. Watkins. pl.61. 95 × 140mm. May 7, 1830.

23 p 59 Fleet Market, from Holborn Bridge./now removed. T. Barber. pl.50. 95 × 145mm. Built by George Dance senior, 1734–7.

24 Ludgate Hill, from Fleet Street. T. Barber. pl.51. 103 × 150mm. *ML* Z 8. April 10, 1830.

25 p 61 St. Stephen Walbrook. pl.15. 98 × 65mm. Pencil drawing (98 × 72mm) in Guildhall Library. *ML* A 23070/2.

26 St. Mary Woolnoth, Lombard St. R. Acon. pl.16. 98 × 65mm. *ML* A 23073/1, dated 1829.

27 The Mansion House, from the Bank. W. Wallis. pl.17. 100 × 150mm. Pencil drawing in Guildhall Library. Jan 1, 1830.

28 p 65 King Charles 1st. Porter & Dwarf, Newgate Street. pl.8. 105 × 70mm.

29 A Figure and Tablet, in Pannier Alley, Newgate St. T. Barber. pl.9. 103 × 60mm.

30 Exeter 'Change, Strand./now pulled down. T. Barber. pl.10. 100 × 147mm. *ML* 58.115/2, dated 1829. Nov 7, 1829.

31 p 66 St. Leonard's Shoreditch. pl.3. 97 × 64mm. Pencil drawing in Bishopsgate Institute and sepia wash drawing in GLC (both 96 × 65mm).

32 St Clement Danes, Strand. S. Lacy. pl.4. 97 × 64mm. *ML* A 16159/5.

33 St Dunstan in the West, Fleet Street. J.B. Allen. pl.5. 95 × 145mm. John Shaw started building the new church in 1831. Published Nov 1, 1829 by Jones & Co. London.

34 p 67 Trinity House, Tower Hill. pl.13. 90 × 140mm. Pencil drawing (137 × 206mm) in Guildhall Library.

35 Town Hall, Borough High Street. pl.14. 98 × 140mm.

R. Winkles. Pencil drawing (92 × 144mm) in Guildhall Library. Jan 1, 1830.

36 p 68 St. Paul's, Covent Garden. pl.21. 100 × 143mm. Pencil drawing (100 × 160mm) in Westminster Public Library.

37 Buckingham Water Gate, Strand. pl.22. 98 × 148mm. J. Henshall. Jan 1, 1830.

38 p 69 Guy Earl of Warwick, Warwick Lane. pl.18. 95 × 72mm.

39 London Stone, Cannon Street. J.B. Allen. pl.19. 95 × 70mm. Pencil drawing (146 × 100mm), dated 1 August 1829, in Guildhall Library.

40 St John's Gate, Clerkenwell. J.B. Allen. pl.20. 98 × 148mm. Pencil drawing (105 × 154mm) in GLC. Dec 19, 1829.

41 p 71 Cheapside, Poultry, & Bucklersbury. W. Wallis. pl.30. 95 × 145mm.

42 Aldgate. W. Wallis. pl.31. 95 × 148mm. Jan. 18, 1830.

43 p 72 South Sea House, Threadneedle St. A. Cruse. pl.36. 98 × 150mm.

44 Excise Office, Broad St. A. Cruse. pl.37. 98 × 150mm. Feb 13, 1830. Sepia wash drawings of both subjects (102 × 153 and 66 × 100mm) in Westminster Public Library (St Marylebone).

45 p 73 Sir Paul Pindar's House, Bishopsgate Street. pl.27. 95 × 65mm. Sepia wash drawing (95 × 65mm) in Bishopsgate Institute.

46 Mercers' Hall, Cheapside. M. Barrenger. pl.28. 95 × 165mm. Pencil and sepia wash drawings (both 95 × 65mm) in Guildhall Library.

47 Skinners' Hall, Dowgate Hill. M. Barrenger. pl.29. 100 × 150mm. Jan 16, 1830.

48 p 74 St. Dionis Backchurch, Fenchurch Street. J.B. Allen. pl.40. 100 × 140mm.

49 St. John the Baptist, Savoy. J.B. Allen. pl.41. 95 × 143mm. Pencil drawing (105 × 168mm) and sepia wash drawing (95 × 147mm) in GLC. Feb 20, 1830.

50 p 75 Drapers' Hall, Throgmorton St. W. Watkins. pl.25. 93 × 143mm.

51 Stationers' Hall, Stationers' Hall Court. W. Watkins. pl.26. 93 × 145mm. Jan 9, 1830.

52 p 76 Clothworker's Hall, Mincing Lane. W. Wallis. pl.45. 95 × 145mm.

53 Goldsmith's Hall, Foster Lane. W. Wallis. pl.46. 95 × 143mm. Sepia wash drawing (95 × 144mm) in GLC. March 13, 1830.

54 p 77 Middlesex Hospital. J. Rogers. pl.81. 95 × 150mm.

55 Pensioner's Hall, Charterhouse. J. Rogers. pl.82. 93 × 143mm. ML A 23080/2. Sept 25, 1830.

56 p 78 Middle Temple Hall. J. Hinchliff. pl.79. 93 × 147mm.

57 Clifford's Inn Hall, Fleet Street. J. Hinchliff. pl.80. 105 × 148mm. Augt 14, 1830.

58 p 79 St. Lawrence, King Street. J. Tingle. pl.85. 108 × 148mm. ML A 26063/3.

59 Crosby Hall, Bishopsgate Street. J. Tingle. pl.86. 100 × 145mm. ML A 16160/1. (Longford 434) Oct 9, 1830.

60 p 80 The King's Weigh House, Little East Cheap. R. Acon. pl.83. 100 × 142mm.

61 Coal Exchange, Thames Street. R. Acon. pl.84. 105 × 143mm. Septr 25, 1830.

62 p 81 St. Mary Aldermary. pl.73. 95 × 65mm. Pencil sketch (190 × 140mm) and sepia wash drawing (95 × 65mm) in Guildhall Library.

63 St Michael's Cornhill. W. Watkins. pl.74. 95 × 65mm. Sepia wash drawing (94 × 64mm) in Guildhall Library.

64 St. Olave Jewry, Old Jewry. W. Watkins. pl.75. 103 × 145mm. Pencil drawing (115 × 185mm) in Guildhall Library. July 24, 1830.

65 p 83 Piccadilly, from Coventry Street. pl.32. 93 × 150mm.

66 Middle Row Holborn. T. Barber. pl.33. 98 × 145mm. Pencil and sepia wash drawing (105 × 167mm) in Guildhall Library. Jan 1, 1830.

67 p 84 Gray's Inn Hall, Chapel, and Library. W. Watkins. pl.52. 95 × 148mm.

68 Lincoln's Inn Hall, Chapel, and Chancery Court. W. Watkins. pl.53. 98 × 150mm. April 17, 1830.

69 p 85 Christ Church, Spitalfields. pl.47. 95 × 63mm. Pencil drawing (87 × 65mm) in Bishopsgate Institute.

70 St. Dunstan's in the East. S. Lacey. pl.48. 95 × 65mm. Sepia wash drawing (95 × 64mm) in Guildhall Library.

71 Cornhill, and Lombard Street, from the Poultry. S. Lacey. pl.49. 102 × 148mm. ML 23064/2. March 20, 1830.

72 p 87 St. James's Clerkenwell. J. Henshall. pl.65. 100 × 63mm.

73 St. Margaret Pattens, Rood Lane. J. Henshall. pl.66. 100 × 63mm.

74 St. Giles's Cripplegate, Fore Street. J. Henshall. pl.67. 102 × 143mm. March 13, 1830.

75 p 89 Barber Surgeon's Hall, Monkwell Street. pl.42. 100 × 67mm.

76 Fishmonger's Hall, Thames Street. J. Greig. pl.43. 100 × 67mm.

77 Cordwainer's Hall, Distaff Lane. J. Greig. pl.44. 95 × 147mm. Pencil drawing (116 × 162mm) in Guildhall Library. March 13, 1830.

78 p 90 St. Edmond the King, Lombard Street. pl.70. 100 × 67mm. ML A 23071/2.

79 St. Antholin, from Watling Street. A. Cruse. pl.71. 100 × 65mm. ML A 23071/3.

80 St. Martin Outwich, Bishopsgate Street. A. Cruse. pl.72. 100 × 148mm. July 17, 1830.

81 p 92 Innholder's Hall, College Street. pl.76. 105 × 63mm. Pencil drawing (98 × 64mm) in GLC.

82 Girdler's Hall, Basinghall Street. J. Greig. pl.77. 103 × 63mm.

83 Dyer's Hall, College Street. J. Greig. pl.78. 105 ×

145mm. Pencil drawing (123 × 164mm) in Guildhall Library. July 24, 1830.

84 p 93 Allhallows, Bread Street. pl.92. 102 × 65mm. Pencil drawing (119 × 77mm) in GLC.

85 St. James's, Garlick Hill. R. Acon. pl.93. 102 × 67mm.

86 St. Mary, Aldermanbury. R. Acon. pl.94. 110 × 148mm. Novr. 20, 1830.

87 p 95 Waterman's Hall, St Mary's Hill. pl.87. 102 × 64mm. *ML* A 23008.

88 Painter Stainer's Hall, Little Trinity Lane. J. Tingle. pl.88. 100 × 64mm. *ML* A 23016.

89 Winchester House, Winchester Street. J. Tingle. pl.89. 108 × 150mm. *ML* A 23059/4. Novr 20, 1830.

90 p 96 St. James's Piccadilly. pl.95. 100 × 65mm.

91 St. Peter le Poor, Broad Street. T. Barber. pl.96. 98 × 67mm. Pencil drawing (94 × 66mm) in Guildhall Library.

92 Northumberland House, Charing Cross. T. Barber. pl.97. 98 × 153mm. Dec 18, 1830.

93 p 98 Serjeants' Inn Hall, Chancery Lane. W.H. Bond. pl.90. 103 × 150mm.

94 Staples Inn Hall, Holborn. W.H. Bond. pl.91. 95 × 150mm. Novr 20, 1830.

95 p 99 The Monument, Fish Street Hill. pl.110. 98 × 68mm. Pencil and sepia wash drawing (145 × 95mm) in Westminster Public Library (St Marylebone).

96 St. Austin, Watling Street. S. Lacey. pl.111. 98 × 68mm. Pencil drawings (113 × 70mm and 98 × 66mm) in Guildhall Library.

97 Sessions House, Clerkenwell Green. S. Lacey. pl.112. 93 × 145mm. *ML* A 23059/2. 1831.

98 p 103 Lyon's Inn Hall. pl.107. 100 × 66mm. Signed sepia wash drawing (100 × 65mm) and a pencil drawing (185 × 140mm) in Westminster Public Library.

99 Barnard's Inn Hall. W. Symms. pl.108. 100 × 68mm. Pencil and sepia wash drawings (131 × 77mm and 104 × 70mm) in GLC.

100 Fleet Street. W. Henshall. pl.109. 95 × 148mm. From St Dunstan's to Temple Bar. 1831.

101 p 105 The Tower of London, from Tower Hill. J. Rogers. pl.116. 90 × 150mm. Pencil drawing (95 × 150mm) in Guildhall Library.

102 Prerogative Will Office, Doctor's Commons. pl.117. 98 × 65mm.

103 Ben Johnson's Head, Devereux Court, Strand. M.J. Starling. pl.118. 98 × 65mm. Pencil drawing (95 × 67mm) in Guildhall Library. 1831.

104 p 106 St. Anne's Soho. pl.123. 92 × 65mm.

105 Fore Street, and Cripplegate Church. J. Tingle. pl.124. 90 × 62mm. *ML* A 16159/8.

106 St. Mary, Whitechapel. J. Tingle. pl.125. 98 × 145mm. *ML* A 16160/3. 1831.

107 p 108 Allhallows Staining, Mark Lane. pl.119. 100 × 68mm. *ML* A 16189/2, dated 1830.

108 St. Martin, Orgar, Martins Lane, Cannon St. J.B.

Allen. pl.120. 100 × 68mm. Pencil drawing (105 × 79mm) in Guildhall Library. *ML* A 16159/4.

109 St. Nicholas, Cole Abbey, Fish Street. pl.121. 96 × 68mm. Pencil drawing (115 × 175mm), dated 20 March 1831, in Westminster Public Library.

110 Allhallows, London Wall. A. Cruse. pl.122. 96 × 65mm. Built by George Dance junior, 1765. Pencil drawing (122 × 86mm) in Guildhall Library. 1831.

111 p 110 Westminster Hall. W. Watkins. pl.128. 103 × 145mm. From the North. Pencil drawing (90 × 145mm), dated 22 April 1831, in Westminster Public Library.

112 St. John's Church, Westminster. W. Watkins. pl.129. 95 × 145mm. St John, Smith Square. 1831.

113 p 111 The Duke of York's School, Chelsea. T. Barber. pl.126. 88 × 145mm. (*Longford* 392)

114 Earl Spencer's House, Green Park. T. Barber. pl.127. 100 × 145mm. 1831.

115 p 112 The Albany, Piccadilly. R. Acon. pl.103. 105 × 145mm.

116 Shaftesbury House, Aldersgate Street. M.S. Barenger. pl.104. 95 × 145mm. March 5, 1831.

117 p 113 Broad Street, Bloomsbury. W. Woolnoth. pl.105. 92 × 148mm. *ML* A 23064/4.

118 Holborn Bridge. W. Woolnoth. pl.106. 102 × 148mm. *ML* A 23064/3. 1831.

119 p 114 St. Mildred, Bread Street. pl.98. 108 × 68mm. Pencil sketch (108 × 68mm) in GLC. *ML* A 23070/3.

120 St. Bartholomew, the Great, West Smithfield. T. Higham. pl.99. 108 × 65mm. *ML* A 23073/3.

121 St. Mary, Lambeth. T. Higham. pl.100. 95 × 145mm. *ML* A 16160/5. Jany 1, 1831.

122 p 115 Westminster Bridge. M.J. Starling. pl.132. 97 × 155mm.

123 London Docks, looking West. M.J. Starling. pl.133. 98 × 155mm. 1831.

124 p 116 Russell Square, and statue of the Duke of Bedford. C. Motram. pl.130. 95 × 148mm. Sepia wash drawing (98 × 147mm) in BM (*Crace* 28.65).

125 Bloomsbury Square, and statue of Fox. C. Motram. pl.131. 98 × 148mm. *ML* A 23061/3. 1831.

126 p 117 Compter, Giltspur Street. R. Acon. pl.136. 100 × 150mm. Designed by George Dance junior, 1787.

127 Newgate, Old Bailey. R. Acon. pl.137. 95 × 148mm. 1831.

128 p 118 City of London Lying-in Hospital. J. Gough. pl.134. 105 × 145mm. Sepia wash drawing (107 × 147mm) in Guildhall Library.

129 Lunatic Hospital, St. Luke's. J. Gough. pl.135. 88 × 145mm. 1831.

130 p 119 Grocers' Hall, Poultry. W. Radclyffe. pl.146. 95 × 152mm. *ML* A 23065/3.

131 Brewers' Hall, Addle Street. W. Radclyffe. pl.147. 100 × 155mm. Pencil drawing (119 ¹× 178mm) in Guildhall Library. *ML* A 23065/2. 1831.

132 p 120 St. Catherine Cree, Leadenhall Street. J.

Gough. pl.155. 100 × 155mm. *ML* A 23063/1.

133 St. Mildred, Poultry. J. Gough. pl.156. 100 × 143mm. nd.

134 p 121 Lock Hospital, Hyde Park Corner. W. Wallis. pl.142. 93 × 145mm. *ML* 71.109/1.

135 Christ's Hospital, Newgate Street. W. Wallis. pl.143. 95 × 145mm. Sepia wash drawing (96 × 146mm) in GLC. 1831.

136 p 122 St. Swithin, London Stone, Cannon Street. J. Tingle. pl.144. 88 × 145mm. Pencil drawing (91 × 146mm) in Guildhall Library. *ML* A 23063/4.

137 St. Michael, Queen Hythe. J. Tingle. pl.145. 115 × 148mm. Pencil drawing (132 × 161mm) in Guildhall Library. *ML* A 23066/1. 1831.

138 p 123 Christ Church, and Part of Christ's Hospital. W. Wilkinson. pl.152. 103 × 153mm. Pencil drawing (116 × 181mm), dated 12 August 1830, in GLC. *ML* A 23066/4.

139 Bow Church, Cheapside. pl.153. 105 × 68mm. *ML* A 16159/6, dated 1831.

140 St. Mary Magdalen, Old Fish St. W. Wilkinson. pl.154. 105 × 68mm. *ML* A 16160/6. nd.

141 p 127 Cooper's Hall, Basinghall St. J. Hinchliff. pl.148. 103 × 145mm. *ML* A 23065/4.

142 Apothecaries' Hall, Pilgrim St./Blackfriars. J. Hinchliff. pl.149. 95 × 145mm. Pencil sketch (114 × 166mm) in Guildhall Library. *ML* A 20369/2. 1831.

143 p 128 St. Sepulchre's, Skinner Street. S. Lacey. pl.150. 105 × 150mm. Pencil sketch (111 × 171mm) in Guildhall Library. *ML* A 16160/4.

144 St. Olave, Tooley Street. Lacey. pl.151. 100 × 155mm. *ML* A 23066/4. nd.

145 p 129 St. Bartholomew's Hospital. A. Cruse. pl.140. 95 × 147mm.

146 Stock Exchange. A. Cruse. pl.141. 100 × 147mm. 1831.

147 p 130 King's Bench Prison/principal entrance. J. Garner. pl.170. 100 × 150mm. *ML* A 23061/1.

148 Sadler's Wells Theatre. J. Garner. pl.171. 98 × 152mm. *ML* A 23056. nd.

149 p 131 West India Import Dock, Poplar. T. Barber. pl.157. 95 × 152mm.

150 St. Katharine's Docks, from the Basin. H. Jorden. pl.158. 92 × 152mm. nd.

151 p 133 St. Clement's Church, Clement's Lane. pl.159. 95 × 65mm. *ML* A 16159/5.

152 St. Bennet Fink, Threadneedle Street. J.C. Armytage. pl.160. 93 × 65mm. *ML* A 16159/1.

153 Ironmongers' Hall, Fenchurch Street. J.C. Armytage. pl.161. 105 × 145mm. *ML* A 23069/4. nd.

154 p 134 Farringdon St. and the Fleet Prison. J. Henshall. pl.162. 90 × 150mm.

155 Foundling Hospital, Guildford Street. J. Henshall. pl.163. 95 × 160mm. *ML* A 23062/3. nd.

156 p 136 St. George's, Hanover Square. pl.174. 105 × 80mm.

157 St. George's Bloomsbury. W. Deeble. pl.175. 105 × 78mm.

158 Interior Quadrangle, Somerset House. W. Deeble. pl.176. 95 × 155mm. nd.

159 p 137 Canonbury Tower, Islington. pl.162. 105 × 65mm.

160 St. Mary Islington. H.W. Bond. pl.63. 105 × 65mm. Sepia wash drawing (105 × 67mm) in Guildhall Library.

161 Old Queens Head,/Islington. H.W. Bond. pl.64. 108 × 147mm. *ML* A 23061/4, dated 1829. 1830.

162 p 140 Boar's Head, Great East Cheap. pl.113. 58 × 74mm. *ML* A 23072/2.

163 Ancient Tablet near Holborn Bridge. J. Tingle. pl.114. 58 × 64mm. *ML* A 23072/3.

164 Talbot Inn, Borough. J. Tingle. pl.115. 100 × 150mm. 1831.

165 p 142 St. Thomas's Hospital and Statue of King Edward VI. T. Higham. pl.168. 90 × 148mm.

166 Guy's Hospital, and Statue of Thomas Guy, the Founder. T. Higham. pl.169. 93 × 148mm. nd.

167 p 146 Burlington House, Piccadilly. T. Cleghorn. pl.172. 90 × 155mm.

168 Melbourne House, and Part of the Old Treasury, Whitehall. C. Mottram. pl.173. 95 × 150mm. Pencil drawing (87 × 148mm) and Sepia wash drawing (98 × 151mm) in GLC. nd.

169 p 147 House of Correction, Coldbath Fields. W. Watkins. pl.138. 95 × 146mm.

170 The Old Bull & Mouth Inn, St. Martins-le-Grand,/ now pulled down. W. Watkins. pl.139. 105 × 150mm. Pencil drawing (102 × 147mm) in Guildhall Library. 1831.

171 p 149 Old London Bridge, from Southwark. W. Radcliffe. pl.34. 90 × 152mm.

172 Tower of London, from the Thames. W. Radcliffe. pl.35. 90 × 145mm. Pencil drawing (92 × 148mm) in Guildhall Library. Jan 30, 1830.

173 p 150 New London Bridge. R. Acon. pl.191. 95 × 162mm.

174 Vintner's Hall, Upper Thames Street. R. Acon. pl.192. 95 × 148mm. *ML* A 22410. nd.

175 p 152 Merchant Tailors' School. pl.164. 100 × 65mm. *ML* A 16159/7.

176 St. Mary at Hill. Tho. H. Shepherd. pl.165. 98 × 65mm. *ML* A 16159/3.

177 St. Michael, Crooked Lane. pl.166. 100 × 65mm.

178 St. Mary Somerset, Upper Thames Street. J.E. Roberts. pl.167. 100 × 65mm. nd.

179 p 154 Allhallows Church, Upper Thames Street. J. Hinchliffe. pl.179. 100 × 145mm. Pencil drawing (95 × 145mm) in GLC. *ML* A 23063/2.

180 St. Botolph, Bishopsgate. J. Hinchliffe. pl.180. 98 × 148mm. nd.

181 p 155 Pantheon, Oxford St. J. Hinchliff. pl.101. 94 × 155mm.

182 Olympic Theatre, Wych St. J. Hinchliff. pl.102. 98 × 155mm. Feby 1831.

183 p 156 Chelsea Old Church, and Sir Han Sloane's Monument. R. Acon. pl.183. 95 × 150mm. Pencil drawing (117 × 170mm) in GLC. (*Longford* 568)

184 Christ Church, Blackfriars. R. Acon. pl.184. 102 × 148mm. nd.

185 p 157 New Church, Sloane St. Chelsea. pl.185. 100 × 68mm. Dedicated to the Holy Trinity, built by James Savage, 1828–30; demolished 1890. (*Longford* 480)

186 New Church, North Audley St. W. Deeble. pl.186. 100 × 65mm. St. Mark, built by J.P. Gandy Deering, 1825–8.

187 New Church, Saffron Hill. pl.187. 110 × 68mm. Dedicated to St Peter, built by Charles Barry, 1830–2.

188 New Church, Little Queen St. Holborn. T.H. Shepherd. pl.188. 110 × 68mm. Dedicated to the Holy Trinity, built by Francis Bedford, 1829–31. *ML* A 23071/1.

189 p 158 New United Service Club House. J. Tingle. pl.177. 90 × 148mm.

190 East Wing of Carlton House Terrace. J. Tingle. pl.178. 90 × 150mm. Two Nash buildings, built 1827–33. *ML* A 23062/4, dated 1830. Jany 22, 1831.

191 p 189 The New Athenaeum, Waterloo Place. J. Tingle. pl.189. 92 × 145mm. Built by Decimus Burton, 1827–30. *ML* A 22125.

192 Arthur's Club House, St James's Street. J. Tingle. pl.190. 102 × 148mm. Built by Thomas Hopper, 1826–7; subsequently the Carlton Club. nd.

---

162 · ALLEN'S PANORAMA OF LONDON [1830]

Thomas Allen was another, though shorter-lived, Edward Brayley. This London guide is a by-product of his indefatigable labours on the topography and history of English counties, mostly published between 1827 and his death in 1833, as described in the note on his major work, *The History and Antiquities of London* (no 152). He first undertook to publish the *Panorama* himself, in an edition which is noticed in the *Monthly Literary Advertiser* for August 1830. Meanwhile the publication of two of his county histories was carried out by Isaac Taylor Hinton, a probable relation of John Hinton who owned the *Universal Magazine of Knowledge and Pleasure* which ran throughout the second half of the

eighteenth century and, at regular intervals, published line-engravings of London views. The new publisher also took on some of the sheets of the *Panorama*, substituted steel-engravings for wood and added a printed title-page, an index and a plan with a list of references. There is an edition in all respects similar to this but with the imprint of Whittaker, Treacher & Co substituted on the title-page. Later the publisher George Virtue, who reissued *The History and Antiquities of London*, also published this guide with the addition of many plates and a folding map.

The Panorama of London, and Visitors' Pocket Companion, in a Tour through the Metropolis. By Thomas Allen, author of the histories of Lambeth, London, York &c &c. Illustrated by numerous engravings by J. Rogers. London: printed for I.T. Hinton, 4 Warwick Square (Printed for Whittaker, Treacher & Co., Ave Maria Lane) (Printed for G. Virtue, 26 Ivy Lane) 1830.

Small octavo, 145–50 × 110mm.   1830

COLLATIONS

(author's ed) Engr title-page; contents (1 leaf); pp 1–318, Panorama.

(Hinton, and Whittaker, Treacher & Co eds) Title-page; contents (1 leaf); refs to plan (2pp); pp 1–318, Panorama; index (6pp).

(Virtue ed) Title-page; contents (1 leaf); list of engravings (1 leaf); refs to plan (1 leaf); pp 1–318, Panorama; index (4pp).

The steel-engraved frontispiece to the author's edition is by W. Watkins after a T.H. Shepherd drawing, as were some of the plates in *Metropolitan Improvements* (no 154) which set the fashion for this medium in topographical book illustration. Thus Hinton substituted for the wood-engravings of the author's edition plates in the newer medium and employed J. Rogers, another Shepherd collaborator, to engrave title-page, frontispiece and all the views. Rogers was also engraver-in-chief for other books by Allen, particularly the *History of the Counties of Surrey and Sussex* (1829–30, no 158) and the *County of York* (1828–31). For these two books the drawings were almost exclusively the work of Nathaniel Whittock and to them the smaller *Panorama* views bear some resemblance, particularly in the Whittock-Rogers handling of skies and water reflections. If Whittock was indeed the *Panorama* artist it seems that he supplied Virtue, who later published his own *Modern Picture of*

London (no 183), with 45 extra views to make his edition the best illustrated London guidebook on the market.

Thus the 18 views in the author's edition were increased to 32, all engraved on steel in Hinton's edition; and in Virtue's to 72, excluding an engraved title-page, frontispiece and two plans. In the lists that follow the Hinton plates are listed in full, with a note of the page number opposite which they are bound in the Virtue edition, abbreviated *V*. The extra Virtue plates are then detailed.

The engravings are worked within a ruled frame but lack credits or publication-lines. Plate-marks, when visible, approximate at 90 × 125mm. Plates are listed by Virtue alone and are unnumbered.

Author's ed

1a (wood-engr title) The/Panorama/of/London,/or,/Visitors' Guide./By T. Allen, Author of Lambeth, London, &c./with numerous engravings./London: Printed for the Booksellers/—Sears & Trapp, Printers, 11 Budge Row, Walbrook. (Gothic-framed views of St Paul's Cathedral, St James's Palace, Colosseum, Guildhall, etc)

2a front. The Entrance to the Metropolis from the New London Bridge. Drawn by T.H. Shepherd. Engraved by W. Watkins. 78 × 140/110 × 150mm. Engraved on steel.

3a p 32 Old House lately standing on Tower Hill. 110 × 180mm. Vignette.

4a p 33 Whitehall. 95 × 120mm. Vignette of Banqueting Hall.

5a p 48 The British Museum. 80 × 115mm.

6a p 49 Church of St Mary Aldermary, Bow Lane. 105 × 80mm.

7a p 96 Aldgate Church. 110 × 90mm.

8a p 97 Ironmongers' Hall. 75 × 100mm.

9a p 112 Clothworkers' Hall. 80 × 100mm.

10a p 113 Duke's Theatre, Lincolns Inn Fields. 110 × 80mm. ie Dorset Gardens.

11a p 176 Fishmongers' Late Hall Upper Thames Street. 80 × 100mm.

12a p 177 The Horse Guards. 90 × 120mm.

13a p 192 Westminster Hall. 90 × 105mm.

14a p 193 Aldgate, pulled down after the Accession of George III. Sears. 95 × 80mm.

15a p 240 Bank of England, as it appeared in 1820. 85 × 105mm.

16a p 241 Front view of Leadenhall. 80 × 100mm.

17a p 256 Shaftesbury House. 60 × 100mm.

18a p 257 Henry the Sevenths Chapel. 115 × 85mm. Exterior.

Hinton, and Whittaker, Treacher & Co eds

1 (engr title) The/Panorama/of/London/or/Visitors Guide/by/T. Allen,/Author of Lambeth, London, &c/with Numerous Engravings/ (vignette) The Grand Entrance, Hyde Park. Seymour del. J. Rogers sc. 120 × 80/145 × 95mm. *V* title.

2 front. London, from Blackfriars Bridge. Drawn by Campion. Engraved by J. Rogers. 100 × 163/130 × 180mm. Previously published as front. to Allen's *History and Antiquities of London*. *V* front.

3 (tm) A Reference Map to the Squares, Public Buildings & Objects of Interest in London. 128 × 208/140 × 220mm. Refs on separate leaf. *V* 1.

4 pl.1 The Monument. 85 × 55mm. *V* 317.

5 pl.2 The Mint. 55 × 82mm. *V* 230.

6 pl.3 The Bank of England. 58 × 82mm. *V* 237. (*Bank of England* 97)

7 pl.4 Drury Lane Theatre. 58 × 80mm. *V* 309.

8 pl.5 National Scotch Church. 80 × 55mm. Regent Square. *V* 188.

9 pl.6 St Brides Church. 83 × 55mm. *V* 174.

10 pl.7 St. Margaret's Church and Westminster Abbey. 55 × 80mm. From N. *V* 124.

11 pl.8 Royal Exchange. 83 × 58mm. As altered 1820. *V* 245.

12 pl.9 Harrow School. 58 × 82mm.

13 pl.10 Covent Garden Theatre. 55 × 82mm. *V* 310.

14 pl.11 West India Docks. 58 × 85mm.

15 pl.12 Custom House. 58 × 82mm. *V* 235.

16 pl.13 Kingston Bridge. 58 × 83mm. *V* 318.

17 pl.14 Commercial Sale Rooms. 57 × 80mm. Mincing Lane, built 1811. *V* 240.

18 pl.15 Greenwich Hill. 62 × 85mm. *V* 270.

19 pl.16 St Paul's School. 57 × 82mm. *V* 283.

20 pl.17 Catholic Chapel/Moorfields. 84 × 57mm. *V* 190.

21 pl.18 Corn Exchange. 57 × 82mm. *V* 240.

22 pl.19 Sessions House Clerkenwell. 57 × 82mm. *V* 268.

23 pl.20 London Institution. 55 × 82mm. *V* 294.

24 pl.21 Westminster Hall. 57 × 83mm. From N. *V* 198.

25 pl.22 St John's Gate Clerkenwell. 57 × 82mm. *V* 318.

26 pl.23 House of Commons. 58 × 80mm. From the river. *V* 201.

27 pl.24 Surrey Theatre. 60 × 83mm. *V* 314.

28 pl.25 The London Docks. 60 × 85mm.

29 pl.26 Bow Church. 82 × 58mm. ie St. Mary le Bow. *V* 173.

30 pl.27 Guild Hall. 58 × 82mm. *V* 247.

31 pl.28 Asylum for Female Orphans Westminster. 55 × 83mm. *V* 290.

32 pl.29 The Colosseum, Regent's Park¹. 58 × 83mm. Opened to the public in 1829. *V* 305.

Virtue ed (views supplementary to those noted above)

33 Allen's New Plan of London from Actual Survey 1830. Engraved on steel by H. Martin, 4 Swinton Street, Grays Inn Road. Published for the Proprietors by C. Tilt, 86 Fleet Street. 395 × 540mm. (*Darlington and Howgego* 322)

34 p 105 St Paul's. 90 × 60mm. From Ludgate Hill.

35 p 191 St James's Palace. 60 × 80mm.

36 p 195 The King's Palace. 60 × 90mm. Buckingham Palace, Nash front.

37 p 200 The House of Lords. 58 × 85mm.

38 p 204 Tower of London. 58 × 82mm. From the river.

39 p 204 The Admiralty. 55 × 85mm.

40 p 228 The New Treasury, Whitehall. 60 × 85mm. Under construction 1824–7.

41 p 228 Somerset House. 60 × 85mm. From the river.

42 p 241 East India House. 58 × 82mm.

43 p 244 Auction Mart. 58 × 82mm.

44 p 249 Mansion House. 90 × 60mm.

45 p 250 New Post Office. 60 × 85mm. Built by Robert Smirke, 1824–9.

46 p 255 St Katherine's Dock House. 58 × 82mm.

47 p 256 London Bridge. 60 × 90mm.

48 p 257 Blackfriars Bridge. 58 × 82mm.

49 p 257 Westminster Bridge. 58 × 82mm.

50 p 258 Waterloo Bridge. 60 × 90mm.

51 p 260 Iron Bridge Southwark. 58 × 90mm.

52 p 263 Newgate. 58 × 85mm.

53 p 270 Covent Garden Market. 58 × 85mm.

54 p 270 Billinsgate 85 × 60mm.

55 p 272 Chelsea Hospital. 58 × 85mm. From the river. (*Longford* 38)

56 p 273 St Bartholomew's Hospital. 58 × 88mm. The courtyard.

57 p 274 St Thomas's Hospital. 58 × 82mm.

58 p 278 London Hospital. 60 × 88mm.

59 p 279 London University. 58 × 85mm. Built by William Wilkins, 1827–8.

60 p 280 The New Hall, Christ's Hospital. 60 × 84mm. Built by John Shaw, 1825–9.

61 p 282 Charter House. 60 × 82mm.

62 p 285 The Foundling Hospital. 60 × 85mm.

63 p 296 New College of Physicians. 58 × 82mm.

64 p 298 British Museum. 58 × 85mm. Montague House.

65 p 304 The Late Duke of York's House. 55 × 80mm. Stafford House, completed by Benjamin Wyatt in 1826, now Lancaster House.

66 p 308 Egyptian Hall. 58 × 82mm. In Piccadilly.

67 p 312 Hay Market Theatre. 58 × 82mm. Staffage includes a hay-wain.

68 p 313 The Adelphi Theatre. 85 × 55mm.

69 p 313 Astley's Amphitheatre. 82 × 55mm. Westminster Bridge Road.

70 p 314 Royal Cobourg Theatre. 58 × 85mm. 'Victoria Theatre, Waterloo Road'.

71 p 314 Sadlers Wells Theatre. 58 × 82mm.

72 p 318 Temple Bar. 55 × 82mm.

73 p 318 The London Stone. 60 × 87mm.

74 p 318 Lambeth Palace. 58 × 82mm. From the river.

75 p 318 Hammersmith Suspension Bridge. 58 × 82mm. Built by Tierney Clark, 1824–7.

76 p 318 Holland House. 58 × 85mm. Kensington.

77 p 318 Caledonian Asylum. 58 × 85mm.

78 p 318 St George's Church. 82 × 55mm. Southwark.

163 · BAYLEY'S HISTORY OF THE TOWER [1830]

The history of this book is given above (no 136). The second edition is noted separately because the slightly abridged text had virtually to be re-illustrated, as the preface explains: 'This volume will be found to contain with little variation the text of the large and original edition, the plates of which are destroyed; but, in order to bring it into a single octavo, it has been necessary to shorten the notes and appendix'. It was published in August 1830 at £1 1s or £1 7s with plates on India paper.

In point of fact, although all the numbered quarto plates were destroyed the publisher managed to salvage three of the smaller, unlisted plates to add to his otherwise slender resources. The illustrations consist of nine anonymous etchings and a frontispiece which is a reduced version of the original engraved on steel. All bear the publication-line 'Published May 15, 1830 by Robert Jennings & William Chaplin, 62 Cheapside.'

The History and Antiquities of the Tower of London, with Memoirs of Royal and Distinguished Persons, deduced from Records, State-papers, and Manuscripts and from other original and authentic sources. By John Bayley Esq. F.R.S., F.S.A., M.R.I.A.,/&c &c/Second Edition. London: Published by Jennings & Chaplin, 62 Cheapside. 1830. London: Printed by A. & R. Spottiswoode, New-Street-Square.

Octavo, 225 × 140mm.   1830

COLLATION Title-page; dedication to John Caley, Keeper of the Records, dated 13 May 1830 (4pp); preface, list of plates (2pp); pp 1–616, History and Antiquities; pp 617–27, index.

1 front. View of the Tower of London from the River Thames. Engraved & Printed by Fenner. 88 × 133/133 × 220mm. Reduced from quarto front.

2 p 102 White Tower. 132 × 102/160 × 125mm.

3 p 107 St. John's Chapel in the White Tower. 128 × 105/165 × 135mm.

4 p 111 Room adjoining the Council Chamber in the White Tower. 103 × 130/125 × 165mm. Plate from quarto ed p 116 with new publication-line.

5 p 115 Interior of St. Peter's Chapel. 118 × 100/165 × 125mm.

6 p 130 Vaulted Room in the Bell Tower. 128 × 105/158 × 115mm. Plate from quarto ed p 134 with new publication-line.

7 p 132 Prison Room in Beauchamp Tower/Drawn 1802. 95 × 140/120 × 165mm. Reduced from pl.XIII in quarto ed.

8 p 175 Inside View of Bowyer's Tower. The room in which (it is said) the Duke of Clarence was/drownded in a but of Malmsey wine. 118 × 100/160 × 115mm.

9 p 257 Gateway of the Bloody Tower. 95 × 135/110 × 155mm. Plate from quarto ed p 262 with new publication-line.

10 p 258 Bloody Tower. 130 × 98/155 × 120mm.

164 · BAYNES'S PARKS OF LONDON [c 1830]

Thomas Mann Baynes, born in 1794, painter and lithographer, exhibited at the Royal Academy and the Old Water Colour Society; it is possible that he was related to James Baynes (1766–1837), also a painter and Royal Academy contributor. His several London views include a panorama of the north bank of the Thames from Westminster to London

Bridge, lithographs of Cheapside (1823), of St Katherine's Dock (1829), and an impression of what John Goldicutt's unexecuted design of a Naval Monument would have looked like in Trafalgar Square (1833). In 1823 four Numbers with 20 lithographs of *Scenery in the Environs of London* were published, a more imposing collection than this set of lithographs, printed in grey, of views of four London parks.

The lithographic area of each measures 155 × 230mm and the credits and publication-lines are uniform: 'Drawn & Lithogd. by T.M. Baynes. Printed by C. Hullmandel. Published by Ackermann & Co, 96 Strand.' They were certainly published later than 1827, when Ackermann left the 'Repository' and returned to his former address at 96 The Strand. No text accompanies them.

The Parks of London. Four Plates. London: Published by Ackermann and Co., 96 Strand.

Oblong quarto, 275 × 370mm.   c 1830

1 St James Park/looking towards the Horse Guards.

2 View in the Regents Park/Subscription Archery Rooms. (Colosseum in the background)

3 Hyde Park/The Grand Entrance from Hyde Park Corner.

4 The Green Park. (Looking towards Westminster Abbey)

165 · BRITTON'S PICTURESQUE ANTIQUITIES OF THE ENGLISH CITIES* [1830]

This volume, issued by Britton as a pendant to his publication of Robson's *Picturesque Views of the English Cities* (no 156), was intended, 'after more than 30 years devotion to the study and illustration of the Architectural Antiquities of England', to be his final topographical work—with the exception of terminating the *Cathedral Antiquities of England* begun in 1814. Actually one of Britton's most valuable books, the *History of Westminster Palace* (no 181), written in collaboration with his friend

Brayley, was yet to come and, as long after as 1842, he wrote an *Architectural Description of Windsor*. Having introduced the word 'picturesque' into both his English cities titles he thought it necessary to redefine it and to remind his readers of its originators, William Gilpin, Uvedale Price and others. He interpreted it both in the sense of 'picturesque' distant drawings of city architecture and of close-up views of buildings which were picturesque because they had reached a state of dilapidation. Yet other illustrators who used the word in their titles, such as Malton (no 72) and Ireland (no 71), were very little concerned with ruins. In his introduction Britton wrote as follows:

The word *Picturesque*, as applied to the Antiquities of English Cities, it is presumed, will be clearly recognised and understood by readers who are familiar with the works of Gilpin, Alison, Price and Knight. It has become not only popular in English literature, but as definite and descriptive as the terms, grand, beautiful, sublime, romantic, and other similar adjectives....

The present volume presents a series of engravings, representing several interesting ancient buildings, many of which are either in ruins, or so much dilapidated, as to entitle them to the appellation of Picturesque Antiquities. ... Thus the volume now submitted to the reader, with the Series of Engravings of 'Picturesque Views' from Drawings by G.F. Robson, it is believed will furnish the English Topographer and Antiquary with pleasing and faithful representations and descriptive memoranda of the prominent features and charcteristics of the Cities of England.

Thus wrote Britton in his introduction—in which he also inveighed against the law of legal deposit, the 'imperious impost of eleven copies', by which he had been compelled to *give* no less than £1,200 worth of his own publications in the execution of which above £40,000 had been expended on artists, stationers, printers, binders, etc and nearly £2,000 more in government duty and taxes. The work came out in Numbers at £1 4s medium quarto and £2 imperial quarto. The complete book was advertised in November 1830, half-bound, at £7 14s and £12. It proved a financial liability to Britton.

Picturesque Antiquities of the English Cities. Illustrated by a Series of Engravings of Antient Buildings, Street Scenery, etc. with Historical and Descriptive Accounts of each Subject. By John Britton, F.S.A., M.R.S.L.... (vignette) Bishop's Bridge, Norwich. D. Hodgson del. S Williams sc. London: Longman, Rees, Orme, Brown and Green, Paternoster Row; the Author, Burton Street; and J. Le Keux, Penton Place, Pentonville. 1830. (verso) G. Whittingham, Chiswick.

Quarto, 330 × 250mm.   1830

COLLATION Half-title; title-page; dedication dated 20 August 1830 (1 leaf); pp vii–x, introduction; pp xi–xii, list of engravings on copper and wood; pp 1–88, Picturesque Antiquities.

The illustrations consist of 60 antiquarian subjects, in ruled frames, worked on copper with such precision of line as to suggest steel-engraving, and 22 engravings on wood printed with the letterpress. They are unnumbered, except in the analytical list at the beginning of the volume, and each has engraved along the top margin: 'For Britton's Picturesque Antiquities of English Cities', and a publication-line reading: 'London: Published (date) by Longmans Co. Paternoster Row'. The young topographical artist William Bartlett, who drew most of the views, was articled to John Britton from the age of 14 and has been engaged on making drawings for the *Cathedral Antiquities*. The chief engraver, John Le Keux, formerly apprenticed to James Basire senior, had worked for most of Britton's publications and was probably the most gifted architectural engraver of his day. The last four plates and two wood-engravings illustrate the London section of the text on pp 85–8.

1 p 85 Old London Bridge/with Coffer Dams, the tower of St Magnus Church &c./To Henry Carrington Bowles Esq. F.S.A. of Myddleton House, a patron of Archaeological researches this plate is inscribed by his friend./J. Britton, W.H. Bartlett del. Figures by W. Harvey. Etched by J. Le Keux.... May 20, 1829 ... Printed by Hayward. 140 × 200/200 × 255mm. pl.57.

1a on p 86 St John's Gate. W.H. Bartlett del. Branston and Wright sculp. Vignetted wood-engraving, 80 × 95mm, in letterpress.

2 p 86 Ruins of Winchester Palace, Southwark/To John Newman Esqr Architect, this Plate is inscribed by his sincere friend,/the Author From a sketch by the late W. Capon. Figures by W Harvey. Etched by Le Keux. ... Decr 1, 1828 ... Printed by Barnett & Son. 123 × 205/215 × 265mm. A similar engraving to *Londina Illustrata* (no 131), item 47, both perhaps engraved from the same drawing by William Capon. pl.58.

3 p 87 Ruins of Ely Palace & Chapel, Holborn, London. From a sketch by the late J. Carter F.S.A. Figures by W. Harvey. Etched by J. Le Keux.... Decr 1, 1828 ... Printed by Barnett & Son. 138 × 200/205 × 265mm. cf with John Carter's *Views of Ancient Buildings* (no 64), item 3. pl.59.

4 p 87 Fishmongers Hall—London./To John Sell Cotman Esq. Author of several interesting works on the Archaeological Antiquities of Norfolk, Normandy

&c. this plate is inscribed in testimony of many years of friendship by J. Britton. W.H. Bartlett del. Engraved by Rob. Roberts. Published May 1, 1829 by J. Britton, Burton Street. Printed by Barnett & Son. 150 × 200/210 × 263mm. pl.60.

4a on p 88 Ruins of St James's Church Clerkenwell. J. Carter del. 1788. Branston & Wright sculp. Vignetted wood-engraving, 55 × 110mm, in letterpress.

166 · DENHAM'S ST DUNSTAN IN THE WEST [c 1830]

In July 1832 David Roberts made a drawing of the tower of John Shaw's new church of St Dunstan, Fleet Street as it rose from the remains of the medieval aisles. This was engraved and published in George Cooke's *Views in London* (no 149). In 1838 John Britton published a view of the completed building, drawn by Benjamin Ferrey and engraved by T.T. Bury, in his *Illustrations of the Public Buildings* (no 146). This book by the Rev J.F. Denham is illustrated from drawings by the same T.T. Bury, made shortly before the demolition of the old church to preserve the homely but much loved lineaments of a landmark whose crenellated parapet, extruded clock and aedicule containing automated statuary had presided for centuries over the bustle of Fleet Street.

(wrapper title) Views Exhibiting the Exterior & Interior and Principal Monuments of the very Ancient and Remarkable Church of St. Dunstan in the West in the City of London, To which is added an Historical Account of the Church by the Revd. J.F. Denham, B.A. of St. John's College, Cambridge, Curate of St. Dunstan in the West and Sunday Evening Lecturer of St. Bride's, Fleet Street. Drawn on Stone by F.(sic)T. Bury, Lithog. by Engelmann & Co. London. Published by F. Waller, 49, Fleet Street & A. Northcroft, 97, Chancery Lane.

Folio, 410 × 325mm.   nd

COLLATION Engr title-page; contents (1 leaf); pp 1–24, Historical Account; pp 25–33, Monumental Inscriptions.

The illustrations are lithographs printed in grey monochrome on India paper. T.T. Bury, their draughtsman, was articled to Augustus Pugin senior in 1824 and worked in his office with a group of budding architectural and topographical draughtsmen until he set up his own architectural practice in Gerrard Street, Soho in 1830. He had learned to reproduce architectural drawings by means of the engraved line and lithography, notably Pugin's and Owen Jones's, and had become very skilful at applying colour to building designs. The drawings for this commemorative folio must have been his earliest commission; he was still under age when they were executed. At about the same time Ackermann published his coloured views on the Liverpool and Manchester Railway (1831). Besides contributing to Britton and Pugin's *Illustrations of the Public Buildings* he published works of his own on architectural history, assisted Pugin junior, who was only six months younger than him, with interior designs for the new Houses of Parliament, built numerous churches, schools and public buildings, and eventually was elected a vice-president of the Institute of British Architects. William Gauci, who did the lithography, was the younger son in a family of artists and lithographers and had previously (in 1828) published a view on stone of Buckingham Palace showing John Nash's alterations for George IV (*Crace* 13.24).

1 (lithographic title) Views/Exhibiting/The Exterior & Interior & Principal Monuments/of the very Ancient and Remarkable Church of/St Dunstan in the West,/in the City of London/To which is added an Historical Account of the Church by/The Revd. J.F. Denham, B.A./of St John's College, Cambridge,/ Curate of St Dunstan in the West/and Sunday Evening Lecturer of St Bride's, Fleet Street, &c.(mounted lithographic vignette of Temple Bar, 105 × 210mm) London: Published by F. Waller, 49 Fleet Street, & A. Northcroft, 97 Chancery Lane/Printed by Engelmann, Graf, Coindet & Co. 410 × 325mm.

2 Church of St. Dunstan in the West. On stone by W. Gauci from original drawing by T.T. Bury. Printed by Engelmann, Graf, Coindet & Co. 203 × 248/240 × 270mm.

3 Church of St. Dunstan in the West,/the View looking East shewing the Altar. On stone by W. Gauci from original drawing by T.T. Bury. Printed by Engelmann, Graf, Coindet & Co. 240 × 205/280 × 240mm.

4 Church of St. Dunstan in the West,/the View looking West shewing the Organ. On stone by W. Gauci from original drawing by T.T. Bury. Printed by Engelmann, Graf, Coindet & Co. 250 × 208/290 × 235mm.

5 Monuments and Tablets/in St. Dunstan's Church.

Drawn by T.T. Bury., on Stone by W. Gauci. Printed by Engelmann & Co. 280 × 245/315 × 280mm.

6 Monuments and Tablets/from St. Dunstan's Church. Drawn by T.T. Bury., on Stone by W. Gauci. Printed by Engelmann & Co. 288 × 242/330 × 270mm.

167 · LEIGH'S NEW PICTURE OF LONDON [1830,etc]

The earlier history of this guidebook is to be found under the *New Picture* for 1818 (no 26). In the edition published in 1830, the year before he committed suicide, Leigh advertised another London topographical work, an aquatint panorama:

Just published, price £1. 1s. plain or £2. 16s. beautifully coloured, and folded up in a portable form, The Panorama of the Thames, from London to Richmond. The work is upwards of 60 feet in length and on a scale of sufficient extent to exhibit every building on either shore of the river. It is accompanied by Descriptive Notices of the most Remarkable Places and preceded by a General View of London, 5 feet, 5 inches in length.

As well as this aquatint by M. Clark he published a panoramic view of Richmond.

But it was with steel-engravings that the 1830 *New Picture* was illustrated, the miniature views on copper having been discarded after long service, and they were thus prefaced by Leigh: 'Numerous indeed, are the public buildings in London which occupy a distinguished rank for architectural design and masterly execution, and the present work claims some merit for offering views of many of them, which might otherwise be unknown even to a constant resident in the metropolis'. They were slightly larger than their predecessors, two or three to a plate, but generally the same subjects were represented with the addition of some 20 views of buildings put up in the previous decade.

The price remained steady throughout the 1830s and the purchaser was still given the option of having the text plain or illustrated, with or without Busby's 'Costumes' or Rowlandson's brilliant 'Characteristic Sketches'.

The plates are listed as arranged in the 1830

edition, with references to their positions in 1834 and 1839, and later additions appearing at the end.

Leigh's New Picture of London: or, a view of the political, religious, medical, literary, municipal, commercial, and moral state of the British Metropolis. Presenting a brief and luminous guide to the stranger, on all subjects connected with General Information, business, or amusement. To which are subjoined a Description of the Environs and a Plan for Viewing London in eight days. New (Ninth) edition, carefully revised. London: Printed for Samuel Leigh, 18 Strand and Baldwin and Cradock, Paternoster Row, MDCCCXXX. (Printed for Leigh and Son, 421 Strand;/and Baldwin and Cradock, Paternoster Row, MDCCCXXXIV.) (London: Leigh and Co., 421 Strand, MDCCCXXXIX.)

With Plan of London, and Map of the Environs 6s.
Do   Do and 108 views (1834 and 1839: '111 views')   9s.
Do   Do and 24 Costumes   12s.
Do   Do   and Rowlandson's Do 15s.

Duodecimo, 140 × 90mm.   1830, 1834, 1839

COLLATIONS

(1830) Title-page; pp iii–vi, preface; pp vii–viii, contents; pp 1–399, New Picture of London; pp 400–23, index; pp 1–36, index to plan.

(1834) Title-page; pp iii–iv, preface; pp v–viii, contents, errata; pp 1–411, New Picture of London; pp 412–36, index; pp 437–74, index to plan, etc.

(1839) Title-page; pp iii–iv, preface; pp v–vii, contents; pp 1–457, New Picture of London; pp 458–81, index; pp 482–507, index to plan.

1 front. King's Palace St James's Park. 65 × 115mm. Birds-eye view of Buckingham Palace, with marble triumphal arch as designed in 1829, surmounted by Chantrey's equestrian statue of George IV which eventually was erected in Trafalgar Square. Not used after 1830 ed.

2 p 57 Mercer's Hall – Ironmongers Hall – Newgate. 50 × 28,50 × 35,50 × 65mm. 1834 ed p 57,1839 ed p 74.

3 p 74 Giltspur Street Compter – Cold Bath Fields Prison – Penitentiary Millbank. Each 33 × 57mm. 1834 ed p 72, 1839 ed p 36.

4 p 116 St Paul's Cathedral. 95 × 65mm. W. front and Ludgate Hill. 1834 ed p 116, 1839 ed p 231.

5 p 124 Henry VIIths Chapel – Westminster Abbey. 47 × 62,63 × 63mm. E. end and W. front. 1834 ed p 124, 1839 ed p 130.

6 p 133 St Martin in the Fields – St Luke Chelsea. 50 × 55,55 × 55mm. W. front of St Martin's; James Savage's St Luke's consecrated October 1824. 1834 ed p 133, 1839 ed p 141. (*Longford* 470)

7 p 136 St George Hanover Sqre – St Mary le Strand – St

Clement Danes – St George Bloomsbury. 50 × 33,50 × 33,50 × 28,50 × 38mm. 1834 ed p 136, 1839 ed p 142.

8 p 141 Marylebone New Church – Bow Church/Cheapside – St Brides Fleet Street. 48 × 40,48 × 23,62 × 65mm. St Bride's with its Avenue. 1834 ed p 139, 1839 ed p 146.

9 p 142 Christ Church/Spitalfields – St Lawrence – St Leonard Shoreditch – St Paul Covent Garden. 50 × 23,50 × 40,50 × 30,50 × 33mm. St Lawrence Jewry. 1834 ed p 142, 1839 ed p 150.

10 p 146 Stepney Old Church – St Sepulchres – St Andrew, Holborn. 38 × 53,33 × 53,33 × 53mm. 1834 ed p 145, 1839 ed p 152.

11 p 150 Christ Church – Hanover Chapel – All Souls. 53 × 30,53 × 33,53 × 65mm. Christ Church, Cosway Street built by P. Hardwick, 1825; Hanover Chapel, Regent Street built by C.R. Cockerell, consecrated June 1825; Nash's All Souls, Langham Place consecrated 1824. 1834 ed p 141, 1839 ed p 138.

12 p 151 St Pancras New Church – St Philip's Chapel, Regent Street. 60 × 65, 47 × 65mm. 1834 ed p 146, 1839 ed p 153.

13 p 154 Surry Chapel – Tabernacle. Each 50 × 60mm. Not repeated.

14 p 157 St James's Palace – Gower or York House. 53 × 65,50 × 65mm. York House, now Lancaster House, built by Benjamin Wyatt in Green Park, 1825–6, for the Duke of York on whose death in 1827 it was acquired by Lord Gower, later 1st Duke of Sutherland. 1834 ed p 159, 1839 ed p 168.

15 p 160 Kensington Palace – Spencer House – Lambeth Palace. 33 × 63,35 × 63, 33 × 63mm. 1834 ed p 164, 1839 ed p 172.

16 p 166 Hanover Terrace, Regent's Park – St Catherine's Hospital, Regent's Park – London University. 35 × 65,35 × 63,35 × 65mm. Hanover Terrace built by J.M. Aitkens, 1822–3; St Catherine's Hospital built by Ambrose Poynter, 1826; London University built by William Wilkins, 1827–8. In 1834 ed p 281 and 1839 ed p 300 the central view replaced by 'New English Opera House' (37 × 64mm). ie the Lyceum Theatre designed by S. Beazley; destroyed by fire in February 1830, rebuilt 1831–4.

17 p 170 Westminster Hall – House of Lords and Commons. 53 × 65,50 × 65mm. 1834 ed p 174, 1839 ed p 182.

18 p 174 The Tower from Thames Street. 58 × 100mm. 1834 ed p 177, 1839 ed p 6.

19 p 178 The Monument – The Mint. 73 × 50,33 × 65mm. 1834 ed p 182, 1839 ed p 192.

20 p 182 Mansion House – East India House – The Bank. 37 × 63,35 × 63, 33 × 63mm. 1834 ed p 186, 1839 ed p 194. (*Bank of England* 103)

21 p 185 Royal Exchange – Auction Mart – Trinity House. 38 × 63, 35 × 63, 33 × 63mm. 1834 ed p 189, 1839 ed p 199.

22 p 190 Custom House – New Post Office – Guildhall. Each 35 × 63mm. Sir Robert Smirke's General Post Office, completed 1829. 1834 ed p 193, 1839 ed p 202.

23 p 196 Excise Office – Somerset House Strand – Somerset House from the Thames – Adelphi Terrace. 43 × 31,43 × 31, 30 × 63,30 × 63mm. 1834 ed p 194, 1839 ed p 210.

24 p 198 Temple Bar – Charing Cross & Cockspur Street – The Quadrant, Regents Street. 41 × 61,35 × 61,32 × 61mm. 1834 ed p 199.

25 p 199 Council Office, Whitehall – Horse Guards from the Park – Admiralty. 33 × 60,33 × 60,40 × 60mm. Soane's Privy Council, completed 1827.

26 p 200 Sessions House, Old Bailey – Sessions House/Clerkenwell – St Bartholomews Hospl – City of London/Lying in Hospital – Asylum for female orphans. 28 × 38,28 × 28, 43 × 28, 40 × 35, 33 × 65mm. Orphan asylum rebuilt 1825. 1834 ed p 204, 1839 ed p 46.

27 p 204 Whitehall – Richmond Terrace – Northumberland House. 37 × 62, 35 × 62, 37 × 62mm. Richmond Terrace built by T. Chawner, 1822–5. 1834 ed p 208, 1839 ed p 213.

28 p 216 New London Bridge – Southwark Bridge – Blackfriars Bridge. 20 × 105,20 × 105,18 × 105mm. Rennie's London Bridge, opened August 1831. 1834 ed p 209, 1839 ed p 229.

29 p 218 Waterloo Bridge – Westminster Bridge – Vauxhall Bridge. 20 × 105,20 × 105,18 × 105mm. 1834 ed p 219, 1839 ed p 232.

30 p 222 (tm) Panorama of remarkable objects in London. Engraved for Leigh's New Picture of London by Sidy Hall. 210 × 270mm. 1834 ed p 331. (*Darlington and Howgego* 300)

31 p 254 Greenwich Hospital – Chelsea Hospital. 30 × 115,32 × 115mm. River views. 1834 ed p 235, 1839 ed p 249. (*Longford* 43)

32 p 286 St Paul's School. – British Museum – Surgeon's Hall. 34 × 65, 35 × 65, 37 × 65mm. St Paul's School 'pulled down in 1822 and re-erected from designs by Mr. G. Smith'. 1834 ed p 228, 1839 ed p 283.

33 p 305 Union Club House & College of Physicians – University Club House &c Pall Mall East – London Institution. Each 35 × 65mm. The Club and College built by Robert Smirke, 1823; University Club built by W. Wilkins, opened February 1826. 1834 ed p 285, 1839 ed p 344.

34 p 310 Egyptian Hall – British Gallery – Military Asylum – Foundling Hospital. 43 × 40,25 × 40,33 × 65,32 × 65mm. The Royal Military Asylum built at Chelsea, 1801–3. 1834 ed p 231, 1839 ed p 320. (*Longford* 390)

35 p 315 Colosseum – Burlington Arcade – Thames

Tunnel. 32 × 62, 35 × 62, 42 × 62mm. Colosseum built by D. Burton, 1823–7; excavations for Brunel's Thames Tunnel started 1825. 1834 ed p 299, 1839 ed p 322.

36 p 343 Opera House – Covent Garden Theatre – Coburg Theatre. 42 × 63, 32 × 63, 32 × 63mm. 1834 ed p 309, 1839 ed p 335; in the latter 'Coburg Theatre' caption altered to 'Victoria Theatre'.

37 p 344 Drury Lane Theatre – Haymarket Theatre. Each 55 × 65mm. 1834 ed p 308, 1839 ed p 332.

38 p 352 Deaf & Dumb Asylum – New Bethlehem – St Luke's Hospital. 33 × 65, 33 × 65, 43 × 65mm. 1834 ed p 235, 1839 ed p 249.

39 p 360 (tm) Leigh's New Map of the Environs of London. Drawn & Engraved by Sidy Hall, 14 Bury St Bloomsbury. London, Published by Samuel Leigh, 18 Strand. 220 × 265/240 × 290mm. 1834 ed p 373; 'Published by M.A. Leigh, 422 Strand.' (*Darlington and Howgego* 278)

40 p 368 Hampton Court – Eton College – Claremont. Each 35 × 63mm. Claremont, at Esher, built by Lancelot Brown for Lord Clive and from 1816 the residence of George IV's daughter Charlotte until her death in childbirth in 1817; her disconsolate husband, Prince Leopold, lived there until 1831 when he was elected King of the Belgians and it afterwards became a favourite retreat of Queen Victoria. 1834 ed p 386, 1839 ed p 417.

41 p 379 The Maze. 70 × 123mm. Hampton Court, a plan. 1834 ed p 390, 1839 ed p 423.

42 p 391 Windsor Castle – Windsor Cottage – Holland House. Each 35 × 63mm. The view of George IV's 'cottage orné' in Windsor Great Park, expensively enlarged by Nash as the Royal Lodge, is replaced in 1834 and 1839 eds p 405 by 'New Cemetery Harrow Road' (37 × 63mm).

43 p 423 (tm) Leigh's New Plan of London. Engraved by Sidy Hall. Published by Samuel Leigh, 18 Strand. 440 × 590/490 × 600mm. 1834 ed p 474: 'London, Published by M.A. Leigh, 421 Strand.' (Leigh's widow, Mary Ann); 1839 ed p 507: 'Pubd by Leigh & Son, 421 Strand.' (*Darlington and Howgego* 310)

Additional plates (1834 and 1839)

44 front. Royal Palace/St James's Park. 65 × 120mm. Buckingham Palace; substituted for the unexecuted design of Marble Arch illustrated in item 1 above.

45 p 110 Hungerford Market/River Front – Strand Front. Each 50 × 62mm. Charles Fowler's new building of 1831–3. 1839 ed p 114.

46 p 163 King's Palace, as seen from the garden. – Lambeth Palace, Garden Front. 37 × 127, 34 × 110mm. 1839 ed p 173.

168 · MARTIN'S VIEWS OF LONDON BRIDGE [c 1830]

By far the best single graphic record of the transition period between the completion of the new London Bridge in 1831 and the demolition of the old are Edward Cooke's etchings, *Old and New London Bridges* (no 172). The demise of this battered Gothic monument, so rich in historical association, was a matter of great public interest. It gave rise to the publication of a host of prints, some in panoramic form, such as the five-foot long lithograpic 'View of the Northern Approach to London Bridge' by George Scharf junior, who was commissioned by the City's Bridge Committee to record the progress of the works, and some in sets, such as 'Four Picturesque Sketches of Old London Bridge during its demolition in 1831, 32. From Nature on Stone by T. Lindsay. Printed by C. Hullmandel. London, Published by R. Ackermann 96 Strand. Price 1/6 (each) Plain.' (Nos 1–2, 172 × 245mm; nos 3–4, 182 × 275mm). These were all really exercises in pictorial journalism of the sort that later in the century found a home in the pages of the *Illustrated London News*.

The lithographer R. Martin however set out to compile a sumptuous set of prints which would illustrate the bridge from medieval times until it was finally supplanted by Rennie's new structure—an ideal historical memento for presentation to those who had given up their time to forwarding the project and to the magnates concerned with its official opening. They are usually to be found dispersed in topographical collections but a set with an 1830 Whatman watermark, recorded in the Abbey Library (230), retains wrappers for two of its Parts lettered thus: 'Part I (II)/Four Views of London Bridge,/at different periods,/To be continued. R. Martin, Lithog. 124 High Holborn.' Of the continuation promised the Abbey cataloguer supposes that it is the set (Abbey 223) of four more lithographs with wrappers labelled: 'A View of Old London Bridge, 1823,/after the removal of the water works,/from a drawing by Major G. Yates./And Three Views of New London Bridge,/from drawings by Sir John Rennie,/Architect for the Bridge.'

In six of the historical views Martin has very skilfully translated line-engraving into lithographic terms. The drawings on which items 8 and 9 are based are by a painter described variously as Major George Yates and Gideon Yates, a hardworking topographical artist who specialized in large and detailed water-colours of Thames bridges, of which he painted many between 1823 and 1837; there are ten in the Crace Collection alone. The elevations, plans and sections are given official status by the addition of Sir John Rennie's signature in facsimile; they are numbered (tl) I, II and III.

No text was issued with the Parts. Publication-lines of the first eight read: 'R. Martin, lithogr. 124, High Holborn', and of the remaining four: 'R. Martin & Co. Lithog. 26 Long Acre (74 St Martins Lane)'.

PART 1

1 A View of the East Side of London Bridge, with the Chapel of Saint Thomas in the Reign of King Henry VII, circa 1500, from an illumination in a Manuscript in the British Museum, Royal M.S.S. 16.F.ii.XV. 295 × 510mm.

2 A View of the East Side of London Bridge from South to North, in the Reign of Queen Elizabeth, circa 1600, from an engraving by John Norden. 300 × 510mm.

3 A View of London Bridge in the Year 1616, from an Engraving by John Vischer. 300 × 510mm.

4 A View of London Bridge in the Year 1647, from an Engraving by Hollar. 300 × 510mm. (*Hind* 16)

PART 2

5 A View of the West Side of London Bridge in the year 1710, from an Engraving by Sutton Nicholls. 295 × 503mm. Copied from *Nouveau Théâtre de la Grande Bretagne* (no 22), item 57.

6 A View of the West Side of London Bridge, with the Water Works, in the Year 1749, from an Engraving by S. and N. Buck. 298 × 505mm. Copied from no 54, item 10.

7 A View of London Bridge, taken from Saint Olave's Stairs, in the Year 1751, from an Engraving by John Boydell. 300 × 510mm. Copied from Boydell's *Collection of Views* (no 47), item 13.

8 A View of the East Side of London Bridge, in the year 1827, from a Drawing by Major G. Yates. 300 × 510mm. Water-colour in BM (*Crace* 7.33).

PART 3

9 A View of the West Side of London Bridge, in the Year 1823, after the removal of the Water Works, from a Drawing by Major G. Yates. 300 × 505mm.

10 New London Bridge./First stone laid by the Right Honble John Garratt, Lord Mayor, on the 15th of June 1825. 335 × 530mm. 'No. I'. Elevation and plan, signed by John Rennie.

11 New London Bridge. 340 × 555mm. 'No. II'. Longitudinal section, transverse section, plan, signed by John Rennie.

12 New London Bridge. 345 × 575mm. 'No. III'. Elevations and plan of new and old bridge, signed by John Rennie.

169 · PUBLIC BUILDINGS OF WESTMINSTER [1831]

When the publisher John Harris succeeded to the business of the famous children's book publisher Francis Newbery he revived a two-volume child's guide, the *Curiosities of London* (nos 49, 91). Twenty five years later, in his 'Little Library', an attractive series of miniature squat octavos backed in red leather, he published another pair of illustrated volumes, each at 3s 6d, covering the same ground: the first on Westminster and the second on the City of London, appearing respectively in May and October 1831. Both are written by the same author, anonymously, though a reference on the title-page of the first to the 'Wars of the Jews', which has an introduction signed 'Aunt Jane', points the authorship to a lady named Christina Jane Johnstone, according to Halkett and Laing.

The Westminster volume contains a dozen plates and all are credited 'Sands sc.' without the artist's name; the City volume contains a similar number but most have the additional credit 'T.H. Shepherd del.' It seems likely that both sets were engraved on steel from Shepherd's drawings. The engraver was, no doubt, Robert Sands who specialized in architectural delineations and engraved for two Britton books, the *Beauties of England and Wales* (no 104) and *Illustrations of the Public Buildings* (no 145), and for Brayley and Neale's *Westminster Abbey* (no 123).

The Public Buildings of Westminster described. With twelve engravings. By the author of 'Wars of the Jews' &c.

London: John Harris, corner of St. Paul's Church-Yard. 1831.

Small octavo, 130 × 115mm.   1831

COLLATION   Title-page; pp iii–iv, contents; pp 1–210, Public Buildings; pp 211–20, index.

The illustrations, neatly executed steel-engravings within a ruled frame and with captions in copperplate script, are certainly an advance on those of Harris's previous publication. They are unnumbered and unlisted.

The Westminster plates, in addition to their one credit, bear the publication-line 'Pubd. May 1831, by J. Harris, St. Pauls Church Yard London.'

1 front. London University. 72 × 90mm. Wilkins's Bloomsbury building of 1827–8.

2 p 8 Westminster Abbey. 72 × 88mm. From N.E.

3 p 49 Westminster Hall. 72 × 90mm. From N.

4 p 64 House of Lords & Commons. 72 × 90mm. From S.

5 p 80 The Horse Guards. 72 × 90mm. Whitehall.

6 p 82 The Treasury. 72 × 90mm. Whitehall side.

7 p 84 Admiralty. 72 × 90mm. Whitehall side.

8 p 103 New Palace. 70 × 90mm. Buckingham Palace, Nash's front.

9 p 105 Hyde Park Corner. 72 × 88mm. Towards Piccadilly.

10 p 129 Waterloo Bridge. 70 × 88mm. From W.

11 p 136 Somerset House. 72 × 90mm. Strand front.

12 p 167 British Museum. 72 × 90mm. Montague House from Great Russell Street.

---

170 · PUBLIC BUILDINGS OF THE CITY OF LONDON [1831]

The Second volume of John Harris's child's guide to London is similar in most respects to the first, on Westminster (no 169), except that the publication-line is dated in October and that eight of the plates bear, besides the credit of Sands the engraver, the name of the artist, T.H. Shepherd. All the views, except perhaps that of the Excise Office, are of traditional subjects although the actual London

Bridge depicted had only been formally opened two months previously.

In 1838, for the new reign, Harris published a consolidated edition of the 24 London and Westminster plates, retaining their original 1831 publication-lines. Its title-page gives as the author of the text Frederic Shoberl, a prolific journalist and writer on topographical and genealogical subjects who had edited for Ackermann the *Repository of Arts, The World in Miniature* and some of his illustrated annuals:

The Public Buildings of London & Westminster. Described by F. Shoberl. With engravings. London, John Harris, St Paul's Church Yard, 1838.

Sextodecimo, 130 × 100mm.   1838

COLLATION   Title-page; pp v–vi, contents; half-title (1 leaf); pp 1–104, Public Buildings of London; half-title (1 leaf); pp 1–216, Public Buildings of Westminster.

The Public Buildings of the City of London described with twelve engravings. By the author of 'Public Buildings of Westminster Described'. London: John Harris, corner of St. Paul's Church Yard. 1831. (verso) Printed by Samuel Bentley, Dorset Street, Fleet-Street.

Small octavo, 130 × 115mm.   1831

COLLATION   Title-page; contents (1 leaf); pp 1–246, Public Buildings; pp 247–59, index.

The dozen unlisted, unnumbered plates all carry the credit 'Sands sc.' or 'sculp.' and the publication-line 'Pubd. (London, Published) Octr 1831 by J. Harris, St. Pauls Church Yard (London)'.

1 front. Monument. T.H. Shepherd del. 88 × 72mm.

2 p 10 St. Pauls. T.H. Shepherd del. 86 × 68mm. From Ludgate Hill.

3 p 63 New Post Office. 72 × 90mm. St. Martin's-le-Grand, completed 1829.

4 p 113 Mansion House. T.H. Shepherd del. 72 × 90mm.

5 p 116 Guildhall. T.H. Shepherd del. 88 × 72mm.

6 p 125 Royal Exchange. T.H. Shepherd del. 88 × 70mm.

7 p 134 Bank of England. 75 × 90mm. S. front, with St Bartholomew by the Exchange. (*Bank of England* 91)

8 p 169 Tower. T.H. Shepherd del. 72 × 88mm. From Tower Hill.

9 p 220 New Mint. 75 × 90mm. The Royal Mint, completed in 1809 on Tower Hill.

10 p 224 Custom House. T.H. Shepherd del. 74 × 88mm.

11 p 228 Excise Office. 73 × 90mm.

12 p 230 New London Bridge. T.H. Shepherd del. 68 × 88mm. From the W., Rennie's bridge, opened August 1831.

171 · TAYLOR'S A MONTH IN LONDON [1832]

Jefferys Taylor, the author of this book, was the youngest son of Isaac Taylor junior, a celebrated engraver of architecture and a book illustrator who became a nonconformist pastor and engendered 11 children of whom six survived. In passing on to them a selection of his own knowledge of a wide variety of subjects he devised a number of instructive booklets simply illustrated by himself which, in due course, he published. Two of his daughters, Anne and Jane, became celebrated for their writings for the young of an improving, though somewhat less severe, character. His wife also was a writer on moral topics and a novelist. Jefferys, accordingly, simply filled a vacancy in what had become a family industry.

In the course of this book, which addresses itself much less pompously and more directly to the youthful reader than most of the schoolmasterly tracts on London history for children then in circulation, he introduces observations on various mechanical and technical processes, including those of line-engraving, wood-engraving and lithography, skills familiar in the Taylor home. It is not surprising to find that the six small plates on steel with which it is illustrated are the work of a competent artist-engraver, H.S. Melville. They were available in two varieties, plain or very carefully colour-washed, and bound in boards and quarter-leather or publisher's cloth-gilt, the former being advertised in September 1832, price 5s.

A Month in London; or, some of its Modern Wonders Described. By Jefferys Taylor, author of 'The Little Historian', 'Esop in Rhyme', 'The Forest' &c. London: Harvey and Darton, Gracechurch Street, 1832.

Duodecimo, 175 × 105mm.   1832

COLLATION Title-page; pp 1–182, A Month in London.

1 (engr title) A Month/in/London. (vignette) Zoological Gardens. Melville./London:/Printed for Harvey & Darton/Gracechurch Street. 80 × 80mm.

2 front. Colosseum. Melville. 115 × 80mm. 'Page 85'. Interior.

3 p 31 St. Catherine's Docks. Melville. 78 × 115mm. 'page 31'.

4 p 89 The Zoological Gardens. Melville. 75 × 115mm. 'page 89'.

5 p 120 Covent Garden Market. Melville. 78 × 115mm. 'page 120'.

6 p 135 Opening of New London Bridge/ Augt 1st 1831. Melville. 76 × 115mm. 'page 136'.

172 · COOKE'S OLD AND NEW LONDON BRIDGES [1833]

Edward William Cooke, the son and nephew of two outstandingly able engravers, George and William Cooke, was born in 1811, the year in which William's engravings of Thames scenery were first published in book form (no 106). Artistically precocious, at the age of nine he was already employed in making wood-engravings at a Hackney nursery for Loudon's *Encyclopaedia of Plants*. Augustus Pugin, to whom he was sent by his father for lessons in perspective, soon concluded that the boy had been so well grounded at home that there was little left to teach him. He was much influenced however by Clarkson Stanfield, for whom he copied drawings of boats and marine accessories, and he paid frequent visits to the south coast where he eagerly absorbed the details of ship and boat construction. In the course of his life he produced many hundreds of characteristic pencil sketches of frigates, sloops, colliers, barges and fishing smacks and lovingly delineated rigging, tackle, capstans, anchors and fishing gear of all sorts, as may be seen in the Sheepshanks Gift at the Victoria and Albert Museum. His first complete work, *Shipping and Craft*, was published in 1827 and he etched two sets of plates, 'Coast Sketches' and 'The British Coast', before turning to oils and the paintings which eventually won him respect in the art world, the full membership of the Royal Academy and a fellowship of the Royal Society.

Here we are concerned with one of his persistent interests between the ages of 14 and 22: from 1825, when work on Rennie's new London Bridge was commenced, to 1833, two years after its official opening. He was unceasingly fascinated by all the details of the demolition of a bridge of almost geological antiquity and the simultaneous erection on a neighbouring site of a replacement, built on modern engineering principles. Continually on site, he made innumerable dated drawings of all the processes from several angles, a record as accurate and probing as one made by photography but with a sense of occasion which no camera could have transmitted so vividly. A sequel, 'London Bridges', was announced but not carried out.

The circumstances of the publication of this collection, linking it with their nearly contemporaneous *Views in London and its Vicinity* (no 149), is explained in their opening address, by father and son:

The origin was purely incidental. In arranging materials for the illustrations of 'London and its Vicinity', the old Bridge of the metropolis could not be overlooked... The vast preparations rapidly making for the erection of the grand modern structure destined to supersede the ancient edifice, also demanded attention; and in watching the progress of this gigantic undertaking, the expediency of a separate and distinct publication, forming a satisfactory memorial of the two Bridges, gradually but naturally suggested itself. The numerous and highly interesting points of view which the erection of the New Bridge, the demolition of the Old, and the fine combination of both, afforded, impressed us with the deep conviction of the value and interest of such a work; and from upwards of forty drawings (all made on the spot,) the present twelve were selected, as being the most interesting and various.

George Cooke
Edward W. Cooke. Terrace, Barnes April 1833.

Views of the Old and New London Bridges. Drawn and Etched by Edward William Cooke. With Scientific and Historical Notices of the Two Bridges; practical observations on the tides of the river Thames; and a Concise Essay on Bridges, from the Earliest Period; &c. &c. Derived from information contributed exclusively for this work, by George Rennie Esq. F.R.S. F.A.S. &c. &c. (epigraph) London: Published by Brown and Syrett, 17 Old Broad Street: J. and A. Arch, Cornhill, Paul and Dominic Colnaghi and Co, Printsellers to the Royal Family, Pall Mall East; and George and E.W. Cooke, Barnes Terrace, Surrey. 1833

Folio, 465–75 × 320–35mm.   1833

COLLATION   Title-page; address dated April 1833 (1 leaf); pp i–vi, description of plates; pp 1–20, History of Old London Bridge, Historical Account of New London Bridge, Practical Remarks on the Arch, Bridge Buildings, etc; pp 21–4, Table of the Principal Bridges in Europe; Tides in the River Thames.

Fortunately 69 of Cooke's London Bridge drawings are preserved in the Guildhall Library and include those from which he etched these dozen plates. Most of them were exhibited either in 1973, at the London Bridge Progress Drawings exhibition, or in 1969 at the London Bridge in Art exhibition. Reference is made below to the annotated catalogue of the latter with the abbreviation *LBA*. In 1913 the London Topographical Society issued facsimiles of seven of the unpublished drawings.

The etchings are in double-ruled frames and are numbered tr 'Pl.1', etc. Captions are in voided capitals with sub-captions in italics. The credit is invariable: 'Drawn and etched by Edwd Wm. Cooke'. Dates of the publication-lines fall into three Parts of four plates each: June and October 1832 and April 1833; while the original drawings date between August 1831 and July 1832. 'Proof' copies on India paper were sold at £1 1s per Part and 'Super-Royal Folio' at 14s. The complete work cost '£3; or unbound £2. 12s. 6d. A few copies on India Paper at £4. 4s. 0d.'

1 Part of Old London Bridge, St Magnus and the Monument,/Taken at Low-water, August 15th, 1831. London, Pubd June 1832 for the Proprietor, by J. Brown, 17 Old Broad Street. 355 × 268/405 × 315mm. *LBA* 28.

2 The Old and New London Bridges,/Taken from the Steps at the City end (looking South) during the progress of the works, August 27, 1830. London, Pubd June 1832 for the Proprietors by J. Brown, Old Broad Street. 228 × 315/320 × 405mm. *LBA* 49.

3 Arch of Old London Bridge called Long-Entry Lock/taken from the Sterling at Low Water, Oct 1, 1831. Pubd 1832 for the Proprietor, by J. Brown, 17 Old Broad Street. 190 × 253/250 × 305mm. *LBA* 117.

4 Demolition of Old London Bridge; (Low Water)/As it appeared January 24th 1832. London, Pubd June 1832 for the Proprietor, by J. Brown, 17 Old Broad Street. 245 × 343/315 × 405mm. *LBA* 50.

5 Steps of New London Bridge, St Magnus, the Monument/ and part of the Old Bridge. Drawn 13 Aug 1831 & Etched by E.W. Cooke. London, Pubd Octr 1832 for the Proprietor, by J. Brown, 17 Old Broad Street. 295 × 260/355 × 300mm. *LBA* 67.

6 Demolition of the Great or Chapel Pier of Old London

Bridge/With the Derrick used in Drawing the Foundations, Piles &c. March 1832. London, Pubd Octr 1832 for the Proprietor, by J. Brown, 17 Old Broad Street. 235 × 310/300 × 380mm. *LBA* 52.

7 Ruins of the Crypt, or Under Chapel of St Thomas, on Old London Bridge,/As discovered Feb 1832 at the late Demolition of the Bridge. Pubd Oct 1832 for the Proprietor, by J. Brown, 17 Old Broad Street. 175 × 235/215 × 265mm. *LBA* 55.

8 The Southwark End of Old London Bridge./ From a Drawing taken at Low-water 25th Novr 1831. Pubd Oct 1832 for the Proprietor, by J. Brown, Old Broad Street. 260 × 365/315 × 405mm. From the E. *LBA* 81.

9 London Bridge/From the upper landing of the Steps near Tooley Street. London, Published 20 April 1833 by Brown & Syrett, 17 Old Broad Street & J. & A. Arch, Cornhill & G. Cooke, Barnes Terrace, Surrey. 280 × 215/340 × 250mm.

10 Old London Bridge/As it stood since the repair of 1760, until its dissolution in 1831–2. London, Pubd April, 1833 for the Proprietors, by J. Brown, 17 Old Broad Street, & J. & A. Arch, Cornhill. 193 × 305/245 × 352mm.

11 New London Bridge/from Billingsgate (low water) drawn July 31, 1832. London, Pubd April, 1833 for the Proprietors by J. Brown, 17 Old Broad Street, & J. & A. Arch, Cornhill. 228 × 343/285 × 380mm. *LBA* 109.

12 Dilapidation of the Long-Entry Arch, Old London Bridge,/As it appeared March 20th 1832. Exhibiting a portion of the original structure, & the various additions on either side for widening the Bridge. London, Pubd April, 1833 for the Proprietors by J. Brown, Old Broad Street, & J. & A. Arch, Cornhill. 248 × 360/315 × 405mm. Looking towards N. bank.

173 · SMITH'S ST MARYLEBONE [1833]

This is the earliest separately published history of St Marylebone and remains a standard work on the subject. It is also interesting for its illustrations, not that it is profusely illustrated but because, in 1833 when such architectural plates were generally being commissioned from steel-engravers, these were 'drawn on stone', mostly 'from Nature'. Indeed the lithographic printers Graf & Soret who printed them were active in the field of London illustration mostly during the following decade. They provided also most of the draughtsmanship although one view has the credit of Edward Hassell, water-colourist son of the line and aquatint-engraver John Hassell, whose *Excursions of Pleasure and Sports on the Thames* (no 140) was published ten years previously. Four of the six views are of recently constructed churches which T.H. Shepherd had already drawn for the engravings in Elmes's *Metropolitan Improvements* (no 154). All are printed from the stone in black ink on India paper within a triple-ruled frame. The publication-line reads: 'Printed by Graf & Soret, London, Published by John Smith, 49 Long Acre 1833.'

A Topographical and Historical Account of the Parish of St. Mary-le-bone, comprising a Copious Description of its Public Buildings, Antiquities, Schools, Charitable Endowments, Sources of Public Amusement, &c. with biographical views of eminent persons. Illustrated with Six views and a map. The whole compiled and arranged by Thomas Smith. London: Printed and published by John Smith 49 Long Acre.... 1833.

Octavo, 240 × 150mm.   1833

COLLATION   Title-page; dedication (1 leaf); preface (2pp); contents, list of plates (4pp); pp 1–319, Historical Account; p 320, errata.

1 front. (bl) Map of the Parish/of/of St Mary-le-Bone/1833 London. Published by John Smith, 49 Long Acre. Drawn & Printed by Graf & Soret, 1 Gt Castle St. 340 × 280mm.

2 p 32 Mary Le Bone Manor House (now pulled down). Drawn on stone from a sketch in the possession of John Brown Esqr. A.D. 1790. 82 × 138mm.

3 p 89 New St Mary-le-Bone Church. Drawn from Nature and on Stone by Edwd. Hassel. 135 × 82mm. Built by Thomas Hardwick, 1813–17.

4 p 102 St Mary's Church. Drawn & Printed by Graf & Soret, 1 Gt Castle St. 83 × 138mm. Wyndham Place. Designed by Sir Robert Smirke and consecrated 7 January 1824.

5 p 110 All Souls Church. Drawn & Printed by Graf & Soret, 1 Gt Castle St. 140 × 82mm. Built by John Nash in Langham Place and consecrated 25 November 1824.

6 p 115 Christ Church. Drawn & Printed by Graf & Soret, 1 Gt Castle St. 135 × 82mm. In Lisson Grove. Built from the designs of Philip Hardwick and consecrated in 1825.

7 p 118 Trinity Church. 83 × 133mm. Designed by Sir John Soane and consecrated in 1828.

174 · SMITH'S NEW HISTORY AND SURVEY [1833]

This history of London and Westminster, published in shilling monthly Numbers from June 1832 and dedicated to the Lord Mayor in March 1833, was apparently abandoned after the first volume and the reign of Richard III. Its chief illustrations are 15 wood-engraved views by J.W. Armstrong and a map of Roman London which would not qualify for listing but that they are, unusually, printed not with the text but on separate pages with blank versos. In addition a few small cuts of 'antiquities' are printed with the text on pp 99–110 and 204. Although they are attractive, boldly carved wood-blocks the publisher, or author, apparently thought the book deserved something more sophisticated and borrowed from Jones & Co four of the T.H. Shepherd plates published in 1830 for *London and its Environs in the Nineteenth Century* (no 161). These are designated in the list by *L19C* with the page they face in the Jones publication.

There is no list of plates, only an instruction to the binder to place the steel-engravings at the beginning and the woodcuts at the end of the volume 'until the proper list be given'. Here they are arranged as in the British Library copy (796.g.24).

A New History and Survey of the Cities of London and Westminster, and the Borough of Southwark: with Authentic Graphic Illustrations of their Antiquities ... by W. Smith. (epigraph) Vol. 1. London: Published by Effingham Wilson, 88 Royal Exchange.

Octavo, 215 × 130mm.   1833

COLLATION Title-page; dedication to the Lord Mayor dated from Poplar, March 1833 (1 leaf); pp v–vi, preface; pp vii–xii, analytical contents; pp 1–444, History; pp i–xvi, index, corrigenda, directions to binder.

1 front. The Mansion House, from the Bank. Drawn by Tho. H. Shepherd. Engraved by W. Wallis. 98 × 150/125 × 210mm. Steel-engraving. *L19C* 61.

2 p 1 Londina Augusta/From the best authorities. W. Smith Delt. J.W.A. sculp. 155 × 240mm. Refs 1–31.

3 p 66 Ald-Gate/(A.D.1761). 105 × 95mm. Woodcut, vignetted.

4 p 69 Bishops-Gate/(A.D. 1735). 105 × 90mm. Woodcut, vignetted.

5 p 71 Moor-Gate/(A.D.1672). 100 × 80mm. Woodcut, vignetted.

6 p 72 Cripple-Gate/(A.D.1663). 110 × 80mm. Woodcut, vignetted.

7 p 74 Alders-gate/(A.D.1670). 105 × 85mm. Woodcut in border-line.

8 p 75 New-Gate/(A.D.1672). J.W. Armstrong delt. sct. 130 × 90mm. Woodcut in border-line.

9 p 80 Lud-Gate/(A.D.1670). J.W.A.dt et sct. 133 × 83mm. Woodcut in border-line.

10 p 86 The Bridge-Gate/(A.D.1728) 105 × 88mm. Woodcut in border-line.

11 p 119 St Paul's Cathedral/from the River. Drawn by Tho. H. Shepherd. Engraved by J. Tingle. 100 × 158/130 × 215mm. Steel-engraving. *L19C* 37.

12 p 138 Old London Bridge from Southwark. Drawn by Tho. H. Shepherd. Engraved by W. Radcliffe. 90 × 153/125 × 210mm. Steel engraving. *L19C* 149.

13 p 158 Traitors Gate, Tower of London. J.W. Armstrong delt et sculpt. 158 × 100mm. Woodcut in border-line.

14 p 241 Interior of the Temple Church. JWA dt sct. 140 × 95mm. Woodcut in border-line.

15 p 266 The Cross in Cheapside/(A.D.1290). 135 × 72mm. Woodcut in border-line.

16 p 444 Cornhill, and Lombard Street, from the Poultry. Drawn by Tho. H. Shepherd. Engraved by S. Lacey. 102 × 150/125 × 210mm. Steel-engraving. *L19C* 85.

17 p 444 Bank of England. 90 × 150mm. Woodcut in border-line. (*Bank of England* 76)

18 p 444 Old House in Bishopsgate/formerly the residence of Sir Paul Pindar. J.W.A. del et sct. 160 × 95mm. Woodcut in border-line.

19 p 444 Temple Bar/(A.D.1833). 100 × 80mm. Woodcut, vignetted.

20 p 444 Mercers Hall. 105 × 78mm. Woodcut in border-line.

175 · TAYLOR'S ANNALS OF ST MARY OVERY [1833]

William Taylor was a Southwark engraver who contributed plates to many of the topographical works published between 1830 and 1850, including Tombleson's *Thames* (no 178) and Britton and Brayley's *Westminster Palace* (no 181). St Saviour's (now Southwark Cathedral) had had its tower and choir repaired and restored by George Gwilt in 1822–5 and its transept and stone reredos in 1829–30 by Robert Wallace, who contributes two measured drawings to the illustrations. It was therefore a propitious moment to choose for publishing a history of the building and to illustrate both its antiquities and restored fabric, and the subscription list which Taylor opened attracted considerable support, both local and general. The original wrappers bore the title 'History and Antiquities of St. Saviour's Church & Parish'. The price was £1 5s quarto or £2 Large Paper.

Taylor himself contributed most of the drawings and carried out all the etching and engraving on steel besides writing the text. His book was published by the respectable firm of John Bowyer Nichols, printer to the City of London, noted antiquary and specialist in county histories. Plates of antiquities are unmeasured because they lack border-lines; most plate-marks have been cropped by the binder.

Annals of St Mary Overy; an Historical and Descriptive Account of St Saviour's Church and Parish. With numerous Illustrations. By W. Taylor. London: Published for the Author by Messrs Nichols & Son, 25 Parliament Street; and sold by I. & A. Arch, 61 Cornhill, R. Hill, Bookseller, High Street, Southwark. 1833.

Quarto, 280 × 210mm.   1833

COLLATION Title-page; preface, list of subscribers (2pp); list of plates, index (4pp); half-title; pp 5–144, Annals.

1 front. S.-E. View of St Saviour's Church. W. Taylor. 140 × 190mm.

2 p 9 Roman Remains, Plate 1. W. Taylor. London, Pub. by the Author 1831. (details)

3 p 13 Roman Remains, Plate 2. W. Taylor. London, Published by the Author, 1831. (details)

4 p 19 Remains of the Priory of St Mary Overy. Drawn & Engraved by W. Taylor. Plate 1. London, Published by the Author, 1831. 155 × 132/225 × 200mm.

5 p 32 (tm) Seals of the Priory of St Mary Overy, Southwark. B. Howlett del. W. Taylor sculp. (details)

6 p 44 (tm) Priory Remains, Architectural Fragments, etc. W. Taylor. Pub. by W. Taylor, 48 Queens Row Walworth, April 1833. (details)

7 p 45 Interior View of St Saviour's Church Southwark. W. Taylor. Pub. by W. Taylor 48 Queens Row Walworth. 180 × 120mm.

8 p 46 Anglo-Norman Doorway. (North Side of St Saviour's Church). Drawn & Eng'd by W. Taylor.

Pub. by W. Taylor 11 Church St. St Saviour's. 210 × 160mm. Vignetted.

9 p 51 Chapel of the Virgin Mary, or 'Ladye Chapel'. Engraved by W. Taylor from a drawing by the late J. Carter. Pub. by W. Taylor, 11 Church St, St Saviour Southwark. 190 × 150mm. cf with Carter's Views (no 64), item 5.

10 p 54 Chapels East End of St Saviour's Church. Drawn & Engr. by W. Taylor. Pub. by the Author, 1831. 140 × 190mm. Vignetted.

11 p 68 S.-W. View of St Saviour's Church/(Prior to the Restoration). W. Taylor del. et sc. 143 × 212mm.

12 p 69 Elevation of South Transept/ St Saviours Church. R. Wallace Archt. W. Taylor sculp. 190 × 155mm. Measured drawing.

13 p 71 Elevation of North Transept and parts adjoining/ St Saviour's Church. Robt. Wallace Archt. W. Taylor sculp. 195 × 160mm. Measured drawing.

14 p 72 East End of St Saviour's Church. Drawn by R. Billings. Engr. by W. Taylor. Pub. 1831 by M. Taylor, Church St. St. Saviour's. 192 × 150mm.

15 p 82 Monuments in St Saviour's Church. W. Taylor Fecit. (details)

16 p 88 Sepulchral Remains./St Saviour's. Drawn & Etched by W. Taylor. Pub. by W. Taylor, 11 Church St. St Saviour's. (details)

17 p 92 (tm) Stained Glass formerly in St Mary Overy's Church. Drawn & etched by W. Taylor. London, Pub. by W. Taylor 1831. (detail, coloured by hand)

18 p 101 Coffin of Launcelot Andrews (etc.). Drawn & Etched by W. Taylor. Pub. by W. Taylor, 11 Church St. St Saviour's. (details)

19 p 116 Monumental Remains, St Saviour's Church. Drawn & Engraved by W. Taylor. Pub. by W. Taylor, 11 Church St. St Saviour's. (details)

20 p 134 Ancient Houses, Southwark. Drawn & Engraved by W. Taylor. Pub. by W. Taylor. Church St. Boro'. 190 × 150mm. Vignetted.

176 · CRUCHLEY'S PICTURE OF LONDON [1834]

The first edition of this guidebook, whose title plagiarizes the one first published by Phillips in 1802 (no 85) and gives the illusion of being senior to Leigh's *New Picture* (no 126) which started life in 1818, was actually published in 1831. Its price was

4s, 4s 6d, 6s or 9s, according to the size of the accompanying map and as to whether it was uncoloured, partially coloured or fully coloured. For 5s it was offered in Spanish and for 6s or 7s in French. In English it eventually outlived all its homonyms, being still available in the 1860s as *Cruchley's London.*

It does not properly qualify as a guide illustrated with plates since for the first ten years of its life the normal issue was equipped only with a map and thereafter the only illustrations consisted of 59 wood-engravings printed with the text. It so happens, however, that William Darton and Son acquired some sheets of the second edition in 1834 and published them with seven plates of steel-engravings at 6s. It is this edition which is described here.

It has been advanced that Cruchley himself offered for sale two illustrated editions priced as 12s and 15s, but I have not yet come across an example of these. He did however bind up with the first and subsequent editions of his *Picture of London* a substantial catalogue of his wares, in which this publisher and mapseller prominently advertised his services as being concerned with 'Seal and Copper Plate engraving, printing &c. brass plates, for house or office doors, bankers notes, checks, visiting cards, bills of parcels, lithographic circular letters & Arms, Crests &c. found and engraved on Stone, Steel, Silver and Brass'—in fact general engraving and printing with some heraldic research thrown in. It seems unlikely that, while fulfilling all these functions, he could himself, by 1831, have engraved and published all the plans, maps, panoramas and guidebooks listed in this 36 page booklet; it must simply be a record of his Ludgate Street stock-in-trade, including of course his own publications.

After a description of the *Picture of London* in its variously priced issues follows: 'and its environs (with 111 views). Bound 9s.; with views and twenty-four coloured plates, exhibiting the costume of the lower orders. Bound 12s.; with views and fifty-four characteristic sketches by Rowlandson. Coloured. Bound, 15s.' The number of the integral illustrations and the optional extras, the basic price and the two prices for additional plates all tally exactly with extant copies of Leigh's *New Picture of London* and the forms in which it was available between 1819 and 1842. If he always kept Leigh's

publication in stock it may explain why Cruchley did not trouble to illustrate his own *Picture* until 1842, when the wood-engravings first made their appearance.

Cruchley's Picture of London comprising the History, Rise and Progress of the Metropolis to the present period and a sketch of the most remarkable features of its environs necessary to the foreigner or stranger. Also a Route for viewing the whole in seven days; to which is annexed a New Superior map with references to the principal streets. The Second Edition. With Plates. London; William Darton and Son., Holborn Hill, Price Six Shillings. M.DCCC.XXXIV.

Duodecimo, 140 × 85mm.   1834

COLLATION   Title-page; pp v–vii, preface; pp 1–280, Cruchley's Picture.

The steel-engravings have no credits but all have the publication-line 'London, William Darton & Son, Holborn Hill', undated. Each plate has a ruled border-line, about 120 × 70mm. The map was absent from the copy examined.

1 front. Hyde Park. 65 × 70mm. Vignette. With the Achilles statue.

2 p 21 The House of Lords – The Horse Guards – Buckingham Palace. Each 35 × 67mm.

3 p 28 Somerset House – Westminster Hall – Interior of the House of Lords. Each 35 × 67mm.

4 p 30 St. James's Park. 70 × 65mm. Vignette. Towards Duke of York's Column.

5 p 38 Kensington Palace – The East India House – The Custom House. Each 35 × 67mm.

6 p 41 Guildhall – The Bank – Southwark Bridge. Each 35 × 67mm. The Bank with St Bartholomew by the Exchange.

7 p 58 The Lord Mayor's Show – The Tower – Westminster Abbey. Each 35 × 67mm.

8 (tm) Cruchley's New Plan of London/shewing all the new and intended improvements to the present time. Engraved and Published by Cruchley Map Seller, 81 Fleet Street, from Ludgate Street, St Paul's London. 405 × 580mm. Bound in some copies as an alternative to the above views. (*Darlington and Howgego* 320)

412

177 · PARTINGTON'S NATIONAL HISTORY AND VIEWS OF LONDON [1834–5]

C.F. Partington was a lecturer on technological subjects, a copious writer on science and engineering and editor of *The London Journal of Arts and Sciences* and *The British Cyclopaedia*. Nevertheless, whilst lecturing to mechanics' institutes and publishing numerous treatises on steam traction, watch-making, engraving and printing he managed to find the time to write a commentary on a series of miniature views of London drawn by T.H. Shepherd and H. West, engraved, and probably also printed, by J. Shury. Moreover, unlike most of the previous commentators on London views, he was interested enough in the objects portrayed to inform his readers that they were severally by 'Mr. Savage, Mr. James Peacock, Professor Soane, Mr. Tierney Clark' and by other architects and engineers.

The work first came out in Numbers with white paper wrappers printed with a wood-engraving of St Paul's Cathedral and lettered thus:

The Cheapest Illustrated Work Extant. 25 Views and 16 pages of letter-press for One Shilling.

National Views and History of London and its Environs embracing their Antiquities, Modern Improvements, &c. From original drawings by Eminent Artists. Each number of this highly illustrated work will contain 25 views, engraved in a superior style, with 16 pages of letter-press descriptions, price One Shilling, or Royal Octavo, India Paper, price Two Shillings. Edited by Mr. C.F. Partington of the London Institution. London, Allan, Bell & Co., 12 Warwick Square; William Orr, 14 Paternoster Row and Simpkin & Marshall, Stationers Court.... 1832.

A record number of views was achieved by engraving them five to a plate, but in addition the monthly Numbers consisted of five of these plates, one more than the norm, and were thus good value for money.

The engraved title, frontispiece and other plates issued as the first two Numbers, in August and September, included the publication-line 'London; Published by Allan, Bell & Co. July 1832.' Nos 3 and 4, dated simply 1832, presumably came out in October and November; No 5 appeared in December with a new line: 'London, Published by W.S.

Orr, 1832.' The date was altered to 1833 on plates in Nos 6 and 7 and after this the first two publishers severed their connection with the work when they had collected the plates and the text pages so far published into a bound volume. So much for the ambitions proclaimed in their 'Advertisement' dated August 1832:

The proprietors of the 'National Views and History of London' are fully aware that many works have issued from the press which are more or less descriptive of London and delineations of her public edifices ... but they are convinced that, however creditable most of the works above alluded to may be both in point & matter and embellishments none either are, or profess to be complete in every point of view....

The proprietors propose that their work shall not only embrace the Exterior but also the Interior Views of every public and private building worthy of notice; also the venerable objects of Antiquity, the noble Monuments and Curiosities ... &c &c.

Two of the insufficiently complete works they had in mind must certainly have been *Metropolitan Improvements* (no 154) and *London and its Environs* (no 161), illustrated by Shepherd and published in their entirety at the Temple of the Muses only in the previous year. It is therefore strange that Shepherd's contribution to this more exhaustive venture is mentioned neither on the wrapper nor on the title-page, although his credits appear on a majority of the plates.

No doubt it was on the initiative of the firm of Simpkin & Marshall, co-publishers with Allan, Bell and Orr, that the first seven Numbers were collected in book form and distributed through German and French agents. It was also they who in the next year published a second edition, twice as large, of the first volume and followed it up with a similar second volume, the pair being advertised in April 1835 at £1 1s, Large Paper £2 2s. The publishing house of James Black also acquired an interest in this later edition, since their pre-1836 imprint of 'Black, Young & Young, Tavistock Street' is found on the engraved titles. George Virtue, who was in process of acquiring a notable list of books illustrated with steel-engravings, later reissued a selection in one binding, undated and with an amended title.

(wrapper title) National History and Views of London and its Environs: embracing their Antiquities, Modern Improvements, &c. From original drawings by eminent artists. This half-volume contains nearly 180 spirited views of the metropolis and vicinity. Edited by Mr. C.F.

Partington of the London Institution. London, Allan Bell & Co, 12 Warwick Square; William Orr, Paternoster Row and Simpkin & Marshall, Stationers Court.... George Gropius, Berlin; C. Jügel, Frankfurt a.m.; Im Kunstverlag, Carlsruhe and G. Bennis, Paris, 1833. Price Ten Shillings.

Octavo, 215 × 135mm.   1833

COLLATION Title-page; pp i–ii, advertisement; pp 1–112, Historical and Topographical Illustrations (ie Nos 1–7, with engr front. and the initial 35 plates).

National History and Views of London and its Environs; embracing their Antiquities, Modern Improvements, &c.&c. From original drawings by eminent artists. Edited by C.F. Partington Esq., of the London Institution. In two volumes. Vol. I (II), containing: 300 steel engravings. London: Simpkin and Marshall, Stationers' Hall Court; Oliver and Boyd, Edinburgh; and W. Curry & Co. Dublin (or with the James Black 1835 imprint: 'London: Black and Armstrong, Tavistock Street'). Thoms, Printer and Stereotyper, 12 Warwick Square (vol.2: 'Printed by J. Haddon, Castle Street, Finsbury').

Octavo, 225–35 × 140–5mm.   1834–5

COLLATION Vol. 1. Half-title; title-page; pp v–viii, index; pp 1–208, Historical and Topographical Illustrations. Vol. 2. Half-title; title-page; pp v–vii, index; pp 1–216, Historical and Topographical Illustrations continued.

An Illustrated History of London and its Environs; exhibiting every Building of Importance, Ancient and Modern, on three hundred steel engravings from original drawings by eminent artists with historical and descriptive accounts by C.F. Partington. (2 vols in 1) London, G. Virtue

Octavo, 225 × 140mm.   c 1837

(COLLATION as above)

This is undoubtedly the largest collection of London views to be issued in volume form: in all, 670 subjects engraved on 115 plates, and a map surrounded by 32 more. This abundance has been achieved by reducing the majority of the subjects to very small proportions, not much larger than a special issue postage stamp, but the competent engraver on steel—J. Shury, who was also responsible for the map—has managed quite well within these limits. Drawings for the majority of the plates were by T.H. Shepherd, the only other artist being H. West who contributed 30 of the 60 engravings in the first volume but only two in the second (items 1–2, 8–9, 11, 13, 16–21, 23–5, 28–31, 33–43, 45, 62, 68).

The name of Shepherd suggests there may be some relation to his two major London works, *Metropolitan Improvements* and *London and its Environs*, and they certainly were used as a quarry of subjects, of which the Partington volumes have 125 in common with the first named and over 150 with the second. If, however, the small views are compared with the larger there is little evidence of direct copying, although the viewpoint is often necessarily the same. If 'Ludgate Hill' in *London and its Environs* (item 24) is set beside his Partington view (item 22c) it will be seen that constraints of size and proportion have caused Shepherd to simplify by the elimination of detail and much staffage, but that the smaller picture repeats the attractive architectural grouping of the larger. Similarly with 'St. Antholin' (Partington item 86c, *London and its Environs* item 79) and 'St. James Garlick Hill' (Partington item 86a, *London and its Environs* item 85), although in both of these proportions are retained at about one third of the original scale. It seems probable that Shepherd, who was very prolific, made fresh drawings, sometimes adapted from the previous ones by simplification and the thinning out of staffage. This process can be studied by means of the references in the list to the two works, respectively abbreviated *MI* and *L19C*, with item numbers. The scope of the earlier collections was now however greatly enlarged by including sets of views on such subjects as the Zoological Gardens (opened in 1828), Hyde Park, Kensington Gardens and various residential suburbs such as Pimlico, Putney, Barnes, Hammersmith, Hampstead, Enfield, Chingford and Greenwich.

As a tribute to the durability of steel it is worth mentioning that the first half-dozen plates subsequently found their way to Berlin where they were printed on quarto paper (248 × 200mm) and bound in boards with the title:

Pittoreske Wanderungen durch London. Mit 36 englischen Stahlstichen nach Original-Zeichnungen der Vorzüglichsten Künstler, und mit ausführlichen Erläuterungen und historischen Notizien nach C.F. Partington Esq. of the London Institution etc. etc. Berlin, List & Klemann. (nd; the Guildhall Library dates its copy 'c 1835')

All plates, except for the engraved titles and frontispieces, have upon them five views arranged in the form of a quincunx: two pairs of satellite views, of about 58 × 48mm, above (a and b) and below (d and e) a horizontal view (c) of about 48 × 98mm; or, alternatively, two satellite views of about 48 × 58mm to the left (a and b) and to the right (d and e) of a vertical view (c) of about 98 × 48mm. Each view is within a ruled frame and with captions in voided capitals and italic sub-captions. The credits are all 'Engraved by J. Shury' and 'Drawn by T.H. Shepherd', except for those plates marked 'Drawn by H. West'. In the first issue items 3–37 carried Part and plate numbers (tl and tr); items 2–7, 9–22 carried the publication-line 'London: Published by Allan, Bell & Co. (July) 1832.', item 8 the line '... Augt 1832.', item 38 the line '... Augt 1833.', item 44 the line 'Warwick Square 1833.' and items 23–37, 41, 43, 45 the line 'London: Published by W.S. Orr, 1833.', mostly burnished out from the reissues.

VOL. 1

1 (engr title) National/History and Views of London/ With its Environs/Including its Antiquities/Modern Improvements &c/from Original Drawings/by Eminent Artists/(vignette) Entrance to Green Park. Drawn by H. West. Engraved by J. Shury. London/ Black Young & Young/Tavistock Street/1835(1837). 100 × 105/220 × 135mm. Or 'London: Allan, Bell & Co., 51 Fleet Street; and Simpkin & Marshall,/ Stationers Hall Court/1832.'

2 front. View of London,/(from Waterloo Bridge). Drawn by H. West. Engraved by J. Shury. 98 × 165/135 × 215mm.

3 p 10 (a) Bullion Court – (b) East Façade – (c) Bank of England – (d) Lothbury Façade – (e) The Old Bank. 58 × 48,48 × 98/225 × 140mm. *MI* 89, 2, 88 (b, c, d) (*Bank of England* 134, 78, 92, 69, 46)

4 p 12 (a) St Dunstan in the East – (b) St Mary Cree Church – (c) The Tower – (d) Gateway Bloody Tower – (e) Interior Bowyer Tower. 58 × 48,58 × 98/230 × 135mm. (b) is St Katherine Cree. '1,2'. *L19C* 70, 132, 172 (a,b,c).

5 p 17 (a) Lama Hut – (b) Bear Pit – (c) Entrance to the Zoological Gardens, Regents Park – (d) Tunnel – (e) Aviary. 58 × 48,58 × 100/220 × 135mm. '1,3'.

6 p 18 (a) St John's Church, Waterloo Road – (b) St Martin in the Fields – (c) Temple Church – (d) St Mark the Evangelist Clerkenwell – (e) St Mary's Chapel Somers Town. 58 × 48,56 × 98/220 × 135mm. '1,4'. *MI* 98, 118, 55, 39 (a,c,d,e).

7 p 21 (a) Whitehall – (b) Richmond Terrace – (c) Westminster Abbey/(from Tothill Street) – (d) Horse Guards – (e) Melbourne House. 48 × 58,100 × 58/135 × 220mm. '1,5'. *L19C* 4, *MI* 38, *L19C* 11, 168 (a,b,d,e).

8 p 23 (a) House of Lords – (b) King's Entrance, House of Lords – (c) Westminster Hall (entrance) – (d)

House of Commons – (e) St Stephens Chapel, from the River. Drawn by H. West. 58 × 48,60 × 98/220 × 135mm. '2,1'. Pen and wash drawing of St Stephen's Chapel from the river (58 × 48mm) in Westminster Public Library. *MI* 132, 133, *L19C* 111 (a,b,c).

9 p 27 (a) Boat House – (b) Keeper's House – (c) Serpentine Bridge – (d) King's Road Bridge – (e) The Cascade. Drawn by H. West. 58 × 48,58 × 98/225 × 140mm. '2,2'. *MI* 37 (c).

10 p 28 (a) Old Shot Mill, near Waterloo Bridge – (b) New Shot Mill near Waterloo Bridge – (c) Waterloo Bridge – (d) St Paul's Covent Garden – (e) St John's Savoy. 58 × 48,58 × 98/220 × 140mm. '2,3'. *MI* 148, 14, *L19C* 36, 49 (b,c,d,e).

11 p 30 (a) Ophthalmic Hospital – (b) West Strand – (c) Lowther Arcade – (d) Exeter Hall – (e) British Fire Office. Drawn by H. West. 48 × 58,102 × 58/140 × 225mm. '2,4'.

12 p 31 (a) Sir Herbert Taylor's Villa, Regents Park – (b) Villa in the Regents Park – (c) St Katharines Chapel Regents Park – (d) East Gate Regents Park – (e) West Lodge Regents Park. 58 × 48,58 × 100/220 × 140mm. '2,5'. *MI* 42, 31, 41, 5, 140.

13 p 32 (a) Ophthalmic Institute Finsbury – (b) Catholic Church Finsbury – (c) London Institution Finsbury – (d) Finsbury Chapel – (e) Unitarian Chapel Finsbury. Drawn by H. West. 60 × 48,55 × 98/225 × 140mm. '3,1'. *MI* 136, 46, 34, 47, 115.

14 p 37 (a) Temple Bar – (b) Old St Dunstan's Church – (c) Old London Bridge – (d) London Stone, Cannon Street – (e) Figure Commemorative of the Fire of London. 58 × 48,48 × 100/225 × 140mm. '3,2'. *L19C* 0, 171, 39 (a,c,d).

15 p 49 (a) Christ's Church Newgate – (b) Part of Christs Hospital, from the Ct Yd – (c) New Hall Christs Hospital – (d) Part of the Old Building Christs Hospital – (e) The Old Grammar School. 58 × 48,58 × 98/220 × 135mm. '3,5'. *L19C* 138, 135, *MI* 103 (a,b,c).

16 p 50 (a) Villa in the Regents Park – (b) Villa in the Regents Park – (c) Coliseum and Part of Lake Regents Park – (d) Hanover Lodge Regents Park – (e) South Villa Regents Park. Drawn by H. West. 60 × 48,58 × 100/225 × 140mm. '3,3'. *MI* 10, 44, 69, 17, 86.

17 p 52 (a) Northumberland House – (b) Kings Mews – (c) Admiralty – (d) Monument of Charles 1st, Charing Cross – (e) Monument of James IId Whitehall. Drawn by H. West. 60 × 45,58 × 100/230 × 140mm. '3,4'. *L19C* 92, 13, 14 (a,b,c).

18 p 53 (a) Temple of Victory – (b) Ruined Arch – (c) Chinese Pagoda, Kew Gardens – (d) Hermitage – (e) Chinese Temple. Drawn by H. West. 48 × 60,100 × 60/140 × 225mm. '4,1'.

19 p 55 (a) Statue of Charles IId – (b) Monument of Sir Hans Sloane – (c) Battersea Bridge – (d) Chelsea Old Church – (e) Battersea Church. Drawn by H. West. 58

× 48,58 × 98/230 × 140mm. '4,2'. *L19C* 183 (d). (a–d *Longford* 708, 157, 269, 572)

20 p 59 (a) Royal Military Asylum – (b) Botanical Gardens – (c) St Luke's Church Chelsea – (d) Royal Hospital – (e) Hospital from the River. Drawn by H. West. 48 × 58,98 × 58/140 × 230mm. '4,3'. *MI* 54 (c). (*Longford* 393, 112, 463, 83, 70)

21 p 60 (a) Bridge, Kensington Gardens – (b) Temple – (c) Kensington Palace – (d) Summer House – (e) Green House. Drawn by H. West. 58 × 48,58 × 98/225 × 140mm. (e) is the Orangery. '4,4'.

22 p 61 (a) Albion Fire Office – (b) Bridewell – (c) Ludgate Hill – (d) Fleet Prison – (e) Fleet Market/ (now pulled down). 48 × 58,98 × 58/140 × 230mm. '4,5'. *L19C* 24, 23 (c,e).

23 p 65 (a) Grammar School, Pimlico – (b) Royal Mews, Pimlico – (c) Screen Hyde Park Corner – (d) St Peters Church, Pimlico – (e) Patent Bread Works, Pimlico. Drawn by H. West. 58 × 48,58 × 98/225 × 140mm. '5,1'. *MI* 104, 36 (c,d).

24 p 67 (a) Putney Bridge – (b) Barnes Common – (c) Putney Church – (d) Hurlingham House, Fulham – (e) Entrance to Putney, from Barnes. Drawn by H. West. 45 and 48 × 60,98 × 58/140 × 225mm. '5,2'.

25 p 68 (a) St Peter's Church, Hammersmith – (b) Fulham Church – (c) Suspension Bridge, Hammersmith – (d) Hammersmith Old Church – (e) Chiswick Church. Drawn by H. West. 58 × 48,58 × 98/220 × 140mm. '5,3'. *MI* 92 (c).

26 p 73 (a) Old Church – (b) New Church – (c) Royal Hospital Greenwich – (d) Flamstead House/(Observatory) – (e) Naval Asylum. 58 × 48,58 × 98/220 × 140mm. '5,4'. (b) is St Mary, Greenwich Park, built by G. Basevi, 1823–5; demolished 1936.

27 p 77 (a) St James's Clerkenwell – (b) St John's Gate, Clerkenwell – (c) Sessions House, Clerkenwell – (d) Chapel, Charter House – (e) St Luke's Hospital. 58 × 48,58 × 93/225 × 140mm. '5,5'. *L19C* 72, 40, 97 (a,b,c).

28 p 81 (a) St Saviour's Church, 1829 – (b) St Olave's Church – (c) Custom House – (d) Montague Close – (e) Ladye Chapel. Drawn by H. West. 60 × 48,58 × 98/230 × 135mm. '6,1'. Sepia wash drawing of Montague Close (57 × 47mm) in GLC. *L19C* 144, *MI* 113 (b,c).

29 p 84 (a) All Souls Church Langham Place – (b) Trinity Church, New Road – (c) St Mary-le-bone Church, New Road – (d) St Mary's Church, Wyndham Place – (e) Mary-le-bone Chapel. Drawn by H. West. 58 × 48,58 × 98/220 × 140mm. '6,4'. *MI* 7, 82, 35, 83, 90

30 p 90 (a) Henry 7th's Chapel – (b) North Front of Westminster Abbey – (c) Westminster from Lambeth – (d) West Cloister – (e) East Cloister. Drawn by H. West. 58 × 48,58 × 98/225 × 140mm. '6,3'. *L19C* 3 (b).

31 p 93 (a) Admiral Earl How – (b) Cuthbert, Lord Collingwood – (c) St Paul's/(Interior) – (e) Lieut. Gen. Sir Ralph Abercrombie – (e) Lieut-Gen. Sir John Moore. Drawn by H. West. 48 × 58,98 × 58/140 × 225mm. '6,2'.

32 p 95 (a) Statue of the Duke of Bedford/Russell Square – (b) Statue of Fox, Bloomsbury Square – (c) London University – (d) Russell Institution – (e) Foundling Hospital. 58 × 48,58 × 98/225 × 140mm. '6,5'. *L19C* 124, 125, *MI* 108, 119, *L19C* 155.

33 p 99 (a) Horse Guards – (b) Westminster Abbey/(from St James's Park) – (c) View from Western End of the Lake – (d) Cadiz Mortar – (e) Turkish Gun. Drawn by H. West. 58 × 48, 60 × 98/230 × 140mm. '7,1'.

34 p 104 (a) Paddington Church – (b) St John's Church, Paddington – (c) British Institution – (d) Exchange Bazaar – (e) Horse Bazaar. Drawn by H. West. 58 × 48,58 × 98/145 × 230mm. '7,2'. (b) is St John the Evangelist, built by Charles Fowler, 1829–31.

35 p 106 (a) St Mary' Church – (b) Palace Entrance – (c) Lambeth Palace – (d) Fore Street – (e) Potteries, Fore Street. Drawn by H. West. 58 × 48,58 × 98/225 × 140mm. '7,3'. *L19C* 121 (a).

36 p 110 (a) The Holme – (b) Albany Cottage – (c) View in the Regent's Park – (d) Macclesfield Bridge – (e) Doric Villa. Drawn by H. West. 58 × 48,58 × 98/220 × 140mm. '7,4'. *MI* 25, 152, 79, 12, 91.

37 p 112 (a) Astley's Theatre – (b) Royal Victoria Theatre – (c) New Bethlem Hospital – (d) Surrey Theatre – (e) Blind School. Drawn by H. West. 58 × 48,60 × 98/220 × 135mm. '7,5'. *MI* 150, 70, 137 (c,d,e).

38 p 113 (a) St Philips Chapel – (b) St Georges Chapel – (c) Quadrant – (d) Haymarket Theatre – (e) County Fire Office. Drawn by H. West. 58 × 48,58 × 100/220 × 140mm. *MI* 21, 22, 62 (a,b,c).

39 p 119 (a) Mint – (b) Trinity House – (c) Monument – (d) St Catharine's Dock House – (e) East India House. Drawn by H. West. 48 × 58,98 × 58/140 × 225mm. *L19C* 12, 34, 95, 6 (a,b,c,e).

40 p 124 (a) St James's Church Piccadilly – (b) St James's Palace – (c) Treasury Whitehall – (d) British Institution – (e) German Chapel. Drawn by H. West. 58 × 48,58 × 98/225 × 140mm. *L19C* 90, 7, *MI* 64 (a,b,c).

41 p 126 (a) St Lawrence, King Street – (b) St Mildred Poultry – (c) Grocers' Hall, Poultry – (d) Mercers' Hall, Cheapside – (e) Old Mansion House, Cheapside. 58 × 48, 60 × 100/220 × 140mm. *L19C* 58, 133, 130, 46 (a,b,c,d).

42 p 136 (a) Royal Exchange – (b) Mansion House – (c) London from Bankside – (d) St Mary's Aldermanbury – (e) Guildhall. Drawn by H. West. 58 × 48, 58 × 100/225 × 135mm. *MI* 128, *L19C* 27, *MI* 1, *L19C* 86, *MI* 85.

43 p 138 (a) Gas Light Company, Westminster – (b) York Column, St James's Park – (c) Royal Westminster Mews – (d) St Margaret's Church – (e) Statue of

George Canning. Drawn by H. West. 58 × 48,58 × 98/220 × 145mm. *MI* 77 (c).

44 p 141 (a) Old St Paul's School – (b) St Paul's School – (c) New Post-Office – (d) Aldersgate – (e) Half Moon Tavern/Bishopsgate Street. 58 × 48,58 × 95/220 × 140mm. *MI* 33, 101 (b,c).

45 p 143 (a) Cambridge Terrace – (b) Chester Terrace – (c) Colosseum, Regent's Park – (d) Diorama – (e) Part of St Andrew's Place. Drawn by H. West. 58 × 48,56 × 100/220 × 140mm. *MI* 49, 87, 3, 145, 95.

46 p 145 (a) St Stephen Walbrook (b) St Mary-le-Bow, Cheapside (c) St Olave's Jewry (d) St Mary Aldermary (e) St Mary, Woolnoth. 58 × 48,58 × 98/230 × 140mm. *L19C* 25, 139, 64, 62, 26.

47 p 154 (a) University Club House – (b) Egyptian Hall – (c) Italian Opera House – (d) Burlington Arcade – (e) Crockford's Club House. 58 × 48,58 × 98/230 × 145mm. *MI* 81, 65, 111, 112 (b,c,d,e).

48 p 158 (a) Auction Mart – (b) Corn Exchange – (c) New London Bridge – (d) Stock Exchange – (e) King's Weigh House. 58 × 48,58 × 100/230 × 140mm. *MI* 157, 112, *L19C* 173, 146, 60.

49 p 160 (a) Painters Stainers Hall – (b) Clothworkers Hall – (c) Vintners Hall – (d) Masons Hall – (e) Crosby Hall. 60 × 48,58 × 100/220 × 140mm. *L19C* 88, 52, 174, 59 (a,b,c,e). (e *Longford* 429).

50 p 161 (a) Whittington College – (b) Arthurs Club House – (c) British Museum – (d) St Peter le Poor, Broad Street – (e) Sessions House & Newgate Prison. 58 × 48,58 × 98/218 × 140mm. *L19C* 18, 192, 9, 91, 127.

51 p 169 (a) Harmonic Institution – (b) St George's Church, Hanover Square – (c) West India Import Dock – (d) New Church Saffron Hill – (e) New Church, North Audley Street. 58 × 48,58 × 98/220 × 140mm. *MI* 63, *L19C* 156, 149, 187, 186.

52 p 171 (a) Coopers Hall – (b) Girdlers Hall – (c) Guys Hospital – (d) Town Hall, Southwark – (e) St Bartholomews Hospital. 58 × 48,58 × 98/220 × 145mm. *L19C* 41, 82, 166, 35, 145.

53 p 175 (a) College of Physicians – (b) College of Surgeons – (c) Penitentiary Millbank – (d) St Clement's Church, Eastcheap – (e) Barber Surgeons' Hall. 58 × 48,58 × 98/220 × 140mm. *MI* 72, 57, 151, *L19C* 151, 75.

54 p 178 (a) House of Correction/Coldbath Fields – (b) Trinity Church (Cloudesley Square) – (c) Caledonian Asylum – (d) Sir Paul Pindar's House/Bishopsgate Street – (e) Bishopsgate Church Without. 58 × 48,58 × 98/220 × 135mm. *L19C* 169, *MI* 142, 120, *L19C* 45, 180.

55 p 183 (a) Watermans Hall – (b) Sadlers Hall – (c) Haberdashers Alms Houses – (d) Innholders Hall – (e) Old Fishmongers Hall. 58 × 48,58 × 98/225 × 140mm. (e) sepia wash drawing (57 × 47mm) in GLC. *L19C* 87, 21, *MI* 50, *L19C* 81, 76.

56 p 188 (a) Pantheon, Oxford Street – (b) Drury Lane Theatre – (c) Covent Garden Theatre – (d) Olympic Theatre – (e) Sadlers Wells Theatre. 58 × 48,58 × 98/225 × 140mm. *L19C* 181, *MI* 71, 51, *L19C* 182, 148.

57 p 192 (a) St Clement's Dane – (b) New St Pancras Church – (c) St Thomas's Hospital – (d) St Bennet's Fink – (e) St George's Bloomsbury. 58 × 48,58 × 98/230 × 135mm. *L19C* 32, *MI* 8, *L19C* 165, 152, 157.

58 p 199 (a) Haggerston New Church – (b) Shoreditch Church – (c) Highgate Archway – (d) Hendon Church – (e) Highgate New Church. 58 × 48,58 × 98/230 × 135mm. *MI* 40, *L19C* 31 (a,b).

59 p 203 (a) Hampstead Church – (b) Enfield Church – (c) Hornsey Church – (d) King's Cross – (e) Garden Gate to Manor House/(Stoke Newington). 58 × 48,58 × 98/225 × 140mm.

60 p 204 (a) St Paul's Balls Pond – (b) St Mary's Islington – (c) Canonbury House – (d) White Conduit House – (e) Old Queens Tavern/Islington. 58 × 48,58 × 98/225 × 140mm. *MI* 114, *L19C* 160, 161 (a,b,e).

VOL. 2

61 (engr title) National/History and Views of London/With its Environs/Including its Antiquities/Modern Improvements &c/from Original Drawings by Eminent Artists/Vol. II. (vignette) North Entrance into London/Islington. London/Black Young & Young/Tavistock Street. 95 × 85mm. nd. Anon vignette.

62 front. St. Paul's Cathedral./(South West Front). Drawn by H. West. Engraved by J. Shury. 98 × 154/135 × 215mm.

63 p 1 (a) St Bride's Avenue – (b) St Michael's Crooked Lane – (c) Interior of the Auction Mart – (d) South Sea House – (e) Merchant Taylors Hall. 58 × 48,58 × 98/225 × 140mm. *MI* 129, *L19C* 177, 43, 22 (a,b,d,e).

64 p 7 (a) Middle Temple Hall – (b) Lyons Inn Hall – (c) Chapel, Library & Hall, Lincolns Inn – (d) Serjeants Inn Hall – (e) Cliffords Inn Hall. 58 × 48, 58 × 98/220 × 135mm. Serjeants' Inn, Chancery Lane. Unsigned wash drawing of Lyons Inn Hall (55 × 45mm) in Westminster Public Library. *L19C* 56, 98, 68, 93, 57.

65 p 11 (a) Guildhall, Westminster – (b) Exeter Change/(as it formerly appeared) – (c) Sussex Place, Regent's Park – (d) Old Goldsmith's Hall – (e) Exchange Bazaar/Grays Inn Road. 58 × 48,58 × 100/220 × 135mm. *MI* 96, *L19C* 30, *MI* 135, *L19C* 53 (a,b,c,d).

66 p 15 (a) Vauxhall Bridge – (b) St Catharine's Dock – (c) Earl Spencers House, Wimbleton Park – (d) Stoke Newington Church – (e) St Pancras Old Church. 58 × 48,55 × 100/220 × 140mm. *MI* 149, *L19C* 150 (a,b).

67 p 23 (a) York House (in Green Park) – (b) King's College – (c) Buckingham Water Gate – (d) City Lying-in Hospital – (e) Somerset House/from the Strand. 58 × 48,60 × 100/215 × 140mm. (d) Brown wash drawing of City Lying-in Hospital (57 × 46mm) in GLC. *MI* 52, *L19C* 37, 128, 5 (a,c,d,e).

68 p 27 (a) Pantechnicon Pimlico – (b) Gallery of British Artists – (c) United Services Club House – (d) Six Clerks' Office/Chancery Lane – (e) Earl Spencers House/Green Park. Drawn by H. West. 58 × 48,58 × 98/225 × 140mm. *L19C* 189, 114 (c,e).

69 p 28 (a) Marquis of Westminster's Gallery/(late Earl of Grosvenors—Park Lane) – (b) West Wing of Carlton House Terrace – (c) Athenaeum Club House – (d) Staples Inn Hall – (e) Barnards Inn Hall. 58 × 48,58 × 98/230 × 140mm. *MI* 56, *L19C* 190, 191, 94, 99.

70 p 30 (a) Trinity Chapel/Sloane Street – (b) Gothic Chapel/Stepney – (c) Wimbledon Park Surrey – (d) Royal York Baths/Regents Park – (e) Coal Exchange. 58 × 48,58 × 98/220 × 140mm. *L19C* 185, *MI* 102, 134, *L19C* 61 (a,b,d,e). (a *Longford* 478)

71 p 38 (a) Trinity Church/Little Queen Street Holborn – (b) St Bartholomews the Great/West Smithfield – (c) New Hungerford Market – (d) Covent Garden Market/West Facade – (e) Oxford Market. 58 × 48,58 × 98/225 × 140mm. Pencil drawing, 'Oxford Market from Castle Street 1829' (115 × 205mm), ascribed to T.H. Shepherd, in Westminster Public Library. *L19C* 188, 120, 16, *MI* 156 (a,b,c,d).

72 p 42 (a) Furnivals Inn – (b) New St Georges Hospital – (c) Interior of Freemasons Hall – (d) Alhallows/Staining Lane – (e) Female Orphan Asylum/Westminster. 58 × 48,58 × 98/220 × 135mm. *MI* 76, *L19C* 107, *MI* 80 (a,d,e).

73 p 45 (a) Kew Palace – (b) Chace Lodge, Enfield – (c) Langham House S. Front (Langham Place) – (d) Chingford Church – (e) Chingford Hall. 58 × 48,58 × 98/225 × 140mm.

74 p 49 (a) St Stephen's Church/Wallbrook – (b) Royal Vestibule/House of Lords – (c) Interior of House of Lords – (d) Old Physicians College – (e) Old Bull and Mouth Inn. 58 × 48,58 × 98/230 × 135mm. Interior of St Stephen, Walbrook. *L19C* 17, 170 (d,e).

75 p 54 (a) St Mary at Hill – (b) St Martin Orgar/Martin Lane, City – (c) Burlington House/Piccadilly – (d) Statue of Achilles/Hyde Park – (e) Statue of Major Cartwright/Burton Crescent. 58 × 48,58 × 98/220 × 140mm. *L19C* 176, 108, 167, *MI* 15 (a,b,c,d).

76 p 57 (a) Shaftsbury House/Aldersgate Street – (b) Tallow Chandlers Hall/Dowgate Hill – (c) The Albany Piccadilly – (d) Charles 2nd Porter & Dwarf – (e) Guy, Earl of Warwick. 60 × 48,58 × 98/220 × 140mm. *L19C* 116, 115, 28, 38 (a,c,d,e).

77 p 60 (a) Merchant Tailors School – (b) Sion College – (c) Salters Hall – (d) King's Bench Prison/Entrance – (e) Prerogative Will Office/Doctors Commons. 60 and 58 × 48,58 × 98/220 × 140mm. Sepia wash drawing of Sion College (58 × 46mm) and wash drawing of King's Bench Prison entrance (41 × 67mm) in GLC. *L19C* 175, *MI* 84, *L19C* 130, 102 (a,c,d,e).

78 p 70 (a) Heralds College – (b) New Parliament Chambers – (c) Frognall Priory Hampstead – (d) Entrance to Lollards Tower/Lambeth Palace – (e) Entrance to St Erasmus Chapel/Westminster Abbey. 58 × 48,58 × 98/220 × 145mm. *L19C* 19, *MI* 159 (a,b).

79 p 75 (a) Apsly House – Piccadilly – (b) Ironmongers Hall – (c) The New City Club Ho. Broad St – (d) Drapers Hall – (e) Giltspur St Compter. 58 × 48,58 × 98/220 × 140mm. Wash drawing of Drapers' Hall (58 × 47mm) in GLC. *MI* 153, *L19C* 153, 50, 126 (a,b,d,e).

80 p 77 (a) St Vedest Foster Lane – (b) Spitalfields Church – (c) New Fishmongers Hall – (d) Talbot Inn, Boro' – (e) St Swithin's, London Stone. 60 × 48,58 × 98/220 × 135mm. *L19C* 69, 76, 164, 136 (b,c,d,e).

81 p 81 (a) Bishop Bonners/Palace – (b) Old White Hart Tavern – (c) New Goldsmiths Hall – (d) Temple Church/Interior – (e) Somerset House/Vestibule. 58 × 48,58 × 100/220 × 140mm. *L19C* 8 (b).

82 p 90 (a) Brewers Hall – (b) Pensioners Hall/Charterhouse – (c) Poets Corner, Westminster Abbey – (d) Carpenters Hall – (e) Stationers Hall. 50 × 60 and 48 × 58,98 × 58/135 × 215mm. *L19C* 31, 55, 10, 51 (a,b,d,e).

83 p 95 (a) The Fountain/Green Park – (b) Imperial Gas Works/Maiden Lane Regents Canal – (c) London Orphan Asylum/Clapton – (d) Apothecaries Hall – (e) Serjeants Inn/Fleet St. 58 × 48,58 × 98/220 × 140mm. *MI* 154, 147, *L19C* 142 (b,c,d).

84 p 96 (a) Park Village East/Regents Park – (b) Grecian Villa/Regents Park – (c) Grays Inn Hall, Library and Chapel – (d) Albion Chapel,/Moorfields – (e) The Ancient Conduit/White Conduit Fields. 58 × 48,55 × 98/220 × 140mm. Wash drawing of Park Village East (59 × 47mm) in Guildhall Library and of Albion Chapel (60 × 45mm) in Museum of London. *MI* 131, 94, *L19C* 67, *MI* 121 (a,b,c,d).

85 p 98 (a) Repository – (b) Deer Stables – (c) Elephant Stables – (d) Ostrich House – (e) Stable for Brahmin Bull. 58 × 48,58 × 98/220 × 140mm. Zoological Gardens.

86 p 103 (a) St James's/Garlick Hill – (b) St Antholin's/Watling St. – (c) Crosby Hall/Interior – (d) Part of Regent St. West Side – (e) Part of Regent St East Side. 58 × 48,58 × 98/220 × 140mm. *L19C* 85, 79, *MI* 123, 127 (a,b,d,e). (c *Longford* 455)

87 p 111 (a) St Mary's/Whitechapel – (b) St Michael's/Queenhithe – (c) House of Commons/Interior – (d) Part of Regent Street, East Side – (e) Part of Regent Street, West Side. 58 × 48,58 × 100/220 × 135mm. *L19C* 106, 137, *MI* 138, 122 (a,b,d,e).

88 p 112 (a) St John's Church/Holloway – (b) St John's Church/West Hackney – (c) Smithfield Market – (d) Lock Hospital/Hyde Park Corner – (e) Hanover Terrace/Regents Park. 58 × 48,58 × 98/220 × 135mm. *MI* 158, 27, *L19C* 15, 134, *MI* 9.

89 p 118 (a) Old Church/Croydon – (b) St James Chapel/or New Church – (c) Croydon Palace/Interior

– (d) Abscomb House – (e) Croydon Palace/Remains of. 58 × 48,58 × 100/230 × 140mm.

90 p 120 (a) Clarence Terrace/Regents Park – (b) Cornwall Terrace/Regents Park – (c) New Westminster Hospital – (d) York Terrace/Regents Park – (e) Chester Terrace/Regents Park. 58 × 48,58 × 98/215 × 135mm. *MI* 6, 18, 32, 87 (a,b,d,e).

91 p 122 (a) Ulster Terrace/Regents Park – (b) Church Missionary College/Islington – (c) St Dunstan/in the West – (d) Copenhagen House – (e) Highbury College. 50 × 58,98 × 58/140 × 225mm. *MI* 26, 19, 20 (a,b,e).

92 p 128 (a) St Giles/Cripplegate Within – (b) St Sepulchre – (c) Westminster Bridge – (d) Weavers Hall/Aldermanbury – (e) Dyers Hall/College Hill. 58 × 48,58 × 98/230 × 140mm. *L19C* 74, 143, 122, 83 (a,b,c,e).

93 p 133 (a) Allhallows the Great/Thames St. – (b) Allhallows Bread St. – (c) Improvements Lambeth Palace – (d) North side, Belgrave Square/Pimlico – (e) Aldgate. 58 × 48,58 × 98/220 × 140mm. *L19C* 179, 93, *MI* 116, *L19C* 42 (a,b,d,e).

94 p 136 (a) Old Salters Hall – (b) Hornsey Wood Ho. – (c) Wittingtons Alms Houses/Highgate – (d) Christ Church/Gt Surrey St. – (e) St Dionis Back Church/Fenchurch St. 58 × 48,58 × 100/220 × 140mm. *MI* 66, *L19C* 184, 48 (c,d,e).

95 p 141 (a) Deaf & Dumb Asylum/Kent Road – (b) Brewers' Alms Houses/Mile End Rd. – (c) Antient Crypt (Aldgate) – (d) Winchester Houses – (e) Staples Inn/Holborn. 58 × 48,58 × 98/225 × 135mm. *MI* 67, *L19C* 89, 94 (b,d,e).

96 p 146 (a) Faringdon Market – (b) New Cattle Mart/Balls Pond – (c) Southwark Bridge/from Queenhythe – (d) Part of the Savoy – (e) Traitors Gate/Tower. 58 × 48,58 × 98/220 × 135mm.

97 p 150 (a) St Mary Magdalen/Fish Street – (b) St Martin Outwich/Bishops Gate St – (c) Old Salters Hall Chapel – (d) Blackwell Hall – (e) Old Furnivals Inn. 58 × 48,58 × 100/220 × 135mm. *L19C* 140, 80 (a,b).

98 p 151 (a) New Bull & Mouth Inn (St Martin le Grand) – (b) Middle Row/Holborn – (c) Library/London Institution – (d) Rotunda/Bank – (e) Egyptian Hall/Mansion Ho. 58 × 48,58 × 98/220 × 140mm. *L19C* 66 (b). (d *Bank of England* 171)

99 p 153 (a) Jews Hospital – (b) Universal Infirmary for Children (Waterloo Rd) – (c) The Lady Chapel/Interior – (d) Tomb of Bishop Andrews – (e) Monument of Gower. 60 × 48,58 × 98/220 × 135mm. (c),(d) and (e) in St Saviour, Southwark (Southwark Cathedral).

100 p 159 (a) Chapel of Ease/Stafford St – (b) St Johns Ch./Hoxton – (c) New Palace/Pimlico – (d) Park Crescent/New Road – (e) Piccadilly and Regent Circus. 58 × 48,58 × 98/220 × 140mm. *MI* 35, 28, 144, 53 (a,b,d,e).

101 p 166 (a) Stepney Church – (b) Old Monastery/of Grey Friars – (c) Somerset House/Interior Quadrangle – (d) Statue of William III – (e) Statue of William Pitt. 58 × 48,58 × 98/220 × 135mm. (d) in St James's Square, (e) in Hanover Square. *L19C* 158 (c).

102 p 168 (a) Statue of Sir Joseph Banks – (b) Statue of James Watt – (c) City Basin/Regents Canal – (d) Cordwainers Hall – (e) Stone Buildings/Lincolns Inn. 58 × 48, 58 × 98/220 × 130mm. *MI* 58, *L19C* 77 (c,d).

103 p 170 (a) Grosvenor Chapel, Halken St, Belgrave Sq. – (b) St Mary's Chapel/Park St – (c) Double Lock/Regent Canal – (d) Gateway/Essex St Strand – (e) Ancient Houses/Drury Court. 58 × 48,58 × 98/215 × 135mm. *MI* 117, 24 (a,c).

104 p 172 (a) An Antient House/High St Boro' – (b) Floor-Cloth Manufactory/High Field Kentish Town – (c) Entrance to the Limehouse Dock/Regent Canal – (d) Allhallows/London Wall – (e) St Nicolas Cole Abbey. 58 × 48,58 × 98/215 × 135mm. *MI* 155, 23, *L19C* 110, 109 (b,c,d,e).

105 p 174 (a) Monument/of Sir Isaac Newton – (b) Monument/in Westminster Abbey – (c) Thames Tunnel – (d) Monument of Alderman Beckford – (e) Monument of the Earl of Chatham. 58 × 48,58 × 98/220 × 135m. (d) and (e) in the Guildhall.

106 p 180 (a) St Andrews/Holborn – (b) Spa Fields Chapel – (c) Jack Straw's Castle/Hampstead Heath – (d) The Clerk's Well/Clerkenwell – (e) Entrance to the New Jail/Clerkenwell. 58 × 48,58 × 98/220 × 140mm.

107 p 181 (a) The Rosemary Branch/Hoxton – (b) The Thatched House/Islington – (c) Chalk Farm – (d) Ancient Houses/Fetter Lane – (e) Ancient Houses/Leather Lane. 60 and 58 × 48,55 × 98/230 × 140mm.

108 p 186 (a) Austin Friars – (b) St Botolph (Aldersgate) – (c) Merlin's Cave – (d) The Sir Hugh Middleton's Head – (e) New River Head. 58 × 48,58 × 98/225 × 135mm.

109 p 195 (a) The English Opera Ho. – (b) Hoare's Banking House/Fleet Street – (c) Bagnidge Wells – (d) Excise Office – (e) Vicar Generals Office/Doctors Commons. 58 × 48,58 × 98/230 × 135mm. (a) the Strand Lyceum, burnt out in 1830 and rebuilt. *L19C* 44 (d).

110 p 202 (a) St Andrews Undershaft – (b) St Ethelbergher/Bishopsgate Without – (c) Blackfriars Bridge – (d) Clerkenwell Close – (e) Hatton Gardens. 58 × 48,55 × 98/225 × 140mm.

111 p 206 (a) Jews Synagogue/Duke St. – (b) Sir George Whitmore's/Hoxton – (c) Fishmongers' Alms Houses/London Road – (d) Curious Font/St Mary's Church Hayes – (e) Curious Font/Stepney Church. 60 and 58 × 48,58 × 100/230 × 135mm.

112 p 209 (a) Elephant & Castle – (b) Bricklayers Arms – (c) Fitzroy Square – (d) Q.Eliz's Hunting Lodge/Epping Forest – (e) Old Church/Highgate. 58 × 48,55

× 98/225 × 140mm. Pencil and wash drawing of Elephant and Castle (58 × 51mm) in GLC.

113 p 212 (a) West Twyford Church/Middlesex – (b) Leadenhall Market – (c) Mr. Soane's Museum – (d) Lee Church & Parsonage – (e) Newgate Market. 48 × 58,100 × 58/140 × 225mm.

114 p 214 (a) Brass Crosby Esq. Obelisk – (b) Waithman's Obelisk – (c) Surrey Zoological Gardens – (d) Marine Society's House (Bishopsgate St.) – (e) Residence of the late Richard Bentley. 58 × 48,58 × 98/220 × 140mm. The obelisks stood in Blackfriars Road and at the foot of Ludgate Hill respectively.

115 p 215 (a) St John's Clerkenwell – (b) Engine House/New River Head – (c) Artillery House (Finsbury) – (d) Paternoster Row – (e) Residence of Dr Goldsmith/Green Arbor Court. 58 × 48,58 × 98/225 × 135mm.

116 (tm, with royal arms tc) Plan of London from Actual Survey 1833/Presented Gratis to the Readers of the United Kingdom Newspaper. Engraved and Printed by John Shury, 16 Charterhouse Street, Charterhouse Square, London. 380 × 590/560 × 820mm. The side margins of the map are ornamented with ten views each, measuring about 45 × 66mm, and the lower margin has 12 measuring about 65 × 40mm centered on a thirteenth of Buckingham Palace measuring 65 × 80mm. Most of the subjects engraved duplicate those represented on the plates of views:

(left-hand margin) East India House – Custom House – Mint – St James's Palace – New Hall Christ's Hospital – Colosseum – New Post Office – Bank of England – Hanover Terrace – Corn Exchange.

(right-hand margin) House of Lords – London Bridge – House of Commons – Waterloo Bridge – Drury Lane Theatre – Horse Guards – Kings College – Covent Garden Theatre – Somerset House – Gloster Terrace.

(lower margin) St Katherine's Chapel – The Royal Exchange – The Mansion House – Caledonian Church – Temple Bar – Guildhall – Buckingham Palace – St Paul's Cathedral – The Monument – St Bride's Church – Lambeth Palace – Westminster Abbey – Entrance to the Green Park.

(*Darlington and Howgego* 343)

178 · TOMBLESON'S THAMES [1834]

In 1827 William Tombleson engraved a view of the City of London from beneath the arch of Waterloo Bridge for Robson's *Picturesque Views* (no 156)

and, during the next two years, 15 plates after T.H. Shepherd's drawings for *Metropolitan Improvements* (no 154) and *London and its Environs* (no 161). These were on steel and it was as a designer, draughtsman and publisher for other engravers on steel that Tombleson was to emerge. His set of 69 views of the Rhine, interpreted by a number of engravers, was published in Numbers from 1832 and completed by December 1833, with Carlsruhe, London and Paris imprints. It was available in English or German with a text by W.G. Fearnside and included a map of the river to locate the beauty spots shown. Besides those of Tombleson in Paternoster Row and Creuzbauer in Carlsruhe the imprints included the name of George Virtue, who specialized in issuing topographical works in Numbers illustrated with copper and steel-engravings. The complete volume was advertised in the *Monthly Literary Advertiser* for December 1833 by 'Tombleson & Co., 11 Paternoster Row, where may be had the Views on the Thames etc.' The same periodical in October 1834 announced that the *Thames and Medway* was now complete and could be had bound in cloth for 25s in the ordinary edition or 50s for India paper.

The Thames collection also appeared in monthly Numbers under the imprints of Tombleson and Creuzbauer. Each pair of leaves is numbered consecutively from 1 to 22, and on p 72 Fearnside, who was again the author of the text, excuses its brevity on the grounds that the 'prescribed limits of the present work, which the proprietors are unwilling to extend, as they are desirous of preserving their faith with the public, in not exceeding the specified numbers of monthly parts, have necessarily prevented digression, and materially abridged the descriptive'. Four pages of text and an average of four plates must have been issued with each of the 22 Numbers. As with the previous work a strip map of the course of the rivers was provided and the text made available in English and German. After the author's own edition the book was taken up by the publishers Thomas Holmes and James Black, the latter under the imprint Black & Armstrong. This imprint was adopted in 1836, and under it also was reissued Partington's *National History* (no 177). In addition Black & Armstrong were by this time 'Foreign Booksellers to the Queen', so the republication must have occurred between June 1837 and 1843, when their imprint changed again.

Tombleson's/Thames – La Thamise – Die Themse./
(vignette) The Source of the Thames. Published by
Tombleson & Compy 11 Paternoster Row (London:
Published by Tombleson & Compy 11 Paternoster
Row./Germany:/Creuzbauer & Co. Carlsruhe).

Quarto, 272 × 210mm.   (1834)

COLLATION Engr title-page; dedication to Lord
Brougham (1 leaf); pp i–iv, preface; pp 1–84, The
Thames, index of plates (p 84). (German ed: Engr
title-page; pp i–iv, Vorrede; pp 1–84, Die Themse, index
of plates (p 84).)

Eighty Picturesque Views on the Thames and Medway,
engraved on steel by the first artists. The historical
descriptions by W.G. Fearnside Esq. London, Published
by Black and Armstrong, Foreign Booksellers to Her
Majesty. Price Two Guineas.

Quarto, 265–75 × 210–15mm.   ?c 1838

COLLATION Title-page; list of engravings (1 leaf); pp
1–84, The Thames, index to plates (p 84).

All but four of the views (items 49, 51, 57, 60, by
T.H. Shepherd and Calvert) are drawn by Tombleson. The chief engraver is Henry Winkles. As an
architectural illustrator he had contributed to
Britton's *Illustrations of the Public Buildings of
London* (no 146) in 1824, the year in which he went
to Germany and opened a studio for steel-engravers
at Carlsruhe. There he probably made the acquaintance of the publisher Creuzbauer and when he
returned to England in 1832 he was engaged by
Tombleson to engrave 23 of his views of the Thames
and Medway. The only other considerable contributor was James Tingle who also had gained experience in working on steel for Britton's *Public
Buildings* and for many of the Shepherd views in
Metropolitan Improvements and *London and its
Environs*. Indeed of about 30 engravers engaged on
this work at least one third had contributed plates to
one or other of the Temple of the Muses publications.

Although so many individuals were involved
there is a uniform quality about these attractive
plates which suggests that their execution was
carefully supervised, and perhaps edited, by one
senior engraver—Winkles, no doubt. A feature
which indicates coordination by a skilled craftsman
is the selection of delightful and variegated frames
which set off each view. Illustrations with decorative
framework had been a feature of books in the
rococo period, as witness the copper-engraved

borders to the plates of Thornton's *History* of 1784
(no 61), but they were often so self-important as to
swamp the line-engravings they were designed to
enhance. In this revival, however, the hardness of
the steel plate has enabled it to retain for the
requisite number of impressions such delicate lines
that decoration is quite subordinated to the engraved view; so much so that only a second glance
reveals the intricacy and prettiness of the design
which fills much of the space between border-lines
and plate-marks, and that it often echoes the theme
it surrounds. Somerset House (item 50) is adorned
with the instruments of the Arts and Sciences,
Hungerford Market (item 47) with fish, flowers and
a beehive, Billingsgate (item 57) with nets, lobster-
pots, oyster barrels, dolphins and crustacea, St
Catherine's Docks and Rotherhithe (items 60–1)
with rigging, sails, anchors, oars, guns and a
figure-head, the Adelphi (item 43) with Adam-style
ornament, and so on. The inventiveness of these
apposite backdrops is more likely to have been the
chief engraver's than the artist's, since Tombleson's
similar views of the Rhine were printed without
adornment.

Captions are engraved in voided capitals and
italics. Those marked with an asterisk below are,
somewhat superfluously, provided with translations
into German and French. The artist's credit, with
the three exceptions mentioned above, is 'Tombleson', 'Tomblesons' or 'W. Tombleson delt.' Engravers' credits are quoted as given. The undated
publication-line is normally 'London, Published by
Tombleson & Co. (Compy), (11)Paternoster Row',
to which, as indicated ('Creuzbauer'), is sometimes
added 'Germany, Creuzbauer & Co. Carlsruhe'.

1 (engr title) Tombleson's/Thames – La Thamise – Die
  Themse./*The Source of the Thames. Published by
  Tombleson & Compy 11 Paternoster Row. 85 ×
  63/225 × 175mm. (German ed: 'London: Published by
  Tombleson & Compy 11 Paternoster Row,/Germany:
  Creuzbauer & Co. Carlsruhe.') Translations bur-
  nished out in later eds.

1a front. View from/London Bridge. Tombleson del.
  Le Petit sculpt. London, Published by Tombleson &
  Co., 11 Paternoster Row. 113 × 158/175 × 225mm.
  Issued with Tombleson's and Creuzbauer's original ed
  to face p 74.

2 p 19 *Mill at Kempsford/Gloucestershire. H. Winkles
  sc. 150 × 105/230 × 170mm.

3 p 42 Oxford. W. Lacey sc. 115 × 150/180 × 230mm.

4 p 51 Nuneham Courteney,/Oxon./Lord Harcourts.
  J.C. Varrall sc. 105 × 145/180 × 225mm.

5 p 54 Wallingford,/Berks. T. Howard sculp. 110 × 148/180 × 225mm.

6 p 58 Park Place,/Henley/—Maitland Esq. A.H. Payne sc. 98 × 148/175 × 225mm.

7 p 58 Henley,/Oxon. Sands sc. 105 × 150/178 × 225mm. 'Creuzbauer'.

8 p 58 *Island, near Henley,/Berks. R. Sands sculpt. 105 × 153/180 × 230mm. 'Creuzbauer'.

9 p 59 Fawley Court,/Henley/—Freeman Esqre. H. Winkles sc. 100 × 150/180 × 225mm.

10 p 59 *Medmenham Abbey. Jas Tingle sculp. 105 × 150/180 × 230mm. 'Creuzbauer'.

11 p 59 *Lady Place, Hurley,/Berks. 105 × 150/180 × 230mm. 'Creuzbauer', but no engraver. Listed as 'Manor House', and sometimes thus captioned.

12 p 59 *View near Hurley,/Berks. J. Tingle sculpt. 100 × 155/180 × 230mm. 'Creuzbauer'.

13 p 60 *Bisham Abbey./Berks. H. Winkles sculpt. 105 × 150/180 × 225mm. 'Creuzbauer'.

14 p 60 *Suspension Bridge,/Gt.Marlow, Bucks. H. Bond sc. 105 × 148/175 × 228mm. 'Creuzbauer'.

15 p 60 Cookham/Berks. J. Rolph sculpt. 102 × 150/175 × 225mm. 'Creuzbauer'.

16 p 61 Hedsor/Lord Boston's. W. Taylor sculp. 105 × 150/180 × 230mm.

17 p 61 Cliefden. H. Winkles sculp. 105 × 150/175 × 230mm. 'Creuzbauer'. Captioned also as 'Cliefton'.

18 p 61 *View from/Cliefden Park. W. Taylor sc. 100 × 140/175 × 230mm.

19 p 61 *View from Maidenhead Bridge. Le Petit sculp. 95 × 150/175 × 225mm. 'Creuzbauer'.

20 p 62 Bray/Bucks. J. Tingle sculp. 105 × 150/180 × 230mm.

21 p 63 *Windsor Castle,/Berks. H. Winkles sculp. 105 × 150/175 × 225mm. 'Creuzbauer'.

22 p 63 *Dorney Church,/Bucks. Sands sc. 105 × 155/175 × 225mm.

23 p 63 Eton College./Berks. H. Winkles sculpt. 100 × 150/175 × 230mm. 'Creuzbauer'.

24 p 63 *Windsor Bridge. J. Carter sculp. 105 × 155/175 × 230mm.

25 p 63 *Datchet Bridge/Bucks. T. Harris sculp. 100 × 150/180 × 230mm.

26 p 63 *Old Windsor Locks. W. Lacey sculpt. 110 × 145/180 × 230mm.

27 p 64 *Chertsey Bridge. J. Smith sculp. 113 × 160/180 × 225mm. No publication-line. 'Chertsea' in list.

28 p 65 Shepperton/Middlesex. H. Winkles sculp. 105 × 153/180 × 225mm. 'Creuzbauer'.

29 p 65 *Walton Bridge. Winkles sculp. 95 × 150/175 × 225mm.

30 p 65 *Sunbury Locks. W. Lacey sculp. 108 × 148/175 × 225mm.

31 p 65 *Garrick's Villa/at/Hampton. H. Sands sc. 105 × 152/180 × 230mm.

32 p 66 *Hampton Court Bridge. J. How sculp. 108 × 148/180 × 228mm.

33 p 66 Teddington Locks. H. Winkles sc. 108 × 150/175 × 225mm. 'Creuzbauer'.

34 p 67 Strawberry Hill,/Lord Waldegrave's,/Twickenham. T. Jeavons sc. 105 × 148/175 × 230mm.

35 p 67 Seat of—Drummond Esqr./Twickenham. Westwood sculp. 102 × 145/175 × 225mm.

36 p 67 *Seat of the/Duke of Buckingham/Richmond. S. Lacey sc. 107 × 150/175 × 230mm. Listed as 'Duke of Buccleugh'; it is Buccleuch House. (*Gascoigne* 106)

37 p 68 *View from/Richmond Hill. 105 × 155/175 × 225mm. No engraver mentioned. (*Gascoigne* 107)

38 p 68 *Richmond Bridge. H. Winkles sc. 103 × 153/175 × 230mm. 'Creuzbauer'. (*Gascoigne* 108)

39 p 68 *Seat of the Marquis of Ailsa. W. Taylor sculpt. 108 × 150/175 × 228mm. 'Creuzbauer'. Listed as 'Marquis of Aylesbury'; sometimes captioned 'Seat of Lord Halesby'.

40 p 69 *Kew Bridge. J. Taylor sc. 105 × 148/175 × 225mm.

41 p 69 *Hammersmith Bridge. Jas Tingle sculpt. 95 × 152/175 × 230mm. 'Creuzbauer'.

42 p 71 *Chelsea Hospital/Middlesex. S. Lacey sculp. 95 × 150/175 × 230mm. (*Longford* 54)

43 p 72 *View near Battersea,/Surry. J. Cox sculp. 110 × 150/175 × 230mm. 'Creuzbauer'. With windmill.

44 p 72 *Vauxhall Bridge. H. Winkles sculpt. 105 × 150/180 × 230mm.

45 p 72 *Lambeth Palace. H. Winkles sculpt. 110 × 160/180 × 230mm. 'Creuzbauer'.

46 p 73 *Westminster Bridge. C. Hall sculpt. 105 × 150/175 × 230mm.

47 p 73 *Hungerford/New Market. Payne sculp. 100 × 150/180 × 225mm.

48 p 73 Adelphi Terrace. H. Winkles sculpt. 100 × 150/180 × 230mm.

49 p 73 *Waterloo Bridge. T. Shepherd delt. Abreck sculpt. 103 × 150/175 × 230mm.

50 p 73 *Somerset House/London. H. Winkles sculpt. 110 × 150/175 × 225mm. 'Creuzbauer'.

51 p 73 *Black Friars Bridge. T. Shepherd delt. C. Finke sculpt. 102 × 150/175 × 230mm.

52 p 73 St. Pauls from Bankside. J. Tingle sculp. 105 × 155/175 × 230mm.

53 p 74 *Southwark/Bridge. J. How sculpt. 100 × 150/175 × 230mm.

54 p 74 Southwark. Jas Tingle sculp. 110 × 160/180 × 230mm. Viewed from City.

55 p 74 *London Bridge. H. Winkles sculp. 105 × 150/175 × 230mm.

56 p 74 View from/London Bridge. Le Petit sculp. 112 × 158/175 × 225mm.

57 p 74 Billingsgate. Calvert delt. Carter sculp. 100 × 152/175 × 230mm. 'Creuzbauer'.

58 p 75 *Custom House. Jas Tingle sculp. 105 × 155/175 × 230mm. No artist mentioned.

59 p 75 *Tower of London. H. Winkles sculp. 102 × 152/175 × 225mm.

60 p 75 *St. Catherine's Docks. Calvert delt. J. Tingle sculpt. 100 × 152/175 × 230mm. 'Creuzbauer'.

61 p 75 Rotherhithe. J. Carter sculp. 102 × 148/180 × 230mm.

62 p 75 *Thames Tunnel. H. Winkles sculp. 150 × 105/230 × 175mm.

63 p 76 Greenwich Hospital. H. Winkles sculp. 105 × 155/175 × 225mm.

64 p 76 *View from Greenwich Park. H. Winkles sculp. 98 × 150/180 × 230mm. No publication-line.

65 p 76 *View near Greenwich. W. Taylor sculpt. 115 × 150/180 × 230mm. 'Creuzbauer'.

66 p 77 Erith/Kent. Acon sculpt. 102 × 150/175 × 225mm.

67 p 77 Greenhithe/Kent. J. Varrall sculp. 98 × 150/175 × 225mm.

68 p 77 Northfleet/Kent. Wallis sculp. 102 × 150/175 × 225mm. 'Creuzbauer'.

69 p 77 Gravesend. 105 × 150/175 × 230mm. Engraver burnished out.

70 p 78 *Nore Lights. W. Taylor sculp. 102 × 148/175 × 225mm. 'Creuzbauer'.

Medway

71 p 81 *Teeston Bridge/Kent. Winkles sculp. 108 × 152/175 × 225mm. 'Creuzbauer'. Listed as 'Teston Bridge'.

72 p 81 East Farleigh/Kent. T. Bishop sculp. 105 × 148/175 × 230mm. 'Creuzbauer'.

73 p 81 Maidstone/Kent. A. McClatchie sculp. 110 × 158/175 × 230mm. 'Creuzbauer'.

74 p 81 *Allington Castle,/Kent. H. Winkles sculpt. 102 × 155/175 × 230mm. 'Creuzbauer'.

75 p 81 *Allington Locks,/Kent. J. Tingle sculp. 110 × 150/175 × 230mm.

76 p 82 Aylesford,/Kent. G. How sculpt. 110 × 150/180 × 225mm. 'Creuzbauer'.

77 p 82 *Wouldham Church, Kent. Payne sculp. 100 × 147/175 × 225mm. Listed as 'Woldham Church'.

78 p 82 *Rochester/Castle./Kent. H. Winkles sculp. 104 × 143/180 × 220mm. 'Creuzbauer'.

79 p 83 Chatham,/Kent. Payne sculp. 103 × 145/175 × 228mm.

80 p 83 Gillingham,/Kent. H. Winkles sculp. 100 × 153/175 × 230mm.

81 p 84 (tr) Tombleson's/Panorama Map of the/Thames and Medway. 2 sheets, each 630 × 255mm. On l. refs 1–10.

179 · TROLLOPE'S HISTORY OF CHRIST'S HOSPITAL [1834]

The author of this history, a classical master at Christ's Hospital in Holy Orders, was the son of Arthur William Trollope, who was headmaster there to within a year of his death in 1827. His portrait is included as an illustration in this book, worked by a well-known portrait-engraver, J.H. Robinson. William Trollope also wrote biblical exegesis and he eventually obtained a living in Tasmania.

A History of the Royal Foundation of Christ's Hospital. With an Account of the Plan of Education ... and memoirs of eminent Blues: preceded by a narrative of the rise, progress and suppression of the convent of Grey Friars in London. By the Rev. William Trollope ... late one of the Classical Masters of Christ's Hospital. London: William Pickering, 1834.

Quarto, 280 × 210mm. 1834

COLLATION Title-page; dedication (1 leaf); pp v–viii, preface, list of engravings; pp ix–xvi, contents; pp 1–358, The History; pp i–cxviii, appendix; index (10 pp).

The drawings for the steel-engravings are mostly the work of Henry Shaw, one of John Britton's protégés, who specialized in architectural drawing and engraving, ornament and illumination and who became an FSA in 1833. From the choice of this artist one might guess at a relationship with the John Shaws, father and son, who between them designed all the recent additions to the Hospital, including the infirmary, the great hall and the Mathematical Grammar Schools. Indeed the Grammar School, the range of dormitories and the main entrance from

Newgate Street were still under construction under the direction of John Shaw junior when this book was published. Another engraver employed was Augustus Fox who had previously worked for the same publisher on headpieces in his annual *The Bijou* (1828) and was a contributor to T.H. Shepherd's *Modern Athens* (1829).

1 front. King Edward the Sixth presenting the Charter to Christ's Hospital/from an original picture by Hans Holbein, in the Great Hall. Engraved by Augustus Fox. London, Published by William Pickering, Chancery Lane, Dec. 10, 1833. 100 × 220mm.

2 p 105 The Old Hall, Whittington's Library, & the Cloisters Christs Hospital. Henry Shaw sc. 100 × 170mm. Vignetted.

3 p 106 (Ruins of the Old Hall) 94 × 140mm. Woodcut, with letterpress.

4 p 114 Christ's Hospital, Hertford. Augustus Fox sc. 100 × 135mm. Vignetted. Built as a preparatory school, 1683–95.

5 p 140 The New Grammar & Mathematical Schools, Christ's Hospital. Drawn & Engraved by Henry Shaw. London, Published by William Pickering, Chancery Lane, 1833. 145 × 210mm. In ruled frame. Completed by John Shaw senior, 1832.

6 p 141 The Reverend Arthur William Trollope .../Late Head Master of Christ's Hospital./From the original picture by Tannock ... Augustus Fox sc. 115 × 95mm.

7 p 165 James Palmer Esqr/late Treasurer of Christ's Hospital/from the original picture by Sir Thomas Lawrence,/in the Court Room. Engraved by H.J. Robinson. Published by William Pickering, Chancery Lane, Dec 1, 1833. 115 × 95mm.

8 p 170 The Hall of Christ's Hospital London/Sir William Curtis Bart. President/Thomas Poynder Junr. Esqr. Treasurer/ John Shaw F.A.S. Architect/1825. 105 × 260mm. Opened 25 April 1825. Elevation.

9 p 347 Exterior View of the New Hall, Christ's Hospital. Drawn & Engraved by Henry Shaw. Published by William Pickering, Chancery Lane, 1833. 155 × 210mm. In ruled frame.

10 p 352 Interior of the New Hall, Christ's Hospital. Drawn & Engraved by Henry Shaw. Published by William Pickering, Chancery Lane, 1833. 160 × 200mm. Outline etching, in ruled frame.

180 · THE YOUTH'S NEW PICTURE OF LONDON [c 1834]

This London guide for young people affords slight relief from the usual lecture tour by the father or guardian of an imaginary family in that all the members of the Curwen family, including the 15 year old son who has read up London history in his Cumbrian school library, are allowed to contribute their quota of information in conversation. The imprint is undated but the address of the printer of the earlier edition, together with the latest dated reference in the text to the opening of the new Hungerford Market on 2 July 1833, suggests that it was originally issued not later than 1834.

The wood-engraved title-page of this issue announces 40 engravings, its cloth-gilt binding, a map and 30 plates; but the copy examined contained only 20 steel-engravings gathered at the end, the other illustrations being wood-engravings, either printed in the text or full-size on separate pages with subjects such as the King's levee or Queen Adelaide's 'drawing room'. Another edition, containing 27 plates and a map, has a later address for the printer but the text and captions still refer to the King; it could hardly have been issued later than June 1837.

(wood-engr title) The Youth's New Picture of London; Illustrated with Forty Fine Engravings. London: Edward Lacey, 76, St. Paul's Church Yard. (verso) Sears & Trapp, Printers, 11, Budge Row, Walbrook, London.

The Youth's New Picture of London, An Interesting Account of the rise, progress and present state of the 'Great Metropolis', its public Buildings, their uses &c—great men—trades—charitable Institutions—Religion—important Societies—Shipping—Commerce—Exhibitions—Amusements, and all that can inform the youthful mind respecting the First City in the World. Written in an easy and familiar manner. Illustrated with a Map and numerous plates. London: Edward Lacey, 76 St. Paul's Church-Yard and sold by all booksellers. (verso) W.J. Sears, Printers, 3 & 4 Ivy Lane, Paternoster Row.

Small octavo, 130 × 110mm.   c 1837

COLLATION   Title-page; pp 1–284, New Picture.

The steel-engravings in both editions are identical with those in Whittock's *Modern Picture of London* (no 183) and in nine cases with those in Allen's *Panorama of London* (no 162). The publisher, Edward Lacey, had also been joint publisher of Allen's *Surrey and Sussex* (no 158), also illustrated by Whittock. Five of the 20 views in the earlier edition are not reused in the later one and in neither are the plates listed. References are abbreviated to *MPL* and *PL*, together with relevant item no.

c 1837

1 front. Bank of England. 58 × 82mm. *MPL* 5, *PL* 6. (*Bank of England* 97)

2 p 10 St. Paul's. 90 × 60mm. *MPL* 7.

3 p 20 Temple Bar. 55 × 82mm. *MPL* 17.

4 p 30 New Post Office. 60 × 83mm. *MPL* 2.

5 p 40 The Late Duke of York's House. 55 × 80mm. And 1st ed. *MPL* 66.

6 p 50 Auction Mart. 56 × 80mm. And 1st ed. *MPL* 6.

7 p 60 St. Margaret's Church and Westminster Abbey. 55 × 80mm. *MPL* 40, *PL* 10.

8 p 70 House of Commons. 58 × 80mm. And 1st ed. *MPL* 43, *PL* 26.

9 p 80 The House of Lords. 55 × 83mm. And 1st ed. *MPL* 42.

10 p 90 Corn Exchange. 58 × 80mm. *MPL* 23, *PL* 21.

11 p 100 Mansion House. 88 × 58mm. *MPL* 25.

12 p 110 St. Katherine's Dock House. 58 × 82mm. And 1st ed. *MPL* 36.

13 p 120 Hay Market Theatre. 56 × 80mm. And 1st ed. *MPL* 59.

14 p 130 The New London Bridge. 60 × 90mm. And 1st ed. *MPL* 26.

15 p 140 The London Docks. 60 × 85mm. And 1st ed. *MPL* 37, *PL* 28.

16 p 150 The Kings Palace. 60 × 90mm. And 1st ed. *MPL* 64.

17 p 160 The Foundling Hospital. 58 × 85mm. And 1st ed. *MPL* 73.

18 p 170 St. James's Palace. 55 × 82mm. *MPL* 61.

19 p 180 The Admiralty. 57 × 82mm. And 1st ed. *MPL* 46.

20 p 190 East India House. 55 × 80mm. *MPL* 20.

21 p 200 Harrow School. 58 × 82mm. *MPL* 88, *PL* 12.

22 p 210 The West India Docks. 60 × 85mm. And 1st ed. *MPL* 38, *PL* 14.

23 p 220 Hammersmith Suspension Bridge. 58 × 82mm. And 1st ed. *MPL* 89.

24 p 230 London Institution. 55 × 80mm. *MPL* 9, *PL* 23.

25 p 240 Kingston Bridge. 57 × 83mm. And 1st ed. *PL* 16.

26 p 250 Windsor Castle. 57 × 82mm. And 1st ed. *MPL* 86.

27 p 260 Richmond Bridge. 58 × 80mm. *MPL* 85.

28 p 289 A Map of the Country/Ten Miles Round London. E. Lacey, 76, St. Paul's London. 100mm. Roundel.

c 1834 (extra plates)

29 Hornsey Church. 58 × 80mm. *MPL* 92.

30 Egyptian Hall. 58 × 82mm. *MPL* 60.

31 Lambeth Palace. 58 × 82mm. *MPL* 78.

32 St. Luke's Hospital. 55 × 88mm. *MPL* 67.

33 King's Theatre. 56 × 82mm. *MPL* 58.

34 London, Westminster & Southwark. Engraved for The Stranger's Guide through London. 120 × 370mm. Map. (*Darlington and Howgego* 351)

181 · BRAYLEY AND BRITTON'S WESTMINSTER PALACE [1836]

On the afternoon of 16 October 1834 the Clerk of the Works of the Houses of Parliament directed some of his workmen to burn about two cartloads of old wooden tally sticks, discarded by the Exchequer, in the furnaces which warmed the House of Lords. Having done this they went home, leaving the flues red hot, and by evening the complex of buildings surrounding the Lords was ablaze. In Brayley's words:

An immense multitude of spectators assembled at Westminster to witness the ravages of the fire, the lurid glare of which was distinctly visible for many miles around the metropolis. Even the river Thames, in the vicinity of the spot was covered with boats and barges full of persons whom curiosity had attracted to the scene; and the reflections of the wavering flames upon the water, on the neighbouring shores, and on the many thousands thus congregated, composed a spectacle most strikingly picturesque and impressive. In Old Palace Yard the progress of the fire exhibited a 'Tableau Vivant' of not inferior interest.

In one of the boats was the painter Turner busy immortalizing this spectacular bonfire.

Three regiments of guards, police, firemen and working parties kept order and played water on the flames. On the next day officials of the Office of

Woods, responsible for the maintenance of public buildings, started assessing the damage incurred. The Houses of Lords and Commons and the Painted Chamber had been consumed to the bare walls and their surrounding outworks of buildings quite burnt out, while the cloisters of St Stephen's Chapel, the Courts of Law and the Speaker's House were badly damaged. Only Westminster Hall remained, happily, unscathed.

No sooner had the Office of Woods made their inspection than, with journalistic flair, John Britton's pupil, the 21 year old Robert Billings, moved in with his sketching-block and, surrounded by charred Gothic ruins, started recording the depredations of the flames. Four of his drawings for this book actually bear the date of October 1834 while that of the Upper Cloister of St Stephen' Chapel (item 17) is dated 21 October when the ashes must still have been hot under foot. The work is indeed as much Billings's as it is Britton's or Brayley's since he provided the drawings for all but a handful of the 41 plates. But Britton and Brayley also reacted fairly promptly to this surprise opportunity and before the end of the year were able to announce:

On the 1st January 1835 will be published Number 1. of an Original Work to be completed in Ten Monthly Parts, illustrated by numerous Embellishments: viz: 'A History and Description of the late Houses of Parliament ... by Edward W. Brayley and John Britton Esqrs ...' London: Published by John Weale (Taylor's Architectural Library), 59 High Holborn, and by the Authors.... It is proposed to complete the Work in a single volume about 400 pages of letter-press, and Forty Engravings; and as cheap publications are 'the order of the day' it will be issued on the following terms, viz. Royal 8vo, with proofs at 4s., and demy 8vo at 2s. per Number, including Four Illustrations on steel and wood.

The complete volume was soon available at £1 1s royal octavo, £2 2s quarto and £4 4s de luxe.

Josiah Taylor, who had been Britton's publisher for the *Architectural Antiquities* (no 97) and the *Illustrations of the Public Buildings of London* (no 146), had been succeeded at the Architectural Library by the publisher John Weale. By January 1836 the authors were able to dedicate the completed volume to Earl de Grey, President of the Institute of British Architects which had just been founded. They were also able to state that 'no fewer than ninety-seven sets of Designs have been made for the proposed new Houses of the Legislative Bodies' and, in their preface, to announce that the four designs selected by the Commissioners for the rebuilding competition were those of Charles Barry, J.C. Buckler, D. Hamilton and W. Railton, Charles Barry's designs 'being recommended to be carried into effect'.

The History of the Ancient Palace and late Houses of Parliament at Westminster: embracing Accounts and Illustrations of St. Stephen's Chapel, and its Cloisters,— Westminster Hall,—the Court of Requests,—the Painted Chamber, &c. &c. By Edward Wedlake Brayley, and John Britton, Fellows of the Society of Antiquaries &c.&c.&c. Illustrated by Engravings. (wood-engraving: 'Seal of St Stephen's College. R.W. Billings del. S. Williams sc.', 65 × 95mm) London: John Weale, Architectural Library, 59, High Holborn. 1836.
(Additional engraved title reads: 'Palatial/and/Parliamentary/Edifices of Westminster'. See item 14 below.)

Octavo, 218 × 140mm. (Large Paper 240 × 150mm)
1836

COLLATION Title-page; pp iii–viii, dedication; pp ix–xvi, preface; pp 1–464, History; pp 465–8, list of illustrations; pp 469–76, index.

The 41 steel-engravings fall into two categories: firstly, romantic visions of Gothic ruins such as item 15 which shows the Cloister Court of St Stephen's Chapel and the sun shining through the perpendicular tracery from within the roofless building, reflected from the lake made by the fire-engines, or item 8 where rooks circle above the gaunt walls and turrets of the ruined chapel; secondly, numerous carefully measured outline-drawings of fan vaulting, panelling, tracery and other architectural detail. Similar measured drawings of Soane's additions to the House, now completely destroyed, had been published by Britton in 1826 in the second volume of *Illustrations of the Public Buildings of London* and the same type of plate, but etched on copper, had illustrated his *Architectural Antiquities* nearly 30 years earlier. The greatest number are engraved by Thomas Clark although there are a few credits for engravers such as William Woolnoth and J. Hawksworth who had been employed in Britton publications in the early years of the century. Fourteen of the original drawings are in the House of Commons Library.

The title-page and chapter-head woodcuts are engraved by S. Williams and N. Whittock after Billings and William Capon.

The plates, bound together at the back of the volume, were published at an average of four a month (except June and November) throughout 1835. The numbering, tr, in Roman numerals, relates neither to the order in which they were published nor to their arrangement, which is set out in a list at the end of the volume which, for further information, refers back to a commentary in the 'Arranged list of engravings' on pp 447–64. In some copies they are not arranged in the prescribed order but between pp 418–64 opposite the pages which comment upon them. Each plate is headed 'Britton & Brayley's Westminster' and has this uniform publication-line: 'Published (date) by J. Weale, 59, High Holborn—Gad & Co. Printers.'

1 pl.2 Parliamentary & other offices, courts, &c./ Westminster/The part within the dotted line shews the extent of the fire Octr. 16, 1834. Drawn by E.W. Billings. Engraved by G. Gladwin.... Feby 1, 1835. 110 × 175/140 × 230mm. Plan.

St Stephen's Chapel

2 pl.26 Plans of Chapel & Crypt, St Stephen's Chapel./ Westminster. R.W. Billings del. Saml. Bellin sculp.... April 1, 1835. 100 × 182/140 × 230mm.

3 pl.3 Crypt under St. Stephen's Chapel. /Western end—looking West. R.W. Billings del. July 9, 1835. T. Woolnoth sc.... Octr 1, 1835. 105 × 165/145 × 225mm. Pencil and wash drawing (236 × 355mm) in House of Commons Library.

4 pl.19 St. Stephen's Chapel. /Entrance from Cloisters to Crypt. R.W. Billings del. W. Woolnoth sc.... Decr. 1, 1835. 162 × 100/230 × 140mm.

5 pl.18 Window of the Crypt to St. Stephen's Chapel./ Westminster, Measured & Drawn by R.W. Billings, July 1835. T. Clark sc.... Septr 1, 1835. 180 × 100/235 × 135mm. Section, elevation, plan.

6 pl.25(i) Section of St. Stephen's Chapel and Crypt./ As fitted up for the House of Commons, 1834. R.W. Billings del. G. Gladwin sc.... March 1, 1835. 105 × 182/140 × 230mm.

7 pl.28 St. Stephen's Chapel—East Front./Westminster. R.W. Billings del. J. Carter sc.... Feby. 1, 1835. 155 × 110/230 × 140mm. Water-colour (369 × 280mm), dated November 1834, in House of Commons Library.

8 pl.12 E. End Painted Chamber & S. Side of St. Stephen's Chapel/Westminster. R.W. Billings del. Jany 15, 1835. Thos. Clark sc.... March 1, 1835. 107 × 163/140 × 225mm. The Chapel gutted. Pencil drawing (265 × 409mm), dated 9 January 1835, in House of Commons Library.

9 pl.6 St Stephen's Chapel—One compartment. R.W. Billings del. J. Hawksworth sc.... Octr 1, 1835. 195 × 112/215 × 140mm. Elevation of one bay, with section and buttress.

10 pl.29 Vestibule to St. Stephen's Chapel./Westminster. R.W. Billings del. Thos. Clark sc.... Feb. 1, 1835. 165 × 110/230 × 140mm. Water-colour (389 × 257mm), dated November 1834, in House of Commons Library.

11 pl.11 Elevation, Section and Plan of one compartment (of three)/of the screen St. Stephen's Chapel, Westminster. Drawn & Engraved by R. Billings.... Octr. 1, 1835. 190 × 95/230 × 140mm.

12 pl.27 St. Stephen's Chapel, looking East./Westminster. R.W. Billings del. Novr. 1834. J. Le Keux sc.... May 1, 1835. 153 × 97/228 × 145mm. Water-colour (430 × 302mm), dated November 1834, in House of Commons Library.

13 pl.16 Stairs and Passage/from St. Stephen's Chapel to Cloister. R.W. Billings del. E. Jones sc.... Augt 1, 1835. 165 × 98/230 × 145mm.

14 pl.1 (engr title) Palatial/and Parliamentary/Edifices of Westminster—Parts of St. Stephen's Chapel & Cloister/Westminster. R.W. Billings del. Thos Clark sc. J. Britton dirext.... Jan 1, 1835. 160 × 105/228 × 135mm. Composite design of frieze, window, spandrels and niches, with lc a vignette of the Palace in flames, viewed from the river.

15 pl.17 Plan of Cloisters St. Stephen's Chapel, Westminster. J. Hewitt del. F.P. Becker sc.... Augt 1, 1835. 180 × 130/230 × 140mm.

16 pl.25(ii) Cloister Court/St. Stephen's Chapel. R.W. Billings del. W. Woolnoth sc.... Aug. 1, 1835. 110 × 165/140 × 230mm.

17 pl.30 Upper Cloister, Part of St. Stephen's Chapel, &c./Westminster. R.W. Billings del. Oct. 21, 1834. Thos. Clark sc.... Jany 1, 1835. 182 × 120/230 × 140mm. The fire broke out on Thursday evening, 16 October, and was still burning on Friday; Billings was sketching on site by the following Tuesday. Water-colour (385 × 298mm) in House of Commons Library.

18 pl.36 Cloister, St. Stephen's Chapel, South Walk, Looking E./Westminster. R.W. Billings del. Thos. Clark sc.... April 1, 1835. 160 × 108/230 × 140mm. Pen and pencil scaled drawing (439 × 298mm) in House of Commons Library.

19 pl.34 Cloister—N.W. Angle./ St. Stephen's Chapel. R.W. Billings del. May 1835. J. Woods sc.... July 1, 1835. 152 × 105/230 × 140mm.

20 pl.22(i) Compartment of Cieling at North and South Sides./Cloister of St. Stephen's Chapel. J. Hewitt del. F. Mansell sc.... Octr. 1, 1835. 103 × 167/140 × 230mm.

21 pl.33 Two Compartments South East Angle/Cloister of St. Stephen's Chapel. R.W. Billings del. J. Hawksworth sc.... July 1, 1835. 100 × 163/145 × 230mm.

22 pl.35(i) St. Stephen's Chapel./Plan of half of one window of Cloister & details. J. Hewitt del.... Decr 1, 1835. 105 × 165/140 × 230mm.

23 pl.21 Details of the Cloister of St. Stephen's Chapel. J. Hewitt del. F. Mansell sc.... Octr 1, 1835. 165 × 105/230 × 145mm. Spandrel, columns, window elevation.

24 pl.23(i) Details of the Cloister of St. Stephen's Chapel. J. Hewitt del. F. Mansell sc.... Octr. 1, 1835. 165 × 110/230 × 140mm. Elevation of piers between windows, centre part of ceiling over the piers, etc.

25 pl.31 Ground Plan of Chantry-Chapel &c. St. Stephen's Chapel./Westminster. J.R. Thompson del. May 1835. Saml. Bellin sc.... July 1, 1835. 170 × 110/230 × 140mm.

26 pl.32 Chantry Chapels & Cloister./Section from E. to W. J.R. Thompson del. J. Hawksworth sc.... July 1, 1835. 120 × 165/145 × 230mm.

27 pl.22(ii) Chantry-Chapels./No.1 Section looking W. & elevation of East end, No.3. J.R. Thompson del. T. Clark sc.... Septr 1, 1835. 118 × 176/140 × 230mm.

28 pl.23(ii) Chantry Chapel in Cloisters/St. Stephen's Chapel. J.R. Thompson del. T. Woods sc.... Septr. 1, 1835. 175 × 120/230 × 145mm.

Court of Requests, late House of Lords

29 pl.5 Three Windows, S.end; Court of Requests./Westminster. R.W. Billings del. Octr. 27, 1834. Thos. Clark sc.... Feby 1, 1835. 110 × 170/145 × 225mm.

30 pl.37 Ruins of the House of Lords, &c./Westminster. Drawn by R.W. Billings Octr. 1834. W. Woolnoth sc.... April 1, 1835. 108 × 185/145 × 230mm. Water-colour drawing (282 × 415mm), dated 22 October 1834, 'from Old Palace Yard', in House of Commons Library.

31 pl.38(i) Long Gallery, looking North./Westminster. Drawn & Engraved by T. Clark.... April 1, 1835. 165 × 105/228 × 145mm.

Painted Chamber

32 pl.15 Painted Chamber, looking East./Westminster Palace. R.W. Billings del. Octr. 25, 1834. Thos. Clark sc.... Jany 1, 1835. 155 × 110/230 × 140mm. For 'East' read 'West'. Companion water-colour (387 × 297mm), of the same date, a 'View of the Painted Chamber looking into the House of Lords', in House of Commons Library.

33 pl.14 Painted Chamber, looking East./Westminster. Drawn Oct. 1834 & Engraved by Thos. Clark.... March 1, 1835. 150 × 110/230 × 140mm. cf with drawing (390 × 301mm), signed and dated 'T. Clark Octr 27 1835', in House of Commons Library.

34 pl.13 Stair Case at S.E. Angle, Painted Chamber./Westminster. R.W. Billings del. W. Taylor sc.... March 1, 1835. 163 × 100/230 × 140mm. Pencil drawing (292 × 301mm), dated 1 January 1835, in House of Commons Library.

Westminster Hall

35 pl.10 Westminster Hall./South End, and part of West side. R.W. Billings del. Hawkesworth sc.... Aug. 1, 1835. 150 × 108/230 × 140mm. Interior.

36 pl.8 Westminster Hall. Compartment, E.side, near S.end. Drawn & Engraved by R.W. Billings, Novr 6, 1834.... Jany 1, 1835. 108 × 158/140 × 230mm. Water-colour (278 × 395mm), dated 3 November 1834, in House of Commons Library.

37 pl.9 Westminster Hall./Buttress &c. East side. R.W. Billings del. May 1835. T. Clark sc.... July 1, 1835. 106 × 155/135 × 230mm.

Ancient Capital and Ceiling

38 pl.35 Capital carved in stone of the time of William Rufus./Part of the Cieling of the ancient Palace of Westminster. W. Capon delt. J. Woods sculp.... Octr 1, 1835. 160 × 110/230 × 140mm.

Star Chamber, and Houses of Lords and Commons

39 pl.20 Interior of Star Chamber./Westminster. R.W. Billings del. May 1835. J. Woods sc.... July 1, 1835. 105 × 155/145 × 230mm.

40 pl.38(ii) House of Lords/as fitted up in 1835. R.W. Billings del. Feb. 1835. Thos. Clark sc.... May 1, 1835. 158 × 102/230 × 140mm. Water-colour (325 × 212mm) in House of Commons Library.

41 pl.39 House of Commons./as fitted up in 1835. R.W. Billings del. Feb. 1835. Wm. Taylor sc.... 155 × 105/225 × 140mm. Pencil sketch (242 × 185mm) in House of Commons Library.

---

182 · MALCOLM'S ONE HUNDRED AND NINETEEN VIEWS* [1836]

John Bowyer Nichols, the son of the printer of Malcolm's *Views within twelve miles round London* (no 82) and *Londinium Redivivum* (no 83), who had joined his father in 1815 in an appeal for assistance for Malcolm's impoverished widow and mother, must have retained the plates etched for these works. As sole proprietor of the *Gentleman's Magazine* he also had access to other Malcolm plates and so issued this retrospective collection in 1836. In his 'Memoir' he says: 'Many pleasing specimens of Mr. Malcolm's skill as an Engraver are to be found in the *Gentleman's Magazine* for 1792 to 1815. But his more finished productions appeared in his *Excursions through Kent &c* and in Mr. Nichols's *History of Leicestershire*'. It is of interest to note that in the 'Advertisement', dated 1 October 1836, the selling point was still extra-illustration: 'As almost all the subjects delineated in the present Work are particularly noticed and described in Pennant's 'London' or Lyson's 'Environs of London' it is hoped they will form pleasing Embellishments to those Publications; for which purpose an Index to the Prints is added, referring to the pages of these popular authors'. This, taken with his decision to reissue J.T. Smith's illustrations for *The Antiquities of Westminster* (no 98) in 1837, suggests that grangerizing persisted as a popular hobby into the early Victorian era.

Nichols now offers separately two of Malcolm's 'more elaborate engravings', E. and N. views of Middle Temple Hall (about 355 × 455mm) at 6s the pair (they were first issued in 1800, under Middle Temple auspices, at 15s each). The Leathersellers' Hall plates (items 18–20) were originally published in 1799 at 5s the set.

The plates themselves are unnumbered but details are given of the first 33 as these are mainly of central London. Those originally published in *Londinium Redivivum* are referred back to that work by *LR* with volume and page number.

One Hundred and Nineteen Views in London, and in the vicinity of the Metropolis, drawn and engraved by James Peller Malcolm, F.S.A. Author of Londinium Redivivum, &c. With a Memoir of the Author, written by himself and a descriptive index (epigraph) London, J.B. Nichols and Son, 25, Parliament Street, 1836.

Quarto, 305 × 240mm.   1836

COLLATION Title-page; p2, advertisement dated 1 October 1836; pp 3–6, Memoir of the author; pp 7–12, descriptive index.

1 (front. to the *History of Leicestershire*) Malcolm. 170 × 140/200 × 160mm. Vignette.

2 Remains of the Old Palace called the Marshalsea, N.E. View. 100 × 180/120 × 200mm. Refs a and b.

3 Marshalsea before the new Buildings were erected. 100 × 153/120 × 170mm.

4 Middle Temple. Malcolm. Published Nov 1, 1800 by J.P. Malcolm, 22 Somers Place. Publish'd January 20th 1803 by W. Richardson, York House, No 31 Strand. 215 × 285/273 × 330mm. The Hall, from the S.W.

5 Ely Chapel. Malcolm del. et sc. Published Jan 1 1805 by J.P. Malcolm in Somers Town. 170 × 115/185 × 125mm. *LR* 2,230.

6 St Bartholomews. Malcolm. 185 × 220/205 × 255mm.

Interior of St Bartholomew the Great, looking E. *LR* 1,293.

7 St Bartholomew's South Transept. 110 × 165/123 × 170mm. *LR* 1,291.

8 S. View of Part of the Grey Friars Monastery/Now Christ's Hospital, London. 103 × 140/123 × 150mm.

9 Sir W. Weston. Schnebbelie del. 1787. 205 × 138mm pl.mark. Monument in St James's Church, Clerkenwell. *LR* 3,212.

10 (Portrait of Queen Elizabeth from painted glass in St Dunstan in the West) Published May 1, 1800 by J.P. Malcolm, Somers Place. 108 × 70/180 × 95mm. *LR* 3,456.

11 London Wall & St Giles's Cripplegate. 155 × 95/175 × 110mm. (tr) 'Gent. Mag. May 1817, Pl.II, p 401.' Originally published in 1803 in *LR* 3,271.

12 Monument of Francis Beaumont Esq. at the Charterhouse ... of William Lambe at Lambe's Chapel ... 135 × 230 pl.mark. *LR* 2,317.

13 (along tm) Finsbury-Fields/North. (bl) To his/affect. friends ... and all other lovers of/Archerie ... Will. Hole. (tl, arms of the Goldsmiths' Company) 210 × 128/225 × 145mm. Plan of Butts. *LR* 4,26.

14 St John's Chapel in the White Tower London. Malcolm del. et sc. Published Mar. 7, 1799 by J.P. Malcolm, 34 Chalton St, Somers Town. 140 × 195/150 × 200mm. *LR* 4,629.

15 Death of Whittington. 90 × 80/140 × 110mm. From a MS belonging to Mercers' Company. *LR* 4,515.

16 Dr. Donne – East End of the North Crypt of St Paul's/dedicated to St Faith. Malcolm. 130 × 33, 135 × 108/160 × 200mm. (tr) 'Gent. Mag. Feb. 1820, Pl.II, p 113.' Donne's effigy in a shroud. *LR* 3,61.

17 Crosby Hall. Malcolm del et s. Published Jan. 1, 1805 by J.P. Malcolm. 230 × 170/245 × 190mm. *LR* 3,565.

18 Leatherseller's Hall, London. Malcolm del et s. Publish'd Jan 1, 1799 by J.P. Malcolm, 34 Chalton St. Somers Town. Publish'd Feby 1, 1805 by W. Richardson, York House, No 31 Strand. 133 × 200/145 × 220mm. The courtyard.

19 Leather-seller's Hall. Malcolm del et sc. Publish'd Mar. 1, 1799 by J.P. Malcolm, 34 Chalton St. Somers Town. 175 × 240/190 × 260mm. Interior looking towards screens. *LR* 3,563.

20 St Helens Leatherseller's Hall. London. Malcolm del. et sc. Publish'd Jany 1, 1799 by J.P. Malcolm, 34 Chalton Street, Somers Town. Publish'd Feby 1, 1803 by W. Richardson, York House, No 31 Strand. 140 × 240/155 × 250mm.

21 St Helens. Malcolm del. et s. Publish'd Nov. 1, 1801 by J.P. Malcolm, 52 Chalton St, Somers Town. 110 × 178/125 × 185mm. Exterior. *LR* 3,555.

22 Inside of St Helen's. Malcolm del. et s. Publish'd Dec. 1, 1801 by J.P. Malcolm, 52 Chalton St, Somers Town. 120 × 150/140 × 160mm. *LR* 3,553.

23 (Grate for the nuns in St Helen's Church, etc) Publish'd Oct. 10, 1800 by J.P. Malcolm, Somers Place. 150 × 200mm pl.mark. *LR* 3,554.

24 Remains of the Holy Trinity Aldgate: Destroyed circa 1803. 90 × 108/100 × 120mm. The priory in the parish of St Katherine Cree. *LR* 4,1.

25 (The Crypt of the Church of Holy Trinity at Aldgate, etc) Publish'd Nov. 1, 1801 by J.P. Malcolm, 52 Chalton St., Somers Town. 120 × 165mm pl.mark. *LR* 1,282.

26 St Bartholomew Parva. Publish'd May 1, 1802 by Malcolm, Somers Town. 130 × 160/150 × 175mm. *LR* 1,303.

27 Bangor House, London. Publish'd Feb. 1, 1805 by J.P. Malcolm, Somers Town. 150 × 95/165 × 110mm. (tr) 'Gent. Mag. May 1819, Pl.II p 401.' *LR* 2,228.

28 Westminster 1650. CB pinx. Malcolm sc. Publish'd Dec. 1, 1797 by J.P. Malcolm, Middlesex St, Somers Town. 113 × 185/128 × 190mm. *LR* 4,303.

29 Somerset Place,/1650. CB pinx. Malcolm sc. Publish'd Dec. 1, 1797 by J.P. Malcolm, Middlesex St, Somers Town. 115 × 185/130 × 200mm. (tr) 'Pl.1. p. 89.' *LR* 4,289.

30 Altar in the Chapel of St Blase, at Westminster Abbey. 200 × 160/215 × 180mm. (tr) 'Gent. Mag. Dec. 1821, Pl.II, p 497.' *LR* 1,155.

31 (Specimens of the mosaic pavement in King Edward the Confessor's Chapel, Westminster Abbey, etc) Malcolm del. et sc. Publish'd Jan 1, 1802 by J.P. Malcolm, 52 Chalton St. Somers Town. 220 × 150mm pl.mark. *LR* 1,89.

32 Old Buildings of the Exchequer. PF fecit. 90 × 165/105 × 175mm.

33 Earl Spencer's St James's Park. Schnebbelie del. Malcolm sc. Publish'd Jan 16, 1798 by J.P. Malcolm, 34 Chalton St, Somers Town. 100 × 160/115 × 165mm. *LR* 4,247.

183 · WHITTOCK'S MODERN PICTURE OF LONDON [1836]

The more usual occupation of Nathaniel Whittock, the author of this book, was in the making of topographical drawings to illustrate the writings of others. In 1829 he contributed 30 views to Thomas Allen's two-volume *History of the Counties of Surrey and Sussex* (no 158) and in 1831, with H.

Gastineau, over 140 views to engrave on steel for the same topographer's three-volume *History of the County of York*. He was a self-styled 'tutor in drawing and perspective to the University of Oxford' and published descriptions of that city in 1829 and 1830. His drawing-books were published by George Virtue, including the *Youth's New London Drawing Book* in 1836. He practised lithography, most notably to reproduce his own very free ten-foot long rendering in pen and ink of Wyngaerde's panoramic drawing of Elizabethan London, then in the Bodleian Library, now in the Ashmolean Museum. Virtue was on the lookout for works of travel and topography suitable for publication with steel-engraved illustrations, so Whittock's credentials must greatly have appealed to him.

This book contains not the 100 engravings claimed on the title-page but 92, with the addition of an engraved title and map. Of these only the title-page and frontispiece carry credits: those of the artists Seymour and Campion and the engraver J. Rogers. Campion and Seymour had both also contributed to two of Thomas Allen's London books, the *History and Antiquities* (no 152) and *Panorama of London* (no 162), and from the latter the title and 73 views, all engraved by Rogers, are reused here by Whittock. They are designated below with the abbreviation *PL* followed by the item number. Rogers was also the engraver-in-chief of Whittock's drawings for Allen's county histories mentioned above. On stylistic grounds, detailed in the note on the *Panorama of London*, it is likely that Whittock and Rogers between them are responsible both for the 73 transferred plates and for the 19 extra engravings that go to make up the illustrations of the present volume and that Virtue profited from Whittock's dual role of author-illustrator. It will be seen that nearly all these extra views are of buildings completed after the publication of the *Panorama* in 1830.

Both title-pages are undated but there is reference, on p 152 of the text, to January 1836. The views are in ruled frames with captions in capitals below; they have no publication-lines and are unnumbered except in the check-list. Plate-marks are cropped in the binding.

The Modern Picture of London, Westminster, and the Metropolitan Boroughs containing a correct Description of the most interesting Objects in every Part of the

Metropolis: forming a complete Guide and Directory for the Stranger and Resident, to the Churches, Palaces, Public Buildings, Courts of Law, Scientific and Commercial Establishments, Places of Amusement, &c. By N. Whittock. Illustrated by upwards of One Hundred Engravings on Steel. London: Printed by W. Johnston, Lovell's-Court, St Pauls, for George Virtue, 26 Ivy Lane, Paternoster Row.

Duodecimo, 140 × 90mm. (1836)

COLLATION Title-page; pp iii–iv, preface; pp v–vi, contents; pp 1–572, New Picture of London; pp 573–9, index; list of engravings (3pp).

0 (engr title) The/New Picture/of/London/or Visitors Guide/by/N. Whittock/with Numerous Engravings. (architectural frame, vignetted) The Grand Entrance, Hyde Park. Seymour del. J. Rogers sc. 115 × 80/130 × 85mm. *PL* 1.

1 front. London from Blackfriars Bridge. Drawn by Campion. Engraved by J. Rogers. 100 × 165/125 × 175mm. *PL* 2.

2 p 168 New Post Office. 60 × 83mm. *PL* 45.

3 p 175 Goldsmith's Hall. 60 × 92mm. Built by Philip Hardwick, 1829–35; view unframed.

4 p 193 Billingsgate. 85 × 60mm. *PL* 54.

5 p 204 Bank of England. 58 × 82mm. *PL* 6. (*Bank of England* 97)

6 p 209 Auction Mart. 56 × 80mm. *PL* 43.

7 p 217 St. Paul's. 90 × 60mm. *PL* 34.

8 p 233 Guild Hall. 58 × 85mm. *PL* 30.

9 p 241 London Institution. 56 × 80mm. *PL* 23.

10 p 242 Catholic Chapel/Moorfields. 84 × 57mm. *PL* 20.

11 p 245 Bow Church. 83 × 58mm. *PL* 29.

12 p 247 Royal Exchange. 82 × 58mm. *PL* 11.

13 p 260 The New Hall Christ's Hospital. 60 × 82mm. *PL* 60.

14 p 262 St. Paul's School. 58 × 82mm. *PL* 19.

15 p 264 St. Bride's Church. 83 × 55mm. *PL* 9.

16 p 267 Blackfriars Bridge. 58 × 80mm. *PL* 48.

17 p 268 Temple Bar. 55 × 82mm. *PL* 72.

18 p 272 St. Bartholomew's Hospital. 58 × 88mm. *PL* 56.

19 p 274 Newgate. 58 × 85mm. *PL* 52.

20 p 278 East India House. 56 × 80mm. *PL* 42.

21 p 283 Custom House. 58 × 83mm. *PL* 15.

22 p 284 Commercial Sale Rooms. 58 × 80mm. *PL* 17.

23 p 284 Corn Exchange. 58 × 82mm. *PL* 21.

24 p 287 The London Stone. 60 × 88mm. *PL* 73.

25 p 287 Mansion House. 88 × 58mm. *PL* 44.

26 p 288 The New London Bridge. 60 × 88mm. From the Pool. Opened in August 1831.

27 p 292 The Monument. 85 × 55mm. *PL* 4.

28 p 296 Fishmongers Hall, &c. from New London Bridge. 60 × 90mm. Unframed. Built by Henry Roberts, 1831–3.

29 p 298 St. Thomas's Hospital. 56 × 82mm. *PL* 57.

30 p 303 St. George's Church. 84 × 55mm. In Southwark. *PL* 78.

31 p 308 Surrey Theatre. 60 × 83mm. *PL* 27.

32 p 312 Iron Bridge Southwark. 58 × 88mm. *PL* 51.

33 p 313 Thames Tunnel. 60 × 87mm. Work started on Brunel's tunnel in 1825; it was then closed by flooding but recommenced in 1835.

34 p 319 The Tower of London. 57 × 80mm. *PL* 38.

35 p 326 The Mint. 57 × 80mm. *PL* 5.

36 p 327 St. Katherine's Dock House. 58 × 82mm. *PL* 46.

37 p 328 The London Docks. 60 × 85mm. *PL* 28.

38 p 333 The West India Docks. 58 × 85mm. *PL* 14.

39 p 337 London Hospital. 60 × 85mm. *PL* 58.

40 p 346 St. Margaret's Church and Westminster Abbey. 55 × 80mm. *PL* 10.

41 p 360 Westminster Hall. 58 × 83mm. *PL* 24.

42 p 364 The House of Lords. 58 × 85mm. *PL* 37.

43 p 365 House of Commons. 58 × 80mm. *PL* 26.

44 p 372 Westminster Bridge. 60 × 87mm. *PL* 49.

45 p 373 The New Treasury, Whitehall. 60 × 85mm. *PL* 40.

46 p 374 The Admiralty. 55 × 85mm. *PL* 39.

47 p 376 West Strand. 60 × 93mm. Nash's 'pepperpots' and St Martin's Parochial Buildings, erected about 1827–30.

48 p 381 The Adelphi Theatre. 83 × 55mm. *PL* 68.

49 p 382 Covent Garden Market. 58 × 85mm. *PL* 53.

50 p 383 Covent Garden Theatre. 55 × 82mm. *PL* 13.

51 p 388 New English Opera House. 60 × 90mm. Unframed. Destroyed by fire in 1830 and rebuilt by Samuel Beazley, 1831–4; subsequently called the Lyceum Theatre.

52 p 391 Waterloo Bridge. 60 × 90mm. *PL* 50.

53 p 391 Somerset House. 60 × 83mm. *PL* 41.

54 p 393 King's College Strand. 60 × 95mm. Built by Robert Smirke, 1830–1.

55 p 399 Drury Lane Theatre. 58 × 80mm. *PL* 7.

56 p 401 The New National Gallery. 62 × 95mm. Built by William Wilkins, 1834–8.

57 p 403 New College of Physicians. 58 × 85mm. *PL* 63.

58 p 404 King's Theatre. 56 × 82mm. ie the Royal Opera House, Haymarket.

431

59 p 405 Hay Market Theatre. 58 × 80mm. *PL* 67.

60 p 408 Egyptian Hall. 58 × 80mm. *PL* 66.

61 p 409 St. James's Palace. 58 × 80mm. *PL* 35.

62 p 413 Duke of York's Column. 58 × 90mm. Unframed. Built by Benjamin Wyatt, 1831–4.

63 p 415 New Westminster Hospital. 60 × 90mm. Built by H.W. and C.F. Inwood, 1832–3.

64 p 420 The King's Palace. 60 × 90mm. *PL* 36.

65 p 420 New St George's Hospital. 60 × 90mm. Built by William Wilkins, 1828–9.

66 p 423 The Late Duke of York's House. 55 × 80mm. *PL* 65.

67 p 433 St. Luke's Hospital. 55 × 90mm. Old Street. (*Bank of England* 226)

68 p 439 Sessions House Clerkenwell. 57 × 83mm. *PL* 22.

69 p 440 St. John's Gate, Clerkenwell. 55 × 82mm. *PL* 25.

70 p 445 Sadlers Wells Theatre. 58 × 80mm. *PL* 71.

71 p 453 Caledonian Asylum. 58 × 85mm. *PL* 77.

72 p 460 British Museum. 58 × 85mm. *PL* 64.

73 p 469 The Foundling Hospital. 58 × 85mm. *PL* 62.

74 p 476 National Scotch Church. 80 × 55mm. *PL* 8.

75 p 481 London University. 58 × 85mm. *PL* 59.

76 p 491 The Colosseum, Regent's Park. 58 × 83mm. *PL* 32.

77 p 517 Charter House. 58 × 82mm. *PL* 61.

78 p 520 Lambeth Palace. 58 × 82mm. *PL* 74.

79 p 522 Astley's Amphitheatre. 82 × 55mm. *PL* 69.

80 p 526 Asylum for Female Orphans Lambeth. 55 × 83mm. *PL* 31.

81 p 528 Vauxhall Gardens. 60 × 87mm.

82 p 531 Royal Coburg Theatre. 58 × 84mm. *PL* 70.

83 p 544 Chelsea Hospital. 58 × 83mm. *PL* 55. (*Longford* 38)

84 p 546 Greenwich Hill. 63 × 85mm. *PL* 18.

85 p 554 Richmond Bridge. 58 × 80mm. (*Gascoigne* 110)

86 p 556 Windsor Castle. 55 × 80mm.

87 p 558 Chiswick Church. 58 × 85mm.

88 p 559 Harrow School. 58 × 80mm. *PL* 12.

89 p 560 Hammersmith Suspension Bridge. 58 × 82mm. *PL* 75.

90 p 561 Holland House Kensington. 58 × 85mm. *PL* 76.

91 p 562 Highgate Archway. 58 × 85mm.

92 p 562 Hornsey Church. 58 × 80mm.

93 p 572 (tm) The New Plan of London, from Actual Survey. G. Virtue, London. 405 × 535/430 × 540mm. (*Darlington and Howgego* 349)

184 · WINKLES'S CATHEDRAL CHURCHES OF ENGLAND WALES* [1836]

The publication of this work in Numbers was announced with the following prospectus: 'On the 1st January 1835 will be published in Imperial 8vo, Price one Shilling, No. 1 of Architectural and Picturesque Illustrations of the Cathedral Churches of Great Britain containing 3 highly finished steel engravings by H. & B. Winkles'. By the end of 1838 36 monthly Parts in paper wrappers (at 1s, or 2s India paper) and a total of 121 plates had been published by Effingham Wilson, forming the first two volumes priced at £2 2s imperial octavo or £4 4s quarto on India paper). After an interval a third was published by Tilt & Bogue in 1842. The views in the first volume, with which we are here concerned, were issued from January 1835 to June 1836 in groups of three consecutively numbered plates; in June 1836 unnumbered ground plans of the seven buildings described were added to complete its illustration.

Winkles's Architectural and Picturesque Illustrations of the Cathedral Churches of England and Wales; the drawings made from sketches taken expressly for this work. By Robert Garland, Architect. With descriptions by Thomas Moule ... Volume I. London: Effingham Wilson, Royal Exchange: and Charles Tilt, Fleet Street. 1836.

(engr title) Cathedral Churches/of/Great Britain/Vol.1./By H. & B./Winkles. (vignette) Salisbury Cathedral/Entrance to the Chapter House. Drawn by H. Winkles. Engraved by B. Winkles. London/Published Jany 1, 1835, by Effingham Wilson, Royal Exchange.

Large octavo, 305 × 235mm.   1836

COLLATION Title-page; index (2pp); pp i–xx, introduction; pp 1–140, The Cathedrals (illustrated by 59 plates of Salisbury, Canterbury, York, St Paul's, Wells, Rochester, Winchester).

The text, by Thomas Moule, is played down on the title-page, dominated as it is by the Winkleses, a family of steel-engravers with connections in Carlsruhe various of whose members had been concerned with Tombleson's *Thames* (no 178), *London in the Nineteenth Century* (no 161) and Britton's *Public*

Buildings of London (no 146). Although there are only half a dozen views of St Paul's Cathedral, on plates numbered 25 to 30 published in September and October 1835, they are carefully drawn by good artists: Robert Garland, a young architect who exhibited drawings at the Royal Academy from 1826 to 1831, the future Dickens illustrator Hablot Browne ('Phiz'), who had been apprenticed to Finden and was cutting his teeth on topographical work, and J.W. Archer, another Finden trainee. Assisting the Winkleses were two other former engravers of Shepherd drawings, John Cleghorn and William Deeble, and the perennial William Woolnoth. Credit for the careful printing of some of the plates, which were available both on India and plain paper, is given to the Storer family.

Credits include the formula 'for Winkles's Cathedrals' and the plates are numbered bl. The publication line reads: 'London, Published (date) by Effingham Wilson, Royal Exchange.'

1 p 65 St. Paul's Cathedral/View of the Southern Front from Southwark Bridge. Drawn by Hablot Browne. Engraved by B. Winkles.... Sept., 1835. Printed by Whitcher. 150 × 115/285 × 200mm. pl.26.

2 p 70 St. Paul's Cathedral. Drawn & Engraved by J. Cleghorn.... June 1, 1836. 285 × 205mm pl.mark. Plan, with refs A–W,1–13.

3 p 72 St. Paul's Cathedral/The Western Front. Drawn by J. Archer.... Engraved by B. Winkles.... Octr 1, 1835. 145 × 110/290 × 200mm. pl.28.

4 p 74 St. Paul's Cathedral/North Eastern View. Drawn by Hablot Browne. Engraved by B. Winkles.... Octr 1, 1835. 111 × 138/200 × 285mm. pl.30.

5 p 75 St. Paul's Cathedral/the Crypt, monument of Admiral Viscount Nelson under the Dome. Drawn by R. Garland. Engraved by B. Winkles.... Sept. 1, 1835. Printed by Storer. 113 × 140/205 × 285mm. pl.27.

6 p 76 St. Paul's Cathedral:/Interior of the Dome looking towards the Northern Transept. Drawn by R. Garland. Engraved by Wm Woolnoth.... Sepr 1, 1835. Printed by Storer. 150 × 108/280 × 205mm. pl.25.

7 p 78 St. Paul's Cathedral/the Nave and Choir. Drawn by Hablot Browne. Engraved by W. Deeble.... Oct. 1, 1835. Printed by Storer. 145 × 110/285 × 200mm. pl.29.

185 · BILLINGS'S TEMPLE CHURCH [1838]

Robert William Billings, the architect, was taught to draw by the notable antiquary John Britton and, at the early age of 24, was commissioned by his former master to produce over 100 drawings for a series launched by an even younger architect, George Godwin, entitled *The Churches of London* (no 189). Among the illustrations he made for this collection are seven views of the inside and outside of the Temple Church which were engraved variously on steel and wood and published in June and July 1837. These were picturesque-topographical rather than architectural drawings, since the book was aimed at London lovers in general, but while he was working on them it occurred to Billings that there was no recent architectural account of this most venerable of the London churches and so he decided to make a set of measured drawings of the interior and exterior and a detailed record of columns, buttresses, arcades, stairways, capitals and corbel grotesques. Being himself also a skilled engraver he was able to turn these drawings into beautifully finished outline-engravings on steel plates in the manner of those executed by John Le Keux for the *Illustrations of the Public Buildings* (no 146, items 31–3).

James Savage, the official architect to the Society of the Middle Temple, was working on designs for the restoration of the church. This task was completed in 1841 by Sydney Smirke and Decimus Burton with a result described as follows by its latest restorer, W.H. Godfrey:

Nothing could have been more thorough than the way in which every ancient surface was repaired away or renewed so that in the end the result was a complete modern simulacrum of this superb monument. Very little of this painful accomplishment has survived the serious fire occasioned by the air-raid of 1941, and it has devolved on me to reconstruct the church for a second time. (*Archaeologia* 15, 1953, p 123)

Billings, then, was in the very nick of time to record the appearance of the twelfth century church with its thirteenth century choir and the detail of its ornaments before they were overlaid by relentless Victorian restoration and ultimately shattered by fire-bombs. In a justificatory address preceding the work he mentions the paucity of Temple Church engravings, quoting his own done for Godwin, the four views by G. Shepherd and J. Coney in *Architectura Ecclesiastica Londini* (no 129), and the set of drawings published by the Society of Antiquaries in the *Vetusta Monumenta* of 1835 (no 36).

Architectural Illustrations and Account of the Temple Church, London. By Robert William Billings, Associate of the Institute of British Architects. London: Published by Thomas and William Boone, 29 New Bond Street and Robert William Billings, Manor-House, Kentish Town. 1838. (verso) J.B. Nichols & Son, 25 Parliament Street.

Quarto, 335 × 260mm.   1838

COLLATION Title-page; pp v–vi, address dated May 1838; contents, directions to binder (1 leaf); pp 1–26, Essay on the Templars by Edward Clarkson; pp 27–48, Historical Account; pp 49–55, descriptions of plates

All plates are credited 'Drawn & Engraved by R.W. Billings', and have the uniform publication-line 'London, Published by T. & W. Boone, 1838'. They are numbered tr and bound after the text in that order, except for pl. 1, the engraved title, and pl. 15 which appears as a frontispiece. The first line of each caption. in voided capitals, reads: 'Temple Church, London', and is followed by a specific description of the particular plate.

1 (engr title) Illustrations/of the/Temple Church/by Rob. Willm. Billings/1838. (vignette) Knights Templar, and view of Effigies in the/Temple Church, London. 240 × 165/285 × 225mm.

2 Ground Plan, & plan of windows, &c. 140 × 225/225 × 288mm.

3 South Elevation. 145 × 225/225 × 290mm.

4 1. Section through Column & Buttresses – 2. Transverse Section looking W. – 3. Transverse Section looking E. – 4. East End. 155 × 220/225 × 290mm.

5 Longitudinal Section. 145 × 230/230 × 290mm.

6 Central Window, East End. 210 × 165/290 × 225mm.

7 Side Window-plans, elevation, section & details. 200 × 165/290 × 225mm.

8 Section of Ribs. 200 × 145/290 × 230mm.

9 Details. 160 × 210/230 × 290mm.

10 Details of Pier—Circular Portion. 145 × 190/225 × 290mm.

11 Compartment of Arcade—Circular Portion. 155 × 210/225 × 285mm.

12 Details. 190 × 160/290 × 220mm.

13 Circular Doorway. W. end. 160 × 190/225 × 285mm.

14 Entrance to Circular Staircase. 210 × 155/290 × 225mm.

15 Interior of the Circular Portion, looking West. 210 × 165/290 × 225mm.

16 View of Aisle, Circular Portion. 210 × 160/290 × 225mm.

17 Interior looking East. 190 × 145/290 × 225mm.

18 View of the North Aisle, from the Circular portion. 210 × 160/285 × 225mm.

19 View across the West end, looking North. 215 × 160/290 × 220mm.

20 South East View. 137 × 225/225 × 290mm. Exterior.

21 A. Plan relative to the Essay by Edward Clarkson Esqr. – B. Plan of fourteen steps at 'a' – C. Cell on the circular staircase. 140 × 225/225 × 290mm.

22–4 Capitals, Circular Portion. Pl. 1 (2–3). Each 190 × 150/290 × 225mm.

25–31 Grotesque Heads, Pl. 1 (2–3, IV, 5–7). 190 × 150, 190 × 150, 190 × 143, 190 × 145, 190 × 145, 190 × 140, 190 × 150/290 × 225mm.

---

186 · DUGDALE'S ENGLAND AND WALES DELINEATED* [1838–43]

On the back wrapper of the first of Tallis's *London Street Views*, which was probably published in 1838 (see 'Street Views' in introductory History), appears the following advertisement: 'England and Wales Delineated: Historical, Entertaining and Commercial, &c. &c. Illustrated by Engravings and a Coloured Map of each County. By Thomas Dugdale, Antiquarian; assisted by William Burnett, Civil Engineer. In parts price 2s. each. London Published by Tallis & Co., 15 St. John's Lane, St. John's-gate'. This was repeated at intervals throughout the course of the 88 *Street Views* until 1840 and full-size specimen front wrappers were offprinted on the back wrappers of views nos 54 and 61 as an advertisement. It has not been possible to establish exactly the frequency or dating of the first issue of Dugdale but it may be assumed that the Parts were issued monthly. The second, revised edition came out in 50 Parts and, if this was also true of its predecessor, the monthly issues would have run from 1838 to 1843. These inclusive dates tally with the evidence of the imprints of the bound volumes.

There are 11 of these, in embossed grey-green cloth bindings with titles on the spines: 'Dugdale's England and Wales Delineated, with Maps and Plates. Price 6s. 6d. vol. 1 (etc)'. Each of the first ten volumes consists of a batch of from 20 to 30 topographical engravings on steel, including a frontispiece and engraved title (they have no printed titles), followed by about 160 pages of text in gazetteer form. Sets of county maps are also included in the first six volumes. The first volume begins with 'Abberbury' and the tenth volume ends with 'Zeel'; the pagination and signatures are likewise continuous from volume to volume.

Only the eleventh volume has a printed title-page (undated), but this was published independently of the others, having separate pagination and signatures. A chronology by Leonard Townsend, this volume must have come out in advance of the others since its imprint includes the address of Green Arbour Court, Old Bailey, which the publisher left for St John's Lane in 1838. This reissue, however, has an additional engraved title with the imprint of L. Tallis, 3 Jewin Street, which came into use only after the death in February 1842 of John Tallis senior.

The engraved titles of the first two volumes have the 1838 or post-1838 address of 15 St John's Lane and in the second volume there is a view of the National Gallery, opened in 1838, and a caption referring to Victoria as Queen. The fact that the remainder of the engraved titles have the Jewin Street imprint does not prove, however, that the Parts comprising the next eight volumes were not issued until 1842 or after. Publishers normally delayed the production of such preliminaries until all the Parts were ready for binding. It would rather indicate that all the binding was carried out after 1842 when Townsend's chronology (advertised around 1840, in No 88 of the *Street Views*, as being available at '4s 6d. with cloth boards' from 15 St John's Lane) was reissued as an extra, in uniform binding at 6s 6d.

The arrangement of these bound volumes is however rather puzzling, since the views or maps included in each are unrelated, except by chance, to the text with which they have been bound; moreover no sort of check-list or 'directions to binder' seems to have been printed. Once again one may infer from the way in which the second edition was later published—in 50 Parts at 1s or nine Divisions at 6s 6d each—that this was also applicable to the original issue. The existence of copies of both editions, rebound into two or three volumes, with the plates and maps facing the articles they illustrate, suggests that the issue in Divisions was a means of selling the work on easy terms after its Parts had run their course, and that the elaborate, though not very strong, binding was destined to be scrapped when all the Divisions had been collected—so that the plates could be integrated with the text in a rebinding.

The second edition, as has been stated, came out in 50 monthly Parts. These were enclosed in numbered wrappers with the following notice on the back: 'The large sale, exceeding 27,000 copies, which the early edition of this established work obtained, encourages the proprietor to believe that an *enlarged* and *improved* issue would be peculiarly acceptable to the public ... the topographical descriptions will be entirely re-written'. On the front of the blue wrappers, ornamented with wood-engravings of Windsor Castle and the Great Exhibition, was the following lettering:

In Monthly Parts, Royal 8vo, Price one Shilling. Guaranteed to be completed in Fifty Parts at 1s. each or Nine Divisions at 6s 6d. handsomely bound. Part 1 (etc)—One Shilling/ England/and/Wales delineated/ historical, entertaining/and commercial/London/Published by L. Tallis 1 Crane Court, Fleet Street. (Also by booksellers in Newcastle, Manchester, Birmingham, Wolverhampton, added after Part 6, and Nottingham after Part 7.)

Each Part consisted of about 30 pages with a variable number of plates and the text, as claimed by the publisher, was considerably amended; references to the year 1855 are to be found on p 324, p 378 and p 587, to 1856 on p 1100 and to 1857 on p 1164. As preliminaries there were two printed title-pages with the imprint of 'L. Tallis, 21 Warwick Square' and a number of engraved title-pages and frontispieces intended to front the Divisions; as only two of each of the latter were eventually needed discarded ones may be rebound at the back of the consolidated volumes. The binder was given instructions as to the title, frontispiece and map which were to precede each of these but was only told that the other 56 maps were to go opposite the descriptions of their respective counties and that the views, in alphabetical order, were to face their letterpress descriptions.

(engr) Curiosities of Great Britain./England & Wales/

delineated./Historical, Entertaining & Commercial/ alphabetically arranged/By Thomas Dugdale, Antiquarian/Assisted by William Burnett, Civil Engineer ('Vol.II' to 'Vol.X' and an engraved view)/London Published by John Tallis, 15 St John's Lane, Smithfield (Published by L. Tallis, 3 Jewin Street, City).

An Alphabetical Chronology of Remarkable events, from the earliest authentic period to the present time, with copious explanatory notes. By Leonard Townsend. London: Tallis and Co., Green Arbour Court, Old Bailey.

Octavo, 220 × 140mm.   ?1838–43

COLLATION Vol. 1 (published by John Tallis, 15 St John's Lane, Smithfield). Engr title-page; pp 5–164, Abberbury to Bicester; 30 plates, 10 maps. Vol. 2 (same imprint). Engr title-page; pp 165–324, Bickleigh to Bury; 30 plates, 10 maps, Vol. 3 (published by L. Tallis, 3 Jewin Street, City). Engr title-page; pp 325–484, Bury to Claverton; 20 plates, 10 maps. Vol. 4 (2nd imprint). Engr title-page; pp 485–644, Claydon to Dorchester; 20 plates, 10 maps. Vol. 5 (2nd imprint). Engr title-page; pp 645–804, Dorking to Freshwater; 20 plates, 10 maps. Vol. 6 (2nd imprint). Engr title-page; pp 805–964, Freshwater to Hinckley; 20 plates, 8 maps. Vol. 7 (2nd imprint). Engr title-page; pp 965–1124, Hindon to London; 30 plates. Vol. 8 (2nd imprint). Engr title-page; pp 1125–284, London to Oxwich; 30 plates. Vol. 9 (2nd imprint). Engr title-page; pp 1285–444, Oystermouth to Surrey; 30 plates. Vol. 10 (2nd imprint). Engr title-page; pp 1445–586, Sussex to Zeel; 20 plates. Vol. 11 (printed by William Henry Cox, 5 Great Queen Street, Lincoln's Inn Fields). Engr title-page; pp i-iv, preface; pp 1–144, Alphabetical Chronology; 24 portrait plates.

Dugdale's England and Wales Delineated, edited by E.L. Blanchard. Volume I (II). London L. Tallis, 21 Warwick Square, Paternoster Row.

Octavo, 245 × 160mm.   ?1851–60

COLLATION Vol. 1. Title-page; pp i-ii, preface; directions to binder (1 leaf); half-title; pp 1–812, Abberbury to Gyffin (Parts 1–26). Vol. 2. Title-page; pp 813–1582, Halcombe to Zennor (Parts 27–50).

Most of the plates are anonymous but several of the handsome title-pages and frontispieces, together with a few other views, are credited to T.H. Shepherd and some without credits are of equal quality. Twenty five of the engravings served the publisher twice over since they are to be found also printed, sideways on, with his fascinating *Street Views*. Reference is made to the Numbers on which they appear with the abbreviation *TSV*. The *Street Views* themselves are not described here as their publication has been thoroughly studied in Peter

Jackson's introduction to the (slightly enlarged) facsimile edition (1966).

The plates of the first edition are set out as bound up in the 11 volumes, the plate numbers being supplied to denote their order; the rare appearance of Dugdale's book-title and the occasional, undated publication-line are noted. Only 16 of the original 65 London plates were included in the Parts of the subsequent edition, some with the addition of Dugdale's book-title; these are signified against their first edition issues. Twenty one more, engraved for the second edition, are appended to the list. In view of the haphazard distribution of the illustrations and of the variations in their placing (because of the imprecision of the binder's instructions and lack of a check-list) the following can only claim to be a list of plates actually seen; many copies contain only a selection of these and there may be others in which additional views have been bound.

VOL. 1

1 (pl. 6) The Queen's Palace, Pimlico/Middlesex. 67 × 103mm. Ruled frame. With Marble Arch and Nash's front courtyard. *TSV* 83.

2 (pl. 7) Westminster Abbey. 83 × 130/97 × 140mm. N. view. *TSV* 73.

3 (pl. 19) Bank of England/London. 65 × 108/82 × 140mm. *TSV* 88. (*Bank of England* 98)

4 (pl. 21) Greenwich Hospital. 70 × 130/110 × 140mm. From the river.

5 (pl. 22) West Side of Temple Bar London/At this gate the chief Magistracy receive the Royal Family on State Occasions. 60 × 82/110 × 140mm. Ruled frame. *TSV* 10.

6 (pl. 25) Goldsmith's Hall/Foster Lane, Cheapside London. 65 × 105/110 × 140mm. *TSV* 87.

7 (pl. 26) The Spaniards Tavern, Hampstead/Middlesex. 78 × 115mm.

8 (pl. 27) Chalk Farm, Primrose Hill/Middlesex. 76 × 122/130 × 180mm.

9 (pl. 28) Middlesex Hospital/Charles Street Mary-le-bone.... The present substantial building was completed in 1835. 63 × 115/115 × 135mm. *TSV* 65.

10 (pl. 29) Battersea Bridge./Surrey. 65 × 105mm. (*Longford* 267)

VOL. 2

11 front. The Residence of Sir Paul Pindar/In the Reign of James I/169 Bishopsgate St. Without, London. 105 × 65/140 × 90mm. Double rule frame. *TSV* 67.

12 (pl. 7) Corn Exchange, Mark Lane, London. 70 × 105/105 × 140mm. *TSV* 74.

13 (pl. 13) Canonbury Tower. Leath Del. Smith sc. 98 × 75/200 × 120mm.

14 (pl. 16) St. Paul's Cathedral/London. 83 × 58/140 × 180mm. Double rule frame. Recaptioned 'West View of Saint Pauls Cathedral' for *TSV* 6.

15 (pl. 19) The Royal Palace, Kensington/Middlesex/The Palace in which Queen Victoria was born May 24, 1819. 65 × 105/110 × 130mm. *TSV* 72.

16 (pl. 22) The National Gallery, Trafalgar Square/London. 60 × 105/80 × 140mm. The National Gallery was opened in 1838.

17 (pl. 25) North Entrance of Burlington Arcade, London. 75 × 108/110 × 140mm. *TSV* 71.

18 (pl. 28) Regent Circus, Oxford Street, London. 65 × 98/100 × 140mm. ie Oxford Circus. Captioned 'Williams & Hatton' in *TSV* 41.

19 (pl. 29) The Royal Observatory, Greenwich Park/Kent. 65 × 105mm. Reprinted in 2nd ed Pt 25, p 793.

20 (pl. 30) The Castle of the British Sovereign, Windsor/Berkshire. 65 × 102mm. Reprinted in 2nd ed Pt 49, p 1538, adding book-title.

VOL. 3

21 (pl. 3) Darford/Kent. London, J. Tallis 15 St John's Lane. 65 × 102mm. Ruled frame. Reprinted in 2nd ed Pt 17, p 522, eliminating publication-line and substituting book-title.

22 (pl. 9) Copenhagen House, Islington/Middlesex. 75 × 120mm. Ruled frame.

23 (pl. 10) Kew. McHenry sc. 70 × 110/115 × 145mm. Ruled frame. Kew Bridge.

24 (pl. 13) Northfleet, near Gravesend/Kent. 65 × 105mm. Ruled frame. Reprinted in 2nd ed Pt 40, p 1255, adding book-title.

25 (pl. 20) Royal Military Academy, Woolwich/Kent. 65 × 102mm. Ruled frame. Reprinted in 2nd ed Pt 49, p 1555, adding book-title.

VOL. 4

26 front. The Nelson Column/Trafalgar Square. T.H. Shepherd delt. C. Fenn sc. Drawn and Engraved for/Dugdales England and Wales/Delineated. 130 × 80mm. Reprinted as one of four frontispieces issued with 2nd ed Pts 1–25. Railton's column was completed in 1843.

27 (pl. 4) Kew Palace/Surrey/The Birth-place of George IV. 70 × 105mm. Ruled frame. Reprinted in 2nd ed Pt 31, p 975.

28 (pl. 6) London & Birmingham Railway Terminus/Euston Square/London. T.H. Shepherd delt. H. Bond sc. 82 × 120mm. Ruled frame. Completed by Philip Hardwick, 1839.

29 (pl. 9) Thames Tunnel/(from the Circular Staircase)/London. Drawn and Engraved for Dugdales England and Wales Delineated. 90 × 120mm. Ruled frame. Reprinted in 2nd ed Pt 35, p 1100.

30 (pl. 10) St Martin's Church, St Martin's Lane,/London. 115 × 70/140 × 75mm.

VOL. 5

31 front. The Monument/London. T.H. Shepherd Delt. C. Fenn sc. Drawn and Engraved for/Dugdale's England and Wales Delineated. 130 × 85/210 × 135mm.

32 (pl. 6) Whittington's Alms Houses/Highgate Hill/Middlesex. T.H. Shepherd Delt. J. Davies sc. Drawn & Engraved for Dugdale's England & Wales Delineated. 87 × 135mm. Reprinted in 2nd ed Pt 28, p 889.

33 (pl. 16) Interior of Burlington Arcade, London. 77 × 108/90 × 180mm. *TSV* 71.

34 (pl. 20) High Street, Southwark/London. 65 × 110/80 × 135mm. Double rule frame. Recaptioned 'A View of Bennett's Cloth Mart' in *TSV* 39.

VOL. 6

35 front. The Duke of York's Column/from St James's Park/London. T.H. Shepherd Delt. J. Brown sc. 133 × 82mm. Reprinted as a front. in 2nd ed.

36 (pl. 5) Gravesend/Kent. Drawn & Engraved for Dugdale's England and Wales Delineated. 80 × 120mm. Ruled frame. Reprinted in 2nd ed Pt 25, p 782.

37 (pl. 8) Church Street, Hampstead,/Middlesex/Hampstead is 400 feet above the level of the Sea.... 68 × 103mm. Ruled frame.

38 (pl. 9) Greenwich/Kent. Drawn & Engraved for Dugdale's England and Wales Delineated. 78 × 122m. Ruled frame. From the Isle of Dogs.

39 (pl. 13) Willesden Church/Middlesex. Wood del. J.C. Griffiths sc. 72 × 105/110 × 140mm.

40 (pl. 19) Near Hampton./Middlesex. Bartlett del. Smith sc. 82 × 125/125 × 195mm. Ruled frame.

41 (pl. 22) Scene from Richmond Hill/Surrey. 65 × 108mm. Ruled frame. (*Gascoigne* 131)

VOL. 7

42 (pl. 11) London Orphan Asylum, Hackney Road/Middlesex. Drawn & Engraved for Dugdale's England & Wales Delineated. 65 × 105mm. Reprinted in 2nd ed Pt 14, p 429. The Orphanage was at Clapton until 1869.

43 (pl. 15) Highbury College, Islington/Middlesex. 65 × 108mm. Ruled frame.

44 (pl. 17) Westminster Abbey. 83 × 130/97 × 140mm. Repeat of pl. 7 in vol. 1, with book-title added.

45 (pl. 23) Morley's Hotel/and the/Nelson Column, Trafalgar Square, London. 77 × 105/95 × 140mm. Site of present South Africa House. *TSV* 76.

46 (pl. 27) St James's Palace/Pall Mall London. Drawn & Engraved for Dugdale's England & Wales Delineated. 67 × 108mm.

47 (pl. 28) Shoreditch London. 62 × 105/100 × 140mm. Ruled frame. Captioned 'James Corss Tailor & Draper' in *TSV* 60.

48 (pl. 29) St Bride's Church/Fleet Street, London. 100 × 57/135 × 170mm. Ruled frame. *TSV* 15.

VOL. 8

49 (engr title) Vol. VIII./The Marble Arch/Buckingham Palace,/London. T.H. Shepherd Delt. C.H. Matthews sc. 93 × 98mm.

50 (pl. 14) The Blind Asylum/Southwark/London. A.W. Wray delt. H. Wallis sc. Drawn & Engraved for Dugdales England & Wales Delineated. 77 × 122mm. Ruled frame. Reprinted in 2nd ed Pt 32, p 997. St George's Circus; built by John Newman, 1834–8.

51 (pl. 19) Eton College, Berkshire,/from the Thames. Drawn & Engraved for Dugdale's England and Wales Delineated. 63 × 105mm. Ruled frame.

52 (pl. 24) The Grand Hotel, Covent Garden/London. 80 × 90/95 × 135mm. Vignetted. Opened in 1774 in Lord Orford's former town house (for which see *London Described* (no 29), item 27).

VOL. 9

53 (engr title) Vol. IX./The Quadrant/Regent Street,/London. T.H. Shepherd Delt. C.H. Matthews sc. 80 × 108mm.

54 (pl. 14) Italian Opera House/London. Drawn and Engraved for Dugdale's England and Wales Delineated. 85 × 123mm. Ruled frame. Recaptioned 'Her Majesty's Theatre/London, formerly Italian Opera House' in 2nd ed Pt 35, p 1110.

55 (pl. 17) (tm) Christs Hospital Hall. (bm) Newgate Street, London. 48 × 105/70 × 143mm. *TSV* 5.

56 (pl. 27) The Spaniards Tavern, Hampstead/Middlesex. 78 × 115mm. Repeat of pl. 26 in vol. 1, with book-title added.

57 (pl. 28) All Souls Church, Langham Place,/London. 105 × 62/140 × 80mm. *TSV* 16.

58 (pl. 29) (tm) English's St James's Royal Hotel. (bm) St James's Street, London. 65 × 110/95 × 132mm. On W. side of St James's Street, facing up Pall Mall. *TSV* 14.

59 (pl. 30) Chalk Farm, Primrose Hill/Middlesex. 76 × 122/130 × 180mm. Repeat of pl. 27 in vol. 1, with book-title added.

VOL. 10

60 (pl. 4) Formerly residence of Sir Richard Steel, Haverstock Hill, Hampstead/Middlesex. L. Tallis London. 87 × 128mm. Ruled frame. Reprinted in 2nd ed Pt 27, p 831.

61 (pl. 9) Gracechurch-Street London 53 × 105/90 × 135mm. Ruled frame. Recaptioned 'Martin & Co. Export Ironmongers' in *TSV* 24.

62 (pl. 12) (tm) Holborn Hill, London. (bm) St Andrew's

Church. 50 × 85/75 × 140mm. Double rule frame. *TSV* 3.

63 (pl. 13) West Side of Temple Bar. 60 × 82/110 × 140mm. Repeat of pl. 22 in vol. 1.

64 (pl. 18) Holborn Bars, on the summit of Holborn Hill. 65 × 90/100 × 140mm.

65 (pl. 19) Cheapside, London. 62 × 107/105 × 140mm. Recaptioned 'Rigge's Foreign & English Perfumery Warehouse' in *TSV* 42.

VOL. 11

66 (engr title) An/Alphabetical Chronology/of/Remarkable Events/with copious explanatory notes/by/Leonard Townsend./The New Gresham College/London. T.H. Shepherd Delt. J. Tingle sc. Published by L. Tallis, 3 Jewin Street, City. 110 × 105mm. The View was reprinted with the title of one of the Divisions of the 2nd ed. Gresham College built by George Smith, 1842–3.

67 (pl. 15) Oliver Goldsmith. J. Rogers sc. (vignette) Canonbury Tower, Islington, Middlesex/Formerly the Residence of Oliver Goldsmith. Vignette 50 × 95mm.

2nd ed (extra plates)

VOL. 1

68 front. Interior of the House of Lords/London. L. Tallis. 150 × 112mm.

69 p 789 Greenwich/from the Park. T. Shepherd Pinx. H. Bond sc. Drawn & Engraved for Dugdale's England & Wales Delineated. 85 × 120/150 × 230mm. Pt 25.

VOL. 2

70 p 1081 St James' Bazaar./London. L. Tallis, London. 85 × 130mm. Pt 34.

71 p 1091 Saint Paul's Cathedral/London from the S. West. 85 × 130mm. Ruled frame. Pt 35.

72 p 1093 New Post Office. St Martins-le-Grand/London. 85 × 120mm. Pt 35.

73 p 1094 The Mansion House/London. T.H. Shepherd delt. R. Acon sc. 85 × 120mm. Pt 35.

74 p 1095 New Royal Exchange/London. 85 × 120mm. Pt 35. Sir William Tite's building, opened 1844.

75 p 1098 London Bridge/London. Drawn & Engraved for Dugdale's England & Wales Delineated. 82 × 120mm. Ruled frame. Pt 35.

76 p 1098 The Custom House/London. T. Shepherd Pinx. H. Bond sc. Drawn & Engraved for Dugdale's England & Wales Delineated. 83 × 120/145 × 230mm. Pt 35. From the river.

77 p 1100 Royal Mint/Tower Hill/London. Drawn & Engraved for Dugdale's England & Wales Delineated. 83 × 120/145 × 230mm. Ruled frame. Pt 35.

78 p 1101 Religious Tract Society's Repository, Paternoster Row/London. L. Tallis, London. 90 × 133/150 × 225mm. Pt 35.

79 p 1104 Somerset House/London. Drawn & Engraved for Dugdale's England & Wales Delineated. 85 × 120/140 × 220mm. Ruled frame. From the river. Pt 35.

80 p 1106 The Admiralty/Whitehall. T.H. Shepherd Delt. H. Wallis sc. 85 × 132/145 × 230mm. Ruled frame. Pt 35.

81 p 1114 Apsley House/the town residence of the Duke of Wellington. 85 × 120/135 × 230mm. Ruled frame. Pt 35.

82 p 1118 Royal Italian Opera House/London. 85 × 120/150 × 230mm. Ruled frame. Pt 35.

83 p 1119 The New Hall and Library/Lincolns Inn Fields, London. London, L. Tallis. 87 × 130mm. Ruled frame. Designed by Philip Hardwick, 1843–5. Pt 35.

84 p 1137 New Bridge Street Blackfriars. 65 × 108/80 × 140mm. Recaptioned, tm, 'Crown Life Assurance Company' in *TSV* 78.

85 p 1137 Interior of Lowther Arcade, Strand, London. 105 × 78/138 × 90mm. *TSV* 81.

86 p 1137 The New Houses of Parliament. T.H. Shepherd delin. H. Wallis sc. Drawn & Engraved for Dugdale's England & Wales Delineated. 82 × 133mm.

87 front. The Statue of Nelson./Trafalgar Square/London. W.H. Wray Delt. C. Fenn sc. Drawn & Engraved for Dugdale's England & Wales Delineated. 135 × 85mm.

88 (at end) The Wesleyan Theological College, Richmond. T.H. Shepherd Delt. W.M. Dore sc. 85 × 133mm.

but the publication-line throughout is: 'London, William Darton & Son, Holborn Hill.' There are two vignettes and six triple views, each measuring 35 × 65mm within a border-line of 115 × 70mm.

A Visit to London: containing a Description of the Principal Curiosities in the British Metropolis. By the Author of 'The Visit to a Farm-House'. A New Edition. London: Darton & Clark, Holborn Hill. (verso) J. Green, Printer, Bartlett Buildings.

Duodecimo, 140 × 85mm.   c 1838

COLLATION   Title-page; pp iii-vi, preface, contents; pp 1–192, A Visit to London.

1 front. Hyde Park. 65 × 65mm. Vignette of Achilles statue and Ionic screen.

2 p 35 Christ's Hospital – The Artillery Ground – St Paul's.

3 p 79 The Lord Mayor's Show – The Tower – Westminster Abbey. (The Abbey from the N.)

4 p 93 Guildhall – The Bank – Southwark Bridge.

5 p 104 Somerset House – Westminster Hall – Interior of the House of Lords. (Somerset House from the river)

6 p 110 The House of Lords – The Horse Guards – Buckingham Palace. (Horse Guards and Palace views from St James's Park)

7 p 151 St. James's Park. 70 × 65mm. Vignette showing Duke of York's Column, completed 1834.

8 p 176 Kensington Palace – The East India House – The Custom House.

187 · A VISIT TO LONDON [c 1838]

The publisher of this book, which had been in circulation in various editions since 1805 (no 94), decided to improve upon its archaic appearance in celebration of the accession of Queen Victoria. The text was revised to enable that long-lived mentor, Mr Sandby, to tell his children what had passed at the Queen's coronation. Fresh illustrations were provided, together with a brown, cloth-gilt binding with the City arms and regalia embossed on the spine. By now there were eight plates engraved on steel and a number of attractive wood-engravings, some printed with the text to illustrate it, of say a Christ's Hospital boy or a Greenwich one-legged pensioner, and some used as purely decorative head and tailpieces. The steel-engravings have no credits

188 · WOODS'S HISTORY OF LONDON [1838]

This collection of 30 steel-engravings is clearly in the line of succession to *Metropolitan Improvements* (no 154) and *London in the Nineteenth Century* (no 161) and the link is supplied by T.H. Shepherd who drew the frontispiece and contributed five of the views. As was so often the case at that period and with this type of book the text is a mere makeweight and largely irrelevant to the plates. It was supplied by W.G. Fearnside who, four years before, wrote the descriptions of the illustrations in Tombleson's *Thames* (no 178) but, as the foreword explains, was not completed owing to his untimely death. Thomas

Harral covered the centuries from 1399 to the accession of Queen Victoria in a mere 50 pages and the book was then published at 15s.

The History of London: illustrated by Views in London and Westminster, engraved by John Woods, from original Drawings, by Shepherd, Garland, Salmon, Topham, Clarke, Browne, Roberts &c. Edited by William Gray Fearnside, and (in continuation) by Thomas Harral. (epigraph) London: Published by Orr and Co., Amen Corner, Paternoster Row; Simpkin Marshall, and Co., Stationers' Hall Court; Ackermann and Co, 96 Strand; J. Woods, Woodland Cottage, Pond Lane, Clapton; and to be had of all booksellers in the United Kingdom. MDCCCXXXVIII. Entered at Stationers' Hall.

Octavo, 250 × 180mm.   1838

COLLATION Title-page; pp iii–iv, preface; pp 1–201, History; p 202, directions to binder; index (1 leaf).

This provides a most useful visual account of the London scene in the year of Queen Victoria's accession and about a decade after Shepherd's twin masterpiece was published, especially as he and his fellow artists maintain his excellent tradition of sketching in plenty of human and animal activity in the foreground of each view. The plates, by John Woods and three assistant engravers, are of high quality and the steel consistently produces clear-cut impressions. Half of the plates have, added to the artist's credit: 'from a sketch by R. Garland'. Robert Garland was a young architect, trained at the Royal Academy Schools and exhibiting drawings at the Academy between 1826 and 1831. It seems that his role must have been that of Pugin's in the *Microcosm of London* (no 99) and that he drew the architectural settings while Hablot Browne and Salmon added foreground, staffage and skies . On plates by Shepherd, who was skilled in all branches of topographical drawing, there is no mention of Garland. Ten of the drawings are by J. Salmon, who was later to draw the opening by Prince Albert of Bunning's Coal Exchange, a print published in 1849 (*Crace* 20.101). Besides the six by Shepherd there are nine by Hablot Browne who, along with Garland, contributed to Winkles's *Cathedrals* (no 184) and won fame as 'Phiz' illustrating Dickens's novels.

All but five of the plates were dated; they were published monthly in groups of three, from June to December 1837, with further instalments in February, March and June 1838. Although listed they are unnumbered. Captions are in voided capitals and

the publication-lines, burnished out in later issues, read: '(London) Published (date) by (W.S.) Orr & Co. Amen Corner (Paternoster Row).' A later issue in the Royal Library, printed on Large Paper (225 × 210mm) and bound up sumptuously with Trotter's *Topography* (no 190), lists illustrations after the preface and has an index on the reverse of the last page (p 203); its running-title is *The Great Metropolis*, the plates face different pages and there is one extra of the New Royal Exchange (opened 1844).

1 (engr title) Woods's/Views in/London, Westminster,/ and/Their Vicinities. (vignette) Monument/and/St Magnus Church. J.H. Shepherd del. J. Woods sc. London, Published by W.S. Orr & Co., Amen Corner, Paternoster Row, June 1st/1837. 130 × 100/230 × 155mm. '1837' burnished out in later issues.

2 p 2 King William Street,/and/St. Mary Woolnoth. T.H. Shepherd delt. I. Woods sc. 103 × 153/160 × 240mm. nd.

3 p 16 West India Dock./Import. Drawn by W. Topham from a sketch by R. Garland. Engraved by J. Woods.... Dec 1, 1837. 103 × 151/160 × 243mm.

4 p 18 The Upper Pool. J. Salmon delt. J. Woods sc.... Feb 1, 1838. 103 × 151/160 × 230mm. Looking towards London Bridge and St Paul's.

5 p 20 Cheapside/and/Bow Church. T.H. Shepherd del. W.E. Albutt sc.... July 1st, 1837. 103 × 153/160 × 240mm.

6 p 28 Custom House. Drawn by Hablot Browne from a Sketch by R. Garland. Engraved by J. Woods.... Sepr. 1, 1837. 103 × 150/160 × 240mm. Garland's ochre wash drawing (100 × 150mm) sold at Sotheby's 13 January 1972, item 63.

7 p 29 High Street, Whitechapel. T.H. Shepherd del. T. Cox sc.... July 1, 1837. 98 × 155/155 × 250mm.

8 p 41 Billingsgate. J. Salmon delt. I. Woods sc.... July 1st, 1837. 103 × 160/160 × 240mm.

9 p 43 Southwark, Church &c. Drawn by Hablot Browne from a Sketch by R. Garland. Engraved by J. Woods.... Octr 2nd 1837. 105 × 150/160 × 245mm. Southwark Cathedral viewed from the S.

10 p 48 Westminster Hospital/and/Abbey Church. Drawn by J. Salmon from a Sketch by R. Garland. Engraved by I. Woods.... June 1837. 103 × 150/133 × 225mm. From the W. The hospital built by William Inwood, 1832–3.

11 p 68 London Bridge. Drawn by Hablot Browne from a Sketch by R. Garland. Engraved by J. Woods.... Octr 2nd 1837. 105 × 150/165 × 240mm. From the S.W.

12 p 70 Fishmongers' Hall. Drawn by F.W. Topham from a Sketch by R. Garland. Engraved by J. Woods.... Augt 1, 1837. 105 × 150/160 × 240mm. E.front.

13 p 73 Somerset House,/Strand. H. Browne delt. W.E. Albutt sc.... Novr 1st, 1837. 105 × 150/160 × 240mm.

14 p 116 St Martin's Church/from/Charing Cross. Engd by I. Woods.... Feby 1, 1838. 155 × 103/225 × 155mm.

15 p 129 Cumberland Terrace,/Regents Park. Drawn by I. Salmon from a Sketch by R. Garland. Engraved by I. Woods.... June 1838. 103 × 150/132 × 225mm.

16 p 145 View in Westminster Abbey/from the altar. Drawn by I. Salmon from a Sketch by R. Garland. Engraved by I. Woods. 150 × 102/240 × 150mm. nd.

17 p 147 Mansion House. Drawn by Hablot Browne from a Sketch by R. Garland. Engraved by I. Woods.... Augt 1, 1837. 105 × 155/160 × 245mm. From the N.E., showing conspicuously the attic storey removed five years later.

18 p 148 Leadenhall Street. T.H. Shepherd delt. J. Hopkins sc.... Augt. 1, 1837. 105 × 150/165 × 240mm. Looking E. towards East India House.

19 p 168 General Post Office/St Martins le Grand. Drawn by Hablot Browne from a Sketch by R. Garland. Engraved by I. Woods.... Septr 1, 1837. 102 × 150/160 × 240mm. Looking towards St Paul's Cathedral.

20 p 176 Royal Exchange/and/Cornhill. J.H. Shepherd del. J. Woods sc.... June 1st, 1837. 103 × 150/160 × 235mm. Later issues: 'The Late/Royal Exchange'.

21 p 177 Royal Exchange/destroyed by Fire Jany 10th 1838. R. Garland delt. for Woods's London. J. Woods sc.... Feb 1, 1838. 105 × 145/160 × 225mm. Inner courtyard. 'R. Ackermann Strand' added to publication-line.

22 p 178 City of London School./Milk Street. Drawn by Hablot Browne, from a Sketch by R. Garland. Engraved by J. Woods.... Septr 1, 1837. 148 × 107/240 × 165mm. Designed by J.B. Bunning, 1835; opened 1837.

23 p 191 Limehouse Church. Drawn by Hablot Browne from a Sketch by R. Garland. Engraved by J. Woods.... Octr 2nd 1837. 145 × 105/240 × 160mm. Hawksmoor's St Anne, Limehouse.

24 p 193 Quadrant/Regent Street, J. Salmon. I. Woods. 103 × 150/135 × 220mm. nd.

25 p 194 Buckingham Palace. Drawn by H. Browne from a Sketch by R. Garland. J. Woods sc. 100 × 150/165 × 245mm. nd. Nash's front and forecourt.

26 p 196 View in St. James's Park. J. Salmon del. J. Woods sc.... Nov. 1, 1837. 100 × 152/160 × 250mm. Garland's ochre wash drawing (100 × 150mm) sold at Sotheby's 13 January 1972, item 63.

27 p 197 Horse Guards. T. Clark delt. J. Woods sc.... December 1, 1837. 105 × 148/160 × 245mm.

28 p 198 Duke of York's Column. I. Salmon delt. I. Woods sc. 100 × 145/130 × 225mm. nd. From Carlton House Terrace, looking towards Waterloo Place.

29 p 199 Coliseum/Regents Park. Roberts delt. Cox sc. 103 × 150/160 × 240mm. nd.

30 p 200 St. Katherine's Hospital/Regents Park. Drawn by I. Salmon from a Sketch by R. Garland. Engraved by I. Woods.... March 1, 1838. 100 × 148/140 × 225mm.

31 front. The New Royal Exchange. 103 × 150mm. No credits. This view of Tite's building, opened in 1844, is found in later issues of the book.

189 · GODWIN'S CHURCHES OF LONDON [1839]

The title-page of this book, beneath the name of its author, George Godwin junior, a promising 24 year old architect, states that he was 'assisted by' John Britton, fellow FSA and celebrated antiquarian, then in his sixty-ninth year and having a long list of architectural and topographical works to his credit. He it must have been who encouraged this cultivated young man, an architect's son, winner of the first RIBA medal and founder member of the Art Union of London, to embark on this private survey of the 75 surviving City churches. The appending of his name was not the extent of his generosity for, as will be seen, he persuaded two of his artist friends to draw nearly all the views and another life-long connection to engrave the majority of the steel plates. He probably also contributed some of the historical notes which fill out the architectural descriptions of each building, with the aim described in the preface: 'We have endeavoured, by connecting each building with various remarkable events and persons, to render the churches store-houses of pleasant memories, and to invest them with an interest in the minds of their frequenters, distinct from, although connected with, their sacred character'.

The entire work was issued in shilling Parts between January 1837 and July 1839, normally at monthly intervals, each consisting of a 16 page octavo gathering of text illustrated by one or two plates and a wood-engraving. Sometimes, however, the text of a particular subject straddles the signatures of two gatherings, suggesting that both of them with their accompanying illustrations came out after an interval of two months. Indeed the first issue, a 48 page essay on St Paul's Cathedral, demanded three gatherings and eight illustrations but it was exceptional, being designed also for separate publication in paper boards:

A History and Description of St. Paul's Cathedral; by George Godwin Jun. Architect.... Illustrated by Plates from Original Drawings by Robert William Billings. Engraved by Le Keux, Challis, and Turnbull. London, 1837. C. Tilt; J. Hatchard & Son; L. & G. Seeley; J. Weale; and J. Williams.

The completed series was supplied with alternative printed title-pages for binding into one large volume dated 1839, or two dated 1838 and 1839 each costing 16s. Although the pagination started afresh for each new subject the signatures run without break through both volumes, from B to 2S. The bound Parts fall into date sequence, and contents lists for each volume confirm this order and state the number of views of each church supplied. A hope expressed in the preface that the series would later embrace the churches of Westminster, Southwark and the suburbs was unfortunately never fulfilled.

The Churches of London: a History and Description of the Ecclesiastical Edifices of the Metropolis. With biographical anecdotes of eminent persons, notices of remarkable monuments, etc. By George Godwin, Jun. Architect, F.R.S. & F.S.A. Assisted by John Britton, Esq. F.S.A. Illustrated by numerous Plates, engraved by J. Le Keux and others, from drawings by Frederick Mackenzie, and Robert William Billings. London: C. Tilt; J. Hatchard & Son; L. & G. Seeley; J. Weale; and J. Williams. MDCCCXXXIX.

Octavo, 215 × 145mm.   1838–9 or 1839

COLLATION   Vol. 1. General title-page (1839); title-page to vol. 1 (1838); dedication to the Bishop of London (1 leaf); pp v–vi, preface; contents of vol. 1 (1 leaf); descriptions, separately paginated for each church (sigs B–R). Vol. 2 (1839); contents (2pp); half-title; descriptions, separately paginated for each church (sigs S–2R); glossary (1 leaf); pp i–xvi, outline of contents, errata.

These views not only supplement greatly the 40 City church drawings by Shepherd published in *London and its Environs* (no 161) but also show most of those 40 buildings from a varying standpoint or with different architectural emphasis. The notion of building up a personal graphic record at this particular period was, as subsequent events proved, an inspired one. Within a few years of its publication two of the churches, St Bartholomew by the Exchange and St Benet Fink, had been demolished

to make way for commerce, and in the years from 1870 to the beginning of World War II no fewer than 21 more went the same way. Had the spirit of prophecy been alive among the ecclesiastical authorities it might have foretold that German high-explosive and fire bombs in the early 1940s would add another eight churches to the phalanx then falling to road-widening schemes and commercial greed, and that moreover if they held on to their property they would in due course be able to reap larger financial rewards with greater seemliness. In fact 31 of the churches represented by Godwin's plates and descriptions are no more, and of those no fewer than 24 were designed by Wren.

R.W. Billings, the chief illustrator, was an architect even younger than Godwin and very much a protégé of Britton's to whom he had been articled in 1826 at the age of 13. He was later to become an authority on Gothic architecture and restorer of Scottish castles which he recorded in a four-volume work, *Baronial and Ecclesiastical Antiquities of Scotland* (1845–52). The principal engraver, John Le Keux, was another Britton associate of long standing, having worked for *The Beauties of England and Wales* (no 104), *Architectural Antiquities* (no 97), *Illustrations of the Public Buildings* (no 146) and most recently the *Westminster Palace* (no 181) in which nearly all the drawing was Billings's work.

The other important draughtsman, whose name appears on the additional title-page to volume 2 as chief illustrator, was Frederick Mackenzie whose work had appeared in some of the Britton publications with which Le Keux was associated, particularly the *Architectural Antiquities*, and whose talent for architectural drawing had contributed much to Ackermann publications such as the aquatint *Westminster Abbey* (no 108).

The vignettes, mostly after Billings's drawings, are probably all by Samuel Williams, an experienced wood-engraver and draughtsman, in demand as a book illustrator, who contributed ornamental chapter heads to *Westminster Palace*. In fact these comprise nearly half the total number of views and, because they form an integral part of the illustration and are not merely ornaments, they are recorded in detail.

A handful of lesser contributors to the engraving include Le Keux's son, John Henry, whose name alternates with his father's in the later Parts of the work, William Deeble and James Carter, who both worked for *Metropolitan Improvements* (no 154), E. Challis and Thomas Turnbull.

Where the names of either the artist or the engraver are not cited in entries for steel-engravings it must be taken that these read, as in most cases they do: 'Drawn by R.W. Billings. Engraved by J. Le Keux.' The date only is quoted from the publication-line which, otherwise, is invariably 'London, Published by C. Tilt, Fleet Street (date).' Plates are unnumbered and most plate-marks have been cropped by the binder.

VOL. 1

St. Paul's Cathedral. London (48pp, sigs B–D)

1 front. St. Paul's Cathedral,/The Whispering Gallery. Engraved by E. Challis. Jany. 1st 1837. 155 × 96mm.

2 p 3 St. Paul's Cathedral,/S.W. View. Feby. 1. 1837. 96 × 153mm.

3 p 7 St. Paul's Cathedral,/View of the Choir. Engraved by Thos. Turnbull. Feby. 1. 1837. 158 × 94mm.

4 p 7 View of St. Paul's Cathedral from S.E. before the Fire in 1666./Engraved by S. Williams from a print by Hollar. 65 × 95mm. Vignetted wood-engraving. cf with Dugdale's *St Paul's* (no 8), item 34.

5 p 9 St. Paul's Cathedral,/View of the East End. Jany. 1. 1837. 162 × 100mm.

6 p 41 Monument to Lord Viscount Nelson. S. Williams. 110 × 80mm. Vignetted wood-engraving.

7 p 42 Monument to the Marquis Cornwallis. S. Williams 110 × 80mm. Vignetted wood-engraving.

8 p 43 Monument to Bishop Heber. S. Williams. 110 × 80mm. Vignetted wood-engraving.

St. Bartholomew the Great, Smithfield (16pp, sig E)

9 pl St. Bartholomew's the Great,/Western Entrance in Smithfield. Mar. 1. 1837. 155 × 100mm. Billings has set his name above the shop on the r.

10 p 9 St. Bartholomew's the Great,/View of the Interior. March 1. 1837. 160 × 100mm.

11 p 14 (vignette of Norman retro-choir) R.W. Billings. 85 × 80mm. Wood-engraving.

St. Sepulchre's Church, Skinner Street (16 pp, sig F)

12 p 1 St. Sepulchre's Church,/View from Skinner Street. Apr. 1. 1837. 163 × 98mm.

13 p 5 St. Sepulchre's Church,/Entrance in Skinner Street. April 1. 1837. 150 × 102mm.

14 p 6 (vignette of interior) 73 × 90mm. Wood-engraving. No credits. Shows above pulpit in the centre of the church 'a singular sounding-board in the shape of a large parabolic reflector'.

Church of St. Peter, ad Vincula, in the Tower of London (16pp, sig G)

15 p 1 St. Peter's Church,/In the Tower. May 1 1837. 102 × 148mm. Exterior.

16 p 1 St. Peter's Church,/In the Tower. May 1st. 1837. 100 × 147mm. Interior, looking towards altar.

17 p 13 (vignette of tomb of Sir Richard Cholmondeley, Lieutenant of the Tower) R.W. Billings. S. Williams. 60 × 85mm. Wood-engraving.

The Temple Church, London (32pp, Sigs H–I)

18 p 1 Temple Church,/View of the Circular part. June 1. 1837. 163 × 105mm. Exterior.

19 p 14 (vignette of the exterior from S.E.) R.W. Billings. S. Williams. 65 × 95mm. Wood-engraving.

20 p 15 Temple Church,/View of the Interior from the Vestry Door. July 1. 1837. 165 × 95mm.

21 p 18 Western doorway. R.W. Billings. S. Williams. 65 × 95mm. Vignetted wood-engraving.

22 p 19 Temple Church,/View across the East End. June 1. 1837. 163 × 103mm.

23 p 20 Part of Arcade in the Circular Aisle. S. Williams. 95 × 65mm. Vignetted wood-engraving.

24 p 23 Temple Church,/Interior of the Circular part. July 1 1837. 165 × 102mm.

Church of All-Hallows, Barking (16pp, sig K)

25 p 1 Allhallows—Barking,/S.W. View. Aug. 1. 1837. 100 × 150mm

26 p 7 Allhallows—Barking,/East End. Aug. 1 1837. 100 × 150mm. Interior.

27 p 13 (vignette of the Easter Sepulchre) R.W.B., S.W. 80 × 55mm. Wood-engraving.

St. Andrew's Under-Shaft, Leaden-Hall Street (15pp, sig L)

28 p 1 St. Andrew's Undershaft,/Leadenhall Street. Septr. 1. 1837. 165 × 100mm.

29 p 7 (vignette of W. end as seen in St. Mary Axe). R.W. Billings. S. Williams. 90 × 75mm. Wood-engraving.

30 p 10 St. Andrew's Undershaft,/Stow's Monument and the Font. Septr. 1. 1837. 167 × 95mm.

St. Bartholomew's, by the Royal Exchange (6pp, sig M)

31 p 1 St. Bartholomew's./By the Bank. Octr. 1. 1837. 150 × 100mm. Demolished four years later.

32 p 3 St. Bartholomew's,/By the Bank. Octr. 1. 1837. 95 × 140mm. Interior from S. aisle.

Church of All-Hallows, Bread Street (10pp, sig M)

33 p 3 (vignette of exterior) R.W.B., S.W. 115 × 80mm. Wood-engraving.

Church of St. Olave, Hart Street (10pp, sig N)

34 p 1 St. Olave's. /Hart Street. Novr. 1. 1837. 100 × 150mm. Exterior from S.E.

35 p 5 St. Olave's./Hart Street./View from the Organ Gallery. Novr. 1. 1837. 150 × 90mm.

St. Antholin's, Watling Street (6pp, sig N)

36 p 4 (vignette of exterior) R.W.B., S.W. 110 × 80mm. Wood-engraving.

St. Dunstan's in the East (12pp, sig O)

37 p 1 St. Dunstan's in the East. Decr. 1. 1837. 155 × 98mm. Exterior from S.E.

38 p 10 St. Dunstan's in the East. Decr. 1. 1837. 155 × 98mm. Interior from N.W.

39 p 11 (vignette of lierne vaulted porch) R.W.B., S.W. 95 × 65mm.

St. Mary's Aldermanbury (4pp, sig O)

40 p 1 (vignette of exterior from N.E.) R.W.B., S.W. 90 × 70mm. Wood-engraving.

St. Dunstan's in the West, Fleet Street (14pp, sig P)

41 p 1 St. Dunstan's in the West./Fleet Street. Jany. 1. 1838. 158 × 95mm. John Shaw's church, completed in 1833.

42 p 3 (The old church) I. Dod. 70 × 95mm. Wood-engraving. Copied from West and Toms's *Perspective Views* (no 32), item 17.

43 p 7 St. Dunstan's in the West,/Fleet Street. Engraved by T.Turnbull. Mar. 1. 1838. 152 × 93mm. Interior from S.

St. Michael's, Cornhill (4pp, sigs P–Q)

44 p 1 St. Michael's./Cornhill. Jany. 1. 1838. 157 × 95mm. Exterior from S.

St. Albans, Wood Street (6pp, sig Q)

45 p 1 St. Alban's,/Wood Street. Feby. 1. 1838. 165 × 97mm. Exterior from S.W.

46 p 5 St. Alban's,/Wood Street. Engraved by J. Lemon. Feby. 1. 1838. 155 × 95mm. Interior from W. The artist's portfolio and hat on the bench in foreground.

St. Michael's, Wood Street (4pp, sig Q)

47 p 1 (vignette of E. end, exterior) R.W.B., S.W. 90 × 75mm. Wood-engraving.

St. Augustine's, Watling Street (4pp, sig Q)

48 p 1 (vignette of S.E., exterior) R.W.B., S.W. 110 × 85mm. Wood-engraving.

St. Giles', Cripplegate (10 pp, sig R)

49 p 1 St. Giles',/Cripplegate. March 1. 1838. 150 × 98mm.

St. Bene't's, Paul's Wharf (6pp, sig R)

50 p 5 (vignette of exterior from N.E.) R.W.B., S.W. 120 × 80mm. Wood-engraving.

VOL. 2

St. Vedast's, alias Foster, Foster Lane (8pp, sig S)

51 p 1 St. Vedast's,/Foster Lane. April 1. 1838. 148 × 90mm. Exterior from W.

St. Mary's, Somerset,/Thames Street (4pp, sig S)

52 p 1 St. Mary Somerset,/Thames Street. April 1. 1838. 150 × 198mm. Exterior from S.E.

St. Nicholas', Cole Abbey, Fish-Street Hill (4pp, sig S)

53 p 3 (vignette of exterior from N.E.) R.W.B., S.W. 115 × 70mm. Wood-engraving.

St. Catherine's, Cree-Church, Leadenhall Street (10pp, sig T)

54 p 1 St. Catharine Cree,/Leadenhall Street. May 1. 1838. 148 × 98mm. Exterior.

55 p 1 St. Catharine Cree,/Leadenhall Street. Engraved by Jas. Carter. May 1. 1838. 160 × 95mm. Interior, E. end.

St. Clement's, East Cheap (6pp, sig T)

56 p 4 (vignette of exterior) R.W.B., S.W. 110 × 65mm. Wood-engraving.

Christ Church, Newgate Street (12pp, sig U)

57 p 1 Christ Church/Newgate Street. Engraved by J.H. Le Keux. June 1. 1838. 160 × 105mm. Exterior from N.E.

St. Dionis Backchurch (4pp, sig U)

58 p 1 St. Dionis-Backchurch,/Fenchurch Street. Engraved by J.H. Le Keux. June 1. 1838. 155 × 103mm. Exterior from S.

St. Helen's, Bishopsgate (11pp, sig X)

59 p 1 St. Helen's,/Bishopsgate. July 1. 1838. 140 × 95mm. Interior, with tomb of Sir John Crosby.

60 p 11 (vignette of exterior from S.W.) R.W.B., S.W. 80 × 70mm. Wood-engraving.

St. Michael's, Paternoster Royal. Thames Street (5pp, sig X)

61 p 1 St. Michael Paternoster,/College Hill. Drawn by I.R. Thompson. Engraved by J.H. Le Keux. July 1st 1838. 150 × 100mm. Exterior from S.E.

Allhallows the Great, Thames Street (6pp, sig Y)

62 p 1 Allhallows the Great,/Thames Street. Engraved by T. Turnbull. August 1. 1838. 100 × 153mm. E. view, showing chancel screen and pulpit sounding-board now in St Margaret, Lothbury. Church demolished 1876–94.

63 p 6 (vignette of exterior) R.W.B., S.W. 100 × 85mm. Wood-engraving.

St. Margaret's Pattens, Fenchurch Street (5pp, sig Y)

64 p 1 St. Margaret Pattens,/Fenchurch Street. August 1. 1838. 153 × 93mm. Exterior from S.W.

St. Mary's Abchurch, Abchurch Lane (5pp, sig Y)

65 p 5 (vignette of exterior from S.) R.W.B., S.W. 110 × 85mm. Wood-engraving.

St. Andrew's Holborn (14pp, sig Z)

66 p 1 St. Andrew's,/Holborn. Septr. 1. 1838. 150 × 100mm. Exterior from S.

St. Peter's, Saffron Hill (6pp, sigs. Z-2A)

67 p 1 St. Peter's,/Saffron Hill. Septr. 1. 1838. 160 × 100mm. A church built from the designs of Charles Barry and consecrated in 1832. Billings illustrates the character of the neighbourhood by including, on the left, no 107, the premises of H. Myers, a dealer in old clothes.

St. Michael's, Queenhithe, Upper Thames Street (4pp, sig 2A)

68 p 2 (vignette of exterior from S.E.) R.W.B., S.W. 95 × 90mm. Wood-engraving.

St. Mary's, Le-Bow, Cheapside (10pp, sig 2B)

69 p 1 St. Mary le Bow,/Cheapside. Drawn by F. Mackenzie. Engraved by J. Debell. Octr. 1. 1838. 158 × 95mm. Exterior from Cheapside.

Trinity Church, St. Bride's, Gough Square (4pp, sig 2B)

70 p 1 Trinity Church/Gough Square. Drawn by G. Mackenzie. Engraved by W.F. Starling. Octr. 1. 1838. 152 × 100mm. Built by John Shaw junior and completed June 1838, in 'Anglo-Norman style'; demolished c 1905.

St. Martin's, Outwich, Bishopsgate Street (6pp, sigs 2B–2C)

71 p 4 (vignette of exterior) J.R. Thompson, S.W.120 × 80mm. Wood-engraving.

St. Edmund's, the King and Martyr, Lombard Street (4pp, sig 2C)

72 p 3 (vignette of exterior) S.W. 115 × 65mm. Wood-engraving

St. Mary's Woolnoth, Lombard Street (7 pp, sig 2D)

73 p 1 St. Mary Woolnoth,/Lombard Street. Drawn by F. Mackenzie. Novr. 1st 1838. 155 × 95mm. Exterior from W.

74 p 4 St. Mary Woolnoth,/Lombard Street. Drawn by F. Mackenzie. Engraved by W. Deeble. Novr. 1 1838. 155 × 95mm. Interior from W.

St. Olave's, Jewry (9pp, sig 2D)

75 p 4 (vignette of exterior from W.) R.W.B., S.W. 110 × 80mm. Wood-engraving.

St. Swithin's, London Stone, Canon Street (5pp, sig 2E)

76 p 2 (vignette of exterior from S.W.) S.W. 100 × 75mm. Wood-engraving.

St. Magnus' the Martyr, London Bridge (6pp, sig 2E)

77 p 1 St. Magnus,/London Bridge. Drawn by F. Mackenzie. Decr. 1st 1838. 158 × 95mm. Exterior from N.W.

St. Mildred's, Bread Street (5pp, sig 2E)

78 p 1 St. Mildred's,/Bread Street. Drawn by F. Mackenzie. Engraved by J.H. Le Keux. Decr. 1st 1838. 150 × 102mm. Interior looking E.

79 p 5 (vignette of exterior from W.) R.W.B., S.W. 115 × 70mm. Wood-engraving.

St. Lawrence, Jewry (5pp, sig 2F)

80 p 1 St. Lawrence Jewry. Drawn by F. Mackenzie. Engraved by T. Turnbull. Decr. 1 1838. 150 × 100mm. Exterior from S.E.

St. Margaret's, Lothbury (3pp, sig 2F)

81 p 3 (vignette of exterior from S.E.) S.W. 105 × 60mm. Wood-engraving.

St. James', Garlick Hithe (4pp, sig 2F)

82 p 3 (vignette of exterior from W.) S.W. 110 × 75mm. Wood-engraving.

St. Peter's, le Poor, Old Broad Street (5pp, sig 2F)

83 p 1 St. Peter le Poor,/Broad Street. Drawn by F. Mackenzie. Jany 1st 1839. 155 × 100mm. Exterior from W.

St. Botolph's Aldersgate (5pp, sigs 2F-2G)

84 p 5 (vignette of exterior from E.) I.A. Wheeler sc. 85 × 75mm. Wood-engraving.

Allhallows, Lombard Street (4pp, sig 2G)

85 p 3 (vignette of exterior from S.W.) I.A. Wheeler sc. 100 × 75mm. Wood-engraving.

St. Bartholomew's the Less, Smithfield (8pp, sig 2H)

86 p 1 St. Bartholomew the Less,/West Smithfield. Drawn by F. Mackenzie. Engraved by T. Turnbull. Feb. 1. 1839. 150 × 105mm. Interior looking towards altar.

87 p 5 (vignette of exterior from S.W.) S.W. 95 × 80mm. Wood-engraving.

St. Bene't's, Fink, Thread-Needle Street (4pp, sig 2H)

88 p 1 St. Benét Fink,/Threadneedle Street. Drawn by F. Mackenzie. Engraved by J.H. Le Keux. Feby 1st. 1839. 155 × 100mm. Exterior from S.E. Demolished 1843.

Allhallows' Staining, Mark Lane (7 pp, sigs 2H–2I)

89 p 4 (vignette of tower and bay of W. end, all that remained) 95 × 80mm. Wood-engraving. No credits.

Allhallows', London Wall (5pp, sig 2I)

90 p 2 (vignette of exterior from W.) 110 × 80mm. Wood-engraving. No credits.

St. Andrew's by the Wardrobe, St. Andrew's Hill, Earl Street (8 pp, sig 2K)

91 p 1 St. Andrew's by the Wardrobe./Blackfriars. Drawn by F. Mackenzie. Engraved by J.H. Le Keux. March 1. 1839. 153 × 102mm. Interior from W.

92 p 8 (vignette of exterior from S.E.) S.W. 70 × 80mm. Wood-engraving.

St. Ethelburga's, Bishopsgate Street (4pp, sig 2K)

93 p 1 St. Ethelburga./Bishopsgate Street. Drawn by F. Mackenzie. Engraved by T. Turnbull. March 1st. 1839. 148 × 105mm. Interior looking E.

St. Mary's at Hill, Thames Street (4pp, sig 2K)

94 p 4 (vignette of exterior from E.) 95 × 70mm. Wood-engraving. No credits.

St. Bride's, Fleet Street (11pp, sig 2L)

95 p 1 St. Brides,/Fleet Street. Drawn by F. Mackenzie. Engraved by J.H. Le Keux. Apl. 1st 1839. 160 × 98mm. Shows St Bride's Lane and the church tower; on the l. the publisher Charles Tilt's office.

96 p 7 St. Bride's./Fleet Street. Drawn by F. Mackenzie. Engraved by T. Turnbull. April 1. 1839. 153 × 100mm. Interior looking E.

St. Catherine's Coleman, Fenchurch Street (3pp, sig 2L)

97 p 3 (vignette of exterior from N.W.) 95 × 75mm. Wood-engraving. No credits.

St. Anne and Agnes', Aldersgate Street (3pp, sig 2L–2M)

98 p 3 (vignette of exterior from S.) 95 × 80mm. Wood-engraving. No credits.

St. Bene't's, Grace-Church Street (4pp, sig 2M)

99 p 3 (vignette of exterior from N.W.) 105 × 70mm. Wood-engraving. No credits.

St. Michael's, Bassishaw (3pp, sig 2M)

100 p 3 (vignette of exterior from E.) S.W. 85 × 75mm. Wood-engraving.

St. Mary's, Aldermary. Bow Lane (6pp, sig 2N)

101 p 1 St. Mary's Aldermary,/Watling Street. Drawn by G. Mackenzie. May 1. 1839 160 × 100mm. Exterior from W.

102 p 1 St. Mary's Aldermary,/Bow Lane. Drawn by F. Mackenzie. Engraved by T. Turnbull. May 1. 1839. 155 × 100mm. Interior from S. aisle, looking E.

St. Martin's, Ludgate (4pp, sig 2N)

103 p 3 (vignette of exterior from Ludgate Hill) 100 × 70mm. Wood-engraving. No credits.

St. Matthew's, Friday Street (3pp, sig 2N)

104 p 2 (vignette of E. end, exterior) S.W. 100 × 70mm. Wood-engraving.

St. George's, Botolph Lane (3pp, sig 2N)

105 p 2 (vignette of E. end, exterior) S.W. 90 × 75mm. Wood-engraving.

St. Alphage's, London Wall (4pp, sig 2O)

106 p 3 (vignette of E. end, facing Aldermanbury) S.W. 100 × 75mm. Wood-engraving.

St. Stephen's, Coleman Street (4pp, sig 2O)

107 p 2 (vignette of E. end, exterior) S.W. 90 × 73mm. Wood-engraving.

St. Stephen's, Wallbrook (7pp, sig 2P)

108 p 1 St. Stephen's/Walbrook. Drawn by F. Mackenzie. Engraved by T. Challis. July 1. 1839. 152 × 103mm. Interior looking E.

109 p 5 (vignette of tower from S.W.) S.W. 110 × 75mm. Wood-engraving.

St. Botolph's, Bishopsgate (5pp, sig 2P)

110 p 4 (vignette of exterior from S.E.) 95 × 80mm. Wood-engraving. No credits.

St. Mildred's, Poultry (3pp, sig 2P)

111 p 2 (vignette of S. side on Poultry) 110 × 80mm. Wood-engraving. No credits.

St. Mary Magdalen's, Old Fish Street (5pp, sigs 2P–2Q)

112 p 3 (vignette of exterior from S.E.) 100 × 80mm. Wood-engraving. No credits.

St. Peter's, Cornhill (5pp, sig 2Q)

113 p 3 (vignette of exterior from S.E.) 105 × 75mm. Wood-engraving. No credits.

St. James's, Duke's Place (3pp, sig 2Q)

114 p 1 (vignette of exterior from N.W.) 100 × 80mm. Wood-engraving. No credits.

St. Botolph's, Aldgate (6pp, sigs 2Q–2R)

115 p 3 (vignette of exterior from N.W.) 80 × 75mm. Wood engraving. No credits.

---

190 · TROTTER'S SELECT ILLUSTRATED TOPOGRAPHY [1839]

Charles Marshall, scene painter at Covent Garden, Drury Lane and the Surrey Theatre, was also a landscape artist and creator of panoramas and was thus most suitably picked to assist in the décor of Westminster Abbey for the coronation of Queen Victoria. This book of London and suburban views is really 'Marshall's Select Topography' since 25 of the 34 were drawn by him and Trotter's text is no more than an explanatory gloss. The editor's preface says that it commenced publication in Numbers in April 1837. In November 1838 the complete volume was available, 'elegantly bound' at 15s, but reduced to 8s 6d by 1840.

Select Illustrated Topography of Thirty Miles Round London; comprising Views of various places within this Circuit engraved by W. Floyd, C. Bentley, C. Mottram, J.C. Varrall, and W. and J. Henshall, after original drawings of Charles Marshall, J.W. Allen, G.B. Campion, and other artists; with topographical and historical notices of each place. By William Edward Trotter. Thirty-four views and a map of the district. London, The Proprietor, 1 Cloudesley Terrace, Islington: Simpkin, Marshall & Co. Stationers' Court; C. Tilt, Fleet Street: Ackermann and Co, Strand and G. Virtue, Ivy Lane, 1839.

Octavo, 238–55 × 160–200mm.   1839

COLLATION Title-page; pp iii–iv, editor's preface dated from Kensington, September 1838; pp v–vi, introduction; contents, errata (2pp); pp 1–158, descriptions.

Marshall is said to have introduced limelight to the stage and his gift for illusionist scenery is hinted at by the scene in Vauxhall Gardens (item 17) in which acrobats are shown performing within a giant illuminated cavern; his taste for the panoramic is instanced in the birds-eye view of Green Park from the summit of the recently erected Duke of York's column (item 25). Of the other artists, George B. Campion was a founder member of the New Water Colour Society and C. Campion was a contributor to Thomas Allen's *History* (no 152) and *Panorama* (no 162) of London and to Whittock's *Modern Picture* (no 183). The chief engravers were J. Henshall, who had worked 16 of the plates in *Metropolitan Improvements* (no 154) and *London in the Nineteenth Century* (no 161), and W. Henshall; between them they engraved 16 of these views. Another four were by Charles Mottram, who made a living by book illustrations and by copies in line or mezzotint of the works of Victorian painters such as John Martin and Landseer. Others were drawn from the 'pool' of steel-engravers whose names can be found on the plates of most of the topographical

books of the era; such were J.C. Bentley and J.C. Varrall. A later issue, bound up with Woods's *History* (no 188) and with a reset introduction, is in the Royal Library.

The plates are unnumbered. Plate-marks are often cropped but, when present, measure 145–50 × 230–40mm. Captions are in voided capitals but, as in Tombleson's *Thames* (no 178), are sometimes translated into French and German. Also as in Tombleson a German publisher's name is added to some of the plates giving an alternative publication-line:

(a) 'London, Simpkin Marshall & Co., C. Tilt and the Proprietors, 1 Cloudesley Terrace, Islington/A. Asher, Berlin.'

(b) 'London, Simpkin Marshall & Co., C. Tilt and the Proprietors, 1 Cloudesley Terrace, Islington.'

1 (engr title) Select/Illustrated Topography/of/Thirty Miles around London. (vignette) London. Drawn by C. Marshall. Engraved by W. Henshall. London, Simpkin Marshall & Co., C. Tilt and the Proprietors, 1 Cloudesley Terrrace, Islington. 130 × 110/235 × 150mm. The introduction says of this vignette: 'The preceding vignette may be taken as somewhat allegorical of our task. It displays a view of London from a gallery near the summit of the shot-manufactory in Belvidere-road, which tower, with a little poetic licence, may be deemed the centre around which we draw our magic circle'.

2 p 1 Windsor Castle. (and in French and German) C. Marshall. W. Henshall. (a) 100 × 145mm.

3 p 9 Epsom/Surrey. J.W. Allen. J. Henshall. (a) 100 × 145mm.

4 p 15 St Alban's Abbey/Hertfordshire. (and in French and German) C. Marshall. W. Henshall. (b) 95 × 145mm.

5 p 20 Greenwich Hospital. (and in French and German) C. Campion. W. Henshall. (b) 100 × 148mm. From the Isle of Dogs.

6 p 26 Tottenham Mills/Middlesex. (and in French and German) C. Marshall. J. Henshall. (b) 100 × 148mm.

7 p 26 Millers Bridge/Hughes (Ferry Boat) River Lea. C. Marshall. C. Mottram. (b) 100 × 145mm.

8 p 27 Barking Church/Essex. (and in French and German) C. Marshall. J.C. Bentley. (b) 98 × 142mm.

9 p 30 The Town Hall, &c St Albans,/Herts. (and in French and German) C. Marshall. J. Henshall. (a) 102 × 145mm.

10 p 33 St Michael's Church, St Albans/Herts. (and in French and German) C. Marshall. C. Bentley. (b) 98 × 145mm.

11 p 35 Woolwich. (and in French and German) C. Marshall. W. Henshall. (a) 98 × 145mm.

12 p 44 Broxbourn Bridge/Herts. (and in French and German) C. Marshall. J. Henshall. (a) 100 × 145mm.

13 p 46 Hampton/Middlesex. (and in French and German) C. Marshall. W. Floyd. (a) 100 × 145mm.

14 p 49 Hampton Court/Middlesex. C. Marshall. J. Henshall. (a) 100 × 145mm.

15 p 62 Rochester. C. Marshall. W. Henshall. (a) 98 × 145mm.

16 p 78 Rochester Castle/Kent. C. Marshall. W. Henshall. (a) 100 × 145mm.

17 p 80 Vauxhall Gardens. C. Marshall. C. Mottram. (a) 100 × 140mm.

18 p 84 Hornsey Church/Middlesex. C. Marshall. W. Henshall. (a) 100 × 145mm.

19 p 89 Gate House Highgate/Middlesex. J. Henshall. T. Cox. (b) 95 × 155mm.

20 p 96 London/from Highgate. C. Marshall. (a) 100 × 145mm. No engraver's credit.

21 p 98 Leatherhead Church/Surrey. J.W. Allen. C. Mottram. (b) 98 × 142mm.

22 p 102 Dorking Church/Surrey. J.C. Allen. J. Henshall. (a) 98 × 147mm.

23 p 107 Hall of Mirrors, Colosseum/Regents Park. C. Marshall. J. Turnbull. (a) 105 × 143mm.

24 p 108 Westminster/from Chelsea Fields. C. Marshall. J.C. Varrall. (a) 98 × 143mm. (*Longford* 646)

25 p 110 View looking from the Gallery of the/Duke of York's Column/St James's Park. C. Marshall. J.C. Varrall. (a) 100 × 148mm. The column was erected in 1833.

26 p 111 Richmond/Surrey. G.B. Campion. C. Mottram. (a) 95 × 145mm. (*Gascoigne* 112, with the note: 'originally published as a part work "Henshall's Illustrated Topography of Twenty-Five Miles round London", from April 1837'.)

27 p 119 Twickenham Ait/Middlesex. C. Marshall. M. Wilson. (b) 100 × 145mm.

28 p 127 Sunbury/Middlesex. C. Marshall. J. Henshall. (b) 98 × 145mm.

29 p 131 Walton Bridge/Surrey. C. Marshall. W. Henshall. (b) 98 × 145mm.

30 p 137 Shepperton Lock,/Middlesex. C. Marshall. J.C. Varrall. (b) 100 × 145mm.

31 p 139 Staines Bridge/Middlesex. C. Marshall. J. Henshall. (a) 100 × 148mm.

32 p 146 Chalk Farm Bridge/Birmingham Railway. J. Fussell. (b) 92 × 150mm. No artist's credit.

33 p 147 Ingatestone/Essex. J. Meadows. J. Henshall. (b) 95 × 145mm.

34 p 149 Gravesend/from the Terrace Pier. T.C. Dibdin. J. Henshall. (b) 90 × 125mm. Vignetted.

35 p 158 (tm) Railway Map of the Environs of London, extending 30 Miles, 1839. Drawn and Engraved by J.R. Jobbins. London, Simpkin Marshall & Co.... 240 × 330mm. (cf with *Darlington and Howgego* 381; also 367, an 1838 map to accompany Henshall's *Illustrated Topography of Twenty-five Miles around London*.)

36 (p 68) Hillyers Bridge/Hughes' (Ferry Boat) River Lea. C. Marshall. C. Mottram. 98 × 140mm. Found in later eds; variant of item 7.

191 · LAURIE'S VIEWS OF THE CITY OF LONDON [c 1840]

John Boydell's *Collection* of 1790 (no 47), originally intended as a celebratory review of his own work, was a personal compilation. Francis West's in the next century (no 193) assembled plates by various artists with the common factor that they had all been originally published by the house of Bowles. Laurie's *Views* is akin to the second compilation since it presents 71 engravings published over the years by Robert Sayer and his partners and successors trading from the Golden Buck in Fleet Street. The copy described here is in the GLC History Library.

Their 1880 title-page assigns them to the years between 1730 and 1770 but they actually occupy a much longer time span, commencing with 14 of the *Perspective Views of Ancient Churches*, first published independently by their artist and engraver, Robert West and W.H. Toms, in 1736–9 (no 32) and reissued by Sayer, and ending with two of Richard Laurie's plates, published in August 1838, which commemorate William IV's visit to Greenwich and Woolwich to launch a man of war.

Most of the plates, however, were engraved between 1750 and 1753, years when the production of London views was at a peak both in quality and quantity, and were put out at that time either by Robert Sayer at the Golden Buck, or by Sayer and Henry Overton at the same address, or by John Bowles sharing with Sayer. The collection is therefore invaluable since it incorporates in a single voume a number of mid-eighteenth century prints usually only to be found in topographical collections scattered throughout many portfolios. Twenty two views bear the republication date of 1794, the year in which Robert Laurie entered into partnership with James Whittle; nine others are undated or bear intermediate republication dates.

On their reprinting in 1880 these 45 plates engraved between 1736 and 1753 were still in a remarkably good state of preservation, having presumably been undisturbed in store for 86 years; even if a certain amount of re-engraving was done these impressions on thick wove paper are clean and firm and have an air of authenticity. Turning over the pages one cannot but be impressed by the confidence of the draughtsmen in interpreting the views and the technical skill of the engravers of that period. Moreover they afford a unique composite picture of Georgian London and a reconstitution of the portfolios which the prospective purchaser of London views would be shown at Sayer's shop in the 1760s. The catalogue which he issued in partnership with Bennett in 1775 (reprinted by the Holland Press, 1970) lists on p 41 and pp 58–60 under the heading 'Perspective Views' these 45 plates of which 22 still retain the serial number there assigned to them.

Subsequent plates engraved for Laurie & Whittle or for R.H. Laurie are, with one or two exceptions, anonymous and artistically and technically inferior; some even resort to mechanically ruled skies. Many, like the commemorative plates cited above, were issued as souvenirs to mark the opening of a bridge or roadway or for peace celebrations or a coronation.

Robert Sayer traded from the Golden Buck between 1745 and 1794, with J. Bennett as his partner from 1774 to 1782. His business and premises were then taken over by Robert Laurie, who was an engraver of mezzotints and sporting aquatints and who ran it in partnership with James Whittle, as Laurie & Whittle, until 1812, when his son Richard Holmes Laurie succeeded him and the firm became Whittle & Laurie. Whittle died in 1818 and R. H. Laurie carried on alone until his death in 1858, so that the title-page of this book is posthumous by over 20 years. Carrington Bowles, the son of the founding Bowles, John, inherited his uncle Thomas's premises at 69 St Paul's Churchyard and traded from there between 1764 and 1793; his son Henry succeeded him and published under the name of Bowles & Carver until 1832.

There are Canaletto credits for 11 of the views, engraved variously by Grignion, N. Parr, E. Rooker, John Stevens, J.S. Müller, George Bickham and Thomas Bowles. These are all noted in W.G. Constable's *Canaletto* (2nd ed, 1976, referred to below as *Constable*), although most of the drawings on which they are based are as yet untraced. Bowles, the print publisher, besides engraving two of the Canalettos also drew very creditably and engraved nine other plates. The well-known 'View from One Tree Hill' with which the collection opens was based on a painting by Peter Tillemans, an immigrant from Antwerp who was for a time a scene painter at the Haymarket Opera House, and the two Richmond views (pl. 64–5) were engraved by Grignion after paintings by a local resident, Augustin Heckel, son of an Augsburg goldsmith, who spent his prosperous retirement painting Thames scenery. Of the Laurie & Whittle views the only outstanding ones are Daniel Turner's 'Blackfriar's Bridge' (pl. 31), Audinet's aquatint of Temple Bar (pl. 8) and a soft-ground etching by the drawing-master Benjamin Green of the entrance to the Tower of London (pl. 69); the latter, with the accompanying roundels (pl. 70), must have been etched for one of the drawing-books of which a large number are listed in Sayer & Bennett's 1775 catalogue and which include 'Landscapes in Rounds, pleasant for Youth to draw after'.

Views of the City of London shewing some of its principal streets, churches, and public edifices; with places of interest in the City of Westminster & Suburbs, as existing in the xviiith Century. On 69 Original Engraved Plates, executed about 1730 to 1770. N.B.—The Imprint is not the earliest date of publication. Re-Published by R.H. Laurie, 53 Fleet Street, London, E.C. (At the sign of the 'Golden Buck', 1880. Price £4. 4s. 0d.)

Oblong folio, 385 × 550mm.   1880

The map, old stock, is printed on contemporary laid paper. The plates are serially numbered, tr outside plate-marks, with a stamp, as indicated in the contents list. References to the West and Toms *Perspective Views* are abbreviated *WT* together with a series and item number. References to the 'Perspective Views' in Sayer & Bennett's 1775 catalogue (pp 58–60) are abbreviated *SPV* with item number.

0 (tm) A Plan of London on the Same Scale as that of Paris: In Order to ascertain the Difference of the Extent of these two Rivals. (and in French) ... 1762/with New Improvements to the Year 1766/with improvements to 1769./Printed for Robert Sayer, No 53 in Fleet Street, & Carrington Bowles, No 69 in St Pauls Church Yard, London ... by ... John Rocque. R. Parr sculp. 438 × 622/508 × 673mm. (*Darlington and Howgego* 101)

1 A View of London and Westminster, &c/from one Tree Hill in Greenwich Park. (and in French) Tillemans Pinxt. Stevens delin. et sculp. Republished 12th May 1794 by Laurie & Whittle, 53 Fleet Street London. 230 × 390/265 × 400mm. BL Maps: *K. top.* 21.48: 'Printed & Sold by Robt. Sayer at the Golden Buck opposite Fetter Lane Fleet Street & Henry Overton at the White Horse, without Newgate. Publish'd ... April 2, 1752.' *SPV* 4.

2 A North View of London. (and in French) Canaleti Delin. Stevens sculpt. Publish'd ... 1754. Republished 12th May 1794 by Laurie & Whittle, 53 Fleet Street London. 228 × 385/260 × 400mm. BL Maps: *K. top.* 21.50: 'Printed & Sold by Robt. Sayer at the Golden Buck opposite Fetter Lane Fleet Street & Henry Overton at the White Horse, without Newgate. Publish'd ... 1753.' A Canaletto drawing of this view from Pentonville, of this approximate size, is in BM (1862-12-13-51) (*Constable* 731). *SPV* 3.

3 A General View of the City of London next the River Thames. (and in French) T. Bowles delin. et sculp. Publish'd ... August 12th 1757. Re-published 12th May 1794 by Laurie & Whittle, 53 Fleet Street London. 230 × 388/260 × 400mm. BL Maps: *K. top.* 21.45: 'Printed for Robt. Sayer at the Golden Buck opposite Fetter Lane Fleet Street. Publish'd ... August 20, 1751.' *SPV* 2.

4 A West View of London with the Bridge/taken from Somerset Gardens. (and in French) Canaleti Pinxt in the Collection of Mr Thos. West. E. Rooker sculp. Publish'd ... 1767. Republished 12th May 1794 by Laurie & Whittle, 53 Fleet Street London. 230 × 390/260 × 400mm. BL Maps: *K. top.* 21.46a: 'Printed for Robt Sayer at the Golden Buck opposite Fetter lane Fleet Street. Publish'd ... August 20, 1751.' Sayer first published this on 1 August 1750; in *Crowle Pennant* 6,74. The Canaletto painting on which this was based is almost certainly that sold at Christie's on 26 November 1965(68), now in the Paul Mellon Collection (*Constable* 429b). *SPV* 5.

5 A North West View of St Pauls Cathedral London. (and in French) T.M. Müller sculp. Publish'd ... 1763. Republished 20th May 1823, by R.H. Laurie, 53 Fleet Street. 238 × 395/260 × 405mm. BL Maps: *K. top.* 23.35q: 'Published ... 1753, Printed for and Sold by Robert Sayer opposite Fetter Lane Fleet Street & Henry Overton without Newgate.' *SPV* 10.

6 An inside View of St Paul's in London. (and in French) Müller Junr. Sculpt. Published 12th May 1794 by Laurie & Whittle, 53 Fleet Street London. 230 × 393/260 × 400mm. Eastward view much reworked. BL Maps: *K. top.* 23.36c: 'Published ... 1753. London, Printed for & Sold by Robt Sayer at the Golden Buck opposite Fetter Lane Fleet Street & Henry Overton at the White Horse without Newgate.' *SPV* 11.

7 A Curious Perspective of the inside of St Pauls Cathedral/Shewing Part of the Dome ... (and in French) Published 12th May, 1794 by Laurie & Whittle, 53 Fleet Street London. 260 × 415/290 × 425mm. *SPV* 12.

8 (on label bm) West View of Temple Bar/Inscribed to the Memory of the late Aldn Pickett. B. Cooper junr. delt. 1797. P. Audinet sculpt. Published Septr 1st 1797 ... by B. Cooper No 4 Earl Street, Chatham Square London. 325 × 250/380 × 305mm. Aquatint.

9 The Church of St Mary le Bow in Cheapside London. (and in French) Bowles delin et sculp. London, Printed for Bowles & Carver, 69 St Paul's Church Yard, Robert Wilkinson, 58 Cornhill & Laurie & Whittle, 53, Fleet Street. 1757. 227 × 410/250 × 423mm. *SPV* 18.

10 A View of the Mansion House apointed for the Residence of the Lord Mayor of London ... begun 1739. (and in French) T. Bowles delin. et sculp. Publish'd ... 1753. Re-Published 12th May 1794 by Laurie & Whittle, 53, Fleet Street. 230 × 388/260 × 405mm. BL Maps: *K. top.* 24.14c: 'Publish'd Augt 20, 1751. Printed for and sold by Robt Sayer at the Golden Buck opposite Fetterlane Fleet-street & Henry Overton without Newgate.' *SPV* 9.

11 An Inside View of the Church of St Stephen Walbrooke London. (and in French) T. Bowles Delin et Sculp. London Printed for Bowles & Carver, 69 St Paul's Church Yard, Robert Wilkinson, 58 Cornhill & Laurie & Whittle, 53, Fleet Street. 230 × 390/260 × 400mm. A post-1794 publication-line. BL Maps: *K. top.* 24.4d: 'Publish'd ... 1753. London, Printed for & Sold by T. Bowles in St Pauls Church Yard, John Bowles & Son in Cornhill, Robt Sayer in Fleet Street & Hen. Overton without Newgate.' *SPV* 14.

12 A View of the Royal Exchange London. (and in French) T. Bowles delin et sculp. Re-Published 12th May 1794 by Laurie & Whittle, 53 Fleet Street London. 230 × 392/260 × 400mm. From S.E. along Cheapside; St Paul's Cathedral closes the vista. BL Maps: *K. top.* 24.11d: 'Published August 20, 1751. Printed for & sold by Robt Sayer at the Golden Buck, opposite Fetter lane Fleet Street.' *SPV* 7.

13 (bm, voided capitals) Interior of the Royal Exchange, London. Published July 12th, 1822 by R.H. Laurie, 53 Fleet Street, London. 250 × 420/280 × 430mm. Modern staffage, merchants in stove-pipe hats, substituted for *SPV* 8.

14 A View of the Monument erected in Memory of the dreadfull Fire in the Year 1666.... (and in French) Signr. Canaleti Delin. G. Bickham Sculpt. Published

... 1754. Re-published 12th May 1794 by Laurie & Whittle, 53 Fleet Street, London. 222 × 390/260 × 400mm. BL Maps: *K. top.* 24.16e: 'Published ... 1752. London Printed for and Sold by Robt Sayer at the Golden Buck, opposite Fetter Lane Fleet Street & Heny Overton at the White Horse without Newgate.' The original Canaletto drawing so far untraced (*Constable* 739). *SPV* 27.

Perspective Views of all the Ancient Churches

15 The South-East Prospect of the Church of Alhallows London Wall. R. West Delin. 1736. W.H. Toms sculpt. Publish'd March 16, 1736. (tr) 47. Printed for Robt. Sayer in Fleet Street. 235 × 303/280 × 315mm. *WT* 1,3.

16 The South-East Prospect of the Chapel Royal of St Peter in the Tower. R. West Delin. 1737. W.H. Toms sculpt. Publish'd March 18, 1739. (tr) 48. Printed for Robt. Sayer in Fleet Street. 230 × 308/278 × 315mm. *WT* 2,11.

17 The North-East Prospect of the Church of St Botolph without Aldersgate. R. West Delin. 1737. W. H. Toms sculpt. Publish'd March 18, 1739. (tr) 49. Printed for Robt. Sayer in Fleet Street. 230 × 308/278 × 315mm. *WT* 2,3.

18 The North West Prospect of the Church of St Andrew Undershaft. R. West Delin. 1736. W.H. Toms sculpt. (tr) 50. Printed for Robt. Sayer in Fleet Street. 240 × 303/290 × 315mm. *WT* 1,5.

19 The West Prospect of the Church of St Bartholomew the Great. R. West Delin. 1737. W.H. Toms sculpt. (tr) 51. Printed for Robt. Sayer in Fleet Street. 230 × 300/280 × 310mm. *WT* 2,1.

20 The North-East Prospect of the Church of St Olave Hart-Street. R. West Delin. 1736. W.H. Toms sculpt. (tr) 52. Printed for Robt. Sayer in Fleet Street. 235 × 300/280 × 315mm. *WT* 1,11.

21 The South East Prospect of the Church of Alhallows Barking. R. West Delin. 1736. W.H. Toms sculpt. (tr) 53. Printed for Robt. Sayer in Fleet Street. 235 × 300/280 × 310mm. *WT* 1,1.

22 The South-West Prospect of the Church of St Katharine Creechurch. R. West Delin. 1736. W.H. Toms sculpt. (tr) 54. Printed for Robt. Sayer in Fleet Street. 235 × 305/285 × 320mm. *WT* 1,9.

23 The East Prospect of St Leonard Shoreditch. R. West delin. 1735. W.H. Toms sculp. (tr) 55. Printed for Robt. Sayer in Fleet Street. 220 × 290/265 × 300mm. Not included in the original series.

24 The South-West Prospect of the Church of St Giles without Cripplegate. R. West Delin. 1737. W.H. Toms sculpt. (tr) 56. Printed for Robt. Sayer in Fleet Street. 230 × 305/280 × 315mm. *WT* 2,6.

25 The South Prospect of the Church of St Olave in Southwark. R. West Delin. 1736. W.H. Toms sculpt.

(tr) 57. Printed for Robt. Sayer in Fleet Street. 235 × 298/280 × 310mm. *WT* 2,7.

26 The South-East Prospect of the Church of St Dunstan in the West. R. West Delin. 1737. W.H. Toms sculpt. (tr) 58. London, published by R.H. Laurie, No. 53 Fleet Street. 230 × 305/275 × 310mm. *WT* 2,5.

27 The South Prospect of the Church of St Sepulchre. R. West Delin. 1737. W.H. Toms sculpt. (tr) 59. Printed for Robt. Sayer in Fleet Street. 230 × 305/280 × 310mm. *WT* 2,9.

28 The South-West Prospect of the Church of St. Helen. R. West Delin. 1736. W.H. Toms sculpt. (tr) 60. Printed for Robt. Sayer in Fleet Street. 230 × 300/280 × 210mm. *WT* 1,7.

29 View of the Vauxhall Iron Bridge. Published Augt 20, 1816 by Whittle & Laurie, 53 Fleet Street, London. (tr) 171. 260 × 425/290 × 445mm. Title in voided capitals. Opened 4 June 1816.

30 A View of the Waterloo Bridge. Published July 12, 1823 by Richard H. Laurie, 53 Fleet Street, London. (tr) 170. 260 × 430/290 × 440mm. Title in voided capitals. Opened 18 June 1817; only the centre block of Somerset house is shown as complete.

31 View of Blackfriars Bridge and St Pauls from the Patent Shot Tower Manufactory on the South Side of the River. Drawn & Etch'd by Danl. Turner. Aquatinted by Thos Sutherland. Publish'd Septr 1 1803 by Laurie & Whittle, 53 Fleet Street, London. (tr) 52. 260 × 400/300 × 415mm.

32 The Southwark Iron Bridge ... Published 3rd April 1822 by Richard H. Laurie, 53 Fleet Street, London. (tr) 174. 260 × 420/288 × 438mm. Title in voided capitals. Opened 24 March 1819.

33 The New London Bridge as it appeared ... on the 1st of August 1831.... Published by Richard H. Laurie, 53 Fleet Street, London. (tr) 177. 260 × 428/305 × 450mm. Line, with aquatint, incomplete.

34 View of the New Custom House, taken from the River Thames. Published 12 Augt 1822. (tr) 172. 265 × 425/290 × 440mm. Title in voided capitals. Built by David Laing, 1813–17. According to the Crace catalogue (8.31) this print was first issued in 1817.

35 The Thames Tunnel. Published 9th Novr 1830 by Richard H. Laurie, 53 Fleet Street, London. (tr) 176. 260 × 420/310 × 455mm. Grey aquatint. Title in voided capitals. Brunel's tunnel, begun in 1825 but not opened for traffic until 1843.

36 A View of Greenwich Hospital taken from the River. Sr. Christr Wren Architect. Millam sculp. Published 12th May 1823 by Richard H. Laurie. No 53 Fleet Street, London. (tr) 33. 230 × 380/265 × 395. BM: 'Marx' Pennant 9,194: 'Printed for Robt Sayer opposite Fetter Lane Fleetstreet.' May well be a re-engraving of *SPV* 33.

37 Royal Aquatic excursion to Greenwich Hospital. Published Augt 1, 1838 by Richard H. Laurie, 53 Fleet

Street, London. (tr) 180. 245 × 440/310 × 505mm. Grey aquatint. Title in voided capitals. Refs 1–15, including King's barge.

38 Launch of a First Rate Man of War at Woolwich. (inset below) The New Bason. Published Augt 1st 1838. (tr) 178. 248 × 430/310 × 505mm. Grey aquatint. Title in voided capitals.

39 A North East View of Westminster with the/New Bridge, taken from Somerset Gardens. (and in French) Canaleti Pinxt. in the Collection of Mr Thos West. J.S. Müller sculp. Published … 1754. Re-published 12th May 1794 by Laurie & Whittle, 53 Fleet Street London. 230 × 395/260 × 405mm. BL Maps: K. top. 21.46b: 'London, Printed for Robt Sayer at the Golden Buck opposite Fetter lane Fleet Street. Publish'd … August 20, 1751.' Original painting now in the Paul Mellon Collection (*Constable* 429a). *SPV* 6.

40 A View of Somerset House with St Mary's Church in the Strand London. (and in French) T. Bowles Delin et Sculp. London Printed for Laurie & Whittle, 53, Fleet Street. Bowles & Carver, 69 St Paul's Church Yard, Robert Wilkinson, 58 Cornhill. 330 × 385/260 × 395mm. BL Maps: K. top. 23.28.1f: 'Published … 1753. London, Printed for & Sold by T. Bowles in St Paul's Church Yard, John Bowles in Cornhill, Robt Sayer in Fleet Street & Hen. Overton without Newgate.' *SPV* 17.

41 South Front of Somerset-Place, taken from the River Thames. London Published 1st Jany 1800 by Laurie & Whittle, No 53 Fleet Street. (tr) 53. 260 × 418/295 × 435mm.

42 St Paul's Covent Garden/As it appeared on Fire, at eight o'clock, on Thursday Evening, 17th Septr 1795. Drawn by B.F. Scott. Engr. by John Scott. Published 5th Novr 1795 by Laurie & Whittle, 53 Fleet Street, London. (tr) 22. 230 × 390/275 × 415mm.

43 A View of Northumberland House, Charing Cross, &c. Canaleti Pinxt & Delint. T. Bowles Sculpt. Publish'd … 1753. Printed for and sold by Robert Sayer, at the Golden Buck, opposite Fetter Lane, Fleet Street. 230 × 390/260 × 400mm. BL Maps: K. top. 27.9a adds to publication-line: '& Henry Overton at the White Horse without Newgate.' Original painting owned by the Duke of Northumberland (*Constable* 194). *SPV* 23.

44 A View of the Parade of St James Park, the New Buildings for the Horse Guards, the Admiralty, with His Majesty going to the House of Lords &c. (and in French) Canaleti delin. T. Bowles Sculpt. Re-published 12th May 1794 by Laurie & Whittle, 53 Fleet Street, London. 230 × 390/260 × 400mm. BM: *Crowle* Pennant 4,112: 'Publish'd … Novr. 2 1752. Printed & Sold by Robert Sayer and Henry Overton' without cupola. BL Maps: K. top. 26.7g: 'Publish'd … Novr. 2nd 1753. London, Printed for & Sold by Robt Sayer at the Golden Buck opposite Fetter Lane Fleet

Street & Heny Overton at the White Horse without Newgate.', with cupola added. Original untraced (*Constable* 418). *SPV* 37.

45 A View of the Royal Palace of Hampton Court. (and in French) Rigaud delin. Parr sculp. Published 12th May 1794 by Laurie & Whittle, 53 Fleet Street, London. 230 × 390/260 × 400mm. BL Maps: K. top. 29.14h: 'Publish'd … August 20, 1751. Printed for & Sold by Robt Sayer at the Golden Buck, opposite Fetter Lane Fleet Street & Heny Overton without Newgate.' *SPV* 44.

46 (before letters) (Relief of the guard at St James's Palace; the band with a percussion section of three negro bandsmen with turbans marching into the courtyard) 310 × 460/315 × 465mm.

47 A View of St James's Park taken near the Stable Yard/Comprehending St James's Palace, Westminster Abby, Whitehall &c. (and in French) J. Maurer Delin. J. Smith sculpt. Re-Published 12th May 1794 by Laurie & Whittle, 53 Fleet Street, London. 235 × 398/285 × 405mm. BL Maps: K. top. 26.7b: 'Publish'd … January 1750. London, Printed for R. Sayer Map and Printseller facing Fetter Lane Fleetstreet.' *SPV* 35.

48 Veüe du Mall dans St James's Park (and in English) Chatelain delin. W.H. Toms sculp. Publish'd … 1757. Published 12th May 1794 by Laurie & Whittle, 53 Fleet Street, London. 235 × 395/262 × 410mm. BL Maps: K. top. 26.7k: 'Publish'd … 1752. Printed & Sold by Robt Sayer at the Golden Buck opposite Fetter Lane, Fleet Street & Heny Overton without Newgate.' *SPV* 39.

49 The Chinese Pagoda and Bridge,/erected over the Canal in St James's Park, for the Grand Jubilee of the 1st of August 1814. Published Septr 9, 1814 by James Whittle & Richard Holmes Laurie, No 53 Fleet Street London. (tr) 162. 265 × 420/295 × 440mm. Crude engraving with title in voided capitals.

50 A View of the Temple of Concord/erected in the Green Park to celebrate the glorious Peace of 1814, exhibiting the Fire works on the 1st of August. Published Septr 9, 1814 by James Whittle & Richard Holmes Laurie, No 53 Fleet Street London. (tr) 161. 260 × 420/295 × 440mm.

51 A South View of Westminster Abbey & St Margarets Church. (and in French) T. Bowles Delin. et Sculp. Published by R.H. Laurie, 53 Fleet Street, London. 233 × 390/263 × 400mm. BL Maps: K. top. 24.4g: 'Published … 1753. London, Printed for and sold by T. Bowles in St Pauls Church Yard, John Bowles & Son in Cornhill, Robt Sayer in Fleet Street & Hen. Overton without Newgate.' The viewpoint is the same as that of the engraving of 1750 by J. June BM: *Crowle* Pennant 2,153) copied by Cole for Maitland's *History* (no. 38), p. 1328 (ie from N.W.). *SPV* 15.

52 Westminster Abbey, St Margaret's Church & New Square from Parliament Street. Published 20th July

1822 by R.H. Laurie, 53 Fleet Street, London. (tr) 147. 270 × 440/300 × 455mm. BL Maps: *K. top.* 24.4q.1: 'Published May 18,1812 by Robt Laurie & Jas Whittle.'

53 The Inside of Westminster Abby. (and in French) T. Bowles delin. T. Bowles sculp. Published by R.H. Laurie, 53 Fleet Street, London. 260 × 415/290 × 425mm. BL Maps: *K. top.* 24.4r: 'Published ... Aug. 1753. London, Printed for Tho: Bowles in St Paul's Church Yard, John Bowles & Son in Cornhill, Robt Sayer in Fleetstreet & H. Overton without Newgate.' Looking E. *SPV* 16.

54 The Inside View of King Henry VII Chappel in Westminster Abbey. (and in French) Published by R.H. Laurie, 53 Fleet Street, London. (tr) 16*. 260 × 413/290 × 425mm. BL Maps: *K. top.* 24.4bb: 'Printed for Jno Bowles & Son at the Black Horse in Cornhill.'

55 Coronation Procession of His Majesty George the Fourth, 19th July 1821. Drawn & Etched by W. Heath. Published by R.H. Laurie, 53 Fleet Street, London. 260 × 410/230 × 430mm. Etching and aquatint. Dated in error 19 July 1813. Shows grandstands only, without topographical context.

56 (tm) Westminster Hall. The First Day of Term. A satirical poem. (bm) When Fools fall out for every Flaw ... Gravelot del. Mosley Invt et sculp. Re-Published 6th November 1797 by Laurie & Whittle, 53 Fleet Street, London. (tr) 16*. 265 × 315/315 × 343mm.

57 A View of the Canal, Chinese Building, Rotundo &c/in Ranelagh Gardens, with Masquerade. (and in French) Canalet delint. C. Grignion sculp. Publish'd ... 1759. Printed for & Sold by Robt Sayer at the Golden Buck opposite Fetter Lane Fleet Street. tr 74. 225 × 390/265 × 415mm. BL Maps: *K. top.* 28.4w: 'Publish'd ... Feby 28 1752. Printed for and Sold by Heny Overton at the White-horse without Newgate, Robt. Sayer at the Golden Buck opposite Fetter Lane Fleet Street.' Original drawing untraced (*Constable* 741b). *SPV* Ranelagh, etc. 7. (*Longford* 325)

58 An Inside View of the Rotundo in Ranelagh Gardens. (and in French) Canaleti delin. N. Parr sculp. Publish'd ... 1759. Re-Published 12th May 1794 by Laurie & Whittle, 53 Fleet Street, London. (tr) 72. 235 × 390/260 × 400mm. BL Maps: *K. top.* 28.4x: 'Publish'd ... Decr 2, 1751. Printed for and Sold by Robt Sayer at the Golden Buck opposite Fetter Lane, Fleet Street & Heny Overton at the White-horse without Newgate.' Original drawing untraced (*Constable* 420). *SPV* Ranelagh, etc 5. (*Longford* 342)

59 A View of the Rotundo House & Gardens at Ranelagh, with an exack representation of the Jubilee/Ball as it appeared May 24th 1759 being the Birth Day of his Royal Highness George Prince of Wales. Printed for Robert Sayer, Fleet Street, London.(tr) 73. 235 × 390/263 × 405mm. An earlier ed, dated 24 May 1751, in BM (*Crace* 13.70).

Engraved by N. Parr after an untraced drawing by Canaletto (*Constable* 741a). *SPV* Ranelagh, etc 6. (*Longford* 332)

60 A View of the Royal Hospital at Chelsea &/the Rotunda in Ranelaigh Gardens (and in French) T. Bowles delin et sculp. Published 12th May 1794 by Laurie & Whittle, 53 Fleet Street, London. 235 × 390/265 × 405mm. BL Maps: *K. top.* 28.4i: 'Publish'd ... August 20 1751. London: Printed for & Sold by Robt Sayer at the Golden Buck opposite Fetter Lane Fleet Street.' *SPV* 32. (*Longford* 6)

61 A View of the Grand Walk &c. in Vauxhall Gardens, taken from the Entrance. (and in French) Canaleti delint. E. Rooker sculp. Publish'd ... 1753. Re-Published 12th May 1794 by Laurie & Whittle, 53 Fleet Street, London. (tr) 68. 235 × 390/265 × 415mm. BL Maps: *K. top.* 41.27d: 'Publish'd ... Decr 2, 1751. London, Printed for & Sold by Robt. Sayer at the Golden Buck opposite Fetter Lane, Fleet Street & Heny Overton at the White Horse without Newgate.' Based on a painting in Lord Trevor's collection (Guildhall Art Gallery, *Canaletto in England*, 1959, no 8), but as the engraving is in reverse and differs in various respects they may both be based on a preparatory drawing (*Constable* 431). *SPV* Ranelagh, etc 1.

62 A View of the Grand South Walk in Vaux Hall Gardens/with the Triumphal Arches, Mr Handel's Statue, &c. (and in French) Canaleti delin. J.S. Müller sculp. Publish'd ... 1753. Re-Published 12th May 1794 by Laurie & Whittle, 53 Fleet Street, London. (tr) 70. 230 × 388/263 × 400mm. BL Maps: *K. top.* 41.27e: 'Publish'd ... Decr 2, 1751. London, Printed for & Sold by Robt Sayer at the Golden Buck opposite Fetter Lane Fleet Street & Heny Overton at the White Horse without Newgate.' Original untraced (*Constable* 748b). *SPV* Ranelagh, etc 3.

63 A View of the Temple of Comus &c. in Vauxhall Gardens. (and in French) Canaleti delin. Müller sculp. Publish'd ... 1753. Re-Published 12th May 1794 by Laurie & Whittle, 53 Fleet Street, London. (tr) 69. 233 × 385/260 × 400mm. BL Maps: *K. top.* 41.27f: 'Publish'd ... Decemr 2, 1751. London, Printed for & Sold by Robt Sayer at the Golden Buck opposite Fetter Lane Fleet Street & Heny Overton at the White Horse without Newgate.' Original untraced (*Constable* 748c). *SPV* Ranelagh, etc 2.

64 A West View of Richmond &c in Surry from the Star and Garter on the Hill. (and in French) A. Heckel Delin. Grignion sculp. Published 12th May, 1794 by Laurie & Whittle, 53 Fleet Street, London. (tr) 61. 230 × 390/260 × 400mm. 'Publish'd ... 1752. London, Printed for & Sold by Robt Sayer at the Golden Buck opposite Fetter Lane Fleet Street & Henry Overton at the White Horse without Newgate.' *SPV* Richmond 1. (*Gascoigne* 401)

65 A View from Richmond Hill up the River. (and in French) A. Heckel Delin. Grignion sculp. Published

12th May 1794 by Laurie & Whittle, 53 Fleet Street, London. (tr) 62. 233 × 385/260 × 400mm. 'Publish'd … 1752. London, Printed for & Sold by Robt Sayer at the Golden Buck opposite Fetter Lane Fleet Street & Henry Overton at the White Horse without Newgate.' *SPV* Richmond 2. (*Gascoigne* 400)

66 (duplicates item 45)

67 Aquatic Theatre Sadlers Wells. Publish'd Augt 23, 1813 by Jas Whittle & Richard H. Laurie, 53 Fleet Street. (tr) 156. 270 × 430/300 × 445mm. Title in voided capitals.

68 South East View of Copenhagen House. London; Printed for R. Sayer and J. Bennett, Map and Printseller, No 53 Fleet Street … 20 March 1783. 195 × 300/225 × 330/255 × 360mm. Stipple in sepia with stippled frame.

69 (composite plate) The Old Gateway of the Tower. B. Green ft 1780. Published Novr 2nd 1794 by Laurie & Whittle, 53 Fleet Street London. 165 × 215/200 × 240mm. – N.W. of Cannonbury House – S.E. of Cannonbury House. Drawn & Engraved by B. Green. Roundels, each 100/190 × 250mm. The first is a soft-ground etching from a Benjamin Green drawing-book; there are also copies with the lines 'Published Novr 2nd 1784' and 'Published Novr 2nd 1801 by Laurie & Whittle, 53 Fleet Street', the latter with the nos '38' tl and '1' tr. The other two subjects are also probably from his drawing-book sketches, etched in roundels.

70 (composite plate) Chaple at Kingsland – Queen Elizabeth's Gate at Islington. Drawn & Engraved by B. Green. Roundels, each 100/185 × 250mm. Probably drawing-book material as above.

71 The Highgate Archway from the Turnpike Gate at Holloway. Published 20th March, 1823 by Richd. Holmes Laurie, 53 Fleet Street, London. 265 × 425/305 × 440mm. The Archway Road was opened in 1813. A copy of this print, thus dated and published by Whittle and Laurie, is in BM (*Crace* 36.107).

---

192 · SMITH'S HISTORICAL AND LITERARY CURIOSITIES* [1840]

Charles John Smith, the son of a Chelsea surgeon, was taught engraving by James Pye and became a proficient illustrator of topographical and antiquarian works, with a special aptitude for facsimile engravings of illuminated manuscripts and autograph letters. This led him to publish in 1829 a series of 'Autographs of Royal, Noble and Illustrious Persons' with memoirs by John Gough Nichols. His preoccupation with the memorabilia of notables extended to their former residences: the engraving he made of Dr Johnson's house in Gough Square became a standard book illustration as did a romantic little plate of Goldsmith's Canonbury Tower lodging. Born later he would surely have edited a Blue Plaque guide. These various strands of interest were woven together in the present work issued in Numbers which he did not live to see completed. In 1836 it was published by Smith himself, in 1837 by William Pickering, later by Nichols's father, John Bowyer Nichols, as an occasional publication, and finally as a bound volume by Henry Bohn. The somewhat nebulous scope of the collection and Pickering's attempts to issue it on a regular basis may be deduced from this prospectus:

The Proprietors of this Work have the gratification of informing their Subscribers and the Public, that the Fifth Number will be produced on Tuesday, the 31st of January, 1837 embellished in a novel and extended manner; on which plan also it is proposed that the future Parts of the collection shall be published at regular intervals of Two Months each.

In addition to the very interesting Original Letters and Documents in Fac Simile, and of the Vignette Etchings, of which these Numbers have hitherto consisted, the Work will hereafter comprise entire Plates illustrative of the remarkable scenes of Historical Events … together with Views of the Birth-Places, Residences, and Monuments of celebrated literary characters. It will also sometimes embrace Illustrations of the Old Theatres, Places of Amusement, and Topography of London, Memorials of the Frost Fairs and other memorable scenes of the Metropolis; and, occasionally, Portraits of famous and extraordinary Persons. It is farther intended to introduce Coloured specimens of splendid and remarkable Illuminations …

The separate Numbers of the Collection will … continue to be published at 7s 6d in Demy Quarto, comprising Twelve Plates, with the accustomed Descriptive List in the Letter-press.

A total of eight Numbers and 100 plates was finally published, including a fair number of topographical drawings reproduced by means of steel or wood-engraving or lithography; those of London interest are listed below.

Smith was elected a Fellow of the Society of Antiquaries in 1837 and died in the following year at the age of 35.

Historical and literary curiosities, consisting of fac-similes of original documents; scenes of remarkable events and interesting localities; and the birth-places, residences, portraits and monuments, of eminent literary characters; with a variety of reliques and antiquities connected with the same subjects: selected and engraved by the late Charles John Smith, F.S.A. London: Henry G. Bohn, Covent Garden, MDCCCXL.

(extra title) Facsimiles of Historical and Literary Curiosities, accompanied by etchings of Interesting Localities, engraved and lithographed by and under the direction of Charles John Smith. To be continued occasionally. Published by J.B. Nichols and Son, Parliament Street: sold by J. and A. Arch & Co., Cornhill, London.

Quarto, 275 × 220mm.   1840

COLLATION   Title-pages; 8 Numbers, each consisting of about 12 assorted plates accompanied by unpaginated descriptions (the plates unlisted and unnumbered).

1 (pl. 7) Monmouth House, Larence Strt Chelsea, taken down 1833/the residence of Dr Smollet/see Faulkner's Chelsea. Drawn and Etched by R.B. Schnebbelie. Published by C.J. Smith, Engraver 12 Southampton Street. Sold by Thos Faulkner, Chelsea, 1835. 85 × 110mm. Vignette. Pt 1. (*Longford* 502)

2 (pl. 24) Cottage Haverstock Hill, near Hampstead, the Residence of Sir Richard Steele. From a drawing taken 1804. Published by Charles John Smith, Engraver, London, 1836. 90 × 130mm. Vignetted lithograph. Pt 2.

3 (pl. 25) Interior of observatory, St Martins Street London. Etched & Published by C.J. Smith, Engraver, London, 1836. 70 × 50mm. Vignette. Newton's observatory. Pt 3.

4 (pl. 44) Tomb of William Hogarth at Chiswick. Published by Chas. J. Smith Engraver, London, 1836. 90 × 90mm. Vignette. Pt 4.

5 (pl. 49) House occupied by the Royal Society Crane Court Fleet Street. C.J. Smith sculp. William Pickering, Chancery Lane. 130 × 90mm. Pt 5.

6 (pl. 51) The Residence of Sir Isaac Newton, St Martins Street/Leicester Square. C.J. Smith sculp. Published by William Pickering, Chancery Lane, London, 1837. 115 × 75mm. Pt 5.

7 (pl. 62) Don Saltero's Coffee House, Cheyne Walk, Chelsea. London, 1837, W. Pickering for Smith's Historical & Literary Curiosities. 98 × 62mm. Pt 6. (*Longford* 560)

8 (pl. 63) Residence of Charles Macklin, Tavistock Row, Covent Garden. Bartlett. C.J. Smith. London, 1837. W. Pickering for Smith's Historical & Literary Curiosities. 130 × 85mm. Pt 6.

9 (pl. 73) Frost Fair on the River Thames, 1684. (tr) Monday February the 4th Ao 168¾. 80 × 240mm. Lithograph based on BM drawing (235 × 712mm), by J. Wyck, originally in *Crowle* Pennant, 7.

10 (pl. 76) Exterior View of Astley's Amphitheatre/as it appeared in 1777 from an original drawing by William Capon. Charles John Smith F.S.A. sculp. 140 × 228mm. Pt 7.

11 (pl. 77) Interior View of Astley's Amphitheatre/as it appeared in 1777 from an original drawing by William Capon. Charles John Smith F.S.A. sculp. 138 × 230mm. Circus ring with stands for spectators. Capon's original water-colours for pl. 76–7 (both 140 × 230mm) in BM (*Crace* 35.69,71). Pt 7.

12 (pl. 88) Upper Flask Tavern, Hampstead Heath. Bonner sc. 60 × 88mm. Wood-engraving. Pt 8.

13 (pl. 97) Exterior View of the Italian Opera House/in the Haymarket/As it appeared before the Fire June 17, 1789 from an original drawing by William Capon. Charles John Smith F.S.A. sculp. 165 × 222mm. Original water-colour (197 × 210mm) in BM (*Crace* 11.112). Pt 8.

14 (pl. 98) Residence of John Hoole/the translator of 'Tasso' and 'Ariosto'/Great Queen Street, Lincolns Inn Fields. 130 × 85mm. Shows the 17th century pilastered façade of Great Queen Street houses. Pt 8.

193 · WEST'S COLLECTION OF VIEWS [c 1840]

This album of views must have been assembled some time between 1833, the date which appears on item 14, and 1850 when Francis West, a Fleet Street optician for whom printselling must have been a sideline, moved to 39 Southampton Street. He had somehow acquired a number of copper plates of London views engraved for John Bowles in the previous mid-century and reissued between about 1780 and 1820 by his son's firm, Bowles & Carver, and a successor, Robert Wilkinson. Wilkinson's trade stock of engraved plates, maps and prints was sold at Sotheby's on 29 September 1825 and these particular plates were very likely to have been among the unspecified lots. The oldest among them (pl. 49–50, 52, 55), which were advertised in Bowles's 1728 catalogue and included in his *London Described* (no 29), show the coronation of George II and the latest is a view of the new East India House, first published by Bowles & Carver in 1802. Most however are left-overs from Bowles's mid-century prolific output; 38 of them are certainly listed in his 1753 catalogue.

The popularity of these 'Perspective Views' at that period, the extraordinary variety available from one of the two leading printsellers and the uses to which they were put may be seen in an extract from that catalogue:

PERSPECTIVE VIEWS: The following Sets consisting of a great variety of Perspective Views, are not only in esteem for furniture in frames and glasses, but are much used in proper colours without frames, for viewing in the Diagonal Mirror, in which method of looking at them, they appear with surprising beauty, and in size but little inferior to the real places....

50. *Perspective Views in and about London*, being a collection of pleasant views of the most noted places in London and the adjacent parts, drawn in Perspective by Gravelot, Rigaud, Heckell and Morier; and engraved by Mons. Vivarez, Canot, Major and other best hands. Each print is 11 inches deep, and 17 inches wide and may be had together or separate. Pr. 1s. each black, 2s. coloured, viz.

1. The North Prospect of London and Westminster taken from the Bowling-green at Islington.

2. The south west prospect of London, being a view on the Thames from Somerset House to London Bridge. Shewing not only the buildings next the Thames, but a bird's view over the whole city.

3. The south east prospect of Westminster, being a view on the Thames from Somerset House to Westminster Bridge...

*4. The south east prospect of London from the Thames, shewing the Tower, Custom House, London Bridge etc.

*5. Westminster Bridge.

*6. The royal palace of St James.

*7. The royal palace of Kensington.

*8. The royal palace of Hampton Court.

*9. The royal palace of Windsor Castle.

10. Greenwich Park, being an extensive view from One-tree Hill in Greenwich Park over the Thames and the adjacent country to London.

*11. Greenwich Hospital, as seen from the Thames.

*12. Chelsea Hospital, as seen from the Thames.

*13. The village of Chelsea, as seen from the Thames.

*14. Lambeth House, as seen from the Thames.

*15. Somerset House, with a view of the Thames.

*16. St James' Park, and the City, from Buckingham House.

*17. The magnificent Building erected for the Fire Works in the Green Park, on account of the general peace in 1749, with a view of Buckingham House and the country as far as Chelsea.

*18. A pleasant view of the Canal in St James's Park.

*19. The Parade in St James's Park, with a view of the Treasury and Admiralty Office.

*20. The new Building at the Horse Guards in St James's Park, with the procession of his Majesty going to the Parliament House.

*21. Westminster Abbey and St Margaret's Church.

22. The inside of Westminster Abbey.

23. The inside of King Henry the VIIth's Chapel ...

24. Whitehall, shewing the Banquetting house on one side, and the Horse Guards on the other.

25. The Privy Garden, with that side of the Banquetting house next the River.

26. The entrance of St James's palace, with a view of Pall Mall.

27. Charing-cross and Northumberland-house.

28. A perspective view of Grosvenor Square.

29. A perspective view of St James's Square.

30. A perspective view of Leicester Square.

31. A perspective view of Covent Garden.

32. A perspective view of Lincolns Inn new Square.

33. St Mary's Church in the Strand, and the entrance of Somerset House.

34. The Temple, with a view of the Thames.

35. The beautiful church and spire of St Brides in Fleet Street.

36. Bow Church and Steeple, with a view of Cheapside.

*37. The north west view of St Paul's Cathedral.

38. The inside of St Paul's Cathedral from the West entrance to the organ.

39. The choir of St Paul's Cathedral.

*40. The inside of St Martin's Church.

41. The inside of St Stephen's Church in Wallbrooke.

*42. The Lord Mayor's Mansion House.

*43. A perspective view of the Royal Exchange.

44. The inside view of the Royal Exchange.

45. Ironmongers Hall and Fenchurch Street.

*46. The Monument in memory of the conflagration 1666.

47. The Custom House, with part of the Tower.

48. The north west view of the Tower.

49. Bethlehem hospital and Moorfields.

*50. A perspective view of the Foundling hospital.

*51. The house of Moses Hart Esq. at Isleworth, with a view of the Thames.

*52. A view of Richmond Hill and my Lord Cholmondely's house from the Thames.

*53. A pleasant view of Richmond Hill on each side of the Thames down the River.

*54. A pleasant view of Richmond hill on each side of the Thames up the River.

55. Lord Stafford's house and the village of Twickenham from the opposite shore of the Thames.

*56. The Countess of Suffolk's house, near Twickenham, as viewed from the Thames.

*57. The house of Governor Pitt at Twickenham, with a pleasing view of the Thames.

*58. The Earl of Radnor's house at Twickenham, from the opposite shore of the Thames.

*59. Dr Batty's house at Twickenham, viewed from the opposite shore of the Thames.

60. The house of the late celebrated Poet Alexander Pope Esq. at Twickenham, viewed from the Thames.

61. Prior Park, the elegant seat of Ralph Allen Esq., near Bath ...
62. Blenheim House.

51. *Vauxhall and Ranelagh Gardens*. Being eight views of the admired Buildings and Gardens of Vauxhall and Ranelagh. Pr. 1s. each black. 2s. coloured.

*1. A general prospect of Vauxhall gardens ...
*2. The inside of the rotunda in Vauxhall gardens.
   3. The Grand Walk at the entrance of Vauxhall Gardens, shewing the Orchestra, and musicians playing ...
*4. The Triumphal Arches, and Mr Handel's statue in the fourth grand walk of Vauxhall Gardens.
*5. The Chinese Pavilions in Vauxhall Gardens.
*6. The Rotunda at Ranelagh, with the representation of a jubilee ball ...
*7. The inside of the magnificent Rotunda at Ranelagh with the company at breakfast.
*8. The Chinese House on the canal in Ranelagh garden, with the Rotunda, and company in masquerade.

To these 38 views, marked with an asterisk in the list above, and the four older coronation engravings were added three smaller plates, issued also at mid-century by Bowles's rival, Robert Sayer, and advertised in the 1775 Sayer & Bennett catalogue (reprinted, Holland Press, 1970) among the 'Sets of Small Prints' at 1s 6d per dozen, thus described:

All the foregoing Sets of Prints may be had ready coloured in sheets, or upon paste-boards, for viewing in the concave glasses or optical pillar-machines, in which they have a very agreeable effect. They likewise make genteel furniture when framed and glazed, and are all near of a size, being about 7 inches high by 10 and a half wide.

Eleven further plates, mostly of more recent date, bring the total up to 56.

The plates from which this album was printed have more markedly deteriorated than those later republished by Laurie from Sayer's collection (no 191) but both sets are valuable as a partial record of the two leading printsellers' stock of London views at mid-century. They contain 17 rival versions of the same subjects and many more appear in their lists. Some of the artists and engravers, including Thomas Bowles, worked for both but only Sayer could lay claim to designs by Canaletto.

Very popular with printsellers in the 1740s and 1750s was John Maurer. In this collection nine of the drawings are his (pl. 2–3, 12, 23, 28, 30–1, 33, 36), engraved by himself, Bowles, Canot and Vivares, and he contributed at least eight other items to Bowles's 'Perspective Views' (see above, nos 24–7, 32, 47–9). At the same time he was working for

Sayer, being responsible for a number of the small views listed in the 1775 Sayer & Bennett catalogue (pp 86–7). Original drawings of his, preserved in the Royal Collection at Windsor, are: St James's Park 1741, St James's Palace 1741, Buckingham House 1746 and Horse Guards 1750 (*Burlington Fine Arts Club Catalogue* 1919, 42 a,b and 48 a,b). Samuel Wale was a pupil of Francis Hayman, the artist responsible for pictorial decoration of Vauxhall Gardens, and contributed the drawings on which the four Vauxhall prints (pl. 44–7) are based. The up-river views of Richmond and Twickenham (pl. 25–7, 38–43) are engraved from paintings by Augustin Heckel, a retired goldsmith and local resident and Antonio Joli, Italian scene-painter and emulator of Canaletto who was in London between 1744 and 1748.

The description of each print is followed by particulars of earlier states seen either in BL Maps: King's Topographical Collection (abbreviated *K. top.*), BM Crowle Pennant (abbreviated *P*) or the Guildhall Library. Finally the Bowles catalogue references are given either as *B 1753* or *B 1728*.

A Collection of Views of old London and its environs. Printed for F. West, 83 Fleet Street, London.

Oblong Folio, 390 × 550mm.   c 1840

Most plates carry the undated publication-line 'Published by F. West, 83 Fleet Street, London.' Therefore only alternatives are specifically mentioned.

1 A view of Northumberland House, Charing Cross, &c. (and in French) London, Printed for F. West, 83 Fleet Street. 150 × 225/180 × 275mm. (tr) '11'. In Sayer & Bennett's catalogue p 86, set 8. See items 36 and 53 below.

2 A view of Chelsea. (and in French) J. Maurer Delint. I. Vivarez Sculpt. 240 × 395/270 × 420mm. *K. top.* 28.4b: 'Publish'd ... 1 August 1744. Printed for Thos. Bowles in St Pauls Church Yard & Jno Bowles at the Black-Horse in Cornhill.' The ghost of the burnished-out date still remains and also that of the intermediate publication-line of Bowles & Carver and Robert Wilkinson. *B 1753* 50/13. (*Longford* 250)

3 A view of the Royal Hospital at Chelsea and the Rotunda in/Ranelagh Gardens in Middlesex. (and in French) 245 × 407/275 × 420mm. *P* 2,173: 'J. Maurer Delin. Vivarez Sculpt. Publish'd ... 1 August 1744.' *B 1753* 50/12. (*Longford* 11)

4 A view of Cain & Abel Bird-Cage, and the Grand Temple/Walks in Lord Burlington's Garden at Chis-

457

wick. (and in French) 235 × ⁻383/265 × 400mm. (bl) '30'.

5 A view of the Orangery at Chiswick/Lord Burlington's Garden. (and in French) Rysbrake Delin. 235 × 385/265 × 400mm. (bl) '31'. No publication-line.

6 A view of Gravesend in Kent, with troops passing the Thames to Tilbury Fort. 280 × 440/300 × 450mm. *K. top*. 16.57c: '... 27th July 1780.' Published by Bowles 1781.

7 A Perspective View of the Magnificent Structure, erected in the Green Park for/the Royal Fireworks exhibited the 27 of April 1749 on account of the General Peace. (and in French) 230 × 400/260 × 410mm. Guildhall Library: 'Printed for John Bowles and Printed for Robert Wilkinson and Bowles & Carver.' (ie after 1792). *B* 1753 50/17.

8 A View of the Royal Hospital at Greenwich. (and in French) 250 × 410/280 × 425mm. *B* 1753 50/11.

9 A View of the Bridge over the Thames at Hampton Court. (and in French) 255 × 415/285 × 430.

10 Le Palais Royale de Hampton Court. (and in English) I. Rigaud delin. Si. Torres sculp. Publish'd ... May 30th 1800 by Fras. West, 83 Fleet St. London. 218 × 400/250 × 415mm. Nathaniel Parr engraved this drawing of Jean Rigaud's for Robert Sayer who published it in 1751 as one of Laurie's *Views*, pl. 45. *B* 1753 50/8.

11 The Royal Palace of Kensington. (and in French) 250 × 415/280 × 430mm. *B* 1753 50/7.

12 Lambeth/The Archbishop of Canterbury's Palace. (and in French) Maurer delin. Canot Sculp. 235 × 400/270 × 430mm. *K. top*. 41.1f: 'Publish'd ... 28 July 1745. Printed for John Bowles & Son, at the Black Horse in Cornhill.' *B* 1753 50/14.

13 North West View of the Cathedral Church of St Paul, London. (and in French)/ This Beautiful Fabrick ... Printed for & Sold by F. West 83 Fleet Street, London. 260 × 410/280 × 430mm. (bl) '45'. *B* 1753 50/37.

14 A View of the East India House, Leadenhall Street, London/Richard Jupp Esq. Architect. London, Printed for F. West, 83 Fleet Street. Published 26 Feb. 1833. 260 × 430/305 × 450mm. *P* 12,77: 'Printed for Bowles & Carver, no 69 St Paul's Church Yard, 26th February, 1802.' The new building was completed by Henry Holland in 1800.

15 The Foundling Hospital. (and in French) 260 × 420/290 × 430mm. Guildhall Library: 'Printed for R. Wilkinson in Cornhill & Carington Bowles, at No 69 in St Paul's Church Yard.', a reissue perhaps in the 1780s. *B* 1753 50/50.

16 A General View of the City of London, next/the River Thames. 250 × 410/280 × 425mm. (bl) '39'. *B* 1753 50/4.

17 The Lord Mayor's Mansion House/shewing the Front of the House & the West Side. (and in French) Published by Fras. West, 83 Fleet Street, London. 250 × 410/285 × 425mm. Guildhall Library: 'Printed for John Bowles and Carington Bowles.' *B* 1753 50/42.

18 The Monument of London in remembrance of the dreadfull Fire in 1666/Its height is 202 feet. (and in French) Bowles delin. Bowles sculp. Published by Fras. West, 83 Fleet Street. London. 240 × 405/265 × 410mm. BM (*Crace* 24.16) catalogues a copy as '1752'. *B* 1753 50/46.

19 A View of the Royal Exchange, London. (and in French) ... opened 1669. 235 × 400/265 × 420mm. (bl) '62'. *B* 1753 50/43.

20 A View of the Bank of England, Threadneedle Street, London/the Centre erected 1733. G. Sampson Architect. Sir Robert Taylor ... Architect of the Wings. London, Printed for Bowles & Carver, No. 69 St Paul's Church Yard ... 270 × 428/305 × 440mm. *P* 12,88–9: 'Published by Bowles and Carver, 25th July 1797.' The wings were added 1766–83. (*Bank of England* 32)

21 (between inverted 'C' scrolls) A South View of the Church of St Pancras/in the County of Middlesex. 253 × 415/280 × 430mm. (bl) '40'. The old church. BM (*Crace* 31.48) catalogues as 'Printed for Bowles & Carver 1789.'

22 The Chinese House, the Rotunda, & the Company in masquerade/in Ranelagh Gardens. (and in French) Bowles delin. Bowles sculp. 260 × 405/290 × 415mm. (tr) '7'. BM (*Crace* 13.79) catalogues as '1759' and *Crace* Supplement 13.6 has: 'Printed for R. Wilkinson in Cornhill and Bowles & Carver, 69 St Paul's Church Yard.' *B* 1753 51.8. (*Longford* 328)

23 Ranelagh House & Gardens with the Rotunda/at the time of the Jubilee Ball. (and in French) J. Maurer delin. T. Bowles Fecit. 240 × 405/290 × 435mm. (tr) '6'. *P* 14,57: 'Published 6 May, 1745.' *B* 1753 51/6. (*Longford* 333)

24 The Inside View of the Rotunda in Ranelagh Gardens/with the Company at Breakfast. (and in French) Bowles delin. et sculp. 260 × 400/290 × 410mm. (tr) '8'. Guildhall Library: 'Publish'd ... 1754.' BM (*Crace* Supplement 13.7): 'Printed for R. Wilkinson in Cornhill & Bowles & Carver, No 69 St Paul's Churchyard.', on wove paper with watermark 'Whatman 1816'. *B* 1753 51/7. (*Longford* 340)

25 A View of Richmond Hill from the Earl of Cholmondelly's. (and in French) A. Heckell Delint. J. Mason sculp. 260 × 420/295 × 455mm. *K. top*. 41.18d: 'Publish'd ... 13 Feby 1749. Printed for John Bowles at the Black Horse in Cornhill.' *B* 1753 50/52. (*Gascoigne* 398)

26 A view from Richmond Hill down the River. (and in French) Jolly delint. et Pinxt. F. Vivarez sculpt. 260 × 425/295 × 445mm. 'Publish'd ... 13 Feby 1749. Printed for John Bowles at the Black Horse in Cornhill.' *B* 1753 50/53. (*Gascoigne* 394)

458

27 A view from Richmond Hill up the River. (and in French) Jolly Pinx. F. Vivarez sculpt. 260 × 420/290 × 435mm. 'Publish'd 13 Feby 1749. Printed for John Bowles at the Black Horse in Cornhill.' *B* 1753 50/54. (*Gascoigne* 395)

28 A Perspective View of ye Royal Palace of Somerset next ye River. (and in French) J. Maurer delin. et sculp. 215 × 410/255 × 420mm. *K. top.* 26.4a2: 'Printed for John Bowles at the Black Horse in Cornhill, 1742.' *B* 1753 50/15.

29 A View of Somerset Place, and the Church of St. Mary-le-Strand, London/Sir William Chambers, Architect of Somerset Place. 263 × 425/305 × 445mm. (tr) '64'. *P* 6,94: 'Printed for Bowles & Carver, No 69 St Paul's Churchyard.' BM (*Crace* 17.120) catalogues as '1797'.

30 View of the Canal in St James's Park. (and in French) Maurer delint. Canot sculp. 235 × 405/280 × 410mm. *K. top.* 26.7h and *P* 4,186: 'Publish'd … 26 May 1746. Printed for John Bowles & Son at the Black Horse in Cornhil.' View from Buckingham House to Horse Guards, originally published in the year in which Carington Bowles became a partner. *B* 1753 50/18.

31 A Perspective View of/the Parade in St James's Park/Showing the New Buildings for the Horse Guards, the Treasury, and the Admiralty. J. Maurer delin. et sculp. London, Printed for F. West, 83 Fleet Street. 210 × 410/263 × 430mm. Refs 1–6 and title and refs in French also, bl. An updated version of *K. top.* 26.7f: 'Printed for John Bowles at the Black Horse in Cornhill … 1740.' The central block of the Horse Guards was rebuilt by Kent, 1750–3. *B* 1753 50/19.

32 Veüe du Parc de St Jacques. (and in English) I. Rigaud delin. Nathl Parr sculp. 217 × 400/240 × 415mm. *P* 4,185: 'Printed for Thomas Bowles in St Pauls Church Yard and John Bowles in Cornhill.' A birds-eye view from the top of Buckingham House with its forecourt and fountains in the foreground, Westminster Abbey in the middle distance on the r. with a central spire in addition to its two W. towers and St George, Bloomsbury in the background. Sayer also published a print after Rigaud (*K. top.* 26.7d1) but engraved by S.T. Torres in 1752. Both probably had as common source the large French print after a drawing by Jean Rigaud made in 1736 (*K. top.* 26.7a) when the extent of the Abbey additions was still a matter of conjecture. Original pen and wash drawing (335 × 785mm) in Guildhall Library. *B* 1753 50/16.

33 A Perspective View of ye Parade in St James's Park/The Treasury, the New Buildings, for the Horse Guards and His Majesty/going to the House of Lords. (and in French) J. Maurer delin. et sculp. 210 × 410/255 × 425mm. BM (*Crace* 12.46) catalogues this as '1754', updating an earlier state dated '1742' (*Crace* 12.40). *B* 1753 50/20.

34 The Royal Palace of St James's next the Park. (and in French) Printed for Robert Wilkinson in Cornhill, and Bowles & Carver, 69 St Pauls Church Yard London. 248 × 415/283 × 425mm. The publication-line suggests a date after 1792 for this state. BM (*Crace* 12.16) catalogues this as 'H. Roberts sculp. 1751.' Shows the Mall, looking E. with wooden side walls for playing pall-mall. *B* 1753 50/6.

35 A View of the Garden Entrance of St James's Palace. (and in French) 250 × 420/270 × 430mm. Imperfectly burnished out: '… 69 St Paul's Church Yard London.' A satirical print showing George III with attendant ladies making his way towards a side door.

36 A Perspective View of St James's Square. (and in French) J. Maurer delin. et sculp. 1753. 140 × 273/180 × 285mm. (tr) '9'. *K. top.* 22.31b: 'Printed for Robt Sayer at the Golden Buck facing Fetter Lane, Fleet Street.' In Sayer & Bennett's catalogue p 87, set 10. See items 1 above and 53 below.

37 The Inside of St Martins Church in the Fields. (and in French) T. Bowles delin. et sculp. 260 × 420/290 × 430mm. *K. top.* 25.1c: 'Printed for John Bowles at the Black Horse in Cornhill. Published … 1751.' View to the W. cf with Boydell's *One Hundred Views* (no 47), pl. 38. *B* 1753 50/40.

38 A Perspective View of Twickenham. (and in French) A. Heckell delint. E. Rooker sculp. 260 × 428/293 × 458mm. Guildhall Library: 'Printed for John Bowles at the Black Horse in Cornhill. Publish'd … 13 Feby 1749.'

39 Dr Batty's House at Twickenham as View'd from the opposite Shore … (and in French) 230 × 400/260 × 415mm. *K. top.* 30.19g dated '1749'. *B* 1753 50/59.

40 A View of the Countess of Suffolk's House near Twickenham. (and in French) A. Heckell Delint. Mason sculp. 230 × 405/265 × 420mm. *K. top.* 30.19aa and Guildhall Library: 'Publish'd … 13 Feby 1749. Printed for John Bowles at the Black Horse in Cornhill.' The house called Marble Hill. *B* 1753 60/56.

41 Governor Pitt's House (late Secretary Johnson) at Twickenham. (and in French) A. Heckell Delint. J. Mason sc. Published by Fras West, 83 Fleet St. London. 225 × 405/260 × 415mm. *K. top.* 30.19o and Guildhall Library: 'Publish'd 13 Feby 1749.' The riverside Orleans House, occupied by George Morton Pitt, formerly Governor of Fort St George. cf with Boydell's *One Hundred Views*, pl. 29. *B* 1753 50/57.

42 A View of the Earl of Radnor's House at Twickenham. (and in French) A. Heckell delint. A. Walker sculp. 223 × 400/260 × 415mm. Guildhall Library: 'Publish'd May ye 1st 1750.' cf with Boydell's *One Hundred Views*, pl. 30. *B* 1753 50/58.

43 The House of Moses Hart Esqr. between Twickenham & Isleworth. (and in French) A. Heckell delint. Ant. Walker sculpt. 215 × 400/250 × 420mm. *K. top.* 30.9m: 'Publish'd … 1750.' *B* 1753 50/51.

44 The Inside of the Elegant Music Room in Vaux Hall Gardens. (and in French) S. Wale delin. H. Roberts

sculp. 268 × 425/295 × 440mm. (tr) '5'. Publication-line over burnished-out 'Robert Wilkinson'. BM (*Crace* 35.146): 'Printed for John Bowles at the Black Horse in Cornhill & Carington Bowles in St Paul's Church Yard.' *K. top.* 41.27h: 'Publish'd ... June 24 1752. Printed for Tho. Bowles in St Pauls Church Yard & John Bowles & Son, at the Black Horse in Cornhill.' *B* 1753 51/2.

45 A General Prospect of Vaux Hall Gardens/Shewing at one View the disposition of the Whole Gardens. (and in French) Wale delint. I.S. Müller sculp. 260 × 400/290 × 410mm. (tr) '1'. BM (*Crace* 35.131): 'Publish'd 21 Novr. 1751. Printed for John Bowles at the Black Horse in Cornhill.' *B* 1753 51/1.

46 The Triumphal Arches, Mr. Handel's Statue &c. in the South Walk of Vauxhall Gardens. (and in French) S. Wale delint. I.S. Müller sculp. 260 × 400/280 × 413mm. (tr) '4'. *K. top.* 41.27c and Guildhall Library: 'Publish'd ... 1751. Printed for Tho. Bowles in St Paul's Church Yard & John Bowles & Son at the Black Horse in Cornhill.' cf with Laurie's *Views*, pl. 62. *B* 1753 51/4.

47 A View of the Chinese Pavillions and Boxes/in Vaux Hall Gardens. (and in French) S. Wale delint. T. Bowles sculp. 258 × 403/280 × 420mm. (tr) '3'. BM (*Crace* 35.141): 'Publish'd ... 1751. Printed for Thos Bowles in St Paul's Church Yard & John Bowles in Cornhill.' *B* 1753 51/5.

48 A View of the Bridge over the Thames at Walton in Surry ... (and in French) 250 × 410/280 × 425mm.

49 (along tm) A Prospect of the Inside of the Collegiate Church of St Peter in Westminster,/from the Quire to the East End ... the whole taken from Sandford. 280 × 233/283 × 235mm. (tr) '3'. *London Described* pl. 8. *B* 1728 no 14.

50 (along tm) The Inthronization of their Majesties. A View of the West end of the Church of St Peter Westminster. 285 × 233/287 × 235mm. (tr) '2'. *London Described* pl. 8. *B* 1728 no 14.

51 A North West View of the Westminster Abby and St Margaret's Church. (and in French) Printed for and sold by F. West, 83 Fleet Street, London. 230 × 380/265 × 405mm. (br) '47'. BM (*Crace* 14.81) catalogues as 'T. Bowles del. et sculp. 1751.' *B* 1753 50/21.

52 A Perspective of Westminster Abbey from the High Altar to the West End/Shewing/The manner of their Majesties' Crowning ... from Sandford. 285 × 233/287 × 235mm. (tr) '1'. *London Described* pl. 8. *B* 1728 no 14.

53 A North View of Westminster Bridge. (and in French) London, Printed for F. West, 83 Fleet Street. 153 × 255/175 × 275mm. (tr) '3'. *K. top.* 22.37h: 'Labelye Architect. Bowles Sculp. 1753. London Printed for Robert Sayer opposite Fetter Lane Fleet Street & Heny Overton without Newgate.' In Sayer & Bennett's catalogue p 86, set 8. See items 1 and 36 above.

54 A View of Westminster Bridge from Lambeth. (and in French) 250 × 410/280 × 425mm. Refs in French and English. *P* 3,281a: 'J. Maurer Delint. P. Fourdrinier sculp. Printed for Thomas Bowles in St Paul's Church Yard & Jno Bowles at the Black Horse in Cornhill. Published ... 1 August 1744.' *B* 1753 50/5.

55 A Prospect of the Inside of Westminster Hall. Shewing how the King and Queen and the Nobility did sit at Dinner on the Day of the Coronation ... from Sandford. 285 × 233/287 × 235mm. *London Described* pl. 8. *B* 1728 no 14.

56 The Royal Castle and Palace at Windsor in Berk-shire. (and in French) Published by Fras West, 83 Fleet Str. London. 240 × 410/280 × 430mm. *B* 1753 50/9.

194 · CRUCHLEY'S ILLUSTRATED LONDON [1841–54]

George Frederick Cruchley was one of the leading publishers of maps of London and its environs in the second and third quarters of the nineteenth century. His 'New Plan of London', first issued in 1826, because of its clarity and pleasing appearance retained its popularity for some 20 years, and his 'New Plan of London and its Environs' at five inches to the mile was likewise a public favourite from 1829 until the year of the Great Exhibition. His guide-book *Cruchley's Picture of London*, first published in 1831, also ran into many editions and was translated into French. He moved from Ludgate Street to 81 Fleet Street in 1834 and ten years later took over the stock of business rivals George and John Cary.

The present collection of steel-engravings is the fruits of yet another takeover: from the Fenchurch Street publishers J. & F. Harwood who originally issued them as individually numbered items in series, of which three have survived in the Guildhall Library with the following engraved titles:

Harwood's/Scenery of Great Britain/(vignette) Buckingham Palace. Augt 11th 1841. /First Series/London./J. & F. Harwood, 26 Fenchurch Street. Vignette 88 × 133mm.

Harwood's/Scenery of Great Britain/(vignette) Greenwich Hospital. No. 232. Octr. 1, 1841./Second Series/London./J. & F. Harwood, 26 Fenchurch Street. Vignette 82 × 133mm.

Harwood's/Scenery of Great Britain/(vignette) Windsor Castle from the Long Walk. Decr. 1st 1842./Third Series/London./J. & F. Harwood, 26 Fenchurch Street. Vignette 100 × 150mm.

These volumes between them contain, including the titles, 150 vignetted views of which only a few have credits; they are unlisted and their three-figure numbering is unrelated to their arrangement. In about 1852, after further series had been published, Harwood collected together 30 of the London views and published them as *Illustrations of London*, according to a bookseller's catalogue.

July 1854 is the date of the latest engraving in Cruchley's collection, so some time after this he must have culled his London plates from however many series Harwood had by then published. Reference is made in the list to the origins of the ten views extracted from the first three series. The collection, in oblong octavo (132 × 225mm), is bound in blue cloth-gilt with embossed views and titled *Cruchley's Illustrated/London* and, in lieu of title-page, prefaces the plates with a three-column contents list and the imprint 'G.F. Cruchley, Map Publisher and Globe Manufacturer, 81 Fleet Street, London.' Neither this volume nor the Harwood series adds any text to the views.

All the steel-engravings, with the exception of item 33, are vignetted and in the GLC copy (and that recorded under no 247 in the Abbey catalogue) they are carefully tinted with water-colour washes so that the bound collection makes a very pretty souvenir picture book of London at mid-century. They have some resemblance to the countless little anonymous vignettes in a numerical series put out at about this time by the firm of Rock & Co (nos 204–5, 214) but their more generous proportions have given the artist slightly more scope. Not all are dated but those that are fall between February 1841 and July 1854, with numeration between 108 and 807. Twenty five are anonymous and 20, numbered between 633 and 664, are credited to J. Shury as engraver (and draughtsman in the case of item 38); the first is attributed to 'Sands'.

John Shury was a past master at small engravings, for his are the nearly 700 tiny views after T.H. Shepherd that decorate Partington's *National History* (no 177) and also those that surround the 'Plan of London' bound with that work but originally engraved by him for presentation in 1832 to the readers of the *United Kingdom Newspaper* (*Darl-ington and Howgego* 343). He also made larger plates for the 1821 *Stationers' Almanack* and a number of topographical books published since that time. His drawings of the House of Commons before the fire of 1834 were lithographed by A. Picken.

Plates are arranged according to the contents list. Captions are in copperplate script, 13 also being given in French and German. The publication-line, which usually includes the date, varies thus: '(London:) J(ohn) (& E.) (& F.) Harwood, 26 Fenchurch St. (date).'

1 Adelaide Wharf, London Bridge. Sands. May 24, 1842. 100 × 145mm. No 294. Harwood ser 3.

2 Admiralty. J. Shury sculpt. 100 × 155mm. No 659. Captions in French and German.

3 Apsley House. May 26 1842. 100 × 145mm. No 288. Harwood ser 3.

4 Bank of England. J. Shury sculpt. 100 × 165mm. No 664. S. front and Bank buildings after demolition of St Bartholomew by the Exchange in 1841. Captions in French and German. (*Bank of England* 107)

5 Blackwall Railway Terminus. Aug. 20 1842. 110 × 155mm. No 265. Harwood ser 3.

6 Buckingham Palace. July 26 1849. 120 × 165mm. No 786. Showing Blore's new front of 1846–7.

7 Buckingham Palace./Fourth Series. Augt 11th, 1841. 100 × 135mm. Previous to Blore alterations. Harwood ser 1.

8 New Hall Christs Hospital. J. Shury sculpt. 100 × 140mm. No 643. French caption: 'College de Jesus Christ.'

9 Covent Garden Market./From King Street. J. Shury sculpt. 95 × 155mm. No 652. French caption: 'Marché da Covent Garden'.

10 Duke of Wellingtons Statue. Nov. 1 1846. 138 × 150mm. No 616. James Wyatt's 30 ft high statue erected on Constitution Arch in 1846.

11 Entrance to the House of Lords. May 4 1842. 110 × 150mm. No 618.

12 Guildhall. J. Shury sculpt. 90 × 140mm. No 647. French caption: 'London/Hotel de la Corporation.'

13 Hammersmith Suspension Bridge. Jan 20 1843. 95 × 140mm.

14 Hampstead. 100 × 155mm. No 108.

15 Hampton Court Palace. J. Shury sc. 110 × 165mm. No 635. Captions in French and German.

16 Highgate. 110 × 145mm. No 247.

17 Highgate Cemetery. J. Shury sc. 100 × 165mm. No 633.

18 Horse Guards. J. Shury sculpt. 90 × 155mm. No 658.

19 Interior of the House of Commons. Sept 23 1850. 100 × 140mm. No 796.

20 Islington. June 12 1843. 110 × 150mm. No 545.

21 Kensal Green Cemetery. J. Shury sculp. 110 × 170mm. No 668. Captions in French and German.

22 Licensed Victuallers School/Kennington. 110 × 165mm. No 647.

23 Port of London/Looking West. J. Shury sculpt. 90 × 165mm. No 638. Captions in French and German.

24 London, from Greenwich. May 6 1844. 105 × 162mm.

25 London from the Monument. Feb 20 1841. 100 × 155mm. No 160. Looking towards Blackfriars Bridge and St Paul's. Harwood ser 2.

26 Ludgate Hill. Sept. 2d 1842. 100 × 140mm. No 426. Harwood ser 3.

27 Mansion House London. Sep 16 1841. 110 × 150mm. Harwood ser 2.

28 National Gallery. J. Shury sculp. 95 × 150mm. No 656. Looking towards St Martin in the Fields. Captions in French and German.

29 Nelsons Column Trafalgar Square &c. J. Shury sculp. 110 × 170mm. No 657. Captions in French and German.

30 The New British Museum. July 19 1854. 95 × 175mm. No 194.

31 The New Hall & Library Lincolns Inn/From the S.E. Aug. 10 1845. J. Shury sct. 105 × 160mm. No 665. Buildings completed by P.C. Hardwick, 1843–5; also Gothic gateway into Lincoln's Inn Fields.

32 New Houses of Parliament. J. Shury sc. 105 × 165mm. No 662. Seen from Lambeth. Captions in French and German.

33 Port of London. May 11 1847. 100 × 155mm. No 621. Oblong view towards London Bridge and St Paul's. Not vignetted.

34 The New Royal Exchange. J. Shury sculp. 100 × 160mm. No 640. Captions in French and German. Publication-line dated 23 October 1842 in Harwood ser 3.

35 Sion House Isleworth/Seat of the Duke of Northumberland. Sep 1 1841. 110 × 170mm.

36 Somerset House. June 1 1842. 90 × 145mm. No 645. Strand front with Church of St Mary.

37 St. Pauls Cathedral. J. Shury sculpt. 90 × 140mm. No 645. Captions in French and German.

38 Thames Tunnel/Rotherhithe. J. Shury del. et sct. 120 × 160mm. No 636. 'Length 1200 feet, shaft 50 in diameter and 70 ft. in depth'. Captions in French and German.

39 Mint. J. Shury sculp. 75 × 155mm. No 639. Captions in French and German.

40 The Monument. 110 × 145mm. Harwood ser 1.

41 The New Market Billingsgate. 105 × 140mm. No 807.

Engraving signed 'W.T.' Rebuilt to the designs of J.B. Bunning, City Architect, 1850.

42 The Ornamental Water/with Sussex Place/Regent's Park. Aug 1 1844. 90 × 155mm. No 579.

43 Tower of London. 95 × 150mm. No 249. Harwood ser 2.

44 Treasury. J. Shury sculp. 80 × 150mm. No 660.

45 View of London/from Waterloo Bridge. J. Shury sculp. 75 × 150mm. No 655. Captions in French and German.

46 Westminster Abbey. 90 × 145mm.

195 · LONDON INTERIORS [1841–4]

The publishers, in their preface to this work, say they can lay claim to 'some credit as being the first to undertake a series of engravings consisting exclusively of INTERIOR VIEWS, and which, therefore, so far from being merely new versions of subjects which may have been repeatedly delineated before, are almost without exception entirely fresh to the pencil and supply a mass of Illustration hitherto unattainable'. As far as London is concerned this is strictly true, although Pyne's *Royal Residences* (no 132), published in 1819, actually contains some 20 more interiors than there are here and all but a handful of the 100 plates in Ackermann's *Microcosm of London* (no 99) are indoor views, while his *Westminster Abbey* (no 108) consists largely of internal details. Clearly this is a steel-engraved Victorian echo of the magnificent Regency album of aquatints, the *Microcosm*.

It originally came out in monthly Parts, at first from the firm of George Virtue, specialists in such publications, at 1s 6d or 2s 6d for 'India Proofs' but by the third issue only the 1s 6d edition was advertised. On the wrapper of the fourth Part Virtue's name was superseded: 'This work is publishing in Monthly Parts, each Part contains two highly-finished Engravings on Steel, with eight pages of letter-press, Price 1s. Twenty Parts will complete a Volume. London, Published for the Proprietors, by Joseph Mead, 10 Gough Square, Fleet Street'. The front of the buff wrappers, despite the change of publishers, remains otherwise uniform throughout the series, with further adjustment to the letterpress only for the number of each Part, printed tr, for the numbered titles of the plates enclosed in each wrapper and, on the verso, for the announcement of forthcoming Parts and their illustrations, with the month of their expected publication:

London interiors, with their costumes and ceremonies: A grand national exhibition of the religious, regal, and civic solemnities, public amusements, scientific meetings, and commercial scenes of the British capital: beautifully engraved on steel from original drawings made expressly for this work, by permission of the public officers, trustees, and proprietors of the metropolitan edifices. Forming a splendid work for the library, and adapted for the Portfolio, Print Books, Topographical Illustrations &c. &c. &c. Contents of Part I (etc). London, Published for the Proprietor, by George Virtue, 26 Ivy Lane, and sold by all book and print sellers. (Pts 4–7: 'By Joseph Mead, 11 Bouverie Street, Fleet Street.' Pts 8–38: 'By Joseph Mead, 10 Gough Square, Fleet Street.')

On the wrapper of Part 8 (announced for publication in May 1842) a number of provincial agents were added to the imprint and from Part 19, issued in April 1843, the imprint and the publication-line of most of the plates were extended by 'Paris, M.M. Aubert & Co, Leipzig, T.O. Weigel.', and the captions were translated accordingly into French and German.

Meanwhile, on the back wrapper of Part 13, subscribers are assured that 'To secure the utmost accuracy in the details of these splendid scenes, repeated visits have been made to the Palace, and to its various ceremonial meetings. The publisher has, therefore, every confidence that for fidelity and beauty these plates cannot be surpassed. As representations of the Court Life of Queen Victoria, they are unique'. On that of the next Part the Queen's patronage was claimed, and it was quaintly added that 'thus though it is notorious that the hopes of literary speculators are seldom fulfilled, ours have been more than realized; the public having given them the *Coup de grace* by receiving London Interiors most extensively into favour'. Then followed the announcement that 'Twenty-Four Parts will complete a volume'.

In spite of the 'coup de grâce', the royal connection and public respect in which the young Queen was held brought success to the publication and the anonymous commentator on the Queen's drawing room plate, published in September 1843, purrs delightedly, if somewhat inconsequentially: 'The high tone of refinement prevalent at Court has unquestionably, if not a direct, a beneficial influence on the upper and middling classes of society; and the value of such influence is proved by the absence of it in America'. Yet another extra brought the first volume to a close: 'The Proprietors have to inform their Subscribers that the Supplementary Number promised to be issued with Part XXIV is, from various unavoidable delays in the preparation of the Palace Engravings, postponed until 1st September. On that day, therefore, Part XXV completing Vol. I will be published'. This supplement included the fiftieth plate, usually bound up as a frontispiece, a printed title-page, the dedication to the sovereign, an index and the essay on costume. Immediately it was published the completed, bound volume was also available for purchase.

The issue of the second series seems to have run into difficulties over the timing of the plates since views promised for publication in particular Parts had often to be postponed; indeed two, of Lambeth Palace Hall and Library announced as Part 36, never materialized. It ran out of steam after 26 more plates had been published and was brought to an end with Part 38 which, provided monthly issues were maintained, would have appeared in October 1844. It included a separate title-page and a subject index was printed uniform with that of the first collection, but three Parts (39–41) and six promised plates (Lambeth, Whitehall and the Royal Exchange) were never published.

Complete sets of both series were sold, bound together in a red cloth-gilt binding, and in this and later issues the first 37 plates (issued with Parts 1–18) were brought into line with the subsequent ones by the addition of French and German captions and the names of the Paris and Leipzig agents. An alteration was also made in the commentary on the Chapel Royal, St James's (p 80) by the addition of the words 'Up to 1844' to the sentence 'Every Sunday when her Majesty was in town'. With these amendments the work was reissued later in the century by D. Omer Smith of 76 St Paul's Churchyard and, also, the text and plates of Parts 26–38 were bound up with an odd assembly of engravings and lithographs in an album entitled *The Parlour Table-book; or Pictorial Miscellany* published by William Woodward.

London Interiors: A Grand National Exhibition of the religious, regal, and civic solemnities, public amusements, scientific meetings, and commercial scenes of the British Capital; Beautifully Engraved on Steel, from drawings made expressly for this work By Command of Her Majesty, and with permission of the Proprietors, and Trustees of the Metropolitan Edifices. With descriptions written by official authorities. Vol. I (II). London: Published for the Proprietors by Joseph Mead, 10, Gough Square, Fleet Street.

Quarto, 270 × 210mm.   (1841–4)

COLLATION   Title-page; pp iii–iv, dedication to the Queen; pp v–vi, index; second index (1 leaf); pp vii–viii, preface; pp ix–xx, London Costume; pp 1–192 and 1–104, London Interiors.

The name of Thomas Hosmer Shepherd conjures up countless carefully drawn street scenes, in topographical collections such as the Crace or engraved upon steel in works such as *Metropolitan Improvements* (no 154) and *Modern Athens*. It was therefore a new departure for him when, approaching his fiftieth year, he became the chief contributor to a volume which set out to illustrate only the interiors of buildings. These, the publisher hinted, gave better value for money:

They require more exact and more elaborate drawing, and not only greater delicacy of detail, but a far greater proportion of it, and oftentimes the most laborious sort of all, where there is positively none as to drawing in external views. In taking the last, the work of the draftsman is confined to the building itself, or what answers to the walls of an interior; but in addition to that, he has, in the other case, to delineate ceilings, floors and furniture—all perhaps, of intricate pattern, and requiring to be carefully made on the spot, whereas skies, ground and fore-ground may be put in afterwards, and with little of actual drawing.

This sounds like Shepherd's own line of thought; it is to be hoped that he and his fellow artists received their just rewards from the publisher. Of the originals J.F.C. Phillips says (*Shepherd's London*, p 105): 'His pencil drawings for *London Interiors* (1841–44) are vigorous and break new ground in that attention is focused on the human activity portrayed as well as on its architectural setting. I have been unable to trace any wash drawings prepared for this series'.

Other artists contributing to the first volume were Harden S. Melville, a painter of domestic interiors (pl. 26, 31, 33, 36, 40, 42), George Cattermole (pl. 40–1) and—two links with the execution of Ackermann's aquatint interiors—Frederick Mackenzie

(pl. 28, 49, 56), illustrator of his *Westminster Abbey* and *History of the Colleges* (no 116), and George Belton Moore (pl. 30, 38–9, 43), the pupil of A.C. Pugin of the *Microcosm of London*. With the last named publication there is a direct connection in pl.47 where the artist's credit is given as 'Rowlandson'; it should really be 'Pugin' as the engraver has exactly reproduced the architectural setting of pl. 3 of the *Microcosm*, simply substituting for Rowlandson's portraits of the Board of Admiralty their Victorian successors and adding to the room a ship model on a table by the window. Other plates influenced by the *Microcosm* are items 1, 4, 13, 25, 41, 57–8, 65, 72.

Shepherd had no concern with the second collection and the chief artist from September 1843 was the 26 year old John Gilbert, water-colourist and historical painter who became a prolific book illustrator and later received a knighthood. He was an obvious candidate for depicting the setting and costumes of royal drawing rooms and levees; a dozen of the drawings were his.

The bulk of the engraving was carried out by H.S. Melville who worked no fewer than 50 of the plates, as well as contributing drawings himself, and to a lesser degree by the Radclyffes, father and son, who between them engraved 14.

The illustrations are arranged in order of their publication which, with one exception, coincides with the order in which they were eventually bound. The plate numbers are those assigned on the Part wrappers; the plates themselves are unnumbered. Credits are quoted as they appear in the bm: artist bl, and engraver br. Possible publication-lines are as follows:

any pl.: 'London, Published for the Proprietor(s) by J(oseph)Mead, 10 Gough Square (11 Bouverie Street), Fleet Street. (à) Paris (chez) M.M. Aubert & Co, (and) Leipzig (bei) T.O. Weigel.'
pl. 1–45: 'London, Published for the Proprietor by J. Mead, 10 Gough Square, Fleet Street.'
pl. 1–17: 'London, Published for the Proprietor, by J. Mead, 11 Bouverie Street, Fleet Street.'
pl. 1–7: 'London, Published for the Proprietor, by George Virtue, 26 Ivy Lane.'

VOL. 1

1 (engr title) London Interiors/with their Costumes & Ceremonies/from drawings made by permission/of the Public Officers, Proprietors & Trustees of/The Metro-

politan Buildings. (vignette, 98 × 80mm) Entrance to the National Gallery. London/Published for the Proprietor by George Virtue, 26 Ivy Lane, Paternoster Row./1841. (or 'by J. Mead, 11 Bouverie Street, Fleet Street', or '10 Gough Square Fleet Street', or with the addition to either of these: 'William Ball, Aldine Chambers, Paternoster Row./A Paris chez M.M. Aubert & Co. and Leipzig bei T.O. Weigel') pl. 3, Pt 1. ? October 1841.

2 p 1 Guildhall/Installation of the Lord Mayor on the 8th of November. T.H. Shepherd. H. Melville. 168 × 145mm. pl. 1, Pt 1. ? October 1841.

3 p 5 Jewish Synagogue, Great St. Helens./Celebration of the Feast of Tabernacles. T.H. Shepherd. H. Melville. 185 × 138mm. pl. 2, Pt 1. ? October 1841.

4 p 9 Freemasons Hall/Dinner of the Royal Humane Society with the Procession of Persons saved during the Year from Drowning. T.H. Shepherd. H. Melville. 128 × 185mm. Pt 2. ? November 1841.

5 p 13 Long Room in the Custom House/Payment of the Customs. T.H. Shepherd. H. Melville. 130 × 195mm. Pt 2. ? November 1841.

6 p 17 Egyptian Hall, Mansion House/The Wilson Banquet. T.H. Shepherd. H. Melville. 130 × 185mm. In April 1839 the Lord Mayor, Samuel Wilson, invited nearly 200 connections of the Wilson family above the age of nine years to a banquet, the Hall being 'decorated with unusual splendour'. Pt 3. ? December 1841.

7 p 21 King's College/Distribution of the Prizes in the Theatre, by the Archbishop of Canterbury. T.H. Shepherd. H. Melville. 130 × 185mm. Pt 3. ? December 1841.

8 p 25 House of Lords/Her Majesty opening the Session of Parliament. T.H. Shepherd. H. Melville. 128 × 185mm. Pt 4. ? January 1842.

9 p 29 British Museum—The Reading Room. T.H. Shepherd. H. Melville. 128 × 185mm. Opened in 1838 in Smirke's N. wing, approached from Montague Place; now used as Music and Catalogue Room. Pt 4. ? January 1842.

10 p 33 Exeter Hall/The great Anti Slavery Meeting, 1841. T.H. Shepherd. H. Melville. 130 × 180mm. Exeter Hall was opened on the site of Exeter 'Change in 1831. The meeting was on 1 June, presided over by Prince Albert, his first public appearance. Pt 5. ? February 1842.

11 p 37 Court of Common Council Guildhall/Presentation of a Petition. T.H. Shepherd. H. Melville. 130 × 185mm. Pt 5. ? February 1842.

12 p 41 St George's Church, Hanover Square./Celebration of a Noble Marriage. T.H. Shepherd. H. Melville. 170 × 125mm. Looking towards E. windows. Pt 6. 1 March 1842.

13 p 45 Banquetting House, Whitehall./Distribution of Her Majesty's Maundy. T.H. Shepherd. H. Melville. 130 × 180mm. The distribution of silver pieces to the needy on Maundy Thursday by the Royal Almoner, not by the monarch in person. Pt 6. 1 March 1842.

14 p 49 Lincolns Inn Hall./The Lord Chancellor's Court. T.H. Shepherd. H. Melville. 128 × 182mm. The old Hall with Hogarth's painting 'Paul before Felix' hanging above the Lord Chancellor's dais. The new Hall was to be built in 1843–5. Pt 7. 1 April 1842. Preparatory pencil drawing (120 × 165mm) in Westminster Public Library.

15 p 53 Roman Catholic Chapel, Moorfields./Celebration of High Mass on Christmas Day. T.H. Shepherd. H. Melville. 130 × 178mm. Shows the 'Calvary' behind the altar: 'the work of Agustine Aglio, is painted in fresco on a circular wall, and illuminated by a subdued light concealed in the roof'. St Mary, Blomfield Street. Pt 7. 1 April 1842.

16 p 57 Middle Temple Hall./The Benchers and Members taking Commons. T.H. Shepherd. H. Melville. 120 × 170mm. 'In 1830–1832 it underwent a total renovation'. Pt 8. 1 May 1842.

17 p 61 Lord Mayors Table, Guildhall. /Grand Banquet on the 9th November. T.H. Shepherd. J. Shury. 112 × 175mm. Pt 8. 1 May 1842.

18 p 65 Royal Naval Museum, Somerset House./Exhibition of Models. T.H. Shepherd. H. Melville. 175 × 132mm. The 'Model Room' attached to the office of the Surveyor-General of the Navy. Pt 9. June 1842.

19 p 69 The Rotunda, Bank of England./Payment of Dividends. T.H. Shepherd. J. Shury. 173 × 130mm. Sir John Soane's hall, 1794–5. Pt 9. June 1842. (*Bank of England* 172)

20 p 73 Ceremony of Laying the First Stone of the New Royal Exchange/By Prince Albert, Monday, Jany 17, 1842. T.H. Shepherd. H. Melville. 135 × 188mm. Performed by the Prince Consort in a circus tent. Pt 10. July 1842.

21 p 77 Chapel Royal—St. James' Palace./Celebration of Service before Her Majesty & Prince Albert. T.H. Shepherd. W. Radclyffe. 122 × 175mm. Pt 10. July 1842. Pencil sketch (110 × 190mm), dated 1840, in Westminster Public Library.

22 p 81 Tomb of Queen Elizabeth./Henry VIIth Chapel, Westminster Abbey. T.H. Shepherd. W. Radclyffe. 175 × 125mm. Pt 11. August 1842.

23 p 85 Thatched House Club./Dinner of the Dilettanti Society. T.H. Shepherd. J.H. Le Keux. 130 × 190mm. At the Thatched House Tavern in St James's Street; demolished for the building of the Conservative Club, 1843–5. Pt 11. August 1842.

24 p 89 The Throne Room, Buckingham Palace./Presentation of an Address from the University of Oxford. H. Melville. 128 × 180mm. Pt 12. September 1842.

25 p 93 Central Criminal Court, Old Bailey. T.H.

Shepherd. H. Melville. 125 × 180mm. Pt 12. September 1842.

26 p 97 The Picture Gallery, Buckingham Palace./ Duchess of Cambridge (as Anne of Bretagne) and Her Court, in Her Majesty's Bal Costumé of Queen Philippa. H. Melville. 125 × 180mm. 'at the Fancy Ball, May 12th, 1842'. Pt 13. October 1842.

27 p 101 House of Commons./The Speaker repremanding a person at the Bar. T.H. Shepherd. H. Melville. 128 × 180mm. The House in its temporary accommodation pending the completion of Barry's new Palace of Westminster. Pt 13. October 1842.

28 p 105 St. Paul's Cathedral./Anniversary Meeting of the Children of the Charity Schools of London. F. Mackenzie. W.H. Fuge. 183 × 133mm. View under the dome, looking E. Pt 14. Novemer 1842.

29 p 109 Horse Guards./The Commander in Chief's Levee. T.H. Shepherd. T. Turnbull. 132 × 188mm. 'Our present tableau exhibits the widow of an officer who has fallen in the field, soliciting for her son a presentation to Sandhurst College'. Pt 14. November 1842.

30 p 113 Westminster Abbey./Consecration of the Colonial Bishops. G.B. Moore. H. Melville. 188 × 128mm. 'on the 24th August of the present year'. Pt 15. December 1842.

31 p 117 Council Chamber, Vintner's Hall./Vintner Sheriff receiving the Congratulations of his Company. H. Melville. E. Radclyffe. 143 × 198mm. The cosiest of all the 'interiors'. Pt 15. December 1842.

32 p 121 The Athenaeum./Drawing Room. J. Holland. W. Taylor. 136 × 188mm. 'In 1830 the present mansion, built from the designs of Decimus Burton, Esq., at a cost of forty-five thousand pounds, was opened to the members'. Pt 16. January 1843.

33 p 127 Barber Surgeon's Hall. /The Company admitting a New Member. H. Melville. T.H Ellis. 125 × 180mm. In Monkwell Street. 'The Hall, discoloured by damp, and loaded with dust, presents a very cheerless, cobwebbed appearance'; but the engraving is of the cheerful, sparkling Court Room. Pt 16. January 1843.

34 p 129 Hunterian Museum./Royal College of Surgeons. T.H. Shepherd. E. Radclyffe. 183 × 138mm. Top of engraving rounded off to conform with the ceiling vault. Pt 17. February 1843.

35 p 133 Nelson's Tomb, Crypt of Saint Pauls. T.H. Shepherd. 186 × 138mm. Pt 17. February 1843.

36 p 137 Madame Tussaud's Exhibition./Bazaar, Baker Street. Melville. Melville. 130 × 185mm. Opened in 1833. Pt 18. March 1843.

37 p 141 Drury Lane Theatre./Wrestling Scene in 'As You Like It'. T.H. Shepherd. T.H. Ellis. 135 × 170mm. Pt 18. March 1843.

38 p 145 Reform Club./The Corridors of the Saloon.

G.B. Moore. E. Radclyffe. 128 × 180mm. Built by Sir Charles Barry, 1838–41. Pt 19. April 1843.

39 p 150 Reform Club./The Kitchen. G.B. Moore. W. Radclyffe. 123 × 178mm. Presided over by Monsieur Soyer. Pt 19. April 1843.

40 p 153 Temple Church. Cattermole & Melville. H. Melville. 132 × 172mm. The chancel, looking E., showing restorations by James Savage, Sidney Smirke and Decimus Burton, 1841–3. Pt 20. May 1843.

41 p 157 Westminster Hall./Trial of Warren Hastings. Cattermole & Dayes. H. Melville. 125 × 180mm. Copied by Cattermole from the aquatint 'A View of the Tryal of Warren Hastings Esqre before the/Court of Peers in Westminster Hall … February 13, 1788. London, Publish'd Jany 3, 1789 by R. Pollard, Engraver. Engraved by R. Pollard Asst by F. Jukes. Drawn by E. Dayes.' (405 × 650mm). With a key to participants. Pt 20. May 1843.

42 p 161 St. James' Palace. The Audience Chamber. /Proclamation of Her Majesty the Queen. H. Melville del. et sc. 137 × 180mm. On 21 June 1837. Pt 21. June 1843.

43 p 165 Hall of the Athenaeum. G.B. Moore. W. Radclyffe. 123 × 180mm. Pt 21. June 1843.

44 p 169 Buckingham Palace./The Princess Royal sitting for a Portrait. Gilbert. W. Radclyffe. 183 × 138mm. Winterhalter is shown painting a portrait of the Queen's first born, Victoria Adelaide Mary Louisa, born at Buckingham Palace on 21 November 1840, as she sits propped up in a chair set upon the plush covered table under the gaze of her admiring parents. The Princess Royal was married in 1858 to Frederick III of Prussia. Pt 22. July 1843.

45 p 173 Kensington Palace./The Sussex Library. Jarvis. Melville. 185 × 135mm. The 'lamented Duke of Sussex', sixth son of George III, who had died on 21 April, is shown at work among the 45,000 volumes he had collected; they were mostly on theological topics. Pt 22. July 1843.

46 p 177 Westminster Abbey, Edward the Confessor's Chapel./Coronation Chair, Sword & Shield of Edward 3rd. Holland. Melville. 180 × 133mm. In the publication-line 'Aubert' is misspelled 'Gubert'. Pt 23. ? August 1843.

47 p 181 The Admiralty—Board Room./Meeting of the Lords of the Admiralty. Rowlandson. Melville. 137 × 187mm. The credit 'Rowlandson' acknowledges the debt to Ackermann's *Microcosm of London*, in particular to pl.3 which is exactly reproduced, even to the position of the dial of the wind vane and the pattern of the carpet; only the costumes of the Lords have changed, and a model sailing ship is added to the furnishings. Pt 23. ? August 1843.

48 p 185 Drawing Room of Queen Victoria./Ceremony of Presentation. J. Gilbert. H. Melville. 137 × 183mm. Pt 24. September 1843.

49 p 189 The Bank Parlour./ Court of the Governor and Company. F. Mackenzie. H. Melville. 135 × 190mm. Pt 24. September 1843. (*Bank of England* 155)

50 p 192 (or front.) The Throne,/St James's Palace— Investiture/ of the Knights of the Garter. Gilbert. Melville. 168 × 145mm. Garter insignia with the caption. Supplementary Pt 25. September 1843.

VOL. 2

51 p 1 The Royal Closet, St. James's./Her Majesty giving audience to an Ambassador. Gilbert. Melville. 165 × 142mm. Pt 26. ? October 1843.

52 p 5 The Royal Closet, St James' /The Archbishops and Bishops congratulating her Majesty on Her Birthday. Gilbert. Melville. 130 × 190mm. Pt 26. ? October 1843.

53 p 9 Bank of England. Five Pound Note Office. Gilbert. Melville. 132 × 180mm. The text criticizes the architecture of this room, designed by Sir John Soane as the Accountant's Office, 1805–6. Pt 27. ? November 1843. (*Bank of England* 188)

54 p 13 Stock Exchange. Gilbert. Melville. 137 × 188mm. As designed by James Peacock, 1810–12, and before the modifications of 1853–4. Pt 27. ? November 1843.

55 p 17 Goldsmith's Hall. The Grand Staircase. H. Jewett. H. Melville. 190 × 125m. Engraving with segmental top. Built by Philip Hardwick, 1829–35. Pt 28. ? December 1843.

56 p 21 Goldsmiths Hall on a Ball Night. F. Mackenzie. H. Melville. 138 × 188mm. Scene in the Grand Banqueting Hall. 138 × 188mm. Pt 28. ?December 1843.

57 p 25 Christ's Hospital. The Great Hall./Delivery of the Annual Orations. I.I. Jewitt. Melville. 140 × 185mm. A later version of the occasion depicted in the *Microcosm of London* pl.10, now taking place in John Shaw's Hall of 1825. Pt 29. ? January 1844.

58 p 29 St. James's Palace. Birthday Drawing Room. Gilbert. Melville. 133 × 180mm. Showing the presentation to the sovereign of six selected Christ's Hospital boys who were admitted to the Throne Room just before the beginning of the ceremony. Pt 29. ? January 1844.

59 p 33 The United Service Club./The Great Hall. W. Lee. H. Melville. 145 × 180mm. The text makes no mention of the additions then being made to the club by Burton. Pt 30. ? February 1844.

60 p 37 The United Service Club./The Map Room. I.I. Jewett. H. Melville. 177 × 140mm. The engraving designed as a four-centered arch. Pt 30. ? February 1844.

61 p 41 Somerset House. /Meeting of the Royal Society. Fairholt. Melville. 143 × 190mm. Pt 31. ? March 1844.

62 p 45 Somerset House./Meeting of the Royal Antiqua-rian Society. Fairholt. Melville. 140 × 190mm. Pt 31. ? March 1844. ie the Society of Antiquaries.

63 p 49 Buckingham Palace—The Library./Foreign Levée. Gilbert. Melville. 133 × 195mm. Diplomats being received. Pt 32. ? April 1844.

64 p 53 Buckingham Palace. The Yellow Drawing Room. MacManus. Melville. 135 × 185mm. Pt 32. ? April 1844.

65 p 57 Tower of London./The Great Horse Armoury. Gilbert. Melville. 135 × 185mm. Pt 33. ? May 1844.

66 p 61 Tower of London./The Crown Jewel Room. H. Jewitt. H. Melville. 135 × 180mm. The jewels were kept near the Armoury but when this was burnt out in October 1841 they were saved from the flames and are shown here installed in the new Jewel Office which 'looks very much like a neat modern lodge in Gothic style, designed for a park entrance'. Pt 33. ? May 1844.

67 p 65 General Post Office./ Inland Office. Gilbert. Ellis. 123 × 178mm. Sir Robert Smirke's building of 1824–9. Pt 34. ? June 1844.

68 p 69 General Post Office. /Letter Carriers Room arranged for dispatch of Newspapers. Gilbert. Ellis. 140 × 180mm. Pt 34. ? June 1844.

69 p 73 Tower of London:—The Norman Chapel. B. Sly. Melville. 185 × 133mm. Pt 35. ? July 1844.

70 p 77 Tower of London:—The Norman Armoury. B. Sly. Melville. 185 × 132mm. Engraving designed as four-centered arch. Pt 35. ? July 1844.

71 p 81 Public Exhibition of Frescoes of Sculpture in Westminster Hall. B. Sly. Radclyffe. 185 × 140mm. 'In 1843 … Westminster Hall … was opened for an exhibition of Cartoons, and again in the present year there is a second one of Frescoes and sculpture'. Works submitted for the new Palace of Westminster. Pt 36. ? August 1844.

72 p 85 Exhibition of the Royal Academy.—Private View. Sargent. Radclyffe. 125 × 180mm. Pt 36. ? August 1844.

73 p 89 British Museum.—Egyptian Room. B. Sly. Radclyffe. 140 × 190mm. Pt 37. ? September 1844.

74 p 93 British Museum.—Zoological Gallery. I. Jewitt. Radclyffe. 132 × 208mm. Pt 37. ? September 1844.

75 p 97 British Museum,—Elgin Room. I. Jewitt. Radclyffe. 185 × 140mm. Completed by Sir Robert Smirke, 1831. Pt 38. ? October 1844.

76 p 101 British Museum,—Additional Library. I. Jewitt. Radclyffe. 190 × 140mm. The 'Arch Room' built by Smirke, 1840–1 for storing incunabula. Pt 38. ? October 1844.

196 · BOYS'S LONDON AS IT IS [1842]

Thomas Shotter Boys, born in Pentonville in 1803, was in 1817 apprenticed by his salesman father to the engraver George Cooke and was soon absorbed by that family of gifted artists and engravers, making friends with young Edward who later became notable for his drawings and etchings of shipping on the Thames and south coast. In about 1823, in common with a number of English artists of the period such as William Callow, whom he was to teach, Samuel Prout and Richard Parkes Bonington, with whom he became intimate, he went to Paris and set up as an engraver. He also learned the arts of painting in water-colour and of lithography and, on the invitation of the publisher of Baron Taylor's and Charles Nodier's *Voyages Pittoresques*, between 1833 and 1837 he supplied 24 views executed in lithograph for that publication. Another publication with the title *Architecture Dessinée d'après Nature*, which came out in 1835, consisted exclusively of work by himself and a French fellow artist, A. Rouargue. From Paris in September 1833 he wrote to an artist friend, Henry Mogford: 'I intend to do "Paris *as it is*". I flatter myself I have some picturesque bits, but I am soured with publishers, and so must do it myself'. Indeed a portfolio containing lithographs of these sketches was published in 1839 not by a Parisian publisher but by his cousin of the same name, Thomas Boys of the firm of Moon, Boys & Graves, under the title *Picturesque Architecture in Paris, Ghent, Antwerp, Rouen. Drawn from Nature & on Stone*. The chromolithographic printing was carried out by Charles Hullmandel, an exacting task as Boys in his 'Descriptive Notice' explains:

The whole of the Drawings composing this volume are produced entirely by means of lithography: they are printed with oil-colours, and come from the press precisely as they now appear. It was expressly stipulated by the Publisher that not a touch should be added afterwards, and this injunction has been strictly adhered to. They are Pictures drawn on Stone, and re-produced by printing with Colours: every touch is the work of the Artist, and every impression the product of the press.

This implies that four or five colours were printed in register from a succession of stones, working up from the primary colours to gradations of tint resulting from overprinting.

In the following year, in a letter to the editor of the periodical *The Probe*, he is rebutting any suggestion that Hullmandel was to be credited with the invention of this method: 'I am, sir, *entirely* the originator and *inventor* of my work, as set before the public; within myself the idea originated of producing a work by lithography printed in colour, using the primitive colours for the first tints, and producing variety of tints by their successive super- or juxta-position'. Nevertheless he must have remained on good terms with Hullmandel since it was to him that was entrusted the printing of his next major illustrative work, the *London as it is*, also published by his cousin. Unlike the lithographs of *Picturesque Architecture* these were printed in monochrome, perhaps in order to cut down the original cost of production. No water-colour sketches for this series survive because none were made; there are in existence, however, a couple of preparatory tracings in outline, examples probably of what Boys used to transfer the lines of his design to the first stone from which each view was printed, without shading or tone to begin with. On a second stone, without any drawn lines, were worked the masses and tones required to build up the composition; this was printed in register with the line stone completing the monochrome lithograph. The stages of this process can be observed in a copy of the work in the Guildhall Library which contains both the finished product and proofs of the line and tone images of which each subject is composed. Although designed as monochrome views the lithographs lend themselves admirably to hand colouring and they are most generally known in this form from reproductions of copies said to have been tinted delicately by Boys himself, after the printing. The sets were offered for sale either 'with Sepia tints, £4. 4s. bound' or 'a few copies coloured by hand and mounted in a Portfolio, £10. 16s.' Thus, with Parrott's *London from the Thames* (no 198), this was the last important collection of London illustrations to revert to the mode of Malton's *Picturesque Tour* (no 72) and Ackermann's *Microcosm* (no 99), in which plates were individually finished by hand, before chromolithography, oleographs and mechanical colour printing finally took over from the colourists.

By now Boys's work was widely known, and he had been elected to the New Water Colour Society. The London views were enthusiastically received by the critics although one drew attention to what he called the 'French character of most of the figures'. No doubt the publisher's official standing as 'Printseller to the Royal Family' helped to ensure its success; a copy sent to France's King Louis Philippe was acknowledged in flattering terms and with the gift of a fine watch.

Original Views of London as it is. Drawn from Nature expressly for this Work and Lithographed by Thomas Shotter Boys. Exhibiting its Principal Streets and Characteristic Accessories, Public Buildings in Connexion with the Leading Thoroughfares &c. &c. &c. With Historical and Descriptive Notices of the Views by Charles Ollier. London: Published by Thomas Boys, Printseller to the Royal Family, 11 Golden Square, Regent Street 1842.

Folio, 540 × 370mm.   1842

COLLATION Title-page; dedication to Lord Francis Egerton (1 leaf); 26 leaves of description in English and French, printed on recto only and interleaved with the 26 lithographs.

The notes by Charles Ollier, publisher of Keats, Shelley and Leigh Hunt, provide historical jottings on the scenes chosen by Boys. There is a peacefulness about these more suggestive of Malton's late Georgian city than the bustling Victorian metropolis. The skies, like Malton's also, are mostly those of a serene English summer but the atmosphere is suggested by a haze of cirrus clouds and distances sometimes shadowed by the London smoke pall. Figures represented are well drawn and, in spite of the critic's strictures, suitable to their settings. Their attitudes, when not elegant, are usually quite relaxed in great contrast to the multifarious and almost maniacal activity of the human beings introduced at times by Rowlandson into the *Microcosm* plates.

In his *Picturesque Architecture* the artist cunningly insinuated his signature into views in the form of a shop or tavern sign or on a poster. He similarly set his seal on some of the *London as it is* views: as an inscription on the base of the statue in item 20, with his address on the carriage in item 21, on a sandwich-board in item 18 with an exhortation to vote for him, and as an initialled baker's basket in item 22. In item 3 he includes a self-portrait in tailcoat and top-hat, complete with sketching block

and folding stool, while next to him, a pun on his name, are two inseparable fat boys who were surely Tenniel's inspiration for Tweedledum and Tweedledee. These plates became so popular that forgeries were circulated. Recent facsimiles include a set published by Charles W. Traylen in 1954 and a series being issued by the Greater London Council.

Captions appear in capitals just within the work bl or br and credits just below the work in the margin of the opposite corner. There is no publication-line. The lithographs were available either uncoloured with the commentary in a cloth binding or coloured by hand or, in a very limited edition, coloured and mounted on thick card in a portfolio together with the text pages in specially printed wrappers. On the front boards of both the casing and the portfolio the title was stamped in gilt: 'London/as it is/By Thomas Shotter Boys/1842', with a vignette of London Stone.

1 (bl) Doorway Temple Church. (graffito on the wall to the right of the doorway) London/as it is—/drawn and/Lithographed/by Thos. Shotter Boys/90 Great Portland St. 475 × 325mm. (or, alternatively, 440 × 320mm, vignetted, with the addition of: 'Printed by C. Hullmandel London Published by T. Boys, 11 Golden Square.') The graffito has just been completed by one of a group of three boys, a species of canting heraldry on the artist's name.

2 (bl) Mansion House, Cheapside &c. T. Shotter Boys del et lith. 318 × 430mm. St Mildred, Poultry and St Mary le Bow in the background. Sturdy dustman and wooden-legged crossing sweeper in the foreground.

3 (bl) The Tower and Mint,/from Great Tower Hill. T.S. Boys del et lith. 198 × 435mm. Boys depicts himself sketching in the foreground, almost on the site of the old Tower Hill scaffold. He completed this picture before the fire of October 1841 which gutted the turreted Armoury seen to the l. of the White Tower. The presence of the Thames is signified by masts and rigging silhouetted against the blue distance of the Surrey hills. The monochrome set in the Guildhall Library contains an additional view, which apparently remained unpublished, showing the scene after the fire (see item 27).

4 (br) The Custom House. T.S. Boys del et lithog. 430 × 320mm. The river front, with the spire of St Magnus in the background. In the foreground an official carriage, horseless. An erased signature is still visible in the work bl.

5 (bl) London Bridge &c from Southwark Bridge. T.S. Boys del et lithog. 180 × 460mm. Low tide with sailing and steam craft on the river and barges and other shipping beached on the unembanked foreshores of the City and Bankside. The vista to a forest of masts

469

rising from the Pool of London is not yet intercepted by intervening bridges.

6 (br) London from Greenwich. T. Boys del et lithog. 295 × 435mm. The classic view from a point by Flamsteed House just below the Wolfe memorial statue showing, between banks of lush foliage, the Queen's House and the Royal Naval College, then known as the Naval Asylum, the winding Thames, the Isle of Dogs, and the City of London as a smoky backcloth. To the l. of the viewer is a tripod holding a telescope with which to scan the horizon.

7 (bl) Blackfriars from Southwark Bridge. T.S. Boys del et lithog. 175 × 455mm. Sailing barges loaded with straw are in the foreground while to the r. the afternoon sun gleams on the white stone of St Paul's Cathedral and also catches the towers of St Mary Somerset and St Michael, Queenhithe leaving a further cluster of Wren church towers in the shadow. The gleaming Thames stretches beyond the arches of Blackfriars Bridge towards the distant buildings bordering on the Strand.

8 (br) Westminster from Waterloo Bridge. T.S. Boys del et lithog. 175 × 460mm. In the foreground is a train of empty barges, one catching the eye with its orange sail in the coloured version. To the l. are the Shot Tower and Red Lion Brewery and closing the vista are Labelye's Westminster Bridge, St John (Smith Square), the Abbey and Westminster Hall, the only conspicuous part of the Palace remaining after the fire of 1834. Above the orange sail are the arms of a telegraph used to convey messages to Whitehall.

9 (br) Westminster Abbey, Hospital &c. T.S. Boys del et lith. 325 × 442mm. The Abbey W. front and St Margaret, Westminster with Westminster Hall beyond. Ollier, in his note, congratulates the hospital architect on assorting the façade to the prevailing Westminster Gothic; it was built by William and H.W. Inwood, 1832–3. Westminster scholars are prominent in the scantly populated Sanctuary.

10 (bl) Board of Trade, Whitehall &c. from Downing Street. T.S. Boys del et lithog. 420 × 322mm. Sir John Soane's colonnaded government offices on the l. were about to be transfigured by Sir Charles Barry in 1844. There is a foreshortened view of the Banqueting House on the r. and the vista is closed by the spire of St Martin in the Fields.

11 (bl) Buckingham Palace from St. James's Park. T.S. Boys del et lith. 250 × 450mm. Family groups on the gravel walk are feeding the ducks and geese emerging from the water of the lake which is being cleared of its refuse by two men in a punt. The light of a hazy autumn afternoon bathes the S. wall of the Palace which, four years before its alteration by Blore, is still as Nash left it in 1836 with the Marble Arch, which was to be re-erected at the north end of Park Lane in 1851, still in position as an entrance gateway.

12 (br) N. front to St. James's Palace from Cleveland Row. T.S. Boys del et lith. 405 × 315mm. The gatehouse at 2.40 pm on a summer afternoon; a pair of elegant ladies walk with their small dogs while nursemaids carrying children line up to chat with the guardsman on sentry-go.

13 (bl) The Club Houses &c. Pall Mall. T. Shotter Boys del et lith. 315 × 448mm. In Pall Mall one may still imagine oneself in Boys's London. Of the club houses on the r. only Sir Robert Smirke's Carlton Club, of 1835–6, has been replaced. Beyond all the buildings survive: Sir Charles Barry's Reform Club of 1837–41, just completed when the lithograph was made, his earlier Travellers' Club of 1829–31, Decimus Burton's Athenaeum of 1827–30, and Nash's United Services Club of 1827 which Burton was about to transform into a building worthy of its Waterloo Place partner. Closing the vista, as they still do, are the modest dome of the National Gallery and the spire of St Martin in the Fields. Only the private houses on the N. side of the street have been swept away in favour of larger units.

14 (bl) The Horseguards &c. from St. James's Park. T. Shotter Boys del et lith. 250 × 455mm. The artist was standing on the same spot as when he sketched item 11 but has turned his back on Buckingham Palace. The lake is bridgeless as Nash's Chinese erection had been removed and its successor not yet built and the panorama shows Carlton House Terrace, the Duke of York's Column, the Admiralty telegraph, Kent's white Horse Guards dome rubbing shoulders with the grey form of that of St Paul's Cathedral, the roof of the Banqueting House and the Shot Tower S. of Waterloo Bridge.

15 (br) Hyde Park Corner. T.S. Boys del et lith. 305 × 430mm. From Knightsbridge looking towards Piccadilly. On the l. Decimus Burton's Ionic screen entrance to Hyde Park, Apsley House and Park Lane; on the r. the corner of St George's Hospital and, aligned with it, Burton's Constitution Arch of 1828 before its crowning in 1846 with M.C. Wyatt's giant equestrian statue of the Duke of Wellington. On removal of the arch S. in 1883 the statue was banished and eventually replaced with the familiar 'quadriga'. The centre of the composition is marked by a 6d omnibus making for Piccadilly.

16 (bl) Hyde Park near Grosvenor Gate. T.S. Boys del et lith. 245 × 470mm. This, the most populated of the plates, shows the Sunday afternoon parade of high society in open landaus or on horseback with pedestrian spectators in their 'Sunday best'. Park Lane is to the r. with the colonnaded screen and picture gallery of Grosvenor House just completed by Thomas Cundy for the Marquess of Westminster. Closing the vista is one of Decimus Burton's pretty white Grecian lodges, at Grosvenor Gate.

17 (bl) Piccadilly looking towards/the City. T.S. Boys del et lith. 320 × 432mm. All is changed yet the lively scene depicted, looking E. from the end of Old Bond

Street, has an air of familiarity. Just beyond the shop on the l. is the old entrance to Burlington House. On the S. side of the street the spire of St James, Piccadilly overtops Messrs Fortnum & Mason's shop while, close at hand, Bullock's Egyptian Hall appears to be advertising a panorama consisting of red indians by Catlin. The attention is drawn above street level to balloons in a milky sky, to which a group of passers-by and some workmen laying drains are pointing.

18 (bl) Regent Street looking towards the Quadrant. T.S. Boys del et lithog. 305 × 420mm. The variegated frivolity of the Regent Street commercial façades, insubstantial in the morning light, are set off by the sombre Ionic portico and tower of C.R. Cockerell's Hanover Chapel in the foreground to the r. This lay between Princes Street and Hanover Street before its demolition in 1896. Shopping is in full swing with attendant beggars and crossing sweeper and cockaded footmen attending their mistresses. To the l. a diminutive sandwich-man (or boy) carries a poster, 'Vote for Boys'; there is a state in which the last word has been deleted.

19 (bl) Regent Street looking towards the Duke of York's column. T.S. Boys del et lithog. 315 × 428mm. On either side of the entrance to Lower Regent Street as we look towards Waterloo Place are two stucco segments of a circle never to be completed but clearly marked 'Regent Circus'. On the r., half way down, is the Doric temple front of St Philip's Chapel, built by G.S. Repton in 1820 for his clergyman brother. Closing the view, in front of distant glimpses of the park and Westminster, is the granite column erected by Benjamin Wyatt in 1831–4 to sustain a statue by Sir Richard Westmacott of George IV's brother.

20 (br) Entry to the Strand from Charing Cross. T.S. Boys del et lith. 270 × 450mm. The works for constructing Trafalgar Square were completed in 1841, enabling the portico of St Martin in the Fields to be seen from this viewpoint. Beside it is Morley's Hotel and beyond that the corner turret of Nash's West Strand improvement. S. of the Strand, with twin lead-capped turrets and a central lion, is Northumberland House which survived until 1874. Inscribed on the pedestal of King Charles 1's statue is 'T.S. Boys 1841' and a quota of boys is on the pavement below. To the l. of this is a water cart laying the summer dust, a hansom cab and a striking pair of equestrians.

21 (bl) The Strand. T.S. Boys del et lith. 428 × 315mm. This is a stately procession of three churches advancing to the W. with St Mary le Strand in the lead, St Clement Danes following and the Gothic-crowned new St Dunstan in the West bringing up the rear. To the r. is a fleeting perspective of Somerset House and beside it curvaceous shopfronts. Among the staffage are a Welsh milkmaid and a carrier's cart marked 'T.S. Boys 90 Gt Portland St.'

22 (bl) Temple Bar, from the Strand. T.S. Boys del et lith. 430 × 323mm. This illustrates the congestion caused by the narrow archway of old Temple Bar as a horse pantechnicon travelling W. tries to worm its way through the arch and to circumnavigate a long dray with two huge baulks of timber and two hansom cabs. A baker sits philosophically on his barrow in the foreground, his basket marked 'T.S.B.'

23 (br) St. Dunstans &c. Fleet Street. T.S. Boys del et lith. 428 × 318mm. A portrait of John Shaw's new church at 10.10 am on a sunny day. The E. side of Temple Bar closes the vista and in the foreground is a carrier's cart marked 'T.S. Boys, Goods Removed, Town and Country'.

24 (bl) St. Paul's from Ludgate Hill. T.S. Boys del et lithog. 435 × 310mm. Another church portrait, of the beautiful tower and spire of Wren's St Martin, Ludgate, with the Cathedral a brooding presence in the afternoon sunlight. There is a tangle of traffic on the hill and two Christ's Hospital scholars walk demurely along the pavement. To the r. above the shop front a sign advertises 'Boys'.

25 (bl below the work) Guildhall. T.S. Boys del et lithog. 298 × 400mm. The figures of Gog and Magog keep watch over a few decorous sightseers while the summer sunshine streams through the clerestory windows and is reflected in the white coffered ceiling installed by Wren and so out of keeping with the Gothic arches below. A third of the way up the pier on the l. is carved 'T.S. Boys'.

26 (br) The Bank, looking toward the Mansion House. T.S. Boys del et lithog. 430 × 318mm. View of S. front from the corner of Bartholomew Lane, looking W. To the r. of the Mansion House the spire of St Antholin, Budge Row. The Bank beadle gives directions to a countrified pair. (*Bank of England* 106)

Extra lithograph not usually included in sets, a pendant to item 3

27 (br) The Tower of London, as seen October 31st 1841, the morning after the Fire. Thomas Shotter Boys del et lith. London Published Novr. 5th 1841 by Thomas Boys 11 Golden Square Regent Street. 185 × 440mm.

---

197 · CATER AND OLIVER'S FIRE AT THE TOWER [c 1842]

On the night of 30–1 October 1841 an overhead flue set light to the Bowyer Tower to the north of the Tower of London and the flames soon spread to the neighbouring Armoury. This was a pleasant brick and stone erection, designed by Wren and built 1685–92, with a pediment bearing the arms of William III over the central bay and a small domed lantern which is a conspicuous feature of most pre-1841 views of the Tower. The buckets, hand pumps and light engines provided by the Office of Works were in a deplorable state of dilapidation and neglect and failed to control the blaze which gutted the building, destroying as it went thousands of valuable items of small arms and armour and the wheel of Nelson's *Victory*. The Crown Jewels themselves were only saved by the presence of mind of a policeman who prized open the bars of the cage in which they were kept and brought them out, but for charred wrappings, intact. The Duke of Wellington replaced the burnt-out Armoury with a barracks, designed as a fortress and capable of holding 1,000 men.

William Oliver, whose *Scenery of the Pyrenees* (1842) was lithographed by Thomas Shotter Boys and others, must have been a local resident, as he was on the spot to draw the conflagration while it was in progress whereas Boys was only able to reach it next morning, when the flames had died down (*London as it is*, no 196, item 27). His lithotint of this scene is extra to the listed views of *Fire at the Tower* but is to be found in the set at the Tower of London Library. Neither printed title nor text were published but the lithographic grey paper wrappers, which measure 555 × 375mm, read:

Six Views taken after the Great Fire at the Tower of London. On the 31st Oct 1841; by Messrs. J. Cater & W. Oliver. (six titles listed) London, Colnaghi and Puckle, 23, Cockspur Street. C. Hullmandel's Patent.

The plates are inscribed within the design 'J. Cater and W. Oliver' and bear the credits 'Willm Oliver lithotint, C. Hullmandel's Patent', and the publication-line 'Colnaghi & Puckle, 23, Cockspur Street.' The Tower Library set is printed in grey but that in the Abbey catalogue (241) is described as 'coloured lithotints'.

1 Armoury from the Terrace. 270 × 365mm.

2 Entrance to the Armoury &c. 255 × 360mm.

3 Long Room leading to the Brick Tower. 230 × 340mm.

4 Inside of the Brick Tower. 365 × 260mm.

5 Interior of the Armoury. 255 × 365mm.

6 Ruins from Avenue on the Parade. 255 × 365mm.

7 Conflagration of the Tower of London:/on the night of the 30th October 1841./Drawn upon the spot by William Oliver Esqr. 260 × 375mm.

198 · PARROTT'S LONDON FROM THE THAMES [1842]

These fine lithographs were probably first published as a set in 1842, the same year as *Original Views of London as it is*. (no 196). Between them they hand down a vivid picture of London in the earliest years of Queen Victoria's reign and posterity should be truly grateful to William Parrott and Thomas Shotter Boys for transferring their lively impressions of street and river scenes with such immediacy onto stone.

The 12 plates were issued in Parts to begin with and two of the four wrappers, which each contained three of them, with their numbers left blank, survive in the Guildhall Library:

London from the Thames; being a Series of Views of the Metropolis, from that Noble River. From Original Drawings by W. Parrott, Esq. To be completed in Four Parts, each containing Three Views. Price, Plain, 12s. per Part; coloured, 21s. Published by H. Brooks, 319, Regent Street, Portland Place.

No text accompanied the plates and it is difficult to establish their sequence in the Parts since they were neither numbered nor listed. Their dates, however, run as follows:

Items 4, 11–12	Undated
Item 7	March 1840
Item 3	October 1840
Items 6, 8	April 1841
Item 10	May 1841
Item 9	June 1841
Items 1, 2, 5	November 1841

It seems likely that the superb trio of plates published in November 1841 crowned the set and were followed only by the vignetted title-page issued for binding purposes or as a portfolio curtain-raiser.

Thick cartridge paper, about 360 × 525mm, was

used for the printing and the large oblong folio was bound in brown cloth lettered in gilt around a vignette of St Paul's Cathedral: 'London from the Thames/by/Wm. Parrott/H. Brooks, 87 New Bond Street.'

William Parrott, an Essex farmer's son, was born in 1813. He was apprenticed to John Pye the engraver, who had been taught his craft by Charles Heath, had contributed to *Beauties of England and Wales* (no 104) and had gained a considerable reputation for his plates on steel after Turner. However, Parrott soon became a painter and from 1835 exhibited at the Royal Academy, the British Institution and the Society of British Artists in Suffolk Street. These lithographs show that he was skilful in painting landscape and architecture and in drawing figures and that he had affinities with his illustrious seniors, Samuel Prout and Richard Parkes Bonington, with T.S. Boys and his contemporary William Callow. Like them he followed up his success on the English scene by visiting France where he produced a parallel set of 12 lithograph views of Paris and the Seine, published in 1843. He later travelled to Italy and Germany and went on sketching tours in Normandy and Brittany. His London residence was in the 'Quartier Latin' of Warren Street; he died in or after 1869.

His lithographs are in the tradition of topographical illustration which allowed the artist to control the means of reproduction, either by carrying out his own engraving and aquatinting, as did Thomas Malton (no 72), or by being closely involved in the processes as were Rowlandson and Pugin (no 99) and, later, T.H. Shepherd (no 154). This was soon to be overtaken by mass production methods of steel and wood-engraving and by oleographs, in which the artist had very little say and could be entirely dispensed with in favour of daguerreotypes or photographs. Like Boys he made two stones for each view, one for outline and one for tint, and these combined in register produced the lithotints in the uncoloured versions of *London from the Thames*. They were so designed that the tint stone served to enhance the beauty of the hand-colour washes applied to the 'de luxe' copies, in the same way as the engraver could make printed aquatint blend with applied colour so skilfully as to make them almost indistinguishable.

The book itself is a great rarity but in recent years two sets of excellent colour facsimiles have been issued, one in the United States (by Newton Gregg of Novato, California) and one by the Greater London Council.

Captions are written onto the stone by the artist, br or bl, balanced by his signature in the opposite corner, bl or br: 'W. Parrott, del. et lith.' Publication-lines are printed below. The plates were printed variously by M. & N. Hanhart and C. Hullmandel. The order followed below is that of the uncoloured copy in the GLC History Library and differs from that of the Guildhall Library copy and from Abbey (no 237).

1 (lithographic title) London from the Thames/by/W. Parrott/Dedicated by especial permission/to the Rt. Honble. the/Lord Mayor./ (vignette) Embarcation of the Right Honble. the Lord Mayor from the Tower. W. Parrott lithog. London./Henry Brooks./87, New Bond Street./ Printed by C. Hullmandel. 330 × 420mm. The vignette is flanked by the figures of a Yeoman Warder and a waterman. The whole composition is enclosed in an ornamental border, crowned by the City arms.

2 (br) London Bridge from the Pool. Published Noveber 1841 by Henry Brooks, 319 Regent Street Portland Place./M. & N. Hanhart lith Printers. 272 × 442mm. Through an arch of the sparklingly new London Bridge, Southwark and Blackfriars Bridges are glimpsed. On the wherry l. foreground the initials 'WP' are reversed.

3 (bl) Chelsea with Part of the Old Church & Sir Hans Sloane's Tomb. Published November 1841, by Henry Brooks, 319, Regent St. Portland Place./M. & N. Hanhart, lith. Printers. 226 × 392mm. Congregation leaving service on a summer morning; Chelsea Reach to the r. (*Longford* 136)

4 (bl) West India Docks from the South East. 245 × 425mm. No publication-line but date 'Oct. 1840' scribbled in bl above caption. Sailing ships under repair.

5 (bl) Westminster & Hungerford from Waterloo Bridge. 215 × 410mm. No publication-line. Next to Hungerford Market a jetty protrudes into the river; Brunel's Hungerford Suspension Bridge was not built until 1844–5. A group of boys is bathing and fishing on the unembanked foreshore below Waterloo Bridge. Sepia and body colour drawing (215 × 410mm) in Museum of London (A 22150).

6 (bl) Lambeth & Westminster. From Millbank. Published November 1841 by Henry Brooks, 319 Regent St. Portland Place./M. & N. Hanhart, lith. Printers. 225 × 408mm. Panorama from Westminster Abbey and St John, Smith Square across to Lambeth Palace on the opposite shore; bl a dray with a load of timber.

7 (bl) Southwark Bridge from London Bridge. Published by Henry Brooks, 319 Regent Street, Portland

Place, and 87, New Bond Street, April 15th 1841./ Printed by C. Hullmandel. 230 × 412mm. Paddle steamers waiting to dock at the Old Swan Pier with the lattice work of Rennie's Southwark Bridge and the dome of St Paul's in the background.

8 (br) Ship Building at Limehouse, the President on the Stocks. Published March, 1840, by Henry Brooks, 319 Regent St. Portland Place./M. & N. Hanhart, lith. Printers. 238 × 415mm. Forest of masts with Hawksmoor's St Anne, Limehouse in the background.

9 (br) The Pool. From London Bridge. Morning. Published by Henry Brooks, 319, Regent Street, Portland Place and 87, New Bond Street, April 15th, 1844./Printed by C. Hullmandel. 225 × 412mm. Laden paddle steamers against a background of the Custom House and the Tower of London. Towers of St Dunstan in the East on the r. and St Olave, Tooley Street on the l.

10 (br) Waterloo Bridge from the West with a Boat Race. Published by Henry Brooks, 319, Regent Street, Portland Place, and 87, New Bond Street, June 25th 1841./Printed by C. Hullmandel. 225 × 405mm. Hungerford Market, Buckingham Watergate and Somerset House can be distinguished on the opposite shore; the royal barge rows into the picture on the r.

11 (br) The Pool. Looking towards London Bridge. Published May, 1841 by Henry Brooks, 319 Regent St. Portland Place./M. & N. Hanhart, Lith. Printers. 223 × 418mm. Bumboats and paddle steamers against a background of St Paul's Cathedral, the Monument, St Dunstan in the East and the Tower. A sepia wash and body colour drawing (205 × 405mm) in Guildhall Library is taken from the same viewpoint, a trifle closer in, but the shipping includes more sailing vessels than paddle steamers.

12 (br) Greenwich and the Dreadnought. 225 × 410mm. No publication-line. Behind the hulk of the Dreadnought, in use as a naval hospital, rise the steeple of St Alphege Church and, on the hill above, Flamstead House; on the l. the Royal Naval Hospital.

13 (br) Somerset House. St Pauls & Blackfriars Bridge from Waterloo Bridge. 239 × 495mm. No publication-line. Strollers on the terrace of Somerset House peer over the parapet at the Thames foreshore which, at low tide, has a seaside look, peopled with citizens watching the passing river traffic and with beached sailing and rowing boats.

199 · 'SUMMERLY'S' HAND-BOOK OF WESTMINSTER ABBEY [1842]

Under an assumed name, Henry Cole is the author of this well produced little Abbey guidebook; he used the same pseudonym in publishing other popular guides to institutions such as the National Gallery. From being Assistant Keeper at the Record Office he became an active member of the managing committee of the Great Exhibition and of several later exhibitions in London and abroad. In 1852 he set up the Museum of Manufactures on the first floor of Marlborough House and, as Secretary of the Science and Art Department, was able to supervise its incorporation in the new Victoria and Albert Museum in 1857. Alongside his career as a busy and distinguished civil servant he yet found the time to edit periodicals, paint in water-colour, etch, engrave book illustrations (some of the wood-engravings in this book are his) and work for the improvement of public taste in the graphic arts and book design.

Ignoring the pseudonym the preface to this book is signed 'Henry Cole, March 22, 1842' and says:

Four years ago, I ventured to urge, in a quarterly Review, that wood engraving was a very suitable occupation for ladies; and that the world would probably allow the practice of this art to be one of the few employments not degrading to them. Since that time, the lady-professors of this delicate art have increased at least six-fold.

The lady draughtsmen and wood-engravers, some titled, are listed exhaustively at the beginning of this volume; the best of the latter have been set to engraving the drawings of David Cox junior, with very creditable results. Most of the tiny vignettes, however, are little more than ornaments to relieve the type page; only David Cox junior's four etchings, each vignetted on a separate page but with plate-marks cropped, are detailed. They have no captions, credits or publication-lines.

A Hand-book for the Architecture, Sculptures, Tombs and decorations of Westminster Abbey: with forty-six embellishments on wood, engraved by ladies; and Four Etchings by David Cox jun. By Felix Summerly. (epigraph) London: George Bell, Fleet Street. MDCCCXLII.

Duodecimo, 162 × 100mm.   1842

COLLATION Half-title; title-page; pp vii–viii, contents; pp ix–x, list of illustrations; p xi, index of artists' names; pp xiii–xiv, preface; pp 1–144, Hand-book; pp 145–8, index to monuments.

1 front. (S.W. view of the Abbey from Dean's Yard) 90 × 140mm.

2 p 33 (S.E. view of the cloisters) 80 × 122mm.

3 p 48 (Ambulatory seen from the Henry VII ante-chapel) 85 × 135mm.

4 p 86 (Interior of Henry VII Chapel, looking E.) 125 × 85mm.

200 · DELAMOTTE'S PRIORY AND HOSPITAL OF ST BARTHOLOMEW [1844]

This short history of the Priory and Hospital is illustrated with a few indifferent wood-engravings by T. Gilkes and zincographs by William Alfred Delamotte, a painter and etcher of Huguenot descent who exhibited at the Royal Academy between 1796 and 1848. In the previous year he had published lithographs of his original views of Oxford. The book was first published by Cunningham in 1844 and reissued in 1846 by W.S. Ford, who stuck his label over the original imprint and sold it at four shillings.

An Historical Sketch of the Priory and Royal Hospital of St. Bartholomew: illustrated by W.A. Delamotte. London: Cunningham, 1844 (William Simpson Ford, 18 Holywell Street Strand. MDCCCXLVI).

Quarto, 270 × 210mm.   1844, 1846

COLLATION Title-page; dedication (1 leaf); pp v–vi, list of subscribers; pp vii–ix, preface; list of engravings (1 leaf); pp 1–42, The Royal Priory.

The credits read: 'On zinc by W.A. Delamotte. Chabot, Skinner St.'

1 front. St. Bartholomew the Great. 205 × 165mm. View from presbytery looking W. and including the tomb of Rahere.

2 (zinc title) The/Royal Hospital/of St. Bartholomew &/Priory/by W.A. Delamotte,/Librarian to the Hospital/Published by William S. Ford, 18 Holywell St.

Strand. Designed and drawn on zinc by W.A. Delamotte 1844. 230 × 170mm. Design with Hospital and Priory arms, supported by Hope and Faith between two croziers.

3 p 1 The Hall St. Bartholomew's Hospital. 163 × 205mm. Interior on a prize day.

4 p 13 St. Bartholomew the Less. 195 × 165mm. Interior facing E.

5 p 33 Quadrangle, St. Bartholomew's Hospital. 158 × 228mm.

201 · MEMORIALS OF CHARTERHOUSE [1844]

Thirty years had passed since the buildings of Charterhouse School had been drawn by W. Westall and A. Pugin for aquatint engravings in Ackermann's *History of the Colleges* (no 116) when this more exhaustive graphic record was published with its 14 lithographic views as against the previous five aquatints. They were all both drawn and transferred to stone by Charles Walter Radclyffe for printing by the Queen's lithographer, Day & Haghe, and for publication with explanatory text by James Moore, a local bookseller in Carthusian Street. Radclyffe, a native of Birmingham and member of the Birmingham Society of Artists, came of an artistic family. His father, William, was a successful line-engraver from water-colour landscapes by masters such as Turner, David Cox senior and De Wint and a contributor of steel-engravings to topographical books such as *Metropolitan Improvements* and its sequel (nos 154, 161), his brother William was a portrait painter and another brother, Edward, followed his father as an engraver. Charles himself painted in water-colour and exhibited his landscapes at the Royal Academy and British Institution from 1847 to 1887. He also practised lithography and a lithographic view of his, dated 1842, 'St. Paul's South Front, looking towards Watling Street', is in the British Museum (*Crace* 19.172). The 14 views of Charterhouse must have been published either shortly before or shortly after a similar, undated, collection on Westminster School. They are printed in grey outline overlaid with a buff tint stone and touches of white. The views are surrounded by a ruled frame between which and the view itself are the credits 'C.W. Radclyffe del. & lith. Day & Haghe Lithr. to the Queen.' Captions in voided capitals appear beneath the frame. They are unnumbered and unlisted, although each has its own commentary. The text includes two woodcuts, of the baptistery and the tomb of Francis Beaumont.

Memorials of Charterhouse. A Series of Original Views taken and drawn on stone By C.W. Radclyffe, Esq. (shield of arms, crest and motto) London: Published by James Moore, 4 Carthusian Street, Charterhouse Square. MDCCCXLIV.

Folio, 540 × 365mm.   1844

COLLATION   Title-page; list of subscribers (2pp); pp i–x, Charterhouse (with lists of governors, masters, etc and school list for 1844); descriptions interleaved with lithographs (14 leaves).

1 front. Memorials/of Charterhouse./Drawn & Lithographed by/C.W. Radclyffe, Esqre. (swelled rule, then in view bl) Entrance Gate/London, Published by James Moore Carthusian Street, 1844/ Day & Haghe, Lithrs. to the Queen. 325 × 235mm.

2 The School Master's House and Scholars' Rooms. 212 × 310mm.

3 The Preacher's Court/ Looking North. 215 × 310mm.

4 The Great Hall. 228 × 315mm. Interior.

5 The Porter's Lodge and Gateway, as seen from the entrance court. 200 × 285mm.

6 The Great Chamber or old Governors' Room. 210 × 322mm.

7 The School from the Upper Green. 198 × 315mm.

8 The Entrance-Court. 200 × 290mm. Credits and title below ruled frame.

9 Wash-House Court. 200 × 280mm.

10 The Master's Lodge, with the new additions/as seen from Charter House Square. 225 × 320mm.

11 The Preacher's Court, looking East. 215 × 322mm.

12 The School Room. 205 × 325mm. Interior.

13 The Chapel and adjoining buildings. 200 × 322mm.

14 The Chapel. 205 × 325mm. Interior.

202 · MEMORIALS OF WESTMINSTER SCHOOL [c 1844]

This collection of a dozen lithotints is a more satisfactory record of the school buildings and dependencies than Ackermann's earlier *Colleges* (no 116) in which only three aquatint views, based on drawings by Pugin, were published. The artist and lithographer Charles Walter Radclyffe has already been noticed for his similar publication on the Charterhouse (no 201). The lithographs are just as satisfactory as those of Charterhouse, with a tint stone and highlights similarly added to the outline, but the publication itself is less professional. It was undertaken by the school bookseller who has neglected to print a title-page or to date any imprint or publication-line. There is, however, a list of headmasters, with the last appointment in 1841. No doubt the Charterhouse folio, and another on Eton published in the same year, came to the notice of this 'High Man' and, determined not to be outdone, he commissioned Radclyffe to draw a similar series of views of his own school.

The captions are in voided capitals beneath the views, within the rules with which they are framed. The credits read throughout: 'C.W. Radclyffe del. et lith. Day & Haghe. lithr. to the Queen.'

Folio, 540 × 360mm.   c 1844

COLLATION   Lithotint title-page; dedication (1 leaf); list of subscribers (2 pp); advertisement (1 leaf); pp 1–5, Historical Sketch, List of Headmasters; descriptions interleaved with lithographs (11 leaves); heraldic appendix (1 leaf).

1 (lithotint title) Memorials/of/Westminster School,/Drawn & Lithographed by C.W. Radclyffe. Published by Ginger, School Bookseller,/College Street, Westminster/Day & Haghe Lithogr. to the Queen. 335 × 245mm. View of archway leading from Dean's Yard into Little Dean's Yard.

2 The School Room. 205 × 280mm.

3 The Library. 280 × 203mm.

4 Little Dean's Yard,/Facing the South. 203 × 310mm.

5 The Cloysters. 215 × 290mm. E. walk.

6 The Dormitory. 200 × 312mm. College.

7 The Dormitory and College Garden. 202 × 298mm. Burlington's building, with S. view of the Abbey.

8 Roberts' Boat House – The Fields. Each 152 × 223mm. The boathouse on the Surrey shore near Lambeth Palace; playing fields in Vincent Square.

9 College Hall. 200 × 315mm. Interior. Hall adjoins the Jerusalem Chamber.

10 College Hall/Exterior. 205 × 310mm.

11 Great Dean's Yard. 200 × 310mm.

12 Little Dean's Yard,/Facing the North. 205 × 290mm.

203 · DESCRIPTION OF THE COLOSSEUM [1845]

This building, opened to the public by Thomas Hornor in 1829, is described in a note on *A Brief Account of the Colosseum* (no 159). It changed hands in 1831 and again in 1843 when it was bought by D. Montague who had alterations made to Decimus Burton's fabric by an architect named W. Bradwell. He obtained Prince Albert's support in its revival as a place of wholesome family entertainment and so the new guidebook, published in 1845, was able to claim the Queen's patronage and to display her arms in a wood-engraving on the title-page and worked in gold on the cover.

The 'pièce de résistance' was still Parris's immense panoramic painting of London, which again is illustrated, but other attractions also are described and illustrated by wood-engravings: namely, a sculpture gallery called the Glyptotheca, the Hall of Mirrors, Gothic Aviary and Stalactite Caverns and, in the grounds, some artificial ruins, a Swiss chalet and a replica of Mont Blanc. In after years were added a panorama of Paris and a 'cyclorama' of the Lisbon earthquake, before the building was closed for good in 1863.

A Description of the Colosseum as re-opened in M.DCCC.XLV. Under the Patronage of Her Majesty the Queen and H.R.H. Prince Albert. With numerous illustrations and eight coloured sections of The Panorama of London, embossed by Messrs. Dobbs, Bailey & Co. This Catalogue has been prepared for the Proprietor by Messrs. Kronheim and Skirving, Engravers and Designers and the Illustrations and Letter-Press are printed from Stereotype Plates cast by the Patent Process of Messrs. Kronheim & Co., 3, Earl-street, Blackfriars,

London:—Printed by J. Wertheimer and Co., Finsbury Circus. M.DCCC.XLV.

Small oblong quarto, 185 × 220mm   1845

COLLATION   Title-page; pp 3–6, The Colosseum and Glyptotheca; pp 7–24, Grand Panorama of London, etc; 8 embossed plates of panorama and 6 wood-engravings of 'attractions'.

The nature of the illustrations is explained on the title-page. The 16 plates are in fact reduced copies of the eight lithographed sections of Hornor's panorama sketches, printed with the outline of specific objects in relief to give a three-dimensional effect. Each section is given in two versions: one printed in shades of brown with an elaborate ornamental frame in the same tone, the other in outlines of brown with overprinted layers of sickly blue, pink and yellow, suggesting cheap confectionery rather than the colours of nature. A seventeenth edition published in 1846 reverted to plain impressions of the views printed in black and white. The naming of the sites on the plates follows Hornor's but the lists of numbered references printed beneath each embossed view are slightly abridged. The coloured plates have the credit 'Kronheim & Skirving sc. Dobbs & Bailey & Co.' The views, less frames and references, each measure 123 × 147mm. They are arranged in the same order as in the earlier guidebook.

1 1–2 (S.W. turret of St Paul's – Blackfriars Bridge – Shot Tower – Wimbledon) Refs 1–43.

2 3–4 (N.W. turret of St Paul's – Ludgate Hill – Bloomsbury – Colosseum) Refs 1–47.

3 5–6 (Newgate – Clerkenwell – Pentonville – Highgate Archway) Refs 1–40.

4 7–8 (Paternoster Row – Aldersgate – Aldgate – Shoreditch – Bethnal Green) Refs 1–42.

5 9–10 (St Paul's School – St Mary le Bow – St Lawrence Jewry – Moorfields – London Docks – Stratford, Essex) Refs 1–46.

6 11–12 (St Augustine, Watling Street – St Swithin – the Tower – Southwark – Woolwich) Refs 1–32.

7 13–14 (St Nicholas Cole Abbey – St Mary Somerset – Southwark Bridge – Southwark Cathedral) Refs 1–18.

8 15–16 (St Benet, Paul's Wharf – Herald's Office – Bankside – Christ Church, Southwark – Streatham – Clapham) Refs 1–22.

Rock Brothers, who published hundreds of small topographical steel-engravings, some of which were collected in booklets (nos 205, 214), took into partnership the engraver A.H. Payne, illustrator of Bicknell's *Illustrated London* (no 207). Under their joint imprint appeared a concise, vest-pocket guide to London which ran into several editions and was illustrated with half a dozen miniature engravings from the Rock series. Those in the September 1845 issue are noted below; this was reprinted several times and illustrated with the same plates, save for one substitute in 1847. None of the plates has credits and three of them, apart from the absence of a serial number, are exactly as published in *Rock's Illustrations of London* (no 214), referred to as *RI*. Publication-lines, br or bl, read simply 'Rock & Co. London.'

Rock's Illustrated Guide to the Sights and Amusements of London, with lists of Bankers, Cab fares and Steamers leaving London &c. &c. &c. Sixth ed. Corrected to Sept. 1845. London: Rock Brothers and Payne.

Sextodecimo, 110 × 70mm.   1845, etc

COLLATION   Title-page; pp 1–48. Illustrated Guide

1 front. Post Office. 55 × 95mm. *RI* 8.

2 p 14 Monument. 65 × 90mm. *RI* 3.

3 p 20 Thames Tunnel. 60 × 90mm. *RI* 1.

4 p 28 Mansion House. 60 × 90mm.

5 p 36 Lake, in Regent's Park. 60 × 90mm.

6 p 44 Buckingham Palace. 55 × 95mm. Before the Blore E. front of 1846–7.

Additional 1847 plate (substitute for item 5)

7 p 4 Bank of England. 55 × 100mm.

The firm founded by William Frederick Rock in 1834 specialized in the publication of Christmas cards and topographical steel-engravings, vignetted and of a size suitable for printing on letterheads, on sets of cards or for binding into little picture-books. Hundreds of examples of these separate British views survive, most of them numbered in a series which ran into thousands. The booklet collections are also to be found: for instance, one of Cambridge of about 1851 and another of Bury St Edmunds of 1854 locally published and two of London dated approximately 1845 and 1851 (no 214).

The views in the earlier collection are rather larger than usual, which suggests they were published to rival similar sized vignetted views which were being issued in series by J. & F. Harwood of Fenchurch Street from August 1841 (no 194). One of the views is of Sir William Tite's rebuilt Royal Exchange, opened in October 1844, and the captions include a reference to May 1845 when Hungerford Suspension Bridge was opened. The engraving is vignetted throughout, with a plate-mark of about 165 × 230mm. Plates are unnumbered and unlisted but all carry, either bl or br, the single credit 'Rock & Co. London' and on items 7 and 11 the address 11 Walbrook is added. There is no text nor a title-page but the green cloth-gilt binding is lettered 'Views/of/London/ 2/6 /Rock. London.' The overall oblong folio size is 210 × 280mm.

1 The Royal Exchange London./Tite, Architect. 100 × 160/165 × 230mm.

2 Post-Office, London. 105 × 150mm. Looking towards St Paul's Cathedral.

3 St Paul's Cathedral. 105 × 150mm.

4 The British Museum. 90 × 160mm.

5 Exeter Hall—May Meeting. 110 × 160mm.

6 Westminster Abbey. 110 × 155mm. W. front.

7 Westminster Hall. Rock & Co. 11 Walbrook London. 90 × 140mm. The walls are hung with pictures, perhaps in connection with the competition for designing fresco paintings to cover them which was being promoted in the early 1840s and is referred to in *London Interiors* (no 195) vol.1, p 160.

8 View from Lambeth Palace. 90 × 170mm. In bm: 'Westminster Abbey – Houses of Parliament – Westminster Bridge'.

9 The New Houses of Parliament/Barry, Architect. 90 × 165mm.

10 Lambeth Palace/the Residence of the Archbishop of Canterbury. 100 × 160mm. From river.

11 Hungerford Suspension Bridge/Opened 1 May 1845. Rock & Co. 11 Walbrook London. 95 × 170mm. Designed by Sir I.K. Brunel.

12 Port of London. 85 × 145mm.

13 Thames Tunnel/1200 feet long 76 feet below high watermark, was 8 years building & cost £446,000/Opened 25 March 1843. 110 × 140mm. Designed by Sir I.K. Brunel.

14 The Thames Tunnel with a view of Rotherhith/Shewing the relative positions of the tunnel & the river./The Thames Tunnel is 1200 feet long, 76 feet below high water mark, & cost £446,000. Opened 25 March 1843. 120 × 150mm.

206 · JESSE'S LITERARY AND HISTORICAL MEMORIALS [1847]

John Heneage Jesse was a well-connected young man who obtained a clerkship in the Admiralty on the recommendation of the Duke of Clarence. This gave him the leisure to write verse on historical subjects and, in due course, some entertaining historical memoirs based on manuscript letters of the Stuart and Hanoverian monarchs. Richard Bentley, in publishing his *Literary and historical Memorials of London,* at 28s for two volumes, illustrated it with a modern plan of sites of historic buildings and reduced facsimiles by J. Cook of nine plans and engravings more or less contemporary with the events described. The credit throughout is 'J. Cook sc.' and the publication-line 'Richard Bentley 1847'.

Literary and historical Memorials of London. By J. Heneage Jesse.... In Two Volumes. Vol. I (II) London, Richard Bentley, 1847.

Octavo, 220 × 140mm.   1847

COLLATION   Vol. 1. Title-page; pp v–viii, contents, list of illustrations; pp 1–448, Memorials. Vol. 2.

Title-page; pp v–vii, contents, list of illustrations; pp 1–456, Memorials continued.

VOL. 1

1 front. Palace of Whitehall in Charles the Second's Reign: Anno 1680. 145 × 230mm. Reduced copy of Fisher's ground plan as engraved by George Vertue for *Vetusta Monumenta* (no 36), item 63.

2 p 1 (in compartment) London/and/Westminster/in the reign of/Queen Elizabeth/Anno Dom: 1563. 190 × 515/210 × 525mm. Based on Vertue's pewter engraving of the map attributed to Ralph Agas for *Vetusta Monumenta*, items 61–2. (*Darlington and Howgego* 8, note)

3 p 84 (in cartouche tl) The Parish of/St James, Westminster./From a Survey taken in/1755. 220 × 183mm. Refs 1–47 and 1–18. Reduced from Stow's *Survey* (no 37) vol. 2, p 655.

4 p 121 St James's Palace and part of the City of Westminster/taken from the Nth side of Pall Mall/ ... 1660. Hollar del. 78 × 192mm. Probably reduced from the engraved copy of Hollar's drawing in Grose's *Antiquarian Repertory* (no 56) vol.1, p 197.

5 p 313 Old Palace Yard, in the reign of Charles the First. Hollar del. 90 × 183mm. Reduced from Hollar's *Prospects* (no 5), 6. (*Hind* 90)

VOL. 2

6 front. The Tower of London in the Reign of Henry the Fifth. Charles Duke of Orleans. 125 × 100mm. Round-headed. From a miniature in the MS poems of Charles of Orleans (BL: Royal MSS, 16.f.2).

7 p 102 (in compartment) Plan of/St Giles's/in the Fields. (lm) From an original sketch made in the Reign of Queen Elizabeth. 75 × 102mm. Refs 1–9. See note to item 2 above.

8 p 213 The Palace of Whitehall. Hollar del. 82 × 175mm. From the drawing in the Pepysian Library, Cambridge engraved for *Londina Illustrata* (no 131), item 88.

9 p 233 Plan of the River Thames, showing the corresponding sites of adjacent and modern buildings. 110 × 257mm.

10 p 258 The Tower and its Liberties/Taken from correct surveys made in the Reign of Queen Elizabeth. 125 × 183mm. Refs A–Y, etc. Reduced from the George Vertue engraving of a 1597 draught by William Haiward and J. Gascoigne made for *Vetusta Monumenta*, item 7.

479

207 · PAYNE'S ILLUSTRATED LONDON [c 1847]

This London guide is usually referred to by the name of the engraver rather than that of the author, one W.I. Bicknell, who contributes a bland topographical commentary and a history of England in two sections up to the accession of Queen Victoria. Its aim is sufficiently explained by an eloquent prospectus:

Never in the history of our country were building operations in fuller activity than at present, or greater beauty of design displayed. Localities consisting of dark and narrow lanes or alleys, where the light of Heaven was scarcely admissible, and where vice reigned almost uncontrolled, have been swept away; and in their place elegant structures reared, on which the architect has exerted his utmost skill. Ground which but a short time since from its low and marshy situation, remained unproductive or, what was worse, exhaled its baneful *miasma*, is now covered with magnificent squares and noble mansions;—tenanted by persons of the highest rank.

Yet amidst the mighty enterprise of capital by which these improvements in London—the Emporium of the World—have been brought about, the visitor, and even the inhabitant of the metropolis, has been at a loss how to guide his steps, or how to preserve the recollection of what he has seen.... Under this feeling the Proprietors of *The Illustrated London* undertook the present publication with the idea of giving a concise yet comprehensive View of London as it now is, and is about to become.

In short, a successor to *Metropolitan Improvements* (no 154), combining in one publication a history, a guidebook and a celebration of the aesthetic, social and philanthropic benefits which had accrued from the not unprofitable endeavours of early Victorian land developers, architects and builders.

The work was originally issued in Numbers at a popular price, as advertised on the back of its wrappers:

Payne's Illustrated London will be published in Fortnightly Numbers, price Sixpence, containing five highly-finished Steel Engravings and from 16 to 24 pages of Letter-press, historical and descriptive; and in Monthly Parts at One Shilling, containing 10 highly-finished Engravings, and from 32 to 48 pages of Letter-press. The whole to be completed in about 20 Parts.

The first Number was advertised in the *Monthly Literary Advertiser* for February 1846; this and the next five Numbers consisted of eight to 16 pages of history and eight pages of topography which related to the four or five views (on two or three plates). Otherwise, in the absence of publication-lines on the plates or imprint date, dating must depend on internal evidence: there are at least two references in the text to the year 1847 (in describing the British Museum on p 305 and in connection with the rates of insurance premiums on p 343) and also there is an interior view of the House of Lords, only ready for occupation in that year. This suggests that the Numbers and Parts were coming out during 1846 and the late summer of 1847.

The collation is variable since the text is in three distinct paginations which the binder either divided into two volumes, interpolating the plates as near to relevant text as possible, or collected into a single volume, segregating plates and engraved title in a separate supplement.

Illustrated London, or a Series of Views in the British Metropolis and its Vicinity, engraved by Albert Henry Payne, from original drawings. The historical, topographical and miscellaneous notices, by W.I. Bicknell. (epigraph) London: E.T. Brain & Co. 88, Fleet Street.

Octavo, 180 × 120mm.   c 1846–7

COLLATION Title-page; preface (2pp); pp 1–408, Illustrated London; index (4pp); Part 1, pp 1–171, History of London (to Henry IV); Part 2, pp 1–76, History of London continued (to Victoria).

One hundred and eighty nine views illustrate this work, 43 measuring about 85 × 140mm on single-view plates and 146 about 60 × 85mm on double-view plates. Only one plate (item 10) has a draughtsman's credit and all were engraved by Payne or his apprentices. It may be that he also made the drawings, for he was a painter as well as an engraver, working both in London and Leipzig where he set up a studio. It is certain, however, that he was much influenced by T.H. Shepherd's image of London and the debt owed by a considerable proportion of the views to plates in *Metropolitan Improvements* and *London in the Nineteenth Century* (no 161) is apparent. Sometimes the Shepherd view is exactly followed, only with a reduction in size, sometimes it is extended a little to the right or left of the original and sometimes it is brought up to date with new trade names on shop fronts, architectural accretions or modification, and the maturing of trees and shrubs. In every case the staffage is revised and often buildings are bathed in a lurid storm light (as in item 85, Cripplegate Church and St Dionis). Attention is drawn to such parallels by the abbreviations *MI* and *L19C* in the following list.

Payne added many subjects to the Shepherd repertoire, both from the London environs and from central London. In the latter he shows a number of buildings erected within the 20 years since 1827, such as London Bridge Station completed in 1841, the Royal Exchange and St Michael, Chester Square completed in 1844, the Conservative Club and Hungerford Bridge completed in 1845, and the British Museum and House of Lords completed in 1847. Of his own inspiration are some romantically conceived river and park views (at items 6, 14, 18, 24, 37–8, 48, 51, 65). He also included a view of his publisher's premises (item 111).

The total number of views in any given copy varies and those in the list may be taken as the optimum number for the original issue. Later plates, taken over from *Tallis's Illustrated London* (no 215) have found their way into some copies, for example a view of the 1851 Great Exhibition building, used as a frontispiece. Not only is there no check-list of illustrations but, as with *London in the Nineteenth Century,* the binder was left to decide whether to place double-view plates against the text referring to the first of the views or the second, a further source of variation in bound copies. The only lettering on most of the plates is the caption in plain capitals.

1 (engr title) Payne's/Illustrated London./(vignette) St Pauls from the River. London: Brain & Payne, 12 Paternoster Row. Vignette 90 × 90mm.

2 front. The Royal Exchange. A.H. Payne del. et sc. 90 × 140mm. Designed by Sir William Tite, opened October 1844. From Poultry.

3 p 3 The Quadrangle, Royal Exchange. 85 × 140mm.

4 p 4 The Corn Exchange/Mark Lane – The Custom House. Each 60 × 87mm. Corn Exchange view derived from *MI* 112.

5 p 8 Richmond Bridge – Hampton Court. Each 60 × 85mm (*Gascoigne* 138)

6 p 10 Hampton Court. 87 × 140mm.

7 p 11 Somerset House. 88 × 138mm. The water laps the rusticated basement; the City is seen in the distance.

8 p 13 Christ's Hospital/New Hall – Goldsmith's Hall. Each 60 × 85mm. Goldsmith's Hall built by Thomas

Hardwick, 1829–35. Christ's Hospital view derived from *MI* 103.

9 p 20 Post Office – Albert Gate. Each 60 × 85mm. Albert Gate, Knightsbridge.

10 p 39 The National Gallery. C. Warren del. A.H. Payne sc. 90 × 140mm.

11 p 50 King's College, Strand – Somerset House, Strand. Each 60 × 85mm.

12 p 64 Hungerford Bridge – Duke of York's column. Each 60 × 85mm. Bridge designed by Brunel and opened in the spring of 1845.

13 p 65 Buckingham Palace. 85 × 140mm.

14 p 67 Buckingham Palace. 85 × 140mm. Nash front and Marble Arch from the lake in St James's Park.

15 p 68 The Admiralty – Banqueting House, Whitehall. Each 62 × 85mm. Banqueting House view derived from *L19C* 4.

16 p 70 St. Martin's Church – Northumberland House. Each 63 × 85mm.

17 p 70 St. Martin's Church/Trafalgar Square. 90 × 140mm. From S.E.

18 p 77 Waterloo Bridge. 85 × 140mm. With Somerset House.

19 p 80 Lambeth Palace – Westminster Hall. Each 60 × 87mm.

20 p 87 Westminster Bridge – Horse Guards. Each 60 × 87mm. Whitehall view of Horse Guards, as *L19C* 11.

21 p 93 King William St. – Cheapside. Each 63 × 88m.

22 p 95 The Mansion House. 85 × 140mm.

23 p 102 New Gresham St. – Merchant Tailor's Hall. Each 63 × 88mm.

24 p 103 The Ornamental Water/St James' Park. A.H. Payne. 83 × 140mm.

25 p 108 Burlington Arcade – Egyptian Hall. Each 63 × 88mm. Two Piccadilly views, as *MI* 81, 111.

26 p 110 The New Atheneum,/Waterloo Place – Crockford's Club House. Each 63 × 87mm.

27 p 129 The Conservative Club House. 88 × 138mm. In St James's, built by Sydney Smirke and George Basevi, 1843–5.

28 p 138 New United Service Club House – Arthur's Club House,/St James' St. Each 60 × 87mm. Derived from *L19C* 189, 192.

29 p 140 The Bank. 85 × 138mm. (*Bank of England* 111)

30 p 164 Statue of King William – The Monument/Fish St. Hill. Each 63 × 87mm. The statue, by Samuel Nixon, erected between William IV Street and Gracechurch Street December 1844.

31 p 165 Lothbury – Cornhill. Each 60 × 85mm. Cornhill, looking W.

32 p 173 The Sessions House/Clerkenwell – Old Bailey. Each 63 × 85mm.

33 p 175 Giltspur St. Compter – St John's Gate,/ Clerkenwell. Each 63 × 85mm. Building added to St John's Gate, otherwise both as *L19C* 40, 117.

34 p 177 Penitentiary,/Millbank – Vauxhall Bridge. 65 × 87, 63 × 87mm. Penitentiary view derived from *M1* 151.

35 p 179 Hungerford Market – Buckingham Water Gate. Each 60 × 85mm. Water Gate view as *L19C* 37.

36 p 198 Greenwich Park – Observatory, Greenwich Park. Each 60 × 90mm.

37 p 199 Greenwich Hospital. 85 × 140mm.

38 p 206 Chelsea Hospital/(from Battersea Fields). 82 × 140mm. (*Longford* 58)

39 p 206 Chelsea/from Battersea Bridge – Royal Military Asylum, Chelsea. Each 63 × 85mm. (*Longford* 135, 394)

40 p 210 Middlesex Hospital – The Foundling Hospital. Each 60 × 85mm. Additions to the front of the Middlesex and a tree by the Foundling Hospital is taller, otherwise as *L19C* 54, 155.

41 p 218 St Lukes Hospital – St Georges Hospital. Each 60 × 85mm. In some copies this plate is Westminster Hospital, mislabelled. St Luke's derived from *L19C* 129. (*Bank of England* 227)

42 p 219 Bethlem Hospital – Westminster Hospital. Each 60 × 85mm. In some copies this is St George's Hospital, mislabelled.

43 p 231 Guys Hospital – St Thomas's Hospital. Each 60 × 85mm. Derived from *L19C* 166, 165.

44 p 237 Hospital for Consumption and Diseases of the Chest (Brompton). 82 × 140mm. Founded 1841, opened to patients May 1850, built by Horace Francis. (*Longford* 531)

45 p 239 Smithfield. 82 × 140mm. Looking towards St Bartholomew's Hospital.

46 p 246 Covent Garden Market. 83 × 140mm.

47 p 252 Entrance to Hyde Park – Apsley House. Each 62 × 86mm.

48 p 254 The Thames/from the cliffs at Rosherville. 90 × 140mm.

49 p 259 Windsor Castle/from the Terrace – Virginia Water/Fishing Temple. Each 60 × 85mm.

50 p 261 Eton College – The Long Walk/Windsor. Each 60 × 87mm.

51 p 262 Richmond Hill. 85 × 140mm. (*Gascoigne* 139)

52 p 262 Twickenham/Orleans House – Near Teddington. Each 62 × 87mm. Teddington Weir.

53 p 263 Sion House/Seat of the Duke of Northumberland – Isleworth Church. 63 × 85, 60 × 85mm.

54 p 265 Kew Bridge – Hammersmith Suspension Bridge. 63 × 85mm.

55 p 265 Fulham – Barnes Church. Each 60 × 85mm.

56 p 266 Wandsworth – Putney. Each 63 × 83mm. River views.

57 p 273 London Docks. 82 × 138mm.

58 p 273 St. Katherine's Docks. 90 × 140mm.

59 p 274 The Thames Tunnel. 85 × 140mm.

60 p 274 Blackwall – The Dreadnought, Deptford. Each 62 × 90mm. This battleship hulk was moored off Greenwich and had, since 1831, been used as an international hospital for mariners.

61 p 278 Rosherville Gardens, Gravesend – (ditto). Each 60 × 85mm. Two different views.

62 p 278 Gravesend – Terrace Pier Gravesend. Each 60 × 85mm.

63 p 279 The Tower – Billingsgate. 65 × 88, 62 × 88mm.

64 p 286 Trinity House – The Mint. Each 63 × 85mm. Mint as *L19C* 12.

65 p 293 London Bridge. 83 × 138mm. From the S.E.

66 p 299 The British Museum. 90 × 135mm. Smirke's façade, completed 1847.

67 p 299 Egyptian Room British Museum. 87 × 140mm.

68 p 313 London & Westminster Bank/Lothbury. 85 × 140mm.

69 p 322 New Lodge, Victoria Park/Bonners Fields – Temple Bar. Each 60 × 85mm. Victoria Park founded 1842. Temple Bar view derived from the title-page vignette of *L19C*.

70 p 323 Temple Gardens – Adelphi Terrace. Each 60 × 85mm. Both from river.

71 p 324 Regents Park Zoological Gardens. 83 × 138mm.

72 p 325 Surrey Zoological Gardens, Mount Vesuvius & Bay of Naples. 83 × 138mm. This zoo occupied about 13 acres between Walworth and Kennington Common.

73 p 328 East India House. 85 × 140mm. Derived from *L19C* 6.

74 p 333 Highgate Church (from the cemetery) – Kensall Green Cemetery (Entrance Lodge). Each 60 × 85mm. Kensal Green Cemetery opened 1838.

75 p 336 Kensall Green Cemetery. 85 × 140mm.

76 p 338 Bridge over the Serpentine – Royal Humane Society, Serpentine. Each 60 × 82mm. The Humane Society Receiving House, to deal with bathing accidents, was designed by J.B. Bunning, 1834; enlarged 1837.

77 p 340 The National Mercantile Assurance Life Office/corner of the Poultry. 88 × 140mm.

78 p 343 South Western Railway Station,/Nine Elms – South Eastern & South Coast Railway Station,/ London Bridge. Each 60 × 85mm. London Bridge Station built by George Smith and Henry Roberts, 1843–4.

79 p 357 St. Pauls Cathedral. 130 × 90mm. From foot of Ludgate Hill.

80 p 357 St. Olave, Tooley Street – St. Swithin's London Stone/Cannon Street. Each 60 × 85mm. Derived from *L19C* 144, 136.

81 p 357 St. Clement Danes/Strand – St. Pancras/New Church. Each 83 × 60mm.

82 p 358 St. Saviour Southwark. 130 × 90mm.

83 p 359 North View of St. Paul's Cathedral. 92 × 135mm.

84 p 359 St. Botolph, Bishopsgate – St. Mary, Whitechapel. Each 60 × 85mm. Derived from *L19C* 180, 106.

85 p 360 Cripplegate Church – St. Dionis Backchurch/ Fenchurch St. Each 60 × 85mm. Derived from *L19C* 74, 48.

86 p 361 St. Michaels Chester Sq. – Lowndes Square. Each 60 × 85mm. St Michael's built by Thomas Cundy, 1844; Lowndes Square built 1837–9. (*Longford* 625)

87 p 364 St. Paul's Covent Garden – St. Sepulchre. Each 60 × 85mm. Derived from *L19C* 36, 143.

88 p 365 St. John's Westminster – Temple Church. Each 60 × 85mm. Derived from *L19C* 112, *MI* 118.

89 p 369 Westminster Abbey. 85 × 138mm. W. front.

90 p 369 St. Michael's Queenhithe – Allhallows Ch. Upper Thames St. Each 60 × 85mm. Derived from *L19C* 137, 179.

91 p 370 St. Johns Church (Upper Holloway) – Highbury College. Each 60 × 85mm.

92 p 370 New Church/Waterloo Road – St. Mary, Islington. Each 85 × 63mm. St Mary's view derived from *L19C* 160.

93 p 376 Unitarian Chapel, South Place Finsbury – Roman Catholic Chapel Moorfields. Each 60 × 85mm. Derived from *MI* 115, 46.

94 p 377 London Institution, Finsbury Circus – Albion Chapel, London Wall. 63 × 85, 60 × 85mm. Derived from *MI* 34, 121.

95 p 383 Cranbourne St. – New Coventry St. Each 60 × 85mm.

96 p 383 The Treasury, Whitehall. 85 × 140mm. Sir John Soane's building, completed in 1827 and illustrated in *MI* 64, had by 1846 had its façade dismantled by Sir Charles Barry, the Corinthian order raised up on a basement and urns added to the parapet.

97 p 383 Hanover Terrace/Regents Park – Cornwall Terrace/Regents Park. Each 60 × 85mm.

98 p 383 Kensington Palace – Queens Road Palace Gardens Bayswater. 60 × 83, 60 × 80mm.

99 p 384 Macclesfield Bridge/Regents Park – Centre of Cumberland Terrace/Regents Park. Each 60 × 85mm. The terrace, with added foliage, as *MI* 141.

100 p 384 Adelphi Theatre – Exeter Hall. Each 85 × 60mm.

101 p 385 Ironmongers Hall – Stationers Hall. Each 60 × 85mm. Derived from *L19C* 153, 51

102 p 385 Salters' Hall/St Swithins Lane – Drapers' Hall/Throgmorton Street. Each 60 × 85mm. Derived from *MI* 84, *L19C* 50.

103 p 385 Vintners' Hall/Upper Thames Street – Skinners' Hall/Dowgate Hill. Each 60 × 85mm. Derived from *L19C* 174, 47.

104 p 385 The Guildhall. 83 × 140mm.

105 p 387 Polytechnic Institution – Princess' Theatre. Each 60 × 85mm. The Polytechnic, Regent Street founded 1838; the Princess's Theatre in Oxford Street.

106 p 393 Haymarket Theatre – Covent Garden Theatre. Each 60 × 85mm.

107 p 394 Lyceum Theatre – Drury Lane Theatre. Each 60 × 85mm.

108 p 384 The Italian Opera House. A.H. Payne. 83 × 138mm.

109 p 399 Royal College of Surgeons – Apothecaries Hall. Each 60 × 85mm. A comparison of this view of the Royal College with *MI* 57 shows how Sir Charles Barry relieved the porch of its ponderous ornaments and crowned the building with a seemly entablature. Apothecaries' Hall as *L19C* 142.

110 p 399 The London University. 80 × 140mm. Derived from *MI* 108.

111 p 400 Crosby Hall/Bishopsgate Street – Office for Payne's Illustrated London. 60 × 85mm. The second view is of 88 Fleet Street, the shops of E.T. Brain & Co and, next door, Tilt & Bogue, booksellers and publishers. (*Longford* 435)

112 p 403 Interior of the House of Lords. 138 × 90mm. The House moved into Barry's building in 1847.

113 p 403 The New Library (Temple) – Furnivals Inn. Each 60 × 85mm. The Gothic Inner Temple Library built by Sir Robert Smirke, 1824–8; Furnivals Inn view derived from *MI* 76.

114 p 403 New Hall & Library Lincoln's Inn. 85 × 140mm. Built by P.C. Hardwick, 1843–5.

115 p 404 Grays Inn Hall – Middle Temple Hall. Each 60 × 85mm. E. end of Middle Temple Hall, with alterations, but Gray's Inn Hall unchanged. Derived from *L19C* 67, 56.

116 p 407 Licensed Victuallers' School – School for the Indigent Blind. Each 60 × 88mm. The former in Kennington, the latter in St George's Fields.

117 p 408 Whittington's Alms Houses, Highgate. 87 × 140mm.

208 · EINE WOCHE IN LONDON
[c 1849]

Albert Henry Payne was a draughtsman and engraver whose collection of small engravings, *Illustrated London* (no 207), was published by E.T. Brain in 1846–7. He spent much of his time in Germany, where he set up an engraving establishment in Leipzig from which he published this German seven-day tour of London, describing the chief buildings in some detail and giving information on transport facilities. It was issued, undated, in yellow wrappers printed in red and includes Payne's own steel-engraved plan of London with vignetted views, assigned by Darlington and Howgego to about 1846 (see item 1 below). Also there is a group of four plates, each with a number of small views, delicately engraved on steel and separated from each other by ornamental borders. The first plate combines, somewhat anachronistically, a view of Bunning's Coal Exchange (of which the foundation was laid at the end of 1847 but which was not officially opened until 1849) and one of Buckingham Palace, but not as a German tourist would have found it in 1849 since it shows the Marble Arch, removed in 1847, still in place and also Nash's east front to the Palace which by that time had been transformed by Blore.

The plates are unnumbered and have no credits but are headed by the word 'London' in voided capitals.

Eine Woche in London oder so sieht man die Riesenstadt mit allen ihren National-Anstalten und Instituten, offentlichen Gebäuden, Merkwürdigkeiten etc. in sieben Tagen—Mit 32 Ansichten in Stahlstich und 1 Plan von London. Leipzig und Dresden. Englische Kunstanstalt von A.H. Payne. London, W. French, 67 Paternoster Row.

Small octavo, 180 × 120mm.   c 1849

COLLATION   Title-page; pp iii–iv, contents; pp 1–78, Historische und beschreibende Skizze.

1 (tm) Payne's Illustrated Plan of London. Published for the Proprietors by A.H. Payne, Dresden and Leipzig. 410 × 750/440 × 780mm. With two views in vignettes: (tr) ? view of London from Hampstead ponds (80 × 145mm, (bc) showing the Palace of Westminster from Lambeth (50 × 140mm). (*Darlington and Howgego* 402)

2 St Paul's – Royal Exchange – Coal Exchange/ – Buckingham Palace (park front)– **Buckingham** Palace (garden front). 50 × 40, 50 × 80, 50 × 40; 50 × 80, 50 × 80/180 × 210mm. Of the two Palace views the first is Nash's E. front.

3 Horse Guards – Colosseum – London Bridge/ – Duke of York's Column – New Houses of Parliament – Limehouse Church/ – Bow Church – Mansion House – Fishmongers Hall. 28 × 50, 28 × 50, 28 × 50; 50 × 20, 50 × 110, 50 × 20; 28 × 50, 28 × 50, 28 × 50/180 × 210mm.

4 Regents Park – St James's Park – Whitechapel/ – Monument – Custom House – St Martin's Church/ – East India House – Somerset House – Quadrant. Leipzig d. Engl. Kunst Anstalt. 28 × 50, 28 × 50, 28 × 50; 50 × 33, 50 × 80, 50 × 33; 28 × 50, 28 × 50, 28 × 50/180 × 210mm. St Martin in the Fields; Somerset House seen from the Strand.

5 King William Street – The Upper Pool – Southwark Church/ – Westminster Hospital – Lambeth Palace – City of London School/ – Somerset House – General Post Office – The Bank of England. 28 × 50, 28 × 50, 28 × 50; 50 × 35, 50 × 80, 50 × 35; 30 × 50, 30 × 50, 30 × 50/180 × 210mm. Lambeth Palace courtyard; Somerset House from the river; the Bank from the S.

209 · ACKERMANN'S SERIES
[1851]

This set of ten lithographs was issued by Rudolph Ackermann, the eldest son of the publisher of the aquatints of *The Microcosm of London* (no 99) and of many other London views. Rudolph junior opened his own print shop in 1825 at no 191 of the newly completed and very fashionable Regent Street. Adjacent was his picture gallery, the Eclipse Sporting Gallery, shown to advantage on the last plate of the series. It was named after a famous racehorse of the day, for he addressed himself predominantly to the tastes of the hunting, shooting, boxing, horse-racing and driving fraternity in the pictures he showed and the prints he published. Pierce Egan's Tom and Jerry would have been among his customers and no less the Rawdon Crawleys since he also stocked military prints of the gorgeously accoutred soldiers of the Queen.

The Great Exhibition, however, brought to Regent Street crowds of provincial shoppers and visitors from the Continent who belonged to none of the categories of his usual squirearchical clientèle but were simply bent on drinking in the wonders of the capital, perhaps catching a glimpse of the young Queen being driven down the Mall, and bringing home with them a memento of what they had experienced. Seeing publishers and booksellers vying with each other in producing '1851' guide-books, maps and souvenir albums, Ackermann decided to enter into competition with his brother's firm, which still traded in the Strand after the father's death in 1834, and to offer the public a set of London views printed by lithography, which was then at the height of its popularity as a reproductive medium.

Not unnaturally his thoughts turned to a family of artists who were then pre-eminent in the field of London topographical illustration, the Shepherds. George and Thomas Hosmer, father and son, had early been employed on his own father's *Repository of the Arts* and *Westminster Abbey* (no 108) but Thomas had an even more accomplished elder brother, George Sidney Shepherd, and it was to him that Ackermann turned for representative views of the metropolis suitable for reproduction. They were printed by the Queen's lithographers, Messrs Day & Son, having been transferred to stone by Thomas Picken. In the following year Picken lithographed four of 12 much larger London views drawn by E. Walker for the same publisher.

The printing, as was usual with lithotints, was carried out by means of two stones, one printing in black line and the other adding an overall tint to the picture. Copies coloured by hand were available for those who cared to pay the extra. A more detailed account of the series is given by Ralph Hyde in his preface to a facsimile published by the Guildhall Library in 1972. Credits throughout read: 'Drawn by G.S. Shepherd. T. Picken lith.' and 'Day & Son Lithrs to the Queen'. Captions (bm) and the series note (tm), 'R. Ackermann's Series, No. ( )', are in voided capitals. Reissues, published by W.H.J. Carter, have his name added above the captions.

1 Windsor Castle. 180 × 280mm.

2 View from Richmond Hill. Published March 1st 1851 by Rudolph Ackermann. 185 × 280mm. (*Gascoigne* 734)

3 St. Paul's Cathedral. Published March 20th 1851 by Rudolph Ackermann. 202 × 275mm. The precinct is still completely surrounded by the iron railings erected in 1714. Sir John Kinnersley Hooper's name appended to a public notice suggests the drawing was made during his mayoralty, 1847–8.

4 Westminster Abbey. Published March 20th 1851 by Rudolph Ackermann. 195 × 275mm. View from N.W.

5 The Royal Exchange, and Bank of England. Published May 8th 1851 by Rudolph Ackermann. 220 × 280mm. W. front of Tite's Royal Exchange, opened 1844.

6 The Mansion House./Looking towards Cheapside. Published May 8th 1851 by Rudolph Ackermann. 205 × 278mm. From the same standpoint as Boys's in *London as it is* (no 196), item 2. Apart from the up-to-date staffage the only notable differences are that on the l. an extra bay of the Lombard Street building is included, the attic excretion on the roof of the Mansion House is missing (having been demolished in 1842), the house at the Walbrook-Poultry corner has been rebuilt, and the bell-turret has been removed from St Mildred, Poultry.

7 The Club Houses, Pall Mall. Published May 8th 1851 by Rudolph Ackermann. 208 × 278mm. From the same standpoint as Boys's in *London as it is*, item 13, but embraces a bay extra of the buildings to the N. and S. of Pall Mall.

8 The Horse Guards. Published May 8th 1851 by Rudolph Ackermann. 205 × 280mm. As seen from the park with a troop of Horse Guards making their way towards Wellington Barracks.

9 Buckingham Palace./Her Majesty's Escort—16th Lancers. Published May 8th 1851 by Rudolph Ackermann. 202 × 290mm. A close-up view of Blore's remodelling of the E. façade of the palace, completed 1847, when Nash's marble entrance archway was dismantled to be re-erected at Cumberland Gate in 1851. The Queen and Prince Consort are being escorted in an ordinary carriage-and-four.

10 View of Regent Street./Drawing Room Day. Published May 8th 1851 by Rudolph Ackermann. 222 × 305mm. Immediately to the l. of the spectator is Ackermann's bow window hung with prints and the Eclipse Sporting Gallery. Also visible are Lewis & Allenby's Lace Warehouse, which occupies nos 193, 195 and 197, and Cramer the music publisher at no 201. Beyond, the openings of Conduit Street, Maddox Street and Hanover Street are bathed in the afternoon sunshine. Almost closing the vista are the Ionic portico, twin towers and central dome of C.R. Cockerell's Hanover Chapel. A procession of Horse Guards is making its way towards the Palace.

485

210 · ARCHER'S VESTIGES OF OLD LONDON [1851]

A collection of drawings, which included over 450 of London architecture and antiquities housed in 17 portfolios, was bought by the British Museum in March 1874. They had belonged to William Twopenny of the Temple, who had commissioned from John Wykeham Archer about 20 each year and went on amassing this remarkable topographical hoard until the day of his death. Archer, an artist-antiquarian, was born in Newcastle-upon-Tyne but was trained as an engraver by John Scott of Clerkenwell, a specialist in animal portraits. He then returned north and worked a series of views of Fountains Abbey and plates for Mackenzie and Ross's *History of Durham* (1834). Back in London in about 1831, he worked for the engraver brothers Finden, well known both for their separate plates and their many book illustrations, and then set up on his own as an engraver on steel for the publishers of magazines and books. Plates of his are to be found in Ritchie's *The Wye and its Associations* (1841) and Beattie's *Castles and Abbeys of England* (1845). When the medium lost its popularity he became a wood-engraver for the *Illustrated London News* and works such as Charles Knight's *London* (1841–4).

He was also an associate member of the New Water Colour Society and his habit of exploring the London streets, sketching block in hand, must have become known to his patron. He died, by chance, in the same year as that other great London perambulator, T.H. Shepherd, who had drawn hundreds of views for another patron, Frederick Crace, much as Archer had done for Twopenny. The circumstances are outlined in the preface: 'The author having found matter for nearly three hundred drawings of remains, interesting for their architectural character, and historical associations, the greater part of which still exist in London, Middlesex and Southwark. By the favour of William Twopenny Esq., in whose collection these drawings are deposited, a careful selection has been made'.

Each of Archer's historical notes is printed as a separately paginated section, with the engraved view as a frontispiece. Only the first and longest note has its six plates distributed through the text. The work was published in Parts, the first being advertised by Bogue in December 1849: quarto 6s, on India paper 10s or coloured 12s.

Vestiges of Old London, A Series of Etchings from Original Drawings, Illustrative of the Monuments and Architecture of London. In the First, Fourth, Twelfth and Six succeeding Centuries. With Descriptions and Historical notes by John Wykeham Archer. London: David Bogue, 86 Fleet Street. MDCCCLI. (verso) Henry Vizetelly, Printer and Engraver, 15 and 16 Gough Square, Fleet Street.

Folio, 370 × 250–80mm.   1851

COLLATION   Half-title; title-page; contents (1 leaf); preface (1 leaf); pp 1–8, introduction; descriptions separately paginated.

The plates, etched on steel, recall by their subjects the work of J.T. Smith in *Antiquities of London* (no 70) and *Ancient Topography of London* (no 115). It is interesting to note how some of the 'antiquities', without any particular official effort to conserve them, have weathered 50 years and apparently remained intact. One of the London Wall towers in the Old Bailey, for example, had survived simply because it was discovered, and left standing at the end of his yard, by a local builder.

That said, however, it must be admitted that Archer was more successful at drawing the figures of people and animals (especially cats) which he introduces than was Smith and, although he did not diversify his medium, as Smith did, with aquatint and lithography, he was on the whole a more skilful engraver and was helped by the refinement of steel. Nevertheless these fine engravings must have seemed rather old-fasioned when they were published—in an age of lithographs, lithotints and various experiments in colour printing. This may account for their being coloured by hand in carefully applied washes, at first of pallid shades of ochre, green, pink and blue and later in the series with those same patches of stronger reds and blues on wearing apparel which T.S. Boys used in colour printing lithographs.

Captions and the invariable credit, 'J.W. Archer fect.', are printed in reddish-brown ink and quasi-Gothic lettering. Plates are unnumbered (except in the list) and undated and all bear the publication-line 'London, D. Bogue Fleet Street.' *BM* references are to the original drawings in the Archer portfolios at the Department of Prints and Drawings, together with their dates where known.

1 front. Monument of John Stow/St Andrew Undershaft, Leadenhall Street. 230 × 150mm. Vignetted.

pp 1–24, 1–2, The Wall of London

2 p 5 London Wall/Tower Postern. 155 × 220/230 × 310mm. *BM* 1.18 (1843).

3 p 13 London Wall/St Martin's Court, Ludgate Hill. 205 × 160/290 × 230mm. *BM* 1.20 (May 1848).

4 p 15 London Wall/Base of a tower in the church yard of St. Giles Cripplegate. 190 × 160/280 × 230mm. *BM* 1.25 (1841).

5 p 15 London Wall/Cripplegate Postern. 215 × 165/280 × 230mm. Fragment of Cripplegate pulled down 1760, in White Horse Inn Yard, showing a parish mark 'St G.C. 1841'. *BM* 1.26.

6 p 17 London Wall/South Wall of Cripplegate Postern. 215 × 145/280 × 225mm. *BM* 1.27 (1845).

7 p 21 London Wall/Remains near Trinity Square. 155 × 218/230 × 280mm. Depicted before 1850; forms part of Atkinson's hemp warehouse. *BM* 1.30.

8 p 1 Interior of a Tower belonging to the Wall of London. Old Bailey. 145 × 210/235 × 280mm. *BM* 1.21 (1845).

pp 1–4, Roman Altar of Diana

9 p 1 Altar of Diana—discovered in Foster Lane. 230 × 280mm. Details of altar discovered December 1830. *BM* 1.1 (1846).

pp 1–6, Vestiges of Roman London

10 p 1 Roman Vestiges. 285 × 230mm. *BM* 1. 15, 16.

pp 1–6, Lambeth Palace

11 p 1 Crypt under the Chapel/Lambeth Palace. 145 × 205/230 × 285mm. *BM* 8.6 (March 1841).

pp 1–4, 1–4, 1–12, Remains of the Priory of St Bartholomew

12 p 1 + The Tomb of Rahere/ In the Priory Church of St. Bartholomew Smithfield. 165 × 220/230 × 275mm. *BM* 4.9 (1841).

13 p 1 Room in the Coach and Horses /Bartholomew Close. 215 × 165/285 × 230mm. Occupies the N. end of the cloisters. *BM* 4.19 (August 1841).

14 p 1 West Gate of St Bartholomew's Priory/ Smithfield. 195 × 140/280 × 230mm. *BM* 4.15.

pp 1–4, Tower of London

15 p 1 Salt Tower—Tower of London. 220 × 160/285 × 230mm. Portion disclosed by demolition of neighbouring house, 9 November 1846. *BM* 2.1.

pp 1–2, Bermondsey Abbey

16 p 1 + Remains of the East Gate + Bermondsey Abbey +. 218 × 155/290 × 230mm. *BM* 7.23 (1842).

pp 1–4, St Bartholomew's, Kingsland

17 p 1 + Chapel of St Bartholomew + Kingsland. 152 × 220/225 × 285mm. Building removed 1846. *BM* 16.5 (1841).

pp 1–2, Milborn's Alms Houses

18 p 1 The Drapers Alms Houses Crutched Friars. 220 × 152/290 × 230mm. Founded by Sir John Milbourne, 1535; removed 1861. *BM* 2.11 (1843).

pp 1–2, Tothill Street, Westminster

19 p 1 Room in the King's Arms/ Tothill Street Westminster. 138 × 205/230 × 285mm. *BM* 13.6 (February 1845).

20 p 2 Wood carving and original sign of the House/ Cock Inn. Tothill Street, Westminster. 290 × 230mm. Details. The sign is a Tudor 'King's Arms', the original name of the house, and the carving is an 'Adoration of the Magi'. *BM* 13.7 (February 1845).

pp 1–2, Cock and Magpie

21 p 1 The Cock and Magpie,/Drury Lane. 212 × 160/280 × 220mm. Includes view of St Mary le Strand steeple. *BM* 10.23 (March 1847).

pp 1–2, Monument from Old St. Paul's

22 p 1 Monuments belonging to Old St. Pauls. 155 × 225/230 × 280mm. Effigies of Sir William Cockayne, Sir Christopher Hatton, Dr Donne, Sir Nicholas Bacon, Dr Nowell and Lady Cockayne. *BM* 3.27 (1843).

pp 1–6, Southampton House

23 p 1 Staircase of Southampton House, Holborn. 230 × 180/280 × 230mm. Top corners of engraving rounded off. *BM* 11.17 (January 1846).

pp 1–4, Sir Paul Pindar's House

24 p 1 House of Sir Paul Pindar/ Bishopsgate Street Without. 220 × 150/280 × 225mm. *BM* 6.15 (1843).

pp 1–2, Old Mansion, Petticoat Lane

25 p 1 Door of an old Mansion/ in Gravel Lane Hounsditch said to have been a residence of Count Gondomar. 210 × 150/285 × 225mm. Pulled down 1844. *BM* 6.21 (1844).

pp 1–2, Gray's Inn

26 p 1 Room in Fulwood's Rents/ Grays Inn. 165 × 218/230 × 285mm. *BM* 14.17 (1850).

pp 1–2, Clerkenwell

27 p 1 Chimney in the Baptists Head/ Clerkenwell. 158 × 218/230 × 280mm. On E. side of St John's Lane. *BM* 14.27.

pp 1–2, St. Saviour's, Southwark

28 p 1 Tomb of Bishop Andrews/ in the Lady Chapel St Saviours, Southwark. 192 × 155/290 × 225mm. *BM* 7.19 (1839).

pp 1–12, Milton's House, Petty France

29 p 1 The House of Milton and Tree planted by him/ in Petty France, Westminster. 225 × 162/280 × 225mm. Milton lived at no 19, 1652–60. *BM* 13.9 (14 May 1845).

pp 1–2, Dryden's House, Fetter Lane

30 p 1 The House of John Dryden, Fetter Lane. 220 × 155/285 × 225mm. Shows Fleur de Lis Court. *BM* 9.19 (1842). (*BM* 13.27 shows Dryden's residence at 43 Gerrard Street, Soho drawn by Archer in 1858.)

pp 1–6, Temple Bar

31 p 1 Old Bulk Shop, Temple Bar. 220 × 165/280 × 225mm. The pent roof to this shop, Short & Son, fishmongers, was removed in 1846 and the house demolished in 1865. A sandwich-board passing under Temple Bar advertises the Egyptian Hall exhibition of Benjamin Robert Haydon's painting 'The Banishment of Aristides' the failure of which caused him to commit suicide in 1846. *BM* 9.20 (1846).

pp 1–2, Clarendon House, Piccadilly

32 p 1 Remains of Clarendon House/ Three Kings Livery Stables, Piccadilly. 210 × 150/290 × 230mm. The house itself demolished 1683. *BM* 13.17 (November 1847).

pp 1–6, 1–10, Fleet Ditch

33 p 1 Old Houses with the open part of the Fleet Ditch/ near Field Lane. 180 × 165/280 × 230mm. The Ditch was soon after covered over. *BM* 11.13 (1841).

34 p 7 Interior of the Fleet Ditch/ at the back of Field Lane. 125 × 230/225 × 270mm. Covered-over section, Holborn Bridge beyond. *BM* 11.12.

pp 1–4, 1–2, 1–2, Street Monuments, Signs, Badges, &c.

35 p 1 1, Mercers' Company Badge – 2, Chained Swan, Cheapside – 3, Panyer Alley – 4, Seven Stars, Cheapside – 5, Sun, Cheapside. 225 × 280mm. *BM* 17.14 (1842).

36 p 1 1, Gryphon's Head – 2, Boar's Head, Eastcheap – 3, Four Doves Alley, St Martins le Grand – 4, Pelican, Aldermanbury – 5, The Old George, Snow Hill. 225 × 280mm. *BM* 17. 3, 11, 12, 14, 17.

37 p 1 1, Medallion, Old Jewry – 2, Arms of Oxford University, Little Distaff Lane – 3, Adam and Eve, the Fruiterers' Company – 4, The Bear, Addle Street – 5, The Ape, Philip Lane – 6, The Unicorn, 39 Cheapside. 225 × 280mm. *BM* 17.2, 7, 17.

211 · HOLMES'S GREAT METROPOLIS [1851]

Thomas Holmes, who succeeded to the bookselling business of Edward Lacey in 1847, when in search of a London memento attractive to visitors to the Great Exhibition decided to reissue W.G Fearnside's text for Woods's *History of London* (no 188), first published in 1838 with 30 plates mostly engraved by John Woods; to freshen it up he added ten pages of comment on more recent events but the original index remained unrevised. For illustrations he used its original plates, including the title-page which was simply re-engraved 'Holmes's' instead of 'Woods's Views', but removed the W.S. Orr publication-lines and most of the credits. To arrive at a round number of 50 he added to these 15 plates from another, similarly dated book, *Select Illustrated Topography of Thirty Miles Round London* (no 190), together with five fresh views intended to give the whole an appearance of contemporaneity. They were of the Exhibition building itself and of notable rebuildings in the intervening years: Sir Charles Barry's Treasury Buildings and House of Lords, Sir William Tite's Royal Exchange and Bunning's Coal Exchange. These additional plates have no publication-lines and only one has credits.

Plate-marks have been cropped by the binder. References in the list below are to items in Woods's *History* (abbreviated *WHL*) and to *Select Illustrated Topography* (abbreviated *SIT*). Plates are unnumbered and the publisher's check-list gives no clearer indication of those culled from *SIT* than '&c., &c., &c.'

Holmes's Great Metropolis: or Views and History of London in the Nineteenth Century being A Grand National Exhibition of The British Capital. With historical and topographical Notices of each place. Edited by William Gray Fearnside, Esq., and Thomas Harrel. Illustrated with fifty splendid steel engravings. London: Published by Thomas Holmes, (Successor to Edward Lacey,) Great Book Establishment, 76 St Paul's Church-yard.

Octavo, 240–85 × 145–220mm. (1851)

COLLATION Title-page; list of plates (1 leaf); pp 1–211, History; p 212, index.

1 (engr title) Holmes's/Views in/London, Westminster,/ and/Their Vicinities. (vignette) Monument/and/St Magnus Church. J.H. Shepherd del. J. Woods sc. London, Published by W.S. Orr & Co., Amen Corner, Paternoster Row, June 1st. 130 × 100mm. *WHL* 1.

2 front. Mansion House. 105 × 155mm. *WHL* 17.

3 p 1 Exhibition. 105 × 152. The building in Hyde Park.

4 p 1 The New Royal Exchange. 103 × 150mm. Opened 1844. *WHL* 31.

5 p 4 London/from Highgate. C. Marshall. 100 × 145mm. *SIT* 20.

6 p 8 General Post Office/St Martins le Grand. 102 × 150mm. *WHL* 19.

7 p 14 City of London School./Milk Street. Drawn by Hablot Browne, from a Sketch by R. Garland. Engraved by J. Woods. 148 × 107mm. *WHL* 22.

8 p 20 Quadrant/Regent Street. 103 × 150mm. *WHL* 24.

9 p 24 View looking from the Gallery of the/Duke of York's Column/St James's Park. C. Marshall. J.C. Varrall. 100 × 148mm. *SIT* 25.

10 p 26 Leadenhall Street. 105 × 150mm. *WHL* 18.

11 p 32 Southwark, Church &c. Drawn by Hablot Browne from a Sketch by R. Garland. Engraved by J. Woods. 105 × 150mm. *WHL* 9.

12 p 38 High Street, Whitechapel. 98 × 155mm. *WHL* 7.

13 p 44 Hornsey Church/Middlesex. C. Marshall. W. Henshall. 100 × 145mm. *SIT* 18.

14 p 46 Buckingham Palace. 100 × 150mm. *WHL* 25.

15 p 52 London Bridge. 105 × 150mm. *WHL* 11.

16 p 56 Westminster/from Chelsea Fields. C. Marshall. J.C. Varrall. 98 × 143mm. *SIT* 24.

17 p 60 Horse Guards. 105 × 148mm. *WHL* 27.

18 p 64 Gate House Highgate/Middlesex. J. Henshall. T. Cox. 95 × 155mm. *SIT* 19.

19 p 66 Fishmongers' Hall. 105 × 150mm. *WHL* 12.

20 p 72 Chalk Farm Bridge/Birmingham Railway. 92 × 150mm. *SIT* 32.

21 p 74 Westminster Hospital/and/Abbey Church. 103 × 150mm. *WHL* 10.

22 p 80 Cheapside/and/Bow Church. 103 × 153mm. *WHL* 5.

23 p 88 Duke of York's Column. 100 × 145mm. *WHL* 28.

24 p 92 Woolwich. 98 × 145mm. *SIT* 11.

25 p 94 View in Westminster Abbey/from the altar. Drawn by I. Salmon from a Sketch by R. Garland. Engraved by I. Woods. 150 × 102mm. *WHL* 16.

26 p 100 Barking Church/Essex. C. Marshall. J.C. Bentley. 98 × 142mm. *SIT* 8.

27 p 102 King William Street,/and/St. Mary Woolnoth. 103 × 153mm. *WHL* 2.

28 p 108 St. Katherine's Hospital/Regents **Park. Drawn** by I. Salmon from a Sketch by R. Garland. Engraved by I. Woods. 100 × 148mm. *WHL* 30.

29 p 112 Hampton/Middlesex. C. Marshall. W. Floyd. 100 × 145mm. *SIT* 13.

30 p 116 Custom House. 103 × 150mm. *WHL* 6.

31 p 122 Coliseum/Regents Park. 103 × 150mm. *WHL* 29.

32 p 128 Hampton Court/Middlesex. 100 × 145mm. *SIT* 14.

33 p 130 Cumberland Terrace,/Regents Park. 103 × 150mm. *WHL* 15.

34 p 136 The Upper Pool. 103 × 151mm. *WHL* 4.

35 p 144 Somerset House,/Strand. 105 × 150mm. *WHL* 13.

36 p 148 Staines Bridge/Middlesex. C. Marshall. J. Henshall. 100 × 148mm. *SIT* 31.

37 p 150 The Late/Royal Exchange/and/Cornhill. 103 × 150mm. 'The Late' added to the original caption. This building was destroyed by fire in January 1838; see item 4 above for its replacement. *WHL* 20.

38 p 158 St Martin's Church/from/Charing Cross. Engd by I. Woods. 155 × 103mm. *WHL* 14.

39 p 164 Royal Exchange/destroyed by Fire Jany 10th 1838. 105 × 145mm. The inner courtyard. *WHL* 21.

40 p 172 West India Dock,/Import. 103 × 151mm. *WHL* 3.

41 p 180 View in St. James's Park. J. Salmon del. J. Woods sc. 100 × 152mm. *WHL* 26.

42 p 184 Limehouse Church. Drawn by Hablot Browne from a Sketch by R. Garland. Engraved by J. Woods. 145 × 105mm. *WHL* 23.

43 p 188 Vauxhall Gardens. C. Marshall. C. Mottram. 100 × 140mm. *SIT* 17.

44 p 192 Billingsgate. 103 × 160mm. *WHL* 8.

45 p 196 Twickenham/Ait/Middlesex. 100 × 145mm. *SIT* 27.

46 p 200 Greenwich Hospital. 100 × 148mm. *SIT* 5.

47 p 204 Windsor Castle. C. Marshall. W. Henshall. 100 × 145mm. *SIT* 2.

48 p 207 Treasury, Whitehall. 105 × 150mm. 'Has assumed a very different character under the transforming hand of Mr. Barry'. Built 1844–5.

49 p 208 House of Lords. Boyd and Cannavan sc. 105 × 153mm. Building of the new Houses of Parliament had commenced in 1840 and was still in progress.

50 p 210 Coal Exchange. 105 × 150mm. Built by J.B. Bunning, 1849.

212 · ROZENBOOM'S LONDEN EN ZIJNE MERKWAARDIGHEN [1851]

The Great Exhibition was the pretext for enterprising European publishers to compile and print guides to London in the vernacular and the existence of this one, from De Jong of Arnhem, indicates that there was sufficient flow of visitors from Holland at mid-century to make it worth while to publish a pocket guide to its sights, transport and, in particular, its hotel and eating facilities. The author's name is printed on the buff paper wrappers, as transcribed, but not on the similar title-page.

Four quite adequate steel-engravings, with no individual credits but the general ascription 'd. Kunst-Verlag', are there to remind the Dutch tourist of the highlights of the visit.

Londen en Zijne Merkwaardighen bewerkt, Volgens de Beeste Bronnen (door H.J. Rozenboom). Met 4 Staalgravuren. Arnhem, P.A. de Jong, 1851.

Octavo, 208 × 165mm.   1851

COLLATION   Half-title; title-page; pp v–vi, preface; pp vii–viii, contents; pp 1–68, Londen.

1 front. Het Greenwich Hospitaal. 95 × 148mm. From N.E.

2 p 23 St Pauls Kerk/van de Theems de zien. 95 × 148mm. From S. Bank.

3 p 27 Londen-Brug. 98 × 140mm. From Tooley Stairs.

4 p 45 Tower van Londen. 95 × 137mm. From the river.

213 · MIGHTY LONDON [1851–5]

Of all the collections of London illustrations this, issued by Mary Read & Co of Johnson's Court, Fleet Street, has proved the most inscrutable. About a quarter of the total number of plates carry numerals relating to some sequence and the text is broken up into short articles, each one intended to refer to an individual plate; this suggests original publication in Numbers. These were then collected into two Series, each with its separate index: 'The Publishers of Mighty London finding it is the intention of many Subscribers to bind the Work up in two volumes, have printed the Index in a convenient form for that purpose ... Covers complete for the Work, either in One or Two Volumes, can be had on application to the Publishers'. The individual check-lists of plates were discarded when the two Series were bound together in a single volume and, as a result, it is impossible to predict which particular illustrations will be found where in any given copy. Especially this applies to the Great Exhibition and Crystal Palace, Sydenham views which, although carefully numbered in a separate sequence, are rarely included as a complete set with either of the two Series.

Further to complicate collation at least five different title-pages, all undated, were issued: one each, printed, for the two Series; an additional engraved title for the first Series; a printed title for the Manchester issue of the book; and an arresting title printed in display types of blue and gold for the later, consolidated edition. All have significant variations of wording but references from the publication-lines of the plates are invariably to 'Mighty London Illustrated' or 'Mighty London'.

The text of the first Series may approximately be dated by a reference, on p 44, to 29 September 1851, on which date 'Commissioners appointed to choose a site for a new National Gallery have just published a Report', and that of the second Series by references, on p 165, to the launching of the *Royal Albert* in May 1854 and to the opening of the Crystal Palace on Sydenham Hill on 10 June 1854. The consolidated edition contains a map dated 1860.

Of the two copies recorded in the Abbey collection (2881, 3584) the first, an oblong quarto measuring 260 × 370mm, comprises two Series of 42 and 48 plates each, without text but with the title 'Views of Mighty London'. The second copy, a quarto of 292 × 238mm, consists of 110 plates interpolated in 236 pages of text, with an engraved title corresponding to item 0 below.

(*Title-page* pl. 0)

Quarto, 290 × 238mm   nd

COLLATION   Engr title-page; list of plates (1 leaf); pp

490

1–112, Mighty London; index (2pp); title-page (of second Series, ed by H.S. Brooke); list of plates (1 leaf); pp 113–236, Mighty London continued; index (2pp).

A variant title-page (BL: 10350.3.6) reads:

The World's Metropolis or Mighty London, Illustrated. Including the most interesting Buildings Twenty miles round, the Royal Palaces of Great Britain &c. &c. Second Series. Edited by H.S. Brooke Esq., London; Read & Co., Publishers, 10 Johnson's Court, Fleet Street, Paris: H. Mandeville, 16 Rue Dauphiné.

The Manchester edition makes no mention of 'The World's Metropolis':

The History of Mighty London and its Environs: Illustrated. James Ainsworth & Co. No 93, Piccadilly, Manchester. Read & Co. 10 Johnson's Court, Fleet Street, London

The blue and gold title of the later, consolidated edition also makes no mention of 'The World's Metropolis':

London and Its Environs Twenty Miles Round. Including besides its General History, Interior & Exterior Views of Royal Palaces of England, the Houses of Parliament, the New Crystal Palace at Sydenham, the Great Exhibition of 1851 and all the most interesting public & private buildings, streets, Parks, Places of Note &c. &c. in and around the Great Metropolis. Read & Compy, 10 Johnson's Court, Fleet Street, London. H. Mandeville, 42 Rue Vivienne, Paris. R. Mosley, New York.

Quarto, 270 × 205mm.   c 1860

COLLATION Title-page; pp 1–236, Mighty London; index to first Series (2 pp); index to second Series (2 pp)

This work is sometimes found in catalogues under the name of the artist, T.H. Shepherd, since he is mentioned on the engraved title-page. Although by no means the sole illustrator, the 25 drawings he contributes form an interesting supplement to his earlier and more extensive work for *Metropolitan Improvements* and its sequel (nos 154, 161) and enable him to record subsequent 'improvements' such as Nash's Marble Arch, now at Cumberland Gate, and Burton's completed Constitution Arch, Carlton House Terrace, Trafalgar Square and the new façade applied to Buckingham Palace by Blore. Indeed the credits that most frequently recur, in pairs, are those of 'Read', perhaps an artist member of the publisher's family, and either Albutt or 'Chavanne', who was perhaps the Lyons engraver, painter and sculptor who thus signed himself. Twelve anonymous lithotints mark special occa-

sions, such as the re-erection and reopening of the Crystal Palace at Sydenham Hill (items 93–101) and the visit to London of Napoleon III and his Empress in April 1855 (items 28, 33), and depict the royal residences of Balmoral and Holyrood. Two steel-engravings showing St Clement Danes and Newington Causeway (items 27, 85) were presumably added as a makeweight since their captions are in copperplate script in place of the otherwise uniformly voided capitals.

Publication-lines which contain sometimes only the London publisher and at other times add the agents in Paris and New York, are set out in full. They are undated, with rare exceptions: the portrait of the Prince Consort (20 June 1854) and the Napoleonic visit referred to above, which advances the dating of the second Series to May 1855.

The Great Exhibition for its duration dominated the London scene and John Tallis and a number of other publishers issued detailed illustrated accounts of it in Parts, later to be bound. Consequently *Mighty London*, whose real theme was topography and architecture, was extended by the publisher to include views of Paxton's great glass Palace and of some of the national displays to be seen inside it. By the time the second Series was drawing to an end the Exhibition in Hyde Park had closed, so this was supplemented by illustrations of the Crystal Palace as re-erected on Sydenham Hill where it was opened again on 10 June 1854 in the presence of the Queen, the Prince Consort and the King of Portugal. There is some disagreement among binders as to where these extra plates should appear; in the list below they are grouped towards the end of each of the Series. Other plates are usually bound as close as possible to the text which refers to their subjects. All engravings and lithographs met with in several copies of *Mighty London* are here listed but are unlikely to be found in their entirety in any one copy. Indeed some editions contain no more than a selection. Such is *Les Beautés Architecturales de Londres* issued by the French agent Mandeville, and by Read at £1 1s in November 1853, with only 35 steel-engravings: 24 of London generally and 11 of the Great Exhibition.

Colour has been added to the steel-engravings and lithotints in rare instances only.

SER 1

0 (engr title) The World's Metropolis,/or/Mighty Lon-

don,/illustrated by a Series of Views beautifully Engraved on Steel./Of its/Palaces, Public Buildings, Monuments & Streets,/from original drawings by Thomas H. Shepherd, Esqr./To which is added/A Comprehensive History from the earliest Period to the Present Day./(vignette) Residence of the late Sir Robert Peel, Bart./Whitehall Gardens./London./Published for the Proprietors. Read & Co. Engravers & Printers, 10 Johnson's Court, Fleet St. 145 × 190mm. Vignetted. Sir Robert Peel died on 2 July 1850. In some copies this vignette is also found, without the title lettering, facing p 196. An original Shepherd water-colour (152 × 216mm) in BM (*Crace* 16.60) and a pencil drawing (135 × 185mm) in Westminster Public Library.

1 front. Victoria R. 240 × 175mm. Stipple portrait with signature in facsimile. No credit or publication-line.

2 front. Albert. 240 × 175mm. Stipple portrait of the Prince Consort with signature in facsimile. In first state without publication-line but found also facing p 113, to introduce the second Series, with the line: 'London, Read & Co. 10 Johnson's Ct. Fleet St. June 20, 1854'.

3 p 1 New Houses of Parliament./From Lambeth Palace. Read. Lacey. London, Read & Co. 10, Johnson's Ct. Fleet St./Paris, H. Mandeville. 155 × 230mm. No 47. The perspective of this view makes it appear that the Palace is within a stone's throw of Barry's Parliament building, as does that of a larger engraving by T.A. Prior, 'Westminster from Bishop's Walk Lambeth', published in J.C. Anderson's retrospective *English landscapes & views* (1883). cf with item 68 below, an alternative view.

4 p 6 Hyde Park Gardens./From Victoria Gate. Read. Lacey. London, Read & Co. 10 Johnson's Ct. Fleet St./Paris: H. Mandeville. 155 × 230mm. No 61.

5 p 9 The Marble Arch./Hyde Park Corner, Oxford St. T.H. Shepherd. Lacey. *Engraved for Mighty London Illustrated.* Read & Co. 10 Johnson's Ct. Fleet St. 157 × 235mm. ie at Cumberland Gate, where it was re-erected in 1851. An original water-colour (178 × 267mm) in BM (*Crace* 29.119).

6 p 10 The Crystal Palace./From the Serpentine./No. 1. Engraved for the Publisher, Read & Co. 10, Johnson's Ct. Fleet St. 158 × 228. No credits.

6a p 10 The Crystal Palace in Hyde Park for the Great International Exhibition of 1851./The Building was designed by Joseph Paxton Esq. of Chatsworth.... Engraved & Printed by Read & Co. 10 Johnson's Court, Fleet Street. 190 × 485mm. Rounded top corners. The caption includes the dimensions. This alternative for item 6 is found in the Royal Library, Windsor copy.

7 p 14 Kensington Palace. Shepherd. Wrightson. *Engraved for Mighty London Illustrated.* Read & Co. 10 Johnson's Ct. Fleet St. 156 × 225mm.

8 p 16 Triumphal Arch & Duke of Wellington's Statue./Constitution Hill. Shepherd. Albutt. *Engraved for Mighty London Illustrated.* Read & Co. 10 Johnson's Ct. Fleet St. 163 × 230mm. The 30 ft high statue of Wellington by James Wyatt, cast in bronze in 1846, was immediately an object of ridicule which did not cease until it was removed from the arch in 1883.

9 p 18 Apsley House & Entrance to Hyde Park./Piccadilly. Shepherd. Wrightson. *Engraved for Mighty London Illustrated.* Read & Co. 10 Johnson's Ct. Fleet St. 157 × 228mm. Built by Robert Adam; refaced by Benjamin and Philip Wyatt, 1828.

10 p 23 Buckingham Palace./(New Front). T.H. Shepherd. Le Pettit. *Engraved for Mighty London.* Read & Co. 10 Johnson's Ct. Fleet St. 153 × 235mm. E. front as remodelled by Edward Blore, 1846–7.

11 p 24 Buckingham Palace./From the Private Grounds./London: Read & Co. 10 Johnson's Ct. Fleet St. Paris; H. Mandeville/New York: H. Moseley. 155 × 227mm. No 57. No credits.

12 p 28 The Horse Guards/From facing St. James's Park. Williams. Le Pettit. *Engraved for Mighty London Illustrated.* Read & Co. 10 Johnson's Ct. Fleet St. 155 × 235mm.

13 p 28 Conservative Club & St. James's Palace./St. James's Street. Read. Woods. London, Read & Co. 10, Johnson's Ct. Fleet St./Paris, H. Mandeville. 158 × 230mm. No 49. Built by G. Basevi and S. Smirke, 1843–5.

14 p 34 Regent's Circus, Oxford St./ T.H. Jones. Lacey. London, Read & Co. 10, Johnson's Ct. Fleet St./Paris, H. Mandeville, 42 Rue Vivienne. 155 × 225mm. No 41.

15 p 34 The Quadrant, Regent's Street. Shepherd. Chavanne. *Engraved for Mighty London Illustrated.* Read & Co. 10 Johnson's Ct. Fleet St. 155 × 225mm. No 26. cf with item 90 below, an alternative view.

16 p 35 Carlton House Terrace & Duke of York's Column./From St. James's Park. Shepherd. Allan. *Engraved for Mighty London Illustrated.* Read & Co. 10 Johnson's Ct. Fleet St. 155 × 235mm. The terrace built by John Nash, 1827–33, the column by Benjamin Wyatt, 1831–4.

17 p 36 Pall Mall./Wellington's Funeral Procession passing the Senior United Services Club. Read. Chavanne. London, Read & Co. 10, Johnson's Ct. Fleet St./Paris, H. Mandeville. 160 × 222mm. No 52. September 1852.

18 p 36 Army & Navy Club./Pall Mall. Shepherd. Patten. *Engraved for Mighty London Illustrated.* Read & Co., 10 Johnson's Ct. Fleet St. 158 × 230mm. Opened on 25 February 1851, built by Parnell and Smith; now demolished.

19 p 37 Marlborough House./The Residence of the late Queen Dowager (now the Vernon Gallery). Shepherd. Le Pettit. *Engraved for Mighty London Illustrated.* Read & Co. 10 Johnson's Ct. Fleet St. 158

× 225mm. From 1849 a temporary home for paintings to be housed in 1859 in the South Kensington Museum.

20 p 40 The Italian Opera House./(Her Majesty's Theatre)/Haymarket. Read. Albutt. London, Read & Co., 10, Johnson's Ct. Fleet St. Paris, H. Mandeville. 165 × 227mm.

21 p 42 Trafalgar Square. T.H. Shepherd. Alais. *Engraved for Mighty London Illustrated.* Read & Co. 10 Johnson's Ct. Fleet St. 150 × 228mm.

22 p 47 Northumberland House, Trafalgar Sqre./(From St. Martin's Lane.) Jones. Albutt. *Engraved for Mighty London Illustrated.* Read & Co. 10 Johnson's Ct. Fleet St. 195 × 225mm. No 36. Morley's Hotel on the l.

23 p 48 Hungerford Suspension Bridge. T.H. Shepherd. H.S. Barnard. *Engraved for Mighty London Illustrated.* Read & Co. 10 Johnson's Ct. Fleet St. 155 × 228mm.

24 p 49 Theatre Royal Covent Garden. London, Read & Co. 10 Johnson's Ct. Fleet St. 155 × 225mm. No 80. No credits.

25 p 52 Somerset House./From Waterloo Bridge. Clark. *Engraved for Mighty London Illustrated.* Read & Co. 10 Johnson's Ct. Fleet St. 160 × 225mm.

26 p 52 Somerset House & St. Mary le Strand./Strand. Read. Chavanne. London, Read & Co. 10, Johnson's Ct. Fleet St./Paris, H. Mandeville, 42 Rue Vivienne. 165 × 220mm. No 39.

27 p 54 St. Clement Danes, Strand. 160 × 230mm. No credits or publication-line. The view includes many trade names, eg the *Illustrated London News.* Caption in copperplate script.

28 p 54 Temple Bar, Fleet St./Visit of the Emperor Napoleon III & the Empress Eugénie to the City Thursday, April 19th, 1855. London, Published May 2nd, 1855 by Read & Co. 10, Johnson's Ct. Fleet St. 150 × 220m. Lithograph.

29 p 61 St. Paul's Cathedral./from Ludgate Hill. T.H. Shepherd. Redaway. *Engraved for Mighty London Illustrated.* Read & Co. 10 Johnson's Ct. Fleet St. 212 × 175mm. This plate sometimes as front. to first Series.

30 p 65 St. Paul's Cathedral./South Side, from Cannon Street. Lambert. Lambert. No 75 of Read's View of London. Published by Read & Co. 10 Johnson's Court, Fleet Street, 157 × 223mm.

31 p 71 General Post Office./St. Martins-le-Grand. Read. Wood. London, Read & Co. 10, Johnson's Ct. Fleet St./Paris, H. Mandeville. 155 × 225mm. No 56.

32 p 81 The Guildhall./King St. Shepherd. Lacey. *Engraved for Mighty London Illustrated.* Read & Co. 10 Johnson's Ct. Fleet St. 154 × 227mm. No 33.

33 p 81 Interior of the Guildhall./The Lord Mayor & Corporation presenting their address to the Empress & Emperor of the French, April 19th, 1855. Published May 2nd 1855 by Read & Co. 10, Johnson's Ct. Fleet St. 150 × 223mm. Lithograph.

34 p 86 The Mansion House./(Official Residence of the Lord Mayor.) Shepherd. Albutt. *Engraved for Mighty London Illustrated.* Read & Co. 10 Johnson's Ct. Fleet St. 158 × 228mm.

35 p 94 Goldsmith's Hall./Foster Lane. Read. Albutt. London, Read & Co. 10 Johnson's Ct. Fleet St./Paris, H. Mandeville. 155 × 225mm.

36 p 97 Bank of England. Shepherd. Albutt. *Engraved for Mighty London Illustrated.* Read & Co. 10 Johnson's Ct. Fleet St. 160 × 225mm. (*Bank of England* 117)

37 p 100 The Royal Exchange. Read & Co. Engravers & Printers, 10 Johnson's Ct. Fleet St. 160 × 230mm. No credits.

38 p 106 King William St./London Bridge. Jones. Hopkins. *Engraved for Mighty London Illustrated.* Read & Co. 10 Johnson's Ct. Fleet St. 163 × 233mm. No 35.

39 p 107 The Monument./Fish St. Hill. Shepherd. Clark. *Engraved for Mighty London Illustrated.* Read & Co. 10 Johnson's Ct. Fleet St. 153 × 230mm.

40 p 112 Custom House & London Bridge. T.H. Shepherd. Chavanne. *Engraved for Mighty London Illustrated.* Read & Co. 10 Johnson's Ct. Fleet St. 158 × 228mm.

41 p 112 Exterior View of the Great Exhibition of all Nations./From the Serpentine. Read. Chavanne. *Engraved for Mighty London Illustrated* & Published by Read & Co. 10 Johnson's Ct. Fleet St. 165 × 230mm.

42 p 112 Interior of the Great Exhibition./No. 2./North Transept. Chavanne. *Engraved for Mighty London Illustrated.* Read & Co. 10, Johnson's Ct. Fleet St. 165 × 237mm.

43 p 112 Interior of the Crystal Palace,/or/Great Building for International Exhibition, Hyde Park./No. 3. T.H. Shepherd. Chavanne. *Engraved for Mighty London Illustrated.* Read & Co. 10, Johnson's Ct. Fleet St. 165 × 230mm.

44 p 112 Interior of the Great Exhibition./No. 4./From the Transept looking East. Read. Clark. London: Read & Co. 10, Johnson's Ct. Fleet St. 165 × 232mm.

45 p 112 Interior of the Great Exhibition./No. 5./From the Transept looking West. Chavanne. Chavanne. *Engraved for Mighty London Illustrated.* Read & Co. 10, Johnson's Ct. Fleet St. 168 × 230mm.

46 p 112 Interior of the Great Exhibition./No. 6./American Department (East End). Read. Chavanne. *Engraved for Mighty London Illustrated.* Read & Co. 10, Johnson's Ct. Fleet St. 170 × 230mm.

47 p 112 Interior of the Great Exhibition./No. 7./South Transept. Read. Chavanne. Engraved for the Pub-

493

lishers. Read & Co. 10, Johnson's Ct. Fleet St. 170 × 225mm.

48 p 112 Interior of the Great Exhibition./No. 8./ British Department. Read. Chavanne. Engraved for the Publishers, Read & Co. 10, Johnson's Ct. Fleet St. 168 × 228mm.

49 p 112 Interior of the Great Exhibition./No. 9./From Dante's Temple. Clark delt. et sculpt. *Engraved for Mighty London Illustrated.* Read & Co. 10, Johnson's Ct. Fleet St. 167 × 230mm.

50 p 112 Interior of the Great Exhibition./No. 10./Grand State Opening May 1, 1851. Read. Chavanne. Engraved for the Publishers, Read & Co., 10 Johnson's Ct. Fleet St. 163 × 230mm.

51 p 112 Her Majesty's Boudoir./In the Great Exhibition of 1851./No. 11./Read. Chavanne. *Engraved for Mighty London Illustrated.* Read & Co. 10 Johnson's Ct., Fleet St. 168 × 225mm.

52 p 112 The Great Exhibition of all Nations./West End./No. 12. Read. Chavanne. *Engraved for Mighty London Illustrated.* Read & Co. 10 Johnson's Ct. Fleet St. 170 × 223mm.

53 p 112 Interior of the Great Exhibition./French & Belgium Departments./No. 13. Read. Chavanne. Engraved for the Publishers, Read & Co. 10 Johnson's Ct. Fleet St. 168 × 227mm.

54 p 112 Interior of the Great Exhibition./West end, looking East./No. 14. Read. Chavanne. *Engraved for Mighty London Illustrated.* Read & Co. 10 Johnson's Ct., Fleet St. 170 × 225mm.

55 p 112 Interior of the Great Exhibition./Italian Department./No. 15. Read. Chavanne. London, Read & Co. 10 Johnson's Ct. Fleet St. 168 × 225mm.

56 p 112 Interior of the Great Exhibition./Zollverein Department./No. 16. Read. Chavanne. London, Read & Co. 10 Johnson's Ct. Fleet St./Paris. H. Mandeville, 42 Rue Vivienne. 165 × 225mm.

57 p 112 Interior of the Great Exhibition./Egypt, Turkey & Greece./No. 17. Read. Chavanne. London, Read & Co. 10 Johnson's Ct. Fleet St./Paris. H. Mandeville. 170 × 222mm.

58 p 112 Interior of the Great Exhibition./Indian Department/No. 18. Read. Chavanne. London, Read & Co. 10 Johnson's Ct. Fleet St. Paris. H. Mandeville. 172 × 222mm.

59 p 112 Interior of the Great Exhibition./Russian Department./No. 19. Read. Chavanne. London, Read & Co. 10 Johnson's Ct. Fleet St. Paris, H. Mandeville. 173 × 223mm.

60 p 112 Interior of the Great Exhibition./Ceylon, Malta & Canadian Departments./No. 20. Read. Chavanne. London, Read & Co. 10 Johnson's Ct. Fleet St. 175 × 222mm.

61 (tm) New Map of London. Drawn & Engraved from authentic documents & actual survey, by B.R. Davies,

16 George Str. Euston Square. 425 × 685/482 × 735mm. (R. Hyde, *Printed Maps of Victorian London*, 12—4)

SER 2

62 p 113 The Tower of London. Patten. Patten. *Engraved for Mighty London Illustrated.* Read & Co. 10 Johnson's Ct. Fleet St. 153 × 220mm.

63 p 150 The Royal Mint./Tower Hill. Read. Albutt. London, Read & Co. 10 Johnson's Ct. Fleet St. Paris, H. Mandeville. 158 × 230mm. No 71.

64 p 153 The Thames Tunnel. Jones. Lacey. *Engraved for Mighty London Illustrated.* Read & Co. 10 Johnson's Ct. Fleet St. 158 × 227mm.

65 p 160 Greenwich Hospital/River Front. Read. Chavanne. London, Read & Co. 10 Johnson's Ct. Fleet St. Paris, H. Mandeville, 42 Rue Vivienne. 160 × 228mm.

66 p 160 London from Greenwich Park. Read. Chavanne. London, Read & Co. 10 Johnson's Ct. Fleet St./Paris, H. Mandeville. 158 × 220mm. No 43.

67 p 170 Interior of Westminster Hall. London, Read & Co. 10 Johnson's Ct. Fleet St. 195 × 150mm. No 76.

68 p 171 New Houses of Parliament. Read & Co. Engravers & Printers, 10 Johnson's Ct. Fleet St. 152 × 225mm. cf with item 3 above, an alternative view.

69 p 173 Victoria Tower./Royal Entrance to New Houses of Parliament. Jones. Grieffeld. *Engraved for Mighty London Illustrated.* Read & Co. 10 Johnson's Ct. Fleet St. 225 × 167mm. No 37.

70 p 174 Her Majesty Proroguing Parliament./ House of Lords. Read. Woods. London, Read & Co. 10 Johnson's Ct. Fleet St./Paris, H. Mandeville. 195 × 150mm.

71 p 175 Interior of the House of Commons. Read. Chavanne. London, Read & Co. 10 Johnson's Ct. Fleet St./Paris, H. Mandeville. 195 × 150mm. No 55.

72 p 181 Westminster Abbey./(From the West). Read & Co. Engravers & Printers, 10 Johnson's Ct. Fleet St. 155 × 228mm. No credits.

73 p 194 The Treasury Buildings. Whitehall. T.H. Shepherd. Redaway. *Engraved for Mighty London Illustrated.* Read & Co. 10 Johnson's Ct. Fleet St. 157 × 223mm.

74 p 195 The Banqueting House Whitehall./(Now used for a Chapel). Shepherd. Clark. *Engraved for Mighty London Illustrated.* Read & Co. 10 Johnson's Ct. Fleet St. 158 × 228mm.

75 p 198 The Admiralty./Whitehall. Brown. Le Petit. *Engraved for Mighty London Illustrated.* Read & Co. 10 Johnson's Ct. Fleet St. 160 × 235mm.

76 p 200 The British Museum./(New Front). Read & Co. Engravers & Printers, 10 Johnson's Ct. Fleet St. 150 × 230mm. No credits.

77 p 209 London University. Read. Albutt. London,

Read & Co. 10 Johnson's Ct. Fleet St./Paris, H. Mandeville. 155 × 230mm. No 60.

78 p 210 St. John's Gate, Clerkenwell./Part of the Ancient Hospital of the Knights of St. John of Jerusalem. Read. Albutt. London, Read & Co. 10 Johnson's Ct. Fleet St./Paris, H. Mandeville. 158 × 228mm. No 74.

79 p 212 New Hall & Library./Lincoln's Inn. Read. Albutt. London, Read & Co. 10 Johnson's Ct. Fleet St./Paris, H. Mandeville. 158 × 228mm. No 50.

80 p 215 The New Record Office./Rolls Buildings. Read. Albutt. London, Read & Co. 10 Johnson's Ct. Fleet St./Paris, H. Mandeville. 160 × 220mm. No 64. Copies also seen with 'Pl. 27' tr. This shows Sir James Pennethorne's building of 1851–66 with a lofty clock tower as originally designed.

81 p 219 London New Cattle Market, Copenhagen Fields. London, Read & Co. 10 Johnson's Ct. Fleet St. 155 × 225mm. No 77. The Smithfield Cattle Market was abolished by Act of Parliament in August 1851. This is a birds-eye view of its replacement on the Caledonian Road, opened by Prince Albert 13 June 1855. No credits.

82 p 221 East India House./Leadenhall Street. T.H. Shepherd. W. Wallace. *Engraved for Mighty London Illustrated.* Read & Co. 10 Johnson's Ct. Fleet St. 160 × 230mm.

83 p 222 The Corn Exchange./Mark Lane. Read. Albutt. London, Read & Co. 10 Johnson's Ct. Fleet St./Paris, H. Mandeville. 158 × 217mm.

84 p 228 School for Indigent Blind./And Bethlehem Hospital St George's Fields, Southwark. Read. Albutt. London, Read & Co. 10 Johnson's Ct. Fleet St./Paris, H. Mandeville. 160 × 225mm. No 62.

85 p 228 Newington Causeway. London, Publish'd for the Proprietors by W. Sprent, 47 King Square E.C. 160 × 230mm. Caption in copperplate script. No credits. Shows the old Elephant and Castle public house.

86 p 230 Lambeth Palace./Town residence of the Archbishop of Canterbury. T.H. Jones. W. Lacey. London, Read & Co. 10 Johnson's Ct. Fleet St./Paris, H. Mandeville. 158 × 232mm. No 38. View from river.

87 p 230 Chelsea Hospital./River Front. Jones. Wood. London, Read & Co. 10 Johnson's Ct. Fleet St./Paris, H. Mandeville. 158 × 225mm. No 44. (*Longford* 53)

88 p 230 Suspension Bridge at Chelsea./Leading from near Chelsea Hospital to the New Park Battersea. Read. Wrightson. London, Read & Co. 10 Johnson's Ct. Fleet St./Paris, H. Mandeville. 155 × 222mm. No 63. Erected from the designs of Thomas Page and opened on the same day as Battersea Park, March 1858. (*Longford* 303)

89 p 231 Wyld's Monster Globe,/Leicester Square. T.H. Shepherd. Chavanne. *Engraved for Mighty London Illustrated.* Read & Co. 10 Johnson's Ct. Fleet St. 142 × 225mm. Exhibited in Leicester Square 1851–62, 60 ft high and lighted by gas, showing on the inner surface the physical features of the earth. The 1851 drawing by Shepherd (165 × 255mm) in BM (*Crace* 18.23).

90 p 231 Regent St. from the Quadrant./looking North. Shepherd. Hopkins. *Engraved for Mighty London Illustrated.* Read & Co. 10, Johnson's Ct. Fleet St. 158 × 225mm. No 25. cf with item 15 above, an alternative view.

91 p 232 Zoological Gardens./Regent's Park. T.H. Shepherd. Le Pettit. *Engraved for Mighty London.* Read & Co. 10 Johnson's Ct. Fleet St. 155 × 240mm.

92 p 233 Dulwich College./and Picture Gallery. Read. Lacey. London, Read & Co. 10 Johnson's Ct. Fleet St./Paris, H. Mandeville. 155 × 230mm. No 66.

93 p 233 The New Crystal Palace at Sydenham. Read. Lacey. London, Read & Co. 10 Johnson's Ct. Fleet St./Paris, H. Mandeville. 155 × 228mm.

94 p 233 The Crystal Palace at Sydenham/No. 1/South Wing and Transept from the Park, West. London, Read & Co. 10 Johnson's Ct. Fleet St. 188 × 240mm. Rounded top corners. Anon lithograph.

95 p 233 The Crystal Palace at Sydenham./No. 2./Garden Front of the Great Central Transept. London, Published by Read & Co., 10 Johnson's Court, Fleet Street. 240 × 190mm. Rounded top corners. Anon lithograph.

96 p 233 Interior of the Crystal Palace at Sydenham./No. 3./View from the South Transept. London, Read & Co. 10 Johnson's Ct. Fleet St. 250 × 190mm. Rounded top corners. Anon lithograph.

97 p 233 Interior of/the Crystal Palace at Sydenham. No. 4./The Egyptian Court. Published by Read & Co., 10 Johnson's Court, Fleet Street. 245 × 190mm. Rounded top corners. Anon lithograph.

98 p 233 Interior of/the Crystal Palace at Sydenham./The Byzantine Court./ opened by Her Majesty June 10th 1854/Central Transept. 240 × 187mm. Rounded top corners. Anon lithograph. Another state omits the words 'The Byzantine Court'.

99 p 233 Interior of the Crystal Palace at Sydenham./The Byzantine Court. 240 × 185mm. Rounded top corners. Anon lithograph.

100 p 233 Interior of/the Crystal Palace at Sydenham./ No. 7./The Nubian Court. Published by Read & Co., 10 Johnson's Court, Fleet Street. 240 × 190mm. Rounded top corners. Anon lithograph.

101 p 233 Interior of/the Crystal Palace at Sydenham./ No. 8./The Nineveh Court. London, Published by Read & Co. 10 Johnson's Court, Fleet Street. 240 × 190mm. Rounded top corners. Anon lithograph.

102 p 233 Harrow School & Church./Harrow on the Hill. Mason. Mainwaring. London, Read & Co. 10 Johnson's Ct. Fleet St./Paris, H. Mandeville. 155 × 222mm. No 54.

103 p 234 Great Palm House, Kew Gardens. London, Read & Co. 10, Johnson's Ct. Fleet St./Paris, H. Mandeville, 42 Rue Vivienne. 160 × 222mm. No 40. Completed to the designs of Decimus Burton, 1848.

104 p 234 The Wesleyan Institution./Richmond./ Read. Wrightson. London, Read & Co, 10 Johnson's Ct. Fleet St./Paris, H. Mandeville, 155 × 222mm. No 65. (*Gascoigne* 150)

105 p 234 Hampton Court Palace./From the Thames. Wrightson. Wrightson. London, Read & Co. 10 Johnson's Ct. Fleet St./Paris, H. Mandeville. 155 × 224mm. No 70.

106 p 234 Hampton Court Palace. Read. Albutt. London, Read & Co. 10 Johnson's Ct. Fleet St./Paris, H. Mandeville. 158 × 225mm. No 42.

107 p 235 Windsor Castle./The Queens Private Apartments. Read. Albutt. London, Read & Co. 10 Johnson's Ct. Fleet St./Paris, H. Mandeville. 155 × 228mm. No 45.

108 p 235 Windsor Castle./From Victoria Bridge. Read. Chavanne. *Engraved for Mighty London Illustrated.* Read & Co. 10 Johnson's Ct. Fleet St. 153 × 228mm.

109 p 235 Windsor Castle./Entrance from the Town. Read. Albutt. London, Read & Co. 10 Johnson's Ct. Fleet St./Paris, H. Mandeville. 158 × 230mm. No 28.

110 p 235 Ruins at Virginia Water./Near Windsor. Read. Wrightson. London, Read & Co. 10 Johnson's Ct. Fleet St./Paris, H. Mandeville. 155 × 220mm. No 67. An artificial construct composed of incongruous fragments of classical architecture from the British Museum removed by George IV.

111 p 235 Osborne House./Her Majesty's Marine Villa, Isle of Wight. Read. Albutt. London, Read & Co. 10 Johnson's Ct. Fleet St./Paris, H. Mandeville. 160 × 228mm. No 51. Designed and built in 1848 by Thomas Cubitt, one of the guarantors of the Great Exhibition.

112 p 235 The New Palace of Balmoral./Her Majesty's Highland Residence. London, Read & Co. 10 Johnson's Ct. Fleet St./Paris, H. Mandeville. 152 × 225mm. No 72. Lithotint. No credits.

113 p 235 The Ancient Royal Palace of Holyrood./ Edinburgh. London, Read & Co. 10 Johnson's Ct. Fleet St./Paris, H. Mandeville. 152 × 220mm. No 73. Lithotint. No credits.

114 (tl) Reynolds's/Map of/Modern London/divided into quarter mile sections/Published by James Reynolds, 174 Strand 1860. Drawn & Engraved by R. Jarman. 480 × 730mm. (R. Hyde, *Printed Maps of Victorian London*, 54—4)

214 · ROCK'S ILLUSTRATIONS OF LONDON [c 1851]

William Rock's speciality in small, vignetted topographical engravings has been described in connection with the earlier collection *Views of London* (no 205). This is a collection of his smaller, numbered series which according to their numeration ran into thousands and were also issued as separate card views, sometimes delicately tinted in water-colour. The 29 views in this binding certainly do not represent all the small-scale London views issued by Rock, which extend over a considerable number of years and sometimes record the same building, eg Buckingham Palace, at two different stages in its architectural history. There is no text, title-page or listing. Captions are in copperplate script or small capitals and the only credit, bl or br, is 'Rock & Co. London'. The binding is brown, embossed cloth-gilt with the lettering 'Rock's /Illustrations/ of/London/ 2/6.' The small oblong folio size is 100 × 180mm.

1 The Thames Tunnel, with a view of Rotherhith. 60 × 90mm. No 613. Reduced from Rock's *Views*, item 14.

2 Coal Exchange, London. Sept. 29th 1849. 65 × 90mm. No 1227. Bunning's building, opened by the Prince Consort 30 October 1849.

3 Monument. 65 × 90mm. No 634.

4 The Thames/Custom House, Tower &c. 60 × 90mm. No 616.

5 St. Katherine Cree Leadenhall St. London. April 10th 1850. 65 × 85mm. No 1383.

6 The Royal Exchange, London. 60 × 95mm. No 598.

7 Guildhall. 65 × 90/85 × 130mm. No 608.

8 Post Office. 55 × 95/80 × 130mm. No 614. Reduced from Rock's *Views*, item 2.

9 St. Mary Woolnoth, Lombard St. London. April 10th 1850. 75 × 65mm. No 1382.

10 Mansion House, London. May 20th 1850. 60 × 90/90 × 130mm. No 1400.

11 Saint Mildred's Poultry. Feby 10th 1850. 60 × 90/90 × 130mm. No 1336.

12 St. Mary le Bow, Cheapside. Feby 10th 1850. 85 × 60mm. No 1335.

13 Bank of England. London. May 20th 1850. 60 × 95mm. No 1399.

14 Christs Hospital. 55 × 90mm. No 594.

15 St. Paul's Cathedral. 85 × 65mm. No 609.

16 Theatre Royal, Drury Lane. May 20th 1850. 60 × 90mm. No 1371.

17 Somerset House, facing the River. 55 × 95mm. No 615.

18 Theatre Royal, Covent Garden. May 20th 1850. 60 × 90mm. No. 1370.

19 House of Lords Westminster. 75 × 65mm. No 629. Interior.

20 Saint James' Palace, London. April 20th 1850. 60 × 90mm. No 1388.

21 Houses of Parliament Westminster. 55 × 90mm. No 630. Reduced from Rock's *Views*, item 9.

22 Buckingham Palace, London. April 20th 1850. 60 × 95mm. No 1387. From the lake in St James's Park.

23 Wellington Barracks, St. James's Park. 60 × 95mm. No 1044. Built by Sir F. Smith in consultation with Philip Hardwick, c 1833.

24 Athenaeum. April 20th 1850. 60 × 90mm. No 1385.

25 Universities Club House. April 29th 1850. 60 × 90mm. No 1386.

26 Wellington Statue, Hyde Park Corner. 70 × 85/95 × 150mm. No 596.

27 The Exhibition of the Industry of all Nations London/ Designed by Jos. Paxton Esqr. FCS. Oct. 14th 1850. 65 × 100mm. No 1479.

28 The Industrial Exhibition for 1851. Octr. 14th 1850. No 1478. Elevation with measurements.

29 Hospital for Consumption/Brompton. 55 × 90mm. No 591. (cf with *Longford* 718)

215 · TALLIS'S ILLUSTRATED LONDON [c 1851–2]

For the Great Exhibition of 1851 John Tallis issued two publications in particular: one a lavish souvenir of the Exhibition itself, *Tallis's History and Description of the Crystal Palace* (from 1854 to 1855 in six 'Divisions', bound in blue cloth with the Exhibition building in gilt, price 10s 6d each Division), illustrated with steel-engravings of which many were based on daguerreotype originals; the other this *Illustrated London*, a combined historical guidebook and, for visitors to the Exhibition, souvenir of the metropolis and its environs. The author,

William Gaspey, rises above the insipid generalizations of most guidebook writers of his time, really relating his text to the subjects illustrated. He has also gone to the trouble of ascertaining historical dates, providing architectural descriptions and quoting the names of the architects of the buildings shown.

As with Dugdale's *England and Wales Delineated* (no 186) and the Crystal Palace history, Tallis issued this book in what he called 'Divisions'. There were four, each bound in red cloth with the Exhibition building embossed in gilt and this lettering on the spine: 'Tallis's Illustrated London in Commemoration of the Great Exhibition. Div. I (II–IV). 6/6 by W. Gaspey.' Each Division consists of a collection of plates followed by a half-text, broken off in mid-sentence, of one of the two volumes. With the first and third was also published an engraved title-page, for use when the temporary bindings had been discarded.

The 'preliminary chapter' speaks of 'The Grand Exhibition of the Industry of all Nations, of which London is to be the stage, in the spring of 1851'. None of the title-pages is dated but the text abounds with references to 1851 and specifically 'certain alterations which are now (1851) being carried on' (vol. 1, p 261) and 'the present year (1851)' (vol. 2, p 216). In the second volume, however, we are told (p 264) that New Billingsgate Market 'was erected after the designs of Mr. Bunning, the city architect, in 1852'. The assumption is that this book, like Dugdale's, was issued in Numbers by Tallis before being accumulated into Divisions, probably from 1850 to 1852.

Some idea of the scale of Tallis's business is to be gleaned from a textual note on the illustrations of Highbury Barn Tavern (items 143–4):

Notwithstanding the humble designation of 'Barn' the establishment is by no means of an humble character, containing three noble assembly-rooms. Of these, two are detached from the main building, and are placed advantageously in the grounds.... In this attractive place of resort, Messrs. John Tallis and Co., the publishers of this work, give their annual banquet and festival during the Whitsuntide holidays, to the persons in their employment, numbering upwards of two hundred.

Tallis's Illustrated London; in commemoration of the Great Exhibition of all nations in 1851. Forming a complete guide to The British Metropolis and its environs. Illustrated by upwards of two hundred steel engravings from original drawings and daguerreotypes.

With Historical and Descriptive Letter-press, by William Gaspey, Esq. Vol. 1 (II). John Tallis and Company, London and New York.

Octavo, 185 × 125mm. c 1851–2

COLLATION   Vol 1. Title-page; pp iii–vii, contents; pp 1–320, Illustrated London. Vol. 2. Title-page; pp iii–vii, contents; pp 1–304, Illustrated London continued.

When Tallis published Dugdale's *England and Wales Delineated* he frugally made further use of 25 of the plates from his *Street Views* to illustrate the London article (see 'Street Views' in introductory History). In his introduction to the present work he claimed:

In order to impart more effectually a correct idea of the magnitude, and the superb edifices of the British metropolis, the publishers have, at a great cost, engaged artists of eminence to furnish graphic representations of whatever is most deserving of notice in London and its tributary neighbourhoods. The letter-press, thus aided and rendered more significant by the choicest labours of art, will impart to those unacquainted with, and residing at a distance from, London, more accurate notions of its grandeur and dimensions than has been supplied by any previous publication.

Impressing the country cousins did not however cost him as much in engravers' fees as he implied. Having acquired the business of E.T. Brain, the publisher of an earlier *Illustrated London* (no 207), he inherited with it 116 of the plates engraved for that publication by Albert Henry Payne which, taking into account double-view plates, placed at his disposal for the Great Exhibition guidebook 189 separate views, none of them more than about four years old. They had the considerable advantage of having been issued without tell-tale publication-lines or numeration and the engravers' credits were so rare as not to be worth burnishing out. They are cited below as *PIL*, with item number.

To this ready-made store he added a 'top dressing' of 44 anonymous single-view plates, making a total of 160 plates or 233 views. As is usual, however, with books of this period which have an index but no check-list of views, copies containing the full tally are rare. The extra plates matched the original Payne engravings in size, style and captions and were likewise unnumbered and without publication-lines or credits. They are mostly illustrative of buildings recently erected; indeed one of those shown, the Infant Orphan Asylum at Wanstead (item 151), was not completed until 1854. They include also views of the Great Exhibition, of the two Zoological Gardens and of Kew Gardens.

VOL. 1

1 (engr title) Tallis's/Illustrated/London/in commemoration of/The Great Exhibition of 1851. By W. Gaspey, Esq. /(vignette) St. Paul's from the River. John Tallis & Company, London & New York. Vignette 90 × 90mm. *PIL* 1.

2 front. The Royal Exchange. A.H. Payne del. et sc. 90 × 140mm. *PIL* 2.

3 p 7 London. Drawn by N. Whittock. Engraved by J. Rogers. J. Tallis, London, Edinburgh & Dublin. 125 × 208mm. View from London Bridge in engraved strapwork frame surmounted by shields of Westminster, the City and Southwark.

4 p 7 North View of St. Paul's Cathedral. 93 × 135mm. *PIL* 83.

5 p 17 St. Paul's Cathedral. 130 × 90mm. *PIL* 79.

6 p 25 The Sessions House/Clerkenwell – Old Bailey. Each 63 × 85mm. *PIL* 32.

7 p 44 The New Library (Temple) – Furnivals Inn. Each 60 × 85mm. *PIL* 113.

8 p 49 Grays Inn Hall – Middle Temple Hall. Each 60 × 85mm. *PIL* 115.

9 p 51 New Lodge, Victoria Park/Bonners Fields – Temple Bar. Each 60 × 85mm. *PIL* 69.

10 p 53 St Clement Danes/Strand – St Pancras/New Church. Each 83 × 60mm. *PIL* 81.

11 p 56 King's College, Strand – Somerset House, Strand. Each 60 × 85mm. *PIL* 11.

12 p 57 Somerset House. 88 × 138mm. *PIL* 7.

13 p 62 Waterloo Bridge. 85 × 140mm. *PIL* 18.

14 p 72 Covent Garden Market. 83 × 140mm. *PIL* 46.

15 p 73 St. Paul's Covent Garden – St. Sepulchre. Each 60 × 85mm. *PIL* 87.

16 p 86 Temple Gardens – Adelphi Terrace. Each 60 × 85mm. *PIL* 70.

17 p 88 Hungerford Market – Buckingham Water Gate. Each 60 × 85mm. *PIL* 35.

18 p 89 Hungerford Bridge – Duke of York's column. Each 60 × 85mm. *PIL* 12.

19 p 92 St Martin's Church – Northumberland House. Each 63 × 85mm. *PIL* 16.

20 p 94 The National Gallery. C. Warren del. A.H. Payne sc. 90 × 140mm. *PIL* 10.

21 p 96 Nelson Column/Trafalgar Square. 135 × 90mm. The statue by E.H. Baily was set up in November 1843 but the bronze lions also are shown, in advance of their arrival in 1867. The column was designed by W. Railton.

22 p 97 St. Martin's Church/Trafalgar Square. 90 × 140mm. *PIL* 17.

VOL. 2

Gaspey, Esq. (vignette) London from Greenwich Park./ John Tallis & Company, London & New York. Vignette 90 × 80mm.

76 front. Buckingham Palace. 85 × 140mm. *PIL* 13.

77 p 15 New Hall & Library Lincoln's Inn. 85 × 140mm. Three figures added, in foreground l., otherwise as *PIL* 114.

78 p 26 Egyptian Room British Museum. 87 × 140mm. *PIL* 67.

79 p 26 The British Museum. 90 × 135mm. *PIL* 66.

80 p 48 St Saviour Southwark. 130 × 90mm. *PIL* 82.

81 p 58 Licensed Victuallers' School – School for the Indigent Blind. Each 60 × 88mm. *PIL* 116.

82 p 59 Bethlem Hospital – Westminster Hospital. Each 60 × 85mm. *PIL* 42.

83 p 91 Greenwich Hospital. 85 × 140mm. *PIL* 37.

84 p 93 Greenwich Park – Observatory, Greenwich Park. Each 60 × 90mm. *PIL* 36.

85 p 107 The Thames/from the cliffs at Rosherville. 90 × 140mm. *PIL* 48.

86 p 108 Windsor Castle/from the Terrace – Virginia Water/Fishing Temple. Each 60 × 85mm. *PIL* 49.

87 p 109 Eton College – The Long Walk/Windsor. Each 60 × 87mm. *PIL* 50.

88 p 110 Hampton Court. 87 × 140mm. *PIL* 6.

89 p 112 Twickenham/Orleans House – Near Teddington. Each 62 × 87mm. *PIL* 52.

90 p 113 Richmond Hill. 85 × 140mm. *PIL* 51. (*Gascoigne* 148)

91 p 114 Richmond Bridge – Hampton Court. Each 60 × 85mm. *PIL* 5.

92 p 116 The Palm House, Kew Gardens. 90 × 140mm. Designed by Decimus Burton, completed 1848.

93 p 117 Kew Palace. 87 × 140mm.

94 p 117 Sion House/Seat of the Duke of Northumberland – Isleworth Church. 63 × 85, 60 × 85mm. *PIL* 53.

95 p 120 Kew Bridge – Hammersmith Suspension Bridge. 63 × 85mm. *PIL* 54.

96 p 122 Fulham – Barnes Church. Each 60 × 85mm. *PIL* 55.

97 p 123 Wandsworth – Putney. Each 63 × 83mm. *PIL* 56.

98 p 125 Lambeth Palace – Westminster Hall. Each 60 × 87mm. *PIL* 19.

99 p 129 The Houses of Parliament. 90 × 130mm. 'The New Senate House, commenced in 1836 is still (1851) in progress'.

100 p 135 Interior of the House of Lords. 138 × 90mm. *PIL* 112.

101 p 142 London Bridge. 83 × 138mm. *PIL* 65.

102 p 143 The Corn Exchange/Mark Lane – The Custom House. Each 60 × 87mm. *PIL* 4.

103 p 145 The Tower – Billingsgate. 63 × 88,62 × 88mm. *PIL* 63.

104 p 151 The Wellington Barracks/in the Tower of London. 85 × 135mm. Built by Anthony Salvin, 1845.

105 p 158 Rosherville Gardens, Gravesend – (ditto). Each 60 × 85mm. *PIL* 61.

106 p 159 Gravesend – Terrace Pier Gravesend. Each 60 × 85mm. *PIL* 62.

107 p 163 St. Katherine's Docks. 90 × 140mm. *PIL* 58.

108 p 164 London Docks. 82 × 138mm. *PIL* 57.

109 p 170 Guys Hospital – St Thomas's Hospital. Each 60 × 85mm. *PIL* 43.

110 p 172 St Lukes Hospital – St Georges Hospital. Each 60 × 85mm. *PIL* 41.

111 p 173 Middlesex Hospital – The Foundling Hospital. Each 60 × 85mm. *PIL* 40.

112 p 174 The New London Fever Hospital/Liverpool Road. 85 × 135mm. Built by Charles Fowler, 1848.

113 p 174 Hospital for Consumption and Diseases of the Chest (Brompton). 82 × 140mm. *PIL* 44. (*Longford* 531)

114 p 174 The New Small Pox Hospital Highgate. 90 × 135mm. Built 1850.

115 p 174 The New Consumption Hospital/now building near/Victoria Park. 90 × 133mm. The City of London Hospital for Diseases of the Chest, opened by the Prince Consort 1855.

116 p 175 Kensall Green Cemetery. 85 × 140mm. *PIL* 75.

117 p 176 Highgate Church (from the cemetery) – Kensall Green Cemetery (Entrance Lodge). Each 60 × 85mm. *PIL* 74.

118 p 178 The New City Prison Holloway. 90 × 140mm. 'Commenced 25th April 1849, to be completed May 1852'. Built by J.B. Bunning.

119 p 183 London & North Western Station Euston Square. 90 × 135mm. Built by Philip Hardwick, 1836–9.

120 p 183 New Hall London & North Western Railway Station Euston Square. 90 × 130mm. Built by P.C. Hardwick, opened 1849.

121 p 184 South Eastern Railway Station/London Bridge. 87 × 132mm. Built by Samuel Beazley, 1850.

122 p 185 South Western Railway Station,/Nine Elms – South Eastern & South Coast Railway Station,/ London Bridge. Each 60 × 85mm. *PIL* 78.

123 p 192 Salters' Hall/St Swithins Lane – Drapers' Hall/Throgmorton Street. Each 60 × 85mm. *PIL* 102.

124 p 196 Christ's Hospital/New Hall – Goldsmith's Hall. Each 60 × 85mm. *PIL* 8.

125 p 197 Vintners' Hall/Upper Thames Street – Skinners' Hall/Dowgate Hill. Each 60 × 85mm. *PIL* 103.

126 p 202 Ironmongers Hall – Stationers Hall. Each 60 × 85mm. *PIL* 101.

500

127 p 209 Royal College of Surgeons – Apothecaries Hall. Each 60 × 85mm. *PIL* 109.

128 p 210 The Conservative Club House. 88 × 138mm. *PIL* 27.

129 p 212 The New Atheneum,/Waterloo Place – Crockford's Club House. Each 63 × 87mm. *PIL* 26.

130 p 213 New United Service Club House – Arthur's Club House,/St James' St. Each 60 × 87mm. *PIL* 28.

131 p 214 Army and Navy Club House/Pall Mall. 90 × 130mm. Built by Parnell & Smith, 1848–51.

132 p 216 The Italian Opera House. A.H. Payne. 83 × 138mm. *PIL* 108.

133 p 217 Haymarket Theatre – Covent Garden Theatre. Each 60 × 85mm. *PIL* 106.

134 p 218 Lyceum Theatre – Drury Lane Theatre. Each 60 × 85mm. *PIL* 107.

135 p 227 Adelphi Theatre – Exeter Hall. Each 85 × 60mm. *PIL* 100.

136 p 228 Polytechnic Institution – Princess's Theatre. Each 60 × 85mm *PIL* 105.

137 p 229 Sadlers Wells Theatre. 88 × 132mm.

138 p 231 Surrey Theatre. 90 × 135mm. Blackfriars Road.

139 p 237 Zoological Gardens Regents Park. 85 × 135mm.

140 p 238 Regents Park Zoological Gardens. 83 × 138mm. The Camel House. *PIL* 71.

141 p 240 Surrey Zoological Gardens. 90 × 135mm. Between Walworth and Kennington Common.

142 p 240 Surrey Zoological Gardens. 87 × 138mm. Another view.

143 p 241 The Gardens, Highbury Barn Tavern. 90 × 133mm.

144 p 241 The Gardens, Highbury Barn Tavern. 88 × 132mm. Another view.

145 p 242 The Ornamental Water/St James' Park. A.H. Payne. 83 × 140mm. *PIL* 24.

146 p 246 Marble Arch, Oxford Street. 90 × 135mm. Removed from outside Buckingham Palace in 1851; 're-erected in the present year at the north east entrance of Hyde Park'.

147 p 247 Entrance to Green Park. 130 × 90mm. Constitution Arch, built by Decimus Burton, 1846.

148 p 251 Macclesfield Bridge/Regents Park – Centre of Cumberland Terrace/Regents Park. 60 × 85mm. *PIL* 99.

149 p 251 Hanover Terrace/Regents Park – Cornwall Terrace/Regents Park. Each 60 × 85mm. *PIL* 97.

150 p 256 Leicester Square/with the building in which Mr Wyld's model of the Earth is exhibited. 88 × 140mm. 'The Great Globe, erected this year (1851) by Mr. Wyld, the great mapseller, and member of Parliament for Bodmin'.

151 p 263 The Infant Orphan Asylum Wanstead. 90 × 135mm. Built by John Henry Taylor, 1854.

152 p 263 Lady Owens Alms Houses/St John Street Road. 85 × 132mm. Goswell Road.

153 p 264 Billingsgate Market. 90 × 135mm. 'erected after the designs of Mr. Bunning, the City Architect', 1852.

154 p 264 Colney Hatch Lunatic Asylum/from the Railway Bridge. 85 × 135mm. Opened 17 June 1850.

155 p 264 Colney Hatch Lunatic Asylum. 85 × 135mm. Another view.

156 p 264 The Orphan Working School/Haverstock Hill, Hampstead. 93 × 128mm.

157 p 266 Prince Albert's Model Lodging House/erected in Hyde Park 1851. 88 × 135mm. 'Two model houses, constructed after the plans of Prince Albert, for four families, and adjacent to the cavalry barracks at Knightsbridge. The leading feature of the design was that of the receding and protected open central staircase, with the connecting gallery on the first floor'. Designed by Henry Roberts and still to be seen in Kennington Park re-erected as a lodge.

158 p 273 The Building for the Great Exhibition Hyde Park 1851. 88 × 135mm.

159 p 277 The Transept of the Great Exhibition/looking South. Engraved by W. Lacey from a daguerreotype by Mayall. 150 × 198/180 × 225mm.

160 p 277 The Transept of the Great Exhibition/looking North. Engraved by W. Lacey from a daguerreotype by Mayall. 150 × 198/180 × 225mm. The last two plates in the book mark the advent of photography, albeit at one remove, into London illustration. Daguerre's process, invented in 1833, became generally available in 1839. Both are also used in the first bound 'Division' (price 10s 6d) of Tallis's *History and Description of the Crystal Palace*.

216 · THOMPSON'S OLD LONDON [c 1851]

The chronological extremes meet in this set of etchings published by subscription about 1851 (the British Museum set (173.b.1) is on Whatman paper dated 1847). They were executed by Peter Thompson, carpenter and builder who, in 1835, had sent in a Tudor Gothic design for the new Houses of Parliament and published them in lithograph in 1836 as *Designs ... Submitted to the Committee of Taste*.

No title-page or text were issued but a printed prospectus, listing the subjects of the prints and quoting their prices, is headed: ' "Old London". Now Publishing by Subscription "Facsimiles of a Set of Drawings shewing the Fortifications round London as directed to be done by the Parliament in 1643" '. With this went a subscription-list, headed by the Prince Consort and including the Guildhall Library, and an invitation to further subscribers to send their names 'to Mr. Thompson, 1 Osnaburgh Place, Trinity Church' where the drawings on which the engravings were based might be inspected.

They may now be inspected bound in an album at the British Museum. Thompson gave them out to be the work of one John Eyre, born at Bakewell in Derbyshire in 1604, who obtained, he said, a captaincy in the London Train-Bands and, although originally a Royalist, ultimately espoused the Parliamentary cause, fought at Chalgrove Field and at Marston Moor—where 'while charging at the head of his regiment' he was mortally wounded— and died on 23 July 1644. It was indicated that between 1639 and 1641 he was much in the company of Wenceslaus Hollar and sketching monuments in London churches. As evidence of the association the album contains pen, ink and wash drawings of Old St Paul's tombs not featured in the illustrations to Dugdale's *St Paul's* (no 8): those of Robert Fitzhugh, W. Harrington, Francis Walsingham and Margaret, Countess of Shrewsbury, all signed 'W. Hollar del.', with dates 1642 or 1643; and there is a drawing of Brooke House, Hackney similarly signed. The biographical details are said to be supplied from a conveniently found manuscript commonplace book and are consolidated by an elaborately drawn up pedigree with hearaldic illuminations, tracing the Captain's descent to Simon Eyre, shoemaker and Lord Mayor of London in 1445.

The London fortification drawings bear no signatures but are claimed as the work of Eyre, from among 'some 300 specimens of his labour' which came to light after his death.

The hoax, if hoax it was and not simply a dishonest plan to make money by the sale of the 'originals' after they had been established through the etchings, took in an FRS and two FSA subscribers but the Guildhall Library had second thoughts and cancelled its subscription to the prints. Some care had been taken in selecting old paper and

brownish ink for the drawings and the captions are in a bogus seventeenth century hand, an attempted authentication reminiscent of the Ireland and Chatterton forgeries. The general layout of the fortifications could have been provided by Vertue's 'Plan of the City and Suburbs of London as fortified by Order of Parliament', engraved in 1738 for Maitland's *History of London* (no 33), and the elevations in the views of specific forts, batteries, redoubts and bulwarks are quite credible, as also is the background of the gabled houses of pre-fire London, old St Paul's, the Tower of London and Gothic churches such as St Mary, Whitechapel. No pupil or associate of Hollar's, however, would have been content with perspective so primitive, skies so featureless or such amateurish drawing of the figures of citizens and Cromwellian soldiers peopling the streets. Of the etchings, which are close facsimiles of the drawings, a manuscript note in the British Museum collection states that '50 sets were printed, the coppers were destroyed, about 30 sets were distributed to private subscribers'. Subjects, not separate plates, are given numbers by the engraver.

1 Plan of Fortifications. 205 × 270/220 × 295mm. Refs 1–22. 2s 0d.

2 1 A Redoubt with two Flanks, near St Giles's Pound.
2 A Small Fort at the east end of Tiburn Road.
3 A Large Fort with 4 Half Bulwarks across the Tiburn Road. 205 × 340/220 × 360mm. 2s 6d.

3 4 A small Bulwark at Oliver's Mount (against) Tiburn Brook. 155 × 195/165 × 240mm. 1s 0d.

4 5 A Large Fort with 4 Bulwarks on the Reading Road beyond Tiburne Brook.
6 A Small Redoubt and Battery on the Hill from St James's Park. 205 × 330/220 × 345mm. 2s 0d.

5 7 Court of Guard on Chelsey Road.
8 A Battery and Breastwork in Tothill Fields. 280 × 200mm. 1s 0d each.

6 9 A Quadrant Fort with 4 Half Bulwarks at Foxhall. 200 × 330/225 × 345mm. 2s 6d.

7 10 A Fort with 4 Half Bulwarks in St Georges Fields. 200 × 280/230 × 370mm. 2s 0d.

8 11 A large Fort with 4 Bulwarks at the end of Blackman Street. 210 × 330/220 × 370mm. 3s 0d.

9 12 A Redoubt with 4 Flanks at the end of Kent Street. 210 × 325/230 × 345mm. 2s 6d.

10 13 A Bulwark and half on the Hill at the end of Gravel Lane. 200 × 340/220 × 360mm. 3s 6d. Tower of London and London Bridge beyond.

11 14 A Hornwork near the Church of Whitechapel Street. 215 × 330/225 × 340mm. 3s 0d.

12 15 A Redoubt with 2 Flanks at Brick Lane. 150 × 195/155 × 240mm. 1s 0d.

13 16 A Redoubt at the Hackney Corner of Shoreditch. 17 A Redoubt at the Corner of the Road for Edmonton at Shoreditch. 205 × 335/230 × 350mm. 3s 0d.

14 18 A Battery and Breastwork on the Road to Islington. 208 × 330/230 × 340mm. 3s 0d.

15 19 A Battery and Breastwork at the end of St Johns Street. 208 × 340/220 × 360mm. 3s 0d. Old St Paul's at the lower end.

16 20 A View of London from the North showing the Fortification from Whitechapel to Tothill Fields/ 1642 & 1643. 205 × 1020/250 × 1060mm. 10s 0d. The most ambitious of the views and one which must have demanded the greatest exercise of the imagination. Presumably the perpetrator worked largely from post-Fire views: Hollar's set of engravings from Islington (*Hind* 70–7) and, in the next century, Thomas Bowles's, North Prospect (BL Maps: *K. top.* 21.42) and those of John Stevens (*K. top.* 21.50) and John Swertner (*K. top.* 21.56).

17 21 A Battery east Grays Inn Lane. 202 × 340/220 × 365mm. 2s 6d.

18 22 Two Batteries at Southampton House. 200 × 325/220 × 360mm. 2s 0d.

19 Capt. John Eyre. Oval, 80 × 70mm. 1s 0d.

217 · SAYER'S AND OVERTON'S VIEWS* [1753]

The set of 'Prospects' published by Henry Overton (no 26) with the alternative title *Britannia Illustrata* was representative of the lesser topographical prints he issued during the decade 1720 to 1730. In 1753 reprints of some of these plates, together with London views of a similar size which were then being published by Robert Sayer, were bound into an oblong album (230 × 360mm) which was acquired by the Prince of Wales, the future George IV, and is now preserved in the Royal Library at Windsor. Its title-page has reference only to the first 30 plates, engraved by John Harris:

(engr title in cartouche) Views/of all the Cathedrall Churches of/England and Wales &c./neatly Engrav'd (and in French) /Sold by Henry Overton at ye White Horse/without Newgate London. 130 × 175/155 × 195mm.

These were all included also in the earlier collection from which are now likewise reprinted 11 of the Prospects of London (referred to as *OP*) lacking both credits and publication-lines.

The total number of plates is brought up to 62 by the addition of others from three sets of Sayer views, two of which are dated 1753 and the rest 1752, amended in manuscript to 1753:

(a) Views of London and Westminster Bridges, engraved by Thomas Bowles with the publication-line: 'London, Printed for Robt Sayer opposite Fetter Lane Fleetstreet & Henry Overton without Newgate.'

(b) Nine London views drawn and engraved by John Maurer, with the publication-line: 'London, Printed for Robt Sayer at the Golden Buck facing Fetter Lane (End) Fleet Street.'

(c) Ten Hampstead and Highgate views engraved by J.B. Chatelain, each measuring 160–5 × 260/190 × 275–80mm, with the publication-line: 'London, Printed for & Sold by Heny Overton at the White Horse without Newgate & Robt Sayer at the Golden Buck opposite Fetter Lane, Fleet Street. 1752.' These were originally issued with the credits 'Chatelain Delint. W.H. Toms sculp.', with the line 'Published March 25th 1745 ... & Sold by the Proprietor W.H. Toms Engraver in Union Court near Hatton Garden, Holborn.', and with 'Hampstead' in the caption, spelt thus.

These are identifiable as 'Sets of Small Prints' listed in Sayer & Bennett's catalogue of 1775 (pp 86–8): the Bowles engravings in Set 8, 'Twelve Views of the City of London'; the Maurer in Set 10, 'Twelve perspective Views of the principal churches, streets, and squares in the cities of London and Westminster'; with two survivors from the Chatelain views relegated to Set 13, 'Views of Villages, Noblemen and Gentlemen's Seats'. The abbreviation *SSP* refers to this catalogue in which the sets of a dozen were priced at 1s 6d, while all 30 cathedral plates cost only 3s.

The Chatelain plates are numbered consistently tr 1 to 10; the occasional number engraved on the other Sayer plates is used neither in this collection nor in the 1775 catalogue.

1 The North West view of St Pauls. 150 × 240/170 × 245mm. *OP* 2.

2 A Perspective View of Westminster Abbey &/St. Margaret's Church. (and in French) J. Maurer de. & sc. 1752. 160 × 270/190 × 290mm. Earlier state dated '1746' in BL (Maps: *K. top.* 24.4f). *SSP* 10/8.

3 Lambeth House/in Surry, ye Palace of the Arch Bishop of Canterbury. 140 × 240/155 × 245mm. br '4'. *OP* 16.

4 A View of London Bridge. (and in French) Bowles Delin. et Sculp. 1753. 153 × 268/175 × 275mm. tr '4'. *SSP* 8/2.

5 A North West View of Westminster Bridge. (and in French) Labelye Architect. Bowles sculp. 1753. 152 × 270/175 × 280mm. tr '5'. *SSP* 8/3.

6 The City Gates. 150 × 240/165 × 245mm. *OP* 12.

7 Guild Hall, In King Street Cheapside. 150 × 240/170 × 245mm. *OP* 8.

8 The Royal Exchange in Cornhill. 150 × 240/170 × 245mm. *OP* 6.

9 The Custom House. 150 × 242/165 × 245mm. Plate worn. *OP* 5.

10 The Admiralty Office at White Hall. 140 × 235/160 × 240mm. *OP* 19.

11 The South Sea House in Threadneedle Street. 145 × 230/160 × 240mm. *OP* 4.

12 New Bedlam in Moorfields. 145 × 240/165 × 245mm. *OP* 7.

13 Christ's Hospital in Newgate Street. 153 × 240 × 170 × 245mm. *OP* 9.

14 A Perspective View of Temple Barr and/St Dunstan's Church. (and in French) J. Maurer de. & sc. 1752. 160 × 270/190 × 290mm. BL (Maps: *K. top.* 22.23a) dated '1753'. *SSP* 10/12.

15 A Perspective View of St Clements/Church in the Strand. (and in French) J. Maurer del. et sculp. 1752. 165 × 270/190 × 285mm. BL (Maps: *K. top.* 23.12.1a) dated '1753'. *SSP* 10/2.

16 A Perspective View of St Mary's Church in the Strand/near the Royal Palace of Somerset London. (and in French) J. Maurer del. et sculp. 1752. 165 × 270/190 × 285mm. BL (Maps: *K. top.* 23.28.1e) dated '1753'. *SSP* 10/7.

17 A Prospect of Westminster Hall. 150 × 232/165 × 245mm. Cut down plate, revised caption and br '5'. *OP* 17.

18 A Perspective View of the Royal Stables/at Charing Cross. (and in French) J. Maurer delin. et sculp. 1752. 165 × 272/190 × 285mm. BL (Maps: *K. top.* 24.15.1b) dated '1753'. *SSP* 10/5.

19 A Perspective View of Whitehall & Whitehall Gate. (and in French) J. Maurer de. et sc. London 1752. 140 × 270/165 × 285mm. Looking N. to St Martin in the Fields. Earlier state dated '1746' in BL (Maps: *K. top.* 26.5m). *SSP* 10/9.

20 A Perspective View of Buckingham House in St./James's Park. (and in French) J. Maurer de. et sc. London 1752. 140 × 270/170 × 285mm. Earlier state dated '1746' in BL (Maps: *K. top.* 26.3a). *SSP* 10/4.

21 Powis House in Ormond Street. 150 × 240/165 × 245mm. br '9'. *OP* 21.

22 A Perspective View of Grosvenor Squar. (and in French) J. Maurer de. et sc. London 1752. 140 × 270/165 × 285mm. Earlier state dated '1746' in BL (Maps: *K. top.* 22.29a). *SSP* 10/10.

23 A Perspective View of St James's Square. (and in French) J. Maurer delin. et sculp. 1752. 140 × 270/180 × 290mm. BL (Maps: *K. top.* 22.31b) dated '1753'. *SSP* 10/3.

24 A Prospect of Greenwich, Deptford & London, taken from Flamstead Hill in Greenwich Park. 143 × 230/165 × 240mm. *OP* 10.

Vues diverses des Villages pres de Londres

25 1. A View of Hampsted from the foot way next the Great Road, Pond Street. (and in French) Chatelain Delin. et sculpt. London, Printed for & Sold by Heny Overton at the White Horse without Newgate & Robt Sayer at the Golden Buck opposite Fetter Lane, Fleet Street. 1752. 165 × 260/190 × 275mm. Title to set tm. *SSP* 13/11.

26 2. A View of Hampsted from the Top of Pond Street. (and in French)

27 3. A View of Hampsted, from ye corner of Mrs Holford's Garden. (and in French)

28 4. A View of ye Long Room at Hampsted from the Heath. (and in French)

29 5. A View of Hampsted from the Pond. (and in French)

30 6. A View of Hampsted from the Heath near the Chapel. (and in French)

31 7. A View of St Pancras Church &c. (and in French)

32 8. A View of Highgate, from Traytors Hill. (and in French)

33 9. A View of Highgate from Upper Holloway. (and in French) *SSP* 13/12.

34 10. A View of Highgate from the great Road at Kentish Town. (and in French)

218 · ENGLAND DISPLAYED*
[1769]

This illustrated general description of England and Wales was published in the same year as Newbery & Carnan's anonymous *Description of England and Wales* (no 46), by a group of booksellers headed by S. Bladon of 28 Paternoster Row who later took a share in Entick's edition of Maitland's *History of London* (no 38). It came out in 80 weekly Numbers of between six and 12 pages each, to be bound in two volumes, and was written, it was claimed, by that 'Society of Gentlemen' so readily available to the Paternoster Row fraternity. Associated with Bladon is John Coote of 16 Paternoster Row, neighbour and sometime partner of John Cooke, at no 17, who was then engaged in publishing Chamberlain's *History* (no 48) and soon after issued a *Complete English Traveller* (no 52) and a *Modern Universal British Traveller* (no 60), all in sixpenny Numbers. Numbers 14 to 21 (pp 150–219) treat of Middlesex.

England Displayed. Being a New, Complete and Accurate Survey and Description of the Kingdom of England, and Principality of Wales.... By a Society of Gentlemen ... The Particulars respecting England, revised, corrected and improved, by P. Russell, Esq; And those relating to Wales, By Mr. Owen Price (epigraph). Vol. 1 (2). London: Printed for the Authors, by Adlard and Browne, Fleet-Street. And Sold by S. Bladon, No 28, T. Evans, No 54 and J. Coote, No 16 in Paternoster Row: W. Domville and F. Blythe, at the Royal Exchange. MDCCLXIX

Folio, 365 × 200mm.   1769

COLLATION   Vol. 1. Title-page; advertisement, royal warrant (2pp); pp v–viii, preface; pp 1–392 (Pts 1–42), England Displayed. Vol. 2. Title-page; pp 3–314 (Pts 43–80), England Displayed continued; contents, directions to binder, list of subscribers (4pp).

The views, line-engravings, though listed are unnumbered. They are in beaded frames, similar to those used by the engravers for Chamberlain's *History* with which this book has a map in common, by Thomas Bowen. The captions are in copperplate, as is the running title (tm) 'Engraved for England Displayed'.

1 p 150 (tm) A New and Correct Map of the Countries Twenty Miles Round London. By Thos Bowen. 320 ×

365/340 × 385mm. (cf with *Darlington and Howgego* 147)

2 p 151 (tm) Middlesex. 150 × 195/170 × 205mm. Map.

3 p 160 View of St Paul's Cathedral London. 135 × 220,160 × 235 (frame)/175 × 255mm.

4 p 189 View of the Queen's Palace in St James's Park. 123 × 230,150 × 250/170 × 275mm.

5 p 200 View of Holland House, near Kensington. 130 × 255,150 × 255/180 × 275mm.

6 p 214 View of Dr Batty's House at Twickenham. 110 × 220,135 × 245/180 × 260mm.

7 p 215 View of the Duke of Argyll's House at Whitton. 120 × 220, 145 × 245/180 × 260mm.

219 · FUNERAL AND INTERMENT OF LORD NELSON [1806]

The *Monthly Literary Advertiser* for April 1806 carried the following announcement:

Four Prints on Nelson's Funeral, Price £2. 2s.

Mr Cundee has the Honour to inform the Public that the Four Descriptive Prints, in Colours, of the Ceremonies which took place previous to the Funeral, and at the Interment of the illustrious Lord Nelson, are now ready for Delivery. The Drawings for these Prints were taken from actual observation, by C.A. Pugin Esq.... and are engraved in aquatinta by Messrs Lewis, Merigot and Hill.

The Four Prints are all of uniform size, each measuring 13 by 17 and a half Inches, carefully printed in colours on a superfine imperial Paper: Outline of Subjects: 1.... These interesting Prints are accompanied with concise Letter-press Descriptions ... and delivered gratis.

In topographical collections these prints are usually found distributed but in a British Library volume which collects Nelson funeral material (648.a.29) they are bound together, but without letterpress.

Their publication-lines read: 'Pubd ... April 1, 1806 by James Cundee, Albion Press, Ivy Lane, Paternoster Row, London.'

1 Remains of Lord Nelson laying in state in the Painted Chamber at Greenwich Hospital. Engraved by M. Merigot from a drawing by C.A. Pugin, executed during the period of exhibition. 325 × 440/400 × 500mm.

2 Funeral Procession of the late Lord Viscount Nelson from Greenwich to Whitehall/on the 8th January 1806. Engraved by I. Hill from a Drawing made by C.A. Pugin during the time of the Procession. 320 × 440/400 × 500mm.

3 Funeral Procession of the late Lord Nelson, from the Admiralty, to St Pauls, London/on the 9th of January, 1806. Engraved by M. Merigot from a drawing made by C.A. Pugin during the time of the Procession. 345 × 445/400 × 500mm. This shows the enormous funeral car drawing up by the W. end of St Paul's Cathedral, outside the railings. It was designed by Rudolph Ackermann, the carriage-maker and fine art dealer, and his aquatint engraving of the hearse, after a drawing by McQuin, is bound up in the BL vol.

4 Interment of the Remains of the late Lord Viscount Nelson in the Cathedral of St Paul, London,/on the 9th of January 1806. Engraved by F.C. Lewis from a drawing made by C.A. Pugin during the time of the Ceremony. 320 × 435/395 × 550mm. View looking E. from under the dome.

1 p 43 Lord Nelson's Funeral Procession by Water from Greenwich Hospital to White-Hall; Jany 8th 1806/ Taken from Bank-Side, Exhibiting a View of St Paul's, London Bridge, &c. Turner pinxt. J. Clark & H. Merke sculp. Published & Sold March 1, 1806, by Edwd Orme Engraver-Printseller to the King and Royal Family, 59 Bond Street, London. 300 × 475/350 × 480mm. Aquatint. pl.8.

2 p 48 The Funeral Procession of Lord Viscount Nelson, Jany 9th 1806. W.M. Craig del. J. Godby sculp. Published & Sold Jany 12, 1806, by Edwd Orme Engraver-Printseller to the King and Royal Family, 59 Bond Street, London. 265 × 400/330 × 430mm. Aquatint. pl.9. Seen from Ludgate Hill.

3 p 54 The Ceremony of Lord Nelson's Interment in St Paul's Cathedral. Jany 9th 1806. Drawn by Wm Orme from a Sketch made on the spot by the Reverend Holt Waring. J. Clark & J. Hamble sculpt. 440 × 305/475 × 355mm. Aquatint pl.10.

4 p 66 (tm) The Remains of Lord Nelson proceeding from Greenwich Hospital. Published and Sold May 1, 1806 by Edwd Orme, 59 Bond Street, London. 90 × 250/110 × 260mm. Line-engraving. Also published as a headpiece to a broadsheet commemorative poem by the patriotic Navy pay clerk, W.T. Fitzgerald.

220 · ORME'S LIFE AND DEATH OF NELSON* [1806]

On the death of Nelson commemorative prints were much sought after and Edward Orme's graphic life of the hero, with a text by F.W. Blagdon, was collected from the stock of his print shop engravings celebrating the naval victories, together with three aquatints in colour and a line-engraving specially commissioned to record the funeral ceremony after the lying-in-state at Greenwich.

Orme's Graphic History of the Life, Exploits, and Death of Horatio Nelson … containing fifteen engravings; and intended as an accompaniment to the three celebrated whole-sheet plates of His Lordship's splendid victories … The Memoirs by Francis William Blagdon. London, Printed for … and sold by Edward Orme, 59 Bond Street the corner of Brook Street: and by Longman, Hurst, Rees, and Orme, Paternoster Row. J.G. Barnard, Printer, 57, Snow Hill, 1806.

Quarto, 360 × 255mm.   1806

COLLATION Title-page; dedication to the King (1 leaf); verse tribute (1 leaf); pp 5–66, Memoirs; list of plates (1 leaf).

221 · ACKERMANN'S 'VIEWS OF LONDON' [1811–22]

Eighteen fine large aquatints, coloured by hand, of which 17 are in the Guildhall Library, have been identified by Ralph Hyde as forming the series advertised in 1819 by Rudolph Ackermann on the back wrapper of his *Observations on Ackermann's Patent Moveable Axles for Four Wheeled Carriages*: 'A View of Southwark New Iron Bridge, being a continuation of the "Views of London", price 15s. in colours, size 14 by 19 inches'. The advertisement goes on to list 12 more of the series, but not the first two dated 1811 and by then, no doubt, out of print, nor the Waterloo Bridge view of 1818, nor the last two which were yet to be published in 1822. The intermediate prints were published at the rate of three or four per annum from 1816 to 1819.

The set was inaugurated by the artists and engraver who only the previous year had completed the final plates for Ackermann's *Microcosm of*

London (no 99)—Pugin, Rowlandson and Bluck—but after these two initial views the dominant artist was T.H. Shepherd, then in his early twenties. Nine of his already characteristic drawings were engraved for the series. The other artist, John Gendall, was only three years his senior. After being recommended by Sir John Soane to Ackermann he became one of his resident artists, helping to run the business and experiment with lithography. Of the other engravers Joseph Stadler and Thomas Sutherland had made important contributions to the *Microcosm* and Daniel Havell was engraving aquatint views for Ackermann's *History of the Colleges* (no 116) and Pyne's *Royal Residences* (no 132), books contemporary with these London views.

A generation later five of the of the same subjects were treated in a series of coloured lithographs by Thomas Picken (no 209); it was published by Ackermann's son and based on drawings by T.H. Shepherd's elder brother, George Sidney—a demonstration of the family continuity in London topographical illustration. Earlier, in 1836, this same Ackermann had published aquatint replacements for two of the original plates: that of the Royal Exchange, whose tower had by then been rebuilt, and that of the Horse Guards, both with up-to-date staffage.

Fortunately a number of the pencil drawings on which the T.H. Shepherd aquatints were based survive to witness to the care taken by the artist over details of architecture and costume and the faithfulness of these fine engravings to their originals. A coloured outline-engraving of one of the plates in the Museum of London shows the method of building up from these drawings to the final aquatinted and hand-coloured print. There is no text and the plates are unnumbered and unlisted. Publication-lines read: 'London Published (date) at Ackermann's Repository of Arts, 101 Strand.' Plate-mark dimensions are given wherever possible but not all have survived as the plate were generous in size.

1 A Bird's eye view of Covent Garden Market,/taken from the Hummums. 1st January 1811. Pugin & Rowlandson delt. Bluck sculpt. 355 × 493/425 × 530mm. View looking W.

2 A Bird's eye view of Smithfield Market,/taken from the Bear & Ragged Staff. Pugin & Rowlandson delt. Bluck sculpt. 1st January 1811. 355 × 550/425 × 530mm. Original water-colour drawing (280 × 440mm) in Guildhall Library (Pr 621/WES).

3 A View of the Royal Exchange,/Cornhill. T.H.Shepherd delt. Dl Havell sculpt. July 1st 1816. 370 × 495/445 × 530mm. The pencil drawing (390 × 480mm) in BM (*Crace* 22.83) differs slightly, most notably in the figures of the news vendors running towards the S. entrance, with their horns. A replacement plate (360 × 490mm), published in 1836 without credits by Ackermann & Co, 96 Strand, shows the building from the same angle but with the new entrance front and tower built by George Smith, 1820–6 (and burned down in 1838) and with up-to-date staffage, including a sandwich-man with board advertising 'Diorama de London' (open 1823) (*Crace* 22.89). This plate is sometimes found with only two aquatinted colours, blue and grey, uncoloured by hand.

4 A View of the Bank of England. T.H. Shepherd delt. Dl Havell sculpt. Augt 1st 1816. 350 × 490/435 × 530mm. From the Shepherd drawing (345 × 580mm) in BM (*Crace* 22.21), with minimal change of staffage to l. of centre. (*Bank of England* 43)

5 A View of the Horse Guards/from Whitehall. T.H. Shepherd delt. J.C. Stadler sculp…. Octr 1st 1816. 348 × 490/430 × 530mm. Pencil drawing (348 × 480mm) in BM (*Crace* 16.86). A replacement plate (357 × 492/442 × 530mm) has the same caption and the publication-line 'London, Publish'd April 15th 1836 by Ackermann & Co., 96 Strand.' The staffage has been brought up to date. The Guildhall Library copy (W.W2/HOR) is printed in two aquatint colours, blue and grey.

6 A South View of the New Custom House./Reduced from a Drawing by D. Laing Esqr the Architect. J.C. Stadler sculpt. April 1, 1817. 355 × 490/430 × 530mm. Built 1814–17.

7 A South View of Somerset House,/from Waterloo Bridge. J.H. Shepherd delt. J.C. Stadler sculpt. April 11 1817. 350 × 492/435 × 535mm. Pencil drawing (310 × 490mm), signed 'T. Hosmer Shepherd 1817', with slightly different staffage in foreground, in BM (*Crace* 6.231).

8 East India House. T.H. Shepherd delt. J.C. Stadler sculpt. June 1st 1817. 347 × 485/435 × 535mm. Pencil drawing (300 × 480mm) in BM (*Crace* 23.59).

9 North East View of/Westminster Abbey. J. Gendall delt. J.C. Stadler sculpt. Septr 12th 1817. 345 × 485/430 × 530mm. Gendall's drawing was shown at the RA in 1818.

10 View of Waterloo Bridge/From the East end of Somerset House Terrace. J.H. Shepherd delt. J.C. Stadler sculpt. April 12th 1818. 335 × 485mm. Opened 18 June 1817.

11 South East view of St Paul's Cathedral. J. Gendall delt. D. Havell sculpt. 1st May 1818. 360 × 495mm.

12 View of the Admiralty. J. Gendall delt. J.C. Stadler sculpt. Octr 1st 1818. 355 × 480mm.

13 Southwark Iron Bridge,/as seen from Bank-side. J. Gendall delt. T. Sutherland sculpt. Jany 1st 1819. 335 × 485/425 × 530mm. Opened on 24 March 1819.

14 View of Somerset House,/from the Strand. T.H. Shepherd delt. J. Bluck sculpt. Jany 1st 1819. 340 × 490/? × 530mm. Pencil drawing (330 × 480mm) in BM (*Crace* 17.122). In the Museum of London is an outline-etching of this subject, coloured by hand as a guide to the aquatint engraver and colourists.

15 Westminster Hall & Abbey/as seen from Westminster Bridge. J. Gendall delt. D. Havell sculpt. Jany 1 1819. 350 × 490mm.

16 View of the Tower of London. J. Gendall delt. D. Havell sculpt. Octor 1819. 355 × 495mm.

17 The Quadrant, Regent Street. T.H. Shepherd delt. J. Bluck sculpt. May 1 1822. 340 × 495mm. Pencil drawing (340 × 490mm) in BM (*Crace* 10.149). Opened in the late summer of 1819.

18 Regent Street,/from Piccadilly. T.H. Shepherd delt. J. Bluck sculpt. July 1, 1822. 340 × 490mm. The Shepherd pencil drawing (315 × 490mm) in BM (*Crace* 10.161) is also taken from 'Regent Circus' but views what is now Lower Regent Street from a slightly different angle, thus completely obscuring the façade and coupled columns of Carlton House. This façade is, however, the centrepiece of the aquatint which also differs in its staffage, so it is likely that Shepherd made another drawing when it was pointed out to him that he had omitted the vista intended as the culmination of the new route linking the Regent's park to his palace. A smaller drawing (120 × 195mm) in Guildhall Library (W.2 REG) does indeed show Carlton House but it is taken from a point closer to Nash's own house on the l. and St Philip's Church on the r. The Circus was completed by about 1820. Another pencil drawing (320 × 405mm) in Westminster Public Library shows Carlton House faintly sketched in, from the viewpoint of the aquatint. (*Crace* 10.162)

---

222 · BRITTON'S FINE ARTS OF THE ENGLISH SCHOOL* [1812]

John Britton must have intended this work, issued in numbered Parts, to be a general survey of British painting, sculpture and architecture, printed in folio to sort with large illustrative engravings, but only 110 pages of text and 23 plates survive so it must have been short lived. We are here concerned with its first issues, announced in the *Monthly Literary Advertiser* for February and August 1810:

Number I of the FINE ARTS of the ENGLISH SCHOOL:... Edited by John Britton ... Contents:... 4. An elevation of the West Front of St Paul's Cathedral ... 5. A Plan of the Substructure of the same Building ... both drawn by James Elmes—Number II (to be continued quarterly) ... A Geometrical Section of the dome, transepts, &c....

The essay on the Cathedral was by the architect Edmund Aikin, who had already published a collection of villa designs and whose father was the learned author and physician John Aikin who in 1811 published a *History of the Environs of London* (no 107). The four plates were drawn by another architect, almost his exact contemporary, whose earliest publication this seems to have been: James Elmes, who later wrote the first documented life of Sir Christopher Wren. They were very finely engraved by two of Britton's most expert craftsmen, John Le Keux and Richard Roffe.

The Fine Arts of the English School, illustrated by a Series of Engravings from Paintings, Sculpture, and Architecture of eminent English Artists with ... essays by various authors edited, and partly written by John Britton, F.S.A. (epigraph) Printed at the Chiswick Press, by C. Whittingham for Longman, Hurst, Rees, Orme and Brown, Paternoster Row: J. Taylor, High Holborn, the Editor, Tavistock Place and W. Bond, Newman Street, London. 1812.

Folio, 415 × 320mm.   1812

COLLATION   Title-page; engr title-page (with a view of the Strand front of Chambers's Somerset House); dedication to the Prince Regent dated January 1812 (1 leaf); contents (1 leaf); preface (2pp); pp i–iv, introductory address by J. Britton dated January 1812; pp 1–66, Fine Arts (January 1812); pp 1–26, Fine Arts (February 1812); pp 1–18, An Essay towards a History and Description of the Cathedral Church of St Paul, London by Edmund Aikin (illustrated by plans from drawings by James Elmes).

The four plates, each dedicated to a senior architect, are engraved tm with the plate number and 'Class 3—Architecture—for the Fine Arts of the English School', and have as their publication-line 'London, Published (date) by Longman & Co Paternoster Row, J. Taylor (59) High Holborn (and W. Bond, Newman Street).' A fifth plate, a plan, without the superscription and with different credits, was added, together with a four-page preface by Britton, to a separate reissue in the following year:

Plans, Elevation, Section and View of the Cathedral Church of St. Paul, London: engraved by J. Le Keux, from drawings by J. Elmes, with an Historical and Descriptive Account by E. Aikin, architect. London: Longman, Hurst, Rees, Orme and Brown ... 1813.

The plates survived for another 35 years, after which they were reissued (less the printer's credits) with an abridged text:

A History and Description of the Cathedral Church of St. Paul, London. With a concise account of the edifices which have previously occupied the same site. By Edmund Aikin, Architect. Illustrated by Plates from Drawings by James Elmes, Architect. Published by A.E. Evans and Sons, 1 Great Queen Street, Lincolns-Inn Fields, London. 1848.

Folio, 375 × 265mm.   1848

COLLATION   Title-page; pp 1–7, History; p 8, description of plates; 5 plates.

1 St. Pauls Cathedral Church/London/Plan of the basement or substructure:... Sir Christopher Wren Architect. James Elmes delint. from actual measurements. Richd Roffe sculp. Nov 1, 1809. 180 × 330/300 × 420mm. Refs A–K.

2 St. Pauls Cathedral Church/London/Geometrical Elevation of the Western front./To John Soane ... inscribed. Sir Christopher Wren Architect. James Elmes delint. John Le Keux sculp. Printed by Cox & Barnett. Nov. 1, 1809. 290 × 225/400 × 320mm.

3 St. Pauls Cathedral Church/London/Geometrical Section of the Dome, Transepts &c from North to South./To William Porden ... inscribed. James Elmes delint. John Le Keux sculp. Printed by Hayward. May 1, 1810. 285 × 220/410 × 320mm.

4 St. Pauls Cathedral Church/London/Perspective View of the North and East Sides/To Charles Heathcote Tatham ... inscribed. James Elmes delint. John Le Keux sculp. Printed by Hayward. Jan 1, 1811. 205 × 255/320 × 410mm.

1813 and 1848 reissues

5 Ground Plan of St. Paul's Cathedral Church,/London./ The dotted lines shew the ornaments of the Vaultings. Sir Christopher Wren, Architect. W.B. Hue del. from Measurements. H. Le Keux sculp. London, Published Aug. 1, 1813 by Longman & Co. Paternoster Row & J. Taylor, 59 High Holborn. 220 × 330mm. Refs A–W,a–i,1–12.

223 · STORER'S CATHEDRAL CHURCHES OF GREAT BRITAIN* [1814–19]

This work, published between 1814 and 1819, was a contemporary of John Britton's series the *Cathedral Antiquities of London* which, however, came out in extensive monographs on single cathedrals and continued for a further 16 years. James Storer may have intended his work to be published in a similar fashion since there is a separate text for each cathedral description, with half a dozen or more plates listed and grouped at the end, and each separate section of the letterpress is paginated by an italic alphabet with only an irresolute attempt to co-ordinate the contents of the volume by means of signatures. Each of the four volumes appeared with a uniform title-page so presumably the work was published in Numbers with provision for binding. The series includes an 18 page essay on St Paul's Cathedral with eight views and a ground-plan listed and numbered. No letters, apart from this numbering, were added to the plates which are printed on India paper so the captions have been taken from the plates list. In a later work, Winkles's *Cathedral Churches* (no 184), the St Paul's plates are mostly also printed by Storer.

History and Antiquities of the Cathedral Churches of Great Britain. Illustrated with a Series of Highly Finished Engravings, Exhibiting general and particular Views, Ground Plans, and all the architectural Features and Ornaments in the various Styles of Building ... By James Storer. (epigraph) In Four Volumes. Vol. III (IV). London: Published by Rivingtons; Murray; Hatchard; Clarke; Taylor; and Sherwood, Neely, and Jones. MDCCCXVII (MDCCCXIX). Coe, Printer, Little Carter Lane, St Paul's.

Quarto, 265 × 200mm.   1817–19

COLLATION   (of the essay on St Paul's, bound at the binder's whim in either vol. 3 or vol. 4) Leaves a–r (less 'j' but including 'r' verso, ie 18pp), History and Antiquities of the Cathedral Church and See of St Paul, London, index ('r' verso); 9 plates.

1 A View of the Southern Front ... 110 × 85/180 × 125mm.

2 Interior of the South Transept with part of its Western Aisle ... 110 × 80/185 × 125mm.

510

3 View from the end of Cheapside, looking south-west. 95 × 100/125 × 185mm.

4 A distant view of the Western and Southern Fronts of the Cathedral taken from the River Thames ... 80 × 115/130 × 185mm.

5 The South Eastern End of the Cathedral ... 110 × 80/180 × 130mm.

6 View of the interior, shewing the Eastern end of the Nave ... 115 × 80/175 × 130mm.

7 View of ... part of the Crypt ... the burial place of Nelson. 90 × 105/130 × 180mm.

8 The Western Front. 115 × 80/175 × 130mm.

9 (plan of the Cathedral with, tm) St Paul's Cathedral/ Shewing the Groining of the Roof. Pubd by Sherwood & Co. Nov. 1, 1817. 185 × 120/203 × 130mm.

224 · BRIEF ACCOUNT OF THE CORONATION OF GEORGE IV [1821]

This souvenir of the coronation, published by Walther of Covent Garden, consists of a brief, anonymous text described as 'a judicious compilation from accounts already before the Public', presumably newspaper reports, together with eight plates, six of which are small aquatints coloured by hand, listed from 2 to 7. These are early works by W. Read, an extremely versatile engraver. Publication-lines where present read: '(London) Published by D. Walther, Bridges Street Covent Gar(de)n.' The unnumbered plates, other than the frontispiece, are gathered at the end of the work.

A Brief Account of the Coronation of His Majesty, George IV. July 19, 1821. London: Printed for D. Walther, Brydges Street, Covent Garden. 1821. (verso) G. Richards, Printer, 100 St Martin's Lane, Charing-cross.

Octavo, 240 × 155mm.   1821

COLLATION   Title-page; pp 1–32, Brief Account.

1 front. His Most Gracious Majesty,/George the IV. 85 × 60,115 × 95/235 × 140mm. Black and white stipple-engraving.

2 The Procession from Westminster Hall to the Abbey. Drawn & Engraved by W. Read. 117 × 183/140 ×

235mm. A birds-eye view with the awnings eliminated to show the procession.

3 The New Imperial Crown,/worn by his Majesty George the Fourth at his Coronation. W. Read sc. 150 × 105/210 × 140mm. No publication-line.

4 Coronation of His Majesty George the Fourth./July 19 1821. W. Read Fecit. 190 × 135/230 × 145mm. W. view of interior of the Abbey from the sanctuary, the crowning in progress.

5 Ceremony of Homage at the Coronation/of His Majesty George the Fourth./from a drawing taken on the spot. W. Read sculp. Published Sepr. 1st 1821 ... 185 × 135/230 × 145mm. E. view inside the Abbey, looking towards the sanctuary.

6 The entrance of the Champion with the ceremony of the Challenge. W. Read fecit. 210 × 125/235 × 140mm. Westminster Hall, N. entrance.

7 The Grand Coronation Banquet/in Westminster Hall, July 19th 1821. 185 × 130/225 × 145mm. No credit or publication-line.

8 The Regalia. 185 × 125/225 × 145mm. Refs 1–11. Black and white engraving.

225 · HUISH'S HISTORY OF THE CORONATION OF GEORGE IV [1822]

This coronation souvenir was published by Robins & Co to compete with Walther's *Brief Account* (no 224). Walther's book consists of a brief résumé of the ceremonial illustrated by eight plates of which six are coloured aquatints while Robins engaged a miscellaneous writer on topics such as bee-keeping to produce a more substantial text which includes an historical survey but is illustrated by half a dozen plates in black and white only. The engravings are unnumbered but have a publication-line: 'Published by J. Robins & Co. Albion Press, London (date).' Their dates extend from July, two days after the coronation, to October 1821 but it is apparent from the advertisement on the back wrapper that the book was not published until January 1822.

An Authentic History of the Coronation of His Majesty King George the Fourth: with a full and authentic detail of that august solemnity ... To which is prefixed a concise

History of the Coronations of the Kings of England. By Robert Huish Esq. London: J. Robins and Co. Albion Press, Ivy Lane, Paternoster Row. 1821.

Octavo, 220 × 130mm.   1821

COLLATION Half-title; title-page; pp i–iv, introduction; pp 1–314, History; list of plates (1 leaf).

1 front. Westminster Hall,/as it appeared at the Coronation of George IV/With the ceremony of the Champion's Challenge. R.B. Schnebbelie delt. J. Chapman sculpt. Augt 4, 1821. 160 × 100/210 × 125mm.

2 p 47 1. The Crown of State. Sept 1, 1821. 210 × 125mm pl. mark. With the other regalia.

3 p 207 The Coronation Procession of King George the Fourth. R.B. Schnebbelie del. H. Summons sculp. Octr 6, 1821. 95 × 175/120 × 205mm.

4 p 232 King George the fourth. Engraved by R. Page. Aug 2 1821. 165 × 110/215 × 120mm. Stipple portrait in coronation robes.

5 p 255 Westminster Hall,/as it appeared at the Coronation of George IV/The Royal Banquet. R.B. Schnebbelie delt. J. Shury sculpt. Augt 9 1821. 165 × 105/220 × 125mm.

6 p 262 The King's champion. Engraved by R. Page. July 21, 1821. 160 × 100/220 × 125mm.

226 · AN IMPARTIAL HISTORICAL NARRATIVE [1823]

The 'cause célèbre' of George IV's attempts, on his accession in 1820, to rid himself of his Queen, Caroline of Brunswick, produced a spate of polemical literature, mainly directed against the King. He had married her in 1795 but deserted her in the following year soon after she had borne him a child, Princess Charlotte. His persecution of her and his attempt to obtain a Bill of Divorcement against her on grounds of adultery made her the object of much popular sympathy to which fuel was added when she was ignominiously turned away from her husband's coronation at the very door of the Abbey. Robert Bowyer, miniature painter to the Queen, printseller and bookseller, published a number of prints illustrating these events to which he added a narrative for publication in book form.

An Impartial Historical Narrative of those Momentous Events which have taken place in this country during the period from the year 1816 to 1823. Illustrated with Engravings by the first artists. London. Printed by Thomas Bensley, Crane Court, Fleet Street; for Robert Bowyer, 74 Pall Mall. 1823.

Folio, 490–520 × 365–90mm.   1823

COLLATION Title-page; pp 1–56, Impartial Historical Narrative and Description of the Engravings.

The eight plates include three large aquatints, hand coloured, engraved by M. Dubourg who had previously illustrated Edward Orme's similar historical memento of the 1814 Peace celebrations (no 112). Of these the coronation scene in the Abbey, with its solitary throne, was painted by Stephanoff of Pyne's *Royal Residences* (no 132). He is also here the delineator of the House of Lords interior during the investigation into the Queen's conduct, an engraving in line and stipple. The publication-line reads: 'Pubd by R. Bowyer, 74 Pall Mall, London.'

1 p 8 A Tribute of Respect to His late Majesty King George the Third./Medallions of Her Royal Highness the Princess Charlotte & Queen Caroline./Mr Wyatt's Cenotaph to the Memory of Her late Royal Highness the Princess Charlotte. T. Stothard & I. Stephanoff delt: G. Murray & W. Morrison sculp.... 1822. 400 × 275/475 × 350mm. Line-engraving.

2 p 23 Arrival at Brandenburgh House of the Watermen &c. with an address to the Queen on the 3d. October 1820. Dubourg sculpt ... 1 Octr. 1821. 275 × 365/355 × 470mm. Aquatint. Brandenburg House was rented by Queen Caroline in May 1820 and she occupied this Hammersmith riverside home during her trial until May 1822, when she died there.

3–4 p 26 View of the interior of the House of Lords, during the important investigation in 1820. Painted by J. Stephanoff: Engraved by John George Murray ... June 1, 1823. 335 × 470/370 × 490mm. Line and stipple-engraving. The separate etched outline-plate forms a key to the above and includes a small 'View of the Villa d'Este on the Lake of Como, the Residence of Her late Majesty Queen Caroline' (115 × 135mm).

5–6 p 40 Facsimiles of the Autographs of the Royal Family/Also of the Peers who voted during the investigation of the Charges against Queen Caroline/ in the House of Lords, 1820 ... Augt. 1, 1822. 405 × 300mm. Etched, on two sheets.

7 p 40 The Queen Returning from the House of Lords. Dubourg sculpt ... 1 Octr 1821. 275 × 365/360 × 490mm. Aquatint. Scene outside the Houses of Parliament.

8 p 45 The Coronation of His Majesty, George the Fourth: taken at the time of the Recognition. July 19,

1821. Stephanoff Pinxt. Dubourg sculpt.... June 4, 1822. 330 × 460/375 × 490mm. Aquatint.

227 · 'GOLDSMITH'S' NATURAL AND ARTIFICIAL WONDERS* [1825]

Richard Phillips, the radical bookseller and founder of the *Leicester Herald* and *Monthly Magazine*, included among the list of his early avocations that of schoolmaster. This enabled him, once he was established in London as a publisher of guidebooks and as Sheriff and future Lord Mayor, to supplement his income by writing textbooks. In 1805, a year after the publication of *Modern London* (no 189) under his imprint, the first edition of *A Grammar of Geography* appeared and was to become an educational bestseller with revised editions coming out over a period of 60 or more years. For this and other schoolroom books, however, he adopted the persona of the Rev J. Goldsmith, for good commercial reasons, surely, since it hinted at the authorship of some learned clerical tutor to the sons of the squirearchy. Under this pseudonym, and in his fifty-eighth year, was published this three-volume geographical and topographical survey of the United Kingdom of which the first two volumes were concerned with England and Wales and the third with Scotland and Ireland.

It is illustrated with small, undistinguished line-engravings, mostly two to a page, by W. Read, who could turn his hand to any medium: stipple and mezzotint portraits, the aquatinting of Rowlandson's illustrations for *The Adventures of Johnny Newcome in the Navy* (1818), and the charming aquatints for Shaw's *History of Moray* (1827); He also turns up as printer of some of the steel-engravings in *Metropolitan Improvements* (no 154).

There are ten London illustrations in the first volume and five in the second. The publication-line reads: 'Published by G.B. Whittaker. 1825.'

The Natural and Artificial Wonders of the United

Kingdom: with engravings. In three volumes. Vol. I (II). England and Wales. By the Rev. J. Goldsmith ... London: Printed for G.B. Whittaker, Ave Maria Lane. MDCCCXXV.

Duodecimo, 170 × 100mm.   1825

COLLATION Vol. 1. Title-page; pp iii–v, preface dated 1 March 1825; list of plates (2pp); pp 1–360, British Antiquities, etc. Vol. 2. Title-page; list of plates (2pp); pp 1–360, Commercial Establishments, etc.

VOL. 1

1 p 143 Westminster Abbey. Read sculp. – St Pauls. W. Read sculp. 57 × 75,55 × 75/165 × 95mm.

2 p 272 Mansion House – Guildhall. W. Read sc. Each 55 × 75/165 × 95mm.

3 p 261 Somerset House. W. Read sc. – Westminster Hall. W. Read sc. Each 53 × 78/165 × 95mm. Somerset House from river; Westminster Hall from the N.

4 p 277 Theatre Covent Garden – Opera House. W. Read sc. 55 × 78, 50 × 78/165 × 95mm. Italian Opera House, Haymarket.

5 p 299 Greenwich Hospital. Read sc. – Chelsea Hospital. Read sc. 53 × 75, 50 × 75/165 × 95mm. Both from the river. (*Longford* 37)

VOL. 2

6 p 1 East India House. W Read sc. – Royal Exchange. W. Read sc. Each 50 × 78/165 × 95mm.

7 p 11 Custom House. 78 × 115/95 × 165mm. Anon.

8 p 57 Waterloo Bridge. 75 × 120/95 × 165mm. Anon.

9 p 64 Southwark Bridge. W. Read sc. 75 × 125/95 × 165mm. Built by John Rennie, 1815–19.

228 · HAKEWILL'S ZOOLOGICAL GARDENS [1831]

James Hakewill succeeded to his father's decorating business in 1791 and some of his designs were shown at the Royal Academy from 1800. In 1813 he published a *History of Windsor* illustrated from his own drawings and, in 1817–18 and 1825, 'Picturesque Tours' of Italy and of Jamaica with aquatints based on his sketches. In 1826 the Zoological Society of London was instituted and the architect Decimus Burton engaged to design the buildings and cages needed to house the animals, a work which occupied him at intervals until 1841. It fell to Hakewill to record for the Society what Burton achieved in the first five years of his commission and his ten lithographs of the Gardens were published in folio (410 × 305mm), without text, in 1831. Most copies are printed in grey but the Abbey catalogue (233) gives details of a set with added colour and the original titled brown wrappers with the prices 'Prints 18/- Proofs on India 25/-'.

All plates but one have the credits 'Drawn from Nature and on Stone by James Hakewill. Printed by C. Hullmandel.', with a plate number tr. The running title 'Zoological Gardens, Regent's Park (Southern Portion)' is on all the plates, either as part of the caption or along the tm.

0 (title, in decorative frame with dedication to William IV) A Series/of/Ten Views/in the Southern Portion of the Gardens of/The Zoological Society in the Regent's Park./laid out from the Designs of/Decimus Burton Esqr. (list of views)/The Views made from Nature, and/Drawn on Stone by James Hakewill.... Published Feby 24th, 1831 by James Hakewill No 9 Manchester Strt, Manchester Sqr./Printed at C. Hullmandel's Lithographic Establishment, 49, Gt Marlborough Strt. Roundel, 170mm.

1 Entrance Terrace looking towards the Bear Pit. 140 × 260mm, within a frame of classical architecture 180 × 280mm.

2 View from the Bears Pit./Towards the Emu House. 210 × 310mm.

3 View from the Emu House. 220 × 315mm.

4 Llama House & Macaw Cage. 215 × 315mm.

5 Arch-Way to the North Garden. 215 × 315mm.

6 The Brahmin Bull, Bison, &c. 215 × 310mm.

7 The Goat House. 220 × 315mm.

8 The Otters and Seals. 215 × 315mm.

9 The Monkey Cage. 220 × 320mm.

10 Proposed Terrace for the Nobler Animals. Drawn on Stone by James Hakewill.... 210 × 310mm.

229 · SCHARF'S ZOOLOGICAL GARDENS [1835]

George Scharf was born in Bavaria and studied drawing and lithography in Munich. In 1810 he left for an adventurous life in France and the Low Countries, supporting himself by painting miniatures. He joined the English army, was present at the Battle of Waterloo and finally, in 1816, settled in London for life and there found employment in portrait painting and illustrating scientific works. His most notable work is in the field of London topography, and in the collection of his drawings in the British Museum he has left a valuable and detailed record of streets and houses in Georgian London, including the original Museum building itself. Particularly impressive are the drawings and lithographs commissioned by the City Bridge Committee which show the approaches to old London Bridge before and during the demolitions entailed by the building of the new bridge from 1830 to 1831.

Among the drawings in the Museum are some of the Zoological Gardens made in the 1830s when he was preparing the present set of lithographs. This set consists of five, printed in grey or coloured by hand, and shows the animals and their visitors against a background of the cages, Decimus Burton's buildings and the Regent's Park. These are credited 'G. Scharf del. et sculp. Printed by C. Hullmandel' and have the publication-line 'London, Published by the artist, 14 Francis Str., Tottenham Court Road.', mostly dated 1835. The captions are general, without reference to the specific animals or locations depicted.

Two extra plates, dated 1835 and 1836, show only the chimpanzees and the giraffes with their keepers but include no topographical detail. The series usefully complements Hakewill's similar collection (no 228), which also consists of lithographs printed by the firm of Hullmandel.

1 Zoological Gardens, Regent's Park. 202 × 310mm. Showing the aviaries.

2 Zoological Gardens, Regent's Park. 202 × 315mm. The bear pit. There are two versions of this print; in the second the bear's pole has been moved to a safer distance from the spectators.

3 Zoological Gardens, Regent's Park. 215 × 315mm. The camel house and zebras.

4 Zoological Gardens/Regent's Park. 200 × 315mm. The elephant enclosure.

5 Zoological Gardens/Regent's Park. 205 × 310mm. The monkey house.

6 Chimpanzee or African Orang Utan, Zoological Gardens/ Regent's Park. 190 × 250mm. Vignetted.

7 The Giraffes, with the Arabs who brought them over to this country./Zoological Gardens,/Regent's Park. Octr. 1836. 210 × 340mm. Vignetted.

230 · BURY'S VIEWS ON THE LONDON AND BIRMINGHAM RAILWAY [1837]

Rudolph Ackermann junior, whose father and grandfather had been in the carriage building business and whose firm's publications portrayed the London of the cabriolet and stage-coach, ushered in the new reign with a series of aquatints of the railroad that was now forging northward from Euston Square. Only three months after her accession he hailed the age of Victoria as the Railway Age; so soon indeed that he had still to describe himself as printseller not only to Her Majesty but also to her mother the Duchess of Kent.

Part 1 of this work most enticingly shows the terminus, cuttings, tunnels and bridges as far as Kings Langley in Hertfordshire. The artist was the architect Thomas Talbot Bury, a pupil of A.C. Pugin who specialized in tinted architectural drawing, engraving and lithography, had contributed to Pugin's *Illustrations of the Public Buildings of London* (no 146), and had recorded old St Dunstan in the West for lithography (no 166) before its demolition in 1832. Another artist, J.C. Bourne, had been drawing the progress of the railway since 1836, but although Ackermann brought out the first set of Bury aquatints well before the Bourne lithographs (no 231) were available the earlier publication seems to have succumbed to the later, whose 32 views along the entire route were collected in 1839. These were likewise available from Ackermann's (in the Strand) as one of their distributors.

Three very competent engravers translated Bury's drawings into aquatint and delightful colour was added to the half dozen plates, no doubt under his direction. There is no text or list of plates but each is numbered tr and carries the credit 'T.T. Bury delt.' and publication-line 'London, Published September 18th, 1837 by Ackermann & Co., 96 Strand.'

Six Coloured Views on the London and Birmingham Railway, from Drawings made on the Line. With the Sanction of the Company. By Mr. T.T. Bury. Part 1. London: Published by Ackermann and Co., 96 Strand, and to be had of R. Ackermann, 191, Regent Street; Printsellers by Appointment to Her Majesty and Her Royal Highness the Duchess of Kent. 1837. Price Twelve Shillings.

Folio, 350 × 300mm.   1837

1 The Station at Euston Square. J. Harris sculpt. 210 × 270/250 × 305mm.

2 View taken from under the Hampstead Road Bridge/ looking towards the station at Euston Square. C. Hunt sculpt. 213 × 270/250 × 305mm.

3 View taken from the Bridge over the Canal, Camden Town. N. Fielding sculpt. 210 × 270/250 × 300mm.

4 Viaduct at Watford. J. Harris sculpt. 215 × 270/250 × 300mm.

5 Entrance to the Tunnel at Watford. N. Fielding sculpt. 265 × 213/305 × 250mm.

6 Bridge over the Canal near Kings-Langley. J. Harris sculpt. 215 × 280/250 × 305mm.

231 · BOURNE'S DRAWINGS OF THE LONDON AND BIRMINGHAM RAILWAY* [1839]

John Cooke Bourne's drawings of the London to Birmingham Railway were made between 1836 and 1838 and then issued as lithographs. He published them jointly with Ackermann & Co, in Numbers, of which four, completing the work, were available in 1839 at £4 14s 6d, including a commentary on work in progress by John Britton. The first Number, which came out in September 1838 priced at one guinea, is detailed here. It consists of the title-page, a double map of the railway line and seven plates of the excavation and works in the London area; views in the other Numbers are of the Home Counties and beyond. The placing of captions and credits varies from plate to plate. Lithographic printing was shared between Day & Haghe and C. Hullmandel. The Publication-line reads: 'Published (date) by J.C. Bourne 19 Lamb's Conduit St. & Ackermann & Co. Strand.'

Folio, 545 × 380mm.   1839

COLLATION Lithotint title-page; pp 1–2, list of drawings, tabular view of the railway; pp 3–26, historical and descriptive accounts; maps, 37 plates.

0 (lithotint title in decorative frame with roundels showing building progress 1830-6 as corner-piece) Drawings/of the/London and Birmingham/Railway,/By/John C. Bourne,/with/An Historical and Descriptive Account/by John Britton F.S.A./Inscribed to the Directors and Engineers of the Company. (vignette) Arrival and Departure Shed Euston Square. London/Published by the Proprietor J.C. Bourne, 19 Lambs Conduit St./Ackermann and Co. Strand and C. Tilt, Fleet Street./1839./Designed and Drawn by Jno C. Bourne. 405 × 305mm.

1 London and Birmingham Railway. 2 line-engraved maps, each 185 × 330mm.

Middlesex

2 (br in work) Entrance Portico—Euston Grove Station. J.C. Bourne del. et lith…. Sepr 1 1838. Printed by Day & Haghe, lithrs to the Queen. 230 × 295mm. The 'Propylaeum' with pavilions, sketched 1838.

3 (bl) Hampstead Road Bridge: Sept 5. 1836. J.C. Bourne del. et lith…. Sepr. 1, 1838. 260 × 415mm. S. side.

4 (br in work) Building retaining wall near Park Street, Camden Town Sepr 17th 1836. J.C. Bourne del. et lith…. Decr. 1838. 280 × 420mm. Park Village excavations.

5 (br in work) Railway bridge over the Regent's Canal. J.C. Bourne del. et lith…. Sepr 1, 1838. 240 × 380mm. E. side, sketched May 1837.

6 (br in work) Building the Stationary Engine House, Camden Town April 28th 1837. J.C. Bourne del. et lithog…. 1839. Printed by C. Hullmandel. 290 × 435mm.

7 Eccentric for shifting rail – Locomotive engine-house – Chimnies of Stationary Engine-House. J.C. Bourne del. et lith…. July 1838. 235 × 340mm. Looking S. towards engine house.

8 (br in work, on each view) Entrance to locomotive engine house Camden Town – Primrose Hill Tunnel. J.C. Bourne del. et lithog…. 1839. Printed by C. Hullmandel. Each 170 × 260mm. Sketched 1839 and 1837.

516

232 · NAYLER'S CORONATION OF GEORGE IV* [1839]

Publication of one series of *The Ceremonial of the Coronation of King George the Fourth* was initiated by John Whittaker in 1821 and of another by Sir George Nayler, Garter King of Arms, in 1823. The King died in 1830, as did the two sponsors of the work in the following year, leaving it incomplete. Henry G. Bohn was at the time building up a trade in rare books at 4 York Street, Covent Garden and in 1835, when Nayler's executors put up for sale the unsold copies of the two Parts already published, together with the copper plates of the illustrations and the copyright, he purchased them and also acquired some of Whittaker's plates. He then lost no time in printing off unpublished matter and having the plates coloured and bound with accompanying text into a folio volume. The 'Advertisement' he prefixed to this is dated 6 April 1837, although the date on the title-page is 1839. The work, which he originally published at £50 8s, was reduced to £12 12s in his 1841 catalogue.

The original drawings were mostly done by members of the Stephanoff family, a name prominent among the credits of Pyne's *Royal Residences* (no 132), and by Charles Wild who also contributed to that publication. Much of the engraving, in both aquatint and mezzotint, was carried out by R. Havell junior, William Bennett, William Bond and H. Meyer. All but three of the 45 plates have beautiful colour added to them, that of the costumes being particularly rich and satisfying.

Nearly all the topographical plates with which this work is concerned were published in the 1839 collection in the first instance and will be described in this context. But less than three months after the dating of Bohn's 'Advertisement' George IV's successor had in his turn died and in 1838 a further coronation was impending. The public interest generated by the accession of a schoolgirl Queen encouraged Bohn to go on expanding the work originally planned by Whittaker and by Nayler into what he was to describe as 'the finest book in the world'. He supplemented his first selection with many extra full-length portraits of the coronation participants by Sir Thomas Lawrence, PRA and

Nayler and rounded it off with a view of the coronation of the young Queen's uncle and predecessor. When this extended, de luxe edition, bound in two elephant folios, was published in 1841 not only was the number of plates increased from 45 to 72 but every sumptuous detail of the book exuded regal pomp and splendour. It was, in the words of Abbey, in whose catalogue (260) it is described minutely, 'a unique book that is painted, enamelled, gilt and bejewelled, and printed upon vellum and satin as well as upon paper'. Bohn's 1841 catalogue valued it at £250, a 1979 bookseller's catalogue at £9,000.

The Coronation of His Most Sacred Majesty King George the Fourth solemnized in the Collegiate Church of Saint Peter Westminster upon the Nineteenth Day of July MDCCCXXI undertaken by His Majesty's Especial Command, by the late Sir George Nayler, Garter Principal King at Arms and since his decease completed from the official documents. London Published by Henry George Bohn, York Street Covent Garden. MDCCCXXXIX.

Folio, 570 × 420mm.   1839

COLLATION Title-page; dedication to George IV (1 leaf); advertisement dated 6 April 1837 (1 leaf); list of plates (1 leaf); pp i–lvi, The Court of Claims; pp 1–134, Coronation preparations and ceremonial; indices (8pp).

The plates are themselves unnumbered but their list order is noted. Publication-lines read, unless otherwise stated: '(London) Published ... (date) by Sir George Nayler Garter.' Of the dozen topographical plates the eight carrying this line are dated either January 1824 or January 1827 and were presumably issued with the first and second Parts of the work, published respectively, according to Bohn's 'Advertisement', in 1825 and 1827. The remainder were no doubt among Bohn's additions.

1 His Majesty/George the Fourth/Proclaimed King/of the/United Kingdom of Great Britain and Ireland,/at Carlton House, on Monday 31st January 1820. C. Wild Delint. R. Havell Junr. sculpsit.... Jany 1824. 190 × 240/460 × 360mm. pl.1. Carlton House façade.

2 His Majesty George the Fourth/Proclaimed King at the Royal Exchange London. 31st January 1820 ... Jany 1827. 250 × 332/350 × 450mm. pl.2.

3 The Court of Claims,/in the Painted Chamber of the Palace at Westminster./1821. J. Stephanoff delt. S.W. Reynolds engraver to the King sculp.... Jany 1824. 242 × 330,250 × 340/420 × 550mm. pl.3.

4 Procession/of the Dean and Prebendaries of Westminster with/The Regalia./July 19th 1821. Charles

Wild delt. M. Dubourg sculp.... Jany 1824. 320 × 445/420 × 560mm. pl.4. Westminster Hall.

5 The King/seated in St. Edward's Chair, Crowned by the Archbishop of Canterbury/ 19th July 1821. Figures by J. Stephanoff. Architecture by Augs. Pugin. F.C. Lewis sculpsit.... Jany 1824. 360 × 480/420 × 560mm. pl.38. Westminster Abbey interior, looking W.

6 The Ceremony of the Homage./19th July 1821. Architecture by Augs. Pugin. Figures by J. Stephanoff. W. Bennett sculpt.... Jany 1824. 350 × 480/420 × 560mm. pl. 39. Looking towards the S. transept of the Abbey.

7 The Royal Banquet./The bringing up of the First Course/ 19th July 1821./Plate 1st. Chas. Wild delt. R. Havell Junr. aquat.... Jany 1824. 320 × 450/415 × 560mm. pl. 40. Westminster Hall, looking W.

8 The Royal Banquet/ First Course continued. Chas. Wild delt. W.I. Bennett sculpt.... Jany 1824. 320 × 450/415 × 560mm. pl. 41. Westminster Hall, looking N.

9 Explanatory Key to the Grand Historical Print of the Coronation of His Most Gracious Majesty King George the Fourth. Published by G. Humphrey, 27 St James's Street, London, Jany 25th 1822. 165 × 480,220 × 510/235 × 530mm. Coloured aquatint. pl. 42. Panorama, viewed from the N., of Westminster Hall, Parliament and the Abbey with stands for the spectators.

10 Interior of Westminster Hall as prepared for the Banquet. B. Winkles Etched. 340 × 460/420 × 560mm. Uncoloured outline-etching. pl. 43.

11 Longitudinal Section of Westminster Hall. 420 × 550mm pl.mark. Uncoloured outline-etching. pl. 44.

12 The Ancient Coronation Chair. 2 The Chair of State. 3 The Chair in which the King sat. 4 Fald Stool 5 Fald Stool. 245 × 340/350 × 450mm. Uncoloured outline-etching. pl. 45.

233 · PHILLIPS'S HISTORY OF BERMONDSEY [1841]

J. & W. Robins of Tooley Street, Bermondsey, the publishers of many London illustrated books and of some of the *Stationers' Almanack* engravings of London, issued this book jointly with J. Unwin who provided the five lithographs printed in grey. There are no artistic credits but the undated publication-line reads: 'Published for G.W. Phillips, Unwin litho Bucklersbury.'

The History and Antiquities of the Parish of Bermondsey. By G.W. Phillips. London; J. Unwin, 31 Bucklersbury ... J. & W. Robins, Tooley Street ... 1841.

Octavo, 225 × 140mm.   1841

COLLATION   Title-page; pp 1–115, History.

1 front. South West View of St. Mary Magdalen, Bermondsey/as it appeared in the year 1804. 110 × 170mm.

2 p 8 North Gate-House of Bermondsey Abbey. 160 × 110mm.

3 p 35 Ancient Houses in Long Walk, Bermondsey/ formerly occupied by the Conventual Buildings. 110 × 175mm.

4 p 53 West front of St Mary Magdalen, Bermondsey. 165 × 110mm.

5 p 87 St James's Chapel of Ease. 160 × 105mm. Built in Spa Road by James Savage with G. Allen, 1827–9.

5 The Library. 215 × 160/270 × 200mm.

6 General View,/shewing the proposed New Hall and Library, Stone Buildings &c. 183 × 305/245 × 350mm.

235 · ARCHITECTURAL ANTIQUITIES AND PRESENT STATE OF CROSBY PLACE [1844]

Crosby Place, built by Sir John Crosby, grocer and wool merchant, was on the east side of Bishopsgate Street, on land leased to him in 1466 by the prioress of St Helen's Nunnery. It is associated with Richard III, when Duke of Gloucester, and was lived in by Sir Thomas More in about 1518, and later by his son-in-law William Roper. In the Great Fire all but the fine medieval hall, 69 feet long with a splendid open timber roof and an oriel at the dais end, was burnt. This hall became successively a nonconformist meeting house, a temporary home for the East India Company and, from 1810, was leased to a firm of packers who greatly damaged the building by dividing it into floors. On expiration of their lease in 1831 an appeal was launched for restoration which, when the funds had been raised, was carried out by E.L. Blackburne (whose account of it, illustrated only with a frontispiece and plan, was published in 1834) and by John Davies, the architect also of a synagogue in neighbouring Great St Helen's built between 1837 and 1838.

234 · LINCOLN'S INN HALL AND LIBRARY [1842]

Philip Hardwick completed Sir Robert Taylor's Stone Buildings in Lincoln's Inn in 1835 and drew up plans for a new Gothic Hall and Library in 1842. The actual building operation was supervised by his son, Philip Charles, and the block as it now stands on the west side of the Inn was completed in 1845. This set of lithotints, bound in green cloth in the Royal Library at Windsor, is without text, title-page or contents list but is dated July 1842. On paper measuring 530 × 355mm, each plate has the pin-marks by which correct register of the tint stone was ensured and in some cases the size of the stone can be deduced from the burnishing of the paper beyond the inked surface. Each plate has the credit 'P. Hardwick Archt. Day & Haghe, Lithr. to the Queen.'

1 Plan of Principal Floor. July 1842. 220 × 340mm, stone.

2 South East View. 175 × 300/240 × 340mm.

3 North West View. 170 × 285mm.

4 Interior View from South to North of Great Hall. 346 × 180mm.

The present account of the restored hall is thoroughly illustrated with measured drawings by Henry Hammon and was distributed by the Architectural Library. After restoration the hall was leased to a literary institute and then served successively as a wine merchant's warehouse and a restaurant. It was removed altogether from the City in 1927, being re-erected in Cheyne Walk, Chelsea as part of an international hostel for women designed by Walter Godfrey. No fewer than 38 engravings of the hall on its original site, published between 1790 and 1864, are illustrated in Longford's *Images of Chelsea*.

The plates, steel-engravings, are numbered tr. They have no publication-lines but all have the credit '(Measured and)Drawn by Henry J. Hammon Archt.'

The Architectural Antiquities and Present State of Crosby Place, London, as lately restored by John Davies Esq., Architect. Delineated in a series of plans, elevations, sections and parts at large; with perspective views, from original drawings. By Henry J. Hammon, Architect. With an historical and descriptive account. London: Printed for the author; and sold by John Weale, Architectural Library, 59 High Holborn; W. Pickering, 177 Piccadilly and Smith, Elder & Co., Cornhill. 1844.

Quarto, 320 × 245mm.   1844

COLLATION Title-page; pp 3–4, dedication dated May 1844; pp 5–7, list of subscribers; pp 8–13, introduction; pp 14–16, description of plates.

1 (br) General Ground Plan of/Crosby Place/London. 270 × 375/305 × 300mm.

2 View of Crosby Place from the 'Priory Close'/as it is supposed to have existed about 1475. Engraved by W.S. Wilkinson. 160 × 230/180 × 260mm.

3 Interior of 'The Hall'/1520 circa the occupancy of Sir Thomas More afterwards Lord High Chancellor. Engraved by W.S. Wilkinson. 226 × 165/260 × 180mm.

4 West Front. Engraved by W.S. Wilkinson. 220 × 135/260 × 180mm.

5 (bl) North Side of Quadrangle/a Court, No. 1 on plan. Engraved by A.R. Freebairn. 160 × 230/180 × 260mm.

6 West Elevation in Quadrangle./ No. 1 on Plan. Engraved by A.R. Freebairn. 160 × 235/180 × 260mm.

7 North Front. Engraved by W.S. Wilkinson. 215 × 155/255 × 180mm.

8 Longitudinal Section through 'The Hall'/Looking West in its present state 1844. Engraved by George Winter. 235 × 390/300 × 420mm.

9 Elevation of North end of the Hall. 230 × 160/260 × 180mm. No engraver's credit.

10 Elevation of South Side of Throne Room and Council Room. Engraved by George Winter. 155 × 220/180 × 260mm.

11 Elevation of West end of Throne Room and Council Room. Engraved by J.H. Le Keux. 225 × 155/260 × 180mm.

12 Details of Roof of Hall. Engraved by W.S. Wilkinson. 240 × 158/260 × 180mm.

13 Details of Roofs, &c. Engraved by Geo. Winter. 235 × 160/260 × 180mm.

14 Ancient Fire Place. Engraved by Geo. Winter. 235 × 160/260 × 180mm.

15 Antient Doorways. 165 × 250/180 × 260mm. No engraver's credit.

236 · 'LIMNER'S' CRIES OF LONDON [1851]

This book revives a tradition dating back to the 1711 collection of engravings of Laroon's itinerant dealers, by way of the platitudinously copied Francis Wheatley paintings of London cries originally engraved in 1793–7. Prettified as they were, the latter gave their workaday subjects a picturesque bloom which had great popular appeal. It led Robert Phillips to add a supplement of street trades to his *Modern London* (no 89) and the guidebook publisher Samuel Leigh to offer, either separately or bound up with his *New Picture of London* (no 126), colour plate editions of Busby's *Costumes of the Lower Orders* (1820) or, alternatively, of Rowlandson's inimitable *Characteristic Sketches* (1820) of pedlars, hawkers and con-men, plucked from the rumbustious crowds which people the streets in his *Microcosm* (no 99). More recently, in 1839, a posthumous continuation of J.T. Smith's celebration of London mendicants, *Vagabondiana*, had been illustrated by his etchings of street vendors.

Where this book differs from its predecessors is in the careful delineation of the topographical settings in which the traders are placed. Each of the 24 architectural backgrounds is carefully drawn and engraved by 'Luke Limner', a pseudonym for John Leighton of the family of Holborn wood-engravers and lithographers whose firm printed this charming collection.

The work was issued in alternative editions: as a collection of plain wood-engravings, or with a greenish-yellow lithotint superimposed on the 'cries' in all but the highlights. The plain edition, in wood-engraved wrappers, is dated 1851, the other is undated and bound in publisher's cloth with elaborate designs back and front. Border-lines of the 'cries' measure uniformly 110 × 95mm. They carry no credits.

The design of the figured publisher's binding of the lithotint edition is derived from that of the wrapper. It shows a background of City buildings, including St Paul's and the Monument between confronted 'L's' for Leighton. While the 'cries' themselves have an overall lithotint only, touches of red and grey are added to the title-page. There is an additional title-page (item 27) based on the frontispiece of the plain edition.

COLLATION Engr title-page; pp 1–24, descriptions interleaved with plates.

0 (wood-engr wrapper title) The/Cries/of/London/and Public Edifices/By/Luke Limner/Esq. In Twenty-six illustrations. (in banderole, against background of St Paul's Cathedral flanked by shields of Westminster and Southwark arms; below, various street traders, mending cane chairs and bellows, selling rabbits, etc)

1 (wood-engr title) London Cries/&/Public Edifices/by Luke Limner Esq./Grant and Griffith/successors to Newbery and Harris/Corner of St Paul's Church Yard, London./1851. (against vignette of Ludgate Hill and the W. front of St Paul's Cathedral)

2 front. (The artist in fanciful costume, surrounded by studio 'props' and drawing from a very animated collection of lilliputian hawkers) 130 × 115mm.

3 p 1 The Tower of London—Pots & Kettles to Mend, Bellows to Mend.

4 p 2 The East India House—Rhubarb.

5 p 3 The Bank of England—Matches.

6 p 4 The Royal Exchange—Oranges, Sweet St Michael Oranges.

7 p 5 The Mansion House—Buy a Cage for your fine singing bird.

8 p 6 Old College of Physicians Warwick Lane—Old Chairs to Mend.

9 p 7 Smithfield/St Bartholomew Hospital, Church, & Cathedral of Saint Paul—Cat's Meat, Dog's Meat.

10 p 8 St John's Gate, Clerkenwell—Dust Oh.

11 p 9 Temple Bar—Buy a Lace of the Poor Blind.

12 p 10 Somerset House—Umbrellas to Mend, Any Old ones to Sell.

13 p 11 Covent Garden Market—Cherry Ripe! Round & Sound 4d. a Pound.

14 p 12 Covent Garden Theatre—The Costardmonger/ Hearth Stones, & Flanders Brick.

15 p 13 Trafalgar Square/ with part of the National Gallery and Saint Martin's Church—Images, Buy Images. (Italian vendor with tray of plaster statues.)

16 p 14 Charing Cross/with Northumberland House, and Statue of King Charles the First—Baked Potatoes all Hot.

17 p 15 Whitehall—Bow Pots. (ie bay pots; the girl near the Banqueting Hall is selling sprigs.)

18 p 16 Burlington House, Gateway—Wild Duck Rabbit or Fowl./ Strawberries. (The famous gateway onto Piccadilly designed by Lord Burlington.)

19 p 17 Saint George Hanover Sq.—New Mackerel.

20 p 18 Saint James' Palace—Old Clothes./Buy a Box, Buy a Box.

21 p 19 Westminster Abbey/and Tower of St Margaret's Church—Milk Below. (A Welsh milkmaid with a chimney hat.)

22 p 20 Lambeth Palace—Water Cresses.

23 p 21 New Hall Lincolns Inn—Knives & Scissors to Grind./ Buy a Mat, A Rope or Parlour Mat. (The new hall built by Philip Hardwick, 1843–5).

24 p 22 Foundling Hospital—Sweep.

25 p 23 North Western Railway—Muffins, Crumpets. (Philip Hardwick's Euston Arch.)

26 p 24 Coliseum—Buy a Broom. (The Colosseum, Regent's Park.)

27 (additional wood-engr title) The/London/Cries/&/ Public/Edifices/from Sketches/on the/Spot/By Luke Limner Esq. Printed at the Litho press of Leighton Taylor, 19 Lambs Conduit Street. 130 × 115mm.

237 · LAMI'S SOUVENIRS DE LONDRES [1826]

Guidance for the foreign visitor to the capital, in the form of an illustrated itinerary in French, was provided from time to time by continental publishers, commencing with the London volume of Beeverell's *Délices de la Grande Bretagne* (no 20). At the time of the Napoleonic Wars the Parisian printer Crapelet published a *Souvenirs de Londres* (no 119) cheaply illustrated with engravings taken over from an earlier work. A decade later this same title was used by another Parisian, the bookseller and publisher Lami-Denozan, for a set of a dozen delicately hand coloured lithographs. These were intended as a memento for tourists from the Continent of their trip to London, illustrating the journey, the sights, and typical Anglo-Saxon diversions. The illustrator was Eugène Lami who later collaborated with Henri Monnier in a more extensive work published in Parts and entitled *Voyage en Angleterre* (1829–30); this shows some London characters and street scenes, including a turnpike road and the Billingsgate fish market.

The *Souvenirs* has an interesting view of Pall Mall with its row of pioneer gas street lighting well to the fore. All the plates, numbered tr, carry the credits 'Eug(ène) Lami', plain, or with 'del.', 'delt.' or 'pinxt', and 'Lith. de Villain'. The first only carries the undated publication-line 'A Paris, chez Lami Denozan, editeur, Rue de Seine, St Germain, No. 10.' There is no printed title, list or text, only brown paper wrappers (245 × 322mm), lithographically printed, on which the title is enclosed in a moiré ribbon with silver buckles:

Souvenirs/De Londres/M.DCCC.XXVI. Lami Denozan, Editeur, Rue de Seine No. 10. /Sazerac et Duval, passage de l'Opéra—Alp. Giroux, Rue du Coq St. Honoré, No. 7. (The date in the Guildhall copy is amended in MS to read '1828' and the imprint is covered with a blue label reading: 'Lami-Denozan, Librarie,/Rue des Fossés-Montmartre, No. 4.') Lami De Nozan Invt. 1826.

1 La traversée sur le Paquebot. 105 × 220mm. A rough crossing.

2 Le stage. 103 × 210mm. The stage-coach from Dover.

3 Pall-Mall. 110 × 220mm. Prominent are the 13 gas standards installed on the S. side on principles derived from the French scientist Le Bon.

4 Visite à l'Abbaye de Westminster, Chapelle d'Henri VII. 103 × 223mm.

5 La Tour (Galerie des Fusils). 105 × 220mm.

6 Une Chasse. 115 × 220mm. Fox hunting.

7 Une Course. 115 × 220mm. Horse racing.

8 Un Combat de Coqs. 120 × 225mm. The Cockpit, with Westminster Abbey towers visible through open doors.

9 Les Boxeurs. 115 × 222mm. Unidentifiable interior.

10 Un Prêche. 110 × 215mm. Interior of the Banqueting Hall, Whitehall at service time.

11 Course sur la Tamise. 105 × 215mm. Boat race with Westminster Bridge and Lambeth in background.

12 Douvres. 110 × 220mm. Stage-coach with Dover Castle in background.

---

238 · WOOD'S LINCOLN'S INN [c 1845]

Philip Hardwick, the architect of the new buildings at Lincoln's Inn, lent his name to a set of plates lithographed by Day & Haghe in 1842; an official record of work completed and in progress in that year (no 234). This further set of lithotints by L.J. Wood, an experienced landscape artist and lithographer, printed by M. & N. Hanhart, shows the architecture as finally built including the Gothic gateway into New Square from the Fields, with its barley-sugar chimney. Printed in black and yellow, it is the best published representation of these fine Victorian buildings which are dated 1843 under the gable of the Hall, and the scene shown is remarkably close, staffage apart, to what can now be seen from the gardens, the square or the Fields. The fabric fortunately sustained little war damage and has been skilfully cleaned and restored. There are no printed title, list or text. Plates, which are unnumbered, are uniformly credited 'Drawn by L.J. Wood. On Stone by L.J. Wood. M. & N. Hanhart Lith. Printers.', or 'On Stone by T.C. Dibdin', as in the Abbey catalogue (232). Publication-lines, undated, read:

(a) 'Published by John Weale, 49 High Holborn'.
(b) 'Published by John Weale, 59 High Holborn'.

Oblong folio, 350 × 530mm.   c 1845

0 To the Treasurer/and/Masters of the Bench/of the/ Honble Society of Lincoln's Inn,/these drawings/of the Hall & Library,/are with the permission of their worships/most respectfully dedicated/By their Obedient Servant/L.J. Wood/M. & N. Hanhart Lith. Printers. 435 × 305mm.

1 The New Hall and Library, from the East Gardens Lincoln's-Inn. (a) 230 × 340mm.

2 The East End of the New Library, from the East Gardens Lincoln's-Inn. (b) 230 × 340mm.

3 The South East View of the New Hall Lincoln's-Inn. (a) 245 × 358mm. Gothic gateway visible.

4 South End of the New Hall from/the Vice Cha_ellor of England's Court, Lincoln's-Inn. (b) 235 × 355mm. ie view from the old Hall, with full view of the Gothic gateway.

5 The East Terrace New Hall Lincoln's-Inn. (a) 245 × 355mm.

6 The Hall and Gateway from Lincoln's-Inn-Fields. 245 × 355mm. No publication-line.

7 The Western Side of the New Hall Lincoln's-Inn-Fields. (b) 245 × 355mm.

TOPOGRAPHICAL INDEX: CENTRAL AREA

[The first number given is that assigned to a particular book in the catalogue. It is divided by a stroke from the item numbers for individual plates. Single numbers in bold type indicate that all the plates in a given book illustrate the subject in question. Churches, etc are grouped together, in alphabetical order, under **Churches, Chapels, Monastic Houses,** as are general London views under **London.**]

Addle Street (inn sign)	210/37
Adelaide Wharf, London Bridge	194/1
Adelphi	38/129; 51/36; 55/4; 57/63; 61/71; 72/29–32; 73/3; 75/61; 124/3; 126/79; 134/22; 151/23; 167/23; 178/48; 183/48; 207/70; 215/16
Adelphi Theatre	131/197; 148/12; 162/68; 207/100; 215/135
Admiralty	
(1)	22/39
(2)	26/19; 29/15; 38/73; 41/6; 44/31; 48/13; 51/35; 57/14; 58/7; 61/90; 62/30; 72/18; 73/2; 76/8; 80/1; 89/8; 90/50; 98/109; 101/10; 103/12; 126/1; 130/28; 134/5; 138/21; 145/16; 151/12; 161/14; 162/39; 169/7; 177/17; 180/19; 183/46; 186/80; 193/31; 194/2; 207/15; 215/24; 217/10; 221/12
—interior	99/3; 195/47
Albany Cottage	*see* Regent's Park
Albany, Piccadilly	126/80; 161/115; 177/76
Albemarle House, Piccadilly	*see* Clarendon House
Albion Fire Office, Ludgate Hill	177/22
Albion Mills, Blackfriars	99/35
Aldermanbury (sign)	210/36

Aldersgate	13/4,6a; 14/4; 25/4; 26/12; 29/9; 33/3; 37/4; 38/1; 48/3; 51/4; 57/40; 61/43; 63/5; 67/11; 93/10; 96/13; 111/44; 114/5; 174/7; 177/44
Aldersgate Street	131/102; *see also* Shaftesbury House
Hall—Holy Trinity Brotherhood	104/39; 155/94
Aldersgate Ward	25/38; 37/54; 38/10; 51/5; 61/44
Aldgate	13/2,2a; 14/2; 25/4; 26/12; 29/9; 33/3; 37/4; 38/1; 51/4; 61/43; 63/5; 93/10; 96/11; 111/42; 114/5; 161/42; 162/14a; 162/14a; 174/3; 177/93
Aldgate Street	64/11; *see also* Church of St Michael
Aldgate Ward	25/22; 37/29; 38/13; 51/6; 57/40; 61/39
Apothecaries' Hall	161/142; 177/83; 207/109; 215/127
Apsley House, Hyde Park Corner	72/95; 154/153; 177/79; 186/80; 194/3; 207/47; 213/9; 215/31
Army and Navy Club	213/18; 215/131
Arthur's Club, St James's	161/192; 177/50; 207/28; 215/130
Artillery Ground, Finsbury	177/115; 187/2
Arundel House, Strand	**74**; 98/87–8
Ashburnham House, Westminster	146/86–7
Aske's Hospital, Hoxton	
(1)	25/15; 28/29; 37/16; 38/75; 79/7
(2)	154/50; 177/55
Astley's Amphitheatre	99/4,66; 131/198; 146/56; 148/8; 162/69; 177/37; 183/79; 192/10

524

George I, statue — *see* King George I

Gerard's Hall, Basing Lane — 70/73; 118/16; 127/55; 131/130; 143/1

Gibbons's Tennis Court, Vere Street, Clare Market — 131/193

Giltspur Street Compter — 96/35; 111/21; 126/9; 161/126; 167/3; 177/79; 207/33; 215/49

Girdlers' Hall, Basinghall Street — 161/82; 177/52

Globe Theatre, Bankside — 77/10; 120/7; 131/168–70

Gloucester Gate Terrace, Regent's Park — 177/116

Godolphin House, St James's Park — 22/39

Golden Lane, Barbican — 70/51; 127/6–7

Golden Square — 26/32; 29/11; 37/121

Goldsmiths' Arms, Southwark — 131/158

Goldsmiths' Hall
(1) — 37/55; 38/11; 48/36; 57/46; 61/55; 104/10; 121/23; 134/12; 151/10; 155/24; 161/53; 177/65
(2) — 152/51; 177/81; 183/3; 186/6; 195/55–6; 207/8; 213/35; 215/124

Goodman's Fields Theatre, Ayliffe Street — 131/190–1

Goswell Street — 100/22

Gracechurch Street — 1/3; 131/6; 186/61; *see also* Church of St Benet

Gravel Lane, Houndsditch — 210/25

Gray's Inn — 25/55; 29/22; 37/66; 41/36; 48/60; 61/79; 81/15; 88/18–20; 93/70; 161/67; 177/84; 207/115; 215/8

Gray's Inn Lane, Meux's Brewhouse — 100/24

Great Burlington Street General Wade's — 24/39

Great Exhibition of 1851 — *see* Crystal Palace

Great Queen Street — 117/25; 192/14

Great St Helen's — *see* Church of St Helen, Bishopsgate

Green Arbour Court, Old Bailey — 177/115

Green Park, Westminster — 98/89; 104/28, 91; 107/21; 112/2; 114/26; 117/8–9; 147/23; 152/49; 164/4; 177/83,116; 191/50; 193/7; 215/147; *see also* Spencer House

Greenwich — 26/10; 28/55; 47/11; 54/5; 57/83; 60/1; 61/89; 62/2,29; 75/64–5,67; 89/3; 106/69; 139/58; 149/47; 178/65; 186/38,69; 196/6; 198/12; 217/24; *see also* Churches of St Alfege, St Mary; Duke of Norfolk's Almshouses

Greenwich Hospital — 20/3; 21/34; 22/47–8; 23/2; 24/23–6,38; 25/17; 26/44; 28/55; 29/45; 37/19; 38/122; 41/38; 44/38; 47/16–17; 48/50; 53/6; 55/8; 57/82; 61/90; 62/30; 65/8; 66/3; 71/55; 72/79–81; 90/5; 99/97; 101/15; 103/32; 105/36; 107/33; 119/9; 126/104,119; 130/18; 134/13; 147/33; 149/48; 157/22; 167/31; 177/26; 178/63; 186/4; 190/5; 191/36–7; 193/8; 198/12; 207/37; 211/46; 212/1; 213/65; 215/83; 219/1–2; 220/4; 227/5

Greenwich Observatory — 22/51; 28/55; 89/1,4; 177/26; 186/19; 198/12; 207/36; 215/84

Greenwich Palace — 36/13

Greenwich Park — 48/51; 52/3; 60/5; 61/97; 75/66; 85/58; 89/4; 90/10; 92/1; 94/7; 107/34; 121/99; 130/19; 133/2; 139/59; 147/7; 162/18; 178/64; 183/84; 186/69; 191/1; 194/24; 196/6; 207/36; 213/66; 215/75,84

Queen's House — 24/7–8; 117/26

Vanbrugh Castle — 100/23

Gresham College Bishopsgate Street — 41/39; 44/15; 48/38; 57/19; 61/56; 155/16

Gresham Street — 186/66; 207/23; 215/40

Grocers' Hall
(1) — 26/54; 38/23; 48/36; 51/17; 57/46; 61/55
(2) — 84/3–4; 104/9; 155/86; 161/130; 177/41

Grosvenor House, Millbank — 131/104

Grosvenor House, Park Lane — 154/56; 177/69; 196/16

Grosvenor Square — 24/48; 37/122; 72/91; 117/16; 134/7; 217/22

Grosvenor Street — 100/43

Grove House — *see* Regent's Park

Grub Street ('General Monk's', etc) — 96/28; 111/54; 115/20–1,31; 127/44

Guildhall (The) — 13/18; 15/3; 17/9; 19/6; 20/12; 21/18; 22/64; 23/8; 25/35; 26/8; 28/17; 30/9; 33/8; 35/5; 36/57; 37/50; 38/24; 41/40; 43/8; 44/17; 48/25; 49/7; 51/18; 53/7;

TOPOGRAPHICAL INDEX: ENVIRONS AND BEYOND

554

556

INDEX TO ARTISTS, ENGRAVERS, ARCHITECTS, AUTHORS, BOOK TITLES AND SELECT PUBLISHERS

Becker, F.P., engr,
fl.1835–50 — 181/15
Bedford, Francis, archt and
dr, 1784–1858 — 154/98; 158/7; 161/188
Beeverell, James, author,
c 1707 — **20**
Bellin, J.N., author, c 1759 — **39**
Bellin, Samuel, engr,
1799–1893 — 181/2,25
Benazech, Peter, engr,
c 1730–c 1783 — 47/41
Bennett, W.J., engr,
1787–1844 — 116/6; **132;** 232/6,8
Benning, R., engr,
fl.1714–61 — 41/17,79–80; 47/45–6
Benoist, Antoine, dr and
engr, 1721–70 — **44;** 61/12; 155/27–8,56
Bentley, Charles, engr,
1806–54 — **157;** 190/10
Bentley, Joseph Clayton,
engr, 1809–51 — 190/8; 211/26
Bentley, Richard, publ,
1794–1871 — **206**
Bernini, G., sculptor,
1598–1680 — 67/A14,B2,C3
Beschreibung von London — **67**
Beugo, A., publ, c 1810 — 98/120
*Bibliotheca topographica
Britannica* — 83/12–14
Bickham, George, engr,
1684–1769 — 191/14
Bicknell, W.I., author,
c 1847 — **207**
Bierling, Adam A, dr,
c 1646 — **74;** 98/88
Billings, R.W., dr and engr,
1813–74 — 98/121; 175/14; **181; 185;
189**
Birch, William, engr,
1755–1834 — 56/9; **69;** 77/26
Bird, Francis, sculptor,
1667–1731 — 13/20; 27/153; 29/32
Birrell, Andrew, dr and
engr, fl.1794–1805 — **96; 111**
Bishop, H., dr, c 1823 — 146/34–6
Bishop, T., engr, c 1834 — 178/72
Black, Young & Young,
publ, 1822–35 — **177**
Black & Armstrong, publ,
1836–9 — **178**
Bladon, S., publ — **38; 218**
Blagdon, F.W., author,
1778–1819 — **112; 220**
Blanchard, E., editor,
c 1851–60 — **186**
Blome, Richard, dr and
surveyor, fl.1667–1705 — **25**
Blore, Edward, archt and
engr, 1787–1879 — 98/118; **136;** 139/45–6; **146;**

194/7; 209/9; 213/10
Bluck, J., engr,
fl.1791–1831 — **99; 108;** 116/4,9,11; **221**
Blyth, Francis, publ,
fl.1766–88 — **56**
Bogue, David, publ, c 1851 — **210**
Bohn, Henry G., publ,
1796–1884 — **192; 232**
Bohn, James, publ — **122**
Boitard, L.P., engr,
fl.1738–63 — 33/2; 38/2
Bol, Cornelys ('IV'), dr,
c 1666 — 82/2–3; 83/29–30; 131/95;
182/29–30
Bond, H., engr, fl.1834–51 — 178/14; 186/28,69
Bond, H.W., engr,
fl.1829–31 — 154/124–5,146–7;
161/159–61
Bond, J.L., archt and dr,
1764–1837 — 97/4,22
Bond, W., engr, fl.1821–8 — 136/26; 154/27–8,82
Bond, W.H., engr, fl.1831 — 161/93–4
Bonner, G.W., engr,
1796–1836 — 192/12 (?)
Bonner (or 'Bonnor'),
Thomas, engr,
fl.1773–1807 — 61/58; 104/73,145,147
Bonomi, Joseph, archt,
1739–1808 — 72/93; 100/34
*Book of the prospects of the
remarkable places, A* — **15**
Boone, T. & W., publ,
c 1838 — **185**
Booth, John, publ,
1794–1855 — **98; 115; 129**
Bosley, B., engr, c 1826 — 146/98,126
Boswell, Henry (pseud),
author — **63**
Bourne, John Cooke, dr,
1814–96 — **231**
Bourne, T. engr, fl.1821–40 — 131/19,80
Bowen, Emmanuel, engr,
fl.1744–76 — 33/6; 40/1; 55/10
Bowen, Thomas, engr,
fl.1750–90 — 48/68; **51;** 55/10; 57/96;
218/1
Bowles, Carington, publ,
1724–92 — 44/14; 191/0; 193/15,30,45
Bowles, John, publ,
1701–79 — **22; 27; 28; 29; 37; 105; 191;
193**
Bowles, Thomas, engr and
publ, fl.1712–67 — **22; 27; 29; 30;** 33/3; **37;** 38/1;
191; 193; 217/4–5
Bowles & Carver, publ,
1793–1832 — 191/9,40; **193**
Bowyer Robert, publ,
1758–1834 — **226**
Boyd, engr, c 1851 — 211/49

559

SELECT BIBLIOGRAPHY

Reference Books, Monographs, Unpublished Work

Barker, Richard Felix and Jackson, Peter. *London: 2000 years of a city and its people.* London, 1975.

Barley, Maurice Willmore. *A guide to British topographical collections.* London, 1974.

Bénézit, Emmanuel. *Dictionnaire critique et documentaire des peintres, sculpteurs, dessinateurs et graveurs de tous les temps et de tous les pays.* 8 vols. Paris, 1954–5.

Bridson, D.G.R. and Wakeman, G. *A guide to nineteenth century colour printers.* Loughborough, 1975.

Britton, John. *Autobiography.* 3 vols. London, 1848–50.

Brown, Philip A.H. 'London publishers and printers, 1800–1870'. Unpublished typescript in British Library Reference Division.

Bryan, Michael. *Dictionary of painters and engravers.* 4th ed. 5 vols. London, 1903–5.

Colvin, Howard M. *A biographical dictionary of British architects, 1660–1840.* London, 1954 (rev ed 1978).

Colvin, Sir Sidney. *Early engravings and engravers in England 1545–1695.* London, 1905.

Constable, William G. *Canaletto: Giovanni Antonio Canal 1697–1768.* 2nd ed, by J.G. Links. 2 vols. Oxford, 1976.

Courtauld Institute of Art. *A checklist of painters, c 1200–1976, represented in the Witt Library, Courtauld Institute of Art, London.* London, 1978.

Cox, Edward Godfrey. *A reference guide to the literature of travel.* Vol. 3: 'Great Britain'. Seattle, 1949.

Cox-Johnson (Saunders), Ann L. *Handlist of painters, sculptors and architects associated with St Marylebone 1760–1960.* Marylebone Public Libraries, London, 1963.

Cunningham, George H. *London.* London, 1927.

Darlington, Ida, and Howgego, J.L. *Printed maps of London, circa 1553–1850.* London 1964 (rev ed 1979).

Dictionary (The) of national biography from the earliest times to 1900. 22 vols. Oxford, 1885–1900.

Dolphin, P., Grant, E and Lowis, E. *The London region, an annotated geographical bibliography.* London, 1981.

Evans, Joan. *A history of the Society of Antiquaries.* Oxford, 1956.

Finberg, Hilda F. 'Canaletto in England'. *Walpole Society* 9–10 (1920–2), 22–76, 75–8.

Gascoigne, Bamber. *Images of Richmond: a survey of the topographical prints to the year 1900.* Richmond-upon-Thames, 1978.

Glaister, Geoffrey Ashall. *Glossary of the book.* 2nd ed. London, 1979.

Gough, Richard. *British topography or, an historical account of what has been done for illustrating the topographical antiquities of Great Britain and Ireland.* 2 vols. London, 1780.

Gray, Basil. *The English print.* London, 1937.

Gunnis, Rupert. *Dictionary of British sculptors, 1660–1851.* London, 1953.

Halkett, Samuel and Laing, J. *Dictionary of anonymous and pseudonymous English literature.* New ed. 7 vols. Edinburgh, 1926–34.

Hamilton, Harlan W. *Doctor Syntax; a silhouette of William Combe Esq. (1742–1823).* Kent, Ohio, 1969.

Hammelman, Hanns Andreas and Boase, T.S.R. *Book illustrators in the 18th century.* New Haven, 1975.

Harben, Henry A. *A dictionary of London: being notes topographical and historical relating to the streets and principal buildings in the City of London.* London, 1918.

Hardie, Martin. *English coloured books.* New York, 1906 (repr 1973).

Water-colour painting in Britain. Vol. 1: 'The 18th century'. Ed by D. Snelgrove, J. Mayne and B. Taylor. London, 1966.

Hind, Arthur M. *Engraving in England in the sixteenth and seventeenth centuries.* Vol. 2: 'The reign of James I'. London, 1955.

Wenceslaus Hollar and his views of London and Windsor in the seventeenth century. London, 1922.

Holloway, Merlyn. *Steel-engravings in nineteenth century British topographical books.* London, 1977.

Hughes, Therle. *Prints for the collector: British prints from 1500 to 1900.* London, 1970.

Hunnisett, Basil. *Steel-engraved book illustration in England*. London, 1980.

Hutchison, Sidney C. 'The Royal Academy Schools, 1768–1830'. *Walpole Society* 38 (1962), 123–88.

Hyde, Ralph. *Ward maps of the City of London*. Map Collectors Circle, London, 1967.

Ivins, William Mills junr. *How prints look: photographs with a commentary*. New York, 1943 (repr 1968).

Jackson, Peter. *John Tallis's London street views 1838–1840*. London, 1969.

Lane, Charles. *Sporting aquatints and their engravers*. Leigh-on-Sea, 1978.

Lockie, John. *Topography of London*. 2nd ed. London, 1813.

Longford, Elizabeth. *Images of Chelsea*. Catalogue by J. Ditchburn. Richmond-upon-Thames, 1980.

Lowndes, William Thomas. *The bibliographer's manual of English literature*. 6 vols. London, 1857–64.

Marks, Stephen Powys. *The map of sixteenth century London*. London, 1964.

Maxted, Ian Francis. *The London book trades 1775–1800: a preliminary checklist of members*. Folkestone, 1977.

Millburn, John R. *Benjamin Martin*. Leiden, 1976.

Morgan, William. *London &c actually survey'd and a prospect of London and Westminster*. Introductory notes by R. Hyde. Lympne, 1977.

Norman, Philip. 'Seven Drawings of London Bridge by E.W. Cooke'. *London Topographical Record* 9, 1914. (The drawings themselves reproduced as publication 33 of the London Topographical Society, 1913.)

Oppé, Adolf Paul. *The drawings of Paul and Thomas Sandby in the collection of H.M. the King at Windsor Castle*. Oxford, 1947.
English drawings, Stuart and Georgian periods at Windsor Castle. London, 1950.

Parker, Karl Theodore. *The drawings of Antonio Canaletto at Windsor Castle*. Oxford, 1948.

Pevsner, Sir Nikolaus. *Buildings of England: London*. 2 vols (vol. 1, rev by B Cherry). Hayes, Middx, 1973, 1952 (repr 1974).

Phillips, Hugh. *Mid-Georgian London*. London, 1964.
The Thames about 1750. London, 1976.

Phillips, John F.C. *Shepherd's London*. London, 1976.

Plomer, Henry Robert. *A dictionary of the printers and booksellers who were at work in England, Scotland and Ireland from 1668–1725*. Oxford, 1922.
A dictionary of the printers and booksellers who were at work in England, Scotland and Ireland from 1726 to 1755. London, 1932.

Prideaux, Sarah Treverbian. *Aquatint engraving; a chapter in the history of book illustration*. London, 1909.

Rawlinson, William G. *The engraved work of J.M.W. Turner, R.A.* 2 vols. London, 1908–18.

Ray, Gordon N. *The illustrator and the book in England from 1790 to 1914*. New York, 1976.

Redgrave, Samuel. *A dictionary of artists of the English school*. 2nd ed. London, 1878 (repr 1970).

Robinson, Francis J.G. and Wallis, P.J. *Book subscription lists; a revised guide*. Newcastle-upon-Tyne, 1975.

Roscoe, Sydney. *John Newbery and his successors 1740–1814: a bibliography*. Wormley, Herts, 1973.

Rostenberg, Leona. *English publishers in the graphic arts 1599–1700: a study of the printsellers and publishers of engravings, art and architectural manuals, maps and copybooks*. New York, 1963.

Roundell, James. *Thomas Shotter Boys 1803–74*. London, 1974.

Russell, Ronald. *Guide to British topographical prints*. Newton Abbot, Devon, 1979.

Scouloudi, Irene. *Panoramic views of London 1600–1666*. City of London Corporation, London, 1953.

Sprinzels, Francis. *Hollar Handzeichnungen*. Vienna, 1938.

Stroud, Dorothy. *George Dance, architect 1741–1825*. London, 1971.

Stuchbury, Howard E. *The architecture of Colen Campbell*. Manchester, 1967.

Summerson, Sir John. *Georgian London*. London, 1945 (rev ed 1970).
The life and work of John Nash, architect. London, 1980.

Survey of London. Greater London Council, London, 1900– (in progress).

Thieme, Ulrich, and Becker, F. *Allgemeines Lexicon der bildender Künstler*. 37 vols. Leipzig, 1907–50.

Thorne, James. *Handbook to the environs of London*. London, 1876 (repr 1970).

Tod, William B. *Directory of printers in London and its vicinity, 1800–40*. London, 1972.

Tooley, Ronald Vere. *English books with colour plates 1790–1860*. London, 1954 (repr 1975).

Twyman, Michael L. *Lithography 1800–1850; the techniques of drawing on stone in England and France and their application in works of topography*. London, 1970.

Upcott, William. *A bibliographical account of the principal works relating to English topography*. 3 vols. London, 1818 (repr 1978).

Vaughan, John Edmund. *The English guide book c 1780–1870; an illustrated history*. London, 1974.

Vertue, George. 'Notebooks, vol. VI: The history of engraving'. *Walpole Society* 30 (1948–50), 181–204.

Walker, Richard J.B. 'The Palace of Westminster after the fire of 1834'. *Walpole Society* 44 (1972–4), 94–122.

Wallis, Peter John. *An eighteenth century book trade index*. Newcastle-upon-Tyne, 1977.

Webb, David. 'Guidebooks to London before 1900: a history and bibliography'. Unpublished thesis for FLA. 1975.

Wheatley, Henry Benjamin and Cunningham, P. *London past and present: its history, associations and traditions*. 3 vols. London, 1891.

Wiles, Roy KcKeen. *Serial publication in England before 1750*. Cambridge, 1957.

Young, Elizabeth and Young, Wayland. *Old London churches*. London, 1956.

584

Catalogues

Abbey, John Roland. *Scenery of Great Britain in aquatint and lithography, 1770–1860*. London, 1952 (repr 1972).

Anderson, John P. *The book of British topography: a classified catalogue of the topographical works in the library of the British Museum relating to Great Britain and Ireland*. London, 1881 (repr 1976).

Bank of England. *An historical catalogue of engravings, drawings and paintings in the Bank of England*. London, 1928.

Bohn, Henry G. *A catalogue of books*. London, 1841.

Bowles, John. *A catalogue of maps, prints, books and books of maps, which are printed for and sold by John Bowles*. London 1728.
A catalogue of maps, prints, copy-books, &c from off copper-plates, printed for John Bowles. London, 1731 (rev ed 1753).

Boydell, John & Josiah. *An alphabetical catalogue of plates engraved by the most esteemed artists which compose the stock of John and Josiah Boydell, engravers and printsellers*. London, 1803.
Sale catalogue of John & Josiah Boydell's (deceased) stock. Sold by Robert H. Evans in June 1818. London, 1818.

British Museum. *Catalogue of British drawings*. Vol. 1: 'Sixteenth and seventeenth centuries'. Comp by E. Croft-Murray and P. Hulton. London, 1960.
Catalogue of drawings by British artists … in the British Museum. Comp by L. Binyon. 4 vols. London, 1898–1907.
Catalogue of the manuscript maps, charts, and plans and of the topographical drawings in the British Museum. 3 vols. London 1844–61 (repr 1962).
An exhibition of forgeries and deceptive copies held in the Department of Prints and Drawings. London, 1961.
London; an excerpt from the British Museum catalogue of printed maps, charts and plans. London, 1967.
Turner in the British Museum: drawings and watercolours. Exhibition cat by A. Wilton. London, 1975.

Burlington Fine Arts Club. *Catalogue of a collection of early drawings and pictures of London*. London, 1919.

Crace, Frederick. *A catalogue of maps, plans and views of London, Westminster and Southwark. Collected and arranged by Frederick Crace*. Ed J.G. Crace. London, 1878.

Daniell, Walter Vernon and Nield, F.J. *Manual of British topography: a catalogue of county and local histories, pamphlets, views, drawings, maps, etc connected with and illustrating the principal localities in the United Kingdom*. London, 1909.

Guildhall Art Gallery. *Canaletto in England*. London, 1959.
Edward William Cooke. London, 1970.
London Bridge in art. London, 1969.
London Bridge progress drawings exhibition. London, 1973.

IPEX 80. *Catalogue of exhibitions of British coloured books 1738–1898*. British Printing Machinery Association, London, 1980.

London County Council. *Members' Library catalogue*. Vol. 1: 'London history and topography'. London, 1939.

London Museum. *Catalogue of oil paintings in the London Museum*. Comp J. Hayes. London, 1970.

Magdalene College, Cambridge. *Catalogue of the Pepys Library at Magdalene College Cambridge*. Vol. 3, pt 1: 'Prints and drawings: general'. General ed R. Latham. Cambridge, 1980.

New York Public Library. *The Arents collection of books in parts and associated literature: a complete check-list*. New York, 1964.

Royal Academy of Arts. *Turner 1775–1851*. London, 1974.

Royal Institute of British Architects. Sir Bannister Fletcher Library, Drawings Collection: Burlington-Devonshire Collection, pt 1. *Catalogue of the drawings of Inigo Jones, John Webb and Lord Burlington*. London, 1960.

Sayer, Robert. *New and enlarged catalogue for the year 1766*. London, 1766.
Sayer and Bennett's enlarged catalogue of new and valuable prints, in sets, or single. London, 1775 (repr 1970).

Smith, Alfred Russell. *A catalogue of ten thousand tracts and pamphlets and fifty thousand prints and drawings illustrating the topography and antiquities of England, Wales, Scotland and Ireland. Collected by the late William Upcott and J.R. Smith*. London, 1878.

Sotheby's. *A catalogue of the books, maps and charts of the late Mr Robert Wilkinson of Fenchurch Street; including his valuable copyrights, copper plates, and impressions of the following … —The 'Londina Illustrata', 2 vol in folio together with the original manuscript. Sold by auction by Mr Sotheby, Thursday 29 September 1825 and three following days*. London, 1825.
Catalogue of the famous collection of London topography formed by John Edmund Gardner (deceased). 3 pts, 1923–4.
Catalogue of the important collection of engravings and drawings of London, the property of Arthur Boney Esq (deceased). London, 1947.
Catalogue of the library of John Burns. London, 1943.
Catalogue of the valuable library of Lord Nathan of Churt. London, 1962.
Londini illustrata: a catalogue of the valuable and choice collection of prints and drawings illustrative of Pennant's History of London, to be sold by auction, February 1822. London, 1822.

Stewart, Bertram. *The library and the picture collection of the Port of London Authority*. London, 1955.

Tate Gallery. *Landscape in Britain c1750–1850*. Comp by L. Parris. London, 1973.

Van der Aa, Pieter. *Catalogue de livres, de cartes géographiques, des villes, chateaux &c de l'univers qui se trouvent chez van der Aa*. Leiden, 1715.

Vertue, George. *A catalogue of the entire and genuine library of books of Mr George Vertue, engraver, late of Brownlow Street, deceas'd, sold by auction 18th, 19th March, 1757. (In Sale catalogues of libraries of eminent persons.* Ed A.N.L. Munby. Vol. 10. London, 1974.)

Victoria and Albert Museum. *Catalogue of water-colour paintings by British artists and foreigners working in Great Britain.* Rev ed and supplement. London, 1927–51.

Watercolours by Thomas Girtin. London, 1975.

Watt, Robert. *Bibliotheca Britannia.* 4 vols. London, 1824.